PENGUIN REFERENCE

Commercial Law

Roy Goode is Emeritus Professor of Law in the University of Oxford and Emeritus Fellow of St John's College, Oxford. A former solicitor, later a barrister and Queen's Counsel, he held chairs at Queen Mary College, University of London, and at Oxford, where he was Norton Rose Professor of English Law until his retirement in 1998. He is an Honorary Bencher of Inner Temple, a Fellow of the British Academy, of Goodenough College and of the Royal Society of Arts and is an Honorary Fellow of Queen Mary. He holds honorary doctorates from the University of London and the University of East Anglia. He was for fifteen years a member, and is currently an honorary member, of the Governing Council of the International Institute for the Unification of Private Law (UNIDROIT). He was knighted in 2000 for services to academic law.

Roy Goode served as chairman or member of several government committees. He has lectured extensively in this country and abroad and is the author of a number of standard textbooks and monographs. His leisure interests include chess, walking and browsing in bookshops. He is married with one daughter and lives in Oxford.

THIRD EDITION

COMMERCIAL LAW

Roy Goode

PENGUIN BOOKS

PENGUIN BOOKS

Published by the Penguin Group
Penguin Books Ltd, 80 Strand, London WC2R 0RL, England
Penguin Group (USA) Inc., 375 Hudson Street, New York, New York 10014, USA
Penguin Group (Canada), 10 Alcorn Avenue, Toronto, Ontario, Canada M4V 3B2
(a division of Pearson Penguin Canada Inc.)
Penguin Ireland, 25 St Stephen's Green, Dublin 2, Ireland (a division of Penguin Books Ltd)
Penguin Group (Australia), 250 Camberwell Road,
Camberwell, Victoria 3124, Australia (a division of Pearson Australia Group Pty Ltd)
Penguin Books India Pvt Ltd, 11 Community Centre, Panchsheel Park, New Delhi – 110 017, India
Penguin Group (NZ), cnr Airborne and Rosedale Roads, Albany,
Auckland 1310, New Zealand (a division of Pearson New Zealand Ltd)
Penguin Books (South Africa) (Pty) Ltd, 24 Sturdee Avenue, Rosebank 2196, South Africa

Penguin Books Ltd, Registered Offices: 80 Strand, London WC2R 0RL, England

www.penguin.com

First published by Penguin Books and Allen Lane 1982
Reprinted with minor revisions by Penguin Books 1985
Second edition published by Butterworths and Penguin Books 1995
This edition published by LexisNexis UK and Penguin Books 2004

5

Typeset by Columns Design Ltd, Reading, UK
Printed in England by Clays Ltd, St Ives plc

For my daughter Naomi

Contents

PART ONE   THE FOUNDATIONS OF COMMERCIAL LAW

PART FOUR   SECURED FINANCING

PART FIVE SPECIFIC FORMS OF SECURED BUSINESS FINANCE

Preface

Part of the fascination of commercial law lies in its seemingly infinite capacity for change. Having studied the subject for nearly 50 years, I still find myself taken by surprise and by the stimulus of re-examining familiar concepts in new and unfamiliar settings. So my interest in indirect holdings of securities, sparked off by a seminar in Oxford and my ensuing involvement with a team of enthusiastic and frighteningly clever colleagues in work on the Hague Convention on the Applicable Law, exposed me to a range of practices and problems of a kind I had not previously experienced. Indeed, some of the subtleties did not surface until long after the diplomatic conference at which the convention was concluded and then only because of constant probing by my fellow rapporteurs in work on the explanatory report, aided by a truly expert and hard-working Advisory Group. So, too, with the equally challenging project entrusted to a Working Group, which I have had the privilege of chairing, set up the Bank of England's Financial Markets Law Committee to draft principles for a substantive United Kingdom law on property interests in indirectly held securities. In both cases the vigorous exchange of ideas between scholars and specialist practitioners sharpened the arguments and led to a much deeper and market-responsive product than would otherwise have ensued.

I have long held the view that the primary objective of commercial (as opposed to consumer) law is to respond to the legitimate needs of the mercantile community and of the markets which are central to its activities. What is striking is the readiness of legislatures and courts of different countries, and of those responsible for drafting international conventions, to modify or even jettison long-established principles in order to produce commercially sensible outcomes and to promote the fulfillment of reasonable expectations. So the House of Lords, in *Re Bank of Credit and Commerce International SA (No 8)* [1998] AC 214, overcame the serious theoretical difficulties involved in a person's taking security over his own obligation to uphold the efficacy of a charge in favour of a bank over its own customer's credit balance. Having myself started this hare by arguing over 20 years ago that in property terms charge-backs were conceptually impossible, and, indeed, securing judicial support for that proposition, I now think that while I was right in the conceptual reasoning, the House of Lords had a better feel for the commercial reality, demonstrating that while concepts are essential to law, we must never allow them to become our masters.

In the nine years since the appearance of the second edition of this work a great deal has happened in the field of commercial law. There has been a huge volume of case law relating to different facets of the law of contract, tort, property, restitution, and corporate insolvency (including, inevitably, yet further cases on floating charges) and a steady stream of jurisprudence on the procedural aspects of cross-border litigation. Parliament too has been very active. The Contracts (Rights of Third Parties) Act 1999 has largely, though not entirely, abolished the doctrine of privity of contract, with implications yet to be fully explored. The Sale of Goods Act 1979 was amended in 1994 to give prepaying buyers of goods to be drawn from a bulk a co-ownership interest in the bulk pending appropriation to their specific contracts, and amended again to give enhanced rights to buyers in consumer sales. The Insolvency Act 1986 has been extensively revised, notably by legislation abolishing Crown preference, requiring a percentage of the assets subject to a floating charge given by a company to be surrendered on its insolvency to form a fund available for unsecured creditors, and – still more dramatically – abolishing administrative receivership except in designated categories of case. There has also been a complete overhaul of the rules on dispute resolution, with the replacement of most of the Rules of the Supreme Court, on which I was brought up, by the Civil Procedure Rules, and the enactment of the Arbitration Act 1996 as a comprehensive code for the conduct and review of arbitral proceedings and awards. These two measures alone have necessitated the complete rewriting of the chapters on commercial litigation and commercial arbitration.

Two important EC directives on financial collateral have been implemented by legislation. These are designed to allow rights in financial collateral to be created without excessive formality, to be perfected without registration and to be protected from avoidance under national insolvency laws, primarily to reduce systemic risk. Meanwhile, the ill-fated EC Insolvency Convention, which collapsed because, of the 15 member states involved, the United Kingdom was alone in refusing to sign up to it – not because of any objection to the convention itself but because Margaret Thatcher decided that in view of what she perceived as the European Commission's intransigence over British beef a little retaliation was called for! It was a short-lived victory, because the convention became a regulation, directly entering the law in all member states,, and provides a set of uniform conflicts rules governing jurisdiction, the applicable law and the recognition of rights in insolvency proceedings in a member state. The Brussels jurisdiction and judgments convention has also been converted into an EC regulation.

There has been equally vigorous activity at the international level. Soon after the appearance of the second edition the United Nations Convention on Independent Guarantees and Stand-by Letters of Credit was concluded. Six years later the 2001 Cape Town Convention on International Interests in Mobile Equipment, with its aircraft equipment protocol, and protocols to follow on rail and space property, brought to fruition a decade of work on a highly ambitious project, which was no less than to create an entirely new *sui generis* form of international interest in railway rolling stock, aircraft objects and space assets, with a set of basic default remedies, an entirely unique international registry to record such interests and a set of priority rules based on the order of registration. This was followed in short order by the UN Convention on the Assignment of Receivables in International Trade and, a year later, by the Hague Convention on the Law Applicable to Rights in Indirectly Held Securities previously mentioned. Thus the three principal international, intergovernmental bodies all produced major international instruments designed to facilitate cross-border trade and to reduce transaction costs.

The scholars, too, have made their contribution to the harmonization of international trade law. The Commission on European Contract Law, under the leadership of Professor Ole Lando, completed the third and final phase of *Principles of European Contract Law* in 2002, while only two months ago the second and final part of the UNIDROIT *Principles of International Commercial Contracts*, prepared by a Working Group under the direction of Professor Joachim Bonell, was formally approved by the Governing Council of UNIDROIT. Meanwhile, a Study Group has been set up by UNIDROIT to prepare a draft convention on substantive rules concerning securities held with an intermediary, and has produced a preliminary draft.

Nor is this all. There have been major changes in business practice in relation to export sales, transportation and documentary credits, demand guarantees and standby credits; the International Chamber of Commerce has published Incoterms 2000 and the eUCP for electronic presentations under letters of credit, and the Institute of International Banking Law & Practice Inc has issued the International Standby Practices (ISP98), a set of rules governing standby letters of credit.

In this new edition I have sought not only to take account of all these developments but also to bring fresh thoughts to a range of issues and to incorporate some of the ideas that came to me while preparing the 1997 Hamlyn lectures, later published under the title *Commercial Law in the Next Millennium*. This has necessitated a substantial amount of rewriting as well as a refinement of a number of thoughts expressed in the previous edition. The task of selection from the mass of material available has become ever harder. Nevertheless, I have striven to adhere to the primary purpose of this book, which is not to capture every case or cover every point but rather to demonstrate the richness of English commercial law, to explain its conceptual framework and the range and diversity of the different branches of law – contract, tort, property, equity, trusts and unjust enrichment – brought to bear on issues arising from commercial transactions, and to show that despite this profusion of sources, the subject has a coherence and an underlying philosophy, its relevance to business being demonstrated through an analysis of typical commercial transactions. Above all, I have striven to capture the sheer intellectual excitement of commercial law as the solving of each mystery unfolds yet other mysteries behind it.

In the preparation of this new edition I have been greatly encouraged by the kind remarks made about its predecessor by students, scholars and practising lawyers not only in this country but also, to my astonishment, in countries overseas whose legal systems are not part of the common law family at all. But this is the last edition for which I shall be responsible. I have reached the view that at the age of 71 it is time to make way for one who is younger and more vigorous and will bring his own perspective Happily, my friend and colleague Professor Ewan McKendrick has kindly agreed to assume responsibility for future editions, and I know that this work, on which I have lavished such care and affection for three decades, will be in good hands.

I am indebted to many people for their help in a variety of ways. They are identified in a separate page of acknowledgments. To each of them I express my deep appreciation. But there is one person above all to whom I owe everything: my long-suffering wife, Catherine, who has with extraordinary tolerance and understanding supported my various endeavours over a period of 40 years and borne with fortitude the burdens of living with the obsessions of an author who in the field of law is at last within sight of laying down his pen.

POSTSCRIPT

The untimely death of my friend and colleague Peter Birks, Regius Professor of Civil Law at Oxford University, soon after this book was completed has robbed the academic world of an outstanding scholar who mapped out the first conceptual structure of the English law of unjust enrichment. Peter was ever generous to those such as myself who from time to time wandered uncertainly into his field. He was an inspirational teacher who galvanized generations of students and colleagues with his passion for teaching and rigorous scholarship and his dedication to legal education. He will live on through his works and the affectionate memories of academic and practising lawyers around the world.

Roy Goode
Oxford
7 July 2004

Preface to the Second Edition

In the title of his famous article 'The Mystery of Seisin' the great legal historian Frederic Maitland neatly depicted the fate of the scholar: to be in continuous pursuit of the ultimate truth about one's subject, sensing at times that one has finally reached it, only to discover, like Tantalus with his overhanging fruits, that it escapes just before the moment of capture. So also with commercial law, a subject which after decades of study still holds endless fascination.

The first edition of this book represented an attempt to lay down the fundamental concepts of commercial law and then apply these to typical forms of business transaction. The warm response from both students and practising lawyers demonstrated a need for such a book and I have adhered to this approach in the new edition. The effective treatment of concepts underlying the rules of commercial law remains a primary objective of the work. The theoretical framework advanced in the first edition appears to have stood the test of time, though further reflection, together with a number of illuminating decisions by the courts, has led me to modify and refine the analysis of certain aspects of property and sales law, particularly in relation to constructive possession and attornment, the identification of the subject-matter of a transfer obligation (which has given rise to several important decisions), tracing into products and proceeds and security in personal property.

I have also had some new ideas on ways of presenting the fundamentals of commercial law to my readers. These result partly from work done in writing monographs on security, payment and corporate insolvency, and partly from my experience in putting together and teaching a new commercial law course in Oxford, where I have found it helpful to begin with a discussion of typical contract structures in order to demonstrate how contractual relationships can be organized in different ways to produce or avoid a particular legal result. The case law of the past decade has also shown both the importance and the limitations of market rules and practices, and I have devoted part of a chapter to the discussion of the role of the market. More generally, there have been several major developments in contract law, and advances in the law of restitution have also had to be taken into account, particularly in relation to tracing claims to money. On the legislative front a great deal has happened since the appearance of the first edition. There have been three sale of goods statutes; insolvency law has been entirely recast; directives have been issued and implemented on unfair contract terms and on self-employed commercial agents; the Carriage of Goods by Sea Act 1992 has made it a great deal easier for a transferee of the shipper's rights to bring proceedings against the carrier; and there have been minor changes in the law concerning cheques. The evolution of electronic funds transfer systems has led to major changes in bank payment mechanisms, which are of considerable importance to the commercial lawyer.

The commercial lawyer of today needs to know not only of his own law but of developments in what has come to be known as transnational commercial law, the corpus of law that grows from international conventions and other instruments of harmonization and from conscious and unconscious parallelism in judicial thinking in different jurisdictions. There has been a substantial volume of activity in this sphere of which I have endeavoured to take account in the chapters on international trade and finance. The International Chamber of Commerce has been particularly active, with two revisions of the Uniform Customs and Practice for Documentary Credits in the past decade, new Uniform Rules for Demand Guarantees and Uniform Rules for Contract Bonds, and major revisions of Incoterms and the Uniform Rules for Collections. The United Nations Commission on International Trade Law has vigorously pursued a number of important projects, including a model law on funds transfers and a draft convention on international guarantees and standby letters of credit. The Institute for the Unification of Private Law has two more commercial law conventions to its credit: the Ottawa Conventions on International Financial Leasing and International Factoring. There have also been two important formulations of contract law principles, the Unidroit *Principles of International Commercial Contracts*, under the direction of Professor Joachim Bonell, and the Commission on European Contract Law *Principles of European Contract Law* under the chairmanship of Professor Ole Lando.

There has therefore been much new material to distil and absorb into the text in such a way as to convey the essence of the changes without obscuring the framework of commercial law which it has been my concern to project. The result is a substantial amount of rewriting. Three entirely new chapters have been added, on commercial contracts, agency in commercial transactions, and concepts of money and payment. The sequence of chapters has been rearranged so as to complete the examination of domestic transactions before moving to international trade. I have reworked (though without changing the structure) the chapters on general contract law and the passing of the property on sale, and have made major revisions to the chapters on implied terms in favour of the buyer and the buyer's remedies for breach to reflect the major changes made by the Sale and Supply of Goods Act 1994. The chapter on corporate insolvency law has been completely rewritten in the light of the Insolvency Act 1986 and resultant case law, as have the chapters on carriage of goods by sea and the conflict of laws. Dispute resolution has been divided into two separate chapters, litigation and arbitration (with brief references to alternative dispute resolution), and indications given of the likely shape of the forthcoming Arbitration Bill. Finally, I have dropped the chapter on product liability – on the basis that this belongs more properly to consumer protection and the law of tort – and have replaced a number of the forms reproduced in the work.

As before, I owe a great debt to many people, in particular my friend and colleague Professor Francis Reynolds for his detailed comments on the chapter on carriage of goods by sea, which saved me from several errors; Terry Allen of the Bank of

England for a similar service in relation to the chapters on payment and payment systems; Ray Battersby of the Simplified Trade Procedures Board (SITPRO), for his helpful comments on the draft chapter on the organization of export sales; Professor Robert Cooter of the University of California, Berkeley, for reassurance as regards my brief treatment of the problem of the lost-volume seller; Professor Joachim Bonell of the University of Rome I 'La Sapienza' for kindly supplying me with the text and digest of cases on the Vienna Sales Convention drawn from the Unilex database which he edits; Sir Anthony Colman, for advance sight of the new edition of his book on the Commercial Court; and Stephen Nathan QC for his help on the specimen forms of pleading shown in the book.

I am indebted to the organizations separately listed for permission to reproduce the standard documents included in the work, and to the numerous individuals who helped me either by supplying such documents or by sending me other forms for consideration, in particular Leslie M. Bland of Close Invoice Finance; Richard Calnan of Norton Rose; Tony Clemas of LEP International; Julie Coen of British International Freight Association; Jeremy Croal of Zurich International; Al Danino of SITPRO; Kevin Hall and William Sheehan of Lloyds Bank; Hugh Homan of Berwin Leighton; Denis Hopkin of Lombard North Central; Janet F. Mathieson of the Solicitors' Law Stationery Society; Jack Miller of HSBC Holdings; John Patrick of the Consumer Credit Trade Association; Pascale Reins of the International Chamber of Commerce, Paris; Leila Riddington of International Factors; Geoff Robbins of P&O Containers; Freddy Salinger; Desmond Sopp of Citibank Consumer Services; Stephen Whish of Midland Bank; and Andrew White of Forward Trust.

I should particularly like to thank my former research assistant, Teun Strycken, for all the help he gave me in literature searches for the new edition as well as a number of helpful comments on the text from the perspective of a civil lawyer, and Regina Asariotis for a similar service admirably provided some years ago before the hiatus caused by my unexpected incursion into the world of occupational pensions. The wonderfully skilful and painstaking work of the editorial consultant, Barbara Horn, has filled me with admiration. I am also deeply grateful to the team at Penguin Books, in particular Mark Handsley and Andrew Cameron, for the great amount of work they put into the publication of this book; to Andrew Marshall of Butterworths and Katharine Brown, Caroline Herd and Ann Morgan of his tables department for the preparation of the tables, to Elisabeth Ingham for preparation of the index and to Tanya Cohen, an Oxford law student, for her invaluable assistance with the proofreading.

Once again I must acknowledge my debt to my colleagues and students in Oxford and elsewhere who sparked off lines of thought and helped to clarify my ideas through discussion and debate; and to the many practising lawyers, bankers and business people who gave so generously of their time to answer my queries and to supply me with information and documents.

Finally, a special word of thanks to my wife, Catherine, who despite the pressures of her own work has given me unfailing support and has once again borne with extraordinary patience and fortitude the intrusion of authorship activities into our domestic life.

The law is stated on the basis of materials available to me at 1 July 1995.

Roy Goode
St John's College
Oxford

1 August 1995

Foreword to the First Edition

No task is easier than that of finding authors wanting to write legal textbooks. As editor of this legal series. I have set myself a very much more difficult problem. My approach is to identify a basic legal subject which, because of changed circumstances, is no longer adequately covered and then to ask whether the writer exists who in my view is capable of filling the gap.

That is how we came to publish Stanley de Smith's *Constitutional and Administrative Law*. Obviously if such rigorous requirements are imposed new books will not appear as regularly as in some other series. De Smith's book is already in its fourth edition as this second book in the series is published Why has it been chosen? Commercial law is a classic example of the weakness of so much textbook writing in Britain. Any reasonably competent legal scholar can mug up the statutes and reported decisions in a field like commercial law and present an acceptable account of their import. The essence of commercial law is in commercial transactions. It by no means follows that the accident of litigation indicates fully how these transactions are carried out. What is called for is a synthesis of the theory underlying commercial relationships and the practice which governs their operation. That synthesis also necessitates a blending of the purely commercial elements with the underlying principles of the law of property and trusts.

It would be unreasonable, if not impossible, to expect this tremendous burden to be borne either by a mere academic commercial lawyer or by a practitioner. I knew of only one English lawyer with decades of experience in the practice of commercial law who also holds a chair in commercial law. I was therefore delighted when I persuaded Professor Roy Goode to write this book. Nobody has previously attempted to combine an analysis of fundamental principles with a description of typical commercial transactions, in which the nature of the business operation, the roles of the parties and the function of the various documents devised are all explained. In this way the student will have the best opportunity ever given to him of learning what happens in commercial legal life. He will certainly become acquainted for the first time with many vital commercial matters which have never been aired in the reported cases. I believe that reading this book will be an equally profitable experience for legal practitioners, especially those who do not specialize exclusively in commercial law, but who are none the less frequently called upon to draft and advise on commercial documents.

H. Street

Preface to the First Edition

When Penguin Books invited me in 1973 to contribute a book on commercial law to the 'Foundations in Law' series edited by Professor Harry Street, I accepted with both enthusiasm and trepidation: enthusiasm, because this is the book I have always wanted to write; trepidation, because of the high standard set by the previous volume in the series and the formidable task of reducing to manageable compass such a vast field of law.

In the event, the task was far harder than I had ever imagined, and a work that was to have been written in five years took me eight, a delay caused in part by my habit of writing my best thoughts on the back of bus tickets and then losing them. I would have liked to spend a further eight years on the text before exposing it to the public gaze, but this might have strained even the legendary patience of Penguin and of their editor, Michael Dover.

Every author builds on the labours of his predecessors. There are several good books on commercial law, and on specific aspects of the subject; I freely acknowledge my indebtedness to those who have gone before me in this field. They are too numerous to mention here, but my principal sources have been identified at appropriate points throughout the book. However, in a number of respects the present volume seeks to break new ground.

In the first place, I have treated as within the purview of commercial law all those legal principles, from whatever branch of law they are drawn, which regularly surface in commercial disputes. It has long seemed to me that there is an unfortunate gulf between the commercial lawyer and the property and equity lawyer. Contract, sale of goods and negotiable instruments are accepted as falling within the domain of the former, equitable interests and conflicting real rights within the latter's field of expertise. But in the world of business, problems do not divide themselves into such neat packages. The seller or buyer of goods is likely to need finance, for which purpose he will usually be asked to furnish security. The financier will be concerned to establish the priority of his security interest and its validity in the event of the debtor's bankruptcy or liquidation. The typical commercial problem is a mixture of contract, sales law, tort, property, equity and trusts. The practitioner has to be familiar with the principles of each of these fields of law in order to be able to give sound advice to his client. So this book devotes a substantial amount of attention to principles of property law and of equitable obligation. Also included are topics which have hitherto been treated as the exclusive preserve of textbooks on company law – in particular, floating charges, receivership and liquidation.

Secondly, despite its size the book is concerned primarily with principles. It is a foundation book, in keeping with the title of the series, but it is not elementary. The greatest difficulty confronting the student lies not in the sophisticated rule but in the fundamental concept. Rules may change, concepts are more permanent. Hence it is the theoretical framework of a subject which demands the closest attention, for it is this that endures when the detailed rule has passed into oblivion. Chapters 2, 3, 6, 16 and 25–28 are the key conceptual chapters. Chapter 2, devoted to basic concepts of personal property, is, perhaps, the most important in the whole book and was also the most difficult to write, if only because so much of personal property law is conceptually obscure, and every time one thinks one has at last discovered the eternal truth it turns out to be a mirage. The full significance of the principles set down in this chapter will not become apparent until the reader has progressed further into the book, and he should return to it regularly to see how those principles are applied in specific situations.

The treatment of security interests in chapters 25–27 marks a departure from the normal method of presenting this topic in English textbooks, though it would in many respects be familiar to an American commercial lawyer. I have also essayed some new thoughts on that most brilliant of creations of the common law, the floating charge, which continues to present a whole range of difficult conceptual problems, despite a century of case law. (Law students seem to experience difficulty with charges. I retain an affectionate memory of the second-year student who, when asked in a property paper to describe the satisfaction of a charge over land, answered that in his experience there was nothing to equal fox-hunting!)

This book falls broadly into two halves, though not so divided sequentially. The first is concerned with theory and is relatively abstract. The second is devoted to what may be termed applied commercial law, in which I have attempted to show how typical financing operations are set up, the parties involved, the documents and forms of security used and the relevance of the principles previously enunciated to the resolution of a variety of common practical problems.

The application of theory to a specific dispute is rarely as clear cut as would be suggested by a reading of the textbooks. It is inevitable, indeed essential, that this should be so. A map which matched the actual ground, point for point, would defeat its purpose. A textbook which sought to encompass all possible variations would be unusable. The surgeon operating on a patient knows that his knife will reveal, not the clear divisions of the body revealed by Gray's *Anatomy*, but a slippery mass of blood, muscle and bone in which a certain amount of searching may be necessary to locate the organ on which he wishes to operate. But Gray's *Anatomy* remains an indispensable tool for the medical student, for the body does possess a structure and it is only by sharpening the principal features in a somewhat unreal way that the student can obtain a perception of their relationship to one another. The same is true of the legal textbook for the student of law.

It is surprising how many legal questions arising in day-to-day practice have not been the subject of a reported case. It is in this situation that resort must be had to first principles. I have not hesitated to explore a number of legal problems which have yet to come before the courts, for in many ways these are the most interesting.

The book is thus designed to assist the practitioner as well as the student. But the analysis of the practical problems has been provided not simply to furnish a solution for the practising lawyer but also to illumine the principle for the student and to show how fundamental legal concepts constantly surface in a new form.

Finally, I have striven to convey the intellectual excitement of commercial law, which has constantly to adapt itself to the challenge of new business methods, new instruments and new technology.

I should like to acknowledge my indebtedness to Professor Street, whose advice has been invaluable and who saved me from several errors. I have many others to thank for the fact that this book has finally seen the light of day: my long-suffering secretary, Mrs Nicky Jones, who was responsible for the typing of much of the earlier drafts; the Rushgrove Secretarial Agency, for their help with the typing in the later stages; Mrs Anne Shotts, who came to my rescue by completing a mountain of typing in an impossibly short space of time; one of my former students, Miss Philippa Hughes, who read the entire text, completed various missing references and pointed out a number of infelicities; Mr Julian Burling, who at an earlier stage helped me greatly with literature searches; business and professional friends and acquaintances, who cheerfully accommodated my propensity for asking questions and gave me a great deal of assistance in answering my inquiries; colleagues and students, past and present, whose ideas and comments contributed to my better understanding of a number of problem areas discussed in the text; Mrs Anne Lyons, who once again has come to my help with a first-class index; Mrs Breda Farrington, who performed a similar service in the preparation of the tables; the printers Hazell Watson & Viney Ltd, who set the text so meticulously; and the staff of Penguin Books, headed by Michael Dover, for all their work and for their endless patience.

I owe a special debt to Queen Mary College, for giving me sabbatical leave to enable me to finish this book; and to my wife, Catherine, and my daughter, Naomi, who for nearly a decade have endured with extraordinary fortitude the obsessions of authorship.

The law is stated on the basis of materials available to me as at 1 May 1982.

Faculty of Laws, R. M. Goode

Queen Mary College,

London

1982

Roy Goode is Emeritus Professor of Law in the University of Oxford and Emeritus Fellow of St. John's College, Oxford. A former solicitor, later a barrister and Queen's Counsel, he held chairs at Queen Mary College, University of London, and at Oxford, where he was Norton Rose Professor of English Law until his retirement in 1998. He is an Honorary Bencher of Inner Temple, a Fellow of the British Academy and of Goodenough College and the Royal Society of Arts, and an Honorary Fellow of Queen Mary, and holds honorary doctorates from the University of London and the University of East Anglia. He was for 15 years a member, and is currently an honorary member, of the Governing Council of the International Institute for the Unification of Private Law (UNIDROIT). He was knighted in 2000 for services to academic law.

Roy Goode served as chairman or member of several government committees. He has lectured extensively in this country and abroad, and is the author of a number of standard textbooks and monographs. His leisure interests include chess, walking and browsing in bookshops. He is married with one daughter and lives in Oxford.

An Expression of Thanks by the Author

I am greatly indebted to a number of people for their assistance in the preparation of this new edition. Colin Beaumont and Robert Keen of the British International Freight Association gave me many useful insights into changes in export practice and documentation. Graham Christianson of Midland Bank and Jeremy Smith and Roger Graham of Lloyds TSB patiently answered my numerous questions on current practices in relation to documentary credits and demand guarantees, as well as supplying specimen documents, some of which are reproduced in the book. Gordon Cragge, Andrew Grainger and Aileen Prendergast of SITPRO not only gave up-to-date information on export trade documentation and procedures but also furnished numerous specimen documents, which have been reproduced. Ross Tozer and Russell Nightingale of P & O Nedloyd brought me up to date on shipping documents and also kindly arranged a visit aboard one of P & O's liner container ships. To Dennis Rosenthal and Julia Owen of Berwin Leighton Paisner and Michael Moloney of First National Motor plc I express my thanks for their helpful comments on the chapters on conditional sale and hire-purchase, leasing and financing against stock and receivables, and for supplying various standard forms. I am similarly grateful to Noel Ruddy of Paul Davidson Taylor for sending me a form of factoring agreement.

From Roger Jones of Lloyds TSB Group and David McFarlane of APACS I received helpful information on the current CHAPS rules and clearing system, while Murray Cohen of BACS gave me similar information about the BACS rules. Andrew McKnight kindly supplied me with copies of some informative legal updates he had prepared and which were relevant to several chapters. Steve Leinster of the Insolvency Service, in the course of discussing proposals to change some of the rules on insolvency set-off, gave me an informal tutorial on the philosophy and effect of the complex provisions of the Enterprise Act 2002 which was very illuminating.

I am indebted to Professor Francis Reynolds of Worcester College, Oxford, for taking away from his own punishing publication schedule to review once again the chapter on carriage of goods by sea and save me from some egregious errors. I also drew on the encyclopedic knowledge of Professor Boris Kozolchyk of the University of Arizona College of Law, Tucson, on some questions of documentary credits law, and am also grateful to |Professor Jim Byrne, Director of the Institute of International Banking Law & Practice Faculty, George Mason University School of Law, who gave me the benefit of his own experience in documentary credits law and furnished me with copies of some of his institute's publications. Mr Justice

Colman kindly reviewed the chapter on commercial litigation, with particular reference to the Commercial Court, on which his own jointly authored work is the standard text. The chapter on commercial arbitration benefited greatly from the knowledge and insights of Johnny Veeder QC, one of the world's leading international commercial arbitration lawyers, and of Georgios Petrochilos, a former postgraduate research student who is now with Freshfields Bruckhaus Deringer, Paris, and whose own recently published work *Procedural Law in International Arbitration*, based on his doctoral thesis at Oxford, is required reading. As always, I benefited from exchanges with Professor Ole Lando, external professor of international and comparative commercial law at the Copenhagen Business School, this time on the vexed subject of mandatory laws, and helpful advice from Edwin Peel of Keble College, Oxford, who kindly looked through the conflicts chapter and made a number of helpful points, while Professor Peter Birks of All Souls College, Oxford, gave me reassurance, in his typically generous way, on my understanding of the gains-based/non-gains-based classification of restitutionary rights On the technical side Margot Levy came to my rescue by completely reformatting one of the chapters in which the footnotes were playing fast and loose and were completely unresponsive to my efforts at control.

Special words of thanks are due to Shaheed Fatima, an Oxford graduate and now a member of Blackstone Chambers, for rewriting the chapter on commercial litigation to reflect the sweeping changes made by the Civil Procedure Rules 1998 and developments in the practice of the Commercial Court, and also for revising the chapter on conflict of laws; to Vanessa Mak and Oren Bigos, both of them Oxford postgraduate students, for the very great deal of work they did so cheerfully and efficiently in combing through the legal literature and case law relevant to the entire field covered by the book, and to Oren for also organizing meetings and documents with outside experts. Without their help I would have been unable to bring this new edition to fruition. I should also like to express my warm thanks to Martin Toseland of Penguin Books, who, as before, are publishing the paperback version; and LexisNexis (who I shall always think of as Butterworths), who, in addition to producing the hardback version, were also responsible for the tables, index and much of the production process. So a big thank you to Julian Roskams, who oversaw production of the new edition, the tablers Kathy Brown (cases) and Sukeina Bhimji (legislation) and the outside proofreader, Caroline Ion, for their painstaking work; and to Brian Watts of Columns Design Limited, the typesetters, for his speed (which was truly amazing), accuracy and helpfulness. Finally, I wish to pay a particular tribute to Barbara Horn, a publishing consultant who performed a signal editorial and co-ordinating service for the second edition and, happily, was again willing to be pressed into service for the third. Barbara is an author's dream. She reads everything with an eagle eye, pays meticulous attention to detail and, though not a lawyer, she has an unerring instinct for inconsistencies not only in style and layout but even in the substance of the text. Sympathetic to the problems of both authors and publishers, she has skilfully and with immense hard work and good humour steered this volume to publication.

The author and the publishers would like to express their indebtedness to the following organizations for their permission to reproduce their standard forms and for supplying copies:

	Form
Barclays Bank plc	22.1
Citibank NA	21.2
Citibank Savings	27.4
Consumer Credit Trade Association	27.2, 27.3, 27.5, 28.1
First National Finance	28.9
First National Motor plc	29.1
Fortis Commercial Finance	29.2
International Chamber of Commerce	35.13, 35.14
HSBC	35.2, 35.6, 35.7
International Bullion	3.2
Laser Engineering	3.1
Lloyds TSB	35.3, 35.10, 35.15
P & O Nedlloyd	32.4, 32.5, 32.11, 32.12
SITPRO	32.3, 35.1

The forms listed above are reproduced without responsibility on the part of the organizations giving permission to do so and for illustration purposes only and should not be used for any other purpose.

List of Figures

Table of Statutes

Table of Statutory Instruments

Table of Codes

Table of EC Treaties and Legislation

Table of Conventions and Model Laws

Table of Uniform Rules, Uniform Trade Terms and Restatements

Table of Cases

B

C

D

E

G

H

I

J

K

L

M

N

O

P

Q

R

S

T

U

W

Y

Z

**Decisions of the European Court of Justice are listed below numerically. These
decisions are also included in the preceding alphabetical list.**

PART ONE
The Foundations of Commercial Law

1 The Nature and Sources of Commercial Law

1. THE LAW MERCHANT

One of the most powerful influences on human activity is the driving force of trade. Governments may be overthrown, wars may break out, large areas of a country may be devastated by natural disaster, but somehow traders find ways of establishing and continuing business relationships. The inventiveness of the scientist and the engineer in matters physical is matched by the ingenuity of the trader in constantly developing new sales techniques, new instruments to accommodate more efficiently the requirements of the commercial community, new methods of surmounting hurdles thrown up by the law or by the actions of government.

In the history of English law there have been few developments that have captured the imagination as strongly as the medieval law merchant, which for hundreds of years subsisted as a distinct source of rights, administered by courts in which the merchants themselves were judges, before ultimately becoming redundant because of the adaptation of the common law itself to commercial needs and usages.[1] The maritime courts, the courts of the fairs and boroughs,[2] and the staple courts, in company with other commercial courts of the Middle Ages, determined disputes involving foreigners not by English domestic law but according to the 'general law of nations' based on mercantile codes and customs such as the Laws of Oléron[3] and reflecting international maritime and commercial practice. To these courts, as to their counterparts elsewhere in the civilized world, came not only our own merchants but foreign traders from all parts of Europe, content to have their disputes resolved by tribunals which, though located in England, were required to

---

1 See generally Selden Society, *Select Cases on the Law Merchant*, (1908–32), vols I (ed Charles Gross) and II and III (ed Hubert Hall); F. R. Sanborn, *Origins of the Early English Maritime and Commercial Law* (1930); W. S. Holdsworth, *A History of English Law*, 17 vols (7th edn, 1956–72): vol 1, pp 562–573; vol 5, pp 60–154; vol 8, pp 99–300; L. Trakman, *The Law Merchant: The Evolution of Commercial Law* (1983); W.A. Bewes, *The Romance of the Law Merchant* (1923, reprinted 1986). The earliest known text on the English law merchant is by the anonymous author of *Lex Mercatoria*, which recent scholarship dates as completed in about 1286 . See for a detailed analysis Basile, Bestor, Coquillette and Donahue, *Lex Mercatoria and Legal Pluralism: A Late Thirteenth Century Treatise and Its Afterlife* (1998).

2 Known as courts of piepowder because they 'were frequented by chapmen of dusty feet, who wandered from mart to mart' (Gross, *Select Cases*, p xiv).

3 Oléron, an island off the west coast of France, was for some while in the ownership of the English Crown as a commune of the province of Guienne (Aquitaine). The decisions of its mercantile community were treated as of the highest authority in England, and the Rolls of Oléron were promulgated by Richard I and reproduced in the Black Book of the Admiralty and in comparable local publications.

have an equal number of English and foreign merchants as jurors[4] and were conversant with foreign mercantile usage and with the concepts of the civil law as well as the common law. The characteristics of these commercial courts were speed in adjudication (a particularly essential requirement for the foreign trader), a realistic attitude towards the proof of facts, a relative freedom from technical rules of evidence and procedure that plagued the common law courts and an acceptance of the fact that the customs of merchants generated rights which required international recognition and which, for the stability of the European markets, needed to be interpreted in a broadly uniform fashion, with an overriding requirement of good faith.[5]

Special statutes were enacted in the Middle Ages for the benefit of the merchant community generally and traders from overseas in particular. These prescribed speedy justice for foreign merchants;[6] the application of the law merchant, and the paramountcy of the merchant courts, in mercantile disputes;[7] and a procedure for formal acknowledgement of indebtedness under writings obligatory (promissory notes) by the taking and enrolment of statutory recognizances which, upon the debtor's default, gave the creditor a statutory title to his lands and chattels until payment, coupled with a right to have the debtor committed to prison indefinitely until the debt was paid.[8]

The adaptability of the *lex mercatoria* was especially notable in the recognition of negotiable instruments. Well before the birth of the English law of contract, the law merchant accepted that a right to a sum of money embodied in a bill of exchange or promissory note could be conferred even though the instrument was not under seal.[9] When the common law did ultimately come to recognize the binding force of

---

4 Carta Mercatoria 1303.

5 A requirement curiously lacking in present law as a prerequisite for the exercise of legal (as opposed to equitable) remedies. See p 95. For a fascinating account of the detailed rules imposed by the market for the protection of the customer, including the prohibition of sales by the back doors of houses or by candlelight, see Walton H. Hamilton, 'The Ancient Maxim Caveat Emptor', (1931) 50 Yale LJ 133.

6 Carta Mercatoria 1303; Statute of the Staple 1353, 27 Edw III, stat 2, c 20. Speedy trial was indeed the essence of disputes among merchants. Dr Charles Gross gives a vivid illustration of the celerity of the procedure by reference to an action tried in the piepowder court of Colchester in 1458 (Gross, *Select Cases*, vol I, p xxvi): 'The plaintiff sued for the recovery of a debt at 8 am and the defendant was summoned to appear at 9 o'clock. He did not come at that hour and the sergeant was ordered to distrain him to come at 10 o'clock, at which hour he made default. Similar defaults were recorded against him at 11 and 12 o'clock. At the latter session judgment was given in favour of the plaintiff, and appraisers were ordered to value the defendant's goods which had been attached. They made their report at 4 o'clock, and the goods were delivered to the plaintiff.'

7 Statute of the Staple, cc 5, 6, 8 and 21.

8 Statute of Merchants (also known as the Statute of Acton Burnell) 1283, 11 Edw I, as amended by the Statute of Merchants 1285, 13 Edw I; Statute of the Staple. But if the defendant remained in prison for more than three months, through failing to avail himself of the statutory right given to him to sell his land and chattels himself within that period in order to pay the debt, the creditor had to pay for the cost of keeping him provided with bread and water for the duration of his stay in prison.

9 The best modern analysis is by James Steven Rogers, *The Early History of Bills and Notes* (1995). See also J. Milnes Holden, *The History of Negotiable Instruments in English Law* (1995); Street, *Foundations of Legal Liability* (1906), vol II, pt III.

executory agreements, it imposed restrictions of a kind not operated by the merchant courts. Thus the common law required that the consideration for a promise should not be a past consideration[10] and should move from the promisee.[11] But such rules were largely bypassed by the *lex mercatoria* which, indeed, went much further, treating a bill of exchange as transferable by mere delivery, with any requisite indorsement (when the common law did not recognize the assignability of debts at all) and even laying down that in given conditions the holder of a bill could acquire a better title to it than his transferor and take free from equities,[12] contrary both to the common law principle *nemo dat quod non habet*[13] and to the equitable rule that the assignee of a chose in action takes subject to equities.[14]

Nevertheless, England contributed relatively little to the evolution of the medieval law merchant. As the centre of European commercial life, Italy had pride of place in the development of the law merchant in the Middle Ages. Not only were its cities powerful and its institutions for the resolution of commercial disputes highly organized but its merchants and lawyers were extremely creative in the development of maritime and commercial instruments , such as the bill of lading and the bill of exchange, and institutions, such as banking and insurance, all of which gave rise to a corpus of substantive rules based on mercantile usage. Such was the emphasis on commercial usage rather than technical law that lawyers were barred from taking part in the proceedings. The influence of the Italian merchants was felt throughout Europe, so that even the great fairs of Champagne were dominated by Italians.[15] By contrast, the trade dynamic that powered the *lex mercatoria* in Italy was lacking in England, which in the Middle Ages was relatively backward in commerce. So the local courts – which were not truly specialized commercial courts but rather courts of general jurisdiction over matters arising in their locality while they were sitting[16] – were concerned mainly with the resolution of disputes concerning smaller internal transactions[17] and dealt with them to a considerable extent within the framework of the common law, albeit with modifications of evidence and procedure, and a few substantive rules, to reflect the need for rapid decisions before the fair or market ended and to ensure the efficacy

10 *Lampleigh v Braithwait* (1615) Hob 105; *Roscorla v Thomas* (1842) 3 QB 234.
11 *Bourne v Mason* (1669) 1 Vent 6, 2 Keb 454, 457, 527; *Crow v Rogers* (1726) 1 Stra 592. But other cases, such as *Dutton v Poole* (1678) 2 Lev 210, were to the opposite effect, and the rule was not conclusively settled until *Tweddle v Atkinson* (1861) 1 B & S 393.
12 Rogers, *Bills and Notes*, ch 8; Milnes Holden, *Negotiable Instruments*, p 64. Lord Mansfield used to try cases with a special jury comprising experienced merchants, whose opinions he greatly valued and whom he frequently invited to dine with him in order to develop a clearer understanding of prevailing commercial practice.
13 See p 416.
14 See p 774. Similarly, the development of the bill of lading as a document of title to sea-borne goods resulted in the courts' acceptance of the right of the indorsee of the bill to recover the goods comprised in it from the shipowner even if title had not passed and the ship had not attorned to the indorsee. See further p 886.
15 Sanborn, *Maritime and Commercial Law*, p 159, citing F. Morel, *Les Juridictions Commerciales au Moyen Age* (1897), p 160, and P. Huvelin, *Essai Historique sur le Droit des Marchés et des Foires*, p 280.
16 Rogers, *Bills and Notes*, p 25.
17 Holdsworth, *English Law*, vol V, p 113.

of commercial contracts. But the central courts were active in commercial matters and though their proceedings could be formalistic and protracted, they were nevertheless building up a body of law applicable to commercial transactions, in addition to which they were often required to give decisions in accordance with the law merchant and for that purpose regularly sought expert evidence from the merchants themselves. Thus modern scholars have tended to reject the traditional, rather romanticized, view of the medieval English law merchant as a separate corpus of law and to regard it instead as 'the factual matrix within which certain types of contract are made'[18] and its rules as largely procedural in character, offering speedy justice and the relaxation of technical requirements of pleading and evidence.[19]

Ultimately, the merchant courts, with the Court of Admiralty, were vanquished by the courts of common law, partly because through the rise of *assumpsit* the courts became able to offer more efficacious contract remedies, partly because of the fact that the proceedings of some of the local courts fell into disrepute and partly because of the general desire of the central courts to increase their jurisdiction. The decline of the Staple Courts and the Court of Admiralty was largely due to one man, Sir Edward Coke, whose passionate devotion to the common law and the common law courts, and whose fierce hostility to all their competitors, resulted in the acquisition by the common law courts of most of the country's commercial litigation. The adaptation of the common law to the requirements of the merchants and the eventual integration of the *lex mercatoria* into the common law were to be brought about by two outstanding commercial lawyers, Chief Justice Holt and Lord Mansfield.

2.   THE FOUNDING OF ENGLISH COMMERCIAL LAW

As has been mentioned, the *lex mercatoria* was international rather than English and when the courts of common law, under the direction of Coke CJ, began to displace the merchant courts in the early part of the seventeenth century, they did not adopt the *lex mercatoria* as a corpus of law for disputes between merchants but, though borrowing certain of its rules, continued in the main to apply the principles of common law with which they were familiar, while making gradual adjustments designed to satisfy the merchant that he could get as good a service from them as he had previously enjoyed from his own courts. But the approach was unsystematic and some of the deviations from the law merchant were unfortunate.[20] The

---

18   John Baker, 'The Law Merchant as a Source of English Law' in *Essays in Honour of Lord Goff* (eds William Swadling and Gareth Jones,1999) at p 96.

19   See, for example, J. H. Baker, 'The Law Merchant and the Common Law Before 1700' (1979) 38 CLJ 295, reproduced in *The Legal Profession and the Common Law: Historical Essays* (ed J. H. Baker, 1986), ch 19; Rogers, *Bills and Notes*, ch 1. It may be noted, however, that the common law was largely procedural in character, and that in the Middle Ages the distinction between substantive and procedural law was less sharp than it is today.

20   One of the most pernicious examples was the invention by the common law of the maxim *caveat emptor*, which had had no place in the law merchant or, indeed, in Roman law or the civil law. See Hamilton, (1931) 50 Yale LJ 133.

moulding of the diffuse collections of rules into a coherent body of commercial law was largely the work of Lord Mansfield, who is rightly considered the founder of English commercial law. Building upon the earlier labours of Holt CJ, who had laid the foundations of the law relating to negotiable instruments, bailment and agency, Lord Mansfield proceeded to reduce the vast mass of case law on commercial disputes to an ordered structure, combining a mastery of the common law with a profound knowledge of foreign legal systems and a deep insight into the methods and usages of the mercantile world. By the time of his retirement, the law merchant had become fully absorbed into the common law, so that a century later the draftsman of the Bills of Exchange Act 1882 and the Sale of Goods Act 1893 was able to provide in both statutes that 'the rules of the common law, *including the law merchant,*' [emphasis added] should continue to apply to bills of exchange and contracts of sale respectively.[21]

In the nineteenth century the formulation of the principles of commercial law in all its major aspects was further developed and refined in the writings of a series of outstanding commercial lawyers, notably Benjamin, Blackburn, Story and Chalmers, who produced leading treatises on the law of sale; Charlesworth and Smith, whose works on commercial law became classics; Byles and Chalmers, who provided a detailed treatment of the law relating to bills of exchange; and Palmer, whose work on company law became the practitioner's vade mecum. It is a testimony to the impact of these intellectual giants that the leading work of several of them continues to be published in current editions under the author's name; and though it is many years since Smith's lucid and trenchant works were last produced, they are still used as a reference for relevant case law. Throughout the nineteenth century a strong influence continued also to be exercised by the works of the great French jurist Pothier, of the previous century, who indeed was not infrequently cited in English judgments as possessing the highest authority on questions of English commercial law.[22]

The close of the nineteenth century was illumined by the fine statutory draftsmanship of Sir Mackenzie Chalmers, whose Bills of Exchange Act 1882 and Sale of Goods Act 1893 were adopted almost verbatim throughout the Commonwealth and, as regards the latter Act, in the United States in its model code, the Uniform Sales Act.[23] Thereafter, English commercial law began to lose its international flavour, less interest being shown in mercantile developments overseas as this country, caught up in a huge expansion of trade, sought to wrestle with

---

21 Bills of Exchange Act 1882, s 97(2); Sale of Goods Act 1893, s 61(2), since replaced by the Sale of Goods Act 1979, s 62(2).

22 See *Cox v Troy* (1822) 5 B & Ald 474, per Best CJ. Sir Mackenzie Chalmers, the draftsman of the Sale of Goods Act, was profoundly influenced by Pothier's *Traité du Contrat de Vente* (1806), as is evident from the frequent references to Pothier in his own work *The Sale of Goods Act, 1893,* notably in the Introduction to the first edition (1894).

23 This Act, drafted by Professor Samuel Williston, was promulgated in 1906 and amended in 1921. It was widely adopted before being replaced by the Uniform Commercial Code (UCC) in 1952. The UCC is subject to ongoing revision, and from time to time new articles are added. The most radical part of the UCC is Article 9, relating to secured transactions, which has attracted much interest throughout the common law world; see further p 674.

commercial problems almost entirely in terms of its own law and trading practices. Inevitably, the assumption of mercantile jurisdiction by the common law courts, applying the rules of common law, resulted in the loss of flexibility and sensitivity to current trade usage that had characterized the old merchant courts. Indeed, despite the enlightened approach adopted by Lord Mansfield and those of his successors who were kindred spirits, the merchant must frequently have wondered whether the common understanding of traders in particular markets as to the effect of typical commercial instruments counted for anything in the courts, which as late as 1873 were subscribing to the view that while it was open to merchants to establish rights by trade usage, they could not subsequently rely on a new usage to displace the rights so established.[24] As we hope to demonstrate, the courts of today, if reluctant to disturb settled rules, the observance of which is so conducive to the certainty for which business people crave, are none the less more receptive to the impact of new trade customs and more alive to the importance of effectuating the presumed intention of the contracting parties.[25] Moreover, with the globalisation of international trade and finance many scholars have detected the emergence of a new *lex mercatoria* as a transnational, autonomous legal system,[26] a subject to which we shall return when discussing international commercial arbitration.[27]

3.   THE NATURE OF COMMERCIAL LAW

Commercial law is that branch of law which is concerned with rights and duties arising from the supply of goods and services in the way of trade.[28] Its scope is not clearly defined, and no two textbooks adopt the same approach as to the spheres of commercial activity that ought properly to be included in a work on the subject. There are, indeed, some who question whether commercial law is a subject at all, suggesting that the apparent monolith is in reality no more than an agglomeration of distinct subjects (sale, negotiable instruments, carriage of goods and the like), the boundaries of which may overlap but which otherwise share little in common beyond the underlying foundations of the law of contract. We shall revert to this contention in the concluding chapter.[29] For the present, it suffices to make the point

---

24 *Crouch v Crédit Foncier of England* (1873) LR 8 QB 374, per Blackburn J at 386, disapproved in *Goodwin v Robarts* (1875) LR 10 Ex Ch 337, per Cockburn CJ at 352.

25 See p 14. See also Alan Rodger, 'The codification of commercial law in Victorian Britain' (1992) 108 LQR 570; R. M. Goode, 'Twentieth century developments in commercial law' (1983) 3 Legal Studies 283.

26 See, for example, Klaus Peter Berger, *The Creeping Codification of the Lex Mercatoria* (1999), ch 2.

27 See ch 39.

28 It is conventional to treat commercial law as confined to personal property and the provision of services. But at certain points it is inescapably entwined with land law. Thus, title to goods may be lost through annexation to land, as a fixture. More important, services include the provision of finance, which is frequently secured on land by a mortgage or by a fixed or floating charge; and no treatment of commercial interests can be considered complete without at least some consideration of the nature of a floating charge and priority problems arising from conflicting security interests in land. See chs 23–25.

29 Chapter 40. In Continental Europe commercial law is considered to include company law, whereas English lawyers treat the latter as a distinct branch of law and regard commercial law as concerned primarily with transactions rather than with institutions.

that the old law merchant has long ceased to be a separate corpus of law[30] and that, unlike most civil law systems, English law does not possess a commercial code, nor does it formally subject transactions between merchants to a regime different from that of the ordinary civil law regulating transactions with or between non-traders.[31]

Nevertheless, as we shall see, principles have developed, and statutory provisions have been enacted, which are peculiar to dealings of a mercantile character.[32] Of cardinal importance in this respect is the impact of usages of trade on the rights of the parties. But this is not the only respect in which the law indirectly marks off commercial from consumer transactions. Thus, a contractual provision which in a contract between merchants may be liberally construed is likely to be subjected to a strict and literal construction when sought to be applied against a consumer. Again, the mercantile character of the contract in dispute may influence the court in deciding whether to strike down an exemption clause, and this approach is now reflected in legislation.[33]

The underlying motif that marks out the legal treatment of commercial trans-actions is a recognition of the need to protect the free flow of trade and to avoid as far as possible the application of rules that will operate to the disadvantage of the bona fide purchaser in the ordinary course of business.[34] It has to be said that on the whole Parliament has been more sensitive to this need than the courts, which on every occasion when legislation has been passed to cut down the scope of the *nemo dat* rule in favour of the innocent purchaser have striven to preserve the rule by a restrictive interpretation of the relevant statute.[35] But the task of maintaining a fair balance is far from easy. The process by which goods are marketed is often complex. Many interests are involved and these may conflict. It is impossible to have a clear perception of commercial law without at least a basic understanding of the mechanism of the transaction under consideration, the parties affected and the documents they employ. Thus, the rules evolved by the courts in relation to c.i.f. contracts will be meaningful to the reader only if he or she is able to visualize the sequence of operations involved in the ordering and movement of goods, the impact of new and speedier methods of transportation, the hazards that may arise for one party or another at different stages of the transaction and the way in which provision may be made against such hazards by the parties in their agreements or by rules of law where the agreements are silent.[36] Again, the law relating to documentary credits and the

---

30 Indeed, it was never an organized body of law at all, rather a diffusion of uncodified usage.

31 Contrast the position in civil law countries, where it is usual to have a commercial code to regulate relations between merchants or those engaging in contracts of a mercantile character. As to the narrowing of the gap between civil law and commercial law, see Boris Kozolchyk, 'The Commercialization of Civil Law and the Civilization of Commercial Law' (1979) 40 Louisiana L Rev 3. See also Geoffrey Samuel, 'Civil and Commercial Law: a Distinction Worth Making?' (1986) 102 LQR 569.

32 See pp 1203 ff for a discussion of the principles and policies of commercial law.

33 See pp 97 ff.

34 For a general discussion of the philosophical foundations of English commercial law, see Roy Goode, *Commercial Law in the Next Millennium* (the 1997 Hamlyn Lectures), pp 12 ff.

35 See pp 21, 416 ff.

36 See chs 34, 36.

rights and duties of parties to negotiable instruments cannot be understood without a basic knowledge of the main stages in the journey of the documents involved, from the time when application is made for their issue to the point of their ultimate destination. All this we shall try to explain in due course.

4.   THE INTERESTS TO BE PROTECTED

Inevitably, commercial law is dominated by the sale of goods; and central to this subject is the contract between seller and buyer. But sales are not the concern of the parties alone. There are many other interests which require protection by the law. The consuming public at large needs safeguards to ensure that products put on the market will not be injurious to life or health; that they will not be held to ransom by monopolies or restrictive trade practices or be deceived by false or misleading advertising; and that trading activity will be controlled to the extent necessary to protect the national economy.[37] The activities of a particular seller are of concern also to sellers in a similar line of business, who are entitled to protection against unfair trading, eg through passing off or infringement of a patent or trade mark or through inducement of a breach of contract subsisting between them and third parties. The owner of goods disposed of without his authority has an interest to protect, as has a purchaser who in good faith buys from one not entitled to sell, or a repairer who in good faith executes work on goods deposited with him for repair by a person not owning the goods or authorized to order repairs. Special classes of buyer may need distinct legislative protection, for example buyers on credit or at auction. The operations of all traders are of concern to their creditors, particularly in the event of insolvency.

It will be obvious, therefore, that the law relating to commercial transactions goes well beyond the law of contract, invading the provinces of property, tort, equity, restitution, company and insolvency law, and entering to a significant degree into the public law sector. Thus, a retail buyer injured by a defective product may have a strict liability claim against the manufacturer by statute[38] or at common law for negligence;[39] a party innocently purchasing goods comprised in an undischarged

37   In bygone years Parliament went to quite extraordinary lengths to fulfil this objective. Thus in the reign of Charles II, in order to deal with a glut of wool resulting from restrictions on the export of this commodity, statutes were passed making it an offence for a person to be buried in a shroud not made entirely of sheep's wool or to be put in a coffin lined or faced with material other than sheep's wool (18 Car 2, c 4 (1666), replaced by Car 2, stat 1, c 3 (1678), as amended by 32 Car 2, c 1 (1680)). This remarkable piece of legislation was not repealed until 1814 (14 Geo 3, c 108).

38   Consumer Protection Act 1987, Pt I, implementing (though imperfectly) the EC Directive on Product Liability 85/374/EEC. The subject of product liability forms part of consumer law and is not discussed in the present work. For a detailed examination of the statutory provisions, see C. J. Miller and R. S. Goldberg, *Product Liability* (2nd edn, 2004), and for a comparative study within the European Community, Christopher Hodges, *Product Liability* (1993). The best theoretical treatment of product liability within the wider context of civil liability as a whole is by Jane Stapleton, *Product Liability* (1994), a perceptive work which poses some fundamental questions as to the purpose and policy of a product liability regime and the stability of the new doctrine.

39   For which the reader is referred to textbooks on the law of tort.

hire-purchase agreement may be exposed to an action for conversion,[40] while a restitutionary claim may be made to the proceeds received by the hirer: a security interest created in a credit transaction may be vulnerable in the event of the debtor's bankruptcy or liquidation;[41] a supplier of goods to which a false trade description has been applied may incur a liability to prosecution,[42] whether or not guilty of any breach of contract. Moreover, commercial law is not confined to goods, but extends to a vast range of transactions relating to documents and services, including finance, carriage of goods and insurance.

In this book the emphasis is on commercial transactions, that is, transactions in which both parties deal with each other in the course of business, whether as merchants or as provider and recipient of financial or other services supplied for business purposes. Though some reference is made to consumer transactions in the context of unfair contract terms,[43] we shall not be concerned with other aspects of consumer protection, a vast subject which merits a volume to itself and to which several excellent publications are now devoted.[44]

5.   THE PRINCIPAL SOURCES OF COMMERCIAL LAW

(i)   Contract

While many branches of the common law affect business transactions, the foundation on which commercial law rests is the law of contract. Commercial transactions are, after all, specific forms of contract, and while each type of commercial contract is governed by rules peculiar to that type, all are subject to the general principles of contract law except to the extent to which these have been displaced by statute or by mercantile usage.[45]

1.   Express and implied terms generally

When considering the law-making capacity of the parties themselves, one must avoid the assumption that they have necessarily negotiated each individual term. Certain basic terms will, of course, be bargained in almost every transaction, such as the *res* which is to be the subject of the contract and the price to be paid for it; and many commercial contracts are indeed hammered out by the parties term by term, and can truly be said to represent their own creation, to which they may be assumed to have addressed their minds. But a large number of commercial agreements are standard-term contracts and are not individually negotiated. Indeed, it would be impossible for business to cope with the enormous volume of bargains conducted daily if every term of every agreement, no matter how consistent

---

40 See p 415.
41 See pp 838 ff.
42 Under the Trade Descriptions Act 1968.
43 See p 97.
44 See, for example, *Cranston's Consumers and the Law* (3rd edn, eds Colin Scott and Julia Black, 2000); Brian Harvey and Deborah Parry, *Law of Consumer Protection and Fair Trading* (6th edn, 2000); and, in relation to product liability, the literature referred to in n 38.
45 See pp 13, 88.

the pattern of business, had to be negotiated step by step between the parties. The standard- term contract is thus an essential feature of business life, and some such contracts are so widely adopted as to become in effect non-parliamentary statutes, attracting detailed analysis in textbooks and a body of case law as disputes are referred to the courts or to arbitration.[46]

Where the supplier is in a substantial way of business, the standard-term contract may be of his own making, or that of his lawyers. But frequently business people use standard contracts devised by others, for example the particular trade association to which they belong,[47] often without much familiarity with the detail of the contract or understanding of its legal implications. The problem becomes still more acute in relation to international transactions,[48] for which many model contracts have been settled by international organizations, such as the United Nations Economic Commission for Europe and the International Chamber of Commerce.[49] In such cases the document is required to accommodate the needs of parties who *ex hypothesi* are operating in different states and are governed by different systems of law, so that the scope for ignorance or misunderstanding of the legal effects of the contract is greatly increased. This does not, however, alter the fact that the parties to the contract, in adopting the standard terms, are making their own law,[50] and such model contracts perform an increasingly valuable function as traders become familiar with them.

Frequently, the parties to a contract do not set out all the terms in the contract itself but find it convenient to incorporate terms by reference to a variety of other documents, eg standard contract terms published by an independent body or group of institutions, a model code of practice or usage, a set of standard trade terms or definitions.

As we shall see, English law has a somewhat extended view of what constitutes a consensual undertaking, in the sense that a contract is considered to embrace not only express terms (including terms incorporated by reference) and terms implied in fact or from a prior course of dealing[51] but also rights and duties implied by law or by mercantile usage, which in other systems would be regarded as constituting independent, non-consensual norms.[52]

---

46 Prime examples are the JCT forms of building contract, to which complete textbooks have been devoted and which have been the subject of many reported cases.

47 For the most important standard commodity contracts, see Clive Schmitthoff, *The Export Trade* (10th edn, eds Leo D'Arcy, Carole Murray and Barbara Cleave, 2000), paras 32–010 ff. Standard forms of contract used in consumer credit transactions are published by the Consumer Credit Trade Association.

48 English law does not in general draw a formal distinction between national and international transactions so far as sources of law are concerned.

49 For example, the ICC Model Commercial Agency Contract (ICC Publication No 496) and Model Distribution Contract (No 518).

50 For a general discussion, see Clive Schmitthoff, 'The Unification or Harmonisation of Law by Means of Standard Contracts and General Conditions' (1968) 17 ICLQ 551.
    When criticizing standard contracts and model codes, it is important to avoid the assumption that faulty drafting or misconceived policy is necessarily the responsibility of the draftsperson. Many such contracts and codes are born only after a lengthy gestation period involving prolonged examination and negotiations. Often the parties settle for less than the best in order to secure a compromise that will save the work as a whole. Those who pour scorn on what are undoubtedly defective features in many contracts and codes would do well to remember that the best is often the enemy of the good.

51 See p 88.

52 See below.

2. Uncodified custom and usage

Of great importance as a source of obligation in commercial contracts are the unwritten customs and usages of merchants.[53] The impact of these on the content and interpretation of contract terms cannot be overstated. It is, perhaps, this feature above all which distinguishes commercial from other contracts, a distinction not formally adopted by the law.[54] The fertility of the business mind and the fact that a practice which begins life by having no legal force acquires over time the sanctity of law are key factors to which the commercial lawyer must continually be responsive. Is a particular document a document of title? The House of Lords may have said no, possibly more than once. But how long ago was the ruling given? Cannot it now be said, in another time, that the acceptance of this document as a document of title in mercantile usage is so entrenched as to justify according it legal recognition as such? Is a payment instrument outside the Bills of Exchange Act negotiable? In principle, yes, if so accepted by the mercantile community, which may happen immediately or only over time.

What is it that gives binding force to unwritten mercantile usage? Is it the express or implied adoption of the usage by the parties in their contract? Or does mercantile usage have independent normative force? The question has been much debated in the context of international commercial arbitration and the controversy as to the existence of an international *lex mercatoria*.[55] In some legal systems the binding force of mercantile usage does not depend on adoption by contract,[56] but in the theory of English law a usage takes effect as an express or implied term of the contract between the parties[57] and is dependent for its validity on satisfying certain external legal criteria, namely certainty and consistency of practice, reasonableness, notoriety, and conformity with mandatory law. Moreover, in order to constitute a usage the practice must be observed from a sense of legally binding obligation, not as a matter of mere courtesy or convenience or a desire to accommodate a customer's wishes.[58]

---

53 See further p 88.

54 A custom is a rule of a particular locality, a usage is a settled practice of a particular trade or profession, but often the two terms are used interchangeably. See generally 12 *Halsbury's Laws of England* (4th edn, 1998 reissue), title 'Custom and Usage'.

55 See p 19.

56 See Clive M. Schmitthoff, *International Trade Usages*, a research report prepared for the Institute of International Business Law and Practice of the International Chamber of Commerce (1987), pp 25 ff.

57 Once a usage has been recognized in decisions, the courts may well be prepared to take judicial notice of it in subsequent cases, but even then it is only upon the basis that the parties must be supposed to have intended to contract with reference to the usage.

58 See *General Reinsurance Corporation v Forsakringsaktiebolaget Fennia Patria* [1983] QB 856, per Slade LJ, at 874; *Libyan Arab Foreign Bank v Bankers Trust Co* [1989] QB 728, per Staughton J at 757, holding that there was no sufficient evidence of a usage that a sum standing to the credit of a Eurodollar account could be withdrawn only through a United States clearing system. As I have pointed out elsewhere, the requirement of belief in the binding nature of the observed practice, which has its counterpart, *opinio juris*, in international customary law, is based on either circularity or paradox, for if the belief is correct, it is not necessary, while if erroneous, it would convert a non-binding practice into a binding one through error. See Roy Goode, 'Usage and Its Reception in Transnational Commercial Law' (1997) 46 ICLQ 1 at p 9. But it is not easy to come up with a meaningful alternative.

3.   Codified custom and usage

It is in the nature of unwritten custom or usage that its meaning and content may be understood differently by different people; indeed, the very existence of an alleged usage may be challenged. In areas of business or finance with a highly developed and widely used body of custom or usage it is particularly important to avoid disputes of this kind. To that end, national and international trade associations and clearing houses may find it convenient to formulate the relevant usages in a published code or set of rules. These will rarely reflect existing usage in every particular, since the opportunity will usually be taken to make improvements to established practice and procedures, but the intended effect of the code or rules is to state or restate best practice. They may be given effect either by making adherence to them a condition of membership of the relevant association or clearing house or by incorporation into individual contracts. At the international level the prime mover in the codification of international trade usage is the International Chamber of Commerce (ICC), an international non-governmental organization serving world business. Working through its specialist commissions, the ICC has produced numerous uniform rules which are adopted by incorporation into contracts. These fall broadly into three groups: banking and insurance, international trade and international transport. The most long-standing and successful of the various ICC formulations is the Uniform Customs and Practice for Documentary Credits (UCP), first promulgated by the ICC in 1933. Bankers throughout the world have adopted the UCP,[59] which is now used almost universally in documentary credit transactions. Other ICC uniform rules in banking and insurance include the Uniform Rules for Collections,[60] the Uniform Rules for Demand Guarantees[61] and the Uniform Rules for Contract Bonds.[62] In the field of international trade extensive use is made of Incoterms,[63] while in relation to transport the ICC has collaborated with the United Nations Commission on Trade and Development (UNCTAD) in producing the UNCTAD/ICC Rules for Multimodal Transport Documents.[64] The ICC has also instantly endorsed the ISP 98 on International Standby Practices.[65]

In English law codified customs and usages, like those which are uncodified, depend for their operation on express or implied adoption in the contract.

---

59 The current edition is that published in 1993 (UCP 500) and now in course of revision. The UCP have been supplemented by the eUCP, published in 2002 and governing the presentation of electronic records. See p 591.

60 Promulgated by the International Chamber of Commerce in 1953 (under the title Uniform Rules for the Collection of Commercial Paper), revised in 1967, 1978 and 1995 (URC 552).

61 ICC Publication No 458, 1992. These rules are designed for demand guarantees and performance bonds under which payment is to be made on written demand and presentation of other specified documents without proof of actual default by the principal obligor. See further p 000.

62 ICC Publication No 524, 1994. These rules are designed primarily for suretyship bonds and guarantees, triggered by proof of actual default, though, where the relevant bond so provides, default may be established by production of a document showing default.

63 A set of rules for the interpretation of commonly used price and delivery terms in international trade. The first edition was published in 1953; the current edition is *Incoterms 2000*. See pp 866 ff.

64 ICC Publication No 481, 1992.

65 Produced by the Institute of International Banking Law & Practice Inc.

(ii) Domestic legislation

Until a few decades ago Parliament adopted a laissez-faire attitude towards commercial transactions, and in so far as legislation was enacted, it tended to be of a declaratory or permissive character, as in the case of the Sale of Goods Act 1893, which in its original form[66] imported implied terms into contracts of sale which the parties were free to exclude or restrict as they chose, within the limits permitted by general contract law. For a long time, commercial transactions were shielded from the statutory intervention that was a growing trend in relation to other fields of human activity, and this relative immunity from control reflected a general philosophy that trade was the life-blood of the nation and that measures that might interfere with the free flow of trade should, if possible, be avoided.

All this has now changed. Exemption clauses in consumer sale and consumer hire-purchase transactions have been outlawed, and even in purely commercial transactions their scope has been restricted[67] by the Unfair Contract Terms Act 1977. Of much greater significance in relation to consumer contracts are the numerous EC consumer protection directives that have been implemented by statutory instrument, including the Unfair Terms in Consumer Contracts Regulations 1999, under which a wide range of unfair terms is rendered void.[68] Rules of competition law may also invalidate anti-competitive agreements and practices.

Hence while there remains substantial scope for free bargaining between parties to a commercial transaction in what is still a mixed economy, the parameters within which they are at liberty to make their own law are steadily shrinking.[69] In analysing commercial law cases it is important constantly to bear in mind the diminishing role of the common law in defining contractual obligations and the growing impact of enacted law and of government intervention and EC directives and regulations. These require a treatise of their own and are outside the scope of the present work.

(iii) External sources of law

1.   International conventions and model laws

With the absorption of the law merchant into the common law, commercial law became less international and more local than once it was, a tendency accentuated by the growth of legislative activity both in this country and elsewhere designed to provide for problems of an internal character. Happily, this trend has not passed unchecked. The sheer volume and complexity of modern international trade have made cooperation at an international level not merely desirable but essential to the free flow of trade among nations. Quite apart from the establishment of free trading

---

66 That is, prior to amendment by the Misrepresentation Act 1967 and the Supply of Goods (Implied Terms) Act 1973. See now the Sale of Goods Act 1979 (repealing and re-enacting the Sale of Goods Act 1893), as amended, the Unfair Contract Terms Act 1977, ss 6, 11 and Sch 2, and the Supply of Goods and Services Act 1982.

67 See pp 97 ff.

68 See p 98.

69 See Grant Gilmore, *The Death of Contract* (1995).

associations, such as EFTA,[70] and the formulation of contractually incorporated uniform rules and trade terms published by international organizations such as the International Chamber of Commerce,[71] much has been achieved in the harmonization of trade law by international conventions.[72] Continuous attention is devoted to measures for the unification of different branches of international trade law. Prominent among the organizations involved in this work are the United Nations Commission on International Trade Law (UNCITRAL),[73] the International Institute for the Unification of Private Law (UNIDROIT),[74] the Hague Conference on Private International Law[75] and organs of the Council of Europe[76] and the European Community.[77]

70 The European Free Trade Association, brought into existence by the Convention of Stockholm in 1960.
71 See p 14.
72 Examples are the various international transport conventions and the mainly private law conventions concluded under the auspices of one or other of the international organizations referred to below.
73 Established by the United Nations in 1968 as a specialized agency for the harmonization of private commercial law, UNCITRAL has been responsible for a variety of UN conventions, including the 1980 Convention on Contracts for the International Sale of Goods, the 1995 Convention on Independent Guarantees and Stand-By Letters of Credit and the 2001 Convention on the Assignment of Receivables in International Trade. There are also numerous UNCITRAL Model Laws, for example, the 1985 Model Law on International Commercial Arbitration, the 1996 Model Law on Electronic Commerce, the 1997 Model Law on Cross-Border Insolvency and the 2001 Model Law on Electronic Signatures. It has also published various legal guides.
74 An international, intergovernmental organization in Rome established in 1926 pursuant to a bilateral agreement between the Italian government and the League of Nations. It was responsible for, among other instruments, the 1988 Conventions on International Factoring and International Financial Leasing and, with the International Civil Aviation Organization, the 2001 Cape Town Convention on International Interests in Mobile Equipment and the Aircraft Equipment Protocol thereto. UNIDROIT has played a prominent role in the preparatory work for conventions later sponsored by other bodies. Examples in the field of contract and commercial law are the 1956 Convention on the Contract for the Carriage of Goods by Road (CMR) and the 1980 UN Convention on Contracts for the International Sale of Goods (UNCITRAL) (see ch 33). UNIDROIT has also produced a highly successful international restatement, *Principles of International Commercial Contracts*, which is not a binding instrument (and therefore did not involve the participation of governments) but has frequently been used in arbitral proceedings as indicative of the best rule or to supplement a more general provision of CISG and as a guide to legislatures in the reform of their contract law. In addition, it has published the *Guide to International Master Franchise Agreements* (1998) and produces a periodical, the *Uniform Law Review*.
75 First held in 1893, the Hague Conference met regularly for many years, but after a period of decline, fell into abeyance during the Second World War. It was revived in permanent form by a treaty coming into force in 1955. The Conference has produced a number of conventions, including, in the field of commercial law, the 1986 Convention on the Law Applicable to Contracts for the International Sale of Goods and the 2002 Convention on the Law Applicable to Certain Rights in Respect of Securities Held with an Intermediary.
76 The Council of Europe came into being in 1949 with the objective of bringing European states into closer cooperation for the purpose of securing the maintenance of essential human rights and the development of social and economic progress. It has produced numerous conventions, including the 1977 European Convention on Products Liability in Regard to Personal Injury and Death, which was effectively superseded by the 1985 EEC product liability Directive (1985/374/EEC).
77 For example, the 1968 Brussels Convention on Jurisdiction and the Enforcement of Judgments in Civil and Commercial Matters, now replaced by Council Regulation (EC) No 44/2001 of 22 December 2000 on jurisdiction and the recognition and enforcement of judgments in civil and commercial matters (commonly referred to as 'Brussels I'), and the 1980 Rome Convention on the Law Applicable to Contractual Obligations. But most harmonization by the EC is now effected through the issue of Directives and Regulations, which are seen as more efficient instruments. See below as to EC law.

Where projects of these bodies are brought to a successful conclusion, the outcome is usually either an international convention or a model law. Conventions are not, as such, sources of law in England, having no force within the country until implemented by legislation; but when implemented, they must be adopted as they stand except to the extent that the relevant convention permits reservations or declarations excluding or modifying particular parts or provisions. By contrast, a state is free to adopt a model law with such additions and amendments as it chooses.

2. European Community law

An entirely new situation arose with the entry of the United Kingdom into the European Communities on 1 January 1973. In taking membership of the Communities, we accepted the provisions of the treaties, regulations and other law-making acts of the Community organs as part of the law applicable in England.[78] Starting with the EC Treaty 1957, which established the European Economic Community, there has been a series of treaties[79] which amended the EC Treaty 1957 and which have been brought together by the Treaty of Nice into the Consolidated Treaty Establishing the European Community. Decisions of the European Court of Justice establish that Community law is not simply an external legal order in the traditional international law sense but a body of law which, though distinct from the national law of a member state, is part of the law applicable in that state, penetrating it by its own force without being dependent on adoption by the state's own legislation — in our case, the European Communities Act 1972 as amended.[80] In any event, that Act expressly requires that all rights and remedies created by or arising under the Treaties and having direct legal effect in accordance therewith are to be recognized and available in law.[81]

It is a well-settled principle of Community law that in the event of a divergence between Community law and national law it is Community law which prevails. It is now clear that as a matter of English law Parliament is no longer sovereign, a point graphically illustrated by the decision of the House of Lords in *Factortame Ltd v Secretary of State (No 2)*,[82] in which, following a ruling by the European Court of Justice, the House of Lords granted an interim injunction against the Crown restraining the Secretary of State from enforcing United Kingdom legislation where

---

78 The phrase 'law applicable in England', used here in preference to 'English law', is borrowed from J.-P. Warner (1977) 93 LQR 349 at 351. It is a convenient way of making the point that while EC law operates in England, it constitutes a legal order distinct from English national law, the former being derived from the Community, the latter from United Kingdom institutions.

79 The Single European Act 1986, the Treaty of Maastricht 1992, which introduced the concept of the European Union (now embodied in Title I of the Treaty of Nice as the Consolidated Treaty on European Union), the Treaty of Amsterdam 1997 and the Treaty of Nice 2001.

80 By the European Communities (Amendment) Act 1993 giving effect to the Maastricht Treaty and the European Communities (Amendment) Act 2002 implementing the Treaty of Nice. See generally Trevor Hartley, *The Foundations of European Community Law* (5th edn, 2003), ch 8, pp 261 ff; Paul Craig and Gráinne de Búrca, *EU Law: Text, Cases and Materials* (3rd edn, 2003).

81 Section 2(1).

82 [1991] 1 All ER 70.

there were strong grounds for contending that this was invalid as incompatible with Community law.[83]

The series of treaties referred to above has given a powerful impetus to the development of the European Common Market and there is a steadily increasing flow of directives and regulations relevant to English commercial law and covering such diverse matters as competition law, company law, banking, insurance, the provision of financial services and consumer protection, as well as regulations on insolvency and jurisdiction. As the result of this growth in the *acquis communautaire*, there has been a substantial increase in the Community's external competence, which is sometimes exclusive and sometimes shared with member states. This restricts the freedom of member states to negotiate and conclude international conventions; increasingly, provision is made in such conventions for regional economic integration organizations (of which the EC is by far the most important) to become parties.[84]

3.   *Transnational commercial law*

We have previously remarked how, with the disappearance of the medieval law merchant, commercial law in England, as elsewhere, tended to lose its international flavour and become predominantly national in character. This has remained true even of those branches of law which might at first sight be thought international, namely private international law (otherwise known as the conflict of laws) and the law of international trade. Thus English courts apply English private international law; and in England international trade law is generally used to denote the English law governing international trade transactions.

Growing recognition of the need for harmonization of principles and rules of commercial law governing international transactions has resulted in the formulation of a wide variety of instruments – conventions, model laws, uniform rules, uniform trade terms, model contracts – designed to reduce the application of purely domestic rules of law in international commercial trading transactions by prescribing rules of international application. But the harmonizing process is not confined to concerted international activity. The common practice of merchants may establish an uncodified international trade usage. The courts of one jurisdiction may decide to adopt a principle established in another or may reach the same point independently. In each case the result is the same, the internationalization of what was at one time a purely local rule. A good illustration is the doctrine of sovereign immunity from jurisdiction, which was at one time regarded as absolute but is now almost universally confined to *acta jure imperii* as opposed to *acta jura gestionis*. When in 1981 the House of Lords decided to abandon the old rule and to bring English law into line with that of other jurisdictions by removing sovereign immunity in relation

---

83 The European Court of Justice has since ruled that the legislation is indeed incompatible in certain respects with EC law.

84 Examples are Article 48 of the Cape Town Convention on International Interests in Mobile Equipment 2001, Article XVII of the Aircraft Equipment Protocol 2001 to that convention, and Article 18 of the Hague Convention on the law applicable to certain rights in respect of securities held with an intermediary, otherwise known as the PRIMA Convention.

to the trading activities of a state,[85] it thereby received into English law a restrictive doctrine of sovereign immunity which had by that time become adopted by almost all influential trading nations.[86]

The product of this process of harmonization through international instruments and conscious or unconscious parallelism has become known as transnational commercial law, a body of codified and uncodified principles and rules which cross national borders.[87]

The growth of international trade and the influence of mercantile usage have led several influential scholars to conclude that there exists a body of uncodified international commercial law, the new *lex mercatoria*, which has normative force in its own right and is dependent neither on incorporation by contract nor on adoption by legislation or judicial reception in a national legal system. The thesis adopted in this book is that while uncodified international usages undoubtedly exist (though they may be hard to identify), they do not have legal force merely by virtue of their existence; they are given effect by the express or implied adoption of the parties or by reception into the law of a national or supranational[88] legal system.[89]

(iv) 'Soft' law

The legal norms described above are buttressed by a variety of forms of 'soft' law, that is, rules which are not legally binding but which in practice will normally be adhered to by those who subscribe to them, whether because of moral suasion, the sanction of expulsion from membership of the trade association promulgating the rules or the fear of adverse legislation or administrative action if the rules are not observed. Among these forms of soft law are voluntary codes of practice,[90] ombudsmen schemes and rules for non-binding mediation adopted by different sectors of industry, commerce and finance. International restatements of scholars of the kind referred to above are also a form of soft law in that they do not themselves

---

85 *I Congreso del Partido* [1983] 1 AC 244. See p 1073.

86 *I Congreso del Partido* [1983] 1 AC 244 per Lord Wilberforce at 261.

87 See Filip de Ly, *International Business Law and Lex Mercatoria* (1992); Klaus Peter Berger, *The Creeping Codification of the Lex Mercatoria*; Jan H. Dalhuisen, *Dalhuisen on International Commercial, Financial and Trade Law* (2000); Norbert Horn and Clive M.Schmitthoff (eds), *The Transnational Law of International Commercial Transactions* (1982). Of particular interest in this regard are the formulations of contract law principles by two different groups of scholars, *Principles of International Commercial Contracts*, directed by Professor Joachim Bonell and prepared and published under the auspices of UNIDROIT (though not involving the imprimatur of governments), and *Principles of European Contract Law*, prepared by the Commission on European Contract Law, a private body, under the chairmanship of Professor Ole Lando. The second and final phase of the UNIDROIT work received the imprimatur of the Governing Council of UNIDROIT in April 2004; the third and final phase of the PECL was published in 2003 and will be absorbed into a wider European Civil Code project under the direction of Professor Christian von Bar.

88 Eg the EC.

89 See further p 1197.

90 In P. Craig and C. Harlow (eds), *Lawmaking in the European Union* (1998) see G. Howells, ' "Soft Law" in EC Consumer Law', p 322, and F. Beveridge and S. Nott, 'A Hard Look at Soft Law', p 288; and see R. B. Ferguson, 'The Legal Status of Non-Statutory Codes of Practice' [1988] JBL 12 and literature there cited.

possess normative force. They are, however, a rather harder version of soft law in that arbitral tribunals not infrequently resort to them as providing the source of a rule of transnational commercial law and they can also be used as a form of model law by legislatures.

6.   THE LIMITATIONS OF JUDICIAL PRECEDENT

It is a common experience of the legal practitioner that things are not as they seem, and that what appears in a textbook as a clear and logical rule of law begins to lose its sharpness when applied to a concrete problem and, under the cold and concentrated scrutiny of lengthy argument, to be exposed as ambiguous, uncertain, capricious and insufficiently refined to distinguish one fact-situation from another.[91]

The world of commerce functions largely on the principle that what are generally accepted by business people as the legal consequences of their actions will be recognized by the courts: and judges, for their part, respond to this need for effectuating commercial usage by striving to reach a result that would commend itself to business people as reasonable. But commercial practice is constantly changing, with old methods of business giving way to new and novel forms of contract constantly evolving. It is thus in commercial law that the impact of the inductive approach of the English judge is most noticeable. The judge does not work like the textbook writer. The former deals with the particular dispute before him and, instead of reasoning from an abstract principle to a concrete result, feels his way to the right conclusion and, within the limits permitted by prior authority, shapes his statement of principle to reach that conclusion. This process may lead him to propound a new principle or to modify an existing principle; and his willingness to do either of these things will depend on his own view of the extent to which previous case law leaves him free to manoeuvre, a matter on which different judges may hold differing opinions. The textbook writer, on the other hand, is not called upon to adjudicate on a concrete dispute. His concern is to extract, criticize and reduce to order statements of principle enunciated in cases already decided and to speculate on the likely or desirable outcome of such other issues as may occur to him. Since his ability to visualize new issues is dependent on information available to him at the time of writing, and on the extent of his own imagination, his exposition of principle is necessarily incomplete, being predominantly concerned with what the courts have decided in relation to previous fact-situations, rather than with the way they will react in the future to new sets of facts, most of which are likely to be outside his field of contemplation. In short, the textbook writer tends to be preoccupied with the pathology of law.

---

91 See *Cordell v Second Clanfield Properties Ltd* [1969] 2 Ch 9, in which Megarry J, having been referred by counsel to a passage in a textbook of which the learned judge himself was a joint author, observed (at 16) that a textbook writer, while a persuasive influence and a valuable fertilizer of thought, 'has to form his ideas without the aid of the purifying ordeal of skilled argument on the specific facts of a contested case. Argued law is tough law … Today, as of old, by good disputing shall the law be well known.'

It is for this reason that the practitioner learns not to place excessive reliance on previous decisions but to apply to his knowledge of these a sense of the court's likely reaction to a given set of facts. For his experience has taught him that not infrequently a judge distinguishes a previous case that will lead him to an undesirable result by relying on some difference in the facts as justifying a different conclusion; and in so doing he may modify the prior statement of principle, holding it to be inapplicable to cases of the type before him. Commercial law is peculiarly susceptible to this technique by reason of the dynamic force of trade. Hence in reading this book the student should bear in mind that there are few absolutes in English law, and that while the propositions stated in this and subsequent chapters are believed to hold good for the majority of situations, there will always be cases in which the stated rule is displaced or requires to be refined. This is as true of general contract principles as it is of the more detailed rules of a particular branch of commercial law.

7.   THE PROBLEM OF LANGUAGE

Much of the work of the courts is taken up with the construction of contracts and statutes. Those whose business it is to work with words soon acquire an appreciation of the limitations of language. The meaning of a word depends on the context in which it is used and the purposes for which its meaning is required to be elucidated. One of the great myths propagated by lawmakers is that everything can be made clear by definition. But a word or phrase can be defined only in terms of other words or phrases; so ought not these in turn be defined? The excessive use of definitions is one of the curses of modern legislation and more often than not seems only to obscure rather than to illumine the meaning. Fortunately, the legislature is sometimes prepared to recognize that certain words are wholly undefinable. Thus the word 'possession' appears in innumerable statutes, but Parliament has wisely chosen not to attempt a definition.

It is, moreover, astonishingly hard to avoid ambiguity. Ambiguity pervades legislation, contracts and even textbooks. Often it passes wholly undetected. Consider, for example, Rule 1 of s 18 of the Sale of Goods Act 1979:

> Where there is an unconditional contract for the sale of specific goods in a deliverable state the property in the goods passes to the buyer when the contract is made …

No ambiguity there, you will say. In order for R1 to apply, the goods must be identified and in a deliverable state at the time of the contract. But is this what the Rule means? What if the goods are agreed to be sold as specific goods but are not in fact identifiable?[92] And might the phrase 'deliverable state' be referring not to the actual condition of the goods but to the assumption made by the terms of the contract?[93]

A related problem is how literal should be the interpretation of a contract or a statute. The purpose of language is to manifest the intention of the maker, whether he be a contracting party, Parliament or some other law-making agency. But the

92 See p 208.
93 See p 233.

courts are bound by the language in the sense that if the meaning of the provision to be construed is clear, it is the duty of the courts to give effect to the provision, even if this means going against the intention of those by whom or on whose behalf the provision was drafted. As the courts are the arbiters of the question whether a provision is or is not unambiguous, a judge in a particular case is usually able to give effect to what he or she conceives to be the intention of the contract or the statute, even where the language appears to suggest otherwise. Even so, the judge will have to make a choice between a literal and a liberal construction, and this cannot be done by reference to the words of the contract or statute itself but only by reference to such extrinsic evidence as is available and admissible, or, if there is none, by making assumptions which in many cases are little more than value-judgments. For example, in *Newtons of Wembley Ltd v Williams*,[94] where B obtained a car from S by false pretences and resold it to an innocent buyer, T, after S had rescinded the contract, the Court of Appeal had to consider whether s.9 of the Factors Act 1889 divested S of his title and vested ownership in T. In the course of his judgment Sellers, LJ, commented:

> Before one takes too favourable a view for the sub-buyer and too harsh a view against the true owner of the goods as to the cases where s.9 can be invoked, one must remember that it is taking away the right which would have existed at common law, and for myself I should not be prepared to enlarge it more than the words clearly permitted and required.[95]

Now whether this reflects a view that, other things being equal, the rights of the original owner are to have priority over the protection of the innocent purchaser, or the still broader view that any statutory provision cutting down a common law right is to be restrictively construed, an assumption of some kind is being made, namely that some special sanctity attaches to ownership, or to rules of common law, which puts on the party seeking to displace the title or the common law rule the onus of showing that this was Parliament's intention. A different court might well have reached the opposite conclusion, based on a value-judgment that in commercial transactions it was important to protect the bona fide purchaser or, more generally, that statutes should in principle be liberally interpreted. It is not necessary for us to say which view is to be preferred; nor, indeed, does it follow that the same approach has to be adopted in relation to all cases. The essential point is that the court found it necessary to adopt some provisional standpoint by reference to facts external to the statute, and thus to reach a conclusion as to where the onus of persuasion lay.

The moral is that no word or group of words has a fixed meaning. Everything depends on the context in which it is used and on the degree to which the court is willing to look behind the language to discover the underlying intention.

8.   THE ECONOMIC ANALYSIS OF LAW

Much valuable work has been done, particularly by scholars in the United States, in testing principles and rules of commercial law against concepts of economic

94 [1965] 1 QB 560.
95 *Newtons of Wembley Ltd v Williams* [1965] 1 QB 560 at 574.

rationality and efficiency and in challenging assumptions commonly made by lawyers as to the appropriate approach to the resolution of particular issues.[96] Questions examined in law and economics literature include the concept and role of the market,[97] the efficiency of breaches of contract and of liquidated damages and penalty clauses,[98] the approach to the computation of damages,[99] and the economic justification for security interests.[100] There is also an extensive use of game theory in the analysis of contracts and remedies for breach. Such literature has had a greater impact in America than in England, where it has proved of limited significance. There is a tendency in law and economics writings to ascribe to the judges a conscious or subconscious application of economic principles in their reasoning when in fact the decisions have been based on quite different considerations, and to postulate hypotheses of rational behaviour on the part of the business person which are untested and may thus fail to take account of a range of factors which in everyday business life, in so far as it is rationally conducted at all, guide commercial decisions. Moreover, the subtlety and complexity of much of the economic argument tend to restrict its utility as a working tool in ordinary litigation. Even so, the law and economics literature has important lessons for the general theory of contract law and contract remedies and offers challenges to the sometimes facile assumptions upon which established contract law doctrines are based.

96 The leading exponent is Richard Posner. See, for example, R. Posner, *Economic Analysis of Law* (6th edn, 2003); Anthony T. Kronman and Richard A. Posner, *The Economics of Contract Law* (1979). His appointment to the judiciary has enabled Judge Posner to apply some of his theories in reaching his decisions.

97 See, for example, Robert Cooter and Thomas Ulen, *Law and Economics* (4th edn, 2004), chs 1, 6 and 7; Hugh Collins, *Regulating Contracts* (1999), ch 5.

98 Charles J. Goetz and Robert E. Scott, 'Liquidated Damages, Penalties and the Just Compensation Principle: Some Notes on an Enforcement Model and a Theory of Efficient Breach' (1977) 77 Colum L Rev 544; Daniel Friedmann, 'The Efficient Breach Fallacy' (1989) 18 J Legal Stud 1; Alan Schwartz, 'The Myth that Promisees Prefer Supracompensatory Damages: An Analysis of Contracting for Damages Measures' 100 Yale LJ 369 (1990).

99 For the particular problem of claims to damages by a lost-volume seller see p 406.

100 Thomas Jackson and Anthony T. Kronman, 'Secured Financing and Priorities Among Creditors' 88 Yale LJ 1143 (1979).

2 Basic Concepts of Personal Property

While the financing of business operations frequently involves the grant of security over land,[1] about which we shall have something to say later,[2] commercial law is primarily concerned with dealings in personal property, tangible and intangible. The sale of goods, the issue and transfer of negotiable instruments and documents of title, the discounting of non-documentary receivables, these lie at the heart of commercial law, generating a mass of fascinating jurisprudential problems, many of which have never been answered, and some, indeed, not even raised.

Most students encountering real property law for the first time go through a period of almost total mystification. What they assumed to be a solid, immovable asset speedily dissolves into abstract tenures and estates, stretched out over an infinity of time, susceptible to peculiar rules and altogether beyond the plane of normal human existence.[3] How different is the world of goods! None of those theoretical abstractions; instead, a familiar picture of tangible objects, absolutely and indivisibly owned, moving from hand to hand in transactions that may be visualized without any great feats of intellectual imagination, reassuringly commonplace as the objects of daily experience.

In fact, the relative simplicity of personal property law is largely illusory. A chattel, it transpires, is not as indivisible as we had supposed. Its ownership may be carved up into legal and equitable rights, it may be exposed to trusts and to successive interests, and it may be subject to two concurrent legal interests and to an indefinite number of concurrent equitable interests. And what are we to make of the intangible forms of personal property? An invisible right notionally embodied in a document or instrument may, miraculously, become the object of a pledge, or a possessory security. A person who disposes outright of a debt, apparently retaining nothing in his hands, physical or metaphysical, yet has power in certain conditions to make an effective transfer of the same debt to a second transferee.[4]

Abstract though these concepts may be, they will be found to possess a practical importance in many of the transactions we are about to consider. The purpose of the present chapter is to set the scene with a brief account of the peculiar characteristics

---

1 As to which see *Megarry's Manual of the Law of Real Property* (8th edn, 2002, ed A. J. Oakley), ch 13; *Cheshire and Burn's Modern Law of Real Property* (16th edn, 2000), ch 21; Kevin Gray and Susan Francis Gray, *Elements of Land Law* (3rd edn, 2001), ch 12.
2 Chapters 22–24.
3 See F.H. Lawson and Bernard Rudden, *Introduction to the Law of Property* (3rd edn, 2002), ch V.
4 See p 652.

of personal property,[5] the different forms it may take, the types of dealing that are possible, and a glimpse of the priority questions and tracing rights that may result from such dealings and will be examined in more detail hereafter.

I. CLASSIFICATION OF RIGHTS

Rights are classified as real (or *in rem*[6]), *ad rem* (more fully, *in personam ad rem*[7]) and purely personal (or *in personam*). Both real and personal rights may be subject to reduction or avoidance by the exercise of powers known as equities.

(i) Real rights[8]

A real right is a right in or over an identifiable asset or fund of assets. In the case of personal property[9] there are three main forms of real right: ownership, possession and equitable charge (hypothecation). The main significance of real rights is that they can be asserted against third parties (other than those acquiring an overriding title) and survive the bankruptcy of the person against whom they are asserted, so that the asset can be held against or reclaimed from his trustee in bankruptcy.[10] Thus if O's goods are stolen or wrongly detained by B, O can recover them from B, and if B becomes bankrupt, from B's trustee; they do not form part of B's estate so as to be available to B's creditors. Similarly, if C takes an equitable charge over D's assets to secure repayment of a loan made by C to D, that charge is enforceable despite D's bankruptcy, and C is entitled to have the assets sold[11] and to look to the proceeds for satisfaction of the debt in priority to D's other creditors. Again, if H is in possession of equipment under a leasing agreement with a leasing company, L Ltd, which goes into liquidation, H is entitled to retain possession against the liquidator for the duration of the agreement so long as he continues to pay the hire charges.

---

5 The most comprehensive textbook treatment of the subject is now to be found in A. P. Bell, *Modern Law of Personal Property in England and Ireland* (1989). See also *Crossley Vaines on Personal Property* (5th edn, 1973). Welcome additions to the literature on personal property are Sarah Worthington, *Personal Property Law: Text, Cases and Materials* (2000), and Norman Palmer and Ewan McKendrick (eds), *Interests in Goods* (2nd edn, 1998). Scots law is particularly strong in its attention to property concepts. For an excellent example, see Kenneth G. C. Reid *et al.*, *The Law of Property in Scotland* (1996).

6 The phrase '*in rem*' is also used to denote rights against the world generally rather than against a particular person and in this sense includes rights given by the law of tort, whether or not relating to property. Civilian writers also used the phrase *ius in re*, which conveniently marks off property rights from other rights available against third parties but has not passed into English usage.

7 The phrase 'rights *ad rem*', at one time in common currency in books on jurisprudence, has fallen into disuse. It is useful nevertheless in focusing attention on the distinction between a right *in* an asset and a right *to* an asset, a distinction not brought out in contrasting real rights with purely personal claims.

8 Also termed proprietary rights. The phrase is avoided here, as it is not apt to describe the equitable charge, which is an incumbrance on an asset but confers no rights of ownership on the chargee.

9 See p 29.

10 Or in the case of a company, liquidation (ie winding-up).

11 Though it will be necessary to obtain a court order for sale if the instrument of charge does not confer a power of sale on the chargee.

(ii) Rights *ad rem*

Claims to an asset may also be made by one who has no existing real right, merely a personal right to have the asset delivered or otherwise transferred to him. Such a person has a mere *ius ad rem*, as opposed to a *ius in re*. For example, if S agrees to let goods to B on hire-purchase and then refuses to deliver them, B has neither ownership nor possession, merely a contractual right to have possession given to him. When this happens, he will as possessor have a real right in the goods, namely the limited legal right of a bailee. Until then, he has merely a personal claim on S, a right to have a real right vested in him by delivery. Similarly, where B contracts to buy goods from S under an agreement for sale, then until ownership passes to B under the contract or possession of the goods is given to him, he has no real rights over the goods, merely a contractual right to call for delivery and transfer of ownership. Again, the holder of a purely possessory title loses his real rights when he ceases to have possession, and his claim against the person who divested him of possession is a mere personal claim.[12] In all these cases the claimant does not acquire a right *in rem* unless and until his right *ad rem* has been effectuated by an actual delivery or transfer by the other party, whether voluntarily or as the result of enforcement of a court order.[13]

An existing real right in an asset is, as one would expect, considerably stronger than a mere personal right to call for its delivery or transfer.[14] The latter does not avail against a subsequent purchaser of the asset who takes for value and without notice of his transferor's breach of duty.[15] Moreover, if the obligor becomes bankrupt, the obligee's right to call for performance of the delivery obligation is extinguished and replaced by a right to prove for damages in the bankruptcy in competition with other creditors,[16] a right which may be valueless. Finally, a mere personal right to possession, though sufficient to confer on the holder possessory remedies in tort against the obligor himself, does not entitle the claimant to pursue such remedies against a third party holding the goods as bailee unless the latter received them after the claimant's own right arose or the bailee has attorned to the claimant.[17]

(iii) Purely personal rights

A purely personal right is one which does not involve the delivery or transfer to the obligee of an identified asset or funds of assets but is to be satisfied by the obligor's personal performance in some other way, such as payment of a debt or damages

---

12 This is subject to the qualification mentioned in n 121.

13 The making of the order does not by itself suffice except where it is expressed to vest the asset in the claimant.

14 The distinction between the two, sharply drawn at common law, has become blurred (1) by the rule of equity which treats the unperfected obligation to transfer as if a transfer had in fact taken place, provided that executed consideration was furnished by the promisee, and (2) by the recognition of the validity of charge-backs. See pp 38, 578.

15 This question is discussed in relation to tracing, p 52.

16 See p 833.

17 See p 44 as to attornment in sale.

from his general assets.[18] Purely personal rights do not survive the defendant's bankruptcy but are converted into rights of proof in competition with other unsecured creditors.

(iv) Equities

An equity is not an existing real right in an asset but rather a personal power in one person to set aside, reduce or extinguish to his own advantage an asset held by another. Equities are broadly of two kinds: those which entitle a person to have revested in him an asset improperly acquired by another, and those which entitle him to reduce or extinguish his personal liability to that other. Typical examples of the first kind of equity are the right to rescind a contract for fraud or misrepresentation or undue influence; to have a transfer set aside for undue influence or breach of fiduciary duty; and to obtain rectification of an instrument which does not truly record the agreement reached between the parties. Thus, if S is induced to sell and deliver goods to B in exchange for a cheque which B knows will not be honoured, S may rescind the agreement on the ground of fraud, and upon his doing so ownership of the goods automatically revests in him. B holds the goods subject to an equity in favour of S by which he can avoid the transaction. Such an equity is an inherent limitation on B's real right, a potential trigger for the reacquisition of the property by S. A prime example of an equity of the second kind is the equitable right to set off against a money claim by one's creditor a cross-claim for money due from that creditor on another account.

Since an equity is an inherent qualification of the real right of the person against whom it subsists, it binds not only that person but his trustee in bankruptcy, for the latter takes the assets of the bankrupt as he finds them, and therefore subject to all equities or incumbrances in favour of a third party. An equity also binds a purchaser for value with notice of the equity and a volunteer, with or without notice. So equities share with real rights the characteristic that they survive the bankruptcy of the person against whom they are asserted and can be asserted against anyone other than a bona fide purchaser for value without notice.[19]

2. PROPERTY AND OBLIGATION

The distinction between real and personal rights may be expressed in another way: as the distinction between property and obligation, between what I *own* and what I *am owed*.[20] The common law observed this distinction strictly. It was obvious that a contract to transfer an asset from A to B was not the same as an actual transfer. Once the transfer had been made in accordance with the formalities required by

---

18 For special problems of characterization arising in relation to claims to money, see p 452.

19 Whether of the legal or the equitable interest. In this respect an equity differs from an equitable interest, which in principle can be cut off only by a purchase of the legal title.

20 See R. M. Goode, 'Ownership and Obligation in Commercial Transactions', (1987) 103 LQR 433.

law,[21] B became the owner; until then he had no proprietary interest of any kind in the asset, merely a contractual right to have it transferred to him, and if A became bankrupt before executing the transfer, B's status was merely that of an unsecured creditor. But the impact of the distinction between contract and conveyance and, more generally, between property and obligation, has been substantially reduced by the development of equitable real rights, in particular through the trust and the principle that equity treats as done that which ought to be done, so that an agreement for transfer is to be treated as if it were an actual transfer.[22] The proprietary interest thus created was as effective as a transfer at law in all respects save one, namely that it would be overridden by a conveyance of the legal estate or title to a purchaser of the asset taking for value in good faith and without notice of the interest in question. Even this weakness has largely been eradicated by statutory provisions for registration of equitable interests, which enable an equitable transferee, by registering his interest, to give notice to subsequent parties and thus reduce[23] the ability of a subsequent legal purchaser to contend that he purchased in good faith and without notice.

There is another sense in which the distinction between property and obligation has become blurred, namely through the recognition that a person to whom a debt is owed can grant a security interest in it not only to a third party but back to the debtor himself. Despite the conceptual problems involved where a debtor becomes his own creditor, the force of commercial practice, both in England and other countries, is not to be denied. So a person holding a bank deposit can, it seems, give a charge back to the bank, and the holder of securities or negotiable instruments, a charge back to the issuer.[24]

The development of equitable proprietary rights, though of limited impact in relation to sales of goods,[25] is nevertheless of cardinal importance in commercial law, for equitable interests play a key role as a form of security in the provision of industrial and commercial finance. In particular, equitable mortgages and charges over property of all kinds are of common occurrence,[26] as are mortgages and charges of equitable interests, eg those arising under contracts to acquire an interest in land, while restitutionary proprietary claims in equity are now a recurrent feature of commercial disputes.[27]

---

21 Land had formerly to be conveyed by a deed embodying formal words of limitation. A deed is still necessary to transfer a legal estate, but words of limitation are no longer required where the grantor intends to convey the whole of his interest (Law of Property Act 1925, s 60(1)). The rule for goods was, and remains, that they may be sold or mortgaged by word of mouth, but a gift of goods must be perfected by deed or delivery of possession.

22 See p 626.

23 Though not entirely eliminate. See pp 647, n 1; 666.

24 See further p 611.

25 For an agreement to sell goods appears not to attract the equitable doctrine (see p 216, 219). Yet it is not without significance in the context of sales law, since in certain conditions a seller who has reserved title may have a right to trace the proceeds in equity. See pp 26, 52.

26 See chs 23–25.

27 See pp 53, 458 ff.

3.   PERSONAL PROPERTY DEFINED

The term 'personal property' is used as the antithesis of real property. In the context of commercial transactions, the main significance of the distinction is that whereas a claim to the latter is a vindicatory action, in the sense that the plaintiff is entitled to possession of the asset itself, chattels cannot be recovered by action[28] as of right, the court having the discretion to award the claimant their value as damages instead.[29]

Apart from leaseholds (which for practical purposes are interests in land though the law continues to regard them as personalty), personal property divides broadly into two groups: tangible movables (goods and money), and intangibles, usually termed 'choses in action'. However, some intangibles are more concrete than others. These are rights to money, goods or securities which are locked up in a document to the extent that the document is considered to represent the right, which thus becomes transferable by transfer of the document itself. Rights so embodied may conveniently be termed 'documentary intangibles', and their significance lies in the fact that the document which manifests them is to most intents and purposes equated with goods and is susceptible to the same remedies of specific delivery, damages for conversion and the like. Into this category of documents fall rights embodied in bills of lading and other documents of title, negotiable instruments, negotiable certificates of deposit and bearer bonds and other bearer securities. We shall examine later those characteristics which assist in determining whether a particular right qualifies as a documentary intangible.[30] Rights which do not so qualify may be called pure intangibles. Most contracts fall into this category, even where evidenced by or arising out of a written contract.[31] The distinction between documentary and pure intangibles is legally significant in various ways discussed hereafter.[32] Intangibles are now far more significant in volume and value than tangibles as objects of security interests.

4.   THE DISTINGUISHING CHARACTERISTICS OF PERSONAL PROPERTY

If we exclude the peculiar case of leaseholds and treat real property as synonymous with interests in land, we can readily perceive why the law has found it necessary to apply different rules to personalty. Save in unusual circumstances, land is immovable and permanent. Its immobility renders it readily susceptible to restrictions on transfer or use, eg by restrictive covenants or by planning legislation. Its permanence facilitates the creation of multiple interests of long duration (long

---

28 But the claimant may be able to have recourse to self-help by taking possession without a court order. See pp 445, 710.

29 At common law the defendant had the option of returning the goods or paying their value. The discretion to order specific delivery of the goods to the plaintiff was first conferred by s 78 of the Common Law Procedure Act 1854, later replaced by rules of court. The discretion is now exercised under s 3(2) of the Torts (Interference with Goods) Act 1977. For the procedure, see CPR, Sch 1, RSC, Ord 45, r 4.

30 See p 48.

31 See p 49.

32 See p 47.

leases, life interests, etc) whereas the relatively short life of goods militates against division of rights in a chattel. These factors render the investigation of title to land more prolonged and its transfer more complex than in the case of goods. Land is acquired primarily for use rather than for resale,[33] and is thus not an asset which is intended to circulate in the stream of trade. Its identity cannot easily be changed, and its fixed location gives it a unique character compared with other land, even if the latter be of precisely the same shape and dimensions. Moreover, as a result of registration systems and conveyancing procedures, title to land can normally be readily established. Personal property, on the other hand, comprises assets of a relatively evanescent character, whose primary value is to be measured in money. Goods deteriorate with use and usually depreciate in value with the passage of time or by reason of obsolescence. They are, for the most part, transferable from hand to hand; title to them is not readily verifiable; their physical movements may be hard to trace; and, in an age of mass production, they are indistinguishable from other goods of the same class. They are objects of commerce and, except to the end-user, their value lies in their convertibility to money by sale or lease. Even in the hands of the end-user, they usually have no unique value and their loss will adequately be compensated by a money payment which will allow the purchase of comparable goods by way of replacement. Similarly, choses in action are of limited duration. Debts are discharged by payment, patents and copyrights expire with the passage of time, shares in companies and partnerships disappear on dissolution. Moreover, debts, the largest category of choses in action, are, like goods, articles of commerce which are freely dealt in by way of assignment or charge.

The effect of these differences between land and other assets is fundamental and all-pervasive. The unique character of a parcel of land means that one who is wrongfully dispossessed or otherwise deprived of it cannot adequately be compensated by an award of damages, so that as against a trespasser he will as a matter of course be given an order for possession,[34] without being subjected to the exercise of any discretion by the court to award damages instead, as is the case in an action for recovery of goods.[35] For the same reason, the court will ordinarily decree specific performance of a contract for the sale of land, whereas this will rarely be given in the case of a sale of goods, where the buyer's interest is essentially financial, since he can go into the market to purchase other goods and is adequately protected by an award of damages for any extra price he has to pay. Again, the disposal of land involves a detailed and lengthy conveyancing procedure, with a substantial interval of time between contract and conveyance to allow for careful investigation of title and related matters, so that the risk of buying from one not entitled to sell is slight and disputes between rival claimants are settled almost entirely by reference to property law. Goods, on the other hand, are much more susceptible to dealings by one who has no right to sell, so that it is necessary for commercial law to evolve distinct rules for the protection of the bona fide

---

33 However, builders and development companies acquire land as stock in trade for the purpose of erecting houses and selling them.

34 For which purpose rules of court provide a summary procedure. See CPR, Pt 55.

35 See n 29 and p 62.

purchaser, in the interests of the free flow of trade. A buyer from one selling in the ordinary course of business cannot fairly be exposed to the full rigour of rules of property law concerning the superiority of legal titles over equitable interests, or the effect of registration of rights in a public register as constructive notice of those rights.[36] Finally, the doctrine of estates, which enables ownership of land to be divided up by slices of time and thus allows a smaller legal title to be carved out of a larger, does not apply to goods.

In short, land is governed primarily by property law concepts, goods and choses in action by commercial law concepts; land law is concerned essentially with status, commercial law with obligations. But as we shall see, many rules of property law apply equally to land and chattels.

5.   LEGAL OWNERSHIP

(i)   Interest and title

Ownership, one of the most elusive concepts of English law, is conventionally defined as the residue of legal rights in an asset remaining in a person, or in persons concurrently, after specific rights over the asset have been granted to others.[37] A person in whom such residue of rights is vested is said to have an absolute interest in the asset. By contrast, one who enjoys merely specific rights, eg possession under a pledge, lien or other bailment, has only a limited interest.[38]

Interest is to be distinguished from title. A person's interest in an asset denotes the quantum of rights over it which he enjoys against other persons, though not necessarily against *all* other persons. His title measures the strength of the interest he enjoys in relation to others.[39] English law attributes great significance to possession. A person in possession with the intention of assuming ownership is treated as owner, and given all the rights and remedies available in tort and property law for the protection of the owner, against everyone except him who has a better title. If O is the true owner but T has taken possession of the asset *animo domini*, both are considered to have title to the absolute interest in the property. O's title, being the best, is indefeasible: T's is a defeasible title, being subordinate to that of

---

36 *Joseph v Lyons* (1884) 15 QBD 280.

37 A. M. Honoré, 'Ownership', in *Oxford Essays in Jurisprudence* (ed A. G. Guest, 1961), p 126; R. W. M. Dias, *Jurisprudence* (5th edn, 1985), ch 14; Bell, *Modern Law of Personal Property*, ch 4.

38 In the case of goods, the only form of limited legal interest known to the law is possession as a bailee. See p 43. The position is otherwise in relation to land, where the law admits not only of the *ius in re sua* represented by a lease but also *iura in re aliena* represented by the servitudes listed in s 1(2) of the Law of Property Act 1925, eg easements and rights of entry.

39 The Sale of Goods Act also uses the term 'property', which denotes title (whether indefeasible or defeasible) to an absolute interest. For an illuminating discussion in the context of the sale of goods, see G. Battersby and A.D. Preston, 'The Concepts of "Property", "Title" and "Owner" Used in the Sale of Goods Act 1893' (1972) 35 MLR 268. Professor Battersby returned to the theme in [2001] JBL 1. See also the thought-provoking article by H.L. Ho, 'Some Reflections on "Property" and "Title" in the Sale of Goods Act' [1997] CLJ 571, and pp 199 ff.

O but effective against all others not claiming under O or defending T's claim with O's authority.[40] There is a statutory exception to this principle, in that the defendant to T's action is now allowed to set up O's title by way of defence, ie to plead the *ius tertii*.[41] But such a plea will cease to be maintainable if O, upon being called on to intervene in the action, fails to do so and is then barred from asserting his title.[42] So strongly does the law adhere to the protection of possession that even a possessor who at the time he acquired possession was aware that the goods had been stolen is entitled to assert his title against all except the true owner. This was so held by the Court of Appeal in *Costello v Chief Constable of Derbyshire Constabulary*,[43] where the facts were as follows.

> The police seized from the claimant a car which they believed to have been stolen. The claimant brought proceedings for delivery up of the car and damages for its detention. The trial judge held that the claimant was aware at the time he acquired the car that it was a stolen vehicle and that this precluded him from recovery. Reversing the decision, the Court of Appeal held that the mere fact that goods had been acquired by unlawful means did not prevent the passing of property in them.[44] Once their statutory power of detention had been exhausted, the police were under a duty to return the goods to the person from whom they had been seized[45] and were not entitled to confiscate the goods in the absence of a statutory power to do so. Even a thief was entitled to bring proceedings against a person unlawfully divesting him of possession.[46]

Title to an absolute interest may be defeasible either because it is the second-best title, as in the case mentioned above, or because, though constituting the best title so long as it continues, it is subject to divestment, as where a mortgage (which confers title to an absolute interest on the mortgagee) is redeemed or the contract under which the title was acquired was a voidable title which has been avoided by the exercise of a right of rescission.[47]

Since title to goods, if not the best, can be acquired only by possession, and since possession, like ownership, is indivisible,[48] it follows that no more than two independent legal titles can exist in goods at any one time.[49] Each of these is separately transferable *inter vivos* or capable of being bequeathed by will.[50] But the holder of a relative title is in a vulnerable position, for in the first place his rights are

---

40 Most law students, asked what interest a trespasser has in land which he occupies *animo domini*, are incredulous at the statement that he acquires a relative title to a fee simple absolute in possession – but that is the law!

41 Torts (Interference with Goods) Act 1977, s 8(1); CPR, r 19.5A; Graham Battersby, 'The Present Status of the Jus Tertii Principle', (1992) Conv N S 100.

42 Under CPR, r 19.5A(3).

43 [2001] 1 WLR 1437.

44 Citing *Bowmakers v Barnet Instruments Ltd* [1945] KB 65. See further p 134.

45 Assuming the true owner had not come forward to claim them.

46 Citing *Webb v Chief Constable of Merseyside Police* [2000] QB 427; *Tinsley v Milligan* [1994] 1 AC 340.

47 As to which see pp 108, 395, 425.

48 Pollock and Wright, *An Essay on Possession in the Common Law* (1888), p 20. See p 42.

49 Ie, the best title and a possessory title. It follows also that a non-possessory legal interest in goods must necessarily be absolute, for since legal ownership must be transferred entire (p 34) a limited legal interest cannot be created directly by transfer of partial legal ownership but can come into existence as a new original interest only by possession under a pledge, hiring or other form of bailment.

50 *Asher v Whitlock* (1865) LR 1 QB 1.

subordinate to those of the true owner and in the second, his possessory title, whether acquired by virtue of his own possession or by transfer from a person still in possession, will automatically be extinguished if the transferor himself loses possession. Only an indefeasible title (or a title which a party is precluded from denying is indefeasible) survives the loss of possession.[51] The erstwhile possessor is left with a purely personal claim for trespass or conversion, subject to the defences of *ius tertii* and *ex turpi causa non oritur actio*. If the transferor of a possessory title delivers possession to the transferee himself, the latter's derivative title is extinguished and replaced by a new, original possessory title based on his own possession.

Absolute ownership exists when the interest is absolute and the title indefeasible.[52] Frequently, however, these two ingredients are not conjoined. A person may have indefeasible title to a limited interest, and he may have relative title to an absolute interest. A good example is the interest enjoyed by a person receiving possession of goods as a bailee of the absolute owner, eg under a rental agreement. He has a right to continue in possession on the terms of the bailment[53] and, since no one else has a better right, he has an indefeasible title to his limited interest as bailee. But suppose that, in defiance of his bailor's rights of ownership, the bailee asserts dominion over the goods by some act inconsistent with the bailor's rights, as by unlawfully offering the goods for sale as if they were his own. The assertion of dominion, though ineffective as against the bailor,[54] is nevertheless good against the rest of the world, since it is supported by possession and possession is recognized by English law as a root of title. The position of the recalcitrant bailee is now reversed. From being the holder of an indefeasible title to a limited interest he has become the holder of a relative title to an absolute interest.

A person cannot, of course, be said to enjoy an interest of any kind unless he has *some* title. If he has neither the best right to the interest he claims nor a possessory title, he has no interest at all. But even without an interest he may still have power to dispose of the asset, for example, as an agent acting within the scope of his actual or ostensible authority[55] or as an assignor of debts which he has previously assigned to another assignee.[56]

---

51 As to possession, see p 42.
52 To avoid possible confusion with absolute title in registered land conveyancing, which is not necessarily immune from attack, we shall hereafter employ the term 'indefeasible' to describe the best title to a chattel.
53 A bailment is a voluntary delivery of possession of goods by one person (the bailor) to another (the bailee) upon terms, express or implied, that the bailee is to return the goods in specie when the bailment comes to an end. It frequently takes effect under a contract, as where goods are pledged by way of security or delivered for repair or storage, but may exist independently of contract, as in the case of gratuitous bailment. For an exhaustive treatment see N. E. Palmer, *Bailment* (2nd edn, 1991).
54 At common law this was so even if the bailor himself was not the true owner, since a bailee was estopped from disputing his bailor's title (*Biddle v Bond* (1865) 6 B & S 225). But the rule has now been abrogated by statute (Torts (Interference with Goods) Act 1977, s 8(1)).
55 See p 168.
56 See pp 56 ff, 654–655, 794–795.

(ii) The indivisibility of ownership of personal property

In legal theory, only personal property is susceptible of private ownership and only land can be the subject of tenure and be governed by the doctrine of estates. Admittedly, the *ingredients* of ownership may be separated and distributed among different persons. Thus, goods may be held on trust or subjected to a mortgage or charge,[57] so that legal title is in one person and beneficial ownership in another; and ownership may be divorced from possession, either lawfully, as where the owner of goods lets them out on hire,[58] or unlawfully, as where he is divested of possession by a trespasser. Hence most of the things that the law permits in relation to land can be achieved also in relation to chattels, except where statute provides otherwise.[59] But whereas in the case of land a smaller legal title can be carved out of a larger (eg a leasehold interest or mortgage by demise can be carved out of a fee simple) and the two interests can exist concurrently as legal interests even though one is not to take effect in possession until a later date, this is not possible in the case of chattels. Legal title to an interest in a chattel (whether it be title to an absolute or a limited interest) can only be held or transferred entire. The legal title may be held by persons concurrently, as joint tenants or tenants in common,[60] and may be transferred as an entity by their collective action, but it is not possible to split that title in the sense of carving a smaller legal title out of it.

Thus, while on a legal mortgage of land the mortgagor and the mortgagee have concurrent legal estates (the former the fee simple, the latter a term of years absolute), a legal mortgage of a chattel necessarily divests the mortgagor of his legal title, leaving him with a mere equity of redemption. Similarly, a charge on chattels is necessarily equitable, since the charge is the creation of equity, and the statutory provision by which a charge by way of legal mortgage creates a legal interest[61] is confined to land. These considerations may be of practical importance in determining priorities where the mortgagor of a chattel in the one case or the chargee in the other purports to dispose of the chattel to a third party.[62] The indivisibility of legal ownership of chattels can be of significance in other transactions also. For example, an agreement by which a chattel is let on lease or rental confers no legal interest on the lessee. Indeed, it gives him no rights *in rem* at all, merely a contractual claim to possession of the chattel for the agreed period of

---

57 See chs 22, 23.
58 For a discussion of equipment finance leasing, see ch 28.
59 As an example of this exception, a legal charge can be created only over land. See below.
60 See p 35.
61 Law of Property Act 1925, s 87(1) (unregistered land); Land Registration Act 2002, s 51 (registered land). The chargee does not in fact obtain a legal estate (a charge being in legal theory an incumbrance, not a grant of a term), but the effect of the section is to put the chargee in the same position as if he had been granted a mortgage by demise (ie, a security lease) for 3,000 years (Law of Property Act 1925, s 87(1)).
62 See p 654.

lease.[63] If, therefore, the lessor before delivery of the chattel sells it to another, the latter acquires the absolute legal interest, and the lessee has at best the possibility of a claim *in personam* against the purchaser for knowingly participating in a breach of contract.[64] It is true that after delivery to him, the lessee does acquire a legal interest, but this is by virtue of possession, not by virtue of the agreement for lease, the sole effect of which is to indicate the character and quantum of the possessory interest, namely a bailment for use limited to the period of the lease. The possessory interest so enjoyed is thus an original interest created by the taking of possession, not a derivative interest carved out of the lessor's ownership.

Hence while a legal interest in a chattel cannot be split, there is nothing to prevent the concurrent existence of two independent legal interests, one derived from an absolute title, the other from possession.[65] The leasing agreement earlier referred to provides an example. After delivery, the lessee as well as the lessor has a legal interest, but there is no infringement of the indivisibility rule, for the lessee's legal interest has possession as its source and does not come about through any transfer by the lessor of part of his ownership. Similarly, if the legal owner of goods deposits them by way of pledge, both he and the pledgee have a legal interest, but again the pledgee's interest is created by possession and is not in any way derived from the ownership of the pledgor, though the fact that the pledgor is the owner and not a thief will obviously be relevant to the strength of the pledgee's title to his interest.

(iii) Co-ownership[66]

While a smaller legal title to goods cannot be carved out of a larger, there is nothing to preclude two or more people from owning goods together as joint tenants or tenants in common. Co-owners are joint tenants where their interest is acquired at the same time as a single interest, that is, without words of severance indicating that

63 English law does not recognize the concept of equitable possession (see pp 41, 627). Hence the view of Browne-Wilkinson V-C in *Re Paramount Airways Ltd* [1990] BCC 130, that for the purpose of s 11(3)(c) of the Insolvency Act 1986 an equipment lessee's contractual right to delivery of possession under the leasing agreement gives him a species of equitable interest in the equipment, is not easy to reconcile with established principles of personal property law. A better ground for this aspect of the decision is that by virtue of his possession the lessee has a limited legal interest in the goods which suffices to constitute 'property' for the purpose of the statutory provisions. Cf the decision of Harman J at first instance [1990] BCC 130 at 136, referring to a 'bundle of rights'.

64 Given that the purchaser was not a bona fide purchaser for value without notice, such a claim could be formulated either as damages for the tort of inducing a breach of contract or as a claim for wrongful interference with goods (yielding relief in the form of an order for delivery and/or damages) on the basis of the common law right to follow the asset (see p 52, and R.M. Goode, 'The Right to Trace and Its Impact in Commercial Transactions' (1976) 92 LQR 360, at p 374, n 59). For the significance of the distinction between real and personal rights, see p 00.

65 See p 42, as to possession.

66 See generally Bell, *Personal Property*, pp 74 ff.; Judith Hill and Elizabeth Bowes-Smith, 'Joint Ownership of Chattels', in Palmer and McKendrick, *Interests in Goods*, ch 10; R. M. Goode, *Proprietary Rights and Insolvency in Sales Transactions* (2nd edn, 1989), pp 6, 21, 71, 86. See also pp 220 ff. as to co-ownership problems that may arise in relation to contracts of sale of goods.

each is to have a distinct share in the goods.[67] Where their interests are acquired at different times, they are tenants in common. A particular characteristic of a joint tenancy is that on the death of one joint tenant the others become sole owners by survivorship. In contrast to land,[68] goods may be the subject of a legal tenancy in common. Full transfer of title to the goods requires the agreement of all co-owners. A purported disposition by one co-owner transfers only his own interest as tenant in common.[69]

Claims to co-ownership are a recurrent source of difficulty in commercial transactions, particularly where a pool of assets is held by a person to meet contractual transfer obligations incurred to several others. Thus it is not always easy to determine whether claimants to a pool of assets which have not been individually earmarked to each of them are co-owners in the proportions of their respective contributions or simply holders of personal rights. There are two paradigm situations. In the first, two or more people contribute materials to be made up by a third party into finished products which are then to be supplied to them in agreed quantities, and the third party becomes bankrupt without having fulfilled his delivery obligations.[70] In the second, two or more people contract to buy goods forming an unidentified part of a defined bulk in a store or warehouse, and the seller becomes bankrupt without having made delivery.[71] Both types of case raise fundamental issues as to the distinction between real and personal rights. In the first situation it is necessary for contributors to the common pool to establish a proprietary base for their claims to an interest in it, as by demonstrating that when they contributed their materials they did not intend to part with their ownership rights except on terms of acquiring an interest in the commingled pool. In the second, claimants must demonstrate that they have acquired a proprietary claim by appropriation to each of them individually or to them all collectively.[72]

(iv) Acquisition and transfer of legal ownership[73]

The acquisition of legal ownership may be original or derivative. It is original where it does not derive from the title of another. Examples are the reduction of a *res nullius* to possession, as where birds or wild animals are taken into captivity, and the acquisition of a defeasible title by possession *animo domino* as previously discussed.[74] Title is derivative where it takes the form of succession to another's

---

67 As where the goods are bought 'in equal shares' or are to be held 'equally'.

68 Law of Property Act 1925, ss 1(6), 34(1), 36(2).

69 This is so whether the co-owner was a joint tenant or a tenant in common, for the effect of a purported sale by a joint tenant is to sever the joint tenancy, so that what passes is the co-owner's resultant interest in common, as would be the case if he had been a tenant in common from the outset.

70 See Goode, *Proprietary Rights and Insolvency,* pp 85–88; and see p 220.

71 See p 221.

72 See pp 220 ff. The preparitory buyers of goods may acquire this by statute. See pp 222 ff.

73 See Palmer and McKendrick, *Interests in Goods*, which includes a fascinating array of the more arcane (though none the less important) objects of acquisition, such as human tissue, treasure trove, wreck and *bona vacantia*.

74 See p 31.

title. The latter may come about voluntarily (eg by gift or sale) or by operation of law (eg by death or bankruptcy). In certain cases a person may, as the result of the acts of himself or another, acquire title without the consent (or even the knowledge) of the prior owner. For example, title may vest in one who in good faith buys goods from a mercantile agent[75] or innocently incorporates them into a larger product as an accession[76] or into land and buildings as a fixture;[77] until recently a bona fide purchaser in market overt also acquired a good title.[78] With its customary pragmatism, English law has never conceptualized such forms of acquisition, so that it is unclear whether they are examples of original ownership or whether the acquirer merely succeeds to the title or titles of one or more prior parties.[79]

By far the most common form of acquisition of ownership is the consensual transfer for value, typically by way of sale or mortgage.[80] The common law had strict rules governing the efficacy of a purported transfer of ownership, and these are still operative. Thus the transferor has to have either a legal title or a power to pass legal title;[81] he has to deliver possession or utilize some other mode of transfer recognized by law;[82] and the dispositive act relied on has to signify an intention to make a present transfer of ownership, not a mere agreement to transfer at a future date. In consequence, the common law does not in general recognize a transfer of after-acquired property as effective by itself to vest ownership in the transferee upon the transferor acquiring the property. There has to be some new act of transfer after the time of acquisition.[83] Moreover, it follows from the indivisibility of ownership that the legal title cannot not be split between one person and another. Thus the common law never recognized the beneficiary under a trust as an owner. If property was conveyed to A upon trust for B, the common law regarded A as the legal owner and ignored the condition that the property was to be held for B. As we shall see, these rigid rules were substantially relaxed by equity, which treats agreements for the transfer of property as if they were transfers, gives effect to assignments of future property without the need for a new act of transfer and regards the beneficiary for whose benefit property is held on trust as being the owner.

---

75 See p 426.

76 R. M. Goode, *Hire-Purchase Law and Practice* (2nd edn, 1970), ch 33.

77 Ibid, ch 32.

78 See p 425.

79 See p 37.

80 Other forms of consensual transfer include gift, exchange, and appropriation by an agent to his mandate from his principal to procure goods in the agent's name but on the principal's behalf. See Goode, *Proprietary Rights and Insolvency*, pp 49–50.

81 See pp 416 ff., as to power to pass title by virtue of actual or ostensible authority or some other exception to the *nemo dat* rule.

82 In the case of land or of a gift of chattels, delivery or a grant by deed was necessary. For other transfers of goods, there were (and are) no special formalities, an oral transfer being sufficient (*Flory v Denny* (1852) 7 Exch 581).

83 *Lunn v Thornton* (1845) 1 CB 379. As regards real property, the law did recognize a limited range of future interests, but this was never so in the case of personalty except in relation to contracts of sale, future produce and progeny, and the like, where (as now) property passed by virtue of the contract. See p 219. As to future interests in copyright, see p 633, n 55.

(v) Loss of legal ownership

Legal ownership may be lost by:

(a)   the voluntary act of the owner, eg by transfer or by exercise of a right to terminate or rescind the agreement under which the asset was acquired;

(b)   re-transfer resulting from exercise by the transferor of a right to terminate or rescind the agreement under which the asset was transferred;

(c)   transfer by operation of law, eg on death, bankruptcy or transfer to the Crown as *bona vacantia*[84];

(d)   displacement by a new original interest, eg that acquired by adverse possession;

(e)   in the case of a tangible asset, destruction of the asset, or loss of its identity through confusion or commingling or through its becoming annexed as a fixture or accession;

(f)   in the case of an intangible asset, expiry through lapse of time (as in the case of a patent right) or discharge (as in the case of payment or other discharge of a debt or other obligation);

(g)   extinction or forfeiture by statute, as in the case of extinction of title by expiry of a period of limitation[85] or the forfeiture of uncustomed goods;

(h)   abandonment.[86]

But loss of ownership does not necessarily deprive the former owner of power to make an effective disposition to a new transferee.[87]

6.   EQUITABLE OWNERSHIP

(i)   The acquisition and transfer of ownership in equity

Equity, though not directly overriding the common law, effectively modified the strict rules of transfer, originally by acting on the conscience of the obligor and ordering him to perfect at law the transfer that he had undertaken to carry out, or the trust he had undertaken to observe, and later by treating as done that which ought to have been done. An agreement to transfer ownership, provided that it was of such a kind as to be enforceable by specific performance,[88] was given effect in equity as if the transfer had already been executed, so that while legal title remained in the intended transferor, beneficial ownership was held to vest immediately in the intended transferee.[89] Similarly, equity gave effect to the trust by insisting that the transferee honour the condition upon which the property was transferred to him. Initially, this too was a

---

84   As where a person dies intestate without heirs or a company is dissolved while still owning property (Companies Act 1985, s 654), though in the latter case application may be made to the court under s 651 to have the dissolution declared void. See generally as to *bona vacantia* Noel Ing, *Bona Vacantia*, and Andrew Bell, 'Bona Vacantia', in Palmer and McKendrick, *Interests in Goods*, ch 8.

85   See Limitation Act 1980, ss 3(2), 17.

86   See A. H. Hudson, 'Is Divesting Abandonment Possible at Common Law?' (1984) 100 LQR 110, and Hudson, 'Abandonment' in Palmer and McKendrick, *Interests in Goods*, ch 23.

87   See p 56.

88   As to the meaning of this requirement, see p 626.

89   The resultant blurring of the distinction between property and obligation is discussed, p 27.

purely personal obligation binding only on the trustee, but over time it was extended to cover purchasers with notice of the trust, donees (with or without notice) and also the trustee's heirs, personal representatives and creditors. Ultimately, it became established that a trust would bind anyone into whose hands the property passed other than a bona fide purchaser of the legal title for value without notice. Hence the interest of the beneficiary under a trust, like that of a party to whom another had contracted to sell or mortgage property, started as a purely personal right against the trustee and later became converted into a full-blooded property interest; and when the object of the trust was ownership itself, as opposed to a limited interest, the beneficiary had now to be recognized as the beneficial owner.[90] Finally, while the common law did not recognize an assignment of future property without a new act of transfer by the assignor after the property had been acquired, equity treated the assignment as effective upon the property automatically upon acquisition.[91]

Equitable title to property (whether land or goods) thus involves divided ownership, legal title being in A and beneficial ownership in B. When A holds the legal title primarily for the benefit of B, the relationship is that of trustee and beneficiary. But division of ownership may also occur without a trust relationship, namely when A holds the legal title primarily for his own interest, as in the case of a mortgage. Divided ownership in one form or another is the essence of equitable title. If both legal and beneficial ownership are vested in the same person, there is no scope for equity to operate on the asset, and no separate equitable interest can be said to exist.[92] One consequence of this is that the legal and beneficial owner cannot transfer a bare legal title while reserving to himself equitable ownership.[93] If he wishes to produce this result, he must do it by way of transfer of his entire interest, followed by a charge or declaration of trust in his favour by the transferee. In other words, the equitable interest must be created by way of grant, not by way of exception or reservation. Another consequence is said to be that equitable tracing rights to proceeds are not available to the legal and beneficial owner of the original asset, but this view, which would have the effect that a victim of theft could not assert a claim to proceeds of the stolen property, stems from the supposed requirement that the claimant should be a person to whom fiduciary duties were owed in respect of the original asset, a requirement now discredited.[94]

---

90 However, what he owns depends on whether the trustee is a bare trustee or has powers of management of the trust fund under an active trust. In the former case the beneficiary is equitable owner of the specific assets comprised in the trust; in the latter, he has an interest in the trust *fund* as it stands from time to time but acquires no interest in the specific assets comprising the fund until he becomes absolutely entitled to the assets and thus acquires the power to terminate the trust and with it the trustee's management powers.

91 See pp 626 ff.

92 *Stamp Duties Commissioner (Queensland) v Livingston* [1965] AC 694, at p 712. It is therefore not clear how, as has been suggested, a thief can be a constructive trustee of the stolen property when the victim of the theft is still the legal and beneficial owner.

93 *Re Bond Worth Ltd* [1979] 3 All ER 919.

94 See Andrew Burrows, *The Law of Restitution* (2nd edn, 2002), pp 93–94; Robert Goff and Gareth Jones, *The Law of Restitution* (6th edn, 2002), paras 2-031 ff. Where the claim is to trace the products or proceeds of property to which the defendant never acquired legal title, there is no role for equity to play, since the claimant recovers by virtue of his legal title (*Trustee of the Property of F.C. Jones & Sons v Jones* [1997] Ch 159).

Though an equitable interest can be carved out of the legal title, the converse is not true. The holder of an equitable interest can transfer only an equitable interest.

Hence equitable ownership may be acquired in any of the following ways:

(a) by an agreement to transfer a legal or equitable title;

(b) by a present transfer which is defective at law, eg for want of compliance with some legally requisite formality, such as execution as a deed;

(c) by creation of a trust, either

    (i) by the intended transferor declaring himself to be a trustee for the intended transferee, or

    (ii) by transfer of the asset to a third party to hold as trustee for the intended transferee;

(d) by a purported present transfer of an after-acquired asset;[95]

(e) by a transfer made by one whose title is purely equitable.

Equitable ownership may be transferred by written[96] assignment or declaration of trust.

(ii)   Equitable title and equitable interest

As in the case of legal ownership, it is necessary, when discussing ownership in equity, to distinguish interest and title, interest denoting the quantum of the right to the asset, title the strength of that right as against others.[97] The range of interests that can exist in equity is considerably greater than the range of legal interests; for whereas almost every interest capable of subsisting as a legal estate or interest can equally subsist in equity,[98] there are many interests which (through a combination of common law rules and statutory restrictions) can exist only in equity. These include future interests, life interests, remainders and executory interests,[99] charges

---

95   In this case the asset, upon being acquired by the transferor, vests in the transferee only in equity, and some new act or instrument is usually necessary in order to endow him with the legal title. See p 37 as to the rule and its exceptions.

96   Law of Property Act 1925, s 53(1)(c), which requires the writing to be signed by the transferor or his duly authorized agent.

97   It is unfortunate that legal terminology concerning equitable ownership tends to obscure the distinction between title and interest. Thus if a legal estate owner contracts to sell or mortgage his estate, we describe the other party's interest as an equitable interest. It would make for clarity if we spoke of his having acquired an equitable title to a legal estate.

98   But as to the interest of a buyer of goods under a contract of sale, see p 216.

99   As regards interests in land, this is the effect of the Law of Property Act 1925, s 1(3). In the case of chattels, it results from the common law rule that legal ownership of a chattel is indivisible, so that a legal term of years cannot be carved out of legal ownership. A purported transfer of a chattel for a given period will, depending on the construction of the transfer, take effect either as a mere hiring agreement, the hirer's legal interest stemming not from the agreement itself but from the possession taken under it, or as a transfer of absolute ownership, with at best a contractual right to the return of the chattel at the end of the stipulated period. Hence the maxim that 'a gift of a chattel for an hour is a gift of it forever' (*Brooke's Abridgement, Done et Remainder*, pl 57).

Where a chattel is supplied for consumption (as is usually the case with wine, grain, money, and the like), it is obviously not returnable in specie, so that the deliveree becomes the full owner, not a mere

on goods and intangibles[100] and any mortgage of goods granted after and during the currency of a legal mortgage given by the same mortgagor.[101]

Equitable interests, like legal interests, may be absolute or limited. Of the items just listed, charges and life interests are limited interests, the others are absolute interests. Though the principle of relativity of title applies to equitable interests, it operates somewhat differently than in relation to legal interests. In the first place, an equitable right or interest can be acquired only by charge or assignment,[102] not by possession, though the delivery of possession may evidence an intention to make a transfer. Secondly, possession is itself a purely legal concept. Whereas there can be equitable ownership, there is no such thing as equitable possession.[103] An agreement to give possession has no effect on real rights at law or in equity. So English law does not recognize such a thing as an equitable pledge.[104] Thirdly, an equitable interest is not as marketable as a defeasible legal interest, for it is on its face subject to a legal interest outstanding in another, and is liable to be overridden by a transfer of the legal interest to a bona fide purchaser for value without notice.[105] Fourthly, whereas there can be only two concurrent legal interests in goods,[106] there is no limit to the number of concurrent equitable interests that can subsist in goods.

(iii) Inchoate interests

Certain types of interest are inchoate, conceived but not yet born. Until birth they receive legal recognition from the law, but once born they are generally treated as having been continuously in existence from the time of conception. They include interests in future property,[107] equitable interests which remain to be perfected by the provision of consideration,[108] and interests which depend on the enforcement of

---

bailee. If it is supplied as a fungible (see p 59), so that the deliveree's obligation is to restore only the equivalent in quality and quantity, the transaction is a loan (*mutuum*) and ownership passes. It is this which distinguishes a loan from a bailment (Wilson, *A Discourse upon Usury* (ed R.H. Tawney, 1925, reprinted 1962), p 276). Where it is agreed that an article of a different kind shall be restored, the contract is one of sale if what is to be given back is money but otherwise is of exchange, or barter, as where grain is lent in exchange for wine.

100 A charge on land expressed to be by way of legal mortgage confers the same rights and remedies as if it were a legal mortgage (Law of Property Act 1925, s 87).

101 This follows from the indivisibility of the legal title; for once a legal mortgage has been granted, the mortgagor is left only with an equitable interest. However, if goods to which O has an indefeasible title are in the possession of P *animo domini*, both O and P have distinct legal titles to an absolute interest and each can grant a legal mortgage. That granted by O will, of course, have priority, in the absence of an applicable exception to the *nemo dat* rule.

102 Except, of course, where it arises by statute or operation of law.

103 Presumably the common law concept of constructive possession (p 43) made it unnecessary for equity to develop a theory of its own.

104 See p 627.

105 See p 38.

106 See p 32.

107 See p 631.

108 For example, interests arising on the exchange of contracts for the sale of an interest in land and before completion. See R. M. Goode, 'Ownership and Obligations in Commercial Transactions' (1987) 103 LQR 433 at p 437

an equity, such as rescission of a contract, crystallization of a floating charge[109] and the election of a tracing claimant to look to the proceeds of an asset to which he has title rather than to the asset itself.[110]

(iv) Floating interests

A person may have an interest not in a specific asset but in a shifting fund of assets.[111] Such is the nature of the interest of a beneficiary under an active (ie managed) trust and of a chargee under a floating charge.

7.   POSSESSION

A person in possession of an asset has, as we have seen, a real right in it. The strength of that right depends on his title; the quantum of the right, on the capacity in which he holds the asset.[112] Possession, like ownership, is incapable of precise definition; indeed, its meaning varies according to the nature of the issue in which the question of possession is raised.[113] Moreover, there is not even an agreed terminology as to the different forms of possession. We can leave the higher theory to the masters of jurisprudence.[114] For our purposes it is sufficient to describe possession of an asset as control, directly or through another, either of the asset itself or of some larger object in which it is contained[115] or of land or buildings on or beneath which it is situated,[116] with the intention of asserting such control against others, whether temporarily or permanently.[117] The common law concept of possession is thus much broader than it is under French law or civil law systems based on French law, where a person holding goods for another is considered to be a mere *détenteur*, having custody but not possession of the goods.

Possession is indivisible. Like ownership, it can only be held and transferred entire.[118] This fact is sometimes obscured by the so-called rule of double possession

---

109 See p 681.

110 See Roy Goode, *Legal Problems of Credit and Security* (3rd edn, 2003), paras 1-62, 1-63.

111 See Christine J. Davies, 'Floating Rights' [2002] CLJ 423; R.C. Nolan, 'Property in a Fund' (2004) 120 LQR 108; and see p 61.

112 See p 31. As to real and personal rights, see pp 25 ff.

113 For an example, see *Re Atlantic Computer Systems plc* [1990] BCC 859, in which the Court of Appeal held that a company which took computers under an equipment lease and let them to the intended end-user under a sublease nevertheless continued to hold possession as between itself and the head lessor, which was the relevant relationship for the purpose of s 11(3)(c) of the Insolvency Act 1986.

114 G. W. Paton, *A Text-Book of Jurisprudence* (4th edn, 1972), ch XXII; D. R. Harris, 'The Concept of Possession in English Law', in Guest, *Jurisprudence*, p 69 ff. For a detailed analysis of possession in relation to goods, see Bell, *Personal Property*, ch 3.

115 But only if the transferor of the larger object was aware of its contents or intended to transfer them known or unknown (*Merry v Green* (1841) 7 M & W 623; *Williams v Phillips* (1957) 41 Cr App Rep 5).

116 *South Staffordshire Water Company v Sharman* [1896] 2 QB 44.

117 However, the law does not usually recognize as possession a contract which is purely fleeting (eg the handling of goods in a shop) or is exercised by a person as employee or guest.

118 Whereas ownership can derive from two separate sources, possession must either be held solely by or shared with the physical possessor and cannot exist independently.

arising from a bailment, where it is said that the bailee, B, has actual, or physical, possession and the bailor, O, constructive possession. Such a formulation is a source of great confusion, as was pointed out by Pollock and Wright in their brilliant essay on possession over a century ago.[119] If B holds possession for an interest of his own, his possession is exclusive. This is so whether he acts as owner himself, that is, in a manner inconsistent with O's title, or holds possession for O subject to a limited interest of his own, eg as hirer under a rental agreement. In the latter case his exclusive possession continues even after the termination of the bailment if and so long as he asserts rights over the asset in defiance of O's entitlement to possession.[120] O may have a *right* to possession sufficient to give him the benefit of tort remedies against third parties dealing with the asset, but he does not enjoy possession itself, directly or indirectly.[121] Similarly, where O's goods are in the hands of a carrier or warehouseman whose charges have not been paid and who intends to exercise a lien over the goods until payment, O does not acquire constructive possession until payment or waiver of the lien.

By contrast, if B holds possession not for any interest of his own but exclusively for O as O's bailee at will, legal possession is shared by B and O.[122] In such a case, to say that O has constructive possession and B actual possession is perfectly legitimate so long as we do not fall into the trap of thinking that there are two distinct possessory titles. There is indeed but one, held by O and B. Their joint interest is to possession what a joint tenancy is to ownership.[123] If B transfers possession to T who agrees to hold for O, then B drops out of the picture and possession is now held together by O and T. Similarly, if O sells the asset to P and B attorns to P (ie, undertakes to hold for), possession is held by P and B. But if, after B's delivery of the asset to him, T claims it as his own or otherwise refuses to hold it to O's order,[124] T acquires exclusive possession. We can no longer speak of

---

119   Pollock and Wright, *Possession in the Common Law*, p 27.

120   See p 34.

121   It follows that if O is not the owner (ie the holder of an indefeasible title), he has no real rights in the asset at all and will be unable to recover it if B becomes bankrupt while still holding possession. However, the position is otherwise if B or his trustee has become estopped from disputing O's title, either because of failure to plead the *ius tertii* or because the true owner, when called upon to intervene to assert his interest, fails to do so and becomes barred by order of the court under CPR, r 19.5A.

122   B may agree to hold possession for O subject to a prior interest of his own. A common case is where B as carrier or warehouseman holds goods for O as current holder of the bill of lading or statutory warehouse warrant subject to B's lien for freight or warehouse charges. In such a case B has exclusive possession until his charges have been paid or the lien waived, at which point his possession becomes shared with O, who acquires constructive possession. Since there is no gap between the cessation of B's exclusive possession and O's acquisition of constructive possession, O is entitled, on acquiring constructive possession, to assert his real right against B's trustee in bankruptcy or liquidator even if the bankruptcy or winding-up occurred while B still had exclusive possession. See further Goode, *Proprietary Rights and Insolvency*, pp 13–14.

123   See p 34.

124   The typical case is where B wrongfully sells the asset to T. But the position would be the same if B delivered it to T with instructions to hold it for O, and in breach of those instructions T asserted a claim to the asset in defiance of O's right to possession. See to the same effect Markby, *Elements of Law* (6th edn, 1905), para 373.

O's 'constructive possession', for this was merely a particular aspect of the indivisible possession held for him by B which B has now lost. Similarly, if O sells to P but T refuses to attorn to P, constructive possession remains with O, and P's real rights in the asset depend entirely on getting the legal title from O. If O was not himself the owner, P acquires no real rights in the absence of attornment by T, and will be unable to recover the asset if T becomes bankrupt.

Hence if the term 'constructive possession' is to be used, it is as well to confine it to cases where the bailee holds possession to the bailor's order, so that possession is shared, by contrast with the case where the bailee has exclusive possession (because he is holding for an interest of his own) and the bailor has merely a right to possess.

We may summarize the foregoing analysis as follows. Possession is either sole or shared, that is, held for another. Sole possession necessarily predicates physical possession or control to the exclusion of others. It follows that two people cannot separately hold sole possession; there can only ever be one possession at any time, sole or shared.

Shared possession is very common in commercial transactions. In some cases B holds possession for O from the outset. In others, he initially holds on his own account or for a third party, T, and later undertakes to O to hold it for him. In order to confer real rights on O, the attornment must identify the goods to which it relates.[125] If B fails to appropriate particular goods to his undertaking (as where B is a warehouseman who holds 100 cases of wine for S and on S's instructions notifies O, as purchaser of 30 cases, that this number will be held to O's order, without further identification being given), his undertaking is a mere 'quasi-attornment'.[126] O has at best a personal claim against B founded on estoppel,[127] not a possessory real right by attornment.[128] Attornment can arise in a wide variety of situations. A seller originally in possession as owner can attorn to his buyer,[129] and a buyer to his

---

125   And since bailment is consensual, it is also necessary that B's possession for O has been expressly or impliedly authorized by O, failing which O does not acquire constructive possession unless and until he assents to B's holding for him (Markby, *Elements of Law*, para 374).

126   This is true also of a bill of lading which does not identify the goods.

127   See N. E. Palmer, *Bailment* (2nd edn, 1991), ch 21.

128   *Re Goldcorp Exchange* Ltd [1995] 1 AC 74. Thus the attornment of a third party to the buyer under a contract of sale requires 'a complete assent of all three parties to the appropriation of specific goods to the buyer under the contract' (Pollock and Wright, *An Essay on Possession in the Common Law*, p 73); and see *Hayman & Sons v McLintock* 1907 SC 936; *Re London Wine Co (Shippers) Ltd* [1986] PCC 121; Goode, *Proprietary Rights and Insolvency*, Appendix; and see p 265.

129   In Pollock and Wright, *Possession in the Common Law*, p 72, the decision in *Marvin v Wallace* (1856) 25 LJQB 369 is cited as authority for the proposition that the seller is considered to have made delivery to the buyer 'whether the vendor's custody is in the character of a bailee for reward or of a borrower'. This, however, is a misreading of the decision, which was based on the fact that after the sale, the seller acknowledged the buyer's title and asked if he could borrow the goods. The buyer could have refused. The seller's assent to hold for the buyer was not under the bailment but preceded it. In *Michael Gerson (Leasing) Ltd v Wilkinson* [2001] QB 514, there was a composite sale and lease back to the seller, so that, in contrast to the position in *Marvin v Wallace*, there was no identifiable point of time at which the buyer was in a position to give the seller instructions concerning the goods. Nevertheless the Court of Appeal held that the effect of the sale and lease back was to give symbolic delivery to the buyer, who otherwise would not be in a position to grant the lease back to the seller, and this sufficed to attract s 24 of the Sale of Goods Act 1979, as to which see pp 430 ff.

seller; a pledgor can attorn to his pledgee; and a third party initially holding the goods for O can later attorn to O's purchaser, P. A person can in a loose sense attorn in advance by issuing a bill of lading, statutory warehouse warrant or other document of title by which he undertakes to surrender the goods to whoever is the lawful holder of the document.[130] Delivery of the document, with any necessary indorsement, thus puts the deliveree in constructive possession, though only if each successive holder was intended by his transferor to be given constructive possession of the goods by the transfer of the document.[131] Attornment may be effected either verbally (in the form of an oral or written undertaking to hold the goods to O's order[132]) or by conduct, eg delivery of the keys to the warehouse where the goods are stored[133] or delivery of one of a collection of articles in the name of the whole,[134] though these are sometimes treated as distinct methods of transfer. It would seem that an attornment can be made only by the physical possessor of the goods, not by a person who himself holds a mere constructive possession, for the physical possessor has not given him any undertaking and, indeed, may be completely ignorant of his existence.[135]

Once acquired, possession is deemed to continue until the asset has passed into the possession of another or has been abandoned.[136] Accordingly, once the requisite degree of control has been established, it is unnecessary to prove its continuance; it is for the party contesting the other's possession to show that this has been transferred to a third party or deliberately surrendered by abandonment.[137] So documents of title taken by way of pledge may be released to the pledgor to enable him to sell as the pledgee's trustee-agent without the pledgee losing legal possession. In such a case, the pledgor holds possession for the pledgee in the same way as under any other shared possession arrangement.

Where possession is doubtful (as in the case of goods used on premises in common occupation), the rule is that possession follows the title.[138]

---

130 Described as a transferable attornment by Lord Hobhouse in *Borealis AB v Stargas Ltd* [2002] 2 AC 205 at 219.

131 For an illuminating examination of this principle, see the judgment of His Honour Judge Diamond QC in *The Future Express* [1992] 2 Lloyd's Rep 79 at pp 95–96, pointing out that transfer of the document of title passes constructive possession only if so intended by the transferor, and thus rests on a principle distinct from that of attornment. This is demonstrated by the fact that decisions on the effect of transfer of a document of title made no reference to the concept of attornment. Accordingly, it would seem that attornment in advance is not recognized by the common law. See *Farina v Home* (1846) 16 M & W 119; *Official Assignee of Madras v Mercantile Bank of India Ltd* [1935] AC 53, per Lord Wright at 58–59.

132 See *Laurie and Morewood v Dudin & Sons* [1926] 1 KB 223, per Scrutton LJ at 237.

133 *Gough v Everard* (1863) 2 H & C 1. Where these give control of the contents of the warehouse, so that the delivery is not merely symbolic, this constitutes an independent form of constructive delivery of the goods.

134 It must be intended that delivery of the part shall count as delivery of the whole (*Kemp v Falk* (1882) 7 App Cas 573, per Lord Blackburn at 586).

135 See Goode, *Proprietary Rights and Insolvency*, pp 11–12.

136 Hudson, *Abandonment*, especially at pp 618–619; Pollock and Wright, *Possession in the Common Law*, pp 18–19; Harris, 'Possession', pp 73–74; Paton, *Jurisprudence*, pp 580–581.

137 See titles cited in n 136.

138 *Ramsay v Margrett* [1894] 2 QB 18; *French v Gething* [1922] 1 KB 236.

8.   DEALINGS IN GOODS

A consensual dealing in goods may take one of three forms:

(a)   an outright disposition of the absolute interest;

(b)   a disposition of the absolute interest by way of mortgage;

(c)   the creation of a limited interest.

Interests in goods may also be transferred by operation of law, as in the case of death or bankruptcy of the holder of the interest, or be subjected to a security created by law, as with a common law or statutory lien.[139] In certain situations the two methods may be combined, the transfer taking place by act of the parties but operating, by virtue of a statutory provision or rule of law, to confer on the transferee a title better than that of his transferor, so that the absolute owner is divested of ownership even though he had not himself participated in the transfer at all.[140]

(i)   Disposition of the absolute interest

An outright disposition of goods *inter vivos* may be effected at law by sale,[141] exchange,[142] gift or loan,[143] or as part of some other transaction, as where materials are supplied under a building contract. In contrast to land, an agreement for the outright transfer of goods is a mere executory contract. Until the transfer takes effect at law, the intended transferee acquires no proprietary interest of any kind.[144] The only way in which an outright disposition of goods can be effected in equity is by declaration of trust.

The position is otherwise in the case of dealings with an absolute interest by way of mortgage,[145] to which the Sale of Goods Act 1979 does not apply even where the mortgage is in the form of a sale,[146] so that an agreement for a mortgage is treated in equity as a mortgage.[147]

(ii)   Limited interests in goods

A limited interest in goods can be created at law only by the taking of possession, under a pledge, rental, lease or other form of bailment, or the retention of

139   See p 621.

140   See pp 619 ff.

141   See chs 7 and 8.

142   See p 202.

143   See p 40, n 99.

144   In the case of sale of goods, this is considered to result from the Sale of Goods Act (p 219); and the court would presumably apply a similar principle to contracts of exchange. An agreement for a gift, or a purported gift not perfected by delivery of possession or by deed, confers no interest on the donee, legal or equitable, for equity does not perfect an imperfect gift, save in exceptional cases, such as those in which the donee can invoke a proprietary estoppel. See Snell's *Equity* (30th edn, 2000), pp 124–125.

145   For this purpose, the reservation of title, eg under a contract of sale, is not considered in law to constitute a security interest; see also p 583. See pp 607–608 as to the effect of extending reservation of title to cover proceeds.

146   Section 62(4).

147   See p 626.

possession in exercise of a lien.[148] This is because, as we have seen, the doctrine of indivisibility of legal ownership precludes a limited legal interest from being created derivatively out of an existing legal interest.[149] Hence a limited interest in goods arising otherwise than by virtue of possession can take effect only in equity.

An equitable interest in goods does not have to be of a type which, if fully perfected, would be recognized at law. A full range of limited interests is available in equity, including a mortgage, a life interest, an entailed interest and an interest for a term of years under a trust.

9.   DEALINGS IN INTANGIBLES

We have previously remarked on the value of debts and other intangibles as assets available for disposal by way of trade or security.[150] As in the case of goods, the absolute interest in an intangible may be disposed of outright or may be made the subject of security. Similarly, a pledge of or other limited interest in intangibles may be created by the delivery of possession, but in English law only documentary intangibles are susceptible to this treatment,[151] since a pure intangible is by definition incapable of physical possession. As the mode and effect of dealings in documentary intangibles differ markedly from those of pure intangibles, these two forms of choses in action require separate discussion.

(i)   Pure intangibles

A pure intangible is a right which is not in law considered to be represented by a document.[152] At common law, such an intangible was generally regarded as incapable of assignment. This was partly because the common law considered rights under a contract to be intended to be personal to the contracting parties and partly through a fear that if the assignment of contract rights were recognized, the path would be open to the evils of maintenance, by which a party having no legitimate interest in pursuing a claim could, by taking it over, pursue remedies which might not have been pursued by the original creditor. The courts of equity, however, were less troubled by these apparent difficulties and were prepared to order the assignor to allow his name to be used by the assignee in a common law action.[153] This rather cumbersome approach is now unnecessary, since it is provided by statute that if certain conditions are fulfilled,[154] the assignee of the debt or other chose in action acquires a legal right to it and can sue in his own name. The

---

148 See p 31.
149 See p 34.
150 See generally Fidelis Oditah, *Legal Aspects of Receivables Financing* (1991).
151 See pp 48 ff, 585.
152 As to the consequences of a right being so represented, and the tests for distinguishing a documentary intangible from a pure intangible, see p 48. For the assignment of debts and other pure intangibles, see p 49.
153 Indeed, the common law courts themselves regularly allowed an assignee to sue in the name of his assignor where this did not appear to be objectionable.
154 Ie, an absolute assignment in writing under the hand of the assignor and written notice to the debtor.

statutory provisions[155] apply equally to an outright sale or gift of choses in action and to a mortgage, that is, an assignment by way of security with a proviso (express or implied) for re-assignment on redemption. But a charge of a chose in action – which, as we have seen, is a mere incumbrance and does not operate to transfer any proprietary interest – is outside the scope of the statute and continues to have effect in equity only.

An agreement to assign an intangible constitutes an equitable assignment, as does an actual assignment which does not conform to all the conditions provided for a statutory assignment. The difference between an equitable assignment and a statutory assignment is procedural rather than substantive: the equitable assignee may in a proper case be required to have the assignor joined as plaintiff.[156] No other disability attaches to an equitable assignment so long as notice of the assignment is given to the debtor before payment by the debtor to the assignor and before the giving of notice by any subsequent assignee.[157] But failure to give notice of assignment can have disastrous consequences for the assignee.[158]

(ii)   Documentary intangibles

Documentary intangibles are of three kinds: documents of title to payment of money (termed instruments[159]), documents of title to negotiable securities (eg bearer bonds and notes), and documents of title to goods. Instruments, bonds, notes, and the like are true documents of title in that ownership of the underlying right to the securities or money may be transferred by delivery of the instrument, bond or note, if so intended. By contrast, documents of title to goods, such as bills of lading, do not in themselves embody ownership rights, merely control giving constructive possession, and it is this control which is transferable by delivery, with any necessary indorsement.[160] The feature characterizing a documentary intangible is that the debt or other obligation is considered in law to be locked up in the document, with the following consequences:

(a)   Delivery of the document, with any necessary indorsement,[161] will, if so intended, operate to transfer to the deliveree legal title to the debt or other right embodied in the document without the need for any instrument of assignment or any notice to the obligor.

(b)   So long as the document remains current, the right to sue on the original consideration for which it was given is suspended.[162]

---

155 Law of Property Act 1925, s 136.
156 Under CPR r 19.4.
157 See pp 773–774.
158 See pp 773–774.
159 See chs 16–19.
160 See Goode, *Proprietary Rights and Insolvency*, pp 59 ff. Older cases tend to treat documents of title to goods as meaning just that, probably because the practice of pledging documents of title was still undeveloped and the transfer of the document of title was usually identified by the contract of sale, expressly or impliedly, as the point at which the property was to pass.
161 See pp 490, 886.
162 See p 526.

(c)   If the obligor tenders payment or other performance to the holder, he obtains a good discharge.

(d)   Conversely, if the obligor tenders payment or other performance to one who is not the holder (eg to the original obligee after he has parted with the document), he does not obtain a good discharge.

(e)   The document is treated as a chattel, with the result that it may be pledged and the person entitled to possession of it is protected by the same tort remedies (conversion, trespass to goods, etc) as are available to protect possession of ordinary chattels.[163]

A document embodying rights transferable by its indorsement and delivery is said to be *negotiable*, and the act of transfer is termed negotiation.[164] It will be apparent that transfer by negotiation is much more convenient than transfer by assignment. Since the obligation is locked up in the document, the delivery of the document, with any necessary indorsement,[165] is all that is needed to transfer the obligation. No separate instrument of assignment is necessary. Further, no notice of transfer or assignment has to be given to the obligor, who knows that the only person to whom he is entitled to make payment or tender delivery is the person who is the holder of the document at the time of its maturity, whether or not he was the original obligee. Finally (and this is limited to negotiable instruments and negotiable securities, as opposed to negotiable documents of title), whereas a mere assignee of a right to a sum of money takes subject to equities, the holder of a negotiable instrument or bearer security who qualifies as a holder in due course takes free from defects in the title of his transferor.

Whether an intangible will be recognized at common law as a documentary intangible depends upon mercantile usage. Is the document one which is treated as representing the obligation? The convenient way of testing this is to ask whether the document is of such a class that in ordinary mercantile usage the obligor's performance would be owed not to the original obligee as such but to whoever is the current holder of the document and in exchange for its surrender. If so, it is highly likely that the intangible is a documentary intangible and capable of transfer or pledge as such. Into this category fall bills of lading, negotiable bills of exchange[166] and a range of other negotiable instruments.[167] If, on the other hand, the document is not of this character, the intangible will be a pure intangible and as such will be capable of being dealt with only by way of assignment or charge, not

---

163   For this purpose an instrument is assessed at its face value (*International Factors Ltd v Rodriguez* [1979] QB 351).

164   There is an unfortunate ambiguity in the term 'negotiable'. In its broad sense, it denotes an instrument or document of title transferable by delivery, with any necessary indorsement. In its narrow sense, it means an instrument which is capable of being held by a bona fide purchaser for value without notice (ie, a holder in due course), free from defects in the title of his transferor. An instrument negotiable in the broad sense is a documentary intangible and as such is pledgeable even if it is not capable of giving rise to holder in due course status. But a payment order or undertaking which is not transferable at all is not a documentary intangible and is not pledgeable except as a scrap of paper.

165   See p 489.

166   A bill of exchange may be rendered non-negotiable by appropriate wording. See p 490, n 57.

167   See chs 18–21.

by negotiation or pledge. Thus, a debt for goods sold and delivered may be recorded in an invoice sent to the debtor, of which a copy is retained by the creditor, but delivery of the copy of the invoice will not transfer title to the debt since it is not a document the possession of which establishes a right to payment. The same applies to sums payable under building contracts and hire-purchase agreements. Even the right to payment under an insurance contract is not a documentary intangible, for though production of the policy is normally required as a condition of payment, the obligation is owed to the name insured, not to the holder of the document as such. The essence of a documentary intangible is that in mercantile usage the right travels with the document.

10. ESSENTIAL ELEMENTS FOR THE CONSENSUAL TRANSFER OF REAL RIGHTS

Whether a transaction relates to tangible or intangible property, four elements are essential if the intended transfer is to be legally effective. First, the person alleged to be the transferor must have had a title to the asset or a power to dispose of it.[168] Secondly, he must have intended to divest himself of his title.[169] Thirdly, he must have taken steps to effectuate that intention by an act of transfer or an agreement for transfer recognized in equity as a transfer. Fourthly, the property claimed to have been transferred must be identifiable as the subject matter of the transfer agreement, either because it has been so identified in the agreement itself or because it has become identified as the result of its subsequent setting aside and appropriation to the agreement by an unconditional act of appropriation made in conformity with the agreement. These propositions may seem self-evident, yet they continue to generate litigation, both as to the validity of the propositions themselves and as to their applicability to the particular facts of the case. Particular problems arise where materials contributed by different people to be made up for them by a third party into finished products are commingled and the third party becomes bankrupt before appropriating the products to any contract with any particular contributor[170] or where a number of buyers contract to purchase given quantities of goods from stock in an identified warehouse and the seller becomes bankrupt before appropriating any of the stock to any particular sale contract.[171]

The need for identifiability applies as much to dealings in intangible property as it does to dealings in tangibles, and as much to declarations of trust as to agreements for sale or charge. For example, the requirement of identifiability is satisfied if A Ltd agrees to transfer to B Ltd all debts due and to become due to A Ltd from third parties,[172] but not if A Ltd agrees to transfer 50% in value of such debts, for such an agreement does not identify the debtors or the debts, and the transfer of ownership depends upon a subsequent act of appropriation of identified debts to the agreement.

168   See p 415.
169   Or be estopped from denying that he intended it.
170   See p 220.
171   See p 221.
172   See *Tailby v Official Receiver* (1888) 13 App Cas 523.

The problem of identification arises only where performance of the transfer obligation relates to fungibles, that is, to one or more legally interchangeable units forming part of a larger collection or bulk and requiring segregation from the bulk in order to become ascertained.[173] Fungibility is thus the antithesis of specificity and presupposes that the property which is the subject of the transfer obligation is divisible by transfer into units capable of ownership separately from the property of which they previously formed part. Thus the question of ascertainment does not arise in relation to the transfer of shares in a single chattel, such as a ship or a racehorse, or shares in a particular issue of securities or part of a single debt, for in all these cases segregation is legally impossible and all that can be transferred is co-ownership of a single, identified asset.[174]

11. CONFLICTING CLAIMS TO PURE PERSONALTY

(i) Types of conflict

There are various situations in which two or more conflicting claims are made to tangible or intangible personalty and the law has to determine which of the claims is to be accorded priority. These divide into four broad groups:

(a) BOTH PARTIES CLAIM AN INDEFEASIBLE TITLE TO THE ABSOLUTE INTEREST IN THE ASSET. In this situation, winner usually takes all, since the upholding of one claim almost invariably destroys the other. The archetypal case is that in which goods belonging to A are wrongfully sold by B to C, as where goods acquired under a hire-purchase agreement are sold by the hirer to a third party. If A's claim is upheld, C will have to return the goods or at least to pay their value. There is no question of C's interest being merely subordinated to that of A, for A's interest is absolute and will thus endure indefinitely. Alternatively, if C's claim is upheld, A is adjudged to have lost the title he formerly enjoyed. A similar dispute can arise in relation to intangibles where A, to whom a debt is owed, sells the debt to B and then fraudulently sells the same debt to C. Exceptionally, the dispute between the two claimants to an absolute interest may be resolved by declaring that they have equal or unequal shares in the goods, as where C wrongfully mingles the property of A with that of B to form a new product. A slightly different type of conflict arises where, for example, B wrongfully sells goods belonging to A and assigns the resulting account for value to T, and A lays claim to the same account as proceeds of his goods. This is dealt with below.

(b) BOTH PARTIES CLAIM A DEFEASIBLE TITLE TO THE ABSOLUTE INTEREST. The typical case is where the owner of an asset mortgages it first to A and then to B. Here both parties have title, but since this is defeasible by repayment of the secured debt, the issue is one of priorities. Assuming that A's first mortgage has priority, B's second mortgage attaches to the debtor's equity of redemption, so that if A's mortgage is paid off without the need for sale of the asset, B's mortgage is promoted, while if

---

173 See p 210.
174 See p 60 and Roy Goode, 'Are Intangible Assets Fungible' [2003] LMCLQ 379.

the asset has to be sold to pay off the debt due to A, B's mortgage will attach to any surplus remaining.

(c) ONE PARTY CLAIMS TITLE TO THE ABSOLUTE INTEREST, THE OTHER TO A LIMITED INTEREST. Here the position is slightly different again, since ownership of the absolute interest is not in issue, and the sole question is whether this is subject to the limited interest claimed by the other party. If the limited interest is upheld, the absolute owner does not lose everything, but his goods remain encumbered by the limited interest until this is discharged. A typical case is where goods which are the property of A have been deposited by B with C for repair in such circumstances that C has a lien on them for the repair charge which is valid against A. Another example is where A sells assets to B which are subject to a charge in favour of C. The rights of B are not extinguished, merely subordinated to the charge. But if the holder of the limited interest is unsuccessful, then he loses entirely, except where the court is able to come to his aid through restitutionary principles.[175]

(d) BOTH PARTIES CLAIM A LIMITED INTEREST. The typical case is where the owner of a chattel charges it first to A and then to B. Title to the absolute interest remains in the debtor; in all other respects the situation is the same as in case (b). The upholding of one claim does not destroy the other but merely subordinates it so that, to the extent to which the value of the debt is sufficient to satisfy both claims, loss is not suffered by the holder of the subordinate interest. In this case both claims are to an equitable interest. It is also possible to have a contest between the holder of a limited legal interest and the holder of a limited equitable interest, as where goods are charged to A and then pledged to B. But there cannot be two concurrent limited legal interests in the same asset. The indivisibility of possession of personalty precludes the possibility in the case of goods, and all limited interests in pure intangibles are equitable in character.

(ii)   Tracing at common law and in equity[176]

The distinction between real and personal rights is well brought out by comparing tracing in equity with its common law counterpart. A person whose asset is wrongfully disposed of by another may, in lieu of following that asset into the hands of its new holder, assert a claim to the proceeds received in exchange for it.

The common law did not recognize the trust; accordingly, if A transferred an asset to B to hold on trust for O, the common law regarded B as the owner and did not recognize the trust in favour of O. If A had wanted to vest ownership in O, he should have done so by a transfer in due form. In consequence, if B, the bailee of O's goods, wrongfully sold them to T, legal title to the proceeds passed to B, not to O, and O's common law remedy was limited to a purely personal claim for the amount received by B or to an *ad rem* claim for delivery up of the proceeds if they

---

175   Eg, by giving him an allowance for improvements. See p 62.

176   See Lionel D. Smith, *The Law of Tracing* (1997); Burrows, *Law of Restitution*, ch 2; Goff and Jones, *Law of Restitution*, ch 2; Graham Virgo, *The Principles of the Law of Restitution* (1999), Pt V; Peter Birks, *Unjust Enrichment* (1985), pp 178 ff and *Introduction to the Law of Restitution* (1985), pp 377 ff.

were non-fungible tangibles. The common law also provided O with similar personal rights against T2, a transferee of the proceeds from B,[177] except where T2 acquired an overriding title to them as a purchaser for value or perhaps where they lost their identity through commingling in a bank account.[178] But since O had no real rights in the proceeds, he could not assert title to them against the trustee in bankruptcy of B or T2 and had to content himself with proving in the bankruptcy in competition with other creditors.

Equity, however, treats B as a trustee of the proceeds resulting from his improper disposition of O's asset, thereby giving O a proprietary right to the proceeds[179] which he can assert against a trustee in bankruptcy and entitling O to follow the proceeds from B's hands into those of T2, except where T2 has acquired an overriding title. But since the equitable remedy is proprietary, not personal, T2 incurs no liability in equity if, having received the proceeds in good faith, he parts with them to T3 before receiving notice of O's rights.[180] In this situation, O is left to pursue his common law remedy against T2 for money had and received (in the case of a money fund) or conversion (where the proceeds take the form of goods), a remedy which will be given only if T2 received the proceeds as a volunteer or with notice of O's rights.

Professor Lionel Smith's work *The Law of Tracing* has done much to clarify both thinking and terminology in this complex subject. First, a distinction is drawn between *following* the original asset and *tracing* its proceeds. Secondly, tracing is not itself a remedy, merely a legal mechanism to establish that a benefit received by the defendant can be identified as resulting from a diminution in the plaintiff's assets. Assuming that this is demonstrated, it is then for the law to determine, according to rules of *claiming*, whether the plaintiff has a proprietary claim to what the defendant received or whether this is barred by an available defence. Thirdly, it is wrong to regard proceeds as the original asset in a changed form, since the original asset continues to exist, and the proceeds represent the exchange value of the asset to the parties to the transaction which produces them. It follows that there is no need to show any physical correlation between the asset the plaintiff lost and the asset the defendant received, merely a loss of *value* by the plaintiff and a receipt of *value* by the defendant. Accordingly, an improper transfer of value by novation[181] is just as traceable as a transfer of value by assignment. These concepts have now been endorsed by the highest authority.[182]

Until recently it had been thought that a claim to proceeds of an unauthorized disposition was based on unjust enrichment, rather than being a vindication of a

---

177 *Banque Belge Pour L'Etranger v Hambrouck* [1921] 1 KB 321. See further p 457, as to tracing claims to money.

178 *Agip (Africa) Ltd v Jackson* [1991] Ch 547, where the Court of Appeal, like Millett J at first instance, [1990] Ch 265, experienced some difficulty with the judgment of Atkin LJ in the *Banque Belge* case suggesting the contrary. See further p 457.

179 For a discussion of proprietary claims to money, see p 458; and for claims to the proceeds of goods supplied under reservation of title, pp 607–608, 720.

180 *Re Diplock, Diplock v Wintle* [1948] Ch 465.

181 See pp 457, 653.

182 See *Foskett v McKeown* [2001] 1 AC 102 per Lord Millett at 128.

pure property right. However, the House of Lords has now held, in *Foskett v McKeown*,[183] that the interest in proceeds is a pure property right flowing from ownership of the original asset and does not derive from the law of restitution. Such a property right, like other property rights, is determined by fixed principles and is not dependent on the court's discretion or on ideas as to what is fair, just and reasonable.[184] Accordingly, the claimant succeeds by virtue of his title and not by way of reversal of unjust enrichment.[185] It is therefore unnecessary for the claimant to show that the defendant has been unjustly enriched; the claimant is entitled to the proceeds as of right, not in exercise of the court's discretion, and defences particular to the law of restitution, such as change of position, are not available.[186] The effect is substantially to reduce the concept of a *restitutionary* proprietary claim.[187] Concern has been expressed that the pure property approach, under which the claimant has an interest simultaneously in the original asset and its proceeds, leads to a geometric multiplication of the claimant's property.[188] The answer is that the claimant has to elect whether to follow the original asset or to trace the proceeds, and once he has elected to pursue one remedy, the other is extinguished.[189]

Tracing in equity presupposes that legal title resides in one person, beneficial ownership in another. Where legal and beneficial ownership are in the same person, there is no separate equitable interest, for the existence of such an interest depends on a division between management and ownership.

(iii) The resolution of conflicting claims

The detailed rules of law by which conflicting claims to goods are resolved are examined at appropriate points in subsequent chapters. But certain principles have evolved at common law and in equity, and these will apply except so far as cut down by statute. They apply equally to tangibles and intangibles, and will constantly recur in our subsequent discussion of priority problems.[190] They are as follows.

---

183 Ibid.

184 Ibid, per Lord Millett at 127.

185 The issue had divided academic writers. See, for example, Peter Birks, [1997] NZ Law Rev 623, advocating the concept of reversal of unjust enrichment; Ross Granthan and Charles E.F. Rickett, [1997] NZ Law Rev 668, and Virgo, *Law of Restitution*, pp 12 ff., contending that the right of recovery is based on property, not unjust enrichment. Mr Virgo's reasoning was in substance adopted by the House of Lords, albeit without acknowledgment.

186 *Foskett v McKeown*, n 182.

187 The concept is not necessarily extinguished altogether, since there are types of proprietary claim which are based not on diminution of the claimant's estate but on equitable wrongdoing, for example, a claim to the disgorgement of benefits received by a company director from pursuing business opportunities which, if he pursued them at all, should have been procured for the benefit of the company, not of himself. See *Cook v Deeks* [1916] AC 554; *Regal (Hastings) Ltd v Gulliver* [1967] 2 AC 134n; Roy Goode, 'Property and Unjust Enrichment' in *Essays on the Law of Restitution* (ed Andrew Burrows, 1991), pp 215 ff. and 'Proprietary Restitutionary Claims' in *Restitution, Past, Present and Future* (eds W. R. Cornish *et al.*, 1998), 63 at pp 73–74.

188 Burrows, *Law of Restitution*, p 92, taking up a point originally made by Birks, *Law of Restitution*, p 394.

189 Smith, *Tracing*, p 324.

190 See ch 24.

(a) NEMO DAT QUOD NON HABET. The rule of the common law is that only the legal owner of goods or one who has been authorized or otherwise held out as entitled to dispose of them can make a disposition which will be effective to divest the legal owner of his title or encumber his interest. In principle, therefore, the owner is entitled to pursue his goods even into the hands of an innocent purchaser for value, and to assert proprietary rights over the proceeds and products of his property.[191] A further aspect of the *nemo dat* rule is that any transfer by the owner himself takes effect subject to existing real rights, so that if the asset is subject to a security interest, the purchaser's rights are qualified by that interest, and if goods are in the possession of a lessee, the purchaser takes them subject to the rights enjoyed by the lessee by virtue of his possession under the lease.[192]

Numerous exceptions to the *nemo dat* rule have been made by statute, but the rule nevertheless retains considerable vigour. Where statute or a rule of law does create an exception to the *nemo dat* rule, the effect is that the transferor effectively conveys not merely his own interest in the asset but that of the person from whom his interest was derived.[193] Thus, a sale by a mortgagee in exercise of his statutory powers transfers to the purchaser not merely the mortgagee's legal interest but full ownership. Similarly, a sale by a pledgee in exercise of his common law power of sale conveys the title of the pledgor. Moreover, in certain cases the exception may result in a person being able to transfer ownership of an asset in which he has not merely a limited interest (eg by virtue of possession) but no interest at all. Thus, where the same debt is assigned to two different purchasers in succession and the second purchaser takes in good faith and is the first to give notice to the debtor, he acquires ownership of the debt in priority to the first assignee despite the fact that as a result of the first assignment the original creditor had nothing left to assign.

(b) SHELTERING. Where, under an exception to the *nemo dat* rule, a person acquires an indefeasible title, he can transfer this in all respects as absolute owner, and those taking from him can shelter under this title and will acquire title in turn even if taking with notice of the prior owner's rights. Thus if H, a person holding a motor car on hire-purchase from the absolute owner, O, wrongfully sells this to P, a private purchaser, who buys in good faith and without notice of the hire-purchase agreement, thereby acquiring a good title under Part III of the Hire Purchase Act 1964,[194] and who then resells the car to T, T will get a good title even though aware at the time of buying the vehicle that it had been fraudulently sold by H at a time when it belonged to O. If the position were otherwise, the title acquired by P would be rendered illusory, for it would not be marketable. There is one exception to the rule as to sheltering – it cannot be invoked by the original wrongdoer, so that if the vehicle were to be reacquired by H from T or an intervening party, H would not be allowed to retain it against O.[195]

---

191 See above.

192 See Goode, *Hire-Purchase Law and Practice*, p 35. For a different view, see W. J Swadling, 'The Proprietary Effects of a Hire of Goods' in Palmer and McKendrick, *Interests in Goods*, ch 20.

193 And in certain cases even the paramount title of a third party.

194 See p 438.

195 2 Bl Comm 450. The same rule applies in equity (*Re Stapleford Colliery Co, Barrow's Case* (1880) 14 Ch D 432 at 445).

(c) A LEGAL INTEREST IS TO BE PREFERRED TO AN EQUITABLE INTEREST. The holder of an equitable interest becomes subordinated to one who subsequently purchases the legal interest in good faith and without notice, at the time he advanced his money, that the equitable interest existed. So if A grants an equitable mortgage of an asset to B and then mortgages that asset in equity to C, who takes in good faith for value and without notice, C, though initially subordinated to B, can jump ahead of B by getting in the legal title, even if by that time he has acquired notice of B's interest.[196] There is one exception. Priority as between successive assignees of a debt or other chose in action is governed by the rule in *Dearle v Hall* and thus goes to the first to give notice to the debtor or fund holder, even if the interest of the person giving notice is equitable and that of the other assignee legal.[197]

(d) WHERE BOTH INTERESTS ARE EQUITABLE, THE FIRST IN TIME PREVAILS. Such a conflict is unusual in the case of goods but sometimes arises where two equitable claims are made to a debt, eg in a contest between a factor and bank holding a floating charge. In the case of debts, however, this priority rule gives way to a stronger equitable principle: that priority goes to the first to give notice of his interest to the debtor if, being the later party, he was without notice of the prior claim. It is only where neither has given notice that the order of creation of the equitable interests is relevant, and in such a case the priority so established is provisional only, since it is liable to be displaced if the holder of the second interest gives notice first. The interest which is prior in time may also be displaced as a result of the second assignee getting in the legal title, in the manner described below.

(e) A LEGAL OR EQUITABLE INTEREST PURCHASED FOR VALUE AND WITHOUT NOTICE PREVAILS OVER A MERE EQUITY. The position concerning mere equities has already been discussed.[198]

(f) A PURCHASER FOR VALUE IS PREFERRED TO A MERE DONEE ('VOLUNTEER'). An interest taken for new value is in principle stronger than one taken for past value or for no value at all. The concept of value and the way in which the deemed order of cash flows on a current account may have the effect of converting past value into new value are discussed later in relation to security interests.[199]

12. THE EFFECT OF TRANSFERS BY A NON-OWNER

(i) Validity and priority

Where, without authority, a person purports to transfer an asset to which he has no title (either because he never had title or because he has lost it), a lawyer asked to

---

196 *Bailey v Barnes* [1894] 1 Ch 25; *Taylor v Russell* [1892] AC 244; *McCarthy & Stone Ltd v Julian S. Hodge & Co Ltd* [1971] 2 All ER 973. As to the circumstances in which the holder of a legal estate or interest may be postponed to a *subsequent* equitable incumbrancer, see p 655.
197 See pp 773, 794.
198 See p 27.
199 See pp 635–637.

consider the effect of such a transfer will often characterize the question as one of validity. Is the transfer valid? Or is it void? If English law did not admit any exceptions to the *nemo dat* rule, such a formulation would be entirely accurate, for an unauthorized transfer by a non-owner would then be inherently impossible as a matter of law and would thus fall into the same category as, for example, a transfer prohibited by statute or a sale to a person of what is already his own property. But because of the various exceptions to the *nemo dat* rule, a transfer by a non-owner cannot be treated in this way. The mere fact that the transferor lacks title is insufficient by itself to tell us whether the transferee will acquire a good title. There can be no doubt that as between transferor and transferee the disposition is 'valid' in any event. The question is in truth one of priority, ie whether the claim of the transferee is superior to that of the original owner.

In just the same way, it is inaccurate to speak of a transfer in legal form by one who has a good title as inexorably valid on that account. It may, for example, be valid as between him and the transferee while void against third parties for want of registration. Hence validity, like invalidity, is a relative concept. The question is, as before, one of priority as between transferee and third parties.

(ii) Nature of interest acquired by transferee

If, by virtue of some exception to the *nemo dat* rule, a person acquiring an asset from one not entitled to dispose of it nevertheless gets a good title, it is pertinent to inquire whose title he gets. Consider the following:

> *Case 1:* S sells goods to B, to whom the property passes under the contract. S, while still in possession of the goods, then sells them a second time, to C, to whom he delivers them. C acquires legal title to the goods, overriding that previously acquired by B.[200]

> *Case 2:* T steals goods belonging to O. The goods are later seized and sold by the sheriff to W to satisfy a judgment against T. W gets a good title overriding that of O.[201]

What, in each case, is the interest acquired? Does S confer on C the interest which S had before he sold to B? Or does C acquire from S the interest of B, through some sort of involuntary assignment resulting from S's second sale? Or does C take a new and original interest? Again, does the sale by T transfer to W the interest (if any) enjoyed by T himself, or the interest of O, or does it confer on W a new and original interest?

We can start to answer these questions by observing that the assumption made in the first question is not quite accurate. S, having sold to B, retains possession and thus a legal interest. The quantum of that interest will depend on S's intention. So long as he intends to possess as bailee, his interest will be limited. Once he assumes the intention to hold as owner, he acquires a full possessory title, subject only to the stronger title of B. Similarly, T, being in possession, has a legal interest and, if

---

200 Factors Act 1889, s 8; Sale of Goods Act 1979, s 24. See p 431.
201 Supreme Court Act 1981, s 138B. See p 443.

holding *animo domini*, has possessory title to an absolute interest, subject only to the stronger title of O. Yet this does not solve our problem. For since the legal title retained by S is subordinate to the indefeasible title of B, and the legal title obtained by T is subordinate to the indefeasible title of O, then if the sale by S to C and the sale by T to W were merely transfers of their existing legal titles, the title acquired by C would be subordinate to that of B and the title acquired by W would be subordinate to that of O.

Clearly, then, our two illustrations are exceptions to the *nemo dat* rule, for while both S and T had a legal title to convey, they effectively conferred more than they themselves possessed, by giving C and W a title paramount to that of B and O. The question is, whose title? Let us start with Case 1. There are at least three different possibilities. The first is that C acquires from S the interest of B, through some sort of involuntary assignment resulting from S's second sale. This is plainly not the case. C's title derives directly from S and is acquired upon the terms of his contract with S; it is not in any way derived from B or affected by the contract between S and B. The second possibility is that S confers on C the interest which S himself had before the sale to B. The third possibility is that C obtains a new and original title not (or not necessarily) limited to that previously held by S. English law does not deal with the problem conceptually, so that we cannot state with certainty whether in jurisprudential terms C obtains a title deriving from that of S himself or a new and independent title. Instead, the law concerns itself with the desired result, treating the issue as one of priorities. This particular exception to the *nemo dat* rule is founded on an underlying estoppel concept; B, by choosing to leave S in possession, assumes the risk of a fraudulent double sale. But if S himself lacks title there is no good reason why the true owner should be deprived of his property. So C gets as good a title as S had himself prior to the sale to B, but no better.[202] Whether C acquires *the* title of S or merely a fresh title as good as that of S is not a question the law answers. C has priority over B but not over the owner, and that is that.

By contrast, the rule operative in Case 2 is not based on the conduct of O but is designed to protect the inviolability of a purchase on a lawful sale by way of execution. Hence W's rights do not merely displace those of T and of any other person who might claim under T, but override O's title as well.[203] We might ask whether W's ownership is original or is derived from O. But the law does not approach the problem in this way; it simply declares that W acquires a title displacing that of O.

In general, the result produced by Case 1 is more typical of the operation of an exception to the *nemo dat* rule, since English law is reluctant to shut out an owner who did not entrust possession or powers of disposition to the wrongful transferor or to an intermediate party. Thus, if B agrees to buy goods from S under a conditional sale agreement and, before becoming the owner, sells and delivers them to T, T will acquire title as against S but not as against a person whose title is

---

202 See p 437.
203 See p 425.

paramount to that of S.[204] Similarly, a mortgagee exercising a power of sale transfers to the purchaser ownership of the asset free from the interests of the mortgagor[205] and those claiming under him[206] but subject to the rights of a prior mortgagee. Again, the issue is resolved in a practical way by a priority rule and does not depend for its resolution on any *a priori* classification of the purchaser's title as original or derivative.

13.   IDENTIFYING THE OBJECT OF A TRANSFER OBLIGATION[207]

In considering the nature of claims to an asset, it is necessary to distinguish

a   an entitlement *in specie*;
b   a claim to a fungible;
c   an interest in a fund; and
d   a right to payment of a debt.

(i)   Interests *in specie*

O has an entitlement *in specie* to an asset in the hands of B when the asset is identifiable[208] and the terms under which B holds it are such that he is under a duty to surrender or transfer the asset itself, and not merely its equivalent in the form of a comparable asset or money, to O or to deal with the asset at O's direction. Entitlements in specie, real or personal, may exist in any kind of asset, tangible or intangible, so long as it is identifiable to the transfer obligation.

(ii)   Claims to fungibles[209]

By contrast, fungibles are assets of which one unit is, in terms of an obligation owed by one party to another, indistinguishable from any other unit, so that a duty to deliver one unit is considered performed by the delivery of an equivalent unit. Fungibles are sometimes described as movables ordinarily valued by number, measurement or weight, eg grain or flour, but this is an inaccurate description. Whether assets are fungibles depends not on their physical characteristics but upon the nature of the obligation owed with respect to them. It matters not whether the subject of the contract is grain, flour or a motor car, or whether it is tangible or intangible. In a contract for the sale of unascertained, or generic, goods, the goods are *ex hypothesi* fungibles, since the duty of the seller is to sell and deliver not a specific chattel identified at the time of the contract but an article (ie *any* article) which answers to the contract description. The same is true of contract relating to

---

204   See pp 437–438.
205   Law of Property Act 1925, ss 2, 88, 89, 104.
206   Including a person to whom the mortgagor has contracted to sell the property (*Duke v Robson* [1973] 1 All ER 481).
207   This topic has been examined in more detail by the writer in (1976) 92 LQR 360 at pp 382 ff and 529 ff.
208   As opposed to being a fungible. See below.
209   See generally Roy Goode, 'Are intangible assets fungible?' [2003] LMCLQ 74.

quasi-specific goods, that is, goods which are not themselves identified but form part of a larger bulk. These are fungibles in that the goods cannot be ascertained until they have been separated from the bulk.[210]

Similar considerations apply to intangibles, such as shares and debts, with the difference that since intangibles do not lend themselves to physical segregation, the test of fungibility is whether they are legally divisible into units capable of separate ownership. Only in this situation is segregation both possible and necessary to identify the subject of the transfer obligation. The failure to appreciate this fact has led to much misunderstanding. Thus the decision of the Court of Appeal in *Hunter v Moss*,[211] in which the court upheld the validity of a trust of part of the issued share capital of a company, has been criticized on the ground that the shares intended to be the subject of the trust had not been segregated, so that the trust should have failed for want of certainty of subject matter. But the criticism is misconceived. Shares of a particular issue are not like potatoes; they are not capable of segregation, either in fact or in law. A person who holds 50 shares in a company which has issued 500 shares is simply a co-owner of the issued share capital to the extent of 10%, and if he transfers 25 shares to another, the transferee in turn becomes a co-owner, to the extent of 5%, of the same issued share capital with the transferor and other shareholders. It is legally impossible to hold or transfer shares separately from the rest of the share capital. There is, in short, no means of segregation, even if the securities are numbered[212] – and the law does not require the impossible. The asset is a single asset, and the question of appropriation does not arise unless there are at least two legally interchangeable units. The same applies even to bearer securities. It is true that the pieces of paper embodying them are capable of physical segregation and thus of separate ownership, but these do no more than represent title to a co-ownership interest in a single asset, namely the totality of the issue of the securities. Likewise, there can be no objection to the assignment of part of a debt – for example, part of a sum standing to the credit of a bank account – for the effect of the assignment is to make the assignee co-owner of a single asset, the debt or deposit.

The position is otherwise, of course, where the terms of the transfer obligation are such that shares of different companies, or of different issues or classes of the same company, are interchangeable, as where a person agrees to provide his broker with collateral by way of margin deposit in the form of quoted securities to a given market value. In such a case the subject matter of the transfer obligation requires to be ascertained by appropriation of particular shares to the agreement. Similarly, where the intended assignment of debts relates not to a single debt but to two or more separate debts, whether due from the same debtor or different debtors, the assignor being free to decide which debts to allocate to the assignment agreement so long as they are of not less than a particular value, ownership cannot pass until such allocation has been made.

---

210   The position is otherwise where, by the terms of the contract or under s 20A of the Sale of Goods Act 1979, the buyer acquires a co-ownership interest in the bulk itself. See pp 222 ff.
211   [1994] 1 WLR 452.
212   Which is no longer the case for UK shares.

(iii) Interests in funds

In legal terms[213] a fund is an asset or collection of assets[214] vested in one person, whom we will call B, to manage on behalf of another, O, upon terms, express or implied, that the asset or assets so given shall be kept by B separate from his own property and that during the currency of his authority B shall be at liberty to change the components of the fund within the limits, if any, specified by his appointment. There are two crucial points to observe about the nature of an interest in a fund. The first is that the fund has an identity distinct from its component parts. O is the beneficial owner of the fund, B the owner of the individual assets from time to time comprising the fund. Unless O has and exercises a power to terminate the manager's authority and thus crystallize the fund, O has neither a possessory nor a proprietary right to any particular component of the fund, nor any right to insist that a specific component in the fund shall remain there. Hence until crystallization of the fund, O has no *locus standi* to pursue against B or a third party an action in conversion, or any other action founded on a right to possession of a specific asset.[215] It is B himself, and no other, who is the person entitled to assert rights over the components of the fund he is managing.[216] Thus the interest of O as beneficiary under an active trust is an interest in the fund of assets from time to time held by the trustee, not in any individual assets; and where O is the holder of a floating charge, his interest is in the fund of assets from time to time held by the company and falling within the scope of the charge, not in the individual assets themselves.[217] But O's interest in the fund is a real right, not simply a personal right, as is evident from the fact that if B were to become bankrupt, the assets comprising the fund would continue to be held for O and would not vest in B's trustee in bankruptcy. The second point to note is that an interest in a fund is more than a purely personal right, for O is entitled to have the fund kept intact (albeit with changing components) and to have misappropriated assets forming part of the fund followed into the hands of third parties other than those acquiring an overriding title. Further, in the event of the bankruptcy of the fundholder, the fund does not form part of his estate available to his creditors but must continue to be held and managed on behalf of O.

---

213 The words 'funds' and 'funds transfer' are also commonly used in a non- technical sense to describe a claim on a bank and the process by which a debtor's instruction to his bank to arrange for payment to his credit by transfer to the latter's bank account is implemented. See pp 464 ff.

214 The term 'fund' is sometimes employed in a narrow sense to denote a fund of money, but for the purposes of the present discussion it matters not whether the managed assets comprise money, goods, shares or pure intangibles. Moreover, while a fund is usually defined as a *collection* of assets, there is no reason why a fund should not be established with a single asset. The test of a fund is not the number of components it comprises but the power given to the manager to change them.

215 English literature on the nature of interests in a fund is surprisingly sparse. See Nolan (2004) 120 LQR 108, Goode (1976) 92 LQR 384, 529, and, for brief discussions, Lawson and Rudden, *Law of Property*, pp 44–46; Bernard Rudden, 'Things as things and things as wealth' (1994) OJLS 81; A. M. Honoré, 'Ownership', pp 132–133.

216 See Goode (1976) 92 LQR, pp 384, 529. Misappropriation of the fund by B himself does not alter its status as a fund, for unless the beneficiary's rights have meanwhile crystallized, the assets recovered from B must be managed by his successor.

217 See p 229.

The concept of a fund is known both to the common law and to equity. An interest in a fund is to be distinguished on the one hand from a real or personal claim to specific assets, as indicated above, and on the other from a mere debt claim, in that the fund is considered to have a distinct and continuous existence, despite the fact that its components are constantly changing,[218] and is thus susceptible to a tracing claim both at law (eg in a personal claim for money had and received, where the fund is a money fund) and in equity, for which a proprietary claim is available. No such claim can be asserted where B's obligation to O is purely in debt, for *ex hypothesi* there is no *res* to which the tracing claim can attach.[219]

14.   THE PROTECTION OF PROPERTY RIGHTS THROUGH THE LAW OF TORTS

The right to property in goods (with which are included documents and instruments[220]) is protected primarily through the law of torts. The owner of a chattel which is in the wrongful possession of another may be able to secure its return by physical repossession, but if he resorts to the courts, he has no ineluctable right to an order for its return. The court has a discretion[221] to make an order for delivery which allows the defendant the option of paying the value of the goods as damages. Further, in making an order for delivery of the goods, the court may impose such conditions as seem just,[222] and may thus, for example, make it a condition of the order that the plaintiff shall compensate the defendant for any increase in the value of the goods resulting from improvements made by him.[223]

Since the tort of conversion involves an interference with another's possession or right to possession, an action in conversion can in general be maintained only by one who was in possession or had an immediate right to possession at the time of the act complained of.[224] Ownership as such does not confer a title to sue[225] except so far as it is the source of, or is combined with, the immediate right to possess.[226]

---

218   Thus the River Thames can be described as an identifiable fund of water. The water at any given moment is not the same as the water a moment earlier, but it is still the River Thames. The Greek philosopher Heraclitus would not have subscribed to the fund theory. So far as he was concerned, you cannot step into the same river twice.

219   It is for this reason that the much-criticized decision in *Sharma v Joory* [1958] 1 QB 448 is plainly erroneous. See Goode (1976) 92 LQR 384 at pp 387–388.

220   See p 50.

221   See p 29.

222   Torts (Interference with Goods) Act 1977, s 3(6). This was so even before the Act. See *Peruvian Guano Co Ltd v Dreyfus Bros & Co* [1892] AC 166, per Lord Macnaghten at 176; *Greenwood v Bennett* [1973] QB 195.

223   *Greenwood v Bennett*, n 222; Torts (Interference with Goods) Act 1977, s 6.

224   See *Markesinis and Deakin's Tort Law* (5th edn, 2003), p 438; *Winfield & Jolowicz on Tort* (16th edn, 2002), pp 604–605; *Clerk & Lindsell on Torts* (18th edn, 2000), paras 14–46. See also *Leigh and Sillivan Ltd v Aliakmon Shipping Co Ltd* [1986] AC 785 (equitable owner of goods having no possessory title could not sue in negligence for damage to the goods without joining the legal owner).

225   See literature cited in n 224.

226   As in *International Factors Ltd v Rodriguez* [1979] QB 351.

On the other hand, a mere contractual right to possession of goods from one who is the owner does not suffice to ground a claim for conversion; it is necessary that the right to possess be allied with a property interest of some kind.[227] So a buyer of goods to whom the property has not yet passed cannot maintain an action for conversion against the seller for failure to deliver them in accordance with the contract of sale.

227 *Jarvis v Williams* [1955] 1 WLR 71.

3 Some Aspects of Contract Law

Commercial law, as we have previously remarked, is grounded in contract. This chapter provides a brief recapitulation of some of the more important principles of contract law,[1] but other sources of obligation, including tort, trusts and restitution, should constantly be kept in mind. English law remains in a state of uncertainty as to the circumstances in which the existence of a contractual relationship should attract a separate duty of care in tort[2] or in which a breach of contract should give rise to separate restitutionary remedies.[3] Indeed, it has been powerfully argued that 'the time is plainly ripe for a new theoretical structure for contract, which will place it more firmly in association with the rest of the law of obligations.'[4] In the present chapter we shall confine ourselves to the fundamentals of contract law as currently understood. The implications of the Human Rights Act 1998 for English contract law have yet to be determined and are not discussed here.[5]

I. THE NATURE AND FUNCTION OF CONTRACT LAW

A contract involves the exchange of equivalents. I agree to buy a television set from my local dealer for £300. The set is obviously worth to me at least slightly more than the £300, for otherwise there would be no point in my parting with my money; while to the dealer, the price is at least a little more than the value of the set to him, for otherwise he would have no incentive to sell it. The figure of £300 is thus seen by each side as a price which yields him a profit: from the seller's viewpoint, in money, from the buyer's, in satisfaction. Where the buyer purchases not for use but for resale, then both parties view the profit in money terms.

---

1 The leading study from an interdisciplinary perspective is Hugh Collins, *Regulating Contracts* (1999). The central themes of contract law are admirably described by Roger Brownsword in *Law of Contract* (2nd edn, ed Michael Furmston, 2003) ch 1.
2 For an illuminating analysis of the concurrence of liability in contract and tort, see the speech of Lord Goff in *Henderson v Merrett Syndicates Ltd* [1994] 3 All ER 506. See also Peter Cane, *Tort Law and Economic Interests* (2nd edn, 1996), pp 326 ff. and *Chitty on Contracts* (29th edn, 2004), paras 1-105 ff.
3 See Andrew Burrows, *Remedies for Torts and Breach of Contract* (2nd edn, 1994), pp 270 ff.; Law Commission Report, *Law of Contract; Pecuniary Restitution on Breach of Contract* (Law Com No 121, 1983).
4 P. S. Atiyah, *The Rise and Fall of Freedom of Contract* (1979), p 778. For recent formulations of contract law principles at an international level, see p 16, n 74; p 1209.
5 See Furmston, *Law of Contract*, paras 1.227 ff.

The primary function of contract law is to facilitate such exchanges by providing a reasonable assurance that each party will be held to his undertaking.[6] Contract law does not in general concern itself with the question whether the television set is in fact worth £300, rather than £100 or £500. It is left to the parties to decide what figure is a sufficient inducement to them to buy and sell, and if television set and price are regarded by the parties as equivalents, they will usually be accepted as such by the law. In the great majority of transactions, the exchange is both simultaneous and immediate. No sooner is the undertaking given than it is performed, as when I buy goods for cash at a store, pay my fare on a bus or at a railway station or consume and pay for a meal at a restaurant. The role of contract law in simultaneous exchange transactions is reduced, for prima facie nothing remains to be performed on either side. In legal terms the contract is almost immediately discharged by performance, and its life is thus very short. But this is not always the case. It may transpire that the parties were contracting under some fundamental mistake which prevented a valid contract from coming into existence in the first place. Alternatively, one of the parties may complain that the other's performance was defective, eg because the goods supplied were not of merchantable quality. If this complaint is well founded, it means that the undertaking to perform has not been fulfilled in conformity with the contract, which to this extent remains executory and susceptible to legal proceedings.

There are, moreover, many transactions in which it is not intended that performance shall be simultaneous and immediate. Often there is a long delay between the making of a promise and its implementation, and performance itself may be spread over a substantial period of time, as in the construction of an office block or an oil tanker. Contracts in which performance on one or both sides is to take place at a future date raise additional questions to which the law of contract is required to furnish answers, such as whether a party is justified in withholding or suspending performance because of default by the other or because of supervening impossibility, and what steps are open to compel performance where none has been tendered.

The law of contract is at its most visible when invoked in litigation, but its influence is felt at every stage in the relationship between the parties. A lawyer drafts a contract very much with the rules of contract law in mind, and will advise his client as to the enforceability and effect of the various provisions. The parties themselves have to take account of their prospective rights and liabilities when assessing their risk in entering into the transaction; and the very existence of the contract as a legally binding agreement may discourage a party from conduct adversely affecting the other's interests. Sensible business people do not conclude contracts in the expectation that litigation will result, but require the assurance of the law's assistance if other parties breach their undertakings. Once concluded, a contract is best put away in a drawer out of sight, except when a party needs to refer to it to

---

6 'A theme that runs through our law of contract is that the reasonable expectations of honest men must be protected. It is not a rule or a principle of law. It is the objective which has become and still is the principal moulding force of our law of contract' (Steyn J in *First Energy (UK) Ltd v Hungarian International Bank* [1993] 2 Lloyd's Rep 194, at 196). Lord Steyn returned to this theme extrajudicially in 'Contract Law: Fulfilling the Reasonable Expectations of Honest Men' (1997) 113 LQR 433.

refresh his memory as to what was agreed or to enforce his rights or resist claims made against him.

2.   CONTRACT, TORT AND RESTITUTION

The primary function of contract law is to secure for each contracting party the benefit of the bargain he has made. So on a breach of contract the innocent party is entitled to the protection of his expectation interest, that is, to be placed in the position he would have had if the contract had been performed. This is achieved either by a decree of specific performance compelling the defendant to perform (relatively infrequent) or by an award of damages representing the money value of the claimant's defeated contractual expectation. But contract law is not the only source of obligation that may arise within a contractual setting. The innocent party may also have claims in tort or restitution. For example, he may have been induced to enter into a contract by the other party's fraudulent or negligent misrepresentation, which is a tort,[7] thus causing loss to himself and unjustly enriching the other party.

The function of tort law is primarily to compensate a party for wrongful harm by putting him back into the position he would have been if the tort had not occurred. So on a claim for damages for fraudulent misrepresentation the measure of damages is not the value of the lost bargain but the amount necessary to restore the claimant to the position in which he was before the contract: in short, to protect his reliance interest. The claim is limited to the loss the claimant has suffered through entering into the transaction.

The role of restitution is different again. Here the measure of recovery is not the loss to the claimant but unjust enrichment of the defendant, who is required to disgorge benefits improperly received at the claimant's expense. So on rescission of a contract for misrepresentation the defendant is required to give back all benefits received under the contract.[8] Restitution may feature in various ways in a contractual context; for example, a party who has done work under a supposed contract which turns out to be void may have a restitutionary claim for the value of the services he provided;[9] and where as the result of a breach of contract the innocent party receives none of the benefit for which he bargained, as on the sale of goods by a party having no title to them, then instead of claiming damages the innocent party may pursue a restitutionary remedy for recovery of money paid on a total failure of consideration.[10] If the defendant has received no benefit, he is not subject to a restitutionary claim, even if the claimant has suffered a loss.[11] So where the defendant's misrepresentation was made in good faith and without negligence and

---

7   The common law has tended to take a restricted view of liability for negligent misstatements causing pure economic loss. In the context of contract s 2(1) of the Misrepresentation Act 1967 creates statutory liability for negligent misrepresentation but this is essentially tort-like in character.

8   See further p 109.

9   *Craven-Ellis v Canons Ltd* [1936] 2 KB 403.

10 See p 119.

11 For an exceptional case in which the defendant was ordered to account for profits received in consequence of his breach of contract see *Attorney-General v Blake* [2001] 1 AC 268, discussed p 116.

he has received nothing under the contract, the claimant has no claim either to damages in tort or to restitution.[12]

These three types of interest, expectation, reliance and restitution,[13] are not mutually exclusive; frequently they overlap. A person who incurs expenditure in negotiations leading up to a commercial contract will normally assume that if he secures the contract and it is duly performed, he will recoup his expenditure and make a profit. His expectation interest thus encompasses his reliance interest, and in certain conditions (eg, where the lost profit is hard to assess) the court may allow recovery of pre-contract expenditure as the measure of damages for breach of the contract.[14] Again, it is often the case that the benefit the defendant receives from his improper conduct corresponds to the loss suffered by the claimant. But this should not obscure the fundamental fact that these three different branches of law are designed to protect different types of interest.

3. PROMISE AND BARGAIN

Not every kind of promise creates a legal obligation. It may be that as a matter of morality a person ought to be held to his undertaking, but law and morality are not coterminous,[15] and there are many promises which are outside the scope of the law: acceptance of an invitation to a game of tennis or to afternoon tea, a voluntary promise to help a friend dig his garden or repair his car. The law concerns itself only with undertakings that are, or are reasonably perceived by the promisee to be, sufficiently serious in intent to justify legal recognition.

English law recognizes various ways of demonstrating seriousness of purpose so as to make a promise binding. One is for the promisor to exact something in exchange ('consideration') as the price of the promise – either performance of an act or an undertaking to perform it at a future date. Another is to put the promise into solemn form, as where a person executes a deed[16] covenanting to make a gift of money or property to a designated donee. A third is by showing that the promisee has relied on the promise.

In English law, only the first of these methods belongs to the realm of contract,[17] and we shall examine it next. Other types of promise owe their binding force to legal principles outside contract law. The promise by deed is enforceable because it

---

12 The court has power to substitute an award of damages for rescission under s 2(2) of the Misrepresentation Act 1967, but this is a limitation on the claimant's right to rescind, not an alternative remedy to which he is entitled.

13 First articulated as such in a seminal article by Lon Fuller and William Perdue, 'The Reliance Interest in Contract Damages', 46 Yale LJ 52, 373 (1936–1937), pts 1 and 2.

14 *Anglia Television Ltd v Reed* [1972] 1 QB 60. The onus is on the defendant to show that the claimant would not have recouped his expenditure if the contract had been fully performed (*CCC Films (London) Ltd v Impact Quadrant Films Ltd* [1985] QB 16).

15 See P. S. Atiyah, *Promises, Morals and the Law* (1981).

16 That is, a document which is signed by the promisor, attested and delivered as a deed (Law of Property (Miscellaneous Provisions) Act 1989, s 1.

17 But this view is not uncontroversial. See p 70.

is in solemn form.[18] The promise which induces unrequested reliance may give rise to a claim in tort for deceit if the promisor never intends to fulfil the promise,[19] and in other cases operates at best as one of the various forms of equitable estoppel,[20] where both the grant of relief and the remedy are matters of judicial discretion. The role of reliance in current legal thinking is hotly debated among scholars and will also be briefly discussed.[21]

(i)   The nature of consideration

The essence of contract, then, is not promise but bargain, a promise made for consideration, whether in the form of a counter-promise or of actual performance. It is this requirement of consideration, or quid pro quo, which distinguishes the common law from the civil law, where the concept of consideration is unknown and gratuitous promises are in principle enforceable.

If S agrees to sell goods to B, and B agrees to buy them from S, at the price of £100, the exchange of undertakings creates a contract which binds the parties even before either has taken a step towards performance. Reliance on a promise is not, therefore, either a necessary or a sufficient ingredient of a binding contract,[22] though it may give rise to a remedy outside contract law.[23] The old authorities defined consideration in terms of benefit to one party and detriment suffered by the other,[24] but this is unhelpful, indeed misleading. Consideration is an act or forbearance which is desired by the promisor, and is fixed by him as the price of his own undertaking. Whether the stipulated act or forbearance does in fact benefit the promisor is immaterial; it suffices that it was undertaken at his request. Similarly with detriment. If I agree to pay my neighbour £100 in consideration of his undertaking to repair the fence separating our two properties, the reason why my promise is enforceable is not because of the detriment he suffers in carrying out the repairs (for I have no interest in causing my neighbour work or expense for its own sake) but because I desire the fence to be repaired. Again, when I promise to pay a man £100 if he refrains from smoking for a month, his self-restraint constitutes good consideration, not because it is a detriment to him but because it is something in which I was sufficiently interested to make it worth my while to spend £100.

By contrast, if I promise to pay someone £500 in the event of his losing a leg in an accident, and I charge no premium or other consideration for my promise, there is no contract and he has no right to sue me for £500 if he loses a leg. Why not?

---

18 At common law it was required to be under seal, but this was abolished by s 1(1) of the Law of Property (Miscellaneous Provisions) Act 1989.

19 See p 81, n 99.

20 See p 106. Common law estoppel relates to representations of fact, not promises for the future (*Jorden v Money* (1854) 5 HL Cas 185). Estoppel by convention is a distinct category. See p 107.

21 See p 69.

22 And see Paul Mitchell and John Phillips, 'The Contractual Nexus: Is Reliance Essential?' (2002) 22(1) OJLS 115.

23 See below.

24 *Currie v Misa* (1875) LR 10 Ex Ch 153.

Because the loss of the leg is not something I requested or desired. On the contrary, it is probably an event I was very much hoping would not occur. I did not say: 'Please lose a leg and I will reward you with £500.' What I said was: 'In the unfortunate event of your losing your leg, I will make you a gift of £500.' The loss of the leg is a condition of my gift-promise, not a consideration which creates a bargain.

A promise by one party to confer an additional benefit on another for the purpose of securing the latter's performance of an existing obligation to supply goods or services which would otherwise be in doubt may be considered given for consideration if the promise was not exacted by economic or physical duress or fraud.[25] But this extension of the concept of consideration has been held not to apply to a promise to pay an existing debt by instalments.[26]

The requirement of consideration applies only to a contract. A completed gift does not require consideration.[27]

(ii) Promise inducing unrequested reliance

The extent to which contract extends or should extend beyond bargain to embrace promises which induce unbargained-for reliance is a matter of hot debate among scholars. The necessity of a bargain is disputed by some writers, who point to various cases in which the courts have declared binding a promise which induced detrimental reliance by the promisee, even though the act of reliance was not one which had been stipulated by the promisor as the price of the promise. However, in almost all these cases the binding force of the promise derives from a principle outside the law of contract, usually one form or another of equitable estoppel which precludes the party making the promise from ignoring its effect.[28] For example, it is well established that if A agrees to grant an interest in land to B and stands by while B, with A's encouragement or acquiescence, incurs substantial expenditure on the land in the belief that it has become or is about to become his own, A may be estopped from disputing that the property has become vested in B.[29] This, however, is not because B's expenditure gives rise to a contract but because A's acquiescence and B's detrimental reliance on it[30] perfects the gift in equity and estops A from asserting his title.[31] Similarly, where A tells B that he will not enforce part of his

---

25 *Williams v Roffey Brothers & Nicholls (Contractors) Ltd* [1991] 1 QB 1. See further p 104 as to the efficacy of this 'practical' consideration in the context of variation of a contract, and Collins, *Regulating Contracts* , pp 144 ff.

26 *Re Selectmove Ltd* [1995] 1 WLR 474, applying the decision of the House of Lords in *Foakes v Beer* (1884) 9 App Cas 605.

27 *Pennington v Waine* [2002] 1 WLR 2075; *T Choithram International SA v Pagarani* [2001] 1 WLR 1.

28 See p 106.

29 See cases cited n 31. This is known as proprietary estoppel.

30 *Gillett v Holt* [2001] Ch 210.

31 See *Dillwyn v Llewelyn* (1862) 4 De GF & J 517; *Inwards v Baker* [1965] 2 QB 29; *Crabb v Arun District Council* [1976] Ch 179. The criticism of the last decision by Professor Atiyah in 'When is and Enforceable Agreement Not a Contract? Answer: When it is an Equity' (1976) 92 LQR 174 was effectively answered by P. J Millett, (1976) 92 LQR, at 342. See also *Western Fish Products Ltd v Penwith District Council* [1981] 2 All ER 204.

legal rights, and B acts in reliance on that statement, A will be precluded from enforcing those rights without reasonable notice,[32] but A's statement does not give rise to a cause of action in contract, merely to a limited defence based on the equitable doctrine of promissory estoppel.

This explanation does not satisfy the critics. They are not content with the result but argue that B should have succeeded in contract.[33] Indeed, they go further and contend that one who relies to his detriment on a gratuitous promise has a stronger moral claim to enforcement of the promise than a person who merely gives a counter-promise in exchange and has not yet begun performance. The case is put with characteristic elegance and persuasiveness by Professor Atiyah, the leading English exponent of the reliance theory of contract:

> Is it not manifest that a person who has actually worsened his position by reliance on a promise has a more powerful case for redress than one who has not acted in reliance on the promise at all? A person who has not relied on a promise (nor paid for it) may suffer a disappointment of his expectations, but he does not actually suffer a pecuniary loss.[34]

As a theoretical conception, in which facts can be assumed without having to be established, the argument is at first sight compelling. Unfortunately, life in the real world is not quite so simple. How do we prove that a person has, or has not, acted in reliance on a promise? B is in the business of buying cement for resale, and engages in a steady flow of purchase and sale transactions. He places an order for 100 tons of cement with S. A week later, he contracts to sell five tons to T. Is this in reliance on S's promise to sell the 100 tons? Who is to say that B would not have contracted to sell five tons of cement to T in any event? Again, if I write to the headmaster of my old school and tell him I propose to make a donation of £100, and a week later the school purchases books for its library, has it relied on my promise? Might it not have bought the books anyway?

The problem of showing reliance becomes even more difficult where the reliance alleged is not positive (performance), but negative (forbearance). A writes to B, promising him a job. B does not reply, but takes no steps to look for employment elsewhere. A few days later he receives a letter from A withdrawing the offer. Is it to be said that B 'acted' in reliance on A's promise? And if so, are we to assume that he has passed up the chance of any one of a dozen different jobs available to him? (And why stop at a dozen? Why not a hundred?)

The difficulty is not purely a practical one. It is far from clear why an act of reliance not requested by the promisor should entitle the promisee to performance of the promise. Surely his remedy, if any, should be limited to compensation for his wasted outlay. Why should he be given by way of damages the value of an undertaking which he did not purchase and which may be worth a great deal more than the expenditure he incurred in relying on the promise? If there is to be a remedy for detrimental reliance, it should be in tort for reimbursement, not in contract for the performance of a gratuitous promise.

---

32   *Central London Property Trust Ltd v High Trees House Ltd* [1947] KB 130. See p 106.
33   See, for example, P. S. Atiyah, 'Contracts, Promises and the Law of Obligations' (1978) 94 LQR 193.
34   Ibid, at 202.

It can hardly be disputed that in English law the reliance basis of enforcing a promise has been established by reference to principles of equitable estoppel outside the law of contract. This is demonstrated by the fact that it is for the court to decide in its discretion whether the case is a proper one for equitable relief and what form that should take. The same is true of proprietary estoppel. It is because of the absence of a contract that the court gives 'the minimum equity to do justice to the plaintiff',[35] so that while in principle the claimant should obtain his expectation interest in specie (or if this is impracticable, in money equivalent) where this was based on a mutual understanding, yet if that expectation is uncertain or extravagant or out of all proportion to the detriment he suffered, the relief given should be more limited, though not necessarily restricted to the detriment suffered by the claimant.[36]

The real issue is whether English law should now discard the historically distinct sets of principles giving effect to promises and subsume them all within a unified theory of contract which treats reliance as an alternative to bargain.[37] No common law system has yet gone so far. The American approach, spearheaded by the American Restatement on Contracts,[38] is to treat reliance as a basis for enforcing a promise, but the rule is carefully qualified both as to the conditions of binding force ('if injustice can be avoided only by enforcement of the promise') and as to the remedy (which 'may be limited as justice requires'), so that it is more akin to, and is often referred to as, a rule of promissory estoppel. More recently, the High Court of Australia has begun to move towards a unified approach to estoppel as grounding a positive claim for recoupment of loss suffered by detrimental loss,[39] but again the binding force of the promise is attributed to estoppel rather than to contract and it is emphasized that 'there must be a proportionality between the remedy and the detriment which it is its purpose to avoid'.[40] Accordingly, even in these jurisdictions it is only in respect of the bargained-for promise that the promisee is assured the protection of his expectation interest. Where American law and Australian law have moved forward is in recognizing that in certain conditions reliance on a promise is a sufficient ground for making the promise actionable and allowing recovery of the expectation loss.

---

35 *Crabb v Arun District Council* [1975] 3 All ER 865, per Scarman LJ at 880.
36 *Jennings v Rice* [2003] 1 FCR 501; and see Simon Gardner, 'The Remedial Discretion in Proprietary Estoppel' (1999) 115 LQR 438.
37 See P. S. Atiyah (1978) 94 LQR 193; Charles Fried, *Contract as Promise* (1981); Hugh Collins, *The Law of Contract* (4th edn, 2003), ch 5.
38 *Restatement, Second, Contracts* 90.
39 *Commonwealth of Australia v Verwayen* (1990) 170 CLR 394; *Waltons Stores (Interstate) Ltd v Maher* (1988) 164 CLR 387. See A. M. Gleeson, 'Innovation in Contract: An Australian Analysis' in *The Frontiers of Liability* (ed Peter Birks, 1994), ch 9, at pp 114 ff. In the more recent decision in *Giumelli v Giumelli* (1999) 106 CLR 101 the High Court of Australia found it necessary to reach a view on the question of an overarching principle of estoppel. There is no such principle in English law (*First National Bank plc v Thompson* [1996] Ch 231, per Millett LJ at 236).
40 *Commonwealth of Australia v Verwayen*, n 39, per Mason CJ at 413. See also Sir Anthony Mason's comments on the Australian developments in 'The Place of Equity and Equitable Remedies in the Contemporary Common Law World' (1994) 110 LQR 238 at 253–256.

(iii) Abstract payment undertakings

Like most propositions of English law, the rule that a contract must be supported by consideration is not absolute. An important exception is the abstract payment undertaking, a promise which the law will enforce as a matter of mercantile usage despite the absence of consideration or even reliance.[41] Prime examples are the documentary credit[42] and the performance bond or demand guarantee.[43] Yet it is clear that these too are bargain-based and are not gift-promises, even though they do not fit the consideration model.[44]

4.   CONTRACT AS A REFLECTION OF THE WILL OF THE PARTIES

Whether viewed in terms of morality or of economic efficiency, the willingness of the law to enforce bargains freely made is rational, for to the extent to which the parties make their own law by the terms of their agreement it is unnecessary to look to outside rules as regulators of their conduct, and they will probably find the results more satisfactory than if such rules were thrust upon them. But the law cannot always stand back and leave it to the parties. In the first place, it takes two to make a bargain, and if the intentions and understandings of one party when making the contract do not coincide with those of the other (as where A thinks he is contracting to buy a Titian painting whereas, so far as B is concerned, the painting is offered merely as being of the school of Titian), the court has to apply an objective test and ask what the reasonable person would have assumed was intended. Secondly, the express terms of the contract are often confined to the barest essentials – the article purchased and the price, for example – and the parties do not trouble to spell out further undertakings, eg as to the quality of the goods or their fitness for the buyer's purpose. Where the court is not able to deduce the intention of the parties from the language and other circumstances in which negotiations were conducted, it may apply rules of law to import into the contract certain implied terms, for example that the goods shall be of satisfactory quality. Such terms, though designated contractual, are in truth prescribed by the law as gap-fillers on the basis of what the law (rather than the parties, who did not address their minds to the question) considers ought properly to be implied into contracts of the kind in question, in the absence of any contrary agreement. Then again, public policy may require the court to refuse enforcement of a contract, or of a particular contractual provision, either because of the circumstances in which it was concluded (eg, under duress or undue influence) or because the terms contravene public policy, as in the case of a covenant unreasonably in restraint of trade or a clause seeking to impose a penalty, rather than mere compensation, for breach of contract.

The result is that while the agreement of the parties is the kernel of their legal relationship, it is for the law to decide, in cases of dispute, what that agreement is,

---

41 See generally Roy Goode, 'Abstract Payment Undertakings' in *Essays for Patrick Atiyah*, (eds Peter Cane and Jane Stapleton, 1991), ch 9.

42 See p 970.

43 See p 1015.

44 See Goode, 'Abstract Payment Undertakings', at pp 222 ff.

whether it is valid and enforceable, and what its legal consequences are. Some would say that terms implied by law fall within the regime of the law of tort rather than the law of contract, for it is a characteristic of the former that duties are imposed by law and of the latter that they are created by agreement. But it is convenient to treat duties imported into a contract by established case law or by statute as forming part of the contract, for their scope is delimited by the contract, and the sanctions for breach and the measure of damages are defined by rules of contract law.

5. FORMATION AND AVOIDANCE

(i) Agreement on essential terms

We can take formation quite shortly, since it is well covered in the textbooks, and, in commercial transactions, disputes as to the existence of a contract are relatively infrequent. Far more common are disputes as to the content and construction of a contract that both parties admit came into being, and as to the fact and consequence of alleged breaches or misrepresentations.

The parties must have agreed on the essential terms or have provided the method by which these are to be determined, and these must be reasonably certain, otherwise there is no contract, merely an agreement to agree or an agreement to negotiate, neither of which is considered to have any legal force.[45] But if the essential terms have been agreed, the fact that the parties have agreed to negotiate as to the remaining terms does not preclude the establishment of a contract; indeed, the court may also be willing to infer an agreement to negotiate in good faith to settle the remaining terms.[46]

Contracts are usually, but not invariably, concluded as the result of offer and acceptance. The offer may call for acceptance either by counter-promise or by conduct. In the former case the contract is termed synallagmatic (ie bilateral or multilateral), in that both parties undertake the performance of future obligations and the contract comes into existence by exchange of promises. In the latter case, only one party (the offeror) undertakes anything. The other accepts by performance or does not perform and thus rejects the offer. Such contracts are unilateral (or 'if') contracts. There are many more unilateral contracts than is commonly supposed. An obvious example is a guarantee. The creditor does not undertake to the surety to make an advance to the principal debtor, but if an advance is made, and each time it is made, a contract comes into existence.[47] Many general or master agreements, intended to regulate continuous dealings between the parties, have no contractual force at the time they are made, despite being signed by both parties. They serve as an umbrella for specific future transactions and will, except so far as modified, apply by express or implied incorporation or course of dealing to each such

45 See p 77.
46 *Donwin Productions Ltd v EMI Films Ltd* (1984) Times, 9 March, Pain J.
47 See p 812.

transaction. For example, the parties may agree on standard terms of sale and purchase without either party committing itself at that stage to make any sale or purchase. In such a case, the contract is merely a set of terms that will govern a sale and purchase if and when made. Block discounting agreements regulating the terms on which a finance house will purchase instalment credit contracts from a dealer are typical master agreements which do not without move create obligations. It is also possible to combine unilateral and bilateral undertakings in one contract, with the result that as to the former the party giving the undertaking is free to withdraw it until the other party has carried out the designated act of performance, while as to the latter there is an immediately binding obligation by exchange of promises.[48]

An offer may be withdrawn at any time before acceptance, even if the offeror has undertaken not to withdraw it, unless the offer is by deed or the offeror receives consideration for his undertaking.[49] A binding offer is termed an option.

(ii)   Formal requirements

Most contracts can be concluded informally, for example, by word of mouth or even by conduct. To this general rule there are various statutory exceptions, including contracts of guarantee,[50] regulated consumer credit agreements[51] and contracts for the sale or other disposition of an interest in land.[52] Contracts of guarantee do not have to be in writing, but merely to be evidenced in writing and signed by or on behalf of the surety.[53] By contrast, regulated agreements and contracts for the disposition of an interest in land must be in writing and must be

---

48 For example, the terms governing the issue of a credit card, in addition to providing for repayment to an issuer of sums paid by the issuer to suppliers from whom the cardholder has purchased goods or services, may stipulate that the cardholder is to keep the card safely and return it on request. A provision of the former kind creates a unilateral obligation, for the cardholder is not obliged to use the card to buy goods or services and incurs the payment obligation only if he does so, whereas a stipulation of the latter type becomes operative from the moment the customer signifies his intention to accept the card.

Where the contract is a 'requirements' contract, in that A undertakes to supply goods to B as and when ordered by B, who does not himself undertake to place orders, A's promise is usually characterized as a continuing offer which crystallizes into a separate contract each time B places an order, but which can be withdrawn at any time except as to orders already placed, in the absence of consideration for an express or implied undertaking to hold the offer open. For a different view, see J N. Adams, 'Consideration for Requirements Contracts' (1978) 94 LQR 73. Even where permissible as a matter of contract law, a refusal to supply may be void under Article 82 of the EC Treaty and s 18 of the Competition Act 1998.

49 *Dickinson v Dodds* (1876) 2 Ch D 463. The Law Commission's Working Paper No 60, *Firm Offers*, provisionally recommended that an offeror who undertook not to revoke his offer for a stated period should be bound by his undertaking, but to date the Commission has not issued a report on the question.

50 Statute of Frauds 1677, s 4.

51 Consumer Credit Act 1974, s 61(1).

52 Law of Property (Miscellaneous Provisions) Act 1989, s 2(1). The Act repealed s 40 of the Law of Property Act 1925 and by making contracts not in writing wholly void it also abolished the equitable doctrine of part performance (*Firstpost Homes Ltd v Johnson* [1995] 1 WLR 1567).

53 Statute of Frauds 1677, s 4.

signed by both parties.[54] In an age of electronic communication the question has arisen whether the requirements of writing and signature can be satisfied electronically. The Law Commission has advised that, in general, electronic mail and transmissions through a web site satisfy the requirement of writing[55] and of a document in that they involve words which are visible on a screen, whereas transmissions by electronic data interchange do not and accordingly fail to qualify as writing.[56] In other words, the digital form of a communication is not writing but its visible representation in words is writing.[57] This formulation is somewhat broader than that adopted in modern international conventions, which in defining writing so as to encompass electronic communications typically incorporate the idea of a record of information capable of being reproduced subsequently.[58] In practice, of course, email and internet messages are usually stored so as to be retrievable, but the Law Commission formulation implicitly treats it as sufficient that an electronic message recording the terms of an agreement is shown in words on a screen, because at that time it is capable of being stored and retrieved, whether or not it is in fact stored so as to be subsequently retrievable and whether or not it is later deleted. Such cases are treated as being the equivalent of a document that has been lost. The function of a signature is to authenticate the document, that is, to demonstrate the signer's approval or apparent approval of its contents. The Law Commission considers that this functional test may be satisfied by any one of four methods of electronic signature, namely a digital signature through a public key/private key encryption/decryption system,[59] a scanned manuscript signature, the typing of a name or initial automatically, and the clicking of a website button.[60] Accordingly, the requirements of Article 9 of the Electronic Commerce Directive[61] and Article 5 of the Electronic Signatures

---

54 Consumer Credit Act 1974, s 61(1); Law of Property (Miscellaneous Provisions) Act 1989, s 2(1), (3).

55 As defined by the Interpretation Act 1978, Sch 1.

56 *Electronic Commerce: Formal Requirements in Commercial Transactions – Advice from the Law Commission* (December 2001), pt 3. See also Hugh Beale and Lowri Griffiths, 'Electronic commerce: formal requirements in commercial transactions' [2002] LMCLQ 467. In relation to the Internet, see Christopher Reed, *Internet Law: Text and Materials* (2000).

57 *Electronic Commerce,* para 3.15.

58 See, for example, Article 1(1) of the 1988 UNIDROIT Convention on International Factoring ('capable of being reproduced in tangible form'); Article 1(nn) of the 2001 Convention on International Interests in Mobile Equipment ('a record of information … capable of being reproduced in tangible form on a subsequent occasion'); Article 5(c) of the 2001 UN Convention on the Assignment of Receivables in International Trade ('any form of information that is accessible so as to be usable for subsequent reference'). See to similar effect the 1996 UNCITRAL Model Law on Electronic Commerce (as amended 1998), art 6 ('accessible so as to be usable for subsequent reference').

59 The Law Commission does not regard it as necessary that the signature itself should be visible. See *Electronic Commerce,* para 3.38.

60 Ibid, paras 3.31 ff.

61 Directive 2000/31 dated 8.6.2000 art 9 requires member states to ensure that their legal systems allow contracts to be concluded by electronic means and to remove legal obstacles to the contractual process. The directive has been implemented in the UK by the Electronic Commerce (EC Directive) Regulations 2002, SI 2002/2013.

Directive[62] are considered satisfied by the existing law. It is not thought either necessary or even desirable to enact legislation to confirm this approach on a global basis, since in some contexts it might be desirable to retain the conventional approach to a document and a writing.[63] The Law Commission's analysis is to be welcomed. However, some care needs to be exercised before treating it as applicable for the requirements of a specific statute, particularly where it is a strong consumer protection statute. For example, it is unlikely that a consumer credit agreement would be treated as satisfying the documentary requirements of the Consumer Credit Act 1974 and regulations merely because it is visible on a screen.[64]

(iii) Other elements

Reference has already been made to the general requirement of consideration.[65] A contract also requires legal capacity to enter into it,[66] an intention to create legal relations[67] and a *consensus ad idem*, though the test usually to be applied is not what each party in fact had in mind but what each ought reasonably to have assumed from the language and conduct of the other.[68] Reasonable certainty of meaning is also a requirement. If the expression of proposed terms is so vague that no clear meaning can be established[69] or so ambiguous that the court is unable to determine which of the possible alternative meanings is the most probable,[70] the matter ceases to be one of mere construction and the whole agreement fails for

---

62 Directive 1999/93/EC dated 13.12.1999. Article 5 requires member states to ensure that advanced electronic signatures which are based on a qualified certificate and which are created by a secure-signature-creation device satisfy the legal requirements of a signature in electronic form in the same manner as a handwritten signature for paper-based data. The directive has been implemented in the UK by the Electronic Communications Act 2000 and the Signatures Regulations 2002, SI 2002/318.

63 *Electronic Commerce,* para 3.43.

64 See *Goode: Consumer Credit Law and Practice*, para 30.103.

65 See pp 67 ff.

66 See now the Minors' Contracts Act 1987, which repealed the Infants Relief Act 1874, leaving the enforceability of contracts entered into by minors to be governed exclusively by common law rules and by the provisions of the 1987 Act relating to ratification. See G. H. Treitel, *Law of Contract* (11th edn, 2003), ch 13; Cheshire, Fifoot and Furmston, *Law of Contract* (14th edn, 2001), ch 13.

67 There are certain situations in which business people find it convenient to fudge the question whether a legal commitment is intended, in order to be able to do the deal. The typical case is the so-called letter of comfort, which may or may not generate a contract, depending upon the intention of the parties as determined from the terms of the comfort letter. Inevitably, agreement is bought at the price of uncertainty. See, for example, *Kleinwort Benson Ltd v Malaysia Mining Corp Bhd* [1989] 1 All ER 785 (letter of comfort held not to be contractual); and, for a similar finding in relation to a letter of intent, *British Steel Corp. v Cleveland Bridge and Engineering Co Ltd* [1984] 1 All ER 504. By contrast, in *Wilson Smithett & Cape (Sugar) Ltd v Bangladesh Sugar & Food Industries Corp.* [1986] 1 Lloyd's Rep 378, the letter of intent was held to be contractual.

68 *Smith v Hughes* (1871) LR 6 QB 597; *Reardon Smith Ltd v Hansen-Tangen* [1976] 3 All ER 570; *The Hannah Blumenthal* [1983] 1 All ER 34; *The Leonidas D* [1983] 3 All ER 737. The position is otherwise where one party's understanding of the contract was known to the other, even though not matching his own (*Hartog v Colin and Shields* [1939] 3 All ER 566).

69 *G. Scammell & Nephew Ltd v Ouston* [1941] AC 251 (balance of purchase to be paid 'on hire-purchase terms over a period of two years' held too vague to enable the meaning of the term to be stated).

70 As in *Raffles v Wichelhaus* (1864) 2 H & C 906.

uncertainty. It is because of the perceived lack of certainty that, in contrast to the position in civil law countries and America, English law does not recognize the validity of a contract to negotiate,[71] though apparently an agreement to use reasonable endeavours to negotiate *is* enforceable,[72] as is a lock-out agreement by which one party agrees for consideration not to negotiate with any third party for a fixed period.[73] Moreover, where the essential terms have been agreed, the court is prepared to imply a term to negotiate in good faith further terms to be inserted into the written agreement.[74] It cannot be said that the argument against recognition of agreements to negotiate, or the distinction between such agreements and agreements to use reasonable endeavours to negotiate, is compelling.[75] Fortunately, an asserted contract rarely fails for uncertainty, for the court is usually able to find a preponderance of evidence in favour of one meaning or another. Moreover, if the fundamental terms of the contract are either agreed or capable of determination, the fact that the subsidiary terms alleged to exist are not stated or are couched in ambiguous language is of little materiality to the existence of a contract, since the court will either rule that the asserted terms were not in fact agreed at all and thus do not form part of the contract or will exercise its gap-filling technique by drawing inferences of fact or law.

(iv) Void, voidable and unenforceable contracts

A *void* contract is one which is utterly devoid of legal effect. Thus at common law a supposed contract may be void because of want of consensus or consideration or because of mistake as to identity[76] or as to the existence or essential character of the subject matter.[77] Mistake as to identity has caused a good deal of difficulty, with

---

71 *May & Butcher Ltd v R.* [1934] 2 KB 17n; *Courtney and Fairbairn Ltd v Tolaini Bros (Hotels) Ltd* [1975] 1 All ER 716; *Scandinavian Trading Tanker Co A.B. v Flota Petrolera Ecuatoriana, The Scaptrade* [1981] 2 Lloyd's Rep 425; *Australian and New Zealand Banking Group v Frost Holdings* [1989] V.R. 695; *Walford v Miles* [1992] 2 AC 128. Whether entry into negotiation attracts any legal obligations is a separate question discussed in the context of good faith, p 95.

72 *Walford v Miles*, n 71.

73 Ibid. But an agreement not to negotiate with a third party for a reasonable period (as opposed to a fixed period) will not be upheld. It is hard to see why not. See Sir Patrick Neill, 'A Key to Lock-Out Agreements?' (1992) 108 LQR 405 at p 413.

74 *Donwin Productions Ltd v EMI Films Ltd*, n 46.

75 See Ian Brown, 'The Contract to Negotiate: A Thing Writ in Water?' [1992] JBL 353.

76 *Cundy v Lindsay* (1878) 3 App Cas 459. But this will usually nullify a contract only if the innocent party intended to contract with the person whose identity was assumed and no other (*Lewis v Averay* [1972] 1 QB 198). The statement in Cheshire, Fifoot and Furmston, *Law of Contract* (p 280) that the claimant must also show he took reasonable steps to verify the identity of the person with whom he was invited to deal is, with respect, erroneous. The proposition is nowhere stated in the cases cited as authority for it, and it is difficult to see for whose benefit the duty of care suggested could be imposed – not for the sake of the other party, who *ex hypothesi* knows of the mistake and is not acting in good faith, nor for that of a subsequent purchaser, since the validity of a contract is to be tested as at the time it is made.

77 *Associated Japanese Bank (International) Ltd v Crédit du Nord SA* [1989] 1 WLR 255. It was at one time thought that a common mistake which was not so fundamental as to render a contract void at common law could be set aside in equity (*Solle v Butcher* [1950] 1 KB 671). But recently the Court of Appeal has declined to follow *Solle v Butcher* on the ground of its inconsistency with the decision of the House of Lords in *Bell v Lever Bros Ltd* [1932] AC 161 and has held that there is no equitable jurisdiction to grant rescission of a contract which is valid at law. See generally Treitel, *Law of Contract*, ch 8.

distinctions drawn between identity and attributes, so that while in *Cundy v Lindsay*[78] the House of Lords held the contract to be totally void, in *Lewis v Averay* the Court of Appeal held it to be merely voidable. The denouement has now come with the decision of the House of Lords in *Shogun Finance Ltd v Hudson*,[79] in which by a bare majority[80] it was held that a distinction is to be drawn between face-to-face contracts, in which the innocent party typically intends to sell to the person present before him and identified by sight and hearing, so that the fraud as to identity merely renders the contract voidable,[81] and a written contract identifying the parties and intended to be made by the innocent party only with the person named in it as the other party, so that where that person exists but his signature is forged by a crook the contract is wholly void.

A contract may also be invalidated by statute, as where it is a wagering contract[82] or relates to the sale or other disposition of an interest in land but is not in writing as required by statute.[83] A contract which is void produces no legal relationship between the parties. A necessary consequence is that payments made and property transferred under the supposed contract are recoverable (subject to the defence of illegality[84]), for neither party has an entitlement to what he has received.

By contrast, a *voidable* contract is one which a party is entitled to rescind, or to have set aside by the court, by reason of some external vitiating factor (deceit, misrepresentation,[85] duress,[86] undue influence,[87] mistake as to identity induced by a fraudulent misrepresentation in face-to-face dealings[88]), but which is valid and binding until rescinded. Rescission cancels the contract from the beginning, so that each party is obliged to return the benefits he has received and, so far as possible, the parties are restored to the position they would have occupied had no contract been entered into.[89] An *unenforceable* contract is a contract which is valid, and

---

78 See n 76.

79 [2004] 1 AC 919.

80 Lords Nicholls and Millett dissenting.

81 Applying *Phillips v Brooks* [1919] 2 KB 243 and disapproving the majority decision of the Court of Appeal *Ingram v Little* [1961] 1 QB 31.

82 Gaming Act 1845, s 18.

83 Law of Property (Miscellaneous Provisions) Act 1989, s 1.

84 See p 130.

85 See pp 107 ff. A contracting party may also have a statutory right of cancellation, eg under s 67 of the Consumer Credit Act 1974 or the Consumer Protection (Cancellation of Contracts Concluded away from Business Premises) Regulations (SI 1987/2117), implementing Council Directive 85/577/EEC. Mistake not induced by misrepresentation and not sufficiently fundamental to render the contract void at law cannot be set aside in equity. See n 77.

86 Physical duress is rare but contracts have sometimes been set aside for economic duress, particularly where the claimant was led to enter into the contract through the exercise of illegitimate pressure by the other party and had no reasonable alternative. The ingredients of actionable economic duress are conveniently set out in the judgment of Dyson J in *DSND Subsea Ltd v Petroleum Geo-Services ASA* [2000] 1 BLR 530.

87 Most of the cases on undue influence concern a wife induced to give a guarantee secured on the matrimonial home to support the extension of credit to her husband. See, for example, *Royal Bank of Scotland plc v Etridge (No 2)* [2002] 2 AC 773.

88 See text to n 79. For mistake as to the subject matter, see n 77.

89 See further p 109.

therefore effective to produce a legal relationship between the parties, but for some reason cannot be legally enforced by one party (and sometimes by the other as well). Illegality usually renders a contract unenforceable rather than void.[90] Other grounds of unenforceability are expiry of a period of limitation for bringing an action; want of capacity; and absence of a signed memorandum of agreement prescribed by statute or breach of some other statutory requirement which, by the terms of statute, is visited with the sanction of unenforceability of the agreement.[91] There are various reasons why certain categories of contract are made unenforceable by the law rather than totally void. Where the defect is purely evidentiary, there is no objection to enforcement of the contract later if the requisite note or memorandum comes into existence after the making of the contract. Moreover, it may be desired to allow enforcement against one party but not the other (eg to allow enforcement against the party who has signed the document evidencing the contract terms but not against the party whose promise is purely oral; or against the party who has broken the statutory requirement but not against the party for whose protection the requirement was imposed). Since an unenforceable contract is nevertheless valid, payments made and property transferred under it cannot be recovered on the basis of a total failure of consideration except where the payee or transferee relies on the unenforceability of the contract to refuse performance of his own obligations.[92] The degree of unenforce-ability will itself vary according to the statute, some statutory provisions rendering the contract unenforceable by action (leaving the parties free to have recourse to self-help), while others prohibit enforcement by any means, judicial or extrajudicial.[93]

(v) Nullity and rescission distinguished from termination

It is a common misapprehension that if one party is in breach of contract – as where the seller of goods tenders goods that do not conform to the contract description – the contract is totally void, or is at least voidable at the option of the buyer.[94] This is not so. A breach of contract has absolutely no effect on the existence and validity of the contract. It gives the innocent party a right to damages, and in certain cases may entitle him to terminate the agreement;[95] but termination is not at all the same thing

90 This follows from the fact that illegality does not as a rule vitiate payments and transfers of property made under the contract. See p 133.

91 One of the main categories was that prescribed by s 40 of the Law of Property Act 1925, namely contracts relating to the sale of an interest in land. But that section has been repealed by s 2 of the Law of Property (Miscellaneous Provisions) Act 1989, which requires such contracts to be in writing, not merely evidenced by writing, and provides that in default the agreement is to be not merely unenforceable but void.

92 *Thomas v Brown* (1876) 1 QBD 714; *Pulbrook v Lawes* (1876) 1 QBD 284.

93 Contrast the former s 40 of the Law of Property Act 1925 with s 65 of the Consumer Credit Act 1974. Most types of contract may be made without formality.

94 A myth cherished by generations of conveyancers until finally exploded by Michael Albery, 'Mr Cyprian Williams' Great Heresy' (1975) 91 LQR 337, whose insistence on a return to basic principles of contract law was later vindicated by the decision of the House of Lords in *Johnson v Agnew* [1979] 1 All ER 883.

95 See p 123. The act of termination is also described, somewhat confusingly, as 'repudiation' or as 'acceptance' of the guilty party's repudiation (acceptance here denoting willingness to treat the repudiation as ending the contract, not as a waiver of rights or remedies).

as rescission. Termination for breach brings the contract to an end at a particular time without affecting accrued rights and liabilities. Rescission is retrospective, cancelling the contract from the beginning, so that it is deemed never to have existed. The rights and duties of the parties are retrospectively obliterated and each must, as far as possible, restore to the other benefits received under the contract. The right to rescind derives not from a breach of the contract but from some external act or event (misrepresentation, duress, undue influence) which precedes the contract and constitutes an improper inducement to enter into it, such that the law will allow the party affected resile from the bargain and cancel it from the beginning.[96]

6.   THE CLASSIFICATION OF STATEMENTS MADE IN A CONTRACTUAL SETTING

A protracted process of inquiry and negotiation may attend a commercial trans-action. A company wishes to explore the desirability of installing a computer at its head office. It writes to a computer manufacturer for information and receives a visit from the sales manager. The latter engages in customary sales talk, discusses the information needs of the company, jots down notes and figures, makes tentative suggestions as to the most suitable type of computer, makes observations on the supply of programs, leaves behind sales literature and promises to follow up with a detailed plan later. This arrives subsequently; there ensue further meetings, tele-phone discussions, correspondence in which the company raises points of difficulty and seeks modifications to strengthen performance or answer a special purpose; costings are obtained, further assurances exacted, formal documents signed and ultimately the purchase of the computer and accompanying software consummated.

Months or even years later the lawyer may be called upon to advise which of the oral and written statements made – from the time of the initial inquiry to the signature of the final document – have legal effect and what legal consequences ensue if an assertion of fact or an expression of opinion proves unfounded or if a forecast of future performance is not fulfilled.

Statements made in a contractual setting are susceptible to elaborate classification, but may be broadly divided into three groups:

(i)   Statements which are altogether devoid of legal effect

Into this category fall, inter alia, mere puffs or commendations and honest expressions of opinion or intention. The former attract no legal consequences[97]

---

96 See p 81.
97 *Scott v Hanson* (1829) 1 Russ & M 128; *Dimmock v Hallett* (1866) 2 Ch App 21. However, the older decisions should be read with circumspection, for they reflected a robust philosophy of *caveat emptor* to which courts at the present time are much less sympathetic. Thus it is unlikely that *Dimmock v Hallett* (in which a description of land as 'very fertile and improvable', when it was in large measure a wilderness and had been abandoned as useless, was held a mere commendation) would be decided in the same way today.

because every trader may be expected to commend his wares and in so doing ought not to be taken too seriously and also because general commendatory expressions ('the best second-hand bookshop in the country', 'a wonderful buy') involve value judgments which cannot readily be tested by the objective standards of the law. Honest expressions of opinion or intention usually do not involve the maker in any legal responsibility, even if the opinion proves ill-founded or the stated intention is not carried into effect.[98] This is because in expressing his opinion, the maker of the statement is merely stating what he believes, not asserting that his belief is well-founded,[99] while the fact that a course of conduct stated to be intended is not in the event performed does not falsify the statement of intention, which *ex hypothesi* was true when made.[100] Comfort letters (eg that a parent company's normal policy is to give adequate financial support to its subsidiary) are usually intended to give reassurance rather than any legal commitment, and the same is often true of letters of intent.[101]

(ii) Representations inducing a contract

A person may make a statement of fact which is not couched simply as an expression of opinion but is made in such definite terms as reasonably to lead the person to whom the statement is made to believe that it is true and, in reliance on its truth, to enter into a contract with the maker. If at the time when it is made the statement is not intended to be or become a term of the contract but is a 'mere' representation, then at common law the falsity of the statement, though giving the representee a right to rescind the contract, does not usually[102] entitle him to damages except where it was made fraudulently or was in fact incorporated as a contract term subsequently. Rescission is allowed because the representee has been led to enter into the contract on a false basis; but the courts have denied a remedy in damages on the ground that since the representation was not made a term of the contract, the representor was not undertaking legal responsibility for the truth of his representation.[103]

The restriction of warranty to a statement forming a term of the contract is of relatively recent origin.[104] The deviation appears to have been influenced by a

---

98 *Bisset v Wilkinson* [1927] AC 177.

99 Ibid. The position is otherwise where the maker of the statement expresses an opinion or intention which he does not in fact hold (*Edgington v Fitzmaurice* (1885) 29 Ch D 459; *Brown v Raphael* [1958] Ch 636 at p 643). Moreover, a statement of belief by a party who was in a position to know the true facts may imply the existence of reasonable grounds for that belief (*Brown v Raphael* [1958] Ch 636; *Esso Petroleum Co Ltd v Mardon* [1976] QB 801).

100 See, in the context of false descriptions under the Trade Descriptions Acts, the judgment of MacKenna J in *R. v Sunair Holidays Ltd* [1973] 2 All ER 1233 at 1236.

101 See p 802, n 19.

102 For exceptions, see p 107.

103 *Heilbut, Symons & Co v Buckleton* [1913] AC 30.

104 It stems from *Heilbut, Symons & Co v Buckleton*, where the House of Lords misinterpreted a statement by Buller J in *Pasley v Freeman* which was concerned to distinguish a warranty (whether or not forming a term of a contract) from a statement not attracting legal responsibility. Buller J himself misstated earlier authority in ruling that an intention to warrant was necessary. See further p 186, n 22.

strong desire to preserve the integrity of the illogical parol evidence rule.[105] The result has been unfortunate in the extreme. English law has thereby become committed to the proposition that a misstatement made without intention to assume contractual responsibility is not actionable, in the absence of fraud, despite the fact that it is a statement of hard fact (as opposed to honest belief or intention), that it is intended by the maker to be relied upon as an inducement to the recipient to enter into a contract, and that it is in fact relied upon for that purpose. It is difficult to conceive of circumstances in which the objective observer, hearing a statement possessing all these characteristics, could reasonably conclude that the maker did not intend to assume responsibility for the truth of his statement.[106]

Conscious of this problem, the courts have tried to deal with it in one of three ways: (a) by postulating that the statement was in the circumstances no more than an expression of the maker's honest belief in the truth of the facts stated[107] (a conclusion which proves too much, for it thereby prevents the statement from amounting even to a 'mere' representation); or (b) by finding that the statement was in truth part of the contract;[108] or (c) where such a finding was blocked by the parol evidence rule, by holding that the statement had independent contractual force as a 'collateral' warranty or contract which induced the recipient of the statement to enter into the 'main' contract.[109] At the root of the difficulty lies the notorious parol evidence rule,[110] but for which the court would have no difficulty, even where the contract was reduced to writing, in holding that responsibility for the truth of the preceding statements of fact was intended to form part of the total obligation undertaken by the representor.

Fortunately, the impact of the rule that a non-fraudulent misrepresentation not imported as a contractual term is not actionable[111] – a rule to which there were exceptions even at common law[112] – has been considerably mitigated by the provisions of the Misrepresentation Act 1967, which entitle the representee to damages for non-fraudulent misrepresentation unless the representor can show that he reasonably believed the representation to have been true.[113]

Mere non-disclosure does not usually constitute a misrepresentation, but it may do so, as where its effect is to distort a positive misrepresentation.[114]

---

105 See p 91.
106 See further p 185, n 18. It is interesting to see that in New Zealand the remedies for misrepresentation and breach of contract have been assimilated by the Contractual Remedies Act 1979.
107 *Oscar Chess Ltd v Williams* [1957] 1 WLR 370.
108 *Dick Bentley Productions Ltd v Harold Smith Motors Ltd* [1965] 1 WLR 623.
109 See p 93.
110 See p 91.
111 *Derry v Peek* (1889) 14 App Cas 337.
112 See p 107.
113 Section 2(1). See p 107.
114 See *Chitty on Contracts*, para 6-013 and, for a comprehensive analysis, Anthony Duggan, Michael Bryan and Frances Hanks, *Contractual Non-Disclosure* (1994).

(iii) Statements constituting terms of a contract

A statement may have contractual force either as a term of the final agreement concluded between the parties or as a prior warranty generating a collateral contract, the consideration for the warranty being the promisee's entry into the main contract.[115] It would seem that a false collateral warranty can also be relied on by the innocent party as a misrepresentation inducing the main contract, entitling him to rescind the main contract as an alternative to claiming damages for breach of the collateral warranty.[116] Even where there is no collateral warranty, a misrepresentation which induces a contract and is incorporated as a term of the contract does not lose its force as a prior misrepresentation, and the innocent party has the choice of treating the statement as a misrepresentation grounding rescission[117] or as a breach of a contractual term attracting a claim in damages and/or (if the breach is serious) a right to treat the contract as repudiated.[118]

(iv) Public statements relating to goods the subject of a consumer sale

In the case of sale to a buyer who deals as consumer any public statements on the specific characteristics of the goods made about them by the seller, the producer or his representative, particularly in advertising or on labelling, are included in the relevant circumstances mentioned in s 14(2A) of the Sale of Goods Act for the purpose of determining whether the goods are of satisfactory quality.[119]

7. ASCERTAINING THE CONTRACT TERMS

The content and meaning of a contract may derive from a variety of sources.

(i) The express language of the contract

1. In general

The language of the contract is obviously the principal tool used by the courts in determining what the parties have agreed. The contract will be interpreted in accordance with any rules of interpretation that may be provided by the contract itself. Subject to this, technical terms will ordinarily be accorded their technical meaning,[120] language accorded a special meaning by custom or usage will be

---

115 See p 93.
116 This, of course, is possible only where the collateral warranty induced entry into a contract with the representor himself or with a third party of whom the representor was the actual or deemed agent for the purpose of making the representation.
117 Misrepresentation Act 1967, s 1.
118 See p 124.
119 Sale of Goods Act 1979, s 14(2D).
120 *Shore v Wilson* (1842) 9 Cl & Fin 355; *Marquis of Cholmondeley v Lord Clinton* (1820) 2 Jac & W 1. Extrinsic evidence is admissible to prove the meaning of technical terms. But if it is clear that the words were not intended in their technical sense; it is the duty of the court to construe them according to their normal and popular meaning.

considered to bear that meaning if the contract was entered into in the light of such custom or usage,[121] and the remainder of the contract will usually be read according to the normal and popular sense of the language used.[122] Extrinsic evidence will as a rule be admitted to resolve any ambiguity in the language, whether latent[123] or patent.[124] Whether, and to what extent, extrinsic evidence is available for other purposes, eg to add to, vary or contradict the contract document, or to show that the contract is subject to some undisclosed condition or is voidable on some ground, depends principally on the scope of the parol evidence rule.[125]

2.   Signed and unsigned contracts

Except where otherwise prescribed by statute,[126] it is not necessary for a contract to be in writing or for a written contract to be signed. However, there is an important difference between signed and unsigned contract documents in that a person signing a contract is bound by all the terms contained in the document,[127] whereas a stipulation that is particularly onerous or unusual will not be given effect as a term of the contract unless reasonable steps were taken to bring it to the notice of the party against whom it is asserted.[128]

3.   Standard-term contracts

The policy aspects of standard-term contracts are adverted to elsewhere. For the present we shall comment on them only in relation to their significance in ascertaining the terms which the parties are to be taken to have agreed.

First, there is the problem of internal consistency where blank parts of a standard-term contract are completed. Not everyone using such a contract is skilled in its handling, and not infrequently blank spaces left for the insertion of terms peculiar to the transaction in question are completed in such a way as to produce inconsistency with the printed words. Since the particular overrides the general, the rule of construction applied is that written words inserted in or added to a printed contract override inconsistent printed provisions.[129]

Secondly, both parties may have their own standard conditions. A buyer may order goods on his own standard-term conditions (fig 3.1) and as likely as not the seller will purport to accept the order on *his* standard terms (fig 3.2), which in all probability will be inconsistent with those of the buyer. The approach of English law is to say that the seller's 'acceptance' of the buyer's order is a counter-offer

---

121   *Smith v Wilson* (1832) 3 B & Ad 728; *Peter Darlington Partners Ltd v Gosho Co Ltd* [1964] 1 Lloyd's Rep 149.
122   *Robertson v French* (1803) 4 East 130. See further p 90.
123   *Chitty on Contracts*, vol 1, paras 12-124.
124   Ibid, para 12-125.
125   See p 91.
126   See p 74.
127   *L'Estrange v Graucob* [1934] 2 KB 394.
128   *Parker v South Eastern Rly Co* (1877) 2 CPD 416; *Thornton v Shoe Lane Parking Ltd* [1971] 2 QB 163; *Interfoto Picture Library Ltd v Stiletto Visual Programmes Ltd* [1988] 1 All ER 348.
129   *Robertson v French*, n 122.

CONDITIONS OF ORDER

(1) The Company will not be liable for orders unless they are issued on its printed order forms duly signed on behalf of the Company.

(2) Unless this order has been accepted within 14 days from the date thereof it shall not thereafter be open for acceptance without our express written confirmation in that respect. Any alteration of or extension to this order must be the subject of confirmation in writing from us.

(3) Delivery of the goods must be completed within the time specified in our order and all work required by our order must be carried out in accordance with our instructions and must conform in all particulars to the requirements of this order and unless otherwise specified to B.S.I. standards where such exist. If this order is not completed to our requirements or in accordance with these Conditions or within the time specified we reserve the right to cancel this order and to purchase the goods elsewhere, charging you with any extra expense without prejudice, however, to any other claim we may have by reason of such non-completion.

(4) An advice note, on which the order number is clearly stated, must be sent to us the same day as the goods, and a delivery note must accompany each delivery. (Failure to send such notes will delay payment of invoices.)

(5) Invoices stating the order number must be rendered immediately the goods are dispatched, and in any case all invoices must be in our hands by the 6th of the month following the month of delivery; otherwise they will be carried forward to the following month's account and payment delayed one month without forfeiture of discount.

(6) This order is subject to a cash discount of 2!s per cent. for payment during the second month following the month of delivery, unless we wish to exercise the option of earlier payment to secure a special cash discount as arranged.

   Statement of Account must be rendered by the 10th of the month following delivery, or in the case of prompt payments, such periods as may be arranged. Failure to comply with this condition will delay payment without forfeiture of discount.

(7) All goods must be packed in such a manner as to reach us in good condition, carriage paid. Packing cases, boxes, reels and drums will not, except under special arrangement, be paid for, but if marked as returnable they will be despatched to you carriage paid.

(8) Payment will be made without prejudice to our rights if the goods you supply to this order prove to b unsatisfactory or not in accordance with specification or approved sample.

(9) Tools or Patterns made by you or supplied by us for the execution of this order are to be used exclusively for the service of this establishment, unless permission to do otherwise is first obtained from us.

(10) You to replace any defective material and to indemnify us against (a) any extra expenses or costs due to your part of the work being defective, or otherwise entailing extra charges upon us; and (b) any claims for infringements of patents or accidents to your workmen or any other workmen, whether engaged at our Works or elsewhere in the execution of this contract.

(11) Any goods or materials we send to you to be processed or for any other purpose to be insured by you against fire or any other loss or damage incurred whilst in your custody.

(12) Any order quoting a Government contract or sub-contract number is subject to the standard contract and conditions and/or any special conditions stipulated by the Government Department concerned, details of which will be supplied on request.

(13) No part of this order is to be sub-let without our permission.

(14) Any modification to the above Terms and Conditions must be in writing and duly authorised.

(15) These Conditions shall have precedence over any printed conditions appearing on any acceptance form, delivery form, letter or the like from you. Nothing in these Conditions shall prejudice any condition or warranty (expressed or implied) or other right or remedy to which we are entitled in relation to the said goods or work, the subject of this order.

(16) In the event of the goods being despatched to te Company under a contract of carriage the effect of which is that the Carrier's responsibility for loss or damage to the goods is limited more than it would otherwise be under the provisions of the Carriers Act 1830, due notification thereof must be given to the Company to enable it, if it so desires, to effect adequate insurance of the goods and any failure to give such notification shall entitle the Company to decline to treat delivery of the goods to the Carrier as delivery to the Company, or to hold the Seller of the goods responsible in damages for any loss or damage to the goods.

(17) Our Inspector or Representative and any Inspector or Representative of our customer or his agent or of any Government department concerned shall be entitled on our authority to inspect the goods or work which are the subject matter of this order at any reasonable time at your Works.

Fig. 3.1. Standard-term conditions of purchase

86

STANDARD CONDITIONS OF SALE
of
INTERNATIONAL BULLION AND METAL BROKERS (LONDON) LIMITED

1. **Definitions**
   In these Terms and Conditions:-
   1.1 "Agreement" means an agreement for the supply of Goods from IBMB to the Purchaser which shall be governed by these Terms and Conditions;
   1.2 "IBMB" means International Bullion and Metal Brokers (London) Limited;
   1.3 'the Delivery Date" means a date notified to the Purchaser by IBMB for the delivery of Goods;
   1.4 "Goods" means goods ordered from IBMB, and includes (where the context admits) each instalment or consignment of the same;
   1.5 "the Purchaser" means the person, firm or company contracting to purchase Goods from IBMB.

2. **Applicability**
   2.1 These Terms and Conditions, with such variations only as a director of IBMB may consent to or specify in writing, shall apply to and govern all Agreements.
   2.2 All terms, conditions, representations and warranties whether express or implied, and whether before or on the date of any Agreement, are hereby excluded, save to the extent that the same appear in these Terms and Conditions or are specifically agreed in writing by a director of IBMB.
   2.3. By placing an order for Goods subsequent to any previous receipt of or referral to these Terms and Conditions, the Purchaser acknowledges that these Terms and Conditions shall prevail over any qualification or condition purported to be imposed by the Purchaser.

3. **Prices**
   3.1 Unless expressly stated otherwise, prices quoted for Goods are net, ex-works and are exclusive of VAT, which is payable by the Purchaser.
   3.2 The price payable for Goods is that current at the Delivery Date.
   3.3 Prices indicated in IBMB's quotations, catalogues, and other advertising material shall not be binding on IBMB.

4. **Payment**
   4.1 The Purchaser shall pay for Goods within 30 days of the date of invoice, or terms as stated on front of invoice, but the allowance of this credit period is subject to the provisions of paragraph 7.4.5.
   4.2 In the event of any delay in payment, IBMB shall be entitled to charge the Purchaser interest, calculated on a daily basis, at the rate of 3% over the base lending rate of HSBC plc from time to time, for the period that payment is overdue.

5. **Delivery**
   5.1 Goods shall be delivered from the premises of IBMB on the Delivery Date and, unless otherwise agreed, the Purchaser shall pay for the carriage of the Goods.
   5.2 Risk in Goods shall pass on delivery.
   5.3 For delivery, time shall not be of the essence.

6. **Inspection**
   The Purchaser shall inspect Goods as soon as practicable after delivery and shall report any shortages in, breakages of or defects in Goods to IBMB in writing within seven days of delivery, failing which the Goods shall be conclusively presumed to have been accepted as being in good order and in conformity with the Agreement.

7. **Title**
   7.1 Until the Purchaser has both:-
      7.1.1 paid in full for Goods; and
      7.1.2 paid in full all other monies it owes to IBMB howsoever such debts have accrued
         those Goods shall remain the sole and absolute property of IBMB as legal and equitable owner.
   7.2 In the event of delivery of Goods prior to the passing of title in them, the Purchaser shall be in possession of them solely as bailee and fiducairy agent of IBMB until such time as the Purchaser has paid for them in full.
   7.3 The Purchaser shall insure to their full value Goods wherein the risk but not the title has passed to it and shall indemnify IBMB for loss, damage to or destruction of such Goods, and shall hold any insurance monies payable in respect of such Goods in trust for IBMB.
   7.4 Until title to Goods has been passed to the Purchaser:-
      7.4.1 the Purchaser shall store and lebel them so that they remain separate from other goods in the Purchaser's possession and are readily identifiable as the property of IBMB;
      7.4.2 the Purchaser shall at the request of IBMB deliver them up to IBMB and allow IBMB to recover them on request and for such purpose IBMB may at any time (through its representatives or agents) enter premises at which they are situtated;
      7.4.3 the Purchaser may as fiduciary agent of IBMB dispose o9f them in the course of its business and pass good title to them to its owner customer (being a bona fide purchaser for value without notice of IBMB rights) provided that such disposal shall be by the Purchaser as principal in relation to its own customer, and shall not commit IBMB to any contractual relationship with or liability to any such customer.
      7.4.4 the permission contained in paragraph 7.4.3 may be revoked at any time by notice by IBMB and shall automatically and without notice be revoked upon the commencement of liquidation proceedings (compulsory or voluntary) of the Purchaser or the appointment of a receiver, administrator, administrative receiver of judicial administrator over any part of the Purchaser's assets;
      7.4.5 In the case of all disposals of Goods under Paragraph 7.4.3, IBMB shall be legally and beneficially entitled to the proceeds of the disposal; the Purchaser shall not use the same in the course of its business and shall account to IBMB forthwith for the proceeds of the disposal notwithstanding that the period of credit allowed to the Purchaser hereunder may not have expired, keeing the same, until paid over to IBMB, identified as IBMB's monies and separately from its own monies and those of third parties, ins a separate bank account in which a credit balance shall be at all times maintained.

8. **Liability**
   8.1 Subject to paragraph 8.3, IBMB hereby excludes all conditions, undertakings and warranties implied by law in relation to Goods.
   8.2 Subject to paragraph 8.3, IBMB hereby excludes all liability for consequential or indirect loss or damage (including loss of profits, economic loss and exploitation loss) suffered by the Purchaser by reason, directly or indirectly, of any breach of IBMB of any Agreement.
   8.3 Nothing in this paragraph 8, these Terms and Conditions, or any Agreement shall exclude or restrict IBMB's liability for:-
      8.3.1 death or personal injury resulting from the negligence of IBMB, its servants or agents; or
      8.3.2 breach of IBMB's implied undertaking as title to Goods.

9. **Force Majeure**
   IBMB shall not be under any liability to the Purchaser in respect of any failure to perform, or delay in performing, any obligation under any Agreement attributable to any cause of whatsoever nature beyond IBMB's reasonable control, and no such failure or delay shall constitute a breach of contract by IBMB.

10. **Termination**
    Without prejudice to its rights and remedies, IBMB may without liability terminate any Agreement forthwith on written notice if:-
    10.1 the Purchaser is in any material breach of the same ; or
    10.2 any distress, execution or other legal process is levied upon any of the Purchaser's assets; or
    10.3 any arrangement or composition is made between the Purchaser and its creditors (whether generally or pursuant to proposals made under Section 1 of the Insolvency At 1986) or there is passed a resolution or there is made an order for the winding-up of the Purchaser, or there is made any administration order in respect of the Purchaser or there is appointed any liquidator or administrative receiver, judicial administrator or receiver or manager in respect of any part of the undertaking or assets of the Purchaser.

11. **No waiver**
    Any failure or delay on the part of IBMB to terminate an Agreement or take any action for the enforcement of an Agreement6 in consequence of any breach by the Purchaser shall not operate as a continuing waiver of the breach in question or prevent IBMB from subsequently enforcing its reights in respect of that continuing or any other breach.

12. **General**
    12.1 If any provision of these Terms and Conditions is held by any competent authority to be invalid or unenforceable in whoe or in part, the validity and enforceability of the remainder of the provisions hereof shall not be effected thereby.
    12.2 Every Agreement to which these Terms and Conditions apply shall be construed and take effect in accordance with the laws of England and Wales and the parties shall accept the non-exclusive jurisidiction of the English Courts.

Fig. 3.2. Standard-term conditions of sale

(since to be effective an acceptance must be the 'mirror image' of the offer, ie must be unqualified[130]); and if the buyer proceeds with the contract without further comment, he is taken to have assented by conduct to the counter-offer thus made. This is so even if the buyer's conditions had contained a clause providing that those were to override any inconsistent provisions in the seller's terms; for *ex hypothesi* the seller, in invoking his own conditions, has rejected the buyer's clause. In short, English law adopts the 'last shot' approach. Acceptance by conduct applies to a counter-offer as much as to an original offer, and is inferred from the counter-offeree's subsequent acts in furtherance of the transaction.[131]

4. Terms incorporated by reference

Instead of setting out all the terms itself, the contract document may incorporate by reference the provisions of other documents. Thus a contract for the sale of land may incorporate the Law Society's Conditions of Sale, which will then take effect as if set out expressly in the contract document.

(ii) Implication[132]

There are various grounds on which the court will be willing to read into a contract terms not expressly spelled out between the parties. They divide into two groups, terms implied in fact and terms implied in law.[133]

I. Terms implied in fact

(a) TERMS IMPLICIT IN EXPRESS TERMS. The court will imply a term where its inference from the language of the contract is such that it can be said to be too obvious to need stating. Thus, the grant of a first refusal of property, though expressed to be given in the event of the owner desiring to sell it, was held to preclude him from making a gift of the property without first offering it to the grantee of the first refusal.[134]

(b) TERMS NECESSARY TO GIVE BUSINESS EFFICACY TO THE CONTRACT. The court will imply a term where it is necessary to give business efficacy to the contract.[135] The court is slow to imply a term on this ground,[136] and it is not sufficient that the court

---

130 *Tinn v Hoffman & Co* (1873) 29 LT 271.

131 *Butler Machine Tool Co Ltd v Ex-Cell-O Corporation (England) Ltd* [1979] 1 All ER 965. For the American approach to the 'battle of the forms', see Uniform Commercial Code, s 2–207: White and Summers, *Uniform Commercial Code* (5th edn, 2000), pp 29 ff. See also the general discussion of the problem reproduced in (1980) 4 Can Bus LJ 263 ff.

132 See E. Allan Farnsworth, 'Disputes Over Omission in Contracts', 68 Col L Rev 860 (1968).

133 See Treitel, *The Law of Contract*, pp 201 ff.; *Scally v Southern Health and Social Services Board* [1992] 1 AC 294.

134 *Gardner v Coutts & Co* [1967] 3 All ER 1064.

135 *The Moorcock* (1889) 14 PD 64, per Bowen LJ at 68; *Southern Foundries v Shirlaw (1926) Ltd* [1940] AC 701.

136 See *Shell U.K. Ltd v Lostock Garages Ltd* [1976] 1 WLR 1187; *Liverpool City Council v Irwin* [1977] AC 239; *B.P. Refinery (Westernport) Ltd v Shire of Hastings* (1977) 52 ALJR 20; *Trollope & Colls Ltd v North Western Regional Hospital Board* [1973] 1 WLR 601.

considers that such a term would be reasonable. The term sought to be implied must be such that, without it, the contract would not be commercially workable. Thus, where an act is required to be performed to a party's satisfaction, it will usually be implied that his approval must not be capriciously withheld.[137] Again, there is in most contracts an implied term that neither party will obstruct performance by the other;[138] and there *may* be an implied term that a party will not take steps that will have the effect of preventing the other from earning his rights under the contract.[139]

(c) TERMS IMPLIED FROM PRIOR COURSE OF DEALING. Where parties have consistently[140] contracted on certain terms, so that it may reasonably be assumed that the transaction under consideration was intended to be governed by the same terms, the court will usually be willing to find that the terms apply, even if not expressly adopted in relation to the transaction.[141]

(d) TERMS IMPLIED BY CUSTOM OR USAGE. A term may be annexed to a contract by local custom or trade usage.[142] To be effective, such custom or usage must not be contrary to the law, and must be reasonable,[143] generally known or known to the party against whom it is invoked, and consistent with the express terms and general tenor of the contract.[144] Thus, the perfect tender rule ordinarily applicable on a contract of sale has been displaced by evidence of a trade usage permitting a limited shortfall in quality or quantity against an appropriate reduction in the price.[145] Custom or usage may be invoked not only to import a term into the contract but also to give a special meaning to express terms.

2. *Terms implied in law*

(a) TERMS IMPLIED AS RULES OF THE COMMON LAW. For certain types of transaction the courts have so regularly implied certain terms that these have become standard and will be implied as a matter of law unless excluded by the parties.[146] Prime

---

137 *Dallman v King* (1837) 4 Bing NC 105; *Braunstein v Accidental Death Insurance Co* (1861) 1 B & S 782. It is in each case a question of construction whether the withholding of approval must be reasonable or whether it suffices that it is honest. See, for example, *Stadhard v Lee* (1863) 3 B & S 364; *Diggle v Ogston Motor Co* (1915) 84 LJKB 2165.

138 *Mackay v Dick* (1881) 6 App Cas 251; *Kyprianou v Cyprus Textiles Ltd* [1958] 2 Lloyd's Rep 60; *Bournemouth and Boscombe Athletic Football Club v Manchester United Football Club* (1980) Times, 22 May.

139 Compare *Turner v Goldsmith* [1891] 1 QB 544 with *Rhodes v Forwood* (1876) 1 App Cas 256 and *Luxor (Eastbourne) Ltd v Cooper* [1941] AC 108.

140 *McCutcheon v David Macbrayne Ltd* [1964] 1 All ER 430.

141 *Henry Kendall & Sons v William Lillico & Sons Ltd* [1969] 2 AC 31; *Vacwell Engineering Co Ltd v B.D.H. Chemicals Ltd* [1971] 1 QB 88; *Circle Freight International v Medeast Gulf Exports* [1988] 2 Lloyd's Rep 427.

142 For the traditional distinction between custom and usage, see 12(1) Halsbury's Laws (4th edn, 1998 reissue), para 605, and p 13, n 54. Nowadays the two terms are often used interchangeably.

143 *North and South Trust Co v Berkeley* [1971] 1 All ER 980; and see *Kum v Nah Tat Bank Ltd* [1971] 1 Lloyd's Rep 439.

144 *Humfrey v Dale and Morgan* (1857) 7 E & B 266, affirmed (1858) EB & E 1004. Custom and usage take effect as implied terms of the contract and are not considered in English to have independent normative force. See p 13.

145 *Peter Darlington Partners Ltd v Gosho Co Ltd*, n 121.

146 *Shell U.K. Ltd v Lostock Garages Ltd* [1977] 1 All ER 481, per Lord Denning MR at 487.

examples are the terms of title, fitness and merchantable quality implied in contracts of sale of goods in the nineteenth century, prior to the enactment of the Sale of Goods Act.[147] Where the courts have not already established such terms as a matter of law, they will do so where as a matter of policy the term in question is one which the law should imply as a necessary incident of a defined contractual relationship.[148] The range of such implied terms is steadily spreading. For example, it has been held to be an implied term in a contract for the supply of services that they will be performed with such care and skill as is reasonable, having regard to the degree of experience which the provider holds himself out as possessing;[149] in a contract for labour and materials, that the materials will be of proper quality and fit for the purpose;[150] and in a contract of agency, that the agent is entitled to be indemnified against expenses and liabilities incurred by him in the performance of his duties.[151]

(b) TERMS IMPLIED BY STATUTE. A statute may act on a contract not merely by restricting its efficacy or by imposing *ab extra* additional duties on the parties to it[152] but by importing obligations into the contract itself as implied terms. The infringement of such a term is in such a case not a breach of statutory duty but a fully fledged breach of contract. Thus, terms as to title, quality, fitness and the like are now imported into sale and hire-purchase agreements by the Sale of Goods Act 1979 and the Supply of Goods (Implied Terms) Act 1973,[153] and into other contracts involving the supply of goods and contracts for the supply of services by the Supply of Goods and Services Act 1982. We may also equate with implied terms duties set out in a statute which, though not designated as implied terms, are intended to describe the contractual obligations of the parties so far as not excluded or modified by the language of the contract.[154]

8. CONSTRUING THE CONTRACT

(i) The nature of the construction process

In its broad sense, construction of a contract denotes determination of the total legal effect of the agreement concluded by the parties. This may involve two entirely distinct processes: (i) interpretation of the language used by the parties, and (ii) implication of terms where the contract is silent.[155]

---

147 See p 185.
148 *Scally v Southern Health and Social Services Board*, n 133.
149 *Bolam v Friern Hospital Management Committee* [1957] 2 All ER 118; and see now the Supply of Goods and Services Act 1982, s 13.
150 *Young and Marten Ltd v McManus Childs Ltd* [1969] 1 AC 454.
151 *Thacker v Hardy* (1878) 4 QBD 685. See *Bowstead and Reynolds on Agency* (17th edn, 2001), art 64.
152 Eg, on an employer, to ensure the health, safety and welfare at work of his employees (Health and Safety at Work etc., Act 1974, s 2); on a landlord under a short lease, to keep the structure and exterior of the premises in repair (Landlord and Tenant Act 1985, s 11).
153 See ch 11.
154 Eg, the delivery obligation of the seller under the Sale of Goods Act. See p 263.
155 See p 87.

I.   Interpretation

The modern approach to the interpretation of contracts is neatly encapsulated in the speech of Lord Hoffmann in *Investors Compensation Scheme Ltd v West Bromwich Building Society*:[156]

> Almost all the old intellectual baggage of 'legal' interpretation has been discarded. The principles may be summarised as follows.
>
> (1) Interpretation is the ascertainment of the meaning which the document would convey to a reasonable person having all the background knowledge which would reasonably have been available to the parties in the situation in which they were at the time of the contract.
>
> (2) The background was famously referred to by Lord Wilberforce as the 'matrix of fact', but this phrase is, if anything, an understated description of what the background may include. Subject to the requirement that it should have been reasonably available to the parties and to the exception to be mentioned next, it includes absolutely anything[157] which would have affected the way in which the language of the document would have been understood by a reasonable man.
>
> (3) The law excludes from the admissible background the previous negotiations of the parties and their declarations of subjective intent. They are admissible only in an action for rectification. The law makes this distinction for reasons of practical policy and, in this respect only, legal interpretation differs from the way we would interpret utterances in ordinary life. The boundaries of this exception are in some respects unclear. But this is not the occasion on which to explore them.
>
> (4) The meaning which a document (or any other utterance) would convey to a reasonable man is not the same thing as the meaning of its words. The meaning of words is a matter of dictionaries and grammars; the meaning of the document is what the parties using those words against the relevant background would reasonably have been understood to mean. The background may not merely enable the reasonable man to choose between the possible meanings of words which are ambiguous but even (as occasionally happens in ordinary life) to conclude that the parties must, for whatever reason, have used the wrong words or syntax: see *Mannai Investments Co Ltd v Eagle Star Life Assurance Co Ltd* [1997] AC 749.
>
> (5) The 'rule' that words should be given their 'natural and ordinary meaning' reflects the commonsense proposition that we do not easily accept that people have made linguistic mistakes, particularly in formal documents. On the other hand, if one would nevertheless conclude from the background that something must have gone wrong with the language, the law does not require judges to attribute to the parties an intention which they plainly could not have had. Lord Diplock made this point more vigorously when he said in *Antaios Compania Naviera S.A. v Salen Rederierna A.B.* [1985] AC 191, 201:
>
> 'if detailed semantic and syntactical analysis of words in a commercial contract is going to lead to a conclusion that flouts business commonsense, it must be made to yield to business commonsense.'

---

156   [1998] 1 WLR 896 at 912–913.

157   By which, as he subsequently explained, Lord Hoffmann meant anything which a reasonable man would have regarded as relevant (*Bank of Credit and Commerce International v Ali* [2002] 1 AC 251, para 39).

2. Implication

Implication is usually stated to be a process by which the court arrives at the presumed intention of the parties,[158] but it is clear that in many cases the intention thus attributed to the parties is fictitious since the facts generating the dispute were not within their contemplation at all and no one can tell with confidence how they would have framed the contract if they had addressed their minds to the question.[159] In such cases the court is in truth reaching a solution by the application of external rules based on considerations of policy, though it may disguise this process by use of labels such as 'construing the contract' or 'deducing the intention of the parties'. Thus, terms implied by law, whether established by prior authority or enunciated *de novo* in the light of the relationship between the parties and other policy factors, will be imported into a contract without the court finding it necessary to consider what the parties would have been likely to agree if they had addressed their minds to the prospect of the terms in question.[160] Similarly, rules for determining whether a contract is frustrated by change of circumstances represent a judicially imposed solution which may be buttressed by appeal to the assumed intention of the parties but which in reality depends on the court's view of the degree of fundamentality of the change.[161]

(ii) The parol evidence rule

If there be a contract which has been reduced into writing, verbal evidence is not allowed to be given of what passed between the parties, either before the written instrument was made or during the time that it was in a state of preparation, so as to add to or subtract from or in any manner to vary or qualify the written contract.[162]

This is the classical exposition of the so-called parol evidence rule, a rule which, in truth, extends to all extrinsic evidence, whether oral or otherwise, and which, moreover, is in some respects a rule of substantive law rather than a mere rule of evidence.[163] Thus it has been held impermissible to construe a contract by reference to the negotiations that led up to it[164] or the conduct of the parties after conclusion of the contract.[165] Such a rigid rule, characteristic of the law of evidence in

---

158 *The Moorcock*, n 135, per Bowen LJ at 68.
159 See Glanville Williams, 'Language and the Law' (1945) 61 LQR 384 at p 401; Wright, *Legal Essays and Addresses* (1939), p 259; *Greaves & Co (Contractors) Ltd v Baynham Meikle & Partners* [1975] 2 Lloyd's Rep 325, per Lord Denning MR at 327.
160 See, for example, *Liverpool City Council v Irwin* [1976] 2 All ER 39, per Lord Edmund-Davies at 54–55, quoting the speech of Viscount Simonds in *Lister v Romford Ice & Cold Storage Co Ltd* [1957] AC 555 at 576.
161 *Hirji Mulji v Cheong Yue S.S. Co* [1926] AC 497, per Lord Sumner at 510; *Davis Contractors Ltd v Fareham U.D.C.* [1956] AC 696. See further p 137.
162 *Goss v Lord Nugent* (1833) 5 B & Ad 58, per Lord Denman at 64; *Bank of Australasia v Palmer* [1897] AC 540, per Lord Morris at 545.
163 See *Wigmore on Evidence*, para 2400.
164 *Prenn v Simmonds* [1971] 3 All ER 237. The position is otherwise if the terms of the contract are ambiguous and the pre-contract documents indicate the parties' intended meaning (*The Karen Oltmann* [1976] 2 Lloyd's Rep 708).
165 *James Miller and Partners Ltd v Whitworth Street Estates (Manchester) Ltd* [1970] AC 583; *Schuler A.G. v Wickman Machine Tool Sales* [1974] AC 235.

England, has little to commend it,[166] and is believed to be widely ignored in practice. Very often the record of negotiations culminating in the contract is the best guide to the intention of the parties, as is their behaviour subsequently. It is well-established that in construing a contract the court looks at the factual matrix, or business setting, in which it was made.[167] It is clear that this is not confined to cases where the disputed term is ambiguously expressed.[168] This being so, it is hard to see why the court should ignore pre-contract and post- contract acts and documents to construe the contract, even where on its face there is no ambiguity.

The parol evidence rule is in any event subject to numerous exceptions. It does not apply where the evidence establishes the existence of a collateral contract,[169] or where it can be shown that the document was not intended as a complete record of the contract terms[170] (a typical case is where the contract is partly in writing, partly oral), or where its existence or operation was dependent on some prior unexpressed stipulation;[171] or that it was procured by misrepresentation[172] or was tainted by illegality;[173] or that it disguised the true nature of the transaction.[174] Further, the court may order rectification of a document which does not correctly record the agreement between the parties.[175] These exceptions have largely destroyed the rule;[176] and today's judges are more reluctant to use it as a short-cut method of excluding extrinsic evidence of doubtful credibility, preferring to avoid the risk of injustice (or even the appearance of injustice) by letting in the evidence while requiring it to be of a compelling nature before accepting it in the face of an apparently comprehensive contract document. As that outstanding contract scholar Corbin said some 60 years ago: 'The writing cannot prove its own completeness and accuracy.'[177]

But where the parties have included an 'entire agreement' clause in their contract stating that it represents the entirety of what they have agreed to the exclusion of all

---

166   See to similar effect Gerard McMeel, 'Prior Negotiations and Subsequent Conduct – The Next Step Forward for Contractual Interpretation?' (2003) 119 LQR 272; Sir Johan Steyn, 'Written Contracts: To What Extent May Evidence Control Language?' (1986) CLP 23.

167   *Prenn v Simmonds*, n 164, per Lord Wilberforce at 239.

168   See, for example, *The Antaios* [1985] AC 191, in which Lord Diplock approved a decision of arbitrators construing 'breach' as meaning fundamental breach.

169   *City and Westminster Properties (1934) Ltd v Mudd* [1959] Ch 129; and see K. W. Wedderburn, 'Collateral Contracts' [1959] CLJ 58.

170   *Harris v Rickett* (1859) 4 H & N 1; *Mercantile Bank of Sydney v Taylor* [1893] AC 317.

171   *Pym v Campbell* (1856) 6 E & B 370.

172   *Dobell v Stevens* (1825) 3 B & C 623, where the misrepresentation was fraudulent; but the principle applies equally to an innocent misrepresentation.

173   *Collins v Blantern* (1767) 2 Wils 341.

174   *Madell v Thomas & Co* [1891] 1 QB 230.

175   *Murray v Parker* (1854) 19 Beav 305; *Craddock Bros v Hunt* [1923] 2 Ch 136.

176   See Law Com Working Paper No 70, *Law of Contract: The Parol Evidence Rule*, para 21. The Working Paper provisionally recommended that the rule be abolished (para 43). Unfortunately, in its report the Law Commission finally decided to make no recommendation for abolition of the rule, primarily on the ground that any attempted description of the rule would be circular. See *Law of Contract: The Parol Evidence Rule* (Law Com No 154, Cmnd 9700, 1986).

177   'The Parol Evidence Rule' 53 Yale LJ 603, 630 (1944), cited by E. Allan Farnsworth, *Farnsworth on Contracts* (3rd edn, 2003), vol II, p 231, who notes that 'the trend clearly favours Corbin' and cites the *Restatement Second* §210 in support.

prior agreements, the court will usually refuse to give effect to prior supplemental or inconsistent terms.[178]

(iii) Collateral contracts[179]

One way of surmounting the parol evidence rule is to find that statements by a party preceding the contract were distinct promises constituting a collateral warranty or undertaking, the consideration for this being the other party's entry into the main contract. The device of the collateral contract has been developed with some vigour by the courts and has been extended to cases where the statement induces the recipient of it to enter into a contract not with the maker of the statement but with a third party. For example, a motor dealer induces a customer to take one of his cars on hire-purchase from a finance house by representing the car to be in excellent condition. If the court is satisfied that the representation was a warranty, that is, that it was given as a promise by which the dealer bargained for the customer's entry into the hire-purchase agreement with the finance house, then if the representation was false, the dealer will be held liable in damages for breach of the warranty embodied in a collateral contract between him and the customer.[180] Of course, liability of this kind cannot logically be confined to cases where the action induced was the representee's entry into a *contract*. *Any* activity bargained for by the warranty suffices to ground an action for damages if the warranty is broken, for *ex hypothesi* the warranty is promissory in nature. In such a case the label 'collateral contract' is misleading since there is no 'main' contract at all, but simply a single contract of a perfectly ordinary nature by which the maker of the statement warrants its truth in consideration for performance of the designated activity by the recipient of the statement.

9. RESTRICTIONS ON WHAT CAN BE VALIDLY STIPULATED

(i) Must a contract be fair?[181]

The parties to a contract do not have unlimited freedom to agree upon any terms they choose. The common law in principle adopts a laissez faire standpoint, but recognizes that some limits have to be set to freedom of contract. In particular, the courts will not enforce contracts involving the infringement of the criminal or civil law, or otherwise contrary to public policy or morals;[182] penalty clauses are likewise unenforceable to the extent that they provide the claimant with more than the amount of his loss;[183] and a party will not be able to exclude liability for the

---

178   *Deepak Fertilisers and Petrochemical Corp. v ICI Polymers and Chemicals Ltd* [1999] 1 Lloyd's Rep 387; *Inntrepreneur Pub Co (GL) v East Crown Ltd* [2002] 2 Lloyd's Rep 611.
179   Wedderburn [1959] CLJ 58.
180   See p 720.
181   See Collins, *Law of Contract*, ch 13; Boris Kozolchyk, 'Fairness in Anglo and Latin American Jurisprudence', (1979) 2 Boston Coll Int & Com L Rev 219.
182   *Chitty on Contracts*, ch 17; Treitel, *Law of Contract*, ch 11; Cheshire, Fifoot and Furmston, *Law of Contract*, chs 10, 11 and 12.
183   See p 123.

consequences of his own fraud.[184] Further restrictions are imposed by equity and by statute.

However, there is no general principle of English law that enables a court to refuse enforcement of a contract solely on the ground that its terms are unfair.[185] Even a substantial disparity between the value of a promise and the value of the consideration for it is rarely invoked with success, the usual judicial approach being that it is for the parties, not the courts, to decide what is an acceptable bargain. Indeed, the suggestion that English law recognizes a general concept of inequality in bargaining power[186] has been firmly rejected.[187] But though the courts have been reluctant to interfere with the terms of contracts,[188] they have shown a much greater willingness to examine the circumstances in which the contract under consideration was made and to set aside contracts for what an American writer has termed 'procedural unfairness':[189] economic duress or other coercion;[190] undue influence arising from the relationship of the parties or from taking improper advantage of another's ignorance, infirmity or dependence;[191] sharp or deceptive practices in negotiating the transaction.[192] Underlying all these ideas, as well as the various forms of estoppel, is the concept of unconscionability.[193] The court has long asserted an equitable jurisdiction to reopen unconscionable bargains,[194] and will not allow a person to retain the benefit of his improper conduct. Moreover, since equitable relief is discretionary, the court has an inbuilt power to refuse, or to impose conditions for granting, such remedies as injunctions, decrees of specific performance, declarations and rescission and rectification of contracts.

---

184   *S. Pearson & Son Ltd v Dublin Corporation* [1907] AC 351.

185   But see pp 97 ff. as to the Unfair Contract Terms Act 1977 and the Unfair Terms in Consumer Contracts Regulations 1999.

186   A concept propounded by Lord Denning in *Lloyds Bank Ltd v Bundy* [1975] QB 326; and see Hugh Beale, 'Inequality of Bargaining Power' (1986) OJLS 123.

187   *Pao On v Lau Yiu Long* [1980] AC 614; *National Westminster Bank plc v Morgan* [1985] AC 686.

188   A notable exception is the case of contracts considered to be in restraint of trade. See p 131.

189   Arthur Leff, 'Unconscionability and the Code – The Emperor's New Clothes' 115 U Pa L Rev 485 (1967); and see White and Summers, *Uniform Commercial Code*, pp 154 ff.

190   *Pao On v Lau Yiu Long*, n 187; *North Ocean Shipping Co Ltd v Hyundai Construction Co Ltd* [1978] 3 All ER 1170; *The Siboen and The Sibotre* [1976] 1 Lloyd's Rep 293; *Atlas Express Ltd v Kafco (Importers and Distributors) Ltd* [1989] 1 All ER 641.

191   *Lloyds Bank Ltd v Bundy*, n 186; *Barclays Bank Ltd v O'Brien* [1994] 1 AC 180; *C.I.B.C. Mortgages plc v Pitt* [1994] 1 AC 200; *Cheese v Thomas* [1994] 1 WLR 129.

192   *Hartog v Colin and Shields*, n 68.

193   See S. M. Waddams, 'Unconscionability in Contracts' (1976) 39 MLR 369; S. Deutsch, *Unfair Contracts Doctrine of Unconscionability*; A. H. Angelo and E. P. Ellinger, 'Unconscionable Contracts – A Comparative Study' (1979) 4 Otago Law Rev 300. The High Court of Australia has made the doctrine of unconscionability a major tool of the development of Australian contract law. See A. M. Gleeson in P. Birks (ed), *Frontiers of Liability* (1994).

194   See Treitel, *Law of Contract*, p 420 ff. However, it is also the case that unconscionability as such (as opposed to particular types of vitiating factor such as undue influence) is rarely invoked with success (see, for example, *Multiservice Bookbinding Ltd v Marden* [1979] Ch 84). English law appears to lack a general concept of unconscionability of the kind that has been developed in other jurisdictions through case law and specific statutory provisions such as the New South Wales Contracts Review Act 1980 and the American Uniform Commercial Code, s 2–302.

(ii) Good faith and its role in English law

The reluctance of English courts to recognize a duty to negotiate in good faith or to interfere with bargains freely made is an aspect of a general mistrust of what are perceived to be over-broad principles not susceptible to clear or consistent application.[195] Thus in contrast to Continental and American legal systems,[196] English law does not possess any general requirement of good faith.[197] A duty of good faith is owed in particular situations or relationships. For example, a person seeking to displace another's title[198] or obtain priority over an earlier security interest[199] must show that he himself took in good faith; an agent or other fiduciary owes a duty of good faith to his principal or other counterparty to the fiduciary relationship; good faith is required in contracts of insurance[200] and other contracts characterized as *uberimmae fidei*. Moreover, since equitable remedies are discretionary, a party seeking the assistance of equity will be expected to have acted in good faith.[201] But many situations which in civil law jurisdictions are resolved by reference to a requirement of good faith are dealt with by the imposition of a separate duty which does not depend on good faith. Thus, the seller of defective goods is liable not because he concealed the defect but because he is under a strict duty to tender goods of satisfactory quality;[202] a party to a contract owes a duty not to impede performance by the other party;[203] and a contract induced by misrepresentation can be rescinded even if the misrepresentation was wholly innocent.

At the heart of judicial caution concerning the introduction of a general concept of good faith is that there is no consensus on its content. The central question is how to resolve the tension between the legitimate pursuit of self-interest by a party who has entered or is negotiating to enter into a contract and a proper regard for the legitimate interests of the other party. English law does, it is true, distinguish between relationships that are essentially adversarial, where the guiding principle is that each party has to look after itself, from those which are essentially cooperative because the relationship between the parties or the circumstances in which they come together imposes on one of them an obligation to subordinate its own interests to that of the other, as in the case of an agent or other fiduciary.[204] But even in

---

195 See *Walford v Miles*, n 71.

196 See, for example, art 242 of the German BGB, art 1134(3) of the French Code Civil and s 1–203 of the American Uniform Commercial Code.

197 See *Interfoto Picture Library Ltd v Stiletto Visual Programmes Ltd*, n 128 at 353; Steyn J, 'The Role of Good Faith and Fair Dealing in Contract Law: a Hair-Shirt Philosophy?' (1991) Denning LJ 131.

198 See pp 416 ff.

199 See pp 654 ff.

200 *Rozanes v Bowen* (1928) 32 Ll L Rep 98. But see R. A. Hasson (1969) 32 MLR, who contends that the expansive view of the duty of disclosure in insurance contracts results from a misreading of the root decision of Lord Mansfield in *Carter v Boehm* (1766) 3 Burr 1905.

201 See p 112.

202 See p 300.

203 *Nissho Iwai Petroleum Co Inc v Cargill International SA* [1993] 1 Lloyd's Rep 80; *The Aello* [1961] AC 135.

204 For a useful discussion of this distinction in the context of joint ventures see Gerard M.D. Bean, *Fiduciary Obligations and Joint Ventures: The Collaborative Fiduciary Relationship* (1995).

relationships classed as adversarial there are some limits on the pursuit of self-interest. Thus, a person buying goods from a non-owner who had no authority to sell them will usually have to establish good faith,[205] by which is meant honesty in fact.[206] For this purpose a person who genuinely believes his conduct is morally justified is not dishonest unless he is also aware that it would not be so regarded by reasonable and honest people.[207] But so far, as regards adversarial types of commercial relationship English law does not appear to have gone further so as to require purely objective good faith in the sense of fair dealing by the standards of reasonable people regardless whether the party in question was aware that his conduct would transgress such standards.[208] Still less does it equate good faith with reasonableness. Moreover, in the absence of fraud[209] there is no duty to conduct negotiations in good faith or to refrain from arbitrarily terminating them.[210] English law has no equivalent of the civilian *culpa in contrahendo*. Over time judicial opposition to a more general concept of good faith may weaken, with the implementation of the EC Directive on Unfair Contract Terms, which introduces into English law for the first time a requirement of good faith in consumer contracts in order to avoid a significant imbalance in the parties' rights and obligations, to the consumer's detriment.[211]

(iii) Exemption clauses[212]

1.   The common law

Clauses by which a contracting party seeks to exclude or limit his liability have come under increasing attack from the courts in recent years, particularly in relation to standard-term consumer contracts. Over time, a battery of judicial weapons against exemption clauses has evolved. Thus, public policy precludes a party from excluding liability for his own fraud,[213] and a contract will not be construed as exempting him from liability for the fraud of his agent unless it so provides in clear and unmistakable terms.[214] Written disclaimers of liability have been struck down on the ground that they are contained in a document which the other party had no reason to suppose was contractual;[215] that the contract was concluded before the

---

205   Sale of Goods Act 1979, ss 24, 25.
206   Ibid, s 51(3).
207   *Twinsectra Ltd v Yardley* [2002] 2 AC 164 (Lord Millett dissenting).
208   Ibid. There is now a substantial literature on good faith, particularly in comparative law. See, for example, Furmston, *Law of Contract*, paras 1.78 ff; Roger Brownsword, Norma J. Hird and G. Howells (eds), *Good Faith in Contract* (1999); Reinhard Zimmerman and Simon Whittaker (eds.), *Good Faith in European Contract Law* (2000); J. Beatson and D. Friedmann (eds.), *Good Faith and Fault in Contract Law* (1995).
209   For example, conducting negotiations with no intention to conclude a contract.
210   *Walford v Miles*, n 71. However, there is a duty to respect the confidentiality of information disclosed on a confidential basis
211   See p 100, and Hugh Collins, 'Good Faith in European Contract Law' (1994) OJLS 229.
212   See generally Richard Lawson, *Exclusion Clauses* (7th edn, 2003); Treitel, *Law of Contract*, pp 216 ff.
213   *HIH Casualty and General Insurance Ltd v Chase Manhatten Bank* [2003] 2 Lloyd's Rep 61.
214   Ibid.
215   *Chapelton v Barry Urban District Council* [1940] 1 KB 532.

disclaimer was brought to the other party's notice;[216] that applying the *contra proferentem* rule, the exemption clause was not, as a matter of construction, apt to cover the particular breach or loss complained of;[217] that the defendant was a stranger to the contract containing the exemption clause;[218] that the effect of the clause was misrepresented;[219] that the term broken was fundamental, the core of the contract, and was thus not to be construed as cut down by the exemption clause;[220] and that exemption clauses would not be construed as covering fraud or intentional breach. Finally, the courts developed the doctrine of fundamental breach,[221] for the purpose of ensuring that a party could not fall back on an exemption clause to safeguard himself from the consequences of a breach so grave as to frustrate the commercial purpose of the contract. However, after a prolonged judicial battle between those who argued that the doctrine was one of construction and those who contended that it was a matter of substantive law, the House of Lords has firmly settled the issue, declaring that there is no substantive rule of law which empowers the court to strike down an exemption clause merely because it is unreasonable, or because the consequences of the breach are serious, and that in each case the question is whether as a matter of construction the clause is apt to cover the breach complained of.[222]

2. The Unfair Contract Terms Act

Substantial inroads on the freedom to exclude or limit liability have been made by the Unfair Contract Terms Act 1977. The title to the Act is somewhat misleading, since it is not concerned with the fairness of contracts generally, only with certain types of contractual provision (primarily exemption clauses), and it is not confined to contracts, being applicable equally to attempts to disclaim by notice liability in tort for negligence. As to the latter, the Act nullifies contractual provisions and notices excluding or restricting business liability[223] for negligence resulting in death

---

216 *Olley v Marlborough Court Ltd* [1949] 1 KB 532; *Thornton v Shoe Lane Parking Ltd*, n 128.
217 *Webster v Higgin* [1948] 2 All ER 127; *Karflex Ltd v Poole* [1933] 2 KB 251.
218 *Scruttons Ltd v Midland Silicones Ltd* [1962] AC 446. But see *The Eurymedon* [1975] AC 154; *The New York Star* [1980] 3 All ER 257; and see p 1060.
219 *Curtis v Chemical Cleaning and Dyeing Co Ltd* [1951] 1 KB 805.
220 *Karsales (Harrow) Ltd v Wallis* [1956] 2 All ER 866; *Smeaton Hanscomb & Co Ltd v I. Sassoon Setty Son & Co* [1953] 2 All ER 1471, per Devlin J at 1473.
221 *Karsales (Harrow) Ltd v Wallis*, n 221; *Harbutt's 'Plasticine' Ltd v Wayne Tank & Pump Co Ltd* [1970] 1 QB 447.
222 *Photo Productions Ltd v Securicor Transport Ltd* [1980] AC 827, explaining and applying *Suisse Atlantique Société d'Armement Maritime S.A. v N.V. Rotterdamsche Kolen Centrale* [1967] 1 AC 361, and overruling *Charterhouse Credit Co Ltd v Tolly* [1963] 2 QB 683, *Harbutt's 'Plasticine' Ltd v Wayne Tank & Pump Co Ltd*, n 221, and *Wathes (Western) Ltd v Austins (Menswear) Ltd* [1976] 1 Lloyd's Rep 14. It has been held that clauses limiting liability are not to be construed with the same rigour as clauses excluding liability (*Ailsa Craig Fishing Co Ltd v Malvern Fishing Co Ltd* [1983] 1 All ER 101 at 102–103; *George Mitchell (Chesterhall) Ltd v Finney Lock Seeds Ltd* [1983] 2 AC 803 at 814). While this approach has not been followed by the High Court of Australia (see *Darlington Futures Ltd v Delco Australia Pty Ltd* (1986) 161 CLR 500), it has a certain logic, for *ex hypothesi* the situation to which it is applied is one in which there *is* a breach not covered by the exception clause so that prima facie the limitation of liability is designed for just such a case.
223 As defined by s 1(3).

or injury,[224] and as regards other forms of loss subjects the provision or notice to the requirement of reasonableness.[225] Under s 3, where a party to a contract deals as consumer[226] or on the other's written standard terms of business,[227] that other cannot, by reference to a contract term, exclude or restrict his liability[228] for breach of contract, or claim to be entitled to render a performance substantially different from that which the other party reasonably expected or, as regards the whole or part of his obligation, no performance at all, except in so far as (in any of the above cases) the contract term satisfies the requirement of reasonableness.[229] For the purpose of this section the court is not obliged (though it is entitled) to have regard to the guidelines laid down in Sch 2 as regards ss 6 and 7, which relate to contracts for the sale or other supply of goods.[230] As regards standard terms formulated by an outside body, a relevant consideration is whether that body is neutral (or, alternatively, includes representatives of the competing interests) and is concerned to balance the rights of the parties[231] or whether it is a trade association concerned primarily to safeguard the interests of its members when formulating the contract terms.

To prevent evasion, s 13 of the Act provides that to the extent that it prevents the exclusion or restriction of liability, it also prevents this being done by making the liability or its enforcement subject to restrictive or onerous conditions,[232] by excluding or restricting any remedy[233] or by excluding or restricting any rules of evidence or procedure, and to that extent it prevents excluding or restricting liability by reference to terms which exclude or restrict the relevant obligation or duty.[234] The ambit of this section is far from clear. In restricting the efficacy of exemption clauses in contracts the Act does, of course, presuppose the existence of a contract in the first place and the assumption of the duty of performance to which the exemption clause is directed. For example, a contract to paint the windows of a house does not attract

224 Section 2(1).
225 Section 2(2). Reasonableness is to be tested as at the date of the contract.
226 As defined by s 12. See p 328.
227 See *McCrone v Boots Farm Sales Ltd* 1981 SLT 103. 'Standard terms of business' covers terms prepared by others and adopted by the party concerned, eg the JCT Building Contract, the Law Society's Condition of Sale.
228 See s 13(1), and see p 99.
229 See the remarks of Griffiths J in *R. W. Green Ltd v Cade Bros Farms* [1978] 1 Lloyd's Rep 602 at 607–608. For decisions on these and other factors to be taken into account see *George Mitchell (Chesterhall) Ltd v Finney Lock Seeds Ltd*, n 222 and (as regards disclaimer of liability in tort, where similar considerations apply) *Smith v Eric S. Bush* and *Harris v Wyre Forest District Council* [1990] 1 AC 831. The approach taken in *George Mitchell* is not easy to reconcile with the non- interventionist line adopted in *Photo Productions,* n 222. For a critical analysis, see John N. Adams and Roger Brownsword, 'The Unfair Contract Terms Act: A Decade of Discretion' [1988] 104 LQR 94.
230 As to which see pp 190 ff.
231 As in the case of the contracts referred to in n 227.
232 For example, by requiring notice of rejection to be given within an unreasonably short time. See *Knight Machines (Holdings) Ltd v Rennie* 1995 SLT 166.
233 Eg, excluding the right of set-off (*Stewart Gill Ltd v Horatio Myers & Co Ltd* [1992] 2 All ER 257) or limiting damages.
234 See Elizabeth Macdonald, 'Exclusion clauses: the ambit of s 13(1) of the Unfair Contract Terms Act 1977' (1992) Legal Studies 277.

the operation of the Act merely because it contains a provision that the painter is not to be responsible for repairing defective window sashes. The difficulty is to distinguish cases where there is no initial obligation at all from those where a promise is given, the effect of which is then sought to be qualified.[235]

What constitutes an exemption clause for the purpose of the 1967 Act continues to give rise to difficulty. In *Watford Electronics Ltd v Sanderson CFL Ltd*[236] the Court of Appeal held that an entire agreement clause providing that no statements or representations by either party had been relied on by the other did not constitute an exemption clause within s 3 of the 1977 Act since

> liability in damages under the 1967 Act can arise only where the party who has suffered the damage has relied upon the representation [and] where both parties to the contract have acknowledged, in the document itself, that they have not relied on any pre-contract representation, it would be bizarre (unless compelled to do so by the words they have used) to attribute to them an intention to exclude a liability which they must have thought could never arise.[237]

But the distinction between an exclusion of liability and negation of a fact that is a necessary ingredient of liability is a very fine one and it is doubtful whether the parties themselves would have intended anything other than the exclusion of what would otherwise have been a basis of liability.[238]

There are other provisions in the Act relating to the sale or other supply of goods,[239] examined in a later chapter,[240] as well as provisions affecting unreasonable indemnity clauses and exemption clauses in manufacturers' guarantees relating to goods.[241]

The Act, which contains various exemptions,[242] does not affect any of the judicial weapons available at common law to deal with exemption clauses, other than what was formerly thought to be the rule that in the case of fundamental breach an exemption clause cannot be relied on if the innocent party terminates the contract.[243] On this the Act provides that the clause may be held reasonable and given effect accordingly even if the contract has come to an end.[244]

---

235 The difficulty was grasped by the Court of Appeal in *Harris v Wyre Forest District Council* [1988] 1 All ER 691 (concerning the disclaimer by notice of a duty in tort) but glossed over by the House of Lords when reversing that decision in the jointly heard appeals in *Smith v Eric S Bush* and *Harris v Wyre Forest District Council*, n 230. See also *Phillips Products Ltd v Hyland* [1987] 2 All ER 620; *Johnstone v Bloomsbury Health Authority* [1991] 2 All ER 293, and Macdonald (1992) Legal Studies 277.

236 [2001] 1 All ER (Comm) 696.

237 Ibid per Chadwick LJ, para 41.

238 See further Furmston, *Law of Contract*, pp 528–529.

239 Sections 5–7 and Sch 2.

240 See pp 326 ff.

241 Sections 5, 10.

242 See ss 1(2), 26, 27 and Sch 1, which exempt (inter alia) international supply contracts, an exemption on which the Law Commissions have invited views (*Unfair Terms in Contracts*, Law Com. Consultation Paper 166, Scot. Law Com. Discussion Paper 119, August 2002, paras 5.65, 5.69, 5.71).

243 *Harbutt's 'Plasticine' Ltd v Wayne Tank & Pump Co Ltd*, n 221.

244 Section 9(1). But the supposed rule has now been repudiated by the House of Lords in *Photo Productions Ltd v Securicor Transport Ltd*, n 222 so rendering s 9(1) redundant.

3.   The Unfair Terms in Consumer Contracts Regulations

The Unfair Contract Terms Act, while covering both consumer transactions and contracts entered into upon a person's written standard terms of business, is relatively narrow in its focus, being directed essentially at clauses excluding or limiting liability. The Unfair Terms in Consumer Contracts Regulations,[245] though confined to contracts between a consumer and a supplier of goods or services,[246] are much more powerful, covering all types of contractual term. A contractual term which has not been individually negotiated is to be regarded as unfair if, contrary to the requirement of good faith, it causes a significant imbalance in the parties' rights and obligations arising under the contract, to the detriment of the consumer.[247] Thus for the first time English law will embody a general principle of good faith in relation to consumer contracts. The concept of significant imbalance in parties' rights is also novel. The regulations offer guidance as to the factors to be taken into account in assessing unfairness,[248] and set out an indicative and non-exhaustive list of the terms which may be regarded as unfair.[249] These include terms excluding or limiting the consumer's legal rights for failure in performance by the supplier, so that in relation to consumer contracts the regulations significantly overlap the provisions of the Unfair Contract Terms Act 1977 to similar effect. In contrast to the 1994 regulations and the directive itself,[250] the regulations do not offer any guidance on good faith, but this has been succinctly described in the following terms in a decision of the House of Lords on the 1994 regulations, and these would seem equally applicable under the 1999 regulations:

> The requirement of good faith in this context is one of fair and open dealing. Openness requires that the terms should be expressed fully, clearly and legibly, containing no concealed pitfalls or traps. Appropriate prominence should be given to terms which might operate disadvantageously to the customer. Fair dealing requires that a supplier should not, whether deliberately or unconsciously, take advantage of the consumer's necessity, indigence, lack of experience, unfamiliarity with the subject matter of the contract, weak bargaining position or any other factor listed in or analogous to those listed in Schedule 2 to the Regulations. Good faith in this context is not an artificial or technical concept; nor, since Lord Mansfield was its champion, is it a concept wholly unfamiliar to British lawyers. It looks to good standards of commercial morality and practice.[251]

A term is always to be regarded as not having been individually negotiated where it has been drafted in advance and the consumer has therefore not been able to

---

245 SI 1999/2083, replacing the Unfair Terms in Consumer Contract Regulations 1994, SI 1994/3159, which implemented the EC Directive on Unfair Contract Terms (93/13/EEC, OJ L95/29).
246 'Consumer' means any natural person who, in contracts covered by the regulations, is acting for purposes which are outside his trade, business or profession, and 'seller or supplier' means any natural or legal person who, in such contracts, is acting for purposes relating to his trade, business or profession, whether publicly owned or privately owned (reg 3).
247 Regulation 5(1).
248 Regulation 6.
249 Schedule 2.
250 Recital 16.
251 *Director General of Fair Trading v First National Bank* [2002] 1 AC 481, per Lord Bingham, para 17.

influence the substance of the term.[252] However, the assessment of fairness is not to be applied to the definition of the main subject matter of the contract or the adequacy of the price or remuneration against the goods or services supplied in exchange.[253] The effect of an unfair term is that it is not binding on the consumer,[254] but the contract continues to bind the parties if capable of continuing in existence without the unfair term.[255] The regulations also provide for the issue of injunctions to prevent the continued use of unfair terms.[256]

It might have been expected that, in relation to consumer contracts, implementation of the directive in the United Kingdom would be accompanied by a repeal of the Unfair Contract Terms Act, but this sensible course has not been adopted. The decision is regrettable and can be expected to cause a good deal of confusion. The Law Commissions are expected to render a report in 2004 recommending a single, simplifying enactment.

10. THE PRIVITY RULE AND ITS CONSEQUENCES

(i) The position at common law

It was a basic principle of the common law that a contract could not effectively confer rights or impose duties on those who are not parties to it.[257] Hence a contract between A and B by which A undertook to pay money to C was not enforceable by C. Similarly, if B bought goods from A which suffered from a dangerous defect, as the result of which B's wife, C, was injured, B might have a remedy against A for breach of the contract of sale but C could not, as a stranger to the contract, rely on it and had to found her claim in negligence. Again, though B had a contractual claim against A, he could not invoke the contract against a negligent manufacturer, M, but usually had to show negligence on the part of M if he was to succeed. This aspect of the privity rule was frequently criticized as unfair and unnecessary[258] and, when they considered it appropriate, the courts were not slow to find ways of avoiding the impact of the rule. Various avenues of escape were possible, eg specific performance,[259] assignment of rights by the promisee to the beneficiary[260] and a

---

252 Regulation 5(2). Even if a specific term or certain aspects of it in a contract have been individually negotiated, the regulations apply to the rest of the contract if an overall assessment of it indicates that it is a pre-formulated standard contract (reg 5(3)).

253 Regulation 6(2).

254 Regulation 8(1).

255 Regulation 8. For detailed analyses of the regulations, see Lawson, *Exclusion Clauses*; Furmston, *Law of Contract*, paras 3.97 ff.

256 Regulation 12. The regulations are vigorously enforced by the Office of Fair Trading, usually by persuading businesses whose standard terms are considered unfair to alter them to meet the OFT's objections. For the new statutory enforcement machinery, see the Enterprise Act 2002, Pt 8.

257 *Tweddle v Atkinson* (1861) 1 B & S 393.

258 For a powerful criticism of the rule as causing a distortion of tort law in order to provide a third party with a remedy denied by the rule, see B. S. Markesinis, 'An Expanding Tort Law – the Price of a Rigid Contract Law' (1987) 103 LQR 354, cited in *White v Jones* [1995] 1 All ER 691.

259 *Beswick v Beswick* [1968] AC 58.

260 As to the requirements for a statutory assignment see p 47.

finding by the court that in entering into the contract the promisee was doing so not only on his own behalf but also as agent of the intended beneficiary of the promise, so that the latter is not in truth a stranger to the contract but a second promisee. A good illustration of the agency approach was furnished by the decision of the Privy Council in *The Eurymedon*.[261]

> Goods were carried from Liverpool to Wellington under a contract of carriage entered into between the shipper and the carrier. The terms of the contract were evidenced by a bill of lading which was expressed to limit the liability not only of the carrier and its servants or agents but of any independent contractor employed by the carrier.[262] On arrival in Wellington the goods were damaged as the result of negligence of the stevedore during unloading.
>
> In an action against the stevedore, the latter relied on the limitation of liability embodied in the bill of lading, and the shipper contended that the stevedore, as a stranger to the contract, was not entitled to rely on the exemptions and immunities conferred by the contract on the carrier.
>
> The Privy Council held that in entering into the contract the carrier did so not only on its own behalf but also on behalf of the stevedore, and that accordingly, in addition to the bilateral contract between shipper and carrier, there was a unilateral contract between shipper and stevedore to the effect that in consideration of the stevedore unloading the goods the limitation of liability provision would apply. The offer thus made by the shipper to the stevedore was accepted by performance of the act of unloading, so bringing into existence the separate unilateral contract with the stevedore, who was therefore entitled to rely on the provision for limitation of liability.[263]

The Contracts (Rights of Third Parties Act) 1999[264] largely abrogated the principle that a third party cannot enforce a contract made for his benefit, though there are certain exceptions to this, one of which is that the Act confers no rights on a third party in the case of a contract of carriage of goods by sea except for reliance on an exclusion or limitation of liability in the contract.[265]

Just as a stranger to a contract could not usually assert rights under it, so also he could not as a rule be made liable on it, and this principle is unaffected by the 1999 Act. Here again, however, ways may be found of fixing him with liability despite the privity rule. For example, one may have the converse of the situation which obtained in *The Eurymedon*. A contract between A and B purporting to impose liability on C may be found to have been entered into by A or B as agent for C, in which case C may be made liable upon it.[266] Another source of liability, considerably developed over recent years, is the collateral contract, described earlier in this chapter.[267] Even where the claimant cannot establish a contractual relationship of any kind with the defendant, he may have a claim in tort, eg for

---

261   *Sub nom New Zealand Shipping Co Ltd v A.M. Satterthwaite & Co Ltd* [1975] AC 154.

262   Clauses to this effect are known as 'Himalaya' clauses. See p 1060.

263   This decision was later applied by the Privy Council in *The New York Star*, n 218.

264   See below.

265   Contracts (Rights of Third Parties) Act 1999, s 6(5). The exception preserves the efficacy of the Himalaya clause. Carriage by sea is dealt with in ch 36.

266   As to the liability of an undisclosed principal, see p 176.

267   See p 193.

fraud or negligence or for unlawful interference with the contract between the claimant and a third party.[268]

(ii) The Contracts (Rights of Third Parties) Act 1999[269]

This Act, which resulted from a Law Commission report,[270] provides that, subject to other provisions, a person who is not a party to a contract may in his own right enforce a term of the contract if (a) the contract expressly provides that he may or (b) the term purports to confer a benefit on him,[271] though in the latter case not if the parties did not intend the term to be enforceable by a third party.[272] This last qualification makes it clear that the Act is not intended to enable parties to a typical chain transaction to bypass their counterparties and pursue someone higher or lower in the chain. For example, where part of construction works is sub-contracted, the fact that the works will benefit the building owner will not, in the normal case, give the owner a right to enforce the sub-contract, for this is not intended. Similarly, where a person sells goods knowing that they are intended to be immediately sub-sold, that fact will not as a rule entitle the sub-buyer to enforce the main sale contract, the benefits of which were intended to be conferred solely on the buyer as promisee.

The third party must be expressly identified in the contract by name, as a member of a class or as answering a particular description but need not be in existence when the contract is entered into.[273] He can enforce the term only subject to and in accordance with any other relevant terms of the contract.[274] Where a third party has become entitled to enforce a contract term, then, subject to any express term of the contract, the parties may not rescind or vary it so as to extinguish or vary that entitlement once the third party has communicated his assent to the term to the promisee or the third party has relied on the term and the promisor is either aware of such reliance or could reasonably have been expected to foresee it.[275] The promisor remains entitled to assert any defences and rights of set-off that would have been available to him against the promisee or would have been available against the third party if he had been a party to the contract.[276] The promisee remains entitled to enforce any term of the contract[277] but the promisor is protected against double liability.[278]

---

268 *Lumley v Gye* (1853) 2 E & B 216; *British Motor Trade Association v Salvadori* [1949] Ch 556.

269 See Treitel, *Law of Contract*, pp 651 ff; Furmston, *Law of Contract*, paras 6.59 ff; Andrew Burrows, 'The Contracts (Rights of Third Parties) Act 1999 and its implications for commercial contracts' [2000] LMCLQ 540.

270 *Privity of Contract: Contracts for the Benefit of Third Parties*, Law Com No 242 (1996).

271 Contracts (Rights of Third Parties) Act 1999, s 1(1). This extends to enforcement of a term excluding or limiting liability (s 1(6)).

272 Ibid, s 1(2).

273 Ibid, s 1(3).

274 Ibid, s 1(4).

275 Ibid, s 2.

276 Ibid, s 3.

277 Ibid, s 4.

278 Ibid, s 5.

11.   VARIATION[279] AND NOVATION[280]

The parties to a contract may freely agree to vary it, though for the variation to be effective and enforceable it must be made in compliance with the same formal requirements as those (if any) prescribed for the original contract.[281] Since a variation is contractual, it involves consideration on both sides.[282] This is usually taken to mean that a purported variation which alters the contract in favour of one party only has no contractual force. Thus expressed, the proposition is too broad. An employer, without requiring the employee to perform additional duties, increases the employee's salary. A building owner, at the request of a builder who finds he has underpriced the contract, agrees to increase the contract figure. A car manufacturer, having in its franchise agreements with its dealers agreed to allow credit of 60 days for cars delivered on consignment, increases the credit period to 90 days. Are we to say that none of these variations has contractual force? Instinct rebels against such a non-commercial interpretation of an everyday occurrence – and it would be right to do so. Contracts involving continuing work or a continuing relationship or flow of dealings between the parties depend heavily on the subsistence of mutual goodwill. Tangible benefits may be expected to flow to the party who generates goodwill by improving his terms. Were the other party to decline to continue performance unless the terms were varied, his promise to perform a pre-existing duty in return for the variation ought to be treated as good consideration, for performance is worth more to the obligee than the fruits of a lawsuit.[283] If, therefore, the obligee is willing to improve the terms voluntarily, why should the law compel the other party to show that he exacted the revised terms by threatening to down tools? That is why the decision of the Court of Appeal in *Williams v Roffey Bros & Nicholls (Contractors) Ltd*[284] that a factual (as opposed to legal) benefit of the promise suffices as consideration is to be welcomed as reflecting commercial reality.[285]

---

279 See Sean Wilken, *The Law of Waiver, Variation and Estoppel* (2nd edn, 2002); Tony Dugdale and David Yates, 'Variation, Waiver and Estoppel – A Re-Appraisal' (1976) 39 MLR 680; P. S. Atiyah, 'Consideration and Estoppel: The Thawing of the Ice' (1975) 38 MLR 65.

280 See Julian Bailey, 'Novation', (1999) 14 JCL 189.

281 *Goss v Lord Nugent*, n 162.

282 For an attack on this requirement see C. Ulyatt, 'Should consideration be required for the variation of contracts?' (2002) 9 Auckland U. L. Rev 883.

283 The fallacy of the proposition that an undertaking to perform that which the promisor is already obliged to perform confers no benefit on the promisee was long ago exploded by Professor Arthur L. Corbin in his superb work on contract law, *Corbin on Contracts*, (rev by Joseph M Perillo, 1993), vol 1A, s 172. It is clearly established that an undertaking to perform an existing duty owed *to a third party* may constitute good consideration (*The Eurymedon*, n 218; *Pao On v Lau Yiu Long*, n 190). But an undertaking to perform an existing duty owed to the other party to the contract is considered by some judges not to be good consideration (see the decision of Mocatta J in *North Ocean Shipping Co Ltd v Hyundai Construction Co Ltd*, n 190 at 1177 and of Lloyd J in *Syros Shipping Co SA v Elaghill Trading Co* [1981] 3 All ER 189), while others take a different view (see, for example, the views of Denning LJ in *Ward v Byham* [1956] 2 All ER 318 at 319 and *Williams v Williams* [1957] 1 All ER 305 at 307). The latter approach is preferable in policy terms.

284 [1991] 1 QB 1.

285 In that case the promisee agreed to pay an additional sum for performance of an existing duty in order to ensure the promisor's performance so that the promisee would not incur a liability to a third party through the promisor's default.

A variation, which leaves the rest of the contract intact, must be distinguished from a novation, which replaces the contract entirely with a new contract. The term 'novation' is now usually employed to denote a change of parties, as where in a contract between A and B it is agreed that B shall be released and C shall take his place as the other party to the contract. Novation need not be left to ad hoc agreement; it is open to the parties to provide for it in advance and in particular to establish a contractual mechanism by which novation takes place automatically on the occurrence of a designated act or event. As we shall see,[286] contractual novation has become a powerful market tool for reducing risk and facilitating the transfer of financial assets.

12. WAIVER AND ESTOPPEL[287]

(i) Waiver

The term 'waiver' has many meanings,[288] and its significance depends on the context in which it is used. In essence, it indicates a voluntary surrender of a right or a remedy, the surrender being voluntary both in the sense that no consideration is given for it and in the sense that the act of waiver is, or is considered by the law to be, intentional and its binding nature derives from the will of the waiving party, not from imposition by law consequent upon the conduct of the other party in reliance on the act of waiver. A promise to surrender a right or remedy may induce action by the other party in reliance on that promise. If the inducement was bargained for by the terms of the promise, there is a contractual variation. If it was not bargained for but was reasonably foreseeable as the consequence of the promise, it generates an estoppel.[289] The party promising to give up a right or remedy is estopped, or precluded by law, from going back on his promise. A party having two alternative rights or remedies may be taken to have waived one by pursuing the other, as where a party having a right to treat a contract as repudiated elects to affirm it. This form of waiver is known as election. Election differs from promissory estoppel in a number of respects. It is not binding unless made with knowledge of the facts giving rise to the choice; it concerns a choice to be made between remedies that have already accrued; it does not depend for its efficacy either on consideration or on reliance.[290]

A party to a contract whose own duty to perform is subject to a condition may voluntarily waive that condition if it is solely for his benefit.[291] Such a waiver,

---

286 See pp 148, 156.

287 See Wilken, *Law of Waiver*.

288 See ibid, ch 3; T Dugdale and D Yates 'Variation, Waiver and Estoppel – A Re-Appraisal' (1976) 39 MLR 680 at pp 681–682; Treitel, *Law of Contract* pp 102 ff, 811 ff. As to whether an apparent repudiation waives the requirement of willingness and ability to perform, see Francis Dawson, 'Waiver of Conditions Precedent on a Repudiation' (1980) 96 LQR 239, and see p 396.

289 See below.

290 *The Kanchenjunga* [1990] 1 Lloyd's Rep 391; and see F. M. B. Reynolds, 'The Notions of Waiver' [1990] LMCLQ 453.

291 *Hawksley v Outram* [1892] 3 Ch 359; *Morrell v Studd and Millington* [1913] 2 Ch 648.

rendering his performance obligation unconditional, requires no consideration to support it, but, if voluntary, it will be effective only where the condition waived does not constitute a substantial part of the consideration given in exchange for the obligation to which the condition was attached.[292]

(ii) Estoppel[293]

Estoppel typically arises in a situation where a statement or promise by one person, A, induces another person, B, to act in reliance on the statement or promise, and such reliance was reasonably foreseeable by A as the result of his statement or promise. In such a case, A is usually precluded from subsequently disputing the truth of the facts he had previously asserted or from going back on his promise. The orthodox rule of estoppel, both at law and in equity, was said to be that it was confined to statements of existing fact, and thus did not extend to promises to perform or refrain from performing an act or invoking a right.[294] The common law regarded such promises, if not made under seal, as *nudum pactum*, there being no consideration. But in the celebrated *High Trees House* case,[295] Denning J tapped a slender line of authority to establish a wider equitable principle by which even a promise not to assert a right would bind the promisor if the other party was thereby led to act in reliance on it; and the act of reliance need constitute only a change of position in some way, not necessarily a detriment. This form of estoppel is conveniently known as promissory estoppel.[296]

Promissory estoppel differs in its effect from earlier forms of estoppel in two respects. First, it does not, as a rule, ground a cause of action; it is merely a defence. In other words, it cannot be used as a sword but may be set up as a shield to prevent the claimant from asserting a right or from alleging a breach of duty when he has previously promised not to assert the right or to enforce the duty.[297] Secondly, promissory estoppel is usually only temporary in its effect, and the party bound by

---

292   This qualification is not adverted to in the English texts but is well made by Corbin (*Contracts*, vol 3A, para 753) and has been adopted in the *American Restatement, Second, Contracts*, s 84(1). Corbin's illustration is of a man, B, who undertakes to pay $10,000 to A for the erection of a building. No court, says Corbin, would enforce a waiver by B of his right to the building as a condition precedent to payment so as to commit B to paying $10,000 for nothing. This is plainly the position in English law also.

293   See also p 69 and Wilken, *Law of Waiver*.

294   *Jorden v Money*, n 20. For a criticism of this case, see David Jackson, 'Estoppel as a Sword' (1965) 81 LQR 84, 223.

295   *Central London Property Trust Ltd v High Trees House Ltd*, n 32, applying *Hughes v Director of the Metropolitan Rly Co* (1877) 2 App Cas 439.

296   It is also termed 'quasi-estoppel' and, confusingly, 'equitable estoppel'. The latter term is to be avoided, for it implies that the traditional estoppel arising from representations of existing fact was known only to the common law, whereas it was equally recognized in equity. Promissory estoppel may be regarded as an extension of the old equitable estoppel. Other forms of estoppel are proprietary estoppel (p 71) and estoppel by convention (below).

297   *Combe v Combe* [1951] 2 KB 215; *Argy Trading Development Co Ltd v Lapid Developments Ltd* [1977] 3 All ER 785.

it can, as a rule, restore himself to his full legal rights by giving reasonable notice to the other party.[298]

These two types of estoppel are the most common, though they are not the only forms recognized by the law. A third form, proprietary estoppel, has already been mentioned.[299] A rather more recent form of estoppel developed in the law of contract is estoppel by convention. This arises where each party to the contract has proceeded with the transaction on the basis of a given assumption of fact or entitlement which is known to and acquiesced in by the other. In such a case neither will be allowed to go back on the agreed assumption where it would be unfair or unjust to allow him to do so.[300] So if the parties to a guarantee contract have proceeded on a common, albeit erroneous, assumption that the guarantee covers certain liabilities which it does not in fact cover, they will not be allowed to interpret the contract otherwise than in accordance with that assumption.[301]

13. REMEDIES FOR MISREPRESENTATION

(i) Rescission and damages

A representation, it will be recalled, is a statement of fact, express or implied, anterior to the contract, which is intended to and does induce the person to whom it was made to enter into the contract but is not at the time of its making intended as a promise, though it may later become incorporated as a term of the contract. Since a representation is not as such a promise, its falsity cannot constitute a breach of contract or give rise to an action for damages for breach of contract. If there is any remedy at all, it must lie in tort or statute. Hence a fraudulent misrepresentation is actionable not because of the character of the statement as a representation inducing a contract but because the law of tort gives a general remedy in deceit for fraudulent statements; and a negligent misrepresentation may be actionable either because it is made in circumstances where the defendant owed the claimant a duty of care[302] or under s 2(1) of the Misrepresentation Act

---

298 See *Tool Metal Manufacturing Co Ltd v Tungsten Electric Co Ltd* [1955] 1 WLR 761. But where the other party's change of position in reliance on the promise has become unalterable or it would otherwise be inequitable to allow retraction of the promise, the estoppel becomes permanent in its effect (*Ajayi v R. T. Briscoe (Nigeria) Ltd* [1964] 1 WLR 1326). This also is the position in the case of proprietary estoppel. See p 71.

299 See p 71.

300 *Amalgamated Investment & Property Co Ltd v Texas Commerce International Bank Ltd* [1982] QB 84; *The Vistafjord* [1988] 2 Lloyd's Rep 343. See generally *Chitty on Contracts*, paras 3-107 ff.

301 *Amalgamated Investment & Property Co* Ltd, n 300.

302 As where the defendant was in a 'special relationship' with the plaintiff (*Hedley Byrne & Co Ltd v Heller & Partners Ltd* [1964] AC 465), which is considered to include *par excellence* a prospective contractual relationship (*Esso Petroleum Ltd v Mardon*, n 99). The conditions in which a duty is owed to a third party is a topic of considerable complexity. The current law is to be found in *Caparo plc v Dickman* [1990] 2 AC 605 and *Smith v Eric S. Bush*, n 229.

1967.[303] In addition, equity gives the representee a right to rescind the contract, whether the misrepresentation was fraudulent, negligent or wholly innocent, for his entry into the contract has been brought about on a false basis. The entire contract must be rescinded; partial rescission is not recognized in English law.[304]

The remedies of the injured party were greatly strengthened by the Misrepresentation Act 1967, which allows rescission even if the misrepresentation has become a term of the contract[305] or the contract has been fully performed;[306] gives the innocent party a right to damages unless the maker of a non-fraudulent misrepresentation can disprove negligence;[307] and renders ineffective clauses excluding or limiting liability for misrepresentation except so far as these satisfy the requirement of reasonableness under the Unfair Contract Terms Act.[308] But the Misrepresentation Act also cuts down the common law rights of the representee in one respect, by empowering the court to make him accept damages in lieu of rescission in the case of a non-fraudulent misrepresentation.[309] However, damages cannot be awarded where the right of rescission has been lost.[310]

(ii) Mode and effect of rescission

Rescission may be effected by notice to the guilty party of the innocent party's intention to rescind, or by conduct equivalent to such notice where the guilty party has absconded and cannot be traced,[311] or by repossession of property delivered under the contract.[312] To safeguard himself in case of doubt or to procure the benefit of remedies which are not available by self-help, such as execution of a conveyance in the name of the defendant, the innocent party may ask for a declaration that the contract has been or ought to be rescinded. But even where a court order is sought, the rescission is the act of the claimant, not of the court, and takes effect on the giving of notice or equivalent conduct, such as the commencement of proceedings.[313] In such a case the order is declaratory only.

---

303 The measure of damages is tortious, not contractual, and is the same as for fraud, namely the sum needed to put the claimant in the position in which he would have been if he had not entered into the contract (*Doyle v Olby (Ironmongers) Ltd* [1969] 2 QB 158; *Royscot Trust Ltd v Rogerson* [1991] 2 QB 297). The latter decision remains controversial.
304 *De Molestina v Ponton* [2002] 1 Lloyd's Rep 271; *TSB Bank plc v Camfield* [1995] 1 WLR 430.
305 Misrepresentation Act 1967, s 1(a).
306 Ibid, s 1(b).
307 Ibid, s 2(1).
308 Ibid, s 3.
309 Ibid, s 2(2).
310 *Government of Zanzibar v British Aerospace (Lancaster House) Ltd* [2000] 1 WLR 2333.
311 *Car & Universal Finance Co Ltd v Caldwell* [1965] 1 QB 525.
312 Ibid.
313 *Horsler v Zorro* [1975] Ch 302, per Megarry J at 310; *Alati v Kruger* (1995) 94 CLR 216 (High Court of Australia).

The effect of rescission is to cancel the contract from the beginning, to avoid it retrospectively so that it is treated as never having existed. Hence a necessary concomitant of rescission is restitution: the restoration by both parties (the innocent as well as the guilty) of benefits received under the contract. Property transferred under the contract automatically revests in the transferor.[314]

Restitution must be distinguished from damages. As stated earlier, the function of damages is to compensate the innocent party so as to put him as nearly as possible in the position in which he would have been if the contract had been performed. If the plaintiff has suffered no loss, he is usually entitled to no more than nominal damages.[315] Restitution is concerned not with compensation for loss of a bargain but with the surrender of benefits obtained at the expense of the claimant which it would be unjust to allow the defendant to retain. The innocent party's loss is therefore recoverable only to the extent to which it has resulted in a corresponding benefit to the other party.[316]

(iii) Bars to rescission

Since rescission involves restitution, the right to rescind is usually lost if restitution has become impossible because, for example, the subject-matter has been irretrievably lost or disposed of or substantially changed in character. The courts do not apply this principle in a mechanistic way, and, in general, rescission will be allowed where the lack of perfect restitution does not give the innocent party a windfall at the expense of the guilty party.[317] Inability to give restitution because of acts of the guilty party is also treated more liberally than where restitution is impossible because of the innocent party's acts. The innocent party also loses the right to rescind if he affirms the contract with knowledge of the falsity of the representation; and lapse of time may also, it seems, destroy a right to rescind, by a conclusive presumption of affirmation, even where the innocent party was without knowledge of the fact that the representation was untrue, and therefore did not in fact elect to affirm the contract.[318]

---

314 In *Alati v Kruger*, n 313, it was said (at 224) that if the rescission was effected in equity it was only the equitable title that revested. That is true in English law to the extent that the retransfer of title requires a formal act such as a conveyance, as in the case of land, which was the subject-matter of *Alati v Kruger*, but it is not true of assets requiring no formality for transfer, such as goods, where legal title revests automatically on rescission whether this is effected at law or in equity (*Car and Universal Finance Co Ltd v Caldwell* [1965] 1 QB 525, per Lord Denning MR at 532; *Newtons of Wembley Ltd v Williams* [1965] 1 QB 560, per Sellers LJ at 571. See to the same effect John Cartwright, *Misrepresentation* (2002), para 3.11.

315 For an exceptional case where the defendant was ordered to account for profits received from his breach, see *Attorney-General v Blake* [2001] 1 AC 268, discussed p 116.

316 This is the true explanation of *Whittington v Seale-Hayne* (1900) 82 LT 49, in which a confusing distinction was drawn between damages and an indemnity, when the real point was that the defendant could be required to restore the value of the benefits he had received (rent, rates, repairs) but not the other items claimed by the claimant (loss of stock, removal and storage expenses, wages, etc.), since these were losses sustained by him which had not resulted in any benefit to the defendant.

317 See Treitel, *Law of Contract*, pp 378 ff.

318 *Leaf v International Galleries* [1950] 2 KB 86.

14.   PERFORMANCE OF THE CONTRACT

When a party undertakes a contractual obligation, he is strictly answerable for performance, in the sense that if he fails to perform or his performance is defective, it is no answer that he made all reasonable endeavours or took all reasonable care to carry out his obligations. Liability thus does not depend on fault. Compared with other legal systems, English law is remarkably reluctant to recognize change of circumstances as qualifying or discharging a contractual obligation. Only in the most extreme cases will supervening events which obstruct performance be considered to frustrate the contract in a legal sense.[319]

Although the duty to perform a contractual obligation is strict, there are, of course, many contracts in which the obligation itself is merely to take reasonable care or exercise reasonable skill. Where a party's contractual expectation is defeated despite the exercise of such care and skill by the other party, the latter is free from liability, not because contractual liability is dependent on fault but simply because his obligation was merely to use reasonable care.

Any shortfall in performance, however minor, is a breach of contract entitling the innocent party to damages, though if he has suffered no loss, damages will be purely nominal. Not every breach, however, entitles the innocent party to withhold performance of his own obligations or to reject as ineffective the performance by the other.[320]

15.   REMEDIES FOR BREACH OF CONTRACT[321]

Where a contract is broken, the innocent party has three principal avenues of redress open to him: self-help, judicial decision and arbitration. By self-help is meant some lawful act which does not involve recourse to the courts or an arbitrator.[322] To obtain redress through judicial decision involves litigation, the institution of proceedings before a court of competent jurisdiction.[323] Arbitration is a process by which, pursuant to an agreement, a dispute is referred for determination by a person or tribunal other than a court of law. It is an important method of resolving commercial disputes and is discussed in a later chapter.[324] Of growing significance is alternative dispute resolution which does not involve a binding award, such as mediation.

---

319   See p 135.
320   For him to do this the two obligations must be correlative.
321   See further, in relation to contracts of sale, chs 14 and 15; Donald R Harris, David Campbell and Roger Halson, *Remedies in Contract and Tort* (2nd edn, 2002); Burrows, *Remedies for Torts*.
322   See below.
323   See ch 38.
324   Chapter 39. A judge may act as an arbitrator, in which case his status is that of any other arbitrator, not that of a court except that an appeal lies direct to the Court of Appeal. See p 1119, n 2.

(i) Self-help

English law is surprisingly indulgent to self-help as a means of securing satisfaction for a breach of contract. Indeed, in a number of ways[325] the law positively encourages the innocent party to bypass the judicial process – a reflection of the wider philosophy that God helps those who help themselves, so that diligence in the pursuit of remedies should be rewarded and, as between two competing interests, the race should go to the swiftest. The advantages of self-help, where this is available, are speed, the avoidance of legal costs and the by-passing of procedural and substantive law obstacles to a judicial remedy.[326]

The principal self-help remedies of which the innocent party may avail himself are: forfeiture of a deposit taken from the guilty party; set-off;[327] lien; stoppage in transit; rescission; resale; extra-curial enforcement of security;[328] repossession of his goods (recaption); withholding of performance of his own obligations while the other party remains in default; and termination of the contract for breach.

(ii) Judicial remedies: some general points

1.   The nature and function of judicial remedies

When a lawyer is consulted about a breach of contract, he may advise the client to take proceedings to enforce the contract. What, however, does he mean by 'enforce'? Physical compulsion in a literal sense is plainly out of the question. The nearest the court can get to it is to make an order directing performance and to apply sanctions if the order is not obeyed. An award of money earned under a contract (ie a judgment for debt) is designed to give the claimant the precise benefit contemplated by the contract and is thus a primary remedy. So also is a decree of specific performance directing the defendant to perform a non-monetary obligation on pain of imprisonment for contempt if he fails to do so. But specific performance is the exception rather than the rule, for most breaches of contract are best dealt with by an award of damages, the most common form of civil remedy after debt. The purpose of damages is to give the claimant the monetary value of his defeated contractual expectation. In contrast to judgments for debt and decrees of specific

---

325   For example, (i) a creditor holding a security which is imperfect (eg, for want of registration) is protected if he enforces it before the appearance of a rival claimant having a *locus standi* to impeach the security (see p 667); (ii) a party may rescind a voidable contract by notice (though in the case of a non-fraudulent misrepresentation the court may order damages in lieu of rescission – see p 108), whereas if he seeks a declaration of his right to rescind the grant of relief is discretionary; (iii) a contract unenforceable by action may lawfully be enforced by self-help remedies unless this is prohibited by statute; (iv) the holder of a subordinate equitable interest who acquired it by purchase without notice of the prior equitable interest can jump ahead by getting in the legal title (p 202); (v) a person entitled to possession of a chattel can enforce his rights by seizure, whereas if he seeks an order for specific performance or specific delivery, the court has a discretion to award him damages instead (pp 112 ff.).

326   See n 325.

327   See p 621.

328   See pp 637 ff.

performance, an award of damages is a substitute remedy. It does not give the claimant that to which he was entitled under the contract, but merely a broad equivalent in money, after making such adjustments as are dictated by legal policy.[329] In practical terms, then, we can say that in the great majority of contract disputes which do not involve pure debt the guilty party has the option of buying himself out of the contract by paying damages. This is not as objectionable as it appears. There is little point in seeking to compel literal performance by an unwilling contractor, and the soothing unguent of damages is usually less expensive and less wasteful of resources. Thus the court will not ordinarily decree specific performance or grant a mandatory injunction where damages would be an adequate remedy, or compel a continuing activity, such as the running of a business, which might involve repeated applications to the court, difficulties in determining what constituted a breach of the order or injunction, and the risk of the defendant being compelled to carry on business at a loss.[330]

2.   Remedies at common law

The common law very much favoured the monetary approach to the settlement of disputes. Indeed, the rule at common law was that the defendant had the option of performing his contract or paying damages. The common law courts did not order specific performance of a contract or specific delivery of goods. The range of orders available at common law was in truth very limited, being largely confined to debt, damages and delivery of possession with an option to the defendant, except in the case of land, to pay damages instead of delivering up possession.

3.   Judicial remedies in equity

Courts of equity, however, were prepared to go much further. They were willing to grant specific performance of contracts, injunctions to restrain an actual or threatened breach of a negative stipulation, orders for an account, for the appointment of a receiver and for the execution of instruments of transfer of title, and a range of other remedies.[331]

4.   Legal and equitable remedies contrasted

Though all civil courts now administer both law and equity, the division between rules of common law and rules of equity continues,[332] and two important distinctions between legal and equitable remedies remain. First, a claimant with

---

329   See p 116.

330   *Co-operative Insurance Society Ltd v Argyll Stores (Holdings) Ltd* [1998] AC 1.

331   See generally I. C. F. Spry, *Equitable Remedies* (6th edn, 2001); J A. Jolowicz, 'Damages in Equity' [1975] CLJ 224; Philip Pettit, *Equity and the Law of Trusts* (9th edn, 2001), chs 26–30; Meagher, Gummow and Lehane, *Equity – Doctrines and Remedies* (4th edn, 2002), pt 5.

332   Despite Lord Diplock's dictum to the contrary in *United Scientific Holdings Ltd v Burnley Borough Council* [1978] AC 904 at 925, a statement widely criticized and rightly described as 'extreme' by Mason CJ extrajudicially in (1994) 110 LQR 238 at p 240.

a common law remedy is entitled to exercise it as of right; the court has no discretion to refuse him relief. Thus a claimant with a right to damages must be awarded damages; a claimant owed money must be given judgment for the amount due in the absence of a defence. But equitable remedies have always been discretionary; the court considers whether justice will better be served by granting an equitable remedy than by leaving the claimant to his remedies at law, and in so doing will have regard to the balance of hardship and convenience and to the conduct of the parties. A claimant whom the court considers to have been guilty of delay or sharp practice may be refused relief. Secondly, there is, surprisingly, no general principle of English law that requires legal remedies to be exercised in good faith. A buyer who lawfully rejects goods for nonconformity with description is entitled to recover the price even though the deviation from the contract description is minor and of no account to him, and his motive in rejecting was to escape from a contract that had become unprofitable, eg through a fall in the market.[333] This irrelevance of good faith to the entitlement to legal remedies is at once the most remarkable and the most reprehensible feature of English contract law. Equally, there is no requirement that a legal remedy must be exercised in such a way as to avoid an unreasonable result. Again, this is a defect in English contract law. The position is quite otherwise where an equitable remedy is sought. He who comes to equity must come with clean hands,[334] and since equitable remedies are discretionary, the court is entitled to have regard to the moral merits on both sides in reaching its decision.

(iii) Specific performance[335] and mandatory injunction

The expression 'specific performance' is used in two senses. In the first, narrow, sense it denotes an order directing execution of a deed or document or performance of some other act to perfect the claimant's rights under an executory contract. In its broader sense it encompasses any order for performance of a contractual obligation, whether the contract is executed or executory.[336] A mandatory injunction is a form of specific performance designed to require the defendant who has acted in breach to restore the status quo. We have seen that in commercial disputes specific performance and a mandatory injunction are exceptional remedies. Specific performance is most commonly ordered in relation to agreements for the sale of land and is rarely sought or given in commercial disputes. We need not consider it further here.[337]

---

333   See *Arcos Ltd v E. A. Ronaasen & Sons* [1933] AC 470.
334   Ashburner, *Principles of Equity* (2nd edn, ed Denis Browne, 1933), ch 27; Snell, *Principles of Equity* (30th edn, 2000), pp 31–32.
335   See Gareth Jones and William Goodhart, *Specific Performance* (2nd edn, 1996); Spry, *Equitable Remedies* ch 3; Burrows, *Remedies for Torts*, ch 8.
336   Spry, *Equitable Remedie* pp 51–52.
337   See p 363, as to specific performance of contracts of sale of goods.

(iv) Prohibitory injunction

The position is somewhat different as regards prohibitory injunctions. Whereas for policy reasons the court leans against compelling positive acts,[338] there is much less objection to an order restraining a defendant from performing acts which he has contracted not to perform. Thus the defendant may be restrained from breaking an undertaking not to disclose trade secrets;[339] from implementing a threat to terminate a contract when he has no ground for termination;[340] from entering into contracts with third parties which are inconsistent with his contractual duties to the claimant.[341] Yet the court has to tread with care, for a prohibitory injunction may have the indirect effect of compelling positive performance, a danger to which the courts are now more sensitive than formerly.[342]

(v) Award of money due under the contract

Where a contract provides for payment of a sum of money in consideration of the delivery of goods or the performance of services by one of the parties, then that party, on completing performance, is entitled to payment of the sum he has earned.[343] His remedy in the case of default is not damages but a debt action to recover the contract sum.[344] Debt lies only where the claimant has performed those acts which, by the terms of the contract, entitle him to payment.[345] If such performance is prevented by the defendant's wrongful act, the claimant cannot sue in debt but must claim damages.[346]

---

338 Though the principles governing the grant of mandatory and prohibitory injunctions are similar, the ordering of positive acts may present difficulties which do not arise in the case of enforcement of a purely negative obligation. For example, the defendant may lack the skill or resources to comply with the order; there may be interminable argument as to whether an order requiring the execution of works has been sufficiently complied with; the performance required may involve the court in continuing supervision for which it is not well equipped. It is for reasons of this kind that the court will not usually decree specific performance of contracts for the performance of services, nor will it give such a decree indirectly by the grant of a mandatory injunction.

339 See *Peter Pan Manufacturing Corporation v Corsets Silhouette Ltd* [1963] 3 All ER 402.

340 *Decro Wall International S.A. v Practitioners in Marketing Ltd* [1971] 2 All ER 216.

341 Ibid.

342 Compare *Lumley v Wagner* (1852) 1 De GM & G 604 and *Warner Bros Pictures Inc v Nelson* [1937] 1 KB 209 with *Page One Records Ltd v Britton* [1968] 1 WLR 157.

343 As to performance against the wishes of the defendant, see p 126.

344 Or if none was fixed, a reasonable amount, on a *quantum meruit* (services) or *quantum valebat* (goods). A claim in debt has considerable advantages over a claim to damages. The claimant does not have to show loss, merely an express or implied agreement to pay, so that rules as to remoteness and measure of damages (p 121) do not come into play, nor is the claimant's claim affected by such matters as a duty to mitigate damage. Though it is widely assumed that damages are the main remedy for breach of contract, claims for debt are by far the most common form of action on a contract.

345 However, the performance of an act not going to the entire consideration for the payment may be waived by the defendant, in which case its non-performance is not a barrier to recovery of the contract sum.

346 *Colley v Overseas Exporters* [1921] 3 KB 302; *Telephone Rentals Ltd v Burges Salmon* [1987] CCLR 419.

Where a claimant's contractual obligations are divisible, in the sense that the contract entitles him to be paid in portions for each stage of performance, he can sue for each part of the contract price as the work relevant to that part is completed. But where the contract obligations are not divisible, so that the contract is 'entire', the claimant cannot recover anything unless he has substantially completed performance. He is not entitled to be paid half the price for completing half the work, for the express or implied term of the contract is that he must finish before he is paid a penny.[347] However, where the amount of uncompleted or defective work is small, the court will allow him the contract sum less a deduction for the work not done or done badly,[348] unless the terms of the contract are such as to require strict and complete performance. Such is also the case in regard to the duty in a contract of sale of goods to supply goods of the contract description. Here the principle of substantial performance is, unless otherwise agreed, displaced by the perfect tender rule. The same applies to tender of documents under a letter of credit. But where the defendant voluntarily accepts the benefit of partial performance, the claimant is entitled to be paid for the value of the work he has carried out or the goods he has supplied.[349]

Because of the importance in trade of a reasonable measure of certainty as to payment, commercial people have devised various instruments designed to abstract the payment obligation from the rest of the contract and embody it in a separate autonomous contract which is not dependent for its enforceability on performance of the underlying transaction. Into this category fall irrevocable letters of credit, performance bonds and, to a lesser extent, negotiable instruments.[350]

(vi) Damages[351]

1. The basis of damages in contract

Whereas damages in tort for inducing entry into a contract by fraudulent or negligent misrepresentation are posited on the claimant's reliance interest, and are thus designed to restore him to the position in which he would have been if he had never entered into the contract at all, damages for breach of contract are designed to

---

347 *Cutter v Powell* (1795) 6 Term Rep 320.

348 *H. Dakin & Co Ltd v Lee* [1916] 1 KB 566; *Hoenig v Isaacs* [1952] 2 All ER 176. The position is otherwise where a substantial amount of work is left outstanding (*Bolton v Mahadeva* [1972] 2 All ER 1322).

349 *Sumpter v Hedges* [1898] 1 QB 673. The position is otherwise if the defendant had no choice, as in the case of work done on or materials incorporated into his property (ibid; *Forman & Co Pty Ltd v The Liddesdale* [1900] AC 190).

350 See chs 18–21.

351 After nearly sixty years, the seminal article on the various norms by which damages fall to be determined remains that by L. L. Fuller and W. R. Perdue, 'The Reliance Interest in Contract Damages', 46 Yale LJ 52, 373 (1936–1937). The leading textbook is *McGregor on Damages* (17th edn, 2003). See also H. Street, *Principles of the Law of Damages* (1962) and A. I. Ogus, *Damages* (1973). For an interesting discussion of the conceptual framework of expectancy damages as developed in American law, see David H. Vernon, 'Expectancy Damages for Breach of Contract: A Primer and Critique', 179 Wash Univ LQ 179 (1976); and generally Farnsworth, *Farnsworth on Contract*, ch 12.

give the claimant as nearly as possible what he would have received had the defendant performed his obligation. In other words, the purpose of damages in contract is to award the claimant the value of his defeated contractual expectation, and thus to compensate him not only for the expenses caused by the breach but also for the gains prevented by it, ie the loss of his bargain.

Since the basis of an award of damages for breach of contract is loss to the claimant, it follows that if the claimant has suffered no loss, he is entitled to no more than nominal damages, even if the defendant has profited from the breach.[352] Recovery for unjust enrichment is a function of the law of restitution, not of contract, and in a contractual setting is admissible only where there is a total failure of consideration,[353] which itself is limited to payments made by the innocent party and does not extend to restitution of benefits obtained by the defendant from other sources, such as entry into a more profitable contract with a third party. However, in *A-G v Blake*[354] the House of Lords ordered that the defendant, a former member of the security services who had escaped from prison while serving a 42-year sentence for selling intelligence secrets and had published his autobiography, should account for the royalties, and this despite the fact that the information had already ceased to be confidential. The decision was clearly influenced by the fact that the defendant was, in the words of Lord Nicholls, 'a self-confessed traitor'. The remedy is exceptional, as Lord Nicholls himself acknowledged, and should, it is thought, be given only where the defendant is, or is in a position similar to, a fiduciary. It has not been followed in Australia.[355]

The requirement of loss presents two other difficulties. The first is where the contractual claim is vested in one party but the loss has been suffered by an associated party for whose benefit the contract was concluded. This has the potential of creating a black hole in relation to remedies; the third party is debarred from suing by the privity rule[356] and the innocent party, having suffered no loss, is entitled to purely nominal damages, so that the guilty party escapes scot-free. It is now established that where, on entry into a contract, the parties contemplated that in the event of a breach loss would be caused not to the innocent party but to an identifed or identifiable third party or a subsequent assignee of the innocent party's rights, then, if so intended, the contracting parties may be treated as having entered into the contract for the benefit of the third party and the innocent party can recover

---

352 *Surrey County Council v Bredero Homes Ltd* [1993] 3 All ER 705. See further Burrows, *Remedies for Torts*, p 308 ff; Richard O'Dair, 'Restitutionary Damages for Breach of Contract and the Theory of Efficient Breach: Some Reflections' (1993) CLP 113.

353 The Law Commission considered, but ultimately rejected, a change in the law to allow recovery of money paid on a partial failure of consideration. See Law Com No 121 (1983), *Law of Contract: Pecuniary Restitution for Breach of Contract*, Part III. See further Andrew Burrows, *Law of Restitution* (2nd edn, 2002), pp 327 ff; Graham Virgo, *Principles of the Law of Restitution* (1999), pp 341 ff.

354 [2001] 1 AC 268 applied in *Experience Hendrix LLC v PPX Enterprises Inc* [2003] 1 All ER (Comm) 830.

355 *Hospitality Group Ltd v Australian Rugby Union Ltd* [2001] FCA 1040, citing the judgment of Mason CJ and Dawson J in *Commonwealth v Amann Aviation Pty Ltd* (1991) 174 CLR 64 at 82.

356 But the third party may now have a right of enforcement under the Contracts (Rights of Third Parties) Act 1999. See pp 102–103 and n 360.

on its behalf the amount of the third party's loss.[357] However, the justification for this exception to the privity rule disappears in cases where the third party has a direct claim against the contract breaker, eg under a separate contract.[358] A striking illustration is provided by the decision of a bare majority of the House of Lords in *Alfred McAlpine Construction Ltd v Panatown Ltd*[359] In that case:

> McAlpine, a subsidiary of Unex Corporation, agreed to carry out construction works for Panatown on land owned by Unex Investment Properties Ltd (UIPL), a co-subsidiary of Panatown, for which purpose Panatown had been put in funds by Unex to place the contract. In a separate deed of care McAlpine acknowledged that it owed a duty of care to UIPL and that it would exercise all reasonable care and attention in performance of the construction contract. The construction works were so seriously defective that it became necessary to demolish them and start again. Panatown then initiated arbitration proceedings, and obtained an award of damages from the arbitrator. The High Court set this aside. The Court of Appeal restored the award but its decision was in turn reversed by the House of Lords (Lords Goff and Millett dissenting) on the ground that UIPL had a direct claim under the care deed so that there was no good reason to apply the exception to the normal rule that a claimant can recover only for its own loss.[360] In powerful dissenting speeches Lords Goff and Millett would have allowed recovery, not on the basis of an exception to the privity rule but on the broader ground previously enunciated by Lord Griffiths in the *St. Martin's* case[361] that the plaintiffs had not received the performance for which they had bargained and had thereby lost the value of the promised performance, measured by the cost (reasonably) incurred by the third party in having the remedial works done. On this broader ground the existence of the deed of care was irrelevant, since that was significant only in the context of an exception to the privity rule.

It is respectfully submitted that the minority approach is to be preferred. The promisee has an interest in performance which is measured by its value, whether the performance is to be given to the promisee itself or to a third party for whose benefit the promise was exacted, and in recovering substantial damages the promisee is recouping its own loss, not that of the third party.

The second difficulty created by the requirement of loss arises where the contract is for the provision of work and materials to be carried out in accordance with a precise specification – for example, the construction of a swimming pool of stated dimensions in a private house – and what is provided is not in accordance with the specification but there is no diminution in value. Should the contractor nevertheless be required to reconstruct the swimming pool even if this will involve great expense and add no value? Or should the building owner be required to pay the full price, with an entitlement to no more than nominal damages, when he has not received the performance for which he bargained? English law views with disfavour the award of a remedy which is economically wasteful. At the same time, there is a

---

357 *The Albazero* [1977] AC 774, applying the rule in *Dunlop v Lambert* (1839) 6 Cl & Fin 600; *St Martin's Property Corp. Ltd v Sir Robert McAlpine & Sons Ltd* [1994] 1 AC 85.

358 *Alfred McAlpine Construction Ltd v Panatown Ltd* [2001] 1 AC 518.

359 Ibid. For a detailed analysis of this case see the inaugural lecture by Professor Ewan McKendrick, 'The Common Law at Work: The Saga of *Panatown Ltd v Alfred McAlpine Construction Ltd*' (2004) 3 OUCLJ 1.

360 Presumably the same reasoning would apply in the case of a third party having a claim under the Contracts (Rights of Third Parties) Act 1999.

361 See n 357.

recognition that a claimant to whom a particular performance has subjective value over and above the utility associated with its market price should receive some compensation if he does not receive that value. This 'consumer surplus' notion[362] was adopted by the House of Lords in *Ruxley Electronics Ltd v Forsyth*.[363] In that case a swimming pool was constructed with a diving area significantly shallower than that called for by the contract but there was no diminution in value. The trial judge awarded compensation for loss of amenity, the Court of Appeal reversed his decision and awarded the cost of reinstatement and the House of Lords restored the original decision, holding that the assessment of damages in such a case was not confined to a choice between the cost of reinstatement and nominal damages and that while it would be unreasonable to award damages on the basis of reinstatement cost, the claimant was entitled to some compensation for loss of amenity.

Though the purpose of damages is to compensate the claimant for his loss, it does not follow that this objective is always (or even usually) achieved. The value of a contract is often not precisely measurable. How does one assess the extra profits that would have been earned by an income-producing machine if it had been delivered on time instead of late? Still more difficult, what value does one place on intangible contract benefits, eg a holiday ruined through a breach of contract,[364] a trade reputation lost by the defendant's failure to perform?[365] Further problems arise where the defendant has failed to perform an obligation to build, repair or restore property and the cost of the necessary work greatly exceeds the value thereby added to the property.[366] Moreover, the law fixes limits to recoverable loss, as well as expecting the innocent party to take proper steps to minimize his loss. We revert to some of these questions later. Suffice it to say at this stage that where damages are awarded, these will rarely represent the claimant's actual loss; rather they will reflect what the law considers it just for him to recover.

2.   Loss flowing from the innocent party's termination of the contract

Where the breach of contract is serious (a concept that will be examined more precisely in a moment), the innocent party may have a right to terminate and thereby put an end to the duty to perform of both sides. The result, of course, is to prevent the innocent party himself from reaping the future benefits that completion of the contract would have brought him; but though his loss directly results from his own election to terminate the contract, it is nevertheless considered reasonable to allow him to recoup it, for the termination was engendered by the defendant's repudiation of his obligations, and the loss resulting from termination can thus properly be laid at the defendant's door. But a contractual provision seeking to give the innocent party damages for loss of bargain consequent upon termination of the

---

362 Donald Harris, Anthony Ogus and Jennifer Phillips, 'Contract Remedies and the Consumer Surplus' (1979) 95 LQR 581.

363 [1996] AC 344.

364 *Jackson v Horizon Holidays Ltd* [1975] 1 WLR 1468.

365 *Anglo-Continental Holidays Ltd v Typaldos Lines (London) Ltd* [1967] 2 Lloyd's Rep 61.

366 *Tito v Waddell (No 2)* (1977) 3 All ER 129 at 313–321; *Radford v De Froberville* [1978] 1 All ER 33; Harris, Ogus and Phillips (1979) 95 LQR 581.

contract under an express term allowing termination for any breach will be struck down as penal unless the breach is of such gravity as to constitute a repudiation.[367] The theory is not, however, particularly convincing. It is for the parties themselves to agree what types of breach are to be treated as repudiatory, and it is at least arguable that the inclusion of an express power to terminate for any breach, coupled with a provision for compensation on the footing of loss of bargain in the event of such termination, indicates an intention that every breach is to be treated as repudiatory.[368] The parties are in any event free to stipulate that a particular term is to be treated as a condition.[369]

If, instead of terminating, the innocent party elects to keep the contract alive, and the other party is willing to continue performance, then whatever other loss may have been caused to the innocent party by the breach, it will not have had the effect of depriving him of the future benefits to accrue from the contract. Hence the measure of damages for breach is materially affected by the election of the innocent party to terminate or to affirm. For example:

> A leases equipment to B for five years at a rent of £100 a month. B persistently fails to pay the instalments due and after six months owes £400. If A elects to keep the contract alive, he can sue for the £400 but must wait for future instalments until they fall due. If, however, he elects to treat the contract as repudiated, he can recover not only the £400 but his loss of profit on the contract as a whole, represented by the discounted value of the future rentals, less such sum as he is able to obtain from disposal of the equipment elsewhere, taking reasonable steps to mitigate his loss.

Acceptance of the guilty party's repudiation may result in the innocent party being able to show that the consideration for which he made payments or transferred property under the contract has totally failed. In this event, as an alternative to claiming damages, he may pursue a restitution remedy and recover his money or property as paid or transferred on a total failure of consideration.[370]

3. Types of recoverable loss

The right to damages for breach of contract is not restricted to cases of pecuniary loss. Damages may be awarded for a variety of forms of non-pecuniary injury, including pain and suffering,[371] physical inconvenience,[372] loss of enjoyment[373] and mental distress.[374]

---

367 *Financings Ltd v Baldock* [1963] 2 QB 104, applied in *Capital Finance Co Ltd v Donati* (1977) 121 Sol Jo 270 (Waller LJ dissenting); *Shevill v Builders Licensing Board* (1982) 42 ALR 305 (High Court of Australia).

368 See R. M. Goode, 'Penalties in Finance Leases' (1988) 104 LQR 25 at p 29, and for a more developed argument, Brian R. Opeskin, 'Damages for Breach of Contract Terminated Under Express Terms' (1990) 106 LQR 327.

369 *Lombard North Central plc v Butterworth* [1987] QB 527.

370 See pp 366, 377 as to the application of this principle in relation to contracts of sale.

371 *Grant v Australian Knitting Mills Ltd* [1936] AC 85.

372 *Bailey v Bullock* [1950] 2 All ER 1167.

373 *Jarvis v Swan Tours Ltd* [1973] QB 233; *Jackson v Horizon Holidays Ltd*, n 364.

374 *Heywood v Wellers* [1976] QB 446; *Cox v Philips Industries Ltd* [1976] 3 All ER 161. See also *Malik v Bank of Credit and Commerce International SA* [1998] AC 20 (damage to an employee's future employment prospects).

Pecuniary loss takes two main forms. First, there is what is called normal pecuniary loss, that is, loss that *any* claimant would be likely to suffer because of the breach. Essentially, this means loss of bargain, represented by the difference between the value of the performance as contracted for and its value as in fact tendered.[375] Thus, on non-delivery of goods the normal measure of damages for the buyer is the excess of market price at the due delivery date over the contract price.[376] The computation of normal loss will depend on whether the breach takes the form of total non-performance, defective performance or delayed performance. This in turn depends on the manner in which the innocent party exercises his options; for if he elects to reject a tender of performance which is delayed or defective, the case becomes one of non-performance.[377] Secondly, there is consequential loss[378] – expenditure or loss of profit over and above the loss of or diminution in the value of the immediate subject matter of the contract. For example, if S contracts to sell to B goods for which there is not a ready market and fails to deliver them, with the result that B has to hire other goods while seeking a substitute and then has to pay a higher price for the substitute goods, the excess of that price over the contract price is the normal loss and the hire charges are recoverable in addition as consequential loss.[379]

Whereas normal loss is calculated according to well-established contract law formulae (eg excess of market price over contract price), consequential loss must be properly pleaded[380] and proved. Moreover, it is assumed in favour of an innocent claimant, unless otherwise proved, that he would have been willing and able to carry the contract through to completion, but for the defendant's breach. It is, of course, necessary for the claimant to adduce evidence as to the loss-producing event, and in this regard there is an important distinction between past events and possible future events. That a past event occurred has to be established on a balance of probabilities, and if it is so established the event is considered proved and no discount is to be made for the possibility that it might not have happened. The approach is all or nothing. But it cannot be proved that an uncertain future event will occur. So when a claimant claims damages for the loss of benefits that might have been expected to flow from future events but for the breach (for example, in the case of a film star whose contract is wrongfully terminated, the prospect of future contracts resulting from favourable publicity if she had been allowed to fulfil the original contract), the claim is for loss of a chance that the future benefits would have accrued.[381] The court will not embark on a valuation of the chance if it is

---

375   He may alternatively recover his abortive pre-contract expenditure (*Anglia Television Ltd v Reed*, n 14). But see p 373.

376   Sale of Goods Act 1979, s 51(3). See p 367. For the theory of the lost- volume seller and the problem of establishing loss of bargain, see p 407.

377   See pp 342, 371.

378   Also termed special damage, but we shall follow *McGregor on Damages* in employing the term 'consequential loss', since 'special damage' is used in so many different senses that confusion may arise.

379   See p 368 as to consequential loss for non-delivery.

380   The importance of pleadings is discussed p 1124.

381   *Mallett v McMonagle* [1970] AC 166, per Lord Diplock at 176; *Davies v Taylor* [1974] AC 207, per Lord Reid at 212–213.

merely speculative, but if it is significant, then an appropriate discount must be made for the possibility that the anticipated benefits would not have accrued.[382]

4. Remoteness of damage

Not all loss suffered consequent upon a breach is recoverable. Contract law requires a sufficient connection between the breach and the loss, and has developed well-defined rules for determining whether the loss is too remote. The loss must be causally connected to the breach, so that if it would have occurred in any event, it is not recoverable. Equally, if the loss resulted from some intervening act of the claimant or a third party which the defendant could not reasonably have foreseen as the consequence of the breach, it will be too remote.[383] The effect of the breach was exhausted and replaced by the intervening act as the 'proximate cause'. Given, however, that the loss *is* sufficiently connected to the breach, satisfying the first test of the rules of remoteness, the law, for policy reasons, restricts the defendant's liability to loss which he ought reasonably to have contemplated, at the time of the contract, would be likely to flow from the breach.[384] This is the famous rule in *Hadley v Baxendale*.[385] Under the so-called first limb of the rule, the defendant is liable for such loss as may fairly and reasonably be considered as arising naturally, ie according to the usual course of things, so that *any* claimant would be likely to suffer the loss in question. Under the second limb of the rule, the defendant is further made liable for such loss as may reasonably be supposed to have been in the contemplation of the parties,[386] at the time of the contract,[387] as the probable result of its breach. The second limb is, in fact, merely a particular application of the first, namely that the defendant is answerable for loss he ought reasonably to have contemplated at the time of the contract would flow from his breach. A good illustration of the working of the rule is *Victoria Laundry (Windsor) Ltd v Newman Industries Ltd*.[388]

5. Measure of damages

Where a head of loss satisfies the remoteness test laid down by the rule in *Hadley v Baxendale*, so that the loss is of a kind which in principle is recoverable, the court

---

382 *Davies v Taylor* [1974] AC 207, per Lord Reid at 212. See Helen Reece, 'Loss of Chances in the Law' (1996) 59 MLR 188; *McGregor on Damages*, paras 8-028–8-032.

383 As to the effect of the claimant's contributory negligence, see p 130.

384 It has been held that if the loss is of a type that could reasonably have been contemplated, the defendant is liable for it even if it is greater in degree than was reasonably foreseeable (*H. Parsons (Livestock) Ltd v Uttley Ingham & Co Ltd* [1978] QB 791), but the decision is difficult to justify. See p 380.

385 (1854) 9 Exch 341.

386 Though this is the traditional formulation of the rule, it seems clear from the cases that it is only what could reasonably have been contemplated by the defendant that is relevant.

387 Loss that could not reasonably have been contemplated at that time is too remote even if it could have been contemplated by the time of the breach. For a sustained attack on the rule in *Hadley v Baxendale* as a static rule which focuses on the time of the contract, and an argument in favour of the concept of proximate cause, which looks to the time of the wrong, see Melvin Aron Eisenberg, 'The Emergence of Dynamic Contract Law', (2000) 88 Cal. Law Rev. 1743, 1771.

388 [1949] 2 KB 528, applied in *Koufos v C. Czarnikow Ltd* [1969] 1 AC 350. See further p 367.

has then to proceed to quantify the loss. For example, if A buys goods from B for the purpose of resale and B fails to deliver, it is clear that A has been deprived of the value of the goods contracted to be delivered to him and that this is a loss flowing naturally from the breach. But how is such value to be computed? Is it the price A agreed to pay (in which case his damages will be nominal)? Or the price at which he contracted to resell? Or is it the extra price (if any) A has to pay to obtain substitute goods? The basis of computation of a recoverable head of loss is known as the *measure of damages*. There are two cardinal rules governing the measure of damages. The first is that the claimant is entitled to such sum as will satisfy his expectation interest by putting him broadly in the position in which he would have been if the contract had been fully performed. This entails, on the one hand, identifying the loss of which he has been deprived and, on the other, of setting against it any expenditure or loss he would have incurred but has avoided as the result of the breach. The second is that after a breach the claimant must take reasonable steps to mitigate his loss.[389] The so-called 'duty to mitigate'[390] has both a negative and a positive aspect. The claimant must refrain from unreasonable acts which would increase his loss; and he must take such positive steps to reduce his loss as are reasonable in the circumstances.[391] Thus, the buyer whose seller fails to make delivery will not be expected to sit idly by and incur a liability in damages to his sub-purchaser, but will be expected to do what a prudent person would do, that is, obtain substitute goods on the market or from some alternative source of supply. Equally, he will be expected to purchase the substitute goods on reasonable terms and not to seek to debit the defendant with an extravagant substitute purchase.

It is, however, important to note that actual performance of steps in mitigation is not a prerequisite of the claimant's right to recover. In this sense, the expression 'duty to mitigate' is a misnomer. The position is simply that damages will be assessed on the assumption that his loss is no greater than it would have been if he had taken reasonable steps in mitigation.[392]

Where the steps taken to mitigate are reasonable, the claimant is entitled to recover any expenses incurred in taking such steps, even if these prove to be greater than the loss thereby avoided.[393]

The duty to mitigate only requires the claimant to act reasonably. He is not obliged to cushion the defendant by taking steps which, though legally available, would jeopardize his commercial reputation,[394] nor is he expected to embark on hazardous litigation against a third party in order to reduce his loss.[395]

---

389   Other aspects of the measure of damages, such as the impact of tax, are not considered here.

390   Which is not a positive duty at all, merely a factor limiting the recoverability of damages (see below) and does not apply to claims for sums earned under the contract. But see p 127, text and n 412.

391   Since failure to mitigate can be said to break the chain of causation, the line between remoteness of damage, measure of damages and mitigation is sometimes hard to draw. For a good illustration see *The Alecos M* [1991] 1 Lloyd's Rep 120.

392   For examples in sales law, see p 368. As to the significance of inflation, see David Feldman and D. F. Libling (1979) 95 LQR 270 and I. N. Duncan Wallace (1980) 96 LQR 101.

393   *Esso Petroleum Co Ltd v Mardon*, n 99.

394   *James Finlay & Co Ltd v N.V. Kwik Hoo Tong* [1929] 1 KB 400.

395   *Pilkington v Wood* [1953] Ch 770.

The innocent party comes under a duty to mitigate as soon as the breach occurs,[396] and this is true even where, though having the right to treat the contract as discharged by the breach, he elects to keep it open for performance. In other words, the innocent party cannot, by forcing continuation of the contract on an unwilling guilty party, defer steps in mitigation that would reduce his loss.[397]

As Professor Atiyah has pointed out,[398] the duty to mitigate represents a major weakening of the claimant's right to protection of his expectation interest. The corollary, of course, is that it strengthens the defendant's position significantly by potentially reducing his liability. Indeed, it could be said that one of the adverse effects of what is in the face of it a desirable rule is that it gives every incentive to the defendant to delay the assessment of damages in the hope that the claimant will meanwhile obtain a substitute contract that reduces or extinguishes his loss.

6. Liquidated damages

It is open to the parties to stipulate in their contract the amount of damages that will be payable on a breach; but a contractual provision of this kind will be enforceable only if it represents a genuine and reasonable pre-estimate of the loss likely to flow from the breach.[399] Moreover, it seems that while a party who accepts a repudiation can recover as part of his damages the loss of profit (suitably discounted) that he would have earned from completion of the contract, a contractual provision designed to give him the same right after exercising a contractual right to terminate for breach will be struck down as penal unless the breach leading to the termination was in fact repudiatory.[400]

(vii) Termination for breach

1. Effect of termination

In certain circumstances a breach of contract may entitle the innocent party not merely to suspend performance of a particular correlative obligation[401] but to treat the entire contract as discharged (terminated). The effect of such discharge is to

---

396 But one must distinguish the onset of the duty from the time when acts of mitigation must be done. The duty arises on breach in the sense that this marks the time from which the claimant must act reasonably to reduce his loss. It may, however, be reasonable for him to defer steps in mitigation, eg until he has had a proper opportunity of discovering the best way of remedying the breach or in the reasonable expectation that the cost of remedial measures will be less if taken at a later date. However, on breach of a contract for the sale of goods for which there is an available market, there is an almost ineluctable rule that the market price at the due date of delivery or acceptance must be taken as the basis for measuring damages. See pp 368 ff, 402 ff.

397 See further p 127. The position is otherwise in the case of an anticipatory breach (p 126).

398 *The Rise and Fall of Freedom of Contract*, p 429.

399 The issue has been litigated with particular vigour in hire-purchase cases. See R. M. Goode, *Hire-Purchase Law and Practice* (2nd edn, 1970), ch 18, for a detailed analysis.

400 See p 118. However, the claimant remains entitled to recover his actual loss (*Jobson v Johnson* [1989] 1 All ER 621).

401 Eg, the withholding of delivery of goods under a contract of sale until the buyer is willing and able to tender the price. See Sale of Goods Act 1979, s 28, and see p 393.

relieve both parties (guilty as well as innocent) of their primary duties of performance and their primary right to demand performance. By the act of termination the guilty party's duty to perform is converted into an obligation to pay damages, while the innocent party's right to demand performance and to earn further sums by reason of his own future performance is converted into a right to damages, but without any secondary obligation in substitution for the primary obligation from which he has been released.[402] Termination, unlike rescission, operates only prospectively; it does not affect the accrued rights and liabilities of the parties. A repudiatory breach has no effect on the continuance of the contract unless and until accepted.[403] But acceptance need not be in any particular form or even in words; any conduct conveying to the party in breach that his repudiation has been accepted suffices, including non-performance by the innocent party.[404]

2.   Grounds for termination

Not every breach entitles the innocent party to treat the contract as discharged. An act which evinces an intention not to perform the contract in some essential respect has always been treated as entitling the innocent party to terminate the contract. But in viewing the impact of default which does not manifest such a repudiatory intention, the law distinguishes major breaches, which go to the root of the contract, from minor breaches, which do not. Whether a breach does or does not go to the root of the contract must in all cases be determined by ascertaining the express or presumed intention of the parties at the time of the contract. There are two quite distinct approaches to the ascertainment of that intention, and at different times first one has predominated, then the other.

The more usual approach is to look not at the nature of the act of breach or the gravity of its consequences but at the importance attached to the broken term by the parties at the time of the contract. If the term is a major term (or 'condition', as it misleadingly became known), then any breach, even if minor, is considered to go to the root of the contract so as to entitle the innocent party to terminate it. This is because it is clear from the language of the contract or the surrounding circumstances that the parties attached importance to strict compliance with the term. If, however, the term broken is a minor term, or warranty, the innocent party's remedy is limited to damages, for the parties have contracted on the basis that performance of the warranty is not a condition precedent to the innocent party's own performance obligation. The condition–warranty dichotomy is enshrined in the Sale of Goods Act as regards terms implied in favour of the buyer under a contract of sale, and *any* breach of a term which the Act labels a condition (eg, correspondence with description, fitness or satisfactory quality of the goods) entitles the buyer to

402   See *Moschi v Lep Air Services Ltd* [1973] AC 331, per Lord Diplock at 350. Rights and liabilities accrued prior to termination are unaffected (*Hyundai Heavy Industries Co Ltd v Papadopoulos* [1980] 2 All ER 29, and see p 80). See also Roy Goode, *Legal Problems of Credit and Security* (3rd edn, 2003), paras 8-09, 8-10.
403   'An unaccepted repudiation is a thing writ in water and of no value to anybody' – per Asquith L.J in *Howard v Pickford Tool Co Ltd* [1951] 1 KB 417 at 421.
404   *Vitol SA v Norelf Ltd* [1996] AC 800.

treat the contract as discharged if he is a consumer buyer. Quite apart from the Act, case law has established that certain terms in commercial contracts are to be presumed conditions unless the contrary is shown. For example, stipulations as to time will usually be treated as conditions, so that even a small delay will give the innocent party a right to terminate the agreement, for the assumption is that in the interests of certainty, to which commercial men attach great importance, a stipulation as to time is to be strictly construed.[405]

However, the courts have pointed out that the condition–warranty label is not exhaustive, and that the language of the contract or the nature of the transaction may show that the parties were concerned not so much with the characterization of the particular undertaking as major or minor as with the consequences of its breach. In other words, if at the time of the contract the parties had been asked whether the breach of a particular term would entitle the innocent party to terminate the agreement or would merely give him a right to damages, they would have replied: 'We cannot answer that question in the abstract. It all depends on the seriousness of the breach. If its effect is to frustrate the commercial purpose of the contract, the innocent party will be entitled to end the agreement; in other cases, he is merely to have a claim for damages.' Such terms have been labelled 'innominate', to denote that the parties have not chosen to classify them as either conditions or warranties. Obligations towards which the courts have adopted this second approach include the duty of a shipowner to provide a seaworthy vessel under a charterparty[406] and to proceed on the voyage with reasonable dispatch.[407]

So a breach of a contract will entitle the innocent party to treat the contract as discharged if (i) the act of breach signifies an intention on the part of the guilty party not to carry out the contract in some essential respect; or (ii) subject to special rules for non-consumer sales, the term broken is considered to be a condition; or (iii) the consequences of the breach are such as to frustrate the commercial purpose of the contract; or (iv) the contract empowers the innocent party to terminate it.[408]

The impact of termination on the assessment of damages has already been noted. We need only reiterate the point that termination pursuant to a contractual provision will not necessarily be treated as equivalent to acceptance of a repudiation for the purpose of assessing damages. In other words, the loss of bargain that is recoverable

---

405   *Bunge Corporation v Tradax SA* [1981] 2 All ER 513 (notice of readiness of vessel); *Hartley v Hymans* [1920] 3 KB 475 (delivery under sale contract); *The Mihalis Angelos* [1971] 1 QB 164 ('expected ready to load' clause in charterparty); and see F. M. B. Reynolds, 'Discharge of Contract by Breach' (1981) 97 LQR 541. But stipulations as to time of payment are prima facie not of the essence. See, for example, Sale of Goods Act 1979, s 10(1).

406   *Hong Kong Fir Shipping Co Ltd v Kawasaki Kisen Kaisha Ltd* [1962] 2 QB 26. In *Astley Industrial Trust Ltd v Grimley* [1963] 1 WLR 584, this was applied to the implied term of fitness in a hire-purchase agreement outside the Hire-Purchase Acts; but the effect of the decision was later negated by s 8 of the Supply of Goods (Implied Terms) Act 1973, which equated hire-purchase with sale in labelling the term a condition.

407   *Clipsham v Vertue* (1843) 5 QB 265; and see *Tarrabochia v Hickie* (1856) 1 H & N 183; *Jackson v Union Marine Insurance Co* (1874) LR 10 CP 125.

408   Where the termination affects the defendant's possessory or proprietary rights, the court has an equitable jurisdiction to grant relief against forfeiture, but this is rarely exercised.

on acceptance of a repudiation is not necessarily recoverable on contractual termination; this will depend on whether the court treats the breach as repudiatory.

3.   Anticipatory breach

At this point we must interject a comment on the so-called *anticipatory breach*. Every contract involves not merely the obligations expressly undertaken but also an implied major undertaking by each party that, from the time of the contract to the time fixed for performance, he will continue willing and able to perform. If at any time before the due date for performance a party signifies his intention not to perform the contract in some essential respect[409] or becomes disabled from performing at the due date, the innocent party is entitled to accept the repudiation, that is, treat the contract as immediately at an end, without awaiting the time for performance. In truth, the breach is not anticipatory at all; the guilty party has broken an existing obligation to hold himself willing and able to perform. There is no formality attaching to acceptance and no need for any express statement of acceptance. Even a mere failure by the innocent party to perform may suffice to show his election to treat the contract as at an end.[410]

4.   The innocent party's options

Where there is an anticipatory repudiation, the innocent party is not obliged to accept it. He may instead hold the contract open for performance at the due date. If he elects to do this, he is not obliged to take steps to mitigate his loss.[411] The innocent party's election to affirm the contract is not without risk, for the continuance of the contract enures for the benefit of both parties, and the guilty party is thus just as much entitled as the innocent party to rely on some intervening frustrating event as discharging the contract.

What is the innocent party's position where the repudiation occurs after the time for performance has arrived? The traditional answer is that, as in the case of an anticipatory breach, the innocent party may elect either to treat the contract as discharged or to affirm it and hold it open for performance. But this is extremely

---

409   To justify treatment as a repudiation, the threatened breach must be one which would be repudiatory if committed after the time for performance has arrived. The phrase 'anticipatory breach' is conventionally used to denote such a breach and thus means an anticipatory repudiation. For the effect of a party's refusal to perform based on an honest but mistaken belief that the contract entitled him to do so, see the controversial majority decision of the House of Lords in *Woodar Investment Development Ltd v Wimpey Construction U.K. Ltd* [1980] 1 All ER 571.

410   *Vitol SA v Norelf Ltd* [1996] AC 800, a decision on actual rather than anticipatory breach but the principle is the same.

411   *Brown v Muller* (1872) LR 7 Exch 319. This principle has little to commend it. If the defendant has made it clear that he does not intend to perform at the due date, there is no good reason why the claimant should be allowed to exacerbate his recoverable loss by futilely holding the contract open for performance. In the case of a repudiation after the time for performance has arrived, the claimant comes under a duty to mitigate (see below). Why should the rule be different in the case of an anticipatory repudiation? The weight of American authority has declined to adopt 'this harsh and unreasonable doctrine' (*Bu-Vi-Bar Petroleum Co v Krow*, 40 F 2d 488 (1930), per Phillip J at 492; *Fowler v A. & A. Co*, 262 A 2d 344 (1970)).

misleading. The option given to the innocent party after the other's default in performance of an accrued obligation is very much more restricted than on an anticipatory breach. Indeed, in many situations it is unrealistic to speak of the innocent party having an option to continue the contract at all.

Where the guilty party requests an extension of time for performance or otherwise assents to the continuance of the contract so as to suggest that he is or may be willing to perform, albeit tardily, the innocent party has a genuine option. He can treat the contract as discharged, or he can affirm it and postpone steps in mitigation until the extended date fixed for performance. But the position is otherwise where the guilty party remains obdurate and gives no indication that he intends to proceed. If the innocent party is able to earn his entitlement without the guilty party's cooperation, because no positive act is required on the part of the latter, then, in general, the innocent party may proceed to perform and recover the contract sum,[412] save where performance is so obviously commercially wasteful and of no benefit to the guilty party that the innocent party cannot be said to have a legitimate interest in continuing the contract.[413] But in the great majority of cases the innocent party *is* dependent on the cooperation of the other and, if this is refused, the innocent party comes under an immediate duty to mitigate his loss. The existence of such duty is not compatible with the continuance of the contract in any meaningful sense, for it means that the innocent party must seek substituted performance elsewhere and cannot recover loss that would have been avoided had he elected to treat the contract as at an end.

The affirmation–termination dichotomy is also open to objection in that, just as it overstates the importance of the option to continue the contract, it understates the range of choices open to the innocent party when the guilty party is willing to perform or to cure a defective performance. For example, the proposition that the buyer of defective goods must either accept the tender and be bound or reject the tender and recover his money and/or damages accords neither with law nor with common experience, for it overlooks what is by far the most common choice of the buyer: to reject the goods but ask for them to be repaired or replaced – in other words, to reject the performance tendered but hold the contract open for performance if a fresh and proper tender of performance is made within a reasonable time.[414]

5. Withholding of performance

This leads on to a consideration whether English contract law recognizes any right of the innocent party to suspend his own performance after breach by the other party. The *locus classicus* on this point is the speech of Lord Ackner in *The Simona*:[415]

412 *White & Carter (Councils) Ltd v McGregor* [1962] AC 413.
413 See, for example, *Attica Sea Carriers Corporation v Ferrostaal Poseidon Bulk Reederei* [1976] 1 Lloyd's Rep 250; *The Alaskan Trader* [1984] 1 All ER 129.
414 See below as to suspension of performance, and p 341.
415 *Fercometal SARL v Mediterranean Shipping Co SA, The Simona* [1989] AC 788 at 805.

When A wrongfully repudiates his contractual obligations in anticipation of the time for their performance, he presents the innocent party B with two choices. He may either affirm the contract by treating it as still in force or he may treat it as finally and conclusively discharged. There is no third choice, as a sort of via media, to affirm the contract and yet to be absolved from tendering further performance unless and until A gives reasonable notice that he is once again able and willing to perform. Such a choice would negate the contract being kept alive for the benefit of *both* parties and would deny the party who unsuccessfully sought to rescind, the right to take advantage of any supervening circumstance which would justify him in declining to complete.

This passage, which was addressed to the case of anticipatory breach but is equally applicable to a repudiatory breach after the time for performance has arrived, might at first blush suggest that the innocent party must either terminate the contract or perform it, and cannot simply keep the contract alive and withhold his own performance. That, however, would be a misreading of Lord Ackner's speech, in which he makes it clear that the innocent party's duty to continue performance arises only after he has elected to affirm the contract, but does not deal with the position arising in the period after the act of repudiation but before its acceptance. It is well established that after a repudiatory breach the innocent party is not obliged to make his election immediately; he is entitled to give the guilty party an opportunity to reconsider his position and to tender a proper performance without being treated as having thereby affirmed the contract.[416] So during the negotiations preceding the innocent party's election to accept the repudiation he is not obliged to continue his own performance. Moreover, there are various circumstances, which did not arise in *The Simona*, in which the innocent party has a right to withhold performance even after acceptance of a repudiatory breach and sometimes even where the breach is not repudiatory at all. We can, in fact, identify at least four cases in which the innocent party may withhold performance:

(1)   Where the contract so provides.

(2)   Where the parties have agreed to suspend the contract or the party in breach has represented that it will not require performance or object to its suspension.[417]

(3)   Where the innocent party' duty to perform is by the express or implied terms of the contract dependent on some prior performance by the other party which has not been given or which the other party has indicated it is unable or unwilling to give. In such a case the innocent party has a right to suspend his own performance whether the other party's performance was an obligation under the contract or was a non-promissory condition of the innocent party's duty to perform and whether in the former case the term broken was a condition (in the sense of a major term of the contract) or a warranty.

(4)   Where the innocent part's performance is obstructed or made more difficult by the other party, whether by that party's failure in performance[418] or the imposition of requirements outside the terms of the contract[419] or by failure to

---

416   *Yukong Line Ltd of Korea v Rendsberg Investments Corp of Liberia* [1996] 2 Lloyd's Rep 604, per Moore-Bick J at 608. The guilty party may also have time to cure a non-conforming tender of performance and thus avoid a repudiatory breach altogether. See p 342.

417   *The Simona*, n 415, per Lord Ackner at 805.

418   *Bulk Oil (Zug) AG v Sun International Ltd* [1984] 1 Lloyd's Rep 531.

419   *BV Oliehandel Jonglarid v Coastal International Ltd* [1983] 2 Lloyd's Rep 463.

provide the co-operation which the contract envisages as necessary for the innocent party's performance.[420]

(viii) Termination without breach

A contract may, of course, come to an end without any breach at all, as on the expiry of a fixed term or of a notice of termination given under the contract or where the parties agree on termination. These cases require no comment. What has, however, caused difficulty is the case where the contract is for an indefinite period. Is it then terminable on reasonable notice or is it to be treated as operative in perpetuity? There are cases in support of both solutions. In every case the question is one of construction of the contract. There is a presumption that every contract is permanent and irrevocable,[421] but this is readily rebuttable where the circumstances indicate that this was not contemplated by the contract, in which case it will be terminable on reasonable notice.[422]

(ix) Loss of the right to terminate

The right to terminate is lost if the innocent party expressly or impliedly affirms the contract after knowledge of the breach.[423] In such case, the condition broken sinks to the level of a warranty, and the innocent party's remedy is in damages.

16. DEFENCES TO A CONTRACT CLAIM

There are many possible defences to a claim on a contract and these may be pleaded alternatively or, so far as not mutually inconsistent, cumulatively. The principal defences are that the defendant did not commit the act alleged to constitute the breach of contract; that the act complained of, though committed, did not constitute a breach of the contract; that the contract is void, voidable or unenforceable and, in the case of a voidable contract, that the defendant seeks rescission or has already rescinded it; that the claimant has failed or refused to perform an obligation the performance of which is a condition of the defendant's own duty to perform; and that the claimant's claim is a money claim against which the defendant has a right to set off his own money cross-claim. All of these defences go to liability. The defendant may also contend that the claimant did not suffer the loss alleged or any loss, or that, if he did, it is legally irrecoverable, eg because it is too remote, does

---

420 See *Chitty on Contracts*, paras 13-011, 24-032.

421 *Llanelly Railway and Dock Company v London and North-Western Railway Co* (1873) LR 8 Ch App 942, per James LJ at 949–950; *Islwyn Borough Council v Newport Borough Council* (1994) 6 Admin. LR 386, per Roch LJ at 414. It has been said that many joint venture agreements 'do not contemplate a party having a unilateral right to terminate or exit from the venture … otherwise than through a pre-emption transfer procedure or by exercise of termination rights upon a specified trigger event' (Ian Hewitt, *Joint Ventures* (2nd edn, 2001), para 11–37).

422 *Spenborough Corp. v Cooke Sons & Co Ltd* [1968] Ch 139; *Staffordshire Area Health Authority v South Staffordshire Waterworks Co* [1978] 1 WLR 1387.

423 *Bentsen v Taylor, Sons & Co* [1893] 2 QB 274; *Suisse Atlantique Société d'Armement S.A. v N.V. Rotterdamsche Kolen Centrale*, n 222.

not represent the appropriate measure of damages or is a contractually agreed loss embodied in a liquidated damages provision which is unenforceable as a penalty. However, contributory negligence is not a defence to a purely contractual claim,[424] though the position is otherwise where there is a parallel claim in tort on the same facts.[425]

17. ILLEGALITY[426]

The effects of illegality on a contract are complex and only the barest outline can be given here.

(i) Initial and supervening illegality

We must start by distinguishing illegality under the law as it stands at the time of contract from illegality engendered by a change in the law brought about by statute or statutory instrument after the making of the contract. The latter will usually frustrate the contract[427] except where the statutory prohibition is likely to be temporary[428] or affects the contract only to a minor degree.[429] But illegality affecting the contract under the law as it stands at the time the contract is made renders the contract unenforceable,[430] though not necessarily unenforceable by both parties.[431]

A contract is affected by illegality if:

(a)   the making of the contract is unlawful;[432] or

(b)   the promise or consideration stipulated is the performance of an unlawful act;[433] or

---

424   *Vesta v Butcher* [1989] AC 852.

425   *Barclays Bank plc v Fairclough Building Ltd* [1995] QB 214. The position is otherwise in Australia (*Astley v Austrust Ltd* (1999) 197 CLR 1).

426   See R. A. Buckley, *Illegality and Public Policy* (2002); Nelson Enonchong, *Illegal Transactions* (1998).

427   *Metropolitan Water Board v Dick, Kerr & Co Ltd* [1918] AC 119.

428   *Andrew Millar & Co Ltd v Taylor & Co Ltd* [1916] 1 KB 402; *National Carriers Ltd v Panalpina (Northern) Ltd* [1981] AC 675.

429   See *Cricklewood Property and Investment Trust Ltd v Leighton's Investment Trust Ltd* [1945] AC 221.

430   It is often said that illegality renders a contract void. This goes too far. It is clear that unless the making of the contract is itself expressly or impliedly prohibited by statute, the illegality does not prevent the creation of legal relations between the parties, for if it did (a) property could not pass under the illegal contract, whereas it is well established that it can (see below); (b) it would not be possible to have a situation in which the contract remained enforceable by the party innocent of the illegality, whereas there are several categories of case in which this is permitted (below).

431   See below.

432   *Re Mahmoud and Ispahani* [1921] 2 KB 716 (contract for purchase of linseed oil without required licence).

433   Eg, the sale of obscene prints (*Fores v Johnes* (1802) 4 Esp 97) or the rigging of a share market (*Scott v Brown, Doering McNab & Co* [1892] 2 QB 724).

(c) though the contract is not in itself unlawful, the purpose for which it is made or for which the subject matter is to be applied is unlawful[434] or the intended method of performance is unlawful;[435] or

(d) though free from any of the above defects, the contract stems from or is collateral to another agreement affected by illegality.[436]

The forms of illegality are many and various and do not readily lend themselves to rational classification.[437] They include contracts to commit a crime or tort or to perform acts prohibited by statute,[438] and contracts of which the making or performance is considered to be contrary to public policy or morals.[439] In general – and this is a serious weakness of the common law – all types of illegality affect the guilty party's rights in the same way, whether the infringement be major or minor and whether it be plainly culpable wrongdoing on the one hand or a slight infraction of a highly technical statutory instrument on the other.[440] An attempt by the Court of Appeal in *Tinsley v Milligan*[441] to introduce a more flexible approach was rejected by the House of Lords.[442] But one class of contract must be separated from the rest, namely contracts which are regarded at common law[443] as in unreasonable restraint of trade. Examples are contracts of employment by which an employee is subjected to unreasonable constraints after his employment ends and contracts which seek to restrict competition to a degree beyond what is necessary for the covenantee's protection.

(ii) Contracts in restraint of trade

Contracts in restraint of trade differ from other classes of contract affected by illegality in that the mischief lies not in what the contracting party does or refrains

---

434 *J. M. Allan (Merchandising) Ltd v Cloke* [1963] 2 QB 340 (hire of equipment for illegal gaming).

435 *Ashmore, Benson, Pease & Co Ltd v A. V. Dawson Ltd* [1973] 1 WLR 828 (carriage of goods on lorries in excess of the maximum load permitted for the lorries in question).

436 *Spector v Ageda* [1973] Ch 30 (loan to discharge indebtedness under prior unlawful loan contract).

437 See *Chitty on Contract*, ch 16; Treitel, *Law of Contract*, ch 11.

438 For the presumptions to be made where the statute is silent as to the effect of infringement on a contract, see *Phoenix General Insurance Co of Greece SA v Administratia Asigurarlor de Stat* [1988] QB 216.

439 Notions of morality change from age to age, so that older cases on the subject need to be treated with some reserve. For example, in *Upfill v Wright* [1911] 1 KB 506, a landlord's action for arrears of rent was dismissed on the ground that to the knowledge of his agent, through whom the property was let, the tenant was intending to live there as the mistress of a man who would be supporting her by paying the rent (in the course of his judgment Darling J invoked, inter alia, the Book of Common Prayer). It is inconceivable that a court would today regard the mere fact of extramarital cohabitation as sufficient in itself to taint the tenancy with illegality even where the landlord knows that the couple are not man and wife. (Obviously the position would be otherwise if the premises were let as a brothel.)

440 There is thus much to be said for legislation along the lines of the New Zealand Illegal Contracts Act 1970, which confers wide powers on the court to give relief by way of restitution, compensation, variation of the contract, validation of it wholly or in part or for any particular purpose, etc. (s 7).

441 [1992] 2 All ER 391.

442 [1994] 1 AC 340, affirming the decision of the Court of Appeal on other grounds.

443 Where a statute regulating restrictive trade practices operates, it is the statute which will govern the consequences of infringement. See below.

from doing but in his *binding* himself to the stipulated act or restraint. Since such restrictive covenants are usually part and parcel of a much wider agreement, the courts are willing to sever the offending covenants and enforce the rest of the contract, provided that the contract is drafted in such a way as readily to permit such severance (the 'blue pencil' test[444]) and the covenants in question do not form such a substantial part of the consideration that their deletion would alter the whole basis of the contract.[445] By contrast, other kinds of illegality render the entire contract unenforceable, and severance is not usually permitted.[446] Competition law is now regulated in detail by Articles 81 and 82 of the EC Treaty of Rome and the Competition Act 1998 as amended by the Enterprise Act 2002 and will not be discussed. The rest of the present chapter is confined to the effect of other forms of illegality.

(iii) The effect of illegality on contract rights

A distinction must be drawn between contracts that are illegal as formed, in that the entry into or performance of the contract necessarily involves an illegal act, and contracts which are capable of being performed lawfully but are intended by one or both parties to be performed in an unlawful manner or for an unlawful purpose or of which the subject matter is to be applied to the implementation of an unlawful design. Contracts illegal in the making are not enforceable by either party, even if acting in good faith; for the parties are presumed to know the law, and ought therefore to be aware that their acts will be unlawful.[447] However, if one party falsely represented to the other that the contract was lawful or undertook to do acts (eg obtaining of a licence) which would enable the contract to be lawfully performed, the other may have a claim in damages for deceit or for negligent misrepresentation or breach of warranty.[448]

The position is more complex if the contract is lawful in the making but unlawful in its actual or intended performance. If the unlawful manner of performance was known to both parties, then neither can enforce the contract and their position is the same as on a contract unlawful in the making. Again, this is so even if one party or both acted in ignorance of the fact that the proposed performance was prohibited by law.[449] But if one of the parties was not aware that the contract was to be performed

---

444   So referred to in *Attwood v Lamont* [1920] 2 KB 146 at 149, 155, though the actual decision was reversed on appeal, [1920] 3 KB 571. Severance has been allowed in many cases. See, for example, *Goldsoll v Goldman* [1915] 1 Ch 292, and *T. Lucas & Co Ltd v Mitchell* [1974] Ch 129.

445   *Amoco Australia Pty Ltd v Rocca Bros Motor Engineering Co Pty Ltd* [1975] AC 561.

446   See *Bennett v Bennett* [1952] 1 KB 249, per Somervell LJ at 253–254.

447   *J M. Allan (Merchandising) Ltd v Cloke*, n 434. The case of *Bloxsome v Williams* (1824) 3 B & C 232 is sometimes said to create a difficulty. It is hard to see why. The case did not, as is commonly supposed, involve a claim to enforce an illegal contract but was, on the contrary, a claim to recover money paid under it on the basis of a total failure of consideration; and as the claimant was not *in pari delicto* with the defendant, there was no bar to recovery (see below).

448   *Strongman (1954) Ltd v Sincock* [1955] 2 QB 525; *Burrows v Rhodes* [1899] 1 QB 816. Moreover, a claimant who is not morally culpable may, it seems, recover damages in tort for fraud even where the deceit is not as to the legality of the transaction but is a swindle in intent and performance (*Shelley v Paddock* [1978] 3 All ER 129).

449   *J M. Allan (Merchandising) Ltd v Cloke*, n 434.

by the other in an unlawful manner or for an unlawful purpose – that is, if he was unaware of the *facts* constituting the illegality[450] – then so far as he is concerned, the contract is lawful, and he is entitled to enforce rights accrued due up to the time when he discovers the illegality.[451] If by that time he has fully earned the contract price, he is entitled to be paid in full. Thus, if a gun used for shooting game is bought by a duly licensed buyer but for the purpose of shooting his neighbour, and the seller was unaware of that purpose at the time of the sale, he is entitled to recover the price, even if by the time he comes to bring proceedings he has become aware of the illegal object. Where the innocent party has not completed performance at the time of discovering the illegality, he can recover sums earned up to that time (or, if the price for partial completion is not severable under the contract, a *quantum meruit*[452]) but cannot continue performance or claim money under the contract for so doing or damages for breach of contract in being disabled from completing. He may, however, be entitled to damages for fraud, negligence or breach of warranty as to legality,[453] the measure of damages being the loss suffered through his legal inability to complete the contract.

(iv) The effect of illegality on property rights

Unless otherwise expressly or implicitly provided by statute, illegality renders a contract merely unenforceable, not totally void. Hence to the extent that the obligations of a party under the contract have been performed, the question of enforcement of those obligations does not arise and the illegality has no impact. The performance is legally effective and is not vitiated by the illegality of the contract. It follows that where money has been paid or property transferred under the illegal contract, title passes to the transferee, despite the illegality.[454] Thus, where goods are sold under a contract of sale by which the property is to pass immediately to the buyer, the agreement for sale is both a contract and a conveyance. Illegality will prevent the party or parties at fault from invoking the assistance of the court to enforce the contract, but such assistance is not required to effect the transfer of property, since this passes by virtue of the contract itself, so that the obligation to transfer has been performed and is no longer extant.[455] In two different cases Lord Denning has advanced two separate policy reasons for such a result. The court ought not to allow the guilty transferor to set up his own illegality in order to defeat the transfer he has made;[456] and if the law were not to recognize such transfers,

---

450   *Archbolds (Freightage) Ltd v S. Spanglett Ltd* [1961] 1 QB 374; *Fielding and Platt Ltd v Najjar* [1969] 2 All ER 150.

451   *Archbolds (Freightage) Ltd v S. Spanglett Ltd*, n 450. The complexities of this area of law are legion. See the works cited in n 414, and for a different approach Furmston, *Law of Contract*, ch 5 (Andrew Phang).

452   *Clay v Yates* (1856) 1 H & N 73.

453   See cases cited n 448.

454   *Singh v Ali* [1960] AC 167; *Belvoir Finance Co Ltd v Stapleton* [1971] 1 QB 210. It also follows that the passing of property under the illegal contract is not dependent on delivery (*Belvoir Finance Co Ltd v Stapleton* [1971] 1 QB 210).

455   The principle applies as much to the transfer of equitable ownership as of legal ownership (*Tinsley v Milligan*, n 441, Lords Goff and Keith dissenting).

456   *Singh v Ali*, n 454 at 176.

anyone could take the property with impunity, since no one could assert a good title to it.[457]

Since illegality does not prevent the passing of property, the only basis of recovery by the transferor is restitution of the property on the ground of total failure of consideration, eg where the defendant has failed to pay the price. It is here that the transferor's illegality proves to be a barrier. The law will not in general[458] assist a party to an illegal contract by giving him a restitutionary remedy where title has passed from him.[459] But if the transferor parted with only a limited interest, eg by delivering the goods on hire or hire-purchase, then while that limited interest vests effectively in the transferee despite the illegality and continues so long as the terms on which it is given are complied with, if those terms are broken, so that the limited interest is brought to an end, the transferor can recover by virtue of his title.[460] It is true that breach of the conditions of the transfer can be established only by looking at the illegal contract; but the authorities show that even an illegal agreement may be adduced in evidence, not for the purpose of reliance on it as an essential element of the claimant's claim but (i) as evidence of the fact that the limited interest set up by the defendant has ceased to exist[461] and (ii) by a third party sued by the holder of the limited interest, to show that the claimant's interest was indeed only a limited one.[462]

In short, the court will not ordinarily allow breach of an illegal contract to be set up as a ground for restoring to the transferor property of which he divested himself, even if he has not received the consideration for the transfer; but it will not go further and deprive him of property rights which he retained under the contract.

In the following cases, by exception to the general rule, the court will lend its aid to a party to recover the money paid or property transferred under an illegal contract:

(a) where the parties are not *in pari delicto*, ie where the claimant is morally innocent and the defendant has been guilty of fraud, oppression or breach of fiduciary duty;[463]

(b) where the illegality consists of breach of a statute which was designed to restrict one party only (the defendant) and to protect the other (the claimant). Thus illegality in a moneylending transaction may preclude enforcement of the security by the moneylender[464] but does not prevent recovery of the security by the borrower;[465]

---

457   *Belvoir Finance Co Ltd v Stapleton*, n 454 at 217.

458   For the exception, see below.

459   *Berg v Sadler & Moore* [1937] 2 KB 158. For a detailed treatment of the effect of illegality on restitutionary claims, see Robert Goff and Gareth Jones, *Law of Restitution* (6th edn, 2002), ch 24.

460   *Bowmakers Ltd v Barnet Instruments Ltd* [1945] KB 65. If the property has been wrongfully disposed of by the transferee, he is liable to the transferor in conversion (ibid ; *Belvoir Finance Co Ltd v Stapleton*, n 454).

461   *Bowmakers Ltd v Barnet Instruments Ltd*, n 460.

462   *Belvoir Finance Co Ltd v Stapleton*, n 454.

463   *Atkinson v Denby* (1862) 7 H & N 934; *Hughes v Liverpool Legal Friendly Society* [1916] 2 KB 482.

464   *Kasumu v Baba-Egbe* [1956] AC 539.

465   *Bonnard v Dott* [1906] 1 Ch 740.

(c)   where the claimant withdraws from the illegal transaction before there has been substantial performance;[466]

(d)   where the claimant can show that his title is not dependent on the illegal contract.[467]

(v) Pleading illegality

Where a contract is illegal on its face, the court is obliged to take notice of the illegality and to refuse to enforce the contract, whether or not illegality has been pleaded.[468] Where, on the other hand, the contract is *ex facie* lawful, so that extrinsic evidence would have to be adduced in order to demonstrate that the contract was affected by illegality, then, as a rule, the court will require the illegality relied upon to be properly pleaded and evidence adduced concerning it. In the absence of such an allegation in the pleading, the court will not normally look itself at the surrounding circumstances alleged to indicate the illegal purpose or mode of performance because, had these matters been pleaded, the claimant would have had an opportunity to call evidence to rebut the contentions.[469] Only where the court is satisfied that all the relevant facts are before it and that even if illegality had been pleaded it could not have been refuted will the court take notice of unpleaded illegality in relation to a contract which is on the face of it lawful.[470]

18. IMPEDIMENTS TO PERFORMANCE AND THE DOCTRINE OF FRUSTRATION[471]

(i) Performance not generally excused by adverse change of circumstances

A contract which seems sensible from a business viewpoint at the time it is made may later become unprofitable to one of the parties for a variety of reasons. Commercial contracts are particularly prone to disturbance through supervening events. Wages payable by one of the contracting parties to his employees may be substantially increased through an arbitral award or industrial pressure; the price of materials needed for the contract may rise dramatically; the factory in which a product undertaken to be produced is to be made may be damaged by fire and put

---

466 *Taylor v Bowers* (1876) 1 QBD 291. But recovery will be denied if the illegal purpose has been substantially achieved (ibid) and the same was said to be true if there was no genuine repentance (*Bigos v Bousted* [1951] 1 All ER 92) but this requirement was disavowed by Millett LJ in *Tribe v Tribe* [1996] Ch 107 at 135.

467 See n 454.

468 *Edler v Auerbach* [1950] 1 KB 359, per Devlin J at 371; *North-Western Salt Co Ltd v Electrolytic Alkali Co Ltd* [1914] AC 461.

469 *North-Western Salt Co Ltd*, n 468.

470 *Snell v Unity Finance Co Ltd* [1964] 2 QB 203; *Birkett v Acorn Business Machines Ltd* [1999] 2 All ER (Comm) 429.

471 For a comprehensive treatment of this difficult topic, see G. H. Treitel, *Frustration and Force Majeure* (1994). As to the relationship between risk and frustration in the case of contracts for the sale of goods, see pp 242 ff.

out of operation; and the export of goods or payment for goods imported may become prevented through the executive action of governments. For a variety of reasons, the contracting party may discover to his dismay that even if he is able to complete the contract, in doing so he will not only be unable to earn his expected profit but will undoubtedly make a substantial loss. Whether impediments to performance created by post-contract events discharge the parties from future performance is determined by reference to the doctrine of frustration.

(ii) The meaning of frustration

A contract is said to be frustrated when a supervening event occurs which so fundamentally affects the performance of the contract that in the eyes of the law the contract comes to an end and both parties are discharged from any future duty to perform. The English law doctrine of frustration is quite different from, say, the French law concept of *force majeure*.[472] Frustration operates as a matter of law to bring the contract to an end, whether or not the parties wish it and, indeed, whether or not they are aware of the frustrating event or its legal effect on the contract.[473] By contrast, *force majeure* under French law is a doctrine under which the impediment excuses a party from non-performance of a particular obligation without as such affecting the continuance of the contract. It is for the party complaining of the non-performance to seek rescission of the contract and for the court to decide whether to grant rescission or to adjust the rights and obligations of the parties to take account of the effect of the impediment.[474] The party invoking the *force majeure* event is required to give notice of it as soon as practicable. *Force majeure* clauses are common in contracts governed by English law, which, however, does not possess any legal concept of *force majeure*. Accordingly, the events constituting *force majeure*, the impact of *force majeure* and the conditions in which it may be invoked stem entirely from the terms of the contract. English law knows no *tertium quid* between frustration and non-frustration. If the contract is frustrated it automatically comes to an end. If it is not, the parties must perform, however burdensome the contract may have become and however much the circumstances may have changed. There is no duty on the parties to renegotiate the contract terms, nor does the court have power to modify the contract on the ground of hardship or change in

---

472 See generally Ewan McKendrick (ed.), *Frustration and Force Majeure* (2nd edn, 1995), and Treitel, *Frustration and Force Majeure*, para 12–017.

473 *Hirji Mulji v Cheong Yue SS. Co* [1926] AC 497, per Lord Sumner at 409. It follows that termination of the contract is not affected by the fact that the parties continue performance in the mistaken belief that the contract is still on foot. It may be possible to show an implied new contract on the same terms but this is not easy if the parties have proceeded on the footing that the old contract is still in existence (*BP Exploration Co (Libya) Ltd v Hunt (No 2)* [1979] 1 WLR 783), nor will such conduct estop a party from relying on the doctrine of frustration (ibid). The remedy of a party who has conferred a *post*-frustration benefit on the other party is to bring a restitutionary claim on a *quantum meruit*. See generally Treitel, *Frustration and Force Majeure*, paras 15–002–15–003.

474 See Jacques Ghestin, C. Jamin and M. Billiau, *Les Effets du Contrat* (3rd edn, 2001), paras 723 ff; Philippe Malaurie and Laurent Aynès, *Les Obligations* (11th edn. 2001), paras 565 ff; Barry Nicholas, *The French Law of Contract* (2nd edn, 1992), pp 206 ff.

the economic equilibrium of the contract,[475] which may be particularly difficult to envisage or take into account in the negotiation of long-term contracts.[476] It is thus left to the parties to provide in hardship clauses for renegotiation.[477]

(iii) The common law approach to impediments to performance

In common with a number of legal systems,[478] the common law is very reluctant to recognize an impediment to performance as a ground for relieving a party of his obligations as to future performance. The general principle is that the parties are free to stipulate those events that are to be considered as frustrating the contract, or as entitling one party or the other to an adjustment of the terms, and if the parties fail to do so, the law will not intervene. This is vividly illustrated by two cases, one old, one new.

Case 1

The plaintiff, who had granted a lease to the defendant, sued for arrears of rent. The defendant pleaded that he had been expelled from the premises by an invading force led by the German Prince Rupert.

It was held that this was not a sufficient defence.[479]

Case 2

Sellers agreed to ship goods from Port Sudan to Hamburg. The route contemplated was through the Suez Canal but that was not a term of the contract. The closure of the Suez Canal meant that the cost of transportation would be greatly increased. The sellers refused to ship the goods, contending that the contract was frustrated.

The House of Lords, upholding the decision of the Court of Appeal, held that closure of the Canal, though making the contract more onerous, did not produce so fundamental a change as to frustrate the contract.[480]

(iv) Events that may frustrate a contract

There are, however, certain types of risk which are either so unforeseeable or so destructive of the commercial purpose of the contract that it would be unjust to hold the parties to the bargain; and in these cases the law declares that the contract is frustrated, that is, terminated automatically by force of law. Among the circumstances which will usually frustrate a contract where there is no fault on either side are:

---

475 Contrast the UNIDROIT *Principles of International Contracts*, arts 6.2.1–6.2.3 and comparable provisions in art 6.111 of *Principles of European Contract Law* formulated by the Commission on European Contract Law. See also *Towards a European Civil Code* (2nd revised and expanded edn, ed A. S. Hartkamp *et al.*, 1998), ch 20.

477 See Ugo Draetta, 'Hardship and *Force Majeure* Clauses in International Contracts' in (2002) International Business Law Journal 347.

478 French law, for example, is even stricter than English law, insisting that the event of *force majeure* must render performance wholly impossible. See Code Civil, art 1184, alinéa 2; Ghestin *et al.*, *Les Effets du Contrat*, para 409; Malaurie and Aynès, *Les Obligations*, paras 827 ff; Nicholas, *French Law of Contract*, pp 202–203.

479 *Paradine v Jane* (1647) Aleyn 26.

480 *Tsakiroglou & Co Ltd v Noblee Thorl GmbH* [1962] AC 93. See to similar effect *Globe Master Management Ltd v Boulos-Gad Ltd* [2002] EWCA 313.

(a)   accidental destruction of the subject matter;[481]

(b)   supervening physical disability in contracts of personal service;[482]

(c)   supervening illegality;[483]

(d)   supervening impossibility through government interference;[484]

(e)   inability to procure a necessary consent of a third party, eg a government department whose approval is required;[485]

(f)   a fundamental change in the basis of the contract.[486]

But the rules providing for frustration in the above cases are far from absolute in their application. The terms of the contract may indicate that the party pleading frustration was assuming a strict responsibility so that, for example, he had bound himself to obtain an export licence and not merely to take reasonable steps to obtain it, and cannot therefore rely on a refusal of his application as producing frustration.[487] Supervening illegality will not frustrate a contract if it is clear that the party from whom performance was due was deliberately taking a chance on not being stopped by legislation.[488] Self-induced frustration does not terminate a contract, so that, for example, a party who fails to take proper steps to apply for an export licence cannot rely on the failure to obtain the licence as a frustrating event,[489] and supervening impossibility that would have been avoided if the party invoking it had not previously broken the contract will not ground a plea of frustration.[490] The underlying principle in all these cases has been stated as that of reasonable control. A party cannot plead frustration if the impediment is one which he had the means and opportunity to prevent but still caused or permitted it to come about.[491] This principle has been applied even to cases where a party has entered into several contracts and the effect of the impediment is that he can perform some, but not all, of them.[492] This is a harsh result, for it means that the defendant, despite his inability to perform through supervening illegality, has no way of avoiding a breach of contract and consequent liability. The reasoning on which this conclusion is based is that there is no eligible frustrating event. It is not the impediment itself, for no one contract can be shown to be incapable of performance; nor can it be the

---

481   *Taylor v Caldwell* (1863) 3 B & S 826. But as to contracts of sale, see pp 260 ff.

482   *Poussard v Spiers and Pond* (1876) 1 QBD 410.

483   See p 130.

484   *Bank Line Ltd v Arthur Capel & Co* [1919] AC 435 (government requisition of ship let on time charter).

485   As to the duty to obtain a licence for the export of goods under a contract of sale, see p 942.

486   *Krell v Henry* [1903] 2 KB 740. But this is not lightly established. See, for example, *Davis Contractors Ltd v Fareham Urban District Council* [1956] AC 696; *National Carriers Ltd v Panalpina (Northern) Ltd* [1981] AC 675.

487   *Peter Cassidy Seed Co Ltd v Osuustukkukauppa,* [1957] 1 Lloyd's Rep 25.

488   *Walton Harvey Ltd v Walker & Homfrays Ltd* [1931] 1 Ch 274; *Peter Cassidy Seed Co Ltd v Osuustukkukauppa,* n 487.

489   *Maritime National Fish Ltd v Ocean Trawlers Ltd* [1935] AC 524; *Agroexport State Enterprise for Foreign Trade v Compagnie Européenne de Céréales* [1974] 1 Lloyd's Rep 499.

490   *The Eugenia* [1964] 2 QB 226.

491   *The Super Servant Two* [1990] 1 Lloyd's Rep 1, per Bingham LJ at 10. See Ewan McKendrick, 'The Construction of Force Majeure Clauses and Self-Induced Frustration' [1990] LMCLQ 153; Andrew Phang, 'Frustration in English Law – A Reappraisal' [1992] Anglo-Am. LR 278.

492   *The Super Servant Two,* n 491.

defendant's act of election to perform some of the contracts, for this is the result of the defendant's own choice. But this is to focus on each contract in isolation, whereas the proper approach is surely to take all of them together. If this is done, the difficulty in applying the doctrine of frustration disappears, for it is clear that the defendant cannot perform all the contracts, and his election not to perform some of them is not a free choice but is forced upon him by the frustrating event. This leaves only the question whether the defendant should have a free hand in deciding which contracts to perform or should perform the earliest contracts first or should pro-rate performance among all the contracts. This last solution, adopted in American case law and thereafter in s 2–615(b) of the Uniform Commercial Code, seems the most satisfactory.[493]

There can be little doubt that the English doctrine of frustration as currently applied is too strict and narrow to produce that degree of adjustment which the commercial community would regard as fair. The premise that the parties could have covered the particular eventuality in the contract is unrealistic, for the range of possible obstructions to performance of a contract is so vast and variable that a contract would have to be of enormous length to encompass them. Moreover, the doctrine is too inflexible, for it involves an all-or-nothing approach. Ignoring cases where the frustrating event is temporary only, so that the contract is merely suspended and not terminated, the impact of a supervening disabling event is either that the contract is frustrated, in which case it comes to an end, or that it is not, in which case its terms are enforceable in all their rigour. What is needed is some legal mechanism for adjusting contract terms so as to divide between the parties on a more equitable basis the cost of serious and unforeseen intervening events, leaving the contract to continue in force as adjusted.

The effect of frustration, as we have seen, is to terminate the contract and discharge the parties from liability for future performance. At common law, a party who had paid money under the frustrated contract could recover it if he could show a total failure of consideration,[494] but a partial failure of consideration did not suffice. The rigours of this rule were mitigated by the Law Reform (Frustrated Contracts) Act 1943, where this applies.[495] The general principle laid down by the Act is that sums paid by one party to another under the contract are recoverable, and sums payable by a party under the contract cease to be payable. But the payee or intended payee may be allowed by the court to retain or recover expenses incurred by him before discharge in or for the purpose of performance of the contract;[496] and a party who has obtained a valuable benefit by reason of any act done by the other party before the time of discharge may be ordered to pay that party such sum, not exceeding the

---

493 For a detailed discussion, see Treitel, *Frustration and Force Majeure*, paras 5–015 ff.

494 *Fibrosa Spolka Akcyjina v Fairbair, Lawson, Combe Barbour Ltd* [1943] AC 32.

495 As to the categories of contract excluded from the Act, see s 2(5).

496 Section 1(2), proviso. The award of expenses and the sum to be awarded are in the discretion of the court, and the onus is on the defendant to show that they were incurred to the amount claimed and that it is just to allow their recovery (*Gamero SA v ICM/Fair Warning (Agency) Ltd* [1995] 1 WLR 1226, per Garland J at 1235). Expenses can, in any event, be awarded only to the extent that the defendant claiming them has to repay or ceases to be entitled to recover sums paid or payable to him.

value of the benefit, as the court considers just.[497] But where a party incurs expenditure which does not result in benefit to the other party, the Act does not enable him to recoup such expenditure except out of monies paid or payable by him to the other party. If he has not made a payment or incurred a liability to make a payment (and if he is the party supplying goods or performing services, it is unlikely that any sum will be paid or payable *by* him), he has to bear such expenses himself.

497   Section 1(3). The effect of the statutory provisions was exhaustively examined by Goff J in *B.P. Exploration Co (Libya) Ltd v Hunt (No 2)*, n 473, astonishingly the first reported case on the Act. The decision was upheld on appeal by the Court of Appeal and the House of Lords. See [1982] 1 All ER 925, where all three stages of the case are reported. Although s 1(3) of the Act necessarily refers to benefit conferred *before* the discharge, yet in considering what sum should justly be awarded the court looks at the value of the benefit immediately afterwards, so that if it has been reduced as the result of the frustrating event (as by expropriation) or extinguished altogether (as by destruction of the subject-matter of the contract) the claimant will receive a reduced sum or, as the case may be, nothing at all in respect of the benefit he has conferred (ibid).

4 Commercial Contracts

I. COMMERCIAL AND NON-COMMERCIAL CONTRACTS

In a number of other European legal systems contracts are formally classified according to whether one or other of the parties enters into them in the course of a business. In French law, for example, contracts are commercial, civil or mixed. A commercial contract is one entered into between merchants acting for business purposes; in a purely civil contract neither party acts as a merchant; while a mixed contract is a contract entered into by a merchant acting for business purposes and one who is not a merchant or does not act for the purposes of a business.

By contrast, English contract law, which is uncodified, does not draw any formal distinction between civil and commercial contracts or, indeed, between civil law and commercial law. But while all contracts are governed by general principles of contract law, the commercial character of a transaction frequently leads to the application of particular principles or rules which would not otherwise apply. Repeat transactions between the same parties are a common feature of commercial life, so that contract terms not expressly stated will readily be implied from a prior and consistent course of dealing between the parties.[1] English law also attaches considerable importance to mercantile custom and usage,[2] and to the need to uphold the reasonable practices of business people and the reasonable rules of the markets on which they trade.[3] The courts are much less willing to restrict freedom of contract in commercial transactions than in contracts between a business concern and a consumer, and most consumer-protection legislation is confined to consumer transactions.[4] Accordingly, the absence of a formal classification of the type adopted in continental Europe has not prevented English contract law from applying distinctive rules to commercial contracts.

Moreover, commercial contracts are not homogeneous. Each type of commercial contract has rules peculiar to that type which are superimposed on the principles and rules applicable to commercial contracts at large and, below them, on the general principles of contract law. So contracts of sale of goods are subject to rules not applicable to other types of commercial contract. Similarly, contracts of

---

1 See p 88.
2 See p 13.
3 See p 159.
4 A striking exception is the Consumer Credit Act 1974, which applies to all credit and hire agreements within the statutory financial ceiling where the debtor or hirer is not a body corporate.

insurance, carriage of goods, finance and guarantee each possess distinctive rules tailored specifically to the nature and purposes of the contract. The present chapter is devoted to commercial contracts as a class, with a specific focus on typical structures of commercial relationships and on the nature and functions of an organized market.[5]

2.   CONTRACT TYPES AND STRUCTURES

When two parties decide to transact business, it will often be found that their commercial objectives can be achieved through any one of a variety of contract types. The legal nature of the relationship will depend upon the particular type of contract selected, but the economic effect of one type may be indistinguishable from that of another. For example, B wishes to acquire goods from S without having to make a lump sum payment, while S does not wish to give up all rights in the goods until he has received payment in full. There are several different ways in which these dual objectives might be attained. S could contract to sell the goods to B under a conditional sale agreement, that is, an agreement providing for payment of the price by instalments and the retention of title by S until completion of payment. Alternatively, S could sell the goods to B outright under a contract providing for payment by instalments, B mortgaging or charging the goods to S by way of security for payment. Other alternatives are for S to let the goods to B on hire-purchase (that is, a hiring with an option to purchase)[6] or to lease them to B under a finance lease.[7] Similarly, a company holding investment securities and wishing to use these as collateral to obtain short-term finance could either mortgage or charge the securities or sell them outright under a sale and repurchase agreement ('repo'), which though not in itself a security agreement nevertheless functions as such in commercial terms because of the buy-back agreement and close-out provisions.[8]

Where a particular transaction or series of transactions involves more than two parties and more than one set of relationships, then again it will usually be found that these relationships can be structured in different ways, each designed to achieve a similar objective. If, in the above illustration, S does not wish to extend credit himself, and a third party financier, F, is brought into the deal, one way of doing the deal is for F to buy the goods from S for cash and supply them[9] to B under a conditional sale, hire-purchase or leasing agreement.[10] Alternatively, S could contract directly with B under a conditional sale agreement and then sell the contract and the reserved title to F, who would then be entitled to collect the instalments as S's assignee.

---

5 For typical forms of commercial contract see R. Christou, *Drafting Commercial Agreements* (2nd edn, 1998).
6 See p 713.
7 See p 721.
8 See p 607.
9 Legally, not physically. The goods would be delivered by S.
10 See figs 27.4, 27.5, 28.1 at pp 711, 715, 725.

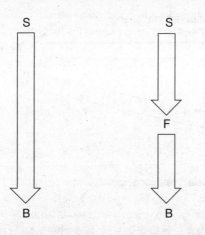

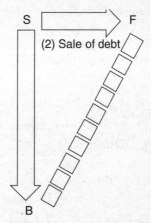

(i) S sells on credit (or lets on hire-purchase) and retains credit burden.

(ii) S sells to finance house which resells on credit (or supplies on hire-purchase).

(iii) S sells on credit (or lets on hire-purchase) then sells contract to finance house or factoring company.

Fig 4.1 Financing of sales on credit

Figure 4.1 shows three ways of financing a sale on credit. In (i) S extends the credit himself; in (ii) S sells to a finance house, which in turn supplies the goods on credit; in (iii) S enters into the supply agreement with B and then sells the contract to F. Where three parties are involved, the relationship may be either a triangular relationship, in which one party (in fig 4.2(i), the assignee) becomes involved with both the other parties in relation to the same contract, or a chain relationship (fig 4.3(i)), in which there is a main sale contract between S and B, and a sub-sale contract between B and SB. In transactions between traders, in the sense of those trading on a market for profit without intending to take physical delivery of goods, a party who has sold goods as the first or intermediate link in a chain transaction may find the opportunity, in a rising market, to buy them back and make a second sale and thereby an additional profit. Figure 4.3(ii) shows a loop transaction in which an intermediate seller buys back the goods; Figure 4.3(iii) shows a complete circle, where the goods come back to the original seller at the top of the chain.

A party to a contract can assign his rights under it but cannot transfer the burden of his obligations to a third party without the consent of the other party to the contract.[11] Even if he purports to transfer the burden of the contract as well as the benefit, this operates only as between himself and the assignee; the assignor remains liable to the other party to the contract. Assignments feature in a wide variety of commercial transactions, including factoring and block discounting of receivables,[12] the assignment by a lead bank of part of its rights under a loan agreement to

11 *Tolhurst v Associated Portland Cement Manufacturers (1900) Ltd* [1902] 2 KB 660.
12 See pp 702, 774.

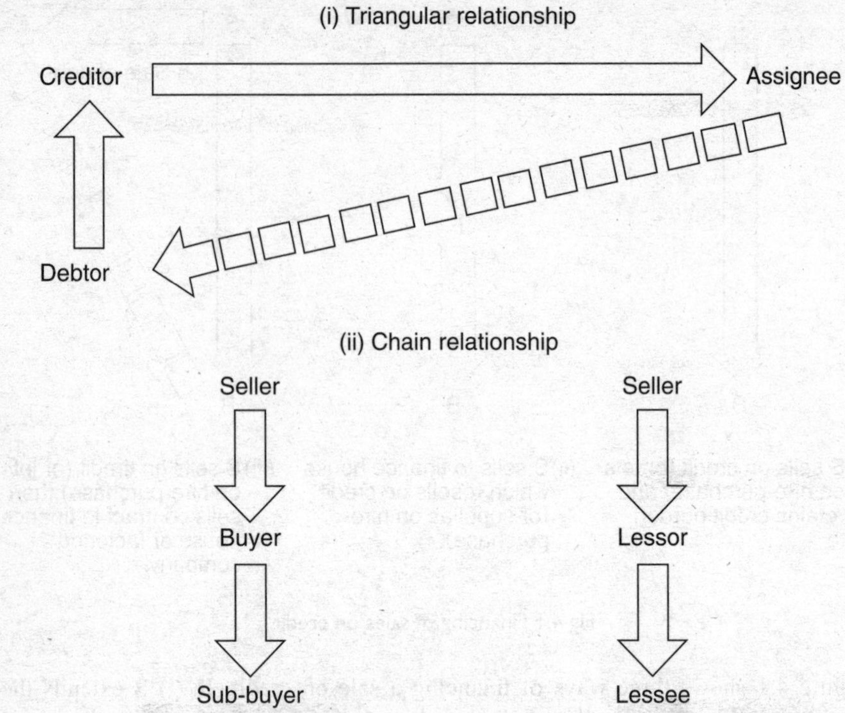

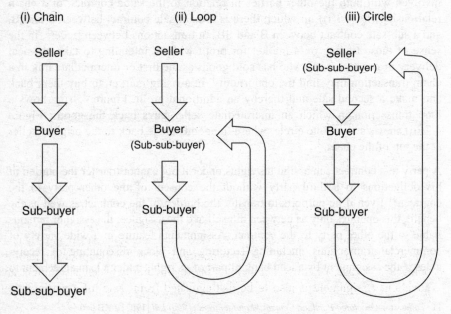

(i) Triangular relationship

Creditor → Assignee

Debtor

(ii) Chain relationship

Seller → Buyer → Sub-buyer

Seller → Lessor → Lessee

Fig 4.2 Tripartite relationships

(i) Chain

Seller → Buyer → Sub-buyer → Sub-sub-buyer

(ii) Loop

Seller → Buyer (Sub-sub-buyer) → Sub-buyer

(iii) Circle

Seller (Sub-sub-buyer) → Buyer → Sub-buyer

Fig 4.3 Chains, loops and circles

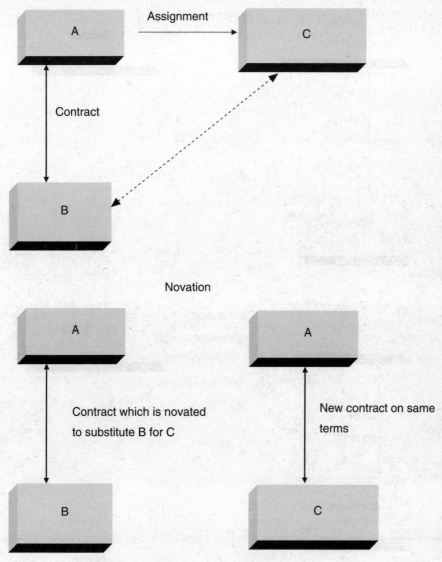

Fig 4.4 The distinction between assignment and novation

other participants under a participation agreement, and securitization of secured or unsecured receivables.[13]

Assignment is to be contrasted with novation, by which the existing contract is replaced by an entirely new contract. Usually novation is used to substitute one party for another, so that where there is a contract between A and B, C is substituted as a party for B, the consideration for C's assumption of liability being B's release. Figure 4.4 illustrates the distinction between assignment and novation. Assignment is also to be distinguished from 'sale' of a participation,

13 See below.

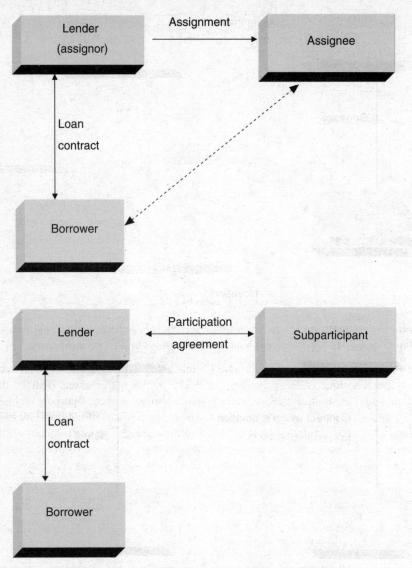

Fig 4.5 The distinction between assignment and a sub-participation

termed a sub-participation, where the lead lending bank does not transfer any part of its rights under the loan agreement to the participant but enters into a back-to-back contract with the participant to pay it an agreed percentage of whatever sum the lead bank receives from the borrower, with whom the participant has no relationship of any kind. Figure 4.5 illustrates the distinction between assignment and a sub-participation.

In operations on an organized market, in which all parties contract on standard terms, it is common to have contractual provisions which avoid the need for a string of deliveries and payments by notionally eliminating the intermediate transactions and providing for delivery direct from the head seller to the ultimate

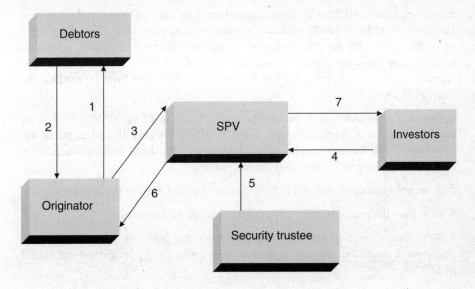

Fig 4.6 Simple securitization by sale of receivables

buyer, the obligations of the various buyers being settled by the payment of differences.[14] It is generally provided that the circle is broken on insolvency.

The packaging of non-marketable assets[15] into marketable securities is achieved through a technique called securitization.[16] The holder of the assets (that is, the original creditor, termed the originator) sells them to a special-purpose vehicle (SPV), usually a single-purpose company, which issues bonds or notes to investors under a trust deed, the assets being charged to the trustee to secure payment of the bonds or notes and the sale price being discharged from the proceeds of the issue.[17] Figure 4.6 provides a simplified illustration of a typical securitization structure.

1 Originator (underlying creditor) makes bulk loans (receivables) to (underlying) debtors. Loans can be trade credit, home loans etc.

2 Underlying debtors owe the debt to the underlying creditor and make periodic repayments of principal and interest.

3 Originator sells the receivables to the SPV (purchaser of receivables) under a transfer agreement. The SPV is often owned by charitable trustees. It is important

---

14 See, for example, the circle clauses in the contract forms issued by the Grain and Feed Trade Association (GAFTA), which publishes a wide range of standard-term contracts, varying from commodity to commodity. The complete set is available for purchase, and the Association kindly supplies a magnifying glass to assist reading it!

15 Typically receivables, such as home mortgage loans or credit cards or leasing receivables.

16 There is an unfortunate similarity between two terms having different meanings, 'security' and 'securities'. In its singular form the word denotes security for performance of an obligation, such as a mortgage or charge. In its plural form it means stocks, shares, bonds, and the like, issued and transferred on a market. 'Securitization' is linked to the latter meaning.

17 Where the assets consist of receivables which are themselves secured by a charge, the security is sub-charged to the trustee.

for the originator and SPV to remain separate and for the sale of receivables to be a clean sale, in order to satisfy capital adequacy, tax and accounting rules. Originator and SPV enter into an administration agreement whereby originator agrees to administer receivables and act as servicing agent for SPV, primarily collecting repayments from underlying debtors on behalf of SPV and then forwarding the moneys to the SPV.

4 Investors lend (funding loan, commonly in the form of subscribing to a bond issue, or making a syndicated bank loan) to SPV to finance the purchase of the receivables. The funding loan is secured by way of a fixed and floating charge over all the assets of the SPV, including the receivables.

5 A security trustee is engaged to hold the security on behalf of the investors.

6 SPV pays the purchase price of the receivables to the originator.

7 SPV repays funding loan to investors from the proceeds of receivables (ie repayments made by underlying debtors and collected by originator on behalf of SPV).

8 Often credit enhancement is used in order to make the securitization more marketable to investors. One method is for the originator to make a high-interest subordinated loan to the SPV. Another method is for a guarantor to give a guarantee to the SPV to meet any shortfall which may occur between the repayments which the SPV receives from the originator and the payments the SPV must make to the investors.

Finally, a substantial volume of business is conducted through a variety of synthetic transactions, in which the parties, instead of engaging in a real transaction for, say, the sale of assets, conclude an agreement which reproduces the effects of the real transaction, in terms of the transfer of economic benefits and risks, but without any actual sale of the assets. Since synthetic transactions do not involve real assets, they provide much greater flexibility and fewer documentation problems. In essence, the originator buys credit protection and releases regulatory capital while retaining the assets to which the transaction is linked. Synthetic transactions typically arise in relation to repos, collateralized debt obligations and securitizations,[18] the credit risk being transferred by a credit derivative such as a credit default swap or a credit-linked note.

3. FACTORS INFLUENCING THE CHOICE

What leads parties to choose one contract type or structure instead of another? One reason is habit. That is the way it has always been done. Another is that the person selling the deal to the customer is an employee of, or has a business relationship with, an organization set up to transact a particular kind of business. So whether B, in our example, enters into a sale, hire-purchase, lease or loan

18 The futures contract is in conception an early form of synthetic transaction, except that, in theory, the parties can, it seems, insist on actual performance. See p 155.

transaction may depend upon whether the person getting the business is from a bank, a finance house or a leasing company, or on whether S himself receives a greater amount of commission on introducing business to one type of financier rather than another.

But where both contracting parties are well informed, the choice of contract type or structure will usually be influenced by commercial necessity or convenience or by legal, accounting or regulatory considerations.

(i) Commercial considerations

There are many different commercial considerations which may influence the choice of the contract type or structure. One of them is the perceived need to avoid disturbing existing relationships. For example, a supplier may not wish his customers to know that he is obtaining finance against the sale transactions. He will therefore wish to avoid bringing the financier into a contractual relationship with his customers and, if discounting his agreements or receivables to a finance house or a factoring company, will insist upon being allowed to collect payments as agent of the finance house or factoring agreement without the assignments being notified to the customers. Similarly, a corporate supplier may decide to sell its book debts rather than borrowing on the security of them, for a charge on book debts is registrable in the Companies Registry,[19] whereas a sale of debts is not. Again, intermediate parties to a chain transaction may insist on being allowed to buy and resell for their own account, or, if acting as agent, to resell in their own names as principals, to avoid the risk of the buyer or sub-buyer cutting them out of future deals by contracting direct with the seller.

Various commercial considerations make securitization attractive, such as reduction in borrowing costs through the transfer of credit risk and an increase in liquidity through an issue on the capital markets.

(ii) Legal and accounting considerations

1. Right to sue and liability to be sued

In a transaction involving three parties and two sets of relationships, the way in which the transaction is structured may determine the right to sue and the liability to be sued. This is primarily because of the requirements of privity of contract. For example, if S sells goods to B for resale to B's customer, SB, S's only claim is against B, there being no privity between S and SB. By contrast, if S appoints B his undisclosed agent to sell in B's own name, S can intervene to enforce the contract against SB.[20] The conventional hire-purchase model by which the finance house, F, buys goods from the supplier, S, and lets them on hire-purchase to the customer, B, brings F into a direct contractual relationship with B, so that if the goods are

---

19 Companies Act 1985, ss 395, 396.
20 See p 176.

defective, B's claim is against F, not against S.[21] This is well illustrated by the decision of the Court of Appeal in *Lowe v Lombank Ltd* [22]

> The plaintiff agreed to acquire a car from a motor dealer. The dealer sold the car to the defendants, who let it on hire-purchase to the plaintiff. The car was completely unroadworthy. The plaintiff sued the defendants for breach of the condition of fitness implied under s 8(2) of the Hire-Purchase Act 1938. Among the various defences advanced by the defendants was that they were bankers, not suppliers of goods.
>
> *Held*: the defendants had chosen to arrange the transaction in such a way that they were in a direct contractual relationship with the plaintiff. They were therefore liable.

F's exposure to liability can be avoided by structuring the deal so that S enters into the hire-purchase agreement with B and assigns it to F.[23]

2.   Assumption or avoidance of an interest in the subject matter

A party may wish to acquire an interest in the subject matter of the contract for greater security. For example, the assignee of debts arising from conditional sale agreements will usually wish to take title (or reserve the right to take title) to the goods in order to be able to repossess and sell the goods on default by the buyer. Conversely, a party may wish to avoid taking title, because of legal liabilities imposed on owners, eg the owner of a ship causing marine pollution[24] or of an aircraft in respect of surface damage.[25]

3.   Characterization of the transaction

Of great importance is the legal characterization of a transaction, upon which may depend liability to tax or stamp duty, public registration requirements, the disclosure of assets and liabilities on a balance sheet, and conformity with statutory or contractual restrictions on entering into certain types of transaction. Particularly significant is the distinction between the purchase of an asset and the advance of a loan on the security of an asset. The sale of goods or book debts by a company is not a registrable transaction, whereas a mortgage or charge on goods or book debts must normally be registered.[26] A loan transaction may breach restrictions on lending or borrowing imposed by statute[27] or contract.[28] There has been much litigation relating to cases where an apparent sale transaction has been attacked, often successfully, as a disguised loan on security.[29] Sales of debts attract *ad valorem* stamp duty;[30] borrowings on the security of debts are exempt.[31] Debts

---

21   In the absence of a misrepresentation or collateral warranty by S. See pp 81, 93, 107.

22   [1960] 1 All ER 611.

23   See p 700.

24   See the Prevention of Oil Pollution Act 1971, s 1(1); *The Huntingdon* [1974] 1 Lloyd's Rep 820.

25   See the Civil Aviation Act 1982, s 76(2), (4). A party may also wish to off-load assets in order to reduce capital adequacy requirements. See p 152

26   See pp 580, 695.

27   See p 580, n 16.

28   As to negative pledge clauses, a breach of which may in turn trigger a cross- default clause, see p 613.

29   See p 605.

30   Under the Stamp Act 1891, Sch 1.

31   Finance Act 1971, s 64(1).

which are sold disappear from the balance sheet; debts which are mortgaged remain.[32]

4. Networking of contracts

The performance of delivery obligations and the settlement of transactions can be made much easier if parties to all relevant agreements contract with reference to a uniform set of terms. This helps to avoid the common problem of a mismatch between the terms of one transaction and those of a linked transaction in a chain, which can leave a party to both transactions exposed to liability on one contract while having no countervailing claims under the linked contract. There are various methods of standardizing terms. One is by the institutional formulation of a set of terms in a way which balances the interests of the different parties, those terms being incorporated by reference into every relevant contract. A prime example is the confirmed documentary credit, which involves at least five sets of contractual relationship. Though each is distinct from the others, the almost universal practice is to incorporate the Uniform Customs and Practice for Documentary Credits into all the contracts. Another method of standardization is through the rules of an organized market, rules which every member undertakes to observe as a condition of his right to continued membership.[33] A similar technique is applied to the settlement of banking transactions, which are governed by Clearing House Rules, to which all members of the clearing subscribe, and which can be imposed by contract on non-members transacting business with or through members.[34]

5. Coordination of fractional interests

Transactions involving large numbers of players could not be conducted efficiently if each player were left to enforce his rights individually without regard to the interests of others. The power of a single participant might be very limited; conversely, precipitate action by a major participant could adversely affect the interests of others. Suppose, for example, that there is a £100 million bond issue, the bonds being available in denominations of £10,000. At any one time there could be literally thousands of bondholders. In the event of delay or default, there would be chaos if the issuer of the bonds had to negotiate separately with each bondholder. Again, many international loans are far too large for any one bank or group of banks to handle. What is required is a mechanism by which several hundred banks can contribute to a loan facility in a way which keeps their loans separate but applies a uniform set of terms to all the loans and gives one bank, within defined limits, the power to act on behalf of all. The development of legal techniques for the coordination of fractional interests is a striking example of the way in which creative lawyers have responded to the commercial needs of their clients.

Two techniques deserve particular mention: the trust for bondholders and the syndicated loan. The trust, though of medieval origin, has proved an immensely

---

32 See further as to the importance of characterization, pp 605 ff.
33 See p 157.
34 On operational matters they will be bound without a contract. See pp 158–159.

powerful and flexible instrument of modern finance. The issuer executes a trust deed in favour of trustees for the bondholders investing the trustees with defined powers, including powers to act in the event of default. Every bond is issued subject to the terms of the trust deed, so that the bondholder, though the legal owner of the right to payment conferred by the bond, confers irrevocable authority on the trustees to exercise their powers under the trust deed for the benefit of all bondholders. A remarkable, if seldom-remarked, characteristic of the trust in this context is that it does not necessarily involve the holding of any trust property in the ordinary sense. What the trustees hold is a collective delegation of authority from the bondholders. The pension fund trust fulfils a similar coordinating function, the trustees being the vehicle for the collective protection and enforcement of the rights of the scheme members, though in this case the trustees also hold the assets of the scheme.

The syndicated loan is another example of the way in which fractional interests can be coordinated. A syndicated loan has been succinctly defined as

> a loan made by two or more lending institutions, on similar terms and conditions, using common documentation and administered by a common agent.[35]

The loan is assembled by one or more arranging banks, which invite other banks to participate in the loan.[36] Each bank accepting the invitation agrees to make available a defined part of the total facility on standard terms. But the syndicated loan is not a joint loan by the different members. Each member of the syndication is committed only to the extent of its agreed participation. The distinctive feature of a syndicated loan is that while each participation is treated as a separate loan and each lending bank preserves its freedom of individual action in the event of default, all the participants enter into common contract documents on similar terms and at a common rate of interest vis-à-vis the borrower, and the entire loan is administered by a common agent, who provides the link between the borrower and the lending banks.

(iii) Regulatory considerations

Prominent among regulatory considerations are capital adequacy requirements. Pursuant to the 1988 Basel Accord,[37] governments have been imposing increasingly stringent requirements concerning regulatory capital designed to ensure that banks maintain a capital base adequate to support the risk assets proving irrecoverable, the risk being weighted according to the risk-category allocated to particular types of asset. There is thus an incentive for banks to engage in transactions which take assets off their balance sheet. So from this perspective it is more advantageous for a bank wishing to raise funds on its investment portfolio to make an outright transfer of title under a repo transaction than to mortgage or charge the securities, which would keep them on its balance sheet and thus attract a capital adequacy requirement in respect of them.

---

35 Stanley Hurn, *Syndicated Loans* (1990), p 1.
36 The bank taking the most substantial participation is known as the lead bank or lead manager.
37 To be replaced by a more stringent set of guidelines, commonly referred to as Basel II.

4.   MARKET CONTRACTS AND THEIR ORGANIZATION[38]

A market, in its broadest sense, is any place or system by which intending buyers of goods or services can find or be put in touch with intending suppliers of those goods or services, and vice versa. The market may be a physical location, such as an open-air market or a trading hall, or it may be little more than an electronic communications system to which all members of the market have access, as in the case of electronic dealings in securities.

(i)   Types of market

The utility of a market is greatly enhanced if it is organized, in the sense of being given an institutional structure for the conduct, monitoring and settlement of dealings on the market. London, as one of the world's leading commodity and financial centres, has developed a whole range of sophisticated markets. Markets fall broadly into two groups: commodities markets, in which commodities are traded with a view to physical delivery, and financial markets, which involve the issue and transfer of contracts embodying, directly or indirectly, an entitlement to investment securities or money. These include commodities futures contracts, which in form are contracts for the sale and delivery of goods but are in almost all cases intended to be converted into purely money obligations by reverse transactions.[39] The financial markets are by far the most important and complex. They include the money market, in which short-term loans are raised against bills of exchange and commercial paper; the capital (securities) markets, which exists to provide medium and long-term finance; the foreign exchange market, for dealings in foreign currencies; and the derivative markets in commodity and financial futures and options, designed essentially for hedging and speculation. A relatively modern phenomenon is the development of international financial markets in Eurocurrency deposits, Eurocommercial paper and Eurobonds.

The financial markets must provide a mechanism both for the issue of securities and for dealings in them after issue. In relation to the issue of securities the market serves as a primary market; in relation to subsequent dealings, as a secondary market. There is no such division in the case of the futures market, which has no issuing function and exists solely for the sale and purchase of contracts.[40]

1.   The physical market in commodities

In the physical (or 'actuals') markets traders buy and sell with a view to taking or making physical delivery. Contracts may be 'spot' contracts, involving delivery in the current delivery month at the prevailing cash price, or forward contracts, in which the price is fixed at the time of contract for delivery in some future delivery

---

38 For a more detailed discussion, see Roy Goode, 'The Concept and Implications of a Market in Commercial Law' (1990) 24 Israel LR 185, reproduced in [1991] LMCLQ 177, and *Commercial Law in the Next Millennium* (the 1997 Hamlyn lectures) (1998), pp 38 ff.

39 See p 154.

40 See p 154.

month.[41] Forward contracts have the advantage to the parties of crystallizing their rights and obligations, so that they have the contractual assurance of delivery and payment regardless of subsequent fluctuations in the market price or lack of availability of the purchased commodity. They thereby enable the trader to safeguard himself ('hedge') against a fall in the price of goods he has bought for future resale, or a rise in the price of goods he has already sold for future delivery. In the former case he enters into an offsetting sale transaction at a price fixed now for future delivery. If the market price falls, the loss he will incur on the original transaction by selling for less than he paid will be compensated, wholly or in part, by the profit he will make on the offsetting transaction, under which the price is higher than that at which he is now able to buy the goods in the market to meet his delivery obligation under that transaction. If the market price rises he will lose on the offsetting transaction but gain on the original transaction. In the converse case where he has sold for future delivery, he enters into a matching purchase for future delivery, so that if the price rises, the loss he makes on the original transaction is matched by the gain on the offsetting transaction, while if the price falls, his loss on the latter is counterbalanced by his gain on the former. The disadvantage of the forward contract is that it is tailored to a specific item of produce that a particular trader in the market wishes to sell or buy at a particular time, rather than an item of standard description available for sale or purchase on a standard contract at any time the trader may wish to sell or buy it. In consequence the trader wishing to hedge may find it difficult to locate a counterparty on the market who is able to enter into a fully matching transaction as regards description, time of delivery and other contract terms.

2.   The futures market in commodities

The ingenious solution adopted by the traders was to create a market in contracts for different kinds of commodity, each contract being on standard terms for delivery of a commodity of standard description in given lot sizes at a stated price denomination per unit in a designated trading month.[42] Contracts for given quantities of a particular commodity are put into the market simply by brokers offering them on the market, without the need to hold any particular goods or possess any particular source of supply. This makes it unnecessary for a buyer or seller to look for a particular counterparty able to make a matching sale or purchase contract to offset the contract he has already entered into. All he has to do is to sell or buy a matching contract on the market. In general those dealing on the futures (or 'terminal') market do not intend to take physical delivery. Their purpose is either to hedge against an adverse movement in the market or to make a profit by

---

41   The contract type is identified, inter alia, by the delivery month, which thus forms part of the contract description. Thus an August contract for soyabeans is not the same as a July contract and can be rejected by the buyer who has contracted for the latter.

42   For an interesting historical account, see A. W. B. Simpson, 'The Origin of Futures Traded in the Liverpool Cotton Market', in *Essays for Patrick Atiyah* (eds Peter Cane and Jane Stapleton, 1991), ch 8.

43   The speculator is an essential player in the futures market, for hedging by one party in order to offload his risk necessarily assumes the willingness of another, the speculator, to assume it.

speculation,[43] though a small amount of business is transacted with a view to physical delivery. Accordingly, a party who has taken a position by buying or selling a futures contract can close his position by a countervailing sale or purchase before the due delivery (terminal) date, thus effectively cancelling out his original transaction and simply paying or receiving the difference between the two prices. For example, if B, having bought a futures contract from S, wishes to liquidate his position, he will sell a corresponding contract to S, receiving the difference between the sale price and the original purchase price if the market goes up and paying the difference if the market goes down. S liquidates his position by the reverse procedure, offsetting his original sale to B with a purchase. Until the liquidation of a party's position by a countervailing transaction and the payment of differences, the contract is said to be an open contract, that is, open for perform-ance by delivery and payment. When a party liquidates his position, so that the prospective delivery and acceptance/payment obligations are replaced by an obligation to pay differences, the contract is said to be 'closed' or 'closed out'. At the terminal date the exchange matches the cancelled transactions, the payments are netted out and differences paid. Since the parties do not usually intend physical delivery, most futures contracts in practice function not as contracts of sale but as contracts for the payment of differences.[44] Nevertheless, a sale on the terminal markets *is* a contract for physical delivery in law,[45] so that a party who fails to close out a contract by the terminal date is obliged to tender delivery if a seller and to accept it if a buyer.[46] This usually takes the form of constructive delivery by the transfer of warehouse warrants.

The financial character of the futures contract by contrast with the physical character of the forward contract is reflected in the fact that dealings in futures are regulated as investments for the purpose of the Financial Services and Markets Act 2000,[47] whereas forward transactions in principle are not.[48]

3. The financial markets

These consist of the money market, in which short-term finance is raised against bills, notes, interbank money transfers, and the like, and the securities (or capital) market for issues and sales of stocks, shares, bonds and debentures.

---

44 In other words, the seller keeps the goods and pays or receives from the buyer the amount by which the market price at the due delivery date exceeds or falls below the contract price.

45 *Gebrüder Metelmann GmbH & Co KG v N.B.R. (London) Ltd* [1984] 1 Lloyd's Rep 614, where the judgment of Mustill J at first instance contains (at 623) a useful description of the essential features of the futures market.

46 Not necessarily the original party, as one of the functions of a commodity exchange is to match traders wishing to tender physical delivery with those wishing to obtain delivery.

47 Financial Services and Markets Act 2000 (Regulated Activities) Order 2001 (SI 2001/544), art 84(1).

48 SI 2001/544, art 84(2), which excludes contracts for future delivery made for commercial and not for investment purposes, the test being whether delivery is to be made within seven days (art 84(4)), ie, those entered into for commercial and not investment purposes. All contracts made or traded on a recognized investment exchange are treated as investment contracts (art 84(3)), as are contracts for differences (art 85(1)), but traded forward contracts are made on a commodity exchange, not an investment exchange, and even where constituting contracts for differences will usually be excluded from regulation as investments under art 85(2)(a).

4.   Derivatives and the derivatives market

Just as the futures market in commodities fulfils the function of hedging against, and speculation on, price changes without (in most cases) performance of a trading transaction, so the derivatives market provides a similar service for financial products, through futures, swaps, options, and through credit-linked notes and other forms of synthetic transaction. They are called derivatives because their pricing is derived from that of conventional securities but they do not involve actual dealings in currency, money instruments or securities – they merely imitate their financial characteristics and are performed by the payment of differences rather than by delivery of and payment for actual instruments.[49] Derivatives are thus flexible instruments which can be used to package financial products which are not available on the market in direct form or which add features to those which are traded on the market. Not all derivatives are traded, or even available, on a market; many, such as swaps, are arranged by bilateral transactions.

(ii)   Characteristics of an organized market

A fully organized market possesses a number of characteristics which have been described elsewhere.[50] They include a formally established exchange with a defined membership and rules, the provision of a trading floor or other communication facilities, the fixing and regular adjustment of prices by reference to supply and demand, the standardization of contracts and the fungibility of the commodities offered,[51] together with a clearing and settlement providing for the netting and settlement of claims.

(iii)   Functions served by an organized market

An organized market fulfils six principal functions. First, it provides a mechanism for matching sellers to buyers, and lenders to borrowers. Secondly, it is a convenient tool for raising large amounts of capital through the primary securities market. Thirdly, it ensures that through the secondary market those who buy commodities or financial assets can readily liquidate their positions and offload their risks on the market with an assurance or reasonable expectation of payment. Fourthly, it enables traders and investors to protect themselves against price fluctuations by an offsetting transaction in the futures market. The ability to hedge is dependent on counterparties who are either hedging in the opposite direction or are speculators having no interest in any underlying trade transaction. Fifthly, by providing the mechanism for an ascertainable market price for a commodity or security of a specified description, an organized market sets a yardstick by which compensation or damages for failure to honour a contract can be objectively measured. This market-price rule is examined in detail in chapters 14 and 15. Finally, through its control of membership and its membership rules, an organized

---

49 See generally Philip R. Wood, *Title Finance, Derivatives, Securitizations, Set-Off and Netting*, ch 15.
50 See the article referred to in n 38.
51 So that each unit is treated contractually as the equivalent of any other unit of the same grade, sample or description.

market helps to ensure the competence and integrity of its members and the observance of fair and efficient standards of trading.

Closely associated with market operations is the system for settlement of bargains through a clearing house. An important function of a clearing house is to net out transactions between the participants, so that instead of large numbers of bilateral settlements, with money going round in a circle, the clearing house establishes which participants are net creditors and which net debtors at the end of the trading cycle, net debtors making a single net payment to, and net creditors receiving a single net payment from, the clearing house. A distinct and valuable function of a clearing house is to provide a means of novating contracts to the clearing house, so that where S sells goods to B on the market, the contract is registered with the clearing house and upon registration the original contract between S and B is replaced by two new contracts, between S and the clearing house for sale and payment, and between the clearing house and B for purchase and payment. In this way the clearing house is substituted as the counterparty to each of the original parties, a procedure which overcomes possible problems of netting and substitutes the resources of the clearing house for those of the individual trader in the performance of payment and delivery obligations.

(iv) The rules and usages of a particular market

Each market develops its own customs and usages. Over time many of these are likely to become codified or replaced by formal rules of the market issued by the exchange, so that members are expected to transact business in accordance with those rules and with the unwritten customs and usages prevailing. The status and effect of market rules and usages may be a matter of some uncertainty. Do they have legal force or are they merely agreed procedures for the efficient administration of the market and not intended to have any legal effect? What, if any, is the legal relationship between the members and the exchange, between the members among themselves and between the exchange and a non-member transacting business through a member? Can a non-member invoke the rules or usages against a member or the exchange? To what extent is a non-member bound by the rules or usages?

1. The legal status of market rules and usages

The legal status of custom and usage has been described earlier.[52] In English law these take effect as implied terms of the contract. The same is true of formal rules issued by the exchange. Unless these are promulgated under statutory powers, they can take effect only by express or implied contract. In the normal case it is a term of membership of the market that members undertake to the exchange and to each other to observe the rules. The effect is to underpin each bilateral sale and purchase contract with a multilateral network of market rules.[53] This, of course, assumes that

---

52 See p 13.
53 An early example of this networking effect of 'club' rules is *Clarke v Dunraven*, *The Satanita* [1897] AC 59.

the rules themselves are intended to have legal force and not simply to be rules of commercial convenience.

2.   The powers of the exchange vis-à-vis members

The power to make those rules is usually conferred on a committee or other executive organ of the exchange and must be exercised in good faith and consistently with the objects of the exchange.[54] To be valid, a decision taken by the exchange or a relevant body established by it must be in conformity with a power conferred by the rules expressly or by necessary implication. The more urgent the need for the decision and the greater the threat to the stability of the exchange if it is not taken, the more likely it is that the court will imply the power to make it. A striking example is provided by the *Shearson Lehman* case,[55] where the facts were extraordinary.

> The International Tin Council was a body established by some twenty-three sovereign states and the EEC, and was based in London. Its primary function was to ensure a stable price for tin, for which purpose it was given funds and a buffer stock of tin, so that it could sell tin when the market was moving too sharply upwards and buy tin when the market was depressed. The market in tin fell sharply and the ITC used up all its funds to buy tin in the hope of restoring the price. But the price of tin continued to fall. The ITC then borrowed money from banks to continue its market-support operations, and exhausted the borrowed funds as well, whereupon it declared itself unable to meet its commitments.[56] The London Metal Exchange thereupon suspended all dealings on the tin market.
>
> Some two months later the LME amended its rules by empowering the relevant committee to publish such settlement prices as they thought fit, and requiring all open contracts having 'prompt' dates (ie due delivery dates) falling on or after the date the market closed to be closed out and balanced by reverse sales and purchases at the price so fixed (the 'ring-out' price). The effect on the plaintiffs, who had sold a quantity of tin prior to closure of the market, was that they would have to keep the tin previously sold and accept by way of payment the excess of the contract price over the 'ring-out' price. The plaintiffs[57] attacked the new rule on various grounds, one of which was that the LME had no power to suspend or affect the performance of contracts already made.
>
> It was held that the committee had both express and implied power to amend the rules to alter rights under existing contracts. The implication of such a power was necessary to avoid possible damage to the Exchange and the endangering of the market.

3.   The position of a non-member vis-à-vis a member

In general, members of a market contract with each other as principals, even where they are entering into transactions for a client rather than for their own account.

---

54 *Shearson Lehman Hutton Inc v Maclaine Watson & Co Ltd* [1989] 2 Lloyd's Rep 570. However, where the objects are not stated, it will be necessary to deduce them from the rules themselves. The objects will then be 'those which, upon a proper construction of the rules read as a whole, are necessary for the fulfilment of such fundamental intention or intentions of the members as can with reasonable certainty be inferred from those rules' (per Webster J at 582).

55 Ibid. For a further illustration of the influence of market rules, see *Money Markets International Stockbrokers Ltd v London Stock Exchange Ltd* [2002] 1 WLR 1151.

56 This default led to a spate of litigation concerning the legal status of the ITC, a fascinating topic, which, unhappily, cannot be explored here. See John Macleod, 'The Saga of the International Tin Council' [1990] LMCLQ 305

57 Who were not members of the LME, a separate point taken by them unsuccessfully and discussed below.

This enables the exchange to exercise control and to ensure that only those seen as fitted to conduct business on the market are directly involved in its operations. It follows that in the normal way a non-member's contract is with the member through whom he concludes the purchase or sale transaction, not with the counterparty to that transaction. Suppose, however, that the non-member is ignorant of the rule or custom to this effect. Here a distinction is drawn between rules relating simply to the conduct of business and those which relate to substantive rights. A person who is not a member of an exchange and who instructs a member to make a purchase on his behalf thereby impliedly assents to the transaction being dealt with in accordance with the normal operational rules of the exchange,[58] for otherwise those rules would become unworkable. But the non-member is not bound by a rule or custom of which he is ignorant which affects substantive rights.[59] So if a non-member instructs his broker to purchase goods as agent, being ignorant of the custom of the market that brokers deal with each other as principals, the non-member is not obliged to accept the transaction, for its effect is to substitute his broker as principal in place of another party.[60]

4.   The position of a non-member adversely affected by acts of the exchange

There is, of course, no contractual relationship between an exchange and a person who is not a member. Accordingly, any claim a non-member may wish to pursue against the exchange for loss suffered by its acts or omissions must lie either in tort, eg for negligence, or in the domain of public law by way of judicial review. It is thought that the court will not readily treat an exchange as under a duty of care to non-members so as to be liable for pure economic loss.[61] On the other hand, it may well be susceptible to judicial review,[62] so that its decisions can be set aside if the procedure adopted is unfair or the decision wholly unreasonable.[63]

5.   THE LEGAL POWER OF THE MARKET

In a world financial centre such as London it would be surprising indeed if the courts were insensitive to the need to uphold reasonable business practice where not otherwise constrained by rules of positive law. In a major market the consequences of a refusal to accept the market's perception of the legal nature and incidents of contracts and financial instruments in widespread use could be severe; indeed, in some cases confidence in the market could be seriously undermined. If, for example, the court were to hold that futures trading was gambling and that dealings

---

58   *Shearson Lehman Hutton Inc v Maclaine Watson & Co Ltd*, n 54; *Cunliffe-Owen v Teather & Greenwood* [1967] 1 WLR 1421.

59   *Robinson v Mollett* (1875) LR 7 HL 802; *Forres (Lord) v Scottish Flax Co Ltd* [1943] 2 All ER 366.

60   *Robinson v Mollett*, n 59.

61   See, for example, *Shearson Lehman Hutton Inc v Maclaine Watson & Co Ltd*, n 54, where the court held it would not be just or reasonable for the members of the committee to be under a duty of care, particularly having regard to LME's status as a self-regulatory body.

62   As was held to be the case in *Shearson Lehman*, though the court concluded that the relevant body had acted fairly.

63   Ibid, where, however, no unfairness was found.

in futures were unenforceable as gaming transactions, London would face the loss of its entire futures market to another international financial centre.

There is therefore considerable scope for the business community to establish law through practice and thus, as it were, to pull itself up by its own legal bootstraps. Thus the concept of negotiability derives its legal support from judicial recognition of mercantile usage in the development of negotiable instruments,[64] the treatment of which is now partially codified in the Bills of Exchange Act 1882.[65] In an action for recovery of payments due to brokers in respect of futures contracts entered into by a speculator, the Hong Kong High Court rejected the defence that futures contracts constituted illegal gaming, holding that a game was something played for sporting, recreational, leisure or pure amusement purposes, and that genuine commercial activities did not constitute gaming even though they involved chance and speculation.[66] The power of the London Metal Exchange to alter its rules even with retrospective effect in relation to open contracts already concluded has been noted above.[67]

But there are occasions when the courts are unable to respect the sanctity of market contracts, despite the adverse effect on the market. This is strikingly illustrated by the decision of the House of Lords in *Hazell v Hammersmith and Fulham London Borough Council*,[68] in which it was held that swaps and similar contracts entered into by local authorities on a massive scale were *ultra vires* and void, so that the local authorities concerned were not liable on them.[69] However much this conclusion may have been compelled by legal principle and by a proper interpretation of the relevant provisions of the Local Government Act 1972, it cannot be denied that the outcome seriously damaged the reputation of the London swaps market. Foreign investors, in particular, must have found it hard to understand how local authorities could be admitted to the market to engage in transactions for profit and then be able to walk away from the bargains they had freely made.

So strong is the perceived need to protect the integrity of the market and to avoid loss of business from abroad that where legal principles or judicial decisions stand in the way of upholding commercially sensible transactions, the government is more often than not likely to intervene with liberating legislation. So the validity of futures contracts was assured by the Financial Services Act 1986, and, at a more general level, subsequent legislation has conferred on market contracts a wide degree of immunity from the effects of insolvency legislation which might otherwise have rendered them vulnerable.[70]

---

64 See p 478.

65 'Partially' because the Act covers only two forms of negotiable instrument. See p 572.

66 *Richardson Greenshields of Canada (Pacific) Ltd v Keung Chak-Kiu and Hong Kong Futures Exchange Ltd* [1989] 1 HKLR 476; similarly *City Index Ltd v Leslie* [1992] QB 98, distinguishing the decision of the House of Lords in *Universal Stock Exchange v Strachan* [1896] AC 166. For the current position in English law, see the Financial Services Act 1986, s 63, and Sch 1, para 9, and *City Index Ltd v Leslie*.

67 See p 158.

68 [1991] 1 All ER 545.

69 In subsequent actions counterparties to swaps transactions with local authorities made claims for restitution of monies paid, which were upheld by the courts or were settled.

70 See p 843 and *Gore-Browne on Companies*, (looseleaf), ch 34A.

Yet it remains the case that capitalist markets generate significant policy tensions.[71] One is between market freedom and market integrity. Markets must be not only free but fair. This means that rules have to be introduced to prevent such malpractices as insider dealing and the creation of a false market by private share-support operations, the publication of untrue or misleading information or the abuse of monopoly power. Another tension is between fairness and stability. The soundness and financial stability of the market are of the utmost importance. In the interests of these it may be necessary to give limited sanction to such stabilization devices as delay in the display of information relating to large-scale share dealings, or the overselling, under-allotment or buying-in of securities. A third tension relates to the mode of regulation. Should the market be regulated primarily by its own members (self-regulation) or by an independent regulator? To what extent is self-regulation within a statutory framework adequate to ensure the integrity of the market? Experience over recent years showed the weaknesses of self-regulation, and the system was replaced by a statutory regime under the Financial Services Act 1986, since repealed and replaced by the Financial Services and Markets Act 2000, which, with subordinate legislation, confers enormous powers on the Financial Services Authority as regulator of the financial services industry.

---

71 See generally Goode, *Commercial Law in the Next Millennium*, ch 2.

5   Agency in Commercial Transactions

A commercial enterprise may use a variety of techniques to ensure that its goods reach the intended market.[1] One is direct selling. The enterprise contracts directly with the various buyers without going through any intermediary. Another is agency. It is often convenient for the enterprise to appoint one or more agents whose business it is to effect sales. This itself may be done in a variety of ways. The agent may simply introduce prospective buyers to his principal, leaving it to the latter to conclude the contract if he wishes. Alternatively, the agent may effect the sale himself on behalf of his principal, either contracting expressly as agent, with or without naming the principal, or contracting in his own name as apparent principal. A third method of selling is to appoint a commission agent whose role is to effect sales without committing his principal to third parties in any way, even as undisclosed principal, so that the agency is a purely internal mandate.[2] A fourth method is to appoint a distributor to buy the goods and resell them on his own account. Yet another is consignment. The enterprise delivers the goods to the consignee to hold in the first instance as bailee but on terms that the consignee is to buy the goods if he notifies his intention to do so and that he is deemed to have elected to buy them if he fails to return the goods within a given time or otherwise adopts the prospective purchase transaction, typically by selling the goods.

A highly specialist form of marketing is franchising. The enterprise grants to others a licence to exploit the franchisor's product or service under his trade mark or trade name on standard terms which, in allowing each franchisee to sell for his own account, impose on him detailed requirements and restrictions designed to enhance the reputation of the franchisor and knowledge of the product or service and to ensure that each franchisee observes proper business practices in selling the product and supplies the franchisor with all the information it needs concerning marketing and sales.[3] The franchisor for its part supplies the product or raw material, the know-how and other ancillary services.

Many factors will be taken into account by the enterprise when considering which of these marketing methods to adopt: cost, commercial convenience, legal considerations, such as the desire to ensure or avoid contractual relations with

---

1 Similar considerations apply to the supply of services. For brevity, 'goods' will be used to include services where this is appropriate.

2 See p 164. For the agency models, see Figure 5.1. Model (iii) is not treated in English law as a true agency.

3 One of the most ubiquitous franchising operations is McDonalds, through whose franchisees hamburgers and fries are purveyed around the world.

(i) Sale through A as agent to T, with or without disclosure of P's identity

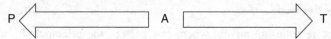

(ii) Sale by A as apparent principal but in reality as agent for an undisclosed principal, P. The contract is between T and A but T may elect to hold P liable and P may intervene to enforce the contract.

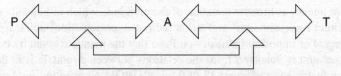

(iii) Sale by A as true principal under a mandate from P ('commission agency' or 'representation') with no relationship betweeen T and P.

Fig. 5.1 Agency Models

buyers, and the tax and accounting implications involved in choosing one method instead of another. On the one hand there may be a desire to sell directly so as to cut out middlemen and agents and keep all the profit. On the other, the enterprise may take the view that it does not want to keep large numbers of staff on its payroll and that anyway its selling may be more effective if conducted through others.

The present chapter is concerned with one type of relationship only, though a highly important one – agency. For the lawyer, agency is a subject of never-ending fascination, subtle and complex. For the business enterprise it is a vital tool in bringing goods and services to the market. But lawyers and business people do not always speak the same language. The lawyer uses the term 'agent' in a fairly precisely defined way,[4] whereas in business the term is frequently used more loosely to include, for example, distribution agreements under which the 'agent' buys and sells for his own account. We shall use the term in its technical legal sense. Only a brief outline can be given here, with the emphasis on relations between the principal or agent and third parties. For fuller details the reader is referred to the standard textbooks.[5]

---

4 See below.

5 The leading English textbook is *Bowstead and Reynolds on Agency* (17th edn, 2001). See also G. H. L. Fridman, *Law of Agency* (7th edn, 1996); B. Markesinis and R. J C. Munday, *An Outline of the Law of Agency* (4th edn, 1998); and for an excellent compilation of text and materials, L. S. Sealy and R. J A. Hooley, *Text and Materials in Commercial Law* (2nd edn, 2003), chs 3–6. For agency agreements, see R. Christou, *International agency, distribution and licensing agreements* (4th edn, 2003).

1.   THE CONCEPT OF AGENCY

(i)   Agency defined

Agency is the relationship arising where one person, the principal (P), appoints another, the agent (A), to bring about, modify or terminate legal relations between the principal and one or more third parties (T). This includes cases where A contracts as principal, so that his agency status is undisclosed, for, as we shall see, the true principal has a right to intervene to enforce the contract and, as a corollary, can be sued on it by the other contracting party. In this respect the common law conception of agency is broader than that of the civil law, which in general confines agency to direct representation[6] and treats indirect representation[7] as incapable of conferring rights or imposing liabilities on P, so that the mandate given by P to A is purely internal and is insulated from the relations between A and T. It is the civil law approach that is adopted in art 13 of the UNIDROIT Convention on Agency in the International Sale of Goods.[8]

An employee may have power to commit his employer to contracts with third parties and in that sense is the employer's agent, but in commercial parlance the designation 'agent' usually denotes one who is self-employed.

(ii)   Agency and authority

Agency may therefore be regarded as a particular form of authority, namely to create or affect legal relations between P and T. Authority to do acts which are not intended to produce this result does not give rise to an agency relationship. So a purely internal mandate by which P instructs or authorizes A to enter into a commitment with a third party not only in A's own name but without involving P even as undisclosed principal does not fall within the English law notion of agency. Sometimes known as a 'commission agency',[9] it constitutes an agency-type relationship between P and A but not one which affects third parties. Such a relationship – designated in civil law jurisdictions as indirect or imperfect representation – can arise in a variety of contexts. One of them is sale. A is authorized to resell goods as 'agent' in the relationship between himself and P but as the principal in his relationship with buyers. In such a case P cannot sue or be sued, even as undisclosed principal, on contracts entered into by A with buyers.[10] Sometimes the law confers a power of sale on A even where he has no authority from P for this, as in the case of apparent authority[11] or of an agency of necessity.[12] Another example of the purely internal mandate is the instruction

6 Ie where A contracts expressly as agent.
7 Where A contracts in his own name for an undisclosed principal.
8 See p 176.
9 The term 'commission' is borrowed from its equivalents in French and German law and denotes the task with which the agent is entrusted, not his remuneration.
10 See generally R. M. Goode, *Proprietary Rights and Insolvency in Sales Transactions* (2nd edn, 1998), ch III.
11 See p 168
12 See p 167.

given by the buyer of goods to his bank to open a letter of credit in favour of the foreign seller. The letter of credit is a payment undertaking which is entirely independent both of the underlying transaction between buyer and seller and of the relationship between buyer and bank. The beneficiary's rights under the letter of credit lie solely against the bank.[13] Where A is authorized to enter into transactions without bringing about or affecting legal relations between P and T, then if such a transaction is concluded, the parties to the contract are A and T, and P can neither sue nor be sued on the contract. But the authority thus given to A may produce effects similar to that of agency in some respects. For example, where A is authorized or instructed to incur on his own behalf a liability to T, the discharge of which is intended to satisfy P's obligation to T – as where A instructs his bank to open a letter of credit in favour of T covering the price of goods sold by T to P – A is entitled to be indemnified against his liability and to be reimbursed for any payment made to T. Again, where A, acting as a commission agent or an agent of necessity, sells P's goods to T, then although P cannot sue or be sued by T, the sale operates to divest P of his ownership and transfer it to T. Similarly, where P takes a floating charge over the assets and undertaking of a company, A, by which it authorizes A to deal with its assets in the ordinary course of business free from the charge, and pursuant to this authority A sells goods to T, then although P is not thereby brought into a contractual relationship with T, he is bound by the sale in the sense that he cannot assert his charge against T.[14]

2. SOURCES OF AGENCY LAW

It will be apparent from what has been said above that agency law has to deal with three distinct relationships: between P and A; between P and T; and between A and T. Any contractual relationship (eg between P and A, or between A and T where A contracts in his own name) is governed by the terms of the contract and general contract law[15] and by particular principles of the common law (including equity) relating to agency. Where A is a self-employed commercial agent, relations between him and P are additionally regulated by the EEC Directive on Commercial Agents,[16] which significantly reduces the ability of the parties to contract out of

13 See p 973.
14 See p 686.
15 Including legislation such as the Misrepresentation Act 1967 and the Unfair Contract Terms Act 1977. But agency is not dependent on contract. It suffices that P consents to the exercise of authority by A and that A consents to exercise that authority (*Yasuda Fire and Marine Insurance Co of Europe Ltd v Orion Marine Insurance Underwriting Agency Ltd* [1995] QB 174). However, to be within the Commercial Agents (Council Directive) Regulations 1993, SI 1993/3053, a commercial agent must have a contract with the principal, which a sub-agent does not (*Light v Ty Europe Ltd* [2003] Eu LR 858).
16 Council Directive on the Coordination of the Laws of the Member States Relating to Self-Employed Commercial Agents, 86/653/EEC, OJ L382/17 dated 31.12.86, p 17. The directive has been implemented in the UK by the Commercial Agents (Council Directive) Regulations 1993 (SI 1993/3053), as amended by SI 1998/2868. See Fergus Randolph and Jonathan Davey, *Guide to the Commercial Agents Regulations* (2nd edn, 2003).

certain of their basic obligations under the directive.[17] Contracts between P or A and T are governed by their terms, general contract law and any common law and statutory provisions applicable to the type of contract in question.[18] Where A is an agent for sale and P and T have their places of business in different states, the relations between P or A and T will be governed by the 1983 UNIDROIT Convention on Agency in the International Sale of Goods, where the applicable law is that of a contracting state. The convention has not been ratified by the United Kingdom and thus has no force in England. It will therefore be referred to primarily for the purpose of comparing its rules with those of English law.

3.   TYPES OF AGENT

An agent may be appointed to act in a specific transaction outside his ordinary course of business (a 'special agent') or in transactions of a designated class or generally (a 'general agent') so as to be within the ordinary course of his business. It was at one time common to distinguish between special (or ad hoc) agents and general agents, and, though the utility of the distinction has been doubted,[19] it has been applied by the House of Lords for the purpose of determining the normal ambit of the doctrine of apparent authority.[20] More significant is whether the agent has power to buy and sell in his own name. A broker is normally expected to deal as such and not as a principal, and if he buys in his own name his principal may be able to disclaim the transaction;[21] a factor may buy and sell both as agent and on his own account,[22] and the same is true of a market-maker as regards dealings in securities. A *del credere* agent is one who guarantees to his principal that the third party will perform his contractual obligations to the principal.[23] A confirming house performs the converse function of giving an assurance of performance to the third party on behalf of its principal by adding its confirmation to the principal's order, thus assuming the same responsibilities as the principal.[24]

Some agency descriptions to be found in nineteenth-century legislation and cases, such as mercantile agents and factors, are nowadays rarely used. The term 'mercantile agent' is defined for the purposes of the Factors Act 1889,[25] while 'factor', which formerly denoted an agent having power to buy and sell in his own name, is currently employed to describe a company which buys debts due from trade debtors and assumes the credit risk.[26]

17 See p 173.
18 Eg contracts of sale are governed by the Sale of Goods Act 1979.
19 See *Bowstead and Reynolds on Agency*, para 1-041.
20 *The Ocean Frost* [1986] AC 717. See p 168.
21 See p 159.
22 As to factors and mercantile agents, see p 420, 427.
23 See *Bowstead and Reynolds*, paras 1-035, 1-038-039.
24 See *Benjamin's Sale of Goods*, paras 23-302 ff.
25 See p 426.
26 See p 774. The modern factor is in fact a derivative of the old-style goods factor. See F. R. Salinger, Factoring. the law and practice of invoice finance (3rd edn, 1999), paras1-11 ff.

4.   AUTHORITY AND POWER OF AN AGENT

(i)   In general

The authority of an agent must be distinguished from his power. A transaction entered into by A within the scope of his actual authority from P will, of course, bind P. But P will also be bound if A acts within his *apparent* authority.[27] In such a case, though A does not have the right to enter into the transaction on behalf of P, the law invests him with the power to commit his principal to the transaction.[28]

(ii)   Agency of necessity

A's power normally derives from some authority conferred by P, but this is not necessarily so. In extreme cases, as where P's property is at imminent risk and A has to take urgent action to save it and is unable to communicate with P or to obtain an adequate response to his request for instructions,[29] the law treats A as an agent of necessity to take the necessary remedial action, as where the master of a ship enters into a salvage agreement with T on behalf of P to save P's cargo,[30] or where A is in possession of perishables belonging to P and sells them for P's benefit before they become rotten.[31]

The doctrine of agency of necessity illustrates the problems that can arise where legal rules develop without being underpinned by a coherent foundation of principle.[32] As Professor Treitel has pointed out,[33] an agency of necessity can produce three quite distinct forms of authority with differing effects. It may enable A to commit P to a contract with T; it may invest A with power to sell P's goods to T without thereby bringing about a contractual relationship between P and T; and it may entitle A to claim recompense or reimbursement for acts done on P's behalf (which may not involve the making of a contract at all). Only the first of these is a true agency.[34] In principle, where T does not know that A is acting for P rather than on his own account, T should be entitled to treat A as the other party to the contract, leaving A to claim reimbursement from P. But there remain a number of problems. For example, should T, on discovering P's existence, have the option of looking to P as an undisclosed principal instead of to A? And what guiding principle distinguishes cases within the second category from those within the first? Moreover, a bewildering number of theories have been advanced as the basis of the claim for reimbursement. These include bailment, restitution, rules of negotiable

---

27 See below.
28 The distinction between authority and power in agency transactions thus corresponds to the distinction between a seller's right to sell and his power of sale, as to which see p 415.
29 *China Pacific SA v Food Corp. of India* [1982] AC 939.
30 *The Winson* [1982] AC 939; *The Choko Star* [1990] 1 Lloyd's Rep 516.
31 See *Sachs v Miklos* [1948] 2 KB 23.
32 See Geoffrey Samuel, 'Legal Reasoning and Liability for People' (1982) 98 LQR 362; Ian Brown, 'Authority and Necessity in the Law of Agency' (1992) 55 MLR 414.
33 *Law of Contract* (11th edn, 2003), p 721.
34 *The Winson*, n 30 at 958.

instruments law governing acceptance for honour and principles of maritime salvage derived from the Roman law concept of *negotiorum gestio*.

It is clear that a distinction is to be drawn between cases where A has an existing agency relationship with P but acts from necessity beyond his express or implied authority and cases where there is no pre-existing agency relationship at all. The law is reluctant to allow claims by the officious intervener who, having no connection with the party on whose behalf he intervenes, chooses of his own volition to take action on that party's behalf. Such cases are controlled not only by strict limits on the doctrine of agency of necessity but also by the general principles of the law of restitution, which restrict recovery to situations where P freely accepts the benefit officiously conferred upon him.[35] The problem is to know what constitutes officious behaviour for this purpose. Now that English law recognizes a general principle of restitution based on unjust enrichment there would be much to be said for subsuming agency of necessity within a broader conceptual framework of remedies for unjust enrichment.

5.   ACTUAL, APPARENT, AND USUAL AUTHORITY

An agent is said to have actual authority when what he does is in fact authorized by his principal, whether expressly or impliedly. Actual authority is to be contrasted with apparent (or ostensible) authority. The phrase 'apparent authority' does not mean merely the appearance of authority; it is legal shorthand for an appearance of authority to which the principal has lent himself by some act by which he represents or holds the agent out as having an authority beyond that which he in fact possesses. Where A acts within the scope of his apparent authority, P is bound to the same extent as if he had actually authorized the transaction. This conforms to the objective theory of contract law.[36] Cutting across the division between actual and apparent authority is 'usual authority', that is, the authority which a person occupying or put into the same kind of position as the agent would normally possess. For example, the manager of a store normally has authority to buy stock, engage sales staff and delegate to them the power to make sales to customers on behalf of the store; an auctioneer has authority to sign a contract of sale on behalf of vendor and purchaser; a solicitor has authority to offer or accept a compromise of proceedings on behalf of a client. An agent has both implied and apparent authority to do what is usual for someone in his position. The implied authority may be restricted by the terms of his instructions from his principal, but a third party dealing with him without notice of the restriction is still entitled to rely on his apparent authority. The difficult case is where A, in concluding a transaction that would be within his usual authority as agent, contracts in his own name without disclosing the existence of a principal, so that the third party assumes he is dealing with a principal. In *Watteau v Fenwick & Co*[37] the doctrine of usual authority was held applicable to such a case also.

---

35   See Robert Goff and Gareth Jones, *Law of Restitution* (6th edn, 2002), paras 17–002 ff.
36   Gerard McMeel, 'Philosophical Foundations of the Law of Agency' (2000) 116 LQR 387 at 389.
37   [1893] 1 QB 346.

H owned a hotel. He sold it to the defendants, who retained him as manager. The licence continued to be held in his name, which remained over the door. The plaintiffs supplied cigars to H, to whom alone they gave credit, believing him to be the owner. They had never heard of the defendants, who had forbidden H to buy cigars on credit. Upon learning that the defendants were the owners of the hotel, the plaintiffs sued them for the amount outstanding. The county court judge gave judgment in favour of the plaintiffs and his decision was upheld by the Divisional Court.

'Once it is established that the defendant was the real principal, the ordinary doctrine as to principal and agent applies – that the principal is liable for all the acts of the agent which are within the authority usually confided to an agent of that character, notwithstanding limitations, as between the principal and the agent, put upon that authority. It is said that it is only so where there has been a holding out of authority – which cannot be said of a case where the person supplying the goods knew nothing of the existence of the principal. But I do not think so. Otherwise, in every case of undisclosed principal, or at least in every case where the fact of there being a principal was undisclosed, the secret limitation of authority would prevail and defeat the action of the person dealing with the agent and then discovering that he was an agent and had a principal.'[38]

Though the decision has never been overruled, it has been disapproved in Canada[39] and doubted in both England[40] and Australia.[41] The problem, of course, is that T does not in such cases rely on the apparent authority of A, for this implies that T is aware of the existence of a principal standing behind A. An analogy has been drawn[42] with the doctrine of apparent ownership of goods or other property, under which a person held out by another as apparent owner is bound by a disposition made by that person to a purchaser for value in good faith and without notice of the true owner's rights. In such a case the ordinary limitation of acting within the scope of apparent authority does not apply, for an owner needs no authority and there is generally no limit to his dealing powers. But the analogy is false. The doctrine of apparent ownership does not operate to expose the true owner to contractual liability of any kind; its sole effect is to preclude him from denying the power of the apparent owner to pass title to a third party. Moreover, it is well established that P cannot ratify an unauthorized act by his agent A who contracts in his own name;[43] and since he cannot sue on the contract, it is unfair that he should be liable on it, particularly since his potential exposure to liability would be almost unlimited. The fallacy of *Watteau v Fenwick* lies in the assumption that there is an agency relationship at all, when the true position is that A is an indirect representative, or commission agent,[44] who has a purely internal mandate from P and is left to

---

38 Ibid, per Wills J at 348–349.

39 *Sign-O-Lite Ltd v Metropolitan Life Insurance Co* (1990) 73 DLR (4th) 541. See G. H. L. Fridman, 'The Demise of *Watteau v Fenwick*' (1991) 70 Can Bar Rev 329.

40 See *The Rhodian River* [1984] 1 Lloyd's Rep 373, per Bingham J at 378–379.

41 *International Paper Co v Spicer* (1906) 4 CLR 739. The decision is also considered 'extremely dubious' by *Bowstead and Reynolds*, para 8–079.

42 See Michael Conant, 'The Objective Theory of Agency: Apparent Authority and the Estoppel of Apparent Ownership' 47 Nebraska LR 678, 686 (1968).

43 See p 70.

44 See p 164.

contract with third parties as the real principal on his own behalf, albeit with a duty to account to P in respect of his dealings.[45]

6.   CONDITIONS NEEDED TO BE ABLE TO INVOKE APPARENT AUTHORITY

(i)   A representation by the principal

An agent who is not authorized to enter into a contract cannot represent his own authority to conclude the contract so as to commit his principal unless he is authorized to make such a representation by the principal himself or by a person having actual or apparent authority from the principal to authorize the making of that representation. P's holding out of A as so authorized may be direct or through another agent, and may also be effected by investing A with a position or function in which he would have usual authority to conduct the transaction which he represents he has authority to conduct. But without some such holding out, A's representation of his own authority to contract does not commit P,[46] though it will expose A to an action by T for damages for breach of warranty of authority.[47] Similarly, if A has no apparent authority to conclude a contract on behalf of P, he will not normally have apparent authority to convey to T the approval of the transaction by P or by someone authorized to approve it on P's behalf.[48]

Apparent authority almost invariably arises in cases where the actual authority given to the agent is general in character.[49]

(ii)   Reliance

T cannot invoke the doctrine of apparent authority unless he acted in reliance on P's express or implied representation that A had authority.[50]

---

45 So, as Professor Tettenborn has pointed out, any defence of *Watteau v Fenwick* must rest on a principle of estoppel which is independent of agency altogether (Andrew Tettenborn, 'Agents, Business Owners and Estoppel' (1998) CLJ 274).

46 *The Ocean Frost*, n 20; *A-G. for Ceylon v Silva* [1953] AC 461, per Mr L. M. D. Silva at 479; *Freeman & Lockyer v Buckhurst Park Properties (Mangal) Ltd* [1964] 2 QB 480, in which the judgment of Diplock LJ contains an illuminating description of the nature and scope of apparent authority.

47 See p 175.

48 *The Ocean Frost*, n 20. For a case where A *was* held to have apparent authority to communicate P's approval, see *First Energy (UK) Ltd v Hungarian International Bank Ltd* [1993] 2 Lloyd's Rep 194, discussed by F. M. B. Reynolds, 'Agency' [1994] JBL 144 at p 146.

49 'It is possible to envisage circumstances which might give rise to a case of ostensible specific authority to enter into a particular transaction, but such cases must be very rare and unusual' (*The Ocean Frost*, n 20, per Lord Keith at 777).

50 *Bedford Insurance Co v Instituto de Resseguros do Brasil* [1984] 3 All ER 766; *Rama Corp. Ltd v Proved Tin and General Investments Ltd* [1952] 2 QB 147; *Freeman & Lockyer v Buckhurst Park Properties (Mangal) Ltd*, n 46.

(iii) Contract within the capacity of the principal

A cannot effectively commit P to a contract which P himself has no power to make, for clearly what a principal cannot do himself he cannot do through an agent. It follows that an act which would not bind P if done by A will not be binding on him if done by a sub-agent.

7.   RATIFICATION OF ACTS DONE WITHOUT AUTHORITY

Where an agent concludes a contract without authority and expresses himself as so doing on behalf of a principal who is then in existence and is named or ascertainable from the description given in the contract, this may be ratified by the principal, in which case it takes effect from the time it was made.[51] But P cannot ratify a contract made by A in his own name[52] or on behalf of a different principal[53] or at a time when P was not in existence.[54]

8.   RELATIONS BETWEEN PRINCIPAL AND AGENT

(i)   Capacity in which agent acts

Where a transaction is effected through an intermediary, it is not always easy to determine for which party the intermediary is acting as agent. There are certain types of relationship where this is settled as a presumption of law or as a matter of business usage in the absence of agreement to the contrary. For example, an insurance broker is prima facie the agent of the insured, not of the insurer, even though it is the latter from whom he receives his commission.[55] In a syndicated loan transaction the lead manager normally acts as agent of the borrower in arranging the syndication, while the agent who manages the syndication after the agreements have been concluded is the agent of the lending banks.[56] But there may be equivocal transactions in which it is far from clear whether the agent, A, is acting for P or on his own behalf or for another principal, P2.[57]

(ii)   Duties of the agent to the principal

In entering into an agency agreement A normally undertakes two distinct sets of obligations to P. The first is the performance of the duties imposed on him by the

51 See generally *Bowstead and Reynolds*, paras 6–032 ff; Treitel, *Law of Contract*, p 726.
52 *Keighley, Maxsted & Co v Durant* [1901] AC 240.
53 *Jones v Hope* (1880) 3 TLR 247n.
54 The typical case is that of a contract expressed to be made on behalf of a company which is about to be incorporated but has not yet been registered (*Kelner v Baxter* (1866) LR 2 CP 174).
55 *Newsholme Bros. v Road Transport and General Insurance Co Ltd* [1929] 2 KB 356; *Anglo-African Merchants Ltd v Bayley* [1970] 1 QB 311; *North and South Trust Co v Berkeley* [1971] 1 WLR 470.
56 Philip Wood, *International Loans, Bonds and Securities Regulation* (1995), para 6–22.
57 See Goode, *Proprietary Rights and Insolvency,* pp 51–56, discussing this problem in the context of an agency for the purchase of goods.

express or implied terms of the agency agreement. A must perform with reasonable care and skill[58] the duties allotted to him by the agreement, must observe any lawful and reasonable instructions given by P so far as they are consistent with the terms of the agreement and must act strictly within the limits of his actual authority. P has the usual contractual remedies for breach of any of these duties. But A's contractual obligations form only part of the total. The law usually (though not invariably) treats A as a fiduciary and thus requires him to fulfil a further range of duties which equity imposes on fiduciaries. The extent to which these apply and the strength of their application vary according to the nature and circumstances of the agency agreement. They will generally include a duty to act towards P loyally and in good faith,[59] to keep and be prepared to render accounts of his dealings on behalf of P, to subordinate his own interests to those of P, to avoid conflicts of interest between P and other principals and to refrain from using his position as agent to acquire for himself property, contracts, business opportunities or other benefits which he ought (if acquiring them at all) to do so for P.[60] A may also, depending on the terms of his agreement with P, be under a duty to keep money and other assets received from or for P separate from his own and be a trustee of any proceeds of sale of P's property.[61] But not all these fiduciary duties apply with full force, or, indeed, at all, to all contracts. For example, it is well understood that an estate agent engaged to find sellers and buyers of properties will be acting for competing principals, for otherwise he could not carry on his business. Accordingly, the estate agent does not commit a breach of fiduciary duty by failing to disclose to the prospective vendor of one property that he is at the same time acting for the prospective vendor of an adjacent property selling to the same purchaser, even though the prospective purchase of both properties by a single buyer could have affected the price,[62] nor is the agent disabled from claiming commission from both vendors.[63]

The rise of financial and commercial conglomerates has made it virtually impossible for any agent, however scrupulous and well-intentioned, to avoid conflicts of interest. All he can hope to do is to manage them. The law allows most of these duties to be excluded or qualified by agreement with P after full disclosure

---

58 The agreement may, of course, impose on A a strict duty of performance, as by requiring him to effect sales of not less than a stated minimum value each year, in which case the fact that A did all he reasonably could to discharge this duty will not be a defence if he fails to achieve sales to the stated value.

59 It goes without saying that an agent may not receive a bribe or secret commission. If he does so, the principal may claim the bribe in an action for money had and received or recover as damages in tort any loss he suffers as the result of entering into the transaction to which the bribe relates. The authorities are in conflict as to whether the remedy for recovery of the bribe is proprietary or purely personal. See p 458, n 52.

60 See *Bristol and West Building Society v Mothew* [1998] Ch 1, per Millett LJ at 18; *Bowstead and Reynolds* para 6–032 ff. An agent's duty to produce accounts relating to the period of his agency continues after the agency relationship has ended (*Yasuda Fire and Marine Insurance Co of Europe Ltd v Orion Marine Insurance Underwriting Agency Ltd*, n 15).

61 *Re Fleet Disposals Services Ltd* [1995] 1 BCLC 345.

62 *Kelly v Cooper* [1993] AC 205.

63 See the Law Commission's Consultation Paper *Fiduciary Duties and Regulatory Rules* (Cons. Paper No 124, 1992), Pt III.

by A of all the material facts.[64] There are, however, certain limits. First, the exclusion or restriction must be one which satisfies the test of reasonableness under the Unfair Contract Terms Act 1977, where applicable.[65] Secondly, an agent or other fiduciary cannot exclude liability for fraud or other wilful default.[66] Thirdly, a commercial agent covered by the EEC Directive on Commercial Agents[67] and the implementing regulations may not derogate from the provisions of art 3 of the directive or regulation 3 of the regulations,[68] which provide as follows:

1. In performing his activities a commercial agent[69] must look after his principal's interests and act dutifully and in good faith.

2. In particular, a commercial agent must:

    (a) make proper efforts to negotiate and, where appropriate, conclude the transactions he is instructed to take care of;

    (b) communicate to his principal all the necessary information available to him;

    (c) comply with reasonable instructions given by his principal.

The remedies available to P for breach of A's contractual duties are the normal remedies available for breach of contract, including damages.[70] The remedies for breach of fiduciary duty vary according to circumstances. They include personal remedies, such as an account and payment of monies received for P, compensation by way of equitable debt for loss caused to P, and confiscation of a bribe or secret commission received by A; and remedies for the enforcement of proprietary rights, such as a constructive trust of money or other assets received by A for himself which he should have received (if at all) for P, and the proceeds of P's property which A has misappropriated.[71] Infringement of A's duties under the directive and regulations is separately actionable as a breach of statutory duty.[72]

---

64 For a discussion of what constitutes adequate disclosure, see ibid, paras 3.4.4 ff.

65 See p 97.

66 *HIH Casualty and General Insurance Ltd v Chase Manhattan Bank* [2003] 2 Lloyd's Rep 61.

67 See n 16. Where the agent carries on his activities within the European Community the application of the directive is mandatory and cannot be excluded by a choice of law clause which selects the law of a state outside the Community and where the principal has its establishment (*'Ingmar' GB Ltd v Eaton Leonard Technologies Inc* [2000] 1 CMLR 9; [2001] 1 All ER (EC) 57, a decision of the European Court of Justice).

68 Directive, art 5; Commercial Agents (Council Directive) Regulations 1993, reg 5.

69 Defined as 'a self-employed intermediary who has continuing authority to negotiate and conclude the sale or purchase of goods on behalf of another person (the principal) or to negotiate and conclude the sale or purchase of goods on behalf of and in the name of that principal' (reg 2(1)). A person cannot be both an agent of his principal and a buyer from or seller to his principal (*Mercantile International Group plc v Chuan Soon Huat Industrial Group* [2002] 1 All ER (Comm) 788). So a distributor who buys and sells on his own account is not a commercial agent (*AMB Imballagi Plastici SRL v Pacflex Ltd* [1999] 2 All ER (Comm) 249), nor is a sub-agent vis-à-vis the principal (see p 165, n 15). But a person may still be an agent, even if not paid a commission, if he earns a mark-up by selling goods on behalf of his principal at a price higher than that which the principal is to receive (ibid).

70 See pp 110 ff.

71 See *Bowstead and Reynolds*, paras 6–074–087.

72 *Garden Cottage Foods Ltd v Milk Marketing Board* [1984] AC 130.

(iii) Duties of the principal to the agent

Hitherto the duties owed by P to A have been left to be determined by the express or implied terms of the agreement. English law has been reluctant to imply terms other than in relation to A's remuneration and security for payment of it, and the case law has for the most part been concerned with such questions as whether A has done what is necessary to entitle him to his commission and whether P owes A a duty to avoid steps (eg withdrawal from a proposed transaction with T or cessation of business) which would prevent A from earning his commission.

With the advent of the EEC Directive on Commercial Agents[73] this has changed. Article 4 of the Directive and regulation 4 of the implementing regulations impose various duties on P from which no derogation is permitted.[74] These are as follows;

1.   In his relations with his commercial agent a principal must act dutifully and in good faith.
2.   A principal must in particular:

   (a)   provide his commercial agent with the necessary documents relating to the goods concerned;
   (b)   obtain for his commercial agent the information necessary for the performance of the agency contract, and in particular notify the commercial agent within a reasonable period once he anticipates that the volume of commercial transactions will be significantly lower than that which the commercial agent could normally have expected.

3.   A principal must, in addition, inform the commercial agent within a reasonable period of his acceptance, refusal, and any non-execution of a commercial transaction which the commercial agent has procured for the principal.

Whether an agent is entitled to be remunerated for his services depends on the express or implied terms of the agency agreement. Agents used in trade and commerce will almost invariably be remunerated, usually by commission, and will be entitled to the agreed remuneration or, if the amount of this is not specified, the remuneration that commercial agents appointed for the goods forming the subject of his agency contract are customarily allowed in the place where he carries on his activities, or if there is no such customary practice, a reasonable sum taking into account all aspects of the transaction.[75] The agent also has a right to be reimbursed his agreed or reasonable expenses, except so far as intended to be covered by his remuneration, and to be indemnified against all liabilities, incurred in the performance of his duties. He is not entitled to reimbursement or indemnity in respect of unauthorized transactions except where the principal ratifies them or accepts a benefit from them, or in respect of transactions which he knows or ought to know are unlawful.[76]

73 See n 16.
74 Directive, art 5; regulations, reg 5. See n 67.
75 EEC Directive on Self-Employed Commercial Agents, art 6(1).
76 See *Bowstead and Reynolds*, paras 7–062 ff.

A's remedies for breach of duty by P may be personal or proprietary. A has a personal right of action for unpaid remuneration and expenses, and has a lien over any property of P in his possession to secure payment of what is owed to him. Further, where A has at P's request incurred on behalf of P a commitment to make a payment to T, A's authority to make the payment becomes irrevocable, and he is entitled to recoup himself from funds of P available to him and for that purpose to debit P's account, even if P has meanwhile become bankrupt or gone into liquidation.[77] This irrevocable right of recoupment by debit to P's account is quite distinct from any lien or right of set-off A may have.[78]

The directive and regulations contain various provisions designed to ensure the payment of commission to A.[79] It is unclear to what extent derogation from these is permitted.[80]

9. POSITION OF THIRD PARTY: AGENCY DISCLOSED

Where A contracts expressly as agent for P as a named or identifiable principal, T's contract is with P, not with A, and only P can sue and be sued on the contract. This is so even where in making the contract A exceeds his authority,[81] though in such a case he becomes liable to T for damages for breach of the implied warranty of authority.[82] But A can expressly undertake liability, either in substitution for or in

---

77 *Yates v Hoppe* (1850) 9 CB 541. Other cases usually cited in support of this proposition are *Crowfoot v Gurney* (1832) 9 Bing 372, *Walker v Rostron* (1842) 9 M & W 411, and *Griffin v Weatherby* (1868) LR 3 QB 753, but these were decided on a different ground, namely an equitable assignment to T of funds in the hands of A and earmarked for the payment.

78 A common law lien in the strict sense is available only over tangible property, such as documents, cheques, securities and the like; and set-off is involved only where money is owed by P to A on a separate account, so that A can set off his right of recoupment on one account against his liability to P on the other.

79 Directive, arts 6–10; regulations, regs 6–10. See p 177.

80 The difficulty arises because the directive contains no express non-derogation rule such as art 5 provides in relation art 3 or art 19 in relation to arts 17 and 18. However, art 11(1) states that the right to commission 'can be extinguished only if and to the extent that' the contract with the third person cannot be executed and the principal is not to blame for that fact, while art 11(3) and reg 11(3) preclude derogation from that provision. In *'Ingmar' GB Ltd v Eaton Leonard Inc* [2001] All ER (D) 448, which followed the decision of the European Court of Justice, Morland J concluded that as there was no equivalent of art 19 in relation to arts 7 and 8, it was open to the parties to derogate from those provisions 'but only so far as they do not thwart the purpose of the Council Directive'. But the judgment makes no reference to art 11.

81 See to similar effect art 14(2) of the UNIDROIT Convention on Agency in the International Sale of Goods: 'Where the conduct of the principal causes the third party reasonably and in good faith to believe that the agent has authority to act on behalf of the principal and that the agent is acting within the scope of that authority, the principal may not invoke against the third party the lack of authority of the agent.'

82 See generally *Bowstead and Reynolds*, paras 9–060 ff. Where P is bound by A's apparent authority, it is not altogether clear whether A escapes liability or is liable in full or is liable for purely nominal damages on the basis that T has suffered no loss, since he can enforce the contract against P. The position is analogous to that arising where S wrongfully sells O's goods to T in circumstances where T acquires an overriding title (p 285), and it is thought that the position should be the same, namely that where it is unclear whether P is bound, T is not obliged to buy a lawsuit and should be allowed to sue A for damages in full, but that where there can be no doubt that P is bound, then although A has still committed a technical breach of warranty, damages will be purely nominal.

addition to that of P. Where A contracts as such but without disclosing P's identity, it is a question of construction of the contract whether T entered into the contract on the basis that he was willing to treat as the other party any person by whom A was authorized to make the contract or whether he looks to the credit of A, not of P. In the former case, T's contract is with P, in the latter, with A.[83] A similar principle is succinctly expressed in art 12 of the UNIDROIT Convention on Agency in the International Sale of Goods:

> Where an agent acts on behalf of a principal within the scope of his authority and the third party knew or ought to have known that the agent was acting as an agent, the acts of the agent shall directly bind the principal and the third party to each other, unless it follows from the circumstances of the case, for example by a reference to a contract of commission, that the agent undertakes to bind himself only.

However, in the case of signed contracts in writing there is an established rule that where A signs in his own name, he is personally liable unless it is clear from the document that he is signing in his capacity as agent.[84] The mere addition of words of description after the signature, such as 'agent' or 'director', will not normally suffice to displace A's liability; it is necessary for him to indicate that he is acting in a representative capacity, eg 'for and on behalf of' P.[85]

Where A contracts as agent but without identifying P, who actually exists, A will not normally be liable, but liability will be imposed where A is in fact the principal,[86] and has sometimes been imposed where P was fictitious or non-existent or where A refused to disclose P's identity, thus preventing T from enforcing the contract against P,[87] or his evidence as to his principal is disbelieved.[88]

10.   POSITION OF THIRD PARTY: AGENCY UNDISCLOSED

Where A makes a contract as apparent principal, so that T is not aware that he is an agent, the parties to the contract are A and T. But if T discovers the facts, he may elect to sue P instead of A,[89] while P for his part may intervene to enforce the contract made on his behalf.[90] This doctrine of the undisclosed principal is generally recognized as anomalous but is firmly entrenched in English agency law. In this respect it differs sharply from the civil law, which treats P's authority to A in such cases as a purely internal mandate which neither confers rights nor imposes liabilities on T.

---

83 *The Santa Carina* [1977] 1 Lloyd's Rep 478.

84 *The Swan* [1968] 1 Lloyd's Rep 5.

85 *Universal Steam Navigation Co Ltd v James McKelvie & Co* [1923] AC 492. But it is difficult to be dogmatic about any particular forms of words, for so much depends on the context and on the commercial understanding of the words used. So 'as agent' has sometimes been held sufficient to indicate a representative capacity, sometimes not.

86 See *Chitty on Contracts* (29th edn, 2004), para 31-094, suggesting, however, that liability on a collateral contract would be a more appropriate basis.

87 *Owen v Gooch* (1797) 2 Esp 567.

88 *Hersom v Bernett* [1955] 1 QB 98.

89 *Browning v Provincial Insurance Co of Canada* (1873) LR 5 PC 263.

90 Ibid; *Siu Yin Kwan v Eastern Insurance Co Ltd* [1994] 1 All ER 213.

However, the doctrine of the undisclosed principal does not apply where

(a) the terms of the contract expressly or impliedly exclude P's right to sue and liability to be sued,[91]

(b) A does not intend to contract on P's behalf,[92]

(c) T makes it clear that he does not wish to contract with anyone other than A[93] or

(d) P stipulates that A is not to commit P to a contract with third parties but is to undertake all transactions on his own behalf.[94]

11. TERMINATION OF THE AGENT'S AUTHORITY

(i) Principal's power of termination

A's authority can be terminated by agreement or by P's unilateral act in giving notice of revocation of the authority, and may also come to an end by operation of law in various circumstances, such as P's bankruptcy.[95] P can terminate A's authority in part or completely, as by determining the agency contract as a whole. But in certain cases, in particular where the authority is given to secure the agent's own interest in some way, it cannot be revoked before that interest has been satisfied and until then continues even after P's bankruptcy. Typical cases of such 'authority coupled with an interest' are where A has been empowered to resort to funds or securities held for P to secure recoupment of expenses or cover for liabilities incurred on P's behalf. But it has been rightly observed that the creation of such a power 'should be regarded as a property disposition rather than as the conferring of authority', for A exercises the power in his own interest.[96] However, P is not precluded from revoking A's authority merely by reason of the fact that this would constitute a breach of the agency agreement. A's remedy is to sue for damages for the breach; he is not entitled to continue acting as if still authorized.[97]

A matter of some importance is the agent's position on termination of the agency agreement. An agent may spend considerable time and effort developing a market for his principal only to find that the principal terminates the agency and takes over the network of contacts without compensating the agent. Until recently, the agent's entitlement to compensation was purely a matter of contract. But under the EEC Agency Directive,[98] on termination of the agency

---

91 *Siu Yin Kwan v Eastern Insurance Co Ltd* [1994] 2 AC 199.

92 *Siu Yin Kwan v Eastern Insurance Co Ltd*, n 91; *Teheran-Europe Co Ltd v S.T. Belton (Tractors) Ltd* [1968] 2 QB 545.

93 *Said v Butt* [1920] 3 KB 497.

94 The so-called commission agency. See further, p 164.

95 See *Bowstead and Reynolds*, ch 10. Article 15 of the EEC Agency Directive contains various rules as to notice of termination.

96 *Bowstead and Reynolds*, para 10–007. A power may be irrevocable both at common law and under the Powers of Attorney Act 1971, though for the latter to apply the power must be expressed to be irrevocable and to secure a proprietary interest of, or some obligation owed to, the donee (s 4).

97 *Frith v Frith* [1906] AC 254.

98 As implemented in the UK by regulations. See n 16.

contract A is entitled to be compensated or, if so provided by the agency agreement, indemnified.[99] The provisions of the directive governing compensation are modelled on French law, those relating to indemnity on German law. Compensation is designed to enable A to recoup his losses resulting from the termination; an indemnity, to reflect the continuing benefit P will derive from new customers introduced by A and loss of the commission A would have earned in respect of sales to those customers.[100] The parties may not derogate from the provisions of Articles 17 and 18 to the detriment of the commercial agent before the agency contract expires.[101]

(ii) Effect of termination on third parties

Termination of the agency agreement, though bringing to an end A's right to commit P to new transactions, does not normally affect third parties who dealt with P before the termination, or who act on the basis of usual authority, and are unaware that A's authority has come to an end.

12.   DISPOSITIONS BY AND TO A

(i)   Dispositions by A

A disposition of P's property by A to T will bind P where effected pursuant to A's actual or apparent authority, in accordance with ordinary agency principles. But A's power of disposal is not confined to true agency situations in which P is brought into contractual relations with T; it applies also where A disposes of P's goods as a commission agent[102] or an agent of necessity.[103] Special statutory provisions apply to dispositions by mercantile agents; these are discussed in chapter 16.

(ii)   Dispositions to A

Where A purchases goods from T at the request of P, it is not always easy to characterize the transaction. Depending on the agreement between the parties, A may purchase as agent for P as a disclosed principal (whether named or unidentified) or as an undisclosed principal or as a commission agent who buys

---

99 Directive, arts 17–19; regulations, reg 17–19. Termination includes expiry by effluxion of time (*Tigana Ltd v Decora* [2003] Eu LR 189). The use of the word 'indemnity' in the English text is unfortunate, conveying a meaning quite different from that in ordinary English usage. It is in essence a payment in respect of value added to P's business by A's activities as agent.

100 Article 17(2), (3). This article, which does not apply where the principal has terminated the agency contract because of the agent's default or where the agent has terminated it without circumstances to justify such termination (art 18), cannot be excluded to the detriment of the agent before the agency contract expires (art 19).

101 Article 19, repeated in reg 19 of the regulations.

102 See p 164.

103 See p 167.

on his own account and immediately resells to P. A may also participate by confirming an order placed by P with T. According to the circumstances title may pass direct from T to P without going through A, or may pass through A to P without any interval between A's acquisition and that of P, or may be held by A on trust for P or as beneficial owner until A has appropriated the goods to his contract with P. The sometimes complex issues arising have been discussed by the author elsewhere.[104]

104 Goode, *Proprietary Rights and Insolvency,* ch III.

PART TWO
Domestic Sales

6　A Brief History of Sales Law

The sale of goods is one of the earliest forms of business transaction, existing from the time when money was first introduced to replace barter. Medieval English law was primarily concerned to protect real rights,[1] and did not recognize the binding force of executory agreements if not under seal.[2] Thus, in the early history of the common law, a bargain and sale of goods, being ineffective by itself to transfer ownership to the buyer,[3] did not as such entitle the seller to sue for the price; it was necessary for him to establish benefit to the buyer by delivery of the goods,[4] so generating the *quid pro quo* which would ground an action in debt and which would not have been sufficiently constituted by the mere promise of performance by the seller. But the manifest commercial importance of sale, and the need for the mercantile community to be able to rely on a principle of *pacta sunt servanda*, drove the common law to accept that if a sale transaction were properly established,[5] ownership would pass to the buyer by virtue of the contract, and he could accordingly maintain an action in detinue, not by virtue of the seller's undertaking to deliver but in exercise of a proprietary right.[6] As a corollary, the seller could sue for the price, though in deference to the principle that a mere executory agreement could not impose liability the courts based the seller's entitlement not on the exchange of promises as such but on the fact that, by virtue of the contract, ownership had passed to the buyer, thus conferring on him the benefit requisite to ground the seller's action.[7]

1　Ie those arising from the delivery of property, the payment of money or the conferment of some other tangible benefit, as opposed to a mere exchange of promises, neither of which was considered by itself a sufficient *quid pro quo* to make the other enforceable.

2　*Anon.* (1338) YB 11 and 12 Edw III (RS) 586. See generally Cheshire, Fifoot and Furmston, *Law of Contract* (14th edn, 2001), pp 1 ff and literature there cited.

3　*Anon.* (1337) YB 50 Edw III, Trin, f 16, pl 8.

4　Fifoot, *History and Sources of the Common Law* (1949), pp 225 ff; David Ibbetson, 'Sale of Goods in the Fourteenth Century' (1991) 107 LQR 480; S. F. C. Milsom, 'Sale of Goods in the Fifteenth Century' (1961) 77 LQR 257 at p 272.

5　Eg by payment of a 'God's penny' (conventionally a farthing) to symbolize the making of the bargain, or of 'earnest money' (a forfeitable deposit as a pledge of good faith), or by part payment of the price, or production of a tally (a stick of wood with notches indicating payments of a given size, which was split in two, each party retaining one half). Frequently a bargain was sealed by a combination of a God's penny and earnest.

6　*Doige's Case* (1442) YB Trin 20 Hen VI, f 34, pl 4, per Fortescue CJ.

7　Ibid. This concept of debt as a proprietary claim was firmly embedded in the language in which debt claims were framed. Even in the Fair Courts and the Courts of the Staple, where merchants were accustomed to the notion of enforceable agreements, a claim for the price of goods traditionally took the form of an assertion that the defendant was 'detaining' the price. Conceptually, there was thus a close link between debt and detinue.

Yet for anything other than these basic rights – the right of the seller to the price, and of the buyer to the goods – the common law had little concern. The main control of sales transactions, apart from the civil jurisdiction of the merchant courts, who applied the *lex mercatoria*,[8] lay through the criminal law, with statutes prohibiting the use of false measures, the watering down of beer and the adulteration of food,[9] and local ordinances regulating the conduct of the market, trade by trade, which were enforced by the trade guilds and the borough courts.[10] Except for sales of food and drink by a dealer in victuals,[11] the seller did not impliedly warrant the quality of the goods he sold,[12] or even have a duty to disclose defects known to him;[13] nor, indeed, did the sale imply that the seller had a good title.[14] In short, *caveat emptor* was the principle that guided the courts. The buyer had eyes; let him use them, or suffer the consequences.[15] If he was unsure of the product or of his seller's title, his remedy was either to make inquiries of others or to exact suitable warranties from the seller.

If the seller knowingly made a false statement as to the nature or quality of the goods, or as to his title to them, he could be sued in tort for deceit;[16] and if he not merely asserted a fact but warranted its truth by express words of warranty, he was liable in deceit even though ignorant of the falsity of his statement.[17] Though the existence of a contract was essential to this warranty liability, it was not necessary

8 See p 3.

9 See, for example, Judicium Pillorie (1266) 51 Hen III, stat 6, which prescribed the punishment of the pillory and tumbrel for bakers giving short weight in bread and for butchers selling unwholesome meat. Cf. *Liber Albus*, Book III, Pt II: 'And if any default shall be found in the bread of a baker of the City, the first time, let him be drawn upon a hurdle from the Guildhall to his own house, through the great streets where there may be most people assembled, and through the great streets that are most dirty, with the faulty loaf hanging from his neck.' For a second offence it was the pillory; for the third, the baker had to forswear his trade within the City forever.

10 See generally Walton H. Hamilton, 'The Ancient Maxim Caveat Emptor', 40 Yale LJ 1133 (1931) at pp 1141 ff.

11 Where liability was imposed by ancient statute (*Burnby v Bollett* (1847) 16 M & W 644).

12 Co Litt 102, *a*.

13 The attitude of the common law was thus in marked contrast to that of the law merchant, which held the seller to a strict duty of good faith, imposing on him a liability for damages if he sold goods to which he had no title or which were not of merchantable quality.

14 See below. In early times such a policy was not unreasonable, for most sales took place at markets and fairs, and a bona fide purchaser in market overt acquired a good title even if the seller had no right to sell, so that there was not a widespread need for an implied undertaking as to title. For the reason underlying the market overt rule, see p 425. It has now been abolished (see p 425).

15 Fitzherbert, *New Natura Brevium* (8th edn, 1755), 94C; P. S. Atiyah, *The Rise and Fall of Freedom of Contract* (1979), pp 178 ff, pp 464 ff. Though of doubtful parentage (see Hamilton, 'The Ancient Maxim Caveat Emptor', 40 Yale LJ 1133 (1931)), this principle became so strongly rooted that as late as 1789 we find in the dissenting judgment of Grose J in *Pasley v Freeman* (1789) 3 Term Rep 51 the proposition, astonishing to modern eyes, that a person causing loss to another by a fraudulent misstatement incurred no liability except in the case of a contract, and even then only if the plaintiff had exacted a warranty, instead of relying on a bare affirmation, of which he ought to have tested the truth himself by appropriate inquiries.

16 See A. W. B. Simpson, *A History of the Common Law of Contract* (1975), pp 240 ff; Milsom (1961) 77 LQR 257 at pp 278 ff.

17 Milsom (1961) 77 LQR 257 at p 280, and *Historical Foundations of the Common Law* (2nd edn, 1971), p 364.

that the warranty should actually be a term of the contract; it sufficed that it was causally connected to the sales transaction by constituting an inducement to the buyer to buy.[18] In short, the seller's liability on a warranty was not in contract but in tort for making a false statement which (albeit made in good faith) deceived the buyer into entering into the contract. But in the absence of fraud, the mere affirmation of a fact by the seller was not enough to involve him in liability for the falsity of his statement unless he expressly warranted its truth, and his use of the word 'warrant' or 'warranty' had to be specifically pleaded in order to establish a cause of action. This was vividly illustrated in the famous case of *Chandelor v Lopus*.[19]

> The plaintiff brought an action upon the case against the defendant alleging that the latter, in selling a stone to the plaintiff, had affirmed it to be a Bezoar stone,[20] which it was not. The majority of the court (Anderson J dissenting) held that the allegation was insufficient to entitle the plaintiff to relief, since the defendant was not liable unless he had given a warranty.[21]

The proposition that a statement of fact could not by itself be a warranty in the absence of express words of warranty was ultimately abandoned;[22] the action for breach of express warranty continued to lie in tort for deceit, not in contract, though

---

18   When a claim for breach of warranty still lay only in deceit, it was laid down that the warranty had to relate to an existing fact and was not actionable if amounting merely to a promise for the future (see Blackstone, 3 Comm. 165, and *Anon* (1472) YB Trin 11 Edw IV, f 6, pl 10), a reasonable conclusion since at the time a promise is made it cannot be said that it is false save where the promisor misrepresents his intention, and the view then was that 'it is common learning that the intent of a man cannot be tried, for the Devil himself knows not the intent of a man', *Anon* (1477) YB 17 Edw IV, Pasch, f 1, pl 2, per Brian CJ). But when *assumpsit* became an alternative basis of the claim, this ground of objection disappeared, since the promise was now a matter of contract. The contractual basis of warranty having superseded the action in deceit for breach of warranty, the promissory nature of the remedy eventually assumed such dominance in the minds of the judges that it came to be assumed that a statement could be a warranty only if it formed part of the contractual undertaking (see n 27). This unfortunate failure to remember the representational function of warranty, as a statement which induced but did not necessarily form part of the contract, is largely responsible for the unhappy distinction now drawn in English contract law between 'mere' representations and terms of the contract. See p 81, and D. W. Greig, 'Misrepresentations and Sales of Goods' (1971) 87 LQR 179. American courts, influenced by that great scholar Samuel Williston, usually avoided falling into this trap. See *Williston on Sales* (rev. edn, 1973–4), paras 181–183, 194–197; and Williston, 'Representation and Warranty in Sales', 27 Harv L Rev 1 (1913), criticizing *Heilbut, Symonds & Co v Buckleton* [1913] AC 30. But cf S. J Stoljar, *Mistake and Misrepresentation*, pp 126–128.
19   (1603) Cro Jac 4. The prolonged influence of this case can be gauged from the fact that it was still being cited in 1957. See *Oscar Chess Ltd v Williams* [1957] 1 All ER 325, per Denning LJ at 327–330.
20   A stone found in the stomach of certain ruminants and reputed to have possessed wondrous medicinal properties.
21   The majority judgments also asserted, erroneously, that the defendant's knowledge of the falsity of his statement was not sufficient, Anderson J again dissenting. The plaintiff should, however, have succeeded on this ground. Subsequently, there was a new trial, in which Popham CJ, at least, was prepared to hold that the seller's concealment of a defect in title or quality would be actionable in deceit even if he had made no affirmation whatsoever. This expression of view appears to have been lost sight of in subsequent cases; and the outcome of the second action in *Chandelor v Lopus* is uncertain, though a statement by counsel in the later case of *Southern v How* (1618) Cro Jac 468 would seem to indicate that the plaintiff was successful. See 8 Harv L Rev 282 (1894).

in the absence of fraud the existence of a contract induced by the warranty was an essential ingredient of the defendant's liability.

Thus, case law on sale up to the seventeenth century, in so far as it emerged at all from the common law courts,[23] was largely devoted to allegations of fraud or breaches of express warranty, arguments that in the absence of these the pleadings were not well founded, and highly technical points arising from formalities imposed by the Statute of Frauds.[24] However, by the sixteenth century the courts were beginning to hold a defendant liable for breach of a contractual undertaking as such, not by way of a claim in tort but by an action on the case in *assumpsit*;[25] and in 1778 there came a significant breakthrough when it was held that a claim for breach of warranty[26] in a contract of sale could be brought in *assumpsit* as an alternative to deceit.[27] The availability of this alternative contractual basis having been established, it was but a short step to hold that in certain circumstances a warranty could be implied.

But only after a struggle was this notion accepted. First to secure recognition were the implied warranties of correspondence with description and sample on the sale of unascertained goods, description here embodying not merely identification in the present narrow sense but quality and performance.[28] This was not achieved without struggle either,[29] and for the first half of the nineteenth century the ambit of the

22 'If the court went on a distinction between the words *warranty* and *affirmation*, the case is not law; for it was rightly held by Holt CJ in the subsequent cases, and has been uniformly adopted ever since, that an affirmation at the time of a sale is a warranty provided it appear on evidence to have been so intended' (*Pasley v Freeman*, n 15, per Buller J). This statement by Buller J became the *locus classicus* for the nature of a warranty, despite the fact that in neither of the decisions of Holt CJ, on which it was based (namely *Crosse v Gardner* (1688) 1 Show 68 and *Medina v Stoughton* (1700) 1 Salk 210) was any reference made to a requirement that the maker of the statement should have intended it as a warranty. However, while adopting the statement, later courts have construed it as importing an objective test of intention.
23 Merchants often avoided the common law courts because of the delay, expense and technicality of the procedure, and resorted to their own courts. See p 4.
24 Most of which has been repealed.
25 *Jordan's Case* (1528) YB 27 Hen VIII, f 24, pl 3. This was carried a stage further in *Slade's Case* (1602) 4 Co Rep 91a, where a bargain and sale was held to imply a promise to pay the price sufficient to ground an action in *assumpsit* without the seller having to prove a distinct and express promise to pay.
26 It should be borne in mind that at this time the word 'warranty' did not have its present technical meaning of a minor term of the contract but denoted an affirmation of material fact (whether or not forming part of the promise) which induced the other party to enter into the contract. It is in this sense that the word is used in the present discussion.
27 *Stuart v Wilkins* (1778) 1 Doug KB 18. Eventually *assumpsit* replaced deceit altogether as the remedy for non-fraudulent breach of warranty, and it became established that no action in deceit would lie in the absence of fraud or recklessness by the defendant in the making of the statement (*Derry v Peek* (1889) 14 App Cas 337). As previously mentioned (n 18), the heavy emphasis that came to be placed on the promissory character of the buyer's remedy had unfortunate consequences for the concept of warranty.
28 See further p 281.
29 Thus in *Parkinson v Lee* (1802) 2 East 314, the court rejected the contention that the innocent seller of hops which rotted because the grain had been watered down by the grower and which therefore did not correspond with the perfectly good sample previously tendered was liable to the buyer, in the absence of an express warranty that the bulk corresponded with the sample.

implied warranties remained uncertain and the case law was confused and conflicting as the courts began uncertainly to move away from the principle of *caveat emptor*.[30] The courts were particularly reluctant to imply a warranty of quality or freedom from defects on the sale of horses, which were treated as a distinct category.[31]

A particular source of difficulty was the all-pervasive influence of land law, which until well into the nineteenth century dominated English law. The general law of contract was largely property orientated, and this was as true of sale of goods as of other contracts. Blackburn's famous work was entitled 'A Treatise on the Effect of the Contract of Sale on the Legal Rights of Property and Possession in Goods, Wares and Merchandise', and was primarily devoted to the property aspects of sales law and the impact of the transfer of property on risk, the right to sue for the price, the ability to bring actions in tort for interference with the goods, and the effect of insolvency of one of the parties on the rights of the other. The vendor's real rights – lien, stoppage in transit, rescission and resale – were treated at length, and considerable space was devoted to equitable interests and assignments, while merchantable quality was dismissed in a few pages and even these examined it in the context of conditions precedent to the passing of property.

Hence only gradually did the courts move away from the *caveat emptor* principle that characterized sales of land, and even then they continued to differentiate sharply between a sale of goods *in esse*, seen or capable of being examined by the buyer, and a sale of unascertained goods, for which the buyer relied on the seller's description. In *Jones v Just*[32] a useful recapitulation of principle came in a famous judgment of Mellor J that emphasized the distinction drawn between a sale of specific existing goods which the buyer was capable of inspecting himself, and which therefore did not attract an implied warranty even as regards latent defects,[33] and a sale by description[34] of goods manufactured or dealt in by the seller which were to be supplied for a particular purpose, or which the buyer had no opportunity to inspect, and in respect of which he therefore relied on the seller's skill and judgement.[35]

---

30 Contrast, for example, *Parker v Palmer* (1821) 4 B & Ald 387, *Lorymer v Smith* (1822) 1 B & C 1 and *Jones v Bright* (1829) 5 Bing 533 with *Barr v Gibson* (1838) 3 M & W 390, *Chanter v Hopkins* (1838) 4 M & W 399 and *Ormrod v Huth* (1845) 14 M & W 651. It is interesting to find that even in the latter half of the nineteenth century the courts had not fully separated tortious from contractual liability. See, for example, the judgment of Lindley J in *Hyman v Nye* (1881) 6 QBD 685, at 689.

31 See Paul Mitchell, 'The Development of Quality Obligations in Sale of Goods' (2001) 117 LQR 645, discussing in detail the evolution of implied terms in the nineteenth century.

32 (1868) LR 3 QB 197. For a criticism of the judgment of Mellor J, see S. J Stoljar, 'Conditions and Warranties on Sale' (1952) 15 MLR 425 at p 434.

33 Citing *Parkinson v Lee* (1802) 2 East 314. Cf. the Second Report of the Mercantile Law Commission in 1855, at p 11, contrasting the rule with that prevailing under Scots law.

34 At this time a sale of specific goods was assumed to be the antithesis of a sale by description. The buyer of specific goods necessarily bought the goods as seen, or as they would have been seen if he had exercised his right to examine. The modern doctrine that even a sale of specific goods is a sale by description if the goods are not bought for their unique qualities compared with other goods of the same class (p 304) had not then taken hold.

35 Citing *Brown v Edgington* (1841) 2 Man & G 279, *Jones v Bright*, n 30 and *Shepherd v Pybus* (1842) 3 Man & G 868.

Acceptance of the implied warranty of title was longer in coming. It was vigorously denied in 1849,[36] but adopted as the normal rule in 1864.[37]

In 1889 the Sale of Goods Bill was presented to Parliament. This had been drafted by Sir Mackenzie Chalmers, who had achieved such success in his codification of the law relating to bills of exchange;[38] and he produced a commentary which was to become a classic work on the Sale of Goods Act.[39] The Bill, after lapsing and being reintroduced in 1891, was radically altered during its passage through Parliament, emerging somewhat confusingly as the Sale of Goods Act 1893 although not in fact passed until 1894.[40] While primarily intended as a codification measure, the Act nevertheless embodied major deviations from the common-law rules; and though the draftsman presumably intended it to preserve the common law distinction between a sale of specific goods and a sale by description, he failed to make his intention sufficiently plain, thus paving the way for the application of a range of implied terms to contracts for the sale of specific goods.[41]

Despite the intense criticism to which the Sale of Goods Act has since been subjected,[42] it was for its time a superb work of draftsmanship, which was to become adopted almost verbatim throughout the common law world.[43] It restated, but also changed, the existing law of sale, and remained entirely unaltered until 1954, when s 4 of the Act[44] was repealed.[45] Further small, but significant, amendments were made by the Misrepresentation Act 1967,[46] the Criminal Law Act 1967[47]

---

36 *Morley v Attenborough* (1849) 3 Ex Ch 500. The argument of the defendant, accepted by the court, was that 'since in the transfer of property circumstances will inevitably occur by which one of the parties must be a loser, the loss, whether arising from defect of title or quality, must fall on the purchaser unless a deceit has been practised or a warranty given. The rule of the common law originated in a desire for peace; for if the rule were otherwise there could be numerous actions by successive purchasers against their respective sellers before the fault could be discovered.'

37 *Eichholz v Bannister* (1864) 17 CBNS 708, where Erle CJ stated that by the very act of selling the seller held out to the buyer that he was the owner of the goods, except where the circumstances were such as to indicate otherwise, eg on a forced sale by the sheriff, who in the nature of things could not be expected to vouch for the debtor's title.

38 Bills of Exchange Act 1882.

39 *Chalmers' Sale of Goods Act 1893* is now (*sub. nom. Sale of Goods Act 1979*) in its 18th edition (1981).

40 The Act is numbered 1894 (56 and 57 Vict) c 71. For a history of the Act, see the Introduction to the first edition (1894) of *Chalmers' Sale of Goods*.

41 See p 291.

42 See p 192 for some problems of language.

43 See p 7.

44 Which (re-enacting s 17 of the Statute of Frauds 1677) provided that, inter alia, contracts of sale for £10 and upwards and agreements not to be performed within a year were not to be enforced by action unless evidenced by a note or memorandum in writing signed by the party to be charged or his agent.

45 Law Reform (Enforcement of Contracts) Act 1954, s 1.

46 Section 4, amending ss 11(1)(c) and 35 of the Sale of Goods Act 1893. See p 340.

47 Repealing s 22(2) of the Sale of Goods Act 1893, which had provided that the provisions of s 22, dealing with sales in market overt, were not to affect the law relating to the sale of horses. The repeal was accompanied by repeal of the Elizabethan statutes relating to the sale of horses (namely the Sale of Horses Act 1555 and 1588) by s 10(2) and Sch 3, Pts I and III, of the Criminal Law Act 1967.

and the Theft Act 1968.[48] More radical textual changes were introduced by the Supply of Goods (Implied Terms) Act 1973[49] and further amendments were made by the Consumer Credit Act 1974[50] and the Unfair Contract Terms Act 1977.[51] Subsequently, these amendments were incorporated into a consolidating enactment, the Sale of Goods Act 1979, and further changes were made in 1994[52] and 1995.[53] Seven years later came the Sale and Supply of Goods to Consumers Regulations 2002[54] which implements the 1999 EC consumer sales Directive.[55] Unfortunately, this too has been effected by incorporation into the Sale of Goods Act instead of in a separate consumer sales enactment. This fact, coupled with the drafting techniques adopted, has resulted in a set of provisions governing consumer sales which are of great complexity in an area of law in which there is a particular need for clarity.[56] But in relation to general sales law the Sale of Goods Act remains for the most part in the form in which it was passed in 1894 – a fitting tribute to its creator but a damning illustration of the imperviousness to change of English sales law.[57]

48 Section 33(3) and Sch 3, Pt III, of the Theft Act repealed s 24 of the Sale of Goods Act, which had provided that the property in stolen goods disposed of in market overt revested in the owner on conviction of the offender. See also s 31(2) of the Theft Act, which makes it clear that conviction of the offender is not to affect the title to stolen property. But the market overt rule has now been abolished by the Sale of Goods (Amendment) Act 1994. See n 52.
49 Which amended ss 12–15, 55 and 62 of the Sale of Goods Act and added ss 55A and 62(1A). See ch 11.
50 Schedule 4, para 3 (making minor terminological changes in s 14(3) of the Sale of Goods Act, as amended by s 3 of the Supply of Goods (Implied Terms) Act 1973 so as to reflect the new terms in the Consumer Credit Act); para 4 (amending s 25 of the Sale of Goods Act 1893 to exclude conditional sale agreements which are consumer credit agreements for the purpose of the Consumer Credit Act – a textual amendment reflecting a similar provision previously contained in s 54 of the Hire-Purchase Act 1965); and Sch 5 (repealing s 14(6) of the Sale of Goods Act 1893).
51 See further, pp 326 ff.
52 Sale of Goods (Amendment) Act 1994, ss 1, 3(2), repealing the market overt exception to the *nemo dat* rule; Sale and Supply of Goods Act 1994, revising the implied term of quality and the rules as to deemed acceptance.
53 Sale of Goods (Amendment) Act 1995, making the prepaying buyer of an individual part of a bulk a co-owner of the bulk.
54 SI 2002/3045.
55 Directive 1999/44/EC of 25 May 1999 on certain aspects of the sale of consumer goods and associated guarantees.
56 For detailed analyses the reader is referred to *Benjamin's Sale of Goods, Special Supplement to the 6th edn* (2003), and Simon Whittaker, *Liability for Products*, ch 18 (publication due March 2005).
57 Cf. the Law Commission and Scottish Law Commission Report *Sale and Supply of Goods* (Cmd. 137, 1987), para 15: '… it is doubtful how far a process of 'patching' the Sale of Goods Act can continue. If further alterations to our law of sale are required, it might … be better to have a new Act or Acts rather than the old Act with amendments.'

7   The Contract of Sale: Its Nature and Function

The contract of sale is by far the most common type of contract. People buy goods for a variety of reasons. The most obvious, of course, is to enjoy their ownership and use. But in commercial dealings traders are not interested in goods as such, only in the profit that can be made, or the loss that can be avoided, by reselling them. In many cases therefore the trader buys goods without ever intending to take physical delivery but to resell at a profit or to hedge against the possibility of a loss. Even in a transaction on the futures market the contract remains one of sale and purchase, and if it is not closed out before the due delivery date, the seller has a duty to tender delivery and the buyer to accept it.[1]

I.   AMBIT OF THE SALE OF GOODS ACT

(i)   The Act as a code

The full title of the Sale of Goods Act 1893 was 'An Act for codifying the Law relating to the Sale of Goods', and in judgments and literature concerning sales law it is not infrequently referred to as 'the Code'. As originally drawn, the Bill 'endeavoured to reproduce as exactly as possible the existing law, leaving any amendments that might seem desirable to be introduced in Committee on the authority of the legislature'.[2] Substantial changes were in fact made to the Bill during its passage through Parliament, so that the resulting enactment represented partly a restatement of existing law in ordered form and partly a departure from common law rules of sale. The Sale of Goods Act 1979, which repealed the 1893 Act and amending legislation,[3] is a pure consolidation measure.

(ii)   The interpretation of the Act

The *locus classicus* for the approach to interpretation of a codifying enactment is the speech of Lord Herschell in *Bank of England v Vagliano Brothers*.[4] From this it is clear that in principle the interpretation of a codifying statute is no different from that of any other enactment. The statute must in the first place be

---

1 See pp 154–155.
2 M. D. Chalmers, Introduction to the first (1894) edition of *The Sale of Goods Act 1893*.
3 See p 189. The one section of the 1893 Act left unrepealed by the Sale of Goods Act 1979 was 26, dealing with the effect of levy of execution against goods. This, however, has since been repealed and re-enacted by the Supreme Court Act 1981, s 147.
4 [1891] AC 107, at 144–145.

construed according to its natural meaning, unaided by reference to prior case law. Only if the statutory provisions are unclear is it permissible to infer that the Act did not intend to change the law, and to resort to the earlier case law in order to establish what the law was previously. This applies equally to an enactment consolidating earlier legislation, even where the enactment is a 'pure' consolidation measure.[5] So decisions on the Sale of Goods Act 1893 should not be used to interpret the Sale of Goods Act 1979 where the meaning of the latter is clear.[6]

While the courts have paid lip-service to the rule of interpretation enunciated by Lord Herschell, they have frequently ignored it when a broad interpretation of the statutory provisions would produce a result running counter to their views of desirable legal policy. Of no provisions is this more true than those dealing with the power of a non-owner to pass a good title to a bona fide purchaser.[7] Issues of this kind could have been resolved purely from the language of the Act itself, by deciding whether s 21(1) giving effect to the common law rule *nemo dat quod non habet* should in a given case be construed as intended to have priority except where a strict construction of the exceptions contained in other sections produced the opposite result. But time and again the courts have approached the matter not by looking at the relationship between s 21 and such other provisions but by harking back to the common-law rule and then going on to hold that to the extent to which the statutory provisions would have the effect of depriving the owner of title to his goods they must be strictly construed.[8]

(iii) Preservation of the common-law rules

In contrast to codes of the continental type, English codifying statutes do not aspire to be all-embracing in the field of law to which they are devoted. In particular, the common law rules survive except so far as expressly or impliedly displaced by the legislation. The Sale of Goods Act expressly preserves a whole range of common law rules and provisions of other statutes.

> 62.(1) The rules in bankruptcy relating to contracts of sale apply to those contracts, notwithstanding anything in this Act.
> (2) The rules of the common law, including the law merchant, except in so far as they are inconsistent with the provisions of this Act, and in particular the rules relating to the law of principal and agent and the effect of fraud, misrepresentation, duress or coercion, mistake, or other invalidating cause, apply to contracts for the sale of goods.
> (3) Nothing in this Act or the Sale of Goods Act 1893 affects the enactments relating to bills of sale, or any enactment relating to the sale of goods which is not expressly repealed or amended by this Act or that.

5 *Farrell v Alexander* [1977] AC 59; *R. v Heron* [1982] 1 All ER 993. The various types of consolidation were described by Lord Simon in the former case and by Lord Scarman in the latter.
6 This is the theory. But since the Sale of Goods Act 1979 closely follows the wording of the 1893 Act, the court may be receptive to an argument that earlier case law can be referred to in order to show that an apparently clear provision in fact raises difficulties of interpretation.
7 See pp 424 ff.
8 See, for example, the passage from the judgment of Sellers LJ in *Newtons of Wembley Ltd v Williams* [1965] 1 QB 560 quoted, p 22.

(iv) What are 'the rules of the common law'?

When s 62(2) provides that 'the rules of the common law ... apply to contracts for the sale of goods', what does this mean? Is the phrase 'common law' employed in the broad sense, in contradistinction to statute law, or in the narrower sense of law as opposed to equity? The question is not simply of theoretical significance, for if the narrower sense is what is intended, the Act must be construed as negating equitable remedies in contracts of sale except to the extent to which these are specifically reproduced. On this basis the Act would not permit equitable rescission for innocent misrepresentation, specific performance of contracts for the sale of unascertained goods, the grant of an injunction to restrain an actual or threatened breach, rectification of a contract document or the setting aside in equity of a contract of sale for mistake.

In England the case for the narrower construction of s 62(2) has in effect gone by default, since while the point has never been argued in any reported case, it has been tacitly assumed in a number of cases that some at least of these equitable remedies are available[9] except to the extent to which these are circumscribed by the express provisions of the Act;[10] and despite two overseas decisions to the contrary,[11] there is little doubt that if the point were now to be raised, an English court would treat 'the rules of common law' as embracing those of equity.

2.   THE LANGUAGE OF THE SALE OF GOODS ACT

Compared with modern legislation, the Sale of Goods Act is delightfully easy to read. Perusal of any section conveys at once the basic idea the draftsman is trying to implant. The tortuousness of recent statutes is avoided, and the impression is given of limpid clarity. But this simplicity is deceptive. The Sale of Goods Act, with its taut phraseology, epitomizes the fundamental problem of language in expressing legal concepts.[12] At various points the draftsman has been so concise as to render an apparently self-evident proposition quite ambiguous. For example, there are several instances of definitions where it is unclear whether the draftsman is describing what a party must be taken to have *contracted* to do or what is the factual situation. Thus, 'specific goods' are defined as goods identified and agreed upon at the time of the contract.[13] Does 'contract for the sale of specific

---

9 *Goldsmith v Rodger* [1962] 2 Lloyd's Rep 249 (innocent misrepresentation) (and cf *Leaf v International Galleries Ltd* [1950] 2 KB 86 and *Long v Lloyd* [1958] 1 WLR 753); *Metropolitan Electric Supply Co Ltd v Ginder* [1901] 2 Ch 799 (injunction); *Behnke v Bede Shipping Co Ltd* [1927] 1 KB 649 (specific performance and injunction); *F. E. Rose Ltd v W. H. Pim & Co Ltd* [1953] 2 QB 450 (rectification).

10 As in the case of specific performance, which is said to be available only where the goods are specific or ascertained, on the footing that s 52 of the Act is exhaustive on this point. See p 363.

11 *Riddiford v Warren* (1901) 20 NZLR 572 (New Zealand Court of Appeal); *Watt v Westhoven* [1933] VLR 458 (Full Court of Victoria). Both of these cases held that a contract of sale cannot be rescinded for innocent misrepresentation except within the narrow limits laid down by the common law (as opposed to equity), viz such a complete difference in substance between what was bargained for and what was obtained as to constitute a total failure of consideration.

12 See p 21.

13 Section 61(1).

goods'[14] mean a contract in which the goods are *presented* as specific, whether or not they are in fact identifiable at the time of contract, or does it mean a contract for the sale of goods which are in fact identifiable? In this particular case it becomes clear that the draftsman is referring to the factual situation, not the undertaking of the parties in their contract.[15] On the other hand, when we raise the same question in relation to the phrase 'deliverable state'[16] we reach a different conclusion. Goods are in a deliverable state when they are in such a state that the buyer would under the contract be bound to take delivery of them.[17] When s 18, r 1 refers to 'an unconditional contract for the sale of specific goods in a deliverable state', it is not talking about a contract for the sale of goods which are *in fact* in a deliverable state but a contract in which the goods are offered as being in a deliverable state, that is, a contract in which the seller has not expressly undertaken to do anything in relation to them prior to the tender of delivery.[18]

Similar problems of ambiguity arise in relation to the word 'description'. This has been held in numerous cases to indicate that which contractually identifies the goods. But it is clear that 'identification' has a different meaning in the case of a contract for the sale of specific goods from that which it has when the contract relates to unascertained goods.[19]

The root of the problem, as with so many difficulties in the law, is the use of a single word to encompass a variety of facts or events. The word thus has to carry more than it is equipped to bear, in that though it is defined (whether in the Act or by judicial interpretation) in language suggesting a unique meaning, it is found to possess meanings which vary according to the circumstances in which it has to be applied, so that the word is not susceptible of consistent interpretation throughout the Act. Among such words are 'description',[20] 'condition',[21] 'delivery',[22] 'accept',[23] 'state'[24] and 'sell'.[25]

The Act contains other linguistic pitfalls. For example, r 1 of s 18 is framed as if, in the conditions stated in the rule, it had executive force, whereas the opening words of s 18 show that the rules are only expressions of presumed *intention*, and the fact that r 1 applies so as to express the presumed intention of the parties does not necessarily mean that such intention is in all cases effective.[26]

Finally, the Act creates categories and situations which it presents as exhaustive, whereas in fact there is often either an inadequate subdivision or a complete *casus omissus*. Thus, 'unascertained goods' is presented as a single species whereas it

14 See ss 6, 7, 17–19.
15 See p 208.
16 Section 18, rr 1, 3, 5.
17 Section 61(1).
18 See p 232.
19 See p 292.
20 See p 291.
21 See pp 231, 279.
22 See p 263.
23 See p 346.
24 See pp 234–235.
25 See p 300.
26 See pp 230–233.

subdivides into wholly unascertained and quasi-specific goods;[27] and ss 6 and 7 are confined to specific goods, the Act saying nothing as to what is the position where the goods are, for example, not specific but 'ascertained'. This silence might lead to the erroneous conclusion that in the cases not described, the legal consequences stipulated would not occur.[28] From this, we may conclude that to construe the Act as if it were complete and self-consistent is a futile exercise. We ought not to ascribe to the draftsman a foresight he cannot have possessed, nor to be excessively pedantic in literal construction, for much of what passes as the internal logic of the Act has been invented by commentators and was not the design of its creator.

3.   THE CONTRACT OF SALE DEFINED

(i)   The ingredients of the contract

The contract of sale is defined in s 2 of the Sale of Goods Act, which is worth setting out in full.

(1)   A contract of sale of goods is a contract by which the seller transfers or agrees to transfer the property in goods to the buyer for a money consideration, called the price.
(2)   There may be a contract of sale between one part owner and another.
(3)   A contract of sale may be absolute or conditional.
(4)   Where under a contract of sale the property in the goods is transferred from the seller to the buyer the contract is called a sale.
(5)   Where under a contract of sale the transfer of the property in the goods is to take place at a future time or subject to some condition later to be fulfilled the contract is called an agreement to sell.
(6)   An agreement to sell becomes a sale when the time elapses or the conditions are fulfilled subject to which the property in the goods is to be transferred.

The root definition in s 2(1), though concisely expressed, contains a number of ingredients the analysis of which enables us to perceive the essential nature of sale and to distinguish it from various cognate transactions. Whether the distinction is in any given case of practical importance is another question, to which we shall revert hereafter.[29] Before we plunge more deeply, we can state the general proposition that the legal objective of a contract of sale is, from the buyer's viewpoint, to obtain ownership and, from the seller's, to receive the price. It is worth emphasizing the word 'legal', because here, as elsewhere in the field of commerce, the objectives of the law and those of the business person are by no means necessarily the same. Indeed, while it would be hard to frame a definition of sale which made no reference to the transfer of 'property' or 'ownership', the preoccupation of English law with ownership as the essential feature for which the buyer bargains is excessive, not to say obsessional.[30]

But there are many transactions involving the transfer of ownership which are not contracts of sale;[31] and while a sale must involve the passing of some form of

27 See p 210.
28 See p 261.
29 See p 203.
30 See p 215.
31 For example, gifts, mortgages (s 62(4)), exchanges (barter), the supply of materials under a contract for work and materials.

ownership, this does not necessarily involve a transfer of absolute title to the goods. There are six key expressions in s 2(1), namely 'contract of sale of goods', 'seller', 'buyer', 'property', and 'money consideration'. Each of these must now be examined in turn.

(ii) 'Contract of sale of goods'

1. Contract of sale

For the purpose of the Act 'contract of sale' includes an agreement to sell as well as a sale.[32] The latter is not merely a contract but a conveyance, operating to transfer the property in the goods to the buyer; the former is a mere agreement, some further act or event being necessary before the property can vest in the buyer under the contract.[33] The agreement must, of course, be a contract.[34]

By s 61(1), 'sale' includes a bargain and sale as well as a sale and delivery, thus emphasizing the point which emerges from s 2, that delivery is not an essential element of a sale contract and that the property may pass to the buyer before delivery.[35]

The Act further provides that its provisions are not to apply to any transaction in the form of a contract of sale which is intended to operate by way of mortgage, pledge, charge or other security.[36] Thus a transfer of goods by way of mortgage to secure a loan is not a sale, even though it involves the transfer of property for a money consideration and even if the mortgage is disguised as a sale.

In order for the agreement to be a sale, it must have as its objective the transfer of property in *goods*.[37] Contracts of sale within the Act are thus to be contrasted with (a) agreements for the transfer of some other form of asset, notably land and choses in action, and (b) agreements the purpose of which is not to transfer an asset as such but to provide services – ie contracts of labour with or without materials.

2. Goods

The Act[38] defines 'goods' as including all personal[39] chattels other than things in action[40] and money,[41] and as including emblements,[42] industrial growing crops[43]

---

32 Section 61(1).
33 See pp 228 ff. 'Agreement for sale' includes a purported sale of future property (s 5(3)).
34 For the ingredients of a contract, see pp 73 ff.
35 See also s 18, r 1, and p 231.
36 Section 62(4). This would in any event follow from the requirements of s 1 that the contract must transfer or provide for the transfer of the property in the goods. See p 199.
37 In addition, the consideration must be a money payment (the price). See pp 202–203.
38 Section 61(1).
39 See p 28.
40 See pp 29, 47.
41 See ch 17.
42 That is, annual crops such as corn, grain, potatoes, produced by agricultural labour, in contrast to *fructus naturales*, ie natural growth of the soil, such as timber and grass, which at common law are not chattels but part of the land on which they grow.
43 See *Benjamin's Sale of Goods* (6th edn, 2002), para 1–093.

and things attached to or forming part of the land which are agreed to be severed before sale or under the contract of sale. It has never been decided whether goods include computer hardware or software. However, in a helpful obiter dictum in *St Albans City and District Council v International Computers Ltd*[44] Sir Iain Glidewell concluded that while goods include hardware, a computer disk on which a program is recorded[45] and a whole computer system covering both hardware and software,[46] a contract for the sale of the program itself is not a contract for the sale of goods.[47] It has also been held in Australia that software supplied by electronic means does not constitute goods.[48] A sale of fixtures or timber to be severed before sale or pursuant to the sale contract is a sale of goods. So also is a sale of crops to be severed, whether they be industrial growing crops or *fructus naturales*. Whether the grant of a right to part of the physical content of land – minerals, soil, underground water, sand and gravel, and the like – is a contract of sale of the materials in question depends upon the circumstances. If the transferor is to extract and to supply at a price, the transaction is usually one of sale.[49] If it is left to the transferee to extract, it will usually be a sale if he is under an *obligation* to extract and to pay for the materials extracted and is not intended to acquire any interest in the materials prior to extraction.[50] If, however, the transferee is simply charged a sum of money for the *privilege* of working the land, being free to work it or not as he pleases,[51] or if, though obliged to extract, he is intended to be given an interest in the materials *in situ* and not as chattels, the transaction amounts to the grant of a profit *à prendre*;[52] and this is the case even if the consideration for the grant is directly related to the quantity of material extracted.[53] Where the transferee acquires rights over the materials as part of the purchase or lease of the land, no contract of sale of goods is involved, the materials merely passing under the conveyance or lease of the land.[54] Where the equipment to which the contract applies is intended to be affixed to land or incorporated in buildings, as in the case of central heating equiment, a lift or swimming pool, and has already been affixed or incorporated at the time of the

44 [1996] 4 All ER 481 at 492.
45 However, it does not follow that all disks are supplied under a contract of sale. In many cases the supplier simply grants a licence to use the disk or retains rights to restrict its use or sale.
46 On this point citing the decision of Rogers J in *Toby Constructions Pty Ltd v Computa Bar (Sales) Pty Ltd* [1983] 2 NSWLR 48.
47 For a more detailed discussion, see P.S. Atiyah, John N. Adams and Hector MacQueen, *The Sale of Goods* (10th edn, 2001), pp 66 ff.
48 *ASX Operations Pty Ltd v Pont Data Australia Pty Ltd* (1990) 27 FCR 460.
49 In this case, the materials to be extracted fall squarely within the definition of 'goods' in s 61(1) of the Sale of Goods Act and the stipulated sum is the consideration for their supply.
50 As in *Amco Enterprises Pty Ltd v Wade* [1968] Qd R 445.
51 See *Egmont Box Co Ltd v Registrar-General of Lands* [1920] NZLR 741 (timber).
52 See *Morgan v Russell and Sons* [1909] 1 KB 357.
53 Ibid.
54 This is a long-standing common law principle; and see Law of Property Act 1925, s 205(1)(ix). However, there are special rules governing coal and coal mines, petroleum, royal metals (gold and silver) and water. See *Cheshire and Burn's Modern Law of Real Property* (16th edn, 2000), pp 172 ff; R. M. Goode, *Proprietary Rights and Insolvency in Sales Transactions* (2nd edn, 1989), ch II.

contract, it does not constitute goods, since title has passed to the owner of the land or building: *quiquid planatur solo, solo cedit.*[55]

3. Services

The distinction between a sale of goods and a provision of services involving the supply of materials is well recognized but not always easy to apply. If, for example, a person undertakes to paint a portrait, to construct a ship, to manufacture furniture to a special order or to install central heating, are these contracts of sale or contracts for work and materials? English courts have wobbled uncertainly from one test to another, first adopting the criterion of relative importance of the labour and the materials,[56] then shifting position to hold that any transaction under which the work results in the production of an article that can be said to be the subject of a sale is a contract of sale,[57] and finally reverting to a modified form of the original test, namely whether the substance of the contract is the exercise of skill and labour, in which the provision of materials is subsidiary, or whether it is the supply of a finished product by way of sale.[58] These tests are not particularly helpful, and the cases are irreconcilable. Where that which is to be supplied is not intended to be furnished as a distinct chattel at all, as where it is to be incorporated as a fixture to land[59] or as an accession to a chattel[60] before the owner of the land or chattel takes control of it, the contract will usually be considered a contract for skill and labour, not a contract for the sale of goods. The same principle applies where the services consist primarily of work that has not gone into the production of the material supplied and the latter is merely subsidiary to the contract as a whole.[61] Where, on the other hand, most of the skill and labour goes into the creation of the article supplied,[62] the strong tendency of the courts is to treat the contract as one of sale, however artistic the product and however valuable or expensive the services of the producer.[63]

---

55 *Wake v Hall* (1880) 7 QBD 295. For a detailed discussion of fixtures in relation to hire-agreements, see R. M. Goode, *Hire-Purchase Law and Practice* (2nd edn) ch 32. Where equipment is leased under an agreement concluded only after it has become a fixture, the lessor is not the owner and cannot claim capital allowances (*Melluish v BMI (No 3) Ltd* [1996] AC 454). See p 237.

56 *Clay v Yates* (1856) 1 H & N 73.

57 *Lee v Griffin* (1861) 1 B & S 272.

58 *Robinson v Graves* [1935] 1 KB 579.

59 As in the case of central heating, built-in machinery in a factory, and the like.

60 As where in the course of repairing or improving goods a part is incorporated in such a way that it cannot be removed without material damage to the goods.

61 *Dodd v Wilson* [1946] 2 All ER 691 (inoculation of cattle with serum by veterinary surgeon held contract for services, not for sale of serum, though ultimately this made no difference to the result of the case – see p 204). But for certain purposes (eg the right to claim or retain an instalment payment under a contract) the court will distinguish a pure contract of sale from one involving a substantial work and materials content. See, for example, *Hyundai Heavy Industries Co v Papadopoulos* [1980] 1 WLR 1129.

62 See *Cammell Laird & Co Ltd v Manganeze Bronze & Brass Co Ltd* [1934] AC 402 (contract to construct two ships' propellers held contract of sale).

63 Thus the courts have held that the supply of a meal in a restaurant is a contract of sale (*Lockett v A. & M. Charles Ltd* [1938] 4 All ER 170), as is the supply of dentures by a dentist (*Lee v Griffin*, n 57).

4.   *Contracts for the making up of goods from another's materials*

Where A supplies materials to B to be made up into a finished product, ownership of the materials to remain in A and B to have no right to use the materials for any purpose of his own, the contract is one of work and labour, unless the bulk of the materials is to be supplied by the manufacturer, in which case the contract is one of sale. Where the agreement is that A shall part with ownership of the materials and acquire the finished product for an agreed money sum, the transaction is one of sale. If several suppliers contribute materials on terms that they are to remain the owners of what they supply and of any amalgam resulting from the commingling of the materials pending appropriation to them of particular units of the finished product, the contract is *sui generis*.[64] The effect of the commingling is that the individual titles previously held by the suppliers to what each contributed are replaced by ownership in common of the amalgam in the agreed proportions pending delivery by the manufacturer to each supplier of the contractual quantity to which that supplier is entitled.[65] Upon each such delivery the supplier to whom it is made acquires title to what is delivered and its interest in the amalgam is either extinguished, if the full contract quantity is delivered, or proportionately reduced, if the delivery is less than the full quantity. If a supplier reserves title to the materials supplied until these have been paid for and then limits its co-ownership to the value of such proportion of the bulk as will equal the sum owing to it, that is likely to be held a floating charge, not an effective reservation of title, and to be avoided in the manufacturer's winding up if not previously registered.[66]

(iii) 'Seller' and 'buyer'

Naturally there must be a seller and a buyer. 'Seller' means a person who sells or agrees to sell goods; 'buyer', a person who buys or agrees to buy goods.[67] An agreement is thus not a contract of sale unless the buyer is bound to buy as the seller is to sell, so that a hire-purchase agreement, by which the hirer has the option to purchase but no obligation to do so, is not a contract of sale within the Act.[68] An agreement between two parties by which one agrees to act as agent in selling the other's goods or in buying goods on behalf of the other is an agency agreement, not a sale contract. The point is an obvious one and the cases have been concerned not with the enunciation of so self-evident a principle but with the problem of determining whether on the facts the relationship between the parties was that of seller and buyer or of principal and agent. The problem is complicated by the fact that in the commercial world the word 'agent' is frequently used in a loose sense to denote a distributor of the supplier, whether in truth selling as agent or on the other

---

64 *Coleman v Harvey* [1989] 1 NZLR 723. See p 221.

65 Where the manufacturer produces a bulk greater in quantity than is needed to satisfy all it contracts, it will be a co-owner to the extent of the excess.

66 *ICI New Zealand Ltd v Agnew* [1998] 2 NZLR 129. See further as to reservation of title, pp 584, 607, and Duncan Webb, 'Title and Transformation: Who Owns Manufactured Goods?' [2000] JBL 513.

67 Sale of Goods Act 1979, s 61(1). But 'seller' is given an extended meaning for the purpose of Part IV of the Act. See s 38(2) and p 409, n 135.

68 *Helby v Matthews* [1895] AC 471. See p 434.

hand buying and reselling on his own account; but the label used by the parties does not alter the legal nature of the transaction.[69] The primary test is whether the alleged agent is obliged to pay for the goods himself, irrespective of whether he makes a sale and without any obligation on him to account for the proceeds of such sale, or whether his duty is to account for the proceeds of sale as such, as opposed to a payment duty arising from a guarantee that a sale will be made or that the buyer will pay the price.[70]

(iv) 'Property'

We now come to a word that has caused a good deal of trouble. An essential ingredient of a contract of sale is a transfer or agreement for the transfer of 'the property' in goods. What does this mean? Does it denote absolute ownership, in the sense of the best possible title, which no one is in a position to challenge, or will the definition be satisfied by something less? And is there a distinction between property and title?

It will be recalled that the Act divides contracts of sale into executed contracts (ie sales) which are immediately effective to transfer the property in the goods to the buyer, and which thus constitute simultaneously a contract and a conveyance, and executory contracts (ie agreements to sell) by which either the parties agree that the property shall pass at a future time, whether automatically or subject to the performance of some condition,[71] or there is a purported sale of future goods.[72] It is clear that unless the parties intend that a legal title (whether or not the *best* title) to an absolute interest in the goods shall pass to the transferee, the agreement is not a contract of sale at all.[73] Thus to be a contract of sale, the transaction must be one in which the transferor is to transfer a legal title. Moreover, an intention to transfer the totality of his actual interest is a minimum requirement to establish even an executory sale contract.[74] The Act itself tells us that 'property' means the general property in goods, not merely a special property,[75] thus excluding agreements the object of which is to transfer a limited possessory interest, eg by way of bailment or pledge.[76] Even a mortgage, which involves more than the conferment of a special property since it passes ownership to the mortgagee, would thus be outside the definition of a contract of sale,[77] independently of the express provision in the Act

---

69 *W. T. Lamb & Sons v Goring Brick Co Ltd* [1932] 1 KB 710; *International Harvester Co of Australia Pty Ltd v Carringan's Hazeldene Pastoral Co* (1958) 100 CLR 644.

70 For various other tests, see *Dixon v London Small Arms Co* (1876) 1 App Cas 632. See further p 205.

71 Sale of Goods Act 1979, s 2(5).

72 Ibid, s 5(3).

73 For a discussion of the relationship between interest and title, see p 31.

74 Thus a sole owner's transfer of only part of his interest so as to create a tenancy in common would not be a sale of goods. Similarly, a transfer by a co-owner of part of his interest would be outside the statutory definition (cf *Benjamin's Sale of Goods*, para 1-121). On the other hand, one co-owner who for a money consideration divests himself altogether of his interest in favour of the other or others is thereby making a sale, a point brought out by s 2(2) of the Act.

75 Section 61(1).

76 Pledge and other security transactions are in any event expressly excluded by s 62(4).

77 See *Beckett v Tower Assets Co* [1891] 1 QB 1.

to that effect,[78] since the mortgagor retains an equity of redemption and is thus not contracting to part with the entirety of his interest.[79]

Next, we must consider the case where the intention of the parties, viewed objectively,[80] is that an indefeasible title shall pass to the buyer, but at a future time. This is not a sale, since no interest in the goods passes to the intended transferee at the time of the contract. It is, however, an agreement to sell. In general, this remains true even if at the time of the contract the seller does not have any title to the goods[81] and indeed even if they do not then exist.[82] Further, the fact that the creation or acquisition of the goods is outside the seller's control does not of itself prevent the contract from amounting to an agreement to sell. What a man promises and what he can perform are two different things. There are exceptional cases in which a contract will not come into existence in these circumstances, as where it is impossible of performance by reason of the fact that the goods already belong to the buyer[83] or are mistakenly believed to exist when they have either never existed at all[84] or have ceased to exist.[85] Even a mistake of one of these kinds will not preclude the contract from constituting an agreement to sell if the mistake was solely that of the buyer[86] or if the seller expressly or impliedly warranted the existence of the goods.[87] In such a case, though a sale is impossible, there is none the less an agreement to sell, for the breach of which the party at risk is liable in damages.[88]

The third possibility is that the seller undertakes an immediate transfer of an indefeasible title (an undertaking which is usually implied[89]) but his title is defective or even nonexistent. Again, it is clear that at the very least an agreement to sell is created,[90] for, as we have just seen, the fact that the seller cannot perform does not mean that he has not contracted to do so. But does the transaction amount

---

78 Section 62(4). The point is not wholly unimportant, for the word 'sale' appears in the Factors Act 1889 but is not there defined.

79 On the other hand, a person with title to an absolute interest in a chattel who, in consideration of a stated price, agrees to hold the chattel on trust for that other thereby brings into existence a contract of sale, even if not expressly agreeing to transfer the legal title, for the beneficiary absolutely entitled can at any time call for the legal title to be transferred to him, under the rule in *Saunders v Vautier* (1841) 4 Beav 115.

80 A basic principle of contract law. See pp 76–77.

81 Sale of Goods Act, s 5; *Rowland v Divall* [1923] 2 KB 500.

82 Sale of Goods Act, s 5; *McRae v Commonwealth Disposals Commissions* (1950) 84 CLR 377.

83 See *Bell v Lever Bros Ltd* [1932] AC 161, per Lord Atkin at 218.

84 See ibid, at 217.

85 Sale of Goods Act, s 6.

86 Who would have an alternative claim in tort for fraud.

87 As in *McRae v Commonwealth Disposals Commissions*, n 83. For a discussion of some of the difficulties arising from s 6 of the Sale of Goods Act, see Atiyah, *Sale of Goods*, pp 93 ff; G. H. Treitel, *Law of Contract* (11th edn, 2003), p 296.

88 If it is the buyer who accepts the risk that the goods do not exist, there is a binding contract, but it is an *emptio spei*, ie a sale of a chance, not a contract of sale of goods, and is thus outside the Sale of Goods Act. Such a contract is to be distinguished from a contract of sale dependent on a contingency (see Sale of Goods Act, s 5(2)), which falls to the ground if the contingency fails to occur within the stipulated time (or if none, within a reasonable time), whereas on the sale of a chance the buyer undertakes to pay the price however the chance turns out.

89 Sale of Goods Act, s 12(1). Such transfer is considered fundamental to the agreement. See p 215.

90 Sale of Goods Act 1979, s 5(3).

to a sale? Beguiled by an uncharacteristic lapse on the part of Lord Atkin in *Rowland v Divall*,[91] some writers have asserted that 'property' means indefeasible title and that a transfer by one whose title is not the best cannot be a sale.[92] Such a conclusion is so at variance not only with the express language of s 5(3) of the Act itself but with the whole legal development of title to chattels that it is difficult to see how the argument has ever taken root. The implied undertaking as to title in s 12 is expressed to arise 'in a contract of sale'; and s 12(1) tells us that the implied condition, in the case of a sale (as opposed to an agreement to sell), is that the seller has a right to sell the goods. But if every sale by definition involves a transfer of the best title, then the implied condition can never become operative on a sale; for if the seller *has* the best title, the implied condition is redundant; and if he has not, then *ex hypothesi* the purported transfer is not a sale and s 12(1) does not apply. The argument that transfer of the best title is essential to a sale thus involves the proposition that a breach of the implied condition that the seller has a right to sell is impossible. Moreover, s 5(1) of the Act includes under the heading of 'existing goods' goods which, though not owned by the seller, are in his possession, and thus implies that a possessory title suffices.[93] Finally, the provisions of ss 24 and 25, enabling a non-owner delivering goods 'under any sale' to pass a good title,[94] would make no sense if the sale by a non-owner were not a sale at all. The same applies to the opening words of s 21(1).

Yet if 'property' does not mean absolute ownership, what does it mean? Plainly *something* must be transferred to the buyer if the transaction is to qualify as a sale. The answer, as was pointed out in a penetrating article previously referred to,[95] is *any* title (however imperfect) if it is a title to the absolute legal[96] interest in the goods, as opposed to some lesser interest. This involves two distinct ingredients. First, the seller must be asserting a right of dominion over the goods, not merely a right to enjoy them for life or for some other limited period, eg under a bailment.[97]

---

91 See n 81 at 506–507. See to the same effect the judgment of May LJ in *National Employers Mutual General Insurance Association v Jones* [1987] 3 All ER 385 at 396, an approach avoided by other members of the Court of Appeal and by the House of Lords [1990] 1 AC 24. See pp 436–437.

92 The question has generated much academic heat, with occasional shafts of academic light. By far the most penetrating analysis to date is by G. Battersby and A. D. Preston, 'The Concepts of "Property", "Title" and "Owner" Used in the Sale of Goods Act 1893' (1972) 35 MLR 268, which effectively destroys the argument that 'property' denotes the best title. See also G. Battersby, 'A Reconsideration of "Property" and "Title" in the Sale of Goods Act' [2001] J.B.L 1, a response to arguments by Lisa McClure, Chantal Stebbings and Gordon Goldberg, 'The History of a Hunt for Simplicity and Coherence in the Field of "Ownership", "Possession", "Property" and "Title"' [1992] Denning LJ 103 and H.L. Ho, 'Some Reflections on "Property" and "Title" in the Sale of Goods Act' [1997] CLJ 571.

93 See further p 229.

94 See pp 431 ff.

95 Battersby and Preston, n 92.

96 As opposed to equitable; see above.

97 The fact that the seller is in truth a mere bailee (eg, under a hiring or hire-purchase agreement) is irrelevant. What matters is the character with which he has chosen to invest his possession. If while in possession as bailee he does an act in relation to the goods which is adverse to his bailor's rights, as by offering to sell them, he thereby asserts an absolute interest and relies on his possession as title to such interest. If, on the other hand, he undertakes merely to transfer his interest as bailee, he is not asserting dominion over the goods and the transfer of his interest cannot be a sale.

Secondly, he must establish some title to that right (though not necessarily the best title). This he does by showing (a) that his title is in fact indefeasible,[98] or (b) that he is in actual or constructive possession,[99] including constructive possession as transferee of a current possessory title where physical possession remains with the transferor.[100] In short, while the seller, unless otherwise agreed, owes a duty to the buyer to transfer an indefeasible title, the contract will still be a sale if he transfers a possessory title. If, however, he is not able to establish any title at all to the asserted right of dominion, he has nothing to convey and the contract is not a sale but an agreement to sell.[101]

The remaining alternative is that the seller undertakes to transfer merely such title as he or a third person may have. Assuming the seller himself has some title and that this is to be transferred immediately, then for the reasons already advanced the transaction constitutes a sale within the Sale of Goods Act, a point now put beyond doubt by s 12(3) of the Act.[102] If the seller's undertaking is to make a future transfer of his limited title, the contract is an agreement to sell. Where the seller undertakes to transfer such title as a third person may have, the contract will be a sale if that third person has some title and the transfer is immediate,[103] but will otherwise be an agreement to sell.

We may conclude, then, that when the Sale of Goods Act refers to 'property' it means title to an absolute interest, and that while a person who has no title may enter into an agreement to sell, he cannot conclude a sale except where having a power of sale despite not having any title himself.[104] The Act uses the term 'property' when describing the passing of ownership 'as between seller and buyer'[105] and 'title' when laying down rules dealing with ownership disputes between a seller or buyer and a third party.[106]

(v) 'Money consideration'

Since in a sale transaction the goods and the money are contrasted, the Act restricts contracts of sale to those contracts in which the consideration for the transfer of the

98 For the modes of obtaining indefeasible title, see pp 36–37.

99 This generates a title which the law will protect against all except the person with a better right to possession. See pp 31–32.

100 That is, a title derived from or through one who has continued to hold possession, being a title which has not been destroyed under some exception to the *nemo dat* rule. See pp 31–32.

101 Section 5(3). It will be noted that without s 5(3) there would have been a lacuna in the statutory provisions, for subss (4) and (5) of s 2 do not between them cover the case of a purported sale by a non-owner.

102 See p 283.

103 Eg where the third party joins in the contract to transfer the property to the buyer by direction of the seller, or where the seller himself, though selling on his own account, transfers the third party's title at the same time under a power of attorney from the third party.

104 See p 00. Hence s 12(3) of the Sale of Goods Act does not imply that a person with no title may sell, merely that he may agree to sell, and even this presupposes that it is intended to transfer at least a defeasible title, for without such intention the contract is not a contract of sale within the Act.

105 See Sale of Goods Act 1979, Pt III, first sub-heading.

106 Ibid, second sub-heading.

property in the goods is a money payment. An exchange of goods for other goods, with no stipulation as to a money price,[107] is a barter and is outside the Act.[108] On the other hand, a part-exchange transaction in which an agreed price is payable partly in money and partly in other goods[109] is a sale.[110] An agreement to provide goods against trading stamps or other tokens is not a sale,[111] and is thus outside the Act,[112] as is a transfer of goods in exchange for land or for the performance of services[113] or for the payment of debts.[114] A supply of goods which is to be followed at a later date by return of their equivalent rather than of the goods *in specie* is a loan.[115]

4. THE SIGNIFICANCE OF THE STATUTORY DEFINITION

We have examined in some detail the ingredients of the statutory definition of the contract of sale. We must now take stock and ask ourselves why it matters. If a contract asserted by one party to be a contract of sale is found not to be, what are the consequences of such a finding? The answer depends on the circumstances. In some cases such a finding will make little or no difference at all to the rights of the

107 The position is otherwise a contract in which A sells goods to B for £100 and B sells other goods to A for £100 and because of the equality in the money consideration the parties agree that the monetary obligation of each shall be satisfied by delivery of the goods bought by the other. Such a transaction is not an exchange but a conjunction of reciprocal contracts of sale (*Davey v Paine Brothers (Motors) Ltd* [1954] NZLR 1122).

108 Though the terms implied in favour of the parties at common law are in many respects similar to those implied under a contract of sale.

109 In most part-exchange transactions, as commonly understood, the goods tendered in part exchange do not on a proper analysis form part of the consideration for the sale at all. The seller quotes an exclusively money price but agrees that he will, if so required by the buyer, purchase the part-exchange goods at a price to be set against that payable by the buyer. (The part-exchange goods then become the subject of a separate contract of sale if and when the buyer accepts the seller's offer of purchase by delivering them to the seller.) See R. M. Goode, *Hire-Purchase Law and Practice* (2nd edn, 1970), p 305.

110 *Aldridge v Johnson* (1857) 7 E & B 885; *G. J Dawson (Clapham) Ltd v H. and G. Dutfield* [1936] 2 All ER 232. The position is otherwise where the parties do not fix a money price to be satisfied partly in cash, partly in kind, but simply provide for the exchange of the goods for other goods and money (*Flynn v Mackin* [1974] IR 101). See E. M. Clare Canton (1976) 39 MLR 589. For a detailed analysis of part-exchange transactions, see Goode, *Hire-Purchase Law and Practice*, ch 14.

111 *O'Dea v Merchants Trade-Expansion Group Ltd* (1938) 37 AR (NSW) 410. But a sale at a money price to be satisfied by trading stamps, or partly by trading stamps and partly by cash (*Chappell & Co Ltd v Nestlé Co Ltd* [1960] AC 87) is a sale. In other words, the same principles apply as where goods are given in exchange or part-exchange. The question in all cases is whether there is an agreed money price. See *Robshaw Bros Ltd v Mayer* [1957] Ch 125, *Simpson v Connolly* [1953] 2 All ER 474.

112 It is, however, governed by the Trading Stamps Act 1964 as amended by the Supply of Goods (Implied Terms) Act 1973, s 16, and the Consumer Credit Act 1974, Sch 4, paras 24–26.

113 *Garey v Pyke* (1839) 10 Ad & El 512.

114 See *Simpson v Connolly*, n 111 (transfer of land in discharge of debt held not to be a sale).

115 Roman law described the transaction as one of *mutuum*. In common parlance a loan is generally taken to refer to the loan of money, but in law the term covers any transaction which treats what is supplied as a fungible (see pp 59–60).

parties.[116] In other situations the impact may be dramatic. Whether a transaction is to be characterized as a contract of sale or some other type of transaction may affect the nature and extent of the rights of the parties *inter se*;[117] the position of a third party who purchases from one of the contracting parties when that party does not have, or has ceased to have, a good title;[118] the liability of the contract document to stamp duty,[119] and the amount of such duty; the tax position of the parties;[120] the existence and extent of statutory duties of which a breach would attract civil or criminal sanctions;[121] the availability of government grants and tax allowances.[122] Two forms of contract deserve special mention, namely contracts for services and agency agreements.

(i)   Services

Whereas in a contract of sale the seller's duty to tender goods of satisfactory quality is strict, so that no amount of care will absolve him from liability if the goods are defective,[123] the obligation of one who undertakes to provide other services is usually limited to the exercise of reasonable care and skill, that is, such care and skill as he professes, either expressly or by implication, in the carrying on of some calling for which a given standard of competence is required.[124] But as regards materials furnished under such a contract, the supplier now has the same duty to supply goods of satisfactory quality as he has under a contract of sale.[125] Moreover, even as regards the pure services element of the contract there is no distinction in principle between a contract for skill and labour and one for the sale of goods. The question in each case is what the supplier has undertaken to provide. If the supplier of services undertakes to produce a given result, as where a contractor agrees to install central heating that will produce not less than a given room temperature, or an engineer to design a structure that will withstand specified stresses,[126] the duty is no less strict than in a contract of sale. The only point of difference is that while in contracts of sale the strict nature of the seller's obligation is assumed unless displaced by evidence of a contrary intention, the normal assumption in a contract for services is that the supplier is not undertaking to produce a given result but

---

116 For example, the terms implied in contracts of hire and contracts of work and labour in so far as they involve the supply of materials are very similar to the terms implied in a contract of sale. See the Supply of Goods and Services Act 1982.

117 See below.

118 See p 434.

119 See *William Cory & Son Ltd v Inland Revenue Commissioners* [1965] AC 1088.

120 For example, on a purchase of goods for the purpose of a business, capital allowances are given to the buyer; on a lease (even a finance lease) to the lessor.

121 Though the tendency in modern legislation is to cover all forms of supply. See, for example, the Consumer Protection Act 1987, s 46.

122 See n 120.

123 See p 320.

124 *Bolam v Friern Hospital Management Committee* [1957] 2 All ER 118. The principle is now embodied in s 13 of the Supply of Goods and Services Act 1982.

125 Supply of Goods and Services Act 1982, s 4, enacting the principle established by the common law. See *Young & Marten Ltd v McManus Childs Ltd* [1969] 1 AC 454; *Dodd and Dodd v Wilson and McWilliam* [1946] 2 All ER 691.

126 *Greaves & Co (Contractors) Ltd v Baynham Meikle & Partners* [1975] 2 Lloyd's Rep 325.

simply to exercise all reasonable care and skill in the performance of work designed to produce that result.

An important difference between a contract of sale of goods and a contract of work and labour involving the supply of materials is that the statutory exceptions to the *nemo dat* rule in the Sale of Goods Act, which in given conditions enable a buyer or seller in possession to pass a good title to a third party even where the buyer lacked or the seller had already parted with title, do not apply to other types of contract.[127] A further difference is that the provisions of s 20A of the Act conferring co-ownership of an identified bulk on prepaying buyers pending delivery under their individual contracts[128] do not apply to contracts of work and labour.

(ii) Agency[129]

Whether a person is to be considered to have purchased goods and resold them on his own account or to have received and disposed of them as agent of the supplier is a question that may be of considerable practical importance, and anyone who proposes to market goods through an agent or distributor will have to consider the legal implications when deciding which form of contract to select, particularly where the goods are to be sold abroad. If A supplies goods to B as agent to sell on A's behalf, there is privity of contract between A and the purchasers of the goods, so that A incurs all the liabilities of a seller if the goods are defective or if B fails to deliver in accordance with the contract. Conversely, A is entitled to sue the purchasers for the price, so that the risk he runs in the event of B's becoming insolvent is somewhat reduced, for instead of having to look at B as the sole purchaser, he is instead entitled to exercise rights against each purchaser separately under the particular contract entered into by that purchaser. If A is in England and B is in a foreign country, A's selection of the form of agreement may be influenced by restrictions imposed by the law of that country on trading by foreigners. A may need a licence to carry on a business through the agency of B, whereas if he merely sells to B for resale, A is not necessarily on that account carrying on business in the foreign country concerned. Again, the delivery of goods to another as agent consignee rather than as purchaser allows deferment of tax.[130]

5.   DOCUMENTARY AND NON-DOCUMENTARY SALES

Special characteristics are possessed by documentary sales, in which the seller agrees to dispatch goods rather than deliver them at their intended destination and to procure for the benefit of the buyer the contract of carriage and any other ancillary contracts that may be agreed, eg of marine insurance, and make over to the buyer the contract documents or other documents embodying their essential terms.[131]

---

127 *Dawber Williamson Roofing Ltd v Humberside County Council* [1979] CLY 212.
128 See p 223.
129 See also ch 5.
130 See p 742.
131 Eg, the parties may agree that the seller is to arrange insurance and to furnish a certificate of insurance rather than the insurance policy itself. See p 896.

Documentary sales involve as a minimum the transfer to the buyer of documents of control over the goods – typically a bill of lading[132] or a warehouse warrant[133] – to enable the buyer to sell or pledge the goods while they are still in transit or in an independent warehouse. Documentary sales are a particular feature of international sale transactions.[134]

6.   CONSUMER SALES

A proliferation of EC directives and UK implementing legislation in the field of consumer law has greatly complicated English sales law, to the point where the law relating to consumer sales has become a subject in its own right. Thus we have directives and implementing UK regulations on:

(a)   misleading and comparative advertising;[135]
(b)   contracts negotiated away from business premises;[136]
(c)   consumer credit;[137]
(d)   unfair contract terms;[138]
(e)   general product safety;[139]
(f)   distance selling;[140]
(g)   price indications;[141]
(h)   consumer sales and guarantees.[142]

Apart from a brief treatment of the last of these, the above directives and implementing regulations are not treated in the present work, which is concerned with commercial transactions, and reference should be made to specialist works on consumer law.[143]

---

132   See pp 885 ff.

133   See R. M. Goode, *Proprietary Rights and Insolvency in Sales Transactions* (2nd edn, 1989), pp 61–62.

134   Examined in detail in chs 32–34.

135   84/450/EEC, implemented by the Control of Misleading Advertisements Regulations 1988, SI 1988/915.

136   85/577/EEC, implemented by the Consumer Protection (Contracts Concluded away from Business Premises) Regulations 1987, SI 1987/2117.

137   87/102/EEC, as amended. There is a proposal to replace this with a new directive based on full harmonization rather than minimum standards, but strong opposition to this may lead to it being either withdrawn or substantially amended. In the UK consumer credit is governed by the Consumer Credit Act 1974 and a large number of statutory instruments.

138   93/13/EEC, implemented by what are now the Unfair Terms in Consumer Contracts Regulations 1999, SI 1999/2083.

139   2001/95/EC, replacing 92/59/EEC, which was implemented by the General Product Safety Regulations 1994, SI 1994/2328.

140   97/7/EC, implemented by the Consumer Protection (Distance Selling) Regulations 2000, SI 2000/2334.

141   98/6/EC, implemented by the Price Marking Order 1999, SI 1999/3042.

142   99/44/EC, implemented by the Sale and Supply of Goods to Consumers Regulations 2002, SI 2002/3045.

143   The leading textbook is John Macleod, *Consumer Sales Law* (2002).

8   The Passing of the Property

The Sale of Goods Act provides that the passing of the property depends on intention; risk of loss or damage goes with the property; and frustration is linked to risk. Hence an examination of the general principles governing the passing of property, risk and frustration is a necessary prelude to our step-by-step analysis of the contract of sale in action; and the starting point of this examination is the problem of identification of the contract goods. In short, what is the subject matter of the contract?

1.   IDENTIFICATION OF THE CONTRACT GOODS

(i)   The need to identify[1]

There are at least five reasons why it may be material to identify the subject matter of the contract. In the first place, the buyer will want to know what he is purchasing; and he cannot as buyer assert property rights over goods without first identifying them as the goods that are the subject of the contract.[2] Secondly, just as ownership depends on identification, so also does possession.[3] Thirdly, and somewhat illogically, identification may be relevant to the availability of specific perform-ance.[4] Fourthly, the buyer cannot maintain an action for conversion against the seller or a third party unless he can show that the act of conversion complained of relates to goods which are or include goods the subject of the contract of sale. Fifthly, if a party wishes to claim that the contract has been frustrated through destruction of the subject matter, he must prove that the goods destroyed were or included the contract goods.

While identification of the contract goods is thus of crucial importance, the *degree* of identification required varies according to circumstances.[5] In particular, where the question is whether the contract goods have been destroyed or disposed of, it suffices to know that the goods called for by the contract formed part of a larger but identified bulk which has been lost or disposed of, for loss or disposal of the whole necessarily involves loss or disposal of the part.

---

1 See also p 50.
2 Sale of Goods Act 1979, s 16. See p 209.
3 See p 42.
4 Sale of Goods Act 1979, s 52(1). See p 363.
5 See pp 210–211.

(ii)   Specific, ascertained, generic and quasi-specific goods[6]

It is convenient to have labels to describe the degree of identification achieved at the time that the contract is made. The Sale of Goods Act makes a twofold classification into specific goods on the one hand and unascertained goods on the other; but, as we shall see, this second class is not a single species but subdivides into two quite distinctive classes, namely quasi-specific goods and wholly unascertained goods.

1.   Specific goods

Where the goods are fully identified at the time of the contract (as where they are handed over or set aside with the buyer's consent at the time he agrees to buy them), they are said to be *specific* goods. In the language of s 61(1) of the Sale of Goods Act, 'specific goods' are 'goods identified and agreed on at the time a contract of sale is made'. Thus, if I go into a shop and buy two pounds of potatoes which I take away with me, or if I try on and purchase a suit which I arrange to be sent to my home, the goods are in each case specific goods, for the precise articles I am buying are known at the time I agree to buy and do not depend on any later selection, made either by the shopkeeper or by me from among the former's stock. The seller would not be entitled to change his mind and require me to take different potatoes or a different suit; nor would I be entitled to change my mind and insist on having the potatoes replaced with other potatoes or the suit replaced with another suit. The definition of specific goods also includes an undivided share, specified as a fraction or percentage, of goods so identified and agreed.[7]

Various provisions of the Act refer to a 'contract for the sale of specific goods'.[8] This phrase is ambiguous. Does it mean that the goods must in fact be identified? Or does it mean merely that the parties must be contracting with reference to the goods on the basis (which may or may not be correct) that they are identified? Suppose, for example, that S contracts to sell 'one of the bottles of wine in my cellar' and there is but one such bottle. The contract is in form a contract for the sale of quasi-specific goods, yet in substance it involves an agreement to sell specific goods, for there is only one member of the designated class. Now let us take the converse case, where S contracts to sell 'the bottle of wine in my cellar', and the cellar contains several bottles of wine. Here the contract is in form a contract for the sale of specific goods, yet in substance it is for quasi-specific goods, for beyond the fact that the contract can be satisfied only by selection of a bottle of wine from those in the cellar, as opposed to wine located elsewhere, we cannot tell which bottle is earmarked to the contract.

Though the Act does not directly tell us whether, for the purpose of definition, we are to look at the form of the contract or the factual situation, it is apparent from the various provisions relating to specific goods – eg ss 6, 7 and 18 – that the Act is concerned with the fact of specificity (or lack of it), not with the contract

---

6 Other classifications will be dealt with at appropriate points in this chapter. The distinction between existing and future goods is relevant to the passing of property and is discussed on p 229.

7 Section 62(1).

8 Sections 6, 7, 17–19.

formulation. If the latter were the determining factor, we could have a contract of sale of specific goods expressed to be existing and located in a particular spot, even though no such goods were located in that spot, or indeed even if no such goods existed at all. But since the Act is concerned with specificity as a fact, we can conclude that a contract for the sale of specific goods requires, first, that the goods be in fact identified, ie unique, at the time of contract, and secondly, as a corollary, that they exist (either as actual or as potential property[9]) at that time. Conversely, if the goods are in fact identified at the time of the contract, the fact that the contract is couched in a form which implies that some act of selection is necessary does not alter the status of the contract as a contract for the sale of specific goods.

2.   Ascertained goods

Section 16 of the Sale of Goods Act tells us that 'where there is a contract for the sale of unascertained goods no property in the goods is transferred to the buyer unless and until the goods are ascertained',[10] that is, identified by some act of appropriation subsequent to the contract. Hence, specific goods are those identified at the time of the contract;[11] ascertained goods are those which were unidentified when the contract was made but become identified subsequently as the contract goods.[12] Section 16 does not simply lay down a rule of law; it is in the nature of things that a person cannot acquire ownership of goods, or indeed any other asset, if it cannot be identified.[13] Nor can the problem be overcome by resort to estoppel or by invoking a trust of the sums paid as the purchase price in the absence of any evidence of an intention to create a trust. A good illustration is the decision of the Privy Council in *Re Goldcorp Exchange Ltd*,[14] where the facts were as follows:

> Goldcorp Exchange was a dealer in gold and other precious metals. It agreed to sell to various customers (referred to throughout in the proceedings as the 'non-allocated claimants') quantities of bullion which, pending physical delivery on seven days' notice, would be stored in the company's vault, each customer being issued with a 'certificate of ownership'. The company became insolvent and there was insufficient bullion to meet customers' entitlements. The unallocated claimants, together with various others, instituted proceedings claiming co-ownership of the remaining bullion. This was rejected by Thorp J at first instance and by the New Zealand Court of Appeal and the Privy Council. All three courts rejected the contention that the problem created by the lack of identification could be overcome by reliance either on estoppel based on the company's literature or on the existence of a trust. Estoppel could not conjure into existence goods which were not there, and the facts were inconsistent with any intention on the part of the company to create a trust for its customers.

> However, in the New Zealand Court of Appeal the majority had accepted a new argument that the purchase price paid by the customers was impressed with a trust in

---

9   As to potential property, see p 229.

10   See further on this point p 213.

11   Section 61(1).

12   Such identification is not necessarily determinative, for if the buyer subsequently exercises a right to reject the goods for nonconformity with the contract, they cease to be the contract goods and unless it is then too late for the seller to re-tender (see pp 342–343), the contract remains on foot as one under which the goods continue to be unascertained pending an effective appropriation. See further, p 213.

13   Hence the opening words of the section suggesting that s 20A provides an exception to the requirement of ascertainment should not be taken at face value. See p 224.

14   [1995] 1 AC 74. Only the central points are examined here.

their favour, namely a trust to apply the purchase price for the purpose for which it was paid, failing which the sums paid were to be held for the customers and were traceable into the company's general assets. The Privy Council robustly rejected this proposition and reversed the decision of the Court of Appeal. Lord Mustill, delivering the opinion of the Board, pointed out that the moneys were paid to the company unconditionally, and that the existence of customers' continuing proprietary interests in the money they had paid was inconsistent with their assertion that they had acquired title under their respective contracts of sale.

Ascertained goods are for the most part governed by the same rules as specific goods. It is true that the rules as to the passing of property in s 18 pick out specific goods for special treatment, but this is simply an indication of the fact that the process of identification is different. Once goods, originally unascertained, have become identified to the contract, we can for most purposes equate these with specific goods. But two important distinctions remain. First, the frustration rules embodied in ss 6 and 7 of the Act are confined to specific goods. Secondly, whereas the buyer's lawful rejection of ascertained goods negates the seller's appropriation of these but leaves him free to make a fresh appropriation if still in time to do so, the seller cannot proffer a substitute for specific goods lawfully rejected, for by definition the contract covers those goods and no other.

3.   Generic or unascertained goods (fungibles)

Frequently, goods are not identified at the time of the contract but depend on some subsequent agreed act of appropriation by the seller or (less commonly) by the buyer. For example, I may order two pounds of potatoes from my greengrocer for delivery later in the day, or a new car from my local motor dealer for which there is an estimated delivery time of two months. In this case there is no existing item of goods which at the time of the contract can be pinpointed as the subject of the contract. I have agreed to buy not a specific and identified item but simply an article (*any* article) which possesses the characteristics I have described to the seller. The contract is thus for the sale of unascertained or generic[15] goods, that is, I have agreed to buy an article which is one of a genus or class and do not mind which one, as long as that which is subsequently selected by the seller (whether from his existing stock or from other sources) possesses the characteristics of the genus. Until that selection (or *appropriation* as it is termed in the Sale of Goods Act) has been made, the contract goods remain unascertained.

4.   The two categories of unascertained goods

When the Sale of Goods Act refers to 'unascertained goods' – a phrase not defined – it fails to distinguish two quite different categories. The goods may be *wholly* unascertained, in that the parties have not even designated a source of supply in their contract, or they may be partially identified as a result of agreement between seller and buyer that they shall be supplied from an identifiable bulk. We shall apply the term 'quasi-specific goods' to denote goods partially identified in this way[16] and in future confine our use of the phrase 'unascertained goods' to goods which are

15 Or fungible. See p 59 as to fungibles.
16 See p 237.

wholly unascertained, while emphasizing that in the Sale of Goods Act itself this phrase is used to cover both categories, with potentially unfortunate consequences.

Contractually, unascertained goods possess neither a present nor a potential location. Indeed, when s 16, in speaking of unascertained goods, tells us that no property in 'the goods' passes to the buyer until ascertainment, it gives a totally misleading impression, for it suggests an undefined but existing collection of articles from which the contract goods are to be selected, whereas the fact is that, unless the parties have at least agreed on the source of supply, 'the goods' have no contractual existence at all! The most that can be said is that somewhere there is, or at some time there may come into being, a source of supply which in the contemplation of either or both of the parties will be drawn on to meet the seller's contractual obligations. But legally that source has no relevance to the contract unless made a term of the contract. If I agree to buy 100 tons of potatoes, then, unless otherwise stipulated, the seller is free to supply them from any existing or future source. I as the buyer have no right to insist that any particular source of supply shall be used. How the seller performs is none of my business as long as he does perform. Conversely, failure of the intended source does not relieve the seller of his delivery obligation; if the anticipated source fails, he must find another.

Goods can move (figuratively) from an unascertained to an ascertained state directly by an act of appropriation sufficient for precise identification. Alternatively, there can be a staged progression, from unascertained to quasi-specific[17] and thence to ascertained goods through appropriation from that bulk.[18]

5. Quasi-specific goods

The significance of quasi-specific goods as a distinct category will readily become apparent. Suppose that the buyer agrees to purchase 100 tons of potatoes forming part of a consignment of 500 tons then on board a named vessel or in a designated warehouse. The goods in this case are not wholly unascertained, for while the particular 100 tons out of the 500 cannot be identified until set aside and appropriated to the contract, it can be said that the seller is neither entitled nor obliged to supply 100 tons from any other source.[19] If the ship were to sink with the loss of all its cargo, or the warehouse were to be set on fire with the destruction of all its contents, we should have no difficulty in saying that the goods the subject of the contract, even though never specifically identified, had perished, since the entire source from which they were to come had been destroyed. Similarly, if the seller, before appropriating 100 tons to the contract, were to sell and deliver to another buyer the whole 500 tons of potatoes, lack of precise identification of the first buyer's 100 tons would not of itself present a barrier to a claim by him for conversion.[20]

17 See p 237.
18 As to appropriation, see pp 213 ff.
19 One must be careful to distinguish a contractually designated source of supply from a mere contractual delivery point. Thus if there is an agreement to sell '100 bushels of wheat ex our warehouse', it is a question of construction whether the seller is required to supply from stock already in his warehouse at the time of the contract or whether he is free to tender wheat obtained from any other source so long as he makes it available for delivery at his warehouse.
20 See p 364.

Just as precise identification of the goods earmarked to the contract may take place either when the contract is made (specific goods) or subsequently (ascertained goods), so also goods may be quasi-specific on the making of the contract or may alternatively become quasi-specific as the result of a provision of the contract allowing a party to designate the source of supply[21] or a subsequent agreement between the parties that the goods shall be supplied from a given source.[22] Further, it is not essential that the source be actually in existence at the time of the contract or of the subsequent agreement. It suffices that it is described with sufficient particularity to enable it to be identified when it does come into existence. For example, the buyer may contract to purchase '1,000 tons of Weston White wheat ex motor vessel *Challenger* expected to load between 16 and 31 December from Oregon or Washington',[23] a sufficient description to identify the contractual source of supply in the absence of some latent ambiguity.[24]

Certain important consequences flow from the status of goods as quasi-specific goods. The identification of the bulk from which they are to be drawn may enable us to test (in contrast to the case of wholly unascertained goods) whether

(a)   they are still in existence,
(b)   their control has passed from the seller to the buyer,
(c)   the seller has wrongfully parted with possession and
(d)   the seller or an independent carrier or other bailee is wrongfully detaining them.

Such identification, though insufficient to pass the property in particular goods,[25] may nevertheless be enough to raise issues of risk,[26] frustration[27] and availability of personal remedies in tort arising from the detention or conversion of the bulk from which the contract goods are to be supplied.[28] In addition, identification of the bulk may lead to ascertainment of the precise contract goods through exhaustion, as by delivery of the rest of the bulk to other purchasers.[29]

So far it has been assumed that the contract provides for a single, identified source of supply. But there is nothing to preclude the parties from agreeing that the seller may supply from either or both of different sources of supply, or indeed from any of a number of identified sources. In such a case two separate acts of appropriation may be involved: an act designating the particular bulk from which the contract goods are to be supplied and a subsequent or simultaneous act of appropriation to identify the particular goods. Until the first of these acts of appropriation, the destruction of one of the possible sources of supply cannot be said to involve destruction of the contract goods for the purpose of the rules as to risk and

---

21   As where a c.i.f. contract provides for the seller to give a notice of appropriation of goods shipped on board a specified vessel. See p 939.
22   See p 935, n 51.
23   *Re Wait* [1927] 1 Ch 606.
24   As in *Raffles v Wichelhaus* (1864) 2 H & C 906.
25   Sale of Goods Act 1979, s 16. However, the prepaying buyer now acquires a co-ownership interest in the bulk. See p 224.
26   See p 242.
27   See p 260.
28   Above.
29   See p 237.

frustration, for the seller still has the remaining source or sources from which to fulfil his contractual obligations. Similarly, the seller does not commit an act of conversion by disposing elsewhere of all the contents of a particular bulk, for this does not preclude him from meeting his delivery obligation from another contractual bulk.

(iii) The process of identification

Where the contract is for the sale of unascertained or quasi-specific goods, two stages of identification separated by an interval of time are involved. At the moment the contract is made, the parties must, as terms of the contract, agree upon the characteristics by which the goods to be supplied are to be identified. This means at least some verbal description[30] in writing or by word of mouth, but in many cases the difficulty of expressing in words all the relevant characteristics of the required article makes it desirable for the description to be supplemented by other methods, eg, a sample, photographs, drawings, specifications expressed in mathematical or chemical formulae, reference to established grades or other standards, and the like. At the second stage, goods possessing the specific characteristics must be set aside and appropriated to the contract, so that the seller ceases to be entitled to proffer or the buyer to take other goods, even if having all the designated characteristics.

(iv) Appropriation to the contract

In the case of a contract for the sale of specific goods no question of appropriation arises, for the goods are identified at the time of sale. Where, however, the contract is for the sale of unascertained or quasi-specific goods, the identification of goods as the contract goods depends on some act of appropriation, after the making of the contract, by the seller with the assent of the buyer, or the buyer with the assent of the seller. Appropriation merely fixes the contract goods; it does not necessarily result in the transfer of ownership to the buyer, though it may be relevant under the rules in the Act as to the assumed intention of the parties concerning the transfer of ownership.[31]

Appropriation may be conditional or unconditional. In the latter case it is irrevocable;[32] in the former, the party making the appropriation reserves the right to substitute, or require the substitution of, other goods in certain conditions.[33] Since appropriation is a contractual act, it is effective only if carried out, or accepted by the other party as having been carried out, in conformity with the contract. So if a seller purports to appropriate to the contract goods of a different description from those specified in the contract, the appropriation is ineffective[34] unless the buyer

---

30 However, not every descriptive statement forms part of the contract description, but only that which is necessary to identify the goods. See p 292.

31 See p 233.

32 Assuming that it is in accordance with the contract and that the buyer does not on some other ground exercise a right to reject.

33 See pp 234 ff.

34 *Varley v Whipp* [1900] 1 QB 513, per Channell J at 517.

has given or subsequently gives his assent to the change of identity.[35] Again if the parties have agreed that notice of appropriation shall be given to the buyer, the appropriation will not normally become operative until such notice has been given.[36]

While an unconditional appropriation made by one party with the assent of the other[37] binds the seller irrevocably,[38] its impact on the buyer is conditional only; for if, though the goods are of the contract description, the tender is not otherwise in conformity with the contract (eg because the goods are unfit or of unsatisfactory quality or because delivery is tendered late in a contract where time is of the essence), the buyer can exercise his right to reject, in which event the original appropriation is nullified and the rights of the parties are for the most part[39] regulated as if no appropriation had been made and no delivery tendered.[40]

What is the position if the seller tenders a quantity of goods in excess of the contract quantity? Does this prevent property passing on the ground that until some act of appropriation it cannot be said which goods belong to the buyer?[41] The answer depends on the intention of the parties. If this is that the property in the entire quantity is to pass in the first instance to the buyer, subject to its right to reject the excess later, the buyer becomes the owner of the whole quantity and when the excess is rejected, the property in it revests in the seller.[42] If, on the other hand, the intention is that the property will pass only when the buyer has separated from the bulk the quantity to be delivered under the contract, the property will not vest in the buyer until it has effected the separation.

2. PROPERTY: SOME GENERAL ASPECTS

(i) Property as the core of the contract

It has long been established that as a matter of contractual obligation the seller's transfer of an indefeasible title is fundamental to the agreement. So relentlessly

---

35 This produces interesting situations where the passing of the property is in issue, for the buyer's right to assert that a purported appropriation was not valid may overlap with his right to reject the goods for non-correspondence with description. The distinction between the two rights is that exercise of the former prevents the property from vesting in the buyer at all, whereas rejection of goods may well not take place until after the property has passed to the buyer and will then result in the property revesting in the seller, so extinguishing the initially valid appropriation (see below). The right to disclaim an ineffective appropriation is narrower than the right to reject the goods, for appropriation goes only to identity, not to attributes, so that if the goods earmarked to the contract are of the contract description and the act of appropriation is one expressly or impliedly authorized by the contract, the appropriation is effective even if the goods are of poor quality or unfit for their purpose.

36 See pp 235, 940 as to a notice of appropriation.

37 As to what constitutes a sufficient act of appropriation, see pp 234 ff.

38 But see n 32.

39 As to the seller's liability to the buyer for expenses incurred by the latter in connection with the abortive tender, see p 345.

40 See p 344.

41 See Janet Ulph, 'The Proprietary Consequences of an Excess Delivery' [1998] LMCLQ 4.

42 *The Elafi* [1982] 1 All ER 208.

does English law apply this principle that possession and enjoyment of the goods, even for a substantial period, are not by themselves considered to confer on the buyer a benefit sufficient to preclude him from asserting a total failure of consideration if he discovers that his seller did not have a right to dispose of the goods. The leading authority is the much-discussed decision of the Court of Appeal in *Rowland v Divall*.[43]

> The plaintiff bought a motor car from the defendant for £334. He resold it to a third party, from whom it was repossessed by the police on the ground that it had been stolen by the person who sold it to the defendant. The plaintiff, having refunded to his own purchaser the resale price he had received, then sued the defendant for recovery of the £334 as money paid for a consideration which had wholly failed.

> The trial judge dismissed the claim on the ground that the plaintiff and his purchaser had together had the use of the car for a period of four months; but this decision was reversed by the Court of Appeal on the ground that the plaintiff had not received any part of that for which he had bargained, namely the property and the right to possession. In rejecting the argument that the depreciation of the vehicle through use precluded *restitutio in integrum* to the seller and thus defeated the plaintiff's claim, the Court of Appeal pointed out that since the seller had no title, he could not recover the car in any event and it did not lie in his mouth to set up by way of defence the impossibility of *restitutio in integrum* when this had resulted from his own breach.

Even more striking was the later decision in *Warman v Southern Counties Car Finance Corporation Ltd*,[44] where on similar reasoning the plaintiff was held entitled to recover all payments made under a hire-purchase agreement though he had used the car for eight months before surrendering it to the true owner; and it was further held that even if, as contended by the defendants, the plaintiff had continued payments under the agreement after discovering the defect in the defendants' title, this did not preclude him from recovering from the defendants on the basis of a total failure of consideration. Thus ' … if at any stage the option to purchase goes, the whole value of the agreement to the hirer has gone with it'.[45]

Hence, the seller's right[46] to transfer the property in the goods to the buyer is conceived to be the core of the contract, with the result not merely that actual enjoyment by itself is not considered to constitute a benefit negating total failure of consideration but that the implied condition of title is considered a fundamental term which at common law could not easily be negated in a contract of sale,[47] though the parties could, of course, expressly bargain for an *emptio spei*, a sale of such interest (if any) as the seller has in the goods.[48]

Rowland v Divall is probably good law, in view of the definition of 'contract of sale' in s 2(1) of the Sale of Goods Act, which talks exclusively of property and

43 [1923] 2 KB 500.
44 [1949] 2 KB 576.
45 Per Finnemore J at 582.
46 The fact that the seller has *power* to transfer the property and effectively exercises this does not normally deprive the buyer of his remedy of rejection if the seller did not also have the *right* to sell. See p 286. The seller's duty to transfer the property comes to an end if the goods are destroyed after the risk has passed to the buyer. See p 243.
47 And see now the Unfair Contract Terms 1977, s 6(1)(a), and p 326.
48 *Payne v Elsden* (1900) 17 TLR 161. See now Sale of Goods Act 1979, s 12(3), and pp 289–290.

makes no mention of possession. But in terms of policy, the result cannot be described as satisfactory.[49] It is a further illustration of the all-or-nothing approach so often encountered in English commercial law,[50] and reflects a divergence between legal principle and commercial reality.[51] In everyday life possession is every bit as important as ownership. The implied warranty of quiet possession,[52] which gives the buyer the right to damages if his possession is in fact disturbed, goes a long way towards providing the buyer with all he needs for his protection. It does not, however, go all the way, for the buyer who is to pay without an assurance of title needs some safeguard against exposure to a claim in conversion by the true owner. Perhaps the most satisfactory solution is to alter the rule that good faith and want of notice in receiving and dealing with goods to which another is entitled are no answer to an action for conversion.[53]

(ii)   The relevance of property to other issues

The excessive importance attached by English sales law to the transfer of property does not merely manifest itself in the rule that such transfer is a fundamental obligation of the contract. The impact of the location of the property is all-pervasive.[54]

1.   No real rights short of property or possession

Until the property passes to the buyer or possession has been delivered to him, his rights appear to rest solely in contract and he apparently has no interest of any kind in the goods pending acquisition of the legal title.[55] Thus he does not, it seems, acquire an equitable interest in the goods[56] or any implied right of security under the contract,[57] nor at common law can he claim an interest in common with the

---

49 The Law Reform Committee recommended that the buyer should recover only the amount of his loss, giving credit for any benefit derived from the goods while in his possession (*Transfer of Title to Chattels* (1966, Cmnd 2958), para 36). The Law Commissions at one time appeared to support this proposal, but eventually came out against any change on the ground that there was no reason why the buyer should have to pay the seller for goods belonging to a third party. See *Sale and Supply of Goods* (Law Com No 160, Scot Law Com No 104, Cm 137, 1987) paras 6.1–6.5.

50 For a further example, see p 222.

51 See Michael Bridge, *Sale of Goods*, pp 391 ff for a powerful criticism, and the Law Commissions' Report *Sale and Supply of Goods*.

52 See p 288.

53 *M'Combie v Davies* (1805) 6 East 538; *Fine Art Society v Union Bank of London Ltd* (1886) 17 QBD 705; and see Torts (Interference with Goods) Act 1977, s 11(2).

54 Prior to the Misrepresentation Act 1967 it even affected the buyer's right to reject. See p 340, n 25.

55 *Re Wait*, n 23 per Atkin LJ at 636; *The Aliakmon* [1986] AC 785, per Lord Brandon at 812–813; *Re Goldcorp Exchange Ltd* [1994] 2 All ER 806; *Re Martin, ex p Avery Motors Ltd* [1991] 3 NZLR 630.

56 Ibid. However, the parties are free to make any bargain they wish outside the contract of sale, eg that until the passing of legal title the seller is to hold the goods on trust for the buyer. See *Re Wait*, n 23 per Atkin LJ at 636.

57 Contrast the position of the buyer under the American Uniform Commercial Code, ss 2–401, 2–502, which gives the buyer a 'special property' in the goods upon their identification to the contract and thus enables him to recover them from the seller, upon tender of the price, even if the latter becomes bankrupt.

seller or other buyers in an identified bulk of which he has agreed to purchase an unidentified part.[58] He acquires real rights only by the transfer of ownership or the delivery of possession.[59]

2. Property, risk and frustration

Unless otherwise agreed, the risk of loss of or damage to the goods goes with the property in them[60] and is not directly related to custody or control.[61] The location of the property may, by virtue of its impact on risk, also be relevant to the question of frustration, the Act providing that where there is an agreement to sell specific goods which perish without the fault of either party before the risk has passed to the buyer, the agreement is avoided.[62]

3. Right to sue for the price

The seller's right to sue for the price is in general dependent on the passing of the property in the goods to the buyer.[63]

4. Insolvency of a party

If the seller becomes bankrupt or goes into liquidation without having delivered specific or ascertained goods agreed to be sold, the buyer's ability to enforce against the trustee or liquidator a right of possession against the seller will normally depend upon the buyer's acquisition of the property in the goods. If property was still in the seller at the date of the commencement of the bankruptcy or winding up,[64] the buyer is restricted to a right to prove in competition with other creditors.[65] Similar principles apply where a seller seeks to assert a right to goods in the possession of a buyer who becomes bankrupt without having paid for them.[66]

5. Assertion of claims against third parties

The buyer's ability to assert claims in conversion against third parties into whose hands the goods may have come depends on his establishing that he had a right to possession at the time of the detention or conversion complained of; and while the

---

58 See p 221. As to the changes introduced by s 20A of the Sale of Goods Act 1979, see p 224.

59 For the effect of delivery of possession, see p 42.

60 Sale of Goods Act 1979, s 20(1). But in the case of sale to a person dealing as consumer risk does not pass until delivery (ibid, s 20(4)).

61 But indirectly there is a close connection, in that constructive delivery, by which the seller loses control, usually constitutes an appropriation of unascertained goods. See p 235.

62 Section 7.

63 Sale of Goods Act 1979, s 49(1).

64 As to which see p 836.

65 See pp 833. The position is otherwise where the buyer is in possession, or has a right to possession subject to the prior possessory right of a third party and takes possession (actual or constructive) upon the termination of that prior right. See R. M. Goode, *Proprietary Rights and Insolvency in Sales Transactions* (2nd edn, 1989), pp 13–14.

66 The position is otherwise where the goods have not yet reached the buyer, for the seller can then exercise his lien or right of stoppage in transit (see p 410).

right to possession does not necessarily either depend on or flow from ownership, yet frequently the acquisition of the property is the source of the right to possess and therefore of the ability to maintain possessory actions in tort.[67] Similarly, from the seller's viewpoint the location of the property may be highly material. If, for example, goods are sold on conditional sale[68] and before the property has passed the buyer wrongfully disposes of them to a third party, the seller may have a claim against that third party.

Until recently, the consignee or indorsee of a bill of lading acquired no rights against the carrier unless the property in the goods had passed to him upon or by reason of the consignment or indorsement.[69] This enactment, which caused great problems, has now been repealed by the Carriage of Goods by Sea Act 1992.[70] However, it remains the case that actions in tort against third parties can be brought only by one who had a proprietary or possessory interest in the goods at the time of the act complained of.[71]

6.   Buyer's right and power of disposal

The buyer's right to dispose of the goods to a third party will usually, though not inevitably, depend on his having acquired the property; and though he may have a power of disposal (in the sense of an ability to pass a good title to another), even where he does not have the right to do so[72] the general principle is that *nemo dat quod non habet*.[73]

7.   Tracing rights

It is not only in respect of the goods the subject of the contract of sale that rights may be available. If the buyer sells goods the property in which is still in the seller, the latter may have a common law personal right to follow the proceeds into the hands of the buyer and subsequent recipients[74] and/or an equitable right to trace.[75] The significance of these rights has only relatively recently come to be appreciated.[76]

The 'lump-concept' thinking which makes so much depend on property in the goods attracted so much criticism in the United States when incorporated into the American Uniform Sales Act that with the advent of the Uniform Commercial Code property was largely jettisoned as the determinant of rights. Instead, the draftsman, that outstanding commercial lawyer and jurist Karl Llewellyn,

---

67 See p 364.
68 See ch 27.
69 Bills of Lading Act 1855, s 1.
70 See p 1033. The Act resulted from the Law Commissions report *Rights of Suit in Respect of Carriage of Goods by Sea* (Law Com No 196, Scot Law Com No 130, 1991, H.C. 250).
71 *The Aliakmon*, n 55.
72 See ch 16.
73 See p 416.
74 See p 52.
75 See p 53.
76 Principally because of the impact of the *Romalpa* case. See p 608.

adopted an issue-by-issue approach, taking each step in a transaction in turn and regulating its consequences in a manner designed to produce results that would commend themselves to the commercial world as fair and reasonable in the typical case.[77]

(iii) How the property interest arises

The effect of the Sale of Goods Act, as interpreted by the courts, is that contracts for the sale of goods are governed by rules fundamentally different from those regulating other types of dealing in personal property. The following points of divergence merit particular attention.

(1)   The principle of equity by which the agreement of the owner of an asset to transfer it to another is not merely contractual but vests an immediate equitable interest in the intended transferee appears to have no application to contracts of sale of goods.[78]

(2)   Conversely, the property passes *at law* when it is intended to pass, by virtue of the contract itself and without the necessity for some new act, even if the seller had no interest in the goods at the time of the contract. This is in contrast to the rule for other types of dealing in personal property, by which an agreement to transfer after-acquired assets takes effect in equity when the assets are acquired but does not operate to transfer the legal title unless some new act is done which is either effective as a legal transfer on its own or else is an act designated by the contract as that which will operate to vest the legal title in the transferee.[79]

(3)   The buyer of unidentified goods forming part of a bulk does not acquire equitable co-ownership of the bulk[80] and, prior to the coming into force of the Sale of Goods (Amendment) Act 1995, obtained no property interest, even if paying for the goods in advance, until these had been separated from the bulk and unconditionally appropriated to his contract. However, the Act now has special rules conferring on the prepaying buyer of goods to be supplied from an identified bulk a co-ownership interest in the bulk pending delivery of his contract entitlement to him from the bulk.[81]

---

77   As Karl Llewellyn pointed out in his evidence to the New York Law Revision Commission when debating art 2 of the Uniform Commercial Code, sellers and buyers doing business under c.i.f. contracts managed perfectly well without using the concept of title (1954 Report, pp 160–161, quoted in James J. White and Robert S. Summers, *Uniform Commercial Code* (5th edn, 2000), pp 181); and art 2 adopts the contractual rather than the property approach (see Official Comments to ss 2–401, 2–509). See further Professor T. B. Smith's discussion of 'The Passing of Risk and 'Property' ' in *Property Problems in Sale* (Tagore Law Lectures, 1977).

78   See p 217.

79   See pp 37, 625.

80   *Re Wait* [1927] 1 Ch 606; *Re Goldcorp Exchange Ltd* [1995] 1 AC 74; and see p 209. It would, however, be open to the parties to make a specific agreement outside the contract of sale that would have this effect, eg by a declaration of trust by the seller in favour of himself and the buyer to the extent of their respective interests.

81   See p 224.

3.   CLAIMS TO GOODS FORMING PART OF A BULK

There are two paradigm situations which enable us to examine the problem from opposite ends. Only the second of these is affected by the Sale of Goods Act; the first remains governed by common law rules.

(i)   Commingling of goods from different suppliers

The first case concerns the effect of the commingling of materials contributed by different people to be made up by a third party into a finished product and sold to them in agreed quantities, where the third party becomes bankrupt before delivering the finished product. Here the question is whether they parted with title and the third party acquired title to the materials, the amalgam created by their commingling and the unappropriated finished products.

Example 1: A delivers silver to a silver refiner, S, to be made up into ingots, of which a given number are to be sold to A. Similar arrangements with S are entered into by B, C and D. Before any ingots have been delivered S becomes bankrupt, having in his possession a quantity of unprocessed silver in the form in which it was supplied to him, other silver contributed by all four parties which has become commingled but not yet made up into ingots, and a number of ingots yet to be delivered. Can A, B, C or D lay claim to any of the unprocessed silver, the amalgam or the ingots?

This question cannot be answered without more facts, and it is quite possible that the position of the various claimants will differ. The first matter to be decided is the intention of each of the three parties when they handed over their silver to be processed. Let us suppose that A intended to part with all his interest in his silver and simply to await its return made up into ingots. In that event A has no proprietary claim to anything. By giving up title to his silver, he has lost any chance of asserting a proprietary right to its product, for if the silver is no longer his, what is made from it cannot be either.[82] If ingots had been delivered to him or otherwise unconditionally appropriated to his contract,[83] he would have had title to them. In the absence of any such appropriation he is an unsecured creditor in the bankruptcy, for none of the ingots can be identified as referable to the contract with him; they might equally be referable to the contracts with the other three suppliers or to a decision by S to keep them for himself.

Suppose now that B, by contrast, stipulated that he was to remain the owner of the silver he supplied and that this was to be kept separate from anyone else's silver and applied exclusively to the making up of ingots for him. So far as B is concerned, S is a bailee of the unprocessed silver and the commingling was unauthorized. Equally, he did not bargain for any interest in silver contributed by other suppliers. Hence B can assert a proprietary claim to the unprocessed silver he supplied, if identifiable, and to co-ownership with S, C and D of the amalgam and any ingots (whether or not appropriated to any of the contracts) to the extent that they contain silver contributed by B, but not otherwise.[84]

---

82   *South Australian Insurance Co Ltd v Randell* (1869) 6 Moo PCNS 341.
83   See p 234.
84   *The Ypatianna* [1988] QB 345; *Lupton v White* (1808) 15 Ves 432.

Now take the case of C and D, who are aware that S intends to commingle all the silver for the purpose of making it up into ingots, so that any particular ingots supplied to C or D may come from their own silver, a mixture of their silver and that of other contributors, including S himself, or silver that does not include any part of C's or D's contribution. Suppose further that C and D agree to this on the basis that each retains ownership of his own silver until it has been commingled. In this situation the position of C and D between themselves and *vis-à-vis* S differs from that of B, for whereas B has no claim to any ingots beyond what he contributed to them, C and D each become sole owner of any ingots appropriated to their contracts even if those ingots consist exclusively of materials contributed by the other or by S.[85] This is because C and D have each agreed that the contract with either of them may be satisfied from the amalgam, regardless of who contributed to it,[86] though they cannot, of course, override the rights of B.

The final possibility is that B, C and D agree to transfer ownership of their materials to S immediately but to acquire a co-ownership interest in the commingled silver and any ingots produced with it pending appropriation to them of their respective individual entitlements. There seems no reason why such an agreement should not be respected.[87]

(ii)   Contracts to sell to different buyers from the same bulk

The second situation involves viewing the matter from the opposite end. In this case a supplier agrees to supply a number of buyers with goods from an identified stock of goods in a warehouse or on board a ship but becomes insolvent without any particular goods being appropriated to the contract of a particular buyer. Here the question is not whether a particular claimant has retained title to what he supplied so as to have tracing rights but whether he can show that prior to the bankruptcy he acquired title in the first instance either to particular goods or to a share in the bulk. The answer to this question now depends on whether the buyer has made a payment for the goods.

1.   Goods forming part of a bulk: the non-prepaying buyer

The position of a person who contracts to buy goods forming part of an identified bulk but does not pay for them in advance remains as it has always been: he acquires no property interest of any kind until the goods have been ascertained,

---

85 Of course, to the extent of any contribution made by B, the ingots are co-owned by him, C and/or D.

86 For good illustrations see *Mercer v Craven Grain Storage Ltd* [1994] CLC 328, noted Lionel Smith (1995) 111 LQR 10; and the decision of the New Zealand Court of Appeal in *Coleman v Harvey* [1989] 1 NZLR 723, discussed in Goode, *Proprietary Rights and Insolvency*, pp 87–88, Norman Palmer in *Interests in Goods* (eds Norman Palmer and Ewan McKendrick, 2nd edn, 1998), pp 126, n 39, 756–757, and Gerard McCormack, ibid, pp 512–513. Before appropriation, C and D will usually be co-owners of the amalgam.

87 The situation in *Re Stapylton Fletcher Ltd* [1995] 1 All ER 192 is a good illustration of a two-stage process in which individual buyers first become co-owners of a bulk pending appropriation to their respective contracts and then acquire title to what is withdrawn from the bulk and appropriated to each individual contract. See below.

whether by separation from the bulk and unconditional appropriation to his contract or by exhaustion.

Example 2: S, a wine merchant, contracts to sell to B on credit 99 bottles of 1966 Chateau Montrose claret from a stock of 100 bottles of such wine on S's premises. Before any bottles have been appropriated to the contract S becomes bankrupt. B cannot lay claim to a single bottle of wine, for it cannot be said of any one bottle that it is not the bottle excluded from the purchase. The position would be otherwise if S had sold all 100 bottles to B or if, before S became bankrupt, one bottle had rolled off a shelf and smashed or had been sold and delivered to another buyer,[88] producing appropriation by exhaustion. So B is deprived of the property in 99 bottles because of the one remaining bottle he had failed to buy.

Example 3: A, B and C each order ten cases of wine from S from a larger quantity of wine held in S's warehouse, payment to be made on delivery. Each of the buyers is issued with a warehouse warrant which is expressed to be negotiable and describes the holder of the warrant as the owner of the quantity and type of wine therein stated. Before any of the wine has been withdrawn or otherwise appropriated to any of the three contracts, S becomes bankrupt. A, B and C are unable to show title to any specific bottles or cases, and cannot claim to be tenants in common of thirty cases[89] even, it seems, if that quantity accounts for the entire stock.

The position would be otherwise if S, though not allocating wine to any particular purchaser, had unconditionally appropriated a quantity of wine to meet the orders of buyers generally. In that situation A, B and C would be co-owners of the appropriated wine in the proportion of their respective entitlements.[90]

Example 4: A company offers for sale a quantity of gold bullion from its stock of bullion in storage. Buyers are issued with certificates of ownership but no bullion is set aside for individual buyers or for buyers collectively. The company becomes insolvent. No payment has been made by any buyer. None of the buyers acquires title under his contract of sale since the goods are not ascertained. The difficulty cannot be surmounted by reliance on attornment by estoppel or trust, for both of these require identification of the subject matter. It would be possible for the seller to declare a trust of the entire stock of bullion for purchasers collectively but this is likely to be inconsistent with the commercial realities of the transaction. The result is that all the buyers are unsecured creditors of the insolvent company.[91]

2.   *Goods forming part of a bulk: the prepaying buyer*[92]

The rule that one who contracts to buy an unsegregated part of a bulk acquires no property rights of any kind, even if he has paid the purchase price in advance, has

---

88   Or otherwise appropriated to that buyer's contract.
89   *Re London Wine Co. (Shippers) Ltd* [1986] PCC121; *Re Goldcorp Exchange Ltd*, n 55. However, where there are several contracts of sale with the same buyer, ascertainment of the totality of the goods suffices; it is not necessary that the goods shall have become earmarked as between one contract and another. See p 238.
90   *Re Stapylton Fletcher Ltd*, n 87.
91   *Re Goldcorp Exchange Ltd*, n 55; and see p 209.

been widely criticized. In America it was long ago discarded and replaced with §2–105(4) of the Uniform Commercial Code.

An undivided share in an identified bulk of fungible goods is sufficiently identified to be sold although the quantity of the bulk is not determined. Any agreed proportion of such a bulk or any quantity thereof agreed upon by number, weight or other measure may to the extent of the seller's interest in the bulk be sold to the buyer who then becomes an owner in common.

So under §2–105(4) an agreement to buy, say, 10 bottles from a bulk of 100 is equated with an agreement to buy a 10% interest in the entire bulk. The Law Commissions advocated the adoption of a similar rule in England,[93] though only as regards the prepaying buyer.[94] These recommendations have now been carried into effect by the Sale of Goods (Amendment) Act 1995, which introduces new ss 20A and 20B into the Sale of Goods Act 1979. These provide as follows:

20A Undivided shares in goods forming part of a bulk

(1) This section applies to a contract for the sale of a specified quantity of unascertained goods if the following conditions are met-

(a) the goods or some of them form part of a bulk which is identified either in the contract or by subsequent agreement between the parties; and

(b) the buyer has paid the price for some or all of the goods which are the subject of the contract and which form part of the bulk.

(2) Where this section applies, then (unless the parties agree otherwise), as soon as the conditions specified in paragraphs (a) and (b) of subsection (1) above are met or at such later time as the parties may agree-

(a) property in an undivided share in the bulk is transferred to the buyer, and

(b) the buyer becomes an owner in common of the bulk.

(3) Subject to subsection (4) below, for the purposes of this section, the undivided share of a buyer in a bulk at any time shall be such share as the quantity of goods paid for and due to the buyer out of the bulk bears to the quantity of goods in the bulk at that time.

(4) Where the aggregate of the undivided shares of buyers in a bulk determined under subsection (3) above would at any time exceed the whole of the bulk at that time, the undivided share in the bulk of each buyer shall be reduced proportionately so that the aggregate of the undivided shares is equal to the whole bulk.

(5) Where a buyer has paid the price for only some of the goods due to him out of a bulk, any delivery to the buyer out of the bulk shall, for the purposes of this section, be ascribed in the first place to the goods in respect of which payment has been made.

(6) For the purposes of this section payment of part of the price for any goods shall be treated as payment for a corresponding part of the goods.

---

92 See generally *Benjamin's Sale of Goods* (6th edn, 2002), paras 18–253 ff.

93 By an addition to the Sale of Goods Act 1979.

94 *Sale of Goods Forming Part of a Bulk* (Law Com No 215, Scot. Law Com No 145, HC 807, 1993). One could make a case for allowing even a buyer who has not prepaid to assert an interest in the bulk, for he could enforce his interest only on paying the price. But there is less need to protect such a buyer, whose loss will usually be no more than the excess of the market price or value over the contract price.

20B Deemed consent by co-owner to dealings in bulk goods

(1) A person who has become an owner in common of a bulk by virtue of section 20A above shall be deemed to have consented to-

(a) any delivery of goods out of the bulk to any other owner in common of the bulk, being goods which are due to him under his contract;

(b) any dealing with or removal, delivery or disposal of goods in the bulk by any other person who is an owner in common of the bulk in so far as the goods fall within that co-owner's undivided share in the bulk at the time of the dealing, removal, delivery or disposal.

(2) No cause of action shall accrue to anyone against a person by reason of that person having acted in accordance with paragraph (a) or (b) of subsection (1) above in reliance on any consent deemed to have been given under that subsection.

(3) Nothing in this section or section 20A above shall-

(a) impose an obligation on a buyer of goods out of a bulk to compensate any other buyer of goods out of that bulk for any shortfall in the goods received by that other buyer;

(b) affect any contractual arrangement between buyers of goods out of a bulk for adjustments between themselves; or

(c) affect the rights of any buyer under his contract.

While it remains the case that the property in particular goods does not pass to the buyer until these have been ascertained, s 20A now gives him a co-ownership interest in the bulk pending delivery to him from the bulk of his contract entitlement and a right to withdraw that entitlement from the bulk without liability to other co-owners.

Although the requirement of ascertainment in s 16 is expressed by the opening words of that section to be subject to s 20A, the latter does not in fact provide an exception. It remains impossible to acquire a property interest in goods that have not been ascertained.[95] What s 20A does is to give an interim property right by way of co-ownership of the bulk itself, though only if this is identified.[96] This co-ownership interest falls outside the rules in ss 17 and 18 as to the time when property passes and the provisions of s 20 as to the passing of risk, for these are directed to property and risk in relation to the goods to be delivered under the contract of sale, whereas in the case of the co-ownership interest arising under s 20A the co-ownership rights arise by virtue of that section as soon as the conditions which it prescribes are satisfied, while the Act contains no provisions on risk of loss, damage or deterioration affecting the bulk.[97]

(iii) Conditions in which section 20A applies

In order for s 20A to apply, five conditions must be satisfied.

1.   Contract must specify quantity of goods to be sold

Section 20A applies only if the contract relates to a specified quantity of goods. The specification may be by number, weight or other measurement. But if the contract is

---

95   For the process of ascertainment, see pp 213, 235.
96   See below.
97   See p 257.

for the transfer of an interest in the bulk itself in terms of a given fraction or percentage, the goods are then specific[98] and the rules in s 18 governing the transfer of property in specific goods apply,[99] the respective shares of the co-owners being governed by their agreement and common law rules.

2.   Goods must form part of a bulk

Section 20A does not apply to a contract for the sale of wholly unascertained goods, only to those to be supplied from a bulk. 'Bulk' is defined as a mass or collection of goods of the same kind which (a) is contained in a defined space or area and (b) is such that any goods in the bulk are interchangeable with any other goods therein of the same number or quantity.[100] The requirement that the goods be 'of the same kind' would seem to be more restrictive than for the concept of fungibility, where contractual interchangeability (element (b) above) suffices regardless whether the units forming the collection are of the same kind or disparate in character.[101] The references to a 'mass or collection' and a 'defined space or area' are intended to distinguish ex-bulk goods from wholly unascertained goods and in particular to exclude the seller's general stock.[102] So 'bulk' should be confined to a heap or collection of goods all of the same kind that are together at one place at the same time.[103]

3.   The bulk must be identified

The section does not apply unless the bulk itself is identified. So if the seller has the choice whether to supply the goods from bulk A or bulk B,[104] the section does not come into operation until he has made an unconditional election. Moreover, since even a 'quasi-appropriation' is contractual in character, it is not sufficient that the seller intends to supply from a particular bulk; this must be agreed by the contract or subsequent agreement, whether specifically or giving one party the power of designation.

4.   The buyer must have prepaid

Prepayment is an essential condition of the application of s 20A. It may be total or partial; the effect of a partial payment is simply to scale down the buyer's co-ownership interest.[105] Payment by the buyer obviously includes a payment by a

---

98 Sale of Goods Act 1979, s 61(1).
99 See p 230.
100 Sale of Goods Act 1979, s 61(1).
101 See p 59.
102 Law Commission and Scottish Law Commission, *Sale of Goods Forming Part of a Bulk* (Law Com. No 215, Scot. Law Com. No 145) para 4.3.
103 Examples given in the Law Commissions' Report (ibid), were: a cargo of wheat on a named ship, a mass of barley in an identified solo, cases of wine (all of the same kind) in an identified cellar, ingots of gold (all of the same kind) in an identified vault, bags of fertilizer (all of the same kind) in an identified storehouse and a heap of coal in the open at a specified location.
104 See p 212.
105 Sale of Goods Act 1979, s 20A(6). However, the position is otherwise if the parties have agreed that the property is to pass only on payment in full. See below.

third party with the buyer's authority which operates in total or partial discharge of the buyer's price obligation, including payment by a bank under a documentary credit.[106]

5.   No contrary agreement

Section 20A does not apply if the parties agree otherwise.[107] So if, in relation to the bulk, the seller has reserved a right of disposal, then just as under s 19(1) this would preclude the passing of property in specific or ascertained goods,[108] so also under s 20A(2) reservation of a right of disposal of the bulk as a whole would preclude conferment of a co-ownership interest. Similarly, it would seem that s 20A is excluded if there is an express or implied agreement that the property is to pass only on payment in full and only a partial payment has been made, for it cannot be supposed that the section is intended to give the buyer from bulk a property interest he would not have on delivery *in specie*.[109]

(iv) Proprietary effects

1.   Buyer becomes owner in common

Unless the parties agree otherwise, as soon as the above conditions have been met or at such later time as the parties may agree (a) property in an undivided share in the bulk is transferred to the buyer and (b) the buyer becomes an owner in common of the bulk.[110] The buyer is co-owner with everyone else having an interest in the bulk, including other buyers and, to the extent that their entitlements do not account for the entire bulk, the seller himself.

2.   Measure of buyer's share

At any given time the buyer's co-ownership share is represented by such share as the quantity of goods bought and paid for bears to the quantity of goods in the bulk at that time.

Example 5: S contracts to sell from his warehouse stock of 1,200 cases of 1996 Chateau Montrose wine 120 cases to B1, 240 cases to B2 and 360 cases to B3. All the wine is paid for by the buyers in advance. The buyers have the following interests in the bulk:

B1	120 cases	10%
B2	240 cases	20%
B3	360 cases	30%
S	480 cases	40%

Example 6: The facts are as in example 5 except that B2 has paid only half the price due from him. His interest is only 10%, while that of S is 50%.

---

106 As to what constitutes payment, see p 460.
107 Sale of Goods Act 1979, s 20A(2).
108 See p 208.
109 See the discussion in *Benjamin's Sale of Goods*, para 18-263.
110 Sale of Goods Act 1979, 20A(2). Limb (b) is a tautology, since an 'undivided share' presupposes an ownership in common.

Since the co-ownership share is always measured by reference to the quantity of the bulk at any given time, it follows that if the bulk shrinks by natural wastage or destruction so that there is insufficient to meet the claims of all the co-owning buyers, the value of each co-owning buyer's interest abates in proportion. This is the effect of s 20A(4). It is interesting that this subsection makes no reference to any retained interest of the seller, from which it may be inferred that any reduction in the bulk is first to be attributed to the seller's retained interest and the abatement of the buyers' interests arises only if there remains a shortfall after excluding that interest. This interpretation is consistent with the view that the risk of shrinkage falls in the first instance on the seller as regards his interest.[111] So in example 5, if 240 cases were accidentally destroyed, reducing the stock to 960 cases, the loss is borne entirely by S, reducing his entitlement from 480 cases to 240, while the number of cases to which the buyers are entitled remains unchanged and accordingly the proportion of their entitlement to the reduced number of cases increases to produce the following redistribution:

B1	120 cases	12.5%
B2	240 cases	25%
B3	360 cases	37.5%
S	240 cases	25%.

The interests of the buyers are reduced only if what is lost exceeds the amount of S's retained interest. So if 516 of the 1,200 cases are destroyed, the loss comes first out of S's 480 cases, extinguishing his interest in the bulk, and the buyers share the loss of the other 36 cases proportionately, leaving them with interests in the remaining 684 cases in the ratio 1:2:3 as follows:

B1	114 cases
B2	228 cases
B3	342 cases

By contrast, an increase in the bulk beyond the total quantity of the buyers' entitlements does not affect them one way or the other, since the increase belongs to the seller or other person entitled to it.

3.   Effect of a buyer's withdrawal from bulk

If one buyer takes out all that is due to him, he ceases to have a share in the bulk and the remaining buyers are co-owners of what is left, measured as above. If the buyer takes out only part of what is due to him, then the delivery to him is to be ascribed in the first instance to the goods he has paid for.[112] This means that he retains an interest in the bulk only if the goods he has paid for exceed in quantity what he has withdrawn, and his continuing interest in the bulk is limited to the proportion of the excess in relation to the remaining bulk.

Example 7: The facts are as in Example 6. B2 withdraws 75 cases, leaving 165 cases still to be supplied to him under the contract and 1125 cases remaining in the

---

111   See p 257.
112   Sale of Goods Act 1979, s 20A(5).

bulk. He had paid for only 120 cases and the 75 cases he has withdrawn are to be attributed to those for which he had paid, reducing his co-ownership interest to 45/1125 (ie the 45 cases in the bulk remaining attributable to his payment divided by the remaining quantity of the bulk), namely 4%.

4.   *Buyer may acquire constructive possession in common*[113]

Section 20A(2), in conferring co-ownership, does not say anything about constructive possession, which, it is thought, can come about only if the seller or other person in physical possession attorns to the buyers in common in respect of the bulk rather than to each individual buyer in respect of his entitlement. Such shared constructive possession does not in any way depend on s 20A and has always been available. It does not, however, appear to add to the buyer's rights and remedies deriving from his ownership and right to physical delivery from the bulk, which together are sufficient to ground an action for conversion against the seller or any third party who interferes with the right to possession.

(v) Right to withdraw from bulk

Each co-owner under s 20A is deemed to have consented to any delivery of goods out of the bulk to any other owner to whom such goods are due under the contract and to any dealing with or removal or disposal of goods in the bulk by any other owner in common.[114] A co-owning buyer who receives no more than his entitlement under his contract is not liable to any other person for having taking his entitlement,[115] and in particular he is not liable to any other buyer who suffers a shortfall because the bulk is inadequate to satisfy all entitlements.[116]

4.   THE TIME WHEN PROPERTY PASSES TO THE BUYER

Before turning to the detail of the rules governing the time when property passes to the buyer, we must briefly mention two other categories referred to in the Act, namely *existing* goods and *future* goods. This classification is distinct from and cuts across the specific/generic/quasi-specific classification previously discussed, and is expressed in s 5(1) of the Sale of Goods Act in the following terms:

> The goods which form the subject of a contract of sale may be either existing goods, owned or possessed by the seller, or goods to be manufactured or acquired by him after the making of the contract of sale, in this Act called future goods.

This definition of future goods is repeated verbatim in s 61(1). It will be seen that goods may be existing goods even if not owned by the seller; the seller's possession

---

113 See Louise Gullifer, 'Constructive possession after the Sale of Goods (Amendment) Act 1995' [1999] LMCLQ 93.
114 Sale of Goods Act 1979, s 20B(1).
115 Ibid, s 20B(2).
116 Ibid, s 20B(3). Thus no buyer receiving what is due to him has to compensate another buyer who suffers a shortfall because of a shrinkage in the bulk or because a third buyer has taken more than his entitlement.

suffices. Since the Act draws a contrast between existing and future goods, and thus presumably does not contemplate the possibility of goods being both existing and future at the same time, it follows that by 'future goods' is meant goods which either do not exist at all at the time the contract is made or, though existing, are neither owned nor possessed by the seller. Hence the word 'acquired' is confined to situations where the seller lacks both ownership and possession at the time of the contract and obtains one or the other, or both, subsequently.

Future goods are usually wholly unascertained but this is not necessarily the case. For example, I may agree to buy from A the first car he makes or a car already in existence which A has contracted to buy from B but has not yet acquired. In the exceptional case of potential property, that is, property which in the course of nature may grow from existing property of the seller (produce from land, offspring of animals, etc), future goods may perhaps be regarded as specific even before they have actually come into existence. Thus if S contracts to sell to B the entire crop of potatoes to be grown on a particular piece of land, the subject matter of the sale is identified at the time of sale even though not yet in existence.[117] But this is so only where the existing asset is specific and the potential product is ascertainable without any subsequent act of appropriation. An agreement to sell 200 tons of potatoes from a particular piece of land is not a contract for the sale of specific goods, for the contract contemplates that the total output from the land may be greater than 200 tons, and if it is, some act of appropriation will be necessary in order to identify the particular 200 tons that are to satisfy the contract.[118]

Future goods may also be quasi-specific, as where S agrees to sell to B 100 tons of potatoes *ex* a named vessel, being part of a larger quantity of potatoes on board the vessel which S has not yet acquired himself.

Existing goods may be specific, unascertained or quasi-specific, depending on the degree of identification achieved at the time of the contract.

The label 'future goods' appears to serve a twofold purpose. First, it is used in s 5(3) to make it clear, in conformity with the general concept of 'property' discussed in an earlier chapter,[119] that since a sale involves a transfer of property, and property means either an indefeasible title or possession with intent to assert dominion, a purported sale of that which the seller neither owns nor possesses (ie future goods) is merely an agreement to sell. Secondly, it features in r 5(1) of s 18,

---

117 The common law recognized this by allowing the legal title to after-acquired potential property to vest in the purchaser automatically upon its coming into existence without any new act of transfer of the kind that would ordinarily be mandatory. See *Grantham v Hawley* (1615) Hob 132; *Petch v Tutin* (1846) 15 M & W 110, and p 631. It is not clear whether potential property constitutes 'future goods' for the purpose of the Sale of Goods Act or whether it can be the subject of an immediate sale, but the point is of little practical importance, for, if so intended by the parties, such property vests in the buyer immediately on coming into existence, without any new act, except where it is growing on land, in which case it probably has to be severed before the property can pass. See *Benjamin's Sale of Goods*, paras 1-100, 5-095.

118 In other words, the same degree of identification is necessary for potential property as for goods contracted to be sold as existing at the time of the contract.

119 See p 55.

though its sole effect is to make that rule applicable to contracts for the sale of future specific goods.[120]

With these preliminary remarks, we can turn to consider the rules embodied in the Sale of Goods Act for the passing of the property from seller to buyer.

(i)   Specific goods

Where the contract is for the sale of specific goods, no problems of identification arise, for by definition the goods are identified on the making of the contract. Hence the time when the property passes to the buyer depends solely on the intention of the parties.

> 17. (1) Where there is a contract for the sale of specific or ascertained[121] goods the property in them is transferred to the buyer at such time as the parties to the contract intend it to be transferred.
>
> (2) For the purpose of ascertaining the intention of the parties regard shall be had to the terms of the contract, the conduct of the parties and the circumstances of the case.

The general provisions of s 17(2) are supplemented by more precise 'rules for ascertaining intention' embodied in s 18, which apply to determine the time of passing of the property to the buyer 'unless a different intention appears'. Section 18 contains five rules, the first three of which are concerned with contracts for the sale of specific goods.

> Rule 1 – Where there is an unconditional contract for the sale of specific goods in a deliverable state the property in the goods passes to the buyer when the contract is made, and it is immaterial whether the time of payment or the time of delivery, or both, be postponed.
>
> Rule 2 – Where there is a contract for the sale of specific goods and the seller is bound to do something to the goods for the purpose of putting them into a deliverable state, the property does not pass until the thing is done and the buyer has notice that it has been done.
>
> Rule 3 – Where there is a contract for the sale of specific goods in a deliverable state but the seller is bound to weigh, measure, test, or do some other act or thing with reference to the goods for the purpose of ascertaining the price, the property does not pass until the act or thing is done and the buyer has notice that it has been done.

It should be emphasized that these and other rules in s 18, supplemented by those in s 19,[122] are merely presumptive rules of intention; they are displaced by any contrary intention evinced by the agreement and by other provisions of the Act which directly or indirectly govern the passing of the property irrespective of the intention of the parties.[123]

---

120   See p 234.

121   The word 'ascertained' is imprecise in this context. More accurate is 'to be ascertained'.

122   See pp 239–240.

123   Eg ss 5(3), 16. The character of s 18 as a mere determinant of intention is masked by the wording of the specific rules, which are framed as if self-executing. Thus r 1 purports to provide that in the conditions stated 'the property in the goods passes to the buyer', whereas what is meant is that the property is assumed to be intended to pass to the buyer, so that it will pass by virtue of s 17(1) of the Act *unless* prevented from so doing by some other provision of the Act, such as s 5(3). See further p 232.

RULE 1 When referring to 'deliverable state', the rule is not concerned with the actual state of the goods on the making of the contract but is simply postulating that the seller has not by the terms of the contract undertaken to do anything to the goods before tendering delivery to the buyer.[124]

It will be apparent that neither delivery nor payment is directly related to the passing of the property. Two questions are posed by r 1. What is an 'unconditional contract' and when are goods 'in a deliverable state'?

(1) *'Unconditional contract'.* The problem created by this phrase stems partly from the much-abused word 'condition', which possesses a variety of meanings,[125] and partly from the fact that the word 'unconditional' is positioned so as to qualify the contract rather than the sale under the contract. It is clear that if the operation of the contract as a whole is subject to a condition precedent – as where there is a contract for the sale of specific goods subject to the seller obtaining a legally required licence – the case is not within r 1. But what if the contract is subject to a condition subsequent, to a resolutive condition by which the contract, though otherwise unconditional, is to become void in stated events, eg if the goods fail to meet a given standard on testing by a designated third party? It is strongly arguable that a condition subsequent, unlike a condition precedent, does not preclude the contract from being 'unconditional' within r 1, for by its nature a condition subsequent does not suspend the operation of a contractual provision but merely produces a restoration to the status quo (in this case revesting of the property in the seller) if the stipulated condition occurs. It is even more clear that 'unconditional' cannot be intended to denote the absence of any condition in a sense of a major term of the contract (ie condition as opposed to warranty), for this construction would obliterate the operation of the rule almost entirely. Hence the accepted view is that 'unconditional contract for the sale of specific goods' means no more than a contract of sale under which the passing of the property to the buyer is not made subject to any condition.[126] Rule 1 would, indeed, have been more happily worded if it had used the phrase 'contract for the unconditional sale of goods'.

This construction means that r 1 is not displaced by a condition subsequent, nor by the inclusion of terms the breach of which attract a right to terminate, nor even by conditions precedent if they are not conditions which suspend the contract as a whole or the passing of the property but merely suspend the operation of other terms, eg payment.[127] On the other hand, a conditional sale agreement by which the property in the goods is not to pass until payment or the performance of some other condition is plainly outside r 1. So also is a contract for a sale of goods expressly stipulated as goods to be acquired by the seller for the purpose of sale to the buyer, for the parties are then implicitly recognizing that the passing of the property is conditional upon the seller acquiring the goods.

---

124 See further p 232.
125 See S. J. Stoljar, 'Contractual Concept of Condition' (1953) 69 LQR 485.
126 *Benjamin's Sale of Goods*, para 5–019; P. S. Atiyah, J. N. Adams and H. L. McQueen, *Sale of Goods* (10th edn, 2001), pp 316–318.
127 This last point is apparent from the concluding words of r 1 itself.

What, however, is the position where a seller contracts to sell specific goods which, though offered to the buyer on the basis that they are currently in the seller's possession or ownership, are in truth future goods? Is this within r 1, so as to pass the property in the goods to the buyer? Some writers, baulking at the prospect of r 1 applying to such a situation, have surmounted the difficulty by treating 'specific goods' as excluding future goods in the context of r 1, thus giving future goods a meaning for the purpose of r 1 different from that which the term bears in s 5. But these verbal gymnastics are neither appropriate nor necessary. The difficulty disappears if we remember that r 1 does not of itself have executive force but merely states the presumed intention of the parties.[128] The sale as existing goods of goods which are in fact future goods is unquestionably within r 1, for the presumed intention is to pass the property to the buyer immediately. It does not follow, however, that this intention is effective. In fact, in this situation it is not effective, for s 5(3) provides in terms that where by a contract of sale the seller purports to effect a present sale of future goods, the contract operates as an agreement to sell the goods with the result that the property will not pass to the buyer unless and until the seller has himself acquired a title, whether indefeasible or relative,[129] or the buyer acquires an overriding right by virtue of some exception to the *nemo dat* rule.

(2) *'In a deliverable state'*. Section 61(5) provides that goods are in a deliverable state when they are in such a state that the buyer would under the contract be bound to take delivery of them. This would suggest that if the goods are in such a state that the buyer is entitled to reject them, as where they are not of satisfactory quality, r 1 does not apply and property does not pass. But if this be right, we are constrained to reach the somewhat startling conclusion that in a contract for the sale of specific goods the property will never pass to the buyer on the making of the contract if the goods are defective. Such a wide view of r 1 has not been canvassed in the courts, which have hitherto been called on to apply the rule only in a very limited range of situations.[130] There can be little doubt that the restricted view assumed in the cases is correct. The trouble with r 1, as with certain other provisions of the Sale of Goods Act, is the excessive compression used in the drafting. The wide view of r 1 would require us to read it as follows: 'Where there is an unconditional contract for the sale of specific goods and the goods are in a deliverable state at the time of the contract ... ' but this reading is not consistent with the case law on which the formulation of the rule is based. Rule 1 applies where, *on the assumption that the goods are what they purport to be*, the seller has not by the terms of the contract undertaken to do anything to them as a prerequisite of the buyer's acceptance of delivery. In short, in speaking of 'deliverable state', r 1 refers not to the actual state of the goods but to the fact that the parties have agreed that the seller may tender delivery of them without first having to do something to them to put them into a state where they are ready for delivery.

---

128   See n 123.

129   See p 31.

130   Of which the most typical is severance from land or buildings to which the goods are affixed at the time of the contract. See, for example, *Kursell v Timber Operators and Contractors Ltd* [1927] 1 KB 298; *Underwood Ltd v Burgh Castle Brick and Cement Syndicate* [1922] 1 KB 343.

RULE 2 This rule, unlike r 1, does not refer to an 'unconditional' contract, for the obvious reason that by the operation of r 2 itself the property is deemed to be intended to pass only when the conditions of deliverable state and notice thereof to the buyer are satisfied. The phrase 'deliverable state' has the same meaning as in r 1, that is to say it refers to the situation in which the seller has undertaken to do something to the goods before tendering delivery of them.

RULE 3 This rule, which applies only where it is the seller who has the obligation to weigh, measure, test, etc, and only when such act is necessary for the calculation of the price, is somewhat curious in view of the fact that ascertainment and payment of the price are not generally prerequisites of the passing of the property. The rule is of little practical importance.

It is to be noted that whereas r 1 is couched in positive terms, so that subject to the other provisions of the Act[131] there is a presumed intention to transfer the property where the requirements of r 1 are satisfied, rr 2 and 3 are negative and thus prescribe the *minimum* requirements that have to be met before an intention to transfer the property can be inferred. Fulfilment of these minimum requirements will not necessarily suffice, however.

Since all the rules in s 18 are subject to the opening caveat 'unless a different intention appears', and since reservation of a right of disposal pending fulfilment of stipulated conditions precedent plainly manifests a contrary intention, the above rules are subordinated to s 19 (reservation of a right of disposal) where that section is applicable.[132]

(ii) Unascertained goods

The overriding provision in the case of wholly unascertained goods is s 16, which states the self-evident proposition that no property can pass until the goods are ascertained.[133] In the nature of things, this is not a rule which can be excluded by contract.[134] Goods become ascertained by unconditional appropriation. In the case of a contract for the sale of unascertained goods by description, the presumed intention of the parties as to the passing of the property is governed by r 5 of s 18, the first two sub-rules of which provide as follows:

> Rule 5 – (1) Where there is a contract for the sale of unascertained or future goods by description, and goods of that description and in a deliverable state are unconditionally appropriated to the contract, either by the seller with the assent of the buyer or by the buyer with the assent of the seller, the property in the goods then passes to the buyer: and the assent may be express or implied, and may be given either before or after the appropriation is made.
>
> (2) Where, in pursuance of the contract, the seller delivers the goods to the buyer or to a carrier or other bailee or custodier (whether named by the buyer or not) for the purpose of transmission to the buyer, and does not reserve the right of disposal, he is to be taken to have unconditionally appropriated the goods to the contract.

131 Eg ss 5(3), 19.
132 See pp 239–240.
133 See p 209.
134 *Jansz v G.M.B. Imports Pty Ltd* [1979] VR 581.

This is by far the most difficult rule to apply and is also one of the most important. A dispute as to the applicability of r 5 typically arises where the seller, having collected the whole or part of the price from the buyer in advance, becomes bankrupt without having made delivery. The buyer's rights are vitally affected by the question whether the goods have become unconditionally appropriated to the contract, for if they have, the buyer becomes the owner of them,[135] whereas if they have not, he is restricted to proving in competition with other unsecured creditors. The following questions arise.

1.   To what classes of sale contract does Rule 5 apply?

This is answered by the opening words of r 5, which refer to contracts for the sale of unascertained or future goods by description. The rule does not distinguish wholly unascertained from quasi-specific goods, and 'unascertained' covers both categories.[136] Future goods, even if specific,[137] are brought within the rule. This may seem illogical, but in practice works well enough, for it is extremely unlikely that future goods will also be specific if they are sold by description, and r 5 is confined to sale by description.[138]

2.   What other conditions must be satisfied?

Given that the contract is of a class falling within r 5,[139] four other conditions must be satisfied before r 5 comes into play. First, there must be an appropriation of goods to the contract. Secondly, the appropriation must be unconditional. Thirdly, the goods must be of the contract description. Fourthly, they must be in a deliverable state. In this context, the phrase 'deliverable state' has a different significance from that which it possesses in relation to rr 1 and 2, for in r 5 it denotes the actual state of the goods as opposed to the state in which the seller has expressly undertaken to put them before tendering delivery. Hence for the purpose of r 5, goods are not in a deliverable state unless (a) they are in fact in such condition that the buyer would not be entitled to reject them when tendered or (b) they are accepted by the buyer as being in a deliverable state. Whether goods conform to the contract description is a question which, as we shall see,[140] involves distinguishing identity from attributes and is considered in detail in a subsequent chapter.[141] For the purpose of r 5 the distinction is less material than in other parts of the Act, for a defect in quality which prevents the goods from being in a deliverable state will render r 5 inapplicable even if the defect is not such as to prevent the goods from conforming to the description in the contract.

---

135 With the result that the goods do not form part of the seller's estate and cannot be retained by his trustee, who is obliged to surrender them to the buyer.

136 But the operation of the rule in relation to quasi-specific goods may be different and is therefore discussed separately, p 237.

137 See p 232.

138 As to the meaning of this, see p 291.

139 See above.

140 See p 292.

141 See pp 292 ff.

This leaves the requirement of unconditional appropriation. What is meant here is some act which earmarks goods as the contract goods and irrevocably commits the parties to those goods, thus depriving the party who performs the act of appropriation of the right to change his mind and substitute other goods of the contract description. An act of constructive delivery[142] which puts the goods out of the control of the seller – as by delivery to a carrier[143] without reserving a right of disposal[144] or by procuring a third party in possession of the goods to attorn to the buyer – almost always constitutes an unconditional appropriation. If there is no loss of control, assent to the specific act of appropriation is usually necessary. Such assent may be given before or after the act of appropriation and may be express or implied. The performance by the seller of what would ordinarily be regarded as acts of internal organization – such as segregating the goods in his warehouse, packaging them and labelling them in the name of the buyer – will not normally constitute appropriation unless the act in question was that specifically designated by the contract, for the seller is entitled to say that what he does with the goods while they are in his control is entirely his own affair, and that having provisionally allocated goods to the contract, he has changed his mind and decided to allocate different goods.[145] The position is otherwise where the contract provides, expressly or impliedly, for an act of appropriation preceding the seller's loss of control, as where the seller agrees to sell 'the first widget I receive' or the contract allows the seller to fix the contract goods by giving a notice of appropriation.[146] An instructive case on these points is *Healy v Howlett & Sons*.[147]

> The plaintiff contracted to sell to the defendants twenty boxes of mackerel. He dispatched 190 boxes of mackerel by rail from Valentia, Ireland, to Holyhead, *consigned to his own order*, giving instructions to the railway company at Holyhead to distribute the fish among his various customers, including the defendants. Due to the train being delayed, the mackerel arrived in Holyhead late and in such condition that it would inevitably be unmerchantable under its contract description when delivered to the defendants in London. The railway officials at Holyhead set aside twenty boxes of mackerel and dispatched them to the defendants, who rejected them as unmerchantable. After disposing of the mackerel elsewhere, the plaintiff sued for the balance of the price, contending that the fish had been appropriated to the contract at Valentia and that the risk of deterioration had thereupon passed to the defendants.

> *Held*, there was no appropriation until the twenty boxes had been set aside for the defendants at Holyhead, by which time the deterioration had occurred, so that the defendants were justified in rejecting the goods.

It is worth observing that the requirement of assent to the seller's appropriation is just as essential in the case of goods which are being made by the seller for the

---

142 As to constructive delivery generally, see p 43.

143 See p 253. But the goods do not pass out of the seller's control by such delivery unless consigned to a particular buyer. If it is left to the carrier himself to make the selection as between one customer and another, he acts as the seller's agent and property does not pass to any particular buyer until earmarked to the contract by the carrier (*Healy v Howlett & Sons* [1917] 1 KB 337, and below).

144 Section 18, r 5(2). See pp 239–240.

145 See *Mucklow v Mangles* (1808) 1 Taunt 318, per Heath J at 319; *Carlos Federspiel & Co S. A. v Charles Twigg & Co Ltd* [1957] 1 Lloyd's Rep 240.

146 See p 935.

147 *Healy v Howlett & Sons*, n 143.

buyer as it is for goods which the seller is to supply from stock or outside sources. This may at first sight seem surprising. If I instruct a boatbuilder to build me a boat of specified type and dimensions, and without further communication from me he proceeds with the work and completes a boat that accords with the specifications I have laid down, then surely, it will be said, neither he nor I can deny that it is *my* boat, in the sense of being the boat appropriated to *my* contract. But even here, the rule requiring assent applies, for as was said over 170 years ago: 'A tradesman often finishes goods, which he is making in pursuance of an order given by one person, and sells them to another.'[148] On the other hand, it would not be unduly difficult to establish an assent to the boatbuilder's appropriation of the boat (and indeed of the incomplete structure). It would suffice if I visited the boatbuilder's yard and made approving comments when he showed me the structure, or even if I telephoned to inquire about progress and the builder gave me details sufficient to identify the boat he was talking about and I did not dissent.[149]

It is important to bear in mind that while an unconditional appropriation is necessary if the property is to pass under r 5, it does not follow that it inevitably signifies an intention to transfer the property; nor is appropriation necessarily connected to actual delivery. Appropriation merely denotes the act by which the contract goods become ascertained and earmarked to the contract. There are many reasons why the parties may wish to reach the point of identifying the contract goods without necessarily intending that property shall pass at that stage. For example, a foreign buyer purchasing goods from an English seller on a c.i.f. basis will not ordinarily acquire the property until he has paid the price and taken possession of the shipping documents,[150] but he will wish to know well in advance of that time on what ship the goods have been loaded so that he can either resell on a c.i.f. basis or calculate the time of arrival of the goods and organize arrangements for their collection. Again, if the goods are of a kind which is in short supply, the buyer may wish to be assured that goods have been earmarked from the seller's existing stock to meet the contract, even if the buyer does not require immediate delivery and is not to obtain ownership until payment at a later date.

3.   Can Rule 5 be excluded?

In theory, since all the rules in s 18 are subject to a contrary intention, r 5 could be excluded by agreement of the parties. But such an exclusion would normally be pointless, since it would then be necessary for the parties to spell out their own rule to govern the passing of the property, and this could just as easily be done within r 5 itself, either by defining the act of appropriation or by reserving a right of disposal

---

148 *Mucklow v Mangles*, n 145. The comment was made to illustrate a somewhat different point, namely the presumed intention of the parties that ownership of goods to be made is not to pass to the buyer until they have been completed, but it is equally apposite to the issue of appropriation. See further n 149.

149 On the facts of *Mucklow v Mangles* there was almost certainly an appropriation, but it would not have helped the buyer to avoid the effect of the seller's insolvency, for appropriation merely identifies the contract goods, it does not as such confer any real right on the buyer.

150 See p 940.

to the seller pursuant to s 19[151] or a right of substitution to the buyer in the contract of sale.[152]

(iii) Quasi-specific goods

Where the contract is for the sale of an unascertained part of an identified bulk, ss 16 and 17 and r 5 of s 18 apply to the same extent as for wholly unascertained goods. But the identification of the source from which the contract goods are to be supplied produces one difference, namely that the goods may become ascertained without any physical act of the seller or buyer, as the result of exhaustion,[153] ie shrinkage of the bulk to a quantity no greater than that stipulated in the contract.[154] This shrinkage may occur in various ways, eg delivery of part of the bulk to another buyer; reduction of the bulk through destruction or evaporation; or damage, deterioration or other change in composition of part of the bulk so that such part ceases to correspond to the contract description. Any of these events may produce the result that the contractual source of supply, being reduced to no more than the contract quantity, becomes referable in its entirety to the contract; and the result appears to be that the seller is to be considered to have made an unconditional appropriation for which the buyer's prior assent suffices even though the seller has not lost control, since it is clear that the seller has lost the power to substitute other goods. If the seller has undertaken to notify the buyer when this stage has been reached, his failure to do so does not affect the ascertainment of the goods (for in this situation the seller has no choice as to the goods to which his notice can relate), though it may have consequences for the seller if the buyer, being unaware that the goods are now identified and available for collection, does not collect them and they are later damaged or destroyed.[155]

Where separate quantities of goods on board a vessel or in a warehouse are agreed to be sold to the same buyer under different contracts, it is not necessary to allocate a particular part of the goods to a particular contract; it suffices that all the goods are intended for the buyer, either from the outset or by exhaustion following deliveries to other buyers.[156]

(iv) Goods delivered on approval or on 'sale or return'

Rule 4 of s 18 provides as follows:

> When goods are delivered to the buyer on approval or on sale or return or other similar terms the property in the goods passes to the buyer:

---

151 See pp 239–240.

152 See p 241.

153 *Wait and James v Midland Bank* (1926) 31 Com Cas 172; *The Elafi* [1982] 1 All ER 208. This has now been given statutory effect under the Sale of Goods (Amendment) Act 1995, which inserts a new r 5(3) in s 18 of the Sale of Goods Act 1979.

154 For the converse case where the seller tends a quantity of goods in excess of that called for by the contract see p 360.

155 See Sale of Goods Act 1979, s 20(2), and p 248.

156 *Re Wait and James*, and *The Elafi*, n 153.

(a)   when he signifies his approval or acceptance to the seller or does any other act adopting the transaction;

(b)   if he does not signify his approval or acceptance to the seller but retains the goods without giving notice of rejection, then, if a time has been fixed for the return of the goods, on the expiration of that time, and, if no time has been fixed, on the expiration of a reasonable time.

We have deliberately left this rule to the end as its very inclusion in s 18 is an oddity. This is because while all the other rules deal with the transfer of property under a contract of sale, the delivery of goods on approval or on a sale-or-return basis is not made pursuant to a contract of sale;[157] the 'seller' is merely making an offer of sale to the 'buyer', coupled with an assent to the latter's retention of possession for a reasonable period while he makes up his mind. In commercial parlance a transaction is usually termed a 'sale on approval' where the recipient is to examine the goods to see if they are suitable for his purpose and a 'sale or return' where the recipient wishes to have the facility of returning the goods for some reason other than disapproval of their suitability, eg because the quantity supplied may prove surplus to requirements or because he takes delivery for the purpose of resale and may be unable to find sufficient buyers; but the legal effect of the two transactions appears to be the same. The delivery of the goods constitutes an offer of sale by the deliveror and the offer is accepted in the conditions prescribed by r 4 or when the deliveree does any act designated by the deliveror as the mode of acceptance.

There being no contract of sale at the time of delivery, the words 'seller' and 'buyer' in r 4 (and the word 'buyer' in the opening lines of s 18 so far as these govern r 4) do not bear their ordinary signification,[158] but are convenient to describe the deliveror and the deliveree under the proposed sale. But though there is no contract of sale, there is nevertheless a contract, the effect of which is to confer on the deliveree a right to possession and an option to buy which he is taken to exercise if he fails to return the goods within the agreed period. Hence the deliveror, as grantor of the option, cannot withdraw his offer of sale.[159]

A delivery on approval or on 'sale or return' is a consensual arrangement[160] and must be distinguished from a delivery of totally unsolicited goods. Nothing in r 4 entitles the deliveror to foist goods on an unwilling recipient and then claim (contrary to the common law rule)[161] that silence implies assent. Before r 4 can

---

157 For a contract of sale involves not merely a commitment to sell but an obligation to buy (*Edwards v Vaughan* (1910) 26 TLR 545; *Helby v Matthews* [1895] AC 471).

158 See s 61(1).

159 *Atari Corp.(UK) Ltd v Electronics Boutique Stores (UK) Ltd* [1998] QB 539; *Kirkham v Attenborough* [1897] 1 QB 201, per Lord Esher MR at 203. The contract in the *Electronics Boutique* case was curious in that it required payment to be made well before expiry of the period allowed for return of the goods. The plaintiffs originally asserted but later rightly abandoned the argument that the right of return was lost once the payment date had passed. The effect of such a contract would seem to be that the buyer is contractually obliged to make payment by the agreed date but can recover it upon exercising his right to return the goods within the period allowed. See also John N. Adams, (1998) 61 MLR 432.

160 A fact reflected in the opening words of s 18, r 4: 'When goods are delivered to the buyer on sale or return or other similar terms ...'.

161 *Felthouse v Bindley* (1862) 11 CBNS 869.

apply it must be shown that the recipient either received the goods as a voluntary bailee or became a willing possessor for a sufficient time before purchase to create a meaningful right of disapproval or return,[162] as opposed to an immediate contract of sale. An involuntary bailee is not under a duty either to return the goods or to communicate non-acceptance in order to avoid an obligation to buy.[163]

Sale-or-return transactions are to be distinguished from apparently similar agreements such as hire-purchase and conditional sale by virtue of the fact that, pending acceptance of the goods, the deliveree is a mere custodian and does not acquire rights over the goods *vis-à-vis* the seller unless and until he becomes committed to the purchase of the goods by accepting them. The commitment to purchase and the passing of the property almost invariably coincide, by virtue of r 4, though it is open to the parties to agree that the passing of the property shall be deferred to a later point of time, eg payment.[164]

(v) Reservation of right of disposal[165] or substitution

The presumption raised by s 18 as to the seller's intention to transfer the property to the buyer will be displaced where the seller reserves the right of disposal pending the fulfilment of stated conditions, of which the most common is payment of the price. Section 19 of the Act deals with reservation of a right of disposal in the following terms:

19 – (1) Where there is a contract for the sale of specific goods or where goods are subsequently appropriated to the contract, the seller may, by the terms of the contract or appropriation, reserve the right of disposal of the goods until certain conditions are fulfilled; and in such a case, notwithstanding the delivery of the goods to the buyer, or to a carrier or other bailee or custodier for the purpose of transmission to the buyer, the property in the goods does not pass to the buyer until the conditions imposed by the seller are fulfilled.

(2) Where goods are shipped, and by the bill of lading the goods are deliverable to the order of the seller or his agent, the seller is prima facie to be taken to reserve the right of disposal.

(3) Where the seller of goods draws on the buyer for the price, and transmits the bill of exchange and bill of lading to the buyer together to secure acceptance or payment of the bill of exchange, the buyer is bound to return the bill of lading if he does not honour the bill of exchange, and if he wrongfully retains the bill of lading the property in the goods does not pass to him.

The reservation of the right of disposal under s 19(1) may be either express or implied. A conditional sale agreement, which provides that property is not to pass until payment and that on default the seller may repossess the goods, offers a good

---

162 It is a matter of construction of the contract whether the buyer has to physically return the goods or simply hold them available for collection.

163 This common law rule is greatly strengthened by the Unsolicited Goods and Services Acts 1971–1975, which preclude demand for payment for unsolicited goods sent to a person otherwise than for the purpose of his business and which enable him, if the goods are not collected within the time prescribed by the Acts, to keep the goods as his own without payment.

164 As in *Weiner v Gill* [1906] 2 KB 574.

165 This topic is further explored in connection with export sales (p 940) and bills of exchange (p 949).

illustration of an express reservation of a right of disposal. Very commonly, however, the reservation is to be inferred from the seller's conduct and almost invariably this takes the form of an act by which the seller preserves control over the goods. Section 19(2) provides an example. Where in a bill of lading the goods are consigned to or to the order of the seller or his agent, the seller retains control, for only he or the agent or a person to whom the bill of lading has been transferred will be entitled to collect the goods on arrival.[166] Even where the seller arranges for the bill of lading to be made out in the name of the buyer as consignee, yet if the express or implied terms of the sale are cash against documents, the seller will be considered to retain a right of disposal at least so long as he holds the documents.[167]

Yet in all these cases the court is seeking to ascertain the intention of the parties. The fact that the seller parts with control does not necessarily mean that he is intending to transfer the property, for his intention may be merely to part with possession. Indeed, in c.i.f. contracts the normal presumption is that where the documents are released by the seller to the buyer in anticipation of immediate payment, the parties intend that, while the buyer is to have possession, the property is to remain in the seller until payment.[168] Conversely, the fact that the seller retains the documents is not always indicative of an intention to reserve the right of disposal, for the seller may consider himself adequately protected by retaining constructive possession while allowing ownership to pass to the buyer.[169]

Where the contract is for the sale of specific goods, the seller must obviously make the right of disposal a term of the contract. If he fails to do this, he cannot unilaterally introduce such a term subsequently. If, however, the contract is for the sale of generic goods (whether wholly unascertained or quasi-specific), the reservation may be made either in the contract or at the time of appropriation, and in the latter case it will be effective to stop the passing of the property, even if the reservation is in breach of the contract.[170]

Section 19(3) lays down a special rule for documentary bills of exchange. The buyer must either honour the bill (by acceptance or payment according to the agreement between the parties) or return the bill of lading. If he retains the bill of lading after dishonouring the bill of exchange by non-acceptance or non-payment,[171] the property does not pass. Section 19(3) does not deal directly with the location of the property in the short interval that may elapse between the buyer's receipt of the documents and his acceptance or payment of the bill of

---

166   *The Ciudad de Pasto* [1988] 2 Lloyd's Rep 208. See also *The Antares III* [2002] 1 Lloyd's Rep 233, and p 885.
167   See pp 934, 939.
168   See p 939.
169   See p 935.
170   *Gabarron v Kreeft* (1875) LR 10 Exch 274.
171   Non-acceptance in the case of a time bill, non-payment in the case of a sight bill (see p 487). An accepted time bill may, of course, be dishonoured later by non-payment but it is obvious that this latter type of dishonour is not intended to fall within s 19(3) and that the property will pass to the buyer upon acceptance of the bill and will not remain in the seller pending payment.

exchange,[172] but the obvious inference is that the bill of lading is delivered conditionally on honouring of the bill of exchange and that meanwhile the property in the goods is to remain in the seller.

Reservation of the right of disposal, though it precludes the passing of the property to the buyer and thus defers his acquisition of the right to deal with the goods, does not necessarily mean that the buyer has no *power* of disposal; for, being in possession of the document, he may be able to give an innocent third party a good title, overriding that of the seller, by virtue of some exception to the *nemo dat* rule.[173]

Section 19 deals only with reservation by the seller of a right to dispose. It does not cover the converse case of retention by the buyer of a right to change his mind after an act of appropriation by him. Such a right may, of course, be expressly or impliedly conferred by the contract. Alternatively, the buyer can, in the event of a contract for the sale of unascertained goods, reserve the right at the time of appropriation, so that in effect his appropriation is conditional only.

172   A bill presented for acceptance need not be accepted instantaneously, and is dishonoured only if not accepted within 'the customary time' (Bills of Exchange Act 1882, s 42), ie, twenty-four hours, excluding non-business days (*Bank of Van Diemen's Land v Bank of Victoria* (1871) LR 3 PC 526). Similarly, a bill presented for payment is not dishonoured by non-payment if the drawee tenders payment later the same day (*Hartley v Case* (1825) 1 C & P 676).
173   See pp 434 ff.

9   Risk and Frustration

Once the buyer has acquired both possession and property in the goods, their subsequent fate, except so far as due to some breach by the seller, is not the latter's concern, and if the goods are damaged or destroyed, it is the buyer's loss, unless the parties have otherwise agreed. But deterioration, damage or loss may occur before this stage is reached, that is, when the buyer has neither possession nor property, or when he has the one but not the other. The parties may expressly agree who is to suffer the loss, but very frequently they fail to make provision for this eventuality. The law has then to resolve two questions: who is to suffer from the loss, and what effect is the loss-making event to have on the contract? The first of these two questions is regulated by the rules relating to risk; the second, by rules as to frustration of the contract.[1] But risk and frustration, though distinct concepts, are connected in that where frustration occurs, the resultant working out of the rights of the parties may mean that the burden of the loss falls more heavily on one than on the other.[2]

One of the principal reasons why English law has been so troubled with questions of risk is that by s 20 of the Sale of Goods Act risk is tied to property, and as we have seen the passing of the property is not dependent on delivery.[3] It follows that the buyer may acquire the property in goods while these are still in the seller's possession, and if the goods are then accidentally destroyed without fault, the loss prima facie falls on the buyer. A more reasonable rule would have been to link risk with control, for the person in control of goods (whether by physical possession or by having the right to give directions as to the goods to a third party holding them) is best able to take proper steps for their protection and to cover loss by insurance.

I.   THE MEANING OF 'RISK'

The statutory provisions as to risk are to be found in ss 20, 32 and 33 of the Sale of Goods Act, with which must be read the rules of frustration embodied in ss 6 and 7. But before we examine these provisions we must get a clearer perception of what is meant by 'risk'. Goods are at a party's risk if he has to bear the loss resulting from their damage or destruction. The impact of this will depend on whether the party in question is the seller or the buyer. As Professor Sealy has rightly remarked:

1 See p 260.
2 See p 261.
3 See p 231.

The truth is that risk is a derivative, and essentially negative, concept – an elliptical way of saying that either or both of the primary obligations of one party shall be enforceable, and that those of the other party shall be deemed to have been discharged, even though the normally prerequisite conditions have not been satisfied.[4]

Where the goods are at the seller's risk, this means that if they suffer a mishap, the seller, being unable to tender delivery in accordance with the contract, cannot recover the price from the buyer and must repay any part of the price paid in advance. It does not necessarily follow, however, that he incurs a liability to the buyer for non-delivery. This second question depends on the impact which the loss-making event has on the contract as a whole and is thus a question not of risk but of frustration.

Where the goods are at the buyer's risk, this means that he must pay the price[5] despite the fact that the goods have been lost or damaged before the buyer has taken possession, or after he has taken possession but before the property has passed to him.[6] In other words, since the risk is on the buyer, destruction of the goods absolves the seller from his duty to deliver the goods or to transfer the property in them to the buyer,[7] and if the goods are merely damaged, the seller is entitled to tender, and the buyer is obliged to accept, delivery of them as if they were in conformity with the contract, while the buyer remains liable for payment of the price in full. In this situation the question of frustration cannot arise, since if the contract were to be treated as frustrated by loss of or damage to the subject matter,[8] the buyer would be discharged from his obligation to pay the price, so that effectively the risk would be thrown back on the seller.

An analogous position arises in the case of goods sent on approval or on 'sale or return'. If they are destroyed or damaged while at the deliveror's risk, the loss falls on him and the intended recipient incurs no liability. If the loss or damage occurs when the goods are at the risk of the intended recipient, he is precluded from rejecting them and thus becomes liable for the price as if he had voluntarily adopted the transaction.[9]

---

4 L. S. Sealy, 'Risk in the Law of Sale' [1972] 31 CLJ 225, at p 226.
5 If he does not, he can in the alternative be sued for damages for non-acceptance, but almost invariably the action for the price is more efficacious. See p 402.
6 This produces the curious result that whereas a seller who is precluded from tendering delivery by reason of the buyer's breach cannot sue for the price (unless he can show that delivery has been waived) but must rest his claim in damages (see p 395), where delivery is prevented by accidental destruction after the risk has passed to the buyer, he is liable for the price.
7 Assuming, of course, that the contract is one under which the risk has passed before the passing of the property, contrary to the normal rule embodied in s 20(1).
8 See p 260.
9 However, the general rule is that the risk does not pass to the deliveree until he has adopted the transaction, whether expressly or by failing to give notice of rejection within the stipulated time or (if none) within a reasonable time. This is the combined effect of s 20 and s 18, r 4. In such a case, the buyer does not become liable for the price merely because of destruction of the goods before he has adopted them (*Elphick v Barnes* (1880) 5 CPD 321). See further, pp 255–256.

2.   THE GENERAL PRINCIPLE OF RISK: *RES PERIT DOMINO*

The draftsman of the Sale of Goods Act appears to have taken as axiomatic the need to link risk not to delivery but to property. If the goods I contracted to buy have become mine, any subsequent loss is my loss; if the loss occurs when the goods are still the property of the seller, the loss falls on him. Some critics of this rule have urged a return to the principles of Roman law. However, in this respect Roman law was far from possessing the virtues now ascribed to it by modern commercial lawyers. True, the general principle of Roman law was that property did not normally pass to the buyer until delivery at the earliest.[10] But this fact loses much of its significance when we discover that Roman law did not tie risk to property at all. On the contrary, from the buyer's viewpoint it was even more stringent than the Sale of Goods Act, stipulating that in the absence of fault, risk passed to the buyer on the making of the contract even if the buyer at that point had neither possession nor property.[11] The English rule is embodied in s 20 of the Sale of Goods Act.

(1)   Unless otherwise agreed, the goods remain at the seller's risk until the property in them is transferred to the buyer, but when the property in them is transferred to the buyer the goods are at the buyer's risk, whether delivery has been made or not.

(2)   But where delivery has been delayed through the fault of either buyer or seller the goods are at the risk of the party at fault as regards any loss which might not have occurred but for such fault.

(3)   Nothing in this section affects the duties or liabilities of either seller or buyer as a bailee or custodier of the goods of the other party.

The general rule, then, is that risk passes with property. This is subject to several qualifications. First, it is displaced by contrary agreement between the parties. Secondly, even where risk is prima facie on one party, it may be shifted, wholly or partly, as the result of fault by the other. Thirdly, where the seller is authorized to send the goods (ie to deliver them to an independent carrier for onward transmission to the buyer), the Act provides special rules for the risks of transit.[12] Fourthly, where the buyer deals as consumer,[13] sub-ss (1) to (3) of s 20 are required to be ignored and goods remain at the seller's risk until they are delivered to the consumer.[14] Fifthly, s 20 does not in terms distinguish specific or ascertained goods from unascertained or quasi-specific goods. But the distinctions are very material, for they influence the passing of the property, which in turn affects the incidence of risk. Moreover, despite the peremptory language of s 20, the location of the property is not the only determinant; the extent to which control has passed from seller to buyer may also be material, a fact of particular relevance where the goods are at the time of the contract, or later become, quasi-specific. Finally, s 20 does not

10 F. De Zulueta, *The Roman Law of Sale* (1957), p 31.
11 Ibid. In practice, the distinction between the Roman rule and s 20 of the Sale of Goods Act is less marked than might appear, since '... the circumstances in which the risk passes in Roman law are much the same as those in which the property passes and with it the risk under our law' (Buckland and McNair, *Roman Law and the Common Law* (2nd rev edn, 1965), pp 288–289).
12 Sections 32(2), (3), 33. See pp 254–255.
13 See the Unfair Contract Terms Act 1977, s 12, applied by the Sale of Goods Act 1979, s 61(5A).
14 Sale of Goods Act 1979, s 20(4).

apply to the risk of loss of goods held in co-ownership by virtue of s 20A of the Act, in respect of which the law remains unsettled.[15]

The scene having been set, we can now examine in detail the impact of risk and frustration, and associated rules of delivery,[16] at different stages of the contract. In the case of goods that have become identified or quasi-specific by the time of the act or event which brings the application of the rules into question, the effect of these can best be seen in relation to the location of the goods at that time. But goods which are still wholly unascertained cannot be treated in this way, for they have no situation. They must therefore be treated as a distinct category, and it is with them that we shall begin.

3. WHOLLY UNASCERTAINED GOODS

Where the contract is for the sale of wholly unascertained goods and the seller is unable to tender delivery because the stock from which he intended to meet the order is destroyed or his anticipated source of supply otherwise becomes unavailable, then in the absence of fault by the buyer causing delay in delivery the loss will fall on the seller, for if the goods have not become ascertained it cannot be predicated that the perished goods were those earmarked for the buyer. The question whether the seller has made an effective appropriation may thus be very material to the incidence of risk. In the language of the Sale of Goods Act, the risk prima facie passes with the property, and the property does not pass until the goods have become ascertained by an unconditional appropriation effected in conformity with the contract.[17] Moreover, the seller will not normally be able to plead frustration, for it is not a term of the contract that the goods shall be taken from the seller's existing stock or any other identified source of supply, and the buyer is thus entitled to say that if one source of supply dries up, then it is for the seller to find another. But the Sale of Goods Act only complements, and does not wholly replace, common law rules of frustration, and it is possible to envisage circumstances in which the destruction of available sources of supply is so total and unforeseeable as to produce frustration at common law.[18] In any event, destruction of the subject matter of the contract is not the only type of frustrating event. Even in the case of wholly unascertained goods, other causes of frustration may arise, eg a change in the law which makes it illegal for the seller to proceed with the contract.

Though risk of loss of his anticipated source of supply prima facie falls on the seller, this principle may, under s 20(2) of the Act, be displaced where delivery has been delayed through the fault of the buyer. Though the reference to 'the goods' in s 20(2) might suggest that this proviso is confined to specific, or at any rate specific and quasi-specific, goods, it has been held equally applicable to unascertained goods. In this case 'the goods' means no more than 'the contractual goods which

---

15 See p 257.
16 The topic of delivery is examined in ch 10.
17 See *Healy v Howlett & Sons* [1917] 1 KB 337, the facts of which are set out at pp 235–236.
18 Eg where the only area in which goods of the contract description are produced is destroyed by earthquake or volcanic lava or is submerged beneath the sea.

have been assembled by the seller for the purpose of fulfilling his contract and making delivery'.[19]

4.   QUASI-SPECIFIC GOODS

The *res perit domino* rule causes particular difficulty in the case of goods which are at the time of the contract, or which later become, quasi-specific as the result of agreement between seller and buyer that the contract goods shall be supplied from a larger and identified bulk. For example, the seller may agree to sell 100 out of 500 crates of whisky in a warehouse. This is an example of goods that are quasi-specific at the time of sale. Or he may contract to sell 100 crates of whisky f.o.b. London and later put on board a vessel at London 300 crates, giving notice to the buyer that these include the 100 crates ordered by the buyer. Here the goods are wholly unascertained at the time of the contract but become quasi-specific through the later act of appropriation. The effect of the goods being quasi-specific is that if the bulk in which they are comprised perishes, we can say that the contract goods, though not precisely identified, have ceased to exist, so that the questions of risk and frustration arise. It is in this respect that the distinction between quasi-specific and wholly unascertained goods possesses particular significance.[20]

From the seller's viewpoint, however, this is of little help in answering his problem. True, he is able to say that the contractual source of supply has perished,[21] thus rendering future performance impossible, so that if the risk has not passed to the buyer, the contract is frustrated and the seller is not liable to the buyer for non-delivery. But this is poor consolation to the seller, who with the loss of the goods is disabled from recovering the price. What the seller needs to show is that the risk has passed to the buyer; but under the normal rule linking risk to property this is precisely what he cannot do, for necessarily quasi-specific goods are unascertained, so that no property passes.[22]

So long as the bulk from which the goods are to be supplied remains under the seller's control, the *res perit domino* rule works reasonably well, for the seller as possessor is best placed to safeguard the goods and to cover the risk of loss by insurance, and in so far as the property is to pass on ascertainment he can normally bring an end to the risk by making the necessary appropriation of goods to the contract. But where the bulk is with a third party and the seller relinquishes control, as by transferring a document of title to the buyer or by authorizing the third party

---

19 *Demby Hamilton & Co Ltd v Barden* [1949] 1 All ER 435, per Sellers J at 437. It is apparent from the next sentence of the judgment that in speaking of 'the contractual goods' Sellers J was not intending to depict identified goods but simply goods kept by the seller for the fulfilment of the contract.

20 See below.

21 The effect of loss of only part of the bulk is unclear. But see pp 227, 257.

22 Section 16. See p 237. However, under s 20A of the Sale of Goods Act a prepaying buyer of goods forming part of a bulk acquires a proportionate interest in the bulk pending withdrawal of his entitlement from the bulk, so that the subject matter of his temporary interest is the bulk itself, which is, of course, identified or ascertained. As to whether s 20 applies in this situation, see p 257.

to attorn to the buyer, the seller's difficulty becomes acute, for the power to appropriate ceases to be in him and lies with the third party and/or the buyer, who between them control the time at which the goods become ascertained and therefore the time at which the property is to pass. In such a case, the court may be willing to infer an intention to exclude s 20, the implied agreement being that risk shall pass to the buyer when the seller has done everything required of him to put the goods into the buyer's hands. A good illustration is *Sterns Ltd v Vickers Ltd*:[23]

> The defendants, who had purchased from the Admiralty 200,000 gallons of white spirit lying in the tank of a storage company, sold 120,000 gallons to the plaintiffs, who resold the same quantity afterwards to a third party. The defendants procured from the storage company and passed to the plaintiffs a delivery warrant for 120,000 gallons of the spirit, and the plaintiffs in turn endorsed this warrant to their purchaser, the third party. When the third party came to take delivery, he found that the quality of the spirit had deteriorated in storage, and claimed damages from the plaintiffs, who claimed over against the defendants, alleging that the spirit was not of the quality warranted by the terms of the contract.
>
> The Court of Appeal, though not deciding whether the property had passed to the plaintiffs prior to the deterioration,[24] held that even if it had not, the risk was on the plaintiffs, for the defendants had done all that they undertook to do, the plaintiffs could have demanded delivery from the storage company as soon as they had received the delivery warrant and if they had done so they would have procured spirit which was then in conformity with the contract. The plaintiffs' claim was therefore dismissed.[25]

This case is usually treated as exceptional,[26] but the principle it embodies is eminently sensible, and it is submitted that, unless otherwise agreed, it applies to any case in which the seller loses control of quasi-specific goods by giving constructive delivery, provided that in so doing he fulfils the delivery obligation imposed on him by the contract. In most cases this proviso will be satisfied, even where the contract provides for physical delivery by the seller to the buyer, for in accepting a document of title or other form of constructive delivery the buyer is implicitly assenting to this mode of performance of the seller's delivery obligation, and is thus estopped from contending that the original delivery term has not been fulfilled. If the buyer contracts for physical delivery, eg at his own premises, and is offered a warehouse warrant or an attornment by a third party in possession, he can decline to accept this on the ground that it is not the mode of delivery prescribed in

---

23 [1923] 1 KB 78.

24 Scrutton LJ considered that the plaintiffs' contention on this point, namely that the property had not passed, was correct.

25 The precise ground for excluding s 20 was not expressly stated but must be taken to rest on the inference of an agreement that risk was to pass to the buyers on transfer of the delivery warrant to them.

26 See, for example, *Benjamin's Sale of Goods* (6th edn, 2002), para 6–004, citing *Comptoir d'Achat et de Vente du Boerenbond Belge S. A. v Luis de Ridder Limitada* [1949] AC 293. But the *ratio decidendi* of that case was not the supposed exceptional character of the decision in *Sterns Ltd v Vickers Ltd* but the fact that the respondent sellers had not given effective control to the buyers, merely a delivery order by one of the sellers' agents to another. Such an order conferred no right against the carrier of the goods without its attornment (p 44) and there was no evidence to indicate that the buyers had bound themselves to accept it as performance of the delivery obligation.

the contract; but if he accepts, he must take the consequences,[27] and cannot expect the seller to continue on risk as to quasi-specific goods over which the seller no longer has control.

It must, however, be emphasized that in *Sterns Ltd v Vickers Ltd* the warehouse had assented to the delivery warrant in favour of the buyer,[28] so that the act of appropriation was in the buyer's control, not the seller's. The position is otherwise where there is no such assent.[29]

5.   IDENTIFIED GOODS

(i)   Goods in the seller's possession[30]

Where specific or ascertained goods are, without fault on the part of the seller, lost or damaged[31] while in the seller's possession, then prima facie the risk is on the buyer if the property in the goods has passed to him and on the seller if it has not.[32] This does not, however, apply to a sale to a person dealing as consumer,[33] where the risk passes to the consumer only on delivery.[34] Moreover, if one of the parties is at fault, the risk may pass to him in some measure, though the extent to which it shifts depends on the nature of the fault. Fault may occur either because the seller fails to observe his duties as a bailee in relation to the goods[35] or because through the wrongful act or default[36] of the seller or buyer delivery is delayed.[37] The two types of fault differ in their effect in that whereas the consequence of fault causing delay in delivery is regulated by s 20(2) and shifts the risk only as regards loss which might not[38] have occurred but for such default, the effect of breach of a duty owed

---

27 Ie, the consequence of control passing. He may, of course, accept on the basis of reserving his right to proceed against the seller for the expense incurred in having to organize physical collection himself.

28 Creating a quasi-attornment rather than a true attornment, which requires that the goods held for the buyer as new bailor be identified. See p 44.

29 For the risk in the case of prepaid unascertained goods forming part of a bulk, in which the prepaying buyers acquire co-ownership interests in the bulk, see p 257.

30 'Seller's possession' is here used to denote possession (actual or constructive) by the seller or his agent, as opposed to possession by an independent warehouseman, carrier or other bailee.

31 Unless otherwise indicated, 'damage' is hereafter used to include deterioration.

32 Section 20(1).

33 See Unfair Contract Terms Act 1977, s 12, as applied by s 61(5A) of the Sale of Goods Act 1979.

34 Sale of Goods Act 1979, s 20(4).

35 In which case the buyer's common law remedies are preserved by s 20(3). As to want of care by the buyer in possession, see p 256. The fact that at the time of the agreement the goods are not in conformity with the contract description or of satisfactory quality or fit for their purpose is not a fault of the seller of a kind within s 20(2) or (3), which is confined to delay in delivery and breach of the seller's duty as bailee. This may appear to create a problem for the buyer if the nonconforming goods are destroyed before rejection by the buyer; but the answer would seem to be that the buyer retains the right to reject, and thus pass the risk back to the seller, even though the loss has already occurred and the risk has thus crystallized. See p 353, n 43, and P. S. Atiyah, John N. Adams and Hector MacQueen, *The Sale of Goods* (10th edn, 2001), p 354.

36 Which is what is meant by fault in s 20(2). See s 61(1).

37 In which case s 20(2) applies.

38 See (1) below.

as bailee is governed by common law rules of bailment, not by s 20, which merely preserves the common law position; and, at common law, a bailee who deviates from his bailment becomes strictly liable as an insurer and is answerable even for wholly accidental loss unless he can show that it would inevitably have occurred even without the breach.[39]

Where there is no delay by the buyer in taking delivery and the seller alone is in default, whether as regards care of the goods or as to making delivery, the position is clear. The seller is disabled from recovering the price, and at the same time is exposed to an action for damages for non-delivery, for his fault precludes him from contending that the contract is frustrated.[40] More complex is the position where the seller has not protected the goods and the buyer is late in taking delivery or has otherwise caused delay in delivery. The problem here is not merely to work out the respective liabilities of the parties where both are at fault. Before we can address ourselves to this question we first have to decide whether both parties are at fault or whether, on the other hand, the default of one has excused performance by the other, so that his apparent default is legally justified. The nature and extent of the duty to deliver and to accept delivery are discussed later[41] and need not concern us at this point. For the present our inquiry reduces itself to three questions. First, what is the extent of the seller's duty as bailee, given that there has been no default by the buyer resulting in delay in delivery? Secondly, what impact, if any, does such default by the buyer have on the seller's responsibilities as bailee?[42] Thirdly, assuming that both parties are in breach and that neither breach excuses the other, what are the respective rights and liabilities of the parties?

1.   The seller's duty as bailee

Where the seller holds the goods for the buyer pending collection or delivery, he must comply with any express terms of the bailment. Thus, if he undertakes to keep the goods in a particular building or in a particular room, he must not store them elsewhere; and if they are to be secured in a designated manner against damage or theft, he must secure them in that manner and no other. If the seller deviates from the terms of the bailment then, like any other bailee, he becomes strictly liable for delivery up of the goods in proper condition and will not be excused even by accidental loss or damage not resulting from his negligence unless he can show that

---

39 See *Lilley v Doubleday* (1881) 7 QBD 510; *Edwards v Newland & Co* [1950] 2 KB 534.

40 *Allied Mills Ltd v Gwydir Valley Oilseeds Pty Ltd* [1978] 2 NSWLR 26 (NSW Court of Appeal). Moreover, he has no right to cure non-performance by the tender of substitute goods of the same description, for once the contract goods are ascertained, then, unless they are rejected by the buyer as not in conformity with the contract, no other goods can be substituted without the buyer's consent. On the other hand, a buyer who unreasonably refuses a tender of alternative goods will not be able to recover by way of damages a loss that he would have avoided if he had taken reasonable steps to mitigate his damage by accepting the tender in question. See *Payzu Ltd v Saunders* [1919] 2 KB 581, and see p 122.

41 See pp 263 ff.

42 The converse question, whether the seller's breach of duty as bailee extinguishes the buyer's obligation to accept delivery, depends on the buyer establishing either that the goods as tendered do not conform to the contract or that the breach of duty so goes to the root of the contract as to constitute an anticipatory repudiation.

it would have occurred even without the deviation.[43] In the absence of express agreement as to the manner of his custody, the seller owes an implied duty to exercise reasonable care.

If, without breach of duty on the part of the seller, the goods perish before the property has passed to the buyer, the risk is on the seller,[44] but the contract of sale is either avoided under s 7 of the Act, where the goods are specific, or frustrated at common law, where they are ascertained, with the consequences previously discussed.

Where, however, the goods are merely damaged but do not perish either in a physical or in a commercial sense, the contract remains afoot, so that the seller will have to repair the goods at his own expense to bring them into conformity with the contract and will incur the usual liability to the buyer if he fails to supply conforming goods or is late with delivery.

In the event of the goods perishing or suffering damage after the property has passed to the buyer and without fault by the seller, the risk is on the buyer, the contract is not frustrated[45] and the buyer must pay the price. The seller continues liable to tender the goods, and the buyer to take delivery and accept them, in so far as delivery remains possible.[46]

2.   *Impact of the buyer's default*

Suppose that because of default by the buyer in taking delivery (whether at the seller's premises or elsewhere) the goods remain in the seller's possession and suffer loss or damage after the due delivery date. Where then does the seller stand? It is clear that if the time of taking delivery was of the essence and the seller had, prior to the loss or damage, properly elected to treat the contract as repudiated, he has no liability to the buyer, even for negligence, for after the seller's acceptance of the repudiation the buyer no longer had an interest in the contract, and the sole effect of the seller's negligence would be to reduce the damages recoverable from the buyer.[47] Where, however, the buyer's breach did not go to the root of the contract because time was not of the essence, or where the seller had not elected to treat the breach as a repudiation, the contract of sale remains afoot for the benefit of both parties, and the buyer's delay in taking delivery would not appear to absolve the seller from all responsibility for the goods,[48] though the extra expense involved

---

43 See cases cited n 39.

44 Section 20(1).

45 See p 243.

46 Where delivery is not possible, the position ought to be that the seller is excused from the delivery obligation. Unfortunately, the Act is silent on the point. For this and other criticisms of s 7, see Glanville Williams, *The Law Reform (Frustrated Contracts) Act 1943* (1944), at pp 81 ff. Professor Williams's strictures on the section were echoed by the Law Reform Commission of New South Wales, in relation to s 12 of the New South Wales Sale of Goods Act (*Working Paper on the Sale of Goods* (WP 13, 1975), pp 255 ff.; *Report on Frustrated Contracts* (LRC 25, 1976), para 8.16). *Semble*, the increased expense of delivery resulting from the adverse event – eg the cost of raising a sunken vessel – is part of the buyer's risk.

47 Under s 37 of the Act. See p 400.

48 But *semble* his status becomes that of an involuntary bailee, with a consequent diminution in the nature of his obligation. See N. E. Palmer, *Bailment* (2nd edn, 1991), ch 12.

in the prolongation of those duties is recoverable as damages and the seller can charge for storage.[49] But if the goods are damaged or destroyed without any breach of bailment by the seller, then to the extent to which the damage or loss might not have occurred if the buyer had taken delivery when he should, any risk that would ordinarily have rested on the seller passes to the buyer.[50] In such a case, even total destruction does not frustrate the contract.

(ii) Goods stored with a third party

Issues of risk and frustration become still more complex where goods identified as the contract goods are stored with a third party, eg in a warehouse or at a railway depot. There are now not two parties involved but at least three: the seller, the buyer and the depository. The goods may have been located in the warehouse[51] at the time of the contract of sale or they may have been delivered there afterwards. The storage may have been effected by the seller or his agents or by some third party, eg the person from whom the seller acquired the goods. The warehouse may be a bonded warehouse in which the goods, after importation, are being held pending customs clearance or it may be an ordinary depository where no question of customs arises, either because the goods are not imported or because they have already been cleared for customs. The goods may be held purely for deposit or they may be held for the purpose of onward transmission, so that the depository is not merely a bailee but also a carrier.

There are four key questions to be resolved:

(1) Did the delivery of the goods to the depository, or their continuance in the depository's possession, involve or result from a breach of duty on the part of the seller?
(2) Did the depository hold the goods as a carrier or other bailee for transmission to the buyer or merely as a warehouseman?
(3) Had the property passed to the buyer?
(4) Even if the property had not passed, had the buyer obtained control? In other words, was the depository the bailee of the seller or the buyer?

1. Breach of duty by seller

This could occur in various ways. The seller may have undertaken to keep the goods at his own premises, in which case their removal to a warehouse is a breach of the terms of the bailment, making him strictly liable for loss.[52] Even if not prohibited from depositing the goods in a warehouse, the seller may have failed to exercise reasonable care to ensure that the warehouse was suitable and competently staffed. Again, assuming that the seller acted perfectly properly in depositing the goods in the warehouse in question, or that the goods were deposited there before

49 See p 400.
50 Section 20(2).
51 For convenience, the term 'warehouse' will be used to denote any kind of store or depot not under the control of the seller or buyer.
52 See pp 244–250.

the seller acquired control of them, the period of storage may have been un-necessarily prolonged as the result of the seller failing to pay storage charges, so subjecting the goods to a warehouse lien and preventing the buyer from obtaining delivery.[53] In each of these cases the seller is in breach of duty with the conse-quences previously described.

2.   Was the depository holding as warehouseman or as carrier or other bailee for transmission?

Goods are not infrequently warehoused by a carrier on his own premises, either while in transit or to await collection by the buyer. Thus, if British Rail undertakes to carry goods from Edinburgh to London, then except in the unlikely event of their being put straight on the train at Edinburgh by the seller and collected at King's Cross by the buyer immediately on arrival, the goods will have to be kept in a depot of some kind when not on the train. Where the carrier holds the goods in store at the end of the journey, nice questions may arise as to when he ceases to hold them as carrier and becomes a warehouseman.[54]

The Sale of Goods Act has special rules regulating delivery to an independent carrier or other bailee for transmission to the buyer. It is thus relevant to know whether, at the time the goods were lost or damaged, the depository held them as a mere bailee holding the goods for collection or as a carrier or other bailee holding them for the purpose of transmission to the buyer. In the latter case, the rules discussed in section (iii), below, apply.[55]

3.   Had the property passed to the buyer?

We are here dealing with identified goods, so that no problems of ascertainment arise. It does not, of course, follow that the property is in the buyer. Even if the goods were sold as specific goods, and were thus identified at the time of the contract, the seller may have undertaken further acts to put them into a deliverable state,[56] or he may by the terms of the contract have reserved title, eg pending payment. If the goods were not ascertained at the time of the contract, an unconditional appropriation is necessary to pass the property, and even this is not sufficient where, by the terms of the contract or of the appropriation, the seller reserves a right of disposal. The reservation of such a right is particularly likely to be manifested where the goods are held by a third party, such as a carrier[57] or a warehouseman,[58] for while the relinquishment of control by the seller to the buyer does not necessarily indicate an intention to transfer the property,[59] the seller's

---

53 This constitutes a twofold breach by the seller: failure to deliver in accordance with the contract and breach of the implied term of freedom from incumbrances.

54 See p 411, n 154.

55 As to who is a carrier, see p 254.

56 In which event the property prima facie does not pass until those acts have been done and the buyer has notice of the fact (s 18, r 2).

57 See p 262.

58 See below.

59 See p 935.

retention of control is evidence of his desire to retain a right of disposal, so as to negate an intention to transfer the property to the buyer. Accordingly, while the transfer of the property and the transfer of control are distinct conceptions, they are closely interlocked. But however the transfer of property occurs, if it has taken place before the loss of or damage to the goods, the risk is prima facie on the buyer, in accordance with the principles previously discussed.

4. Had the buyer obtained control?

The question of control is important not only as a guide to whether the property has passed[60] but also as a distinct issue, for just as the transfer of control to the buyer may pass the risk to him in the case of quasi-specific goods,[61] so also it may have this effect where the goods are or have become wholly identified.[62]

Ex hypothesi physical possession is enjoyed neither by seller nor by buyer but by a third party, the warehouse company. In determining who had control when the loss or damage occurred, the question to be asked is whether at that time the warehouse still held the goods as bailee of the seller or whether the buyer had become the bailor. When the duty of the warehouse to surrender ceases to be owed to the seller and becomes a duty to the buyer, constructive delivery (and thus control) is considered to have been given to the buyer. This will occur, even without the passing of the property, where

(a) the seller transfers to the buyer (by delivery, with any necessary indorsement)[63] a bill of lading or other document of title[64] comprising the goods; or

(b) the warehouse attorns to the buyer, that is, acknowledges that it now holds the goods to the buyer's order.[65]

(iii) Goods in transit

We have so far dealt with cases where the goods are lost or destroyed while in the possession of the seller or the buyer or a third party who holds them as custodian of the seller or buyer but with no duty to transmit. We must now see what happens where identified[66] goods are lost or damaged in transit, that is, after delivery to an independent carrier[67] or other bailee for the purpose of transmission to the buyer[68] but before the buyer or his agent has taken delivery.[69] Delivery to a carrier, in

---

60 This may also operate in reverse, ie the passing of the property, established independently of control, will usually entitle the buyer to possession, subject to any necessary tender of the price where credit has not been given.

61 *Sterns Ltd v Vickers Ltd*, n 23.

62 For the giving of control to the buyer may imply an agreement to exclude the normal rule in s 20.

63 See p 890.

64 Eg, a statutory dock or warehouse warrant.

65 As to attornment generally, see pp 43, 266.

66 The goods may become identified by the act of delivery to the carrier which starts the transit, but this will usually be the case only where they are consigned to a designated buyer. See p 235, n 143.

67 See below.

68 As opposed to deposit with a bailee for collection by the buyer.

69 Sale of Goods Act, s 45. See further, p 410, as to when goods are deemed to be in transit.

addition to marking the commencement of transit of the goods, prima facie constitutes an appropriation of the goods to the contract, in the absence of the seller's reservation of a right of disposal.[70]

Where s 32(1) applies, so that delivery to a carrier is deemed delivery to the buyer, other than a buyer dealing as consumer, the rules governing risk and frustration where the goods are lost or damaged in transit are the same as for goods lost or damaged in the buyer's possession,[71] except so far as modified by the provisions of the Sale of Goods Act designed specifically for goods in transit.[72] These must now be examined.

I.   *Goods otherwise at risk of seller*

Let us suppose that the goods, though in the constructive possession of the buyer by virtue of s 32(1), would ordinarily have remained at the seller's risk, either under the ordinary rule linking risk with property or because the seller had expressly agreed to deliver the goods at his own risk. Nevertheless, as regards the period of transit, the seller's risk is modified by s 33.

> Where the seller of goods agrees to deliver them at his own risk at a place other than that where they are when sold, the buyer must nevertheless (unless otherwise agreed) take any risk of deterioration in the goods necessarily incident to the course of transit.

What does 'necessarily incident to the course of transit' mean? Does it mean, for example, that if I order a china tea set from a shop and it arrives broken, I have to bear the loss and pay the full price for the broken china? The short answer is no. Section 33 is very narrow in scope. It applies only where, by reason of the nature of the goods carried, the contractual mode of transport or other circumstances, there is a normal risk of deterioration *despite the exercise by the seller of all proper care and conformity with the obligations imposed on him by the contract*. Thus, s 33 cannot be invoked by a seller who has failed to ensure that the goods are properly packed or who has not taken reasonable care to select a competent carrier. Nor does the section apply to the sale of perishables, for the implied condition of satisfactory quality requires not merely that they shall be sound when delivered to the carrier but that they shall be in such condition when so delivered that with a normal transit they will arrive sound.[73]

Again, the buyer is not at risk as regards abnormal incidents, eg the collapse of a building on the lorry carrying the goods. In effect, all that s 33 does is to provide that if the buyer, in circumstances where loss or damage is liable to occur despite proper precautions by the seller, still authorizes dispatch, he must take the consequences. It is to be remarked that at the time of the case law from which s 33 was derived, travel and transportation were much more hazardous affairs. Everyone

---

70   Section 18, r 5(2). See p 234.

71   See p 255. This does not, of course, mean that for all the purposes of the Sale of Goods Act delivery to the carrier is equivalent to delivery to the buyer. In particular, the right of stoppage in transit is not normally lost until delivery to the buyer himself or his authorized agent. See p 410.

72   In particular, ss 32(2) and (3). See p 255. For delivery to a carrier, see pp 266 ff.

73   *Mash & Murrell Ltd v Joseph I. Emmanuel Ltd* [1962] 1 WLR 16n; and see p 000. See also B. G. Hansen, 'Inherent Vice and Contracts for the Sale of Goods' (1975) 2 Dalhousie LJ 168.

knew that the roads were badly built, that a coach was liable to be held up by highwaymen, that sailing ships might be diverted and sunk in a storm. The category of risks 'necessarily incident to the course of transit' is much smaller now than it was then. Nevertheless, some such risks can still exist, eg where goods are ordered to be delivered to a farm that can be reached only over a very bumpy track, or where the goods consist of highly inflammable explosives that are very sensitive to disturbance and may explode without warning despite all reasonable care. Whether the prospect of a lorry becoming involved in a road accident is a risk necessarily incident to the course of transit remains to be determined!

2. Goods otherwise at risk of buyer

Where under the ordinary rules the goods in transit would be at the risk of the buyer, the seller will nevertheless have to bear the risk himself if he fails to comply with s 32(2) and (3), where those subsections are applicable.[74]

(2) Unless otherwise authorized by the buyer, the seller must make such contract with the carrier on behalf of the buyer as may be reasonable having regard to the nature of the goods and the other circumstances of the case; and if the seller omits to do so, and the goods are lost or damaged in course of transit, the buyer may decline to treat the delivery to the carrier as a delivery to himself or may hold the seller responsible in damages.

(3) Unless otherwise agreed, where goods are sent by the seller to the buyer by a route involving sea transit, under circumstances in which it is usual to insure, the seller must give such notice to the buyer as may enable him to insure them during their sea transit; and if the seller fails to do so, the goods are at his risk during such sea transit.

Subsection (3) will be considered in relation to export sales.[75] The object of sub-s (2) is to ensure that if the goods are damaged in transit while at the buyer's risk, he will, so far as reasonable, be able to maintain an effective claim against the carrier.[76] Accordingly, the seller must select a competent carrier,[77] and must not accept a contract which unreasonably restricts the carrier's duties or his liability in the event of a breach of duty. Reasonable endeavours by the seller to procure a proper contract of carriage are not in themselves sufficient. What is required is that the contract of carriage itself shall be reasonable in the circumstances. If, despite all endeavours, the seller is driven to accept a contract which is not reasonable for the buyer's protection, the buyer has the remedies given by s 32(2). On the other hand, in determining what the buyer can reasonably be required to accept, regard must be had to the terms of contract prevailing in respect of the types of transport which the seller is authorized or required to use under the contract of sale, and if the contract of carriage which the seller concludes is as good as is normally available, the seller cannot be held at fault because the bargaining power of carriers of the class in

---

74 They do not apply to sales to a person dealing as consumer (Sale of Goods Act 1979, s 32(4)).

75 See p 932.

76 Though the contract is in its inception made between seller and carrier (unless expressed to be taken out by the seller on behalf of the buyer), the buyer will nevertheless have a direct right of action against the carrier in given conditions once the transport document has been transferred to him. See p 1058, with particular reference to sea carriage.

77 This is implicit in s 32(2), for if the carrier is incompetent, no terms of the carriage can be reasonable.

question enables the carrier selected to impose terms of carriage which do not provide the buyer with adequate protection against loss or damage of the goods in transit.[78] Moreover, provided that the seller acts reasonably in selecting the carrier, the fact that the carrier proves unable to meet his liabilities for such loss or damage (eg because he becomes insolvent and has no policy of insurance to which the buyer can have recourse)[79] does not alter the incidence of risk, and it is the buyer who will have to bear the loss.

(iv) Goods in the buyer's possession

Since risk is linked to property, not to delivery, the fact that the goods are in the buyer's possession at the time of loss or damage does not affect the basic rules previously described except in relation to consumer sales. If there has been no fault on either side, then, unless otherwise agreed, the risk is on the buyer if the property has passed and on the seller if it has not; and in the latter case the contract is avoided by s 7 of the Act.[80] In practice, this result is relatively infrequent. In most cases the property will have passed to the buyer on or before delivery. Where it has not,[81] possession will normally be held by the buyer under a written contract – eg a hiring or hire-purchase agreement – which will usually stipulate that the goods are held at the buyer's risk and that he is liable for loss or damage, even if not caused by his negligence. Even where there is no such contractual provision, the buyer must observe his duties as bailee, namely to follow precisely any express terms of the bailment and in any event to exercise reasonable care for the safekeeping of the goods; and a breach of any of his bailment obligations will, if the goods are delayed or destroyed, leave him liable for the price,[82] or at the seller's option for the diminution in or loss of the value of the goods, unless the buyer can show that the loss or damage would inevitably have occurred even if the terms of the bailment had been strictly observed.[83]

The rules are different in the case of a sale to a person dealing as consumer. In this case risk passes only on delivery,[84] and this is so whether or not the property has passed to the buyer.

(v) Goods forming part of a bulk within section 20A

It will be recalled that under s 20A of the Sale of Goods Act the prepaying buyer of unascertained goods forming part of a bulk acquires a proportionate interest in the

---

78 'What is a reasonable contract appears to depend on what is usual in the trade in question' (*Benjamin's Sale of Goods*, para 18–100).

79 Under the Third Parties (Rights against Insurers) Act 1930.

80 See p 250.

81 It will be seen that there is a difference between possession by the seller and possession by the buyer in that the seller, while in possession, is a bailee whether or not he still has the property in the goods, whereas the buyer to whom the property has passed will not as a rule be the seller's bailee but will be free to deal with the goods as he chooses.

82 See cases cited n 39.

83 Ibid.

84 Sale of Goods Act 1979, s 20(4).

bulk pending delivery to him of his entitlement under the contract. The Act contains no specific provision as to the incidence of risk in relation to the bulk. It is thought that s 20 is inapplicable to this situation, since what it addresses is the passing of risk in relation to the goods that are to be transferred to the buyer under the contract of sale, not the buyer's temporary interest in the bulk, and while the definition of 'goods' in s 61(1) includes an undivided share in goods, this too is concerned with the goods that are to be transferred under the contract of sale and does not apply to co-ownership created by the Act itself. What, then, should be the incidence of risk? It is unnecessary in this situation to resort to the principle established in *Sterns Ltd v Vickers*,[85] where the problem arose because the buyer had not acquired a proprietary interest of any kind, merely control over the contractual appropriation, whereas in cases to which s 20A applies, the prepaying buyers become owners in common of the bulk, so that in the case of total loss of the bulk where the seller has retained no interest there is no difficulty in applying the *res perit domino* rule by analogy with s 20. In the case of partial loss, however, the normal presumption that this should be borne rateably by all co-owners, including the seller if he has not parted with the entirety of his interest, would not be appropriate, for the seller has a duty to supply all the buyers from the bulk to the extent of their contractual entitlements. Accordingly, any loss, damage or deterioration affecting only part of the bulk should in the first instance be attributed to such part of the bulk as is retained the seller[86] and only if there remains a shortfall of goods in proper condition should the loss be borne rateably by the various buyers. This conclusion is reinforced by s 20A(4), which in applying the co-ownership interests to the reduced bulk refers only to the aggregate of the undivided shares of the buyers, not to any interest of the seller.[87] But these principles are subject to the provisions of ss 32 and 33 of the Act relating to goods in transit[88] and in the case of documentary sales they will usually be displaced by the special rules applicable to these.[89]

6.   GOODS SUPPLIED ON APPROVAL OR ON 'SALE OR RETURN'

Goods supplied on approval or on 'sale or return' or similar arrangements are, of course, identified from the outset as the potential subject matter of the contract of sale, and while ss 7 and 20 of the Sale of Goods Act do not apply,[90] the principles applicable at common law are similar. If the goods are accidentally damaged or

---

85   [1923] 1 KB 78. See p 247.

86   See the report of the Law Commissions, *Sale of Goods forming Part of a Bulk* (Law Com No 215, Scot. Law Com No 145, 1993), para 4.14.

87   See pp 226–227, and illustrations there given.

88   See pp 254 ff.

89   See pp 936, 440.

90   For until the deliveree adopts or is deemed to have adopted the transaction under s 18, r 4, the contract is not a contract of sale at all (see p 238); and once he has adopted the transaction, the property will pass to him under that rule. It is arguable that s 20 (though not s 7 – see *Edwards v Vaughan* (1910) 26 TLR 545) is wide enough to cover sales on approval and sale-or-return transactions, on the basis that, like s 18, r 4, it employs the words 'seller' and 'buyer' in an extended sense. But even if s 20 does not apply, the rules at common law produce a similar effect (*Elphick v Barnes*, n 9).

destroyed without fault on the part of the 'buyer' or those for whom he is responsible [91] and before he has signified his approval of the goods or otherwise adopted the transaction within r 4 of s 18, the risk is on the 'seller' and he is obliged to accept the return of the goods (if capable of return) without having any claim to the price.[92] Where the loss or damage occurs as the result of fault by the 'buyer', it is usually said that he is to be taken to have adopted the transaction so that the risk is on him. This approach is fallacious. Where the 'fault' alleged is an act inconsistent with the continued possession of the goods on approval or on sale or return, property and risk pass to the 'buyer' not because of his fault but because he has adopted the transaction within s 18, r 4. Indeed, no question of fault can then arise, for in adopting the transaction he becomes the owner of the goods and ceases to owe any duty to the seller. But fault may occur through some act which does not of itself signify an adoption of the transaction, as where the 'buyer' fails to take proper care to safeguard the goods, with the result that they are damaged. In such a case, he incurs the normal liability of a bailee to pay for the diminution in the value of the goods, but there seems no good reason why he should be considered to have adopted the transaction so as to become liable for the price.[93]

7.   INSURANCE

A prudent seller or buyer will not leave the risk of loss to be determined by the uncertain application of the rules embodied in the Sale of Goods Act but will cover his position by insurance. The policy being one of indemnity against loss, it is enforceable by the insured only if he can show that at the time of loss of or damage to the goods he had an insurable interest in them.[94] It is not, however, essential for him to establish an insurable interest at any earlier time, eg when the policy is taken out,[95] unless the terms of the policy so require. Conversely, insurable interest when the policy is taken out will not suffice if the insured has ceased to have an insurable interest at the time of the loss.[96]

The seller has an insurable interest in goods the subject of the contract of sale if at the time of loss or damage he is (a) the owner of the goods,[97] or (b) in possession of them,[98] or (c) at risk under the rules previously discussed,[99] or (d) entitled to exercise a right of stoppage *in transitu*.[100] Cases (a), (c) and (d) are straightforward. Case (b) requires a word of explanation. The interest of the seller in possession may

---

91 This would include persons to whom he has given possession in a manner or on terms inconsistent with his own holding of the goods on approval or on sale or return.

92 *Elphick v Barnes*, n 9.

93 Cf. *Benjamin's Sale of Goods*, para 5–055. The question was adverted to but not decided in *Poole v Smith's Car Sales (Balham) Ltd* [1962] 1 WLR 744.

94 See *MacGillivray on Insurance Law* (10th edn, 2002), ch 1, especially at paras 1-132–1-134; Malcolm Clarke, *Law of Insurance Contracts* (4th edn, 2002), ch 4, especially at para 4–5E.

95 Clarke, *Law of Insurance Contracts*, paras 10, 24, 27.

96 See *Collingridge v Royal Exchange Assurance Corp* (1877) 3 QBD 173, per Lush J at 177.

97 Whether at law or in equity (*Castellain v Preston* (1883) 11 QBD 380 at 398).

98 See below.

99 See pp 244 ff.

100 See p 410.

take various forms. If he is an unpaid seller holding a lien over the goods, the policy safeguards his interests under the lien. Even where he has no lien, his status as a bailee of the buyer entitles him to insure the goods to their full value.[101] He may also insure for the buyer's interest as well as his own,[102] in which event he can recover the full value of the loss or damage from the insurers but is accountable to the buyer for any excess beyond the amount of his, the seller's, interest in the sum recovered.[103]

The buyer acquires an insurable interest as soon as possession, property or risk has passed to him or he has made a payment in respect of the goods,[104] and he can insure against loss of profit on resale as soon as the contract of sale is concluded.[105]

Insurance may be taken out for the particular goods the subject of the contract of sale or it may be comprised in a master or floating policy, eg a policy covering all goods stored on the seller's premises or in transit, to a stated value.

The fact that insurance has been taken out by the seller or buyer does not necessarily render academic questions of risk under the Sale of Goods Act, for on making payment to the insured under the policy, the insurers may become subrogated to the rights of the insured against the other party to the sale contract. For example:

(1) Goods purchased by B but remaining in possession of the seller, S, are insured by S and are later destroyed without fault on the part of S. On making payment to S under the policy, the insurance company becomes subrogated to S's right to collect the price from B, to whom the risk had passed with the property.

(2) S delivers goods to B under a contract of sale, reserving ownership until payment. B insures the goods, which are later destroyed by fire without fault on the part of B. On making payment to B under the policy, the insurance company becomes subrogated to such rights, if any, as B may have against S for non-delivery.[106]

It will be seen that in these cases the existence of insurance has not eliminated issues of risk and liability between seller and buyer but has merely shifted the interest in them from the insured to the insurers.

Whether the insured party has rights to which the insurers can claim to be subrogated depends on the contract of sale and any applicable provisions of the Sale of Goods Act. If, for example, the seller in possession insures both for his own interest and for that of the buyer and, consequent upon damage to the goods while in the seller's possession, a payment is made to him by the insurers, the insurers will not normally be subrogated to the seller's rights against the buyer, for the

---

101 *Hepburn v A. Tomlinson (Hauliers) Ltd* [1966] AC 451.

102 Ibid.

103 Ibid; *Castellain v Preston*, n 97.

104 *MacGillivray on Insurance Law*, para 1–132; Clarke, *Law of Insurance Contracts*, para 4–5E2.

105 *MacGillivray on Insurance Law*, para 1–133; Clarke, *Law of Insurance Contracts*, para 4–5N.

106 If s 7 applies, so that the contract is frustrated, B may not have any rights to which the insurers can succeed by subrogation.

insurance was taken out for the buyer's benefit as well as that of the seller, the risk was one against which the policy was designed to protect the buyer and to allow the insurers a right of subrogation would be to defeat the intention of the parties to the contract of sale.[107]

8.   THE SALE OF GOODS ACT RULES ON FRUSTRATION

(i)   Grounds of frustration

The Sale of Goods Act, in addition to preserving the general rules of the common law,[108] including rules as to frustration, contains two provisions – ss 6 and 7 – dealing in particular with the perishing of specific goods before the property in them has passed to the buyer. Section 6 (which is not a frustration rule but simply an exemplar of the rule of common law rendering a contract void for antecedent impossibility) has been discussed in an earlier chapter.[109] Section 7 provides as follows:

> Where there is an agreement to sell specific goods and subsequently the goods, without any fault on the part of the seller or buyer, perish before the risk passes to the buyer, the agreement is avoided.

The limited scope of this section should be noted. It is confined to agreements to sell specific goods, and thus does not cover quasi-specific goods,[110] nor does it extend to goods that become ascertained after the making of the contract,[111] though why the section should draw this distinction between specific and ascertained goods is not clear. Section 7 does not apply where there is an immediate sale, but only to agreements by which the property is to pass to the buyer at a future date.[112] Its application is excluded by fault[113] on the part of the seller or buyer, and is also excluded where the risk has passed to the buyer, for the buyer must then suffer the loss and pay the price.[114] It is limited to cases in which the goods 'perish', a word which has never been exhaustively defined but which embraces not only total physical destruction but also total loss in the sense of the contract, as where the

---

107   *MacGillivray on Insurance Law*, paras 22–97 ff; Clarke, *Law of Insurance Contracts*, para 31–5D.
108   Section 62(2).
109   See p 200.
110   On the other hand it appears to cover the perishing of part only of specific goods, so avoiding the contract as a whole except where by the terms of the contract the perished part is severable. See *Barrow, Lane & Ballard Ltd v Phillip Phillips & Co Ltd* [1929] 1 KB 574, a case on s 6 of the Act. Under s 20A of the Sale of Goods Act 1979, giving the prepaying buyer of part of a bulk is given a proportionate interest in the bulk (see p 224). Section 7 does not apply to such a case and it is unclear how the risk is to be allocated. See *Benjamin's Sale of Goods*, paras 6-006 ff.
111   The draftsman of the 1893 Act appears to have assumed that ascertained goods were covered by s 7. See *Chalmers' Sale of Goods* (18th edn, 1981), p 100.
112   This is the effect of the words 'agreement to sell' in s 7. See s 2(5) and p 194.
113   'Fault' – that is, a wrongful act or default (Sale of Goods Act 1979, s 61(1)) – would here seem to have a meaning similar to that which it bears for the purpose of s 20, namely (a) a breach of a party's duty as bailee (which exposes him to liability even if the goods perish accidentally – see p 249) or (b) a delay in tendering or taking delivery without which the loss might have been avoided (p 248).
114   See p 243.

goods deteriorate to such an extent as to be unsaleable under the contract descrip-tion[115] or are so damaged as to become goods different from those contracted for,[116] or are irretrievably lost by theft,[117] misdirection or otherwise. Finally, s 7 may be excluded by agreement.[118]

Where s 7 does not apply and the risk has not passed to the buyer,[119] the common law rules of frustration[120] are free to assert themselves; and these may come into play not merely because the goods perish but because of some other unforeseeable event undermining the basis of the contract.[121] Even the common law rules do not apply where there is fault on one side or the other.[122]

The interplay between s 7 and the common law frustration rules may be sum-marized as follows:

(1) Where s 7 applies, the common law rules of frustration are excluded in so far as they concern the effect of the perishing of the goods, but remain operative as regards other grounds of frustration, eg supervening illegality.[123]
(2) Where s 7 does not apply, the common law frustration rules can be invoked if the risk has not passed to the buyer, there is absence of fault on both sides and the other preconditions of frustration at common law are fulfilled.

(ii) Effect of frustration under section 7

Where s 7 does apply, the agreement is 'avoided'. This word is usually employed by contract lawyers to denote avoidance *ab initio*, as where a party elects to rescind a contract that is voidable for misrepresentation;[124] but in s 7 'avoided' probably means 'terminated', so that when the goods perish the contract comes to an end, discharging the parties from performance of future obligations without disturbing accrued liabilities.[125] The Act does not go on to work out the consequential position of the parties, but since the Law Reform (Frustrated Contracts) Act 1943 does not apply in this situation[126] we are thrown back on the rules of the common law. If all the contract goods have perished, the seller is absolved from his duty to deliver and the buyer is discharged from liability to pay the price and can recover any payment

115 *Asfar & Co v Blundell* [1896] 1 QB 123.
116 *Oldfield Asphalts v Grovedale Coolstores (1994) Ltd* [1998] 3 NZLR 479.
117 See *Barrow, Lane & Ballard Ltd v Phillip Phillips & Co Ltd,* n 110.
118 Section 55(1).
119 See p 244.
120 See p 262, and as to frustration in export sales, pp 931–932, 934.
121 See p 135.
122 It seems that for this purpose a party who has agreed to make sales to different buyers under different contracts will be treated as at fault merely because, being disabled from performing all the contracts, he elects to perform some and therefore inevitably defaults on the remainder. See *The Super Servant Two* [1990] 1 Lloyd's Rep 1 criticized pp 138–139.
123 In consequence, frustration at common law is not necessarily excluded by the fact that at the time of the event relied on as causing frustration the goods are still wholly unascertained. See p 245.
124 See pp 78.
125 As at common law. See p 124.
126 Law Reform (Frustrated Contracts) Act 1943, s 2(5)(c).

he has made on the ground of total failure of consideration.[127] If only some of the goods have perished, the position is less clear. It would seem that where the delivery obligation is indivisible, the buyer is not obliged to accept the remaining goods,[128] though he is entitled to call for their delivery if he wishes,[129] but that where the delivery obligation is divisible and the whole of a contractually separate part of the goods has perished, the seller is absolved from his duty to deliver that part, and the buyer is released from liability for the price of it and can, if he has already paid the price, recover it on the ground of total failure of consideration; as regards the remainder of the goods, the seller continues to be liable to deliver and the buyer to accept and pay for them.[130]

9.   EFFECT OF FRUSTRATION AT COMMON LAW

Upon the contract becoming frustrated at common law, the rights of the parties will be governed by the Law Reform (Frustrated Contracts) Act 1943.[131]

---

127 See p 243.
128 For he has a right to reject a short tender. See p 358. But if he does so in the case here postulated, the contract would then become frustrated, for it is impossible for the seller to tender the full contract goods.
129 *H. R. & S. Sainsbury Ltd v Street* [1972] 1 WLR 834, distinguishing *Barrow, Lane & Ballard Ltd v Phillip Phillips & Co Ltd*, n 110.
130 See pp 272–273, as to severable contracts generally.
131 See p 139.

10 Delivery

I. THE CONCEPT OF DELIVERY

The concept of delivery, and its relationship to other duties of the seller, is not easy to grasp. There are several reasons for this. First, the Sale of Goods Act makes a misleading division between implied terms on the one hand[1] and duties of the seller on the other.[2] But 'implied terms' and 'duties' are not distinct concepts. To state that there is an implied term that the goods shall be of satisfactory quality and fit for their purpose is merely another way of saying that it is the duty of the seller to tender goods that are of satisfactory quality and fit for their purpose. The duty to deliver is thus not a distinct and isolated obligation but encompasses all the seller's obligations, express and implied, with respect to the goods, including the implied terms of title, correspondence with description, quality and fitness for purpose.[3] Indeed, we can go further and say that, subject to any express provisions of the contract, the status of these implied terms as *conditions* is relevant only to the buyer's right to reject; for if the buyer elects to accept a defective tender, the broken implied condition sinks to the level of a warranty, thus restricting the buyer to a remedy in damages,[4] while if the buyer rejects the tender on the ground that one of the implied conditions is not satisfied, the case becomes one of non-delivery, and the buyer's right to treat the contract as repudiated depends on his showing that the non-delivery is itself a breach of condition because time of delivery was or has become of the essence and has expired without a proper retender by the seller.[5] In short, it is a repudiatory failure to deliver, not a noncompliance with a statutory implied condition as such, which is the immediate ground of the buyer's right to treat the contract as discharged.

Secondly, the term 'delivery', defined in s 61(1) of the Act as 'voluntary transfer of possession from one person to another', is capable of a number of different meanings and is not confined to the transfer of physical possession. Indeed, the draftsman, wisely avoiding any attempt to define that most nebulous word 'possession', treats possession and delivery as including all forms of so-called constructive possession and constructive delivery, including acts which do not result in the receipt of possession as a real right at all but merely create for the buyer or transfer to him a personal right to obtain possession.

1 Sections 12–15.
2 Sections 27–33.
3 The statutory implied terms are analysed in detail in ch 11.
4 See p 378.
5 See p 341.

Thirdly, the fact of delivery may be significant for a variety of purposes, and what constitutes delivery for one purpose will not necessarily suffice as delivery for another purpose. For example, delivery of the goods to a carrier for transmission to the buyer is deemed to be delivery to the buyer within s 32(1), destroys the unpaid seller's lien and, if made without reservation of a right of disposal, constitutes an unconditional appropriation of the goods to the contract within s 18, r 5(2) so as to pass the property under r 5(1) and thus the risk under s 20. On the other hand, such delivery is not equated with delivery to the buyer for the purpose of the rules as to stoppage in transit, and the transit continues until the carrier himself delivers the goods (whether actually or constructively) to the buyer or his agent or wrongfully refuses to deliver.[6] Again, constructive delivery may suffice to divest the seller of possession but will not constitute performance of a contract calling for actual delivery.

2.   THE RELATIONSHIP BETWEEN IMPLIED TERMS AND THE DELIVERY OBLIGATION

The integration of the implied terms with the seller's duty to deliver becomes still clearer if we consider the following questions:
What must the seller deliver?
When must delivery be made?
How must delivery be made?

The answer to all these questions is to be found in s 27 of the Sale of Goods Act.

> It is the duty of the seller to deliver the goods, and of the buyer to accept and pay for them, *in accordance with the terms of the contract of sale.*

This makes it clear that if the seller is to avoid a breach of the delivery obligation, he must ensure that the goods themselves conform to the requirements of the contract and that delivery is tendered at the time and in the manner prescribed in the contract.[7] Where the contract is silent, the seller's duties are to be found in ss 12–15 (ownership and quality of the goods), 28 (readiness of the buyer to pay) and 29–32 (manner of delivery), as interpreted in various cases.

A tender of delivery which is not in conformity with the contract is not necessarily ineffective. In the first place, not all aspects of the delivery obligation are within the 'perfect tender' rule[8] so as to entitle the buyer to treat the nonconforming tender as bad and reject the goods. Secondly, the right of a buyer not dealing as consumer to reject goods for slight defects is now significantly qualified.[9] Thirdly, even where the buyer is entitled to reject, the tender of delivery will be effective if the buyer elects (or is deemed to have elected) not to exercise his right of rejection. But if the

---

6 Section 45. See p 410.
7 We have seen earlier that in many types of commercial contract – particularly futures contracts – the parties do not intend physical delivery at all. But even in these contracts there is a duty on the seller to tender and on the buyer to accept delivery if the transaction is not closed out prior to the due delivery date. See p 155. For delivery terms in export sales, see p 866.
8 As to which, see p 290.
9 See p 338. Similarly with delivery of the wrong quantity. See pp 358 ff.

buyer does reject, the tender becomes invalid. Hence the seller's failure to deliver can occur either because he tenders no goods at all or because the goods tendered are properly rejected by the buyer as not in conformity with the contract. The buyer's acceptance of nonconforming goods exposes the seller to an immediate action for damages as for breach of warranty.[10] Rejection, on the other hand, does not necessarily place the seller in breach at all as regards his primary delivery obligation,[11] for unless the improper tender signifies an intention or unwillingness to perform (and thus constitutes an anticipatory breach), rejection simply produces non-delivery and the seller may still have time to retender in conformity with the contract.[12] Finally, the taking of delivery must be distinguished from acceptance of the goods.[13]

3. MODES OF DELIVERY

The voluntary transfer of possession[14] may be effected either by actual delivery or by constructive delivery. By actual delivery is meant the transfer of physical possession to the buyer or his agent. This is the most common method of delivery in domestic transactions. Constructive delivery denotes the transfer of control of the goods to the buyer without physical possession. There are six types of constructive delivery.

(i) Transfer of document of title

Where the seller holds a document of title to the goods[15] the transfer of that document to the buyer gives legal control, and thus constructive delivery, of the goods themselves if so intended by the transferor.[16] For the transfer to be effective, the buyer must be given possession of the document, which must in addition indicate that the buyer's possession of it is authorized. This indication may be given either from the fact that the document is made out in favour of the bearer or, if it is to a named person or his order, because it carries the indorsement of the person named and of any subsequent party to whom the document has been specially indorsed.[17] The only common law document of title is the bill of lading, but there are various statutory documents of title, eg statutory dock and warehouse warrants.

---

10 See p 376. So the provisions of the Act relating to damages for breach of the terms of quality and fitness come into play only if the buyer accepts the nonconforming goods, in which case the conditions sink to the level of warranties, and damages are governed by s 53. Where the buyer rejects the goods, then while the breach of the term of quality or fitness may be the ground of rejection, the remedy is damages for non-delivery, not damages under s 53.

11 As to the implied *warranty* that the tender conforms to the contract, see p 340.

12 This question is explored in detail pp 341 ff.

13 See p 391.

14 The definition of 'delivery' in s 61(1).

15 As to the meaning of 'document of title' see p 45, n 131.

16 The importance of the transferor's intention needs to be stressed. See p 45.

17 See p 886.

(ii) Delivery of an object giving physical control

An example is the delivery of the keys to the premises where the goods are stored. This is conventionally treated as constructive delivery of the goods, though in truth it is more akin to physical delivery.

(iii) Attornment

The third method of constructive delivery is attornment. A party attorns to the buyer by lawfully acknowledging that goods which he previously held for himself or another are now held for the buyer.

(a) Where the goods are still in the seller's possession, he attorns by acknowledging that he holds them as the buyer's bailee. The Court of Appeal has held that on a sale and lease-back there is a notional attornment, and thus constructive delivery, by the seller to the buyer even though there is no moment of time at which the buyer is able to give directions to the seller as to what is to be done with the goods.[18]

(b) Where the goods are held by a third party (eg a warehouseman) to the order of the seller, the third party's undertaking to the buyer[19] to hold the goods for the buyer is an attornment, and gives constructive delivery to the buyer, but only if the undertaking so given is lawful, that is, authorized by the seller.

It would seem that to be effective to give constructive delivery, the attornment must relate to identified goods. An 'attornment' in respect of an unidentified part of a bulk gives rise merely to a personal obligation, and does not confer a possessory interest on the buyer,[20] except where the attornment is on the instructions of a seller who is himself a prepaying buyer having a proportionate interest in the bulk under s 20A of the Sale of Goods Act 1979.[21]

(iv) Buyer's continuance of possession in his own right

Where the goods were already in the buyer's possession, as bailee of the seller, before the making of the contract of sale, then upon the buyer becoming entitled to possession in his own right (whether under the contract of sale or otherwise by consent of the seller) there is a notional delivery to him by the seller.

(v) Delivery to a carrier

This constitutes constructive delivery under s 32(1) of the Sale of Goods Act, which provides as follows:

> Where, in pursuance of a contract of sale, the seller is authorized or required to send the goods to the buyer, delivery of the goods to a carrier (whether named by the buyer or

18 *Michael Gerson (Leasing) Ltd v Wilkinson* [2001] QB 514.
19 An undertaking to the *seller* to release the goods to the buyer is not sufficient (*Godts v Rose* (1855) 17 CB 229; Sale of Goods Act, s 29(4)).
20 See p 42.
21 See pp 223 ff.

not) for the purpose of transmission to the buyer is prima facie deemed to be a delivery of the goods to the buyer.

Rather curiously, this provision is strictly confined to delivery to a carrier, and, in contrast with other sections dealing with such delivery,[22] is not extended to cover delivery to some other type of bailee for the purpose of transmission to the buyer. It appears, therefore, that delivery by the seller to, say, an independent packing house for the purpose of packing and dispatch of the goods to the buyer does not suffice to effect constructive delivery to the buyer under s 32(1), though it may be effective as an act of appropriation within r 5 of s 18. Section 32(1) does not apply in relation to a sale to a person dealing as consumer, so that delivery to the carrier is not in such a case to be treated as delivery to the buyer[23] and in consequence will not normally have the effect of transferring risk to the buyer.

Several points of interpretation arise under s 32(1). First, in what circumstances is the seller considered to be 'authorized' to send the goods to the buyer? There is no problem if the contract expressly provides that the goods shall be sent, either by using the word 'send', or some equivalent word such as 'post' or 'dispatch', or by employing a delivery term implying transportation by an independent carrier, such as f.o.b., f.c.a.[24] But frequently the buyer orders goods without addressing his mind to the medium by which they are to be brought to his door. The question then is whether the seller fulfils his duty of delivery by giving possession to the carrier and procuring a reasonable contract of carriage for the buyer's benefit,[25] in which case he incurs no responsibility for the subsequent fate of the goods[26] and can claim the price even if they never reach their appointed destination, or whether he is obliged to go further and ensure that the goods arrive safely at the buyer's address.[27]

Examined against this question, s 32(1) comes perilously close to tautology. 'Carrier' means an independent carrier, not an employee of the seller[28] nor even, so it is said, an agent of the seller; but if he is not the seller's agent, he must be the agent of the buyer, for clearly the contract of carriage must be taken out for the benefit of one or the other. Hence, in the final analysis, s 32(1) says merely that where the carrier (whether or not named by the buyer) is expressly or by implication made the agent of the buyer, delivery to the agent shall be treated as delivery to the buyer – a fairly self-evident proposition and one which gives no guidance as to when, in the absence of a stipulated delivery point, the carrier is to be considered the agent of the buyer rather than of the seller.

We can see, then, that while one who transports goods as the employee of the seller or the employee of the buyer is not a carrier but is simply the alter ego of the seller or buyer himself, to say that a person who carries as agent of the seller is not a

---

22 Sections 18, r 5(2); 19(1); 45; 46.

23 Section 32(4).

24 For an explanation of these terms, see pp 867 ff.

25 See p 255.

26 Subject to compliance with s 32(3) where applicable. See p 255.

27 The question does not, of course, arise when the presumption of delivery at the seller's premises operates (s 29(1)).

28 Or of the buyer. See below.

carrier is to beg the question, namely whether the transporter is or is not the seller's agent. On this question we can derive some assistance, though not complete satisfaction, from the following propositions:

(a)   The transporter is the seller's agent, and not a 'carrier' within s 32(1), as regards every part of the journey preceding the agreed delivery point. Thus there is no problem where the contractual delivery point can be established, for until that point is reached the seller has not discharged his delivery obligation and the transporter must therefore be acting on his behalf and not on behalf of the buyer. The difficulty lies in establishing what *is* the agreed delivery point when the parties themselves have not been explicit on the point.

(b)   If the contract calls for the goods to be 'sent' or 'dispatched' to the buyer, as opposed to being 'delivered' to the buyer, then prima facie as a matter of ordinary usage it is to be assumed that the seller is free to send them by any normal method of dispatch, so that delivery to one who is not the seller's employee and who constitutes a normal type of transporter for the goods in question represents delivery to a carrier, and is thus deemed delivery to the buyer, within s 32(1).

(c)   When the wording of the contract is neutral, using terms which do not necessarily indicate either dispatch on the one hand or delivery on the other, the court has to do the best it can to ascertain the intention of the parties. In an Australian case it has been held that the phrase 'please supply us' prima facie indicates a requirement to deliver at the buyer's premises.[29] If the contract is altogether silent as to the mode and place of delivery, the presumption is that this is to be at the seller's premises,[30] so that unauthorized dispatch or delivery to the buyer's premises would presumably be at the seller's risk.

A person is not a carrier unless he undertakes responsibility as principal for at least some movement of the goods constituting part of their transit, and he is a carrier only as regards the movement so undertaken. Hence a mere depository is not a carrier, nor is a bailee who receives goods for onward transmission without himself having responsibility for transporting them. Again, a freight forwarder who simply undertakes to make arrangements for transportation by others, being himself merely an intermediary, is not a carrier, though the position is otherwise if he assumes responsibility for transportation as a principal,[31] even if in fact he delegates the task of carriage to others.[32]

We have not quite exhausted the problems arising under s 32(1). The word 'send' has generated some discussion. It evidently bears a different meaning from that

---

29   *Wiskin v Terdich Bros Pty Ltd* (1928) 34 ALR 242.

30   Sale of Goods Act, s 29(2). See further pp 391, 394.

31   Freight forwarders often combine the functions of carrier and forwarding agent, so that it is sometimes difficult to determine in what capacity they have acted in a particular transaction (D.J Hill, *Freight Forwarders* (1972), para 25). It has long been common for forwarders to contract as principals for the entire journey even where this is multi-modal. See p 1063; and generally, Hill, *Freight Forwarders*, chs 2 and 3.

32   The question when a carrier ceases to hold the goods as carrier and becomes a warehouseman is considered later in relation to stoppage in transit. See p 411, n 154.

implicit in s 29 of the Act, for that section uses the word 'send' to embrace all forms of delivery (including delivery by the seller's own employees) other than collection at the seller's own premises, whereas in s 32(1) what is contemplated is delivery to a carrier.[33] Such delivery is only prima facie deemed to be a delivery to the buyer. Delivery is a matter of intention and the presumption of delivery is displaced where, in giving possession to a carrier, the seller reserves the right of disposal, either expressly or by implication, as by retaining documents giving control[34] or by instructing the carrier to deliver the goods at their destination not to the buyer but to the agent of the seller.[35]

What constitutes an effective tender in terms of performance is considered in detail in Chapter 12, where we shall examine the 'perfect tender' rule.

(vi) Delivery of part in the name of the whole

This mode of delivery has been described earlier.[36]

4.   THE DELIVERY POINT

The place of delivery, and thus the degree of movement for which the seller is responsible, depends on the terms of the contract,[37] and, in so far as these are silent, the provisions of the Sale of Goods Act.[38] The seller may restrict his delivery burden to the minimum by undertaking merely to hold the goods available for collection by the buyer; or he may agree to deliver to the buyer's own premises or to those of a third party, eg a warehouseman or a subpurchaser; or his obligation may be the intermediate one of *dispatching* the goods, that is, of delivering them to a carrier for onward transmission to the buyer.[39] The contract of carriage is then deemed to be entered into by the seller for the benefit of the buyer.[40]

The stipulation of a delivery point may be relevant for two distinct reasons. It may indicate that the seller is not required to convey the goods at all beyond the delivery point; or it may denote merely that the quoted price covers delivery only up to that point and that any further act of delivery will be at the buyer's expense.[41]

---

33 Including delivery on board a ship under an f.o.b. contract. This straightforward approach was somewhat blurred by the decision of the majority of the Court of Appeal in *Wimble, Sons & Co v Rosenberg & Sons* [1913] 3 KB 743 (Vaughan Williams LJ dissenting), who in order to justify the application of s 32(3) to f.o.b. contracts felt it necessary to argue that in s 32(1) 'send' meant more than delivery on board the vessel. Such a construction of s 32(1) is difficult to sustain.
34 See pp 239, 935.
35 An example is given in s 19(2) of the Act.
36 See p 45.
37 Including any incorporated Incoterms. See p 867 For the meaning of established delivery terms in export sales, such as f.o.b., c.i.f., and the like, see pp 867 ff.
38 Section 29.
39 See pp 253 ff.
40 As to the buyer's rights vis-à-vis the carrier, see p 1058.
41 See p 866.

The Sale of Goods Act rules as to the place of delivery are concisely expressed in s 29(1). In practice, few disputes arise as to the place of delivery, which is usually obvious from the terms or circumstances of the contract. It is unclear whether, when delivery is to be made by transfer of documents, s 29 applies to fix the delivery point of the documents. Again, few problems arise in practice. Frequently, delivery of documents is to be made against payment, in which case the delivery point and place of payment will usually coincide.

5. TIME OF DELIVERY

The seller must tender delivery at the time stipulated in the contract. The buyer can reject a late tender if, and only if, time is of the essence under the contract or, though not originally of the essence, has been made so as the result of notice, or if more than a reasonable period has elapsed since the contractual delivery date.[42]

Where under the contract the seller is bound to send the goods to the buyer but no time for sending them is fixed, the seller is bound to send them within a reasonable time.[43] Demand or tender of delivery may be treated as ineffectual unless made at a reasonable hour. What is a reasonable hour is a question of fact.[44]

6. EXPENSES OF DELIVERY

Unless otherwise agreed, the expenses of and incidental to the tender of delivery must be borne by the seller and the expenses of taking delivery by the buyer.[45] Where the delivery point is stated merely as a price term, expenses of delivery beyond that point are for the buyer's account.[46] Unless otherwise agreed, the expenses of and incidental to putting the goods into a deliverable state must be borne by the seller.[47]

7. EXCUSES FOR NON-DELIVERY

Even where there is an agreed delivery date, the duty to deliver may be suspended; and in certain cases it will be discharged altogether. The duty is in suspense pending

---

42 See *Hartley v Hymans* [1920] 3 KB 475; *McDougall v Aeromarine of Emsworth Ltd* [1958] 3 All ER 431; *Bunge Corp. v Tradax SA* [1981] 2 All ER 513, per Lord Wilberforce at 541–542. In commercial contracts, time of delivery is prima facie of the essence, though the particular circumstances of each case must be taken into account (*Bunge Corp. v Tradax SA*; *The Naxos* [1990] 3 All ER 641; *The Honam Jade* [1991] 1 Lloyd's Rep 38). In the forward and futures markets, where contracts are designated by the delivery month, the stipulated month forms part of the contract description. See p 154, n 41; p 933.

43 Section 29(3).

44 Section 29(5).

45 This is not dealt with by the Sale of Goods Act but is a rule of the common law.

46 See p 866.

47 Section 29(6).

fulfilment of any conditions precedent to its performance, eg the buyer's willingness and ability to pay the price.[48] It is also suspended where through unforeseeable circumstances beyond the seller's control there is some temporary obstacle to performance which, if prolonged, would produce legal frustration of the contract.[49] The seller is altogether discharged from performance of the contract if it becomes frustrated[50] or if the seller accepts a repudiation by the buyer[51] or exercises a contractual right to terminate or rescind.[52] The undertaking to deliver will also be rendered nugatory if the contract is avoided, whether under s 6 of the Act[53] or at common law.[54]

8. THE BUYER'S DUTIES

The seller's duty to tender delivery is matched by the buyer's duty to take delivery and the entirely separate obligation to accept the goods.[55]

9. INSTALMENT DELIVERIES

Where delivery of contract goods is tendered by instalments, a question which not infrequently arises is what effect the buyer's acceptance or rejection of one instalment has on the duties of the parties as to delivery and acceptance of the remaining instalments. If, for example, the first instalment is defective but is accepted by the buyer, does this debar him from rejecting subsequent instalments? If he unlawfully rejects the first instalment, or fails to pay for it, does this rejection or failure discharge the seller from his duty to tender the remaining instalments? These and related questions are to be resolved by reference partly to s 31 of the Act, partly to rules of common law. Section 31 provides as follows:

> (1)   Unless otherwise agreed, the buyer of goods is not bound to accept delivery of them by instalments.

> (2)   Where there is a contract for the sale of goods to be delivered by stated instalments, which are to be separately paid for, and the seller makes defective deliveries in respect of one or more instalments, or the buyer neglects or refuses to take delivery of or pay for one or more instalments, it is a question in each case depending on the terms of the contract and the circumstances of the case whether the breach of contract is a repudiation of the whole contract or whether it is a severable breach giving rise to a claim for compensation but not to a right to treat the whole contract as repudiated.

---

48 *Levey & Co v Goldberg* [1922] 1 KB 688. As to who has to make the first move, see p 394.
49 See p 135.
50 See p 260.
51 See p 396.
52 See p 412.
53 See p 200
54 See p 200
55 See pp 390 ff.

It will be seen from s 31(1) that the buyer is not obliged to accept[56] delivery by instalments unless otherwise agreed. The mere fact that goods are shipped under separate bills of lading for discharge at different ports does not make the contract one for delivery by instalments where the seller's duty is to make a single tender of documents covering the entirety of the goods.[57]

One consequence of the rule embodied in s 31(1) is that if less than the contract quantity is tendered by the seller and the buyer accepts the tender, he is not bound to accept a subsequent tender of the balance.[58] Similarly, if the buyer rejects the nonconforming part of a tender while accepting the rest,[59] he is not obliged to accept a fresh and conforming tender in relation to the rejected part even if this is made in due time. In the absence of circumstances showing a contrary intention, the buyer is entitled to insist on a single tender. Where several deliveries are tendered, then, assuming them to be tendered under the same contract, the seller will be in breach of duty if that contract does not, expressly or by implication, permit tender by instalments. But first we have to be satisfied that the tenders are indeed made under the same contract; for if each is made under a separate contract, it is not a case of tender by instalments at all, the seller will not be in breach of his single-delivery obligations and the rules as to instalment deliveries will not come into play. Where, on the other hand, there is but one contract for delivery by instalments, then, to determine the effect of a breach as regards one instalment on the rest of the contract, it is necessary to ascertain whether the obligation broken is divisible in performance or indivisible.[60]

(i)   Separate contracts or a single contract?

Where each consignment tendered is the subject of an entirely separate, self-contained contract, then unless the parties have agreed, expressly or by implication, that the different contracts are to be in some way interdependent, a breach of one contract, even if so grave as to constitute a repudiation of that contract, will not affect the guilty party's right to enforce the other contracts, except where the breach is such as to show that he is unable or unwilling to perform those contracts also. The problem is to know whether the parties had in fact concluded a single contract or several contracts. While no hard-and-fast rules can be laid down – for in the last analysis everything turns on the intention of the parties – there are various features which will strongly point to a single contract. The first is the documentation employed. If all the goods are ordered on a single order form, that is a clear

---

56 Nor is he entitled to demand. This point is not covered by s 31(1) but is established at common law. See *Honck v Muller* (1881) 7 QBD 92, per Bramwell LJ at 98–99. However, it seems obvious that the seller cannot invoke this common law rule to prevent the buyer from exercising the right now given to him to reject a nonconforming part of a tender (see p 342) and hold the contract open for performance by retender of that part.

57 *Cobec Brazilian Trading & Warehousing Corp. v Alfred C. Toepfer* [1983] 2 Lloyd's Rep 386.

58 *Behrend & Co Ltd v Produce Brokers & Co Ltd* [1920] 3 KB 530.

59 As he is now entitled to do. See p 344.

60 Another pair of labels commonly used is 'severable' and 'non-severable'. Non-severable obligations are also termed 'entire'. The usual approach is to speak of divisible and indivisible *contracts* rather than obligations. The reason for eschewing this approach is given in n 64.

indication of a single contract, even if the order form embraces a range of different items that are individually priced. Thus, an order for stationery may list designated quantities of notepaper, envelopes, fountain-pens and propelling pencils, each item being separately priced, but there is not a separate contract for each class of item, for the parties plainly contemplate that the same contract conditions shall govern the entire order and prima facie delivery is to be made at one time.[61]

Where separate order forms embodying the same conditions are used, a relevant question is whether the forms are dispatched together or otherwise in circumstances indicating that each comprised merely part of a composite order. If different order forms embodying different contract terms (other than merely differences in price or delivery) are utilized, this strongly suggests separate contracts, for the differences would make it difficult, if not impossible, to operate the transaction as a single contract. Again, even where the various orders embodied the same standard terms, if they are dispatched at different times or relate to merchandise of such widely differing character as to negate any inference that delivery of the whole at one time is contemplated, the inference of separate contracts may readily be drawn.

Three typical forms of arrangement between seller and buyer deserve special mention.

1. General selling terms which contemplate specific orders

The parties may agree on a set of general trading terms which are to regulate dealings between them. Such terms will not themselves embody any specific transaction but will be expected to govern all purchases made by the buyer from the seller. Here the position is reasonably straightforward. The general selling conditions do not themselves constitute a contract of sale; they merely state the terms on which contracts of sale subsequently concluded between the parties are to be considered made if not expressly displaced.

2. Call-up of a global quantity by declaration

The seller may agree to sell, and the buyer to buy, a designated quantity (or alternatively a minimum or maximum quantity) of goods during a given period, the buyer being entitled to 'call up' or 'declare' purchases as and when he requires, within the global amount and period and other limits agreed. For example, the contract may provide for the sale of 5,000 yo-yos to be called up within not more than twelve months by declarations each of which is to relate to not less than 1,000 yo-yos. In this case the normal inference is that the parties intend a single contract under which delivery is to be made by instalments at the buyer's option; and this would not be displaced by the fact that the seller has reserved the right to increase the price between orders. The same applies where it is the seller to whom the option of making declarations is given.[62]

---

61 This, of course, depends on the agreement and the course of dealing between the parties. For example, it may have become an established practice for the seller, if temporarily out of stock of an item, to indicate on the delivery sheet that this was to follow, and for the buyer to accept this.

62 *Ross T. Smyth & Co Ltd v T. D. Bailey Son & Co* [1940] 3 All ER 60; *J Rosenthal & Sons Ltd v Esmail* [1965] 1 WLR 1117.

3.   Provision for each shipment or delivery to be treated as a separate contract

Another common practice is for the seller to agree to sell a given quantity of goods with the right to ship or otherwise deliver by instalments, the contract providing that each shipment or delivery is to be treated as a separate contract. Such clauses will not be given literal effect if this would produce an artificial division of what is in truth a single contract, but will be treated as subsidiary clauses of a single contract, their effect being that each delivery may be treated separately for the purpose of performance to the extent that one party's duty to perform as regards a particular delivery is not necessarily dependent on performance by the other party in relation to a prior delivery. In short, documents of this kind will not convert one contract into several[63] but will be treated as making the single contract severable, that is, divisible in terms of performance, so that instead of the contract as a whole being treated as entire, each designated instalment of the contract is regarded as entire, so as to constitute a separate 'contract within a contract'.

(ii)   Divisible or indivisible?

Given that there is but a single contract providing for delivery by instalments, what is the effect of breach by one party on the other's duty to perform? This depends to some extent on whether the obligation in question is divisible (ie severable) or whether it is 'entire' (ie indivisible or non-severable).[64] An obligation is entire when complete performance of it by one party is a condition precedent to the other's duty to perform, and divisible where it is intended that each stage of performance shall be treated separately and carry its own part of the total consideration for the performance, so that a party's default in performance of one stage does not go to the whole consideration so as to entitle the innocent party to withhold his own performance of a later stage.[65]

The distinction between divisible and indivisible obligations is of significance only as regards those obligations of which even a minor departure from the agreed term is a repudiation. As regards other obligations, it matters little whether they are divisible or indivisible, for in neither case does a breach ipso facto constitute a repudiation, while in both cases a breach showing an intention to repudiate the contract as a whole entitles the innocent party to treat it as discharged.[66] So in a case where, for example, time of payment is not of the essence, the principles to be applied in determining whether the buyer's default in payment is a repudiation will be the same whether the payment obligation is divisible or indivisible.

Divisibility of an obligation must be distinguished from the mere right to spread its performance. The essential characteristic of the former is divisibility of

---

63   *Ross T. Smyth & Co Ltd v T. D. Bailey Son & Co*, n 62; *Maple Flock Co Ltd v Universal Furniture Products (Wembley) Ltd* [1934] 1 KB 148.

64   The question is usually posed as one of divisibility of the *contract*. But this is incorrect. Some parts of a contract may be divisible, others indivisible. It is necessary to look at the particular obligation.

65   *Reuter, Hufeland & Co v Sala & Co* (1879) 4 CPD 239, per Brett LJ at 254, 256–257.

66   See, for example, *Warinco A.G. v Samor SpA* [1979] 1 Lloyd's Rep 450.

performance on one side and consideration for each partial performance on the other, thus creating a contract within a contract and making delivery of each individual instalment a separate, self-contained part of the delivery obligation. If the seller has the right to tender by instalments but the price is payable in a lump sum or in some other manner not fixed by reference to the individual instalments to be tendered, the seller's delivery obligation, though it may be distributed over the number of instalments in question, is not divisible, for no part of it can be matched against any corresponding part of the price. Similarly, the buyer's right to pay by instalments does not make the delivery obligation divisible if the terms of the contract indicate that a single delivery is contemplated.[67] The essential correlation between divisibility of performance and divisibility of consideration for the performance is reflected in s 31(2) of the Act.[68]

Moreover, the terms of the contract may give one party the option of dividing his performance, in which case the question whether his obligation is divisible or not is to be answered in the light of his actual election.[69] On the other hand, it seems equally clear that a provision expressly or impliedly requiring or permitting delivery by instalments is not enough to make the delivery obligation divisible unless there is an express or implied term that each instalment is to carry its own price, for in the absence of such a term there is no way of separating the contractual treatment of the individual instalments. Certainly there appears to be no reported case in which an English court has upheld an instalment contract as severable without inferring an apportionment of the price.

We can now turn to consider the consequences for the parties where the obligation is held to be indivisible and the different results that will flow if each instalment is held to be a separate division, or contract, within the main contract.

(iii) Delivery obligation indivisible

Where the contract provides for delivery by instalments but the seller's delivery obligation is indivisible, the following rules apply, except so far as displaced, expressly or impliedly, by the contract.

---

67   Expressed as a general proposition, the right of one party to spread his performance does not of itself imply that he can claim to split the other party's consideration in the same way, nor that the other party is entitled to split his own performance.

68   Set out p 271. That section in terms applies only where the contract provides for delivery by stated instalments which are to be separately paid for, but it is not considered to displace the less rigid rule of common law, which recognizes divisibility even where the contract does not expressly state each instalment or say that it must be separately paid for (see *H. Longbottom & Co Ltd v Bass, Walker & Co Ltd* [1922] WN 245). Thus it suffices if the right to deliver by instalments and the duty to pay a calculable part of the price for each instalment can be inferred from the language of the contract and the surrounding circumstances. It would seem that 'defective delivery' in s 31(2) does not include non-delivery, but the same principles apply at common law. See *Benjamin's Sale of Goods* (6th edn, 2002), para 8–076.

69   *J Rosenthal & Sons Ltd v Esmail*, n 62. The seller is bound by his election (*Reuter, Hufeland & Co v Sala & Co*, n 65).

(a) The seller is not entitled to demand a part of the price against partial delivery unless the buyer elects to accept such delivery,[70] in which case the buyer must pay for the goods accepted.

(b) The buyer's improper rejection of an instalment constitutes a repudiation of the entire contract.[71] The same rule applies to non-payment of an instalment in cases where time of payment is of the essence.[72]

(c) Where the tender of an instalment is too late to be effective[73] or where the buyer lawfully rejects a defective instalment and it is too late for the seller to make an effective retender,[74] the seller's repudiatory breach in relation to that instalment constitutes a repudiation of the entire contract and thus entitles the buyer to treat the contract as discharged, even if the seller is willing and able to make a proper tender of the remaining instalments and has no intention of repudiating the contract as a whole.[75]

(d) The seller's lien or right to withhold delivery for non-payment[76] extends to the whole of the undelivered goods and secures the whole of the price. The buyer is not able to say that his default relates only to the goods already delivered to him, for since the delivery obligation is *ex hypothesi* indivisible, so also is the correlative obligation as to payment,[77] so that the buyer's default constitutes a non-payment for the goods as a whole.[78]

(e) Accidental destruction of part of the goods before the risk has been passed to the buyer[79] may frustrate the entire contract.[80]

Prior to 1995 acceptance of an instalment under an indivisible contract constituted an adoption of the contract as a whole, and thus barred rejection of subsequent instalments, except in certain limited cases.[81] Now, however, acceptance of an instalment or part of an instalment does not preclude rejection of future instalments except in so far as the instalment accepted forms part of the same commercial unit as the later instalments.[82] Accordingly, in this respect there is no difference between a divisible and an indivisible contract.

70 It will be recalled that the buyer is not bound to accept delivery by instalments unless otherwise agreed (Sale of Goods Act, s 31(1)). If, therefore, he rejects a tender by instalments, he is within his rights and the seller cannot demand payment. See pp 271–272.

71 See *Reuter, Hufeland & Co v Sala & Co*, n 65, per Thesiger LJ at 247.

72 Prima facie it is not (Sale of Goods Act, s 10(1)).

73 Ie, because time of delivery was or became of the essence and has expired.

74 See n 73.

75 *Reuter, Hufeland & Co v Sala & Co*, n 65.

76 See p 409.

77 By virtue of the fact that, unless otherwise agreed, delivery and payment are concurrent conditions (s 28). But, as pointed out earlier, such correlation depends in each case on the terms of the agreement, and it is quite possible to have a contract in which the delivery obligation is indivisible but the buyer is given the right to pay by instalments, and vice versa.

78 *H. Longbottom & Co Ltd v Bass, Walker & Co Ltd*, n 68.

79 As to which, see pp 244 ff.

80 See p 260.

81 As to which, see the first edition of this work, pp 229, 314, 316.

82 Sale of Goods Act 1979, ss 11(4), 35(7), 35A, incorporating amendments made by the Sale and Supply of Goods Act 1994.

(iv) Delivery obligation divisible

The consequences of the delivery obligation being divisible are, of course, the converse of those flowing from an indivisible obligation.

(a)   The seller is entitled to require the buyer to accept and pay for each instalment tendered in conformity with the contract and this right is not affected by the seller's breach in relation to other instalments[83] except where such breach constitutes a repudiation of the entire contract which is accepted by the buyer as discharging the contract.[84]

(b)   The buyer's improper rejection of an instalment does not ipso facto constitute a repudiation of the contract as a whole,[85] but will do so only if

  (i)   it is made in such circumstances as to convey to the objective observer either an intention to repudiate or an inability to perform the contract as a whole;[86] or

  (ii)   its effect is so substantial as to go to the root of the contract.[87]

The same rules apply to non-payment for an instalment in a case where time is not of the essence.[88]

(c)   The fact that the seller is out of time for making an effective tender or retender[89] of a defective instalment does not as such constitute a repudiation of the contract as a whole,[90] but will do so only in the same circumstances as described in (b) above. At one time, it was thought that the only criterion was subjective, ie the mental state of the defaulting party, but it is now established that even if he did not intend to repudiate, he will be deemed to have renounced if his default goes to the root of the contract. The main tests to be considered in applying s 31(2) are, first, the ratio quantitively which the breach bears to the whole, and, secondly, the degree of probability or improbability that such a breach will be repeated.[91]

(d)   For the purpose of the seller's rights of lien and withholding of delivery each instalment is a separate contract, so that the buyer's default in payment for one instalment does not entitle the seller to withhold delivery of future instalments[92]

83   *Regent OHG Aisenstadt und Barig v Francesco of Jermyn Street Ltd* [1981] 3 All ER 327; *Jackson v Rotax Motor & Cycle Co* [1910] 2 KB 937, per Farwell LJ at 947, citing with approval (though erroneously attributing it to Lord Esher) a passage from the dissenting judgment of Brett LJ in *Reuter, Hufeland & Co v Sala & Co*, n 65, at 256.

84   *Robert A. Munro & Co Ltd v Meyer* [1930] 2 KB 312.

85   *Warinco A.G. v Samor SpA* [1977] 2 Lloyd's Rep 582, per Donaldson J at 588. The decision was reversed by the Court of Appeal [1979] 1 Lloyd's Rep 450, but purely on the application of the law to the facts.

86   Ibid.

87   *Honck v Muller*, n 56; *Mersey Steel & Iron Co Ltd v Naylor, Benzon & Co* (1884) 9 App Cas 434; per Lord Blackburn at 443–444.

88   *Mersey Steel & Iron Co Ltd v Naylor, Benzon & Co*, n 87; *Freeth v Burr* (1874) LR 9 CP 208.

89   Ie, retender after rejection of a prior tender by the buyer.

90   See authorities cited n 83.

91   *Maple Flock Co Ltd v Universal Furniture Products (Wembley) Ltd*, n 63, per Lord Hewart CJ at 157.

92   *Mersey Steel & Iron Co Ltd v Naylor, Benzon & Co*, n 87.

except where the defect is so grave or persistent as to constitute a repudiation of the contract as a whole. Similarly, the seller cannot exercise a lien over goods comprising an instalment that has been paid for to secure the price of other instalments.[93]

(e)   Accidental destruction of one or more instalments before the risk has passed to the buyer will not frustrate the contract unless its impact is to destroy the commercial basis of the contract.[94]

10.   REMEDIES FOR NON-DELIVERY

The remedies for non-delivery and for tender of nonconforming goods are discussed in a subsequent chapter.[95]

---

93 *Merchant Banking Co of London v Phoenix Bessemer Steel Co* (1877) 5 Ch D 205.

94 Where severable instalments have been delivered prior to the frustrating event, these are to be treated as separate contracts which are not frustrated (Law Reform (Frustrated Contracts) Act 1943, s 2(4)).

95 See pp 366 ff. As to non-delivery of an instalment under a contract providing for delivery by instalments, see above.

11 The Statutory Implied Terms in Favour of the Buyer[1]

We have noted earlier[2] the artificiality of the distinction between duties, such as delivery, and terms implied under the Sale of Goods Act, which are simply duties imposed by law under another name. The present chapter is devoted to these implied terms. As previously noted,[3] consumer sales law has now mushroomed into a distinct subject which can be treated only briefly in a work devoted to commercial transactions.

1. CONDITIONS AND WARRANTIES

English contract law, as we have seen, draws an important distinction between conditions and warranties. A condition is a major term of the contract, a term of such importance that any breach of it is considered to go to the root of the contract so as to entitle the innocent party to treat the contract as discharged. A warranty, on the other hand, is a minor term, collateral to the main purpose of the contract, for breach of which the innocent party has a right to damages while remaining bound to perform his own obligations under the contract.

The condition–warranty dichotomy was created by the Sale of Goods Act. It is true that prior to the Act there was a well-established distinction between a condition and a warranty, but this distinction was of a decidedly different character from that depicted in the Act and now carried into our general contract law. The pre-1894 cases cannot be properly understood without some perception of what the courts then meant by conditions and warranties.[4]

---

1 The remedies available to the buyer for breach of duty, including non-compliance with the statutory implied terms, are discussed in ch 14. The subject of implied terms in consumer sales has now become very complex as the result of a new Part VA inserted into the Sale of Goods 1979 by reg 5 of the Sale and Supply of Goods to Consumers Regulations 2002, S1 2002/3045 and can be touched on only briefly in a work devoted to commercial transactions. For detailed analyses see *Benjamin's Sale of Goods*, Special Supplement to the 6th edn (2003), and Simon Whittaker, *Liability for Products*, ch 18 (publication pending).

2 See p 263.

3 See p 15.

4 The topic is complex. For an admirable treatment see S. J Stoljar, 'Conditions, Warranties and Descriptions of Quality in Sale of Goods' (1952) 15 MLR 425, (1953) 16 MLR 174, and literature there cited. This two-part article was strongly influenced by the writings of Professors Williston and Corbin, whose trenchant criticisms of the condition–warranty labels in the Sale of Goods Act show clearly how English law has been led into error.

(i)   Conditions and warranties prior to the Sale of Goods Act 1893

Originally the term 'condition' denoted not a contractual undertaking by A to B but simply a prerequisite of B's duty to perform, or continue to perform, an obligation to A. Thus A and B agree that *if* A transfers to B the property in goods of a particular description, B will pay the price. Here, A is not *promising* to transfer any goods to B. He is simply stipulating that if he does so, B is to pay the agreed price. In the early days of contract law, after the courts had come to recognize that consideration could be generated by the mutual exchange of promises, they tended to assume that in a bilateral contract the respective promises of the parties were independent of each other, so that the performance of A's promise to B was not a condition precedent to B's duty to perform his own promise to A. This was considered to be the logical consequence of the fact that the consideration for B's promise was not performance by A but simply A's counterpromise, which B had in fact received. Hence a condition was conceived as an act or event external to the contract and not forming part of the promise of either party. Eventually, the courts were driven to accept that in most cases the parties contemplated not merely mutuality in the exchange of promises but also a mutual exchange of performances. Thus A's duty to transfer the property in the goods to B and B's duty to accept the goods and pay the price came to be accepted as mutually dependent obligations, so that performance of A's obligation to B could properly be labelled a condition precedent to B's duty to perform his obligations to A, and vice versa. The condition was not itself a promise, but the performance of the promise was a condition.

Where the goods were specific, that is, earmarked at the time of the contract, then, unless the seller had undertaken to do something to put them into a deliverable state, the property would usually pass to the buyer, so that the seller's fundamental obligation was satisfied, and any superadded undertakings as to description or quality were mere warranties, collateral to the main purpose of the contract, the breach of which thus gave the buyer a right to damages but did not entitle him to reject the goods.[5] The policy reason for this was that as the property had passed, the contract was partially executed and the buyer, having received the primary benefit to which he was entitled, lost the right to treat the contract as discharged, for he could not unilaterally retransfer the property to the seller.[6] This principle, that the transfer of the property in specific goods barred the right to reject, was carried over into s 11(1)(c) of the Sale of Goods Act 1893, where it remained until removed by the Misrepresentation Act 1967.[7] The term 'warranty' was thus largely confined to express statements on the sale of specific goods. In the case of an executory contract for the sale of unascertained goods, a different rule prevailed.[8] In such a case the buyer had not contracted to take the goods that lay before his eyes or were available

---

5   Unless they were wholly useless, in which case there was a total failure of consideration to which the label 'breach of condition' was also misleadingly attached.

6   *Street v Blay* (1831) 2 B & Ad 456; *Behn v Burness* (1863) 3 B & S 751, per Williams J at 755.

7   Section 4(1).

8   *Street v Blay*, n 6. Where the contract was for the sale of specific goods but the property did not immediately pass to the buyer, the position was unclear. In some cases the court treated the sale as a sale by description, in others the statement of quality was treated as a warranty unless its breach rendered the goods of no value.

for his examination but expected to receive goods of the contract description, the term being employed widely to cover both the characteristics necessary to identify the goods in the sense of enabling the parties to know to what the contract related *and* statements as to quality, performance and the like. Put another way, the seller's undertakings as to quality, etc, were considered to go to the identity of the goods so as to render their fulfilment part of the condition precedent to the buyer's obligation to accept the goods. It followed that whether the nonconformity related to identity in the narrow sense or to attributes, the property would not pass to the buyer if the goods did not conform unless the buyer decided to accept them, in which case, of course, he lost his right to reject. The only distinction between statements of description going to identity in the narrow sense and statements of quality and other attributes was that contractual provisions excluding the latter would not entitle the seller to tender goods of an essentially different kind from that contracted for.[9] Cases laying down this rule were thus the forerunners of the modern case law on fundamental breach.

(ii) Conditions and warranties under the Sale of Goods Act

The draftsman of the Sale of Goods Act, having originally intended to adhere to the principles described above, ultimately deviated from this approach,[10] with various consequences, some benign, others unfortunate. He failed to state the common law antithesis between sales of specific goods and sales by description, and thus (a) opened the way for the courts to declare that even a sale of specific goods was by description if the buyer bought in reliance on express or implied words of description, and (b) for the first time imported implied undertakings as to quality and fitness into contracts for the sale of specific goods. The result of the former was to create a curious gap between what was necessary to identify goods at the time of contract for the purpose of their being specific and what was required to ensure that in addition they corresponded with their contract description.[11] Further, instead of recognizing that an undertaking as a term of the contract was quite distinct from performance of the undertaking as a condition, and that it was possible to have a condition without any promise to perform it and, conversely, a promise of which the performance was not a condition, the draftsman used the word 'condition' as a synonym for a major term of the contract, an abuse of language that has rightly incurred severe criticism.[12] Finally, by labelling as an 'implied condition' the seller's duty to supply goods conforming to the contract description, the draftsman implicitly accorded correspondence with description a rank similar to that of fitness and merchantable quality, as terms implied *by law*, whereas the duty to supply goods of the contract description is, of course, a *factual* and *express* undertaking the breach of which, as Lord Abinger had pointed out many years before in *Chanter v*

---

9 *Chanter v Hopkins* (1838) 4 M & W 399.

10 Without apparently realizing it. Much of the resultant confusion arises from Chalmers' mistaken assumption that his condition–warranty dichotomy, which he adopted to denote major and minor promises, was merely another way of expressing the distinction between dependent and independent covenants.

11 See p 291, as to the problems created by this logical difficulty.

12 See Stoljar (1952) 15 MLR 425, (1953) 16 MLR 174, and literature there cited.

Hopkins,[13] is not merely breach of part of the contract[14] but a total non-performance of it.

As we shall see, the end result of all these changes was to transform the buyer's position from that of *caveat emptor* to one in which the denial of a remedy to the buyer for defective or nonconforming goods became the exception rather than the rule. But this result was not achieved without some violence to language and conceptual analysis.

Sections 12–15 of the Sale of Goods Act[15] prescribe a set of seven implied terms in favour of the buyer, namely title,[16] freedom from charges and encumbrances, quiet possession, correspondence with description, quality, fitness for purpose and correspondence with sample.

Of the seven statutory implied terms, five (title, correspondence with description, quality, fitness for purpose and correspondence with sample) are labelled conditions, while the remaining two (freedom from charges and encumbrances, and quiet possession) are termed warranties. The first group thus comprises terms the breach of which entitles the buyer to reject the goods, while the second embraces terms of less importance, the breach of which entitles the buyer to damages only, except where the circumstances are such as to evince repudiation by the seller of his obligations under the contract.[17] In each case the duty to perform is strict; reasonable care does not suffice.

The impact of non-performance of an implied condition varies according to whether the buyer elects to reject the goods or to accept them. If he rejects,[18] the situation becomes one of non-delivery[19] and, unless the seller makes a fresh tender which conforms to the contract or is accepted by the buyer, the seller will be exposed to an action for damages for non-delivery under s 51 or, in exceptional cases, a claim for specific performance under s 52. Where, on the other hand, the buyer elects to accept the goods, or is deemed to have accepted them and thus becomes debarred from rejecting, the broken condition sinks to the level of a warranty,[20] and the buyer's remedy is then, under s 53, to set up the breach of warranty in diminution of the price and/or claim damages for breach of warranty, with possible additional claims at common law for special damage or interest.[21] Sections 53 and

---

13 See n 9.

14 Lord Abinger referred to a breach of warranty, but a breach of the kind he was dealing with would now be labelled a breach of condition, and the same reasoning applies.

15 The Act referred to is the Sale of Goods Act 1979, re-enacting the Sale of Goods Act 1893, as amended. In the case of prescribed feeding stuffs a separate warranty of fitness is implied under s 72 of the Agriculture Act 1970.

16 Strictly speaking, what is implied is not that the seller has title but that he has a right to dispose, not quite the same thing, for he may perfectly legitimately be selling goods to which he has no title, eg, as agent for an undisclosed principal or as bailiff under an execution. The label 'title' is a convenient shorthand to denote a right to dispose and is used in this sense throughout this chapter.

17 See p 124.

18 Assuming he has not lost the right to do so. See pp 346, 346 ff.

19 See p 265, n 10.

20 Section 11(4).

21 These are preserved by s 54.

54 between them appear also to embrace claims for damages for delay in delivery, whether the delay be in the original delivery or in some subsequent delivery made consequent upon the buyer's lawful rejection of the earlier tender. A claim for delay in delivery, as opposed to a claim for non-delivery, arises only where the goods are ultimately delivered.[22]

2. TITLE, FREEDOM FROM ENCUMBRANCES AND QUIET POSSESSION

It is convenient to take these three terms together, despite the fact that the first is a condition and the others mere warranties, for they are closely linked and a breach of the latter will often be a consequence of a breach of the former. These three implied terms are set out in s 12 of the Act, which (omitting subs.(6)) reads as follows:

12(1) In a contract of sale, other than one to which subsection (3) below applies, there is an implied term on the part of the seller that in the case of a sale he has a right to sell the goods, and in the case of an agreement to sell he will have such a right at the time when the property is to pass.

(2) In a contract of sale, other than one to which subsection (3) below applies, there is also an implied term that –

(a) the goods are free, and will remain free until the time when the property is to pass, from any charge or encumbrance not disclosed or known to the buyer before the contract is made, and

(b) the buyer will enjoy quiet possession of the goods except so far as it may be disturbed by the owner or other person entitled to the benefit of any charge or encumbrance so disclosed or known.

(3) This subsection applies to a contract of sale in the case of which there appears from the contract or is to be inferred from its circumstances an intention that the seller should transfer only such title as he or a third person may have.

(4) In a contract to which subsection (3) above applies there is an implied term that all charges or encumbrances known to the seller and not known to the buyer have been disclosed to the buyer before the contract is made.

(5) In a contract to which subsection (3) above applies there is also an implied term that none of the following will disturb the buyer's quiet possession of the goods, namely –

(a) the seller;

(b) in a case where the parties to the contract intend that the seller should transfer only such title as a third person may have, that person;

(c) anyone claiming through or under the seller or that third person otherwise than under a charge or encumbrance disclosed or known to the buyer before the contract is made.

(5A) As regards England and Wales and Northern Ireland, the term implied by subsection (1) above is a condition and the terms implied by subsections (2), (4) and (5) above are warranties.

With this section must be read s 6(1) of the Unfair Contract Terms Act 1977, which bars contracting out.[23] These two sections raise numerous questions, each of which requires separate consideration.

22 See p 374.
23 See pp 326–327.

(i) Implied and express terms are conditions

The implied term of a right to sell is a condition, breach of which entitles the buyer to terminate the contract and recover all payments under it.[24] Unsurprisingly, the Court of Appeal has rejected the contention that an express term as to title is merely a warranty and has held it to be a condition also.[25]

(ii) Seller need not be a dealer

In contrast to s 14, relating to implied terms as to quality and fitness, s 12 is not confined to a seller selling in the ordinary course of business but extends to private sellers.

(iii) The seller's right to sell

We have already seen that the law regards the transfer of property to the buyer as the essence of the contract, so that if the buyer acquires no title because the seller lacks the right to sell, there is a total failure of consideration.[26] The words 'right to sell', though normally equated with title, have both a wider and a narrower significance. On the one hand, it is not essential that title be in the seller himself. It suffices that the sale is made with the consent of the party in whom title is vested, as where the seller, with the approval of the owner, sells in his own name as apparent principal[27] or, having himself agreed to buy the goods from a third party, procures that party to transfer title direct to the sub-purchaser.[28] On the other hand, the fact that the seller has and transfers the property in the goods will not necessarily preclude a breach of the condition, for the sale may infringe some patent, trade mark or other proprietary interest so as to entitle the holder of the patent or other right in question to stop the sale, either altogether or in the form in which the goods are to be supplied under the contract.[29] A good illustration is *Niblett v Confectioners' Materials Co Ltd:*[30]

> The defendants sold to the plaintiffs 1,000 cases of condensed milk in tins bearing the label 'Nissly Brand'. Nestlé and Anglo-Swiss Condensed Milk Co Ltd then threatened proceedings for infringement of their trade mark and exacted an undertaking from the defendants not to dispose of condensed milk with the label 'Nissly'. In order to secure the release of the purchased goods from the Customs the plaintiffs were forced to remove the offending labels and sell the condensed milk unlabelled for the best price they could get.

---

24 See p 377.
25 *Barber v NWS Bank plc* [1996] 1 WLR 641.
26 See p 215. See also p 377.
27 If he expressly sells as agent then it is, of course, the owner who is the seller.
28 *The Elafi* [1982] 1 All ER 208, per Mustill J at 215.
29 If the inability to sell arises from the fact that it is the buyer who has furnished the seller with a specification infringing a patent or trade mark, then, of course, the buyer cannot complain but, on the contrary, will have to indemnify the seller against liability he incurs to the owner of the patent or trade mark.
30 [1921] 3 KB 387.

It was held that the plaintiffs were entitled to damages for breach of the implied condition[31] as to the defendants' right to sell. The obligation of the defendants was not merely to pass a good title but also to ensure that the goods did not infringe the trade mark of a third party so as to enable that third party to interfere with the sale.

The buyer has the right not merely to *a* title but to the best (ie an indefeasible) title.[32] Hence while a seller in possession can, even though not the owner, transfer the property in the goods to the buyer in the sense of conveying the title he holds by virtue of his possession *animo domini*,[33] the buyer is not obliged to accept this, for it is not what he contracted to acquire.

What if a third party makes an unfounded but plausible claim to the goods? Must the buyer take upon himself the burden of defending the proceedings so as to vindicate his seller's title and thus his own? And if it is the seller who is sued by the third party, is the buyer obliged to await and abide by the outcome of the contest, or can he say that the shadow on the seller's title is sufficient ground for pleading a breach of s 12, even though it is ultimately established that the third party's claim was not a good one? There are at least three ways in which the law could resolve the problem, which at present admits of no clear answer.

(a)   It could be argued that the buyer is not obliged to accept a doubtful title, and that his rejection of the goods at a time when the doubt is still unresolved is justified even if it ultimately emerges that the third party's claim was ill-founded. It is a well-established rule of land law that the vendor must prove his title and that the purchaser cannot be forced to accept a doubtful title.[34] There is much to be said for applying this rule to a sale of goods, for the buyer ought not to be expected to suffer uncertainty as to his position or expense in defending the third party's claim. On this view, the buyer who rejects while the seller's title is still in doubt is entitled to treat the contract of sale as repudiated unless the seller succeeds in removing the shadow on the title before his time for tender of delivery has run out.[35] If the buyer, instead of rejecting, elects to defend the third party's claim and is successful, the costs he incurs would then be recoverable from the seller as damages for breach of warranty, to the extent that he does not otherwise recover from the plaintiff.

(b)   An alternative argument is that a shadow on the title is not a defect in title, but that if the buyer is in fact subjected to a claim by a third party, his costs of defending the claim are recoverable from the seller as damages for breach of the implied warranty of quiet possession.

(c)   Finally, it could be argued that the seller has no duty to prove his title and that if the buyer wishes to show a breach of s 12, he must positively establish that the seller did not have a right to sell.

---

31   Atkin LJ considered that the warranty of quiet possession was also infringed, inasmuch as the plaintiffs were not able to assume possession without first stripping off the labels; and Bankes and Atkin LJJ were further of the opinion that the defendants were in breach of the implied condition of merchantable quality.

32   See p 215.

33   See pp 201–202.

34   See J. T. Farrand, *Contract and Conveyance* (4th edn, 1983), pp 87 ff.

35   This depends not only on the contractual time for delivery but also whether time is of the essence and, if not, whether a reasonable time from the delivery date has expired.

In practice, the issues have not been raised in this form, and where a title dispute arises in a chain of transactions, the buyer has simply disputed the plaintiff's claim and, to cover himself against the possibility of defeat, has joined his seller as a third party, claiming an indemnity and damages on the basis of a breach of s 12.[36] This approach works well enough where the claimant institutes proceedings at a time when the buyer is still in possession. The buyer's position is less satisfactory, however, where he is faced with a choice as to what to do where the possibility of a claim by the third party is known but has not yet been asserted. There seems no reason why the buyer should be expected to pay the price on a speculation as to the outcome of a prospective dispute, or to engage in litigation (whether with the seller or with the claimant) to resolve the issue, and if there is a real doubt as to the seller's title which cannot be cured in proper time, the buyer should be held entitled to invoke s 12 and plead a breach of the condition of the seller's right to dispose of the goods. On the other hand, it would not be right to require the seller affirmatively to prove his title, for in the case of goods, in contrast to land, there is no machinery by which this can be done. All that should be required is the absence of a shadow on the title, or if there be a shadow, its removal, if this can be effected in due time.

A right to sell must be distinguished from a power of sale. The seller may, by some exception to the *nemo dat* rule, be able to transfer to the buyer a title overriding that of the true owner, as on a sale by a seller in possession after having made a prior sale to another buyer.[37] Though in such cases a good title passes to the buyer, yet the seller is in breach of the implied condition that he had a *right* to sell the goods, for vis-à-vis the true owner his disposition was unlawful. In *Barber v NWS Bank plc*[38] the Court of Appeal held that where a person holding a motor car as buyer under conditional sale agreement with a finance house discovers that the finance house has no title, he is entitled to terminate the contract for breach of s 12 despite the fact that under Part III of the Hire-Purchase Act 1964 he would have obtained a good title on completion of payment. But that decision turned on the express wording of the statute, s 27(6) of which made it clear that nothing in the section would exonerate the seller from liability. Whether in other cases a buyer who obtains good title can rely on the breach to reject the goods is unsettled, there being no authority directly on the point.[39] If there is any doubt about the effect of the disposition to the buyer, the court should have no hesitation in declaring the seller in breach, for if it be right that the buyer cannot be compelled to take a doubtful title which the seller in fact is able to substantiate, then a fortiori the buyer ought not to have cast upon him the difficulty and expense of proving to others, including a sub-purchaser, that he obtained a good title despite the fact that the disposition to him was unlawful. More difficult is the case where the seller's disposition takes effect in

---

36 For illustrations of such chain disputes see *Butterworth v Kingsway Motors Ltd* [1954] 2 All ER 694; *Bowmaker (Commercial) Ltd v Day* [1965] 1 WLR 1396.

37 Sale of Goods Act, s 24. See p 431.

38 [1996] 1 WLR 641.

39 In *Niblett Ltd v Confectioners' Materials Co Ltd*, n 30 , Atkin LJ said at 401–402: 'It may be that the implied condition is not broken if the seller is able to pass to the purchaser a right to sell notwithstanding his own inability; but that is not the case here, for the Nestlé Company Ltd had the same rights against the appellants as they had against the respondents.'

such circumstances as to leave no doubt that the buyer acquired a good title. The probable answer here is that though the seller is still in breach of s 12, the breach has no operative effect since the buyer is given in fact as well as in law a right just as good as that for which he bargained, so that the remedy for the breach abates.[40]

(iv) At what time is the condition required to be satisfied?

Section 12 requires of the seller that 'in the case of a sale, he has a right to sell the goods, and in the case of an agreement to sell, he will have such a right at the time when the property is to pass'. The words 'in the case of a sale' are obviously meant to cover not only a sale by one who is the owner but whose right to sell is restricted – as in the Nestlé case – but also a purported sale by a non-owner.[41] On a contract for the sale of specific goods, the condition will thus normally have to be satisfied when the contract is made,[42] in the absence of a term postponing the passing of the property to a later date, eg until payment. If the contract is for the sale of unascertained goods, the seller will be required to have the right of disposal by the time the property would vest in the buyer under s 18, r 5, as modified by the contract.

However, the seller's failure to get in the title or otherwise acquire a right of disposal by the time laid down in s 12 is not necessarily fatal. In the first place, if the buyer rejects when the seller is still in time to make a fresh tender,[43] the seller may be able to cure the defect.[44] Secondly, if before the buyer has exercised his right to reject, the seller acquire the right to dispose of the goods, the defective title acquired by the buyer is then 'fed' and perfected, so that the breach of condition is cured and can no longer be relied on by the buyer.[45] There is a similar result if the title is fed after the buyer has elected to adopt the transaction. But if it is the buyer himself who cures the defect, as by discharging an outstanding hire-purchase agreement, he can recover the expense of so doing as damages for breach of warranty.[46]

If the seller has a right of disposal at the time when the property is to pass, the fact that a third party subsequently acquires a right to prevent the buyer using or dealing with the goods does not give rise to a breach of the implied condition of title, for that condition is required to be satisfied only at the time of sale.[47] The buyer may, however, have a remedy for breach of the implied warranty of quiet possession.[48]

---

40 But see *R. v Wheeler* (1990) 92 Cr App Rep 279, in which it appears to have been assumed that even where title passes to the buyer on a sale in market overt the buyer could reject. *Sed quaere.*
41 See p 201.
42 See s 18, r 1.
43 See n 35.
44 See p 342.
45 *Butterworth v Kingsway Motors Ltd*, n 36, per Pearson J at 701.
46 Or, if he has not already paid the price, set up the payment to the true owner in diminution or extinction of the price (s 53(1)).
47 *Microbeads A.G. v Vinhurst Road Markings Ltd* [1975] 1 WLR 218.
48 Ibid. See below.

(v) Freedom from charge or encumbrance

The implied warranty of freedom from undisclosed charges or encumbrances[49] has little practical significance, for a charge can subsist only in equity or by statute and will usually be overridden by a sale to a purchaser without notice, who is in any event adequately protected against charges and other encumbrances by the implied warranty of quiet possession.[50] The measure of damages for breach of the implied warranty is usually the amount necessary to discharge the charge or encumbrance in question.

(vi) Quiet possession

The implied warranty of quiet possession, unlike the implied condition of title, is not a once-for-all term operating only at the time the property is to pass, but is a continuing warranty on the part of the seller. Hence, if at some time after the sale, the buyer's possession is disturbed by the seller himself [51] or by the lawful act of a third party (other than a person entitled to the benefit of a charge or encumbrance disclosed to the buyer before the contract was made), the seller is in breach even though at the time of sale he had a good title, so that the interference with the buyer's possession does not stem from a defect in title.[52] Further, the rule of real property law that the warranty of quiet possession does not extend to interference by those claiming by title paramount has no application to contracts for the sale of goods.[53] But unlawful interference by a third party is not a breach of the warranty, nor is even a lawful interference if this is not due to the fault of the seller or a superior title.[54]

(vii) Contracting out of section 12

Prior to the Supply of Goods (Implied Terms) Act 1973 it was possible to contract out of the implied condition of title,[55] though in view of the fundamental nature of

---

49 Section 12(2).

50 For an exceptional case where the warranty of freedom from encumbrances did have significance, see *Lloyds & Scottish Finance Ltd v Williamson* [1965] 1 WLR 404.

51 Eg, by interfering with the goods so as to prevent their use by the buyer (*Rubicon Computer Systems Ltd v United Paints Ltd* (2000) 2 TCLR 453, where a person acting on behalf of the seller placed a time-lock on a computer preventing access) or by exercising a purported lien which he does not actually have (*The Rio Sun* [1985] 1 Lloyd's Rep 350), which, of course, would be a breach of the contractual duty to deliver quite apart from the section.

52 *Microbeads A.G. v Vinhurst Road Markings Ltd*, n 47. In *The Playa Larga* [1983] 2 Lloyd's Rep 171, Ackner LJ appeared sympathetic (at 180) to the argument that there must be some temporal limit on the operation of the warranty of quiet possession, but it is difficult to see what limit there could be beyond that imposed by the Limitation Act 1980. See Michael Bridge, 'The Title Obligations of the Seller of Goods' in *Interests in Goods* (eds Norman Palmer and Ewan McKendrick, 2nd edn, 1998) 303–327 at p 307.

53 *Microbeads A.G. v Vinhurst Road Markings Ltd*, n 47.

54 *Oeheri International Trading Co v Donald & McCarthy* [1999] SLR 391 (Singapore High Court). See further on quiet possession Bridge, 'Title Obligations of the Seller of Goods'.

55 See the Law Commissions' *Exemption Clauses in Contracts – First Report: Amendments to the Sale of Goods Act 1893* (1969, Law Com No 24, Scot Law Com No 12), paras.12, 17.

this term the courts would no doubt have declined to construe an exemption clause as intended to have this effect unless it was clearly expressed.

Section 6(1) of the Unfair Contract Terms Act 1977 (incorporating provisions previously enacted in s 55(3) of the Sale of Goods Act 1893 as inserted by the Supply of Goods (Implied Terms) Act 1973) renders void any term of the contract of sale, or of any other contract, exempting from all or any of the provisions of s 12. Accordingly, any limitation of the implied condition of title and of the warranties of freedom from encumbrances and quiet possession must now be found in the language of s 12 itself. From this, two different bases of limitation may be extracted.

1. Buyer's knowledge of defect or encumbrance

The fact that at the time of contracting the buyer knew of the seller's want of title is not as such sufficient to displace the implied condition as to title. This may seem surprising but is sensible enough, for, as in the case of land,[56] the normal assumption is that the seller will cure any *removable* defect in title (eg an outstanding mortgage), so that except where the removal of the defect is outside the seller's control no significance is to be attached to the purchaser's knowledge of it.[57] It is thus somewhat curious that the Act adopts a different approach to the implied warranties of freedom from encumbrances and quiet possession. There is no good reason for distinguishing a charge or encumbrance from any other removable defect in title. The fact that it is known to the buyer at the time he makes the contract ought not in itself to be relevant. The crucial question should be whether the intention of the parties is that the buyer shall take subject to or free from the charge or encumbrance in question.[58]

2. Intention to transfer such title as the seller or third party may have

In cases where there appears from the contract or is to be inferred from its circumstances[59] an intention that the seller should transfer only such title as he or a third person may have, s 12(5) replaces the terms that would otherwise be implied under s 12(1) with a set of more limited implied terms, all of which are categorized as warranties.[60] The seller has a duty to disclose charges or encumbrances known to him, except in so far as these are already within the buyer's knowledge.[61] In

---

56 See Farrand, *Contract and Conveyance*, p 69.

57 However, whereas on the sale of land there is almost invariably a significant time-lag between contract and conveyance, thus leaving scope for a contractual obligation to discharge encumbrances before completion, a contract for the sale of goods may, and frequently does, operate simultaneously as a conveyance. Where title is to pass to the buyer immediately upon the contract, there may be difficulty in implying an obligation on the seller to remove charges or encumbrances known to the buyer.

58 In this connection see n 57.

59 Eg, on a sale by an executor or a sale of a judgment debtor's goods by a sheriff or bailiff or by an auctioneer on his behalf (*Payne v Elsden* (1900) 17 TLR 161; *Chapman v Speller* (1850) 14 QB 621).

60 Hence a breach does not normally entitle the buyer to treat the contract as discharged.

61 'Know' signifies actual knowledge, not constructive notice.

addition, the seller gives a limited undertaking as to future conduct on the part of himself and, if he is purporting to transfer such title as a third person may have, that person, the undertaking being that the buyer's possession will not be disturbed by the seller, the third person (if any) or anyone claiming through or under the seller or third person otherwise than under a charge or encumbrance disclosed or known to the buyer before the contract is made.[62]

Can a seller who purports to exclude the implied condition of title fall back on s 12(3) and (5) and say that the effect of the exemption clause is to evince an intention to transfer merely such title as he has? It seems clear that such an argument would not avail. The core of the contract will be taken to be that which the buyer is reasonably entitled to assume from the manner in which the contract terms are presented to him by the seller. If the seller presents the transaction as one in which he is selling as owner, he will be held to what he has apparently offered, and the court will not construe the exemption clause as converting a purported transfer of an indefeasible title into a transfer of such title as the seller may possess.

3.   CORRESPONDENCE WITH DESCRIPTION

Section 13 of the Sale of Goods Act (omitting sub-s (4)) provides as follows:

13. Sale by description.

(1) Where there is a contract for the sale of goods by description, there is an implied term that the goods will correspond with the description.

(1A) As regards England and Wales and Northern Ireland, the term implied by subs.(1) above is a condition.

(2) If the sale is by sample as well as by description it is not sufficient that the bulk of the goods corresponds with the sample if the goods do not also correspond with the description.

(3) A sale of goods is not prevented from being a sale by description by reason only that, being exposed for sale or hire, they are selected by the buyer.

The unhappy designation as an implied condition of that which is in truth an express delineation of the very subject matter of the contract has already been commented upon.[63] Fortunately, the courts contrived to avoid the possible adverse consequences, by recognizing that correspondence with description was not simply, like fitness or merchantable quality, a condition implied by law which was capable of being excluded by agreement,[64] but a fundamental obligation which would not lightly be construed as cut down by an exemption clause.[65] Indeed, the courts have gone further and insisted (as if it were a necessary corollary of the fundamental nature of the conformity with description obligation) that *any* disconformity, however minor, infringes 13, unless purely microscopic.[66] This 'perfect tender'

---

62 Section 12(5).
63 See p 282.
64 Sale of Goods Act, s 55, as originally enacted. But see now p 327.
65 *Vigers Bros v Sanderson Bros* [1901] 1 KB 608; *Montague L. Meyer Ltd v Kivisto Carelia Timber Co Ltd* (1929) 142 LT 480. See now Unfair Contract Terms Act 1977, s 6, pp 326 ff.
66 *Arcos Ltd v E. A. Ronaasen & Sons* [1933] AC 470.

rule has attracted much adverse criticism and is analysed in some detail in a later chapter.

Subsection (3) of s 13 re-enacts provisions added by the Supply of Goods (Implied Terms) Act 1973 in order to remove a doubt[67] as to whether there could be a sale by description where the buyer simply selected the goods himself in a self-service store.

(i) The elements of a sale by description

We saw in an earlier chapter that there is a contract for sale by description where, as terms of the contract, descriptive words are employed, expressly or impliedly, for the purpose of identifying or defining the goods and are at least in some measure relied on by the buyer for that purpose. Each of these ingredients will be separately examined.

(ii) Description as a term of the contract

In order for a contract to be for sale by description, the descriptive statement relied on must be a term of the contract and not a mere representation inducing the buyer to enter into the contract.[68] This highly artificial separation of the external inducement from the internal undertaking was insisted upon by the House of Lords in *Heilbut, Symons & Co v Buckleton*,[69] a decision which has been applied on more than one occasion, though latterly with increasing reluctance.[70] The principle remains intact but the modern tendency is to bypass it by finding as a fact that the descriptive words were indeed part of the bargain and not merely an anterior inducement to enter into the contract.

(iii) The extension of the 'description' concept to specific goods

In the nineteenth century 'sale by description' was used as the antithesis of sale of specific goods; for in the latter case goods were in existence and earmarked, the buyer could inspect for himself, the *caveat emptor* principle meant that the seller was under no duty to disclose defects, and the buyer was thus buying on the strength of his own judgment and not by reference to any description expressly or impliedly annexed by the seller. The earmarking of the goods in a physical sense at the time of the contract, and their availability for physical inspection at that time, were taken to mean that they were identified for all purposes, whether or not they possessed the intrinsic qualities which were the inducement to the buyer to buy. For an article to be thus earmarked it was necessary only that it should be of the *kind* agreed upon (using the word 'kind' in a very broad sense) and should be the sole

---

67 *Final Report of the Committee on Consumer Protection* (1962, Cmnd 1781), para 441; 1969 Law Com Report, No 24, paras 23–25.

68 Hence 'description' for the purpose of the Sale of Goods Act is narrower than for the purpose of the Trade Descriptions Act 1968.

69 [1913] AC 30.

70 See p 81.

article possessing at the time designated by the parties[71] the location in space by reference to which it was described.

Almost certainly the draftsman of the Sale of Goods Act intended that the phrase 'sale by description' should be used in its common law signification, that is, by contrast to a sale of specific goods; for by definition specific goods are those identified and agreed upon at the time of the contract,[72] and if description be taken to mean that which earmarks or identifies in the broad sense stated above,[73] then on a contract for the sale of specific goods noncorrespondence with description ought logically to be impossible. This reasoning is probably the true basis of the decision in *Varley v Whipp*,[74] where it was held that a contract for sale of a particular reaping machine which the buyer had not seen and which was therefore identifiable only by description[75] was not an unconditional contract for the sale of specific goods within s 18, r 5, as the reaping machine did not possess the identity of the goods contracted to be sold. But it has subsequently been held that 'there is a sale by description even though the buyer is buying something displayed before him on the counter: the thing is sold by description, though it is specific, so long as it is sold not merely as a specific thing but as a thing corresponding to a description …'.[76] It is thus apparent that an article may lack conformity with description for the purpose of s 13 even though it is specific within the meaning of the Sale of Goods Act and that description as identification subtly changes meaning when applied to specific goods. Indeed, this raises the whole question: what exactly do we mean by specific goods?[77]

(iv) Distinguishing identity from attributes

Goods do not correspond with the contract description if they are essentially different from the goods for which the buyer bargained, that is to say, are of a different 'kind' or constitute a different 'substance'. The task, then, is to ascertain what 'kind' of goods were the subject of the contract and then to see whether what was tendered was of that kind or of a different kind. The problem is to know how to delineate the contractual genus, the 'core' of the contract. Consider, for example, the following advertisement, on the assumption that its terms are incorporated in their entirety into the resulting contract.

> For sale. 2003 Honda Civic automatic, only one owner, 10,000 miles, headrests, radio, excellent condition.

71 This will usually be the time when the descriptive statement is made, not the time of contract. See below.

72 Sale of Goods Act, s 61(1).

73 This premise is examined below.

74 [1900] 1 QB 513.

75 Williston argued persuasively that this was not a true case of sale by description at all. 'The distinction is artificial between such a case and a case where the buyer sees the goods and agrees to buy what he sees, relying on a description by the seller the truth of which inspection cannot determine. Whether the buyer sees the goods or not, it is the description which induces him to buy but it is not the description which identifies the goods' (*Williston on Sales*, rev edn, vol 1, 1948, para 224).

76 *Grant v Australian Knitting Mills Ltd* [1936] AC 85, at 100.

77 See p 295.

What is the essence of the bargain? What kind of article is being offered? If the seller tendered a caravan, we should be in no doubt that this was not the type of article to which the contract related. The difficulty is to determine how closely we are to regard the genus as defined: that is to say, what parts of the descriptive statement are so crucial to the identity of the subject matter that their absence would make what was tendered essentially different from the goods bargained for? Is the core of the contract a car (ie *any* car), with make and model being mere attributes? Is it a car (*any* car) manufactured by Honda? Or do the other ingredients – year, type of gear-change, prior ownership, mileage and so on – also form part of the essential identity of the subject of the contract? As a matter of impression we should probably reach the conclusion that 'Honda Civic automatic' was clearly part of the contract description, that '2003' would very likely be so regarded,[78] that 'only one owner' and '10,000 miles' are borderline, and that 'headrests', 'radio' and 'excellent condition' are almost undoubtedly mere attributes not going to the identity of what is to be contracted to be sold.

Philosophers have raged for centuries over the distinction between identity and attributes. Indeed, there is a sharp division of opinion on the crucial question whether an article is any more than the aggregate of its constituent parts – whether, in short, identity *can* be distinguished from attributes.[79] It would thus be futile to attempt a definition of 'the core' of a contract.

> ... I do not believe that the Sale of Goods Act was designed to provoke metaphysical discussions as to the nature of what is delivered in comparison with what is sold. The test of description, at least where commodities are concerned, is intended to be a broader, more commonsense, test of a mercantile character. The question whether that is what the buyer bargained for has to be answered according to such tests as men in the market would apply, leaving more delicate questions of condition, or quality, to be determined under other clauses of the contract or sections of the Act.[80]

Applying such a test, the courts have held that there was nonconformity with description where the seller tendered as Long Staple Salem cotton that which was Western Madras cotton;[81] where a mixture of hemp and rape oil was offered in performance of a contract to supply foreign refined rape oil;[82] where what was proffered as oxalic acid was found to contain 10% of sulphate of magnesium and was thus not oxalic acid within the commercial sense of the contract.[83] Similarly, copra cake contaminated with so large an admixture of castor bean as to render it poisonous was held not to be copra cake for the purpose of the contract,[84] and meat and bone meal adulterated to the extent of 5% with cocoa husks was not regarded as meat and bone meal within the contract.[85] Again, the courts have treated as part of the contract description such diverse matters as method of packing,[86]

78 *Beale v Taylor* [1967] 1 WLR 1193.
79 See also p 297.
80 *Ashington Piggeries Ltd v Christopher Hill Ltd* [1972] AC 441, per Lord Wilberforce at 489.
81 *Azémar v Casella* (1867) LR 2 CP 677.
82 *Nichol v Godts* (1854) 10 Exch 191.
83 *Josling v Kingsford* (1863) 13 CBNS 447.
84 *Pinnock Bros v Lewis & Peat Ltd* [1923] 1 KB 690.
85 *Robert A. Munro & Co Ltd v Meyer* [1930] 2 KB 312.
86 *Re Moore & Co and Landauer & Co* [1921] 2 KB 519.

shipment[87] and marking[88] and occasionally quality[89] and quantity.[90] On the other hand, herring-meal containing an ingredient which generated a toxin was not held to have lost its identity as herring-meal;[91] 'fair average quality' of the season was, in the context in which it appeared in the contract, a statement as to quality, not a part of the contract description,[92] and defects in quality do not render the goods not in conformity with the description if the goods remain in substance the goods contracted for.[93]

It is important not to place excessive reliance on decisions as to the effect of particular phrases, for each case turns on the language of the contract and on its commercial setting, and is not a reliable guide to the conclusion that a court will reach in another case on similar facts. Hence instead of listing words and phrases that have attracted judicial rulings in the past, it is more fruitful to concentrate on some fundamental questions, of which the following are but a selection.

1.   Is the distinction between specific and unascertained goods relevant for the purpose of description under the Sale of Goods Act?

If description goes to identity[94] and goods sold as specific goods[95] do not in fact answer the contract description, then they do not possess the identity ascribed to them. How, then, can they be specific at all? Clearly, if we are to make sense of the statutory definition of specific goods, we must recognize that the identification function of 'description' is not the same in the case of specific goods as it is in the case of unascertained goods. The word 'description' when applied in reference to specific goods imperceptibly changes meaning. Whereas on a contract for the sale of unascertained goods the description fixes the identity of the subject matter, so that there is no effective appropriation unless the goods selected do in fact answer to

---

87 *Bowes v Shand* (1877) 2 App Cas 455; *Montague L. Meyer Ltd v Travaru A/B H. Cornelius of Gambleby* (1930) 46 TLR 553.

88 *Smith Bros (Hull) Ltd v Gosta Jacobsson & Co* [1961] 2 Lloyd's Rep 522. The position is otherwise if the mark is designated purely as a convenient means of reference, not as a mode of physical identification (*Reardon Smith Line Ltd v Hansen-Tangen* [1976] 2 Lloyd's Rep 60).

89 See cases cited nn 83–85. But normally quality is treated as a matter distinct from description. It is usually only where the defect is so serious as to alter the nature of the article that it will produce non-correspondence with description. See n 92. The purpose for which the goods are required may also form part of the contract description. See *Teheran-Europe Co Ltd v Belton (Tractors) Ltd* [1968] 2 QB 545, per Diplock LJ at 559.

90 *Canada Law Book Co v Boston Book Co* (1922) 66 DLR 209. But a shortfall or excess of quantity, which is dealt with expressly in s 30 of the Act (pp 381 ff), is even less likely to be treated as going to identity so as to constitute a breach of the implied term of correspondence with description.

91 *Ashington Piggeries Ltd v Christopher Hill Ltd*, n 80. But herring-meal was only one element in the compound which comprised the mink food in that case. It was selected because it was the defective ingredient. Such selection is not, it has been pointed out, the proper way of approaching the issue, which is to look at the entirety of the goods the subject of the dispute (Ingrid Patient (1971) 34 MLR 557 at p 558). A defect in a particular component may be serious enough to alter the character of the component without changing the nature of the goods as a whole.

92 *Ashington Piggeries Ltd v Christopher Hill Ltd*, n 80.

93 Ibid.

94 See p 292.

95 That is, goods identified and agreed upon at the time of the contract (s 61(1)).

the contract description (or at least are accepted by the buyer as so answering),[96] the function of the contract description in a contract for the sale of specific goods is not to identify the article which the buyer has agreed to buy and the seller to sell but to delineate the fundamental obligation of the seller, that is, to define the essence of what he is undertaking to deliver.

In other words, what the description identifies is not the article which is *in fact* selected by the parties and earmarked to the contract but the essential characteristics which the article that has become so earmarked must possess if the seller is to fulfil his fundamental obligation. Instead of correspondence with description being, as in the case of unascertained goods, a condition precedent to identification, the buyer's exercise of a right to reject for nonconformity with description is a condition subsequent. The buyer is not saying: 'I wish to buy an article possessing the characteristic X and if this is such an article I will buy it.' He is saying: 'I wish to buy *this* article on the basis that it possesses characteristic X and if it is not such an article I reserve the right to reject it.'

The distinction is of some importance, for it shows that in the case of specific goods noncorrespondence with description merely gives the buyer the option of treating the goods as not in conformity with the contract and does not alter the fact that the nonconforming goods were nevertheless the unique goods the subject of the contract. Hence if the buyer does reject, the seller has no right to cure the breach by tendering other goods which do conform to the contract description, for though such substituted goods may possess characteristic X, they are not *the* goods the buyer contracted to buy but simply goods possessing the characteristic which ought to have been possessed by the goods the buyer *did* contract to buy.

2.   As at what time is the description of specific goods fixed?

Although on a contract for the sale of specific goods the identification is made at the time of the contract, yet the true contractual identity of the goods is fixed by reference to the state of affairs existing when the description was given, unless that description has changed by the date of the contract or the buyer has otherwise ceased to rely on it. Thus, if I own two paintings, one in my lounge and the other in my bedroom, and I offer to sell 'the painting hanging in my bedroom', the buyer, if relying solely on that description to identify the goods, is entitled to the painting which is in my bedroom at the time of my offer, even though by the time of his acceptance the paintings have been switched round.[97] This, of course, is so obvious as to seem hardly worth stating. Yet it is important to keep the temporal reference point in mind, for it may bear on the question whether there is an ambiguity in the seller's offer which can be resolved only by treating a descriptive statement as part of the identification of the goods.[98]

---

96 See p 213.

97 Of course, if he inspects the painting which I have moved to the bedroom and decides to buy it, we can say that the original description has ceased to be relevant to identification, since the buyer is now buying on the basis of his inspection, not in reliance on my description.

98 See the first edition of this work, pp 251–252, discussing whether the presence or absence of other members of the class of goods described influences the identity content of the descriptive statement.

(v)　Reliance on the description

The mere fact that the seller *offers* to sell by description, in the sense that he intends his words of description to identify the contract goods, does not make the contract one for sale by description unless the buyer accepts the offer on that basis. The seller must not merely offer to sell by description but must contract to do so; and this involves that the buyer must contract to buy by description. If the buyer agrees to buy in exclusive reliance on his own skill and judgment, so that he is not depending on the description to delineate the subject matter of the contract, the sale is not by description and the descriptive words employed by the seller will become inoperative. Thus reliance on the description is an essential ingredient of a contract for sale by description.[99] However, the proof of reliance is not an onerous task. On a sale of unascertained goods, the buyer necessarily relies on the description, for he has no other way of knowing to what the contract relates. Even in a contract for the sale of specific goods, if the goods in question are ordinary articles of commerce, the court will usually presume that the buyer intended to buy in reliance on the goods possessing the characteristics making up their description rather than purchasing a specific article as such. Moreover, reliance need not be total. It suffices if the description is material in influencing the buyer's decision to buy.[100]

However, there are cases in which it is clear that the buyer does not rely in any way on the seller's description when entering into the contract. This is particularly likely to happen in transactions between dealers, who typically (though not invariably) rely on their own expertise. A good illustration is provided by the decision of the Court of Appeal in *Harlingdon & Leinster Enterprises Ltd v Christopher Hull Fine Arts Ltd,*[101] a case which has given rise to much discussion.

> The plaintiffs and the defendants were both art dealers. The defendants offered for sale two paintings which they described as being by Gabriele Muenter, who was a German expressionist. The employee of the plaintiffs who viewed the paintings was told that the defendants knew little about them and nothing about Gabriele Muenter. The plaintiffs themselves were more expert in German expressionist paintings than the defendants. The employee asked no questions about the provenance of the paintings, nor did he request an opportunity to make further inquiries. The plaintiffs bought the paintings, which were later found to be forgeries. The plaintiffs sought to reject the paintings and recover the price on the ground of nonconformity with description in breach of s 13 of the Sale of Goods Act.

> *Held* (Stuart-Smith LJ dissenting): the description did not have sufficient influence on the plaintiffs for it to have been intended to become a term of the contract, and was therefore not relied on by the plaintiffs, so that the contract was not for the sale of the paintings by description.

This decision is plainly correct. In the art world there are frequent disputes and disagreements as to the provenance of particular works, and different expressions

---

99　*Joseph Travers & Son Ltd v Longel Ltd* (1947) 64 TLR 150; *Leggett v Taylor* (1965) 50 DLR (2d) 516. In *Harlingdon & Leinster Enterprises Ltd v Christopher Hull Fine Arts Ltd* [1991] 1 QB 564 (see below) it was said to be theoretically possible for a description which is not relied on to become an essential term of the contract (*per* Nourse LJ at p 574); but it is hard to see how a sale could be 'by description' if the description played no part in influencing the buyer to buy.

100　*Joseph Travers & Son Ltd v Longel Ltd*, n 99. Cf the decisions on fitness for purpose, pp 319–320.

101　See n 99.

conveying varying degrees of confidence in the stated attribution. Much of the success of dealers comes from backing their own judgment over that of others who take a different view.

(vi) Can section 13 be excluded?

It is clear that in principle s 13 as such can be excluded,[102] subject to ss 3 and 6 of the Unfair Contract Terms Act. But the effect of excluding s 13 is minimal. The exclusion negates the *implication by law* of the term of correspondence with description, whereas we have seen that the description is that which identifies the subject matter of the contract and is thus an *express* delineation of the contract goods. Hence a purported exclusion not merely of s 13 as a statutory provision but of the seller's duty to deliver goods conforming to the contract description cannot be effectuated without negating the entire contract. The seller could, of course, contract to sell, for example, 'this article, which may or may not be a car', but the court would expect plain language before interpreting the contract as intended to have this effect, and if such language were used, the contract would not then be a contract for sale by description but an agreement to sell the designated article 'as is'. In short, the requirement of correspondence with description applies only where there is a contract for sale by description, and the effective exclusion of a duty to furnish goods corresponding with the description given would either negate the contract or convert it into one for the sale of a unique chattel.

(vii) The utility of the distinction between identity and attributes

Even supposing that there is a logical distinction between identity and attributes, it is highly artificial from the viewpoint of the buyer of the goods. If he contracts to buy 'a 1994 Honda Civic motor-car in excellent condition', he will expect just that, and will be singularly unimpressed by the argument that the 'identity' of what he is buying is confined to '1994 Honda Civic' and that 'excellent condition' is a mere attribute. Moreover, where as a matter of construction the express statement, though not considered to go to identity, is nevertheless regarded as a major term of which a breach would go to the root of the contract, the buyer has the same right to reject, and other remedies, as for noncorrespondence with description. We may therefore ask whether any useful purpose is served by retaining the concept of 'correspondence with description'.

As the law at present stands, the status of a descriptive statement as part of the contract description is relevant, in at least three ways. First, the duty to provide goods conforming to the description cannot readily be excluded.[103] Secondly, whereas in the case of other terms the doctrine of substantial performance applies unless the parties otherwise agree or the circumstances of the contract otherwise indicate,[104] the courts have held that *any* nonconformity with description, other than purely microscopic, entitles the buyer to reject. Thirdly, whereas the statutory

---

102 Section 55(1); Unfair Contract Terms Act 1977, s 6(3).
103 See pp 290, 327, 330.
104 Eg on a commercial sale, where time of delivery is prima facie of the essence. See p 270, n 42.

implied terms of fitness and satisfactory quality are conditions, express statements as to the goods may be conditions or warranties (depending on the court's view as to the importance which the parties must be taken to have intended to attach to compliance) or, indeed, may be terms which cannot be given any a priori label at all, the legal effect of a breach depending on the gravity of its consequences and not on any classification of the express term broken as a condition or a warranty.[105]

Yet none of these factors makes the present concept of correspondence with description indispensable. We could, for example, drop s 13 altogether (recognizing that a contract description is anyway an *express* term), and provide (a) that the buyer shall be entitled to reject, and/or to pursue other remedies for breach of contract, where as the result of the goods differing in a material respect (whether as to description, quality, quantity or otherwise) from those which the buyer contracted to buy, the commercial value of the bargain to the buyer is substantially impaired, and (b) that any provision purporting to exclude or restrict the buyer's rights under (a) shall be regulated by s 6(2) and (3) of the Unfair Contract Terms Act in the same way as those subsections now regulate contractual provisions purporting to exclude the statutory implied terms. By attaching the same consequences to all material breaches we should avoid the necessity of distinguishing identity from attributes and should thus give effect to the commercial understanding of the transaction. By insisting that the difference from specification be 'material' we should release the seller from the rigours of the present 'perfect tender' rule and bring the law of sale into line with that of other contracts. By looking at the consequences of the breach rather than the nature of the term broken we should escape the artificial classification of the seller's undertakings as conditions or warranties. As to these last two points s 15A now precludes a non-consumer buyer from rejecting for breaches of the implied conditions which are so slight that it would be unreasonable for him to do so.[106]

4.   QUALITY

At common law, the courts were reluctant to imply any terms of fitness or quality, and the general principle was *caveat emptor*.[107] We have seen how this principle gradually came to be eroded.[108] Nevertheless, its impact was such that in the Sale of Goods Act itself, *caveat emptor* is still presented as being the dominant rule.

> 14(1) Except as provided by this section and section 15 below and subject to any other enactment, there is no implied term about the quality or fitness for any particular purpose of goods supplied under a contract of sale.

But the exceptions have become so large and general that, despite the impression given by s 14(1), the *caveat emptor* rule is now a shadow of its former self, and, except in the case of private sales, the seller will in most cases be under a duty to

---

105   *Hong Kong Fir Shipping Co Ltd v Kawasaki Kisen Kaisha Ltd* [1962] QB 26.
106   See p 338.
107   See p 184.
108   See p 187.

supply goods of satisfactory quality and fit for their known purpose[109] save to the extent to which, within the limits permitted by the Unfair Contract Terms Act 1977, the Unfair Terms in Consumer Contracts Regulations 1999[110] and common law principles, he has contracted out of those obligations.

(i)   The duty to supply goods of satisfactory quality

Prior to the Sale and Supply of Goods Act 1994, the epithet used to describe the quality of goods which the buyer, in certain cases, had the right to expect was 'merchantable'. The phrase 'merchantable quality', originally intended to convey that one merchant buying from another would have regarded the goods as suitable,[111] became extended to cover sales by business sellers to consumers, and was first defined by statute in the Supply of Goods (Implied Terms) Act 1973, which inserted a definition in what later became s 14(6) of the Sale of Goods Act 1979. Under that section the test of merchantable quality was whether the goods were as fit for the purpose or purposes for which goods of that kind were commonly bought as it was reasonable to expect having regard to any description applied to them, the price (if relevant) and all the other relevant circumstances. The problem with the fitness for purpose test was that while it clearly covered both saleability and usability, it was less clear that it encompassed such matters as freedom from minor or cosmetic defects or durability, though in the end the decisions of the courts established that the phrase was broad enough to cover these aspects.

It became apparent that, used in this extended sense, neither the word 'merchant-able' nor the reference to fitness for purpose adequately conveyed the concept of acceptable quality, but there was considerable difficulty in finding an appropriate substitute. Among the various alternatives canvassed were 'good', 'proper' and 'acceptable'. The Law Commissions opted for the last of these,[112] but in the 1994 Act the label 'satisfactory' was adopted. In its amended form s 14 of the Sale of Goods Act provides a general standard of quality and then sets out a non-exhaustive list of matters which in appropriate cases are to be considered aspects of the quality of goods. The new definition for the most part restates the quality aspects which the courts had held to fall within the concept of merchantable quality. However, in at least one important respect it departs from the case law, by making it clear that an aspect of quality is fitness of the goods for *all* the purposes for which goods of that kind are commonly supplied, whereas prior to the 1994 Act it had been held sufficient for goods to be fit for any one of those purposes.[113]

We shall first examine the ambit of the duty and then consider the quality standard and the aspects of quality to which the court can have regard. The duty is strict;

---

109 The implied condition of fitness is examined p 315.
110 SI 1999/2083, as amended by SI 2001/1186.
111 See Law Commissions' Report, *Sale and Supply of Goods* (Law Com No 160, Scot Law Com 104, Cmnd 137, 1987), para 3.7.
112 Ibid, paras 3.14 ff.
113 *M/S Aswan Engineering Establishment Co v Lupdine Ltd* [1987] 1 WLR 1, where it had been unsuccessfully argued that the change of wording effected by the 1979 Act had produced this result.

reasonable care is not enough. The remedies for breach of the duty, including the additional remedies provided to consumers,[114] are discussed in ch 14.

(ii) The ambit of the duty

Subsections (1) and (2C) of s 14 provide as follows:

(1) Where the seller sells[115] goods in the course of a business, there is an implied term that the goods supplied under the contract are of satisfactory quality.

…

(2C) The term implied by subsection(2) above does not extend to any matter making the quality of the goods unsatisfactory –

(a) which is specifically drawn to the buyer's attention before the contract is made,
(b) where the buyer examines the goods before the contract is made, which that examination ought to reveal, or
(c) in the case of a contract for sale by sample, which would have been apparent on a reasonable examination of the sample.

By s 14(4) an implied term about quality may be annexed to a contract of sale by usage.

1.   'Goods'

The obligation to supply goods of satisfactory quality is not confined to new goods but covers used and second-hand goods,[116] though the state of the goods and the price at which they are offered will, of course, be relevant to the standard of quality the buyer is entitled to expect.

2.   'In the course of a business'

The implied condition of quality does not in general apply to private sales. For the condition to be attracted, the seller must sell in the course of a business. 'Business' includes a profession and the activities of any government department or public authority.[117] The term is a wide one and denotes any regular activity of a business character carried on by a person on his own account, whether or not for financial or other reward.[118] 'In the course of a business' has a broad meaning. It is not necessary that the transaction should be one of a type conducted with regularity by the seller. Indeed, it is not necessary that he should be a dealer in goods of that type at all. So if the seller sells an item of equipment used in his business with a view to acquiring new equipment in its place, that is a sale in the course of a

---

114   Sale of Goods Act 1979, Pt 5A, inserted by the Sale and Supply of Goods to Consumers Regulations 2002 (SI 2002/3045), reg 5.
115   The word 'sells' is obviously used here loosely to include an agreement for sale.
116   *Bartlett v Sidney Marcus Ltd* [1965] 1 WLR 1013. *Shine v General Guarantee Corporation* [1988] 1 All ER 911, which rather strangely applied s 14(6) of the Sale of Goods Act to a hire-purchase agreement, a type of agreement outside the scope of the Act! The statutory provision which should have been applied was 10(2) of the Supply of Goods (Implied Terms) Act 1973, which is to similar effect. See also *McDonald v Empire Garage (Blackburn) Ltd* (1975) Times, 7 October.
117   Section 61(1).
118   *Rolls v Miller* (1884) 27 Ch D 71.

business.[119] The sale does not have to be *for the purpose* of the business, nor is it necessary that the business should have as its object sales of or other dealings in goods of the kind to which the particular sale relates, or indeed any goods. The status of the buyer is not, of course, material to the application of s 14(2), which protects both business buyers and consumer purchasers.[120]

The restriction of the implied term of quality to sales by those selling in the course of a business is subject to the exception[121] embodied in s 14(5):

> The preceding provisions of this section apply to a sale by a person who in the course of a business is acting as agent for another as they apply to a sale by a principal in the course of a business, except where that other is not selling in the course of a business and either the buyer knows that fact or reasonable steps are taken to bring it to the notice of the buyer before the contract is made.

The purpose of this exception is obvious, namely to avoid a situation in which the buyer is led into thinking that his seller is selling in the course of a business when in fact the seller is acting as agent for a purely private principal. Of course, if the seller, though acting as agent, sells as a principal, the buyer may treat him as the principal and rely on the implied condition of quality, if otherwise applicable. But where the buyer learns that the seller is selling only as agent (whether for a named or an unnamed principal), the buyer is entitled to assume that the principal is making a business sale unless the buyer knows that he is a private seller or reasonable steps are taken to bring that fact to the buyer's notice before the contract is made.

3.   'The goods supplied under the contract'

The words 'supplied under the contract' were originally introduced by the Supply of Goods (Implied Terms) Act 1973 to make clear what had already been established in the cases, that what is required to be of appropriate quality is not merely the contract goods agreed to be *sold* but the whole of what is supplied in purported performance of the contract, including containers and other articles mixed in with the contract goods.[122] Thus where the contract was for the sale of mineral water in a bottle, and through a defect in manufacture the bottle exploded and injured the buyer, she was held entitled to recover for breach of the condition of merchantable quality (as it then was) even though the bottle remained the property of the manufacturer and was not included in the sale.[123] Since the mineral water was obviously to be supplied in the bottle, the bottle was supplied under the contract of sale and had itself to conform to s 14. Similarly, where a ton of 'coalite' was bought

---

119   *Stevenson v Rogers* [1999] QB 1028, distinguishing *Davies v Sumner* [1984] 1 WLR 1301 and *R. & B. Customs Brokers Ltd v United Dominions Trust Ltd* [1988] 1 WLR 321.

120   But the distinction *is* relevant to the efficacy of a contractual provision purporting to exclude s 14(2). See p 326.

121   The restriction and the exception apply equally to the implied condition of fitness for purpose, discussed p 315. The undisclosed principal may be liable as well as the agent (*Boyter v Thomson* [1995] NLJR 922, HL).

122   *Geddling v Marsh* [1920] 1 KB 668; *Niblett Ltd v Confectioners' Materials Co Ltd*, n 39; *Wilson v Rickett, Cockerell & Co Ltd* [1954] 1 QB 598.

123   *Geddling v Marsh*, n 122.

and on being put on a fire exploded through the presence of some explosive substance mixed in with the fuel, the fuel was held to be unmerchantable despite the fact that the lumps of fuel themselves were of proper quality; for the implied condition of merchantable quality applied not merely to the 'coalite' itself but to the whole consignment tendered in performance of the contract, and the presence of the explosive substance meant that what was *supplied* under the contract was unmerchantable.[124]

It may be that instructions for the use of the goods are also to be treated as part of the goods supplied under the contract,[125] but even if they are not, it would seem that where the buyer cannot reasonably be expected to use the goods without adequate instructions and the instructions are inadequate, inaccurate or misleading, the goods will not be of satisfactory quality.[126] The same applies a fortiori if no instructions are supplied at all.

4.   Disclosed defects

Section 14(2C) provides that the implied term of satisfactory quality does not extend to any matter making the goods unsatisfactory which is specifically drawn to the buyer's attention before the contract is made. This part of the statutory provisions stems from the 1973 Act, with modifications under the 1994 Act, and there has been no case law on it. There are thus some unresolved questions. What is meant by 'specifically drawn to the buyer's attention'? This presumably requires that the buyer shall have had pointed out to him the particular defect of which he later seeks to complain, so that it would not be enough for the seller to say, in general terms, that the goods were in rather poor condition or that they were sold subject to defects unparticularized. But how much factual information concerning the defect must be communicated to the buyer before it can be said to have been 'specifically drawn to the buyer's attention'? Is it sufficient if the seller points to the outward manifestation of the defect, leaving it to the buyer himself to make further investigation? Or must the root of the trouble be precisely identified to the buyer? For example, is it enough to tell the buyer of a motor car that there is a malfunction of the engine without revealing that this is due to extensive corrosion? Each case depends on its facts, but the guiding principle would seem to be that it suffices to draw attention to a defect in general terms provided that the buyer is not misled as to the nature of the defect, eg by having it presented to him as arising from a relatively minor factor, X, when X is itself but a reflection of a more fundamental factor, Y. In such a case the buyer is entitled to expect that Y will be specifically drawn to his attention.

Must it be the seller who draws the defect to the buyer's attention? The section does not say so, and it seems clear that if anyone, whether or not employed by or

---

124   *Wilson v Rickett, Cockerell & Co Ltd*, n 122.

125   See the decision at first instance in *Wormell v R.H.M. Agriculture (East) Ltd* [1987] 3 All ER 75, which held goods to be unfit for their purpose on the ground that the instructions were misleading. The decision was reversed on appeal on the facts. For the legal significance of instructions in other respects, see J K. Macleod, 'Instructions as to the Use of Consumer Goods' [1981] 97 LQR 550.

126   In *Wormell v R.H.M. Agriculture (East) Ltd*, n 125, this appears to have been assumed by the Court of Appeal, though the point was not directly addressed.

otherwise connected with the seller, points out the defect, the seller will not be answerable on account of it. On the other hand, some positive act of drawing attention seems to be required, whether it be oral or in writing. The mere fact that the buyer himself spots a defect would not attract this particular exception, though it would ordinarily bring into play the second exception described below.

5. Examination by the buyer

A further effect of s 14(2C) is that where the buyer examines the goods before the contract is made, the implied term of satisfactory quality does not extend to any matter making the quality of the goods unsatisfactory which that examination ought to reveal. The question here is not, as it was at common law,[127] whether the buyer had an opportunity to examine, but whether the examination he in fact conducted should have revealed the defects of which he seeks to complain. Thus the buyer does not lose his right to complain of unsatisfactory quality merely because he contracted to buy without having examined. Yet if the buyer not merely fails to examine but waives his right of examination, and thus expressly or impliedly accepts the risk of defects that would have been revealed if he had examined, he cannot rely on the implied condition of quality;[128] and if, when offered a full examination, he confines himself to a cursory inspection, he cannot rely on defects which the full examination would have revealed to show the goods were not of satisfactory quality. This is the effect of the much-criticized decision in *Thornett & Fehr v Beers & Son*.[129]

> The defendants agreed to purchase from the plaintiffs a quantity of glue in barrels in a warehouse. The plaintiffs offered every facility for examination but the defendants' representatives, being pressed for time, did not have any of the barrels opened but contented themselves with an inspection of the outside of the barrels. Had the defendants opened the barrels, they would have found that the glue was defective.

> It was held by Bray J that the defendants had examined the goods within the language of the Act, for the Act did not require full examination, the defendants had conducted such inspection as satisfied them that the goods were in order and, the price being very low, were willing to take the risk involved in not conducting a more thorough examination. Accordingly, there was no implied condition of merchantable quality.

The decision would have been more satisfactory if expressed as a straightforward case of waiver of examination. In any event, the words 'that examination' in the present section (as opposed to 'such examination' in the original s 14) seem to

---

127 *Jones v Just* (1868) LR 3 QB 197; *Thornett & Fehr v Beers & Son* [1919] 1 KB 486, per Bray J at 489.

128 This rule is not derived from the Act but is an application of the common law principle that a contracting party can waive conditions in his favour and having done so cannot subsequently invoke them. However, it would seem that a contractual exclusion of the opportunity to examine (as opposed to a voluntary waiver of that opportunity) is an exemption clause for the purpose of s 6 of the Unfair Contract Terms Act 1977 (see s 13 of that Act), so that where the buyer deals as consumer (see p 328) he cannot *bind* himself to waive examination, and in other cases exclusion of the opportunity to examine is valid only if satisfying the requirement of reasonableness (see p 328). Rather surprisingly, the provisions of s 35(3) of the Sale of Goods Act expressly preserving the consumer buyer's opportunity to examine for the purpose of the rules as to deemed acceptance (p 348) were not also incorporated into s 14(2C).

129 See n 127.

indicate that what is now relevant is the examination actually conducted by the buyer, so that, for example, a buyer who contented himself with inspecting the exterior of the car he was purchasing would not be debarred from complaining of defects apparent only from an examination of the engine. In deciding what ought to have been revealed by the buyer's examination, the court is presumably to apply an objective test, namely that of the reasonable man, ignoring, on the one hand, any special expertise possessed by the buyer and, on the other, any unusual degree of ignorance.

6.   Sale by sample

Section 14(2C)(c) deals with an inconsistency in the earlier legislation as regards the treatment of sales by sample. Under s 15(2)(c) of the original Act, on a sale by sample there was an implied condition that the goods would be free from any defect, rendering them unmerchantable, which would not be apparent on a reasonable examination of the sample. The implied condition would therefore not operate as to defects that a reasonable examination of the sample would have revealed, even if the buyer did not in fact examine the goods. By contrast, the implied term of merchantable quality under s 14(2), which extended to sales by sample, was not excluded merely because of what a reasonable examination would have revealed, but only where the buyer had in fact examined the goods. The new provision makes it clear that in the case of a sale by sample s 15(2)(c) is to prevail and that if a reasonable examination of the same would have revealed the defect, the implied term as to quality is excluded in relation to that defect whether or not the buyer has in fact examined the sample.

(iii) The quality standard

Section 14(2A) of the Sale of Goods Act 1979 provides as follows:

> For the purposes of this Act, goods are of satisfactory quality if they meet the standard that a reasonable person would regard as satisfactory, taking account of any description of the goods, the price (if relevant) and all the other relevant circumstances.

This is a new formulation introduced by the Sale and Supply of Goods Act 1994. Accordingly, pre-1973 case law offering definitions of merchantable quality under the Sale of Goods Act 1893[130] and case law on the amended definition in the Supply of Goods (Implied Terms) Act 1973[131] must now be regarded as of historic interest only for most purposes.

In determining whether goods are of satisfactory quality the court must have regard to the description, price (if relevant) and other relevant circumstances. The contract

---

130   The three most widely used definitions were those given by Lord Wright in *Cammell Laird & Co Ltd v Manganeze Bronze & Brass Co Ltd* [1934] AC 402 at 430; by Farwell LJ in *Bristol Tramways, etc, Carriage Co Ltd v Fiat Motors Ltd* [1910] 2 KB 831 at 841; and by Dixon J in *Grant v Australian Knitting Mills Ltd* (1933) 50 CLR 387 at 418. In *Henry Kendall & Sons v William Lillico & Sons Ltd* [1969] 2 AC 31, there was a division of opinion as to the respective merits of the three definitions, the majority favouring the test propounded by Dixon J.

131   See, for example, *M/S Aswan Engineering Establishment Co v Lupdine Ltd*, n 113; *Rogers v Parish (Scarborough) Ltd* [1987] 2 All ER 232; *Business Application Specialists Ltd v Nationwide Credit Corp Ltd* [1988] RTR 332.

description goes to the essence of what it is that the seller has contracted to sell, so that whether goods are of satisfactory quality almost inevitably depends on the description under which they are sold.[132] Thus, cloth sold for industrial purposes would not be expected to have the same visual and tactile quality as cloth sold to be made up into dresses,[133] and a commodity sold as being of average quality will not be expected to be of top quality. Price will also be relevant in most cases. Clearly the buyer of an old second-hand car cannot expect of it the performance or absence of visual blemishes required of a car sold as a new car;[134] and an article sold at an unusually low price may be expected to be inferior in quality to an article of similar description sold at a normal price.[135] Thus in *Business Application Specialists Ltd v Nationwide Credit Corp. Ltd*,[136] a decision on the former s 14(6):

> A second-hand Mercedes car, sold at a little under £5,000 with 37,000 miles on the clock, broke down after a further 500 miles because of burnt-out valves and badly worn valve seals. The repairs cost £635. Evidence was given by an independent expert that it would be unusual for defects of this kind to manifest themselves in such a car after only 38,000 miles.
>
> *Held* by the Court of Appeal that following the enactment of s 14(6) of the Sale of Goods Act it was no longer necessarily sufficient for a second-hand car to be safe and roadworthy, the test applied in earlier cases,[137] but that after this usage some degree of wear and tear had to be expected, the cost of repairs was not particularly great in relation to the price and the car when sold was of merchantable quality.

Indeed, there may come a point where the quality standard that can reasonably be expected approaches zero, as where a car suitable only for the scrap-heap is sold for £5. However, there may well be cases where price is of limited or no relevance, as where goods are expressed to be sold at bargain or knock-down prices, particularly on liquidation sales. A 'bargain' is no bargain if the quality is no greater than reflected by the price.

---

132 It is submitted that the phrase 'any description of the goods' in s 14(2A) refers to the contract description, as opposed to descriptive language not embodied in the contract (see p 291). Where a noncontractual description constitutes a misrepresentation, the buyer's remedy is to rescind the contract or, where the misrepresentation was fraudulent or negligent, to claim damages. See p 107.

133 See, for example, *B. S. Brown & Sons Ltd v Craiks Ltd* [1970] 1 WLR 752.

134 In that connection it should not be overlooked that the buyer is not necessarily confined to reliance on the statutorily implied condition of satisfactory quality; he may have another line of attack by claiming breach of an *express* undertaking or an undertaking implied *in* fact. It is arguable, for example, that to describe a car as 'new' implies that it does not possess significant blemishes. See *Cehave N.V. v Bremer Handelsgesellschaft MbH, The Hansa Nord* [1976] QB 44, *per* Lord Denning MR at p 63. (For motor-car enthusiasts, the most detailed discussion of 'new' is to be found in the judgment of Franki J in *Annand & Thompson Pty Ltd v Trade Practices Commission* (1979) ATPR 40–116, ASC 55–046 (Federal Court of Australia), giving at least five possible meanings of the word.)

135 *Feast Contractors Ltd v Ray Vincent Ltd* [1974] 1 NZLR 212; *Cehave N.V. v Bremer Handelsgesellschaft MbH*, n 134, *per* Lord Denning MR at p 63. But this depends on the circumstances. Shops frequently have seasonal and clearance sales and offer special discounts on particular lines of stock. Since a sale implies a genuine price reduction, the buyer is prima facie entitled to expect the same quality as on sale at a normal price, though the position is otherwise, of course, if the goods are sold as shop-soiled or as 'seconds'.

136 See n 131.

137 Eg *Bartlett v Sidney Marcus Ltd* [1965] 2 All ER 753.

'Other relevant circumstances' would include in particular risks voluntarily assumed by the buyer. For example, it is also reasonable to suppose that the buyer will take his chance with products known to carry inherent risk in normal use, eg cigarettes,[138] drink, drugs and butter;[139] and if the buyer, without the knowledge of the seller, buys the goods for use in an environment for which they are known to be unsuitable, he cannot complain that they are on that account of unsatisfactory quality.[140]

(iv) Aspects of quality

Section 14(2B) of the Sale of Goods Act is also largely new and follows the recommendations of the Law Commissions in their 1987 report *Sale and Supply of Goods*.

> For the purposes of this Act, the quality of goods includes their state and condition and the following (among others) are in appropriate cases aspects of the quality of goods –
>
> (a)   fitness for all the purposes for which goods of the kind in question are commonly supplied,
> (b)   appearance and finish,
> (c)   freedom from minor defects,
> (d)   safety, and
> (e)   durability.

The reference to state and condition re-enacts the previous provisions. The rest of s 14(2B) was inserted into the Sale of Goods Act by the Sale and Supply of Goods Act 1994. To a considerable extent s 14(2B) reflects the position already reached by the courts over the past decade, though, as we shall see, the fitness test has been strengthened.

1.   'In appropriate cases'

It is important to appreciate that s 14(2B) does not lay down any absolute rule that goods will fail the quality test if they do not satisfy all the listed criteria. In every case the question is what a reasonable person would regard as satisfactory, having regard to the contract description, the price and other relevant circumstances.

2.   'Fitness for all the purposes'

This is a change in the law. Previously it had been held that the test of merchantable quality was satisfied if the goods were fit for any one of the purposes for which goods of that kind were commonly bought, even if unfit for the other purpose or purposes.[141] That will no longer suffice. In principle, the standard is fitness for *all* normal purposes. Again, however, this is so only 'in appropriate cases', so that the seller can ensure through the contract description or other indications to the buyer

---

138   *Green v American Tobacco Co* 304 F 2d 70, 85 (1962); 154 So 2d 169 (1963); 325 F 2d 673 (1963); 391 F 2d 97 (1968); 409 F 2d 1166 (1969).
139   2 *Restatement, Torts*, 2d, para.402A, Comment *k*.
140   See *M/S Aswan Engineering Establishment Co v Lupdine Ltd*, n 113.
141   *M/S Aswan Engineering Establishment Co v Lupdine Ltd*, n 113.

that any common purpose for which the goods are unfit is excluded.[142] So if a car is sold for scrap, the fact that it is unroadworthy will not prevent it being of satisfactory quality.

3.   'Appearance and finish'

This reflects the existing law.

Starting with the purpose for which 'goods of that kind' are commonly bought, one would include in respect of any passenger vehicle not merely the buyer's purpose of driving the car from one place to another but doing so with the appropriate degree of comfort, ease of handling and reliability and, one may add, pride in the vehicle's outward and interior appearance. What is the appropriate degree and what relative weight is to be attached to one characteristic of the car rather than another will depend on the market at which the car is aimed.[143]

4.   'Freedom from minor defects'

Under the old law the question whether minor defects rendered goods un-merchantable proved very troublesome. On the one hand there was a substantial line of authority which held that defective goods were defective goods and were not to be considered merchantable merely because the defect could be remedied at trifling cost;[144] on the other hand there were cases which held that defects that were repairable readily and cheaply did not render the goods unmerchantable.[145] The purpose of the new formulation is to show that the first approach is the one to be followed, so making it easier for a court faced with facts such as those in *Millars of Falkirk Ltd v Turpie*[146] to reach a different conclusion.[147]

5.   'Safety'

Safety is an obvious element of quality. In principle, goods which are unsafe are not of satisfactory quality. Again, however, it is necessary to look at the circumstances. Goods may be safe for some purposes but not for others; if the seller excludes the unsafe purposes in the contract description of the goods, the buyer will not have grounds for complaint. Again, goods may be safe if used in a certain way or in accordance with particular procedures. In that case it is for the seller to provide adequate instructions. If he does, the goods will not fail the quality test on safety grounds; if he does not, their quality will be unsatisfactory.

---

142   Law Commissions' Report, *Sale and Supply of Goods*, para 3.36.
143   *Rogers v Parish (Scarborough) Ltd*, n 131, per Mustill LJ at 237.
144   *Jackson v Rotax Motor & Cycle Co Ltd* [1910] 2 KB 937; *Rapalli v K. L. Take Ltd* [1958] 2 Lloyd's Rep 469; *Rogers v Parish (Scarborough) Ltd* [1987] QB 933; *Winsley v Woodfield* [1929] NZLR 480; *International Business Machines Co v Sheherban* (1925) 1 DLR 684.
145   *Millars of Falkirk Ltd v Turpie* 1976 SLT (Notes) 66 (defective oil seal easily repairable at small cost).
146   Ibid.
147   Law Commissions' Report, *Sale and Supply of Goods*, para 3.43.

6.   'Durability'[148]

Prior to the 1994 Act it had been urged in a number of reports that there should be an implied term that the goods comprised in a contract of sale shall be durable for a reasonable period of time.[149] The Law Commissions rightly concluded that durability should not be an independent term but should feature as an aspect of quality.[150] It is, however, necessary to examine this concept of durability a little more closely to see what it means and what changes, if any, it makes to existing law.

There is no doubt that even before the 1994 Act the breakdown or malfunctioning of goods within an unusually short time after delivery at least raised a presumption that the goods were not of proper quality and condition at the time of delivery. But is there an implied term that goods in proper condition when delivered shall remain in good order and working condition for a reasonable period thereafter? There is curiously little authority on the point. It has been held that where perishables are to be dispatched by the seller (as opposed to being delivered to the buyer's premises), eg on a sale f.o.b. or c.i.f., they must be delivered to the carrier in such condition that with a normal transit they will arrive sound.[151] This is not a rule of durability; it is merely a commonsense rule to the effect that if at the time of delivery to the carrier the perishables are already in such peak condition that they are likely to arrive in a deteriorated state, then if they do so arrive the requirement of satisfactory quality or fitness as at the time of delivery is not satisfied. The material date remains the date of constructive delivery by the seller to the carrier. Though the rule has been formulated with special reference to the case of perishables in transit,[152] it is

---

148   See ibid, paras 3.47–3.61; Stephen Kapnoullas and Bruce Clarke, 'Countdown to Zero: the Duration of Statutory Rights for Unfit and Unmerchantable Goods' (1999) JCL 154; W. C. H. Ervine, 'Durability, Consumers and the Sale of Goods Act' (1984) JR 147.

149   See, for example, Ontario Law Reform Commission, *Report on Consumer Warranties and Guarantees in the Sale of Goods* (1972), pp 37–38, and the Commission's revised proposals in its *Report on Sale of Goods* (1979), pp 215–216; Law Commission, *Implied Terms in Contracts for the Supply of Goods* (1979, Law Com. No 95), paras 113–114; Law Commission and Scottish Law Commission, *Sale and Supply of Goods*, paras 3.49–3.52. Most of the Canadian provinces have enacted consumer protection legislation prescribing (inter alia) an implied warranty of reasonable durability. The recommendation made by the Law Commissions was that this should be incorporated as part of the requirement of merchantable quality. See their 1987 report, paras 3.52 ff.

150   Law Commissions' Report, *Sale and Supply of Goods*, paras 3.57–3.61.

151   *Mash & Murrell Ltd v Joseph I. Emanuel Ltd* [1962] 1 WLR 16n. The product? Potatoes!

152   See, eg, the judgment of Winn J in *Cordova Land Co Ltd v Victor Bros Inc* [1966] 1 WLR 793. See in this connection the dictum of Lord Diplock in *Lambert v Lewis* [1981] 1 All ER 1185 at p 1191: 'The implied warranty of fitness for a particular purpose relates to the goods at the time of delivery under the contract of sale in the state in which they were delivered. I do not doubt that it is a continuing warranty that the goods will continue to be fit for a reasonable time after delivery, so long as they remain in the same apparent state as that in which they were delivered, apart from normal wear and tear.' Read literally, this passage might suggest an implied term of durability. But the learned Law Lord was considering a different point, namely the stage at which the effect of a breach of warranty became exhausted, as the result of the breach becoming apparent, so as to preclude the buyer from relying on the warranty to secure an indemnity against liability arising from resale of the goods by him after the defect had become evident. It seems clear from the first sentence of the quoted passage that by 'continuing warranty' Lord Diplock meant a continuing obligation for defects which, though manifesting themselves after delivery, resulted from the goods not being in proper condition at the time of delivery.

but a particular application, in relation to perishables, of a general concept of fitness and satisfactory quality applicable in relation to all goods, namely that if at the time of delivery by the seller they are not in such condition that they will endure for a reasonable period of time, assuming no misuse by the buyer or other untoward event occurring after delivery and outside the seller's control, then they are not satisfactory or fit for their purpose. If I buy a car which, without explanation, breaks down after a week, this is strong (though not conclusive) evidence that it was faulty when delivered, and the onus will be on the seller to show that the breakdown did not occur through faulty design or manufacture.

So though the inclusion of a reference to durability in s 14(2B)(e) clarifies the law, it probably does not change it. As before, durability is a quality element which bites at the time of supply.[153] If the goods are at that time in such condition that with proper usage and in normal circumstances they will remain of satisfactory quality for a reasonable time, then they will satisfy the implied term of quality even if, in the events that occur, they develop a malfunction earlier than would ordinarily be expected for goods of the kind in question. As before, premature breakdown raises a presumption that the goods were not of satisfactory quality at the time of supply, but the presumption is rebuttable, as by showing that the buyer's use was excessive or not in accordance with instructions accompanying the goods or that the goods had been damaged by some other act of the buyer or a third party. However, there is now a special rule applicable for the purposes of the additional remedies given to a consumer buyer under Part 5A of the Sale of Goods Act.[154] For these purposes goods which do not conform to the contract at any time within six months starting with the date of delivery to the buyer must be taken not to have conformed at that date unless it is established that they did so conform at that date or the application of the statutory provision would be incompatible with the nature of the goods or the nature of the lack of conformity.[155]

7. Absence of legal impediment to use

Prior to the 1994 Act it had been held that the concept of merchantable quality was not confined to the physical state of the goods or their suitability for a normal purpose; for goods to be merchantable there also had to be no legal impediment to their being used for such a purpose and sold under the contract description. If the buyer could be restrained by injunction from such use or sale, then the goods were not merchantable even if their physical qualities were fully to the standard called for by the contract.[156] The new formulation of quality would not appear to change this. A buyer of goods, whether for use or for resale, reasonably expects to be able to resell the goods freely if he wishes and is unlikely to regard the goods as of satisfactory quality if there is a legal impediment to their resale.

153 Law Commissions' Report, *Sale and Supply of Goods*, para 3.54.
154 Ie the remedies of repair, replacement, price reduction or rescission. See p 389.
155 Sale of Goods Act 1979, s 48A(3), (4).

(v) Effect of commercial usage substituting price abatement for rejection

A distinctive approach to the quality problem, formulated in *Cehave N.V. v Bremer Handelsgesellschaft MbH*,[157] is that goods with minor defects, or of which a part is not up to the contract quality, are not of unsatisfactory quality when the commercial person would consider that the proper way of dealing with the matter was not by rejection of the goods but by an allowance against the price. But this confuses the right with the remedy. It is one thing to say that the buyer is bound by a trade custom by which minor defects entitle him merely to an abatement of the price, not to rejection of the goods,[158] but quite another to hold that such a way of dealing with the matter means that there is no breach of the implied term at all. Either the goods are of proper quality, in which case there is no breach and no remedy, in the absence of some express term or term implied in fact,[159] or they are un-merchantable, in which case the quality term is broken. There is no halfway house: the court cannot hold the goods to be of satisfactory quality *and* award the buyer a reduction in the price.[160] How, then, is the buyer to get the abatement of the price, which, according to *Cehave*, is the commercial person's solution to the problem? *Cehave* is best regarded as a decision turning on its own particular facts, which were indeed extraordinary.

> A German company agreed to sell 12,000 tons of US citrus pulp pellets to a Dutch company for approximately £100,000, delivery to be c.i.f. Rotterdam and shipment to be made in good condition. The buyers paid the price, obtained the documents and had the goods unloaded, when they found that, although the cargo in one hold was perfectly sound, part of the cargo in another hold was severely damaged through overheating. The buyers rejected the entire cargo and when the sellers refused to repay the price, the buyers obtained an order from the Rotterdam county court for sale of the cargo by agents appointed by the court. The agents sold the entire cargo for £32,720 to a Mr Bass, who resold it to the original buyers at the same price. The buyers thus resumed possession of the self-same pellets they had previously contracted to buy from the German company and rejected on arrival, and proceeded to transport them to their plant sixty miles away and use them in almost exactly the way they would have done if the pellets had all been sound, suffering absolutely no loss. Thus, without detriment to themselves, the buyers had reacquired for a little over £30,000 goods they had originally bought for £100,000, yet they insisted they were entitled to recover the full price from the original sellers for breach of the implied condition of merchantable quality.

> This claim, reluctantly upheld by the Board of Appeal of GAFTA, was rejected by the Court of Appeal on the grounds that (i) while the express term as to shipment in good

---

156 *Niblett Ltd v Confectioners' Materials Co Ltd*, n 30.

157 See n 134. See to the same effect *Millars of Falkirk Ltd v Turpie*, n 145.

158 *Re Walkers, Winser & Hamm and Shaw, Son & Co* [1904] 2 KB 152.

159 See n 000.

160 *Jackson v Rotax Motor & Cycle Co Ltd*, n 144; *Rapalli v K. L. Take Ltd*, n 144. It is well established that the mere fact that goods can be made saleable for a trifling expenditure does not prevent them from being unmerchantable (ibid; *Jackson v Rotax*; *Winsley v Woodfield*, n 144; *International Business Machines Co v Sheherban* n 144), a point reaffirmed in *Rogers v Parish (Scarborough) Ltd* n 144. But a trade custom by which minor defects entitled the buyer merely to an abatement of the price, not to rejection of the goods, has been upheld as reasonable (*Re Walkers, Winser & Hamm and Shaw, Son & Co*, n 158).

condition had been broken, it did not constitute a condition of the contract, and the effect of its breach was such as in the eyes of commercial people would justify a deduction from the price, not rejection, so that the remedy was damages; and (ii) though *any* breach of the condition of merchantable quality would entitle the buyer to reject, goods did not have to be perfect in order to be of merchantable quality, and it sufficed that they remained saleable for the purpose for which they would normally be bought, even with some reduction in the price. In this case, the pellets had been bought for use as cattle food and were still usable and had in fact been used as such. The goods were therefore of merchantable quality.[161]

(vi) Additional relevant circumstances in consumer sale

Section 14(2D)–(2F) contains further provisions as to relevant circumstances in the case of sales to a buyer dealing as a consumer. In such a case the relevant circumstances include any public statements on the specific characteristics of the goods made about them by the seller, the producer or his representative, particularly in advertising or on labelling.[162] But a public statement about such matters is not a relevant circumstance if the seller shows that

(a)　at the time the contract was made he was not, and could not reasonably have been, aware of the statement,

(b)　before the contract was made the statement had been withdrawn in public or, to the extent that it contained anything which was incorrect or misleading, it had been corrected in public, or

(c)　the decision to buy the goods could not have been influenced by the statement.[163]

(vii) The time at which the implied condition of quality must be satisfied

We have seen that the duty to see that the goods are of satisfactory quality is not a continuing obligation; it is required to be satisfied only at the point of delivery.[164] But in determining whether the goods *are* of satisfactory quality at the time of delivery, regard must be had to any natural deterioration likely to occur in transit.

161　Understandably, the Court of Appeal was not over-impressed by the fact that the goods had been sold off under the court order for a price nearly £70,000 below the original contract price, a circumstance attributable not so much to the defects complained of as to a fall in the Rotterdam market price at the time of sale, coupled with the good offices of the worthy Mr Bass.

162　Sale of Goods Act 1979, s 14(2D).

163　Sale of Goods Act 1979, s 14(2E). This does not however prevent any kind of public statement from being a relevant circumstance, whether in relation to consumer sales or otherwise, if it would have been so independently of s 14 (2A), (2D) and (2E). See s 14(2F).

164　See the cases cited n 152 and *Bernstein v Pamson Motors Ltd* [1987] 2 All ER 220, per Rougier J at 226. See also *Crowther v Shannon Motor Co* [1975] 1 WLR 30, a decision on the implied condition of fitness, but the same principle applies. Cf. the decision of the Court of Appeal in *UCB Leasing Ltd v Holtom* [1987] RTR 362. The rule that the goods must be of satisfactory quality at the time of delivery, rather than the time of sale, is subject to the qualification that the seller is not liable for any damage to the goods between the time of sale and the time of delivery which occurs without fault on the part of the seller and at a time when the risk has passed to the buyer. As to the passing of risk, see ch 9.

The seller of plums f.o.b. or c.i.f. will not perform his duty to supply goods of satisfactory quality if he puts on board a ship plums which are then at such a peak of perfection that they will inevitably arrive rotten at the port of destination. The rule in the case of perishables[165] is that to be of proper quality they must, at the point of delivery, be in such condition that with a normal voyage they will arrive sound. This does not mean that the satisfactory quality obligation is extended beyond the contractual delivery point. If the goods are indeed in such state that with a normal voyage they will arrive sound, the fact that through other circumstances – eg poor ventilation in the ship's hold, deviation from the shipping route causing delay – they arrive in a deteriorated condition will not put the seller in breach of the duty to supply goods of satisfactory quality. Thus, as we have seen, there is no independent requirement of durability.[166]

(viii) The state of knowledge by reference to which the quality of the goods has to be tested

In considering whether goods are defective and, if so, whether the defect renders them unsatisfactory, nice questions arise as to the degree of knowledge that must be ascribed to the hypothetical purchaser and as to the date by reference to which that knowledge must be tested.

1.   Latent defects

In deciding whether goods are of satisfactory quality, the court must ascribe to the hypothetical buyer a knowledge of any latent defects in the goods. In other words, the seller is not entitled to say: 'The defect was not apparent on examination, therefore there would have been no difficulty in selling the goods.' The question is not whether a person ignorant of the defect would have bought the goods, nor even whether a person did in fact buy the goods because of such ignorance, but whether, had the true facts been known, the goods would have been saleable under their contract description.[167] What is involved, in short, is an objective standard against which the goods have to be tested, not the imperfect perception of the buyer.[168]

2.   Characteristics not known to be harmful at time of delivery

In the preceding paragraph it was assumed that the goods possessed a hidden characteristic which, in the light of the state of knowledge at the time of delivery, was known to be injurious, so that what was unknown was simply the fact that the particular goods possessed that characteristic, not the adverse consequences that would flow if they did possess it. But a defect may be latent in an entirely different sense, in that the concealed characteristic may be one which in the state of

---

165   *Mash & Murrell Ltd v Joseph I. Emanuel Ltd*, n 151. The position in the case of non-perishables is discussed under the topic of durability (p 308), in reference to which the implied condition of fitness is also examined.

166   See p 308.

167   *Grant v Australian Knitting Mills Ltd*, n 76, per Dixon J at 418; *Henry Kendall & Sons v William Lillico & Sons Ltd*, n 130.

168   See Law Commissions' Report, *Sale and Supply of Goods*, para 3.25.

knowledge at the time of the transaction is not recognized as a defect at all. For example, asbestos masks may have been supplied at a time when the risk of cancer from asbestos was not appreciated. Here it might be thought that the situation is somewhat different. An asbestos mask would have been commercially saleable, with full knowledge of its asbestos composition, at the time of the particular transaction. Is the hypothetical buyer to be assumed to possess at that time medical and scientific knowledge which did not exist until a much later date? It appears that he is,[169] though the reasons are scarcely convincing.[170]

3.   *Immunities not known to exist at time of delivery*

This is the converse of 2 above, and raises the same question of principle. What is the position if goods possessing a characteristic which at the time of sale is thought to render them of unsatisfactory quality are subsequently found to be safe and usable if limited to a particular quantity or used for a particular purpose or treated in a particular way? Such was the situation in *Henry Kendall & Sons v William Lillico & Sons Ltd*,[171] where, at some time after the sale of certain groundnut meal, it became known that particular ingredients of the meal were toxic, thus rendering the meal unsaleable, but at a later date still, and before the trial of the action, it was discovered that the meal, though toxic, could safely be included in cattle food in small quantities, so that it became saleable once more for that purpose. The question was whether that which would in fact have been unmerchantable if the defect had been known at the time of sale became retrospectively merchantable, so to speak, because of the later discovery that it could safely be used in the way described above. This produced a sharp division of opinion in the House of Lords. The majority view was that since after-acquired knowledge of the defective nature of the meal was utilized to show want of merchantable quality, it would be artificial to exclude later after-acquired knowledge to demonstrate that the defect was not as serious as had been thought. The minority view was well expressed by Lord Pearce, who, after commenting that in judging merchantability one must obviously assume a knowledge of hidden defects, continued:

> But what additional after-acquired knowledge must one assume? Logic might seem to indicate that the court should bring to the task all the after-acquired knowledge which it possesses at the date of trial. But I do not think that this is always so. For one is trying to find what market the goods would have had if their subsequently ascertained condition had been known. As it is a hypothetical exercise, one must create a hypothetical market. Nevertheless the hypothetical market should be one that could have existed, not one which could not have existed at the date of delivery. Suppose goods contained a hidden deadly poison to which there was discovered by

---

169   *Henry Kendall & Sons v William Lillico & Sons Ltd*, n 130 (and see (3) below). The point could have been raised again in *Ashington Piggeries Ltd v Christopher Hill Ltd*, n 80, but the respondents, rather surprisingly, conceded that the mink food the subject of the contract of sale was unmerchantable, despite the fact that its deleterious features could not have been appreciated, even with the exercise of all care and skill, in the light of the knowledge prevailing at the time of the contract.

170   See (3) below.

171   See n 130. The case is also known as the *Hardwick Game Farm case*, the Hardwick Game Farm being the original plaintiff and Henry Kendall & Sons a later party who then claimed over against their own suppliers.

scientists two years after delivery a simple, easy, inexpensive antidote which could render the goods harmless. They would be unmarketable at the date of delivery if the existence of the poison was brought to light, since no purchaser could then have known the antidote to the poison. Hypothesis is no reason for complete departure from possibility. One must keep the hypothesis in touch with the facts as far as possible ... [172]

Which of these two conflicting views is to be preferred? There is little doubt that *if* after-acquired knowledge that a characteristic is defective is to be admitted, it would be wrong to exclude later knowledge qualifying what had been discovered in relation to the defect. On this aspect, the logic of the majority view is unanswerable. The crucial question is whether after-acquired knowledge of the fact that a sub-stance originally believed harmless is in fact injurious should be taken into account in the first place.

There is much to be said for the view that this is to substitute a hypothetical market for that which actually existed. It presupposes that satisfactory quality is incapable of being tested at a given date (ie the date of delivery) but is subject to shifts and changes with each addition to relevant knowledge right up to the time of trial. This is surely unreasonable. The parties are entitled to know where they stand at the time when they invoke their rights under the contract. It is unreasonable to expose a buyer to a claim for damages because he rejects as unsatisfactory goods which are in fact of unsatisfactory quality at the time of rejection but later are retrospectively declared satisfactory because of the advance of scientific knowledge. Moreover, the hypothesis does not go far enough, for if the after-acquired knowledge is to the effect that *in stated conditions* the goods can be safely used, then it follows that the seller should have given adequate instructions at the time of sale drawing attention to those conditions. The parties must be assumed to have contracted in the light of the state of knowledge prevailing at the time of delivery.[173] After-acquired knowledge, whether as to unsuspected toxicity or as to unsuspected immunity or antidotes, should be ignored.

(ix) Is satisfactory quality a constant concept?

A separate issue again is whether satisfactory quality is itself a constant concept and, if not, what is the relevant date for testing it. It is clear that perceptions of what is satisfactory are not fixed or immutable but change with commercial and consumer attitudes. An article readily saleable despite its faults in one age may be quite unacceptable in another because of rising standards in the market and a greater sophistication on the part of buyers. It seems equally clear that in testing quality in this sense the relevant date is the date of the contract, not the date of delivery, still less the date of the trial of the action. Any other conclusion would have the effect of increasing the standard of the seller's delivery obligation beyond that which was the basis of the parties' bargain.

---

172   Ibid, at 118.
173   Or arguably at the time of contract. But it would not, perhaps, be unreasonable to expect the seller to carry the risks attendant on new knowledge between contract and delivery.

5. FITNESS FOR PURPOSE

Section 14(3) of the Sale of Goods Act reads as follows:

> Where the seller sells[174] goods in the course of a business and the buyer, expressly or by implication, makes known
>
> (a)   to the seller, or
> (b)   where the purchase price or part of it is payable by instalments and the goods were previously sold by a credit-broker[175] to the seller, to that credit-broker,
>
> any particular purpose for which the goods are being bought, there is an implied term[176] that the goods supplied under the contract are reasonably fit for that purpose, whether or not that is a purpose for which such goods are commonly supplied, except where the circumstances show that the buyer does not rely, or that it is unreasonable for him to rely, on the skill or judgment of the seller or credit-broker.

As with quality, the implied condition is confined to cases where the seller sells in the course of a business[177] but, where applicable, extends to all goods supplied under the contract, whether or not the subject of the *sale*.[178]

'Particular purpose' does not necessarily mean a special, or non-normal, purpose but simply a specified purpose, whether ordinary or otherwise.[179]

(i)   Relationship with quality

The implied condition of fitness for a particular purpose to some extent overlaps with that of quality, in that an aspect of quality is fitness of the goods for all the purposes for which goods of that kind are commonly supplied,[180] while the condition of fitness under s 14(3) requires that the goods be fit for such a purpose[181] as well as for any particular, non-normal purpose for which the buyer makes it known they are required.[182] But the two implied conditions must be distinguished. Goods may be fit for the particular purpose required by the buyer yet be unsatisfactory because they are not of a quality which makes them saleable under their contract description. For example, an expensive motor car purchased as new may be perfectly fit for the required purpose of being driven along the road and yet not be of satisfactory quality because of poor finish, dents or other defects that would not be acceptable to the purchaser of a new car, particularly in an expensive price range, though not affecting the car's performance. Conversely, goods may be of satisfactory quality yet not suited to the particular purpose required by the buyer, as where cattle food suitable for animals generally is bought for the particular purpose of being fed to mink and turns out to be injurious to mink.[183]

---

174   See n 116.
175   As defined by s 61(1).
176   Which by s 14(6) is a condition.
177   For the provisions of s 14(5) as to sale through an agent, see p 301.
178   See pp 300–301. As to statutory implied warranty on the sale of feeding stuffs, see n 15.
179   *Preist v Last* [1903] 2 KB 148.
180   See p 306.
181   See (ii). For the position where goods are capable of use for several normal purposes, see pp 317–318.
182   This is now made explicit in s 14(3), enacting the rule established at common law (*Preist v Last*, n 179).
183   *Ashington Piggeries Ltd v Christopher Hill Ltd*, n 80.

(ii) Fitness for normal purpose

It is unfortunate that when the Supply of Goods (Implied Terms) Act was enacted opportunity was not taken to remove the overlap of the implied conditions of quality and fitness. Because of the differences between the criteria laid down in s 14(2) and those enunciated in s 14(3), the possibility is created of goods being fit for their normal purpose so as to be of satisfactory quality within s 14(2) yet being unfit for their normal purpose within s 14(3), and vice versa. This possibility arises because s 14(2) excludes the condition of quality as regards disclosed defects and defects that ought to have been apparent from the examination conducted by the buyer, whereas no such ground of exclusion is provided by s 14(3) in relation to fitness for purpose. Similarly, s 14(3) negates the implied condition of fitness where the buyer does not rely, or cannot reasonably rely, on the seller's skill and judgment, whereas want of reliance on the seller's skill and judgment is not a relevant factor for the purpose of s 14(2).

When the goods are of a kind having only one normal purpose, the seller's knowledge that the buyer requires the goods to be fit for that purpose will usually be assumed;[184] but where the goods are of a kind capable of being used for more than one normal purpose, it is for the buyer to make known[185] which normal purpose he requires the goods to serve, otherwise the seller will fulfil his duty by tendering goods which answer any one of the normal purposes, whether or not it happens to be the particular normal purpose for which the buyer requires them.[186]

(iii) Fitness for special purpose

If the goods are bought for some particular purpose of the buyer – that is, a purpose which is not their normal purpose or is more exactly defined than would normally be the case – then that purpose must be expressly or impliedly communicated to the seller if he is to be made responsible for ensuring that the goods are fit for the particular purpose.[187]

(iv) Communicating the purpose

In deciding whether a particular purpose has been effectively made known to the seller, three questions arise: *by* whom must the purpose be communicated, *to* whom must it be communicated, and *how* must the purpose be described to the seller?

I.   *By whom the purpose must be made known*

Section 14(3) requires that it be the buyer who, expressly or by implication, makes known to the seller any particular purpose for which the goods are being bought.

---

184 *Grant v Australian Knitting Mills Ltd*, n 76, at 99.
185 As to the means by which such knowledge may be communicated, see pp 316–317.
186 *Preist v Last*, n 179. Contrast the position as regards the implied term of quality (p 298). Different normal purposes must, it seems, be distinguished from different specific applications of a single normal purpose. See pp 317–318.
187 *Preist v Last*, n 179.

This would, of course, cover communication by the buyer's agent. In practice, the courts interpret this requirement liberally and, if the particular purpose is known to the seller or is apparent from the circumstances of the contract, this will suffice as an implied communication of purpose by the buyer.[188]

2.   To whom the purpose must be made known

The purpose is sufficiently communicated if made known to the seller or to any person having actual or ostensible authority to receive communication of the purpose on behalf of the seller. But s 14(3)(b) provides a further category of person to whom the buyer may make known the purpose, namely a credit-broker[189] by whom the goods were sold to the seller, being then resold to the buyer upon terms as to payment by instalments. Thus, if A wishes to acquire a car from a motor dealer, B, on credit terms and B sells the car to a finance house, F, which resells on credit sale to A, the car must be fit for any purpose communicated by A either to F directly or to B. This provision reflects B's status under the Consumer Credit Act as a deemed agent of F.[190]

3.   The particularity with which the purpose must be stated

The purpose for which the buyer may require the goods may, as we have seen, be their normal purpose or one of a prescribed range of normal purposes or a non-normal purpose. The seller is entitled to assume that the goods are required for their normal purpose, or one of their normal purposes, unless otherwise indicated by the buyer. Accordingly, if the buyer requires the goods for a non-normal purpose, he must take steps to acquaint the seller of this fact before the contract is made, otherwise the seller, if unaware of the special purpose for which the goods are bought, will not be considered to undertake that they are suitable for that purpose.[191] Hence where an article is purchased for installation in other goods, the seller is not liable for a failure of the article to meet its intended purpose where this is caused by some abnormal feature in the goods in which it is installed. Instructive on this point is the decision of the House of Lords in a Scottish case, *Slater v Finning Ltd.*[192]

> The pursuers, on the advice of the defenders, ordered a new camshaft for their motor fishing vessel. Noises started coming from the engine and parts became badly worn. The camshaft was twice replaced but problems with the engine continued. Eventually the old engine was sold and installed in the purchaser's vessel, which logged many thousands of miles without incident. In proceedings by the pursuers for damages for breach of the implied condition of fitness under s 14(3) of the Sale of Goods Act it

---

188 *Manchester Liners Ltd v Rea Ltd* [1922] 2 AC 74, per Lord Atkinson, at 84; *Shields v Honeywill & Stein Ltd* [1953] 1 Lloyd's Rep 357; *Ashington Piggeries Ltd v Christopher Hill Ltd*, n 80, per Lord Guest at 477.

189 Defined in s 61(1), which is itself derived from the Consumer Credit Act 1974, Sch 4, para 3. See *Goode: Consumer Credit Law and Practice* (looseleaf), paras [27.41], [48.13] ff, as to credit brokerage.

190 Consumer Credit Act 1974, s 56(2). See *Goode: Consumer Credit Law and Practice*, ch 32.

191 *B. S. Brown & Son Ltd v Craiks Ltd* 1969 SLT 107 and 357 (the subsequent appeal to the House of Lords was against the ruling on merchantable quality only).

192 [1997] AC 473.

was found as a fact that the camshaft failed not because of any internal defect but because of excessive torsional resonance excited by some cause external to the engine and the camshafts.

Held: a seller is not liable for a failure in the goods supplied resulting from some external and abnormal feature not made known to the buyer, and this was so whether or not the abnormality was known to the seller.

More difficult are the cases where goods are required (a) for one of a range of normal purposes, or (b) for a purpose which is a particular and specific application of a wider normal purpose. The distinction between the two categories is one of degree rather than kind. Thus, an antique lamp may be purchased to give illumination or purely for ornament and with no intention to put it to use. That might be considered within category (a), the two purposes being quite unconnected. Again, meat may be bought which is suitable both for human consumption and for feeding to animals. Here the overall purpose of the purchase is to use the meat for food, but within that function it may be purchased with the specific intention of feeding it to animals rather than humans, and to some types of animal rather than others.

The two categories appear to be governed by different principles. As regards the former, it is for the buyer to specify the particular normal purpose for which he requires the goods. If he does not, s 14(3) does not come into play,[193] though if the goods are unfit for one of their normal purposes the buyer may now be able to claim that they are not of satisfactory quality.[194] But where the buyer communicates the purpose for which the goods are required, he is not obliged to specify all the particular applications, within that normal purpose, to which he proposes to put the goods. He is entitled to assume that they will be fit for all applications commonly utilized under the umbrella of the designated purpose.

The distinction is well brought out in the third-party claim in the *Ashington Piggeries* case,[195] in which herring-meal, purchased and made up into a compound for feeding to mink, was toxic and killed large numbers of mink to which the compound was fed. Herring-meal was commonly used both as an animal food and as a fertilizer. The sellers knew the herring-meal was required for use as animal food but did not know that it was to be fed to mink. It appears to have been accepted by the House of Lords that if the sellers had not known whether the meal was required for use as food or as fertilizer no condition of fitness for purpose would have been implied. But the majority view was that the buyers, having intimated that it was required for animal food, did not have to go further and specify all the different kinds of animal to which the food might be given. It sufficed that herring-meal was commonly fed to mink.

Lord Diplock, however, dissented from this view. He did not expressly draw a distinction between a range of purposes and a specific application of a single normal purpose, and considered that feeding to animals comprised not one purpose but a

193   *Preist v Last*, n 179.
194   See p 316.
195   See n 80. For a more detailed description of the facts in relation to the plaintiffs' claim against the defendants, see pp 321–322.

range of purposes, so that if the buyer wished the goods to be suitable for a particular purpose (in this case, if he wished the food to be suitable for mink, as opposed to animals generally), he should either have that purpose incorporated into the contract description of the goods or identify with greater precision the purpose for which he required them.

It would seem that the difference between Lord Diplock's approach and that of the other members of the House is not one of principle but rather of the inference to be drawn from the particular set of facts. In Lord Diplock's view, the purpose for which the buyers actually required the herring-meal was not feeding to animals generally but feeding to mink, while the suppliers could not reasonably have inferred that the herring-meal *was* required for feeding to mink but at most that it *might* be so required, which was not within the language of the subsection. The view of the majority was that the required purpose was the general one of feeding to animals and that use of the herring-meal as mink food was merely a specific, and common, application within the umbrella of the general purpose. The purpose might be wide but that was no great hardship to the seller, for if a particular purpose encompassed a number of different applications, the buyer was entitled only to the satisfaction of suitability requirements common to them all, so that the wider the designated purpose, the greater the dilution of the seller's responsibility.[196] There is, however, a distinction between a wide purpose and a requirement so generalized as not to constitute a specified purpose at all. As pointed out by Lord Reid in the *Hardwick Game Farm* case,[197] the required purpose must be stated with sufficient particularity to show the buyer's (reasonable) reliance on the seller's skill and judgment. It was on that ground that the buyers failed in *Hamilton v Papkura District Council*,[198] where the Privy Council held by a majority[199] that sellers of water required by statute to be of a standard fit to drink were not required to ensure that the water met the higher standard of suitability to enable the buyers' cherry tomatoes, which were particularly sensitive to certain toxins in the water, to be grown hydroponically. The alternative claim in negligence was unanimously dismissed.

(v) 'Reasonably fit for that purpose'

The word 'reasonably' indicates that fitness for purpose, like satisfactory quality, is a relative concept. The question is what a reasonable buyer would expect from the goods, having regard to their price, age, state of wear and other relevant factors. Thus in *Bartlett v Sidney Marcus Ltd*:[200]

> The plaintiff purchased a second-hand Jaguar car for £950, on the basis that the clutch needed repair and that this would be done at his expense, the price being reduced by £25 to take account of this factor. The defect in the clutch proved more serious than had been thought and cost £84 to repair. The plaintiff's claim that the car was not fit for the purpose or of merchantable quality was dismissed by the trial judge, whose judgment

196   See n 80, per Lord Wilberforce at 497.
197   *Henry Kendall & Sons v William Lillico & Sons Ltd*, n 130, at 79.
198   [2002] 3 NZLR 308.
199   Lords Hutton and Rodger dissenting.
200   [1965] 1 WLR 1013. But as the result of what is now s 14(2B) the courts now take a broader view of what can reasonably be expected of a second-hand car. See p 306.

was upheld on appeal. The buyer had acquired the car in as good a condition as he was entitled to expect.

The seller is liable only to see that the goods are fit for their known purpose, not for some other, uncommunicated purpose;[201] and he does not commit a breach of s 14(3) merely by reason of the fact that goods that would be fit for a normal buyer are unsuitable for the particular buyer because, unknown to the seller, the buyer has an unusual sensitivity to goods of such description.[202] But where the seller knows or ought reasonably to know, in the light of the expertise he professes himself as holding, that certain people are unusually sensitive to the product he is selling, then it is his duty to warn the buyer or at least to take reasonable steps (whether by administration of tests or otherwise) to ensure that the buyer is not such a person.[203]

Whether goods are reasonably fit for their known purpose is to be determined objectively and does not in any way depend on the degree of care which the seller may have exercised. Hence the fact that the goods are unfit through some latent defect which no amount of care on the part of the seller could have detected is not an answer to a claim based on s 14(3), for it does not in any way make the goods more suitable for their purpose than if no care had been exercised.[204] The fact that the implied condition is attracted by reliance on the seller's skill and judgment does not mean that the condition is satisfied by the exercise of all reasonable care and skill. As Lord Reid observed in *Henry Kendall & Sons v William Lillico & Sons Ltd*:

> If the law were always logical one would suppose that a buyer, who has obtained a right to rely on the seller's skill and judgment, would only obtain thereby an assurance that proper skill and judgment had been exercised and would only be entitled to a remedy if a defect in the goods was due to failure to exercise such skill and judgment. But the law has always gone farther than that. By getting the seller to undertake to use his skill and judgment the buyer gets under s 14(1) an assurance that the goods will be reasonably fit for his purpose and that covers not only defects which the seller ought to have detected but also defects which are latent in the sense that even the utmost skill and judgment on the part of the seller would not have detected them.[205]

(vi) Reliance on seller's skill or judgment

The implied condition of fitness for purpose does not apply 'where the circumstances show that the buyer does not rely, or that it is unreasonable for him to rely,[206] on the skill or judgment of the seller or credit-broker'. The ingredient of reliance is directly connected to the communication of the purpose for which the goods are required, for the buyer relies on the seller's skill or judgment to supply

---

201 See p 316.

202 *Griffith v Peter Conway Ltd* [1939] 1 All ER 685.

203 There does not appear to be any authority on the point, but there are a number of products to which people are known to be allergic and good practice requires that inquiry be made of them before the product is supplied. Failure to take reasonable precautions might also render the supplier liable in tort. See *Miller's Product Liability and Safety Encyclopaedia III* (looseleaf) [82].

204 *Randall v Newson* (1877) 2 QBD 102; *Henry Kendall & Sons v William Lillico & Sons Ltd*, n 130.

205 See n 130, at 84.

206 See pp 322–323.

goods fit for the known purpose, and if the purpose is not sufficiently communicated, the buyer cannot reasonably rely on the seller's skill or judgment to ensure that the goods answer that purpose.[207]

It is clear that if the buyer relies exclusively on his own skill or judgment to select goods fit for the purpose for which he requires them, he cannot hold the seller at fault if the goods prove unsuitable. But whereas prior to the 1973 Act the onus of showing reliance on the seller's skill or judgment lay on the buyer,[208] it is now for the seller to show affirmatively that there was no reasonable reliance. Hence such reliance will be assumed until the contrary is proved.

The question of reliance can conveniently be considered under a number of different heads.

1. Sale under patent or other trade name

As originally enacted, s 14 excluded the implied condition of fitness where the contract was for the sale of a specific article under its patent or other trade name. But the courts construed this provision restrictively, ruling that it did not apply unless the patent or trade name was specified in such a way as to show that the buyer did not intend to rely on the seller's skill or judgment.[209] The provision was thus reduced to a specific application of the reliance test, and as it served little purpose, it was dropped by the Supply of Goods (Implied Terms) Act 1973, implementing the recommendations of the Law Commission.[210]

2. Partial reliance

It not infrequently occurs that the buyer relies on the seller's skill or judgment as to some aspects of the goods while drawing on his own expertise as to other aspects. In such cases the question is whether the unsuitability of the goods arose in relation to the former aspect or in relation to the latter. If the goods prove unfit for their purpose on account of some fact within the buyer's sphere of expertise, he cannot complain. But the fact that he relied on his own skill or judgment on that aspect does not preclude him from asserting a breach of s 14(3) if the goods are unfit because of some fact within the seller's sphere of expertise on which the buyer relied. This point is well brought out by the decision of the House of Lords in *Ashington Piggeries Ltd v Christopher Hill Ltd*[211]

> Ashington Piggeries Ltd was a mink-farming company controlled by a leading mink farmer and a known expert in mink nutrition. On behalf of his company, the farmer asked Christopher Hill Ltd to make a vitamin-fortified mink food, to be called 'King Size', in accordance with a formula he had prepared. Christopher Hill, though

---

207 *Henry Kendall & Sons v William Lillico & Sons Ltd*, n 130, per Lord Reid, at 80.

208 Ibid, at 81. But reliance on the seller's skill and judgment as to the fitness of the goods for their ordinary purpose is readily inferred. See *Ashington Piggeries Ltd v Christopher Hill Ltd*, n 80, per Lord Guest, commenting on the dictum of Lord Denning MR in *Teheran-Europe Co Ltd v S. T. Belton (Tractors) Ltd*, n 89, at 554.

209 *Baldry v Marshall* [1925] 1 KB 260.

210 *Exemption Clauses in Contracts – First Report*, n 55, paras 32–33.

211 See n 80.

well-known compounders of foodstuff (principally for poultry, pheasant, calves and pigs), had never produced food for mink and knew nothing of the nutritional requirements of mink food. They suggested, and the mink-farming company accepted, two variations of the formula, one of which was to substitute herring-meal for whitefish-meal as one of the ingredients. The ingredients were to be of the best quality available.

The mink food was prepared and marketed, with no complaints that mink had suffered from the compound, but after Christopher Hill had begun to use Norwegian herring-meal in the compounding of 'King Size', heavy losses began to occur to mink fed with the compound. This was later found to be caused by a toxin produced by a chemical reaction generated by a preservative in the compound. At the time of the contract the possibility of the chemical reaction producing the toxin was unthought of, and in the then existing state of knowledge no deliberate exercise of human skill or judgment could have prevented the herring-meal from having its toxic effect on mink. But later publications by an expert indicated that mink were seriously affected by the herring-meal and that other animals were sensitive to the toxin, though they were affected to a much lesser extent and there was no evidence that animals other than mink had suffered from the 'King Size' compounded by Christopher Hill with the Norwegian herring-meal.

Ashington Piggeries, on being sued for the price of 'King Size', counterclaimed damages for loss suffered by the death of the mink, alleging, inter alia, that the compound was not fit for the purpose for which it was supplied, namely being fed to mink.

The House of Lords, reversing the decision of the Court of Appeal, held that while Ashington Piggeries relied on their own skill or judgment to ensure that no idiosyncrasy of mink made the food unsuitable for mink, they relied on the skill and judgment of Christopher Hill to obtain the ingredients, mix them correctly and ensure that they did not contain a toxin or poisonous element rendering the compound unsafe for feeding to animals generally. Christopher Hill had failed to supply a compound fit for the required purpose and were thus liable on the counterclaim.

In short, both the seller and the buyer had areas of expertise and the question was whether the defect complained of fell within the area of expertise of the buyer (in which event the buyer could not complain) or of the seller. If there had not been evidence of the sensitivity of *other animals* to the toxin generated by the herring-meal, the counterclaim for breach of the implied condition of fitness would not have succeeded, for the death of the mink would then have been shown to be due to the peculiar sensitivity of mink, a matter within the sphere of expertise of the buyer. But other animals *were* affected (though to a much lesser degree) by Norwegian herring-meal. It may be asked why the House of Lords should have regarded it as relevant to examine the fitness of the compound for other animals when it was known to be required only for mink.[212] The answer is that their Lordships were not concerned with suitability for other animals in a general sense but with whether the food was safe; and the fact that other animals had been adversely affected by the herring-meal of the type used in the compound showed that the food was unsafe, *regardless of any characteristic peculiar to mink*.

3.   Unreasonable reliance

Even where the buyer relies on the seller's skill or judgment to ensure that the goods are reasonably fit for their required purpose, he will not be able to invoke the

---

212   See Ingrid Patient (1971) 34 MLR 557 at pp 559–60.

implied condition of fitness for purpose if such reliance was unreasonable. The onus of proving unreasonableness is on the seller. The mere fact that the buyer failed to avail himself of an opportunity to examine the goods and would have discovered their unsuitability if he had examined them does not by itself make it unreasonable for him to rely on the seller's skill or judgment. On the contrary, his decision not to examine for himself may well have been taken because of his reliance on the seller.

Where the buyer does examine the goods, and they possess defects apparent on examination which ought to make it clear to the buyer that they are unsuited to their purpose, this may be a ground for holding the buyer's reliance on the seller's skill and judgment unreasonable, but it does not inevitably follow that there should be such a finding. The seller may, for example, have assured the buyer that the defects would not in any way impair the utility of the goods for their required purpose.

If the goods are offered as subject to defects, on the basis that the buyer is to take them as he finds them, he can scarcely claim to be acting reasonably in reliance on the seller's skill or judgment as to the fitness of the goods. The same applies where the buyer knows or ought reasonably to have known that the seller has no expertise in relation to the goods in question, and a fortiori where the seller expressly disclaims such expertise.[213] However, there are disclaimers and disclaimers. Section 6 of the Unfair Contract Terms Act precludes contracting out of the implied condition of fitness in the case of a consumer sale; and the court will obviously not allow that section to be evaded merely by incorporating a contractual provision that the buyer relies on his own skill and judgment and not on that of the seller. Whether such a clause makes the buyer's reliance unreasonable depends on the prominence of the clause or other steps taken by the seller to bring it to the buyer's notice. If the buyer ought reasonably to have read it, then no doubt he will be unable to invoke s 14(3) of the Sale of Goods Act. But we can infer from s 6 of the Unfair Contract Terms Act that this result will not occur simply because the term features as a term of the contract, even if the contract be signed by the buyer.

Where the suitability of the goods for their required purpose is a matter peculiarly within the buyer's own knowledge or sphere of expertise, this will usually make it unreasonable for him to rely on the seller's skill or judgment, though the matter is otherwise where, as in the *Ashington Piggeries* case,[214] the expert buyer relies on the seller to ensure that the goods possess those characteristics which are or ought to be within the seller's sphere of knowledge.

4. The time at which reliance has to be tested

The fact of reliance and the reasonableness of reliance must be established as at the date of the contract.

---

213 As in *Ashington Piggeries Ltd v Christopher Hill Ltd*, n 80, where the defendants would have escaped liability if the food compound which they prepared in accordance with the plaintiffs' specification had been safe but merely unsuitable.
214 Ibid.

(vii) The time at which the condition of fitness must be satisfied

As with quality, the implied condition of fitness is not a continuing duty but is a once-for-all obligation which has to be satisfied at the time of delivery.[215] But if the goods cease to function, or evince defects, within a shorter period than normal, that is evidence that they were not in proper condition when delivered.[216]

6.   CORRESPONDENCE WITH SAMPLE

The first two subsections of s 15, as amended by the Sale and Supply of Goods Act 1994, provide as follows:

(1) A contract of sale is a contract for sale by sample where there is an express or implied term to that effect in the contract.

(2) In the case of a contract for sale by sample there is an implied term

(a)   that the bulk will correspond with the sample in quality;
(b)   [Repealed]
(c)   that the goods will be free from any defect making their quality unsatisfactory which would not be apparent on reasonable examination of the sample.

The sample may be one extracted from the bulk to be purchased or it may be entirely separate from that bulk. The mere fact that a sample is exhibited during negotiations for a sale does not make it a sale by sample. It is necessary that the sample displayed be intended to form the contractual basis of comparison with the goods subsequently tendered. As a working rule, it may be said that a sale is unlikely to be considered a sale by sample unless the sample is released by the seller to the buyer or to a third party for the purpose of providing a means of checking whether the goods subsequently tendered correspond with the sample. The mere fact that I look at a pair of shoes in a shop window and then ask the shop assistant for 'a pair like that' does not make the sale a sale by sample. It will be observed that the implied term of correspondence with description is not confined to sales made by a seller in the course of business. This is logical, for a sale by sample is simply an alternative to a sale by description, and s 15 is thus properly equated with s 13 rather than with s 14.[217]

Section 15(2)(b) needs little comment, being a specific application, in the case of sale by sample, of the more general principle expressed in s 34 as to the buyer's right to examine the goods for the purpose of ascertaining whether they are in conformity with the contract.[218] Prima facie, the contractual delivery point is the place for comparing the bulk with the sample,[219] but this may be displaced by evidence of a contrary intention.

---

215   *Crowther v Shannon Motor Co*, n 164; but see the speech of Lord Diplock in *Lambert v Lewis* [1981] 1 All ER 1185 at 1191. See also A. H. Hudson, 'Time and Terms as to Quality in Sale of Goods' (1978) 94 LQR 566.
216   *Crowther v Shannon Motor Co*, n 164; and see further under 'Durability', p 308.
217   For an argument that most breaches of s 15 are adequately covered by ss 13 and 14, see J. R. Murdoch, 'Sale by Sample – A Distinction Without a Difference?' (1981) 44 MLR 388.
218   See pp 348 ff.
219   *Perkins v Bell* [1893] 1 QB 193.

Paragraphs (a) and (c) of s 15(2) can best be understood if analysed together. We can begin by considering the function of a sample.

> After all, the office of a sample is to present to the eye the real meaning and intention of the parties with regard to the subject-matter of the contract which, owing to the imperfection of language, it may be difficult or impossible to express in words. The sample speaks for itself. But it cannot be treated as saying more than such a sample would tell a merchant of the class to which the buyer belongs, using due care and diligence, and appealing to it in the ordinary way and with the knowledge possessed by merchants of that class at the time. No doubt the sample might be made to say a great deal more. Pulled to pieces and examined by unusual tests which curiosity or suspicion might suggest, it would doubtless reveal every secret of its construction. But that is not the way in which business is done in this country. Some confidence there must be between merchant and manufacturer. In matters exclusively within the province of the manufacturer, the merchant relies on the manufacturer's skill, and he does so all the more readily when, as in this case, he has had the benefit of that skill before.[220]

Hence the buyer is not entitled under s 15(2)(a) to require the bulk to correspond with the sample except as to those qualities, whether of the sample or of the bulk, that would be apparent from such examination as is normal in the trade. From this principle, coupled with the provisions of s 15(2)(c), four propositions may be extracted. First, if the sample contains latent desirable qualities which are not carried over into the bulk, and through their absence the bulk is of unsatisfactory quality, the buyer's remedy is under s 15(2)(c). If the absence of such qualities does not render the bulk of unsatisfactory quality, the buyer has no claim under s 15 at all.[221] Secondly, if the sample contains a latent defect but the bulk does not, the bulk does not on that account disconform to the sample, for the seller does not undertake that the bulk will correspond to the sample as regards those characteristics of the sample that would not be apparent from reasonable examination of it;[222] he merely undertakes, under s 15(2)(c), that they will not be such as to render the quality of the goods unsatisfactory. Thirdly, if the bulk contains a latent defect which was not in the sample, then again there is no breach of s 15(2)(a),[223] and the buyer must show that the defect makes the bulk of unsatisfactory quality, so as to come within s 15(2)(c). Finally, if both the sample and the bulk contain the same latent defect and the bulk is in all other respects in conformity with the sample, s 15(2)(a) is complied with (all too well!), but if the defect is one which renders the quality of the bulk unsatisfactory, there is a breach of s 15(2)(c).[224]

In the commodity trades it is common for the rules of the relevant association to provide for the machinery by which samples are to be taken, with a view to securing that the sample is fairly representative of the bulk,[225] and where those rules are incorporated into the contract, the parties will be bound by them.[226]

---

220 *James Drummond & Sons v E. H. Van Ingen & Co* (1887) 12 App Cas 284, per Lord Macnaghten at 297.
221 *F. E. Hookway & Co Ltd v Alfred Isaacs & Sons* [1954] 1 Lloyd's Rep 491.
222 Ibid.
223 *Steels & Busks Ltd v Bleecker Bik & Co Ltd* [1956] 1 Lloyd's Rep 228.
224 For an illustration see *James Drummond & Sons v E. H. Van Ingen & Co*, n 220, the effect of which decision was incorporated into s 15(2)(c).
225 See, for example, the sampling rules provided by the Grain and Feed Trade Association in GAFTA 100.
226 See p 157.

7.   THE EXCLUSION OF LIABILITY FOR FITNESS, QUALITY AND CORRESPONDENCE WITH DESCRIPTION OR SAMPLE

The laissez-faire policy of the Sale of Goods Act 1893, with its express encouragement to contract out of the statutory implied terms,[227] was allowed to hold sway for a remarkably long time. Indeed, by the middle of last century the courts, evidently despairing of intervention by the legislature, had developed their own weapons for dealing with exemption clauses, through rules of strict construction and the doctrines of fundamental term and fundamental breach.[228] Yet still Parliament delayed, and the protection accorded to a hirer on hire-purchase since 1938[229] remained unavailable to the cash buyer, despite a strong recommendation by the Molony Committee that exemption clauses in consumer sales should be curbed.[230] It was only as the result of the Law Commission's first report on exemption clauses[231] that Parliament was finally persuaded to act, adopting (with certain amendments) the draft Bill appended to the report. The end product was the Supply of Goods (Implied Terms) Act 1973, which revised the implied terms in ss 12–15 of the Sale of Goods Act and also[232] modified and expanded s 55 so as to ban contracting out of the terms implied by s 12 and, in the case of consumer sales, the terms implied by ss 13–15, and empowered the courts to rule such exemption clauses unenforceable in non-consumer sales, in given conditions. In addition, the ability of the parties to displace by a choice of law clause the application of English law to a contract of sale whose proper law would otherwise have been English is excluded by a new s 55A.[233] These provisions were replaced by the Unfair Contract Terms Act 1977 ss 6, 11, 27(2) and Sch 2.

Section 55, as slightly amended by the Sale and Supply of Goods Act 1994,[234] provides as follows:

> (1) Where a right, duty or liability would arise under a contract of sale of goods by implication of law, it may (subject to the Unfair Contract Terms Act 1977) be negatived or varied by express agreement, or by the course of dealing between the parties, or by such usage as binds both parties to the contract.
>
> (2) An express term does not negative a term implied by this Act unless inconsistent with it.

Like the *caveat emptor* statement in s 14(1), the general rule in s 55(1) as to freedom to contract out of the Act is now subordinated to the exceptions in s 6 of the Unfair Contract Terms Act. The restrictions imposed by s 6 are, however, confined to provisions excluding or limiting the operation of ss 12–15 of the Sale of Goods Act. Section 6 leaves untouched contractual provisions purporting (a) to negate duties imposed by other sections of the Sale of Goods Act or by *express*

---

227   Section 55.
228   See p 96.
229   Hire-Purchase Act 1938, s 8(3).
230   *Final Report of the Committee on Consumer Protection* (1962, Cmnd 1781), paras 426 ff.
231   See n 55.
232   Section 4.
233   See F. A. Mann, 'The Amended Sale of Goods Act 1893 and the Conflict of Laws' (1974) 90 LQR 42, for a singular view of the effect of that section.
234   By substituting 'term' for 'condition' in s 55(2).

undertakings, or (b) to exclude terms implied *in fact* or terms purporting to exclude liability in tort, eg for negligence. Exemption clauses of these kinds are controlled only by the common law and by other more general provisions of the Unfair Contract Terms Act, in particular ss 2 and 3,[235] and, in relation to consumer sales, by the more wide-ranging provisions of the EEC Directive on Unfair Contract Terms[236] as implemented in the UK by the Unfair Terms in Consumer Contracts Regulations 1999.[237] We first consider the 1977 Act before turning briefly to examine the impact of the 1999 regulations on exemption clauses.

(i) Exclusion of title, quiet possession and freedom from encumbrances

The terms of title, quiet possession and freedom from encumbrances imported into contracts of sale by s 12 of the Sale of Goods Act cannot be excluded, and any provision in any contract (whether the sale contract itself or a separate contract entered into by the buyer, either with the seller or with a third party such as the manufacturer) purporting to exclude any of these terms is rendered void.[238] This is so whether or not the contract of sale is a consumer sale. Hence the purported exclusion of s 12 is ineffective even where the sale is to a commercial buyer or where the seller is a private seller.

Of course, s 12 itself provides circumstances in which the terms implied under it may be excluded or limited. For example, there is no implied warranty of freedom from disclosed charges or encumbrances;[239] and a seller may contract to transfer only such title as he or a third party may have, in which case the ordinary terms as to title are replaced by a more limited set of implied undertakings.[240] But where there is nothing to indicate that the seller is contracting to transfer only a limited title, he cannot fall back on s 12(2) and (5) to surmount s 6(1) of the Unfair Contract Terms Act.[241]

(ii) Exclusion of other[242] implied terms: consumer sales

As against a person dealing as consumer, a term of the sale or any other contract[243] purporting to exclude any of the provisions of ss 13, 14 or 15 is void.[244] Thus, implied terms of correspondence with description or sample, quality or fitness cannot be effectively excluded as against a person dealing as consumer. Again, ss 12–15 define the circumstances in which terms as to fitness, quality and the like are to be implied. The mere fact that a seller avoids the implication of the terms in

235 See pp 97–98.
236 See p 100. For the penal sanctions against inclusion of invalid exemption clauses, see p 331.
237 SI 1999/2083, as amended by SI 2001/1186. See p 100.
238 Unfair Contract Terms Act 1977, ss 6(1)(a), 10.
239 Section 12(2). See p 283.
240 Section 12(3)–(5).
241 See p 289. See also the Unfair Contract Terms Directive and implementing regulations, p 100.
242 Ie, other than title, quiet possession or freedom from encumbrances.
243 Eg. in a manufacturer's guarantee.
244 Unfair Contract Terms Act, s 6(2).

the first place, eg by drawing defects to the buyer's attention prior to the sale or by giving a warning which makes it unreasonable for the buyer to rely on the seller's skill and judgment, cannot, it is thought, be treated as imposing an exemption clause. But an attempt to exclude the implied term by incorporating a waiver of the opportunity of examination would, it is thought, be treated as an exemption clause within the statutory provisions.[245]

By s 12 of the Unfair Contract Terms Act a person deals as consumer where the following conditions are satisfied.

1.   The buyer neither is nor holds himself out as contracting in the course of a business

The buyer does not deal as consumer if he makes the contract in the course of a business, or holds himself out as doing so. Despite the formulation of the 'private purpose' requirement as a requirement that has to be positively satisfied in order for the buyer to deal as consumer, the onus is in fact on the seller to show that the buyer bought or held himself out as buying in the course of a business, not on the buyer to show the contrary.[246]

What if the buyer buys goods – eg a car – for use both privately and for the purpose of his business? This is a little more difficult. The test is not the *purpose* for which the goods are bought, but whether the buyer makes the contract (or holds himself out as making it) in the course of a business. In other words, is the purchase a purchase by the business or is it a purchase by the buyer as a private individual? If he orders the goods on his business notepaper and requires delivery to his business premises, this indicates a purchase in the course of business. Again, if the cost of the goods is debited as an expense of the business, this may indicate a purchase in the course of a business.[247] But in all cases the purchase must be as an integral part of the business, either because it is a transaction (even an isolated transaction) concluded in the way of trade and with a view to profit or because, though it would be merely incidental to the business if viewed as an isolated transaction, it is a transaction of a type carried on with a degree of regularity that establishes it as an integral part of the business.[248] On this basis it has been held that there is nothing to preclude a company from being a buyer who deals as a consumer.[249]

Conversely, if the buyer holds himself out as buying privately, the fact that he intends to use the goods exclusively in his business does not prevent him from

---

245 See ibid, s 13(1). By s 35(3) of the Sale of Goods Act (see also p 352) such exclusion is now of no effect for the separate purpose of s 35(2) of the Act (preserving the buyer's right to reject until he has had a reasonable opportunity for examination), but there is no comparable provision as regards 14(2C). Hence it is necessary to fall back on the more general provisions of the Unfair Contract Terms Act.

246 Ibid, s 12(3).

247 But it is by no means conclusive. Holding oneself out to the seller as a business buyer is one thing; holding oneself out in this way to the Inland Revenue, having conveyed to the seller that one is buying privately, is something else!

248 See *R. & B. Customs Brokers Co Ltd v United Dominions Trust Ltd* [1988] 1 All ER 847, [1988] 1 WLR 321, applying the decision of the House of Lords in *Davies v Sumner* [1984] 1 WLR 1301.

249 *R. & B. Customs Brokers Co Ltd v United Dominions Trust Ltd* [1988] 1 WLR 321.

qualifying as a consumer. On the other hand, if the buyer, though holding himself out as a private buyer, is in fact purchasing the goods in the course of a business, the requirement of s 12 will not be satisfied.

2. The seller makes the contract in the course of a business

Private sales are excluded; but 'course of a business' has a wider connotation than might at first be apparent. It is not necessary that the seller shall be a dealer in goods of the same kind as those the subject of the contract. Indeed, it is not necessary that he shall deal in goods at all. It suffices that the sale is made in the course of *a* business, of whatever nature. The phrase 'in the course of a business', which features in various provisions of the Trade Descriptions Act 1968, is not confined to sales of stock in which the seller is a dealer but covers any act performed as an integral part of a business activity, and thus includes, for example, regular selling off of fixed assets after their useful life in the business has come to an end[250] or even an isolated transaction if in the way of trade and carried on with a view to profit.[251]

3. The goods are of a type ordinarily bought for private use or consumption

Where the goods are of a type ordinarily used exclusively for business purposes, then even if the buyer is purchasing them for private purposes, he will not be dealing as consumer. On the other hand, s 12 does not say that the goods must be of a type bought *exclusively* for private use or consumption. Accordingly, sales of multi-purpose goods bought for both business and private use, such as motor cars, still fall within s 12 if the other requirements of that section are satisfied.

4. The contract is not a sale by auction

There are good policy reasons for excluding auction sales. The seller at auction is frequently unable to undertake that the goods will comply with the statutory implied terms, as where the transaction is a forced sale by a sheriff or bailiff. It also may be difficult for the auctioneer to know whether the buyer is a business buyer or a private purchaser; and auction sales usually involve an element of speculation, making it undesirable to preclude contracting-out.[252]

5. The contract is not a sale by competitive tender

Such sales are excluded from the definition of consumer dealings because, as in the case of auction sales, they are of a more speculative nature than ordinary sales[253]

---

250 *Havering London Borough Council v Stevenson* [1970] 1WLR 1375.

251 *Davies v Sumner*, n 248.

252 See the Law Commissions' *First Report on Exemption Clauses*, paras 114 ff, showing a division of opinion among the members of the Commissions as to the desirability of the exemption; HL Deb 16 Nov. 1972, col 847; and HC Deb 13 Feb. 1973, col 1159. A sale privately through the auctioneer after the goods have failed to reach their reserve price is not a sale by auction (*D. & M. Trailers (Halifax) Ltd v Stirling* [1978] RTR 468).

253 See HL Deb 16 Nov. 1972, col 847.

and the seller will not necessarily have the means of knowing whether the buyer is a business buyer or a private purchaser.

(iii) Exclusion of other[254] implied terms: non-consumer sales

Where the buyer does not deal as consumer, the implied terms of correspondence with description,[255] fitness, quality and correspondence with sample may be validly excluded or restricted but only so far as the exempting term satisfies the requirement of reasonableness.[256] Schedule 2 provides guidelines to which the court must have regard in determining whether the test of reasonableness is satisfied. In contrast to the position under the 1973 Act, the question is whether the *term* is reasonable, not whether *reliance* on it is reasonable. Reasonableness has to be tested in the light of circumstances prevailing at the date of the contract. In each case the onus is on the seller to show that the exempting term is reasonable.[257]

(a) RELATIVE BARGAINING STRENGTH. The first factor mentioned is the strength of the bargaining positions of the seller and buyer relative to each other taking into account, amongst other things, alternative means by which the customer's requirements could have been met. Thus, where the seller holds a monopoly position he will find it harder to persuade a court to uphold reliance on the exemption clause.

(b) INDUCEMENT TO BUYER TO ACCEPT CLAUSE. A material consideration is 'whether the customer received an inducement to agree to the term or in accepting it had an opportunity of entering into a similar contract with other persons, but without having to accept a similar term'.

(c) BUYER'S KNOWLEDGE OF TERM. Recognizing that parties frequently enter into contracts without reading them, the subsection includes as a relevant factor 'whether the buyer knew or ought reasonably to have known of the existence and extent of the term (having regard, among other things, to any custom of the trade and any previous course of dealing between the parties)'. For the purpose of determining whether a business buyer ought to have known of the existence of the exempting term, certain features are of obvious relevance. A tailor-made, type-written contract is more likely to be read than a printed, standard-term document. A previous course of dealing between seller and buyer will make it more difficult for the buyer to establish ignorance of the standard terms. A trade custom by which the responsibilities of the seller are restricted or qualified is likely to be a significant factor weighing against the buyer, for business buyers are presumed to contract with knowledge of customs affecting the trading activity in which they operate. On the other hand, a lengthy, obscurely worded exemption clause will tilt the scales against the seller, as will a clause which restricts liability in a manner unusual in the trade. Finally, the buyer's knowledge of the existence and effect of the exemption clause

---

254   Ie, other than title, quiet possession and freedom from encumbrances.

255   But see p 282.

256   See *George Mitchell (Chesterhall) Ltd v Finney Lock Seeds Ltd* [1983] 2 AC 803; *R. W. Green Ltd v Cade Bros Farms* [1978] 1 Lloyd's Rep 602, a decision on s 55(4), (5), of the Sale of Goods Act 1893. See also pp 97–98.

257   Unfair Contract Terms Act, s 11(5).

is far from conclusive, for it is only one factor among many, and may be outweighed by evidence of marked inequality in bargaining power adversely affecting the buyer's ability to negotiate.

(d) EXEMPTION IF CONDITIONS NOT COMPLIED WITH. The fourth factor mentioned in Sch 2 deals with the situation where the exempting term excludes all or any of the provisions of ss 13, 14 or 15 if some condition is not complied with. In such a case the question is whether it was reasonable at the time of the contract to expect that compliance with that condition would be practicable. Typical provisions within this paragraph are those which require the buyer to notify a complaint within a specified time or to accompany such notification with the part or parts alleged to be defective. A material factor in such cases is whether the time limit allowed was reasonably capable of being adhered to,[258] whether it was practicable to require dispatch of the defective part (which might require considerable skill to extract without further damage) and so on.

(e) SPECIAL ORDERS. The final matter listed in the guidelines in Sch 2 is whether the goods were manufactured, processed or adapted to the special order of the buyer. Obviously, a special order may create particular difficulties for the seller. He may be willing to accept the order but only on the basis that he is allowed to qualify his responsibility. On the other side of the coin, the buyer may require the goods to be specially made precisely in order to avoid defects of the kind experienced in mass-produced articles, and since he is likely to be paying a significantly higher price for goods made to his order, he may legitimately be able to argue that the exemption clause does not satisfy the test of reasonableness.

The guidelines in Sch 2 to the Unfair Contract Terms Act are not exhaustive. In *George Mitchell (Chesterhall) Ltd v Finney Lock Seeds Ltd*[259] the House of Lords considered relevant, as tending to show the unreasonableness of a limitation of liability clause, not only that the sellers could have obtained liability insurance at a modest cost[260] but also that the sellers had not usually relied on the clause in the past but had negotiated a settlement.

(iv) Penal sanctions for inclusion of a void exemption clause

The nullifying of exemption clauses in consumer sales, though a welcome step, proved only partially effective, since many sellers continued to incorporate void exemption clauses into their contracts, relying on the consumer's ignorance of the statutory provisions. Such sellers would, indeed, go further and, upon receipt of a complaint from an aggrieved consumer about a defective product, would flagrantly

---

258 See case cited p 98, n 232.

259 See n 256.

260 This is the second of the two factors specifically mentioned in s 11(4) of the Act in relation to limitation of liability clauses, but in practice it is taken into account by the courts also when considering the reasonableness of an exemption clause. This factor is, of course, directly linked to the first of the two factors mentioned in s 11(4), namely the resources which the person invoking the limitation of liability clause could expect to be available to him for the purpose of meeting the liability should it arise.

breach the spirit of the legislation by drawing attention to the exemption clause, well knowing that it had no legal effect. The consumer would thus be misled into abandoning a perfectly good claim. This reprehensible practice, which was the subject of a report by the Consumer Protection Advisory Committee,[261] has been made an offence by the Consumer Transactions (Restrictions on Statements) Order 1976.[262]

(v) Control of exemption clauses through unfair contract terms regulation

The wide-ranging provisions of the Unfair Terms in Consumer Contracts Regulations 1999, which have been referred to earlier,[263] also potentially affect exemption clauses in consumer contracts.[264] An examination of these regulations is outside the scope of a work on commercial law and reference should be made to literature on consumer law.[265]

8.   SHOULD FURTHER TERMS BE IMPLIED?

The adequacy of the range of terms now implied by the Sale of Goods Act has come increasingly into question both in this country and in other parts of the Commonwealth whose sales law is modelled on the Sale of Goods Act. The following additional terms, in particular, are worthy of consideration.

(i)   Suitability for immediate use

The Law Commissions at one time considered, but ultimately rejected, the idea of including the suitability of goods for immediate use, not as an independent implied term but as an aspect of quality.[266] As consultees pointed out, there are many cases where goods are quite properly sold when they are not suitable for immediate use, as where they are maturing or where they can be used only after some act by the buyer, such as fixing a plug or removing locking pins.[267]

(ii) Durability

As previously pointed out,[268] the Law Commissions rightly rejected the notion of an independent implied term of durability. Instead, durability features as an aspect of quality, and as such is to be satisfied as at the time of supply.

---

261 *Rights of Consumers – A Report on Practices Relating to the Purported Exclusion of Individual Rights of Consumers and Failure to Explain their Existence* 1974–1975 HC 6.
262 As amended by the Consumer Transactions (Restrictions on Statements) (Amendment) Order 1978.
263 See p 100.
264 See the indicative and non-exhaustive list in Sch 2.
265 See in particular John Macleod, *Consumer Sales Law* (2002) paras [11.12] ff.
266 *Sale and Supply of Goods*, para 3.62.
267 Ibid, para 3.64.
268 See p 308. But as to consumer sales, see p 389.

(iii) Replaceability

There is no implied obligation on the seller (or indeed on the manufacturer) of goods to ensure that, if a purchased article is lost or damaged or wears out, a replacement will be available. This may be of no great moment where the article is used on its own, but creates more difficulty if it is part of a set, for inability to replace it may diminish the value of the remainder of the set, as in the case of a given utensil or a piece of porcelain forming part of a table setting. If at the time of sale of the set the seller warrants that it is a running line for which replacements will be available, he may incur a liability for misrepresentation or breach of warranty if this proves not to be the case. There would be serious practical difficulties in imposing on the seller an undertaking as to replaceability, even for a limited period, for the ability to keep replacements available depends on so many factors outside the seller's control.

(iv) Servicing and spare parts

There is a stronger case for importing into contracts of sale an undertaking that servicing facilities and spare parts will be available for a reasonable period after sale. Many items of equipment are complex and require specialist knowledge; moreover, the parts used in the manufacture are all too often specially made for the product and not standard, and thus are not available except from the manufacturer or its distributors. The absence of servicing facilities or of spare parts thus seriously reduces the effective working life of the purchased article. An obligation to ensure that spare parts and servicing will be available for a limited period was advocated by at least two Canadian reports[269] and is now imposed by several Canadian statutes. No such legislation at present exists in England, and the Law Commission advised against it in its two reports.[270]

(v) Information

The duty to provide information about the goods is generally encompassed within the existing implied terms of quality and fitness for purpose. Thus there is a duty to warn the buyer of safety risks if the goods are, or are not, used in a particular way or for a particular purpose,[271] while the Sale of Goods Act itself contains provisions negating the implied term of quality as regards matters drawn specifically to the buyer's attention before the making of the contract[272] and the implied term of fitness for purpose where the buyer does not rely, or the circumstances show that it is unreasonable for him to rely, on the seller's skill and judgment.[273] Yet there is

---

269 Both by the Ontario Law Reform Commission. See *Report on Consumer Warranties and Guarantees in the Sale of Goods* (1972), pp 40–401, and the Commission's revised proposals in its *Report on Sale of Goods* (1979), pp 216–217.

270 Law Commission, *Implied Terms in Contracts for the Supply of Goods* (1979, Law Com. No 95), paras 115–122; *Sale and Supply of Goods*, para 3.66.

271 See pp 307, 318 ff.

272 Sale of Goods Act 1979, s 14(2C)(a).

273 Ibid, s 14(3).

force in the criticism[274] that to subsume everything under one or other of the implied terms is artificial. If the goods are perfectly suitable but the buyer needs adequate instructions in order to use them, there is much to be said for a free-standing implied duty to provide the necessary instruction, rather than an implication, contrary to the facts, that the goods are not of satisfactory quality or are unfit for their purpose.

9.   THE EFFECT OF REPLACEMENT OR REPAIR OF DEFECTIVE GOODS

(i)   Replacement

A largely unexplored problem is the effect on a contract of sale of the seller's agreement to accept a return of the goods because of defects and to replace them with similar goods. What is the nature of the contract between the parties in relation to the new goods? The analysis to some extent depends on whether or not the repayment was effected pursuant to a guarantee.

1.   No prior guarantee

Suppose that S sells a pair of expensive shoes to B, but after these have been worn for a short time the heel of one of the shoes comes off and S agrees to replace the shoe with a new pair. If this new pair of shoes is then proved to be faulty, what are B's rights?

The agreement for replacement of the shoes could be characterized in various alternative ways. One possibility is that it is merely an agreement to make a fresh tender under the original contract, on the basis that the original tender was not a tender of conforming goods. On this view the agreement to replace is not a rescission or variation of the original sale contract but merely an undertaking to execute a fresh act of performance. Alternatively, it could be argued that the agreement to replace is a rescission of the original contract of sale by mutual agreement and the creation of a new contract of sale relating to the pair of shoes given in replacement. A third possibility is that the agreement is a variation of the original contract of sale, which thus continues in all respects in relation to the new shoes upon the terms previously applicable to the original shoes. A final alternative is that the agreement to replace the shoes is not itself either a new contract of sale or a variation of the original contract but is a settlement of B's claim under the original contract. In other words, in lieu of her remedies as the buyer of defective goods, B agrees to accept a new pair of shoes, and the delivery of these constitutes an accord and satisfaction in relation to S's liability under the original contract. The old contract is discharged, and the new contract is to supply shoes of similar description, but not by way of sale, since the consideration is not a sum of money[275] but the release of S from liability under the sale contract.

---

274   Steve Hedley, 'Quality of Goods, Information, and the Death of Contract' [2001] JBL 114 at p 116.
275   As required for a contract of sale by s 2(1) of the Sale of Goods Act.

The characterization of the new agreement is not without importance, for if it falls into the last of the four possible categories described above, the statutory implied terms will not apply,[276] and while similar terms would be implied at common law,[277] these could be excluded by contract within the limits permitted by the common law and by s 7 of the Unfair Contract Terms Act.

The answer depends on the circumstances. If the original contract was for the sale of specific goods, an agreement by the seller to tender and the buyer to accept other goods in replacement is necessarily either a variation of the original contract of sale or a new contract of sale which (inter alia) rescinds the old contract. Plainly, the tender of goods other than those the subject matter of the original contract is not simply a performance of the original contract. If, on the other hand, the original contract was for unascertained goods, the buyer's lawful rejection of a nonconforming tender means that the rejected goods are not to be treated as the subject of the contract, and the tender of replacement goods is merely a fresh attempt at performance of the original contract. If the new goods are in conformity with the contract, the contract will become completed by performance. If they are not, the buyer will have the same right to reject as before.[278]

In most cases it will make little practical difference whether the agreement to replace constitutes an agreement to retender under the original contract or a variation under that contract by substitution of goods or a replacement of the contract by a new contract of sale. It is, however, possible to envisage circumstances in which the distinction might be material, eg where the making of a new contract would require a licence or would be prohibited altogether by a change in the law. It is only in the unusual case that the agreement to replace is likely to be construed as a compromise agreement not itself constituting a contract of sale. Even assuming that the agreement is to be treated as an accord, the court is likely to ascribe to it the same legal characteristics as the contract it replaces.[279] Moreover, it does not follow that the original contract of sale is extinguished, for the replacement agreement may be construed by the court as making a rescission of the original contract depend on performance of the new undertaking and not merely on the promise of such performance. In that event, the replacement agreement would not itself constitute an accord and satisfaction, but merely an accord, and if it were not performed by the seller, the buyer would have the option of reverting to his rights under the original contract of sale.

---

276 But breach of the new agreement may entitle the buyer to fall back on the original contract. See below.

277 This can be inferred from the general tendency to equate all contracts for the supply of goods so far as implied terms are concerned. See p 204.

278 But he will be in a still stronger position than on the first rejection in that even if the time for delivery under the original contract had not expired, he could argue that two defective tenders amounted to a repudiation by the seller and deprived him of the right to make yet another tender. See p 345.

279 For an illustration in the field of hire-purchase, see *Viking Hire-Purchase Co v Jordan* (1966) 111 Sol Jo 51, and R. M. Goode, *Hire-Purchase Law and Practice* (2nd edn), p 957.

2.　Replacement pursuant to guarantee

Where defective goods are replaced pursuant to guarantee,[280] certain additional factors call for consideration. If the guarantee is furnished by the seller, it is a question of construction whether the guarantee is part and parcel of the contract of sale or is a separate contract. In the former case the tender of new goods in pursuance of the guarantee is simply a new tender made pursuant to the original contract, and the rights of the buyer continue to be governed by that contract.[281] If the guarantee is given not by the seller but by the manufacturer, then in so far as it has contractual force at all, it is necessarily a contract distinct from the contract of sale. This considerably complicates the issues. If the manufacturer implements the guarantee, the supply is made pursuant to the terms of the guarantee and not under a contract of sale,[282] with the result that if the replacement is itself defective, the buyer's remedies against the manufacturer may be qualified or excluded by the guarantee, subject only to s 5 of the Unfair Contract Terms Act.[283]

There was also a problem at common law relating to the consideration for the guarantee. The buyer might be able to treat this as a collateral warranty inducing him to buy the goods, but he might have bought the goods without relying on the guarantee or even knowing of it. In the case of a consumer guarantee this problem has now been resolved by the Sale and Supply of Goods to Consumers Regulations 2002,[284] which gives contractual force to a guarantee to a consumer by a person acting in the course of a business, given without extra charge, to reimburse the price paid or to replace, repair or handle consumer goods in any way if they do not meet the specifications set out in the guarantee statement or in the relevant advertising.

Does a guarantee given in respect of the original goods extend to replacements supplied in pursuance of a guarantee? This is a question of construction. Prima facie, a guarantee would not, it is thought, be construed as a floating guarantee but would be confined to the goods to which the contract of sale related. The buyer's remedy as regards defects in the replacement goods is to claim damages for breach of the contract of guarantee and/or to pursue his remedies, if any, under the original contract of sale.[285]

280　As to the legal status of a manufacturer's guarantee in favour of a retail purchaser, see n 282.

281　But the guarantee will not necessarily apply to the replacement goods. See below.

282　This would seem to be so whether the replacement goods are furnished by the manufacturer direct or through the retailer who sold the original goods.

283　Which in these circumstances would, in the case of goods of a type ordinarily supplied for private use or consumption, prevent the exclusion or limitation of liability for loss or damage arising from the goods proving defective while in consumer use where such loss or damage results from the negligence of the manufacturer or a distributor. In any event, the buyer may still have rights against the seller in respect of the goods originally tendered under the contract of sale.

284　SI 2002/3045, regs 15, 2.

285　It does not follow that he has such a remedy, for the supplier or manufacturer may accept a strict liability under a guarantee for breakdown that could not be established as due to breach of a term of the contract of sale.

(ii) Repair

Where the seller, instead of replacing defective goods tendered under the contract of sale, repairs the goods and sends them back to the buyer, then if the repairs prove to have been ineffective to restore the goods to the condition called for by the contract, the buyer can exercise the same rights and remedies as on the original nonconforming tender.

An interesting question arises where the repair is pursuant to a guarantee. In general, a guarantee is not limited to the first breakdown but covers (within the limits defined by the guarantee) all defects and failures notified during the guarantee period. If a defect remediable under the guarantee is not properly repaired, the effect is to shorten the period for which the buyer can continue to use the goods under cover of the guarantee. For example, if a car covered by a six-month guarantee is returned after one month and is promptly and effectively repaired, the buyer can use the car for a further five months (less the repair period) protected by the guarantee, and thus secure the benefit of the guarantee for the mileage done in that period, whereas if the repairs are not promptly and properly carried out and because of delays he does not get his car back in good working order for three months, the car can be used for only a further two months under guarantee. There seems no reason why the shortening of the period of guarantee cover due to failure to execute repairs properly and promptly cannot be included as an element in the damages to which the buyer is entitled, if the party furnishing the guarantee is not willing to extend it for the appropriate period. In the case of motor vehicles the voluntary Code of Practice for the Motor Industry requires manufacturers to operate fair and equitable policies to permit the extension of a warranty if the car to which it relates is off the road for an extended period for rectification of warranty faults, or the repetition outside warranty of a fault which had previously been the subject of rectification work during the warranty period.[286]

---

286   See Anthea Worsdall, *Consumer Law for the Motor Trade* (4th edn, 1999), pp 154, 215–216.

12   Rejection and its Consequences

Where the buyer rejects goods, he thereby signifies that he is not prepared to accept them pursuant to the contract. Refusal to take delivery may (and usually does) signify rejection, but just as the taking of delivery is not synonymous with an acceptance, so the refusal to take delivery does not inevitably signify rejection.[1] In each case it is a question of fact and intention.

1.   THE RIGHT TO REJECT

The buyer has the right to reject goods tendered under a contract of sale in any of the following cases:

(a)   Where he is permitted to do so by the express terms of the contract.

(b)   Where a right to reject is given by terms implied in fact or by usage of trade or a course of dealing between the parties.[2]

(c)   Where the seller has committed a breach of an express or implied condition of the contract.[3] The old rule was that unless *de minimis*, even a small and non-material breach of condition conferred a right of rejection,[4] and this remains the case as regards sales to consumers. But this excessively rigid rule never applied in Scotland[5] and the non-consumer buyer can no longer reject where the breach is so slight that it would be unreasonable for him to do so.[6]

(d)   Where the seller has by words or conduct evinced an intention to repudiate the contract or has disabled himself from performing it in an essential respect or has broken the contract in such a way as to frustrate its commercial purpose.[7]

The right to reject does not have to be exercised reasonably,[8] so that if, for example, the goods do not correspond to their contract description, the buyer is entitled

---

1 See p 391. As to particular facets of rejection in documentary sales, including the difficult decision of the House of Lords in *Berger & Co Inc v Gill & Duffus S.A.* [1984] AC 382, see pp 944 ff.

2 See pp 87–88.

3 See p 127.

4 *Arcos Ltd v E. A. Ronaasen & Son* [1933] AC 470.

5 Where the test is whether the breach is material. See Sale of Goods Act, s 15B(1)(b), inserted by the Sale and Supply of Goods Act 1994; and David M. Walker, *The Law of Contracts and Related Obligations in Scotland* (3rd edn, 1995), para 19.4.

6 See Sale of Goods Act 1979, s 15A, though only as regards terms implied by ss 13–15.

7 See p 124.

8 *Arcos Ltd v E.A. Ronaasen & Son* [1933] AC 470; *Clegg v Olle Andersson* [2003] 1 All ER (Comm) 721.

to reject them whether or not the non-conformity of the goods affects their saleability.[9]

The buyer is not bound to exercise a right to reject for breach of a condition; he can elect to treat the breach of the condition as a breach of warranty,[10] in which case the contract will remain on foot and the buyer's remedy will be damages for breach of warranty. Moreover, there are various cases in which the right to reject will be lost even where the buyer may wish to reject.

2. TIME OF REJECTION

The buyer may reject the goods either by declining to receive them when delivery is tendered or by giving notice of rejection before a tender of delivery or after receipt of the goods and before acceptance. The distinction between rejection on tender and rejection after receipt appears to have no legal consequences, beyond the fact that a claim by the buyer for expenses to which he has been put as the result of an ineffective tender by the seller[11] is likely to be greater where the buyer has taken the goods into his custody than where he has not. The goods must be rejected within a reasonable time,[12] and in determining what is reasonable it is necessary to consider the interests of the seller as well as those of the buyer.[13]

3. MODE OF REJECTION

The right to reject must be exercised by an unequivocal notice of rejection to the seller.[14] In exercising a right to reject the goods, the buyer is not, unless the contract so provides, bound to return them to the seller. It suffices that he intimates to the seller that he refuses to accept them.[15] It is the duty of the buyer to hold the goods available for collection by the seller at the contractual place for examination.[16] If the buyer is not in a position to do this at the time he gives notice to reject, the notice will usually be ineffective.[17] The notice of rejection need not be in writing, nor need it specifically identify the goods so long as they are identifiable with certainty as the goods to which the notice relates.[18]

---

9 *Arcos Ltd v E.A. Ronaasen & Son*, n 8. But see text to n 6.
10 Sale of Goods Act 1979, s 11(2).
11 The basis of such a claim is that running parallel with any express delivery obligation of the seller is an implied, collateral undertaking (ie a warranty) not to involve the buyer in expense by making a tender which is not in conformity with the contract. See p 344.
12 Sale of Goods Act 1979, s 35(4).
13 *Truk (UK) Ltd v Tokmakidis GmbH* [2000] 2 All ER (Comm) 594.
14 *Graanhandel T. Vink B.V. v European Grain & Shipping Ltd* [1989] 2 Lloyd's Rep 531.
15 Sale of Goods Act, s 36.
16 See p 356.
17 See p 349.
18 *Atari Corp. (UK) Ltd v Electronics Boutique Stores (UK) Ltd* [1998] QB 539. This was a decision on sale or return but the principle is the same.

4.   EFFECTIVENESS OF NOTICE TO REJECT

A notice which leaves the seller in reasonable doubt as to whether the buyer is or is not rejecting is not sufficient.[19] Even if the notice of rejection is unequivocal, the buyer cannot rely on it if at the time he gives it he has already lost the right to reject.[20] On the other hand, the seller is entitled to treat the notice of rejection as binding on the buyer, who cannot himself be heard to deny the effectiveness of his own notice.[21] It is for the seller to decide whether to hold the buyer to the notice or to treat it as ineffective by reason of the inconsistent conduct. In the latter case the property in the goods revests in the seller, and the buyer will be guilty of conversion in dealing with the goods[22] unless he was authorized by the seller to do so or acted as an agent of necessity.[23] The only cases where the buyer is entitled to treat his notice to reject as ceasing to be operative is where the seller agrees or where he refuses to accept the notice and the buyer acts in reliance on that refusal.[24]

5.   LOSS OF RIGHT TO REJECT

The buyer may lose his right to reject by conduct which is inconsistent with rejection before, at the time of or subsequent to his notice to reject.[25] So he cannot reject if at the time of giving notice he has already accepted the goods or is deemed to have done so,[26] or is on some other ground precluded from denying that he has adopted the transaction.[27] Similarly, the buyer's notice of rejection is ineffective if it is inconsistent with his contemporaneous conduct, as where at the time of giving the notice he proceeds to sell the goods or do some other act inconsistent with rejection, for he cannot say one thing and do another.[28] Finally, a notice of rejection which is valid when given may be lost by subsequent conduct which is inconsistent

---

19 *Graanhandel T. Vink B.V. v European Grain & Shipping Ltd*, n 14.

20 See below.

21 This is a case of election, not estoppel, so that the seller does not have to show he relied on the notice (see p 106).

22 This will be the case where the buyer resells the goods and delivers them to the subpurchaser or resells them in circumstances where the subpurchaser acquires a good title. But a sale unaccompanied by delivery and ineffective to pass an overriding title is not a conversion (*Lancashire Waggon Co v Fitzhugh* (1861) 6 H & N 502).

23 *Tradax Export S.A. v European Grain & Shipping Ltd* [1983] 2 Lloyd's Rep 100, per Bingham LJ at 107; *Graanhandel T. Vink B.V. v European Grain & Shipping Ltd*, n 10, per Evans J at 533.

24 There is no authority directly on the point, though it was adverted to in *Graanhandel T. Vink B.V. v European Grain & Shipping Ltd*, n 14, at 533, by Evans J, who did not find it necessary to decide it. In contrast to the buyer's notice of rejection (above), the seller's refusal to accept the notice would not, it is thought, bind him unless and until the buyer acts in reliance on it, for the intimation of such a refusal is not a matter of election but of estoppel.

25 At one time the right to reject was also lost once the property in the goods had passed to the buyer, but this part of s 11 (then s 11(1)(c)) was repealed by s 4(1) of the Misrepresentation Act 1967.

26 Sale of Goods Act 1979, s 11(4). See ch 13.

27 Eg, where, through no fault of the seller, restoration of the goods to the seller is impossible. See p 352. See also p 358, n 79.

28 *Chapman v Morton* (1843) 11 M & W 534; *Tradax Export S.A. v European Grain & Shipping Ltd*, n 23, per Bingham LJ at 107; *Vargas Pena Afezteguia y Cia v Peter Cremer GmbH* [1987] 1 Lloyd's Rep 394.

with the revesting of the goods in the seller.[29] Again, it is only the seller, not the buyer, who can treat the notice of rejection as ineffective.[30]

6.   THE EFFECT OF IMPROPER REJECTION

Where the buyer purports to reject without being entitled to do so, this constitutes a repudiation, which the seller is entitled, though not obliged, to accept as discharging the contract. If the seller elects to hold the buyer to the contract, the purported rejection is ineffective, the property in the goods, if already in the buyer, remains in him and, unless the rejection took a form which involved the seller in loss (as where the buyer returns the goods to the seller's premises), the seller's decision to affirm the contract enures for the benefit of both parties, so that, in the absence of a further breach by the buyer, the seller has no claim for damages beyond the purely nominal damages recoverable for breach of the implied undertaking of the buyer to hold himself ready and willing to perform up to the due date of performance. But the seller cannot, by holding the contract open for performance after the date when the buyer ought to have accepted the goods, defer taking steps to mitigate his loss.[31]

Where the seller accepts the buyer's repudiation, the property (if then in the buyer) revests in the seller, who is entitled to recover the goods and sue the buyer for damages for non-acceptance.

Whether, in the case of an instalment contract, the buyer's improper rejection of one instalment constitutes a repudiation of the whole contract depends on the circumstances.[32]

7.   THE EFFECT OF LAWFUL REJECTION

It has been said, in relation to contracts of sale, that 'a right to reject is merely a particular form of the right to rescind'.[33] This statement, made in a judgment dealing with a case where the seller had quite clearly repudiated his obligations, has been taken out of context and converted into the general proposition that rejection equals rescission. The use of the word 'rescind' is in any event unfortunate, for what is meant is termination for breach, not rescission *ab initio*, as for misrepresentation.[34] But even with this qualification, is the proposition true? What

---

29 *Tradax Export S.A. v European Grain & Shipping Ltd*, n 23, per Bingham LJ at 107. This results from the application of common law principles, not from s 35 of the Sale of Goods Act, which is confined to inconsistent acts committed prior to the notice to reject (ibid).

30 See above, text and n 19.

31 See p 402.

32 See pp 271 ff.

33 *Kwei Tek Chao v British Traders & Shippers Ltd* [1954] 2 QB 459, per Devlin J at 480.

34 This confusion of language probably stems from the fact that the effect of acceptance of a repudiation in a contract of sale seems very similar to the effect of rescission *stricto sensu*, for the property revests in the seller, while the buyer is entitled to withhold payment of the price, or recover it if he has already made payment. There is, however, an important difference in that at common law the corollary of rescission is not damages but restitution (see pp 79–80), whereas the buyer who lawfully rejects is entitled to damages.

in fact is the effect on the contract of a buyer's well-founded election to reject a tender as not in conformity with the contract?

It is generally considered that where defective goods are tendered, the buyer has but two alternatives: to adopt the contract or to reject the goods and thereby treat the contract as discharged. Such an assumption, though deriving some support from s 11(4) of the Sale of Goods Act, is neither consonant with legal principle nor in accord with commercial practice. The typical buyer, confronted with defective goods, does not do either of these things. He tells the seller that the goods are not accepted in the condition in which they are tendered and asks that they be repaired or replaced. The tender is rejected but the buyer holds the contract open for performance by a fresh tender.[35] Even if the buyer does not request or desire repair or replacement of the defective goods, the seller is as a rule entitled to do this if he still has time under the contract. The sole effect of rejection as such[36] is to nullify delivery. The seller is treated as if he had not tendered delivery at all.[37] If, when the buyer gives notice to reject, the time for delivery has already expired, the seller is in breach.[38] If the time for delivery has not then expired, then prima facie there is no breach of the seller's primary delivery obligation.[39]

Unless otherwise agreed, where the buyer exercises a right to reject, the property in the goods revests in the seller[40] and the goods are again at his risk.[41] This would seem to be the case even if the seller has the opportunity to make a fresh and conforming tender.[42]

8.   THE RIGHT TO CURE

This right of the seller to cure a defective tender by making a fresh tender of conforming goods is well illustrated by the decision of the Court of Appeal in *Borrowman Phillips & Co v Free & Hollis*.[43]

35 There are certain forms of redress which at common law cannot be forced on the seller, eg (i) repair of defective goods or other curing of a nonconforming tender; (ii) revocation of acceptance (see p 355). However, under s 48B of the Sale of Goods Act a consumer buyer now has a statutory right to require repair or replacement of goods not conforming to the contract of sale, subject to the power of the court under s 48E to order another remedy.

36 Apart from putting the seller in breach of his implied collateral undertaking not to make an invalid tender. See p 344.

37 With one difference, however, namely that the seller probably incurs a liability in damages for any expense incurred by the buyer in making arrangements to take delivery under the abortive tender. See p 344.

38 Though he may still retender if time is not of the essence.

39 See below and nn 25, 26.

40 *Tradax Export S.A. v European Grain & Shipping Ltd*, n 23, per Bingham LJ at 107; *Gill & Duffus S.A. v Berger & Co Inc*, n 1, at 395. See further p 350, n 18.

41 *Head v Tattersall* (1871) LR 7 Exch 7, per Cleasby B at 19: 'The person who is eventually entitled to the property in the chattel ought to bear any loss arising from any depreciation in its value caused by an accident for which nobody is at fault.'

42 See below.

43 (1878) 4 QBD 500. For an earlier decision to similar effect see *Tetley v Shand* (1871) 25 LT 658.

The plaintiffs, who had taken over a contract to supply to the defendants a quantity of maize, offered a cargo on board a named vessel but were unable to tender the shipping documents pursuant to the contract. An arbitrator having upheld the defendants' contention that the tender was invalid, the plaintiffs offered a further cargo on board a different vessel, together with the necessary documents. This offer was also refused, on the grounds that the plaintiffs could not substitute other goods for those first tendered. The Court of Appeal, rejecting the defendants' argument that the first tender irrevocably identified the contract goods, held that since the defendants had rejected them, the plaintiffs were at liberty to tender another cargo in conformity with the contract, and this had been done. They were therefore entitled to damages for non-acceptance.

Though doubt has been expressed as to whether English law recognizes a general right of cure,[44] the principle has since been enunciated in a number of cases[45] and has received powerful judicial support in the House of Lords decision in *The Kanchenjunga*:[46]

> If the time for delivery has not yet expired, the seller is still entitled to make a fresh tender which conforms with the contract, in which event the buyer is bound to accept the goods so tendered.[47]

It is, however, regrettable that opportunity has not been taken to modernize the Sale of Goods Act by including express provisions as to the right of cure,[48] a right which mitigates the impact of an improperly motivated rejection by the buyer while at the same time tending to avoid economic waste. The right to cure given by s 2–508 of the American Uniform Commercial Code goes somewhat beyond the common law right of retender and could usefully be adopted here.

2–508. Cure by Seller of Improper Tender or Delivery; Replacement

(1) Where any tender or delivery by the seller is rejected because non-conforming and the time for performance has not yet expired, the seller may seasonably notify the buyer of his intention to cure and may then within the contract time make a conforming delivery.

---

44 See, for example, the Law Commissions' Working Paper *Sale and Supply of Goods* (Law Com WP No 85, Scot Law Com Cons Mem No 58, 1983), para 238; Rex J Ahdar, 'Seller cure in the sale of goods' [1990] LMCLQ 364; Antonia Apps, 'The right to cure defective performance' [1994] LMCLQ 525.

45 *Ashmore & Son v C. S. Cox & Co* [1899] 1 QB 436 at 440–441; *H. Longbottom & Co Ltd v Bass Walker & Co* [1922] WN 245, per Atkin LJ at 246; *E. E. & Brian Smith (1928) Ltd v Wheatsheaf Mills Ltd* [1939] 2 KB 302, per Branson J at 314; *McDougall v Aeromarine of Emsworth Ltd* [1958] 3 All ER 431, per Diplock J at 438; *Agricultores Federados Argentinos Sociedad Cooperativa Limitada v Ampro S. A. Commerciale Industrielle et Financière* [1965] 2 Lloyd's Rep 157, per Widgery J at 167; *The Playa Larga* [1983] 2 Lloyd's Rep 171; *Wanganyi Motors (1963) Ltd v Broadlands Finance Ltd* (1988) 2 NZBLC 103.

46 [1990] 1 Lloyd's Rep 391.

47 Ibid, per Lord Goff, at 399, citing *Borrowman Phillips & Co v Free and Hollis*, n 43.

48 See the American Uniform Commercial Code, s 2–508, set out below; John Honnold, 'Buyer's Right of Rejection', 97 U Pa L Rev 457 (1949); Alan Schwartz, 'Cure and Revocation for Quality Defects: The Utility of Bargains', 16 BC Ind & Com LR 543 (1975); G. L. Priest, 'Breach and Remedy for the Tender of Non-Conforming Goods under the Uniform Commercial Code: An Economic Approach', 91 Harv L Rev 960 (1978); White and Summers, *Uniform Commercial Code* (5th edn, 2000), vol 1, pp 332 ff.; Ontario Law Reform Commission, *Report on Sale of Goods* (1979), pp 444 ff. The Law Commissions considered proposing a cure remedy but ultimately came down against it (*Sale and Supply of Goods* (Law Com No 160, Scot Law Com 104, Cmnd 137, 1987), paras 4.13–4.17).

(2) Where the buyer rejects a non-conforming tender which the seller had reasonable grounds to believe would be acceptable with or without money allowance the seller may if he seasonably notifies the buyer have a further reasonable time to substitute a conforming tender.

In the case of a contract for the sale of unascertained goods, a tender lawfully rejected because the goods are defective may be cured either by putting the rejected goods into the condition called for by the contract or by offering different goods which conform to the contract. But where the contract is for the sale of specific goods which are rejected by the buyer, one of these methods of cure is not open to the seller. He can repair the goods so as to put them into proper condition,[49] but he cannot, without the buyer's consent, tender other goods, for the contract itself identified the subject matter of the contract, and it is not open to the seller to change the contract goods by unilateral action.[50]

There are three cases in which the seller is deprived of the right to cure a defective tender.

(i)   Where it is too late to retender

A retender is not necessarily too late merely because the contract date for delivery has passed. The rules as to time for a retender are the same as those for the original tender; and, as we have seen, the buyer is entitled to reject late delivery only where time is of the essence[51] or where a reasonable time has elapsed after the contract delivery date.

(ii)   Where the rejection relates to part of the goods and the seller has no right to tender by instalments

Until recently, a buyer who accepted part of the goods was precluded from rejecting the rest where not conforming to the contract. This is no longer the case.[52] But if, in a contract that does not provide for delivery by instalments, the buyer exercises his right to accept part while rejecting the rest, he cannot be compelled to accept a fresh tender as to the part rejected, for he is not obliged to accept delivery by instalments.[53]

---

49 But if the contract was for the supply of new goods, the curing of the defect by repair is probably not open to the seller where major repairs are required, for it is arguable that the goods will then no longer be new. For an Australian decision on the various meanings of 'new', see p 305, n 135.

50 Of course, if the first tender had been rejected because the article tendered was not the specific article which the buyer had agreed to buy but a different article – as where the seller had sent the wrong goods by mistake – the seller would be entitled to put the matter right by sending the correct goods. The buyer may in any event be expected to accept alternative goods, not by way of performance but in reasonable mitigation of his loss (*Payzu Ltd v Saunders* [1919] 2 KB 581).

51 See p 270.

52 See pp 357–358, 359.

53 Sale of Goods Act 1979, s 31. See pp 271–272, 359.

(iii) Where the seller's conduct is a repudiation

It is clear that if the seller refuses to retender, he commits a breach which the buyer is entitled to treat as discharging the contract. This is so whether the refusal is intimated after the seller has taken back the goods or before, as where he refused to accept their return. But suppose that S, having had his first tender rejected on the ground that the goods are defective, makes a further tender within the contract period which is again rejected because the goods tendered still fail to conform to the contract. What happens next? Is S entitled to an indefinite number of bites at the cherry within the contract period? Clearly not. In every contract there is an implied condition that the party undertaking an obligation shall continue willing and able to perform up to the due date for performance. If, therefore, the seller's contract evinces either an intention to repudiate or an inability to perform, the buyer is entitled to treat the contract as repudiated by what is usually, though inaccurately, termed anticipatory breach. At what point this stage is reached depends on the circumstances. Several imperfect tenders would obviously expose the seller to an allegation that he has repudiated;[54] but even a single defective tender could constitute repudiation if it were so defective, or was made so near the expiry date (in the 'time being of the essence' sense), as to indicate that proper performance by the seller was either not intended or impossible.

We are left with one final problem. If rejection of an imperfect tender made within the contract period is merely non-delivery, and thus not of itself a breach of the delivery obligation, can the buyer recover the loss and expenses he incurred in connection with the abortive tender? There appears to be no authority on this point, but it is submitted that the seller, in addition to his positive delivery obligation (which is, of course, a condition of the contract), owes an implied collateral duty not to make an invalid tender, and that, accordingly, the buyer would be entitled to compensation for any loss suffered[55] and any expenses needlessly incurred in arrangements to collect goods which upon subsequent tender he lawfully rejects.[56]

---

54 *Quaere* whether a justifiable loss of confidence in the seller resulting from the initial defective tender suffices to entitle the buyer to treat the agreement as at an end. No reported English case has yet gone so far.

55 Eg, in delivering perishable goods which deteriorate and have to be destroyed.

56 Sale of Goods Act, s 11(4).

13   Acceptance

1.   THE MEANING OF 'ACCEPTANCE'

The draftsman of the Act has not been consistent in his use of the word 'accept', which is employed in different senses in different parts of the Act. Section 27, which imposes on the buyer the duty to accept the goods in accordance with the contract, suggests some positive act of acceptance, though its effect is probably no more than to require the buyer to refrain from acts signifying rejection.[1] Section 50(3), on the other hand, when referring to the date on which the buyer ought to have accepted the goods, evidently refers not to acceptance in the full sense but to the taking of delivery.[2] Finally, in s 35, which states when the buyer is deemed to have accepted the goods, 'acceptance' means no more than an election or deemed election not to reject for failure to make a perfect tender[3]. It is with acceptance as a bar to rejection that the present chapter is concerned.

2.   ACCEPTANCE AS NON-REJECTION OF AN IMPERFECT TENDER

The analysis of acceptance as an acknowledgement of perfect tender raises two crucial questions. When is the buyer considered to have given such an acknowledgement? And what is the consequence of his so doing? To answer the second question first, the effect of acceptance of the goods is to debar the buyer from rejecting the goods or from treating the seller as having repudiated the contract.[4] But the parties may agree otherwise; and special rules apply where the contract is severable[5] or the goods tendered exceed the contract quantity.[6]

Since acceptance usually precludes subsequent rejection, a crucial issue is what constitutes acceptance for this purpose. At what point does the buyer lose the right to insist on the seller taking back the goods? It is a remarkable circumstance that this, the most common question raised by the consumer buyer, a question on which lawyers and citizens' advice bureaux are daily asked to

---

1 *Benjamin's Sale of Goods* (6th edn, 2002), para 9–002.
2 See p 401.
3 See pp 264, 290, as to the perfect tender rule.
4 Sale of Goods Act, s 11(4). The position is otherwise where the agreement is a conditional sale agreement and the buyer deals as consumer within Part I of the Unfair Contract Terms Act 1977 (Supply of Goods (Implied Terms) Act 1973, s 14, as amended by Sale of Goods Act 1979, s 63(1) and Sch 2). Acceptance of part of the goods no longer bars rejection of the rest. See pp 357–358, 359.
5 Sale of Goods Act, s 11(4). See p 272.
6 Section 30(2). See p 358.

advise, remains the most intractable problem of sales law. There are many everyday disputes between traders and shoppers where it is difficult, if not impossible, to advise the customer whether he or she is still entitled to return the goods and recover the price.[7]

3.   AN OUTLINE OF CHANGES TO THE RULES ON ACCEPTANCE

The rules for determining whether the buyer has accepted the goods are embodied in ss 35 and 35A of the Sale of Goods Act. The statutory provisions relating to acceptance and its effect have undergone several important amendments over the past forty years. Section 35 has always prescribed three types of act on the part of the buyer which are to be deemed an acceptance of the goods: intimation of acceptance, performance of a post-delivery act inconsistent with the seller's ownership, and retention of the goods after the lapse of a reasonable time without intimation of rejection. Under the 1893 Act deemed acceptance under s 35 was qualified only by the special rules contained in ss 30(2),[8] 30(4)[9] and 31.[10] The Misrepresentation Act 1967 introduced a further qualification, by subjecting the second, and probably the third, of the three types of act to the provisions of what was then s 34(1), which provided that the buyer was not deemed to have accepted the goods until he had had a reasonable opportunity of examining them to ascertain whether they conformed to the contract. The Sale and Supply of Goods Act 1994 recast ss 34 and 35 and added a new s 35A. The old s 34(1) has now become s 35(2), expanded to cover sales by sample; intimation of acceptance now constitutes deemed acceptance only where the buyer has had a reasonable opportunity of examination; and retention of the goods for a reasonable time without intimating rejection is now a deemed acceptance in all cases, whether or not the buyer has had a reasonable opportunity to examine.[11] The new s 35(6) also makes it clear that there is no longer a deemed acceptance solely because the buyer asks for or agrees to repair of the goods or because the goods are delivered to another under a sub-sale or other disposition.[12] In addition, s 30(4), relating to delivery of mixed goods, has been repealed.

The effect of acceptance is governed in general by s 11(4),[13] but subject to the overriding provisions of the new s 35A, which give the buyer a right of partial rejection,[14] the new s 15A, which restricts the right of a non-consumer buyer to reject for a slight breach, and the new sub-s30(2A), which imposes a similar

---

7 Rejection does not, however, necessarily carry with it an immediate right to recover the price or otherwise treat the contract as discharged. See p 341.

8 Dealing with delivery of an excessive quantity.

9 Relating to delivery of the contract goods mixed with goods of a different description.

10 Dealing with instalment deliveries.

11 However, such an opportunity, or lack of it, is relevant to the question whether a reasonable time has elapsed (s 35(5)).

12 Sale of Goods Act 1979, s 35(6).

13 Which provides that in the case of a non-severable contract the buyer's acceptance of the goods precludes rejection and restricts him to his remedies for breach of warranty.

14 Which is not, however, available as regards goods forming part of a commercial unit (s 35(7)).

restriction on the consumer buyer wishing to reject for a slight excess or shortfall in quantity.

4.   WHAT CONSTITUTES ACCEPTANCE

Sections 35 and 35A of the Act provide as follows:

35. (1) The buyer is deemed to have accepted the goods, subject to subsection (2) below–

(a)   when he intimates to the seller that he has accepted them,
      or
(b)   when the goods have been delivered to him and he does any act in relation to them which is inconsistent with the ownership of the seller.

(2) Where goods are delivered to the buyer, and he has not previously examined them, he is not deemed to have accepted them until he has had a reasonable opportunity of examining them for the purpose –

(a)   of ascertaining whether they are in conformity with the contract, and
(b)   in the case of a contract for sale by sample, of comparing the bulk with the sample.

(3) Where the buyer deals as consumer or (in Scotland) the contract of sale is a consumer contract, the buyer cannot lose his right to rely on subsection (2) above by agreement, waiver or otherwise.

(4) The buyer is also deemed to have accepted the goods when after the lapse of a reasonable time he retains the goods without intimating to the seller that he has rejected them.

(5) The questions that are material in determining for the purpose of subsection (4) above whether a reasonable time has elapsed include whether the buyer has had a reasonable opportunity of examining the goods for the purpose mentioned in subsection (2) above.

(6) The buyer is not by virtue of this section deemed to have accepted the goods merely because –

(a)   he asks for, or agrees to, their repair by or under an agreement with the seller, or
(b)   the goods are delivered to another under a sub-sale or other disposition.

(7) Where the contract is for the sale of goods making one or more commercial units, a buyer accepting any goods included in a unit is deemed to have accepted all the goods making the unit; and in this subsection 'commercial unit' means a unit division of which would materially impair the value of the goods or the character of the unit.

(8) Paragraph 10 of Schedule 1 below applies in relation to a contract made before 22 April 1967 or (in the application of this Act to Northern Ireland) 28 July 1967.

35A. (1) If the buyer –

(a)   has the right to reject the goods by reason of a breach on the part of the seller that affects some or all of them, but
(b)   accepts some of the goods, including, where there are any goods unaffected by the breach, all such goods,

he does not by accepting them lose his right to reject the rest.

(2) In the case of a buyer having a right to reject an instalment of the goods, subsection (1) above applies as if references to the goods were references to the goods comprised in the instalment.

(3) For the purpose of subsection (1) above, goods are affected by a breach if by reason of the breach they are not in conformity with the contract.

(4) This section applies unless a contrary intention appears in, or is to be implied from, the contract.

We must now examine the three categories of deemed acceptance in more detail, noting *en passant* that these are not exhaustive and that any other conduct of the buyer which would according to general contract principles amount to an election to affirm the contract produces a deemed acceptance.[15]

(i) Intimation of acceptance

The major change introduced by the 1994 Act is that the buyer's intimation of acceptance (for example, by signing an acceptance note at the time of delivery) does not constitute acceptance for the purpose of the statutory provision unless the buyer, at the time of giving the intimation, has had a reasonable opportunity to examine the goods.[16] This resolves the serious problem confronting many buyers in signing away their rights of rejection by signature of an acceptance note.[17] There are many defects which are not apparent from external inspection at the time of delivery and, indeed, may not become apparent until after considerable use of the goods. This is true not only of complicated pieces of machinery such as motor-car engines and computers but also of more mundane articles like carpets, dresses and shoes. This is therefore a sound change in terms of policy.

(ii) Act inconsistent with seller's ownership

Any act by the buyer which is inconsistent with the ownership of the seller constitutes a deemed acceptance within s 35 if it is performed after the goods have been delivered to the buyer and after he has had a reasonable opportunity to examine them.

This second category of deemed acceptance has been a source of great confusion and has generated considerable litigation. We can, however, start by disposing of a dilemma posed by textbook writers, and adverted to in reported cases, which is more illusory than real, namely, if the property in the goods has already passed to the buyer, how can the seller have any ownership with which the buyer's subsequent actions can be inconsistent? It is hard to see why this question should have occasioned such difficulty. Section 35 is plainly not postulating ownership by the seller at all; on the contrary, it is referring to acts by the buyer which implicitly assume his own ownership and negate any revesting of the goods in the seller. In other words, what s 35 is in effect saying is that if, after delivery and a reasonable opportunity to examine, the buyer does an act which is inconsistent with rejection

15 See p 357.
16 Sale of Goods Act 1979, ss 35(1), (2).
17 But see p 97, as to the effect of the Unfair Contract Terms Act 1977.

of the goods (and thus with the revesting of ownership in the seller[18]), then he must be taken to have accepted them. The problem is to know what acts have this effect.

In a sense, all acts of dominion exercised by the buyer over the goods are 'inconsistent with the ownership of the seller', so that, literally construed, the second limb of s 35 would debar the buyer from rejecting if he, having had a reasonable opportunity to examine the goods, did no more than continue in possession *animo domini*, for however short a time, after delivery. Plainly s 35 does not mean this. What, then, does it mean? The problem arises because in his desire to be concise the draftsman has carried ellipsis to its uttermost limit. The second limb of s 35 may on a superficial reading appear to embody a single theme, but in fact it reflects three entirely distinct principles of contract law. The first is that the innocent party cannot both approbate and reprobate: having elected to affirm the transaction, he cannot thereafter change his mind and repudiate it. The second is that even without a knowledge of the facts entitling him to terminate the contract, the innocent party may be estopped from so doing where he acts in such a way as reasonably to lead the other party to believe that he is electing to keep the contract on foot. For example, if a non-consumer buyer were to dispose of the goods after intentionally waiving his right of examination, he could not rely on his lack of knowledge of defects to preserve his right of rejection.[19] Thirdly, the innocent party cannot unscramble a transaction unless he is himself able to give *restitutio in integrum*, except where his inability to do this arises from the wrongful act of the guilty party himself. This third principle usually arises in claims for rescission rather than acceptance of repudiation, but in the case of a contract of sale it applies equally to the latter, for it is inherent in rejection that the property revests in the seller and the goods must be delivered up to him.[20]

The conditions in which the first two principles become operative have little in common with the third. Affirmation is to a considerable extent subjective, depending on the state of knowledge of the innocent party. To be effective as an election, the act of affirmation relied on must ordinarily be done with knowledge of the breach and of the legal right to choose between acceptance and rejection.[21] This applies in sales law as in other contracts, subject only to the modification that the

18   The possibility of this revested ownership was described by Devlin J in *Kwei Tek Chao v British Traders & Shippers Ltd* [1954] 2 QB 459 as the seller's 'reversionary interest', an unfortunate phrase which tends to obscure rather than illuminate, since it suggests a *retention* of residual rights of ownership by the seller rather than a *revesting* of ownership which results from the buyer's rejection after ownership has passed to him. That Devlin J intended the latter meaning, not the former, is apparent from his references to the 'condition' of transfer being a condition subsequent and to the difficulty in the first of the alternative views of Atkin LJ in *Hardy & Co v Hillerns & Fowler* [1923] 2 KB 490 that the right to reject prevented the property from passing to the buyer at all.

19   This is no longer the case as regards a buyer dealing as consumer. See below.

20   See p 338, and *Street v Blay* (1831) 2 B & Ad 456. It is this factor, peculiar to contracts involving the transfer of property, which has led writers and judges to equate rejection with rescission rather than with acceptance of repudiation. But as has been pointed out earlier, the equation is not valid. See p 341, n 34.

21   *Peyman v Lanjani* [1985] Ch 457.

need for some measure of finality in sales transactions has led the law to impose a sharper cut-off point on buyers, by equating reasonable opportunity for examination (and a fortiori examination itself) with knowledge of the defect.[22] Estoppel is based on a representation of the innocent party's intentions (with or without knowledge of the breach) on which the other party reasonably relies. Inability to give restitution, on the other hand, is a state of affairs, and this state of affairs is not affected one iota either by the innocent party's ignorance of the breach or by the absence of any representation by that party or reliance by the other. Conversely, a party who elects to treat a contract as subsisting after knowledge of the breach thereby affirms it, and becomes bound by his election, even though, when he seeks to change his mind, he remains able to restore the goods to the guilty party. Finally, the first and third legal principles to which we have referred are governed by different time factors. Whether an act evinces an intention to affirm depends on whether the innocent party was aware of the breach at the time of the act in question. But in considering whether rejection is barred for inability to restore, the relevant time is not the time of the act which puts the goods out of the innocent party's possession but the time when restoration to the guilty party is due, ie when notice of rejection is given.

Much of the difficulty in reconciling the cases disappears once it is appreciated that they fall into two distinct groups, one group involving cases where the buyer has affirmed the contract or is estopped from disputing that he has affirmed it, the other, cases where he is unable to restore the goods. In determining what acts are to be considered 'inconsistent with the ownership of the seller' we must be careful to distinguish the former group from the latter. Where the buyer is in a position to return the goods to the seller at the relevant time[23] and place[24] and has not affirmed the contract with knowledge of the breach or represented an intention to accept the goods on which the seller has relied, there will rarely, if ever, be scope for s 35(1)(b) to come into play so as to bar rejection.[25] Conversely, nothing in the Sale of Goods Act will entitle the buyer to reject the goods where he would have lost the right to do so at common law.[26]

1. Affirmation

Where the buyer's post-delivery act is done with knowledge of the seller's breach, or the buyer is estopped from denying that he has affirmed the contract, almost any assumption of ownership implicit in the act will suffice to attract s 35(1)(b). Thus it has been held inconsistent with the seller's ownership, and accordingly a bar to rejection, for the buyer to sell,[27] pledge or mortgage[28] the goods, offer them for

---

22 See p 356. This comment applies, of course, only as regards the right to reject, not the implication of terms as to satisfactory quality and the like (see ch 11) and remedies other than rejection.

23 See p 353.

24 See p 353.

25 There may, of course, be other statutory barriers to rejection, in particular those provided by ss 15A and 30(2A), as to which see pp 338, 358.

26 See p 357.

27 *Benaim & Co v L. S. Debono* [1924] AC 514; *Metals Ltd v Diamond* [1930] 3 DLR 886.

28 *Kwei Tek Chao v British Traders & Shippers Ltd*, n 18.

sale,[29] enter them at auction,[30] seek to negotiate a price reduction on account of defects,[31] register a transfer of the goods to him[32] or even merely use them.[33] Indeed, bare retention for any significant period after knowledge of the breach is likely to be construed as indicating an election to accept,[34] even where the period is not such as would attract the operation of s 35(4),[35] though the position is otherwise if the retention of the goods occurs solely because the buyer has asked for, or agreed to, repair of the goods by or under an arrangement with the seller.[36] In these affirmation cases, where the buyer does not deal as consumer, the fact that he may not have had a reasonable opportunity to examine the goods is irrelevant, for *ex hypothesi* he is aware of the defect, so that an examination would be superfluous. His act of ownership thus constitutes a waiver of the right to examine, so that s 34 does not operate. The position is now otherwise in the case of a buyer dealing as consumer.[37]

Similar consequences ensue where a non-consumer buyer, though not in fact aware of the defect in the goods, has had a reasonable opportunity, before performing his act of dominium, to conduct an examination which would have revealed the defect,[38] or alternatively has elected to take the goods as they are despite lack of opportunity for examination.[39] But where the buyer deals as consumer,[40] no agreement, waiver or otherwise can deprive him of his right to rely on s 35(2) preserving his right of rejection until he has had a reasonable opportunity for examination.[41]

2.   Inability to restore

Even if he has not performed an act signifying affirmation of the contract after knowledge of the breach or opportunity for examination, the buyer's right to reject

---

29 *Symonds v Clark Fruit & Produce Co Ltd* [1919] 1 WWR 587. It is thought that s 35(6)(b) of the Sale of Goods Act, which provides that the buyer is not deemed to accept the goods merely because they are delivered under a sub-sale or other disposition, does not come into play to preserve the right of rejection where the buyer has affirmed the contract or is estopped from disputing that he has affirmed it.

30 *Hitchcock v Cameron* [1977] 1 NZLR 85.

31 *Canterbury Seed Co Ltd v J G. Ward Farmers' Association Ltd* (1895) 13 NZLR 96.

32 *Armaghdown Motors Ltd v Gray Motors Ltd* [1963] NZLR 5.

33 *Lee v York Coach & Marine* [1977] RTR 35.

34 *Kwei Tek Chao v British Traders & Shippers Ltd*, n 18. The position is otherwise where the buyer continues to retain and use the goods because of the seller's assurance that they can be made to function properly (*Schofield v Emerson Brantingham Implement Co* (1918) 43 DLR 509; *Barber v Inland Truck Sales Ltd* (1970) 11 DLR (3d) 469); and see Sale of Goods Act 1979, s 35(6)(b).

35 Which does not depend for its application on knowledge of the breach. See pp 353–354.

36 Sale of Goods Act 1979, s 35(6)(a).

37 See below.

38 *Jordeson & Co v Stora Koppabergs Bergslags Aktieborag* (1931) 41 Ll L Rep 201; *Perkins v Bell* [1893] 1 QB 193; and see p 356.

39 See p 303 as to waiver of examination. Whether the buyer had a reasonable opportunity to examine before performing his act of dominium is a question of fact which involves consideration of the time and place at which he could reasonably have been expected to examine. See p 356.

40 References in the Act to dealing as consumer are to be construed in accordance with Part I of the Unfair Contract Terms Act 1977 (Sale of Goods Act 1979, s 61(5A)). See p 328.

41 Sale of Goods Act 1979, s 35(3).

is lost if at the relevant time he is unable to surrender the goods to the seller at the proper place[42] and in the proper condition.[43] Exceptionally, this does not apply to rejection for a defect in the seller's title, which precludes the buyer from returning the goods to the seller anyway.[44] For the purpose of s 35 the relevant time is not the time of the act which divests the buyer of possession or control of the goods but the time when he gives notice to reject.[45] It follows that mere resale, even if followed by delivery to a subpurchaser, does not necessarily constitute an act inconsistent with the seller's ownership under this form of deemed acceptance, for by the time he comes to give notice of rejection the buyer may have recovered the goods and be able[46] to surrender them at the place where the seller is entitled to expect them to be.[47] Section 35(6)(b) of the Sale of Goods Act now expressly provides that the buyer is not deemed to have accepted the goods merely because they are delivered to another under a subsale or other disposition.

Conversely, if at the time when he gives notice to reject, the buyer is unable to recover the goods and surrender them to the seller at the above place, the buyer is deemed to have accepted the goods; and the fact that he regains possession after giving notice to reject does not validate the notice.[48] This rule, which is not affected by s 35(6)(b), has been criticized, but is sensible, for the seller is entitled to know where he stands and cannot be expected to be held up while the buyer endeavours to secure the return of the goods. One can put the matter another way by saying that as regards the buyer's duty to surrender the goods to the seller after giving notice of rejection, time is of the essence.

Inability to restore is not within s 35(1)(b) unless the buyer's notice to reject is given after delivery,[49] as it usually will be. But where notice to reject is given before delivery and the buyer has already divested himself of control of the goods, there may be a deemed acceptance at common law.

(iii) Retention of the goods

Under s 35(4) the buyer is deemed to have accepted the goods when, after the lapse of a reasonable time, he retains the goods without intimating to the seller

---

42 Prima facie this is the place expressly or impliedly fixed for examination of the goods, which may well be the subpurchaser's premises. See p 356.

43 That is, in the condition in which they were on arrival at the contractual place of examination, subject only to such interference as would necessarily arise from a reasonable examination (*Hammer & Barrow v Coca-Cola* [1962] NZLR 723, per Richmond J). But the mere fact that the goods have been damaged or destroyed does not preclude rejection if the buyer was not at fault (*Head v Tattersall* (1871) LR 7 Exch 7).

44 *Rowland v Divall* [1923] 2 KB 500. See p 215.

45 See *Hardy & Co v Hillerns & Fowler*, n 18, per Bankes LJ at 496 and Atkin LJ at 499.

46 As in *Molling & Co v Dean & Son Ltd* (1901) 18 TLR 217. The position is otherwise where the buyer resells with knowledge of his seller's breach, for that constitutes an affirmation of the contract. See pp 351–352.

47 See text and n 42, and p 356.

48 See the judgments referred to in n 45. Hence the timing of the buyer's notice to reject is all-important. If he moves too quickly in giving it, he may put himself out of court. He should get the goods back first, then give notice of rejection.

49 *Hammer & Barrow v Coca-Cola*, n 43.

that he has rejected them. This part of s 35 is no longer dependent on the buyer's having had a reasonable opportunity to examine the goods, though it is relevant in determining whether there has been a lapse of a reasonable time.[50] The word 'retains' is not defined but evidently signifies either physical possession or such form of constructive possession as affords the buyer a reasonable opportunity to examine the goods.

What is a 'reasonable time'? This is one of the most troublesome problems in sales law, and continually arises in relation to complaints by consumers, to whom it is often difficult to give confident advice on the point. Until the 1994 Act, all that the Sale of Goods Act told us, in s 59, was that this was a question of fact. Now, however, s 35(5) provides that one of the material facts in determining whether a reasonable time has elapsed is whether the buyer has had a reasonable opportunity to examine the goods. In deciding whether a notice to reject was given in time, the court must balance the interests of the parties. Particularly relevant on the seller's side is the impact of delay on his ability to resell. If the market is seasonal or fluctuating, protection of the seller's interests requires a speedier notification than where the market is likely to remain constant.[51]

On the buyer's side, relevant considerations are the availability of a reasonable opportunity for examination,[52] the ease or difficulty of examination,[53] the time reasonably taken to try to make the goods work,[54] the conduct of the seller after the defect has been drawn to his attention,[55] the fact that the goods were known to the seller to be bought for resale, so that any defect would be unlikely to be discovered until the goods were in the hands of the subpurchaser,[56] the time reasonably spent in discussions with any subpurchaser to ascertain the facts and to find out whether the subpurchaser himself intends to reject the goods and, if so, whether the whole or part of them.[57] The buyer is also entitled to a reasonable time to decide whether to accept or reject, and for that purpose to ascertain what it would cost to repair the goods, how long repairs would take and whether a replacement is available, either from the seller or from some other source. Remarkably, there is almost no modern English authority on these points, though they are well established both in Canada[58] and in New Zealand.[59] One of the few decisions dealing with loss of the right to

---

50   See below.
51   *Hammer & Barrow v Coca-Cola*, n 43, per Richmond J at 733.
52   Section 35(5).
53   Which obviously varies according to the complexity of the product. See *Public Utilities Commission of City of Waterloo v Burrows Business Machines Ltd* (1974) 52 DLR (3d) 481 (Ontario CA), per Brooke JA at 489.
54   For example, if the seller urges the buyer to give the goods another try or fails to respond to the buyer's complaints altogether, the resultant delay will not be laid at the buyer's door. See the Canadian cases cited in nn 34, 53.
55   *Manifatture Tessile Laniera Wooltex v J B. Ashley Ltd* [1979] 2 Lloyd's Rep 28, and the Canadian cases referred to n 34.
56   *Truk (UK) Ltd v Tokmakidis GmbH* [2000] 1 Lloyd's Rep 543.
57   *Manifatture Tessile Laniera Wooltex v J. B. Ashley Ltd*, n 55; and see I. H. E. Patient, 'Loss of Buyer's Right to Reject' (1980) 43 MLR 463.
58   The authorities are assembled by Professor Michael Bridge in *Sale of Goods*, pp 293–294.
59   For a survey of the relevant authorities, see Michael Hwang, 'Time for Rejection of Defective Goods' [1990] LMCLQ 334.

reject through mere retention and use of the goods, without any other relevant conduct on either side, is the much-discussed decision of Rougier J in *Bernstein v Pamson Motors Ltd*.[60]

> The plaintiff bought a new car from the defendants for just under £8,000 on 7 December and drove it home, a distance of some 10 miles. Because of illness, he was unable to use the car until after Christmas, when he made one or two short trips, during which the car behaved perfectly. On 3 January, when the car had done a little over 100 miles, the plaintiff set off down the M3, but switched off the engine because of an unusual engine noise and was unable to restart the car. This was because the camshaft had seized up as the result of being starved of oil through a blockage in the lubrication system. The car had travelled a total of some 140 miles since leaving the manufacturer's works. On the following day the plaintiff wrote to the defendants to reject the car as not of merchantable quality. But the defendants arranged for it to be repaired under the manufacturer's warranty at no cost to the plaintiff, and after lengthy and expensive repairs, the car was then as good as new. However, the plaintiff declined to take it back and brought proceedings for recovery of the price.
>
> *Held*: the car was not of merchantable quality but even after discounting the period when the plaintiff was ill, the remaining three weeks represented the lapse of a reasonable time and the plaintiff was entitled to no more than damages for breach of warranty. By 'reasonable time' in s 35(1) was meant a reasonable time to examine and try out the goods in general, rather than with an eye to any specific defect.

The decision is generally considered to be harsh,[61] reflecting an extremely stringent approach to the need for finality in sales transactions, and in at least one other case a quite different approach has been taken.[62] Whether or not *Bernstein v Pamson Motors Ltd* was correctly decided, the result would almost certainly be different now, since in deciding what is a reasonable time a material question is whether the buyer had a reasonable opportunity to examine the goods for the purpose of ascertaining whether they were in conformity with the contract.[63] But it remains the case that finality is considered important in sales transactions, where the test of what is a reasonable time has always been much more severe than it is for a hiring or hire-purchase transaction.[64]

The American Uniform Commercial Code offers a convenient alternative solution by conferring on the buyer a specific right to revoke his acceptance.

> 2–608. Revocation of Acceptance in Whole or in Part
>
> (1) The buyer may revoke his acceptance of a lot or commercial unit whose non-conformity substantially impairs its value to him if he has accepted it
>
> (a) on the reasonable assumption that its non-conformity would be cured and it has not been seasonably cured; or

---

60 [1987] 2 All ER 220.
61 See, for example, Ross Cranston and Guy Dehn, 'The Right to Reject' [1990] JBL 346.
62 See the unreported decision of Russell J in *M. & T. Hurst Consultants Ltd v Grange Motors (Brentwood) Ltd* (October 1981), for which I am indebted to Professor F. M. B. Reynolds, 'Loss of Right to Reject' (1988) 104 LQR 16 at p 17–18. However, in a Singapore decision even fourteen days was held to constitute the lapse of a reasonable time. See *Eastern Supply Co v Kerr* [1994] 1 MLJ 10. For earlier authorities see *Benjamin's Sale of Goods*, para 12–061.
63 Sale of Goods Act 1979, s 35(5).
64 See, for example, *Laurelgates Ltd v Lombard North Central Ltd* (1983) 133 NLJ 720.

(b)   without discovery of such non-conformity if his acceptance was reasonably induced either by the difficulty of discovery before acceptance or by the seller's assurances.

(2) Revocation of acceptance must occur within a reasonable time after the buyer discovers or should have discovered the ground for it and before any substantial change in condition of the goods which is not caused by their own defects. It is not effective until the buyer notifies the seller of it.

(3) A buyer who so revokes has the same rights and duties with regard to the goods involved as if he had rejected them.

This concept does, of course, run quite counter to the principle of finality of acceptance embodied in the Sale of Goods Act but reflects the requirements of the market place.

Not uncommonly, the seller will offer either to repair the goods himself or to send them back to the manufacturer for repair. If the buyer accepts this offer, does he thereby adopt the sale so as to bar rejection if the repairs are not satisfactorily carried out? The Sale of Goods Act now makes it clear that he does not.[65]

(iv) The place and time of examination

In deciding whether the buyer has had a reasonable opportunity to examine, it is necessary to establish the place of examination under the contract, for until the goods have reached that place the buyer cannot be taken to have had the opportunity for examination contemplated by the contract. Hence the fact that the buyer could have examined the goods at an earlier point does not affect his right to insist on examination at the contractual place of examination,[66] unless he is a non-consumer buyer and the circumstances show that he has waived that right.[67]

Where the contract does not specify the place of examination, the presumption is that this is to take place at the contractual delivery point.[68] However, the presumption is rebutted where the buyer is not entitled to take physical delivery at that point. Hence it is well established that in c.i.f. contracts, the place of examination is not that at which the documents are handed to the buyer but the port of arrival and that the time for this examination is on or within a reasonable period after their arrival.[69] Accordingly, the buyer's acceptance of the shipping documents does not preclude him from rejecting the goods, after their arrival, for

---

65 Section 35(6)(a).

66 There does not appear to be any authority directly on the point, but there seems no reason why the buyer should be expected to examine before the goods reach the contractual point of examination. Indeed, in the case of perishables a defect which has become apparent by the time the goods reach the place for examination under the contract may not have been detectable from inspection at an earlier point. Cf D. W. Greig, *Sale of Goods* (1974), p 140. This conclusion is fortified by the wording of s 35(2) of the Sale of Goods Act, which evidently contemplates a reasonable opportunity for examining *after delivery*.

67 A buyer dealing as consumer can no longer effectively waive the opportunity of examination (s 35(3)).

68 *Perkins v Bell*, n 38. As to the contractual delivery point, see pp 269, 867 ff.

69 See *Kwei Tek Chao v British Traders & Shippers Ltd*, n 18.

nonconformity with the contract,[70] except where the nonconformity is such as would be apparent on the face of the documents.[71] The presumption that the contractual delivery point is the place of examination may also be rebutted where examination at that point is not suitable and the seller knows that the goods are destined for onward dispatch.[72]

(v) Delivery to a subpurchaser

Considerable litigation has resulted from transactions in which nonconforming goods have been sub-sold by the buyer before delivery and the goods have at his request been delivered by the seller direct to the subpurchaser. In some cases it has been held that in handing over the goods to a carrier for transmission to a subpurchaser the seller has made constructive delivery, so that the buyer should have examined the goods at that point.[73] In others, it has been said that the place of examination was the premises of the subpurchaser, so that the act of delivery to the subpurchaser was not an act inconsistent with the seller's ownership performed after the buyer had had an opportunity to examine under the contract.[74] As stated above, the Sale of Goods Act now makes it clear that mere delivery to another under a sub-sale or other disposition does not of itself constitute acceptance.[75] But the common law barriers to rejection[76] may still be invoked against him where applicable.

(vi) Deemed acceptance under common law rules

Section 62(2) of the Sale of Goods Act preserves the rules of the common law, so far as not inconsistent with the provisions of the Act. It therefore seems clear that even where s 35 does not apply, the buyer loses his right to reject if, after knowledge of the seller's breach, he elects to affirm the transaction or is estopped by his conduct[77] from disputing that he has affirmed the contract, or puts it out of his power to restore the goods to the seller. For example, conduct signifying an intention to affirm but taking place before delivery would not be within s 35 but would nevertheless attract the common law rule.

5. THE EFFECT OF ACCEPTANCE

The general effect of acceptance is laid down by s 11(4), which provides:

> Subject to section 35A below, where a contract of sale is not severable and the buyer has accepted the goods or part of them, the breach of a condition to be fulfilled by the

---

70 Ibid.

71 Ibid; and see p 946, n 132.

72 *Molling & Co v Dean & Son Ltd*, n 46; *Bragg v Villanova* (1923) 40 TLR 154; *A. J. Frank & Sons Ltd v Northern Peat Co Ltd* (1963) 39 DLR (2d) 721.

73 *Hardy & Co v Hillerns & Fowler*, n 18; *E. & S. Ruben Ltd v Faire Bros & Co Ltd* [1949] 1 KB 254.

74 *Hammer & Barrow v Coca-Cola*, n 43.

75 Section 35(6)(b).

76 See p 350.

77 The effect of s 35(6)(b) is that mere delivery to a sub-buyer, etc, would not be sufficient.

seller can only be treated as a breach of warranty, and not as a ground for rejecting the goods and treating the contract as repudiated,[78] unless there is an express or implied term of the contract to that effect.[79]

This subsection, which does not apply to severable contracts[80] or to conditional sale agreements that are agreements for consumer sales,[81] has been so cut down by s 35A,[82] to which it is expressed to be subject, that it has no significance at all unless read distributively as meaning that where the contract is not severable, the buyer who has accepted the goods cannot reject them and the buyer who has accepted a part or an instalment of the goods cannot reject *that part or that instalment.*

(i)   Delivery of the wrong quantity

Section 30(1)–(2B) provides as follows:

(1) Where the seller delivers to the buyer a quantity of goods less than he contracted to sell, the buyer may reject them, but if the buyer accepts the goods so delivered he must pay for them at the contract rate.

(2) Where the seller delivers to the buyer a quantity of goods larger than he contracted to sell, the buyer may accept the goods included in the contract and reject the rest, or he may reject the whole.

(2A) A buyer who does not deal as consumer may not –

(a)   where the seller delivers a quantity of goods less than he contracted to sell, reject the goods under subsection (1) above, or
(b)   where the seller delivers a quantity of goods larger than he contracted to sell, reject the whole under subsection (2) above

if the shortfall or, as the case may be, the excess is so slight that it would be unreasonable for him to do so.

(2B) It is for the seller to show that a shortfall or excess fell within subsection (2A) above.

(3) Where the seller delivers to the buyer a quantity of goods larger than he contracted to sell and the buyer accepts the whole of the goods so delivered he must pay for them at the contract rate.

(4) [Repealed]

(5) This section is subject to any usage of trade, special agreement, or course of dealing between the parties.

---

78 This division of terms into conditions and warranties was at one time thought to be exhaustive not only for contracts of sale but for contracts generally. For the modern view, see p 125.
79 As originally enacted, s 11(1)(c) of the Sale of Goods Act 1893 also barred rejection where the contract was for the sale of specific goods the property in which had passed to the buyer, but this particular limb of the subsection was repealed by s 4(1) of the Misrepresentation Act 1967.
80 See p 272.
81 Supply of Goods (Implied Terms) Act 1973, s 14(1). Section 14(2) is designed to ensure that no common law rule to similar effect can be invoked.
82 Which allows the buyer who has a right of rejection to accept some of the goods, whether or not conforming to the contract, without affecting his right to reject the rest for nonconformity with the contract, and to accept one instalment without affecting his right to reject a future nonconforming instalment.

These provisions may, of course, be modified by express or implied agreement between the parties; and very commonly such a modification is to be spelled out, either from a previous course of dealing or from trade usage permitting a given level of tolerance. Hence no lawyer can safely advise his client on the application of s 30 without ascertaining whether there was some prior course of dealing or a governing usage of trade, a fact emphasized by s 30(5).

Where delivery is to be made by instalments, and the wrong quantity is tendered in a particular instalment, s 30 operates in relation to that instalment, and the consequential effect on the rest of the contract then falls to be resolved by reference to s 31.[83]

Where less than the full contract quantity is tendered, the buyer may retain that part with a view to receiving the balance later, and if such balance is not tendered or if when tendered it is found not in conformity with the contract so as to entitle the buyer to reject, he can reject both that balance and the quantity originally taken, even though as regards the latter he would otherwise be deemed to have accepted it by retention within s 35(4).

We must now say a few words about each of the subsections.

1. Short delivery

A minuscule shortfall has always been disregarded by the court under the *de minimis* rule.[84] Now, however, the buyer who does not deal as consumer may also be precluded from rejecting where the shortfall, though not *de minimis*, is nevertheless so slight that it would be unreasonable for him to reject.[85] Rejection is also barred where the shortfall is within a level of tolerance or degree of approximation sanctioned by the contract or by usage of trade.[86] A shortfall is very common in the shipment of bulk cargo, such as oil and grain, as the result of wastage through evaporation, adhesion to the hold, and the like, and within a level of tolerance specified in the contract or implied by custom it is dealt with by abatement of the price rather than rejection. If the buyer elects to accept the short delivery, he cannot later be compelled (though he remains entitled) to take the balance of the goods ordered, for he is not obliged to accept delivery by instalments.[87] In consequence, if he exercises a right not to take the remaining goods, he can recover the price paid for them[88] and is entitled to damages for any further loss suffered through non-delivery at the proper time except to the extent to which he could reasonably have been expected to mitigate his loss by taking the balance of the goods instead of exercising his right not to do so.[89] If he signifies a willingness to accept a subsequent tender but the tender is not made or is defective in quantity[90] and he can show that his

---

83 *Regent OHG Aisenstadt und Barig v Francesco of Jermyn St Ltd* [1981] 3 All ER 327.
84 *Arcos Ltd v E. A. Ronaasen & Son* [1933] AC 470, per Lord Atkin at 480.
85 Sale of Goods Act 1979, s 30(2A)(a).
86 See *Benjamin's Sale of Goods*, para 8–050.
87 Section 31(1). See p 271.
88 As paid on a total failure of consideration.
89 The principle stated in *Payzu Ltd v Saunders* [1919] 2 KB 581 applies here also.
90 The same would seem to be true if the subsequent tender is defective in quality.

acceptance of the first tender was conditional upon proper tender of the balance, he can reject not only the second tender but also that which he had conditionally accepted.[91]

Short delivery may arise because part of the quantity tendered is lawfully rejected by the buyer as not in conformity with the contract. Again, the buyer cannot be compelled to accept a retender in relation to the part rejected.[92]

2.   *Excessive delivery*

As with short delivery, a trifling excess will be disregarded, at any rate if the seller does not demand payment for it,[93] and a buyer not dealing as consumer will be precluded from rejecting the whole of the goods if the excess is so slight as to make such rejection unreasonable.[94] But there is nothing to stop him from rejecting the slight excess and keeping the contract quantity. If the buyer decides to accept the entire quantity tendered, he thereby waives all remedy for the breach[95] and must pay for them at the contract rate.[96]

(ii)   Severable contracts

Section 11(4) is expressed not to apply to severable contracts. This part of s 11(4) is now otiose, since acceptance of a part or an instalment of the goods no longer bars rejection of the rest for nonconformity, even if the contract is not severable.[97]

---

91 *London Plywood & Timber Co Ltd v Basic Oak Extract Factory & Steam Sawmills Co Ltd* [1939] 2 KB 343.
92 Section 31.
93 *Shipton Anderson & Co v Weil Bros & Co* [1912] 1 KB 574 (excess of 55 lb over agreed 4,950 tons).
94 Section 30(2A)(b).
95 For in tendering the excessive quantity the seller is in effect offering the buyer a new contract, which the latter then accepts (*Gabriel, Wade & English Ltd v Arcos Ltd* (1929) 34 Ll L Rep 306).
96 Section 33.
97 See pp 357–358.

14 The Buyer's Remedies for Misrepresentation or Breach by the Seller

Where the seller is guilty of a misrepresentation or breach of contract, various forms of redress are open to the buyer. The complexity of sales law derives in no small measure from this multiplicity of remedies and from the fact that, whereas some remedies go together so as to be exercisable cumulatively, the buyer who possesses several remedies not so grouped may have to elect which remedy or set of remedies to pursue.[1]

1. THE REMEDIES IN OUTLINE

(i) Rescission and restitution

Where the seller has made a misrepresentation, whether fraudulently, negligently or wholly without fault, the buyer is entitled to rescind *stricto sensu*, that is, to treat the contract as avoided from the beginning.[2] With rescission goes restitution, that is, the surrender by each party of benefits received from the other. Where this is impossible, rescission will usually (though not invariably) be barred.[3] If the property had passed to the buyer prior to rescission, the effect of rescission is to revest the property in the seller.[4] The remedy of rescission operates in the same way in relation to contracts for sale as for other contracts.[5]

(ii) Rejection of the goods

The buyer is entitled to reject goods which do not conform to the contract description or are not of satisfactory quality or fit for their known purpose or are tendered late when time is of the essence or the delay is such as to constitute a repudiation by the seller.[6] The grounds for and effect of rejection – which neither produces rescission in the strict sense nor even necessarily amounts to an

---

1 For the provisions of the Unfair Contract Terms Act 1977 as to unreasonable restrictions on remedies, see p 97; and for the EC Directive on Unfair Contract Terms and the implementing Unfair Terms in Consumer Contracts Regulations 1999, p 100.
2 This is the most common ground for avoiding a contract of sale, though as we have seen (p 78) there are other classes of voidable contract, eg contracts entered into under duress or undue influence.
3 See p 109.
4 See p 108.
5 See p 107.
6 *McDougall v Aeromarine of Emsworth Ltd* [1958] 1 WLR 1126.

election by the buyer to treat the contract as at an end[7] – have been considered in an earlier chapter.[8]

(iii) Suspension of payment

The non-fulfilment by the seller of any obligation to which the duty of payment is correlative entitles the buyer to suspend payment until the obligation has been performed. For this purpose the status of the obligation as a condition or warranty is irrelevant. Whether it be a major or a minor term, it is *ex hypothesi* a condition of payment, and the buyer has the right to insist on simultaneous performance of the correlative obligation. Thus, unless otherwise agreed, payment and delivery are concurrent conditions, and the buyer need not tender payment unless and until the seller is ready and willing to give the possession of the goods in exchange.[9]

(iv) Termination and restitution or damages

The buyer may terminate a contract of sale upon any ground specified in the contract as authorizing termination or if the seller commits a breach of condition or otherwise repudiates the contract. Even a repudiation in advance of the due date for performance[10] entitles the buyer to treat the contract as at an end without waiting until the date in question.[11] Termination of a contract of sale necessarily entitles the seller to recover possession of the goods and the buyer to repayment of the price,[12] and thus produces effects closely resembling those of rescission in the strict sense. It is for this reason that the buyer's acceptance of the seller's repudiation is commonly referred to as rescission. But this usage is misleading, for it conceals the fact that whereas in principle the remedy of the buyer consequent upon rescission is restitution,[13] on termination for breach the buyer is not obliged to pursue a restitutionary remedy for recovery of money paid on a total failure of consideration, but has the option of claiming damages. This will be his preferred choice where he has not paid anything to the seller – so that the question of restitution does not arise and he is seeking compensation for loss of bargain or for special damage suffered – or where he has suffered loss exceeding the price paid to the seller, eg by abortive expenditure on repairs. In such a case the price he has paid will simply feature as an element of his damages, not as money paid on a total failure of consideration.

(v) Acceptance of the goods and damages or offset against the price

The buyer does not have a right to reject for every kind of breach;[14] and even where there is a right to reject, the buyer can elect to adopt the transaction by accepting the

---

7   See p 341.
8   See pp 338 ff.
9   Sale of Goods Act, s 28. For the effect of this provision see p 394.
10 Ie the so-called anticipatory breach. See p 126.
11 See p 366.
12 Section 54 of the Act expressly preserves the buyer's right to recover money paid on a total failure of consideration.
13 See p 79.
14 See p 338.

goods, and in various circumstances will be deemed to have accepted them even if he did not so intend.[15] The effect of acceptance is that the condition broken sinks to the level of a warranty and the buyer can claim damages for breach of warranty and/or set up the breach in diminution or extinction of the price.[16]

(vi) Specific performance

The court has power to order specific performance of a contract to deliver specific or ascertained goods,[17] whether or not the property has passed to the buyer. Specific performance has, indeed, been decreed even of a contract for the sale of unascertained goods,[18] but the decision, though to be welcomed as commercially realistic, is hard to reconcile with s 52(1) of the Sale of Goods Act and with both earlier and subsequent authority.[19] The general rule is that specific performance will not be available where damages would be an adequate remedy;[20] and since most categories of goods are of a type that can either be purchased in the open market or acquired from other sources, specific performance of a contract of a sale of goods will be decreed only in unusual circumstances, eg where the goods are unique or rare or are being made to the buyer's special requirements.[21] But it has to be said that the reluctance to grant specific performance can lead to an over-broad view of what constitutes availability in the market, and as a result a considerable financial burden on the innocent plaintiff. For example, in the *Bronx Engineering* case:[22]

> The defendants had wrongfully repudiated a contract to sell goods to the plaintiffs. The evidence showed that it would take the plaintiffs between nine and twelve months to obtain similar goods from an alternative source. Even this serious delay failed to persuade the Court of Appeal that the case was a proper one for the grant of specific performance, for the goods were of a type 'obtainable on the market in the ordinary course of business'[23] and the additional loss suffered by the plaintiffs as the result of the delay would be covered by an increased award of damages.

It is hard to see why a repudiating seller should be allowed to walk away from actual performance of its contract and leave the innocent buyer to wrestle with the commercial difficulties and added loss and expense of a delay of up to a year when this could so easily have been avoided by an order for specific performance. There is much to be said for relaxing the stringency of the rules as to specific performance, which in civil law jurisdictions is considered a primary remedy. The position is, of

---

15 See pp 349 ff.

16 Sale of Goods Act, s 53(1), (4).

17 Section 52(1). The reference to ascertained goods is another example of the draftsman's compression technique. The contract cannot itself be to deliver ascertained goods, since such goods are not identified until after the making of the contract (see p 209). In longhand, the section means that where there is a contract to deliver goods, and these are either identified at the time of the contract or become identified thereafter, the court can order specific performance.

18 *Sky Petroleum Ltd v VIP Petroleum Ltd* [1974] 1 WLR 576.

19 See *Re Wait* [1927] 1 Ch 606; *Société des Industries Métallurgiques S.A. v Bronx Engineering Co Ltd* [1975] 1 Lloyd's Rep 465. Neither s 52 nor *Re Wait* were referred to in the judgment.

20 See p 113. However, a consumer buyer may obtain specific performance of the duty to repair or replace. See p 389.

21 *Behnke v Bede Shipping Co Ltd* [1927] 1 KB 649.

22 See n 19.

23 Ibid, per Lord Edmund Davies at 469.

course, otherwise where the buyer has paid all or part of the price and the seller has become bankrupt or gone into liquidation. In such a case specific performance would give the prepaying buyer an undue preference over the general body of creditors, contrary to well-established principles of insolvency law.[24]

(vii) Additional remedies for consumer buyers

Where the buyer is a person dealing as consumer, Part 5A of the Sale of Goods Act 1979[25] gives him additional remedies where the goods do not conform to the contract of sale at the time of delivery.[26]

(viii) Tort remedies for non-delivery

Where the buyer has become entitled to possession[27] and the seller fails or refuses to deliver possession, the buyer can sue in tort for specific delivery and damages for detention, or for the value of the goods by way of damages for conversion.[28] The tort of conversion[29] is founded on interference with a right to possession. The plaintiff's ownership is not relevant except as a source of the right to possess.[30] There is little doubt, for example, that if the seller under a conditional sale agreement[31] refuses to deliver the goods to the buyer, the latter has a cause of action in conversion.[32]

(ix) Other tort remedies

The seller who causes loss to the buyer by a fraudulent misrepresentation or other fraudulent conduct is liable in tort for deceit. A negligent misrepresentation, though in principle not giving rise to a claim for damages,[33] was actionable even at common law when it resulted in physical injury to the person or property of the plaintiff[34] or was in breach of a fiduciary duty[35] or a duty created by some other

---

24 The position is usually different in contracts for the sale of land or for the mortgage of goods, for in both cases the contract is generally treated in equity as constituting an assignment, so that the seller or mortgagor has ceased to be the beneficial owner. One consequence of the principle that until the property in goods has passed under a contract of sale the buyer's rights are purely contractual (pp 216–217) is to restrict still further the availability of specific performance in contracts of sale of goods by comparison with other types of contract.

25 Inserted by the Sale and Supply of Goods to Consumers Regulations 2002, SI 2002/3045.

26 See p 389

27 See p 395.

28 There is little advantage in pursuing the tort remedy, for the buyer will not be able to recover greater damages than he could have recovered in contract (*Chinery v Viall* (1860) 5 H & N 288; *The Arpad* [1934] P189).

29 And of detinue before it was merged with conversion by the Torts (Interference with Goods) Act 1977.

30 See p 62.

31 See p 700.

32 See p 212.

33 See p 107.

34 See p 108.

35 *Nocton v Lord Ashburton* [1914] AC 932.

special relationship;[36] and a right to damages is now expressly given by s 2(1) of the Misrepresentation Act 1967.[37]

(x) Damages for breach of collateral contract

Where a seller, by a false statement which is promissory in character, induces the buyer to enter into the contract of sale, the false statement constitutes a warranty giving rise to a distinct collateral contract,[38] the breach of which entitles the buyer to damages. There seems no reason why, as an alternative, the buyer should not be able to treat the collateral warranty as a misrepresentation in relation to the contract of sale and to rescind that contract.[39]

(xi) Declaration

Proceedings for a declaratory judgment may sometimes prove a useful remedy, and this has been granted in several cases.[40]

2.   ANTICIPATORY BREACH

Where the seller, before the time for delivery has arrived, intimates that he is unable or unwilling to proceed with the contract or otherwise disables himself from performing it,[41] the buyer has an option. He can either treat the contract as immediately discharged[42] and claim damages or he can hold the contract open for performance and await the due date for delivery. If he adopts the former course, he comes under a duty to mitigate[43] as soon as he has accepted the seller's repudiation,[44] but, subject to this, the measure of damages is the same as on non-delivery, ie excess of market price[45] at the due delivery date[46] over contract price.[47]

---

36 *Hedley Byrne & Co Ltd v Heller & Partners Ltd* [1964] AC 465.
37 See p 107.
38 The consideration for the warranty being the buyer's entry into the main contract. See p 93.
39 See p 81.
40 See *Benjamin's Sale of Goods* (6th edn, 2002), para 17–100.
41 An intimation that, while ready and willing to perform, he will not be able to perform on time is treated in the same way if time is or has become of the essence. But a threatened breach which if actually committed would not be a repudiation cannot become repudiatory by anticipation.
42 But this statement of principle has to be substantially qualified in relation to documentary sales. See p 929.
43 Eg by buying in a rising market. Provided that the buyer acts reasonably, he is entitled to have damages assessed by reference to the price at which he purchases in taking steps to mitigate his loss even if it later transpires that the price is higher than the market value at the due delivery date (*Melachrino v Nickoll & Knight* [1920] 1 KB 693).
44 Ibid.
45 Or if there is no available market, value (see p 370).
46 The market price at the date of repudiation or acceptance of repudiation is irrelevant; and the concluding part of s 51(3) of the Sale of Goods Act (dealing with the situation where no time was fixed for delivery) is inapplicable to cases of anticipatory breach (*Millett v Van Heek & Co* [1921] 2 KB 369; *Tai Hing Cotton Mill Ltd v Kamsing Knitting Factory* [1979] AC 91).
47 See p 368.

If the buyer elects to hold the contract open, the duty to mitigate is deferred, but if the seller persists in his refusal to perform when the due delivery date arrives, the buyer thereafter keeps the contract open at his peril, for though he is entitled to do this he cannot thereby further postpone his duty to mitigate and will not be able to recover his loss to the extent that this is caused by the failure to act promptly in mitigation of his loss after the due delivery date has passed.[48]

A vexed question is whether what appears to be an anticipatory breach can subsequently be justified by reliance on factors not known to the renouncing party at the time of his renunciation but showing that at that time the other party was himself in a position where he would not be able to perform at the due date. This is discussed in the next chapter in relation to renunciation by the buyer.[49] Exactly the same considerations apply where it is the seller who renounces.

3.   NON-DELIVERY

(i)   Buyer's remedies generally

Upon the seller's failure to deliver the goods, the buyer has various remedies open to him:

(a)   If the failure constitutes a repudiation (either because time of delivery was or has become of the essence or because the delay is so great as to frustrate the commercial purpose of the contract[50]), the buyer may: (i) treat the contract as at an end; and (ii) either recover payments he has made in respect of the price, on the basis of a total failure of consideration, or sue for damages for non-delivery.[51]

(b)   If the failure does not constitute a repudiation, or if though it does the buyer does not wish to accept the repudiation, he may: (i) hold the contract open for performance, in which event it continues in force for the benefit of both parties;[52] (ii) in rare cases, obtain an order for specific performance,[53] but in any event (iii) claim damages for delay in delivery.[54]

---

48 See p 368.
49 See p 396.
50 See p 125.
51 For the measure of damages, see below. Restitution is an alternative to damages, not an additional remedy. Obviously a buyer claiming damages for loss of profit must give credit for the expenses he would have incurred in earning that profit and has avoided as the result of the breach. Hence if he paid the price in advance, he can claim repayment by way of restitution or the excess of value over price by way of damages, but he cannot demand both the value of the goods of which he has been deprived and the sum he has paid, and other expenses he has incurred, in connection with the purchase and prospective delivery of the goods.
52 Exceptionally, the buyer, though the innocent party, may lose this option. See pp 125–160 For delivery of the wrong quantity, see p 358.
53 See p 363.
54 If the seller persists in his failure to deliver and the case is not one in which the buyer can get specific performance, the buyer may ultimately be forced to accept the inevitable and treat the contract as discharged, in which case his claim will be for non-delivery, not delay in delivery. Moreover, once the time for performance by the seller has arrived, the buyer cannot, by holding the contract open for performance, postpone the duty to mitigate imposed on him. See p 368.

(ii)   The measure of damages for non-delivery[55]

The general principles of contract law governing the measure of damages have been set out in an earlier chapter.[56] The Sale of Goods Act builds on these principles – and in particular on the rule in *Hadley v Baxendale*[57] – in its provisions relating to damages for breach.

> 51(1) Where the seller wrongfully neglects or refuses to deliver the goods to the buyer, the buyer may maintain an action against the seller for damages for non-delivery.
>
> (2) The measure of damages is the estimated loss directly and naturally resulting, in the ordinary course of events, from the seller's breach of contract.
>
> (3) Where there is an available market for the goods in question the measure of damages is prima facie to be ascertained by the difference between the contract price and the market or current price of the goods at the time or times when they ought to have been delivered or (if no time was fixed) then at the time of the refusal to deliver.
>
> ...
>
> 54. Nothing in this Act affects the right of the buyer or the seller to recover interest or special damages in any case where by law interest or special damages may be recoverable, or to recover money paid where the consideration for the payment of it has failed.

Section 51(2) states the first limb of the rule of *Hadley v Baxendale*, and s 51(3) sets out the normal measure of damages under that limb. Section 54 preserves the operation of the second limb of the rule in *Hadley v Baxendale*, 'special damages' in this context[58] denoting damages for loss resulting not as the natural consequence of the defendant's breach but from some special circumstance which the plaintiff will have to show ought reasonably to have been within the defendant's contemplation at the time of the contract if the defendant is to be held liable for the loss in question.[59]

Section 51(3) contains two crucial phrases, 'available market' and 'market price'. Why the presence or absence of an available market is so important will shortly be seen. Once the significance of the market concept has been grasped, we can go on to examine more closely what is meant by an 'available market'[60] and what constitutes the 'market price'.[61] For present purposes we can define an available market as a market to which the buyer has reasonable access and in which he can procure goods of a description and quality comparable to those he has contracted to buy and at a price governed primarily by the market forces of supply and demand. The measure of damages to which the buyer is entitled in the event of the seller's failure to deliver depends on whether there is in fact an available market. As we shall see, the

---

55 For excellent discussions of this topic see *McGregor on Damages* (17th edn, 2003), paras 20–002 ff; *Benjamin's Sale of Goods*, paras 17–001 ff. For delivery of the wrong quantity, see p 358.

56 See pp 121 ff.

57 (1854) 9 Exch 341.

58 The term has a variety of meanings, and 'consequential loss' is to be preferred. See p 122.

59 See p 122.

60 See p 382.

61 See p 384.

market-price rule in contracts of sale of goods represents a major departure from the ordinary rules of contract law relating to mitigation of loss.[62]

1.   *Measure of damages where there is an available market*

Where there is an available market[63] the following principles apply.

(a)   Prima facie, the measure of damages is the amount by which the market price at the due date of delivery (or if no date for delivery was fixed, at the date of the seller's refusal to deliver[64]) exceeds the contract price.[65] This is the normal basis for evaluating the loss 'directly and naturally resulting, in the ordinary course of events, from the seller's breach of contract' under s 51(2) following the first limb of the rule in *Hadley v Baxendale*. It is predicated on the assumption that upon non-delivery the buyer can mitigate his loss by buying substitute goods in the open market. To the extent to which he suffers further loss by not going to the market, he cannot hold the seller responsible.

(b)   If the time for delivery has been extended at the request of the seller, the market price is taken at the postponed delivery date.[66] It would seem, however, that the buyer cannot, without the assent of the seller, postpone steps to mitigate by holding the contract open for performance by the seller. If the seller, having refused to deliver, maintains that refusal, the buyer is then expected to buy in the market.[67] To this rule, which applies to contracts generally,[68] there is one qualification. The buyer is in any event entitled to a reasonable time within which to ascertain the seller's intentions after a failure to deliver, with a view to agreeing on a postponed delivery date.[69]

(c)   If the buyer, in addition to a general loss of bargain resulting from excess of the market price over the contract, suffers special damage that ought reasonably to have been within the seller's contemplation at the time of the contract[70] – eg extra freight,[71] the cost of additional time spent in locating replacements,[72] or the cost of adapting the substitute goods[73] – such special damage is recoverable as well under s 54. However, if at the due date of delivery the market price has fallen, so that the effect of the seller's repudiation

62 See p 386.
63 A question which has to be tested as at the due date of delivery. If there was a market at the time of the contract of sale but there has ceased to be a market by the time the seller is due to deliver, he cannot complain if damages are assessed on a different basis.
64 This limb of s 51(3) does not apply in the case of an anticipatory breach by the seller. See n 46.
65 Section 51(3).
66 *Ogle v Earl Vane* (1868) LR 3 QB 272.
67 *Melachrino v Nickoll & Knight*, n 43.
68 See p 121. The rule does not, however, apply to cases of anticipatory breach, for the innocent party is entitled to hold the contract open for performance at the due date. See p 126.
69 Cf the position in regard to the right to reject, p 349.
70 The seller's knowledge of special circumstances may in fact displace the market price altogether, as where he knows that the buyer is committed to sub-selling as specific goods the articles which are the subject of the sale contract. See p 384.
71 In cases where freight is payable by the buyer.
72 *J. & B. Caldwell Ltd v Logan House Retirement Home Ltd* [1999] 2 NZLR 99.
73 *Blackburn Bobbin Co Ltd v T.W. Allen & Sons Ltd* [1918] 2 KB 467.

is to enable the buyer to acquire the goods more cheaply, the reduction in price must be offset against any claim for special damage under s 54.[74]

Where there is an available market,[75] the market-price rule is not easily displaced.[76] In particular, the excess of market price over contract price will be used as the basis for calculating damages even if the buyer:

(a) does not in fact go into the market at all to buy substitute goods but merely does without – for he has still been deprived of a bargain if the market price exceeds the contract price;[77]

(b) goes into the market at a later date and obtains substitute goods at a higher or lower price than the market price prevailing at the due delivery date – for he could have done this even if the seller had performed his contract, and the substitute purchase has no necessary connection with the contract;[78]

(c) is able to buy substitute goods at the due delivery date at less than the market price[79] – for he could have got them in addition to the contract goods and thereby have had the benefit of two bargains, and in any event what the buyer chooses to buy has no necessary connection with the original contract and is thus *res inter alios acta*;[80]

(d) had contracted to resell goods of the same description[81] at a price higher than the market price[82] – the buyer can still perform his subcontract by going into the market, and if he does not do so, he cannot expect the seller to pay the extra loss resulting from the fact that the resale price exceeds the market price;

(e) had contracted to resell goods of the same description[83] at a price lower than the market price[84] – the seller cannot take advantage of this to reduce the

74 There appears to be no authority on the point, but it would seem to follow from general principle.

75 As to this, see p 368.

76 For a criticism of the rigidity of the market-price rule, see p 386.

77 This is merely a specific application of the wider principle of the law of damages that a person who suffers a loss in value through a wrongful act need not take steps to restore the value lost as a condition of recovering damages. Thus where the estimated cost of repairs is taken as a reliable guide to the diminution in value of goods which are not in the condition warranted, the buyer can recover such cost, as representing the diminution in value, even if he chooses not to have the repairs carried out.

78 See *R. Pagnan & Fratelli v Corbisa Industrial Agropacuaria Lda* [1970] 2 Lloyd's Rep 14, per Salmon LJ at 18. But on the particular facts of that case the substitute purchase was held to be connected to the broken sale contract. See p 370.

79 There is no clear authority on the point, but the principle seems clearly to follow from the passage in the judgment of Salmon, LJ, cited n 78.

80 For the exceptional case illustrated by *R. Pagnan and Fratelli v Corbisa Industrial Agropacuaria Lda*, n 78, see p 370. The rule itself is open to criticism as being fundamentally inconsistent with the duty to mitigate, which presupposes that the guilty party is entitled to the benefit of any loss avoidance resulting from steps to mitigate that the innocent party took or ought reasonably to have taken. See further p 386.

81 For the position where, to the knowledge of the seller, the buyer had contracted to resell the identical goods, see p 384.

82 *Williams v Reynolds* (1865) 6 B & S 495; *Mohammad Habib Ullah (Sheik) v Bird & Co* (1921) 37 TLR 405. See further p 384.

83 As to the effect of a contract to resell the identical goods, see p 384.

84 *Williams Bros Ltd v Edward T. Agius Ltd* [1914] AC 510, approving the decision of the Court of Appeal in *Rodocanachi, Sons & Co v Milburn Bros* (1886) 18 QBD 67, a case of failure to deliver goods under a charterparty.

damages, since it is no concern of his what the buyer chooses to do with the goods, and the buyer would have been perfectly entitled to obtain from a different source (eg in the market) the goods necessary to fulfil the subpurchase contract;

(f)   had contracted to resell with a delivery date the same as that under the original sale contract, so that on non-delivery by his seller there is no time left to go into the market to fulfil his obligation to his subpurchaser – for a prudent buyer will in his subcontract allow a margin of time, and if he chooses to rely on his seller for delivery on a date leaving no margin available, he cannot put the resulting loss on the seller.[85]

The market-price principle is in no way displaced by the fact that a resale by the buyer at a higher price was within the knowledge or reasonable contemplation of the seller;[86] for the buyer can cover the subcontract by buying in the market,[87] and his duty to mitigate the loss in this way is unaffected by the seller's knowledge of the subcontract, since the seller is entitled to assume that the buyer will take reasonable steps in mitigation.

In exceptional circumstances the market-price rule is displaced even though there is an available market. An illustration is *Pagnan and Fratelli v Corbisa Industrial Agropacuaria Limitada*,[88] where, after lawful rejection of the goods by the buyers, negotiations between the parties resulted in an agreement by the buyers to purchase the self-same goods from the sellers at a reduced price, the goods being resold by the buyers at a profit. It was held that the purchase by the buyers was not in this case *res inter alios acta* but was between the self-same parties in relation to the same goods and formed part of a continuous dealing between the sellers and the buyers. To ignore it would be to give the buyers damages for a fictitious loss when they had made a profit. In the circumstances it could not be said that the buyers had established a recoverable loss. The buyer may, indeed, be expected to mitigate his loss in an appropriate case by accepting the seller's offer to purchase the goods again.[89]

2.   Measure of damages where there is no available market

Where there is no available market for the contract goods,[90] the rules governing the computation of damages become more complex. An available market presupposes both that substitute goods are readily accessible to the buyer and that it is reasonable for him to go into the market to acquire them. Hence his general damages can be measured by reference to the market price, whether he contracted to buy the contract goods for resale, for use in his business or for any other purpose.

---

85   *Williams v Reynolds* n 82, cited by Salter J in *Patrick v Russo-British Grain Export Co Ltd* [1927] 2 KB 535.

86   *The Arpad* n 28 per Maugham LJ at 230.

87   For the position where the buyer cannot do this because he has contracted to sub-sell the very goods he is buying, see p 384.

88   See n 78.

89   *The Solholt* [1983] 1 Lloyd's Rep 605, per Sir John Donaldson MR at 608.

90   As to what constitutes an available market, see p 382.

The position is quite different if there is no available market. Goods of comparable description to those contracted for will not necessarily be available from another source, and even if they are, it does not necessarily follow that the buyer can reasonably be expected to utilize that source, nor even that he will be considered to have acted reasonably if he does utilize it. Hence damages may have to be computed on the basis that the buyer does not obtain substitute goods (whether of similar description or of a kind most nearly equivalent to the goods contracted for), and the loss resulting from his deprivation of the contract goods will thus depend very heavily on the purpose for which he required them. If they were purchased for the purpose of resale, his loss (though not necessarily his *recoverable* loss) is the loss of profit he would have made on resale. If he required the goods for the purpose of generating income in his business – eg because they comprised machinery used in the manufacture of products or because he intended to let them out on hire – his loss is to be measured by the capitalized value of the income he would have been expected to receive for the goods over the period of their working life. If the goods were to be used in the business but were not directly of an income-producing character, the loss is prima facie represented by the excess of their value over the contract price, that is, the extra sum the buyer could reasonably expect to have to pay in order to purchase goods of comparable description and quality, or their nearest equivalent.[91] The case is otherwise, however, where the goods are unlikely to be used (eg, where they are bought as spares in circumstances where it is improbable they will be required), so that it would be unreasonable for the buyer to go to the expense of procuring a substitute.[92]

These variations of loss do not exhaust the complications, for we also have to consider, in accordance with the rule in *Hadley v Baxendale*, to what extent any particular form of loss could reasonably have been contemplated by the seller as flowing from his breach; and this question (which is relevant, inter alia, to determine whether a buyer can be heard to say that because of a contract to resell the very goods he purchased, there was no available market to him[93]) requires us to ascertain to what extent the buyer's intended application of the goods should reasonably have been present to the seller's mind. This causes particular complications where the seller could reasonably have contemplated more than one possible application of the goods by the buyer. In such a case, is the loss to be measured by reference to the actual application of the goods or can either the buyer or the seller insist upon measurement of the loss by reference to any reasonable hypothetical application?[94]

Some of the cases are not easy to reconcile, but the following rules can probably be extracted from them.

91 Where the nearest equivalent consists of goods of a higher quality, the courts have generally allowed recovery of the full replacement cost without reduction for the element of 'betterment'. See *Bacon v Cooper (Metals) Ltd* [1982] 1 All ER 397; *Harbutt's 'Plasticine' Ltd v Wayne Tank and Pump Co Ltd* [1970] 1 QB 447.
92 *The Alecos M* [1991] 1 Lloyd's Rep 120; G. H. Treitel, 'Damages for Non-Delivery' [1991] 107 LQR 364.
93 See p 384.
94 This problem is discussed on p 382, in relation to the meaning of an available market.

(a)   There being no available market, the normal value of the goods[95] must be substituted for the market price,[96] and the buyer's loss of profit determined accordingly.

(b)   In each of the situations described below, the measurement of value as a basis for computing damages is subject to the buyer's overriding duty to take reasonable steps to mitigate his loss, eg, by buying from an alternative source.

(c)   Where the goods were to be acquired with a view to resale[97] and the seller could reasonably have been expected to be aware that a resale was not unlikely[98] (eg, because the buyer is a merchant dealing in goods of the like description), a normal resale price may be taken as the value. By a normal resale price is meant such percentage addition to the price charged to the buyer as the court considers, on the available evidence, would represent a reasonable mark-up for goods of a like description.[99] Where the buyer has actually contracted to resell, the resale price is prima facie evidence of the normal value, but is not conclusive, since the buyer may have negotiated a resale on uncommonly favourable terms and, unless the seller was aware of this, he will not be answerable for the excess of the profit above the normal profit figure.[100]

(d)   Where the seller was aware not only that the goods were acquired for resale but also that the resale price was higher than normal, then to the extent to which the resale price was known to him or within his reasonable contemplation because of his knowledge of the subcontract, it will be taken as the value of the goods, and damages will be assessed accordingly. This is so whether the resale price is higher or lower than the market price. In other words, the resale price can not only be relied on by the buyer to increase his damages where it exceeds the normal price, it will also go to reduce the seller's liability if it is below the normal price.[101]

(e)   Where the goods are not bought for resale, or for making up into a product intended for sale, but are to be used in the buyer's business with a view to generating income – as where they comprise machinery employed in the manufacture of goods for sale – the computation of damages may become

---

95   Ie the value which could reasonably be expected to be in the contemplation of a seller not aware of any unusual element involved.

96   *J Leavey & Co Ltd v George H. Hirst & Co Ltd* [1944] KB 24, in which the court assessed damages on the footing of the profit the buyer would have made on resale.

97   The principle is the same where they have first to be made up into a finished product, as in *J. Leavey & Co Ltd v George H. Hirst & Co Ltd*, n 96.

98   The correct test is not entirely clear. 'Probable', 'likely', 'an even chance', 'not unlikely', are all phrases that have been used. At one time it was thought that the buyer had to fulfil an additional requirement, namely to show that the seller was not merely on notice of the probability of a resale but expressly or impliedly undertook responsibility for loss of the resale profit if he failed to deliver. See *British Columbia and Vancouver's Island Spar, Lumber & Sawmill Co Ltd v Nettleship* (1868) LR 3 CP 499; *Patrick v Russo-British Grain Export Co Ltd* [1927] 2 KB 535. But this view has now been discredited. See *Koufos v C. Czarnikow Ltd* [1969] 1 AC 350, per Lord Upjohn, at 428; *GKN Centrax Gears Ltd v Matbro Ltd* [1976] 2 Lloyd's Rep 555.

99   *Household Machines Ltd v Cosmos Exporters Ltd* [1947] KB 217.

100   Ibid.

101   There appears to be no direct authority, but the proposition follows from general principle.

more complex, since it depends on the interaction of two variables, a capital element (the extra cost of obtaining substitute goods if these are procurable) and an income element (the loss of profit resulting from depreciation of the goods for the period necessary to obtain substitutes). No single formula meets every case, since the degree of importance of each of the two variables depends on whether substitute goods are in fact ultimately obtained, whether it was reasonable for the buyer to incur expenditure in obtaining them and what is a reasonable period over which to base the claim for loss of income. The overriding principle is that where a claim is made under both heads, capital and income, damages should not be duplicated through overlap. Within this principle there is scope for a plaintiff buyer to elect between one form of claim and another. In this context the decision of the Court of Appeal in the *British Rema* case,[102] where a logical split of the claim between capital and income was disallowed on the erroneous grounds that this would duplicate damages and allow recovery under a head of damages that had not been pleaded, is unfortunate.[103]

(f) The basis of each of the different measures of damages described above is compensation for loss of bargain, the object being to put the buyer as nearly as possible in the position in which he would have been if the contract had been performed. However, in given conditions the buyer may elect for an alternative basis of damages, namely the recovery of abortive expenditure incurred in connection with the transaction,[104] the object here being to restore him to the position he occupied before the contract. Expenditure recoverable on this ground may even include pre-contract expenditure,[105] though it would seem that the plaintiff is not entitled to recover under this head more than he would have recovered for loss of bargain.[106]

3. Consequential loss

To any claim for damages for loss of bargain may be added consequential loss resulting from the breach,[107] eg extra freight or insurance charges in connection with the substitute goods and liability incurred to subpurchasers for non-performance of the sub-sale contract,[108] together with legal costs incurred in reasonably defending the sub-

---

102 *Cullinane v British Rema Manufacturing Co Ltd* [1954] 1 QB 292.

103 See p 381.

104 Where this expenditure is of a kind resulting in a corresponding benefit to the seller, as where it consists in payment of the whole or part of the price in advance, the buyer need not formulate his claim as one for damages but can recover his payment in restitution on the ground of total failure of consideration. Expenditure rendered futile by the breach must be distinguished from consequential loss resulting from the breach. The former is expenditure incurred in order to earn the fruits of the bargain and is recoverable only as an alternative to damages for loss of bargain. The latter is expenditure that would not have been incurred at all but for the breach and is recoverable in addition to damages for loss of bargain. See further below.

105 See p 120, n 375.

106 *Bowlay Logging Ltd v Domtar Ltd* (1978) 87 DLR (3d) 325.

107 Consequential loss features more prominently in claims for delay in delivery or delivery of defective goods. See below and p 379.

108 Limited, again, to what the seller could reasonably have expected (*Grébert-Borgnis v J. & W. Nugent* (1885) 15 QBD 85; *R. & H. Hall Ltd and W. H. Pim Jnr & Co Ltd* (1928) 30 Ll L Rep 159).

buyer's claim.[109] Loss of profit is recoverable to the extent that this is not reflected in the normal measure of damages;[110] and damages are recoverable by the buyer for loss of repeat orders where this loss results from the seller's breach and ought reasonably to have been within his contemplation as the consequence of the breach.[111]

4.   DELAY IN DELIVERY

Damages for delay in delivery arise only where a late tender is made which the buyer either elects or is obliged to accept; for the buyer's lawful rejection of a late tender makes the case one of non-delivery, for which the buyer's remedies will be those earlier described.

The computation of the normal measure of damages for delay in delivery – a matter not specifically dealt with by the Sale of Goods Act – proceeds on a basis entirely different from that applicable to non-delivery.[112] Instead of treating the contract as repudiated for non-performance, the buyer seeks damages for defective performance on the footing that the contract remains alive. The measure of damages is thus akin to that applicable for breach of warranty, whereas in the case of non-delivery damages are assessed as for breach of condition.

The continuance of the contract also has an impact on the buyer's duty to mitigate. In the case of non-delivery, the duty to mitigate comes into play on the due delivery date, and where there is an available market, it is by reference to the market price on that date that the buyer's damages are assessed, for the assumption is that the buyer will cover his position by making a purchase in the market.[113] But where delivery is merely delayed, so that the seller ultimately tenders the goods, then while the buyer, on the due delivery date, is expected to mitigate any anticipated loss of income by hiring substitute goods for the period of the delay,[114] he is not obliged to buy substitute goods in replacement for the contract goods, for *ex hypothesi* the seller has proved willing and able to perform and thus cannot be heard to say that the buyer should have cut his losses on the due delivery date by buying replacement goods.[115] It is for this reason that, where the buyer buys for resale, the price at which he could have bought substitute goods on the *due* delivery date is irrelevant, as his damages are measured by reference to the price at which he could reasonably expect to *sell* them on the *actual* delivery date.[116]

109   *Hammond & Co v Bussey* (1887) 20 QBD 79 (defective quality).
110   *Vanda Compania of Costa Rica v Société Maritime Nationale of Paris* [1974] 2 Lloyd's Rep 502.
111   *GKN Centrax Gears Ltd v Matbro Ltd*, n 98, disapproving the dictum of Scrutton LJ in *Simon v Pawson & Leafs Ltd* (1932) 38 Com Cas 151. The *Matbro* case concerned delivery of faulty goods but the principle is equally applicable to non-delivery; and in each case it is a question of fact as to whether the loss of custom could reasonably have been contemplated by the seller at the time of the sale contract.
112   See pp 366 ff.
113   See p 368.
114   Unless induced not to do so by reason of assurances by the seller that delivery will be made promptly (*Smeed v Foord* (1859) 1 E & E 602).
115   Ibid.
116   *Kwei Tek Chao v British Traders & Shippers Ltd* [1954] 2 QB 459.

As with non-delivery, the measure of damages depends on whether the buyer bought the goods for resale on the one hand or for use in his business as an income-producing asset on the other.[117] The significance of this distinction tends to be overlooked by commentators, whose formulation of the measure of damages by reference to the drop in the capital value of the goods through the delay presupposes that the goods are bought for resale, which is not necessarily the case. Where the goods are bought for use, the buyer's loss will usually take the form of loss of profit-income, not diminution in capital value, and such loss of income, so far as not unusual in degree,[118] will thus represent normal loss directly flowing from the breach, not, as is commonly stated, consequential loss.[119]

(i)   Goods bought for resale

In computing the direct loss through delay suffered by a buyer who buys for resale, the market price or value of the goods at the due delivery date must be compared not with the contract price (as in the case of non-delivery) but with the market price or value at the actual delivery date. In short, where there is an available market at the due delivery date, the normal measure of damages is the amount (if any) by which the market price has dropped between that date and the date of actual delivery.[120] Where there is no available market, the measure of damages is the drop in the value of the goods between the two dates,[121] value being measured in the same way as on non-delivery.[122]

As in the case of non-delivery, resales by the buyer should be ignored where there is an available market. The mere fact that the buyer may have been able, by reselling forward, to avoid the consequence of a fall in the market is not something on which the seller is entitled to rely to reduce the damages, for it is *res inter alios acta*, stemming from the buyer's decision (which could involve him in substantial risk) not to cover his subcontract by buying in the market on the seller's failure to meet the due delivery date.[123] A resale forward at a price which turns out to be below the market price at the due delivery date would not increase the seller's liability, and (so the argument goes) there seems no good reason why the seller should be allowed on the one hand to claim immunity from the consequences of a resale by the buyer on adverse terms and on the other to disregard the market price if it is lower than the resale price. For these reasons, most writers agree that the decision in *Slater v Hoyle and Smith Ltd*,[124] where the below-market price realized by the buyer on resale was ignored, is to be preferred to the contrary decision of the Privy Council in *Wertheim v Chicoutimi*

---

117 Also relevant is whether the purpose of the purchase should have been within the seller's reasonable contemplation.

118 *Victoria Laundry (Windsor) Ltd v Newman Industries Ltd* [1949] 2 KB 528.

119 See below.

120 See *Elbinger AG v Armstrong* (1874) LR 9 QB 473, at p 477.

121 Value being determined by whatever test is the most appropriate in the light of the evidence available. See, for example, *Fletcher v Tayleur* (1855) 17 CB 21.

122 See p 372.

123 For a criticism of this approach, see p 387.

124 [1920] 2 KB 11.

Pulp Co[125] to the effect that the difference between the market price at the due date and the price obtained by the buyer on resale represented the limit of the seller's normal liability.

Consequential loss is recoverable in addition, as in the case of non-delivery.[126]

(ii) Goods bought for use

Where the goods are bought for use, not for resale, the measure of damages is quite different. The complaint of the buyer in this situation is not that he acquired an asset whose realizable value was diminished through the delay – for he did not intend to realize it at the due delivery date – but that he has been deprived of the use of the asset for the period of the delay and has thereby suffered inconvenience and/or lost income or increased expenditure in procuring the temporary use of comparable goods. Apart from pure inconvenience, the buyer seeks to be reimbursed for loss of income-profit and for any expenditure incurred in taking reasonable steps to mitigate such loss.

If the asset is of an income-producing kind – eg because it is a production machine or because it is utilized in the provision of income-producing services or is an asset that the buyer acquired for the purpose of letting on hire – the normal measure of damages is the loss of profit that the seller could reasonably have contemplated as flowing from the breach.[127] The buyer will, in accordance with the normal duty to mitigate, be expected to take reasonable steps to minimize loss of income, eg by hiring substitute goods, where this is possible. Any expenditure reasonably incurred in so doing is recoverable even if it proves to be greater than the loss that would have been suffered if no such steps had been taken.[128]

5. TENDER OF NONCONFORMING GOODS

If the seller tenders goods not conforming to the contract – eg because they do not correspond with the contract description or are unmerchantable or unfit for the known purpose – the buyer may: (i) reject the goods and, if the seller is not able or willing to re-tender in due time,[129] treat the contract as repudiated, and sue for damages for non-delivery;[130] or (ii) reject the goods and, instead of claiming damages, pursue a restitutionary remedy for recovery of the price, if paid; or (iii) accept the goods and thereby treat the breach of condition as a breach of warranty, and sue for damages as for breach of warranty.

125 [1911] AC 301.

126 *Elbinger AG v Armstrong*, n 120.

127 A good illustration is the landmark decision in *Victoria Laundry (Windsor) Ltd v Newman Industries Ltd*, n 118, in which the defendants, who were late in supplying a boiler required by the plaintiffs for their laundry and dyeing business, were held liable for loss of normal profits resulting from the plaintiffs' loss of business but not for the additional loss arising from the fact that certain contracts entered into by the plaintiffs with third parties were on unusually lucrative terms.

128 This is a general principle in the computation of damages. See p 121.

129 See p 341. For the additional remedies of a consumer buyer, see p 389.

130 For the measure of damages, see p 121.

(i) Remedies after rejection

The effect of the buyer's lawful rejection of the goods is to make the case one of non-delivery, and the buyer's remedies under (i) or (ii) above will be available accordingly, pursuant to the principles described earlier in this chapter. The only particular feature deserving mention is that since there is an implied undertaking on the part of the seller not to make a nonconforming tender,[131] the buyer, on rejecting, can, it is thought, include as part of his claim any expenses rendered futile in connection with the tender, eg the costs incurred in taking possession of the goods and installing them prior to rejection. There is no decision directly to this effect, but it has been held that a seller who fails to collect the goods promptly after notice of rejection is liable in damages for storage costs incurred by the buyer.[132] A buyer dealing as consumer has the additional remedies of repair or replacement, reduction of the price and rescission of the contract, described earlier.[133]

(ii) Remedies after acceptance

Where the buyer accepts, or is deemed to have accepted,[134] the goods, the conditions as to quality, fitness, etc, sink to the level of warranties, and damages fall to be assessed accordingly.[135]

6. DEFECT IN SELLER'S TITLE

The implied term as to title is a condition, breach of which entitles the buyer, if he acts before the defect has been cured,[136] to treat the contract as repudiated and:

(a) to recover damages for loss of bargain[137] or alternatively to recover any payment he has made as money paid on a total failure of consideration;[138] and

(b) to recover any consequential loss of a kind that the seller ought reasonably to have contemplated would flow from the breach, including abortive expenditure on repairs, liability incurred to a subpurchaser, and the like.

If the buyer elects to proceed with the contract after discovering the defect in the seller's title, his remedy is restricted to damages for breach of warranty; but, unless the defect in title has been cured by the time the action is heard, the measure of damages is in this particular case very similar to that applicable when the seller's repudiation is accepted, for in the absence of title, the buyer can continue to assert that he has not had the essential benefit contracted for, and that damages are to be assessed accordingly.[139] The buyer is entitled to recover the price in full as paid on

---

131 See p 341.
132 *Kolfor Plant Ltd v Tilbury Plant Ltd* (1977) 121 Sol Jo 390.
133 See p 344.
134 See pp 348 ff.
135 Below.
136 See p 287.
137 If the buyer has paid the price, this will, of course, form an element in the damages.
138 *Rowland v Divall* [1923] 2 KB 500.
139 *Warman v Southern Counties Car Finance Corp. Ltd* [1949] 2 KB 576.

a total failure of consideration even though he has had the goods and used them for a considerable period.[140]

7.   DAMAGES FOR BREACH OF WARRANTY

The measure of damages for breach of the implied warranty of quiet possession depends on the circumstances. Where the buyer is divested of possession, then prima facie the measure of damages is the value of the goods together with any special damage suffered, eg expenditure on repairs which is rendered abortive through the buyer's loss of possession.[141] But the buyer must take reasonable steps to mitigate his loss, so that where, for example, the third party's claim is a charge or encumbrance the amount of which is less than the value of the goods, the duty to mitigate might well require the buyer to avoid loss of possession by discharging the charge or encumbrance.

Where the buyer accepts, or becomes precluded from rejecting,[142] goods not conforming to the contract, his claim is limited to damages for breach of warranty.[143] The measure of damages is the estimated loss directly and naturally resulting, in the ordinary course of events, from the breach of contract,[144] and in the case of breach of warranty as to quality of goods, this is prima facie the amount by which the value of the goods as warranted exceeds their value in the state in which they are delivered.[145] For this purpose, the two values must be taken as at the contractual date for delivery.[146] Where there is an available market at the due delivery date, the market price must be taken as the warranted value.[147] The contract price as such is not relevant (except in so far as it is evidence of the market value), for the question is not how far the delivered value falls short of the sum the buyer agreed to pay[148] but how much more the goods would have been worth if tendered on the due delivery date in proper condition.[149] Where there is no available market, the value of the goods must be ascertained by other means. A working guide to the value as warranted is the price at which the buyer had contracted to resell the goods,[150] though this is not conclusive.[151] Alternatively, the estimated

140 *Rowland v Divall*, n 138. See p 215.
141 *Mason v Burningham* [1949] 2 KB 545.
142 See pp 348 ff.
143 Sale of Goods Act, s 11(4).
144 Section 53(2). This is, of course, the first limb of the rule in *Hadley v Baxendale* (1854) 9 Exch 341.
145 Section 53(3). If the value of the goods is zero, the seller is unable to recover any part of the price, so that the effect is very much the same as on rejection of the goods and termination of the contract. See *Argos Distributors Ltd v Advertising Advice Bureau* (1996) Feb 15 [1996] CLY 5285.
146 *Argos Distributors Ltd v Advertising Advice Bureau*, n 145.
147 *Loder v Kekulé* (1857) 3 CBNS 128.
148 The buyer may have bought at a bargain price amounting to no more than the value of the goods as in fact delivered to him, but he has nevertheless lost the benefit of the bargain, wholly or in part, if they are delivered in a damaged or inferior condition.
149 *Jones v Just* (1868) LR 3 QB 197.
150 See *Clare v Maynard* (1837) 6 Ad & E 519l.
151 Ibid.

cost of putting the goods into their warranted state may be taken as indicative of the diminution in value caused by the breach of warranty,[152] though again this is only a prima facie guide and will not apply where the carrying out of repairs would be uneconomic in the sense that it would not *pro tanto* restore the lost value.[153] The rule in s 53(3) is only a presumption and may be displaced by evidence that the buyer's loss is greater or less than the difference in value.[154]

Consequential loss claims may well arise upon the acceptance of goods which prove defective. Such claims will be governed by the rule in *Hadley v Baxendale*.[155] Loss will be treated as within the reasonable contemplation of the parties if, knowing of the breach, they ought reasonably to have contemplated as a serious possibility[156] the type of loss that in fact occurred, even if the severity of the loss could not reasonably have been envisaged.[157] If the buyer has sub-sold the goods and this was within the reasonable contemplation of his seller at the time of their contract, the buyer may be able to claim an indemnity for liability incurred or compensation paid to his subpurchaser.[158] The buyer must take reasonable steps to mitigate his loss, and must not exacerbate his loss by unreasonable action after discovery of the breach. The principles are easier to state than to apply, as is shown by the decision of the Court of Appeal in *H. Parsons (Livestock) Ltd v Uttley Ingham & Co Ltd*:[159]

> The plaintiffs, who were pig farmers, purchased from the defendants for £275 a bulk-food storage hopper for the purpose of storing pig nuts. Due to the failure of the defendants to open the ventilator at the top of the hopper after delivery, the pig nuts became mouldy. The plaintiffs nevertheless went on feeding the nuts to the pigs, since such nuts were not usually harmful. Subsequently, many of the pigs suffered an attack of an intestinal infection, *E. coli*, as the result of eating the mouldy nuts, and died, causing loss to the plaintiffs of between £20,000 and £30,000.

> Swanwick J held that the defendants had broken the implied condition of fitness for purpose under the Sale of Goods Act, that this implied term was an 'absolute warranty' and that, accordingly, the defendants were liable for all the loss resulting from the breach, whether or not this was within their reasonable contemplation. In case he was held wrong on this point, he went on to find that, at the time the hopper was supplied, neither a farmer in the position of the plaintiffs nor a hopper manufacturer in the position of the defendants could reasonably have contemplated that there was a serious possibility that pigs fed with mouldy nuts would become ill. Therefore if, contrary to

152 *Minster Trust Ltd v Traps Tractors Ltd* [1954] 3 All ER 136. The value of the goods as delivered may also be indicated by the price offered for the goods by a subpurchaser with knowledge of the defects (*Biggin & Co Ltd v Permanite Ltd* [1951] 1 KB 422).

153 However, the reasonable cost of repairs which in the event prove uneconomic may be recoverable as *consequential* loss if the buyer can show that the ordering of such repairs was a reasonable step in mitigation.

154 *Bence Graphics International Ltd v Fasson UK Ltd* [1998] QB 87. However this decision of the Court of Appeal is not free from difficulty, for the reasons trenchantly set out by Professor Guenter Treitel in his case note (1997) 113 LQR 188.

155 See p 121.

156 There is a judicial division of opinion as to the most appropriate expression of the degree of probability required. See n 98.

157 Ibid. In this respect there appears to be no distinction between contract and tort.

158 *Danecroft Jersey Mills Ltd v Criegee* (1987) Times, 14 April.

159 [1978] QB 791.

his ruling, the reasonable contemplation of the parties was relevant, the loss suffered by the plaintiffs would be too remote to be recoverable.

The Court of Appeal rejected the view that the strict duty owed under the Sale of Goods Act excluded the operation of the normal rule in *Hadley v Baxendale*, but upheld the verdict in favour of the plaintiffs on the grounds that:

(a) per Lord Denning MR, there was no distinction between the 'natural contempla-tion' test of remoteness in contract and the 'reasonable foreseeability' test in tort, and that where the loss suffered resulted from physical injury to the person or property of the plaintiff, he was entitled to recover the whole loss even if this was reasonably foreseeable only as a slight, rather than a serious, possibility;

(b) per Scarman LJ (with whom Orr LJ agreed), the cases did not support the distinction drawn by Lord Denning between economic loss and loss resulting from physical injury or damage, but that it was not necessary for the plaintiffs to show that the defendants ought reasonably to have contemplated that pigs would die from being fed mouldy nuts; it sufficed that they should have appreciated the serious possibility of pigs suffering injury or death if fed with nuts stored in a hopper unfit for storage purposes.

It is not easy to reconcile the decision with the rule in *Hadley v Baxendale*. Faced with the finding of the judge at first instance that injury to the pigs could not reasonably have been contemplated as the consequence of feeding them with mouldy nuts, Scarman LJ said that the true question was what should have been contemplated on the more general assumption that the hopper was unfit for storing nuts.

The assumption [to be made] is of the parties asking themselves not what is likely to happen if the nuts are mouldy but what is likely to happen to the pigs if the hopper is unfit for storing nuts suitable to be fed to them. While, on his finding, nobody at the time of contract could have expected *E. coli* to ensue from eating mouldy nuts, he is clearly – and as a matter of common sense, rightly – saying that people would contemplate, upon the second assumption, the serious possibility of injury and even death among the pigs.[160]

Now, contract law is well known for its abstract character, but is this not carrying abstraction too far? It involves ignoring the actual act of breach (failure to open the ventilator), which could not reasonably have been contemplated as attracting a risk of injury, and postulating instead some more generalized breach (failure to supply a hopper fit for the purpose) which could reasonably have been expected to produce injurious consequences. It involves ignoring the particular occurrence (mouldy nuts) that caused the death of the pigs and postulating some other event, within the broad label 'unfit for storing nuts', which did not occur but which would have been within the reasonable contemplation of the parties as an injurious event if it had occurred. The trial judge, for his part, appears to have applied the first limb of the rule in *Hadley v Baxendale* on the ground that 'the natural result of feeding toxic food to animals is damage to their health and may be death'. But it is clear from his findings of fact that for pigs to suffer illness through eating mouldy pig nuts was not usual or likely to happen in the ordinary course of events. Again, an assumption of a more generalized event (toxicity of pig food) is substituted for the actual occurrence (mouldy nuts) for the purpose of determining the consequences that could be said to flow naturally from the breach.

---

160 Ibid, at 812.

Moreover, if the plaintiffs as specialist pig farmers thought it safe to continue feeding mouldy nuts to the pigs, and thereby contributed to their own loss, why should the defendants be saddled with liability for the ensuing sickness and death of the pigs?

Finally, the remoteness test laid down by Scarman LJ seems to obliterate the distinction between the rules of remoteness in contract and those in tort.

Difficult questions arise where goods not conforming to warranty are of an income-producing kind and the buyer seeks to claim both diminution in their capital value and loss of profit. It is, of course, clear that the buyer cannot recover both the full diminution in warranted value as at the contract delivery date *and* the full loss of profit resulting from the nonconformity, for he could earn the profit only by using the goods and thus depreciating their capital value, and to allow him both loss of income-profit and loss of capital value as at due delivery date would be to duplicate his compensation. But in the much criticized decision in *Cullinane v British Rema Manufacturing Co*[161] the Court of Appeal went further and held that the buyer could not even split his claim as between capital-loss and income-loss, eg by confining his claim for loss of income-profit to a period shorter than the working life of the asset (viz to the period to trial of the action) and deducting the residual value of the goods[162] at the end of that period. In the case in question the Court of Appeal, by a majority, held the buyer to the limited number of years' profit claimed but declined to recognize that on this basis the loss of profit awarded did not absorb the buyer's capital loss, measured by the diminution in the capital value through the breach of warranty less the residual value at the end of the period for which the profit was claimed.

The outcome of this manifestly unjust decision appears to have been due to a misunderstanding on the part of the majority of the Court of Appeal (Morris LJ dissenting) as to the basis of the plaintiff's contentions. The duplication of damages which the majority assumed to be the consequence of the claim as pleaded did not exist, for in computing his loss of profit the plaintiff allowed for depreciation, with the result that the claim for loss of capital was effectively restricted to such part of the capital loss as was not referable to the period for which loss of profits had been claimed. It is to be hoped that, if a similar case should arise in the future, the decision in the *'Rema'* case will not be followed.

At the same time, it would be wrong to allow the plaintiff to split his claim in a purely arbitrary fashion. The test for determining at what point the period for loss of profits should end is to be determined by reference to what a reasonable buyer would do, taking proper steps to mitigate his loss. If, after trying to operate a defective machine profitably for a given period, it becomes prudent for him to cut his losses and dispose of the machine, then damages should be calculated on the basis of loss of profit to that date plus loss of capital, as depreciated to that date.

161 See n 102. For two devastating criticisms of this decision in which the mathematics were fully explored, see J. K. Macleod, 'Damages: Reliance or Expectancy Interest' [1970] JBL 19, and S. Stoljar, 'Normal, Elective and Preparatory Damages in Contract' (1975) 91 LQR 68.

162 Either by a lump-sum deduction from the capital loss claim or by an annual deduction from profits for depreciation.

8.   'AVAILABLE MARKET'

We have seen that where there is an available market, the market price is used as the yardstick to measure the damages to which the aggrieved party is entitled; and that where a market exists for goods of the contract description, the mere fact that in the buyer's particular circumstances he has no access to the market for the purpose of mitigating loss resulting from the seller's breach (eg because he has contracted to resell the identical goods he is buying) does not entitle him to plead the want of an available market unless he can show that those circumstances ought reasonably to have been within the seller's contemplation at the time of the contract. In short, the market-price rule will apply not only where there is in fact a market available to the buyer but also where there is a *deemed* available market, the buyer being precluded from relying on barriers to availability not within the reasonable contemplation of the seller.

Two questions now arise for consideration. What constitutes an available market and, given that a market in fact exists which would be available to the buyer but for his particular circumstances,[163] what degree of knowledge of those circumstances must the seller possess in order to debar him from contending that damages are to be assessed on the footing that the market was in fact available to the buyer? It should be borne in mind that the only effect of the absence of an available market is to displace the prima facie market-price rule embodied in s 51(3). The buyer will still be expected to take reasonable steps to mitigate his loss, eg by buying on a market which is not immediately available or by buying from a source which is not a market at all or procuring goods which are not the exact replica of those contracted for.[164]

(i)   The meaning of 'available market'

An available market is a market which either is or is deemed to be available to the buyer in the sense that he can reasonably be expected to have immediate recourse to it at the requisite time[165] and place if his seller fails to tender the contract goods on the due delivery date. The word 'market' has no precise meaning.[166] It is not

---

163 Characteristically, his commitment to resell the self-same goods he is buying, so that he cannot perform his subcontract by buying a substitute on the market. It is this typical situation that is considered in section (ii), below.

164 It is worth making this point, because there is sometimes a temptation to expand the concept of 'available market' for fear that the buyer may otherwise be entitled to claim that the alternative source of supply was not open to him. But whether a buyer should utilize an alternative source of supply depends not on whether this constitutes an available market but on what the buyer can reasonably be expected to do to mitigate his loss.

165 What is the requisite time has occasioned some discussion. In *Charter v Sullivan* [1957] 2 QB 117, Sellers LJ concluded that the market had to be available immediately after the breach. The learned editors of *Benjamin's Sale of Goods* disagree, regarding this as a rather too stringent approach, and offer in its stead 'a reasonable time after the breach, given the nature of the goods in question and the business situation of the plaintiff' (para 16–063). With respect, this is not tenable. For the purpose of computing damages, the market price has to be taken as at the date of the breach; *ergo*, the market must be available at that date. If it is not, value must be substituted for market price in calculating damages. This does not create a problem, for if the goods are able to be disposed of, or substitute goods purchased (as the case may be), soon after the breach, the price is strong evidence of the value of the goods at the date of the breach.

166 *Charrington & Co Ltd v Wooder* [1914] AC 71, per Lord Dunedin at 82.

confined to sales and purchases at a particular place set aside for the bringing together of seller and buyers but extends to any situation in which goods are dealt in as fungibles at prices fluctuating according to supply and demand. Hence, in order for there to be a market, the following conditions must co-exist:

(a) The goods available for purchase must, in relation both to the contract goods and to each other, be fungibles, that is, goods of which any one unit is considered in the locality or trade in question to be the exact equivalent[167] of any other unit of the same grade, sample or description, as opposed to a quantity of articles of which each is unique and varies in price according to its particular qualities. For example, there are well-established markets in designated types and grades of coffee, cocoa, soya beans, etc, and a buyer whose seller fails to deliver coffee of a type dealt in on the market can go into the market to obtain the exact equivalent of what his seller failed to deliver. On the other hand, the Court of Appeal has held that second-hand cars do not satisfy this test of fungibility, for no two second-hand cars are alike and there is thus no 'available market' for second-hand cars.[168] The same will almost invariably be true of goods to be made to the buyer's special order.

(b) The equivalent units must be available in sufficient quantities to meet all demands by would-be purchasers. In other words, the supply must at least equal the demand.[169]

(c) The price must be one which fluctuates with supply and demand, as opposed, for example, to a fixed retail price,[170] though it has been rightly pointed out that this distinction may be academic.[171]

Given that a market exists, it must be 'available' to the buyer in the sense of being within reasonable geographical access[172] to him and capable of being reached immediately after the contractual time for delivery has passed.[173] Where there is more than one such market, the relevant market is that which the seller ought reasonably to have expected the buyer to prefer.[174]

---

167 Within customary degrees of tolerance. If there is no exact equivalent, there is no available market but the buyer's duty to mitigate may require him to procure the *nearest* equivalent.

168 *Lazenby Garages Ltd v Wright* [1976] 1 WLR 459. But expressed in this form, the proposition is surely too sweeping. It may well be that on the particular facts of that case the car in question was unique, but it is certainly not true to say that there is no established market in second-hand cars. On the contrary, there are any number of car auctions, and general motoring and trade journals which give second-hand values for almost all makes and models of cars.

169 Where the action is by the seller for damages for non-acceptance, then naturally the converse applies, ie the demand must at least equal the supply (*W. L. Thompson Ltd v Robinson (Gunmakers) Ltd* [1955] Ch 177).

170 *Charter v Sullivan*, n 165, per Jenkins LJ at 128.

171 *McGregor on Damages*, para 20–109.

172 *Benjamin's Sale of Goods*, para 16–064.

173 *Contra*, ibid, para 16–063; but see n 165.

174 It is submitted that the buyer is not merely entitled but obliged to have the relevant market determined in this way. He is not allowed simply to pick the market where the price is highest and then assume as a matter of course that this is the price by reference to which his damages are to be assessed. The question in each case is whether the selection of the market is reasonable. Where two or more markets fit this description but the buyer does not in fact go into the market at all to make a substitute purchase, damages will presumably be assessed on the basis of the lowest price.

Even where the above conditions are satisfied, the market may not in fact be available to the buyer as an alternative source of supply because, for example, he has contracted to resell the self-same goods he is buying, ie the goods he is buying are fixed by his subcontract as the source of supply. But whether this is a circumstance which the buyer is entitled to invoke against the seller depends on the degree to which the seller ought to have contemplated it, a matter to which we will shortly turn.

(ii) 'Market price'

The relevant market price is the price to the buyer of buying at the due delivery date[175] in a market to which he can reasonably be expected to resort[176] for goods of a similar description and available, as far as possible, in similar conditions. Determining the appropriate market price on this basis is sometimes a matter of considerable difficulty. Indeed, it may prove impossible to locate on the market a transaction which conforms to the same contract description as that of the broken contract.[177]

9.   THE RELEVANCE OF SUBCONTRACTS BY THE BUYER

The mere fact that the buyer had contracted to sell goods of the same description as those which he is buying and intends utilizing the latter to meet the order placed by his own purchaser does not, as we have seen, displace the market-price rule so as to reduce the damages payable to the buyer if he had sold below the market price[178] or to increase them if he had sold above the market price,[179] for if the seller fails to deliver, then, unless the buyer has contractually committed himself to reselling the identical goods he has bought – an arrangement which, though not uncommon, is not the norm – he can perform his subcontract by buying equivalent goods in the market.[180] It makes no difference that the seller knew or ought to have realized that the goods were being bought for the purpose of resale; for this does not by itself indicate that those self-same goods will be designated in the subcontract as the specific contract goods. In order for the buyer to displace the market-price rule because of subcontracts he must establish:

175   Or if the seller is allowed a period for delivery, the last day of the period available to him for tender of delivery.
176   Which may well be the same market as that in which he originally contracted to buy the goods from the seller. But this is not necessarily the case. What has to be determined is the market available to the buyer, and the price of the goods on that market, in the situation in which the buyer finds himself at the date the goods should have been delivered, not the market in which the seller sells and the price on that market. Of course, the converse is true where the claim is by the seller against the buyer for non-acceptance.
177   For a good illustration in relation to an f.o.b. contract which could not be replaced by a similar contract, the contractual delivery month having effectively expired, see *The Golden Rio* [1990] 2 Lloyd's Rep 273.
178   *Williams Bros Ltd v Edward T. Agius Ltd*, n 84; p 369.
179   *Williams v Reynolds*, n 82; *Mohammad Habib Ullah (Sheik) v Bird & Co*, n 82. See p 369.
180   *Kwei Tek Chao v British Traders & Shippers Ltd* [1954] 2 QB 459, per Devlin J at 489.

(a)   that he purchased for resale;

(b)   that at the time of his contract to purchase he had committed himself or intended to commit himself to deliver to his subpurchaser the whole or part of the self-same goods he was buying, and not merely goods of equivalent description and quality;

(c)   that both (a) and (b) were known to the seller, or ought reasonably to have been within his contemplation, at the time of the head contract.

If the seller, though aware of (a), did not know and could not reasonably have contemplated (b), then he is entitled to assume that the buyer will be able to use the market to satisfy the sub-sale contract if the seller himself fails to deliver, so that the market-price rule will still apply.[181]

Where, however, the seller ought reasonably to have contemplated not merely that the buyer would resell the goods but that he would contract to pass on to his subpurchaser the identical goods he himself was buying, then the seller cannot contend that on non-delivery the buyer has an available market, and, accordingly, if the seller fails to deliver, the buyer's claim is for loss of profit[182] on the subcontract, or an indemnity for liability to his subpurchasers,[183] and will not be restricted to the excess of the market price over the contract price.[184] The problem is to know what suffices to bring the terms of the existing or projected subcontract into the seller's field of reasonable contemplation. Considerable confusion has been caused by certain loose dicta in some of the speeches in the House of Lords in *R. & H. Hall Ltd v W. H. Pim (Junior) & Co Ltd*,[185] which appear to suggest that it suffices if the contract entered into by the seller contemplated that the buyer might sub-sell the identical goods purchased. Thus Viscount Haldane stated:

> I think further that the contract and the conditions which it incorporates show that it was contemplated that the cargo might be passed on by way of sub-sale if the buyer did not choose to keep it for himself, and that the seller in such a case contracted to put the buyer in a position to fulfil his subcontracts if he entered into them. They were regarded by the terms of the original contract as subcontracts which the original buyer was to be in a position to enter into, with stipulations which bound the original seller to enable the original buyer to fulfil them. Whether the latter was likely to enter into such subcontracts and pass the cargo down a chain of resales is not material. It is enough that the contract contemplated by its terms that he should have the right to do so if he chose.[186]

This passage is undoubtedly responsible for much of the ensuing criticism of *Hall v Pim*, for, in suggesting that the only relevant factor is whether the seller ought

---

181   Ibid; *Aryeh v Lawrence Kostoris & Son Ltd* [1967] 1 Lloyd's Rep 63.

182   *R. & H. Hall Ltd v W.H. Pim (Junior) & Co* Ltd (1928) 30 Ll L Rep 159. But not necessarily the full loss. The seller is liable only for loss of the profit that the buyer might reasonably have been expected to make on a resale on normal terms, except where the seller was aware of the favourable terms of the resale contract. See p 376, n 127.

183   *Bence Graphics International Ltd v Fasson UK Ltd* [1998] QB 87, which, however, is open to the objection that, among other things, that it was not a case in which the buyer was committed to supply to his subpurchaser the selfsame goods he had contracted to buy.

184   Ibid.

185   See n 108.

186   (1928) 30 Ll L Rep 159 at 161.

reasonably to have contemplated resale of the goods,[187] the passage in question fails to make it clear that this alone would not convey to the seller that the resale contract could be satisfied only by the self-same goods purchased by the buyer himself. In other words, Viscount Haldane's speech appears to run counter to a long line of prior authority by omitting to mention that in order to displace the market rule, the circumstances must be such that the seller ought reasonably to have contemplated not merely *any* resale but a resale on terms requiring the buyer to deliver the very goods that he himself was buying.

But the speech must be read in context; and when one examines the particular facts in *Hall v Pim*, admirably set out in the speech of Lord Blanesburgh, it is apparent that what was involved was not a mere contemplation of resale but a standard-term trade association contract which expressly contemplated resale along a string and which was followed by resale and sub-sale contracts in identical form except as to dates, price and parties, these contracts in turn being supplemented by subsidiary agreements, suggested by the original sellers for their own intended advantage, by which all three preceding contracts were to be treated as string contracts relating to the identical cargo. A further fact which strongly influenced the House was the sharp practice of the sellers in so manipulating events as to produce by artificial means an apparent deferment of their breach of contract, with the aim of reducing their damages on a falling market.

We may therefore safely conclude that nothing in *Hall v Pim* displaces the rule established by previous authority, that for the seller to be charged with the buyer's loss of profit on a subcontract in a situation where there is otherwise an available market, it must be shown that the seller knew or ought reasonably to have contemplated a resale on terms appropriating to the resale contract the identical goods to be supplied to the buyer under the head contract.

10.   A CRITIQUE OF THE MARKET-PRICE RULE

The market-price rule is designed to put the buyer in broadly the same position as if the seller had tendered delivery on the due date; and the assumption is that the buyer will mitigate his loss by going into the market to buy substitute goods on the very day on which he ought to have had delivery of the contract goods from the seller. It is for this reason that the court disregards changes in market price after the due delivery date, the theory being that if the buyer delays making a substitute purchase, he makes his own speculation on the future movement of the market and can neither increase his damages because of a rise in the market price nor suffer a reduction in them if the market falls.

But the market-price rule is founded on an abstraction. It is concerned not with the factual situation of the plaintiff buyer but with the position of the notional, reasonable buyer, who is hypothesized as locked into remedial action on a single, statutorily defined date, the due delivery date. The market price at this due date is the yardstick for measuring damages whether the buyer 'covers' against the seller's

---

187   See n 98.

default before the due delivery date or defers his substitute purchase until well after that date or decides not to buy substitute goods at all. The market-price rule is not concerned with the price the buyer actually paid for the substitute goods but with the price he would have paid if he had purchased them on the contractual date for delivery of the original goods. Moreover, the rule, far from being an application of the duty to mitigate, is a distortion of it. In general contract law, though the duty to mitigate arises at the time when performance falls due,[188] in the sense that the due date of performance marks the time from which the innocent party comes under a duty to take reasonable steps to mitigate, reasonable action does not necessarily mean immediate action. Indeed, it may be prudent for the innocent party to delay steps in mitigation until he can secure substitute performance on more favourable terms. But the market-price rule entirely disregards prudence and reasonableness, and inflexibly fixes the due delivery date as the date at which mitigating action is expected, regardless of circumstances. If, for example, the contract price of goods is £1,000 and the market price at the due date is £1,100 but the buyer, holding back on a falling market, purchases his substitute goods a month later for £900, the courts insist that he is still entitled to recover £100 damages, ie the excess of £1,100 over £1,000, though he has lost nothing. The seller, it is said, is not entitled to have his damages diminished by the buyer's own efforts to mitigate his loss. But in general contract law that is precisely what the guilty party is entitled to demand. If steps in mitigation reduce the innocent party's loss, this enures for the benefit of the guilty party, and this is so even where the mitigating action in fact taken was not such as the guilty party could reasonably have required the innocent party to take. The innocent party cannot recover more than the loss which ultimately results from the breach. The strict adherence to the market-price rule goes against this fundamental principle.[189]

Yet the market-price rule does, on further examination, have much to commend it. It is true that in the case of contracts other than of sale, successful steps in mitigation, even if taken some time after the due date of performance, go to reduce the plaintiff's loss. But the defendant has to show that such steps were in truth connected to the breach in that they were designed to reduce its impact, and were not merely acts independent of the breach which the innocent party had intended to perform anyway; and the longer the gap between the due performance date and the date of the action alleged to be in mitigation, the harder it becomes for the guilty party to show that such action was connected to the breach at all. Where a commercial buyer makes regular purchases on the market, it becomes extremely difficult to say that a purchase made, say, a week after the original seller's failure to deliver was intended as a substitute for the original contract goods rather than as a wholly independent transaction.[190] Moreover, if a series of such purchases is made, which of them is to be taken as a substitute for the goods which the original seller

---

188   Unless there is an earlier anticipatory breach which the buyer elects to accept. See p 365.

189   For a recent criticism, see John N. Adams, 'Damages in Sale of Goods', [2002] JBL 553.

190   Article 2 of the American Uniform Commercial Code, in giving an aggrieved seller a comparable right of 'cure' through resale, requires him to identify the resale contract (s 2–706); but, rather curiously, there is no similar requirement that a buyer plaintiff should identify his substitute transaction to the contract broken by the seller.

failed to deliver? The market-price rule, rigid though it is, cuts through the difficulties of causal connection by ignoring events occurring after the due delivery date, and looking only at the market price at that date. It has the advantage of simplicity and of a greater measure of certainty, avoiding the formidable problems associated with internal calculation of profits and overheads, and the proof of these to the satisfaction of the court.[191] Sales law is probably the one area in which, because of the continuous course of dealing involved in market operations, the mitigation principles that apply to other contracts cannot on the whole work effectively, because the task of establishing the causal connection between breach and acts supposedly in mitigation is so great.

There is, however, one situation in which the rigidity of the market-price rule bears unfairly on the buyer, namely where he accepts the seller's anticipatory repudiation. A buyer whose seller repudiates before the due delivery date may not wish to take the chance of waiting until that date before covering his position by a substitute performance, for in waiting he runs the risk of a significant rise in the market price. True, if the price does rise, the quantum of his damages against the seller is correspondingly increased, but a right to sue for damages is not at all the same as money in the bank. If, by immediate cover, the buyer can show that he was taking reasonable steps to mitigate his loss, then his damages will indeed be measured by the excess of the actual price of the substitute goods over the contract price, even if, contrary to expectations, the market has gone down by the due delivery date.[192] But the buyer has no assurance that the court will approve his premature new purchase as a reasonable step in mitigation, particularly since, in its formulation of the market-price rule, the Act plainly contemplates that in ordinary circumstances the buyer will not go into that market until the date when the original goods should have been tendered.

Article 2 of the American Uniform Commercial Code protects the buyer in two ways. First, upon the seller's non-delivery or repudiation (whether before or after the due delivery date), the buyer is permitted (though not obliged) to 'cover' by making in good faith and without unreasonable delay any reasonable purchase of or contract to purchase goods in substitution for those due from the seller, and to recover as damages the excess of the 'cover price' over the contract price, together with any incidental or consequential loss, after deducting any expenses saved in consequence of the seller's breach.[193] The substitute purchase need not be made on an available market in order to qualify as reasonable; and if the purchase is reasonable, the relevant figure is the actual purchase price, not the market price as such. Secondly, if a buyer chooses not to 'cover' in this way, he can fall back on the market-price rule, which, however, takes as the relevant market price not the price on the due delivery date under the broken contract but that prevailing at the time when the buyer learned of the breach. In other words, though, like the English rule, the Code's market-price formula is abstract in that it is not concerned with the price

---

191   See p 405.
192   *Melachrino v Nickoll & Knight*, n 43.
193   Section 2–712. For a perceptive analysis, see White and Summers, *Uniform Commercial Code* (5th edn, 2000), para 6–3.

the buyer actually pays for substitute goods (or, indeed, whether he buys them at all), it is more realistic than the English rule in that it envisages a reasonable buyer as going into the market as soon as he learns of the breach[194] rather than waiting until the delivery date fixed by the original contract, and assumes that if the buyer had in fact covered, the cover price would have been the same as the market price.[195] There is much to be said for applying the Code provisions to the computation of damages where the seller commits an anticipatory breach.

11. ADDITIONAL REMEDIES OF THE CONSUMER BUYER

Part VA of the Sale of Goods Act 1979 gives a buyer dealing as consumer[196] a set of additional remedies where the goods do not conform to the contract of sale at the time of delivery. For this purpose goods do not conform to a contract if there is a breach of an express term or a term implied by s 13, 14 or 15 of the Act;[197] and goods are deemed to be non-conforming at that time if they do not conform at any time within six months starting with the date of delivery to the buyer[198] unless it is established that they did conform at that date or the application of the presumption is incompatible with the nature of the goods[199] or the nature of lack of conformity,[200] in which case the deeming provision does not apply.[201] Where the goods are non-conforming, the buyer is given the right to require the seller to repair or replace the goods or, alternatively, to require the seller to reduce the price by an appropriate amount or rescind the contract with regard to the goods in question,[202] The option whether to repair or replace lies with the buyer but is not exercisable if the remedy is impossible or disproportionate in comparison with the remedy of price reduction or rescission.[203] The remedy of price reduction is given only where the buyer is precluded from requiring repair or replacement or the seller has failed to repair or replace the goods as required.[204]

---

194 Though it would, perhaps, be preferable to substitute the time when the buyer accepted the repudiation. For a discussion of the difficulties attendant on 'learned of the breach' in cases of anticipatory breach, see White and Summers, *Uniform Commercial Code*, para 6–7.

195 Even under these provisions life is not all roses. In particular, the confluence of s 2–712 and s 2–713 may give the clever buyer an opportunity to have his cake and eat it, by making a new purchase which he will rely on as a substitute purchase by way of cover if the market price goes down but will ignore, and rely on the market price, if the market price goes up. For the differing views on whether he can do this, see White and Summers, *Uniform Commercial Code*, para 6–4.

196 As defined by s 12 of the Unfair Contract Terms Act 1977 (see p 328), applied by virtue of the Sale of Goods Act 1979, s 61(5A).

197 Sale of Goods Act 1979, s 48F.

198 Section 48A(3).

199 For example, if they are perishable foodstuffs.

200 As where they possess defects resulting from misuse by the buyer.

201 Sale of Goods Act 1979, s 48A(4).

202 Sections 48A(2), 48B, 48C. Under s 48E the court may order specific performance of the obligation to repair or replace.

203 Section 48B(3). As to when a remdy is to be considered disproportionate, see s 48B(4).

204 Section 48C(2).

15 Duties of the Buyer and Remedies of the Seller for Misrepresentation or Breach

1. DUTIES OF THE BUYER

In addition to any other obligations expressly or impliedly imposed by the contract the buyer must:

(a) from the date of the contract hold himself continually willing and able to perform his obligations at the due date;[1]

(b) take delivery of the goods when tendered in conformity with the contract;

(c) accept the goods, ie refrain from conduct signifying rejection;[2]

(d) pay for the goods in accordance with the contract.

These obligations are cumulative. Thus payment for the goods does not of itself absolve the buyer from his duty to take delivery, for the seller, in addition to being paid, is entitled to have the goods taken off his hands.[3]

2. THE SELLER'S REMEDIES IN OUTLINE

The seller's remedies for breach by the buyer, like those of the buyer for breach by the seller, fall broadly into two groups: those which enable the seller, if he wishes, to disengage from the transaction, and those which assume continuance of the contract. Into the first category fall rescission (that is, cancellation from the beginning) on the ground that the contract was induced by misrepresentation, economic duress or some other vitiating factor; acceptance of the buyer's anticipatory repudiation, thus ending the contract while preserving a right to damages; acceptance of the buyer's repudiation after performance has fallen due, with similar consequences; and resale of the goods under the provisions of the Sale of Goods Act or of the contract by reason of the buyer's default in payment. All these remedies have the effect of divesting the buyer of the property in the goods and revesting it in the seller. In this respect contracts of sale of goods are unique, for, in general, termination for breach, in contrast to rescission, does not affect accrued rights and liabilities, whereas in the case of sale the buyer's property rights are divested as much on termination as on rescission,[4] though not

---

1 Breach of this duty is an anticipatory breach, the remedies for which are discussed at p 396.

2 This is an obligation distinct from the duty to take delivery (see p 391) and its breach may attract different sanctions. For example, whereas unjustified non-acceptance is necessarily repudiatory, this is not always true of the failure to take delivery. See p 401.

3 See p 401.

4 See p 123.

with retrospective effect. Into the second group of cases fall claims by the seller for payment (in an action for debt), damages and the rarely granted specific performance[5] or mandatory injunction.[6]

Cutting across the above classification is the division of remedies into real and personal. Real remedies are those asserted against the goods themselves: lien, stoppage in transit, resale.[7] The first two of these represent remedies by way of security for the price and presuppose the continuance of the contract of sale; the third, by contrast, has the effect of terminating the contract.[8]

3.   TAKING OF DELIVERY

The taking of delivery is not as such an acceptance of the goods,[9] though it is usually the first step towards acceptance; and s 37 of the Sale of Goods Act inferentially imposes on the buyer the positive duty to take delivery[10] as an obligation distinct from the negative duty to accept, ie to refrain from unjustifiably rejecting.[11] The legal significance attached to the taking of delivery is indeed quite different from that annexed to acceptance. In taking delivery, the buyer does no more than give up his right to treat the act of tender as ineffective because made at the wrong time or place or in the wrong manner, and is not to be taken as signifying satisfaction with or willingness to retain the goods, as in the case of acceptance.

Whether it is for the seller to dispatch or deliver the goods or for the buyer to attend on the seller to collect them depends on the contract. Prima facie, the delivery point is the seller's place of business.[12]

---

5   A judgment for payment of the price can be regarded as a form of specific performance, though not so styled. However, if the right to the price depends on some act by the buyer which he declines to perform (such as nomination of a vessel to receive the goods, without which the seller cannot make delivery) and which is a concurrent condition of the right to payment under s 28 – see p 393 – the court will not ordinarily order performance of that act by the buyer but will leave the seller to his remedy in damages.

6   A mandatory injunction to perform an act needed to enable the seller to obtain payment is in essence an order for specific performance. For a case where it was granted, see *The Messiniaki Tolmi* [1982] QB 1248, where the documents to be presented by the seller under a letter of credit included a notice of readiness to be countersigned by the buyer, and the latter having refused to countersign the notice, the Court of Appeal upheld a mandatory injunction directing the buyer to do so, in default of which the notice was to be countersigned by a Master of the High Court. The case later went to the House of Lords on other issues. See [1983] 2 AC 787.

7   The revesting of the goods in the seller which results from rescission or termination of the contract does, of course, have proprietary effects, but is more accurately classified as the restoration of a real *right* resulting from the exercise of a personal power (or equity), rather than as a remedy.

8   See p 411.

9   See p 392.

10   Under s 27, the obverse of the seller's duty to deliver is the buyer's duty to accept. It is only indirectly, by making the buyer liable for loss to the seller caused by the buyer's refusal to take delivery, that s 37(1) indicates this as a duty.

11   See below.

12   Sale of Goods Act, s 29(2).

Any ground that would be available to the buyer for refusing to accept the goods provides equal justification for refusing to take delivery of them. Thus the buyer is not obliged to take goods that do not conform to the contract, nor need he take delivery where the property in the goods ought to have passed to him under the contract at or before the time of delivery but at that time the seller still lacks the right to dispose of the goods. But the buyer may be entitled to refuse delivery on grounds quite independent of any right to reject, in the sense of refusal to accept. So a tender of delivery may be treated as ineffectual if not made at a reasonable hour, or otherwise at the time or place or in the manner stipulated by the contract. Refusal of delivery in such a case is not the same as rejection of the goods *qua* non-acceptance. It is simply an objection to the mode of performance of the attempted act of delivery itself, and it is an objection which may properly be taken, even if the buyer has, by an actual or deemed acceptance, lost the right to reject the goods for nonconformity with the contract.

4.   ACCEPTANCE

Section 27 of the Act tells us that it is the duty of the buyer to accept and pay for the goods in accordance with the terms of the contract of sale.[13] Though framed in terms of a positive act, the duty to accept is no more than a negative obligation, ie, to refrain from conduct signifying rejection. Where refusal to take delivery is an intimation of rejection (as is usually the case), it will constitute a breach of the duty to accept; but rejection is not inevitably to be inferred from refusal to take delivery,[14] nor, of course, is such refusal the only form that rejection can take.

5.   PAYMENT

(i)   The payment obligation

It is the duty of the buyer to pay for the goods in accordance with the terms of the contract of sale. Payment must prima facie be in legal tender,[15] but this is not usually found convenient or insisted upon in transactions of any size, so that the presumption that payment is to be by legal tender is readily displaced. In any event, payment[16] by cheque is a good tender if it is not objected to by the seller[17] and the

---

13 The seller's remedies for non-acceptance are discussed at p 401.

14 See n 2.

15 See p 451.

16 It is therefore commonly said that the giving of a cheque is conditional payment. This, like the phrase 'payment by cheque' itself, is not an accurate statement of the effect of giving a cheque, which is simply to make a fresh promise of payment in documentary form and with the effects prescribed by the Bills of Exchange Act 1882. Payment results from the honouring of the cheque and the consequent release of funds to the payee. See p 460.

17 Moreover, if in previous transactions between the same parties the seller has always taken payment by cheque, payment by this method may be implied into the contract from the prior course of dealing.

cheque is duly honoured.[18] With modern methods of transfer of money – Giro, direct debit, banker's payment – nice questions may arise as to the precise moment at which payment is to be treated as having been made.[19] Payment must usually be made at the seller's place of business,[20] but the contract may otherwise provide, and contractual provisions as to the time of payment may by necessary implication govern the place of payment. Thus if the contract provides for 'C.O.D.' (cash on delivery), payment must be made against delivery at the contractual delivery point. It is normally the duty of the buyer (like any other debtor) to see the money gets into the hands of his seller,[21] so that the buyer takes the risk of this failing to occur, eg because of miscarriage of the post or through failure of the buyer's bank to honour the buyer's cheque when in funds[22] or to comply with the buyer's instructions to remit the price to the seller.

(ii) Time of payment

The seller is entitled to be paid at the time expressly or impliedly laid down in the contract. This, however, is subject to the qualification that any conditions precedent to the right to be paid which are prescribed by the Sale of Goods Act or the contract must first be complied with.[23] The time of payment is prima facie not of the essence, even on a commercial sale.[24] This reflects the fact that the most the seller is likely to lose from delay in payment is interest on his money,[25] so that forfeiture of the buyer's right to proceed with the contract would be a penalty disproportionate to the injury suffered by the seller through non-payment.[26]

(iii) Conditions of payment

The seller's right to be paid the price is prima facie dependent on the fulfilment of two conditions. First, he must be ready and willing to tender delivery of the goods in exchange for the price.[27] Secondly, he must show either that the property in the

---

18 If it is dishonoured, whether because of lack of funds in the drawer's account or because of the drawee bank's insolvency, the seller has the option of suing on the cheque or on the original consideration, the former being almost invariably more advantageous (see p 513). He also becomes an unpaid seller for the purpose of the Sale of Goods Act, with real rights over the goods so long as the buyer has not acquired both possession and property. See p 409. By contrast, payment by credit card is absolute in that the seller of the goods is considered to accept the card issuer's promise of payment as discharging the buyer's liability for the price, whether or not the issuer fulfils its promise. See *Re Charge Card Services Ltd* [1988] 3 All ER 702 and p 462.

19 See ch 17.

20 *Benjamin's Sale of Goods* (6th edn, 2002), para 9–046.

21 Ibid.

22 As to the buyer's rights against his bank in this situation, see p 554.

23 See below.

24 Contrast the position as regards the seller's duty of delivery (p 271).

25 Where, however, the money is needed to enable the seller to complete some other transaction and that fact is known to the buyer at the time of his contract with the seller, time of payment may by implication be of the essence, and the seller may even be entitled to claim as part of his damages the extra expenses incurred in completing the transaction (*Wadsworth v Lydall* [1981] 2 All ER 401).

26 Blackburn, *Contract of Sale* (3rd edn, 1910), p 507.

27 Sale of Goods Act, s 28.

goods has passed[28] or that under the terms of the contract the price became payable on a certain day irrespective of delivery and that that day has arrived.[29]

1.   Payment and delivery as concurrent conditions

Unless otherwise agreed, delivery of the goods[30] and payment of the price are concurrent conditions; that is to say, the seller must be ready and willing to give possession of the goods to the buyer in exchange for the price, and the buyer must be ready and willing to pay the price in exchange for possession of the goods.[31] What s 28 requires is not coincidence of performance of the delivery and payment obligations but coincidence of willingness to perform. If one party is unable or unwilling to perform, the other party need take no steps towards performance. If neither party is able or willing to perform, there is a stand-off, and the contract is in suspense as regards the delivery and payment obligations.

Given that each party is ready and willing to perform, then whether the first step has to be taken by the seller or by the buyer depends on the contractual delivery point. Prima facie, this is the seller's premises,[32] and if this presumption is not displaced, it is for the buyer to present himself there with the price and collect the goods in exchange. Where delivery is to be made to the buyer's premises, it is obviously the seller who must make the first move. If the contractual delivery point is elsewhere, the parties must meet there to exchange at the appointed hour.

2.   The right to sue for the price

Section 49 of the Act (omitting sub-s (3)) provides as follows:

> 49(1) Where, under a contract of sale, the property in the goods has passed to the buyer and he wrongfully neglects or refuses to pay for the goods according to the terms of the contract, the seller may maintain an action against him for the price of the goods.
>
> (2) Where, under a contract of sale, the price is payable on a day certain irrespective of delivery and the buyer wrongfully neglects or refuses to pay such price, the seller may maintain an action for the price, although the property in the goods has not passed and the goods have not been appropriated to the contract.

Section 49(1) is a curious provision. It emphasizes the obvious point that in order for the seller to be able to sue for the price, the price must have become due under the terms of the contract. But if this requirement is satisfied, why is there need of more? Why should the subsection add a further stipulation that the property in the goods shall have passed to the buyer? This would seem to be simply faulty drafting. Obviously, the seller is free to bargain for payment of the price in advance of the passing of the property, and indeed this is the case with almost every conditional sale agreement.[33] Hence s 49(1) is probably to be treated as if it did no more than

---

28 Ibid, s 49(1).
29 Ibid, s 49(2).
30 Ie, delivery in accordance with the contract. Thus s 28 involves a willingness to give possession of goods fulfilling, inter alia, any terms implied under ss 12–15 of the Act.
31 Section 28.
32 Section 29(2).
33 See p 709.

ascribe to the parties a prima facie intention not to require payment of the price until the passing of the property to the buyer. This is not unreasonable, for no buyer who is not taking on credit ordinarily expects to pay for goods unless he is getting ownership as well as possession, and if it is intended that he shall pay in advance of acquiring the property, then the contract should so provide.

Where the buyer's refusal to pay is associated with his failure to accept the goods, then, in lieu of suing for the price, the seller can claim damages for non-acceptance, though it is only in unusual circumstances that he will wish to pursue the latter course. But if the passing of the property, or indeed any other condition precedent to the seller's right to the price, is obstructed by the buyer, the seller's remedy is in damages. Thus in *Colley v Overseas Exporters (1919) Ltd*:[34]

> On a contract for the sale of unascertained goods f.o.b., the buyer failed to name the vessel on which the goods were to be shipped, with the result that they had to be left at the dock. The sellers sued for the price.

Held: the property in the goods had not passed, and the action failed.

The drafting of s 49(2) is at first sight equally odd. Why should a contractual provision making the price payable irrespective of delivery carry with it the further implication that the price is payable irrespective of the passing of the property? The answer would seem to be that in most cases delivery is the act which appropriates unascertained goods to the contract, and since the property in such goods cannot pass until they are ascertained[35] a provision for payment in advance of delivery would usually be stultified if the seller were still to have to show that the property had passed.

6.   RESCISSION OF THE CONTRACT

The grounds for rescission *stricto sensu*[36] are the same as in other classes of contract. The most common event triggering off the seller's right to rescind is the buyer's fraud – typically, in misrepresenting his identity[37] or giving a cheque for the price knowing that there are no funds to meet it.[38] But the seller will usually have to act swiftly if rescission is to be effective. All too often he finds his right barred because of a resale by the buyer to an innocent third party.[39]

The remedy of rescission is available to the seller even if both the possession and the property in the goods have passed to the buyer[40] and even if the buyer has become bankrupt,[41] for the seller's right to rescind is an equity which binds the buyer's trustee in bankruptcy.[42]

---

34   [1921] 3 KB 302.
35   Sale of Goods Act, s 16.
36   That is, cancellation *ab initio* (eg, for misrepresentation), as opposed to termination for breach. See p 123.
37   See p 77.
38   See, for example, *Car & Universal Finance Co Ltd v Caldwell* [1965] 1 QB 525.
39   See p 425.
40   As in *Car & Universal Finance Co Ltd v Caldwell*, n 38.
41   *Re Eastgate* [1905] 1 KB 465; *Tilley v Bowman Ltd* [1910] 1 KB 745.
42   See p 27.

7.   ANTICIPATORY BREACH

Where, before the tender of delivery, the buyer signifies his refusal or inability to proceed with the contract,[43] the seller may either accept the repudiation, that is, treat it as immediately discharging the contract, and sue for damages, or hold the contract open for performance, in which case it continues in force for the benefit of both parties.[44]

(i)   Acceptance of the repudiation

1.   *Relevance to buyer's liability of seller's own inability to perform*[45]

The first question which arises is whether the buyer can justify his apparently repudiatory act by showing that the seller would have been unable to perform the contract even if it had proceeded. Where the buyer's refusal to accept delivery is expressly grounded on the seller's own future inability to perform, there is no difficulty, for the buyer is entitled to treat that inability as an anticipatory breach, so that his own act is not a renunciation of his duty to accept the goods but an acceptance of the seller's own repudiation.[46] But what if the buyer was unaware that the seller would not be able to perform the contract? In principle, this should make no difference, for it is a well-settled rule of contract law that if a party purports to terminate a contract on an unjustified ground, he can subsequently, on discovering the existence of facts that would have entitled him to bring the agreement to an end, rely on those facts as validating his apparent repudiation.[47] The difficulty arises because of the decision of the Court of Appeal in the curious case of *Braithwaite v Foreign Hardwood Co Ltd*:[48]

> The sellers contracted to deliver a quantity of rosewood by ship to Hull in two instalments. After shipment of the first instalment but before its arrival, the buyers wrote to say that they would not accept it, contending that they were entirely discharged from their obligations under the contract by reason of the sellers' breach of an alleged collateral oral agreement not to sell rosewood to anyone else. The buyers maintained their refusal to accept the first consignment after tender[49] of the bill of lading, where-upon the sellers resold the goods and claimed as damages the difference between the

---

43   Not every threatened breach is repudiatory. The test is whether the breach would be repudiatory if committed after the time for performance has arrived. For example, an advance warning that the buyer will not be able to take delivery until a few days after the contractual delivery date will not usually constitute a repudiation of the contract.

44   See pp 126–127.

45   This question arises also in relation to the assessment of damages, as to which see p 398, n 63.

46   For the assessment of damages in such a case, see p 365.

47   *Boston Deep Sea Fishing & Ice Co v Ansell* (1888) 39 Ch D 339; *Taylor v Oakes, Roncoroni & Co* (1922) 127 LT 267. For the special position of documentary sales, see p 944.

48   [1905] 2 KB 543. For excellent discussions of this case, see M. G. Lloyd, 'Ready and Willing to Perform: The Problem of Prospective Inability in the Law of Contract' (1974) 37 MLR 121; *Benjamin's Sale of Goods*, paras 9–012 ff, 19–162 ff.

49   The report of the decision in the *Law Reports* suggests that Collins MR thought the sellers' agents had merely indicated a readiness to hand over the bill of lading (see [1905] 2 KB 543 at p 549), which is how Salmon LJ interpreted the facts in *Esmail v J Rosenthal & Sons Ltd* [1964] 2 Lloyd's Rep 447 at 466; but the headnote to that report and the judgments as set out in the other reports leave little room for doubt that the bill of lading was actually tendered. The ensuing analysis assumes that this was the case.

contract price and the market price. The same happened when the bill of lading for the second consignment was tendered. Subsequently, the buyers discovered that a small percentage of the first consignment of rosewood was of a quality inferior to that stipulated in the contract.

The buyers, having failed to establish the oral agreement, claimed that damages for their renunciation in regard to the first consignment[50] should be nil, because at the time of such renunciation the sellers, by reason of the defective portion of the first consignment, were not able to show that they were ready and willing to perform at the time of the buyers' renunciation.

It was held that the buyers, having adhered to their repudiation of the contract, had waived performance of the conditions precedent to the sellers' right to enforce the contract and could not, by reason of their after-acquired knowledge, set up a defence they had previously elected not to make.

The decision has generated much controversy. It has been applied[51] and doubted[52] but never reversed. Much of the controversy stems from the difficulty of extracting the true ratio of the decision from the judgments,[53] and indeed of determining to what extent the court had addressed its mind to issues of fact that ought to have been material to the inquiry.

The first point to make is that, though the case has often been treated as one of anticipatory breach accepted by the innocent party, in fact on the buyers' initial renunciation after shipment of the goods and before their arrival, the sellers elected to hold the contract open for performance as regards each consignment until the tender of the bill of lading relating to that consignment, so that what ultimately happened was that the sellers accepted the buyers' actual breach[54] in refusing to accept a tender of the bills of lading. It is, however, convenient to discuss the case at this point, since the issues it raises are the same whether the accepted repudiation[55] took place before or after performance fell due. Secondly, it is well settled that ignorance of an available ground for rejecting an actual or prospective tender of performance does not preclude the party allegedly in breach from relying on that ground when he later discovers it.[56] Thirdly, while it is true that renunciation by one party which is accepted by the other absolves that other from future

50 The contract was considered severable and the nonconformity affected only the first consignment.
51 *Taylor v Oakes, Roncoroni & Co*, n 47; *British & Beningtons Ltd v North Western Cachar Tea Co* [1923] AC 48.
52 See *British & Beningtons Ltd v North Western Cachar Tea Co*, n 51, per Lord Sumner at 70; *Benjamin's Sale of Goods*, para 19–164. See also *Gill & Duffus S.A. v Berger & Co Inc* [1984] AC 382; *The Simona* [1989] AC 788, per Lord Ackner at 805.
53 See *Benjamin's Sale of Goods*, paras 19–162 ff.
54 If it was a breach. See below as to the effect of the sellers' earlier act in shipping nonconforming goods.
55 There is no doubt that the repudiation in each case was accepted, and this has been assumed in subsequent cases. See *Taylor v Oakes Roncoroni & Co*, n 47, per Scrutton J at 271; *The Simona*, n 52, per Lord Ackner at 803. In *The Simona* Lord Ackner expressed surprise (at 803) at the statement by Collins MR in *Braithwaite* (n 48 at 551) that the contract had been kept alive. But it is clear that what Collins MR was referring to was not the repudiation on tender of the bills of lading but the earlier renunciation after shipment, when the sellers elected to keep the contract on foot. See further p 398.
56 See cases cited n 51.

performance,[57] it does not render irrelevant that other's willingness and ability to perform at the time of the renunciation of which he complains, for if at that time he was not himself able and willing to perform, then it is he who is guilty of an anticipatory breach which (whether or not known to the renouncing party) makes the renunciation justified.[58] Whether, on the facts in *Braithwaite*, the sellers were indeed unable to perform or whether they could have rectified their breach by a fresh tender, if necessary,[59] remains unclear.[60] If they had still been ready and willing to do so, the buyers would not have been entitled to maintain their repudiation, but the issue was never discussed. The buyers seem to have assumed that the shipment of the nonconforming goods would not merely have been a ground for their rejection but would have constituted a repudiation of the contract, an assumption not in conformity with legal principle.[61]

The assumption in *Braithwaite* that a party's renunciation of a contract precludes him from relying on a prior repudiation by the other party has rightly been characterized as heretical.[62] Its consequence is that a seller who would inevitably have been in breach if the contract had continued until the due date for performance is compensated for a loss calculated on a wholly unreal basis.[63]

The final point concerns the onus of proof. It is questionable whether in modern law a party alleging a breach of contract is under any initial onus to show that he himself was ready and able to perform. Such a contention is implicit in his pleading[64] and it is submitted that it is for the defendant not only to plead the contrary but also to discharge the legal burden of proving it at the trial.

The decision in *Braithwaite* was unsuccessfully invoked in *The Simona*[65] as authority for the proposition that a party who elects to *affirm* a contract after an anticipatory repudiation is nevertheless entitled to withhold his own performance

---

57 The impossibility of such performance through subsequent events that would have been outside his control goes only to the measure of damages to which he is entitled and does not affect his right to succeed on liability.

58 See *British & Beningtons Ltd v North Western Cachar Tea Co*, n 51, per Lord Sumner at 71–72.

59 It is doubtful whether the deviation in quality would have justified rejection by the buyer.

60 The question was adverted to by Lord Sumner in *British & Beningtons Ltd v North Western Cachar Tea Co*, n 51 at 71.

61 See p 341. The failure to distinguish a shipment of nonconforming goods from a total renunciation of the contract through an unwillingness or inability to perform at the due date which manifests itself before performance is due may account for the decision of the House of Lords in *Gill & Duffus S.A. v Berger & Co Inc*, n 52 and p 396.

62 Michael G Lloyd, 'Ready and Willing to Perform: The Problem of Prospective Inability in the Law of Contract' (1974) MLR 121 at 129. However, the actual decision could now be justified on the entirely distinct ground, not argued in the case, that in a c.i.f. contract the buyer's right of rejection of nonconforming goods does not arise until their arrival and therefore cannot be invoked to justify a refusal to take up and pay for the documents. See *Gill & Duffus S.A. v Berger & Co Inc*, n 52, a decision which is itself not free from difficulty and is discussed pp 944–945.

63 A point forcefully made (though without reference to *Braithwaite*) in *The Mihalis Angelos* [1971] 1 QB 164, where the Court of Appeal, having declined to treat as unlawful a repudiation made on a wrong ground when a legitimate ground for termination existed, held that if that view were wrong, damages would in any case be purely nominal.

64 This was expressly stated in the former RSC Ord 18, r 7(4) but there is no equivalent in the CPR.

65 See n 52.

until the repudiating party gives notice of his change of heart and his willingness to perform the contract. Lord Ackner pointed out that in *Braithwaite* the innocent party had elected to accept the repudiation; if that was not the case, then the decision was wrong.[66]

2. Measure of damages

This is laid down by s 50, which is the exact counterpart of the provision in s 51 relating to non-delivery, and the observations made in relation to s 51 apply *mutatis mutandis*, except that, of course, the measure of damages for non-acceptance where there is an available market is the excess of the contract price over the market price, whereas in the case of an action for non-delivery it is the excess of the market price over the contract price.[67] The relevant rules are examined a little later, in relation to refusal to accept after the time for acceptance has arrived.[68] The main difference in cases of anticipatory breach is that the second limb of s 50(3) would appear to be inapplicable,[69] so that where the time for acceptance is not fixed, damages for the buyer's anticipatory repudiation are determined by reference to the date on which he would have been obliged to accept the goods,[70] subject to his duty to mitigate, which arises immediately upon his acceptance of the repudiation.[71]

Where there is no available market for the goods, some other suitable measure of damages must be selected, eg excess of contract price over the seller's actual resale price if he can resell them or, if another buyer cannot be found, excess of contract price over cost of manufacture or acquisition, credit being given for the scrap value of the goods.[72]

(ii) Affirmation of the contract

Where the seller elects to affirm the contract, it continues for the benefit of both parties, and the buyer (unless committing a further act of renunciation which the seller accepts) is entitled to tender performance on the due date notwithstanding his earlier repudiation.[73] The seller for his part, having affirmed the contract, is not entitled to withhold his own performance until the other party indicates a willingness to perform. The effect of his affirmation is to negate the earlier renunciation, and he is not entitled to treat this as continuing in force until the other party's intimation of a willingness to perform. Such willingness must be assumed unless and until there is a fresh repudiatory act by the other party.

Having elected to affirm the contract after the buyer's anticipatory repudiation, the seller is not obliged to take steps to mitigate his prospective loss, even if the buyer

66 *The Simona*, n 52. See also pp 944, 126.
67 For the text of s 50, see p 402.
68 See p 402.
69 By analogy with the position under s 51(3). See p 365, n 46.
70 For problems in determining the due date of acceptance, see p 346. See also p 402.
71 *Benjamin's Sale of Goods*, para 16–077 and pp 122, 126.
72 Nice questions of assessment arise where the buyer orders goods to be specially made for him and repudiates when they have been partially manufactured.
73 See p 126.

indicates that he is maintaining his renunciatory attitude, unless the reiterated anticipatory breach is accepted by the seller. In short, the buyer cannot force the seller to abandon the contract, or to take precautionary steps in anticipation of such abandonment, prior to the due date of acceptance of the goods. In this respect the seller's position on the buyer's anticipatory breach differs from that arising when the time for acceptance of the goods has arrived. Apart from this, the seller's election to affirm does not alter the basis of assessing damages if the buyer ultimately fails to accept the goods, because even where the buyer's anticipatory breach is accepted, damages are measured by reference to the state of affairs at the due date for acceptance.[74]

8.   REFUSAL TO TAKE DELIVERY

Where the buyer's failure or refusal to take delivery signifies an intention to reject the goods, the seller is entitled to pursue his remedies for non-acceptance as described in the ensuing section.[75] Similarly, if the buyer's breach is a repudiation, as where the time of taking delivery is of the essence, the seller can treat the contract as discharged and recover damages at common law.[76] In such a case he cannot, except at the request or with the consent of the buyer, postpone his duty to mitigate by holding the contract open for performance. If he does elect to affirm the contract, his extra loss suffered through so doing will not be recoverable from the buyer.[77]

Section 37 provides as follows:

> (1) When the seller is ready and willing to deliver the goods, and requests the buyer to take delivery, and the buyer does not within a reasonable time after such request take delivery of the goods, he is liable to the seller for any loss occasioned by his neglect or refusal to take delivery, and also for a reasonable charge for the care and custody of the goods.

> (2) Nothing in this section affects the rights of the seller where the neglect or refusal of the buyer to take delivery amounts to a repudiation of the contract.

It is to be observed that in referring to 'loss occasioned by his neglect or refusal to take delivery', s 37(1) is not contemplating a loss of bargain situation of the kind arising from the buyer's repudiation (an eventuality separately dealt with in s 37(2)) but is essentially dealing with delay in taking delivery. Damages for refusal to take delivery altogether, though theoretically claimable under s 37, would in practice be picked up as part and parcel of general damages either under s 50 for non-acceptance or at common law for repudiation of the contract.[78] The purpose of s 37

---

74 As a corollary, by electing to hold the contract open for performance, the seller runs the risk of an intervening event which frustrates the contract and thus releases the buyer from liability.

75 See p 401. As to instalment deliveries, see pp 271 ff.

76 It follows that the provisions of the Sale of Goods Act relating to non-acceptance do not cover every case where the contract falls through on account of the buyer's repudiation; for the buyer may indeed accept the goods for the purpose of the Act (eg by waiving examination and accepting in advance of delivery) but later repudiate the contract by declining to take delivery. In such a case, the seller's right to damages arises at common law and is not governed by s 50.

77 Cf the position on non-acceptance, p 402.

78 See n 76. In addition, special damages are recoverable under s 54.

is to give the seller a right to special damages for loss resulting from the buyer's failure to take delivery on time, eg the expenses incurred by the seller in making an abortive tender,[79] or the extra costs of prolonging insurance cover.[80] The section also entitles the seller to reasonable storage charges.[81]

9. NON-ACCEPTANCE

As we have seen, non-acceptance must be distinguished from the mere failure to take delivery.[82] Non-acceptance denotes rejection of the goods. Failure or refusal to take delivery may signify an intention to reject, but it may denote no more than that the buyer is not yet ready to receive the goods. The distinction is not without importance, for a failure or refusal to take delivery when tendered is not necessarily repudiatory (since the time of taking delivery is not always of the essence), whereas it is implicit in s 50 that a neglect or refusal to accept the goods (ie a wrongful rejection of them) is a repudiation, at least as to that part of the contract relating to the goods in question.[83]

The buyer's refusal to accept the goods may be intimated either before tender of delivery or on or after such tender. The time of refusal to accept does not affect the basis on which damages are assessed, though it may influence the quantum of the seller's recoverable expenses or other consequential loss. For example, if non-acceptance is intimated before tender of delivery, the seller has the opportunity to avoid the expense of an abortive tender, whereas if the buyer signifies non-acceptance at the time of tender of delivery, the seller will wish to recover any packing and transportation costs incurred in making the tender and in taking the goods back to his premises, while if non-acceptance is not intimated until after delivery has been taken the seller (if not entitled to leave the goods with the buyer and to sue for the price[84]) will incur still greater expense in collecting them.

Though the taking of delivery does not by itself constitute acceptance,[85] it represents in most cases the first and positive stage of acceptance, and it would seem that it is to this positive stage that s 50(3) of the Act refers when it speaks of 'the time or times when the goods ought to have been accepted'. In other words, for the purpose of s 50(3) the due date of acceptance means the date on which the buyer

---

79 For example, wasted transportation costs.
80 Loss resulting from accidental destruction of the goods following the buyer's failure to take delivery would be dealt with not by damages under s 37 but by transfer of risk under s 20(2), as to which see p 251.
81 *Somes v British Empire Co* (1860) 8 HL Cas 338. An unusual alternative route, successfully followed by the plaintiffs in *Penarth Dock Engineering Co v Pounds* [1963] 1 Lloyd's Rep 359, is an action in tort for mesne profits for trespass to the plaintiff's property, the measure of damages being the value of the benefit to the defendant from his unauthorized use rather than the loss suffered by the plaintiff.
82 But the Act is not entirely consistent in the meaning it gives to 'acceptance'. See text and n 86.
83 For the position on instalment contracts, see p 271.
84 See below and p 394.
85 See p 391.

ought to have taken delivery.[86] Similarly, non-acceptance must be taken to occur where the buyer performs a positive act of rejection, eg by refusing a tender of delivery with intention to reject or by communicating his intention not to accept.

If the property in the goods has already passed to the buyer at the time he rejects them, the seller has the option of claiming damages for non-acceptance or simply suing for the price.[87] Almost invariably, the latter remedy, where available, is to be preferred, for not only does it avoid problems of computation of damages and the duty to mitigate but also, in the absence of at least an arguable defence, the seller can obtain final summary judgment under Ord 14 of the Rules of the Supreme Court.

Where the seller elects to claim damages, or is obliged to do so because he has not become entitled to the price, he gains little by seeking to hold the contract open for performance against the wishes of the buyer, for this will not justify a delay in taking steps to mitigate his loss.[88]

The measure of damages for non-acceptance is provided by s 50 in the following terms:

> (2) The measure of damages is the estimated loss directly and naturally resulting, in the ordinary course of events, from the buyer's breach of contract.

> (3) Where there is an available market for the goods in question the measure of damages is prima facie to be ascertained by the difference between the contract price and the market or current price at the time or times when the goods ought to have been accepted or (if no time was fixed for acceptance) at the time of the refusal to accept.

Section 50(2) represents the first limb of the rule in *Hadley v Baxendale*[89] and this is crystallized by s 50(3). In addition, special damages may be recoverable under s 54. As in the case of claims by the buyer, the computation of damages for non-acceptance depends on whether or not there is an available market in which the seller can sell elsewhere.

(i) Available market

Where there is an available market, the assumption is that the seller will have recourse to it by selling in the market the goods his buyer refused to accept. Hence s 50(3) fixes the measure of damages as prima facie the amount by which the

---

86 Any other conclusion is fraught with difficulty. If, for the purpose of s 50(3), 'accept' were to be construed as denoting the complete act of acceptance, ie not only the taking of delivery but retention of the goods for such period or in such circumstances as to result in loss of the right to reject, then (a) it would be extremely difficult to fix the due date of acceptance (there being no way of establishing the due date of a negative, ie the date on which the buyer ought not to have rejected), and (b) rejection of delivery with the intention of non-acceptance would constitute an anticipatory breach, not an actual breach, of the duty to accept – an approach that has never been adopted.

87 See p 394.

88 See pp 126–127. If the buyer decides after all to accept the goods after the due date for acceptance, then if the seller affirms the contract, his remedy is to sue for damages for delay. See pp 400, 407.

89 (1854) 9 Exch 341.

contract price exceeds the market or current price at the due date for acceptance.[90] In addition, the seller is entitled to be compensated[91] for any expenses or other special damage reasonably incurred, eg in bringing the goods back from the original buyer's premises and in storing, insuring and reselling them. Where at the due date for acceptance[92] the market price has risen, so that the effect of the buyer's repudiation is to enable the seller to resell at a higher price, the increase must be offset against any claim by the seller for special damages under s 54.[93]

What is an available market so far as the seller is concerned? If the seller actually offers the goods for sale, there is no available market unless there is one actual buyer on that day at a fair price. If there is no actual offer for sale but only a notional or hypothetical sale for the purposes of s 50(3), there is no available market unless on that day there are in the market sufficient traders potentially in touch with each other to evidence a market in which the actual or notional seller could, if he wished, sell the goods.[94]

As in the case of actions by the buyer,[95] the market-price rule is not readily displaced, given an available market. In particular, the excess of contract price over market price will be used as the basis for calculating damages even if the seller:

(a)   does not in fact go into the market to resell the goods but retains them[96] – for he still has on his hands goods of which the value at the due date of acceptance is less than the buyer contracted to pay;

(b)   has contracted a liability to his own supplier – for his remedy is to sell the goods in the market, and if instead he chooses to repudiate the contract with his supplier, he cannot expect an indemnity from his buyer;

(c)   resells the goods in the market at a later date for a higher or lower price than that prevailing at the date on which the original buyer ought to have accepted the goods – for his extra profit or loss results from his own speculation in holding the goods, not from the buyer's breach, so that the buyer is neither entitled to credit for the seller's extra profit nor liable for his extra loss;[97]

90 Ie, for taking delivery (see text and n 86). If this has been postponed at the request or with the consent of the buyer, the postponed date for acceptance becomes the relevant date (*Hickman v Haynes* (1875) LR 10 CP 598); but if the buyer makes it clear that he does not intend to accept the goods, the seller cannot, by holding the contract open against the buyer's wishes, defer performance of his duty to mitigate and postpone the normal date at which the market price is to be taken under s 50(3).

91 Under s 54.

92 See text and n 86.

93 Thus if the rise in the market price at the due date of acceptance is greater than the amount of the special damage, the seller has no claim, though he is not, of course, accountable to the buyer for the surplus, but a rise in the market price *after* the due date for acceptance is irrelevant and does not reduce the seller's claim for general or special damages. See below.

94 *Shearson Lehman Hutton Inc v Maclaine Watson & Co Ltd (No 2)* [1990] 3 All ER 723, per Webster J at 730.

95 See p 369.

96 The cases on sale at a later date (n 97) are equally relevant where the seller does not resell at all.

97 *Campbell Mostyn (Provisions) Ltd v Barnett Trading Co* [1954] 1 Lloyd's Rep 65, applying *Jamal v Moolla Dawood, Sons & Co* [1916] 1 AC 175. But this reasoning is open to objection as running counter to the effect of the mitigation rule in general contract law. See pp 121, 405.

(d) resells the goods at the due date for acceptance, to a third party at a price higher or lower than the market price – for if he is able to find a new buyer willing to pay above the market price the seller is entitled to retain for himself the benefit of his skill or exertion and, conversely, if he chooses to resell below the market price he cannot expect to charge the original buyer with the extra loss resulting;[98]

(e) has, in order to meet his contract, purchased the goods himself for a higher price than the market price prevailing at the date on which his own buyer should have accepted – for his loss results from a fall in the market and would have been incurred to this extent even if the buyer had fulfilled his obligations.

But the market-price rule in s 50(3), strong though it is, provides only a prima facie measure of loss and will not be applied where it would operate unrealistically or unfairly.[99] The governing principle is that set out in s 50(2).[100] Thus, if supply exceeds demand, the seller can argue that resale to another buyer does not mitigate his loss, since but for the original buyer's breach the second sale could have been made from the seller's other stock, so that he would have had profit from two sales instead of one.[101] For the same reason, the fact that the seller is able to persuade his own seller to accept the return of the goods without payment of compensation does not, it is said, reduce or extinguish his loss of profit,[102] but merely saves him the outlay he would otherwise have incurred. The problem of the lost-volume seller (to use American terminology) is in fact considerably more complex than is suggested by the English cases, and we shall return to it a little later.[103] Where demand exceeds supply, the lost-volume argument will not run, for the seller is then in a position to dispose of all his stock, including the goods not accepted by the buyer, and thus cannot claim to have lost a bargain.[104]

Moreover, the loss of bargain principle presupposes that the goods thrown back on the seller's hands as the result of the buyer's repudiation are sufficiently similar to other items in stock to enable the seller to say that the resale of such goods has deprived him of the opportunity to utilize another item of stock to satisfy the second sale. This will not be the case where the goods taken back are 'unique', as has been held to be the case in relation to second-hand motor-cars.[105]

---

98 But where the market price or value is difficult to establish, the actual resale price may be evidence of it.

99 *W. L. Thompson Ltd v Robinson (Gunmakers) Ltd* [1955] Ch 177.

100 See *Bem Dis A Turk Ticaret S/A TR v International Agri Trade Co Ltd* [1999] 1 All ER (Comm) 619 and cases there cited.

101 Ibid; *Re Vic Mill Ltd* [1913] 1 Ch 465. An alternative basis for displacing the market-price rule in such a case is that if supply exceeds demand, there is not an available market. As to whether the assumptions underlying the loss of bargain argument are justified, see p 406.

102 *W. L. Thompson Ltd v Robinson (Gunmakers) Ltd*, n 99.

103 See p 406.

104 *Charter v Sullivan* [1957] 2 QB 117.

105 *Lazenby Garages Ltd v Wright* [1976] 1 WLR 459. For a comment on this case, see p 383, n 168. See also *J Sargent (Garages) Ltd v Motor Auctions (West Bromwich) Ltd* [1977] RTR 121.

(ii) No available market

The principles determining whether there is an available market are similar to those applicable to claims by the buyer,[106] except, of course, that we are now concerned with a market in which the seller can sell, not a market in which the buyer can buy. In the absence of an available market, the measure of damages will usually be the amount by which the contract price exceeds the value of the goods; and a useful indication of such value (though not, of course, conclusive) is the price at which the seller resells them,[107] assuming that the other terms of sale are similar to those of the original contract. In addition, the seller is entitled under s 54 to recover any special damage, eg the cost of adapting the goods to make them suitable for resale to another buyer where this step is reasonable.[108] As an alternative to the excess of the contract price over the value of the goods, the seller may recover expenditure wasted as the result of the breach.[109]

Resale does not necessarily reduce the seller's claim for loss of profit, for he may be able to show that even in the absence of an available market he would, but for the defendant's breach, have made two sales instead of one.[110]

(iii) Critique of the market-price rule

The operation of the market-price rule in relation to claims by the seller is open to much the same criticisms as those previously made in regard to claims by the buyer. In computing his damages, the seller is tied down to the market price at the due date of acceptance, so that in the case of the buyer's anticipatory breach, the assumption is that the seller will wait until that date before reselling and will not try to cover his position by an earlier resale. Again, if the seller, through prudent deferment of resale beyond the due date for acceptance by the original buyer, is able to reduce his loss because of a rising market, his buyer is not able to claim the benefit of this, any more than a seller can claim reduction in damages against him because of the buyer's postponed purchase of substituted goods in a falling market.[111] Mitigation is assumed to take place on the due date of performance by the buyer, whether in fact this occurs earlier or later, and the financial impact of such earlier or later steps to mitigate is ignored, whether increasing or reducing the loss established by the due-date price. Again there is much to be said for adopting provisions along the lines of s 2–706 of the Uniform Commercial Code, which gives the seller a right to cover his position by resale immediately on the buyer's breach, without having to wait until the date fixed by the contract for the taking of delivery by the buyer.

---

106 See p 368.
107 *Harlow & Jones Ltd v Panex (International) Ltd* [1967] 2 Lloyd's Rep 509.
108 *Re Vic Mill Ltd*, n 101.
109 *Bem Dis A Turk Ticaret S/A TR v International Agri Trade Co Ltd* , n 100.
110 Ibid; *W. L. Thompson Ltd v Robinson (Gunmakers) Ltd*, n 99; *Hill & Sons v Edwin Showell & Sons Ltd* (1918) 87 LJKB 1106. But see below.

(iv) The problem of the lost-volume seller

In awarding damages for loss of profit on the second sale (ie the extra sale the plaintiff would have made if the contract goods had not been thrown back on his hands) the courts have been content to look at the state of the market at the relevant date and, if it is shown that supply exceeded demand, assume that the second sale would have produced as much profit as the sale frustrated by the contract. In the two leading cases[112] this assumption has not been challenged, and the seller's profit calculations have been either agreed by the other side or accepted by the court.

However, in the United States a growing volume of literature[113] has demonstrated the complexities inherent in such calculations. In the first place, the excess of supply over demand does not of itself establish that the seller could and would have made the extra sale. Suppose that at the relevant time he was out of stock. Then he would have had to manufacture the extra unit or acquire it elsewhere. As a manufacturer, he might have reached the optimum level of production beyond which it would not pay to acquire the additional staff, accommodation or equipment needed to produce that unit. Alternatively, manufacture might have been prevented through illness, industrial action or one of the myriad other events that can interfere with the smooth running of business. Similar considerations apply to the seller's willingness and ability to purchase the additional unit required to meet the second order. To award as damages for loss of profit a sum equal to that which would have been made if the defaulting buyer had honoured his bargain is thus to ignore these hazards and equate loss of opportunity to make a sale with loss of an established contract.

Secondly, even assuming that the seller could show that he would have been willing and able to make or obtain the extra unit to satisfy the second contract, it by no means follows that he would have made the same profit as on the sale to the defaulting buyer. Beyond a certain point, the law of diminishing returns applies; the additional resources required to make or acquire the extra unit, to store it and to process its addition to stock reduce, and may even extinguish, the profit margin.

Thirdly, the extent to which overheads attributable to that part of the broken contract which the seller no longer has to perform (ie by reason of the buyer's breach) should be deducted in computing the seller's loss of profit is conjectural. The calculation of overheads is not an exact science. The amount of overheads attributable to each unit of stock depends on more or less arbitrary management accounting decisions and will vary according to the quantity of stock produced; and the saving of overheads resulting from the termination of the contract may be illusory, in that the costs are more properly to be treated as fixed costs which will have to be reallocated to the remaining contracts, reducing their profitability.

---

111   See p 387.

112   *Re Vic Mill Ltd*, n 101; *W. L. Thompson Ltd v Robinson (Gunmakers) Ltd*, n 99.

113   The leading analyst in this economic minefield, which the amateur would do well to bypass, is Professor Robert J Harris, whose principal writings on the subject, together with those of other scholars, are listed in White and Summers, *Uniform Commercial Code* (5th edn, 2000), p 275.

These considerations lead to the conclusion that the court should not be too ready to assume the full loss of a bargain merely because of evidence of an excess of supply over demand, and that, at the very least, some discount should be made from the assumed profits of the second sale to take account of the possibility that this would not have taken place or would have been less profitable than the broken contract.

10. DELAY IN TAKING DELIVERY

Whether the buyer's delay in taking delivery is to be treated as a repudiation entitling the seller to regard the contract as discharged depends on the circumstances. Where time is of the essence[114] or the buyer has failed to comply with a notice requiring him to take delivery within a reasonable time, the seller may treat the contract as ended, in which event the case becomes one of non-acceptance. Where, however, the seller does not take this step or the buyer's breach is not repudiatory and the buyer ultimately takes delivery, the seller is entitled to damages for the delay, and to charge for storage, pursuant to s 37.[115]

11. REMEDIES FOR NON-PAYMENT

(i) Strength of the buyer's payment obligation

The buyer's obligation to pay the price is the correlative of the seller's obligation to deliver the contract goods.[116] Yet while the duties of delivery and payment are concurrent conditions[117] – so that the seller's ability and willingness to tender delivery are prima facie prerequisites of his right to demand tender of the price – the two obligations are not necessarily of equal strength. The only consequence to the seller of non-payment of the price is that he is deprived of the use of money, a matter that can readily be compensated by an award of interest in addition to the contract sum. But non-delivery of goods in a commercial transaction may be disastrous. If the goods are of an income-producing kind bought for use in the buyer's business, he may suffer a substantial loss of profit, not to mention damage to his commercial reputation and the possible loss of repeat orders. If the goods are bought for resale and there is no available market, the seller's default may place the buyer in breach of his contractual obligations to his own purchaser.

The law recognizes in various ways the distinction between the payment interest of the seller and the delivery interest of the buyer. Thus, whereas on a commercial sale time of delivery is prima facie of the essence,[118] time of payment is usually not.[119] Again, the perfect tender rule obliges the seller to comply strictly with the

114 See p 401.
115 See p 401.
116 Sale of Goods Act, s 27.
117 Section 28. For the meaning of this provision, see p 394.
118 See p 270.
119 Section 10(1).

obligation to furnish goods in accordance with the contract description,[120] and of the correct quality,[121] but a deviation from the agreed mode of payment,[122] though a breach of contract which entitles the seller to reject the payment tendered,[123] is not prima facie a repudiation entitling him to treat the contract as discharged.

(ii)   Personal remedies

Once the price has become due,[124] the seller's remedy is not damages but an action for the price and interest.[125] However, in certain cases the seller may be able to rely on the default as entitling him to resell and recover damages[126] or as constituting a repudiation which he can treat as discharging the contract, with a right to recover the goods and damages.[127] Further, where the buyer has failed or refused to accept the goods, the seller may as an alternative sue for damages for non-acceptance.

(iii)   Real remedies under the Sale of Goods Act

The Sale of Goods Act confers on the unpaid seller the following rights over the goods, in conditions laid down by the Act:

(a)   Where he is in possession, a lien on the goods or (if the property has not passed to the buyer) a coextensive right to withhold delivery.

(b)   A right to stop the goods in transit.

(c)   A right of resale.

These real remedies may be reinforced by the express provisions of the contract, though not without legal pitfalls.[128]

Three preliminary points may be made concerning the seller's statutory rights over the goods. First, they are available only where the seller is an unpaid seller within the meaning of the Act[129] and one or more of the other conditions precedent to the exercise of the remedy is satisfied.[130] Secondly, the rights are not affected by the buyer's bankruptcy, being equally available against his trustee in bankruptcy. Thirdly, if both property and possession have passed to the buyer, the seller's rights

---

120   See p 291.

121   See p 298.

122   As to the proper mode of payment, see *Benjamin's Sale of Goods*, paras 9–028 ff.

123   See ibid.

124   See p 394.

125   Interest (simple or compound) may be payable under the contract, and simple interest may be payable under s 35A of the Supreme Court Act 1981 (High Court) or s 69 of the County Courts Act 1984 or, in the case of a qualifying debt, statutory interest under the Late Payment of Commercial Debts (Interest) Act 1998 where there is no contractual agreement for payment of interest constituting a substantial remedy (s 8) as defined by s 9.

126   See p 411.

127   Below. But the seller will not usually be entitled either to resell or to treat the agreement as repudiated where both possession and property have passed to the buyer. See below.

128   See p 414, n 176.

129   See p 409.

130   See p 409.

over the goods are lost, and he is restricted to his personal remedies, unless (a) ownership or possession is restored to the seller by the voluntary act of the buyer,[131] or (b) the seller has grounds for rescission *stricto sensu*, eg for misrepresentation.[132] The seller cannot himself secure a revesting of the property by purporting to accept the buyer's repudiation, for the contract is executed and, as in land law, one cannot, by claiming to treat a contract as terminated for repudiation, undo the effect of a conveyance.[133] On the other hand, he may be able to achieve his objective in some measure by a contractual provision entitling him to repurchase in the event of the buyer's default.[134]

We shall not devote overmuch space to the seller's real remedies, for in modern commerce they are of limited practical importance. There are several reasons for this. A large number of sales are on credit terms, and both possession and property pass to the buyer before payment. Where the seller is not sure of his buyer's financial position or reliability, he may stipulate for payment in advance or on delivery or by a documentary letter of credit. Hence the exercise of rights over the goods is now likely to arise only in the relatively infrequent case where goods to be paid for on open account are still in the seller's possession or in transit when the buyer becomes insolvent.

1. The meaning of 'unpaid seller'

Under s 38(1) of the Act the seller[135] is deemed to be an unpaid seller within the meaning of the Act where the whole of the price has not been paid or tendered or where a bill of exchange or other negotiable instrument taken as conditional payment has been dishonoured or the condition on which it was received has otherwise not been fulfilled.[136] In other words, a seller is unpaid until he has received full and unconditional payment. The fact that the buyer may not be in default is irrelevant.[137] Thus, a seller is an unpaid seller even if he has agreed to give credit and the credit period has not expired. Equally, he is unpaid during the currency of a bill of exchange taken by him in respect of the price.[138]

2. Lien or right to withhold delivery

The term 'lien' denotes rights over another's property, and in the case of sale of goods is thus appropriate where the property has passed to the buyer, for the seller

---

131 As in *Commission Car Sales (Hastings) Ltd v Saul* [1957] NZLR 144.

132 See p 395.

133 *Total Oil Great Britain Ltd v Thompson Garages (Biggin Hill) Ltd* [1972] 1 QB 318.

134 See p 414.

135 In this part of the Act 'seller' includes any person who is in the position of a seller, as, for instance, an agent of the seller to whom the bill of lading has been indorsed, or a consignor or agent who has himself paid (or is directly responsible for) the price (s 38(2)).

136 See also s 19(3), discussed pp 395, 949.

137 *R. V. Ward Ltd v Bignall* [1967] 1 QB 534, *per* Diplock LJ at 550. This is a point of some importance where the buyer becomes insolvent before the price falls due.

138 Thus until maturity of the bill, the seller is an unpaid seller within s 38(1)(a). If the bill is dishonoured, he becomes an unpaid seller additionally under s 38(1)(b), which seems superfluous.

cannot exercise a lien over his own goods. The point is purely technical, for where the property has not passed, the seller is given a right of withholding delivery similar to and coextensive with his rights of lien and stoppage in transit.[139]

By s 41(1) the unpaid seller has a lien for the price[140] only if he is in possession of the goods[141] *and* (a) the goods have been sold without any stipulation as to credit; or (b) the goods have been sold on credit but the term of credit has expired;[142] or (c) the buyer becomes insolvent.[143]

The assertion of a lien does not in itself affect the continuance of the contract of sale,[144] and except where the seller becomes entitled to resell under the Act or the contract he remains fully liable for performance, subject only to his lien. This is so even where the buyer becomes insolvent. Insolvency does not constitute either an act of repudiation by the buyer or an inability to perform, for the buyer's obligations may still be carried out by his trustee in bankruptcy.[145]

Since the lien depends on the seller's continued possession, it is lost where the seller delivers the goods to a carrier or other bailee for transmission to the buyer without reserving a right of disposal,[146] or where the buyer or his agent lawfully obtains possession of the goods or the seller waives the lien. Delivery of part of the goods, though not in itself destroying the seller's lien over the remaining goods, may indicate an intention to waive the lien altogether.[147] In addition, though not in general affected by resale or other disposition by the buyer,[148] the lien may become overriden by or subordinated to the right of a bona fide transferee from the buyer of documents of title to the goods.[149]

3.   Stoppage in transit

The seller's right to stop goods in transit is much more restricted than his lien. Having started the delivery process, the seller is not entitled to halt it merely because of the buyer's default in payment. He must go further and show that the buyer has become insolvent.[150] The right of stoppage is exercised by repossession

---

139   Section 39(2). The right to withhold delivery thus encompasses both (a) retention of possession by the seller and (b) stoppage in transit so as to prevent the goods from coming into the possession of the buyer.

140   A lien prima facie secures only the price, not expenses incurred by the seller, eg storage. But the lien can be extended by contract to cover such expenses.

141   He need not be in possession in his own right; possession as agent or bailee of the buyer suffices (s 41(2)).

142   This will rarely apply, for the essence of credit is that the buyer obtains possession before payment.

143   By s 61(4) of the Sale of Goods Act 1979, as amended by s 235 and Sch 10, Part III, of the Insolvency Act 1985, a person is deemed to be insolvent within the meaning of the Act if he has either ceased to pay his debts in the ordinary course of business or he cannot pay his debts as they become due.

144   Section 48(1).

145   *Re Edwards* (1873) 8 Ch App 289.

146   But the seller will have a right of stoppage in transit.

147   Section 42.

148   Section 47(1).

149   Section 47(2).

150   Section 44.

by the seller or by notice to the carrier and is available only so long as the goods are still in transit. Goods are in transit from the time when they are delivered to a carrier[151] or other bailee for the purpose of transmission to the buyer[152] until the buyer or his agent takes delivery from the carrier or other bailee.[153] 'Delivery' here means actual delivery, not, of course, the constructive delivery which results from the act of delivery to the carrier himself.[154] Where the goods are delivered to a ship chartered by the buyer, it is a question of fact depending on the circumstances of the particular case whether they are in the possession of the master as carrier or as agent to the buyer.[155]

The right to stop goods in transit is given on the basis that the carrier or other bailee is still lawfully in possession. The Act therefore provides that where he wrongfully refuses to deliver the goods to the buyer or his agent, the transit is deemed to be at an end. Thus the carrier cannot by his own wrongful act prolong the buyer's exposure to the seller's right of stoppage. The effect of part delivery is the same as for the lien.[156] The right of stoppage is not affected by the buyer's resale, but is subordinated to the rights of a third party taking documents of title to the goods in good faith and for value, and if he is an outright buyer (as opposed, for example, to a mere pledgee), the right of stoppage is lost altogether.[157]

The carrier is entitled to act on a notice of stoppage even if it transpires that the seller had no right to stop the goods in transit. The buyer's remedy for wrongful stoppage is against the seller, not the carrier.[158]

Exercise of a right of stoppage, like assertion of a lien, does not affect the subsistence of the contract. The seller, having recovered the goods, must hold them available for the buyer pursuant to the contract, against payment of the price, unless and until the contract comes to an end.

4.   Resale

Resale by the unpaid seller is dealt with in s 48 of the Act, a confusing and badly drafted section, for it mixes indiscriminately powers of resale and rights of resale, its first two subsections[159] show an intention to deal with the effect of exercise of rights of lien and stoppage in transit, while the last two subsections have no necessary connection with these rights, and its treatment of the impact of resale

---

151 Section 46(1), (2). The carrier must then redeliver the goods to, or according to the directions of, the seller, at the seller's expense (s 46(4)) and subject to the carrier's lien for unpaid freight (see p 1055).

152 As to the meaning of this, see p 253.

153 Section 45(1).

154 Under s 32(1). But the carrier's attornment to the buyer ends the transit (s 45(3)) unless the buyer rejects the goods (s 45(4)). Thereafter the carrier is in the nature of a warehouseman.

155 Sale of Goods Act 1979, s 45(5).

156 See s 45(7) and p 410.

157 Section 47(2)(a).

158 *The Tigress* (1863) 1 New Rep 449; *The Constantia* (1807) 6 Ch Rob 321. Alternatively, the carrier can interplead.

159 And in the original Act, the heading also ('sale not generally rescinded by lien or stoppage in transitu').

upon the original contract leaves something to be desired. The section provides as follows:

> 48 (1) Subject to this section a contract of sale is not rescinded by the mere exercise by an unpaid seller of his right of lien or retention or stoppage in transit.
>
> (2) Where an unpaid seller who has exercised his right of lien or retention or stoppage in transit re-sells the goods, the buyer acquires a good title to them as against the original buyer.
>
> (3) Where the goods are of a perishable nature, or where the unpaid seller gives notice to the buyer of his intention to re-sell, and the buyer does not within a reasonable time pay or tender the price, the unpaid seller may resell the goods and recover from the original buyer damages for any loss occasioned by his breach of contract.
>
> (4) Where the seller expressly reserves the right of resale in case the buyer should make default, and on the buyer making default re-sells the goods, the original contract of sale is rescinded but without prejudice to any claim the seller may have for damages.

Certain important features must now be examined.

(a) RIGHT OF RESALE AND POWER TO RESELL DISTINGUISHED. There are various situations in which one who is not the owner of goods can effectively pass a good title to an innocent third party even though in disposing of the goods to the third party he does not have the authority of the owner. The disposer has the power of sale but not the right to sell. This distinction should be borne in mind in relation to s 48, sub-s (2) of which gives the seller a power to resell and gives a good title to the second buyer without thereby implying that the seller is acting lawfully *vis-à-vis* the original buyer.

(b) RIGHT TO RESELL. Section 48 confers on the unpaid seller the right to resell in two cases.[160] The first is where the goods are of a perishable nature and the buyer does not within a reasonable time pay or tender the price.[161] The second is where the unpaid seller gives notice to the buyer of his intention to resell and the buyer does not within a reasonable time pay or tender the price.[162] This last provision is merely a statement of the common law rule that where time of payment is not initially of the essence of the contract, it can be made of the essence by service of a notice.[163] It would seem that in neither case does the statutory right apply where both property and possession have passed to the original buyer.[164] Where the seller has delivered the goods to the buyer while retaining the property, the statutory right of resale is exercisable, but s 48 gives no guidance as to recovery of possession from the original buyer. On general principles, the 'rescission' produced by the resale would seem to entitle both the seller and the second buyer to maintain tort claims against the original buyer and/or recapture the goods.

(c) POWER OF RESALE. Under s 48(2), where the unpaid seller, having exercised the right of lien or stoppage in transit, resells the goods, the buyer obtains a good title

---

160 For the real remedies arising independently of the provisions of the Act, see p 414.
161 Section 48(3).
162 Ibid.
163 *Chitty on Contracts* (29th edn, 2004), para 22–014.
164 *Benjamin's Sale of Goods*, para 15–117.

against the original buyer.[165] This provision is concerned with those cases in which the property in the goods has already passed to the original buyer, for where the seller has retained the property, he can obviously transfer it to the second buyer without any need for s 48(2).[166] Hence s 48(2) is an exception to the *nemo dat* rule.[167] It is equally clear that unless one of the later subsections of s 48 applies or the seller has a right to resell at common law,[168] a resale under s 48(2), though effective to pass a good title to the second buyer, is a breach of the seller's duty to the original buyer, for, since the exercise of a right of lien or stoppage does not rescind the original contract,[169] it is the duty of the seller who has exercised such a right to hold the goods for the buyer pending tender of the price. Hence by reselling, the seller incurs a liability to the original buyer for damages for breach of contract, or for conversion. As a further alternative, the original buyer could waive the tort, treat the sale as made on his behalf and claim the proceeds of such sale as money had and received, subject to a set-off in respect of his liability for the price payable under the original contract. Strangely, the overriding title acquired by the second buyer is not made dependent on his good faith or want of notice of the first sale. Even if he bought with notice, he is immune from liability to the first buyer in conversion; and it seems probable that the subsection also protects him against liability for interference with the original sale contract, for if he could be sued in tort on this ground, the benefit of his title would be rendered illusory. Section 48(2) appears to be confined to cases where the seller still has possession of the goods, or a right as against the original buyer to immediate possession of them, at the time of resale.[170]

(d) EFFECT OF RESALE ON THE ORIGINAL CONTRACT. Section 48(4) expressly provides that resale pursuant to an express contractual right rescinds the original contract of sale, but without prejudice to any claim the seller may have for damages.[171] It has been held that a resale under s 48(3) has the same effect.[172] 'Rescinded' in this context denotes termination for breach, not rescission *ab initio* as for misrepresentation. It would seem to carry with it a right to recover possession from the original buyer if the goods have been delivered to him, provided that the property has not passed as well.[173]

---

165 Section 48(2).

166 *R. V. Ward Ltd v Bignall*, n 137, per Diplock LJ at 549. For a critical comment on this case see G.D. Goldberg, 'Resale: Performance or Rescission' [1995] LMCLQ 470.

167 For another case where the seller can pass a good title despite having parted with the property in the goods, see p 430. If the second buyer cannot invoke s 48(2) (eg, because the seller was not an unpaid seller within the meaning of the Act) he may be able to fall back on one of the other exceptions to the *nemo dat* rule, eg s 24 (see p 431). The title acquired by the second buyer under s 48(2) is, it is submitted, no greater than that acquired by a second buyer under s 24, ie, such title as was vested in the seller immediately prior to the second sale, and ignoring the first sale for this purpose. See p 57.

168 See p 414.

169 Section 48(1).

170 *Benjamin's Sale of Goods*, para 15–102.

171 Damages would prima facie be assessed as for non-acceptance (see p 402).

172 *R. V. Ward Ltd v Bignall*, n 137, overruling *Gallagher v Shilcock* [1949] 2 KB 765.

173 See text to n 164, and below.

(iv) Real remedies at common law

The rights which the Sale of Goods Act gives to the seller over the goods are not exhaustive.

1. Retention of title

A seller who in his contract of sale reserves title until payment continues as owner pending payment unless and until his title is displaced by virtue of some exception to the *nemo dat* rule.[174] But it does not necessarily follow that he has an immediate right to recover possession; and the existence of such a right is an essential prerequisite to the seller's ability to pursue tort remedies against the buyer or a third party through a claim in conversion. The seller will have a right to repossess if (a) the contract so provides, or (b) the contract empowers the seller to rescind or terminate it for default in payment and he exercises that contractual right, or (c) the buyer's default in payment constitutes a repudiation of the contract (whether under the express terms of the contract or because time of payment is impliedly of the essence or the delay in payment is so grave as to be repudiatory) and the seller elects to accept the repudiation.

2. Acceptance of repudiation

If the seller has parted with possession while retaining the property or has retained possession while transferring the property, he can, if the buyer's default in payment is repudiatory, reacquire full rights over the goods by accepting the repudiation. Where the seller has retained possession while transferring the property, acceptance of the repudiation revests the property in him.[175] If he has lost possession while retaining the property, then by accepting the buyer's repudiation, he becomes entitled to resume possession. But if both property and possession have passed, the seller loses all real rights, and cannot rely on the buyer's repudiation as revesting the property in him unless the buyer voluntarily restores possession to him.[176]

3. Agreement for repurchase

There would seem to be no reason why the seller should not reserve the right to repurchase the goods in the event of the buyer's default and then set off the unpaid balance of the original purchase price against the repurchase price. Such a transaction is not in the nature of a security, for the buyer has no right of redemption and the goods come back to the seller not by way of enforcement of the buyer's price obligation but by way of repurchase.

---

174   See ch 16.

175   *R. V. Ward Ltd v Bignall*, n 137.

176   See p 408. If the seller, having transferred both property and possession, seeks to rely on a contractual provision for repossession he is likely to be met with the defence that the right to repossess makes the document a bill of sale which, in so far as it purports to give rights over the goods, will be void for noncompliance with the Bills of Sale Acts. See 4 Halsbury's Laws (4th edn, 1998 reissue), title 'Bills of Sale'.

16 Title Conflicts between Seller or Buyer and Third Parties[1]

Most sales of goods are made either by their owner or by his duly authorized agent, but sometimes the seller is neither the owner nor authorized by the owner to sell. He may be an agent who has exceeded his authority, eg by selling without securing his principal's prior approval to the terms; or a buyer who, having received possession from his seller, has wrongfully resold the goods before himself acquiring title; or a thief who has stolen and disposed of them before they have been traced. In all these cases the question arises whether the owner can recover his property and, if so, on what terms, or whether, on the other hand, the person into whose possession the goods have come is entitled to retain them.

As we shall see, a person who has neither title nor authority to sell may sometimes confer a good title on a third party. He lacks the *right* to dispose, for his action is unauthorized, yet has the *power* of disposal in that in given conditions the law will treat his disposition as effective, binding the true owner even though he did not consent to it.[2] Where, in such a case, the disposition is an outright transfer of the goods, the original owner necessarily loses all his interest in them, though he will have personal claims against the transferor. But not all cases are of this kind. The unauthorized disposition may be intended to confer a purely limited interest in the goods, as where they are bailed to the third party or subjected to a lien or pledge or some other type of security interest. Here the owner does not lose all his rights; his interest merely becomes encumbered by or subordinated to the limited interest conferred on the third party.

Where the unauthorized disposition is ineffective, the owner is entitled to recover the goods or payment of their value;[3] but if the defendant took them in good faith and has added to their value by making improvements, the court may give him an allowance for the value so added.[4] Accordingly, if the court makes an order for delivery of the goods it will usually be upon terms that the plaintiff is to pay the defendant the value of the improvements, while if the order is for payment of

---

1 See also p 714.
2 This chapter is confined to cases where title is lost through a sale or other disposition by a non-owner. For loss of title by operation of law through the goods becoming fixtures or accessions or through confusion, commingling or specification, see Peter Birks, 'Mixtures', in *Interests in Goods* (2nd edn, Norman Palmer and Ewan McKendrick eds, 1998), ch 16; R. M. Goode, *Hire-Purchase Law and Practice* (2nd edn, 1970), chs 32, 33.
3 See p 443.
4 This was a well-established rule at common law and is now embodied in ss 3 and 6 of the Torts (Interference with Goods) Act 1977.

the value of the goods by way of damages, the sum awarded will be the value of the goods in their unimproved state.

1.   THE COMPETING CLAIMS FOR PROTECTION

In the typical case A, in possession of goods with the consent of their owner O, wrongfully sells them to an innocent third party, T, and then disappears or becomes insolvent. The question which must then be answered is which of the two innocent parties, O or T, must suffer the loss.

> In the development of our law, two principles have striven for mastery. The first is for the protection of property: no one can give a better title than he himself possesses. The second is the protection of commercial transactions: the person who takes in good faith and for value without notice should get a good title. The first principle has held sway for a long time, but it has been modified by the common law itself and by statute so as to meet the needs of our own times.[5]

The common law has always strongly favoured the preservation of proprietary rights. It is an article of faith in the common law that only in exceptional cases should the owner of goods be deprived of his title to them otherwise than by his own voluntary act. *Nemo dat quod non habet*: the transferor of goods cannot pass a better title than he himself possesses. The fact that the transferee takes possession in good faith and for value is in most cases irrelevant. It is for him to check on his seller's title, if he can, not for the owner to take steps to safeguard his own property.

This sanctification of vested property rights was not peculiar to the common law. The *nemo dat* rule was a well-established principle of Roman law[6] and, though a different rule prevailed in Europe during the first half of the Middle Ages, the revival of the influence of Roman law in the thirteenth century led to the reinstatement of the *nemo dat* rule, which lasted well into the eighteenth century.[7] But with the growth of commerce and the gradual development of credit came a recognition on the part of the civilians that if goods were to move freely in the stream of trade, proper protection had to be given to the innocent purchaser. The new idea became enshrined in art 2279 of the French Civil Code: '*En fait de meubles la possession vaut titre*'. So the buyer in good faith acquires an overriding title provided that he takes possession.

In principle, the protection of the innocent buyer is a more sensible and more realistic approach. If the owner of goods voluntarily parts with possession of them, he takes upon himself certain risks. He can make his own judgment as to the creditworthiness of the party to whom he gives possession, and if his trust turns out

5 *Bishopsgate Motor Finance Corp. Ltd v Transport Brakes Ltd* [1949] 1 KB 322, per Denning LJ at 336–337.

6 *Nemo plus iuris ad alium transferre potest, quam ipse habet* (Ulpian D 50. 17. 54). See also F. De Zulueta, *Roman Law of Sale* (1957), p 36; Buckland and McNair, *Roman Law and Common Law* (2nd rev edn, 1965), p 77; François Guisan, *La Protection de l'Acquéreur de Bonne Foi en Matière Mobilière* (Lausanne, 1970).

7 For a good historical account of this development see Guisan, *La Protection de l'Acquéreur de Bonne Foi*, chs 1 and 2.

to be ill-founded, he ought not to put the consequences of his own mistaken judgment on to the shoulders of a blameless third party. There is no effective way either of deducing or of investigating title to chattels,[8] and if the goods are to move freely down the distributive chain, it is important that buyers should be able to purchase with confidence in the strength in the seller's title. Yet the civil law approach goes too far, for in giving such sweeping protection to the innocent purchaser, it fails to take account of the needs of those selling on credit to take security for the price.

Over the last hundred years the civil law and the common law have moved closer together. In England the *nemo dat* rule has been steadily eroded by statutory exceptions, while in France and elsewhere certain forms of statutory purchase-money security are now protectable by registration.[9] Yet a gulf remains. *Nemo dat* is still the general rule in England and the exception in France. Only the United States, in art 9 of the Uniform Commercial Code, has managed to produce a set of provisions which fairly balance the conflicting interests.[10]

2. THE *NEMO DAT* RULE AND ITS COMMON LAW EXCEPTIONS

The *nemo dat* rule, which is heavily relied on by sellers to secure payment of the price by reserving title until payment,[11] is enshrined in s 21(1) of the Sale of Goods Act, which also preserves one of the two principal exceptions to it at common law.

> Subject to this Act, where goods are sold by a person who is not their owner, and who does not sell them under the authority or with the consent of the owner, the buyer acquires no better title to the goods than the seller had, unless the owner of the goods is by his conduct precluded from denying the seller's authority to sell.

It will be recalled that a sale by a non-owner is perfectly valid as between the parties, so that the effect of such a sale is a question of priorities, not of validity.[12]

The common law exceptions to *nemo dat* embody three distinct ideas. The first is the agency concept: a non-owner can pass a good title if he has actual or apparent authority[13] from the owner to make the sale. This is the concept referred to in s 21(1). It applies where O has by his conduct held out A as having O's authority to sell to T, so that O is precluded from denying that authority. The holding out must be voluntary and not, for example, at gun point.[14] The second idea is that of apparent ownership: O by his conduct holds out A as being himself the owner of the goods. As before, T is led to deal with A in the belief that A is entitled to dispose of

---

8 Contrast the position in the case of land, p 30.
9 See R. M. Goode, 'A Credit Law for Europe?' (1974) 23 ICLQ 227, at pp 258–262
10 See p 675.
11 See pp 579, 584, 607, and for a comparative treatment see Robert R. Pennington, 'Retention of Title to the Sale of Goods under European Law' (1978) 27 ICLQ 277. See also the International Chamber of Commerce publication *Retention of Title* (2nd edn, 1993), which gives a brief survey of the legal position on retention of title in a number of countries, with specimen clauses.
12 See p 56.
13 'Ostensible authority' is a synonym for apparent authority. See p 168.
14 *Debs v Sibec Developments Ltd* [1990] RTR 91.

the goods, but this time on the basis that A is himself the owner, so that no question of any possible limits to his power to act is involved – an important point, as we shall see. The third idea is the sanctity of purchases made in market overt, a principle later taken over by statute but recently abolished.[15]

A fourth exception to the *nemo dat* rule has from time to time been canvassed, namely estoppel by negligence. O, it is said, must not be so negligent in safeguarding his own property as to facilitate A's fraud in representing to T that he, A, is the owner. Lord Denning was a strong proponent of this theory, maintaining a rearguard action with considerable success even after the theory appeared to have been generally discarded. But in *Moorgate Mercantile Co v Twitchings*[16] the House of Lords, by a bare majority, did at last put to rest the notion that mere inactivity by O in regard to safeguarding his property – in that case, a finance company's failure through carelessness to register a hire-purchase agreement with HP Information Ltd – can debar him from asserting his rights. In general, he owes no duty of care to third parties to protect his own property. The position is the same where non-registration is due not to carelessness but to deliberate policy.[17] To be estopped, he must either represent A as the owner or as authorized to sell or in some way lend himself to such a representation by A. If he does either of these things, he will be estopped whether or not he acted negligently. If he does neither, the fact that he might by suitable means have prevented A from disposing of his goods to T is not sufficient to deprive O of his ownership; nor can T obtain relief through the back door via an action against O for negligence.[18]

It is equally clear that a representation by A as to his own authority or ownership does not bind O unless O has in some way lent himself to that representation.[19]

(i)   Apparent authority

Where T buys from A goods belonging to O in reliance on A's apparent authority to sell them, O is bound and T acquires a good title. As we have seen, this exception to the *nemo dat* principle is preserved in s 21(1) of the Sale of Goods Act. Of course, T does not get a good title unless A sold him the goods. If A merely agreed to sell the goods to T and the transfer of the property was dependent on T's payment of the price, then until he pays the price, T does not acquire ownership. The proposition

---

15 See p 425.

16 [1977] AC 890.

17 *Dominion Credit and Finance Ltd v Marshall (Cambridge) Ltd*, 2 March 1999, unreported. The rules of HPI do not oblige a member to register its hire-purchase agreements. The position might possibly be different if (a) registration were a requirement of membership, and (b) the party claiming to have acquired title was aware that the other party was a member and reasonably relied on the absence of any registration.

18 Ibid; *Debs v Sibec Developments Ltd*, n 14. The rule is somewhat different in equity, at any rate as regards interests in land, where the holder of the legal title can find himself postponed to a subsequent equitable interest through his neglect to obtain or retain possession of the title deeds. See p 655.

19 *A.-G. for Ceylon v Silva* [1953] AC 461 at 479.

would seem self-evident, but was nevertheless challenged in *Shaw v Metropolitan Police Commissioner.*[20]

> O gave possession of his car to A, a rogue, in circumstances where O clearly held out A as authorized to sell the car. A agreed to sell the car to T, to whom he delivered it. Ownership was to pass on payment. T gave a banker's draft to A, who disappeared. But alerted to the fraud, the bank issuing the draft did not pay it. The car was then taken into custody by the Metropolitan Police. O claimed the car; T contended that he had acquired title.

> *Held* by the Court of Appeal that s 21(1) applied only to a sale, not to an agreement for sale, and since T had never paid for the car, the property had not passed to him.

It is important not to read too much into this decision. T's claim was wholly unmeritorious, for he was seeking to assert title to a vehicle for which he had not paid a penny, since the bank had withheld payment of its draft. The common law rule preserved by s 21(1) would therefore not have given title to T, for A never purported to transfer title to him. The position would have been otherwise if A, when contracting to sell the car to T, had not reserved title pending payment. But it would be wrong to treat the decision as meaning that the common law estoppel protects only a buyer to whom the goods have been sold. T failed because he was claiming a title that had never been transferred to him. But he could have relied on A's apparent authority to sell as protecting him in his possession if he had perfected his rights by retendering the price.[21] By conferring on A apparent authority to deal with the goods, O becomes bound by transactions entered into within the scope of that authority, whether they are sales or any other types of transaction. So if A were to pledge the goods to T as security for a loan, the pledge would bind O if within the scope of A's apparent dealing powers. Similarly, O would be bound by a mere agreement to sell to T, for having held out A as authorized to enter into the agreement O could not be heard to say that it was unauthorized. But that agreement would not by itself give T title; it would merely confer on him the right to acquire title by paying the price.

Care should be taken not to confuse apparent authority with the mere appearance of authority. As we have seen,[22] the phrase 'apparent authority' is a convenient legal shorthand to denote an appearance of authority *to which O has lent himself by some express or implied representation to T*, whether made directly or through A. Almost invariably, O's representation is not given directly to T but derives from an instruction given by O to A, so that apparent authority is in most cases an extension of actual authority. O authorizes A to perform certain acts in relation to O's goods and thereby provides A with a springboard which enables A to represent his authority as still wider.

In determining whether T can successfully invoke the apparent authority of A to dispose of O's goods, at least five factors are likely to be relevant:

---

20 [1987] 3 All ER 405.
21 There was, of course, the difficulty that A had disappeared. This could no doubt have been resolved by paying the money into court. But T was too ambitious; he wanted the car for nothing!
22 See p 418.

(a)   A's own status as an agent – in particular, whether he is a professional, a 'mercantile agent' in the language of the Factors Acts, or is merely an ad hoc agent not in the business of buying or selling for others;

(b)   the capacity in which he was instructed to act;

(c)   whether he was given possession of the goods and/or of any indicia of title to them;

(d)   the capacity and manner in which he in fact acted;

(e)   whether T acted in good faith and in the reasonable belief that A was authorized to sell.

1.   A as a mercantile agent

The law sharply distinguishes the professional agent from the amateur. If A is a mercantile agent[23] and is instructed as such by O, then in the absence of any indication to the contrary, T, if dealing with A when acting in the ordinary course of business as a mercantile agent, is entitled to assume that A's authority from O extends to all acts which would be usual for an agent in A's position to be authorized to perform,[24] and T will not be bound by undisclosed limitations imposed by O on such authority. By entrusting his business to a professional agent, whose constant business activity comprises the purchase and sale of goods on behalf of others, O is required to accept the risk of the agent exceeding his authority, while T for his part is entitled within certain limits to rely on appearances when dealing with A.[25] This is sound policy; for a huge volume of business, both domestic and international, is conducted through agents, and both buyers and sellers need assurance that they can safely rely on the agent's authority if he is carrying out the transaction in a normal manner and on usual terms. If the rule were otherwise, large-scale business would be difficult to conduct effectively.

On the other hand, the law does not penalize O *merely* because of appearances. O must have lent himself to the act of the mercantile agent by instructing him to act in that capacity.[26] If I ask a second-hand car dealer, A, to sell my car for not less than £750 and in breach of his instructions he sells it for £500, I must put a brave face on it; I can sue A for deviating from his instructions but I cannot disclaim the

---

23 See p 426. On the reluctance of the courts to recognize a mercantile agency, see L. Rutherford and I. Todd, 'Section 25(1) of the Sale of Goods Act 1893: The Reluctance to Create a Mercantile Agency' [1980] 38 CLJ 346.

24 The American *Restatement* treats this case as an example not of apparent authority but of the 'inherent agency power' to affect relations between O and T. See *Restatement, Agency* (2d), paras 8A, 161. However, there seems no reason why it should not be treated as a form of apparent authority generated by the status which A holds as a mercantile agent and the fact that he has been instructed by O to act in that capacity.

25 A principle embodied and extended in what is now the Factors Act 1889. See p 425.

26 This is so both at common law and under the Factors Act. See p 428. The remedy of a third party who in good faith relies on an appearance of authority to which the principal has not lent himself is to sue the agent for damages for breach of warranty of authority. *Semble*, an action for breach of warranty of authority does not lie where, by virtue of the agent's apparent authority, the principal is bound; in this situation, the third party's proper course is to hold the principal to the contract. See *Rainbow v Howkins* [1904] 2 KB 322.

sale.[27] The position would be the same if, though not giving A unqualified instructions to sell, I entrusted the goods to him for a dispositive purpose, by asking him to invite offers, whether expressly or by exposing the goods for sale in his showroom, and he then sells without my authority.[28] But if I leave my car with him for repair and not for sale, I am not bound by his unauthorized disposition. The purchaser, it is true, is just as misled as in the previous case, but I have not lent myself to A's dispositive act because I have never entrusted the car to him with a view to sale in the first place. T is thus held strictly to the limits of A's actual authority.[29] A fortiori the mere fact that A is given possession of my goods for safe keeping or for his private use does not result in my being estopped from disputing his right to sell, even if by elementary inquiry I could have discovered that he was untrustworthy.[30] The courts have time and again insisted that the owner of the goods owes no duty to third parties to be careful in the protection of his property,[31] and the fact that the person with whom I have deposited them is a mercantile agent does not affect the matter unless I instructed him to act in that capacity. This is a hard rule; for how is the innocent purchaser to know that A, contrary to appearances, is holding the goods in a private capacity or for a purpose other than that for which he usually takes possession of goods?

By a spurious logic, the same rule is applied to the delivery of documents of title to goods.[32] If the mere deposit of the goods themselves with the mercantile agent does not confer on him apparent authority to sell, how can the deposit of indicia of title have any greater effect? But it is fallacious to equate in this way documents of title to goods with the goods themselves. The possession of documents of title is a great deal less ambiguous in character than the possession of goods. Goods may be delivered and held for use, for repair, for letting out on hire or for safe custody. Documents of title, on the other hand, are not taken for any of these purposes except safe custody; and the range of persons whose business it is to hold documents for safe keeping is very much narrower than in the case of goods. I might entrust documents of title to my bank for custody; it is extremely unlikely that I should deposit them for that purpose with a warehouse, a commercial agent or a repairer. Nevertheless, in keeping with decisions concerning the deposit of title deeds to land,[33] the authorities establish that the delivery of documents of title to goods to an

---

27 See *Rainbow v Howkins*, n 26 (sale by auctioneer below reserve price at which vendor had instructed him to sell). Similarly, one who instructs an agent to make a purchase at not more than a stated price is bound if the agent buys at a higher price (*Todd v Robinson* (1825) Ry & M 217).

28 *Turner v Sampson* (1911) 27 TLR 200.

29 See *Astley Industrial Trust Ltd v Miller* [1968] 2 All ER 36, per Chapman J at 40; *Pearson v Rose & Young Ltd* [1951] 1 KB 275, per Denning LJ at 288.

30 Ibid.

31 *Central Newbury Car Auctions Ltd v Unity Finance Ltd* [1957] 1 QB 371; *Mercantile Credit Co Ltd v Hamblin* [1965] 2 QB 242; *Moorgate Mercantile Co v Twitchings*, n 16.

32 *Cole v North Western Bank* (1875) LR 10 CP 354, per Blackburn J at 363. In the light of this well-established common law principle, it is somewhat surprising that in *Central Newbury Car Auctions Ltd v Unity Finance Ltd*, n 31, the court felt that the case turned on whether the vehicle registration book was a document of title, for at common law that would not by itself have made any difference at all.

33 *Martinez v Cooper* (1826) 2 Russ 198. Cf *Northern Counties of England Fire Insurance Co v Whipp* (1884) 26 Ch D 482; *Brocklesby v Temperance Permanent Building Society* [1895] AC 173.

agent otherwise than for the purpose of selling the goods or raising money on them does not confer on the agent the power to bind the owner by an unauthorized disposition.[34] Even the fact that A was entrusted with possession with a view to sale does not suffice to confer a good title on T. He must go further and show[35] that A's disposition was made in the ordinary course of business[36] and that he, T, took in good faith and in the belief that A was entitled to sell.[37]

2.   *A as an ad hoc agent*

Where A is not a mercantile agent, different considerations apply. If I ask my friend Alec the greengrocer to sell my car for me for not less than £750, he cannot, in the absence of other factors, commit me beyond the extent of the authority I have given him. If he purports to sell the car to T for £500, I can disclaim the sale. Alec may incur liability to T for breach of warranty of authority,[38] but that is the most that T can secure by way of redress. By dealing with an amateur, T takes his chance. A good illustration is *Jerome v Bentley & Co.*[39]

> The plaintiff entrusted a diamond ring to one Tatham to sell on his behalf for £550. Tatham was to be entitled to keep any surplus above £550 for himself but was to return the ring if not sold within seven days. In breach of his agreement, Tatham sold the ring to the defendants eleven days later for £175, representing himself as the owner. The defendants subsequently resold the ring. In an action by the plaintiff against the defendants for conversion, it was held that the defendants could not rely on the principle of usual authority successfully invoked in *Watteau v Fenwick,*[40] for in the present case Tatham belonged to no well-known class of agent but was merely a private individual carrying on no calling and simply entrusted with the sale of the ring. Accordingly, his authority came to an end at the end of the seven days, and since he was not a broker or other person engaged in buying and selling goods for others, the defendants were not entitled to assume the continuance of an authority that had in fact come to an end.

But the fact that A is not a full-blooded mercantile agent does not necessarily put T out of court; it simply means that O's delivery of the goods to A for the purpose of sale is not by itself sufficient to create apparent authority going beyond A's actual authority. Something more is needed that will enable T to show that O has expressly or impliedly represented A's authority as wide enough to cover the transaction with T. If O has employed A as his agent on other occasions, this may give T an argument; and the greater the regularity with which O has instructed A to act, the

---

34 A similar rule applied at common law where a dealer sold goods but was allowed by his buyer to remain temporarily in possession of the goods and documents of title to them (*Johnson v Crédit Lyonnais Co* (1877) 3 CPD 32).

35 The onus of so doing lies on T. If he adduces no evidence beyond the fact that A was a mercantile agent when the goods were entrusted for the purpose of sale, T will lose. See *Suttons Motors (Temora) Pty Ltd v Hollywood Motor Pty Ltd* [1971] VR 684.

36 *General Distributors Ltd v Paramotors Ltd* [1962] SASR 1. The meaning of this requirement is discussed in relation to the Factors Act, p 429.

37 It is not, however, necessary for T to show that his belief was reasonable, for the doctrine of constructive notice does not normally apply to commercial transactions. See, for example, *Feuer Leather Corp. v Frank Johnston & Sons* [1981] Com LR 251 and p 666.

38 See *Bowstead on Agency* (17th edn, 2001), pp 459–549.

39 [1952] 2 All ER 114.

40 [1893] 1 QB 346. See p 169 for a criticism of this case.

stronger become T's prospects of showing that O has held A out as having a general authority to act on his behalf in similar dealings. This would suffice to confer apparent authority on A even if O was his sole principal.

(ii) Apparent ownership

The concept of apparent authority is limited to situations in which A is held out as an agent, whether for a named or an unnamed principal. But frequently O and A find it advantageous to conduct business on the basis that while as between themselves A is to sell the goods as O's agent, he is to present himself to the third parties as a principal selling in his own name and on his own behalf. This, indeed, was the traditional role of the factor.

The principles underlying A's power to dispose of goods as apparent owner and thereby deprive O of title even where A acts in breach of his mandate are in some respects akin to those previously discussed in relation to apparent authority. The starting point is, as before, that O owes no duty to third parties to be careful in the protection of his property. The fact that he allows another to take possession and omits steps that would alert third parties to the fact that the possessor has only a limited interest is not sufficient to deprive him of his title in favour of an innocent purchaser who is thereby misled.[41] If, however, O either authorizes A to sell as principal or knows that it is usual for agents in the position of A to sell as principal, a disposition by A as owner will bind O, and this is so whether or not A is given possession of goods.[42] Thus at common law a factor had usual authority to sell goods in his own name,[43] though not to pledge them.[44]

It is at this point that the effect of apparent ownership diverges from that of apparent authority. Where A is held out as authorized to sell, the disposition by him will bind O only so far as it is within A's apparent authority. But where A is held out as owner, the question of apparent authority does not arise, for T has no reason to suppose that A needs the approval of any third party to the disposition.[45] T is thus entitled to assume that A's power to deal with the goods is as unfettered as that of

---

41 *Moorgate Mercantile Co Ltd v Twitchings*, n 16, in which the House of Lords by a bare majority upheld the title of the plaintiff finance house to a motor vehicle let on hire-purchase and wrongfully disposed of by the hirer, despite the fact that as the result of the plaintiff's failure to register the hire-purchase agreement with H.P. Information Ltd (a company set up by the hire-purchase industry to maintain a register of hire-purchase and similar agreements) a motor dealer had in good faith purchased the vehicle in reliance on a clear search from HPI. In the Court of Appeal, Lord Denning's valiant rearguard action had persuaded the majority of the court to the opposite conclusion. An interesting feature of Lord Denning's judgment is the ingenuity with which, having stated the proposition that mere carelessness by the owner in protecting his property did not estop him from asserting his title, the Master of the Rolls then proceeded to elevate what was in truth mere inactivity of the plaintiff in failing to register into a positive representation that it had no interest in the vehicle. See further p 418.

42 *Eastern Distributors Ltd v Goldring* [1957] 2 QB 600.

43 *Baring v Corrie* (1818) 2 B & Ald 137.

44 Ibid.

45 *Motor Credits (Hire Finance) Ltd v Pacific Motor Auctions Pty Ltd* (1963) 109 CLR 87; *Lloyds & Scottish Finance Ltd v Williamson* [1965] 1 WLR 404.

any other owner. So the fact that A sells on unusual terms or does not sell in the ordinary course of business is irrelevant except in so far as it bears on T's good faith and the reasonableness of his belief that A was the owner.[46] Indeed, where A was in fact authorized by O to hold himself out as owner, it would appear sufficient that T genuinely believed A to be the owner, and the reasonableness of such belief is immaterial.[47]

3. STATUTORY EXCEPTIONS TO THE *NEMO DAT* RULE

Trade depends on the rapid movement of goods from hand to hand, and the reluctance of the common law to override the rights of the owner who parted with possession to an agent became a growing source of inconvenience with the expansion of trade in the nineteenth century.

Statutory encroachments on the *nemo dat* rule began with the Factors Act 1823, later amended by the Factors Acts of 1825, 1842 and 1877, all of these being repealed by the Factors Act 1889, still in force, which consolidated and to some extent extended the earlier Acts.[48] The previous Acts progressively extended the power of an 'agent entrusted' with goods or documents of title to goods to pass a good title or pledge of the goods to a third party; but 'agent entrusted' was interpreted by the courts as denoting not any agent but only commercial agents (factors, brokers and the like) ordinarily having power as such to sell or pledge goods, and then only to cases where the agent was entrusted with the goods in that capacity. The Factors Act 1889 substituted the phrase 'mercantile agent' for 'agent entrusted', but the meaning would appear to be the same. The Act, re-enacting and extending the previous legislation, is not confined to dealings by factors and other mercantile agents but also (repeating provisions contained in the Factors Act 1877) covers dispositions by a buyer in possession and by a seller who remains in possession after sale. These provisions in the 1889 Act were re-enacted almost verbatim in s 25 of the Sale of Goods Act 1893 (now s 25 of the Sale of Goods Act 1979). Since that time, the list of statutory exceptions to the *nemo dat* rule has gradually expanded, the most significant addition being the provisions embodied in Part III of the Hire-Purchase Act 1964, which enable the hirer or buyer of a motor vehicle under a hire-purchase or conditional sale agreement to pass an overriding title to a bona fide private purchaser.[49] As we shall see, the statutory provisions, developed piecemeal and interpreted restrictively by the courts, do not in policy terms represent either a rational or a cohesive set of rules for balancing the conflicting interests.

With the exception of statutes authorizing confiscation and forfeiture of goods,[50] all the statutory exceptions to the *nemo dat* rule require that the owner shall have

---

46 Ibid.

47 For having authorized A to represent himself as owner, O cannot be heard to contend that T's belief in A's ownership is unreasonable. The position is otherwise where, in so representing himself, A exceeds his authority.

48 For a useful historical account, see the judgment of Blackburn J in *Cole v North Western Bank*, n 32.

49 See p 438.

50 See p 443.

voluntarily parted with possession, to the buyer or to a mercantile agent. A thief is therefore incapable of passing a good title.[51]

(i)   Sale in market overt

Until recently, where goods were sold in market overt according to the usage of the market, the buyer acquired a good title[52] to the goods, provided he bought them in good faith and without notice of any defect or want of title on the part of the seller.[53] The market overt rule, peculiar to English law, originated in the Middle Ages when shops were few, most goods were sold at markets and fairs, and private sales were severely discouraged as being likely to involve stolen goods. One who received stolen goods and was not able to show that he had acquired them in open market stood in considerable danger of being hanged. In recent times, however, a rule designed to promote honesty among buyers and the integrity of the market came to be seen as providing a charter for thieves and fences, a perception highlighted by the theft of paintings by Gainsborough and Reynolds from Lincoln's Inn and their sale in Bermondsey market. The market overt exception to the *nemo dat* rule has now been abolished.[54]

(ii)   Sale by seller with voidable title

Section 23 of the Act provides that where the seller of goods has a voidable title thereto, but his title has not been avoided at the time of the sale,[55] the buyer acquires a good title to the goods, provided that he buys them in good faith and without notice of the seller's defect in title. For example, A is induced by S's fraud to sell goods to S, who resells them to B before A has discovered the fraud and rescinded the contract. B acquires a good title. This is not at first sight a true exception to the *nemo dat* rule, for S's title, though voidable at the instance of A, is nevertheless a good title until avoided and can be transferred to B as buyer in good faith. But B does in fact acquire a better title than S, for the sale to him extinguishes A's right to rescind the original sale agreement. Hence B's title, unlike that of S, is not voidable at the instance of A. In property terms, B takes the goods free from A's equity. This is merely a specific application of the general rule of contract law that the right to rescind a contract is lost when an innocent third party has acquired an interest in the subject-matter of the contract.

Though B prevails if he buys before A rescinds, the converse is not necessarily true, for though A's rescission revests the property in him, S may still be able to pass a

---

51   The other exception to this principle, sale in market overt, has now been abolished. See below.

52   Ie, the best title, overriding the rights of all prior parties.

53   Sale of Goods Act, s 22(1).

54   Sale of Goods (Amendment) Act 1994, s 1. The other great merit of this enactment is its brevity: two sections occupying three lines. Would that this were the characteristic of the rest of the statute book! For details of the market overt rule, see the first edition of this work at p 401, and Brian Davenport and Anthony Ross, 'Market Overt' in Palmer and McKendrick, *Interests in Goods*, ch 14.

55   Ie, by the seller's own supplier rescinding the contract under which the seller acquired title – typically, for misrepresentation or fraud. For the mode of rescission, see p 108.

good title to B by virtue of some other exception to the *nemo dat* rule, eg under s 9 of the Factors Act as a buyer in possession.[56]

If B, at the time of his purchase, knows that S's title is only voidable, then B himself obtains only a voidable title. Nevertheless, this is still a good title until avoided, so that if before rescission by A there is a resale by B to C, who takes in good faith and without notice of the defect in B's title, s 23 operates again, for the protection of C, and A loses title.

Section 23 applies only where S does in fact acquire title (albeit voidable) in the first instance. If A supplied the goods to S on conditional sale, s 23 does not come into play. A has reserved title and no act of rescission is needed on his part, nor would rescission assist him to defeat s 9 if S subsequently resold the goods to a buyer taking in good faith and without notice of S's want of title. Similarly, if S, instead of buying the goods from A, had stolen them from him, S would not acquire a voidable title; he would have no title at all.

(iii) Disposition by mercantile agent

The common law, as we have seen, developed the general principle that if the owner of goods entrusted them, or documents of title to them, to a professional dealer, a mercantile agent, he took his chance on the dealer's integrity and could not complain if in selling the goods the dealer exceeded his authority. But the common law rule was confined to sales by the mercantile agent; it did not extend to unauthorized pledges of the goods or documents. The Factors Acts extended the common law rule to cover all types of disposition by a mercantile agent and these are now regulated by s 2 of the Factors Act 1889. By s 2(1):

> Where a mercantile agent is, with the consent of the owner, in possession of goods or of the documents of title to goods, any sale, pledge, or other disposition of the goods, made by him when acting in the ordinary course of business of a mercantile agent, shall, subject to the provisions of this Act, be as valid as if he were expressly authorized by the owner of the goods to make the same; provided that the person taking under the disposition acts in good faith, and has not at the time of the disposition notice that the person making the disposition has not authority to make the same.

Where s 2(1) applies, the effect of the disposition by the mercantile agent on the rights of the original owner will, of course, depend on whether it is absolute or by way of security. An absolute disposition, if within the provisions of the section, deprives the owner of his title altogether, and transfers the title (such as it is[57]) to the third party; a disposition by way of pledge[58] or other security merely subordinates the owner's interest to that of the pledgee or other secured party,

---

56 See p 434. Withdrawal by A of his consent to S's continued possession does not affect the operation of s 9 of the Factors Act, for by s 2 such withdrawal is not to affect a person taking without notice of it.

57 The third party will acquire only such title as the owner himself had, so that if this is defeasible, it will remain so in the hands of the third party.

58 A pledge of the documents of title to goods is deemed a pledge of the goods (s 3). The word 'pledge' is widely defined in s 1 and appears to embrace mortgages and charges.

preventing him from recovering the goods or documents until the pledge or other security has been redeemed.[59] In order to invoke s 2(1) successfully the innocent third party must establish the following:

1.   Possession of goods or documents of title by a mercantile agent

The expression 'goods' includes wares and merchandise[60] and appears to have the same meaning as in the Sale of Goods Act. Section 1 of the Factors Act gives an enlarged meaning to 'documents of title', for while at common law the only document recognized as a document of title is a bill of lading, s 1 of the Act extends the term to include 'any bill of lading, dock warrant, warehouse-keeper's certificate, and warrant or order for the delivery of goods, and any other document used in the ordinary course of business as proof of the possession or control of goods, or authorizing or purporting to authorize, either by endorsement or by delivery, the possessor of the document to transfer or receive goods thereby represented'.[61] A motor-vehicle registration book[62] has been held not to be a document of title,[63] serving entirely different functions.[64]

'Mercantile agent' is defined[65] as 'a mercantile agent having in the customary course of his business as such agent authority either to sell goods, or to consign goods for the purpose of sale, or to buy goods, or to raise money on the security of goods'. Despite the title of the Act, it is not necessary that the agent should be a factor, that is, one having usual authority to buy, sell, etc, in his own name. Moreover, the courts have held (stretching the language of s 1 somewhat) that a person can be a mercantile agent even though his business is that of buying and selling on his own behalf, and not as agent at all, and even if he carries on an entirely different kind of business or no independent business, so long as in the particular case the owner entrusted the goods to him in a business capacity for the purpose of dealing with them in the way in which they would be dealt with by a mercantile agent. In other words, acting for a single principal in a single agency transaction may constitute a person a mercantile agent.[66] But s 2(1) does not apply

---

59 However, if the pledge was for an antecedent advance, the pledgee's priority does not extend to the full advance as such but is limited to the enforceable rights of the pledgor to the goods at the time of the pledge (s 4), so that if, vis-à-vis the owner, the mercantile agent had no claim over the goods at all, none will be held by the pledgee against the owner, and if the mercantile agent's claim over the goods was limited to a lien for his charges, the interest of the pledgee will be correspondingly limited.

60 Factors Act 1889, s 1.

61 See R. M. Goode, *Proprietary Rights and Insolvency in Sales Transactions* (2nd edn, 1989) p 62.

62 Now replaced by a vehicle registration document.

63 *Joblin v Watkins & Roseveare (Motors) Ltd* [1949] 1 All ER 47; *Bishopsgate Motor Finance Corp. Ltd v Transport Brakes Ltd*, n 5; *J Sargent (Garages) Ltd v Motor Auctions (West Bromwich) Ltd* [1977] RTR 121; *Beverley Acceptances Ltd v Oakley* [1982] RTR 417 (Lord Denning MR dissenting).

64 Namely, to establish the payment of the vehicle licence fee and to assist the police in tracing stolen vehicles.

65 Factors Act, s 1.

66 *Weiner v Harris* [1910] 1 KB 285; *Lowther v Harris* [1927] 1 KB 393.

if possession is given to a person otherwise than in the capacity of mercantile agent, for example, as a buyer under a conditional sale agreement.[67]

A third person is to be deemed in possession of goods or of the documents of title to goods where the goods or documents are in his actual custody or are held by any other person subject to his control or for him or on his behalf.[68] Hence a mercantile agent who, having received goods from the owner, deposits them in a warehouse which undertakes to hold them on his behalf is considered to be still in possession of the goods.

2. Consent of the owner

To be within the section, the third party must show that the goods were in the mercantile agent's possession with the consent of the owner and that the consent was to possession by the mercantile agent in his capacity as such.[69] If I deliver my car to a motor dealer for sale or with a view to sale,[70] I entrust my car to him as a mercantile agent. If I leave my car at his garage for the purpose of repair, then even though he is a mercantile agent I have not consented to his possessing the car in that capacity and s 2 will not apply to a wrongful disposition made by him.[71] Similarly, s 2(1) does not apply to delivery to a person as hirer under a hirer-purchase agreement[72] or as buyer under a conditional sale agreement.[73] Consent obtained by fraud is nevertheless an effective consent within the meaning of the section.[74]

Consent to possession of the goods by a mercantile agent receiving them as such carries through automatically to any documents of title which the agent thereby obtains.[75] Thus if the agent, having received the goods with the owner's consent, has them loaded on to a ship and receives a bill of lading in exchange, he is deemed to have received the bill of lading with the consent of the owner of the goods, and the effect of any dealing with the bill of lading will be treated on that basis.

Consent is presumed in the absence of evidence to the contrary;[76] and withdrawal of the consent is not effective as against a third party who takes without knowledge of the withdrawal of consent and under a disposition which would have been valid if the consent had continued.[77]

---

67 See below.

68 Factors Act, s 1.

69 *Astley Industrial Trust Ltd v Miller*, n 29, which contains a useful survey of the relevant authorities.

70 As at common law, it is not necessary that I should authorize the agent to sell; it suffices that I deposit the goods with him for the purpose of inviting offers. See *Turner v Sampson*, n 28.

71 *Pearson v Rose & Young* Ltd, n 29, per Denning LJ at 288.

72 *Astlery Industrial Trust Ltd v Miller*, n 29.

73 *Traders Group Ltd v Gouthro* (1969) 9 DLR (3d) 387; *Sun Toyota Ltd v Granville Toyota Ltd* 2002 BCD Civ J 1265.

74 *Pearson v Rose & Young Ltd*, n 29.

75 Factors Act, s 2(3).

76 Ibid, s 2(4).

77 Ibid, s 2(2).

3. Sale, pledge or other disposition

Any form of disposition is protected if it is for consideration[78] and the other requirements of s 2 are fulfilled, and, in contrast to the position under ss 8 and 9 of the Act, it is not necessary that possession shall have been given to the third party. On the other hand, the mercantile agent must himself be in possession at the time of the disposition. It is not sufficient that he was previously in possession.[79] Moreover, the transaction between the mercantile agent and the third party must be one which has a dispositive effect, as opposed to being a mere contract.[80] If, therefore, the agent contracts to sell the goods to a third party but reserves title (eg until payment) and does not deliver possession, then at that stage the third party has no real rights in the goods but merely a personal contractual right and the owner will be entitled to recover them. The position is otherwise once title has passed or possession has been given or some other real right has been conferred on the third party, eg by an agreement that the goods shall stand mortgaged or charged with payment of a sum of money, which takes effect as an equitable mortgage of charge.[81]

4. 'In the ordinary course of business of a mercantile agent'

This means merely that the agent must, in disposing of the goods, act in the manner in which a mercantile agent would act if authorized to carry out the transaction.[82] Factors tending to negate this are: disposition of a kind not normal for a mercantile agent of the type in question;[83] sale at a substantial undervalue[84] or outside normal business hours[85] or otherwise than at or from proper business premises;[86] sale of a vehicle without delivery of the registration document[87] or ignition key;[88] a forced sale designed to allow the buyer to set off the price against an existing indebtedness of the seller to the buyer.[89]

---

78 Section 2 does not expressly require consideration, but this is implicit in s 5, which states what suffices as consideration. Under that section the pledge may be for cash, goods, documents of title or negotiable securities, but in the last three cases the pledgee's rights over the goods are limited to the value, at the time of pledge, of the goods, documents or instruments given in exchange.

79 *Beverley Acceptances Ltd v Oakley*, n 63.

80 This is not merely the natural construction of the words 'sale, pledge or other disposition' but seems to follow from the fact that in s 2, unlike ss 8 and 9, those words are not followed by the phrase 'or under any agreement for sale, pledge or other disposition thereof'.

81 See p 626.

82 *Oppenheimer v Attenborough & Son* [1908] 1 KB 221.

83 *Lloyds & Scottish Finance Ltd v Williamson*, n 45.

84 *Heap v Motorists' Advisory Agency Ltd* [1923] 1 KB 577.

85 *Motor Credits (Hire Finance) Ltd v Pacific Motor Auctions Pty Ltd*, n 45, approved on appeal on this point [1965] AC 867. The decision did not involve the question of mercantile agency, but the principle is the same.

86 *Oppenheimer v Attenborough & Son*, n 82, per Buckley LJ at 230–231.

87 *Stadium Finance Ltd v Robbins* [1962] 2 QB 664; *Pearson v Rose & Young Ltd*, n 29. But see n 88.

88 *Stadium Finance Ltd v Robbins*, n 87. The suggestion in these cases that non-delivery of the registration document or ignition key *ipso jure* prevents the sale from being in the ordinary course of business is not, it is submitted, in accordance with commercial reality. There may be many reasons for a short delay in delivering the document or the keys. Non-delivery at the time of sale should simply be regarded as a relevant fact, not a conclusive determinant in law.

89 *Motor Credits (Hire Finance) Ltd v Pacific Motor Auctions Pty Ltd*, n 45.

5.   Good faith and want of notice

To be protected, the third party must show that he took in good faith and without notice of the agent's want of authority. These two requirements are not synonymous. Good faith denotes honesty in fact, even if the honest belief was unreasonable or the party holding that belief was negligent.[90] Sale to him at an undervalue may be evidence of want of good faith but is not conclusive. On the other hand, the third party will probably be considered to have notice of want of authority if, though acting in good faith, he acquires the goods in such circumstances that no reasonable man would have taken them without further inquiry.[91]

(iv) Consignment[92]

By s 7(1) of the Factors Act:

> Where the owner of goods has given possession of the goods to another person for the purpose of consignment or sale, or has shipped the goods in the name of another person, and the consignee of the goods has not had notice that such person is not the owner of the goods, the consignee shall, in respect of advances made to or for the use of such person, have the same lien on the goods as if such person were the owner of the goods, and may transfer any such lien to another person.

Nothing in the section limits or affects the validity of any sale, pledge or disposition by a mercantile agent.[93]

(v) Disposition by seller remaining in possession[94]

The decision in *Johnson v Crédit Lyonnais Co*[95] resulted in immediate legislation in the shape of the Factors Act 1877, the relevant provisions of which are now embodied in s 8 of the Factors Act 1889, which provides as follows:

> Where a person, having sold goods, continues, or is, in possession of the goods or of the documents of title to the goods, the delivery or transfer by that person, or by a mercantile agent acting for him, of the goods or documents of title under any sale, pledge or other disposition thereof or under any agreement for sale, pledge or other disposition thereof, to any person receiving the same in good faith and without notice of the previous sale, shall have the same effect as if the person making the

---

90 Cf Sale of Goods Act 1979, s 61(3).

91 However, the meaning of 'notice' is unclear. See the discussion by K. C. T. Sutton, *Sales and Consumer Law in Australia and New Zealand* (4th edn, 1995), pp 507–508. What is established is that the equitable doctrine of constructive notice does not apply to commercial dealings in goods. Hence a bona fide purchaser is not fixed with notice of his seller's breach of trust or other breach of duty merely because of a failure to make inquiries as to the seller's right to sell (*Manchester Trust v Furness* [1895] 2 QB 539, applied in *By Appointment (Sales) Ltd v Harrods Ltd* (1977), unreported CA (Bar Library transcript No 465) and *Feuer Leather Corp. v Frank Johnston & Sons*, n 37). The onus is on the third party to show that he took in good faith and without notice (*Oppenheimer v Attenborough & Son*, n 82; *Heap v Motorists' Advisory Agency Ltd*, n 84).

92 For the use of consignment in motor-vehicle stocking arrangements, see p 770.

93 Section 7(2).

94 The ensuing pages are based on the somewhat more extended treatment in Goode, *Hire-Purchase Law and Practice* (2nd edn, 1970), pp 602 ff.

95 See n 34.

delivery or transfer were expressly authorized by the owner of the goods to make the same.

Section 24 of the Sale of Goods Act 1979, re-enacting s 25(1) of the Sale of Goods Act 1893, is in identical terms except that the words 'or under any agreement for sale, pledge or other disposition thereof' are omitted. Since s 8 of the Factors Act is, by reason of the inclusion of the above words, somewhat wider in scope, it is that provision which will be analysed in the following paragraphs. In most cases where s 8 is applicable, s 24 of the Sale of Goods Act will apply also.

1. 'Having sold goods'

The section applies only to a disposition by a person who has sold. It does not cover the case where the first disposition is only an agreement to sell (the property remaining in the seller) or a hire-purchase agreement. In these cases the statutory provision is unnecessary since the seller's retention of the property in the goods enables him to pass title on the second disposition.[96]

Although s 8 is silent on the point, it would seem that the seller cannot, on making his second disposition, transfer a better title than he had before he sold to the first buyer. In other words, 'owner' in the phrase 'expressly authorized by the owner' must be taken to denote the first buyer, and it is only the latter's title that is overridden by the second disposition made by the seller. If, for example, the goods were stolen and the thief sold them to A, A would not acquire the title. It would be absurd if, having sold to A while remaining in possession, the thief could then qualify as a seller in possession and pass title by reselling the goods to B. In that situation, if the section were to apply, the first purchaser from the thief would acquire no title while the second purchaser would. It seems clear that 'owner' is to be read as denoting the relevant owner, ie the first buyer.[97]

2. 'Continues or is in possession'

In order for title to pass under s 8 it is necessary that the seller 'continues or is in possession' of goods, or of documents of title to them, at the time of the second disposition.[98] In *Pacific Motor Auctions Pty Ltd v Motor Credits (Hire Finance) Ltd*,[99] it was held (disapproving earlier cases on the point) that as long as there was no break in the seller's possession after the first sale by him and before he resold, the section applied, even though the character of the seller's possession had changed from that of seller as such to that of bailee, eg under a hiring back from the original buyer on hire or hire-purchase. This decision was followed in *Worcester Works Finance Ltd v Cooden Engineering Co Ltd*,[100] in which, somewhat surprisingly,

---

96 *Semble*, this is so even if the purchaser took with notice of the prior sale or hire-purchase agreement.

97 See *National Employers' Mutual General Insurance Association Ltd v Jones* [1990] 1 AC 24, per Lord Goff at 62, in which Lord Goff expressed a similar view (albeit obiter) on s 8 as part of his reasoning for his decision on s 9, as to which see p 000.

98 *Pacific Motor Auctions Pty Ltd v Motor Credits (Hire Finance) Ltd* [1965] AC 867. See also *Mitchell v Jones* (1905) 24 NZLR 932, and Goode, *Hire-Purchase Law*, pp 604–605.

99 See n 98.

100 [1972] 1 QB 210.

a repossession by the seller's own vendor with the seller's consent was held to constitute a 'disposition' within s 25(1) of the 1893 Act.[101]

It is not necessary that the seller should have remained in possession with the consent of the first buyer. In this respect s 8(1) differs from the comparable provisions of s 9 governing dispositions by a buyer in possession.[102]

3.   Delivery or transfer of goods or documents of title

The second buyer will not acquire title unless there is a delivery or transfer of the goods or documents of title to him. This has been interpreted[103] as meaning that goods must be delivered or documents of title transferred. In *Gamer's Motor Centre (Newcastle) Pty Ltd v Natwest Wholesale Australia Pty Ltd*[104] the High Court of Australia held, by a majority of three to two, that physical delivery was not necessary and that constructive delivery sufficed. So where dealers, having acquired motor vehicles under a floor-plan agreement by which title remained in the seller until payment, resold the vehicles to the plaintiffs but retained possession for the purpose of display, the character of the dealer's possession changed to that of bailee for the plaintiffs, who had thereby obtained constructive delivery and thus title under the statutory provisions. The decision is not easy to support, for every seller of specific or ascertained goods is a bailee of the buyer, so that this construction deprives the delivery requirement of any meaning. Further, it disregards the underlying policy of the statutory provisions, which is not simply delivery to the buyer but divestment of possession by the seller. This is clear from the definition of 'delivery' in s 61(1) as 'voluntary transfer of possession from one person to another'. However, the decision in *Gamer* was applied by Clarke J in *Forsythe International (UK) Ltd v Silver Shipping Co Ltd*.[105] An interesting point arose in *Michael Gerson (Leasing) Ltd v Wilkinson*,[106] where a company in possession of equipment under a leasing agreement sold it to a finance house which let it back to the seller on lease. The sale and lease-back were interdependent, so that there was never a time at which the buyer was in a position to give instructions to the seller as to the goods.[107] Nevertheless, the Court of Appeal rejected the argument that there was never any assent by the seller to hold the goods for the buyer rather than for an interest of its own as lessee and held that there had to have been constructive

---

101   For a criticism of this case, see R. M. Goode, 'The Dispositive Effect of a Seller's Repossession' (1972) 35 MLR 186.

102   See p 435.

103   *Nicholson v Harper* [1895] 2 Ch 415; *Kitto v Bilbie, Hobson & Co* (1895) 72 LT 266.

104   (1987) 163 CLR 236.

105   [1994] 1 WLR 1334.

106   [2001] QB 514.

107   In this significant respect the case differed from *Marvin v Wallace* (1856) 25 LJQB 369, in which the seller acknowledged the buyer's title and asked if he could borrow the goods. The decision is incorrectly cited by Pollock and Wright, *An Essay on Possession in the Common Law* (1888), p 72, as authority for the proposition that there is constructive delivery whether the vendor's custody is in the character of a bailee for reward or of a borrower, whereas in fact the seller's assent to hold for the buyer was not under the bailment for reward but preceded that bailment, leaving it open to the buyer to refuse to allow the seller to have the goods as bailee. What happens after the assent has been given is irrelevant.

delivery to the buyer in order for it to grant a lease back of the goods, and it was not necessary to identify the point at which the constructive delivery occurred.[108]

4.   The wrongful disposition

Where the second disposition is an outright sale, title passes to the second buyer; where it is an agreement for sale, then the second buyer has priority over the first and will acquire title when the property passes to him in accordance with the rules laid down in the Sale of Goods Act;[109] where it is a pledge, then while the first buyer still has title, he holds this subject to the rights of the pledgee. Where the seller, after selling the goods, lets them on hire-purchase and delivers possession to the hirer, the hire-purchase agreement binds the first buyer and if the hirer exercises his option to purchase,[110] he acquires a good title.

5.   Good faith

In order to obtain title under s 8 the party to whom the goods or documents of title are disposed of must have received these in good faith and without notice of the previous sale. This good faith and want of notice must exist at the date of delivery of the goods, or transfer of documents of title, as well as at the date of the disposition. If, therefore, the seller wrongfully resells the goods to an innocent purchaser but, before the delivery of the goods to him, that purchaser becomes aware of the previous sale, then he is subordinated to the rights of the original buyer and does not acquire title. His remedy is, of course, to rescind the contract of sale and/or claim damages for breach of the condition of title.[111]

(vi) Lien and stoppage in transit

The unpaid seller's rights of lien and stoppage in transit are defeated by the buyer's sale to a bona fide transferee for value of a document of title to the goods,[112] and if the buyer, instead of reselling, pledges or otherwise disposes of the document, the unpaid seller's rights are subordinated to those of the transferee.[113]

(vii) Sale by seller who has exercised his right of lien or stoppage

Where an unpaid seller who has exercised his right of lien or stoppage resells the goods, the buyer acquires a good title as against the original buyer.[114] This appears

---

108   Which would have been difficult, for the delivery must take place after the sale and the only relevant act, namely signature of the leasing agreement, would establish that the lessee held for an interest of its own, not at the direction of the buyer-lessor. This difficulty was not addressed in the judgments.

109   Section 18. See pp 260 ff.

110   For the complex position arising where he does not, eg because the hire-purchase agreement is terminated for default, see Goode, *Hire-Purchase Law*, pp 606–607.

111   See pp 361, 378.

112   Sale of Goods Act, s 47(2)(a); Factors Act, s 10. See also Sale of Goods Act, s 25 and Factors Act, s 9.

113   Section 47(2)(b).

114   Section 48(2).

to be the case whether or not the second buyer has notice that the resale by the seller is in breach of his duty to the first buyer. On the other hand, the section is limited to resale by the seller and does not extend to a charge, pledge or other form of disposition.

(viii) Disposition by buyer obtaining possession

Section 9 of the Factors Act 1889 provides as follows:

> Where a person, having bought or agreed to buy goods, obtains with the consent of the seller possession of the goods or the documents of title to the goods, the delivery or transfer, by that person or by a mercantile agent acting for him, of the goods or documents of title, under any sale, pledge or other disposition thereof, or under any agreement for sale, pledge or other disposition thereof, to any person receiving the same in good faith and without notice of any lien or other right of the original seller in respect of the goods, shall have the same effect as if the person making the delivery or transfer were a mercantile agent in possession of the goods or documents of title with the consent of the owner.

Section 25(1) of the Sale of Goods Act 1979 repeats this provision verbatim except that, like s 24, it omits the words 'or under any agreement for sale, pledge or other disposition thereof'. Again, therefore, we shall analyse the slightly wider provisions of s 9 of the Factors Act.[115]

As with other statutory exceptions to the *nemo dat* rule, the courts have consistently taken the view that s 9 must be strictly construed. This has resulted in such a restrictive and literal interpretation of s 9 that it has become extraordinarily difficult for any innocent party to bring himself within its provisions. We shall consider first the various conditions that have to be satisfied in order for s 9 to apply at all and then the effect of its application.

1.   The buyer

Section 9 covers dispositions not only by one who has agreed to buy goods but one who has bought goods, ie title has passed to him. This is at first sight a somewhat odd provision since if the buyer has already acquired title, then there is nothing to prevent him from disposing of the goods without the assistance of s 9. However, it needs to be borne in mind that the buyer himself may not have acquired a full and indefeasible title. It may be that his seller lacked title or power to dispose of the goods. In that case, s 9 operates as against the seller but not as against the true owner.[116] Another case covered by s 9 is that of a buyer whose title is voidable[117] and who resells after his title has been avoided. In this situation it seems that even though s 23 of the Sale of Goods Act[118] would not assist the second buyer, s 9 of the Factors Act will protect him.[119]

---

115 This and the ensuing paragraphs are a shortened version of the treatment in Goode, *Hire-Purchase Law and Practice*, pp 608 ff.

116 See p 437.

117 Eg, because he obtained the goods by fraud or misrepresentation.

118 See p 425.

119 See p 436, n 128.

Section 9 does not apply to a disposition by a hirer under a hire-purchase agreement since from the nature of the agreement he is not compelled to exercise his right to purchase and is not, therefore, a person who has 'agreed to buy' for the purpose of the section;[120] nor does it extend to a disposition by one who has acquired materials under a contract for labour and materials, since, again, this is not an agreement to buy.[121]

Moreover, even dispositions by a buyer holding under a conditional sale agreement are excluded from s 9 if the agreement is within the Hire-Purchase Act 1965[122] and will likewise be excluded in the case of such an agreement within the Consumer Credit Act 1974,[123] for in each such case it is provided that the buyer shall be deemed not to be a person who has bought or agreed to buy goods.[124]

2.   Possession of the goods

In order to pass title under s 9 the buyer must be in possession of the goods or documents of title to them. But he need not be in physical possession; constructive possession suffices. So where the buyer resells the goods and arranges with his seller to deliver them direct to the sub-buyer, such delivery is considered to be a constructive delivery to the buyer,[125] and in turn a constructive delivery by the buyer to the sub-buyer.[126]

3.   Consent of the seller

Unlike dispositions by a seller in possession under s 8, a disposition by a buyer in possession does not attract the operation of s 9 unless the buyer was in possession with the consent of the seller.[127] Such consent is effective for the purpose of s 9 even if obtained by fraud; and where consent is once given, its withdrawal does not

---

120 *Helby v Matthews* [1895] AC 471. The same applies to a disposition by one who has taken the goods on sale or return (*Percy Edwards Ltd v Vaughan* (1910) 26 TLR 545). However, such a disposition constitutes an adoption of the sale, so that if it was on terms such that title was to pass to the deliveree on adoption (which is the presumption under s 18, r 4(a) of the Sale of Goods Act) this would, of course, be effectively transferred to the third party (*Kirkham v Attenborough* [1897] 1 QB 201). The position is otherwise where the terms of the agreement for sale on approval or sale or return are inconsistent with the property passing on adoption of the transaction, as where it is stipulated that the property is not to pass until payment (*Percy Edwards Ltd v Vaughan*, above). See generally Ann Spowart Taylor, 'Goods on Sale or Return and the *Nemo Dat* Rule' [1985] JBL 390.

121 *Dawber Williamson Roofing Ltd v Humberside* (1979) 14 BLR 70 (the point is more clearly brought out in the summary of the case in [1979] CLY 212).

122 Hire-Purchase Act 1965, s 54, as amended by Sale of Goods Act 1979, Sch 2, para 6.

123 Factors Act, s 9, as amended by Consumer Credit Act, Sch 4, para 2; Sale of Goods Act, s 25(2)

124 Ibid.

125 *Four Point Garage Ltd v Carter* [1985] 3 All ER 12.

126 See p 436. The objections raised earlier (p 432) to the acceptability of the buyer's constructive delivery as a means of satisfying s 24 of the Sale of Goods Act do not apply here, for the head seller has lost possession, the sub-buyer has acquired it, and the only question is whether the intermediate seller received constructive delivery and is to be treated as having himself made delivery to the sub-buyer. It is clear on general principle that delivery by the head seller at the request of the intermediate seller constitutes delivery by the intermediate seller himself.

127 'Seller' in this context appears to mean a seller whose consent is necessary, ie one who himself has title or a right to dispose.

affect the buyer's power to pass title under s 9 to a transferee taking without notice of the fact that the consent has been withdrawn.[128]

4.   Documents of title

It seems that where the buyer is in possession of documents of title with the consent of the seller, then the transfer by him of documents of title to the goods attracts the operation of s 9 even though the documents of title transferred are not the same documents of title as those of which the buyer obtained possession with the consent of the seller.[129]

5.   Delivery or transfer

As in the case of s 8, it would seem that there must be physical delivery of goods and that the alternative 'transfer' is limited to documents of title.[130] But, as under s 8, the goods need not be physically delivered by the buyer in possession himself. Delivery by a mercantile agent acting for him suffices, as does delivery by his own seller direct to the sub-buyer at the buyer's direction.[131] The delivery must be voluntary; a seizure of the goods from the buyer does not constitute delivery to the person seizing them for the purpose of s 25.[132]

6.   Sale, pledge or other disposition

The same observations apply as to s 8.[133]

7.   Good faith

The requirement of good faith is expressed slightly differently in s 9 from that stated in s 8. Under s 8 the third party must receive the goods in good faith and without notice of the previous sale. Under s 9 he must receive the goods in good faith and without notice of any 'lien or other right of the original seller in respect of the goods'. The reference to lien is curious since it is difficult to see in what circumstances the seller could have a subsisting lien when he has voluntarily given possession of the goods to the buyer.

Where the above conditions are satisfied, the disposition in favour of the third party has 'the same effect as if the person making the delivery or transfer were a mercantile agent in possession of the goods or documents of title with the consent of the owner'. Although these words admittedly differ from the concluding words of s 8, it had always been assumed until 1965 that they were to be taken as meaning that title passed to the third party. It was assumed that when s 9 said that the

---

128   *Cahn v Pockett's Bristol Channel Steam Packet Co* [1899] 1 QB 643; *Newtons of Wembley Ltd v Williams* [1964] 1 WLR 1028. So the fact that the seller under a conditional sale agreement rescinds the agreement before resale by the buyer does not protect the seller from s 9 (*Newtons of Wembley Ltd v Williams*, above).

129   *D. F. Mount Ltd v Jay & Jay (Provisions) Ltd* [1960] 1 QB 159.

130   See p 432.

131   *Four Point Garage Ltd v Carter*, n 125.

132   *The Saetta* [1993] 2 Lloyd's Rep 268.

133   See pp 433, 437.

disposition was to take effect as if the person making the delivery or transfer were a mercantile agent in possession of the goods, this was an elliptical method of stating that the disposition was to take effect as if the goods had been delivered by a mercantile agent disposing of them in the ordinary course of business of a mercantile agent; for unless these additional words were to be regarded as imported by implication into s 9, it would be rendered almost wholly nugatory. This assumption, adopted in at least two Commonwealth decisions, one in Australia[134] and the other in New Zealand,[135] was somewhat surprisingly rejected by the Court of Appeal in *Newtons of Wembley Ltd v Williams*,[136] where it was held that although on the facts of that case s 9 applied, this did not conclude the matter, for that section impliedly incorporated the requirements of s 2, with the result that a disposition by a buyer under s 9 would pass a good title only if made in the manner in which it would have been made if the buyer had himself been disposing of the goods as a mercantile agent. It is submitted, for reasons elaborated elsewhere,[137] that this is an erroneous interpretation of s 9, and so drastically reduces its scope as to deprive the section of any rational policy basis.

So far, we have assumed that the disposition in favour of the third party is by outright sale or by pledge or mortgage. But suppose that B, having contracted to buy goods from S on terms that B is not to acquire title until payment, enters into an agreement for sale to T on similar terms before title has passed to him from S, and delivers the goods to T. T does not at that stage acquire a good title. None the less, the sub-sale agreement is binding on S, so that T is entitled to hold possession against S so long as he observes the terms of the sub-sale agreement, and title will vest in T on his completing payment under that agreement.[138]

One other problem remains. Though the consent to possession necessary to attract s 9 is the consent of the *seller*, the delivery or transfer is given the same effect as if the person making it were a mercantile agent in possession with the consent of the owner. From this it has been deduced[139] that s 9 can operate even if the original seller lacked title. Such an interpretation would produce the result, absurd in policy terms, that while a thief could not pass title in the stolen goods to his purchaser, yet that purchaser could pass title on a resale. This conclusion, which had rightly been rejected by courts in Kenya,[140] Canada[141] and New

---

134 *Langmead v Thyer Rubber Co Ltd* [1947] SASR 29.

135 *Jeffcott v Andrew Motors Ltd* [1960] NZLR 721.

136 [1965] 1 QB 560.

137 Goode, *Hire-Purchase Law and Practice*, pp 613–614; 'Sale by Seller with Voidable Title' (1965) 115 LJ 4; and see Jacob S. Ziegel (1965) 43 Can Bar Rev 639.

138 For discussion of a similar point arising under s 21(1) of the Sale of Goods Act see pp 418–419. The difference is that s 9 requires delivery to T, whereas the common law rules as to the binding effect of transactions entered into with apparent authority do not.

139 W. R. Cornish, 'Rescission Without Notice' (1964) 27 MLR 472.

140 *Mubarak Ali v Wali Mohamed & Co* (1938) 18 KLR 23, discussed by Aubrey L. Diamond, 'Sale of Goods in East Africa' (1967) 16 ICLQ 1045 at p 1054.

141 *Brandon v Leckie* (1972) 29 DLR (3d) 633. See D. G. Powles, 'Stolen Goods and the Sale of Goods Act 1893 s 25(2)' (1974) 37 MLR 213, and G. Battersby and A. D. Preston, 'Stolen Goods and the Sale of Goods Act 1893 s 25(2) – A Rejoinder' (1975) 38 MLR 77. See also the discussion by P.S. Atiyah, John N. Adams and Hector MacQueen, *The Sale of Goods* (10th edn, 2001), pp 406–408.

Zealand,[142] has also been decisively repudiated in this country by the House of Lords in *National Employers' Mutual General Insurance Association Ltd v Jones*.[143]

(ix) Disposition under Part III of the Hire-Purchase Act 1964[144]

Part III of the Hire-Purchase Act 1964, as amended by the Consumer Credit Act 1974,[145] regulates the rights of third parties who purchase motor vehicles while these are still comprised in a hire-purchase or conditional sale agreement.[146] The broad scheme of Part III is that a disposition of a motor vehicle made by a debtor under a hire-purchase or conditional sale agreement[147] is to be effective to transfer to a 'private purchaser' taking in good faith and without notice of the agreement such title as was vested in the person who had supplied the goods under that agreement.[148] This is so whether the private purchaser takes direct from the debtor or through the medium of a 'trade or finance purchaser'.[149] If the private purchaser is not an outright buyer but himself takes the vehicle on hire-purchase or conditional sale, his possession is protected and he will acquire the original owner's title on completing his payments and (in the case of a hire-purchase agreement) exercising his option to purchase.

These statutory provisions constitute a substantial inroad into the common law rule *nemo dat quod non habet* which has hitherto been the cornerstone of English hire-purchase law. They override s 21 of the Sale of Goods Act[150] but are without prejudice to the provisions of the Factors Act or of any other enactment enabling the apparent owner of goods to dispose of them as if he were a true owner.[151] It should, however, be borne in mind that s 9 of the Factors Act and s 25(1) of the Sale of Goods Act do not in any event apply to dispositions by a debtor holding under a hire-purchase or conditional sale agreement which is within the Hire-Purchase Act 1965 or the Consumer Credit Act 1974.[152]

---

142   *Elwin v O'Regan & Maxwell* [1971] NZLR 1124.

143   See n 97, approving the statement in P. S. Atiyah, *The Sale of Goods* (7th edn, 1985), at pp 302–303. See also the first edition of the present work at pp 413–414.

144   See Goode, *Hire-Purchase Law and Practice*, pp 617 ff and Supplement.

145   Sch 4, para 22.

146   Part III is not limited to cases where the agreement is itself within the Hire-Purchase Act or the Consumer Credit Act.

147   As to when a hire-purchase agreement is to be considered concluded, see *Carlyle Finance Ltd v Pallas Industrial Finance Ltd* [1999] RTR 281. If a purported hire-purchase agreement is void for mistake of identity on a face-to-face dealing between parties, the statutory provisions do not apply (*Shogun Finance Ltd v Hudson* [2004] 1 AC 919). See p 78. *Semble*, the position is the same if the agreement is voidable and has been avoided prior to the disposition.

148   For the legislative scheme originally projected, see Goode, *Hire-Purchase Law and Practice*, p 617, n 14.

149   For the meaning of this, see p 439.

150   Hire-Purchase Act 1964, s 27(5), as amended by the Consumer Credit Act 1974, Sch 4, para 22, and Sale of Goods Act 1979, Sch 2, para 4.

151   Ibid.

152   See nn 122, 123.

1.   Goods to which Part III of the 1964 Act applies

The provisions of Part III are limited to motor vehicles,[153] that is to say, mechanically propelled vehicles intended or adapted for use on roads to which the public has access.[154]

2.   Disposition to a private purchaser

Where the debtor,[155] before the property in the vehicle has become vested in him under the hire-purchase or conditional sale agreement,[156] disposes of the vehicle to a private purchaser who takes in good faith and without notice of the agreement, the disposition is to have effect as if the title of the creditor[157] to the vehicle had been vested in the debtor immediately before that disposition.[158] The following points require to be noted in connection with this provision.

(a) DISPOSITION. By 'disposition' is meant any sale or contract of sale (including a conditional sale agreement), any bailment under a hire-purchase agreement and any transfer of the property in goods in pursuance of a provision in that behalf contained in a hire-purchase agreement, and includes any transaction purporting to be a disposition (as so defined); and 'dispose of' is to be construed accordingly.[159]

It will be seen that the letting of goods on hire-purchase constitutes a disposition and if the new hirer subsequently exercises his option to purchase under the new hire-purchase agreement, that constitutes a separate disposition. But a mortgage is not a disposition.[160]

(b) PRIVATE PURCHASER. This term is used in contradistinction to 'trade or finance purchaser'. A trade or finance purchaser is a purchaser who, at the time of the disposition made to him, carries on a business which consists, wholly or partly:

(i)   of purchasing motor vehicles for the purpose of offering or exposing them for sale;
(ii)   of providing finance by purchasing motor vehicles for the purpose of bailing them under hire-purchase agreements or agreeing to sell them under conditional sale agreements.[161]

153 Section 27(1).
154 Section 29(1).
155 Ie, the hirer or conditional buyer (Hire-Purchase Act 1964, s 29(4), as amended by the Consumer Credit Act 1974, Sch 4, para.22). A person does not qualify as a debtor for this purpose if the agreement is void *ab initio* 439.
Shogun Finance Ltd v Hudson [2004] 1 AC 919) or, *semble*, though originally voidable, has been avoided prior to the wrongful disposition. One of two joint and several hirers is a debtor and has power to pass a good title under the statutory provisions (*Keeble v Combined Lease Finance plc* [1999] GCCR 2065).
156 This will usually be when he has completed his payments.
157 Ie, the owner or seller (Hire-Purchase Act 1964, s 29(4), as amended by the Consumer Credit Act 1974, Sch 4 and para 22).
158 Hire-Purchase Act 1964, s 27(2), as amended.
159 Section 29(1).
160 For a case in which it was unsuccessfully argued that the transaction was a mortgage see *Dodds v Yorkshire Bank Finance Ltd* [1999] GCCR 1621.

A private purchaser means a purchaser who, at the time of the disposition made to him, does not carry on any such business.[162] Broadly, therefore, a trade or finance purchaser means a motor dealer or a finance house, and a private purchaser means a purchaser other than a motor dealer or finance house. The term 'person' is not confined to natural persons so that a body corporate can be a private purchaser for the purpose of the Act in the same way as an individual.[163]

The intention of the provision is to protect members of the public who buy as consumers but not motor dealers or finance companies, who can be presumed to be capable of looking after themselves.[164] However, although a trade or finance purchaser cannot acquire title under these provisions, a purchaser from him will obtain title in certain circumstances.[165]

The expression 'private purchaser' being defined by reference to the business carried on by him at the time of purchase and not by reference to the circumstances in which he made his purchase, it follows that a trade purchaser such as a motor dealer cannot avail himself of the title-passing provisions, even in regard to a purchase made by him in a private capacity.[166]

(c) NOTICE. In order to acquire title the private purchaser must take in good faith and without notice of the hire-purchase or conditional sale agreement affecting the vehicle. If the private purchaser has notice, then title cannot pass to him, nor can it pass to persons claiming under him even though such persons take without notice.[167] A person is to be taken to be a purchaser without notice for this purpose if, at the time of the disposition to him, he has no actual notice that the vehicle is or was the subject of any hire-purchase or conditional sale agreement.[168] Constructive notice is not sufficient, so that, for example, the mere fact that a hire-purchase agreement relating to a motor vehicle is registered with H.P. Information Ltd[169] does not of itself constitute notice to a purchaser unless he is aware of the registration.

Moreover, the Court of Appeal has held[170] that a purchaser does not have notice of a hire-purchase agreement so as to defeat his title under s 27 if, though told that the vehicle had been on hire-purchase, he was led to believe that the hire-purchase agreement had been settled. The phrase '... he has no actual notice that the vehicle is or was the subject of any hire-purchase agreement' refers to any relevant hire-purchase agreement, that is, a hire-purchase agreement in respect of which the purchaser is on notice that it is still current.

---

161 Hire-Purchase Act 1964, s 29(2).
162 Ibid.
163 See Interpretation Act 1978, Sch 1.
164 In particular, they can utilize the services of H.P. Information Ltd in the case of motor vehicles, caravans and the like, to see whether the goods which are offered to them are already comprised in a current hire-purchase or conditional sale agreement.
165 See pp 441–442.
166 *Stevenson v Beverley Bentinck Ltd* [1976] 1 WLR 483.
167 See below.
168 Hire-Purchase Act 1964, s 29(3).
169 See n 164.

In order to qualify for protection the private purchaser must take in good faith, by which is meant honesty in fact;[171] and this is a requirement entirely distinct from the requirement as to absence of notice. Accordingly, if at the time of the disposition the purchaser is aware of a defect in his seller's title, he will not be able to invoke the provisions of Part III even though he was ignorant of the existence of the hire-purchase or conditional sale agreement.

(d) EFFECT OF DISPOSITION. A disposition by the debtor to a bona fide private purchaser has effect as if the creditor's title to the vehicle had been vested in the debtor immediately before the disposition.[172] By 'creditor's title' is meant such title (if any) as was immediately before the disposition by the debtor vested in the person who was then the creditor in relation to the hire-purchase or conditional sale agreement.[173] So if that person did not himself have title (eg because he was a thief or because his own vendor's title was defective), the private purchaser acquires no title. But such person may himself have acquired title under the provisions of the Act, and in that event this will be transferred to the private purchaser in the same way as if it were a normal title.[174]

(e) THE POSITION OF THE PURCHASER. Is the buyer obliged to accept a Part III title or can he repudiate the contract on the ground that the seller is in breach of the condition implied by s 12(1) of the Sale of Goods Act that he has a right to dispose of the goods? If the buyer tries to tender the vehicle to a dealer in part exchange, the dealer will discover the existence of the hire-purchase agreement from H.P. information Ltd and is unlikely to be impressed with the Part III title offered him. Such a title is therefore less marketable than an established title and, for reasons given earlier,[175] the buyer ought not to be compelled to accept it unless it is virtually indisputable.

Similar considerations would seem to apply where the bona fide private purchaser is not an outright buyer but himself takes the vehicle on hire-purchase or conditional sale.

Nothing in the statutory provisions exonerates the hirer or buyer from any liability (civil or criminal) to which he would otherwise be subject,[176] so that in disposing of the goods to the subpurchaser he commits the tort of conversion,[177] and the crime of theft.[178]

3.   *Disposition to a trade or finance purchaser*

A trade or finance purchaser[179] is not entitled to the protection of Part III of the Act and acquires no title from the debtor, even though taking in good faith and without

---

170 *Barker v Bell* [1971] 1 WLR 983, citing Goode, *Hire-Purchase Law*, p 624, n 3.

171 *Dodds v Yorkshire Bank Finance Ltd* [1999] GCCR 1621.

172 Hire-Purchase Act 1964, s 27(2).

173 Section 29(5).

174 For an illustration, see Goode, *Hire-Purchase Law and Practice*, p 624.

175 See p 286.

176 Section 27(6).

177 Assuming that the disposition is effective or he delivers the goods to the purchaser. An ineffective disposition unaccompanied by delivery is not a conversion (*Lancashire Waggon Co v Fitzhugh* (1861) 6 H & N 502).

178 Theft Act 1968, s 1.

notice of the hire-purchase or conditional sale agreement. Nevertheless, such a purchaser is a conduit pipe for the passage of title to (and through) the first private purchaser who takes thereafter, if he takes in good faith and without notice.[180] But if the first private purchaser takes with notice, there is no passage of title, even though he may subsequently resell to a purchaser without notice.[181] If the first private purchaser himself takes on hire-purchase or conditional sale and as a result of his default the new creditor repossesses and sells the vehicle, it would seem that the person to whom the vehicle is then sold does not qualify for protection under Part III, since he is not the first private purchaser.[182]

The title-passing provisions do not in any way protect a trade or finance purchaser who disposes of goods of which he is not the owner,[183] so that even if he acted in good faith, he is liable to the true owner[184] in conversion.[185] Further, if he accepted the goods for the purpose of sale knowing them to be held on hire-purchase, he may be convicted of handling stolen goods[186] and, upon selling them, of the further offence of obtaining property (ie, the price) by deception.[187]

4.   Presumptions

There may be a lengthy chain of people between the hirer who wrongfully disposed of the goods and the ultimate purchaser whose title is called into question, and the latter may find it extremely difficult to trace his title back to the point where he can establish the right to the benefit of the title-passing provisions. To overcome this problem, s 28 lays down various presumptions for the benefit of the purchaser in question.[188]

The effect of these provisions is that once the purchaser establishes that he or an intermediate party was a private purchaser without notice of the hire-purchase agreement (ie was 'the relevant purchaser'), he succeeds unless the creditor who

---

179   See p 439.

180   Hire-Purchase Act 1964, s 27(3). Where the disposition is itself on hire-purchase, the hirer is protected in the same way as where no trade or finance purchaser is involved (s 27(4)), but by an anomaly no such protection is extended to a buyer under a conditional sale agreement.

181   For an example, see Goode, *Hire-Purchase Law and Practice*, p 627, illustration (3).

182   This is a further anomaly. It is not clear why the Act should limit protection to the *first* private purchaser taking from a trade or finance purchaser when no such restriction is imposed as regards a disposition by the offending hirer or buyer to the private purchaser direct.

183   Section 27(6). See *Barber v NWS Bank plc* [1996] 1 WLR 641.

184   Assuming that the true owner has an immediate right to possession, which is normally an essential qualification for a plaintiff suing in conversion.

185   Indeed, it would seem that the mere receipt of the goods by him constitutes an act of conversion. See *Fine Art Society v Union Bank of London Ltd* (1886) 17 QBD 705.

186   Theft Act 1968, s 1. See J C. Smith, *Law of Theft* (8th edn, 1997); Edward Griew, *The Theft Acts 1968 and 1978* (7th edn, 1995); Glanville Williams, *Textbook of Criminal Law* (2nd edn, 1983), ch 39.

187   Theft Act 1968, s 15. See the textbooks cited n 186.

188   See Goode, *Hire-Purchase Law*, pp 628–630 and Supplement; *Worcester Works Finance Ltd v Ocean Banking Corporation Ltd* (1972), unreported (His Honour Judge Garrard, Uttoxeter County Court, noted Goode, *Hire-Purchase Law and Practice*, Supplement, pp A59, A90); *Soneco Ltd v Barcross Finance Ltd* [1978] RTR 444 (in which the Court of Appeal held that s 28 does not apply

supplied the goods on hire-purchase or conditional sale can establish a break in the chain between the fraudulent debtor and the claimant by proving that the person to whom the debtor disposed of the goods was neither:

(a)   the relevant purchaser; nor ·

(b)   a bona fide private purchaser without notice through whom the relevant purchaser claims; nor

(c)   a trade or finance purchaser who sold to the relevant purchaser or to a bona fide private purchaser without notice through whom the relevant purchaser claims.

(x) Sale or forfeiture under statutory powers

There are many statutory provisions authorizing a person to sell the goods of another without his consent and to pass a good title to the purchaser. Among the persons so authorized are a sheriff's officer or bailiff disposing of goods lawfully taken in execution;[189] a mortgagee exercising a power of sale;[190] the Customs and Excise selling goods condemned as forfeited;[191] the Post Office confiscating and selling an unlicensed television set;[192] a bailee exercising a statutory power to sell uncollected goods[193] or selling such goods under an order of the court;[194] a person selling perishables under an order of the court made pursuant to rules of court.[195]

4.   CONFLICTS AS TO PROCEEDS

It is a curious fact that where goods are sold without the owner's authority,[196] attention is concentrated almost exclusively on the owner's right to recover the goods from the transferee, and little or no thought is given to an alternative method of satisfaction, namely a claim to the proceeds generated by the sale. Where those proceeds are tangibles (goods, documents, money), either at the outset or because of conversion from intangibles to tangibles,[197] the owner has a common law personal right to demand delivery up of the proceeds from the person making the un-authorized sale, and from any subsequent transferee of the proceeds other than one taking for value and without notice.[198] Whether the proceeds are tangible or

at all where all the relevant dispositions are known).

189   Supreme Court Act 1981, s 138B; County Courts Act 1984, s 98; Companies Act 1985, s 621(2)(b). The officer or bailiff is protected from liability unless he had notice or might by reasonable inquiry have ascertained that the goods did not belong to the judgment debtor.

190   See p 639.

191   Customs and Excise Management Act 1979, s 139 and Sch 3.

192   Wireless Telegraphy Act 1949, s 14(3)–(3E).

193   Torts (Interference with Goods) Act 1977, s 12. To pass a good title the sale must be 'duly made under this section' (s 12(6)).

194   Ibid, s 13(2).

195   CPR 25.1, para (1)(c)(v).

196   Claims to proceeds where the owner has authorized sale are governed by somewhat different considerations. See p 720.

197   As by using cash proceeds to buy goods.

198   This has been disputed by Millett J on the ground that the common law right to trace proceeds is confined to the first recipient (*Agip (Africa) Ltd v Jackson* [1990] Ch 265 at 287–288). This, in turn, has been challenged by Professor Peter Birks, 'Gifts of Other People's Money' in *Frontiers of*

intangible, equity gives the owner of the original goods a proprietary claim to the proceeds, provided that these were received by the seller in such circumstances as to create a trust obligation, ie an obligation to hold them for the owner in specie or as a fund under an actual, constructive or resulting trust.[199] The equitable right to trace is available against whoever is currently holding the proceeds, except where that person has acquired an overriding title.[200]

Tracing rights are available even where the proceeds generated by the wrongful sale have become commingled with the assets of the seller or of a third party.[201]

5.   REMEDIES IN A CONFLICT SITUATION

Suppose that B, holding goods as bailee of their owner, O, wrongfully sells the goods to T. T's rights against B have been examined earlier[202] and at this point we shall confine attention to O's remedies against B and T. As a preliminary point, the reader is reminded of the significant changes made by the Torts (Interference with Goods) Act 1977. In particular, detinue was abolished:[203] the remedy of conversion, which had been available in most of the situations where detinue lay, was extended to cover loss or destruction of the goods which a bailee has allowed to happen in breach of his duty to his bailor;[204] and in any action for wrongful interference with the goods (which includes the case of conversion[205]) the court was given the same power to order specific delivery as it had in proceedings for detinue.[206] Hence the abolition of detinue is essentially a technical matter, intended to avoid the overlap with conversion, a tort now expanded to embrace all the old forms of detention and all types of relief previously given in detinue. In addition, the bar on pleading *ius tertii*[207] has been abolished,[208] in accordance with rules of court;[209] and the rights of the innocent improver of another's chattels are crystallized.[210]

(i)   Remedies against B

B's wrongful sale of O's goods to T is not by itself actionable as a conversion[211] unless it is effective to divest O of his title pursuant to an exception to the *nemo dat* rule. The mere denial of O's title implicit in B's unlawful sale is not of itself conversion,[212] and if title remains in O, then the sale neither deprives him of

---

Legal Liability (ed Peter Birks, 1994), vol 1, p 31, n 2.
199   See p 52.
200   See p 53.
201   See p 457.
202   See p 284.
203   Section 2(1).
204   Section 2(2).
205   Section 1.
206   Section 3.
207   See p 32.
208   Torts (Interference with Goods) Act 1977, s 8(1).
209   RSC Ord 15, r 10A, preserved as one of the scheduled rules to the CPR.
210   Torts (Interference with Goods) Act 1977, ss 3(6), 6.
211   See n 177.

ownership nor constitutes an interference with his right to possess. But a sale which passes title is a conversion, whether or not accompanied by delivery;[213] and, equally, delivery pursuant to an unauthorized agreement for sale is a conversion, whether or not title passes.[214] In either of these cases, O will almost invariably have an alternative action for breach of bailment.

If B has lost possession, O's remedy against him is purely monetary. He can sue B for damages for the value of the goods or of O's interest in them, whichever is the lesser,[215] or he can claim the proceeds of sale in B's hands, either through a restitutionary claim for money had and received or by means of a tracing claim in equity.[216] Where the proceeds received by B are in a form other than money, the equitable remedy is equally applicable; and the common law gives O a personal right to delivery up of the proceeds, if tangible.[217] If B, having effectively transferred title to T, remains in possession, O can claim an order for delivery of the goods and the payment of consequential damages, but B can set up the *ius tertii*, namely the superior title of T, in accordance with rules of court,[218] so that in practice O would again be restricted to damages.

(ii) Remedies against T

T, if in possession, can be sued in conversion for any of the forms of relief available for wrongful interference with goods, namely an order for delivery up to O (with or without an option to T to pay their value) and/or consequential damages, or damages for the conversion.[219] T apparently commits a conversion by the mere innocent receipt of the goods, even though he has not thereafter been guilty of any improper dealings with them or any refusal to deliver them up.[220] But where T has improved the goods in the mistaken but honest belief that he had acquired a good title, an allowance would be made to the extent of the value added by the improvement.[221]

O is not exclusively dependent on judicial remedies. He may also recover the goods by physical seizure (recaption) and for that purpose enter on T's land,[222] though he should be careful not to make a violent entry, since this constitutes a criminal offence.[223]

---

212 Ibid.

213 *Street on Torts* (11th edn, 2003), p 57–58; *Winfield & Jolowicz on Tort* (16th edn, 2002), p 601.

214 This is the usual case.

215 See *Wickham Holdings Ltd v Brooke House Motors Ltd* [1967] 1 WLR 295, and Goode, *Hire-Purchase Law*, pp 584, 769.

216 See p 52.

217 See p 53.

218 See n 209.

219 Torts (Interference with Goods) Act 1977, s 3(1).

220 See n 185.

221 Torts (Interference with Goods) Act 1977, s 6.

222 Though the exact limits of this right are unclear. See *Winfield & Jolowicz on Tort*, pp 616–619. The owner or seller of goods comprised in a regulated hire-purchase or conditional sale agreement within the Consumer Credit Act 1974 is not entitled to enter any premises to repossess the goods except under an order of the court (Consumer Credit Act 1974, s 92).

223 Under the Criminal Law Act 1977, s 6, replacing the offence of forcible entry under the Forcible

6.   PROPOSALS FOR REFORM

The present patchwork of legislative provisions detailing the exceptions to the *nemo dat* rule can hardly be described as satisfactory. The legislation has generated a vast amount of case law and has given rise to grave problems of interpretation, often resolved at a highly technical level. In 1989, in a review on behalf of the government directed primarily at security interests in personal property,[224] Professor Aubrey Diamond recommended that the existing statutory provisions be replaced with a broad principle that where the owner of goods has entrusted them to, or acquiesced in their possession by, another person, then an innocent purchaser of those goods should acquire good title.[225] In January 1994 the Department of Trade and Industry issued a Consultation Paper inviting comments on this proposal and on particular exceptions to the *nemo dat* rule. The ensuing abolition of the market overt principle appears to have owed nothing to this Consultation Paper, and it is unclear what provoked its publication. It is to be hoped that no government department will ever in the future seek to deal with such a complex set of issues in such an ill-conceived document, a mere eight pages long,[226] containing no analysis, no reasoning, no discussion of the policy issues and no detailed proposals. Reforms in this area of commercial law are best left to the Law Commissions, which have the resources and the expertise to give them the detailed consideration they deserve.

Entry Acts 1381–1623.

224   *A Review of Security Interests in Property* (1989). Professor Diamond's conclusions largely accord with those reached eighteen years previously by the Crowther Committee in its Report on Consumer Credit (Cmnd 4596, 1971).

225   Ibid, para 13.6.

226   If one excludes the last page inviting consultees to identify and quantify the direct or indirect costs

PART THREE
Money, Payment and Payment Systems

17 Concepts of Money and Payment

Money and payment play a central role in commercial and financial transactions. Every working day millions of transactions are concluded involving the sale and purchase of land, goods and services, the lending and borrowing of money, the issue and transfer of financial instruments. Every working day funds are transferred and payments made in discharge of money obligations, and proceedings are instituted for the recovery of unpaid debts. Less frequent, but far from uncommon, are proprietary claims to money alleged to have been improperly received by the defendant at the claimant's expense.

Yet the legal concepts of money, payment and funds transfer remain elusive. When we speak of money in the bank or the recovery of money paid by mistake or misappropriated, we are likely to have an unclear, if not entirely erroneous, picture of what we mean by 'money'. Similar considerations apply to payment and funds transfer. We speak of 'paying' by cheque or by letter of credit, though in truth these instruments do not represent payment, merely a different form of payment promise. We regularly confuse payment with tender and with commitment to pay, and we sometimes find it difficult to determine what precisely is the act which constitutes payment and when payment is to be considered complete. Again, we speak of funds transfers without having a clear idea of who is transferring what and to whom. We also use terminology which confuses the payment message with the act of payment. Thus bankers refer to wire transfers and to electronic funds transfers, conjuring up a picture of electronic currency, invisible and intangible, hurtling through the ether! Finally, the legal characterization of electronic money (or digital cash) remains obscure.

These concepts are not merely of theoretical interest, for upon the correctness of their analysis may turn the success or failure of legal claims running to hundreds of millions of pounds, and the recognition or denial of proprietary claims to money which, if upheld, protect the claimant *pro tanto* against the consequences of the defendant's bankruptcy or liquidation.

We cannot expect to solve all these conceptual problems in a general textbook on commercial law. What we can do is clarify the meaning of terms, set out the relevant principles of law, and provide a better understanding of the mechanism of payment, without which legal analysis is doomed to failure.

I.   MONEY[1]

(i)   The legal meaning of money

The meaning of the term 'money' depends very much on the context in which it is used. Money serves a purely abstract function as a unit of account. It is also a store of value and a medium of exchange. It is this last function, money as a means of payment, with which we are concerned here. Economists take a much broader view than lawyers of what constitutes money. To the economist, anything constitutes money which is generally acceptable as a medium of exchange or as payment of a debt.[2] In particular, this includes bank money, that is, a claim on a bank established by a credit to the customer's account. For the lawyer, however, this definition is too broad. This is because the economist is thinking in terms of purchasing power whereas the lawyer is focusing on money as currency and on what the creditor is entitled to demand in satisfaction of the debt (namely, legal tender). On this point we cannot do better than quote Dr Mann:

> It is suggested that, in law, the quality of money is to be attributed to all chattels which, issued by the authority of the law and denominated with reference to a unit of account, are meant to serve as universal means of exchange in the State of issue.[3]

Thus in England money in its technical legal sense means physical money, that is, notes issued by the Bank of England and coin distributed by the Mint, when transferred as currency, not as a curio or other commodity.[4] It does not include bank money or electronic money.[5]

(ii)   The legal characteristics of physical money

Physical money has five important legal characteristics. First, its value in law is not its intrinsic value as paper or metal but the sum, or unit of account, in which the note or coin is denominated. So a £5 note has a legal value of five pounds, even though the value of the paper of which it consists is negligible,[6] and the same is true of a £1,000 note even though its value as a collector's item is greatly in excess of its nominal

---

1   The only comprehensive and up-to-date treatment of this subject is the late Dr Francis Mann's superb monograph *The Legal Aspect of Money* (1992), the latest (5th) edition of which was completed shortly before his death. A text much earlier in date but still repaying careful study is Professor Arthur Nussbaum's standard work *Money in the Law: National and International* (rev edn, 1950). See also R. M. Goode, *Payment Obligations in Commercial and Financial Transactions* (1983).
2   See Geoffrey Crowther, *An Outline of Money* (rev edn, 1948), p 20.
3   Mann, *Legal Aspect of Money*, p 8.
4   *Moss v Hancock* [1899] 2 QB 111.
5   As to electronic money, see p 453.
6   The banknote is a curious legal animal. In form it is a promissory note, since it embodies a promise by the Bank of England to pay the bearer the denominated sum on demand, and as such it constitutes a negotiable instrument. But since 1931, when the right of the holder to have the note converted into gold was abolished, the promise has been meaningless, as banknotes are also legal tender, so that presentation for payment is both unnecessary and futile, since at best the holder would receive other banknotes in exchange. As the late Professor Olivecrona wittily observed: 'Paradoxically enough, the claims on the central bank are always good because they can never be honoured. Payment does not come into question, since there are no media of payment available' (Karl Olivecrona, *The Problem of the Monetary Unit* (1957), pp 62–63).

value.[7] Secondly, and as a corollary, money is not bought or exchanged; it is either borrowed or received by way of gift or in discharge of an obligation owed to the recipient.[8] Thirdly, money is fully negotiable, in the sense that one who receives notes or coins in good faith and for value obtains a good title even if his transferor stole them or his title was otherwise defective.[9] Fourthly, unless otherwise agreed, a creditor is not entitled to demand or obliged to accept anything other than money in discharge of the debt owed to him. Fifthly, money is a fungible, that is, any unit is legally interchangeable with any other unit or combination of units of the same denominated value. The loan of money, like the loan of securities or of any other kind of asset, transfers absolute ownership to the borrower, whose obligation is to restore not the identical notes and coins received but their equivalent. So a bank with whom notes are deposited is not a bailee of the notes but becomes the owner, with a duty to restore their equivalent in denominated value. Accordingly, a creditor's right to be paid is a purely personal right; he does not *own* money representing the debt, he *is owed* money.[10]

In describing the legal characteristics of physical money we have made reference to one that is generally considered of fundamental importance, namely the right of a creditor to be paid in legal tender, that is, banknotes and coins which meet the statutory requirements for legal tender.[11] This is no doubt true in the case of small transactions, where payment in legal tender would be a reasonable method of payment; it is undeniably false in the case of transactions of any size, where, in the absence of a clear agreement for payment in legal tender, it would be absurd to suppose that this was the method of payment intended by the parties.[12] Indeed, there is clear authority in cases on charterparties – one of the principal sources of case law on what constitutes payment – that even where the contract provides in terms for payment in cash in a specified currency, the word 'cash' prima facie includes any commercially recognized method of transferring funds which gives the transferee immediate and unconditional use of the funds transferred so as to be the equivalent of cash.[13]

7 On 8 March 1983 a £1,000 banknote issued by the Bank of England in 1933 was sold to Spink's, the London dealers, for £6,800 (Times, 9 March 1983). If the owner, instead of selling the note, had presented it for payment to the Bank of England, he would have been entitled to no more than its face value in notes of current legal tender.

8 Goode, *Payment Obligations*, p 4. The position is otherwise where notes or coins are bought or held not as money but as curios or collectors' pieces; they are then ordinary commodities.

9 *Miller v Race* (1758) 1 Burr 452.

10 However, theory yields to commercial practice in one respect in recognizing the right of a bank to take a charge over its own customer's credit balance. See p 611.

11 Currency and Bank Notes Act 1954; Coinage Act 1971, as amended by the Currency Act 1983. Within the Eurozone euro banknotes are legal tender. See EC art 106(1) and Hans Weenink, 'The Legal Nature of Euro Banknotes' [2003] JIBLR 433. The UK is not at present within the Eurozone and art 106(1) does not apply to it (Protocol 25, para 5).

12 See now, for a decision to this effect, *Homes v Smith* [2000] Lloyd's Rep Bank 139.

13 *The Brimnes* [1973] 1 All ER 769, affirmed [1975] QB 929; *The Laconia* [1976] QB 835, reversed on other grounds [1977] AC 850; *The Chikuma* [1981] 1 WLR 314. All these cases involved payment or attempted payment by the transfer of funds to the creditor's account with its bank. Where it is the bank itself that is the debtor, the court is likely to be much readier to hold that the bank's customer is entitled to withdraw the deposited funds in cash. In *Libyan Arab Foreign Bank v Bankers Trust Co* [1989] QB 728 Staughton J accepted the evidence of a banking expert that a depositor had an inalienable right to withdraw his money in cash, however large the amount, and on that basis ordered payment in cash of $292 million.

Accordingly, much of the debate on what constitutes money in law is rather sterile and has few implications for the rights of parties to commercial transactions, where payment by bank transfer is the almost universal method of settlement. In most developed countries, where bank failures are infrequent, a bank's unconditional commitment to pay is treated as the equivalent of cash. The crucial question, then, is not what constitutes money but what constitutes payment. Any transfer of value in a form according with the express or implied agreement of the parties constitutes payment, whether or not it is money in the legal sense. Though cash remains overall the dominant medium of payment, bank money represents by far the most important method of discharging money obligations in commercial transactions.

2.   INTANGIBLE MONEY

(i)   Types of claim to intangible money

We need say no more about physical money, since claims in specie to physical money (eg stolen banknotes) are relatively rare.[14] This is because, as we have seen, money is a negotiable chattel and title even to stolen money passes to a bona fide purchaser for value without notice.[15] Of much greater interest are claims to money in intangible form. It should be unnecessary to point out that such money is not the same as physical money, which passes by delivery. Unfortunately, it is all too common, in discussions of tracing claims to intangible money, to equate it with physical money and pray in aid decisions on dealings in currency to support the proposition that an interbank funds transfer (with which those decisions had nothing to do) passes a legal title to the transferee or, in the case of transfer to an overdrawn account, his bank.[16] It is important to avoid confusion of this kind. Bank money lacks at least most of the legal characteristics of physical money: it is not issued under the authority of the State, it is not legal tender, it does not serve as a universal medium of exchange, and it is not negotiable. The same is true of electronic money, or digital cash, which has now been defined by statute as:

> monetary value, as represented by a claim on the issuer, which is -
>
> (a)   stored on an electronic device;
> (b)   issued on receipt of funds;
> (c)   accepted as a means of payment by persons other than the issuer.[17]

The courts have so far had to consider only whether the debtor was *obliged* to pay in legal tender. Whether it follows that the debtor is *entitled* to pay in legal tender is unclear. In each case it is a question of construction of the particular contract whether the parties have impliedly excluded legal tender as a means of payment or have simply agreed that it is not the only method available.

14   For a modern example see *Lipkin Gorman v Karpnale Ltd* [1992] 4 All ER 512, where the plaintiffs successfully established a common law personal claim to cash misappropriated by a partner of the defendant firm and used to buy gaming chips at the defendants' casino.

15   The defendants in *Karpnale* would have succeeded if they had been able to show that they had given value for the money paid over to them.

16   See pp 459–460.

17   Financial Services and Markets Act 2000 (Regulated Activities) Order 2001 (SI 2001/544), art 3(1), adopting art 1(3)(b) of the Directive on the taking up, pursuit and prudential supervision of the business of electronic money institutions, 2000/46/EC.

Electronic money is designed as an alternative to payment by cash in retail trans-actions and takes the form either of value stored on a microchip. any part of which is transferable in payment for goods or services, or unitized value in the shape of electronic coins which are transferable electronically.[18] It is not considered further.

Claims to intangible money are susceptible to at least two distinct classifications: personal and proprietary, and gain-based and non-gain-based.

1. Personal and proprietary (real) claims

Claims to intangible money divide into two broad categories. The first consists of claims that are wholly generic, in the sense that the claimant's right is simply to be paid from the defendant's general assets[19] and is not attached to any specific bank deposit or other money asset or fund held by the defendant. Such claims are therefore personal, not proprietary, or real, in character, and the claimant takes his chance as an unsecured creditor in competition with other unsecured creditors. Into this category fall, for example, contractual claims for debt or damages, and personal claims at common law for money had and received[20] or in equity for unjust enrichment or recoupment of loss suffered through a breach of trust. Such claims may arise from improper dealings by the defendant with assets of the claimant but, being personal claims, are not dependent on the defendant's continued possession of those assets and may be asserted even if he has disposed of them.

The second category consists of claims which are specific, in that the claimant can point to a particular intangible (typically a bank deposit) as beneficially vested in him under a trust, whether created by act of parties[21] or imposed by law as a resulting or constructive trust. For example, where B wrongfully sells securities he is holding for O and pays the proceeds into his account with his bank, O can claim beneficial ownership of the claim on the bank in respect of the deposit, B being a constructive trustee of that claim for O. Specific claims to intangible money are by definition proprietary in character and thus can be asserted only against a defendant who still holds the intangible to which claim is laid.[22]

---

18 See *Paget's Law of Banking* (12th edn, 2002), paras 17.137 ff. For a more extended treatment, David Kreltszheim, 'The Legal Nature of Electronic Money' (2003) 14 Journal of Banking Finance Law and Practice 161, 261; Alan Tyree, *Digital Cash* (1997), and for an international perspective, Norbert Horn (ed), *Legal Issues in Electronic Banking* (2002). Issuers of electronic money are required to be authorized under the Financial Services and Markets Act 2000 (Financial Services and Markets Act 2000 (Regulated Activities) Order 2001, art 9B) but fall outside the financial services compensation scheme and the financial promotion rules contained in s 21 of the Financial Services and Markets Act 2000.

19 Where the debtor fails to pay voluntarily, this is achieved by post-judgment levy of execution. See p 1158.

20 See p 456.

21 Ie, an actual trust, express or implied.

22 For present purposes we may ignore an interest in a fund (see p 61), for the beneficiary's interest is solely in the fund itself, not in its constituent parts, and his remedy for misapplication of the fund is not a payment to him but a restoration of the misappropriated assets or their money equivalent to the fund.

The distinction is thus between a right to payment (which is generic and personal) and a right to have an identified money intangible made over to the claimant (which is specific and proprietary). The distinction is of importance primarily in relation to the impact of the defendant's insolvency, for, as we have seen earlier, real rights survive the debtor's insolvency and may be enforced to the exclusion of the general body of creditors whereas personal rights are converted into a right to prove in the insolvency in competition with other creditors.

2.   *Gain-based and non-gain-based claims*

Claims to money[23] may also be classified according to whether they are gain-based or non-gain-based.[24] The significance of the distinction varies according to whether the claim is personal or proprietary. Where it is personal, the distinction is relevant to the measure of the claimant's entitlement. A non-gain-based personal claim to money is either for debt or damages, the measure of recovery in the former case being the amount due and in the latter, the recoverable loss suffered by the claimant. By contrast, a gain-based claim to money is based on, and quantified by reference to, the defendant's illegitimate gain. In most cases the claim is based on unjust enrichment at the claimant's expense,[25] but there are some types of wrong which also lead to a restitutionary remedy. A further distinction, which is also relevant to proprietary claims, is that a non-gain-based claim to money or other property is not dependent on the court's discretion, it is unnecessary for the claimant to show unjust enrichment and the defence of change of position is not available.[26]

(ii)   Non-gains-based claims to money

Non-gain-based claims consist of claims to money or to a particular money asset (a) conferred on the claimant by assent of the defendant, usually under a contract or an

---

23 In the ensuing discussion 'money' denotes bank money or other intangible money unless otherwise indicated.

24 Traditionally, gain-based claims have been labelled restitutionary in character. However, as Professor Peter Birks has pointed out, restitution has become used as a synonym for disgorgement of benefit, blurring the distinctions (1) between restitution based on unjust enrichment and restitution based on other grounds, eg contract or a wrong such as breach of a fiduciary duty, and (2) between restoration of what was always the claimant's property (a right to which lies purely in the field of property law) and the creation of a new right in favour of the claimant to reverse the enrichment caused by interference with his previous property right. See Peter Birks, *The Law of Unjust Enrichment* (2003), pp 10, 13. For our purposes the term 'restitution' is therefore too broad, including, as it does, restitution under contracts and express trusts, while 'unjust enrichment' is too narrow, excluding disgorgement of gains made through a wrong. The label 'gain-based' is here used to capture rights (a) not previously held by the claimant, (b) measured by the defendant's improper gain in breach of a duty to the claimant, and (c) imposed by law rather than by contract or express trust, in each case whether those rights lie in unjust enrichment at the claimant's expense or as a remedy for a wrong through which the defendant obtained an illegitimate gain.

25 The phrase 'at the claimant's expense' is used as a shorthand to demonstrate that a subtraction from the claimant's estate is causally connected to the defendant's improper gain. But the measure of the claim is the gain itself, not the value extracted from the claimant's estate, which may have become augmented in the defendant's hands, as by profitable investment of money improperly obtained from the claimant.

26 See pp 54, 458.

express trust, or (b) representing proceeds of a disposition of the claimant's property.[27] Contract rights, as we have seen, are personal, whereas the claim to a money intangible held on trust for the claimant is real, or proprietary,[28] and the claim to proceeds of the claimant's property will itself be proprietary if the defendant is not entitled to retain them. Non-gain-based money claims are of no particular interest for present purposes, and are not discussed further in the present chapter, though in the contract sphere we are very much concerned with questions as to what constitutes payment[29] and when payment is to be considered complete.[30]

(iii) Gain-based claims to money

Gain-based claims too may be either personal or proprietary. In most cases they are based on unjust enrichment and, as such, their common characteristic is that they depend on showing a causal link between an involuntary loss of value suffered by the claimant through the improper act of the defendant or a third party and a corresponding receipt of value by the defendant in circumstances where he would be unjustly enriched if he were not made to give restitution. Good faith by itself is not a defence to a gain-based claim, but change of position in good faith has now been recognized by the House of Lords as a general defence,[31] and the same is true of bona fide purchase for value without notice.[32] These two defences are available whether the claim is personal or proprietary. Gain-based claims have assumed huge importance in commercial and financial dealings. The law relating to them is complex and, in various respects, unsatisfactory, and only a brief outline can be given here.[33]

---

27 See p 456.

28 Unless the defendant trustee holds under an active trust with management powers, in which case the interest of the beneficiaries is in the trust fund itself, not in the individual assets comprised in it. For the nature of an interest in a fund, see p 00.

29 See p 460.

30 See pp 470 ff.

31 *Lipkin Gorman v Karpnale Ltd* [1991] 2 AC 548. See Robert Goff and Gareth Jones, *Law of Restitution* (6th edn, 2002), ch 40.

32 There is a view that bona fide purchase is not a separate defence at all but merely a paradigm of change of position, and this has powerful proponents. See, for example, PJ Millett, 'Tracing the Proceeds of Fraud' (1991) 107 LQR 71 at p 82; Peter Birks, 'Trusts in the Recovery of Misapplied Assets' in *Commercial Aspects of Trusts and Fiduciary Obligations* (ed Ewan McKendrick, 1992), ch 8, at pp 164–165. But in *Lipkin Gorman v Karpnale Ltd*, n 31, Lord Goff (at 580–581) was in no doubt that the defences were entirely distinct, a view shared by Peter Gibson LJ in *Lloyds Bank plc v Independent Insurance Co Ltd* [2000] QB 110 at 132. See to the same effect Paul Key, 'Bona fide purchase as a defence to the law of restitution' [1994] LMCLQ 421 and Goff and Jones, *Law of Restitution*, ch 42. A separate and unresolved (indeed, largely undiscussed) question is whether the defence of bona fide purchaser is an application of ordinary priority rules of property law (in which case the purchaser must have acquired the legal title in order to obtain priority over an earlier equitable interest) or a distinct principle of the law of restitution. The question is adverted to in Birks, *Unjust Enrichment*, pp 199–200. See further pp 459–460.

33 See J. Edelman, *Gain-Based Damages* (2002). There is now a large volume of literature relating to the law of restitution and unjust enrichment. The leading texts on the English law of restitution in general are Goff and Jones, *Law of Restitution*; Graham Virgo, *The Principles of the Law of Restitution* (1999); Peter Birks, *Law of Unjust Enrichment* and *An Introduction to the Law of Restitution* (1985); Andrew Burrows, *The Law of Restitution* (2nd edn, 2002); and Andrew Tettenborn, *Law of Restitution in England and Ireland* (3rd edn 2002).

I.   Gain-based personal claims to money

The exclusion from the law of unjust enrichment of claims to products and proceeds of the claimant's assets[34] means that the importance of the law of unjust enrichment (as opposed to restitution for wrongs) lies principally in the availability of personal claims. Such claims are made where no identified money asset is involved or where the defendant no longer holds it or is clearly solvent so that a proprietary claim is considered unnecessary. A personal claim may arise either at common law or in equity. The common law claim is for money had and received,[35] and typically arises where the defendant wrongfully disposes of an asset belonging to the claimant and fails to account for the proceeds, or receives from a third party money intended for the claimant and fails to pay it to the claimant. For ease of exposition we shall confine ourselves to the first of these. The action for money had and received is a personal claim based on the claimant's common law right to trace his original asset into any substitution for that asset or its proceeds. For example, if B, as hirer of O's car, wrongfully sells it to T and receives a cheque, then instead of following the car itself into the hands of T,[36] O may assert a personal claim to the cheque or its face value. If B does not hand over the cheque to O but pays it into his own account with his bank, X, which is in credit,[37] O may sue for conversion of the cheque or may look to the second substitution, in which the cheque is replaced by B's claim on X, and sue for the amount credited to B's account in an action for money had and received.

Though the claim for money had and received is personal, it is not like a debt claim, for quite apart from the fact that it is not contractual, it depends for its success on the claimant's showing that he started with an asset of some kind and that what the defendant now holds can be identified (or 'traced') as derived from that asset. Tracing is not a cause of action or a remedy, it is simply a legal technique by which value received by the defendant[38] is shown to be causally linked to value lost by the claimant. The common law takes a robust view of causal linkage. It is not necessary to show that the money asset acquired by the defendant was in direct exchange for the claimant's asset or its proceeds. It suffices that the claimant has suffered a loss of value which is reflected in a corresponding receipt of value by the defendant. Accordingly, where the defendant wrongfully procures a transfer (whether by cheque or otherwise) from the claimant's bank account to his own account, the transfer being effected through the bank clearing,[39] the common law has no

---

34 See pp 54, 458.

35 Where the money proceeds result from the defendant's improper disposal of goods or documentary intangibles (as to which see p 48) the claimant has an alternative claim in conversion for the value of the asset disposed of. The claim for money had and received is advantageous where the sum received by the defendant exceeds the value of the converted asset.

36 Which might not be possible, as where T acquires an overriding title or has disappeared.

37 If it is overdrawn, X will usually acquire an overriding title, since payment into the account *pro tanto* reduces X's claim on B and thus makes X a purchaser for value of the sum paid into the account.

38 It is immaterial whether he retains it. His receipt is all that is required to found the action. By contrast, a proprietary claim in equity is confined to value surviving in the hands of the defendant. The two measures of recovery are thus potentially different. Professor Birks refers to value received as the first measure of restitution and value surviving as the second measure of restitution (*An Introduction to the Law of Restitution*, ch III).

39 See pp 464, 535.

difficulty in recognizing that the sum credited to the defendant's account represents the proceeds of the corresponding sum previously in the claimant's account,[40] despite the fact that receipt of funds by the defendant's bank does not as such constitute receipt by the defendant himself [41] and that the payment process does not involve any assignment of the claimant's claim on its bank, so that the sum credited to the defendant's account cannot be regarded as the proceeds of such an assignment but is simply the mirror image of a corresponding debit to the claimant's account to which that credit is causally connected.[42] Similarly, if the defendant borrows money from his bank and uses it to open an account with a second bank, repaying the loan with money improperly obtained from the claimant, the common law recognizes the claimant's ability to trace the misappropriated sum into that account, even though in the first instance the claim on the second bank was acquired with funds advanced by the first bank rather than by the claimant. The law looks to the substance of the transaction and treats the second bank as having been paid with the claimant's money.[43]

Two limitations have been suggested on the scope of the common law right to trace. First, it has been said that any attempt to trace money through the clearing system 'obviously presents insuperable practical difficulties',[44] and, as a tacitly assumed corollary, that while the claimant can trace money representing the proceeds of a collected cheque, he cannot trace money reaching an account through an electronic funds transfer passing through the clearing.[45] It is hard to see what the difficulties are. As stated above, the identification process involves no more than establishing that a debit to the transferor's account with his bank is linked to a credit to the transferee's account with his own bank. The ability to do this has nothing to do with the medium of the payment.[46] Moreover, cheques are collected through the clearing system, so if that is not a barrier in the case of a cheque payment,[47] why should it be in a paperless transfer? Secondly, it is asserted that the common law does not allow tracing into a mixed fund.[48] This is plainly incorrect where the defendant who received the money does the mixing, for liability in an action for money had and received is purely personal and is based on receipt, not retention, so that what the defendant does with the money after he has

---

40 *Agip (Africa) Ltd v Jackson* [1992] 4 All ER 385.

41 See p 470.

42 Hence the general surprise at the decision of the House of Lords in *R v Preddy* [1996] AC 815 to the effect that a person who fraudulently procures the transfer of funds from another person's account to his own could not be convicted of theft, since the interbank transfer did not involve any assignment of the claimant's credit balance, merely a debit at one end reflected by a credit at the other. The decision necessitated emergency legislation in the shape of the Theft (Amendment) Act 1996.

43 *Agip (Africa) Ltd v Jackson*, n 40, per Millett J at 397, approved on appeal [1992] 4 All ER 451, per Fox LJ at 462.

44 Millett (1991) 107 LQR 71 at p 74.

45 Ibid, a proposition which Millett J then applied judicially in *Agip (Africa) Ltd v Jackson*, n 40 at 399.

46 Indeed, on this point the Court of Appeal does not appear to have agreed with Millett J See [1992] 4 All ER 451, per Fox LJ at 465. See also Richard Hooley, 'Payment in a Cashless Society' in *The Realm of Company Law* (ed Barry A.K. Rider, 1998) at pp 243–245.

47 *Banque Belge pour l'Etranger v Hambrouck* [1921] 1 KB 321.

48 *Taylor v Plumer* (1815) 3 M & S 562, per Lord Ellenborough at 567; *Re Hallett's Estate* (1880) 13 Ch D 696, per Jessel MR at 717; *Re Diplock* [1948] Ch 465, per Lord Greene M.R. at p 518–520.

received it is irrelevant.[49] But even the fact that the money has become commingled before reaching the defendant should not be a bar to tracing, for there is no reason why the ability of the common law to identify the money as having come from the claimant should be any less at common law than it is in equity.[50]

2.   Gain-based proprietary claims to money

The category of gain-based proprietary claims has now been substantially narrowed by the ruling of the House of Lords in *Foskett v McKeown*[51] that a claim to the products of an improper disposition of the claimant's property by the defendant is a pure property claim, not an unjust enrichment claim. The effect is to remove from the sphere of gain-based rights those proprietary claims which are based on unjust enrichment at the claimant's expense – that is, are derived by subtraction from the claimant's pre-existing proprietary base – and to restrict such rights to those based on a wrong, for example, the receipt of a bribe or the pursuit of business opportunities by the defendant for his own benefit which, if he had undertaken them at all, should have been exploited for the claimant's benefit, not his own.[52] However, while a proprietary claim to the money or asset first acquired through a wrong is gain-based, property subsequently acquired with such asset falls within the *Foskett v McKeown* principle as a pure property right. Gain-based proprietary claims to money usually arise in the form of a constructive trust or an automatic resulting trust.[53] Examples of such claims arising under a constructive trust are claims to proceeds of the claimant's property improperly disposed of by the defendant or a third party,[54] proceeds of authorized dispositions of the claimant's

49 *Agip (Africa) Ltd v Jackson*, n 40, per Millett J at 399; [1992] 4 All ER 451, per Fox LJ at 463; *Marsh v Keating* (1834) 2 Cl & Fin 250; R. M. Goode, 'The Right to Trace and its Impact in Commercial Transactions' (1976) 92 LQR 360 at p 394.

50 Prior to *Agip* there appears to have been no reported case in which a plaintiff's claim failed on the ground of mixing, a point made by Thesiger LJ in *Re Hallett's Estate*, n 48 at 723. For a powerful argument that it is contrary to both principle and authority to regard mixing as a barrier to the common law right to trace, see Steven Fennell, 'Misdirected Funds: Problems of Uncertainty and Inconsistency' (1994) 57 MLR 38 at pp 43ff; and Lionel D. Smith, *Law of Tracing* (1997), ch 5. The point is of no great significance where the claimant can and does rely on the more powerful equitable proprietary right to trace, but that is supposedly dependent on a fiduciary relationship between claimant and defendant which will not always be present (see below).

51 [2001] 1 AC 102.

52 *Cook v Deeks* [1916] 1 AC 554 (business opportunities); *Attorney-General for Hong Kong v Reid* [1994] 1 AC 324 (bribes), not following *Lister & Co v Stubbs* (1890) 45 Ch D 1. I have argued elsewhere that the institutional constructive trust should not be recognized where the restitutionary remedy is based on a wrong, and that in the case of bribes in particular the grant of a proprietary remedy is not only based on circular reasoning but in policy terms is objectionable as giving the claimant priority over unsecured creditors which he has done nothing to earn, having suffered no diminution in his estate, given no value and performed no act in reliance on the defendant's conduct, whereas unsecured creditors will have given value. See Roy Goode, 'Proprietary Restitutionary Claims' in *Restitution: Past Present and Future* (ed W. R. Cornish *et al*, 1998), ch 5 and 'Property and Unjust Enrichment' in *Essays on the Law of Restitution* (ed Andrew Burrows, 1991), ch 9.

53 An automatic resulting trust is one which arises by operation of law independent of the presumed intention of the parties. The distinction between resulting trusts and constructive trusts is arbitrary and sometimes difficult to draw. The present text follows conventional usage.

54 *Re Hallett's Estate*, n 48; *Agip (Africa) Ltd v Jackson*, n 40.

property where the person disposing of them was an agent or other fiduciary having no right to retain and manage the proceeds, and money paid by the claimant to the defendant under a mistake of fact.[55] Where money is lent on terms that it is to be applied for a particular purpose which in the event fails, the borrower holds it on a resulting trust for the lender, who can accordingly assert an equitable proprietary claim to it.[56]

A proprietary claim cannot, of course, be asserted against one who no longer has the money or where the money has ceased to exist.[57] A more controversial limitation on the equitable right to trace is that there must have been a fiduciary relationship between the claimant and the defendant or a third party through whose hands the money or property producing it passed.[58] Though in the *Agip* case[59] the trial judge and the Court of Appeal felt obliged to follow *Re Diplock*,[60] there seems no good policy reason why the right should be restricted to cases involving a fiduciary relationship; it should suffice that the claimant has a stronger right to the money than the defendant and is thus entitled to recover it under normal priority rules in property law. In the *Chase Manhattan* decision[61] Goulding J robustly surmounted the problem by holding that the fiduciary relationship was sufficiently generated by the improper receipt itself, an ingenious solution which is, however, unsatisfactory, for it presupposes that which is in issue, namely the defendant's fiduciary duty to hold the sum received for the claimant.[62] It is to be hoped that the House of Lords will take the opportunity to put the fiduciary relationship fallacy firmly to rest.

A proprietary claim to money is defeated where the defendant can show that he has acquired an overriding title as a bona fide purchaser for value without notice of the

---

55 *Chase Manhattan Bank N.A. v Israel-British Bank (London) Ltd* [1981] Ch 105 (mistaken double payment of the same debt). There are also cases where authority to dispose of the claimant's asset is given on terms, express or implied, that the defendant is to hold the proceeds for the claimant, but this is consensual and is not based on unjust enrichment. For an example see *Aluminium Industrie Vaassen BV v Romalpa Aluminium Ltd* [1976] 1 Lloyd's Rep 443, which has, however, been distinguished almost out of existence. See p 608.

56 *Barclays Bank Ltd v Quistclose Investments Ltd* [1970] AC 567, in which the House of Lords held that the relationship of lender and borrower subsisting between the plaintiffs and the first defendants did not preclude a concurrent trust relationship between them. In that case, money was lent to a company for the specific purpose of being paid out to shareholders as a dividend, a purpose which was frustrated by the company going into liquidation. The precise nature of the trust arising in this situation has been the subject of much debate. See the analysis by Lord Millett in *Twinsectra Ltd v Yardley* [2002] 2 AC 164 and the authorities there cited.

57 *Bishopsgate Investment Management Ltd v Homan* [1995] Ch 211 (payment into overdrawn bank account).

58 *Re Diplock*, n 48.

59 [1992] 4 All ER 385 at 402 (where Millett J referred to the requirement as having been 'widely condemned'); [1992] 4 All ER 451 at 466. In that particular case there was clearly a fiduciary relationship, so that no problem arose on that score.

60 See n 48.

61 See n 55.

62 The reasoning leading to that decision, though not the result, was criticized by Lord Browne-Wilkinson in *Westdeutsche Landesbank Girozentrale v Islington London Borough Council* [1996] AC 669 at 714–715 and extrajudicially by Sir Peter Millett, 'Restitution and Constructive Trusts' in Cornish, *Restitution*, p 199 at 212. But *Chase Manhatten* also has its defenders. See Daniel Friedmann, 'Payment Under Mistake – Tracing and Subrogation' (1999) 115 LQR 195.

claimant's rights.[63] The defendant's priority is frequently ascribed to the fact that the innocent recipient has acquired *legal* title to the money by virtue of its status as currency. This cannot be the case, for, as pointed out earlier,[64] a bank deposit or other intangible money is not currency, legal title to which passes by delivery,[65] but arises from debits and credits in the banking system which do not involve even the transfer of a claim to the recipient.[66] The true position would seem to be that the bona fide purchaser of intangible money is protected not because he has legal title (which he does not) but because he has not been enriched.[67]

3.   PAYMENT

If the concept of money is difficult, it has at least been the subject of exhaustive analysis.[68] The same cannot be said of the concept of payment, itself a subject of considerable complexity, upon which the literature in common law jurisdictions remains surprisingly sparse.[69] Yet the topic is of great importance, and we should at least examine the fundamental principles.

(i)   The concept of payment

At this point we are concerned not with what types of act constitute payment but with the more fundamental question: what do we mean by payment? Again, it is necessary to distinguish payment in its strict legal sense from some intermediate step which the parties may label 'payment'. Suppose, for example, that a contract between C and D requires D to pay C £10,000 by 10 May, and that C has always been content to accept D's cheques as the payment vehicle. In such a case the parties may well intend that the contractual time of payment will be considered met if C receives D's cheque by 10 May. That is a matter of construction of the contract. But C's receipt of the cheque does not in itself constitute payment by D, for no

---

63 See p 455.

64 See p 452.

65 A rare case involving a claim based on misappropriation of physical money was *Lipkin Gorman v Karpnale Ltd*, n 31, which was, however, a common law personal claim, not an equitable proprietary claim.

66 See p 469. The case is not one of novation (which would vest legal title to the account in the defendant), for this requires the consent of all three parties. It would, of course, be possible for a person to purchase a bank deposit and take an assignment, but this would not assist him, for even a statutory assignee of a debt takes subject to equities. See p 748.

67 A subsidiary ground is that the right to trace is usually a mere equity rather than an immediate equitable interest (see p 27) and as such is displaced by any transfer to a bona fide purchaser for value, whether or not passing the legal title.

68 See Mann, *Legal Aspect of Money*, and the extensive literature there cited.

69 So far as English law is concerned, the author essayed the first modern conceptual treatment of the subject in *Payment Obligations in Commercial and Financial Transactions*, of which the following passages represent a partial distillation and refinement. See also Michael Brindle and Raymond Cox (ed), *Law of Bank Payments* (3rd edn, 2004); *Chitty on Contracts* (29th edn, 2004), paras 21-039 ff. For an admirably comprehensive treatment of electronic funds transfers, see Benjamin Geva, *The Law of Electronic Funds Transfers* (looseleaf) and his equally impressive *Bank Collections and Payment Transactions: A Comparative Legal Analysis* (2001).

funds have been transferred. All that has happened is that D has given C an instrument embodying a direction to D's bank to pay C. By drawing the cheque, D undertakes that it will be paid by his bank.[70] The effect of giving C the cheque is therefore to suspend D's original promise to pay, and to superimpose on it a second promise in a new form. Payment itself is made only when (and if) the cheque is honoured by D's bank, though when this occurs, payment is deemed to have been made at the time of receipt of the cheque.[71]

Payment in the legal sense means a gift or loan of money or any act offered and accepted in performance of a money obligation. Money must therefore feature in some way, either because payment is in physical money or because the obligation to be discharged by the act of payment is a money obligation, in which case the mode of discharge is immaterial to the status of the act as an act of payment.

(ii) Methods of discharging a money obligation

Though any act accepted in performance of a money obligation suffices as payment, in practice payment (or settlement) usually takes one of five forms. The first, the delivery of physical money, is common in small transactions but is little used in commercial dealings. The second is the acceptance of goods in part exchange, the agreed payment for such goods being applied in reduction of the price of the new goods. This requires no further mention. The third, and that on which we shall focus attention a little later, is the transfer of funds to the transferee's bank account.[72] Typically, the transferor and the transferee are different persons, as where the transferor is the debtor and the transferee the creditor. But this is not necessarily the case. Where a person has two or more accounts with the same bank, he can pay a debit balance on one account by transferring funds from another account which is in credit. For example, where the customer of a bank borrows money from the bank for house purchase and has a separate account for accruing interest, a transfer from the customer's current account to the interest account in discharge of the debit balance on the latter constitutes payment of the interest in law, whether for tax or for any other purposes, and this is so whether the current account was in credit or in debit. The fourth is novation,[73] the replacement of the existing contract under which the indebtedness arises with a new contract, whether with the same creditor or with a new creditor. For example, C may agree to refinance D's indebtedness to him under a loan agreement by granting a fresh advance under a new agreement which is applied in discharge of the existing indebtedness. This is again a pure book entry but it has the effect of discharging the earlier indebtedness.[74] Another common form of settlement by novation is novation netting, which involves the contractual consolidation of unmatured liabilities.[75] Finally, the parties can contract for set-off

---

70 See ch 20.
71 *Homes v Smith* [2000] 1 Lloyd's Rep Bank 139.
72 The word 'transfer' here denotes novation, not assignment. See pp 414, nn 88, 469.
73 See pp 145, 157.
74 By contrast, a mere rescheduling of the existing indebtedness under the existing agreement does not constitute payment.
75 See p 472.

(or netting) of matured liabilities. This is known as payment or settlement netting and does not involve novation.[76] The banker's implied contractual right to combine accounts, though not usually described in netting terms, is similar in character.[77]

Depending on the agreement between the parties, a payment may be either referable to a particular transaction or transactions, or be applied in reduction or discharge of a total net indebtedness arising from a series of mutual dealings recorded in a current (or running) account maintained by one or both for the other. The debit and credit items then lose their individual character, all sums paid in forming part of a single blended fund which, when set against the debit items, produces a single net credit or debit balance.[78] Thus instead of each transaction being settled individually, the parties agree that periodically a balance will be struck and the party who is the debtor will pay. Payment of the debit balance constitutes payment of all the items on the account.[79]

(iii) Payment and commitment to pay

It is easy to confuse payment and commitment to pay. Where a cheque is given, it is reasonably obvious that this is not payment, though it is sometimes referred to, rather misleadingly, as conditional payment, that is, payment conditional on its being honoured. All this means is that upon acceptance of the cheque by the creditor the debtor is not, or is no longer, in default, so long as the cheque is met when presented.[80] Rather less obvious is the effect of a credit to a customer's account.[81] Where this results from a funds transfer by a third party, it will constitute payment by that party, assuming the creditor has not insisted on legal tender. But it is not a payment *by the bank*, merely an acknowledgement by the bank of its indebtedness to the customer and an implied undertaking to pay. Payment would typically come about only by allowing the customer to draw cash or by honouring

---

76 See p 473.

77 In several of the older cases the bank's right to offset a debit balance on one account against a credit balance on another is based on the proposition that there is in truth only one account between banker and customer, even if for convenience divided into separate accounts. See, for example, *Re Willis, Percival & Co., ex p Morier* (1879) 12 Ch D 491, *per* James LJ at 498; *Bailey v Finch* (1871) LR 7 QB 34, per Blackburn J at 40; *Halesowen Pressworks and Assemblies Ltd v National Westminster Bank Ltd* [1971] 1 QB 1, per Buckley LJ at 46. However, the better view, as expressed by Mr Philip Wood (*English and International Set-Off* (1989), paras 3–6, 3–11), is that two accounts are not one account, so that the right to combine accounts is a true case of contractual set-off. The set-off is effected by book entry pursuant to express or implied agreement.

78 Goode, *Payment Obligations*, p 12.

79 Ibid.

80 So if the cheque is honoured, payment is deemed to have been made at the time the cheque was received (*Homes v Smith* [2000] Lloyd's Rep Bank 139). Meeting of the cheque involves no more than failure to return it as unpaid within the limited time allowed. It then becomes too late for the bank to dishonour it, so that the bank is committed to paying it. Since the creditor's bank will already have received funds from the debtor's bank in the clearing process (see p 537), commitment and payment coincide. This is not normally the case where other modes of payment are used.

81 For brevity, the payment process is here described as credit to an account, though in fact it is complete when the bank, with the actual or apparent authority of the creditor, receives payment for his account, whether or not it has initiated or completed the mechanical accounting process.

the customer's instructions to transfer funds to a third party, both of which would operate to reduce the bank's indebtedness to the customer. This example shows how important it is to identify the particular relationship under discussion when considering the effect of credit to an account. The bank's commitment to pay constitutes payment as between debtor and creditor but remains a mere commitment as between bank and creditor. By the same token, a debit to the account is not a payment *to the bank*; it is simply a record of the customer's indebtedness. But there is nothing in law to prevent the customer from paying a debit balance on one account by transfer from another account with the same bank.[82]

(iv) Elements essential to an effective payment

In order for an act of payment to be effective as a *pro tanto* discharge of the debtor's obligation, certain essential conditions must be fulfilled. The payment must be made by the debtor or by a third party having actual or apparent authority to make it on his behalf. The law does not recognize as effective an unauthorized payment by an officious intervener except where the debtor ratifies this, whether expressly or by freely accepting the benefit of the payment.[83] The payment must not only be tendered by the debtor but accepted by the creditor or his authorized agent. An unaccepted tender does not discharge the debt, though if sued, the debtor can pay the money into court with a plea of tender and recover his costs.[84] Where the tender is accepted by a third party (such as the debtor's bank) on behalf of the debtor, that party must have actual or apparent authority to accept it.[85]

Where the agreed method of payment is by transfer of funds to the creditor's account, and the transfer is made subject to a condition precedent (eg the arrival of a stated value date or a written notification by the debtor of the release of the funds), the transfer is not effective as a payment until the condition has been satisfied or waived by the debtor. If this does not occur until after the contractual date for payment, the debtor is in breach. For this purpose a transfer is considered conditional where it does not provide the debtor with the same degree of availability as cash, so that if, though the funds themselves are available, the creditor's right to receive interest on them is deferred, even for only a few days, payment is not complete.[86] Moreover, the creditor can reject a tender of payment made on terms of a condition subsequent, eg repayment where the debtor objects to the action of his bank in making the transfer. So where a bank which is unsure whether documents tendered under a credit will be accepted by its customer as conforming tenders

---

82 See p 461.
83 *Owen v Tate* [1976] QB 402. Both the principle of free acceptance and the decision in *Owen v Tate* are controversial. See Peter Birks, 'In Defence of Free Acceptance', in Burrows, *Law of Restitution*, ch 5; Jack Beatson, *Use and Abuse of Unjust Enrichment* (1991), pp 177 ff; Goff and Jones, *Law of Restitution*, pp 58 ff.
84 CPR 37.3 and supplemental Practice Direction, paras 2 and 3. The payment into court is made under Part 36 of the CPR and the court's permission is required before the claimant can accept the sum in court CPR 36.18(3).
85 *The Laconia* [1977] AC 850; *Cleveland Manufacturing Co Ltd v Muslim Commercial Bank Ltd* [1981] 2 Lloyd's Rep 646.
86 *The Chikuma*, n 13.

payment under reserve,[87] the creditor is entitled to reject the tender, in which event the attempted payment will be ineffective.

We have identified above the elements necessary to constitute an effective payment. A separate question, and one of considerable importance, is to determine when payment is to be considered complete. This will have to be deferred until we have examined the payment process and in particular the way in which funds are transferred in the banking system.[88]

4.   PAYMENT SYSTEMS[89]

Though payments in physical money are far more numerous than other forms of payment, the value of cashless transfers now substantially exceeds the total amount of cash held by the public. The dominant cashless transfer system in terms of value is the electronic funds transfer system operated by CHAPS.[90] The CHAPS system, which uses a SWIFT-based platform,[91] offers two separate clearings, CHAPS sterling and CHAPS euro, denominated in sterling and euro respectively. CHAPS euro covers euro transfers between UK banks and, separately, euro transfers between UK banks and banks in the euro system, effected through the Bank of England as a member of the TARGET[92] payment system. Formerly operated on the basis of an end-of-day central clearing, CHAPS moved to a real-time gross settlement system through its SWIFT interface, settlement being effected across members' accounts with the Bank of England, and this is the current structure.[93] Together, the CHAPS systems process payment orders, including payments through TARGET, to a total value averaging some £350 billion a day.[94]

A developed payment system structure has four key components: an interbank communications network for the on-line electronic transmission of large-value

---

87 That is, on condition that the beneficiary repays if the bank's customer declines to treat the documents as conforming.

88 See pp 464 ff. The phrase 'funds transfer' is commonly used to denote the process by which an instruction given by a debtor to his bank to arrange for payment to the creditor results in a credit to the account of the creditor with his own bank. What the debtor holds is a claim on his bank (or a drawing facility), not a fund in a legal sense, and the process does not involve any transfer of that claim to the creditor, merely a debit at one end resulting in a credit at the other. See p 469.

89 See *Paget's Law of Banking* (12th edn), ch 17; Benjamin Geva, 'The Concept of Payment Mechanism' (1986) 24 Osgoode Hall LJ 1; Benjamin Geva, 'International Funds Transfers: Mechanisms and Laws' in *Cross-Border Electronic Banking* (ed Joseph J Norton, Chris Reed and Ian Walden, 2000), ch 1; Mario Giovanoli, 'Legal Issues Regarding Payment and Netting Systems' in *Cross-Border Electronic Banking* (ed Norton, Reed and Walden), ch 9.

90 Clearing House Automated Payment System, which consolidated the former CHAPS sterling and CHAPS euro systems and was temporarily designated NewCHAPS. See *Paget's Law of Banking*, paras 17.85 ff, and pp 465 ff.

91 As to SWIFT, see p 957.

92 Trans-European Automated Real-Time Gross Settlement Express Transfer system, a European-wide real-time gross settlement system for transfers between EU central banks.

93 See p 465.

94 Even this is dwarfed by payments through the New York CHIPS, which average well over US $1.3 trillion a day.

(wholesale) payment orders and associated messages; a clearing house for the physical exchange of paper-based payment orders (bills, cheques, bank giro payments) and the netting of matured payment obligations; an automated clearing house for the batch processing of large-volume off-line, mainly low-value (retail) payment orders stored in magnetic form on tapes and diskettes; and the involvement of the central bank as the vehicle for settlement of dealings between the banks participating in the clearing (settlement banks) by means of transfers in the books of the central bank, where all settlement banks hold an account.

In England the four main clearing systems belong to their members and are operated by three special-purpose clearing companies under a framework established by the Association for Payment Clearing Services (APACS). They consist of the Cheque Clearing for the physical exchange of sterling paper-based debit payment orders (cheques and other instruments, and direct-debit vouchers), a high-volume clearing system for payments of relatively small value; the Credit Clearing, a similar system for paper-based credit collections (credit transfers, credit-card vouchers, and the like); BACS,[95] for the batch processing of off-line debit and credit transfers on tape or diskette;[96] and CHAPS, the bilateral electronic funds transfer system previously mentioned, which was designed primarily for high-value transfers but in practice is increasingly used for smaller transfers as well, the average value processed during 2003 being £1.90 million. CHAPS operates on the basis of real-time gross settlement, while the other three clearings are net settlement systems[97] and have a three-day payment cycle. There are also separate clearings, the Currency Clearings, for the clearing of paper-based payment orders drawn in foreign currencies on United Kingdom banks. These are controlled directly by APACS. There are also payment networks outside the APACS umbrella, such as those involving payment cards.

The management of interbank settlements is of great importance in controlling risks resulting from the failure of a settling participant: risk to its counterparty and, of still greater concern, possible consequential risk to the system as a whole (systemic risk) as a domino effect of that failure. The net and gross settlement systems will be described in due course.[98] But first we shall briefly explain funds transfer terminology and the use of bilateral contract netting as a means of reducing administrative costs and risks between two participants engaged in mutual dealings.

(i)   Funds transfer terminology

Discussion of the subject of interbank funds transfers has been complicated by the lack of any consistently used terminology. However, this is now changing, under the influence of art 4A of the Uniform Commercial Code and the UNCITRAL

---

95   The initials denote the Bankers' Automated Clearing System, but the acronym is now used both for the operating company and for the system.

96   There are also on-line processes associated with BACS via a telecom link, BACSTEL.

97   See p 473. For the cheque clearing system, see p 535.

98   See pp 473 ff.

Model Law on International Credit Transfers,[99] which use broadly the same terminology to describe the key players in a funds transfer operation. This is admirably described in the Prefatory Note to art 4A:

> X, a debtor, wants to pay an obligation owed to Y. Instead of delivering to Y a negotiable instrument such as a check or some other writing such as a credit card slip that enables Y to obtain payment from a bank, X transmits an instruction to X's bank to credit a sum of money to the account of Y. In most cases X's bank and Y's bank are different banks. X's bank may carry out X's instructions by instructing Y's bank to credit Y's account in the amount that X requested. The instruction that X issues to its bank is a 'payment order.' X is the 'sender' of the payment order and X's bank is the 'receiving bank' with respect to X's order. Y is the 'beneficiary' of X's order. When X's bank issues an instruction to Y's bank to carry out X's payment order, X's bank 'executes' X's order. The instruction of X's bank to Y's bank is also a payment order. The entire series of transactions by which X pays Y is known as the 'funds transfer.' With respect to the funds transfer, X is the 'originator,' X's bank is the 'originator's bank,' Y is the 'beneficiary' and Y's bank is the 'beneficiary's bank.' In more complex transactions there are one or more additional banks known as 'intermediary banks' between X's bank and Y's bank. In the funds transfer the instruction contained in the payment order of X to its bank is carried out by a series of payment orders by each bank in the transmission chain to the next bank in the chain until Y's bank receives a payment order to make the credit to Y's account.

We shall adopt the same terminology here,[100] substituting D (debtor) for X and C (creditor) for Y.

(ii)   Classification of funds transfer methods

Methods of funds transfer may be differentiated in various ways. One is according to the medium of the payment order. The main division is between paper-based orders, such as bills, cheques and other negotiable instruments, bank giro payments and credit and debit card vouchers,[101] and paperless orders, which are implemented between banks by telephone or through electronic media.[102] In the Cheque and Credit Clearings paper-based payment orders are physically cleared by exchange at the exchange centre.[103] Paperless orders may be either on-line or off-line. On-line payment orders are those transmitted through CHAPS over telecommunications lines, so that there is an almost instantaneous communication between the sending bank and the receiving bank. On-line orders are used for individual transfers, particularly those for substantial amounts. They do not, of course, involve any physical clearing in a clearing house. They are characterized by a combination of size and speed. Off-line payment orders are those which are stored in magnetic form, such as tapes or disks, and sent to an

---

99   Adopted by the United Nations Commission on International Trade Law in May 1992. See (1992) I Uniform Law Review 3 for explanatory notes and text.

100   But as stated above this is not yet uniform. In the United Kingdom it would be common to refer to X's bank as the sending bank and Y's bank as the receiving bank.

101   See chs 18–21.

102   As Professor Geva points out, what characterizes the system is the mechanism used for interbank communications. The form of instructions given by the originator to his bank or by the beneficiary's bank to the beneficiary is for the most part irrelevant (Benjamin Geva, *The Law of Electronic Funds Transfers*, para 1.03[4]).

103   Though some items may be exchanged between banks directly under bilateral arrangements.

automated clearing house, BACS, for batching by the addressee bank and onward transmission. They are used where substantial numbers of relatively low-cost payments are involved, eg wages, council tax. In terms of volume, cheques are by far the most important form of non-cash payment, but in terms of value they are insignificant in relation to the value of transfers effected through CHAPS.

A second method of classifying funds transfers is according to whether they are initiated by the debtor's bank or the creditor's bank. A funds transfer initiated by the debtor's bank 'pushes' the funds to the creditor's bank by some form of credit transfer, typically by procuring a credit to the creditor's bank in the books of the central bank (the Bank of England) or some other third bank with whom both the debtor's bank and the creditor's bank hold accounts. A funds transfer initiated by the creditor's bank 'pulls' funds from the debtor's bank by some process of debit collection, such as collection of (payment under) a bill of exchange or cheque, issue of a direct-debit order to the debtor's bank pursuant to an authority from the debtor or the accessing of the debtor's account, on-line or off-line, by means of a debit card at the point of supply of the goods or services to which the funds transfer relates.[104]

Thirdly, payment systems may be classified according to whether they are net or gross,[105] and wholesale (large-value) or retail (low-value), and whether they involve real time gross settlement, intra-day clearing,[106] or multi-day clearing. The CHAPS Clearing was formerly intra-day but is now based on real-time gross settlement, while the other clearing systems work on a three-day payment cycle.

Finally, credit transfers may be effected in one of three ways: in-house, where debtor and creditor bank with the same bank, so that funds are simply transferred from the account of the former to that of the latter; through a payment order given by the debtor's bank to its correspondent; or by interbank transfer through the books of the central bank (the Bank of England) or a common correspondent bank as described below, whether bilaterally or through a clearing system. The mechanisms of credit transfers are basically the same for international transfers as for domestic ones, any clearing being effected through the clearing system of the country of the currency involved. Within the European Community, rules have been made governing the duties owed by credit and other institutions involved in a credit transfer to the originator and the beneficiary.[107]

(iii) The mechanism of interbank credit transfers[108]

A good description of the general procedure was given in the extract from the Prefatory Note to art 4A quoted above. But we need to examine the interbank

---

104   Known as EFTPOS (electronic funds transfer at the point of sale).
105   See p 473.
106   Usually once at the end of the day.
107   EC Directive dated 27 January 1997 on cross-border credit transfers (97/5/EC), implemented in the UK by the Cross-Border Credit Transfers Regulations 1999, SI 1999/1876.
108   See Benjamin Geva, *Bank Collections and Payment Transactions*, pp 186 ff; Ross Cranston, *Principles of Banking Law* (2nd edn, 2002), pp 235 ff; R.M. Goode, *Payment Obligations in Commercial and Financial Transactions*, ch IV; and n 00. For debit collections by presentation of cheques, see p 535.

relationships a little more closely to see exactly what happens in legal terms. As a preliminary point, a bank will normally accept a payment order only from a bank with which it has a pre-existing link or relationship. This typically takes one of three forms. In the first, the two banks are correspondents, each maintaining an account in the name of the other. Within the United Kingdom correspondent bank relationships are usually with banks overseas in order to facilitate local payments. In some countries, such as the United States, they also commonly feature in domestic banking.[109] Correspondent banks maintain accounts for each other and implement each other's payment orders. So Bank A acting for its customer, the originator of the payment instruction, issues a payment order to its correspondent, Bank B, requiring it to make the payment on its behalf. Each bank maintains two accounts in relation to the other, a nostro account, showing what it is entitled to receive from the other bank, and a vostro account, showing what it is liable to pay to the other bank. When Bank B makes the requirement payment, it credits its nostro account and Bank A credits its vostro account; when Bank A makes a payment on behalf of Bank B, the position is reversed, Bank B crediting its vostro account and Bank A crediting its nostro account. Periodically the two banks settle with each other by offsetting the balances on the two accounts, so that it is usually unnecessary for either bank to transfer funds to the other. Where, however, one bank feels unable to accept a payment order without being put in funds, the other must arrange a funds transfer through the books of a common correspondent bank as described below.

In the second form of payment, the two banks, though not correspondents, are settling members of the same clearing system. In that case each will normally accept payment orders from the other, and accounts between them and other members of the clearing will be either gross (as with CHAPS) or netted out (as with the other clearing systems) and in each case paid through the books of the Bank of England, where all clearing banks hold accounts.[110]

In the third form of relationship the originating bank and the beneficiary's bank are not settling members of a clearing system or the same clearing system but each hold accounts with a common correspondent bank (CCB), and the beneficiary's bank is put in funds by an in-house transfer in CCB's books. Thus within the United Kingdom two banks which are not themselves settling members of the Credit Clearing may both maintain accounts with the same clearing agent and settle between themselves by an in-house transfer in the books of that agent.

Let us suppose that D wishes to send £10,000 to C in discharge of a debt, and instructs his bank, DB, to arrange for this sum to be transferred to the credit of C's account with his bank, CB. If DB and CB are correspondent banks, each maintaining an account with the other, DB will credit CB's account and debit B's account, CB will debit DB's account and credit C's account, and no funds transfer will at that stage be involved. C is considered paid by D because CB, by accepting DB's payment order, thereby commits itself unconditionally to crediting C's account. But such a correspondent relationship will exist only by coincidence. In

109 Cranston, *Banking Law*, p 40.
110 For a description of settlement netting, see p 473.

the typical case DB and CB will not be correspondents. If both banks are clearing banks, CB will normally feel able to credit C's account unconditionally where it has received a payment order from DB, which will feature in the daily settlement in the clearing. Where DB and CB both have an account with CCB, then CB will usually expect an in-house transfer in its favour before committing itself unconditionally to C. Where DB and CB are not clearing banks, they may arrange to use their respective clearing agents, so that DB will instruct its clearing agent, DBA, to send a payment order to CB's clearing agent, CBA, for the account of CB. In complex transactions there may be several layers of intermediary bank. So all interbank funds transfers result, sooner or later, in an in-house transfer in the books of an institution where two banks both hold an account,[111] either a CCB or the Bank of England as central bank.

5.   LEGAL EFFECTS OF INTERBANK CREDIT TRANSFERS

It will be apparent from the above description that a so-called funds transfer does not involve the transfer to C of D's claim on DB. There is no assignment by D to C of any part of D's credit balance with his bank, nor does CB's receipt of funds from DB constitute per se a receipt by C in the sense of making C a beneficial owner of DB's claim on the CCB or the Bank of England.[112] All that happens is that the debit of D's account with DB leads to a transfer of value or payment commitment passing between DB and CB or their respective intermediaries which enables CB to decide on an unconditional credit to C's account.[113] Two questions now arise. At what point in this process does it become too late for D to countermand his payment order to DB? And when is C considered in law to have received payment from D?

(i)   When does D's payment order become irrevocable?

English law has not yet evolved any clear rules to determine when a payment order in a credit transfer becomes irrevocable.[114] This depends partly on clearing house rules,[115] where applicable, partly on banking practice[116] and partly on contract.[117] In a paper-based credit transfer, such as a giro payment, the sending bank becomes committed to the receiving bank at the time of delivery, whether direct or through

---

111 As noted by Staughton L J in *Libyan Arab Foreign Bank v Bankers Trust Co* [1988] 1 Lloyd's Rep 259 at 273.

112 See pp 471–472, 540.

113 In *R v King* [1991] 3 All ER 705 it was held that a CHAPS payment order operates both to create and to transfer a property right in the form of the chose in action represented by the bank credit. This ruling was not in fact necessary for the decision and it is respectfully submitted that it is incorrect.

114 An exception is the in-house transfer, where payment and commitment to pay coincide. See p 471.

115 See p 470.

116 The importance of banking practice is rightly stressed by Bradley Crawford and John D. Falconbridge, *Banking and Bills of Exchange* (8th edn, 1986), para 3905.4.

117 Only clearing house members are directly bound by the rules of the clearing. Relationships between a member and a non-member or between two non-members are governed by the terms of their contract.

the clearing. Payment of a cheque may be countermanded at any time before it has been paid or deemed to have been paid.[118] In a payment through CHAPS a payment message becomes irrevocable when entered into CHAPS, which in the ordinary way is the point at which the relevant member's settlement account is debited,[119] ie in the books of the Bank of England. At this point the member sending the payment message cannot revoke it and any error has to be dealt with by a reverse payment, upon which the originator of the payment has no right to insist and which the receiving bank may be unwilling to effect without the payee's authority. As between the originator and the sending bank, and between non-clearing banks or between a non-clearing bank and its clearing agent, the time when a payment message becomes irrevocable is determined by the terms of their respective contracts, not by the CHAPS rules. In the case of a payment through BACS a recall must normally be made, either by the sending bank or by the originator direct, by communication to the receiving bank by 3.30 pm on the second day of the cycle.

In order to reduce systemic risk the EC settlement finality directive requires member states to ensure that transfer orders entered into a system (as defined) before the opening of insolvency proceedings, or after but on the same day as the insolvency proceedings but without awareness of those proceedings, are to be binding notwithstanding the proceedings and no law relating to the setting aside of transactions shall lead to the unwinding of a netting.[120]

(ii)   When does C receive payment from D in an interbank transfer?

Here the law is a little clearer. Payment by D to C becomes complete at the moment when CB unconditionally accepts that C is its creditor for the amount in question. CB may be willing to do this in advance of being put in funds by DB, as where DB and CB are correspondents, or it may require to be put in funds first, typically as the result of a banker's payment received direct or through the clearing or a credit to its account with a third bank where both DB and CB hold accounts. In this case payment to C is complete when CB accepts the payment and decides to credit the beneficiary unconditionally with the equivalent amount.[121] The receipt by CB from DB and the receipt by C from D through a credit to C's account with CB are legally distinct.[122] Though the payment by DB to CB (directly or indirectly) is what enables CB to recognize C as its creditor for an equivalent sum, it is not that

---

118 See p 537.

119 CHAPS Rules, Version 1.3 (effective 3 September 2003), r 3.2.1. Where the Bank of England's systems are not able to process the payment message, so that this has to be transmitted in the RTGS by-pass mode, the payment message becomes irrevocable when the receiving member has transmitted a Positive User Acknowledgment (UAK) to SWIFT (r 6.2.1).

120 Article 3, implemented in the UK by the Financial Markets and Insolvency (Settlement Finality) Regulations 1999 (SI 1999/2979), Pt III.

121 It is not necessary that it shall have completed the credit entry to the account; its decision to do so is all that is required.

122 However, for the purpose of a proprietary tracing claim in equity the courts rightly take a robust view and treat CB's unconditional credit to the defendant as derived from the payment to CB. See p 456.

payment which discharges D's debt to C but the resultant decision to credit C's account. It is true that in banking parlance CB is said to receive payment 'for' or 'for the account of' or even 'as agent for' C, but that does not mean that CB's receipt is C's receipt, or that CB's claim on DB or a third bank is held on trust for C. If it has not already given C value by allowing him to draw against the expected receipt, CB collects as agent for C and instantaneously borrows the money back.[123] What C receives from D as the result of CB's decision to credit him is not what CB received but simply an equivalent amount. There are various reasons why CB, despite having received funds for C's account, may be unable or unwilling to credit that account at the time of receipt. The payment order may not adequately identify C, or CB may wish to check whether it still has authority to accept the payment, or may be concerned that the payment is not one which it can lawfully credit, eg because of legal restrictions.[124]

6.   COMPLETION OF PAYMENT OF AN IN-HOUSE CREDIT TRANSFER[125]

So far, we have dealt with completion of payment on the basis of an interbank transfer. What is the position where D and C bank at the same bank, SB.[126] The principle is the same. Payment is complete at the point where SB unconditionally recognizes C as its creditor. The difference arises from the fact that the transfer is purely in-house and does not involve any clearing process, any payment order or any correspondent relationship. All that is involved is that SB accepts C as its creditor in place of D. Payment is thus considered made once SB has performed some act showing its decision to debit D's account and credit C's account, whether or not the decision has been implemented by debit and credit entries to the two accounts.[127] Attempts by banks to reserve to themselves the right to decide this as a matter of subjective intention without reference to their overt acts have not succeeded. In *Momm v Barclays Bank International Ltd*:[128]

> The defendant bank was instructed by telex from Herstatt Bank to credit funds to the claimant's account by a stated value date. The computer processes to effect the transfer from the originator's account to the plaintiff's account were initiated on that date but the computer print-outs were not available until the following morning, when the computer had completed its overnight processing. On the previous day Herstatt had announced its insolvency and the defendants had become aware of the fact that the funds held for Herstatt were insufficient to cover the transfer. Taking the position that all transfer instructions sent through the computer were provisional only, the defendants reversed the transfer in their internal records. No trace of either the original transfer or the retransfer appeared in the plaintiff's own bank statements and came to light only during the course of the litigation. It was held by Kerr J that payment was completed

---

123   For the position of a bank collecting a cheque, see p 540.
124   Examples in recent times are the trade embargoes on Argentina and Libya, where regulations prohibited banks from crediting the accounts of nationals of those countries. The bank may also wish to defer a credit where it suspects money laundering or is on notice that C may not be the person who is entitled to the payment.
125   As to when a cheque is to be considered paid, see p 537.
126   For ease of exposition it will be assumed that they bank at the same branch.
127   *The Brimnes* [1973] 1 WLR 386, affirmed [1975] QB 929.
128   [1977] QB 790.

when the bank initiated the computer process and that it was not entitled to reverse the transfer.

There could, of course, be other overt acts having a similar effect, for example, a communication to the beneficiary that he could now regard the funds as his own and was free to draw on them unconditionally.

7.   CONTRACT NETTING (NETTING BY NOVATION)[129]

Where parties are continuously engaged in mutual dealings it is both administratively convenient and legally prudent for them to offset or 'net out' their reciprocal obligations, reducing them to a single amount.[130] The term 'netting' is used in two distinct senses. In the first, it denotes the amalgamation of two or more executory contracts into a single new contract to be performed at an agreed future date. This is known as netting by novation, to which we now turn. In its second sense it signifies the netting out of matured obligations for the purpose of computing a payment immediately due. This form of netting is commonly termed payment, or settlement, netting and will be examined in the discussion of settlement.[131]

Contract (or novation) netting, that is, the netting of contracts to be performed in the future, is very common in foreign exchange and swaps transactions, and typically takes place under a master agreement between the parties by which each new contract is automatically consolidated with existing contracts to produce a new contract (novation) involving a single net indebtedness. This form of netting has two distinct characteristics. It has immediate contractual force and it gives rise to a single new indebtedness which does not fall due for payment until a later date agreed between the parties. The netting therefore takes place as each new contract is made and is not deferred until the time of payment. It follows that when payment falls due, only a single sum is involved on one side or the other, and no question of netting (or set-off) arises. Contract netting has both administrative and legal advantages. It obviates the need to settle each transaction separately when payment falls due, with the same beneficial consequences as derive from an effective settlement netting.[132] It also helps to avoid the risk that on the insolvency of one of the parties, its liquidator will be able to challenge a right of set-off and to cherry pick by claiming payment from the solvent party of accounts on which the latter is

---

129   See Wood, *English and International Set-Off*, paras 5–75 ff.; Goode, *Legal Problems of Credit and Security* (3rd edn, 2003), paras 7–18, 7–29 – 7–31; Giavonoli, in Norton *et a.*, *Cross-Border Electronic Banking*; Bank for International Settlements, *Report of the Committee on Interbank Netting Schemes of the Central Banks of the Group of Ten Countries* (the Lamfalussy Report, 1990); Bradley Crawford, 'The legal foundations of netting agreements for foreign exchange contracts' [1993] 22 Can Bus L 163.

130   Netting embraces both money obligations and, in the commodities, futures and securities markets, delivery obligations. In these markets netting may occur either by bilateral agreement or by novation of contracts to a clearing house (see p 157). The latter technique is not used in the case of bank clearings. For the purpose of the present chapter it will be assumed that all obligations are money obligations and that the only relevant clearing will be a bank clearing.

131   See p 473.

132   See below.

the debtor while leaving that party to prove in the liquidation for sums payable on accounts on which it is the creditor.[133]

8. SETTLEMENT

Settlement is the process by which the money obligations of parties engaged in mutual dealings are discharged. Settlement is effected, directly or indirectly, through the clearing banks, who settle with each other across the books of the Bank of England, with which they all hold accounts. Settlement systems are of two kinds, net and gross. In a net settlement system the mutual obligations of the parties involved are set off against each other and only the net balance paid. This form of netting is known as settlement (or payment) netting. In contrast to contract netting, settlement netting is purely an accounting process and does not in itself bring about a contractual consolidation of the separate accounts which have given rise to it. It takes place only at the point when payment falls due, and it is not until the completion of payment that the obligations under those contracts are discharged. Net settlement takes place in two phases. There is the netting itself, that is the computation of balances due, and this is followed by the payment of balances so ascertained. A gross settlement system is a pay-as-you-go system in which the parties settle each payment obligation separately (usually, though not necessarily, in real time) through the central bank without regard to other obligations that may flow in the opposite direction.

(i) Net settlement

Net settlement may be bilateral or multilateral. In a bilateral settlement, such as CHAPS, a participant's entitlement or exposure is by agreement with its counter-party, measured solely by reference to its net position with that counterparty, not by reference to the system as a whole, though for administrative convenience it is the multilateral (net net) balances which are established at the end of the day and paid by transfers in the books of the Bank of England.[134] In a multilateral settlement, such as that used in the paper-based clearings, each participant's position is established in relation to all other participants in the clearing, that is, in relation to the system as a whole, under the rules of the clearing by which participants are bound. Thus each participant ends up as a net net debtor or a net net creditor in relation to all other participants with whom it has dealt during the day and settlement.

Net settlement possesses a number of advantages over gross settlement. It avoids a multiplicity and circuity of payment orders; it enhances liquidity, since a

---

133 Under English law cross-money claims between the same parties in the same right can usually be set off against each other on a liquidation, but there are certain circumstances in which the admissibility of insolvency set-off is denied or doubtful.

134 Since this multilateral netting and payment is not contractual but is purely for accounting convenience it would presumably follow that if a participant became insolvent, its liquidator would be entitled to have the settlement unwound to the extent necessary to ensure that the insolvent participant received its net credit balances without having these offset by its net debit balances.

participant's commitments in any one day are reduced by its entitlements; and for the same reason it reduces settlement risk, since the number and value of payments are reduced. It does, however, possess one major disadvantage which is particularly serious in relation to large-value transfers, namely receiver risk. This arises because receiving banks act in reliance on payment orders from sending banks throughout the day, giving immediate value to their customers, but do not receive payment until the end of the day,[135] when the multilateral settlement is completed. This daylight exposure may be multiplied many times as the result of customers who receive funds initiating further interbank transfers involving their settlement bank in additional commitments to other banks. If a participating bank were to fail before completion of the daily settlement, other banks which had made payments and incurred commitments in expectation of receiving funds from the insolvent bank might find themselves not only out of pocket but unable to meet those commitments, thus giving rise to a systemic risk.[136]

(ii) Real-time gross settlement

It is because of the potential gravity of this daylight exposure that the Bank of England and CHAPS introduced a real-time gross settlement system (RTGS) for large-value transfers.[137] Under this system each CHAPS instruction has to be covered by a transfer of funds to the sending bank in the books of the Bank of England before the payment order is sent to the receiving bank. The Bank of England will make such a transfer only where the receiving bank's account is in funds for the purpose. The sending bank's message to the intended receiving bank will be held at the sending bank's CHAPS gateway pending confirmation from the Bank of England that the necessary funds have been transferred to the receiving bank, and only at that point will the system release the sending bank's payment order to the receiving bank, which will have the assurance of knowing that it has already been put in funds through its account with the Bank of England to cover the payment it is asked to make. RTGS thus provides the immediacy and finality that are lacking in a net settlement system. To deal with the problem of reduced liquidity the Bank of England makes daylight funds available to the CHAPS banks by means of same-day sale and repurchase agreements (repos), pursuant to which the Bank will, at the request of a clearing bank, purchase government securities, sterling eligible bank bills and sterling eligible local authority bills offered by that bank and sell them back at the end of the day, and banks will be allowed to make intra-day

---

135 If they are net net creditors.

136 The failure of a participant bank may also create problems under insolvency law, for to allow that participant's claims on a particular counterparty to be reduced by the participant's liabilities to other participants infringes at least two principles of insolvency law. It allows set-off of claims in relation to which there is no mutuality, and it contravenes the *pari passu* principle of insolvency law by giving a preference to creditor participants in the clearing over the insolvent participant's general creditors, including trade suppliers (*British Eagle International Airlines Ltd v Compagnie Nationale Air France* [1975] 2 All ER 390). But in relation to transfer orders entered into a designated system the problem has been alleviated by the Financial Markets and Insolvency (Settlement Finality) Regulations 1999 (SI 1999/2979). See p 843.

137 Similar steps have been taken by other Member States of the European Union.

drawings on their cash ratio deposits. RTGS is not cost-free. Either a paying bank has to tie up balances at the Bank of England to meet outflows or its transfer instructions have to be queued to await the point where its inflows enable the transfers to be carried out or it must enter into a repo transaction with the Bank in order to obtain the necessary funds.

18   Instruments Generally[1]

The banking system has devised various methods of payment, described later in this book.[2] The next two chapters are devoted primarily to two long-established and popular payment media, the bill of exchange and the cheque; but since these are merely two members of a class of documents known as *instruments*, it is appropriate to say something now concerning the nature and history of instruments generally.

1.   WHAT IS AN INSTRUMENT?

An instrument is a document of title to money.[3] As a documentary intangible,[4] it is the physical embodiment of the payment obligation, and its possession (with any necessary indorsement in favour of the possessor) is the best evidence of entitlement to the money it represents.[5] The right to receive payment belongs to the holder[6] for the time being, is exercised by production of the instrument to the obligee or his authorized agent and is transferred by delivery, with any requisite indorsement.[7]

Whether a writing is an instrument, that is, whether possession of it is recognized as carrying with it the right to the specified sum of money or security for money, depends on mercantile usage and on statute, and the list of instruments is not closed. In practice, instruments as a class usually possess distinctive characteristics without which a writing is unlikely to be given recognition as an instrument. Thus, the document is traditionally concise and no greater in size than enables it to be conveniently carried and transferred; its terms are limited to payment obligations, security for payment (if given) and (in the case of scrip) the right to exchange it for the specified bonds or debentures.[8] Given that a document is an instrument, the next

---

1 See also p 48.
2 See pp 292 ff.
3 See p 48.
4 The other class of documentary intangible comprises documents of title to goods.
5 For an extensive discussion of this concept of incorporation of the right into the document see Denis V. Cowen, *The Law of Negotiable Instruments in South Africa* (5th edn, 1985), pp 23 ff. For a comparative treatment, see Peter Ellinger, *Negotiable Instruments*, 9 *International Encyclopaedia of Comparative Law* (ed Jacob S. Ziegel, 2000).
6 As to who is a holder, see p 493.
7 For the function of an indorsement, see p 490.
8 However, negotiable bonds are frequently expressed to be subject to the terms of a trust deed under a trust for bondholders. This is not considered to affect their status as negotiable instruments.

question is whether it is negotiable or non-negotiable,[9] which again depends on mercantile usage and statute.[10]

2.   CLASSES OF INSTRUMENT

Instruments may be negotiable or non-negotiable. A negotiable instrument is one which, by statute or mercantile usage, may be transferred by delivery and indorsement to a bona fide purchaser for value in such circumstances that he takes free from defects in the title of prior parties.[11] A non-negotiable instrument is one which, though capable of transfer by delivery (with any necessary indorsement) in the same way as a negotiable instrument, can never[12] confer on the holder a better right than was vested in the transferor. The full significance of negotiability will be described later.[13] Suffice it to say for the present that the status of a 'holder in due course' of a negotiable instrument is essentially that of a bona fide purchaser acquiring an overriding title.

There are many classes of negotiable and non-negotiable instrument, but they all fall into one of two categories, namely, an undertaking to pay a sum of money and an order to another to pay a sum of money, whether to the person giving the order or to a third party.[14] Instruments taking the form of an express or implied undertaking include promissory notes, banknotes,[15] treasury bills, bearer bonds and bearer debentures, share warrants,[16] bearer scrip certificates and negotiable certificates of deposit (all of which are negotiable instruments) and (non-negotiable) letters of allotment. Instruments taking the form of an order to pay are cheques and other bills of exchange, dividend and interest warrants, bankers' drafts[17] and circular notes (all of which are negotiable), travellers' cheques (probably negotiable), and postal orders, money orders, pension warrants, child benefit orders and the like (non-negotiable).

Orders to pay do not as such create any obligation between the payee and the person directed to make payment (the drawee). If the order is to pay on demand, the drawee either pays or refuses to pay. In the latter case, the payee's remedy is not against the drawee but against the party ordering payment (the drawer). If the order

---

9   See p 49 and below.

10   See below.

11   As pointed out in an earlier chapter (p 49, n 164), the term 'negotiable instrument' is not always used in the strict sense, being sometimes employed to denote any instrument embodying a monetary obligation and transferable by indorsement and delivery, whether or not capable of being transferred free from equities.

12   In the absence of some exception to the *nemo dat* rule falling outside the law relating to instruments.

13   See p 495.

14   A mere receipt showing what is repayable is not negotiable (*Claydon v Bradley* [1987] 1 All E R 522).

15   Strictly, a banknote *is* a promissory note, but with special incidents. In particular, the promise is valueless, for a banknote is legal tender and the holder no longer has the right to require the Bank of England to give him gold, silver or other metal in exchange. See p 450, n 6.

16   It is, perhaps, slightly anomalous that these are classified as instruments, but this can be justified on the basis that the ultimate right of a shareholder is to his share of any surplus moneys on winding up.

17   Which may at the option of the holder be treated as promissory notes.

is to pay at a future date, the drawee is asked to 'accept' the instrument, ie to add his signature by way of an undertaking to pay the instrument at maturity. If he refuses, the instrument is dishonoured, but again the payee's remedy is against the drawer alone. Instruments payable on demand are not accepted. There is no point in the drawee *undertaking* to perform a payment obligation which is due for immediate performance. He either pays or declines to pay.

The Bills of Exchange Act 1882, which regulates bills of exchange and promissory notes, governs some but not all of the instruments described above.[18]

3.   HISTORICAL BACKGROUND[19]

We shall briefly depict the historical development of three types of instrument: the promissory note, the bill of exchange and the cheque. The evolution of these instruments shows the ingenuity of the mercantile community at its very best.

(i)   The promissory note

The promissory note, that is, a document in which A promises to pay a sum of money to B, is of long standing as a credit instrument. But the creditor might find it inconvenient to collect payment himself at the due date and might wish to appoint an agent for that purpose. If the note provided simply for payment by A to B, then in any proceedings B's agent would have to produce a formal authority from B to collect payment. But if the note itself provided for payment to B or his nominee, or to B or other producer (ie holder) of the note, then A could not contest the right of the producer to collect payment, for A himself had provided for it in the terms of his undertaking.

Later it became apparent that the promissory note to some extent partook of the nature of money, and would thus be a very convenient method by which the payee, B, could discharge his own indebtedness to C. On taking a note payable to bearer, or to B or his nominee, B could pass the note over to his own creditor, C, who would thus collect for his own benefit, not merely as agent for B. The development of the promissory note as a negotiable instrument was abruptly halted by Lord Holt, who vigorously denied the negotiable character of the promissory note, saying that it was a new kind of specialty not known to the common law and relegated it to a mere contract.[20] Such was his influence that other judges who had been favourably

18   The Review Committee on Banking Services Law (Chairman: Professor Robert Jack) recommended the enactment of a comprehensive Negotiable Instruments Act covering all forms of instrument possessing stated minimum requirements. A draft Act, prepared by the Committee's consultant, Professor A. M. Shea, is included in Appendix C to the Committee's Report (Cm 22, 1989, rec 8(1)). But the recommendation has not been adopted.

19   See James Steven Rogers, *The Early History of the Law of Bills and Notes* (1995); J Milnes Holden, *History of Negotiable Instruments in English Law* (1955); Street, *Foundations of Legal Liability* (1906), vol II, Pt III. For a description of negotiable investment securities, see p 570.

20   *Clerke v Martin* (1702) 2 Ld Raym 757. Professor Rogers has shown (op cit, pp 177 ff) that Lord Holt's objections have been misunderstood and that much of the criticism levelled against him was misconceived.

inclined to the note felt obliged to follow his lead, and it was necessary to pass legislation, in the form of the Bills of Exchange Act 1704, to restore the promissory note to its earlier position as recognized by the custom of merchants.

(ii)　The bill of exchange

Though instruments resembling bills of exchange have been known for over a thousand years, the development of the bill of exchange in the form in which we now know it begins with the great fairs, international meeting places where merchants from all over Europe transacted business in accordance with that body of law, evidence and procedure established by international usage and known as the law merchant.[21]

Each merchant selling goods desired to be paid in his own currency. The currency exchanges were effected at the fairs by professional money-exchangers, who were conversant with exchange rates and thus provided a currency clearing house, which is the progenitor of the modern foreign-exchange system. It was natural for creditors who wished to collect, and debtors who wished to pay, to appoint exchangers to do it for them. But since the physical transportation of money was inconvenient and hazardous, and since exchangers had many dealings to settle among themselves, the unnecessary inconvenience of continual payments and repayments of monies soon became obvious. The merchants of Lombardy therefore devised a system by which exchangers could, through using correspondents in the creditor's country, localize payment and avoid physical transportation of money.

Suppose that B in Milan wished to pay S in London for goods bought by B from S. The following procedure could be adopted.

(a)　B went to X, a Milan money-changer, and put him in funds, in lire, for the price and X's charges.

(b)　X drew a bill, ie a written request or instruction on Y, his foreign correspondent in London, requiring Y to pay the sum named to S. X sent this bill to S.

(c)　S presented the bill to Y, who paid him in sterling.

(d)　Later, X and Y, who would have had numerous dealings between themselves, struck a balance on their account and settled up.

The advantages of this system were manifold:

(a)　The risk and expense of transporting gold from one country to another were avoided, the payment being localized through the bill procedure, while the number of settlements was greatly reduced.

(b)　If B were being given credit, the embodying of his obligation in a bill would provide S with an instrument he could sell before maturity.

(c)　If X knew B and Y knew S, each would be able to extend credit to its own national in respect of the bill.

21　See p 3.

The bill of exchange was in its inception confined largely to the financing of foreign trade, but was imported into domestic use in this country in about the mid-fifteenth century.

A later development was the acceptance credit. Some merchants, having surplus funds, were willing to provide finance not necessarily linked to a specific trading transaction, by allowing the party requiring funds to draw a bill on them which they could accept and he could then discount. Eventually, these 'merchant bankers' moved exclusively into what had been their secondary activity, with the result that the modern merchant banker is a financier, not a merchant.

(iii) The cheque

The goldsmiths, whose premises were equipped with safes and strongrooms for their bullion, offered as a service the acceptance of deposits from customers, paying interest. The deposit receipts issued by the goldsmiths were an acknowledgement of indebtedness. Later, the practice developed by which the goldsmiths would accept instructions from a depositor to pay a given sum of money to a named third party out of the funds held on deposit. This instrument was the forerunner of the cheque and has a still closer modern equivalent in the negotiable certificate of deposit.[22] The deposit receipt was recognized as a bill of exchange, and was transferable as such, but, since it involved immediate payment (ie was a species of sight bill), it was not 'accepted', there being no executory obligation. Thus the goldsmith was the progenitor of the modern banker, accepting deposits at interest, putting out the money at interest for his own account and honouring cheques drawn on him by his customers. A cheque is now defined by s 73 of the Bills of Exchange Act 1882 as a bill of exchange drawn on a banker payable on demand.

4.   THE AUTONOMY OF THE PAYMENT OBLIGATION

Every instrument, of whatever character, constitutes an independent contract embodying a payment obligation distinct from that of any other contract or duty relationship by virtue of which the instrument was issued. If B orders goods from S and pays the price by bill of exchange or cheque, the price-obligation contained in the contract of sale is suspended and revives if and only if the instrument is dishonoured by non-acceptance[23] or by non-payment at maturity.[24] Since the instrument itself constitutes a separate contract, it must in principle be honoured regardless of any breach by S of the related sale agreement.

This autonomy of the payment obligation[25] is essential to the marketability of instruments, for it provides the assurance of payment upon which purchasers of instruments rely, and is advantageous even in the hands of the original holder.[26] In

22 See p 570.
23 See p 487.
24 See pp 510, 513.
25 Which is not, however, absolute. See p 523.
26 See p 523.

this respect, an instrument fulfils much the same functions as a bond and a letter of credit, both of which embody a duty to pay distinct from, and independent of performance of, the contract pursuant to which they are issued.

But the merger in the instrument of the right to payment under the underlying transaction is not absolute, for the holder of a lost bill can call for a duplicate[27] or apply to the court for an order that the loss is not to be set up in proceedings on the bill if a satisfactory indemnity is given.[28]

5.   CERTAINTY AND UNCONDITIONALITY?

Is it an essential prerequisite of an instrument in general or of a negotiable instrument in particular that the payment obligation should be both certain and unconditional? This was evidently the view of the draftsman of the Bills of Exchange Act, and no instrument can be a bill of exchange within the Act which embodies a payment obligation that is in some respect conditional or dependent on an event external to the instrument itself. But the usages of financial institutions are not to be so rigidly confined. In recent years numerous investment securities have evolved – the bearer bond, the certificate of deposit, the floating rate note – under which the payment obligation is in some measure both uncertain and conditional, yet such documents are invariably accepted as having the quality of instruments and as being negotiable in character, and they would almost certainly be held by the courts to be negotiable instruments, albeit outside the scope of the Bills of Exchange Act.[29]

6.   THE NEGOTIABLE INSTRUMENT AS AN ABSTRACT
PAYMENT UNDERTAKING

The independence of a negotiable instrument from the underlying transaction has led some commentators to treat it as a form of abstract payment undertaking, operating by force of its own issue without more. But this is to overstate the substance and effect of the autonomy principle. In the first place, a negotiable instrument is itself a form of contract which requires to be supported by consideration, and while in the case of a bill of exchange the rules as to consideration are relaxed,[30] it is necessary that consideration shall have been given by someone in order for a party to a bill to be liable on it. Secondly, the autonomy of a negotiable instrument is not absolute, for a breach of the underlying contract giving rise to a total or partial failure of consideration for a bill is *pro tanto* a defence to a claim on the bill except as against a holder in due course.[31] The negotiable instrument thus lacks the essential characteristic of an abstract payment

27 Bills of Exchange Act 1882, s 69.
28 Ibid, s 70.
29 See p 570.
30 In particular, consideration need not have moved from the holder so long as value has been given by some party intermediate between him and the defendant. See p 494.
31 See p 523.

undertaking, that it does not require to be supported by consideration and, as a corollary, is not susceptible to a defence of failure of consideration.[32]

7.   DECLINE IN THE IMPORTANCE OF INSTRUMENTS

The development of electronic funds transfer systems has significantly reduced the importance of negotiable instruments both in domestic and in international trade. Though their use remains considerable, it is to be expected that over time there will be a further decline in their significance. Yet the advantages of negotiability cannot be denied.[33] They are therefore likely to be with us in substantial volume for the foreseeable future.

32 See Roy Goode, 'Abstract Payment Undertakings' in *Essays for Patrick Atiyah* (eds Peter Cane and Jane Stapleton, 1991), ch 9, pp 215–217.
33 See further pp 494, 527. The promissory note remains the basic instrument for forfaiting operations, as to which see *Chalmers and Guest on Bills of Exchange* (15th edn, 1998), pp 80–81.

19   Bills of Exchange

Many of the observations made in this chapter are not confined to bills of exchange but apply, in varying degrees, to other instruments. But the bill of exchange epitomizes the use of instruments as a financing mechanism, particularly in international trade, and for this reason is given a chapter to itself.

The common law rules relating to bills of exchange, cheques and promissory notes were codified by Sir Mackenzie Chalmers in the Bills of Exchange Act 1882, a model statute which was subsequently adopted throughout the common law world.[1] The Act preserves such rules of the common law relating to bills of exchange, promissory notes and cheques as are not inconsistent with its express provisions.[2]

I.   THE STATUTORY DEFINITION

Section 3 of the Bills of Exchange Act provides as follows:

(1) A bill of exchange is an unconditional order in writing, addressed by one person to another, signed by the person giving it, requiring the person to whom it is addressed to pay on demand or at a fixed or determinable future time a sum certain in money to or to the order of a specified person, or to bearer.

(2) An instrument which does not comply with these conditions, or which orders any act to be done in addition to the payment of money, is not a bill of exchange.

This definition, which we shall examine more closely when looking at the structure of a bill, encapsulates two fundamental characteristics of a bill, namely certainty and autonomy. If a bill is to fulfil its mercantile function, the amount and time of payment must be clear and unqualified, the instrument must speak for itself as a complete and integrated writing[3] and the rights and duties of the parties must not be

---

1 But in the United States it was eventually replaced by art 3 of the Uniform Commercial Code. Civil law jurisdictions have taken as their model the Uniform Law on Bills of Exchange and Promissory Notes embodied in the Geneva Convention 1930. A regime specifically designed for international bills and notes is the United Nations Convention on International Bills of Exchange and International Promissory Notes of 1988. This Convention is reproduced in *Chalmers and Guest on Bills of Exchange* (15th edn, 1998), Appendix C.

2 Section 96(2). Thus usages of trade, so far as not displaced by the language of the Act, may still govern the rights of the parties.

3 Notwithstanding the broad interpretation of 'writing' and 'signature' to cover electronic messages and signatures (see p 75), the general view is that the definition in s 3 requires that a bill of exchange must be paper-based and the paper signed. See Hugh Beale and Lowri Griffiths, 'Electronic commerce: formal requirements in commercial transactions' [2002] LMCLQ 467 at 483.

obscured or made uncertain by the inclusion of non-monetary obligations. Hence the bill must be in the form of an order to pay in the sense that, even if courteously framed as a request, it signifies a command or direction to the drawee, not a mere invitation or expression of desire which the drawee is to be free to refuse or ignore.[4] The obligation must be expressed in money (English or foreign[5]), not goods, stock or other money's worth. The order must not direct payment out of a particular fund,[6] for this makes the duty to comply with it dependent on the adequacy of the fund and thus prevents the order from being unconditional as required by the definition.[7] The time of payment must be fixed or ascertainable,[8] and, unless the bill is made payable to bearer, the payee must be named or otherwise indicated with reasonable certainty.[9] And the bill must be complete and not require (whether as a condition of payment or otherwise) the performance of obligations set out in some other document,[10] though there is no objection to its containing a reference to another document purely for information, eg to identify the transaction to which it relates.[11]

The ingredients of the statutory definition are expanded by the ensuing provisions of the Act,[12] some of which will be referred to hereafter.[13]

---

4 Strictly, the drawee cannot, within the terms of the definition, be the drawer himself or a fictitious person or a non-person such as 'cash' or 'wages'. But in the first two cases the Act gives the holder the option of treating the instrument as a bill of exchange or a promissory note (s 5(2)). A bill may also be drawn payable to the order of the drawee (s 5(1)). This is not as surprising as it seems. Where, for example, I ask my bank to purchase shares on my behalf I *could* reimburse the bank by drawing a cheque on my account, which is simply a method of enabling the bank to recoup itself from a particular account.

5 Exchange controls, which formerly restricted dealings in foreign currency and instruments, were abolished in October 1979.

6 Section 1(3).

7 But an unqualified order to pay with an indication of the particular fund out of which the drawee is to reimburse himself or a particular account which is to be debited with the amount is treated as unconditional (ibid). Thus if A draws a bill for £100 on B Bank in favour of C and stipulates that the amount is to be debited to A's No 2 account with B Bank, C is entitled to be paid the face value of the bill, even if A's No 2 account only has £50 in it. The direction to debit that account is not intended to limit the amount of the bill (and thereby render it uncertain) but simply means that B Bank is to recoup itself from the No 2 account as far as possible. The position is otherwise if the bill states: 'Pay C or order the sum of £100 from my No 2 account.' For an interesting argument that a distinction is to be drawn between conditions, which decrease the certainty of payment, do not meet the criteria of conclusivity of details and affect the autonomy of the instrument by subjecting payment to an external event, and stipulations, which require additional action by the drawee or payee that does not have any of these adverse effects, see Smadar Ottolenghi, 'A Conditional Order/Promise – or just a Stipulation?' [1999] JBL 22.

8 So that, for example, a bill payable 'three months after date' must be dated in order to establish the due date for payment (but in given conditions the holder may insert the date himself – see p 487).

9 Section 7(1). Payment to the holder of an office for the time being (eg 'Treasurer of the Barset Chess Club') is permissible (s 7(2)).

10 *Wirth v Weigel Leygonie & Co Ltd* [1939] 3 All ER 712.

11 Section 3(3)(b). It is common practice for a bank issuing a letter of credit to require that drafts drawn under the credit bear a reference identifying the transaction. See p 960, n 51.

12 See, eg, ss 5–11.

13 See pp 492 ff.

An instrument which fails to comply with the requirements of the definition is not a bill of exchange.[14] But an omission is not normally fatal, for it can usually be cured by the holder. Thus, where the maturity of a bill is to be determined by reference to the date of its issue or acceptance,[15] any holder may insert the true date,[16] and an incorrect date inserted by the holder in good faith and by mistake is to be treated as the true date.[17] Again, the person in possession of an inchoate instrument has a prima facie authority to fill it up as a complete bill and to rectify the omission of any material particular.[18] But he can do this only if the person delivering the document has signed it. An unsigned document cannot be a bill of exchange; and a forged or unauthorized signature cannot transfer title to the bill itself, though a party may incur a liability for having impliedly warranted, or through being estopped from disputing, the genuineness of the signature.[19]

2. ISSUE AND ACCEPTANCE

Let us suppose that John Jones has agreed to lend William Brown £450 for six months, repayment to be made, with £50 interest, by a bill of exchange drawn upon Basil Green, who has agreed to provide William Brown with a line of credit and to accept bills drawn on him by William Brown up to the agreed credit limit.[20] The

£500   London
6 January 2000

Six months after date pay to John Jones or order the sum of five hundred pounds, value received.

Accepted payable at Canon's Bank, Henry Street, Leeds

To Basil Green
Leeds

Fig 19.1 Bill of exchange (face)

---

14 Section 3(2). However, it may still be enforceable as a promissory note (*Novaknit Hellas SA v Kumar Bros. International Ltd* [1998] Lloyd's Rep Bank 287).

15 See p 487.

16 Section 12.

17 Ibid, proviso.

18 Section 20(1).

19 See further p 500 as to the distinction between the right to enforce a bill by virtue of a valid title to it and a right arising against a party solely on account of an implied warranty or estoppel.

20 This example is given purely to illustrate a three-party bill. In practice, most term bills are two-party bills drawn to the drawer's own order and then negotiated or discounted by him.

face of the bill would look something like figure 19.1. We will examine each feature of this bill in turn.

(i)   Parties

The person who draws the bill[21] – in this case, William Brown – is termed the *drawer*. He is the person who directs the intended paymaster, Basil Green, to make payment in six months' time to John Jones. Basil Green, the person *on whom* the bill is drawn, is at this stage called the *drawee*. The party in whose favour the bill is drawn, ie John Jones, is known as the *payee*. When the bill is delivered to him, he becomes the first *holder*. Until then, the document is not legally operative, for the commencement of its legal life depends on its issue, ie first delivery, complete in form, to one who takes as a holder;[22] and so long as William Brown retains possession, he cannot incur any liability to John Jones on the bill itself, though if he fails to deliver the bill he may thereby commit a breach of the underlying contract.

Delivery of the instrument to John Jones puts it in issue as a bill, but at that stage, despite Basil Green's name on the bill, there are only two parties to it: William Brown, who by reason of his signature is liable as drawer, and John Jones, who as holder[23] will be entitled to payment of the bill on its maturity. Basil Green has not yet become a party, for he has not accepted the bill, that is, signed it to denote his willingness to comply with the payment instruction given by William Brown, and until he signs it, he cannot be liable upon it,[24] though his refusal to sign may constitute a breach of some prior contract between himself and William Brown. It is thus necessary for the holder, John Jones, to *present* the bill to Basil Green for his acceptance.[25] By signing it as *acceptor*, Basil Green undertakes to pay the amount of the bill on maturity to John Jones or whoever else is the holder. Having accepted the bill, Basil Green, previously termed the drawee, is hereafter called the acceptor. It is customary to insert words of acceptance (as in fig 19.1), but this is not essential; Basil Green's signature in the normal place for acceptance suffices.[26]

21 By 'drawing' a bill is meant signing it by way of an instruction to another to make payment of the designated sum. Hence the term 'draft' is another name for a bill. The drawer may make out the bill himself but this is not necessary; it is equally effective if he signs a bill prepared for him by another, eg, the intended payee.

22 Bills of Exchange Act, s 2. Further, every contract on a bill, whether it be the drawer's, the acceptor's or an indorser's, is incomplete and revocable until delivery of the instrument in order to give effect thereto (s 21(1)), subject to the qualification that where an acceptance is written on a bill and the drawee gives notice to or according to the directions of the person entitled to the bill that he has accepted it, the acceptance then becomes complete and irrevocable (s 21(1)).

23 See p 492.

24 Section 23.

25 Thus bills, or drafts, are also termed 'acceptances'. But an acceptor is not an essential party to a bill. There must always be a drawer, a payee and a drawee, but an unaccepted bill is fully negotiable and is enforceable by the holder against the drawer and prior indorsers. If the drawer draws the instrument on himself, it is not a bill of exchange but the holder may treat it at his option as a bill of exchange or a promissory note. See *Chalmers and Guest on Bills of Exchange*, pp 37–40.

26 Section 17(2)(a).

What if Basil Green refuses to accept the bill? As we have seen, he incurs no liability to the holder for so doing, but the bill becomes *dishonoured by non-acceptance*, with the result that John Jones acquires an immediate right of action against William Brown,[27] despite the fact that the bill has not yet matured, and can recover damages calculated in accordance with s 57 of the Act.[28]

Basil Green's acceptance is necessary only because the bill is a term or 'usance' bill,[29] that is, a bill payable at a future date. If the bill had been expressed to be payable on demand or at sight,[30] then clearly it would be pointless for Basil Green to *promise* to pay it; he would either pay on presentation or refuse to pay.

(ii) Date

Where, as in this case, the bill is payable on the expiry of a fixed period after date, it is obviously necessary to know the date of issue in order to fix the time for payment. Similarly, if it is payable 'six months after sight',[31] dating of the drawee's acceptance is necessary to establish the maturity date. But even in these cases omission of the date is not fatal, for any holder may insert the true date, and if he acts in good faith, the date he inserts will be taken as the true date even if erroneous.[32] Dating of the bill is not, of course, necessary where the bill actually specifies the date on which it is to fall due; and in no case is a bill invalidated by reason of the fact that it is undated,[33] antedated or post-dated.[34]

A demand bill is one which is expressed to be payable on demand or at sight[35] or on presentation.[36] A bill is also payable on demand if no time for payment is specified.[37] A bill accepted or indorsed when overdue is deemed payable on demand as regards the acceptor or indorser.[38]

(iii) Place of drawing

This is customarily shown in the right-hand corner of the bill and is indicated in figure 19.1. Sometimes the drawer's full address is given. It is not essential to show

27 Section 43(2).
28 See p 509. Where the drawer has drawn the bill to his own order, the question of proceedings on the bill does not, of course, arise, and his claim against the drawee is simply for breach of the underlying contract (if any) to accept the bill.
29 Also called a tenor bill.
30 'At sight' means on presentation (s 10(1)).
31 By which is meant six months after acceptance or, if acceptance is refused, noting or protest (s 14(3)).
32 Section 12. However, he cannot thereby become a holder in due course, though the position is otherwise if the date is not necessary to fix the maturity of the bill. See p 496.
33 Section 3(4).
34 Section 13(2).
35 To be distinguished from a bill payable at a given period 'after sight'.
36 Section 10(1).
37 Ibid.
38 Section 10(2).

the place of drawing of a bill but the practice is convenient, for it helps to show whether the bill is an internal or a foreign bill.[39]

(iv) Amount

The amount payable under a bill, ie its 'face value', is usually expressed both in figures and in words, the latter prevailing in the event of inconsistency.[40] The designation of a 'sum certain in money' is an essential ingredient of a bill,[41] but the amount need not be designated in English currency.[42] A sum payable is a sum certain within the meaning of the Act although it is required to be paid with interest, or by stated instalments (with or without a provision that upon default in payment of any instalment the whole shall become due) or according to an indicated rate of exchange or a rate of exchange to be ascertained as directed by the bill.[43]

In export transactions the bill will usually be expressed in sterling but may carry an exchange clause providing for conversion into foreign currency or specifying an exchange rate on which the bill is based or by reference to which payment is to be made.

(v) Time of payment

The bill must be payable on demand or at a fixed or determinable future time. It fulfils the latter alternative if it is expressed to be payable at a fixed period after date or sight,[44] or on or at a fixed period after the occurrence of a specified event which is certain to happen, though the time of happening may be uncertain.[45] But an instrument expressed to be payable 'by' a particular date does not fulfil the statutory requirements, for it leaves the acceptor the option to pay at an earlier unspecified date;[46] and an instrument expressed to be payable on a contingency is not a bill, and the happening of the event does not cure the defect.[47]

---

39 A fact very material to the procedure to be followed in the event of the bill being dishonoured. See p 513.
40 Section 9(2). With modern technology geared to the scanning of figures there may be a case for reversing this rule.
41 Section 3(1).
42 But where it is so designated, it must be stated in decimal currency; the bill will be invalid if the sum payable is expressed wholly or partly in shillings and pence (Decimal Currency Act 1969, s 2(1)). There seems no reason why a bill should not be payable in euros instead of a particular national currency even though the UK is not as yet within the Eurozone.
43 Section 9(1).
44 Section 11.
45 Ibid.
46 *Claydon v Bradley* [1987] 1 All ER 522, where the Court of Appeal felt obliged, with apparent reluctance, to follow its earlier decision in *Williamson v Rider* [1963] 1 QB 89.
47 Ibid.

(vi) Signature

A document cannot be a bill of exchange unless it carries the signature of the drawer.[48] No action lies on the bill against a person who has not signed it; and no title can be derived from a forged signature, though the person in possession can acquire a status as holder through a subsequent indorsement and, if a holder in due course, will then have claims against those who became parties subsequent to the forged signature, on the basis of their being estopped from disputing its genuineness.[49] A person may sign as agent for another – eg a director may sign on behalf of his company – but care is needed to ensure that his representative capacity is made clear and that the statement of the intended principal's name is not to be read as merely descriptive of the signatory himself, for if it is, then he will be treated as principal and be liable on the bill accordingly.[50]

(vii) Place of acceptance

It is usual for the bill to be presented and paid at the acceptor's designated bank; and for this reason the name and address of Basil Green's bank are shown in the margin of the bill above his signature. But this is not essential. The phrase 'payable at Canon's Bank, Henry Street, Leeds' indicates that the bill must be presented at that address if the holder wishes to make the drawer or an indorser liable on it;[51] but the acceptor, as the principal debtor, remains under a duty to seek out his creditor, and the phrase in question is not sufficient to qualify the acceptance so as to impose on the holder the duty vis-à-vis the acceptor to present the bill for payment.[52] To do this it would be necessary to make it clear in the words of acceptance that payment was to be made *only* at the stated address and not elsewhere.[53]

3.   TRANSFER

So far, we have been concerned only with the original parties to the bill, namely the drawer, the payee and the acceptor. But John Jones, the payee in our illustration, may not wish to wait six months for his money. He may prefer to get in the cash by discounting the bill, that is, selling it at a discount. A bill can, like any other chose in action, be transferred by assignment, with notice of assignment to the acceptor, but such a procedure has nothing to commend it, for since the acceptor is not obliged to make payment to anyone other than the holder, he can safely disregard a notice of assignment, and all that the assignee acquires is an equitable title to the

---

48 Section 3(1). But signature by an agent suffices (s 91(1)). As to facsimile signatures, see p 531.

49 See p 501. Note that where a payee or named indorsee is a non-existent or fictitious person, the bill may be treated as payable to bearer, so that indorsement becomes superfluous and the fact that a subsequent indorsement was forged immaterial. See p 521.

50 This has caused a problem in several cases and is discussed further p 519.

51 Failure to do so discharges them (s 45).

52 Sections 19(2)(c), 45, 46(4). See further p 510.

53 Section 19(2)(c). As to the reason for imposing on the holder a general duty of presentment to the drawer or indorser but not the acceptor, see p 510.

instrument, so that he takes subject to equities and cannot sue in his own name.[54] He thereby loses one of the main advantages of an instrument, ie that it can be transferred from hand to hand so as to pass legal title to the sum payable under it. This process of transfer is termed negotiation. 'A bill is negotiated when it is transferred from one person to another in such a manner as to constitute the transferee the holder of the bill.'[55]

Before considering the method by which a bill is transferred we must examine the status of the payee. The bill could simply be made payable to 'bearer'. The rights under it would then vest in whoever was for the time being in possession, and the first holder could transfer it by mere delivery without indorsement. The risks involved in issuing a bearer bill will be obvious. Anyone into whose hands the bill comes (whether lawfully or otherwise) is the holder and as such is able to present the bill for payment to the acceptor on its maturity; and provided that the acceptor acts in good faith and without notice of a defect in the holder's title, the acceptor gets a good discharge by payment of the bill, even if the person to whom he made payment stole the bill or is otherwise unlawfully in possession of it.[56]

So in practice a bill is rarely drawn as a bearer bill. Instead, it is, as in our illustration, drawn to 'John Jones or order'. This means that payment is required to be made either to John Jones himself or to any transferee to whom he might direct payment to be made. The words 'or order', though usual, are in fact unnecessary, since the law implies that John Jones can transfer the bill and direct the acceptor to pay the transferee.[57]

The manner in which the payee makes his direction to the acceptor to pay a third party is by *indorsing* the bill, that is, placing his signature on the back of the bill, and delivering it to the third party concerned. The payee then becomes the first *indorser* and the transferee is the first *indorsee*. If, when indorsing the bill, the indorser names the indorsee, the acceptor must pay that indorsee or any other party to whom the indorsee, by putting his own signature on the bill, directs payment to be made. Such an indorsement is termed a *special indorsement* and preserves the character of the bill as an order bill.[58] Where, as is quite common, the payee as indorser simply puts his signature on the back of the bill without naming an indorsee, this *indorsement in blank*, as it is called, is a direction to the acceptor to pay whoever is currently in possession of the bill, ie the bearer. In short, an indorsement in blank converts the bill into a bearer bill, which is thereafter (unless reconverted into an order bill) transferable by manual delivery, without the need for any indorsement. The only distinction between a bill which becomes a bearer bill in

---

54 This is so under the general law and is reinforced by s 31(4) of the Bills of Exchange Act in the case of a transfer for value, where the transferee acquires the additional right to have the transferor's indorsement.

55 Section 31(1). The word 'negotiate' is also used in financial circles in a narrower sense, to denote transfer of a bill before acceptance, as opposed to the discount of a bill, which signifies transfer after acceptance.

56 Section 59.

57 See s 8(4). Similarly, a bill payable 'to the order of John Jones' is payable to him or his order at his option (s 8(5)). A bill may be drawn to prohibit negotiation (Bills of Exchange Act 1882, s 8(1)).

58 If, in addition, the holder makes the indorsement a *restrictive* indorsement, by directing payment to the named indorsee *only*, or makes it clear that the indorsement is for the purpose of collection by the

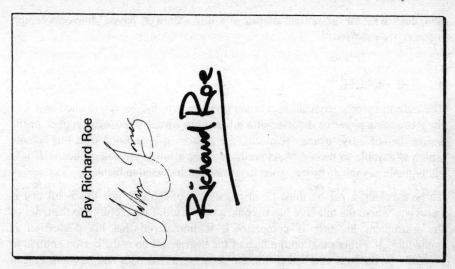

Fig 19.2 Bill of exchange (back)

this way and a bill which starts life as a bearer bill is that an order bill converted to a bearer bill may at any time be reconverted to an order bill by a special indorsement by the holder when transferring it, whereas a bill which is a bearer bill *ab initio* cannot be converted to an order bill, and any indorsement which is designed to transform it into an order bill will be disregarded as ineffective for the purpose.[59] Figure 19.2 illustrates the reverse side of the bill shown in figure 19.1 after it has been indorsed by the payee, John Jones.

In indorsing the bill, John Jones directs payment to be made to Richard Roe. This is a special indorsement, and its effect is that only Richard Roe or a person to whom he has indorsed the bill can present the bill for payment. No other person, even if in possession of the bill, qualifies as the holder,[60] and the bill continues as an order bill. However, Richard Roe, having taken the bill, himself indorses it in blank, thus converting it into a bearer bill. The holder will thus be the person for the time being in possession. Suppose that Richard Roe delivers the bill to Stanley Small, and that he, as holder, indorses the bill specially to Tom Thumb. The bill is reconverted into an order bill, and, in the absence of any further indorsement by Tom Thumb, only he can present it for payment.

To be effective to transfer title to the bill an indorsement must be made by the holder. The Act does, however, make provision for signature by a stranger to the bill, sometimes called a *quasi-indorser*,[61] for the purpose of imposing liability on him despite the fact that he is not in the chain of title. With this exception, we have

indorsee and not with a view to transferring the bill, it ceases to be negotiable (ss 8(1), 35(1)).

59 *Miller Associates (Australia) Pty Ltd v Bennington Pty Ltd* [1975] 2 NSWLR 506. But the indorsement is not totally nugatory, for though the bill continues as a bearer bill the indorser incurs all the liabilities imposed on an indorser under the Act. See p 508.

60 See further below.

61 See p 504.

now dealt with all the normal parties to a bill – drawer, payee, drawee/acceptor, indorser and indorsee.[62]

4.   THE HOLDER

The right to enforce payment of a bill is given only to the *holder*, defined by s 2 of the Act as 'the payee or indorsee of a bill or note who is in possession of it, or the bearer thereof'. By 'bearer' is meant 'the person in possession of a bill or note which is payable to bearer'.[63] As we have seen, a bill is payable to bearer if it is either made payable to bearer when first drawn or indorsed in blank.

To be a holder, a person must be in possession of the bill, and this is all that is necessary where the bill is or has become a bearer bill, for according to the tenor of the instrument his title is complete. It is immaterial that his possession is unlawful.[64] It suffices that on the face of the instrument he is the person entitled to be paid – in the case of a bearer bill, the possessor. This does not, of course, mean that a thief has a legal right to demand payment from the acceptor; what it does mean is that if the thief presents the bearer bill for payment and the acceptor pays him in good faith and without notice of a defect in title, he gets a good discharge.[65] But if the bill is an order bill, mere possession is not necessarily sufficient; the possessor must show that according to the tenor of the bill he is the person entitled to payment. If he is the original payee and the bill has not been indorsed, he is the holder. Where, however, the bill has been specially indorsed,[66] only the named indorsee in possession can be the holder. Thus if a bill payable to A is indorsed by him 'Pay B', B, if in possession, is the holder. If C has possession, the bill is without a holder. B is not the holder, for he lacks possession; C is not the holder, for, though in possession, he is not the named indorsee.

Where an inchoate instrument is delivered, the deliveree has prima facie authority to complete it and thus convert himself into a holder.[67]

The Bills of Exchange Act designates three categories of holder. These are, in ascending order of importance, a mere holder, a holder for value and a holder in due course. With the last of these must be bracketed a holder claiming title through a holder in due course and not himself a party to any fraud or illegality affecting the bill. We consider each of these four types of holder in turn.

---

62 There remain a few bizarre characters found only in the pages of textbooks, ie, referees in case of need and acceptors and payers for honour *supra protest*. See Bills of Exchange Act 1882, ss 15, 65–68.

63 Section 2.

64 *Chalmers and Guest on Bills of Exchange*, pp 13–14.

65 For the instrument itself is then discharged (s 59).

66 If it is indorsed in blank it becomes a bearer bill. A person who indorses a bill to a bank purely for collection and not with the intention of transferring rights does not cease to be a holder (*Novaknit Hellas SA v Kumar Bros. International Ltd* [1998] Lloyd's Rep Bank 287). Note that a cheque does not now have to be indorsed to a bank for collection on behalf of the holder (Cheques Act 1957, s 1), and if the bank gives value or has a lien on such a cheque it has the same rights as if the cheque had been indorsed in blank (ibid, s 2). See further pp 544–546.

67 Section 20.

(i) 'Holder'[68]

The holder of a bill who is not a holder for value nevertheless has certain privileges denied to a non-holder. The latter cannot negotiate an order bill,[69] nor can he, except on behalf of the holder, present the bill for acceptance[70] or payment.[71] The holder can retain possession of the bill and can sue on it in his own name[72] and give a good discharge to a drawee or acceptor whose payment is otherwise in due course.[73] The holder may, in a bill payable after date, insert the date of issue or acceptance of the bill where this has been omitted.[74] Any holder is entitled to convert an order bill into a bearer bill by indorsement in blank and to convert a bearer bill into an order bill by a special indorsement.[75] The holder of a bill lost before it is overdue may apply to the drawer for a duplicate against a written indemnity, and the latter may be compelled to accede to the request.[76]

Despite these advantages, a holder otherwise than for value is (except where claiming title through a holder in due course[77]) in a very precarious position compared with one who has given or is deemed to have given value. Though a holder is prima facie deemed to be a holder in due course,[78] yet if it is established that he is not a holder for value,[79] his claim cannot succeed, for in the absence of consideration the 'contract' generated by the bill is *nudum pactum*.

(ii) 'Holder for value'

The first question is what is meant by 'value'? Section 27(1) of the Act tells us that valuable consideration for a bill may be constituted by (a) any consideration sufficient to support a simple contract, and (b) any antecedent debt or liability, this being deemed valuable consideration whether the bill is payable on demand or at a future time. Paragraph (b) of s 27(1) is usually referred to as an exception to the common law rule as to past consideration. But except in relation to a bill taken as collateral security for a past indebtedness, this assumption is misconceived. So far as concerns a bill taken as absolute or conditional payment of a pre-existing debt, s 27(1)(b) merely re-states the well-established common law rule that a payment or transfer in satisfaction of an existing debt is made for value, for the creditor's right

---

68 In the ensuing paragraphs the word 'holder' is used to denote one who is a *mere holder*, at the very bottom rung of the ladder, as opposed to a holder for value or a holder in due course.

69 Section 31(3).

70 Section 41(1)(a).

71 Section 45(3).

72 Section 38(1).

73 Sections 38(3), 59(1).

74 Section 12.

75 Section 34(4).

76 Section 69.

77 See pp 495 ff.

78 Section 30(2). But the burden of proof shifts if in an action on the bill it is admitted or proved that its acceptance, issue or subsequent negotiation is affected with fraud, duress or illegality (ibid).

79 As to the meaning of which see below.

to payment of the debt is thereby extinguished,[80] and in the case of a term bill there is the additional fact that the creditor's rights on the underlying contract are suspended pending maturity of the bill.[81]

Hence for most purposes 'value' in the Bills of Exchange Act has exactly the same meaning as in the case of an ordinary contract. However, the common law rules as to consideration are modified in two respects. First, every signatory to the bill is prima facie deemed to have become a party to it for value.[82] Secondly, where value has at any time been given for the bill, the holder is deemed to be a holder for value as regards the acceptor and all parties to the bill who became parties prior to such time.[83] Put more simply, it is not essential to 'holder for value' status that the holder shall himself have given value[84] or that his proposed defendant shall have received value for the bill. It suffices that value was given by some party in the chain between the holder and his intended defendant. Two illustrations will make this clear.

(1) S draws a bill on B to the order of S for the price of goods sold by S to B and, having procured B's acceptance, indorses the bill to T by way of gift. T can sue B, value having been given by S, for, as acceptor B, is liable to the holder if value has been given at any time, by whatever party; it is immaterial that T himself was a donee. But T cannot sue S.

(2) B draws a bill in his own favour on A, who accepts gratuitously. B cannot sue A, no value having been given. B indorses to C, who takes for value. C can sue A, even though A received no benefit, since C gave value. C then indorses the bill to D by way of gift. D can sue A, even though A received no benefit and D gave nothing for the bill, for value has been furnished by C and this suffices to make A liable as acceptor. D can also sue B, for the value given by the intervening party, C, makes D a holder for value vis-à-vis B. But D cannot sue C, for D did not give value and there is no intervening party between C and D. Similarly, if D indorses the bill to E by way of gift, E cannot sue C, for E did not give value, nor was value given by D, the party standing between C and E.

In short, a donor, though he cannot be sued by his donee, can be sued by the first holder to give value and by any subsequent holder, whether or not he gave value.

Since the requirement of consideration is by definition satisfied, a holder for value is obviously in a better position than a holder not for value, for his claim cannot be defeated by a plea of want of consideration. But unless he is a holder in due course, a holder for value does not enjoy the full benefits of negotiability, for he acquires no better title than his transferor and thus takes the bill subject to equities and to any defect in the title of any of his predecessors.

---

80 *Currie v Misa* (1875) LR 10 Exch 153; *Taylor v Blakelock* (1886) 32 Ch D 560; *Oliver v Davis* [1949] 2 KB 727 and cases there cited. The position is otherwise if the bill is taken not as absolute or conditional payment but as security for an existing debt. In this case, the creditor gives nothing in exchange for the bill, which but for s 27(1)(b) would be void as given upon a past consideration.

81 See p 441.

82 Section 30(1).

83 Section 27(2).

84 The position is considered to be otherwise if he wishes to qualify as a holder in due course. See p 497.

(iii) 'Holder in due course'

To become a member of the bill-holding aristocracy, the holder must ensure that he is not a mere holder nor even just a holder for value, but a *holder in due course*. This phrase broadly denotes a bona fide purchaser for value without notice. Just as the bona fide purchaser of goods for value and without notice will in certain conditions obtain an overriding title, by way of exception to the *nemo dat* rule, so also will the holder of a bill, if fulfilling certain requirements, be a holder in due course and thus acquire a title to the bill free from equities and defects in the title of his transferor. The conferring of this 'holder in due course' status is the crucial factor which distinguishes a negotiable from a non-negotiable instrument.

The holder in due course is in a powerful position. He can acquire a good title from or through a thief. He is not affected by the fact that any predecessor obtained the bill by fraud or pursuant to a fraudulent or otherwise illegal purpose,[85] or that the consideration given for the bill by a predecessor has wholly failed, as where the original holder took the bill as payment for goods which he failed to deliver or which were lawfully rejected. The holder in due course is not subject to personal defences that might be raised by prior parties, nor is his claim reducible by the exercise of a right of set-off to which the transferor may have been subject.[86] The estoppels binding signatories of a bill operate only in favour of a holder in due course or one claiming through a holder in due course and cannot be invoked by any other kind of holder.[87] The only limitation on the rights of the holder in due course is that where a signature on the bill has been forged or is otherwise of no legal effect, he has no rights against those who were parties to the bill prior to the ineffective signature, for vis-à-vis those parties he is not a holder at all.

What, then, must the holder of a bill do to achieve the exalted status of a holder in due course? Section 29(1) answers this in the following terms:

(1) A holder in due course is a holder who has taken a bill, complete and regular on the face of it, under the following conditions: namely,

(a) that he became the holder of it before it was overdue, and without notice that it had been previously dishonoured, if such was the fact;

(b) that he took the bill in good faith and for value, and that at the time the bill was negotiated to him he had no notice of any defect in the title[88] of the person who negotiated it.

We shall look at each of these ingredients in turn, noting that any holder is prima facie deemed to be a holder in due course.[89]

---

85 *Bank für Gemeinwirtschaft Aktiengesellschaft v City of London Garages Ltd* [1971] 1 WLR 149. See also p 523.

86 As to set-off in relation to a claim on a bill, see pp 515; 516, n 225.

87 An exception is the estoppel binding on an indorser vis-à-vis his own and subsequent indorsees as to the validity and subsistence of the bill and of his title to it. See s 55(2)(c) and p 504.

88 See p 498.

89 Bills of Exchange Act, s 30(2).

1.   'Holder'

Obviously a person cannot be holder in due course unless he is a holder. But not every holder can qualify. As we have previously remarked, a holder in due course is in effect a bona fide *purchaser* of the bill. The original payee, though the holder if in possession, cannot as payee be a holder in due course,[90] a point obliquely made in s 29(1)(b) in the phrase 'at the time the bill was negotiated to him'. Hence only the second or subsequent possessor of a bearer bill or an indorsee in possession of an order bill can be a holder in due course. But though the payee cannot *as such* be a holder in due course, if after he has negotiated it, the bill is renegotiated back to him, he can then qualify, not *qua* payee but *qua* indorsee.[91] This point is of practical importance in providing the payee with machinery to exercise rights against a quasi-indorser, that is, a non-party backing the bill by way of guarantee.[92]

2.   Bill not overdue

A person taking a bill after it has matured cannot be a holder in due course. The reason for this rule is, of course, that as a bill must normally be promptly presented for payment, the fact that it is still outstanding in the hands of the holder after its due date suggests that all is not well.

3.   'Complete and regular on the face of it'

If any material particular is omitted from the bill at the time of its negotiation to the holder, he cannot qualify as a holder in due course, even if he proceeds to exercise his right as holder to complete the instrument.[93] Thus, one who takes an inchoate instrument cannot be a holder in due course. What are the material parts of a bill? It is commonly asserted that omission of the date renders the bill incomplete; but it is hard to see why this should be so, except where the date is necessary to fix the maturity of the bill,[94] for the Act makes it clear that the statement of the date is not an essential ingredient of a bill,[95] and the absence of a date ought not by itself to be regarded as a circumstance arousing suspicion. Similarly, the place of issue of a bill is not, it is submitted, a material part such that its absence will render the bill incomplete. The fact that the bill has not been accepted does not affect its completeness, for a bill is fully negotiable before acceptance. On the other hand, a bill will be incomplete if it fails to identify the payee or the sum payable or if a signature necessary to establish the chain of title is missing. Of course, in the last case the person in possession will not be the holder at all.

---

90   *R. E. Jones Ltd v Waring & Gillow Ltd* [1926] AC 670. But prior to this decision (which has been criticized by several overseas writers) a payee-holder was generally considered to be capable of being a holder in due course.

91   See *Jade International Steel Stahl und Eisen GmbH & Co KG v Robert Nicholas (Steels) Ltd* [1978] QB 917 (drawer to whom bill subsequently negotiated back held to be a holder in due course).

92   See p 504.

93   See p 485.

94   See p 485.

95   Section 3(4)(a).

In addition to being complete, the bill must be 'regular' on the face of it, that is, in apparent good order, with nothing calculated to arouse suspicion.[96] Unauthenticated alterations and erasures should put a person on his guard and will prevent the bill from being regular.[97] Similarly, a significant discrepancy between the name of the payee on the face of the bill and that shown by his indorsement on the back makes the bill irregular.[98]

4. No notice of previous dishonour

The meaning of 'notice' is discussed a little later, for it has proved a vexed question in relation to 'holder in due course' status. If the previous dishonour was by non-payment, then, of course, the holder could not be a holder in due course, even if taking without notice, for the bill would necessarily have been overdue at the time of negotiation.

5. Good faith

The holder must have taken the bill in good faith, that is, honestly, whether or not he was guilty of negligence.[99] Thus it is not a bar to 'holder in due course' status that the holder would have discovered a defect in his transferor's title if he had exercised more care.[100] On the other hand, evidence of an unusual degree of carelessness may lead to the conclusion that the holder deliberately turned a blind eye to suspicious circumstances external to the bill,[101] and this is equated with mala fides.[102]

6. Value

Until recently it had been generally assumed that the special meaning attributed to 'holder for value' by s 27(2) of the Act[103] did not apply where 'holder in due course' status is concerned, and that to be a holder in due course it was necessary that the holder should himself have furnished value, so that he could not rely on value provided by his predecessors. This construction seemed to be plainly indicated by the phrase 'he takes the bill in good faith and for value', and was supported by the great preponderance of writers.[104] Despite this, the view has

---

96 *Arab Bank Ltd v Ross* [1952] 2 QB 216, per Denning LJ at 226.
97 *Byles on Bills of Exchange and Cheques* (27th edn, 2002), para 18–07. As against parties other than a holder in due course, material alteration of a bill renders it void (Bills of Exchange Act 1882, s 64(1)). See p 522.
98 *Arab Bank Ltd v Ross*, n 96, where the omission of the word 'Company' was held to render an indorsement irregular.
99 Section 90(1).
100 *Jones v Gordon* (1877) 2 App Cas 616, per Lord Blackburn at 628.
101 If on the bill, they would, of course, prevent it from being complete and regular.
102 *Jones v Gordon*, n 100, per Lord Blackburn at 628–629.
103 See p 493.
104 See the first edition of this work at p 448; *Chalmers and Guest*, pp 271–272; Jacobs, *Bills of Exchange* (1943), p 184; Bernard B Riley, *The Law Relating to Bills of Exchange in Australia* (2nd edn, 1964), p 119; Denis V. Cowen, *Law of Negotiable Instruments in South Africa* (5th edn, 1985), p 58; and other writers referred to by L. S. Sealy and R. J. A. Hooley, *Commercial Law: Text, Cases and Materials* (3rd edn, 2003), pp 527–528.

been expressed in two cases that 'value' has the ordinary meaning given to it by s 27(2).[105] But in the first case the view expressed was obiter and in neither was reference made to the relevant literature supporting the view that a holder in due course had to have given value himself. It is submitted that this view remains correct.

7.   No notice of defect in title

What is meant by 'no notice' is discussed hereafter.[106] A list of matters constituting defects in title is given by s 29(2), which provides that the title of a person who negotiates a bill is defective within the meaning of the Act when he obtained the bill, or its acceptance, by fraud,[107] duress or other unlawful means or for an illegal consideration or when he negotiated it in breach of faith or under such circumstances as to amount to a fraud.[108] It will be observed that the title of a person negotiating a bill can be defective either because of the manner in which he took the bill or because of the circumstances in which he transferred it.

The list is far from exhaustive, being confined to defects arising from an unlawful act performed, or unlawful consideration given, by the person negotiating the bill to the party claiming 'holder in due course' status. But the negotiator may himself have acted in perfect good faith in taking and transferring the bill, and the defect in title may arise through some unlawful act of a prior holder of which he was unaware. Moreover, it is thought that a defect in title exists whenever the right of the holder to deal with the bill is restricted, even though no breach of duty has occurred on the part of anybody. For example, a person holding a bill as collateral security may without breach of duty negotiate it provided that he informs his indorsee that it is held as collateral security and provided further that he is able to secure its return upon redemption by the debtor; but there can be little doubt that the indorsee would not be a holder in due course, for his right to deal with the bill is curtailed by the same limitations, so that the bill does not have the characteristic of free and unfettered transferability which is the hallmark of a bill of exchange in the hands of a holder in due course.[109]

---

105 See *M. K. International Development Co Ltd v Housing Bank* [1991] 1 Bank LR 74, per Mustill LJ at 80; *Clifford Chance v Silver* [1992] 2 Bank LR 11; L. P. Hitchens, 'Holders for Value and Their Status; *Clifford Chance v Silver*' [1993] JBL 571; and Mark Snedden, 'Deemed Holder for Value of Cheque or Bill of Exchange as Holder in Due Course' (1989) 17 ABLR 400.

106 See p 524.

107 This means fraud in the common law sense, ie dishonesty. The fact that negotiation of a bill constituted what was a fraudulent preference within s 44(1) of the Bankruptcy Act 1914 (since repealed) was held not to mean that the bill was obtained by fraud for the purpose of s 29(2) of the Bills of Exchange Act (*Österreichische Länderbank v S'Elite Ltd* [1981] QB 565).

108 In addition, where a person negotiates a cheque in contravention of s 123(2) of the Consumer Credit Act 1974, his doing so constitutes a defect in title within the meaning of the Bills of Exchange Act (Consumer Credit Act 1974, s 125(2)).

109 For the author's comment to the same effect in relation to bills of exchange taken in connection with hire-purchase agreements, see R. M. Goode, *Hire-Purchase Law and Practice* (2nd edn, 1970), p 679, n 17, and cases there cited. As these stand, the point cannot be regarded as settled.

(iv) Holder claiming under holder in due course

A holder (whether for value or not) who derives his title to a bill through a holder in due course, and who is not himself a party to any fraud or illegality affecting it, has all the rights of that holder in due course as regards the acceptor and all parties to the bill prior to that holder.[110] This is a specific application of the wider common law rule that where, by an exception to the *nemo dat* rule, a party acquired an overriding title to an asset, his transferee can shelter behind that title even if not himself giving value and even if aware, at the time he acquired his interest, that the original owner had been wrongfully deprived of the asset, except where the transferee himself was the party guilty of or involved in such deprivation.[111] Thus 29(3) does not deprive a holder claiming under a holder in due course from enforcing the bill merely because at the time he took it he had notice of some prior fraud or illegality. It is necessary to show that he was a party to the fraud or illegality in question.

5. ACCOMMODATION PARTIES AND ACCOMMODATION BILLS

The ability to discount a bill, and the discount rate it can command in the discount market, depend on the quality of the names on the bill. Sometimes a person in need of finance 'raises the wind'[112] by persuading a friend or acquaintance of known financial standing to 'accommodate' him gratuitously by signing the bill in order to make it acceptable for discount. Thus where A is seeking the finance and his friend B agrees to draw, accept or indorse a bill without receiving value, the bill is said to be drawn, etc, for A's accommodation (A may or may not be a party to the bill himself) and B is an accommodation party. In the language of the Act:

> An accommodation party to a bill is a person who has signed a bill as drawer, acceptor or indorser, without receiving value therefor, and for the purpose of lending his name to some other person.[113]

An accommodation party is liable to a holder for value even though known by the holder to be an accommodation party.[114] Where B, the accommodation party, comes in as the acceptor, the bill is said to be an *accommodation bill*. The significance of this is that since B accepts for the accommodation of A, the party primarily liable is considered to be A, B being deemed merely a surety for A with the result that payment of the bill by A discharges it, whereas in the ordinary way a bill is discharged only by payment by the party named as acceptor.[115] A party may lend his name to a bill as drawer or indorser, and will be an accommodation party, but the bill will not be an accommodation bill, for in such a case the acceptor is intended to remain the party primarily liable, whereas the characteristic of an

---

110 Section 29(3).
111 See p 55.
112 Or 'flies a kite'.
113 Section 28(1).
114 Section 28(2). But he may set up any defences that would have been available to the party accommodated.
115 See p 525. Payment by B will also, of course, discharge the bill.

accommodation bill is that the party intended to be primarily liable is the party accommodated, and payment by him thus constitutes a good discharge of the bill.

6.   LIABILITIES OF PARTIES

(i)   In general

Sections 53–58 of the Bills of Exchange Act deal with the liabilities of the various parties to a bill. Section 53 emphasizes the point, previously made, that a drawee incurs no liability on a bill until he has accepted it.[116] The bill does not operate as an assignment of funds in the hands of the drawee, and the latter is thus not obliged to regard the holder as his new creditor. Further, no one is liable as drawer, indorser or acceptor of a bill who has not signed it as such.[117] But while liability *on the bill* is confined to signatories, it does not follow that a party who has not signed is totally immune from action. The holder of a bearer bill who negotiates it by delivery is not liable *on the bill*,[118] for he has not signed it; but by delivering it, he warrants to his immediate transferee, if the latter is a holder for value, that the bill is what it purports to be,[119] that he has a right to transfer it and that at the time of transfer he is not aware of any act which renders it valueless.[120] Breach of this warranty, though not making the transferor liable for the amount of the bill as such, exposes him to a claim for damages, or alternatively (and more efficaciously) for recovery of the sum paid to him as money paid on a total failure of consideration.[121]

Once a party signs a bill, he incurs to subsequent parties the liability for its payment and is precluded from denying to a holder in due course the genuineness of the signature of prior parties. In certain cases a party may also be estopped, as against a holder in due course, from disputing the existence, capacity and authority of a prior party.[122]

(ii)   Real rights and personal rights[123]

If for the moment we turn our attention away from the liabilities of the parties and look instead at the rights accorded to the holder (for convenience, we shall assume him to be a holder in due course), we must observe the important distinction between the holder who acquires a valid title to the bill and can thus

---

116 However, his refusal to sign may constitute a breach of contract exposing him to a claim for damages. Thus if the seller of goods which are to be paid for by the buyer's acceptance of a term bill draws the bill on the buyer, who refuses to accept it, there is no dishonour of the bill as such, for there is no party liable on it. S's remedy against B is for breach of contract.

117 Section 23.

118 Section 58(2).

119 Ie, that it is genuine.

120 Section 58(3).

121 The transferor's awareness of a fact which merely *diminishes* the value of the bill is not within s 58(3) and does not entitle the transferor to recover the price paid, for there is only a partial failure of consideration.

122 See pp 502 ff.

123 As to real and personal defences to a claim on a bill, see pp 514 ff.

enforce it as owner against all prior parties and the holder who, because of a defect in the bill or its transfer, does not get a good title but acquires rights against a particular party by virtue of some estoppel resulting from the latter's signature or delivery of the bill.[124]

For example, title cannot be derived from or through a forged signature, but as against a holder in due course, the acceptor is precluded from denying the genuineness of the drawer's signature[125] and an indorser is precluded from denying that the signature of the drawer and any prior indorser is genuine.[126] Thus the holder in due course may enforce the bill against the acceptor despite the fact that the drawer's signature was forged and can sue an indorser on the bill despite the forgery of the signature of a prior indorser.[127] But since a party to a bill obviously is estopped from disputing the genuineness of the signature only of *prior* parties, even a holder in due course cannot sue the acceptor if an indorsement is forged,[128] nor an indorser where the signature of a subsequent indorser is forged.[129] In short, the estoppels generated by signature may give the holder personal rights against the signatory *as if* the bill were a fully operative instrument, but the forged signature prevents the holder from acquiring a title valid against those who became parties prior to the forgery,[130] for this breaks the chain between them and the holder.

(iii) Estoppels and warranties

Under some provisions of the Act a party warrants a fact, under others he is estopped from disputing a fact. There is an important distinction between the effects of an estoppel and that of a warranty . A party estopped from disputing a fact upon which the validity of a bill depends – eg the genuineness of a prior party's signature – can be sued on the bill as if it were valid, even if in truth it is not. On the other hand, a person committing a breach of warranty is liable only in damages for breach of warranty and is not, by reason only of that breach, liable to be sued on the bill. In such a case the plaintiff has to prove his loss in the usual

---

124 The position of a signatory who is *estopped* must be distinguished from that of a transferor by delivery who is deemed to *warrant*. The signatory's estoppel has the effect of making him liable on the bill for the full amount payable. Breach of warranty by the transferor does not do so, but simply makes him liable for damages or, if there is a total failure of consideration, for repayment of the price received for the bill. See further below.

125 Section 54(2).

126 Section 55(2).

127 It may be asked how a person in possession of a bill can be a holder in due course (or indeed a holder of any kind) if the chain of title to him is broken by a forged signature. The answer is that where a party signs the bill subsequent to the forgery, this is treated as equivalent to the drawing of a new bill (*Chalmers and Guest*, p 449).

128 *Robarts v Tucker* (1851) 16 QB 560. The position is otherwise where it is the drawer's signature which is forged, for he signs before the acceptor, and the latter, by accepting the bill, is estopped from disputing the genuineness of the drawer's signature (s 54(2)).

129 Section 55(2)(b): 'is precluded from denying to a holder in due course the genuineness and regularity in all respects of the drawer's signature and all *previous* indorsements' [emphasis added].

130 The position is otherwise as against one who signs the bill subsequently, because since his signature is, for title-passing purposes, treated as equivalent to delivery of a new bill (n 127), the holder has a real title and real rights back as far as that signatory, though not earlier.

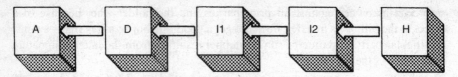

Fig 19.3 The liability chain under a bill of exchange

way, whereas in a claim on the bill the damages are prescribed by the Act and are deemed to be liquidated.[131]

The indorsee of a bill does not, by presenting it for acceptance or payment, warrant its genuineness, and if, unknown to the indorsee, one of the signatures is forged, the acceptor who pays the bill cannot on that ground alone recover the payment.[132]

(iv) The chain of rights and liabilities

Under the Bills of Exchange Act rights flow backwards, liabilities forwards. That is to say, claims on a bill can be brought only against prior parties, while liabilities are incurred only to subsequent parties. Thus the chain of rights runs back from the current holder through prior indorsers (if any) to the acceptor. Each party in the chain can claim against any or all prior parties. The first party whose liabilities are dealt with in the Act is the acceptor. This is because, except where the bill is an accommodation bill,[133] the acceptor is regarded as the party primarily liable on the instrument, the drawer and indorsers being in a position analogous to that of sureties.[134] Thus on a bill which has been twice indorsed, the rights flow backwards as in figure 19.3

So, if we revert to the bill illustrated earlier, the current holder, H (who may be either the immediate indorsee of Richard Roe or a subsequent transferee by delivery), may claim against all prior parties (Richard Roe, John Jones, William Brown and Basil Green) or any of them. Any party sued by H may, after making payment to H, recover from all or any of his own predecessors, and each of them in turn, having paid the bill, may recover from his predecessors.[135] The acceptor, Basil Green, has no one against whom to claim, for he is the last in the chain.[136]

131   Section 57.
132   *Price v Neal* (1762) 3 Burr 1354; *Guaranty Trust Co of New York v Hannay & Co* [1918] 2 KB 623. The rule in *Price v Neal* represents one of the most important qualifications to the right of a party to recover money paid under a mistake of fact. Denial of the remedy to a drawee or acceptor who pays a bona fide holder on a forged signature appears to reflect two distinct policy considerations: first, that the holder, having given value and being himself without fault, has not been unjustly enriched and there is no good reason to order him to repay what he has received; secondly, that the drawee is better placed to know whether the drawer's signature has been forged. But if none of the signatures is genuine, the instrument is a nullity and the rule does not apply. See further p 564.
133   See p 499.
134   An important consequence of this is that they enjoy many of the forms of protection given to sureties against conduct by the creditor which may prejudice them. See pp 503–508.
135   Section 57.
136   Ibid. The matter would be otherwise, however, if he were an accommodation party, for the position as between him and the drawer, William Brown, would then be reversed.

(v) Liability of the acceptor

By s 54 the acceptor, by accepting the bill, engages that he will pay it according to the tenor of his acceptance,[137] and is precluded from denying to a holder in due course:

(a) the existence of the drawer, the genuineness of his signature, and his capacity and authority to draw the bill;

(b) in the case of a bill payable to drawer's order, the then capacity of the drawer to indorse, but not the genuineness or validity of his indorsement;

(c) in the case of a bill payable to the order of a third person, the existence of the payee and his then capacity to indorse, but not the genuineness or validity of his indorsement.

Two points should be observed. First, the statutory estoppels, as one would expect, apply only to facts existing and events accruing up to the time of the acceptance. In other words, estoppels run backwards, not forwards. It is for this reason that the acceptor is not estopped from disputing the genuineness or validity of an indorsement; and even the estoppel as to the payee's capacity to indorse relates only to capacity at the time of the acceptance of the bill, and does not preclude the acceptor from asserting that the payee had become legally incapable at the time he indorsed the bill. Secondly, the estoppels operate only in favour of a holder in due course.

(vi) Liability of the drawer

By s 55(1) the drawer of a bill by drawing it:

(a) engages that on due presentment it shall be accepted and paid according to its tenor, and that if it be dishonoured he will compensate the holder or any indorser who is compelled to pay it, provided that the requisite proceedings on dishonour be duly taken;

(b) is precluded from denying to a holder in due course the existence of the payee and his then capacity to indorse.

It will be observed that the drawer's liability is secondary, not primary; he does not engage himself to pay the bill, merely to ensure that it is accepted and paid and to compensate the holder or any indorser compelled to pay as a result of the bill being dishonoured by non-acceptance or non-payment. The drawer being in the nature of a surety, his liability is dependent on the holder taking the prescribed steps consequent on dishonour,[138] and may also be reduced or extinguished by prejudicial acts or omissions of the holder in the same way as a surety's liability may be affected by prejudicial steps on the part of the creditor. Thus, if without the consent of the drawer, the holder binds himself to grant time to the acceptor, the

---

137 Thus if acceptance is qualified, eg by being local, the holder must perform the qualifying conditions if he is to be able to demand payment from the acceptor. It should be observed that the acceptor's engagement is absolute and is not, like that of other parties, dependent on compliance with procedures laid down consequent upon dishonour. See pp 510, 511.

138 See p 509.

drawer is released, for the prolongation of his period of liability may adversely affect him.[139]

No estoppel is prescribed in relation to the genuineness of the payee's signature, for this is an act occurring after the drawing of the bill and, as we have seen, estoppels run backwards, not forwards.

The estoppels as to the existence of the payee and his capacity to indorse[140] operate only in favour of a holder in due course.

(vii) Liability of an indorser

By s 55(2), the indorser of a bill by indorsing it:

(a)   engages that on due presentment it shall be accepted and paid according to its tenor, and that if it be dishonoured he will compensate the holder or a subsequent indorser who is compelled to pay it, provided that the requisite proceedings on dishonour be duly taken;

(b)   is precluded from denying to a holder in due course the genuineness and regularity in all respects of the drawer's signature and all previous indorsements;

(c)   is precluded from denying to his immediate or a subsequent indorsee that the bill was at the time of his indorsement a valid and subsisting bill, and that he had then a good title thereto.

The estoppel specified in s 55(2)(c) is peculiar to an indorser (for, of course, neither the drawer nor the acceptor has title to the bill) and is the only statutory estoppel capable of being invoked by a holder who is not a holder in due course.

(viii) Liability of a quasi-indorser

The function of an indorsement *stricto sensu* is to transfer title to an order bill. Obviously, such an indorsement can be made only by the holder. But not infrequently a person signs his name on the back of a bill not for the purpose of transferring it but simply to guarantee payment by the prior parties. In other words, he 'backs' the bill, coming in as a surety to reinforce the undertaking of the acceptor (and of the drawer also, if the bill is not drawn to his own order) and thereby give better protection to the payee and, perhaps, enable him more readily to discount the bill. For example, Richard Smith & Co Ltd, having agreed to sell £10,000 worth of goods to Vegetable Imports Ltd, may be willing to take payment by a three-month bill of exchange provided that it is backed by the directors of the buyer company, Jack Andrews and Simon Thomas. So the bill, in addition to being accepted by Vegetable Imports Ltd, will be signed on the back by Jack Andrews and Simon Thomas. After being handed back to Richard Smith & Co Ltd, it will look like figure 19.4.

---

139   *Latham v Chartered Bank of India* (1874) LR 17 Eq 205; *Oriental Financial Corporation v Overend* (1871) 7 Ch App 142.

140   Ie, capacity at the time of delivery of the bill.

Fig 19.4(a) Bill of exchange with quasi-indorser (face)

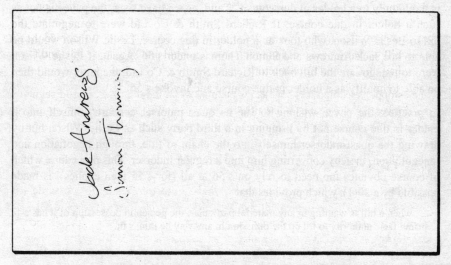

Fig 19.4(b) Bill of exchange with quasi-indorser (back)

Now Jack Andrews and Simon Thomas are not regular indorsers, for their function is to act as sureties, not to transfer title, and since they are not holders, their signatures have no impact on the chain of title. They are what are sometimes termed *quasi-indorsers*. In the civil law and in Roman Dutch law their signatures constitute an *aval*, a particular form of suretyship undertaken by indorsement of a bill of exchange and running with the bill so as to render the surety liable not only to subsequent but to prior holders in the event of default by the party for whose account it is given.[141] English law does not recognize the concept of the

141 For a description of the *aval*, see Cowen, *Law of Negotiable Instruments in South Africa*, ch XIII; *Chalmers and Guest on Bills of Exchange*, pp 455–457.

aval,[142] though the government has indicated its intention to introduce it in accordance with the recommendations of the Jack Report.[143] Hence a bill structured as depicted in figure 19.4 creates a difficulty for the holder. Neither Jack Andrews nor Simon Thomas can be held liable as indorsers under s 55 of the Bills of Exchange Act; nor, despite their intention to give a guarantee, can they be sued as *avalistes*; nor again can they be made liable as sureties independently of the bill in the absence of a separate note or memorandum satisfying the Statute of Frauds.[144]

There are two ways in which a person intended to fulfil a suretyship role can be made liable on the bill. The first is to utilize s 56 of the Act relating to quasi-indorsers. The second is to avoid the problem altogether by structuring the parties in such a way as to make them regular indorsers under s 55.

Section 56 of the Act provides that:

> Where a person signs a bill otherwise than as drawer or acceptor,[145] he thereby incurs the liabilities of an indorser to a holder in due course.

This would not help Richard Smith & Co Ltd at this stage, for the quasi-indorser is liable only to a holder in due course[146] and, as we have seen, the payee is not as such a holder in due course. If Richard Smith & Co Ltd were to negotiate the bill to Leslie Wilson, who took as a holder in due course, Leslie Wilson would be able to sue Jack Andrews and Simon Thomas under s 56. Again, if Leslie Wilson were to renegotiate the bill back to Richard Smith & Co Ltd, the latter would then be able to qualify as a holder in due course and invoke s 56.

In practice, the payee wishing to sue as quasi-indorser converts himself into a holder in due course not by bringing in a third party such as Leslie Wilson but by drawing the quasi-indorser himself into the chain of title, through negotiation and renegotiation, thereby converting him into a regular indorser. This procedure, which of course obviates the need to rely on s 56 at all (for s 55 then applies), is made possible by s 20(1), which provides that

> … when a bill is wanting in any material particular, the person in possession of it has a prima facie authority to fill up the omission in any way he thinks fit.

---

142   *G. & H. Montage v Irvani* [1990] 2 All ER 225.

143   *Banking Services: Law and Practice* (Cm 1026, 1990), Annex 6, para 6.8.

144   *Steele v M'Kinlay* (1880) 5 App Cas 754.

145   Curiously, the section makes no mention of a regular indorser within s 55; but the heading 'Stranger signing bill as indorser' makes it clear that the section is not intended to cover a regular indorser.

146   Unless, of course, words of guarantee are added, in which case he can be sued not on the bill as such but on the independent contract of guarantee as evidenced by the wording and signature on the bill. The assumption in all the cases that s 56 makes the quasi-indorser liable only to a holder in due course is almost certainly wrong. The natural construction of the phrase 'incurs the liabilities of an indorser to a holder in due course' is that the quasi-indorser incurs the same liabilities as those incurred by a regular indorser to a holder in due course. This view, expressed by the author informally, has now been adopted by *Byles on Bills of Exchange and Cheques*, p 198. Certainly the Canadian courts have taken it for granted that s 56 was intended to introduce the principle of the *aval* into English law (*Robinson v Mann* (1901) 31 SCR 484).

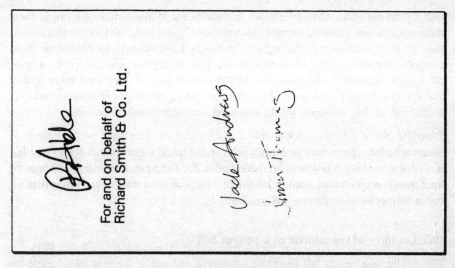

Fig 19.5 Bill of exchange: negotiation and renegotiation (back)

Thus it has been held that the quasi-indorser, by signing the bill, impliedly authorizes the payee to complete it by inserting his own indorsement above[147] that of the quasi-indorser himself. So the payee of the bill shown in figure 19.4 could complete the bill by indorsing above the signatures of Jack Andrews and Simon Thomas. The back of the bill would then look like figure 19.5.

We now have a bill which shows a negotiation by Richard Smith & Co Ltd to Andrews and Thomas and (by virtue of their own signatures) a renegotiation back to Richard Smith & Co Ltd,[148] who thus, *qua* indorsees, qualify for the 'holder in due course' status denied to them as payees. Andrews and Thomas can now be sued as regular indorsers. It might be asked why this is not blocked by s 37 of the Act. In the ordinary way, if A negotiates a bill to B, who later negotiates it back to A, A cannot sue B, for this would produce circuity, since B could claim over against A himself on his earlier indorsement. But the courts have held that extrinsic evidence is admissible to show the true relationship of the parties,[149] so that the payee is entitled to adduce evidence to show that his indorsement was not intended to confer rights on the quasi-indorsers but that, on the contrary, they were to be liable as sureties.

Since indorsements are usually made in descending order, it is not uncommon for the payee mistakenly to insert his signature below that of the quasi-indorser

---

147 This is the correct method, but an insertion below suffices. See below.

148 Strictly, renegotiation of a bill requires delivery as well as indorsement (s 31(3)), and Richard Smith & Co would not in fact have parted with the bill to Andrews and Thomas but would have retained it throughout. Fortunately, the courts do not strain at this particular gnat and are willing to assume a notional delivery. Similarly, s 20 is considered to authorize the completion of a bill with retrospective effect, so that the fact that the signature of the quasi-indorser was placed on the bill when it was incomplete does not affect its regularity after completion. See *National Sales Corp. Ltd v Bernardi* [1931] 2 KB 188; *Lombard Banking Ltd v Central Garage & Engineering Co Ltd* [1963] 1 QB 220.

149 *Macdonald v Whitfield* (1883) 8 App Cas 733.

rather than above it. This, of course, dislocates the chain of title, for prima facie indorsements are made in order of appearance,[150] and the first indorsement ought thus to be by the payee; but again the courts have refused to accede to these technical arguments and have treated the bill as regular and complete despite the irregularity of the sequence of indorsements.[151] Indeed, they have gone further and upheld the bill despite the fact that the payee inserted a restrictive indorsement,[152] the effect of which was to negate further negotiation of the bill.[153]

Even the use of s 56 does not enable a quasi-indorser to be sued by the drawer or others who became parties to the bill prior to the quasi-indorsement. It follows that if a person backing a bill is to be made liable, for example, to the drawer under an *aval*, words of guarantee must be added, in which case the drawer's claim is then on the instrument *qua* guarantee, not *qua* bill.[154]

(ix) Liability of transferor of a bearer bill

The holder of a bearer bill need not, of course, indorse it, for it is transferable by mere delivery. If he does indorse it, he incurs all the liabilities of an indorser. If he merely delivers the bill, he is not liable on it as such[155] but may be sued for damages for any breach of the warranty implied under s 58(3).[156]

(x) Exclusion of liability

It is open to a drawer or indorser to insert an express stipulation excluding or limiting his own liability to the holder,[157] eg by adding after his signature words such as '*sans recours*' or 'without recourse to me'.

7.   PREREQUISITES OF ENFORCEMENT

As we have seen, since a demand bill matures immediately, the payee or other holder simply presents it to the drawee for payment. In the case of a term bill, on the other hand, the first stage is to secure the drawee's engagement, that is, his acceptance of the bill, for which purpose the bill must be presented to him. If he declines to accept, the bill is dishonoured by non-acceptance and the holder can (subject to certain formalities to be described) proceed immediately to enforce his

---

150 Section 32(5).

151 *Lombard Banking Ltd v Central Garage & Engineering Co Ltd*, n 148, and cases there cited.

152 *Yeoman Credit Ltd v Gregory* [1963] 1 WLR 343, in which the payee indorsed the bill to a designated bank for collection and signified this intention by the words 'value on collection'.

153 Section 35. Megaw J avoided the difficulty by holding that the instrument could be treated as having been made in blank initially, the restrictive words being added only because the bill had notionally come back into the payee's hands after the deemed renegotiation by the quasi-indorser.

154 See n 146.

155 Section 58(2).

156 See p 500.

157 Section 16(1). The negotiation of bills without recourse is not uncommon in the export trade and is known as forfaiting. See p 1013.

rights against the drawer and any prior indorser without waiting for the bill to mature. If the bill is accepted, it must on maturity be presented for payment.

If the drawee refuses to accept, the holder must promptly notify the drawer and any prior indorser by giving them notice of dishonour, for as quasi-sureties they have an interest in being given early warning that they will not, as expected, have the acceptor to fall back on. Similarly, if the acceptor fails to honour the bill on maturity, notice of dishonour must be given promptly to the drawer and indorsers, so that they have an early opportunity to take such steps as may be open to them to protect themselves vis-à-vis the acceptor.[158] In the case of a foreign bill there is an additional requirement, namely that dishonour by non-acceptance or non-payment must be formally established by protesting the bill.[159] As we shall see, English law is very strict as to the time and manner of performance of these duties by the holder, and even a small delay may destroy his rights against parties to the bill.

(i)   Presentment for acceptance

Given that the presence of an acceptor (as opposed to a drawee) is not essential to a bill,[160] it follows that presentment for acceptance is not usually necessary.[161] The bill must, however, be presented for acceptance when its terms so require[162] or when presentment is necessary to fix the maturity of the bill, ie because it is payable a designated time after sight.[163] Presentment is also necessary where the bill is drawn payable elsewhere than at the drawee's residence or place of business.[164] This is because such residence or place of business is prima facie the place for payment[165] and if the drawee is to be required to pay elsewhere, he must be given the opportunity of agreeing to do so by his acceptance.[166]

(ii)   Presentment for payment

This is not necessary if the bill has been dishonoured by non-acceptance.[167] In other cases presentment for payment is necessary to establish dishonour by

---

158 In this respect, the duty on the holder of a bill to give notice of dishonour to the drawer and indorsers in order to hold them liable goes beyond that which is generally imposed on a creditor towards a surety under an ordinary contract of guarantee, where no such notice is required.

159 See p 512.

160 See p 486, n 25.

161 Section 39(3). This is considered curious by *Byles on Bills of Exchange and Cheques*, p 112, where it is argued that other parties have an interest in the acceptance. But the drawer, if committed by contract to paying by a bill of exchange, would have to do so whether or not there was an acceptance and, indeed, by drawing the bill undertakes to procure its acceptance, while indorsement of the bill is purely voluntary, and if a holder does not want to negotiate an unaccepted bill, he is not obliged to do so.

162 Section 39(2).

163 Section 39(1).

164 Section 39(2).

165 Section 45(4).

166 Denial of this opportunity does not, of course, prejudice the drawee himself, for until acceptance, he is not liable on the bill anyway. But to the extent that the stipulation of a place for payment other than that designated by the Act makes it less likely that he will be willing to honour the bill there, it is in the interests of other parties that they should know this as soon as possible.

167 Section 43(2).

non-payment[168] and to hold the drawer and indorsers liable.[169] The duty to present for payment is briefly as follows.[170]

1.   The acceptor

Where a bill is accepted generally, presentment for payment is not necessary to render an acceptor liable on a bill.[171] The reason advanced for this curious rule is that, unless the bill be qualified by local acceptance,[172] it remains the duty of the acceptor, like that of an ordinary debtor, to seek out his creditor where he may be found.[173] This, of course, is arrant nonsense, for until the bill is presented, the acceptor cannot be sure who his creditor is. The onus ought therefore to be on the holder to present,[174] not on the acceptor to discover the identity and whereabouts of the current holder.

2.   Drawer and indorsers

Presentment for payment, unless waived or excused,[175] is necessary in order to charge the drawer or an indorser on a bill, and if the bill be not duly[176] presented, these parties are discharged from liability on the bill.[177] Indeed, according to some authorities the holder loses even his right to sue the drawer on the consideration for which the bill was given.[178] But such a draconian rule (which would, for example, enable the buyer of goods tendering a bill of exchange in payment to acquire the goods for nothing if the seller failed duly to present the bill to the acceptor) does not, it is submitted, represent the law today, if indeed it ever did, which is doubtful.[179] The appropriate solution is to treat the drawer as

---

168   Section 45.

169   Section 47(1).

170   See generally *Byles on Bills of Exchange and Cheques*, ch 12; *Chalmers and Guest on Bills of Exchange*, pp 355 ff.

171   Section 52(1).

172   The rules as to place of presentment are set out in s 45(4).

173   *Robey & Co v Snaefell Mining Co Ltd* (1887) 20 QBD 152.

174   Cf *Chitty on Bills of Exchange* (11th edn, 1878), pp 253–255.

175   See p 511.

176   Ie in accordance with the requirements of the Act as embodied in s 45.

177   Section 45.

178   *Byles on Bills of Exchange and Cheques*, p 120, n 9.

179   The authorities primarily relied on in support of the proposition that failure to present extinguishes the liability of the drawer and indorsers even on the original consideration are *Soward v Palmer* (1818) 8 Taunt 277 and *Peacock v Pursell* (1863) 32 LJCP 266. Neither of these cases appears to establish the supposed rule. The true ratio of *Soward v Palmer* is that since the plaintiff had not presented the bill on the due date, the defendant's tender of the amount due on the next day (which was refused) and his subsequent payment of it into court constituted a good tender, which prevented the plaintiff from recovering the (larger) amount of the original consideration. In *Peacock v Pursell* the bill was taken as *collateral security* and by reason of the failure to present, it was rendered valueless. The court upheld the argument that in these circumstances the defendant should be put in the same position as if the bill had been paid and that *to that extent* the obligation secured by the bill should be treated as discharged. In other words, the plaintiff's *laches*, having prevented the reduction in the defendant's liability which would have occurred if the bill had been duly presented, *pro tanto* reduced that liability but did not affect the plaintiff's rights of recovery as regards the balance of the indebtedness.

discharged from liability on the underlying contract to the extent to which he has suffered prejudice.

Usually the bill is expressed to be payable at the acceptor's bank, and the procedure is for the holder or some person authorized to receive payment on his behalf to produce the bill to an officer of the bank in question and ask for payment,[180] giving up the bill in exchange.[181] Payment in due course[182] discharges the bill,[183] which thereupon ceases to be operative. Non-payment after due presentment constitutes dishonour of the bill.[184] Presentment for payment of a term bill must be made on the due date,[185] otherwise the drawer and indorsers are discharged. Presentment of a demand bill must be made within a reasonable time after its issue in order to render the drawer liable or within a reasonable time after its indorsement in order to render the indorser liable.[186]

A party may waive presentment for payment[187] (eg by writing on the bill 'presentment for payment waived'), and presentment is excused in various other cases.[188]

(iii) Notice of dishonour

Where a bill has been dishonoured by non-acceptance or non-payment, notice of dishonour must, unless excused, be given to the drawer and each indorser,[189] and any drawer and indorser to whom notice is not given is discharged.[190] Mere knowledge of dishonour gained *aliunde* by a drawer or indorser is not equivalent to notice, which must be intimated by or on behalf of the holder or of an indorser liable on the bill[191] but need not be in writing or in any particular

180 Sections 45(3), 52(4).
181 Section 52(4). The acceptor's bank will usually return the bill to him afterwards.
182 Ie payment made at or after the maturity of the bill to the holder thereof in good faith and without notice that his title to the bill is defective (s 59(1)).
183 Ibid.
184 Section 47(1).
185 Section 45(1).
186 Ibid(2).
187 Section 46(2)(e).
188 Section 46(2).
189 Notice to the acceptor is not necessary (s 52(3)), for he is, of course, the party who has dishonoured the bill.
190 Section 48. This provision is particularly draconian in view of the short time-limit for giving notice of dishonour and the fact that the discharge of the drawer and indorsers is not made dependent on their having suffered prejudice. As the late Karl Llewellyn rightly observed (*The Common Law Tradition* (1960), pp 404 ff), the concept of risk and prejudice which was present in Lord Mansfield's mind at the time he formulated the principle (in *Blesard v Hirst* (1770) 5 Burr 2670) was not appreciated by judges of lesser vision. In the result, what Lord Mansfield had intended as the very salutary rule that a drawer or indorser was discharged if, through failure or delay in being given notice of dishonour, he lost the opportunity to recoup himself from the acceptor while the latter was still in funds, became crystallized into the rigid penalty now embodied in s 48. The Uniform Law contained in the Geneva Convention on Bills of Exchange reflects much more accurately the wisdom of Mansfield. By art 45, failure to give notice of dishonour does not affect the holder's right to enforce the bill against all parties but he becomes liable for the loss caused by his negligence, up to the amount of the bill.
191 Section 49(1).

form.[192] There is a strict time limit: notice of dishonour must be given within a reasonable time after dishonour, which in the absence of special circumstances means that where the person giving and the person to receive notice reside in the same place, the notice must be given or sent off in time to reach the latter on the day after the dishonour of the bill and where they reside in different places, the notice must be sent off on the day after dishonour of the bill, if there be a post at a convenient hour on that day, or, if not, by the next post thereafter.[193] The consequences of failure to give due notice of dishonour are as disastrous as on failure to make due presentment.[194]

Once given, notice inures for the benefit of the holder, all indorsers in the chain between the holder and the party to whom the notice is given and all subsequent holders.[195]

Notice is dispensed with in various cases.[196] As against a drawer, there are two typical situations in which notice of dishonour is excused.[197] The first is where the drawee or acceptor owes him no duty to accept or pay the bill.[198] The second is where the drawer has countermanded payment. In an action on the bill, care should be taken to plead the facts excusing notice of dishonour where such notice has not yet been duly given.[199]

(iv) Protest

By 'protesting' a bill is meant formally establishing its dishonour[200] by a notarial act. Only foreign bills need be protested,[201] though an inland bill may be.[202] Protesting is carried out in two stages. First, the bill is re-presented by a notary public to the acceptor for payment, and if it is again dishonoured, the notary indorses a memorandum to that effect on the bill, with an indication of the reason given for non-payment. This stage is called 'noting' the bill and is the vital stage, so far as compliance with time limits is concerned.[203] The second stage is the execution of a formal declaration of protest by the notary in the presence of

192 See ibid, s 49(5). If in writing, the notice need not be signed (ibid, s 49(7)).
193 Ibid, s 49(12).
194 See p 510. There is authority for the view that the holder who fails to give notice of dishonour loses his right to sue on the original consideration (*Bridges v Berry* (1810) 3 Taunt 130). But this is open to the same objection as the supposed rule to similar effect in the case of failure to present. See n 179.
195 See s 49(3).
196 Section 50(2). In addition, delay in giving notice is excused where due to circumstances beyond the control of the party giving it (s 50(1)).
197 Section 50(2)(c). These provisions are particularly useful in the case of dishonoured cheques.
198 Usually because the drawer's account is not sufficiently in funds and the drawee/acceptor has not agreed to give sufficient credit to cover the bill.
199 If this is not done, the claim is liable to be struck out as disclosing no cause of action.
200 Or, in the case of a protest for better security (s 51(5)), the refusal of such security.
201 Section 51(2). The object of the procedure is to provide evidence of dishonour which will be accepted by all courts, here and abroad.
202 Section 51(1).
203 A bill must be noted on the day of dishonour or at latest on the next succeeding business day (s 51(4), as amended by the Bills of Exchange (Time of Noting) Act 1917).

witnesses. This is known as 'extending the protest'[204] and takes effect as from the time of noting.[205]

8.   REMEDIES FOR DISHONOUR

Where a bill of exchange is dishonoured by non-acceptance or non-payment, the holder may sue all parties liable on it. Where he took the bill from a party in discharge of that party's liability to him under a separate contract, he has the option of suing on that contract, as dishonour of the bill restores the contractual duty of payment which was suspended by the giving of the bill. For example, if B draws a bill on C in favour of S for the price of goods and C refuses to accept the bill or, having accepted it, fails to pay it at maturity, S need not sue on the bill itself but can treat its dishonour as reviving his rights under the original contract of sale and sue for the price. However, exercise of this latter option will almost invariably be disadvantageous. The issue or transfer of a bill of exchange generates a contract quite distinct from that pursuant to which the bill was given; and since the courts are reluctant to do anything which will adversely affect the autonomy of a bill,[206] they will rarely allow an unliquidated claim,[207] whether for breach of the underlying contract or otherwise, to be set up by way of defence to a claim on the bill or as a reason for staying execution of a judgment on it pending trial of the cross claim;[208] nor will an arbitration clause in a contract normally be treated as covering disputes on a bill given under it.[209] So a claim on a bill of exchange will almost always end in summary judgment for the plaintiff.[210]

The amount of a bill is, of course, recoverable by way of debt and need not be treated as damages. This is true, too, of any interest stipulated by the bill.[211] But non-payment of money is also a breach of contract and, since the holder may not have stipulated for interest on the bill and may in addition require recoupment of other losses and expenses resulting from dishonour, the Act makes provision for dishonour in terms of damages.[212]

204 See s 51(4).
205 Ibid.
206 See p 528.
207 The position is otherwise for a liquidated claim. See p 523.
208 See p 523.
209 *Nova (Jersey) Knit Ltd v Kammgarn Spinnerei GmbH* [1977] 1 WLR 713.
210 See p 529.
211 The position is otherwise where interest is claimed under s 57(1) of the Act without there being any stipulation for it in the bill itself (*ex p Charman* [1887] WN 184).
212 Section 57. This is not disadvantageous to the holder, for as the damages are liquidated (ibid) he need not prove more than the fact of dishonour and compliance with any applicable dishonour procedure (p 509) and is not under a duty to mitigate his loss.
      The damages here referred to are damages awarded to the holder against a party to the bill. A separate question is whether the drawer whose bill is wrongly dishonoured by the acceptor has a claim against the acceptor for injury to his credit. Such a claim has traditionally been reserved for proceedings against a bank for dishonour of its customer's cheque (see p 554), but there seems no reason why such a claim should not lie against an acceptor where it has contracted with the drawer to honour drawings and thus to preserve the drawer's credit. If the acceptor assigns a reason for non-payment which is defamatory of the drawer, the latter may have an alterative claim for defamation.

The measure of damages is the amount of the bill, interest from the time of presentment for payment if the bill is payable on demand and from the maturity in any other case,[213] and the expenses of noting or, where protest is necessary and has been extended,[214] in protesting the bill.[215]

The primary right of action on the bill is, of course, given to the holder, but a drawer who has been compelled to pay may recover from the acceptor, and an indorser who has been compelled to pay may recover from the acceptor, the drawer or a prior indorser.[216] In other words, each party liable on the bill can recover from his predecessors but only after he has discharged his own liability.[217] If, of course, the holder succeeds in forcing payment against the acceptor, intervening parties will not be required to make payment and no question of claims over by them arises.

In practice, the prudent holder will usually sue all parties liable on the bill in one action.

9.   DEFENCES TO A CLAIM ON A BILL

(i)   Real and personal defences

We have previously remarked on the distinction between real rights created by a bill, through the acquisition and transfer of title to it, and personal rights of action derived not from title but from some estoppel resulting from signature or delivery of the bill. In relation to possible defences to a claim on a bill, a comparable distinction is to be drawn between real and personal defences. A party sued on a bill may assert that as between himself and the plaintiff it is a complete nullity, and thus not capable of imposing liability upon him. Such a defence is termed a real defence, for it is founded on the inherent invalidity of the *res* itself, ie the bill, as opposed to a defence based on the personal relationship between plaintiff and defendant. Matters which affect the validity of a bill, so as to be capable of generating real defences, are forgery of a signature, lack of capacity of a signatory,[218] want of authority in the drawing or transfer of the bill, material alteration, the occurrence of an event causing discharge of the bill, and fraud or illegality of a kind rendering the bill void as opposed to merely voidable.

---

213   Ibid.
214   See p 512.
215   Section 57(1). Section 57(2) dealing with damages for recovery of a bill dishonoured abroad was repealed by s 4(2) of the Administration of Justice Act 1977 consequent on the decision of the House of Lords in *Miliangos v George Frank (Textiles) Ltd* [1976] AC 443 that in given conditions a plaintiff can obtain a judgment expressed in foreign currency.
216   Bills of Exchange Act, s 57(1).
217   However, when sued, he can, as a matter of procedure, claim over against prior parties, though his right to recover depends on his making payment.
218   It is interesting to contrast the approach of the Uniform Law embodied in the Geneva Convention on Bills of Exchange as to the effect of forgery, incapacity and the like. By art 7, the fact that for these or other reasons a signatory is not bound does not invalidate the obligation of the persons signing the bill. This is a more realistic approach. In any event the distinction between real and personal defences is of little significance in the last analysis. See below.

By contrast, a personal defence is one which is not founded on the invalidity of the instrument but derives from factors external to the bill which affect the relationship between plaintiff and defendant. Among such defences are total or partial failure of consideration for the bill, eg through non-performance of the underlying contract or other obligation in respect of which it was given; rights of set-off; the right to avoid liability on the bill on the ground that its delivery was induced by misrepresentation rendering it voidable as between misrepresentor and misrepresentee. Defects in title partake of the characteristics both of real and personal defences and are perhaps best treated as a distinct category.[219] On the one hand they relate to rights in the instrument as such, which are, of course, real rights; on the other, they do not as such invalidate the instrument[220] but merely preclude the particular claimant from having a *locus standi* to enforce it.

The distinction between real and personal defences is of significance only as regards parties who became signatories to the bill prior to the forgery or other vitiating factor. As against such parties, the document is not a bill at all, so that even a holder in due course has no right of action. But subsequent indorsement of the bill is treated as equivalent to a fresh drawing,[221] and the indorser is precluded from denying to his immediate or any subsequent indorsee the validity and subsistence of the bill at the time of his indorsement.[222]

A mere personal defence does not vitiate the bill itself and therefore produces no break in the chain of title. The only question is whether the defence is one which affects the current holder of the bill. The answer to this is usually said to depend on whether, in relation to the defendant, the holder is an immediate party or a remote party, for in the former case he supposedly takes subject to equities, whereas in the latter, it is said, he does not.[223] There appears to be no sound basis for this distinction, and several of the authorities relied on, when loosely referring to a remote holder for value, appear to have in mind a holder in due course. The true rule would seem to be that equities may be raised against any party, whether

---

219 Bradley Crawford and John D. Falconbridge, *Banking and Bills of Exchange* (8th edn, 1986), p 1524. See also Bradley Crawford, *Payment, Clearing and Settlement in Canada* (2002), vol 2, §23.03.4. For the meaning of 'defect in title', see p 498.

220 Of course, if the defect in title arises because of a forged signature that is another matter. See below.

221 See n 128.

222 Section 55(2)(c).

223 Crawford and Falconbridge, *Banking and Bills of Exchange*, p 620; *Chalmers and Guest on Bills of Exchange*, pp 332–333; *Byles on Bills of Exchange and Cheques*, p 231. Immediate parties are those adjacent to each other in the chain of liability on the bill (see p 502). Thus, acceptor and drawer, drawer and payee, indorser and his indorsee are immediate parties *inter se*, while acceptor and payee, drawer and indorsee, indorser and an indorsee other than his own are all remote parties in relation to each other. But one who initially holds a bill as immediate party in relation to another may become a remote party as the result of parting with the bill and later reacquiring it, as where the drawer discounts the bill to his bank and then buys it back when the acceptor dishonours it. In such a case the erstwhile drawer becomes a holder claiming through a holder in due course and it is in that capacity that he sues the acceptor as a remote party without being subject to equities (*Jade International Steel Stahl und Eisen GmbH & Co KG v Robert Nicholas (Steels) Ltd* [1978] 2 Lloyd's Rep 13).

immediate or remote, who is not a holder in due course,[224] except that failure of consideration may not be raised against a holder for value merely because the acceptor received no consideration.[225] Thus, if I is induced by F's misrepresentation to indorse a bill to F, and F re-indorses the bill to G for value but in circumstances such that G does not qualify as a holder in due course,[226] then in an action by G against I, the defendant is entitled to set up F's misrepresentation as a defence in just the same way as if he had been sued by F himself. On the other hand if B, having bought goods from S, accepts a bill drawn on him by S for the price and S indorses the bill to T, B cannot set up against T a claim against S for unliquidated damages for breach of warranty, for this is not an equity but a mere personal cross-claim not giving rise to a set-off.[227]

(ii) Forged or unauthorized signature

The general effect of forgery of a signature on a bill has been described earlier.[228] The signature is inoperative and no title to the bill can be derived from it, but payment of the bill can nevertheless be enforced against a party who is precluded from setting up the forgery.[229] The particular case of insertion of a fictitious or non-existent person as payee or indorsee is considered below. Special rules are applicable to cheques, in that bankers paying on a forged indorsement are given a measure of statutory protection.[230]

1.   The meaning of 'forged'

Forgery is not defined in the Bills of Exchange Act, and it is a nice question whether for the purposes of that Act the word 'forgery' is to be interpreted according to the Forgery Act 1861, which was the forgery enactment in force at the time the Bills of Exchange Act was passed, or it is now to have the meaning accorded by subsequent legislation in the criminal law field.[231] At least one judgment[232] takes it for granted that the modern statutory definition is the relevant one, and this seems the better view, for the draftsman of the Bills of Exchange Act, in using a technical term, no doubt intended it to bear the statutory meaning current at the time the relevant section of the Bills of Exchange Act was invoked. If this be right, then for the

---

224 A conclusion also reached by Professor Benjamin Geva in his two excellent articles: 'Equities as to Liability on Bills and Notes: Rights of a Holder not in Due Course' (1980) 5 Can Bus L J 53 and 'Absence of Consideration in the Law of Bills and Notes' [1980] CLJ 360.

225 See Bills of Exchange Act, s 27(2), and p 494.

226 See p 495, as to the conditions to be satisfied in order to secure 'holder in due course' status.

227 The reason is that an unliquidated claim arising under one contract cannot be set off against a liquidated claim on another, unless at any rate the two contracts are closely intertwined; and since a bill of exchange is considered a contract separate from that of the underlying transaction (see pp 522–524) an unliquidated claim for breach of the latter cannot usually be set up against a claim on the former. See *Nova (Jersey) Knit Ltd v Kammgarn Spinnerei GmbH*, n 209 and p 523.

228 See p 489.

229 Sections 54(2)(a), 55(1)(b), (2)(b).

230 See p 556.

231 In particular, the Forgery and Counterfeiting Act 1981, repealing the Forgery Act 1913, s 1(1).

232 That of Scrutton LJ in *Kreditbank Cassel GmbH v Schenkers Ltd* [1927] 1 KB 826 at 840.

purposes of the Bills of Exchange Act as well as of the Forgery and Counterfeiting Act, forgery is the making of a false instrument with the intention of inducing someone to accept it as genuine and thereby to act to his or another's prejudice;[233] and an instrument is false within the meaning of the Act if, inter alia, it purports to have been made by or on the authority of a person who did not make it or authorize its making in the form or terms in which it is made.[234]

2. Forged distinguished from unauthorized

This definition blurs the distinction between a forged signature and a merely un-authorized signature, particularly since an intent to defraud or deceive is not an ingredient of the definition of forgery but merely a prerequisite of its constituting an offence. On the other hand, the definition would seem to require a knowledge that the document was false, so that the signature of a bill of exchange in the honest but mistaken belief that it was authorized would not constitute forgery. What, however, is the position where the signatory was in fact authorized to sign but does so for his own fraudulent purposes and not in pursuance of the interests of his principal? In *Morison v London County and Westminster Bank Ltd*[235] such a misuse of authority was held not to render the instrument a forgery within s 24 of the Forgery Act 1861, and the enlargement of the statutory definition[236] does not appear to have altered the position.

So far as the Bills of Exchange Act is concerned, the distinction between a forged signature and a genuine but unauthorized signature is largely academic, since for most purposes the effect is the same, namely that the signature is a nullity except as against a party estopped from disputing that it was genuine or authorized. Section 24, it is true, suggests that forgery of a signature cannot be ratified, but what the section contemplates is the case where one person affirms his signature as that of another and thus does not purport to act on that other's behalf, an essential prerequisite to ratification by the latter. The definition of forgery in the Forgery and Counterfeiting Act 1981 covers signature on behalf of another without his authority and there seems no reason why this form of forgery should not be capable of ratification.[237] The other supposed distinction between a forged and an unauthorized signature is that the former is said to be outside the scope of the rule in *Turquand's* case,[238] but this suggestion seems contrary to principle.[239]

3. Forgery and the indoor management rule

Under the rule in *Turquand's* case, persons dealing with a company are not bound to inquire into its indoor management and will not be affected by irregularities of

---

233 See Forgery and Counterfeiting Act 1981, s 1.

234 Ibid, s 9(1).

235 [1914] 3 KB 356.

236 In what is now the Forgery and Counterfeiting Act 1981, replacing the Forgery Act 1913 as amended by the Criminal Justice Act 1925, s 35. The new definition of 'false' is set out in s 9 of the 1981 Act.

237 I. D. Campbell, 'Contracts with Companies' (1960) 76 LQR 115 at p 130; *Chitty on Contracts* (29th edn, 2004), vol II, p 18, n 71.

238 See below.

239 See below.

which they had no notice.[240] The rule is complex and has many facets[241] but, despite dicta suggesting otherwise,[242] it is in truth merely a specific application of the general principle of agency law that acts by a person clothed with usual or apparent authority to perform them on behalf of another will bind that other, notwithstanding some internal limitation on the actor's actual authority, unless the party dealing with him had notice of the limitation.[243] Despite suggestions to the contrary,[244] there seems no good reason why the application of the rule should be excluded in cases of forgery;[245] and, indeed, so far as bills are concerned s 24 of the Bills of Exchange Act expressly preserves the efficacy of the bill as against a person precluded from setting up the forgery. One such case is that of a company precluded by the rule in *Turquand's* case from disputing the authority of its officers to sign a bill of exchange on its behalf or otherwise put forward the bill as genuine.

4.   Want of authority generally

Leaving aside the particular position of companies under the rule in *Turquand's* case, signature of a bill of exchange on behalf of or in the name of another without his authority will not bind that other unless the signatory had actual, apparent or usual authority[246] to sign as he did. By s 25 of the Bills of Exchange Act a signature by procuration operates as notice that the agent has but a limited authority to sign, and the principal is bound by such signature only if the agent in so signing was acting within the actual limits of his authority. The scope of this section is unclear. The first question is what suffices in general to denote signature by procuration? Plainly, those words themselves, their Latin equivalents and their abbreviations, 'per pro' and 'p.p.', are sufficient. Presumably this is true also of any other phrase denoting formal authority, eg 'under power of attorney'.[247] Less clear is whether phrases such as 'for and on behalf of' will suffice. Though the abbreviation 'p.p.' is today usually used as synonymous with 'for and on behalf of', this is incorrect, for 'p.p.' means 'through the agency of', and one who signs 'p.p.' should state the name of his principal before the abbreviation and add his own signature after the abbreviation, not vice versa. Moreover, procuration in the strict sense would seem to denote a relatively formal conferment of authority, of the type exemplified by a power of attorney, to act in a manner in which the agent appointed would not normally have authority to act. The phrases 'by procuration', 'per pro' and 'p.p.' are thus intended by the Bills of Exchange Act to signify that the signatory's powers

---

240   *Royal British Bank v Turquand* (1856) 6 E & B 327. For an application of the rule, see *Freeman and Lockyer v Buckhurst Park Properties (Mangal) Ltd* [1964] 2 QB 480. See also the decision of the High Court of Australia in *Northside Developments Pty Ltd v Registrar-General* (1990) 64 ALJR 427.

241   For which the reader should consult the company law textbooks.

242   Eg, those of Greene MR in *Uxbridge Permanent Benefit Society v Pickard* [1939] 2 KB 248 at 257.

243   See *Bowstead and Reynolds on Agency* (2001), art 74, and p 168.

244   *Ruben v Great Fingall Consolidated* [1906] AC 439; *Kreditbank Cassel GmbH v Schenkers Ltd*, n 232.

245   *Bowstead and Reynolds on Agency*, p 324.

246   See p 168.

247   *Byles on Bills of Exchange and Cheques*, p 64.

derive not from the usual authority of an agent but from some special authorization the terms of which should be inquired into.[248]

(iii) Want of capacity

Capacity to incur liability as a party to a bill is co-extensive with capacity to contract.[249] Now that it is becoming increasingly difficult for companies to plead that contracts entered into by them are ultra vires, the question of the capacity of parties to a bill of exchange is of diminished importance. In any event, a party's want of capacity as drawer or indorser does not affect the holder's right to receive payment of the bill and to enforce it against other parties;[250] the acceptor is precluded from denying to a holder in due course the capacity of the drawer to draw the bill;[251] and the drawer is precluded from denying to a holder in due course the payee's capacity to indorse at the time of the drawing of the bill.[252]

(iv) Signature in representative capacity

A person who expressly signs a bill as agent of another incurs no personal liability on it[253] even if he acted without authority,[254] though in the latter case he may be sued for damages for breach of warranty of authority.[255] But the fact of agency must appear from the wording of the signature: if it does not, the signatory, even though in fact acting as agent and signing within the limits of his authority, will be personally liable on the bill[256] unless the holder elects to look to the principal for payment. In this connection, s 26 of the Bills of Exchange Act is of some importance.

> (1) Where a person signs a bill as drawer, indorser or acceptor, and adds words to his signature, indicating that he signs for or on behalf of a principal, or in a representative character, he is not personally liable thereon; but the mere addition to his signature of words describing him as an agent, or as filling a representative character, does not exempt him from personal liability.

> (2) In determining whether a signature on a bill is that of the principal or that of the agent by whose hand it is written, the construction most favourable to the validity of the instrument shall be adopted.

248 *Midland Bank Ltd v Reckitt* [1933] AC 1. Section 25 has rightly been criticized on the ground that there is no reason why signature by procuration should be a unique exception to the rule that a person is bound by the acts of his agent acting within the scope of his apparent authority (*Chalmers and Guest on Bills of Exchange*, pp 209–210).

249 Bills of Exchange Act, s 22(1).

250 Section 22(2).

251 Section 54(2).

252 Section 55(1).

253 But there are statutory exceptions, as where in signing as agent of a company the agent incorrectly states the company's name, and he may be liable for breach of the implied warranty of authority (*West London Commercial Bank Ltd v Kitson* (1883) 12 QBD 157, per A. L. Smith J at 161–162).

254 *Chalmers and Guest on Bills of Exchange*, p 213.

255 *Polhill v Walter* (1832) 3 B & Ad 114; *West London Commercial Bank v Kitson* (1884) 13 QBD 360.

256 *Leadbitter v Farrow* (1816) 5 M & S 345.

Thus, a signature 'John Jones, Director, Excelsior Ltd' involves John Jones in personal liability, for the words after the name 'John Jones' are descriptive only and do not sufficiently indicate that John Jones is signing in a representative capacity.[257] More difficult is the case where the signatory writes the name of his firm or company on the back of the bill and places his signature below it. This is capable of several interpretations. The signature may be intended to be both representative and personal, committing the firm or company and the signatory, or it may be solely a representative signature or solely a personal signature. Here the position would appear to be that if the name of the individual signatory is accompanied by a description of his position with the firm or company, the inference is that the bill was signed by the firm or company itself acting through the named signatory, and the same is true where he signs below the pre-printed name of the company without addition;[258] whereas if his name appears unaccompanied by such description the court will probably hold that both he and the firm or company are liable as parties.[259]

Where the principal is a company, there is a further pitfall to be avoided, in that while the bill is effectively accepted or indorsed on behalf of a company if accepted or indorsed in the name of, or by or on behalf of or on account of the company by any person acting under its authority,[260] yet if the name of the company is omitted or misstated, the officer or other person signing on behalf of the company is personally liable unless the company pays,[261] even if it is clear that he signed only in a representative capacity. Exceptionally, he can escape this liability if the plaintiff is estopped from complaining of the error or omission, as where it is he who was responsible for the error, by inscribing the words of acceptance or indorsement himself and presenting the bill to the defendant for signature.[262]

---

257 *Elliott v Bax-Ironside* [1925] 2 KB 301.

258 *Bondina Ltd v Rollaway Shower Blinds Ltd* [1986] 1 WLR 517.

259 Signature for and on behalf of the company will usually negate any personal obligation of the signatory, but in appropriate circumstances the words may be disregarded as meaningless, eg if the company is already liable on the bill as acceptor, so that the signatory's indorsement is plainly intended to involve him in personal liability (*Rolfe Lubbell & Co v Keith & Greenwood* [1979] 2 Lloyd's Rep 75). Signature in the name of a firm is equivalent to the signature by the person so signing of the names of all persons liable as partners in that firm (s 23(2)).

260 Companies Act 1985, s 37. 'Authority' includes apparent authority (*Dey v Pullinger Engineering Co* [1921] 1 KB 77). *Semble*, a party purporting to sign as agent for an unformed company is personally liable on the bill unless he expressly disclaims liability, by virtue of what is now s 360(1) of the Companies Act 1985. See *Phonogram Ltd v Lane* [1981] 3 All ER 182, a decision which, like the subsection itself, is concerned with an ordinary contract but appears equally applicable to the contract generated by signature of a bill of exchange.

261 Companies Act 1985, s 349(4); *Maxform SpA v Mariani & Goodville Ltd* [1979] 2 Lloyd's Rep 385, affirmed [1981] 2 Lloyd's Rep 54. The fact that the misstatement was too minor to be noticed is irrelevant (*Durham Fancy Goods Ltd v Michael Jackson (Fancy Goods) Ltd* [1968] 2 QB 839), though 'Ltd' instead of 'Limited' is considered acceptable (ibid) and 'Co.' instead of 'Company' (*Banque de l'Indochine et de Suez S.A. v Euroseas Group Finance Co Ltd* [1981] 3 All ER 198), but not the omission of the word 'Limited' or its abbreviation (*Lindholst v Fowler* [1988] BCLC 166).

262 *Durham Fancy Goods Ltd v Michael Jackson (Fancy Goods) Ltd*, n 261.

Signature by way of acceptance raises special considerations, since only the drawee can accept. Accordingly, if a bill is drawn on the principal, a purported acceptance by the agent in his own name is nugatory. It does not bind the company, for the agent had not indicated his representative capacity; and it does not impose liability on the agent, for he lacks the ability to give an effective acceptance.[263] Similarly, if the bill is drawn on the agent, his purported acceptance on behalf of the company is of no effect and neither he nor the company is liable.[264]

(v) Fictitious or non-existing party

1. *Payee or indorsee*

Section 7(3) of the Act provides as follows:

> Where the payee is a fictitious or non-existing person the bill may be treated as payable to bearer.

By virtue of s 34(3), this provision extends to the case where an indorsee under a special indorsement is a fictitious or non-existing person. The bill can then be treated as having been indorsed in blank.

The effect of the above provisions is that if the bill carries an indorsement purporting to be that of the payee or indorsee in question the indorsement can be disregarded, s 24 of the Act (relating to forged signatures) will not apply to it and the instrument will be enforceable by a bona fide holder for value as if it were a valid bill payable to bearer. Similarly, the acceptor who pays the holder in good faith and without knowledge of the forgery will get a good discharge.

As an alternative to invoking s 7(3), a holder in due course can, in proceedings against the drawer, treat the drawer as estopped from denying the existence of the payee,[265] and in proceedings against an indorser, treat him as estopped from denying the genuineness and regularity of the signature of prior indorsers[266] and thus necessarily the fact of their existence.

There has been much controversy as to the meaning of the phrase 'fictitious or non-existing person', but the authorities now establish the following. A named payee or indorsee who never existed or who had died before the drawing or indorsement naming him is both non-existent and fictitious.[267] A named payee or indorsee who does exist will nevertheless be fictitious if he was not intended by the drawer or indorser as the person to receive payment.[268] If, however, the drawer or indorser did intend the payee or indorsee to receive payment, the fact that this

---

263 *Polhill v Walter*, n 255. But he may be liable to an action for damages for breach of warranty of authority (ibid).

264 Ibid.

265 Section 55(1).

266 Section 55(2).

267 *Clutton v Attenborough* [1897] AC 90.

268 *Bank of England v Vagliano* [1891] AC 107, discussed P. E. Salvatori, 'Vagliano: Case Revisited' (1979) 3 Can Bus LJ 296; *Boma Manufacturing Ltd v Canadian Imperial Bank of Commerce* [1996] 3 SCR 727.

intention was induced by another's fraud or misrepresentation does not render the payee or indorsee fictitious.[269] The distinction between a fictitious and a non-existent payee is without practical consequences, s 7(3) treating both in exactly the same way.[270]

2.   Drawee

Where the drawee is a fictitious person, the holder may treat the instrument, at his option, either as a bill of exchange or as a promissory note.[271]

3.   Drawer or indorser

A person signing a bill in an assumed name is liable on it as if he had signed in his own name.[272]

(vi) Unauthorized alteration

Material alteration[273] of a bill without the consent of the parties liable on it avoids the bill except as against a party making, authorizing or assenting to the alteration or subsequent indorsers;[274] but where the alteration is not apparent, the bill may be enforced by a holder in due course according to its original terms.[275]

(vii) Breach of the underlying transaction

A bill of exchange generates a contract quite distinct from the transaction in respect of which it is given. Great importance is attached by the court to the unconditional character[276] of a bill of exchange, for its utility as an instrument of

---

269   *North & South Wales Bank v Macbeth* [1908] AC 137; *Vinden v Hughes* [1905] 1 KB 795; *Royal Bank of Canada v Concrete Column Clamps (1961) Ltd* (1976) 74 DLR (3d) 26.

270   There may, however, be significance in the distinction where the party concerned is the drawer or an indorser, for a fictitious but existing drawer or indorser may be estopped by conduct from disputing the genuineness of his signature and may thus incur the liability of a signatory. For a criticism of s 7(3), see Michael Yong Haron, 'Revisiting 7(3) of the Bills of Exchange Act 1882: An Economic Analysis' [1998] Cambrian L. Rev. 53.

271   Section 5(2).

272   Section 23(1). A bill so signed is a false instrument for the purpose of the Forgery and Counterfeiting Act 1981. See s 9(1).

273   Any alteration which changes the business effect of the instrument is likely to be considered material (*Suffell v Bank of England* (1882) 9 QBD 555). In particular, the following are material: any alteration of the date, the sum payable, the time of payment, the place of payment, and, where a bill has been accepted generally, the addition of a place of payment without the acceptor's consent (s 64(2)).

274   Bills of Exchange Act 1882, s 64(1). In consequence, where a cheque is stolen and fraudulently altered by deleting the name of the payee and substituting that of a third party who pays it into his account, the collecting bank is not liable to the true owner for more than nominal damages for conversion of the cheque, because by the time of collection the cheque had already become void (*Smith v Lloyds TSB Group plc* [2001] QB 541).

275   Section 64(1). See, for example, *Rapid Discount Corp. v Thomas E. Hiscott Ltd* (1977) 76 DLR (3d) 450.

276   See pp 481, 484.

commerce vitally depends on the assurance of payment to the holder.[277] It is thus regarded as akin to cash,[278] and the courts are very reluctant to allow a breach of the underlying transaction to be set up as a defence to a claim on a bill. The issue usually arises in proceedings for summary judgment on the bill, where the defendant has to show an arguable defence,[279] and in nine cases out of ten the plaintiff holder will be given judgment without stay of execution pending trial of the defendant's cross-claim.[280]

In a claim on a bill of exchange the defendant's ability to set up a breach of the underlying transaction by way of defence is substantially restricted. Even as between the original parties (payee and acceptor), the breach is a defence only so far as it gives rise to a liquidated claim for total or partial failure of the consideration for which the bill was given, as where the bill was delivered in payment of the price of goods sold under a contract of sale which were lawfully rejected for nonconformity with the contract.[281] The acceptor cannot, however, set up an unliquidated claim for damages for breach of warranty as a defence to a claim on the bill.[282] As against a holder for value, the defence of failure of consideration is not available even though there is a failure of consideration as between payee and acceptor. Finally, a holder in due course is not affected even by illegality in the underlying transaction.[283]

These rules are well illustrated by two cases:[284] *Bank für Gemeinwirtschaft AG v City of London Garages Ltd*[285] and *Cebora S.N.C. v SIP. (Industrial Products) Ltd.*[286] In the first case the court held, inter alia, that illegality arising from the exportation of foreign currency bills without Treasury consent and in breach of the Exchange Control Act did not affect the rights of a holder in due course.[287] In the second:

> The plaintiffs applied for summary judgment on a series of bills given by the defendants in payment of the price of goods purchased from the plaintiffs under a distribution agreement. The defendants, having served a counter-claim for (inter alia) damages for non-delivery of and defects in goods to which the bills related, sought leave to defend or a stay of execution pending trial of their counter-claim.

> Dismissing the defendants' appeal, the Court of Appeal held that while as between the parties total failure of consideration afforded a defence, a counter-claim for unliquidated

---

277 *Cebora S.N.C. v S.I.P. (Industrial Products) Ltd* [1976] 1 Lloyd's Rep 271, per Sir Erich Sachs at 278–279; *All Trades Distributors Ltd v Kaufman Ltd* (1969) 113 Sol Jo 995, per Lord Denning MR at 996.

278 *James Lamont & Co Ltd v Hyland Ltd (No 2)* [1950] 1 KB 585; *Brown Shipley & Co Ltd v Alicia Hosiery Ltd* [1966] 1 Lloyd's Rep 668; *All Trades Distributors Ltd v Kaufman Ltd*, n 277; *Cebora S.N.C. v S.I.P. (Industrial Products) Ltd*, n 277.

279 See p 1131.

280 See the cases cited n 278.

281 *Forman v Wright* (1851) 11 CB 481; *Thoni GmbH & Co KG v R.T.P. Equipment Ltd* [1979] 2 Lloyd's Rep 282.

282 *Cebora S.N.C. v S.I.P. (Industrial Products) Ltd*, n 277.

283 *Bank für Gemeinwirtschaft Aktiengesellschaft v City of London Garages Ltd*, n 85.

284 For a further illustration, see *Nova (Jersey) Knit Ltd v Kammgarn Spinnerei GmbH*, n 209.

285 See n 85.

286 See n 277.

287 Whether the plaintiff is a holder in due course is, however, a separate question. See further below.

damages where there was no total failure of consideration did not, save in exceptional circumstances, justify either leave to defend or a stay of execution.

It will be apparent that where the bill sued on was given by the defendant as the price of goods purchased from the plaintiff and the defendant seeks to set up defects in the goods as a defence, the ability to do so will depend on whether he effectively rejected the goods on the one hand or accepted (or must be deemed to have accepted) them on the other. Lawful rejection entitles the buyer to recover the price of the goods rejected, creating a liquidated claim which *pro tanto* affords a defence to an action on the bill[288] except as against a holder in due course. Acceptance restricts the defendant to a claim for unliquidated damages for breach of warranty, and these cannot be set up either by way of a substantive defence, or by way of set-off, even if exceeding the amount of the bill.[289]

(viii)Attacks on 'holder in due course' status

Given that the position of a holder in due course is well nigh impregnable, the defendant's efforts are better directed to impeaching the plaintiff's holder in due course status. The prerequisites of such status have been examined earlier. Two of these merit particular attention at this point, namely the holder's good faith and his want of notice of any defect in the title of the person who negotiated the bill to him. Good faith, as we have seen, denotes honesty in fact,[290] and 'notice' signifies knowledge, actual or imputed,[291] as opposed to constructive notice. Hence a holder is not precluded from being a holder in due course by reason of the fact that he was negligent and would, by making reasonable inquiries, have discovered the defect in his transferor's title. But a suspicion of something wrong coupled with a wilful neglect of the means of knowledge – in other words, deliberately turning a blind eye to the suspicious circumstances – is equivalent to knowledge and thus negates good faith.[292]

Where bills are negotiated to the holder in pursuance of a regular business relationship between him and his indorser, who himself takes the bills as the price of goods or services which he undertook to provide, the court may be less willing to treat the holder as insulated from the underlying trading transaction than if there were no such relationship, and may on that account deny the indorsee 'holder in due course' status. English courts have not yet had occasion to pronounce upon this in any reported case, but the issue has arisen several times in North America, particularly in relation to finance houses that discount instalment bills and notes for dealers and retailers pursuant to a prior arrangement;[293] and there is now an

---

288   *Thoni GmbH & Co KG v R.T.P. Equipment Ltd, n* 281, applying *Forman v Wright*, n 281.

289   *James Lamont & Co Ltd v Hyland Ltd (No 2)*, n 278.

290   Bills of Exchange Act, s 90.

291   Knowledge is imputed where it is acquired by an agent who is under a duty to transmit it to his principal or who acquires it as the result of a notification which he has actual or apparent authority to receive.

292   *Jones v Gordon* (1877) 2 App Cas 616, *per* Lord Blackburn at 628–629.

293   The leading case is *Federal Discount Corp. v St Pierre* (1962) 32 DLR (2d) 86. For a discussion of this and subsequent cases, see Jacob S. Ziegel, 'Comments – *Range v Corporation de Finance Belvédère'* (1970) 48 Can Bar Rev 309.

increasing tendency in common law jurisdictions to legislate against the use of bills and notes in consumer credit transactions.[294]

10. DISCHARGE

A party to a bill is discharged from liability if, inter alia, the amount due on the bill is paid either by him or by a prior party or if, he being the drawer or an indorser, the bill was not duly presented for acceptance or payment, or notice of dishonour was not duly given.[295] But discharge of a party does not necessarily mean discharge of the bill. A bill is discharged – that is, treated as having exhausted its legal effect – where no party remains who can sue or be sued on it. This may occur in various ways. The most obvious, of course, is by payment of the bill in due course by or on behalf of the drawee or acceptor.[296] The acceptor (unless he is an accommodation party) is the party primarily liable on the bill, the principal debtor to whom the other parties stand in the relation of sureties. Only the acceptor, or some person having actual or ostensible authority from him, can effectively discharge the bill by payment. This is simply an application of the wider rule of law that no one is entitled to intervene officiously to pay another's debt, and if he does so the payment is ineffective for the purpose.[297] If payment is made by the drawer, the bill remains operative for the purpose of giving him his indemnity against the acceptor. Similarly, if payment is made by an indorser, the bill remains current, the indorser having rights over against prior indorsers, and against the drawer and the acceptor. The indorsee does not pay the bill; he pays *for* the bill.

It is not every payment by the acceptor that will discharge the bill. His payment must be lawful in the sense of being a payment which gives him a good discharge. It must thus be made to the person apparently entitled to receive it[298] and it must not be made before maturity of the bill.[299]

A bill may be discharged in a variety of other ways, eg where, despite its remaining unpaid, there is no one who can sue on it;[300] where the holder at or after its maturity absolutely and unconditionally renounces his rights against the acceptor either in writing or by delivery of the bill to the acceptor;[301] or where the bill is intentionally

---

294 For North American developments, see the papers by R. B. Buglass, R. C. C. Cuming, Benjamin Geva and John F. Varcoe delivered at the Canadian Eighth Annual Workshop on Commercial and Consumer Law in Toronto in 1978, the proceedings of which have since been published (ed J. S. Ziegel, 1980).

295 See pp 509 ff.

296 Section 59(1).

297 Goff and Jones, *Law of Restitution* (6th edn, 2002), p 18. For the application of this principle to payment of a cheque after countermand of payment by the drawer, see p 565.

298 In the language of the Act, it must be made to the holder in good faith, and without notice that his title to the bill is defective (s 59(1)).

299 Ibid. A premature payment operates as a purchase of the bill from the holder by the acceptor, who becomes entitled to reissue it and negotiate it further, so long as he is still holding it in his own right at maturity (s 61).

300 This could happen because of failure duly to present a bill in respect of which the acceptor had given a qualified acceptance.

301 Section 62(1), (2).

cancelled by the holder or his agent and his cancellation is apparent thereon.[302] If a party materially alters a bill,[303] it is generally avoided against any prior party who did not assent to the alteration,[304] but is enforceable by a holder in due course where the alteration is not apparent,[305] and remains enforceable against the person who made the alteration and subsequent indorsers.[306]

11.   EFFECT OF BILL ON UNDERLYING CONTRACT

Let us suppose that B, having bought goods from S on three months' credit, gives S a ninety-day bill of exchange for the amount of the price. What effect does this have on S's rights under the underlying contract of sale? This depends on the intention with which the bill was given. If, as is usual, it was taken as conditional payment,[307] then S's right to payment under the contract of sale is suspended pending maturity or earlier discharge of the bill.[308] If the bill is met, the price obligation is discharged. If it is dishonoured, S's rights revive and he has then to decide whether to sue on the bill or to bring an action on the original contract. What if the bill is stolen from the payee? If it is paid in due course,[309] it is discharged[310] and B's liability to S is accordingly extinguished. In any other case S's rights on the original contract remain in suspense, but he may demand a duplicate on giving an indemnity[311] or may seek judgment on the bill against an indemnity, the matter then being in the discretion of the court.[312]

Where the bill is taken as collateral security, the position is reversed. S's primary rights and remedies are on the original contract of sale and the bill is to be resorted to only in the event of B's default in payment of the price. S is entitled to deal with the bill but only in such a manner as will enable him to get it back in time to surrender it to B if B discharges his obligations under the contract of sale. Thus S can sub-pledge the bill, but must ensure that he is ready to hand it back to B when B becomes entitled to it as a result of completing payment under the sale contract.

302 Section 63(1).
303 See p 522.
304 Section 64(1).
305 Ibid, *proviso*. The phrase 'where the alteration is not apparent' is really superfluous, for if it were apparent the holder would not be a holder in due course. The holder in due course can avail himself of the bill as if it had not been altered and enforce it accordingly (ibid).
306 Ibid.
307 It could be taken as absolute payment, so giving up the right to sue on the original contract even it the bill is dishonoured, but the court would need compelling evidence that this was the intention of the parties.
308 Hence if S brings an action against B for goods sold and delivered and, when signing judgment in default, includes in the judgment figure the amount of a bill that has not yet been presented for payment, the judgment is irregular and the defendant can apply to have it set aside *ex debito justitiae* (*Bolt & Nut Co (Tipton) Ltd v Rowlands, Nicholls & Co Ltd* [1964] 2 QB 10).
309 Ie, because it is a bearer bill paid in good faith and without notice of a defect in the holder's title (s 59(1)).
310 Ibid
311 Section 69.
312 Section 70.

12. SECURITY OVER BILLS

The holder of a bill may pledge, mortgage or charge it by way of security. The monetary obligation embodied in a bill of exchange given in the way of trade constitutes a book debt,[313] and security over such a bill is therefore a charge on a book debt which would ordinarily require registration under s 395 of the Companies Act 1985. However, where the security over the bill is created by deposit of the bill with the creditor, the security is treated as not being a charge on a book debt and is thus exempt from registration.[314] The pledgee of a bill which has been duly negotiated to him is entitled to sue on it as a holder for value but he has no right, in the absence of an agreement with the pledgor, to sell the bill.[315]

13. ADVANTAGES OF A BILL

We mentioned in the previous chapter that the bill mechanism avoids the risks and expense involved in the physical transportation of money and from the creditor's viewpoint provides a convenient means of localizing the transaction. We are now in a position to assess why a bill of exchange, though involving no more than a set of personal undertakings, is nevertheless considerably more advantageous to the obligee than an ordinary contract containing a promise of payment. This reflects the superiority of a documentary intangible over a pure intangible.

(i) Ease of transfer

Delivery of possession, with any necessary indorsement, suffices to transfer the legal right to the sum payable under the bill without the need for any separate assignment. Moreover, since the party liable on the bill knows that his duty is to pay only the current holder and (unless presentment is waived) only when the bill is presented to him for payment, it is not necessary that he should be given prior notice of the transfer, whereas to perfect an ordinary assignment of a debt notice of assignment must be given to the debtor.[316]

(ii) Insulation from the underlying transaction

As we have seen, a bill of exchange is considered to generate a contract quite distinct from that which gave rise to the payment obligation in the first place, with the result that the holder will usually be entitled to exact payment even if he or a prior party has committed a breach of the underlying contract in respect of which the bill was given. The bill transaction is thus wholly or partially[317] insulated from the associated trading contract, in much the same way as the old penal bond was insulated from the contract the performance of which it was designed to secure.

---

313 *Re Stevens* [1888] WN 110; *Dawson v Isle* [1906] 1 Ch 633.
314 Companies Act 1985, s 396(2)(f). The reason for this exemption is to avoid interfering with the negotiability of bills of exchange and other instruments.
315 *Byles on Bills of Exchange and Cheques*, p 227.
316 See pp 48, 773.
317 Dependent on the circumstances. See p 523.

This characteristic facilitates both the marketability of the bill[318] and the speed with which judgment can be obtained in proceedings to enforce it.[319]

(iii) Relaxation of ordinary contract rules

A bill of exchange, though a form of contract, has through the force of the law merchant been accorded special privileges now embodied in the Bills of Exchange Act. In particular, the holder of a bill is entitled to enforce it against all prior parties without having want of privity raised against him;[320] and though consideration must be furnished, it need not move from the promisee.[321] Moreover, an accommodation party is liable on a bill to a holder for value despite the fact that he himself received no value for lending his name to the bill.[322]

(iv) Ready addition of obligors

Not infrequently, a contracting party wishes to have the other party's undertakings reinforced by guarantee from a third party. Alternatively, he may want to have a third party added as co-principal with the other. This involves the preparation and signature of a separate document. The advantage of a bill of exchange is that the undertaking of the acceptor can readily be reinforced, and the standing of the bill improved, by the addition of other names to the bill by way of indorsement.[323] Moreover, since there is no particular magic in the way in which the parties to a bill are ordered, the bill does not have to be drawn on the obligor to the underlying transaction but may instead be drawn on and accepted by a good 'name', eg an established merchant bank, which thus becomes the party primarily liable on the bill, with the original obligor coming in as a party in some other capacity, eg as drawer or indorser.

(v) Negotiability

The most significant feature of a negotiable bill of exchange, and indeed of any negotiable instrument, is that in the hands of a holder in due course it is enforceable despite a defect in the title of any prior holder. In other words, the transferor who negotiates a bill to a holder in due course can pass a better title than he himself possesses.[324]

(vi) Marketability

Because of the features previously described, a term bill of exchange bearing a good name or names is readily marketable, enabling the seller or other holder to

318 See pp 528–529.
319 See p 529.
320 See ss 38(2).
321 Section 27(2). See p 494.
322 Section 28(2).
323 See pp 504 ff.
324 See p 495.

convert the bill into cash without holding it to maturity, whereas there is no ready market for rights embodied in an ordinary contract document. Thus it is much easier for an exporter to discount a bill of exchange drawn for the price of the goods sold than to discount the sale contract itself.

(vii) Speed of enforcement

Because of the need to protect the marketable status of bills of exchange, the courts are extremely reluctant to allow defences to be raised to an action on a bill, so that in the great majority of cases summary judgment will be given within a matter of weeks of the commencement of proceedings.[325] This is in marked contrast to an action on an ordinary contract, where a defendant having an arguable defence is entitled to have his case tried, which may hold up the plaintiff for two or three years, or even longer in a complicated case.

---

325   For an outline of the procedure, see p 1131.

20 Cheques and the Duties of Bankers in Relation Thereto

I.   DEFINITIONS AND DISTINGUISHING CHARACTERISTICS

A cheque is a bill of exchange drawn on a banker payable on demand.[1] Being a demand instrument, a cheque is not accepted; the drawee bank either pays or refuses to pay. It will do the latter if its customer has countermanded payment or if the account is not sufficiently in funds or within the limit of an agreed overdraft facility or if the bank decides to exercise a right to set off a debit balance existing on another account.

Except as otherwise provided,[2] the provisions of the Bills of Exchange Act applicable to a demand bill apply to a cheque.[3] But in truth a cheque is a very different kind of animal. In the first place, it is primarily a payment direction, not a credit instrument, and is by its nature intended to be presented and paid almost immediately, not negotiated to a third party. Secondly, it forms an integral part of the banking mechanism and is thus deeply rooted in the banker–customer relationship. Millions of cheques are issued every day and most of these have to be collected and paid through the clearing system.[4] Duty relationships are thus set up between the collecting bank and its customer, the paying bank and its customer,[5] the collecting bank and paying bank, and each of these in relation to a third party claiming title to a cheque or to the proceeds of its

---

1 Bills of Exchange Act 1882, s 73. A dividend warrant directed to the issuing company's bank is a form of cheque, as is a draft by one bank on another, but not a draft drawn by a bank on its own head office. A post-dated cheque cannot properly be paid by the drawee bank until the date stated. Prior to this the instrument is technically not a cheque at all but would appear to become so on maturity. If the bank wrongly pays the cheque before the date shown and prior to such date the customer countermands payment, the bank will have to suffer the loss itself, unless the circumstances are such that the bank is entitled to debit the customer's account despite the breach of mandate (see pp 554–556).
'Banker' is defined, somewhat unhelpfully, as including a body of persons, whether incorporated or not, who carry on the business of banking (s 2). This definition has not been altered by the Banking Act 1979 in relation to bills of exchange.
2 See ss 74–81.
3 Section 73.
4 See p 535.
5 The *collecting* bank is the bank whose customer is the payee or other holder of the cheque and who is entrusted with the collection of the amount of the cheque on the customer's behalf and the crediting of it to his account (in practice, the credit is usually made on a provisional basis when the cheque is given to the bank for collection; see n 30). The *paying* bank is the bank on whom the cheque is drawn, ie the bank where the drawer keeps his account.

collection.[6] Specific forms of instruction to bankers have evolved in relation to cheques through various types of crossing, to which reference will be made later in this chapter. The sheer volume of cheque transactions,[7] leading to the computerization of account systems, has made it necessary to enact legislation for the protection of bankers in order to relieve them of responsibilities which would otherwise fall upon them. In the result, the greater part of the modern law relating to negotiable instruments is concerned with particular problems arising in relation to cheques. The statutory provisions are to be found in the Bills of Exchange Act 1882 and the Cheques Act 1957.

2. FORM OF A CHEQUE

Figure 20.1 is a typical form of cheque. The number in the top right-hand corner is the national sort code of the branch of the bank. The number in magnetic characters at the bottom left is the cheque number (cheques in a book being numbered in sequence). Next to it is a repetition of the sort code and to the right of this is the customer's account number with the branch, allocated in order to avoid confusion between two customers of the same name. The crossing containing the words '& Co' will be explained a little later. The cheque must carry the drawer's signature, but despite doubts that have been expressed,[8] it would seem that this need not be handwritten and that a stamped facsimile suffices. The same would appear to be true even of a preprinted facsimile, though in order to be enforceable by anyone other than a holder in due course such a cheque would need to be completed within a reasonable time and strictly within the authority given.[9]

The cheque is an order cheque and can thus be paid only to the named payee or his indorsee. Being demand instruments, cheques are not usually discounted, though sometimes the payee will indorse them over to a third party either for collection (where the payee does not himself have a bank account) or in part payment of a debt. But, as a rule, cheques are not indorsed except to the holder's bank for the purpose of collection, and even then it is no longer banking practice to require indorsement where the cheque is being collected for the account of the ostensible payee.[10]

---

6 Improper collection of a cheque exposes the collecting bank to liability to the true owner in damages for conversion, and alternative remedies, such as an equitable claim based on knowing receipt or knowing assistance, are usually neither necessary nor available, for a bank is under no liability for collecting (or for paying) money in a purely ministerial capacity as agent for a customer (*Agip (Africa) Ltd v Jackson* [1990] Ch 265, per Millett J at 288), but the position is otherwise where the bank receives and applies money for its own benefit, as where, for example, the bank applies the proceeds in reduction of the account holder's overdraft (ibid; *Stephens Travel Services International Pty Ltd v Qantas Airways* (1988) 13 NSWLR 331). See Michael Bryan, 'When Does a Bank Receive Money' [1996] JBL 165. See also p 540.

7 Though new payment mechanisms (p 464) have taken some of the pressure off the cheque system, countervailing pressures, such as the impact of the cheque guarantee card, led to a continued growth in the use of cheques, which now appears to be slightly declining.

8 Eg by Denning J in *Goodman v J Eban Ltd* [1954] 1 QB 550.

9 Bills of Exchange Act, s 20(2).

10 See p 549.

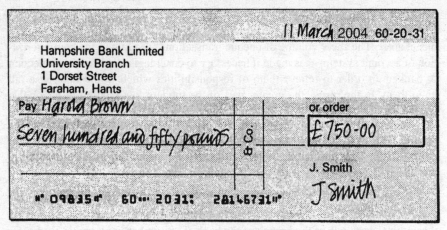

Fig 20.1 Cheque

The order cheque is now the norm, but bearer cheques are still used. As in the case of other bearer bills, they involve the risk of loss or theft, since the drawee bank is entitled to pay anyone who presents the cheque, provided that in making the payment it acts in good faith and without notice of any defect in the title of the holder.[11]

3.   CROSSINGS

Cheque crossings originated in Clearing House practice among bankers. The clerk of the collecting bank would leave in the tray of the paying bank in the Clearing House bundles of cheques for payment, and would write the name of the collecting bank between two transverse lines on each cheque so that the paying bank would know to which bank payment was to be made for account of the payee. Drawers of cheques borrowed this idea, crossing them with the name of the payee's bank to signify that payment had to be made to that bank and not to the payee himself or any other party. The crossing was thus an additional safeguard against fraud. If the drawer did not know the name of the payee's bank, he would simply insert the words '& Co' in the crossing, leaving the name to be completed by the payee himself.

Over time, a variety of crossings developed, each representing a particular form of instruction to the paying bank as to the person to whom payment was to be made. There also emerged a different type of crossing, 'Account payee' and its variants, which constituted a direction to the *collecting* bank not to collect the cheque except for the account of the named payee.

The practice of crossing cheques was formally recognized by Parliament in the Crossed Cheques Act 1856. The current statutory provisions are ss 76–81A of the Bills of Exchange Act and these have been extended, so far as applicable, to other instruments by s 5 of the Cheques Act 1957.

11 Section 59(1).

(i) Crossing a material part of a cheque

A crossing authorized by the Bills of Exchange Act[12] is a material part of the cheque, and it is unlawful to obliterate or, except as authorized by the Act, to add to or alter the crossing.[13] Obliteration or unauthorized alteration thus attracts s 64 of the Act and avoids the cheque except as provided by that section.[14]

(ii) General and special crossings

A crossing made in accordance with the Act constitutes a direction to the bank to make payment only to a banker. If the banker is not named, so that the paying bank is free to pay any bank, the crossing is a general crossing; where the crossing bears the name of the bank to whom payment is to be made, the crossing is a special crossing and the cheque is said to be crossed specially and to that banker.[15]

In order for a cheque to be effectively crossed under s 76 of the Act it must bear across its face either two parallel transverse lines[16] or the name of a banker[17] or both.

(iii) Who may cross a cheque

A cheque may be crossed generally or specially by the drawer.[18] As regards a subsequent holder, the general principle is that he may make the instrument more restrictive but not less. Thus, the holder of an uncrossed cheque can cross it, the holder of a cheque crossed generally may cross it specially, and the holder of any crossed cheque may add the words 'not negotiable', while a banker to whom a cheque is specially crossed may cross it specially to another bank for collection, and a banker to whom an uncrossed or generally crossed cheque is sent for collection may cross it specially to himself.[19] On the other hand, only the drawer himself can uncross a crossed cheque[20] or make a crossing less restrictive than as originally drawn.

(iv) Effect of crossing

A crossed cheque may be paid only to a banker, and a specially crossed cheque may be paid only to the banker to whom it is crossed. A cheque crossed specially to

12 See below.
13 Section 78.
14 See p 522.
15 Section 76(1), (2).
16 With or without the words 'and company' or any abbreviation thereof and/or the words 'not negotiable' (s 76(1)). For the significance of the words 'not negotiable', see p 534.
17 With or without the words 'not negotiable' (s 76(2)).
18 Section 77(1).
19 Section 77(2)–(6).
20 Most order cheques are printed with a crossing on them and if the drawer wishes to draw cash he may be required to open the cheque, eg by writing the words 'pay cash' in the crossing and authenticating them with his signature.

more than one banker may not be paid at all except when crossed to an agent for collection being a banker.[21] If the banker upon whom the cheque is drawn pays it in breach of these restrictions, he is liable to the true owner of the cheque for any loss the latter may sustain.[22] The crossing does not in any way restrict the negotiability of the cheque,[23] so that while a holder in due course who presents the cheque in person and not through a collecting bank is not entitled to payment, yet if the payment is made, it constitutes a payment in due course and discharges the cheque.[24]

If a crossed cheque bears the words 'not negotiable', this does not affect the transferability of the cheque but means that the person taking it cannot transfer a better title than he himself possesses.[25] The marking of a crossed cheque 'not negotiable' thus precludes a subsequent holder from enjoying 'holder in due course' status, though he will enjoy similar benefits if he took from one who qualified as a holder in due course.[26]

(v) 'Account payee'

The words 'account payee', 'account payee only' and the like are frequently used in crossings but were not expressly authorized by the Bills of Exchange Act. Nevertheless, the courts used to give effect to them, not as crossings imposing a duty on the paying bank[27] but as directions to the collecting bank to ensure that it applied the proceeds of the cheque for the account of the named payee only and not some other party, eg an indorsee, except after proper inquiry to satisfy itself that such payment was in order. However, all such crossings now operate to render the cheque non-transferable, so that it is valid only as between the parties.[28]

---

21 Section 79(1).
22 Section 79(2). As to 'true owner', see p 547. As to the protection of the paying bank which in good faith and without negligence pays a cheque which does not appear to have been crossed or has had its crossings altered or obliterated, see s 79(2), proviso.
23 *Smith v Union Bank of London* (1875) 1 QBD 31.
24 The only question then is whether the paying bank is entitled to debit the drawer's account. See p 564.
25 Section 81. The restricted meaning thus accorded to the words 'not negotiable' is confined to cases where they are used in conjunction with a crossing. An uncrossed cheque made not negotiable is not transferable at all and a purported transfer confers no rights on the transferee (*Hibernian Bank Ltd v Gysin & Hanson* [1939] 1 KB 483).
26 Bills of Exchange Act, s 29(3).
27 The paying bank fulfils its duty by paying the collecting bank. It is not concerned with the manner in which the collecting bank applies the payment, this being exclusively the collecting bank's responsibility (*Universal Guarantee Pty Ltd v National Bank of Australasia Ltd* [1965] 1 WLR 691).
28 Bills of Exchange Act 1882, s 81A(1), added by the Cheques Act 1992, s 1, in accordance with the recommendations of the Report of the Jack Committee on Banking Services: Law and Practice (Cm 622, 1989). Section 81A(1) applies to the expressions 'account payee' and 'a/c payee' with or without the word 'only'. For the liability of a bank which collects for a party other than the named payee, see pp 547, 550.

4. THE CHEQUE CLEARING SYSTEM

For a collecting bank to have to make individual presentations of cheques to all the paying banks would obviously be impracticable in the light of the huge volume of cheques passing daily through the banking system. What is needed is a central clearing system in which cheques drawn each day on a particular bank and a particular branch of that bank are batched and presented for payment en bloc and balances are struck among the participating banks so that instead of each bank paying all the banks who are its creditors and receiving payment from all banks who are its debtors, that bank's overall position vis-à-vis the other banks is established and a single debit or credit made to its account. Such a system is one of four distinct clearing systems controlled by the Association of Payment Clearing Systems (APACS).[29] The cheque clearing is now conducted at the exchange centre at Goodmans Fields by the Cheque and Credit Clearing Co Ltd on behalf of its Settlement Members under the overall direction of the Chief Inspector, APACS, and in accordance with the Rules for the Conduct of the Cheque Clearing.

The clearing banks not only process their own articles through the system but also clear effects as agents for banks not having a seat in the Clearing House.[30] Collecting a cheque through the clearing system is an elaborate process,[31] as is shown in figure 20.2, and may take up to a week. This stems from the fact that the Bills of Exchange Act requires the cheque itself to be physically presented for payment.

The mode of payment depends on whether the drawer and the payee bank at different banks, different branches of the same bank or the same branch. It is only in the first case that the cheque goes through the clearing.[32] The payee pays the cheque into his branch, which provisionally credits the payee's account and transmits the cheque, batched with other cheques drawn on the same bank, to its London clearing office. There it is handed over to the paying bank's clearing centre. For accounting convenience the amounts of cheques exchanged in the clearing are netted out at the end of the day and, in advance of the cheques being cleared, value is exchanged between debtor and creditor banks the following morning by debits and credits to their accounts with the Bank of England. Meanwhile, the particular payee's cheque is forwarded by the paying bank's clearing office to the branch on which it is

---

29 See p 464.

30 Cheques and other instruments passing through the clearing system are referred to as 'articles', 'items' or 'effects'. A customer who pays cheques into his account, though provisionally credited with the amount of these as 'uncleared effects', does not receive value until they are cleared, prior to which he needs the consent of his bank to draw against them. If they are dishonoured on presentation, his account will be debited back.

31 It is described in detail in the arbitral award of Bingham J sitting as judge-arbitrator, in *Barclays Bank plc v Bank of England* [1985] 1 All ER 385, in which he held that a collecting bank's duty to its customer is to present a cheque at the branch on which it is drawn, pursuant to s 45 of the Bills of Exchange Act 1882, and that there was no sufficient evidence of banking custom and practice to support the proposition that it was sufficient to present it in the Clearing House.

32 As to the mode of payment for in-house transfers, see pp 538–539.

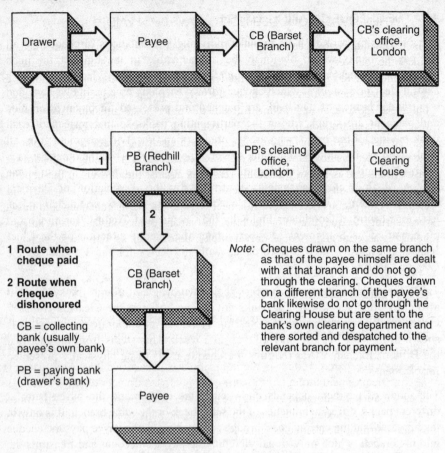

1 **Route when cheque paid**

2 **Route when cheque dishonoured**

CB = collecting bank (usually payee's own bank)

PB = paying bank (drawer's bank)

Note: Cheques drawn on the same branch as that of the payee himself are dealt with at that branch and do not go through the clearing. Cheques drawn on a different branch of the payee's bank likewise do not go through the Clearing House but are sent to the bank's own clearing department and there sorted and despatched to the relevant branch for payment.

Fig 20.2 Journey of a cheque

drawn.[33] If it is honoured, it is cancelled and the drawer's account debited and the credit to the payee's account becomes unconditional. If the cheque is dishonoured, it is returned direct to the branch of the collecting bank where it was paid in, the advance transfer of value between the paying bank and the collecting bank will be reversed and the payee's account will be debited back with the amount of the returned cheque.

In practice, banks regularly use cheque truncation, by which the cheque is physically retained by the collecting bank and details transmitted electronically to the paying bank. This saves time and administration and appears to have no adverse consequences if the cheque is honoured. But the drawer's failure to meet a cheque not physically presented at his branch would not constitute a dishonour within the Bills of Exchange Act.

---

33 Physical presentation of the cheque to the branch is no longer necessary; the process may be truncated by notification of its essential features to the branch by electronic means or otherwise unless presentation of the cheque itself is requested (Bills of Exchange Act 1882, s 74B). Some cheques are currently retained at a central point within paying banks but full truncation (retention at a point within the collecting bank) has not yet been adopted.

5. WHEN IS A CHEQUE DEEMED TO HAVE BEEN PAID?[34]

Since a cheque is not accepted by the drawee bank but merely paid or returned, and since the delivery of a cheque does not (except in Scotland) constitute an assignment to the payee, or other holder, of funds in the drawer's account,[35] the drawee bank does not engage itself to the holder to make payments and, indeed, is obliged to honour an instruction from its customer countermanding payment if it receives this instruction in due time.[36] In ordering his bank not to pay, the customer may be dishonouring the cheque and exposing himself to proceedings by the holder, but the holder has no claim against the drawee bank itself for acting on the drawer's instructions and is left to pursue his remedies against the drawer, in the hope that the latter is not insolvent. It may therefore be important to know at what point a cheque is to be considered paid. It is necessary to distinguish cheques paid through the clearing, cheques drawn on the branch of a bank other than that where the payee holds his account and cheques drawn on the same branch as that where the payee's account is held.

(i) Cheques paid through the clearing

In most forms of payment it is important to distinguish a bank's commitment to pay from actual payment.[37] If a bank which has incurred a commitment to pay goes into liquidation without having completed payment, the person entitled to the payment is merely an unsecured creditor in the liquidation. However, we have seen that in the case of cheques paid through the clearing the interbank transfer of value takes place in anticipation of the cheque being cleared. Accordingly, in this case the time of payment of the cheque coincides with the time the bank becomes committed to pay by not returning the cheque as unpaid within the time allowed.[38]

We may note en passant that if the collecting bank, having been asked to collect the cheque as agent for its customer,[39] goes into winding up before having received the proceeds of the cheque, its implied authority to deal with the proceeds by crediting them to its customer's account, thereby borrowing the proceeds from its customer instead of paying them over to him,[40] comes to an end, and on a subsequent collection of the cheque the proceeds must be held by the collecting bank for its customer and cannot be retained as part of the bank's general assets.[41] If it is the paying bank which goes into winding up before payment of the cheque, then, of course, the cheque cannot be paid, for the assets of the bank come under the control of its liquidator and the bank ceases to be entitled to honour its customers' mandates.

---

34 See R. M. Goode, 'When is a Cheque Paid?' [1983] JBL 164. As to the effect of payment by cheque, see p 462.
35 Bills of Exchange Act, s 53.
36 See below.
37 See p 462.
38 See below.
39 As opposed to collecting on its own behalf after giving value to the customer. See p 542.
40 See pp 470, 541, 543.
41 *Re Farrow's Bank Ltd* [1923] 1 Ch 41.

The drawee bank incurs a commitment to the collecting bank to honour the cheque if:

(a)   it has informed the collecting bank (eg in response to a telephone inquiry) that the cheque will be met on presentment, and the cheque has been duly presented; [42]

(b)   after due presentation of the cheque the paying branch informs the collecting bank (eg in response to a telephone call) that the cheque is being paid;

(c)   the cheque is included in the list of items in the Daily Settlement between the paying bank and the collecting bank;[43] or

(d)   the paying branch fails to return the cheque duly marked with the reason for non-payment within the time laid down by the Clearing House Rules, ie on the day of presentment or, where the need to return the cheque is not noticed through inadvertence on that day, then on the next working day, provided that notice of non-payment is given to the presenting branch of the collecting bank by telephone not later than noon on that day.[44]

In cases (b), (c) and (d) the paying bank is entitled to debit its customer's account with the amount of the cheque. In case (a) it is entitled to do so where its advance assurance of payment was given with the drawer's express or implied authority, but otherwise the bank assumes the risk of countermand of payment by the customer[45] and will in that event have to bear the outlay itself.

(ii)   In-house transfers: different branches

Where the payee banks at the same bank as the drawer but at a different branch, the two branches are treated as if they were separate banks. The payee's branch will receive the cheque for collection, not for payment, for the payee is entitled to payment only from the branch on which the cheque is drawn. Accordingly, the

---

42   Though this is no longer required (see n 33), the usual Clearing House practice is for cheques to be transmitted through the clearing office of the paying bank, which thus acts as a channel of communication between the collecting bank and the drawee branch of the paying bank. Inevitably, some cheques are misdirected by the paying bank's clearing office and thus arrive late at the branch by which payment is to be made. The treatment of wrongly delivered articles is governed by the Clearing House Rules, which do not, however, deal with the question of responsibility for loss resulting from delays in presentation. There seems little doubt that the holder is entitled to look to his bank to make due presentation, and the latter would not be entitled to plead by way of defence the error of the paying bank's clearing office in dispatching the cheque to the wrong bank. Whether the collecting bank would have a right of indemnity against the paying bank is another matter.

43   The Daily Settlement is a ruled sheet completed by each bank showing totals of charges (ie bundles of articles) it has presented on the previous day to each of the other banks for payment (all of which are treated as paid unless returned within the requisite time – see below), together with the totals of unpaid articles and articles wrongly delivered. The figures having been agreed with the other banks, the balance then struck on each clearing bank's Daily Settlement sheet shows whether overall it is a debtor or a creditor in relation to the other clearing banks and the account of each bank with the Bank of England is debited or credited according to whether it is a net net debtor or a net net creditor.

44   In practice, banks tend to ignore the primary time limit and treat the time for return as noon on the following day, no doubt because it would be very difficult to establish that failure to return an item on the day of presentation was deliberate.

45   See pp 554–555.

cheque will be considered paid if not returned by the drawer's branch within the time allowed by the Bills of Exchange Act.[46]

(iii) In-house transfers: same branch

Where a cheque is drawn not only on the same bank but on the same branch as that where the payee holds his account, so that the funds transfer mechanism is purely internal, it is a question of fact whether the bank receives the cheque as agent for collection (albeit from itself) or is acceding to a demand for immediate payment. In the latter event the bank is entitled to deal with the cheque as if collecting from a different bank in the same place[47] and therefore to the lapse of a day before taking a decision whether to honour it or not.[48] There is a presumption that the bank receives the cheque as agent for collection and not for immediate payment.[49] But if the bank does an act indicating its decision to pay, as by initiating the computer processes leading to the transfer from the drawer's account to that of the payee, it will be considered to have paid and will not be entitled to reverse the process without the payee's consent.[50]

6.   THE BANKER–CUSTOMER RELATIONSHIP[51]

The nature of the contract between banker and customer in relation to the customer's account is complex, varying according to the particular banking function which is under consideration.[52]

(i)   Receipt of physical money

As regards money placed on deposit with the banker[53] the primary relationship is that of debtor and creditor. The banker receiving physical money (coins or notes) from or for the account of his customer does so as borrower, not as bailee or trustee.[54] A customer who pays physical money into his account transfers ownership of it to the bank, which is free to use the money for its own purpose and to retain for its own benefit any income from it or accumulation to it. The bank has no duty to hold the money as depository or to keep the money segregated from its other funds.

---

46 See s 49(13).
47 *Boyd v Emmerson* (1834) 2 Ad & El 184.
48 Bills of Exchange Act 1882, s 49(12)(a).
49 *Boyd v Emmerson*, n 46.
50 *Momm v Barclays Bank International Ltd* [1977] QB 790. In that case the payment instruction was by telex, but the same principle would seem to apply to any in-house transfer, whatever the medium of the payment instruction. The situation in *Momm* is not to be equated with a provisional credit to the payee's account of a cheque going through the clearing, for this is mere accounting as between bank and payee and does not involve a debit to the account of the drawer, whose branch will not even know of the issue of the cheque until it has been presented.
51 See generally E. P. Ellinger, E. Lomnicka and Richard Hooley, *Modern Banking Law* (3rd edn, 2002), ch 4; *Paget's Law of Banking* (12th edn, 2002), ch 10.
52 In particular, whether the bank is acting as collecting bank or as paying bank.
53 Whether a deposit or current account.
54 *Foley v Hill* (1848) 2 HL Cas 28; *Joachimson v Swiss Bank Corporation* [1921] 3 KB 110.

It is simply a borrower, with a duty to repay in accordance with the terms of the contract. In this sense, it is misleading to speak of physical money being placed or held 'on deposit' with a bank, for this suggests a deposit of monies by way of bailment in the same way as the deposit of furniture in a store or warehouse, whereas the bank's duty is not to return the coins or notes deposited with it, nor even to account for a money fund, but simply to repay its debt with any stipulated interest.[55]

(ii)   Receipt or collection of 'bank' money

Where a bank collects a cheque for a customer, it is commonly said that the bank receives or collects 'money' or 'funds' for its customer, which it then borrows back. But what precisely does the collecting bank collect? It will be recalled that payment of a cheque is preceded by a transfer of funds from the paying bank to the collecting bank through a net net settlement effected by transfers in the books of the Bank of England.[56] Payment of the cheque results in this transfer becoming final in the sense that the collecting bank is entitled as against the paying bank to retain what it has collected. So at the end of the day what the collecting bank acquires is a claim on the Bank of England, and it is when the transfer that gives rise to this claim becomes final that the collecting bank in turn accepts a commitment to the customer for whom it collected the cheque.

This leads us to the question of the relationship between what the collecting bank receives and what its customer acquires. It is clear that, except to the extent that it has already given its customer value for the cheque in advance, the collecting bank collects as agent for its customer[57] in that it does so on his instructions and for his benefit. But we must not fall into the trap of supposing that the collecting bank's claim on the Bank of England or a common correspondent bank of the paying and collecting bank[58] is held on trust for its customer. The sole legal and beneficial owner of that claim is the collecting bank itself. The effect of its acquiring the claim on the Bank of England is that it becomes contractually committed to crediting its customer's account unconditionally with an equivalent amount. It is only in this sense that the sum credited to the account can be considered as the fruits of the cheque. Thus the debtor–creditor relationship applies to collections for the customer as it does to sums paid into the account by the customer himself. The collecting bank's status as agent for collection is one that leaves it free to treat the actual proceeds of the cheque as its own, with a personal obligation to credit its customer with an equivalent amount.[59]

(iii) Repayment by the customer

Repayment must be made in accordance with the terms of the contract, and it is here that the special incidents of a banking contract become superimposed on the

---

55 For the distinction between a right to payment of a debt and an interest in a money fund, see p 61.

56 See p 535. In the net settlement the collecting bank may be a debtor rather than a creditor.

57 See further p 542.

58 See p 408.

59 Assuming, of course, that the customer is the person entitled.

ordinary debtor–creditor relationship. Thus whereas in general it is the duty of the debtor to seek out his creditor without prior demand for payment and pay him where he may be found,[60] it is an implied term of the banker–customer contract that sums deposited shall be repayable only on demand during banking hours at the branch where the account is kept.[61] In the case of money on current account, the customer's demand is usually signified by the drawing of a cheque in favour of himself [62] or a third party. The cheque can be drawn only on the branch at which the customer keeps his account[63] and if that account is not sufficiently in funds and the branch has not agreed an overdraft facility to cover it, the branch is entitled to refuse payment of the cheque even if the customer has adequate funds with another branch.[64]

(iv) Payment of cheques drawn by the customer

In paying cheques the bank acts as its customer's agent, and it must not only comply with the literal terms of the mandate[65] by ensuring that the cheque is drawn by an authorized signatory, but also exercise reasonable care to see that it is not privy to improper payment.[66] If the payment is in conformity with the mandate, then in making it the bank is simultaneously reducing its indebtedness to its customer. If the payment is not in accordance with the mandate, then the bank cannot in general debit the customer's account, for it has acted without authority.[67] If the payment accords with the language of the mandate but was in fraud of the customer or otherwise improper, so that the customer suffers loss, then if the bank had notice of the facts,[68] it is liable in damages for breach of contract in failing to perform its duty as agent with reasonable care and skill, and may also incur a liability in equity to account as constructive trustee for the money improperly transferred.[69]

In view of the responsibilities undertaken by banks when operating accounts for their customers, it is indeed remarkable that they have traditionally not required any formal agreement regulating the terms of business but rely entirely on terms implied from bank custom and practice and from the course of dealing established with the customer.[70]

---

60 *Walton v Mascall* (1844) 13 M & W 452, per Parke B at 458.

61 *Joachimson v Swiss Bank Corporation*, n 54. Hence until demand, time does not start running against the customer under the Limitation Act.

62 Either by name or, more usually, payable to 'cash'. This is not strictly a cheque, there being no named payee, but is accepted as an instruction to the bank to make payment to the drawer over the counter.

63 *Joachimson v Swiss Bank Corporation*, n 54.

64 *Woodland v Fear* [1857] 7 E & B 519; *Clare & Co v Dresdner Bank* [1915] 2 KB 576.

65 By 'mandate' is meant the customer's instructions to his bank as to the manner in which his account is to be operated, and in particular the names of those who are to be entitled to sign cheques where the account is in joint names or is in the name of a firm, company or society.

66 See pp 559 ff.

67 See p 555, as to the rule and the exceptions to it. For the bank's liability to its customer for wrongful dishonour of the customer's cheque, see p 561.

68 As to what constitutes notice, see p 561.

69 *Selangor United Rubber Estates Ltd v Cradock (No 3)* [1968] 2 All ER 1073; *Rowlandson v National Westminster Bank Ltd* [1978] 1 WLR 798; and see p 560.

70 This has been a feature peculiar to British banking. However, it is becoming more common for banks to reduce the terms of their agreement with the customer to writing.

7.   THE COLLECTING BANK

Receipt of a cheque for collection imposes a range of obligations on the collecting bank[71] and sets up a series of duty relationships between it and others, qualified by certain statutory defences. As a prelude to a consideration of these it is necessary to distinguish the different capacities in which a bank may receive and present a cheque and collect the proceeds. For this purpose it is necessary to differentiate between the handling of the cheque and the receipt and application of the funds. A cheque is a documentary intangible and as such may be the subject of possessory actions in tort, eg for conversion. Money, on the other hand, is not deliverable *in specie* and the remedy of a third party claiming a right to the proceeds of a cheque improperly applied is not an action for conversion of the proceeds but a claim for money had and received or, in given conditions, a proprietary claim in equity based on unjust enrichment.[72]

It is worth taking a moment to consider exactly what we mean when we say that a bank 'receives' the proceeds of a cheque. We have seen that a transfer of value takes place between clearing banks before the cheque is actually presented at the drawer's branch, but at this stage there is no payment by the drawer and no receipt by the payee, so that the transfer is purely internal to the banks. It is only when the cheque is honoured that the value received in advance by the collecting bank can be treated as received from the drawer by the collecting bank so as to be available to the payee.

(i)   The capacity in which the collecting bank acts

I.   *The cheque*

We have previously seen that most cheques are collected through the clearing system and not by the holder personally. The holder will give the cheque to his bank to clear for him, or, if he has no bank account, may ask a friend who has to arrange for clearance by the friend's bank. In both cases the bank receives the cheque as agent of its customer[73] for the purpose of collecting it on the customer's behalf. But the bank may also acquire cheques in its own right, by discounting them (ie by buying them at a discount) or by lending on the security of them. In these cases the bank receives the cheques as a purchaser for value[74] and will collect them on its own behalf. Even where the bank initially receives a cheque as agent for collection,[75] it may acquire an interest of its own by giving

---

71 The collecting bank may also, of course, be the paying bank, as where the drawer of the cheque is a customer of the same bank as the payee. The bank then possesses rights and incurs duties in both capacities.

72 See pp 458 ff. Appropriation of a bank balance belonging to another may also constitute theft under s 15A of the Theft Act 1968.

73 In the sense described p 540.

74 Acquiring an absolute interest if buying outright or the interest of a pledgee or mortgagee if taking the cheque as security.

75 It may do this not only for its customers but also for other banks. Thus the clearing banks act as agents for collection of cheques sent to them by non-clearers.

value for the cheque, eg by allowing its customer to draw against it.[76] In such a case the bank will collect the cheque for its own account to the extent of the value so given.[77]

What consequences flow from the distinction between collection as agent and collection as principal? If the bank collects as agent and the cheque was forged or otherwise irregular, then though the bank may incur a personal liability in tort for conversion[78] it will have a right of indemnity against its customer. The end result is, however, much the same where the bank collects as principal, for it will almost invariably have a right of recourse against its customer or other prior parties. The real point is that a bank collecting solely as agent is not as such a holder for value and, a fortiori, cannot qualify as a holder in due course. Any claim it makes on the cheque if dishonoured is thus liable to be defeated on the ground of want of consideration;[79] and since the bank does not itself acquire an overriding title as holder in due course, it follows that if it does not collect for the true owner it will incur liabilities to the true owner, subject to the statutory defences.[80] Conversely, a bank which collects a cheque on its own account without having credited a customer's account with it[81] does not qualify for the protection given by s 4(1) of the Cheques Act 1957[82] and, unless a holder in due course, will be exposed to a liability which as a collecting agent it might have avoided.[83]

2.   The proceeds

Though the collecting bank, if it has not given value to its customer in advance, collects a cheque as agent for its customer, it does not hold the proceeds on trust for the customer but merely incurs a commitment to credit the customer's account with an equivalent amount. The relationship is that of debtor–creditor, not of trustee–beneficiary.[84] If the bank was a holder in due course of the cheque, it will acquire an overriding title to the proceeds. Where it received the proceeds as agent for its customer and has paid them over[85] in good faith and without notice of the plaintiff's claim, the bank is not liable in an action for money had and received.[86] In other cases its immunity is dependent on the application of s 4(1) of the Cheques Act 1957.[87]

---

76 As to the different ways of giving value, see p 544.
77 So where this is not the full value of the cheque, the bank is simultaneously an agent for collection and a holder for value. See *Barclays Bank Ltd v Astley Industrial Trust Ltd* [1970] 2 QB 527, in which Milmo J rejected the contention that the two capacities were mutually exclusive.
78 See p 548.
79 See p 493.
80 See p 549.
81 This could occur in various ways, eg upon the bank discounting the cheque for the holder.
82 See p 549.
83 See p 552.
84 See p 539.
85 By allowing drawings on the account by the customer, whether in favour of himself or a third party.
86 *Buller v Harrison* (1777) 2 Cowp 565, per Lord Mansfield at 568.
87 See p 549.

(ii) Value

We have seen that it may be important for a collecting bank to establish its status as a holder for value, first because as a holder not for value its claim can be met by a plea of want of consideration, and secondly because if it is not a holder for value, it cannot be a holder in due course so as to acquire an overriding title, and may thus become exposed to a claim by the true owner if the cheque has been improperly dealt with.

What, then, constitutes value for this purpose? Let us start with the common case where, in accordance with normal banking practice, the cheque is credited to the customer's account before clearance, on the basis that it will be debited back if it is dishonoured. In the celebrated decision of the House of Lords in *Capital and Counties Bank Limited v Gordon*[88] it was held that by the mere act of crediting the account the collecting bank became a holder for value collecting on its own behalf and was thus not entitled to the protection then conferred by s 82 of the Bills of Exchange Act on a banker collecting cheques for a customer. The particular effect of the decision was later reversed by legislation,[89] but without altering the principle that the act of crediting the account constitutes the bank a holder for value. However, in a series of subsequent decisions[90] it has been denied that *Gordon's* case laid down any rule that the mere crediting of an account without more constitutes the giving of value, and the case has been explained as turning on the additional fact that by prior arrangement the customer was permitted to draw against the uncleared cheque.

Whatever the merits of this interpretation, it must now be taken as established that the collecting bank does not become a holder for value merely by crediting the cheque to its customer's account before clearance. This is plainly right, for, as we have seen, even an unconditional credit to the customer's account is not payment *by the bank*, merely an acknowledgement of its indebtedness to the customer.[91] Moreover, such a conclusion is much more compatible with the common understanding of the parties than the principle supposedly enunciated in *Gordon's* case. The point is that in ordinary parlance giving value for a cheque involves either buying it or lending on the security of it, and both these acts entail a conscious decision on the part of the bank as buyer/lender and the customer as

---

88   [1903] AC 240.

89   Bills of Exchange (Crossed Cheques) Act 1906, which provided that the protection conferred by s 82 was not lost merely because the collecting bank had credited the cheque to its customer's account. However, this Act having been repealed and replaced by s 4 of the Cheques Act 1957, the present position is again unclear. See p 552.

90   See, for example, *Re Farrow's Bank Ltd*, n 41; *A. L. Underwood Ltd v Barclays Bank Ltd* [1924] 1 KB 775; *Westminster Bank Ltd v Zang* [1966] AC 182; *Fern v Bishop Burns & Co Ltd* [1980] L S Gaz R 1181 (in which Connor J held that, in the absence of a contract between banker and customer entitling the latter to draw against uncleared cheques, the bank was not a holder for value and owed no money to the customer in respect of the uncleared cheque, so that the sum provisionally credited in respect of this was not susceptible to a garnishee order in favour of a judgment creditor of the customer). But see *Sutters v Briggs* [1922] 1 AC 1, and the discussion of the cases in *Paget's Law of Banking*, pp 505 ff. and Chorley & Smart, *Leading Cases in the Law of Banking* (5th edn, 1983), pp 156 ff.

91   See p 462.

seller/borrower. The bank cannot, by the unilateral act of crediting the customer's account, deprive its customer of his property in the cheque by treating him as having sold it. Equally, the customer cannot treat the credit as indicative of a conscious act of purchase by the bank, for the credit is prima facie merely an accounting convenience, a provisional credit which will be adjusted by debit back if the cheque is not met.

On the other hand, it is clear that if the collecting bank gives cash for the cheque, this constitutes value, and the same applies where the customer draws against the uncleared cheque pursuant to a prior or contemporaneous agreement with the bank that he may do so. But such an agreement must be established by evidence, either as an express agreement or as one implied from, eg a course of dealing between banker and customer. It is not to be inferred merely from the crediting of the cheque itself as uncleared effects.[92]

What is the position if, after the cheque has been credited but before it is cleared, the customer is allowed to draw on his account even though there has been no prior arrangement with the bank to do so? If the account was sufficiently in credit to cover the drawing without taking account of the cheque, then clearly the drawing does not constitute value, for under the rule in *Clayton's* case the customer must be taken to have utilized his existing credit balance, not the sum credited as the amount of the cheque. Even where this is not the case – eg because the account was already overdrawn at the time the cheque was credited – it does not follow that the further advance on current account is to be taken as the price of the cheque, for the bank may have been willing to allow for the further drawing in any event, and, indeed, may have given its customer an overdraft facility covering it. In short, there must be a nexus between the cheque and the drawing. It must be shown that the bank intended to collect the cheque on its own behalf as the price of the drawing, ie that (whether by prior arrangement or otherwise) it allowed a further drawing on the strength of the cheque and would or might[93] have refused to allow such drawing if the cheque had not been given.

The principle stated above applies not only where at the time of payment into the account the account is in credit but also where the uncleared cheque is credited to an account which is overdrawn.[94] However, s 27(3) of the Bills of Exchange Act provides that where the holder of a bill has a lien on it arising either from contract or by implication of law, he is deemed to be a holder for value to the extent of the sum for which he has a lien. Since a banker has a lien on uncleared effects to secure the amount of an existing overdraft,[95] he is a holder for value to such amount, and

---

92 *Westminster Bank Ltd v Zang*, n 90.

93 In *Westminster Bank Ltd v Zang*, ibid, Viscount Dilhorne commented that no evidence had been given that further cheques drawn 'would have been dishonoured' but for the cheque credited to the account or that such cheques 'were only honoured in consequence of the uncleared effects'. It is submitted that this dictum is not to be taken too literally. A bank might well allow further dealings on the strength of uncleared effects without necessarily taking the position that it would not have allowed them otherwise. It may simply be that the uncleared effects have made its decision easier.

94 As in *Westminster Bank Ltd v Zang*, n 90.

95 *Re Keever* [1967] Ch 182; *Barclays Bank Ltd v Astley Industrial Trust Ltd*, n 77.

this is so even though he is also the customer's agent for collection.[96] But the banker loses his lien if he returns the cheque to his customer, even if he thereafter gets it back again, and in such a case he loses his status as a holder for value.[97]

(iii) Duties of the collecting banker

The collecting banker, whether collecting for its own customer or as agent for another bank,[98] owes duties to its own customer, to the paying banker and to the true owner of the cheque it collects. These duties, described below, are subject to various defences provided by statute.[99]

1.   Duty to its customer

The collecting banker owes a duty to its customer to collect promptly and diligently all items which are the lawful property of the customer, whether payable to the customer himself or to a third party who has indorsed them to the customer.[100] The holder of a cheque is himself obliged to present it for payment within a reasonable time of issue or indorsement to him in order to be sure of his entitlement to recovery from the issuer or indorser, [101] and in deciding what is reasonable the court would undoubtedly have regard to all reasonable rules of practice of the clearing system.[102]

If the cheque is dishonoured on presentation, the collecting banker must, within the time prescribed by the Act,[103] give notice of dishonour either to the parties liable on the instrument[104] or to its customer,[105] leaving it to the latter to give notice of dishonour to the parties liable. In practice, notice of dishonour of a cheque is rarely

---

96   *Barclays Bank Ltd v Astley Industrial Trust Ltd*, n 77. In general, the bank will be a holder in due course as to this amount but a mere holder as to the balance. The effect is that the bank can sue for recovery of the full face value of the instrument but as regards the amount by which this exceeds the overdraft, it is liable to be met with defences available against a holder who has not given value. See p 544.

97   *Westminster Bank Ltd v Zang* [1965] 1 All ER 1023. This aspect of the Court of Appeal's decision did not feature in the appeal to the House of Lords, [1966] AC 182, which affirmed the decision on the other issues.

98   As in *Honourable Society of the Middle Temple v Lloyds Bank plc* [1999] 1 All ER (Comm) 193. But the degree of care required is lower than that of the correspondent bank for whom the cheque is collected, since the collecting bank does not vet and cannot be expected to know the identity of the correspondent bank's customer and in general is entitled to assume that the correspondent bank will have carried out the appropriate scrutiny. There may, however, be factors which put the collecting bank on enquiry (ibid). The same considerations apply whether the collection is for a domestic non-clearing bank, a foreign bank or a non-bank institution such as a building society.

99   See p 549.

100   This may occur either because the third party is transferring the cheque as part payment of a debt owed by him to the customer or because the third party has no bank account himself and wishes the customer to arrange for collection of the cheque.

101   Bills of Exchange Act, s 74.

102   Under ss 45(2) and 74(2), in determining what is a reasonable time for presentation of a bill or cheque, regard must be had to the usage of trade and of bankers.

103   Section 49(12). See p 512.

104   Ie, the drawer and any indorser. Notice must be given to all parties whom it is sought to hold liable.

105   Section 49(13).

required, since non-payment is almost invariably due either to countermand of payment by the drawer or to the fact that through insufficiency of funds his bank owes no duty to him to honour the cheque, and each of these factors excuses notice of dishonour.[106]

2.   Duty to the paying banker

If the collecting banker receives payment of a forged cheque, then on discovering the forgery the paying bank is in principle entitled to recover the payment as made under a mistake of fact.[107] To this rule there are two qualifications. The paying bank may be estopped from recovering the payment where the forgery was detectable or the bank should otherwise have been put on inquiry or where it is to be taken to have represented the cheque as genuine.[108] It will also be unable to recover if the collecting bank collected as agent and has paid out the money to its principal before receiving notice of the forgery.[109] This is merely a particular application of a general rule of agency law.[110]

The payee has been held liable for repayment where the paying bank, in making the payment, overlooked a prior instruction from its customer to stop the cheque.[111] If this decision is correct,[112] the collecting bank would appear to be exposed to a similar liability, subject to the same estoppel and agency defences as mentioned above in relation to forgery.

The paying bank will also in certain cases have a proprietary claim to the proceeds received by the collecting bank, as where these represent the proceeds of a cheque paid under a mistake of fact, such as a mistaken double payment in discharge of the same debt.[113]

3.   Duty to the true owner of the cheque

The collecting bank's main risk of liability arises from the collection of a cheque for the wrong party, usually because the drawer's signature has been forged or because the signatory is an agent or employee who signed without authority or, though being authorized to sign, drew the cheque for his own benefit in fraud of his principal or employer. A bank which receives a cheque for collection from a party having no title to it is by the very act of receipt[114] liable in conversion to the person then entitled to possession of the cheque.[115] In presenting the cheque for payment

---

106   Section 50(2)(c).
107   *National Westminster Bank Ltd v Barclays Bank International Ltd* [1975] QB 654.
108   Ibid.
109   *Buller v Harrison*, n 86; *Gowers v Lloyds and National Provincial Foreign Bank Ltd* [1938] 1 All ER 766.
110   See *Bowstead and Reynolds on Agency* (17th edn, 2001), art 113.
111   *Barclays Bank Ltd v W. J. Simms, Son & Cooke (Southern) Ltd* [1980] QB 677.
112   See p 564.
113   See p 564.
114   At any rate if the cheque is taken with intent to collect it or otherwise deal with it in a manner which (whether or not known to the bank) is inconsistent with the plaintiff's right to possess. See *Fine Art Society v Union Bank of London Ltd* (1886) 17 QBD 705.
115   See below.

the collecting bank commits a further act of conversion;[116] and having collected the cheque, it exposes itself to an alternative claim for money had and received, for the plaintiff has the option of waiving the tort of conversion and suing instead in unjust enrichment for the proceeds of the property converted.[117] The position is otherwise, of course, where the collecting bank itself acquires an overriding title as a holder in due course.

At common law, the exercise of reasonable care by the collecting bank is no defence to a claim in conversion, for which there is strict liability; and to ameliorate the problem confronting collecting banks a measure of protection was conferred by s 82 of the Bills of Exchange Act 1882, subsequently repealed by the Cheques Act 1957[118] and replaced by s 4 of that Act. This protection was enhanced by the provisions of the Banking Act 1979 enabling banks to plead contributory negligence as a defence.[119]

The person entitled to maintain conversion against the collecting bank is he who at the time of receipt of the cheque by the bank had the best right to possession of it. This would seem to be the same as the 'true owner' referred to in the statutory provisions above mentioned. If the cheque was not indorsed, then prima facie the payee is the person with the title to sue, and this would appear to be the case even if the payee's title to the cheque was voidable,[120] unless avoided by the drawer prior to the cheque coming into the hands of the collecting bank.[121] If the cheque was stolen or otherwise appropriated en route to the payee, the question turns on whether the post office or other carrier received the cheque as agent of the payee on the one hand or of the drawer on the other. In the latter case it remains the property of the drawer, who is the person entitled to sue. Where the cheque has been indorsed, the statements made above in relation to the payee apply with equal force to the last indorsee lawfully[122] in possession prior to the conversion.

Almost invariably, the person with the best right to possession of the cheque will also be the one who has best right to the proceeds of the cheque, and will thus be the party entitled to maintain an action for money had and received if the proceeds are misapplied. In collecting a cheque, the collecting bank acts as agent of the payee or other person entitled to the proceeds and if, after receiving these, the collecting bank pays or credits them to the wrong party in circumstances where the bank cannot invoke the statutory provisions,[123] the right of action is vested in that person, not in the drawer.

---

116 *Fine Art Society v Union Bank of London Ltd*, n 114; *A. L. Underwood Ltd v Barclays Bank Ltd*, n 90; *Lloyds Bank Ltd v Chartered Bank of India, Australia and China* [1929] 1 KB 40.

117 *Bavins Jnr & Sims v London & South Western Bank* [1900] 1 QB 270.

118 Section 6(3) and Schedule.

119 Section 47. Ordinarily, contributory negligence is no defence to a claim for conversion (Torts (Interference with Goods) Act 1977, s 11(1)).

120 Eg, because it was obtained by fraud or misrepresentation. The position is otherwise if the payee's title was totally void.

121 In which case title revests in the drawer.

122 As opposed, for example, to the thief of a cheque indorsed in blank.

123 See below.

(iv) Statutory protection of the collecting banker

Section 4(1) of the Cheques Act 1957[124] provides as follows:

Where a banker, in good faith and without negligence,

(a) receives payment for a customer of an instrument to which this section applies;[125] or

(b) having credited a customer's account with the amount of such an instrument, receives payment thereof for himself;

and the customer has no title, or a defective title, to the instrument, the banker does not incur any liability to the true owner of the instrument by reason only of having received payment thereof.

Further, by subs.3:

A banker is not to be treated for the purposes of this section as having been negligent by reason only of his failure to concern himself with absence of, or irregularity in, indorsement of an instrument.

The fact that cheques marked 'account payee' or 'account payee only' are non-transferable[126] does not deprive the collecting bank of these defences where it exercises reasonable care in collecting for a person other than the payee, nor in general does it appear to render the duty of care more onerous than before the change of law effected by the Cheques Act 1992 in making cheques so marked non-transferable.[127] However, a bank collecting a cheque for a foreign bank does have a duty to inform that bank of the effect of the 1992 Act so that the foreign bank can satisfy its obligation to 'know its customer', given that the collecting bank cannot be expected to have this knowledge.[128]

1. 'Banker'

The protection conferred by the statute is confined to bankers.[129]

2. Good faith

This indicates honesty in fact,[130] a requirement which may be satisfied even where there is negligence.[131] But want of negligence is made a separate condition of immunity.

3. Absence of negligence[132]

Only a banker who has acted without negligence in receiving payment[133] qualifies for full protection, though it is now open to the bank to plead contributory

---

124 Re-enacting with amendments 82 of the Bills of Exchange Act 1882. Section 4(2), which defines the instruments to which the section applies, has been extended to cover cheques which under s 81A(1) of the Bills of Exchange Act 1882 or otherwise are not transferable. These include cheques marked 'account payee'.

125 Including cheques and bankers' drafts. See s 4(2).

126 Bills of Exchange Act 1882, s 81A(1).

127 See *Honourable Society of the Middle Temple v Lloyds Bank Plc* [1999] 1 All ER (Comm) 193.

128 Ibid.

129 See n 1.

130 Bills of Exchange Act, s 90.

131 Ibid.

132 See generally *Paget's Law of Banking*, pp 508 ff.

133 As to what is comprehended by the phrase 'receiving payment', see below.

negligence as a defence,[134] contrary to the usual rule in actions for conversion.[135] As pointed out in a leading work,[136] the reference to negligence in the section imports by implication a duty of care which the collecting banker would ordinarily owe not to the true owner as such but merely to the banker's own customer.

There is a considerable amount of case law dealing with the standard of care which the collecting banker is required to exercise. In general, what is expected of him is not a microscopic examination of an account but the ordinary prudence required of those carrying on a banking business in accordance with normal and proper[137] banking practice.[138] Yet it cannot be denied that over time the attitude of the courts has become increasingly stringent, and there are at least some cases[139] where a bank has been held liable for failing to meet a standard of care which in the view of many bankers is simply impracticable in the light of the huge volume of cheque business conducted.

Those cases in which the collecting banker has been denied the benefit of the statutory provisions by reason of his negligence fall broadly into two groups: failure to exercise reasonable care when opening the account for the person for whom the cheque is later collected; and failure, when collecting the cheque, to take reasonable steps to satisfy himself that the customer was lawfully in possession of the cheque and entitled to receive payment of it.

A person who has improperly obtained possession of a cheque may open the account purely for the purpose of collecting payment and then disappear. Alternatively, the account may be opened with a view to subsequent payment into it of a cheque to which the customer is not entitled. It thus behoves the banker to satisfy himself by reasonable inquiry that the new customer is a fit person to hold the account. For a customer not already known to the bank, this entails obtaining, and taking reasonable steps to verify, details of the customer's address, employment or occupation and similar data, and, as a rule, the taking up of references.[140]

Where the banker is asked to collect the cheque, his overriding concern must be to ensure that the customer is the person entitled to receive payment. If the customer is neither the payee nor the indorsee, that in itself is a fact calling for inquiry and explanation. It may be that the customer has been asked to arrange collection for a third party who does not himself have a bank account; the banker's duty is to take reasonable steps to satisfy himself that the collection of the cheque for the customer was indeed authorized by the third party concerned. If, however, the explanation is satisfactory, he is absolved, even though it later transpires that the customer acted

---

134   Banking Act 1979, s 47.

135   Torts (Interference with Goods) Act 1977, s 11(1).

136   *Paget's Law of Banking*, p 509.

137   Even normal banking practice will not suffice if it is imprudent or otherwise improper.

138   See *Lloyds Bank Ltd v Chartered Bank of India, Australia and China*, n 116; *Orbit Mining & Trading Co Ltd v Westminster Bank Ltd* [1963] 1 QB 794.

139   Eg *Lloyds Bank Ltd v E. B. Savory & Co* [1933] AC 201. It is important to bear in mind that it is for the bank to show that it acted without negligence.

140   *Ladbroke & Co v Todd* (1914) 30 TLR 433. Anti-money-laundering checks are now also required.

fraudulently.[141] Where a cheque is being collected on behalf of a foreign bank, the collecting bank is entitled to assume that the foreign bank has carried out the necessary enquiries to satisfy itself of the identity of its customer, at any rate where the foreign bank has been informed of the effect of an 'account payee' crossing, since that is not something the collecting bank can be expected to know, but the collecting bank remains under an obligation to be alert to circumstances throwing suspicion on the right of the person for whom the cheque is being collected to receive payment of it.[142]

Since it is no longer necessary to indorse a cheque purely for collection,[143] the collecting banker has no duty to call for his customer's indorsement, nor to examine such an indorsement if made,[144] given that the customer is the ostensible payee or indorsee. On the other hand, the banker is still obliged to ensure that the cheque carries all indorsements necessary to establish its customer's title to the cheque. Accordingly, if the customer is not the original payee, the banker must examine the back of the cheque for the indorsements of the payee and of any intervening special indorsee.[145] But this is no longer the case where the cheque is marked 'account payee' or 'account payee only', for it is then non-transferable and the bank is not concerned with any purported indorsement.[146]

Even where the customer is the payee or indorsee, the circumstances may be such as to put the collecting bank on inquiry. The most common case is that of an employee who seeks to pay into his personal account a cheque drawn by his employers, or drawn in favour of his employers and apparently indorsed by them to him. Obviously, there is no problem if a cheque drawn in favour of an employee appears to be his ordinary monthly salary cheque or otherwise conforms to a normal pattern of payments established by the employer. But where there is an element which should put the banker on inquiry, he will not be able to rely on the statute if he fails to inquire. There are many cases in which a director of a company, authorized to sign cheques on its behalf, has fraudulently drawn or indorsed a cheque in his own favour or has otherwise misapplied a cheque intended for the company's own account.

Similar considerations arise where a cheque payable to a partnership firm is sought to be paid into the personal account of a partner or otherwise misappropriated by him;[147] where a cheque payable to the holder of a public office is directed to be paid to his own account;[148] where a cheque payable to a company is indorsed to a private individual and given by him to his bank to be collected for his account.[149]

---

141 *Importers Co Ltd v Westminster Bank Ltd* [1927] 2 KB 297.
142 *Honourable Society of the Middle Temple v Lloyds Bank Plc* [1999] 1 All ER (Comm) 193.
143 Cheques Act 1957, ss 1–3, 4(3).
144 But *semble* the position is otherwise where the cheque is indorsed at the bank's request (*Paget's Law of Banking*, p 398).
145 See the Committee of London Clearing Bankers' Circular dated 23 September 1957, approved on this point by Lord Denning MR in *Westminster Bank Ltd v Zang*, n 97. The Circular is reprinted in J Milnes Holden, *Law and Practice of Banking*, vol 1 (5th edn, 1991), p 522, and in *Questions on Banking Practice* (11th edn, 1978), Appendix C.
146 Bills of Exchange Act 1882, s 81A(1), added by the Cheques Act 1992, s 1.
147 *Baker v Barclays Bank Ltd* [1955] 2 All ER 571.
148 *Ross v London County, Westminster & Parr's Bank Ltd* [1919] 1 KB 678.
149 *A. L. Underwood Ltd v Barclays Bank Ltd*, n 90; *Marfani & Co Ltd v Midland Bank Ltd* [1968] 2 All ER 573.

In all these cases the collecting banker should make proper inquiry; but if the manner in which the account has been conducted by the employer or other principal is such as to lead the bank reasonably to suppose its customer is acting within the scope of his authority, it may be justified in refraining from inquiry, or may be able to contend that the principal is estopped from disputing the authority of the agent or employee to pay the cheque into his account.[150] Relevant features are the amount of the cheque, the status of the agent or employee and the degree of authority normally possessed by one in his position, as well as the measure of authority habitually accorded to him by his principal or employer.[151]

4.   'Receives payment for a customer'

By 'a customer' is meant a person for whom the banker has opened an account.[152] It does not matter how recently the account has been opened, and the existence of the account establishes the banker–customer relationship even if the first and only transaction on the account is the collection of the cheque in question. The statutory protection does not apply where the bank collects the cheque for one who is not a customer.[153] For this purpose, a non-clearing bank which maintains an account with a clearing bank through which it collects its cheques is as much a customer as any other account holder.[154]

5.   'Receives payment thereof for himself'

As an alternative to receiving payment for a customer, the banker may rely on the section if, having credited the customer's account with the amount of the cheque, he receives payment for himself. The effect of this limb of s 4(1) is unclear. In so far as it suggests that a banker ceases to be an agent for collection and becomes a holder for value by the mere crediting of his customer's account, it is against the weight of prior authority[155] and it seems unlikely that the subsection was intended to change the law in this respect. If this be so, it remains a question of fact whether the banker has given value so as to be collecting on his own account, and, as we have seen,[156] the universal practice of crediting uncleared effects does not produce this result. What is plain is that if the banker gives value in circumstances where he does not credit the customer's account, he will be unable to invoke the section, which is intended to apply only to cases where the banker deals with the cheque in a banker–customer relationship.

150   *Australia and New Zealand Bank Ltd v Ateliers de Constructions Electriques de Charleroi* [1967] 1 AC 86; *West v Commercial Bank of Australia Ltd* (1936) 55 CLR 315.
151   See cases cited n 150.
152   *Great Western Rly Co Ltd v London & County Banking Co Ltd* [1901] AC 414; *Taxation Commissioners v English, Scottish & Australian Bank* [1920] AC 683. Probably an agreement to open an account suffices (Chorley, *Law of Banking* (6th edn, 1974), pp 3, 120; Ellinger, Lomnicka and Hooley, *Modern Banking Law*, p 90).
153   In practice, banks do not usually collect cheques for non-customers, though not infrequently they will collect for a customer a cheque given to him for collection by a friend or other third party named as payee who has no bank account of his own. In such a case the collecting bank will require the cheque to be indorsed by the payee.
154   *Importers Co Ltd v Westminster Bank Ltd*, n 141.
155   See p 544.
156   See p 545.

Where the above conditions are satisfied, and the customer has no title, or a defective title, to the cheque, the banker does not incur any liability to the true owner[157] of the instrument by reason only of having received payment thereof.[158] The phrase 'having received payment thereof' has been held to embrace by necessary implication any steps taken in the ordinary course of business and intended to lead up to receipt of the proceeds,[159] and thus covers the handling of the cheque itself. The section therefore protects the bank not only from claims for money had and received but also from claims for conversion of the cheque. Equally it must, it is submitted, extend to retention of the proceeds after their initial receipt and so long as good faith and absence of negligence continue. But s 4 does not by itself give the bank title to the proceeds. It merely enables the bank to receive and retain the proceeds without on that account becoming liable to the true owner, and thus clears the way for the bank to perfect its own title by giving value after their receipt, if it has not done so before, and to the extent of the value so given.[160] But in so far as the bank has not given value at the time it receives notice of the true owner's claim, it must account to him for the amount in question and on failure to do so will be liable in an action for money had and received.

8. THE PAYING BANK

The paying bank owes a duty, first, to its customer as drawer, to comply with the terms of the customer's mandate[161] and to exercise reasonable care and skill in dealing with the customer's affairs; secondly, to the payee or other true owner of a cheque, to make payment to him (or in the case of a crossed cheque, to a collecting bank on his behalf) and not to an unauthorized third party; thirdly, to a person having a superior title to monies standing to the credit of the customer's account, to respect such title.

(i) Duty to the customer to observe the mandate

The nature of the banker–customer relationship and the duties of the banker to his customer have been briefly described earlier in this chapter.[162] Central to the relationship between the parties is the mandate given by the customer to the bank. Money kept on interest-bearing deposit is withdrawable upon a specified period of notice.[163] Sums which the customer requires to be able to withdraw or utilize at will are kept on current account, and the usual method by which the customer conveys

157 This appears to be the same as the person who at common law is entitled to maintain an action for conversion of the cheque or for money had and received in respect of the proceeds.

158 Cheques Act 1957, s 4.

159 *Capital and Counties Bank Ltd v Gordon*, n 88.

160 Such value is to be measured by the amount the customer is allowed to draw on his account after exhausting any credit balance existing at the time the proceeds were credited to the account. This follows from the rule in *Clayton's* case.

161 See p 546, and below.

162 See pp 539, 546.

163 Varying with the interest rate allowed. In practice, banks allow withdrawal on shorter notice against loss of interest.

to his bank a direction to make payment, whether to himself or to a third party, is by the drawing of a cheque on his account. The bank's duty to observe the customer's mandate in regard to the payment of cheques is subsumed under four broad heads.

1.   Honouring the customer's cheques

The paying bank owes a duty to its customer[164] to honour his cheques if properly drawn upon an account in credit or within an agreed overdraft facility and duly presented by the holder. Breach of this duty renders the bank liable in damages to its customer for breach of contract. Such damages may include compensation for injury to the drawer's credit resulting from the wrongful dishonour of his cheque, which are recoverable without the need to prove special damage and in addition to any special damage that may have been suffered. This rule was formerly thought to be confined to traders but has more recently been held by the Court of Appeal to be equally applicable to non-traders.[165] Where the terms on which payment is refused are such as to reflect adversely on the customer's reputation, the customer has an alternative claim for damages for libel. In either case the quantum of damages will, of course, depend on the circumstances, including the plaintiff's general standing and the size of the cheque.[166]

Not all statements of reason for non-payment are defamatory. For example, 'confirmation required', 'words and figures differ', 'indorsement irregular' would not be libellous. 'No account' clearly would be and, despite earlier cases to the contrary,[167] it is thought that 'refer to drawer' or 'R. D.' would likewise be defamatory, since almost invariably these words denote either a countermand of payment or an insufficiency of funds.[168]

2.   Observing a countermand of payment

Just as the bank must honour its customer's cheque when it has no lawful reason to return it, so also it must refuse payment where the customer has given instructions to stop payment and these reach the bank[169] in sufficient time.[170] The bank is, however, entitled to satisfy itself first that the instructions mean what they appear to mean and come from the customer or someone authorized by him. Thus the bank is

---

164 But not to the holder, for the bank does not accept the cheque and thus does not engage itself to the holder to pay the cheque on presentment.

165 *Kpohraror v Woolwich Building Society* [1996] 4 All ER 119. For a critical comment on the case see Nelson Enonchong, 'Contract Damages for Wrongful Dishonour of a Cheque' (1997) 60 MLR 412.

166 Prima facie, the smaller the cheque, the greater the libel.

167 See, for example, *Flach v London and South Western Bank Ltd* (1915) 31 TLR 334.

168 See *Pyke v Hibernian Bank Ltd* [1950] IR 195; *Jayson v Midland Bank Ltd* [1968] 1 Lloyd's Rep 409.

169 The bank must actually receive instructions countermanding payment. The mere dispatch of such instructions through the post is not sufficient. There is no doctrine of 'constructive countermand' (*Curtice v London, City & Midland Bank Ltd* [1908] 1 KB 293, per Cozens-Hardy MR at 298). Moreover, the countermand must be given to the branch on which the cheque is drawn (*London, Provincial and South Western Bank Ltd v Buszard* (1918) 35 TLR 142).

170 Ie before the bank has either paid the cheque or committed itself to pay in a manner consistent with its mandate. See p 537.

not as a matter of law obliged to act on a countermand by unconfirmed telegram, though it may be thereby put on inquiry and thus be expected to utilize the period allowed for giving notice of dishonour[171] to make inquiry of its customer, paying the cheque if before the end of that period it has not received satisfactory confirmation of the instructions. The customer cannot countermand payment if the cheque has come into the hands of a holder in due course or is covered by a cheque card.

A bank which pays a cheque after payment has been countermanded acts in breach of its mandate and is prima facie precluded from debiting its customer's account.[172] But where the payment is effective to discharge an indebtedness of the customer to the payee, then in principle the bank should be entitled to claim subrogation to the payee's rights against the customer and thus to maintain the debit to the customer's account despite the breach of mandate.[173]

3. Paying only against a genuine and authorized signature

In principle, the paying banker's duty to honour his mandate is, like any other contractual duty, a strict one, and where the terms of the mandate are broken, the exercise of reasonable care is no defence. Thus at common law a banker paying out on a forged signature is not entitled to debit his customer's account, however skilful the forgery.[174] As we shall see, such a rule has been modified by statute in the case of forged indorsements.[175]

Similarly, if the customer is other than a single individual (eg is a company, a partnership or other unincorporated body or two or more individuals opening a joint account), the bank must honour cheques drawn only by an authorized signatory, and where the mandate requires two or more signatures, both or all of the signatures so required must appear. However, the customer will in certain conditions be estopped from disputing the genuineness of the signature or the authority of the signatory.[176]

(a) DRAWER'S SIGNATURE FORGED OR UNAUTHORIZED. The statutory provisions conferring protection on the paying banker who pays out against a forged or unauthorized *indorsement*[177] do not extend to cases where it is the drawer's

---

171 See p 511.
172 *Reade v Royal Bank of Ireland* [1922] 2 IR 22. Section 75 of the Bills of Exchange Act expressly provides that the bank's duty and authority to pay are determined by countermand of payment.
173 See p 563.
174 *London & River Plate Bank v Bank of Liverpool* [1896] 1 QB 7; *London Joint Stock Bank Ltd v Macmillan & Arthur* [1918] AC 777. This is not because of any supposed rule that a banker is expected to know his customer's signature but because a document on which the customer's signature as drawer is forged does not constitute his mandate (*National Westminster Bank Ltd v Barclays Bank International Ltd*, n 107, per Kerr J at 666). See also *Jackson v White & Midland Bank Ltd* [1967] 2 Lloyd's Rep 68, where the general principle was accepted but the bank was held entitled to maintain the debit to its customer's account as regards those payments which had effectively discharged the customer's legal liability to the payee.
175 See p 557. For a comparative treatment, see Benjamin Geva, 'Allocation of Forged Cheque Losses – Comparative Aspects, Policies and a Model for Reform' (1998) 114 LQR 250.
176 See below.
177 See below.

signature that has been forged or made without his authority. Indeed, the instrument is not then a cheque at all.[178] But the customer will be estopped from relying on the forgery in three cases. The first is where he draws a cheque in such a way as to facilitate forgery or fraud, as by drawing it in blank or leaving space which allows an alteration to the amount of the cheque.[179] The second is where he discovers that his signature is being forged and neglects to inform the bank.[180] The third is where the signatory has regularly been allowed by his principal or employer to draw cheques in a manner or for a purpose that would ordinarily be regarded as unusual or unauthorized.[181] However, the customer does not owe any wider duty, either in contract or in tort, to take precautions in the management of his business or the appointment or supervision of his staff to prevent forgery or fraud,[182] nor is he under a duty to check his bank statements, though if he does discover that he has been debited with cheques which he has not drawn or which exceed the amount for which he drew them, he must tell his bank promptly. This restrictive approach to the customer's liability is sound policy. If banks wish to impose a wider duty on their customers, they can readily do it by contract. If they decline to do so, or even to put warnings on the bank statements, for fear of losing business, this is all the more reason why they should not be allowed to plead an implied term or a duty in tort or to assert contributory negligence in a manner unrelated to the drawing of the cheque, the discovery of something wrong or the conferment of apparent authority.[183]

(b) FORGED OR UNAUTHORIZED INDORSEMENT. A cheque, like any other bill of exchange, can be transferred by indorsement and delivery; but since it is payable on demand there is obviously little point in discounting it, and except in those relatively infrequent cases where a cheque is indorsed by an agent to his principal or in part payment of a debt owed by the payee to the indorsee, cheques are in practice paid in by the payee himself and are not used as instruments of transfer. At one time the collecting bank would require its customer payee to indorse the cheque for

---

178   For the signature is wholly inoperative (Bills of Exchange Act, s 24), so that the document does not meet the requirements for a bill of exchange (s 3(1)). For a general discussion of the bank's position in the case of forgery, see Nicholas Rafferty, 'Forged Cheques: A Consideration of the Rights and Obligations of Banks and their Customers' (1980) 4 Can Bus L Rev 208.

179   *London Joint Stock Bank Ltd v Macmillan & Arthur*, n 174.

180   *Greenwood v Martins Bank Ltd* [1933] AC 51. Deliberately refraining from making enquiries is equated with actual knowledge, but constructive knowledge, in the sense of having the means to discover the forgery, is not a sufficient defence to the customer's claim (*Price Meats Ltd v Barclays Bank plc* [2002] 2 All ER (Comm) 346).

181   *London Intercontinental Trust Ltd v Barclays Bank Ltd* [1980] 1 Lloyd's Rep 241.

182   *Tai Hing Cotton Mill Ltd v Liu Cheong Hing Bank Ltd* [1986] AC 80.

183   An intermediate position was taken by the Review Committee on Banking Services Law (Jack Committee), which advocated a statutory provision by which a bank could plead contributory negligence where the degree of negligence was sufficiently serious for it to be inequitable to make the bank liable for the whole amount of the debt or damages (*Banking Services: Law and Practice* (Cm 622, 1989), rec 6(1)). In its White Paper on Banking Services Law and Practice (Cm 1026, 1990) the government was disposed to accept this view but deferred any decision pending the Law Commission's Report on contributory negligence, which in the event rejected the introduction of contributory negligence to a claim based on strict liability, such as honouring a cheque which the customer had not issued or authorized (*Contributory Negligence as a Defence in Contract* (Law Com No 219, 1993), paras 4.1, 5.20).

collection, so as to make the bank a holder and perfect its rights to present the cheque for payment. This tedious requirement had the added disadvantage of imposing on the collecting banker the duty to verify the indorsed signature. The main purpose of the Cheques Act 1957 is to remove the necessity for an indorsement except where this is a necessary link in the title of the person for whose account the cheque is being collected.

Section 1 of the Cheques Act 1957 complements ss 60 and 80 of the Bills of Exchange Act,[184] which remain fully in force. It is unfortunate that the opportunity was not taken, when the Cheques Act was enacted, to repeal ss 60 and 80 of the 1882 Act and replace them with a single new provision, for, as they stand, the three sections overlap in considerable measure and in some respects their interrelationship is unclear.[185] It should be noted that all these statutory provisions are confined to cheques. No protection is given to a banker who pays a bill of exchange apparently accepted by his customer and payable at the bank where the acceptance is forged or unauthorized.

Section 60 provides as follows:

> When a bill payable to order on demand is drawn on a banker, and the banker on whom it is drawn pays the bill in good faith and in the ordinary course of business, it is not incumbent on the banker to show that the indorsement of the payee or any subsequent indorsement was made by or under the authority of the person whose indorsement it purports to be, and the banker is deemed to have paid the bill in due course, although such indorsement has been forged or made without authority.

The reason for this statutory provision is that the paying banker has no ready means of verifying the signatures of the payee and subsequent indorsees, who are not (except by coincidence) his customers; and since, in contrast to his position vis-à-vis the drawer, he has no contractual relationship with them, the strict liability that results from a breach of the banker–customer contract does not come into consideration, so that there is no good policy ground for holding the paying banker liable if he fails to detect that an indorsement was forged or unauthorized. Section 60 enables him to assume that such signatures are genuine and authorized provided he pays the bill in good faith and in the ordinary course of business. In such a case he incurs no liability to the true owner and is entitled to debit his customer's account with the amount of the payment. Want of negligence is not stipulated as a condition of the statutory protection, for the obvious reason that even a most careful scrutiny of the cheque would not inform the paying bank whether the signature was forged or genuine, and if s 60 had required the absence of negligence this might have implied a duty of investigation which it would be impracticable for the paying bank to undertake. Section 60, which does not extend to irregular indorsements,[186] is now of diminished importance in view of the fact that cheques that are being collected for the account of the ostensible payee do not require indorsement by him, so that the volume of indorsed cheques is now very much reduced. But in those

---

184 See below.

185 This criticism was endorsed by the Jack Committee in *Banking Services: Law and Practice*, paras 7.25–7.26 and rec 7(5).

186 As to which, see p 558.

cases where indorsement is still required – as where the cheque is being collected for the account of a third party – s 60 materially assists the paying banker.

Section 80 is concerned with a different problem, namely the payment of a crossed cheque to a collecting banker who may (whether in good faith or otherwise) be collecting for one who is not in fact the true owner of the cheque. The paying banker is protected provided that he pays in conformity with the crossing and in so doing acts in good faith and without negligence. Section 80 reads as follows:

> Where the banker, on whom a crossed cheque is drawn, in good faith and without negligence pays it, if crossed generally, to a banker, and if crossed specially, to the banker to whom it is crossed, or his agent for collection being a banker, the banker paying the cheque, and, if the cheque has come into the hands of the payee, the drawer, shall respectively be entitled to the same rights and be placed in the same position as if payment of the cheque had been made to the true owner thereof.

Since a crossed cheque can be paid only to a banker, and since the paying bank is not in a position to check whether the collecting banker is collecting on behalf of the true owner, it is reasonable that a paying banker who pays a crossed cheque to the collecting banker in accordance with the crossing should get a good discharge as if he had made payment to the true owner. But in many cases the paying banker will be able to rely on the stronger protection of s 60, which, unlike s 80, applies irrespective of negligence and is not confined to crossed cheques. On the other hand, s 60 is confined to forged or unauthorized indorsements and does not cover the case where an essential indorsement is missing altogether. In such a case the paying bank must rely on s 80.

From a policy viewpoint, it is not clear why the protection given to a paying banker by s 80 should be confined to crossed cheques. One might have thought that payment of any cheque to another bank should be protected.

(c) UNINDORSED OR IRREGULARLY INDORSED CHEQUES. Section 60 of the Bills of Exchange Act is confined to forged and unauthorized indorsements, and does not apply where the indorsement is irregular or where there is no indorsement at all. These cases are covered by s 1(1) of the Cheques Act 1957, which, pursuant to the policy of dispensing so far as possible with the need for paying banks to examine indorsements,[187] provides:

> Where a banker in good faith and in the ordinary course of business pays a cheque drawn on him which is not indorsed or is irregularly indorsed, he does not, in doing so, incur any liability by reason only of the absence of, or irregularity in, indorsement, and he is deemed to have paid it in due course.

As with s 60, want of negligence is not stipulated as a condition of protection. It is merely necessary that the banker shall pay in good faith and in the ordinary course of business.

In relation to irregular indorsements, the effect of the section is that the paying banker who bona fide and in the ordinary course of business pays against an indorsement in a name that does not exactly match that of the payee or prior

---

187 The *Report of the Committee on Cheque Endorsement* (Cmnd 3, 1956) estimated that only about 3% of cheques were collected otherwise than for the original payee.

indorsee is protected despite the discrepancy. An irregular indorsement is one which on its face does not sufficiently correspond with the description of the payee or named indorsee. For example, if a cheque made payable to 'J. R. Thomas' is indorsed 'J. K. Thomas', the discrepancy in the second initial makes the indorsement irregular, for an initial, unlike a descriptive title (eg 'Major', 'Professor'), is a material part of the signature. Prima facie s 1 absolves the paying banker if he pays against such an indorsement. Section 1 does, however, contain an inherent difficulty, for it applies only where payment is made 'in the ordinary course of business' and, prior to the Cheques Act, a payment against an irregular indorsement would almost inevitably be outside the ordinary course of business. The question would now appear to depend on prevailing banking practice. The circular of the Committee of London Clearing Bankers previously referred to[188] deals with the absence of indorsements rather than with irregular indorsements, but it is reasonable to assume that in those cases where under prevailing banking practice the paying banker is not required to examine a cheque for indorsement, he will equally not be concerned to ensure that an indorsement that does appear on the cheque is regular.

The circular in question would appear to give the banks less freedom than s 1 of the Act envisaged they should have, in that the paying bank continues to be required to examine cheques for indorsement where they are collected otherwise than for the account of the ostensible payee or are cheques presented for payment at the counter.[189] Where a cheque collected through the clearing is crossed, then, in addition to s 1, the paying bank can invoke s 80 of the Bills of Exchange Act.[190]

4.   Complying with payment terms

The paying bank must, of course, comply with the payment terms embodied in the cheque. In particular, payment must be made to the payee or other holder, the requirements of a crossing must be met,[191] the amount paid must correspond with the amount of the cheque and in the case of a post-dated cheque payment made in advance of the date will be at the bank's own expense if the customer countermands payment before that date.

(ii) Duty to the customer to exercise reasonable care and skill

Though the paying banker is under a duty to act in accordance with his mandate, that is, to pay cheques drawn by his customer, or by an authorized signatory on the customer's behalf, in accordance with, and only in accordance with, the customer's instructions, it does not follow that the paying banker is safe in blindly following the terms of the mandate regardless of the nature or purpose of the payment to be made. On the contrary, he has an entirely distinct obligation to act with reasonable care and skill for the purpose of ensuring that monies are not being improperly

188 See n 145.
189 Ibid, para.1(b).
190 See p 558.
191 See p 532.

withdrawn from the account. For example, the managing director of a company may have power to sign cheques on its behalf without limitation, but if he draws a cheque for a large sum in his own favour, it would be extremely imprudent for the bank to pay the cheque without inquiry or confirmation that the payment is in order. Again, if a company's account is drawn on for a purpose which is unlawful, eg to finance the purchase of the company's shares,[192] the bank may incur a liability for breach of contract and/or breach of constructive trust if with notice of the facts[193] it pays the cheque. This was what happened in *Selangor United Rubber Estates Ltd v Cradock (No 3)*,[194] where Ungoed-Thomas J explained that the mandate given to the bank does not relieve it of obligations arising independently of the mandate, in particular the duty to act in accordance with the customer's 'really intended' instructions.

The same judgment affords guidance as to the degree of skill and care required.

> The standard of that reasonable care and skill is an objective standard applicable to bankers. Whether or not it has been attained in any particular case has to be decided in the light of all the relevant facts, which can vary almost infinitely. The relevant considerations include the prima facie assumption that men are honest, the practice of bankers, the very limited time in which banks have to decide what course to take with regard to a cheque presented for payment without risking liability for delay, and the extent to which an operation is unusual or out of the ordinary course of business … What intervention is appropriate in that exercise of reasonable care and skill again depends on circumstances. Where it is to inquire, then failure to make inquiry is not excused by the conviction that the inquiry would be futile, or that the answer would be false.[195]

Few would quarrel with this statement of principle. What caused consternation among bankers was the way in which it was applied in *Selangor* to fix the paying bank with liability for breach of duty, and also in equity as constructive trustee, for paying substantial cheques drawn on a corporate customer which, in a complex series of transactions, were indirectly utilized to finance the acquisition of shares in the company in contravention of s 54 of the Companies Act 1948. Since banks not only handle a large volume of business daily but also have very limited time available to them to hold the cheque before deciding whether to honour it, it is at least arguable that to expect a bank to grapple with complexities of the kind raised in *Selangor*; and to hold it liable despite a finding that any inquiry into the facts would probably have been futile[196] is to raise the standard of care beyond that which is practicable for banks to observe.

(iii) Duty to avoid knowing assistance in a breach of trust[197]

An equally controversial aspect of *Selangor* was the learned judge's ruling that the bank was liable as constructive trustee if it had constructive notice of the improper

---

192   See Companies Act 1948, s 54, since replaced by the Companies Act 1985, ss 151–158.
193   For the test to be applied, see p 561.
194   See n 69.
195   Ibid, at 1118–1119.
196   Contrast *Marfani & Co Ltd v Midland Bank Ltd*, n 149.
197   There is now a prodigious amount of literature on this subject. For an excellent discussion see Charles Harpum, 'The Basis of Equitable Liability', in *The Frontiers of Liability* (ed Peter Birks, 1994), ch 1.

application of its customer's funds (ie a knowledge of facts sufficient to put a reasonable man on inquiry) and that it was not necessary to show that the bank had been guilty of moral turpitude. After numerous decisions in which the courts appeared to veer first towards a requirement of actual dishonesty and then back to constructive notice, it is now established that liability is dependent on 'a dishonest state of mind, that is to say, consciousness that one is transgressing ordinary standards of honest behaviour'.[198] So a person who genuinely believes that what he is doing is not dishonest is not liable for knowing assistance even if in the view of right-minded members of the community he would be considered dishonest. It should, however, be emphasized that only in relation to knowing assistance has want of probity been clearly held a condition of liability. Whether the same degree of knowledge is required to found a personal claim in equity for knowing receipt[199] remains controversial.[200] Indeed, Lord Nicholls has argued convincingly that knowledge itself is entirely irrelevant and that the defendant's liability is strict, albeit restitutionary in character and thus based on unjust enrichment.[201]

(iv) Effect of customer's death or insolvency

1. Death

The death of the customer does not by itself determine his bank's authority to pay a cheque drawn by him before death, but once the bank has notice of the death, it ceases to be entitled to honour the deceased's cheque.[202]

2. Bankruptcy

Where the customer is made bankrupt, all his assets, including amounts on deposit with bankers, automatically vest in his trustee.[203] This by itself would not create excessive difficulty for the banker, for it is unlikely that the making of a bankruptcy order would escape his notice. However, any disposition of property made by the bankrupt in the period between the presentation of the bankruptcy petition (which is not advertised) and the making of the bankruptcy order is void except to the extent that it was made with the consent of the court or was subsequently ratified by the

---

198 *Twinsectra Ltd v Yardley* [2002] 2 AC 164, *per* Lord Hoffmann at 170; *per* Lord Hutton at 172–173, interpreting and applying the language of Lord Nicholls in *Royal Brunei Airlines Sdn Bhd v Tan* [1995] 2 AC 378 at 391. Lord Millett dissented, regarding the same speech by Lord Nicholls as showing that it was unnecessary that the defendant should be conscious that what he was doing was considered dishonest.

199 That is, knowing receipt for the defendant's own benefit, rather than as an agent or conduit pipe.

200 See Harpum, in Birks, *Frontiers of Liability*, p 19.

201 'Knowing Receipt: The Need for a new Landmark' in *Restitution: Past, Present and Future* (eds W. R. Cornish *et al*, 1998) p 231. This extrajudicial view did not find favour with the Court of Appeal in *Bank of Credit and Commerce International (Overseas) Ltd v Akindele* [2001] Ch 437. Nevertheless it is respectfully submitted that on general principles Lord Nicholls' view is to be preferred, a view shared by Andrew Burrows, *Law of Restitution* (2nd edn, 2002) at p 203 and Peter Birks, *Unjust Enrichment* (2003) at pp 139–140.

202 Bills of Exchange Act, s 75.

203 Insolvency Act 1986, s 306.

court.[204] The bank is protected as regards any property or payment received before the commencement of the bankruptcy[205] in good faith for value and without notice of the presentation of the petition or in respect of any interest in property which derives from such a protected interest.[206] However, the statutory protection appears limited to receipts by the bank; payments would require prior authorization or subsequent validation by the court.

3.   Winding up

Similar provisions apply to the winding up of an insolvent company. By s 127 of the Insolvency Act 1986 any disposition of the property of a company made after the commencement of its winding up is void unless the court otherwise orders. In a voluntary winding up the relevant date is the passing of the members' resolution for voluntary winding up, even where a winding-up order is subsequently made.[207] In any other case (that is, where a winding-up order is made without there having been a prior resolution for voluntary winding up) the winding up is deemed to commence at the time of presentation of the winding-up petition.[208] Some time may elapse between presentation and advertisement of the petition, particularly where there are negotiations between the company and the petitioning and supporting creditors as to terms for withdrawal of the petition, and the winding-up order itself may not be made for several months. The court has power to protect bona fide payments and transfers made by the company after the commencement of a compulsory winding up, but will not normally exercise this where the result would be to diminish the assets available for the general body of creditors.[209] The proper course is for the company, on being served with the winding-up petition, to apply to the court for an order validating payments and transfers in the ordinary course of business in the event of the company subsequently going into liquidation.[210]

(v)   Duty to ensure payment to the right party

In addition to observing its customer's mandate, the paying bank owes a duty to the true owner of the cheque (usually the payee)[211] to make payment to him (either directly or, in the case of a crossed cheque, to a collecting bank) and not to anyone else. Breach of this duty exposes the paying bank to an action in tort for conversion of the cheque. Hence careful scrutiny of the cheque by the bank staff is necessary.[212] They must be satisfied that the signature is indeed that of their customer and not a forgery. The cheque must be presented by or on behalf of the holder,[213] so that if it is presented on behalf of someone other than the original

---

204   Ibid, s 284(1).
205   That is, the day the bankruptcy order is made (ibid, s 278).
206   Ibid, s 284(4).
207   Insolvency Act 1986, s 129(1).
208   Ibid, s 129(2).
209   *Re Gray's Inn Construction Ltd* [1980] 1 All ER 814.
210   Ibid; *Re A. I. Levy (Holdings) Ltd* [1964] Ch 19. But see p 843, n 106.
211   See p 548.
212   In practice this is not done where the amount of the cheque is below a given limit set for the customer.

payee, the paying bank must examine the back of the cheque for the requisite indorsement. Where the cheque is crossed, payment can be made only to a banker and the terms of the crossing must be observed.

It is commonly asserted that a bank which pays a cheque to a party not entitled to it incurs a double jeopardy: it cannot debit its customer's account, and it is liable to the true owner of the cheque in conversion for the face value of the cheque. It is, however, submitted that this is true only in those cases where neither the drawer nor the person to whom payment was made has been unjustly enriched as the result of the payment. If the payment was effective to discharge an obligation of the drawer to the party paid, then to avoid unjust enrichment the bank should be subrogated to that party's rights against the drawer.[214] If the payment was not effective for that purpose and the party was acting mala fide or, though acting in good faith, has not changed his position in reliance on the payment, the bank is entitled to recover the money from him as paid under a mistake of fact.[215] The bank should have to bear the loss only where the payment did not discharge a liability of the drawer to the party paid and the latter took in good faith and has changed his position.[216]

(vi) Duty to respect the title of a third party having rights over the account monies

Where the sum standing to the credit of the customer's account represents monies to which another party has a stronger claim,[217] the bank must respect that claim except to the extent to which it has given value for the sum in question before receiving notice of the third party's rights;[218] and if the bank honours payment instructions from its customer with notice of the third party's rights and without having previously given value, it is liable in equity on the basis of knowing receipt. This principle goes much wider than in relation to the payment of cheques and is not discussed further here.[219]

(vii) Recovery by the bank of money paid under a mistake[220]

Where by mistake the bank credits its customer's account with money to which he is not entitled, then in general it may correct the mistake by debiting the sum back; and if the customer has withdrawn the money, he can be made to repay it unless he

---

213 See p 546. If payment is made to the holder in good faith and without notice that his title to the bill is defective, this constitutes payment in due course (Bills of Exchange Act, s 59(1)) and the bank gets a good discharge.

214 Cf the position where the bank mistakenly pays after countermand of payment, p 564.

215 See below as to the analogous position where the bank seeks recovery from the payee after countermand of payment.

216 See below.

217 Eg, under a tracing claim. See *Banque Belge Pour l'Etranger v Hambrouck* [1921] 1 KB 321, and, for a discussion of this case, R. M. Goode, 'The Right to Trace and Its Impact in Commercial Transactions' (1976) 92 LQR 360, at pp 378 ff.

218 For the measurement of such value, see n 160.

219 See p 561.

220 See literature cited n 227.

can show (a) that he was genuinely misled by the error, and (b) that in reliance on the error he changed his position in such a way that it would be inequitable to require him to make repayment.[221]

A bank which pays against a forged signature can recover the payment, as money paid under a mistake, from the payee and also from the collecting bank if it has not parted with the money to or at the direction of its customer.[222]

If the bank inadvertently pays a customer's cheque after receiving instructions not to pay, can it recover the money from the payee? Clearly it can if the money was never due to the payee (eg because he was not the party entitled to the cheque or had already received payment from the drawer on a previous occasion or had furnished no consideration for the payment) or if the payee was aware of the countermand at the time he presented the cheque for payment. But if the amount of the cheque was in fact owed by the drawer to the payee, can the latter still be required to return the payment? Yes, according to *Barclays Bank Ltd v W. J. Sims Son & Cooke (Southern) Ltd*,[223] on the ground that a payment in breach of mandate is not effective to discharge the drawer's indebtedness to the payee, with the result that the payee cannot be treated as having given value for the payment. But, with respect, the question whether the bank's payment is effective to discharge the debt should depend not on whether the bank had a mandate to make the payment but whether the payment was in fact due from the drawer and the bank had ostensible authority to pay. In *Sims* the cheque was for moneys payable under a building contract as certified in an interim certificate by the architect under the contract. There was nothing to indicate that the contractor was not entitled to payment. It is, moreover, fallacious to equate the bank's position with that of a third party who, without any initial authority, officiously pays another's debt. In giving the cheque to the payee, the drawer holds out his bank as authorized to make payment. If the drawer stops payment but does not notify the payee of that fact before he presents the cheque, the payee is entitled to assume, in accordance with well-established principles of agency law, that the bank's authority to pay is still operative. Though the bank's actual authority has been revoked, it has apparent authority to make payment. Why, then, is not the drawer bound by his agent's act? Moreover, in giving up the cheque against payment the payee has changed his position, for if he has to repay the money, he then has neither the money nor cheque and is forced to sue the drawer on the original consideration. This, as has been seen earlier,[224] is a claim much more easily defended than a claim on a negotiable instrument. It is submitted that unless the payee knew of the countermand of payment before he

---

221   *United Overseas Bank v Jiwani* [1976] 1 WLR 964.
222   *National Westminster Bank Ltd v Barclays Bank International Ltd*, n 107, where Kerr J held that a bank which honours a cheque on which its customer's signature was skilfully forged did not by reason of making payment represent to the payee that the signature was genuine.
223   See n 111. See to the same effect the decision of the High Court of Australia in *Australia and New Zealand Banking Group Ltd v Westpac Banking Corp.* (1988) 62 ALJR 292, and the Canadian decision *Royal Bank of Canada v L.V.G. Auctions Ltd* (1984) 2 DLR (4th) 95, affirmed (1985) 12 DLR (4th) 768. *Sims* was also approved by the Court of Appeal in *Lloyds Bank plc v Independent Insurance Co Ltd* [2000] QB 110. See below.
224   See p 513.

collected the amount of the cheque he is entitled to treat the payment as *pro tanto* discharge of the drawer's liability to him, and is thus a bona fide recipient for value and immune from a claim to recovery for mistake of fact.

In *Lloyd's Bank plc v Independent Insurance Co Ltd*,[225] which reached a different conclusion because in that case the bank *had* acted within its mandate, the Court of Appeal, in expressing its approval of *Sims*, rejected the ostensible authority argument on the ground that this was based on estoppel and the necessary ingredients, including reliance, had not been established, the payee relying not on the bank's ostensible authority to pay but on the fact that it was entitled to payment. This seems, with respect, a difficult argument when the payee has given up his cheque in exchange for the payment and has no way of recovering it. For the same reason the outcome of the *Sims* decision seems unreasonable in policy terms. To allow the bank to recover a payment made to a person entitled to receive it from the drawer under the underlying transaction is to destroy the certainty and finality of payment on which the payee, who is the one person not at fault[226] and who has changed his position in reliance on the payment, should be entitled to rely. The bank for its part can be adequately protected by being subrogated to the rights of the payee against the drawer, thus entitling the bank to maintain the debit to its customer's account despite the breach of mandate.[227] It is to be hoped that the occasion will arise in the future for the issue to be determined by the House of Lords.

---

225 [2000] 1 QB 110.

226 The bank should have honoured the countermand; the drawer should have notified the payee of the countermand before he presented the cheque.

227 For the detailed argument in support of these propositions, see R. M. Goode, 'The Bank's Right to Recover Money Paid on a Stopped Cheque' (1981) 97 LQR 254. For other comments on *Sims*, see Andrew Tettenborn, 'Mistaken Payment of Countermanded Cheques' (1980) 130 New LJ 273; P. Matthews, 'Stopped Cheques and Restitution – Another View' [1982] JBL 281 and reply by Goode [1982] JBL 288. See also *Jackson v White & Midland Bank Ltd*, n 174. For a defence of the decision, see Robert Goff and Gareth Jones, *Law of Restitution* (6th edn, 2002), pp 206–207, which, however, observes that the points taken in the above text were not put to Goff J in the course of argument.

21   Other Instruments

Hitherto we have confined our attention to the first of the two main groups of instrument, namely *orders* to pay. There are one or two further instruments of this kind to be considered, but first we shall briefly examine the second group, ie *promises* to pay. There are several instruments within this group,[1] which subdivides into documents of title to money and documents of title to security for money. In this chapter we are concerned only with the former, exemplified by the promissory note.

I.   PROMISSORY NOTES

A promissory note is an unconditional promise[2] made in writing by one person to another signed by the maker, engaging to pay, on demand or at a fixed or determinable future time, a sum certain in money, to, or to the order of, a specified person or to bearer.[3] It is not a bill of exchange[4] but shares most of the characteristics of a bill and is governed by parallel provisions of the Bills of Exchange Act. A typical promissory note looks like Figure 21.1. It will be observed that since the note is a promise to pay, not an order to pay, there is no drawee (and thus, of course, no acceptor). The promisor, Thomas Jones, is termed the *maker of* the note and is for the most part deemed to correspond with the acceptor of a bill.[5] The payee, Jack Robinson, can negotiate the note by indorsement and delivery in the same way as if he were the payee of a bill, and as first indorser he is deemed to correspond with the drawer of an accepted bill payable to the drawer's order.[6] The provisions of the Bills of Exchange Act relating to bills apply, with the necessary modifications, to promissory notes.[7] The modifications derive mainly from the fact

---

1 See p 477.
2 A mere acknowledgement of indebtedness, such as an IOU, is not a promissory note and, indeed, does not constitute an instrument at all (*Claydon v Bradley* [1987] 1 All ER 522). Moreover, it would seem that while the words 'promise to pay' or 'undertake to pay' are not essential, an instrument in which the payment obligation is merely implied is outside the statutory definition of a promissory note (*Akbar Khan v Attar Singh* [1936] 2 All ER 545). *A fortiori* a negotiable certificate of deposit, which does not constitute an undertaking to pay but merely evidences a prior agreement between depositor and depositee, is not a promissory note. See p 572.
3 Bills of Exchange Act, s 83(1).
4 Which is an *order* to pay. See p 483. However, an instrument drawn as a bill of exchange which is invalid may constitute a promissory note (*Novaknit Hellas SA v Kumar Bros International Ltd* [1998] Lloyd's Rep Bank 287).
5 Bills of Exchange Act, s 89(2).
6 Ibid.
7 Section 89(1).

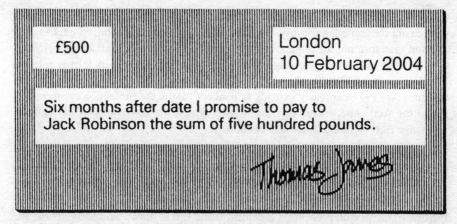

Fig 21.1 Promissory note

that there is no acceptor, so that the provisions as to presentment for acceptance and acceptance itself obviously do not apply. The rules as to presentment for payment broadly follow those applicable to bills but are simpler. The same is true of the liabilities and estoppels of the maker, s 88 of the Act providing that:

The maker of a promissory note by making it

(1) engages that he will pay it according to its tenor;

(2) is precluded from denying to a holder in due course the existence of the payee and his then capacity to indorse.

By virtue of s 89(1) and (2), the indorser of a promissory note accepts the same duties and liabilities as an indorser of a bill under s 55(2), with the omission of references to the acceptor and other necessary modifications.

In certain circumstances the holder of a bill has the option of treating it as a promissory note. This is where there is no genuine drawer, eg where the drawer and drawee are the same or where the drawee is a fictitious person or a person having no capacity to contract.[8]

Promissory notes, though widely employed in the United States, are used relatively infrequently in England except in forfaiting transactions.[9]

2. BANKERS' DRAFTS[10]

A banker's draft is an order to pay drawn either by one bank on another or by a branch of a bank on its head office or another branch. The former type of draft is a cheque, and is distinguished from other cheques only in that the drawer as well as

---

8 Section 5(2).

9 See p 1013.

10 See generally R. R. Pennington and A. H. Hudson, *Commercial Banking Law* (1978), pp 79–80; *Benjamin's Sale of Goods* (6th edn, 2002), paras 22–018 ff.

the drawee is a bank.[11] As regards the latter type of draft, since the drawer and drawee are the same legal entity, the instrument is not strictly a bill of exchange at all (and therefore not a cheque), but the holder of a banker's draft has the right to treat it either as a bill of exchange or as a promissory note.[12] In its former role the banker's draft could be treated by the holder[13] as if it were a cheque,[14] and the Cheques Act 1957 expressly extends to bankers' drafts the protection conferred by s 4 of the Act[15] and, in the case of crossed drafts, the provisions of the Bills of Exchange Act[16] relating to crossed cheques.[17]

What happens if a banker's draft is lost or stolen? The first point to note is that neither the person at whose request the draft was drawn nor the payee is entitled to 'stop' the draft because neither is the drawer. All he can do is to notify the bank which drew the draft so that, if the draft is drawn on itself, it is put on notice as to the title of the person presenting the draft, while if it is drawn on another bank, the drawer bank can stop payment if the draft has not already been paid. Secondly, if the payee had received the draft before it was stolen, so as to become a holder, he can apply for a duplicate, or seek a court order precluding the setting up of the absence of the draft as a defence to payment, on giving the drawer an indemnity.[18] For this purpose, a payee who has expressly or impliedly authorized dispatch of the draft to him through the post constitutes the post office his agent to receive it, so that posting makes him a holder. Thirdly, if the drawee bank has paid the draft in good faith to a person who is not the owner, it will usually have a statutory defence to a claim for conversion and will be entitled to debit the account of the drawer, who, in turn, will be able to debit the account of its customer.[19]

3.   TRAVELLERS' CHEQUES[20]

Travellers' cheques are not like ordinary cheques; indeed, there is dispute as to whether they are cheques at all. The customer does not buy an ordinary cheque; he is issued with cheques, usually in a cheque book, and his account is debited with the amount of a cheque only after it has been presented for payment and honoured. By contrast travellers' cheques are purchased by the customer, and

---

11 The banker's payment, an interbank instrument, is now used only occasionally. See *Paget's Law of Banking* (12th edn, 2002), p 276.

12 Bills of Exchange Act, s 5(2). Bankers' drafts are widely used as the payment instrument on the completion of property purchases, the banker's undertaking to pay being regarded as giving complete safety to the vendor, who might be reluctant to rely on the purchaser's own cheque or even that of his solicitor.

13 But not by other parties (*Capital & Counties Bank Ltd v Gordon* [1903] AC 240).

14 In Australia such drafts are called bank cheques.

15 Section 4(2).

16 Ie, ss 79, 80. See pp 534, n 22; 558.

17 Cheques Act 1957, s 5.

18 Bills of Exchange Act 1882, ss 69, 70.

19 See *Benjamin's Sale of Goods*, paras 22–020 ff.

20 The most detailed treatment is to be found in Denis V. Cowen, *Law of Negotiable Instruments in South Africa* (5th edn, 1985), vol 1, pp 295–313. See also *Chitty on Contracts* (29th edn, 2004), paras 34–173 ff.

debited to his account at the time when they are supplied to him by his bank. Normally, therefore, there can be no question of a travellers' cheque being dishonoured for lack of funds. Moreover, whereas in the case of a cheque which is paid to a person not entitled to it the question is whether the bank can maintain a debit to the drawer's account, in the case of a misappropriated travellers' cheque the issue is whether the customer, who has already paid for it, can obtain reimbursement from his bank.

Travellers' cheques take a variety of different forms. The most common are those in which the issuing bank promises to pay, or draws on itself or others[21] for payment of the amount of the cheque to the order of an unspecified payee, whose name is inserted by the customer when he uses the cheque to make payment.[22] A 'cheque' in the form of a promise to pay is not a cheque but a promissory note; a draft drawn on the bank itself is not a bill of exchange, and therefore not a cheque, but may at the option of the holder be treated either as a promissory note or as a bill of exchange;[23] a draft drawn on others is (subject to the point mentioned below) a bill of exchange and, if drawn on another bank, a cheque.

At the time of issue the customer will be required by the issuing bank to sign his name near the top of the cheque, and when he presents it to the correspondent bank for payment, he will be required to countersign it near the foot in the presence of the correspondent bank's cashier, who will examine the signature to ensure that it matches the original signature. The agreement between bank and customer governing the issue of the travellers' cheques normally makes the signature and counter-signature a condition of the customer's right to be reimbursed if the cheques are lost or stolen. The purpose is, of course, to ensure as far as possible, for the protection of all parties, that the person handing over the cheque in payment is the same as the person who collected it from the issuer.

It is frequently asserted that because payment by the correspondent bank is dependent on the customer's signature and counter-signature the instrument is conditional and is not a bill of exchange or cheque within the Bills of Exchange Act. But this seems excessively technical. The requirement of signature and counter-signature is no more than a prescribed method of verifying the customer's title to the instrument and does not, it is submitted, render it conditional any more than does the requirement that an instrument be duly presented by the holder if payment is to be made.[24] The purpose of the requirement in the Bills of Exchange Act that the order to pay be unconditional is to prevent the imposition of conditions external to the instrument which would impair its autonomy. By no stretch of the imagination can this be said of a stipulation designed solely to ensure that the person presenting the cheque is the party to whom it was issued.

21 Usually the drawee is not specified but, unless otherwise indicated, is taken to cover any of the issuer's correspondents in any part of the world.

22 Another, less common, form involves the customer drawing on the issuing bank in favour of himself or order.

23 See the discussion of bankers' drafts, above.

24 *Contra, Chitty on Contracts,* vol II, para 34–115; Cowen, *Law of Negotiable Instruments,* p 303, citing the South African decision *State v Katsikaris* 1980 (3) SA 580 (AD).

After a long period in which there were no reported English decisions on travellers' cheques there were three reported cases in the 1980s, all dealing with the circumstances in which the customer could claim reimbursement for cheques that had been lost or stolen.[25] The right to reimbursement and the conditions of that right are, of course, governed by the agreement between the issuing bank and its customer. There is, however, a divergence of judicial opinion as to whether, in the absence of an express provision for reimbursement, the customer has an implied right to be reimbursed for lost or stolen cheques. In *Braithwaite v Thomas Cook Travellers Cheques Ltd*[26] Schiemann J opined, by way of obiter dictum, that the customer has no right of reimbursement apart from contract. But in *El Awadi v Bank of Credit and Commerce International SA*[27] Hutchinson J considered a right of reimbursement to be implied as a matter of commercial necessity.[28] Whether the right of reimbursement is lost because of the customer's failure to sign or countersign in accordance with the issuer's instructions or is negligent in some other way again depends on the terms of the contract. In *Thomas Cook*, where there was an express condition that the customer should have safeguarded each cheque against loss or theft, it was held that he had failed to satisfy the condition and was not entitled to reimbursement. In the *BCCI* case there was no such express stipulation, and it was held that it was not to be implied, so that the customer was entitled to reimbursement despite 'the most serious negligence'. In the light of these cases the law must be considered uncertain. On general principle, the law should recognize an implied right of reimbursement where this is not excluded by the terms of the contract but should also imply a duty on the customer to take reasonable precautions to safeguard the cheques issued to him, so that to the extent of his failure to do this, he should not be allowed to claim reimbursement.

4.   NEGOTIABLE INSTRUMENTS AS INVESTMENT SECURITIES

So far, we have examined the negotiable instrument solely in the context of its function as a method of discharging a payment obligation (typically short-term) under a specific transaction between two parties. But the negotiable instrument also plays an important role as a vehicle for raising long-term funds on the market. As such, it is not merely a payment device but also a form of investment security. An early instrument of this type was the bearer debenture, an instrument issued to the public at large, or to selected investors, in which the issuing company undertook to pay to the holder of the instrument its face value at maturity and periodic interest in the meantime. As a bearer security, the debenture was transferable by delivery.

---

25   *Fellus v National Westminster Bank plc* (1983) 133 NLJ 766; *Braithwaite v Thomas Cook Travellers Cheques Ltd* [1989] 1 All ER 235; and *El Awadi v Bank of Credit and Commerce International SA* [1989] 1 All ER 242.

26   See n 25.

27   Ibid.

28   In *Fellus v National Westminster Bank plc*, n 25, Stuart-Smith J observed that issuing banks in general undertake to give refunds but did not address the question whether such an undertaking was to be implied.

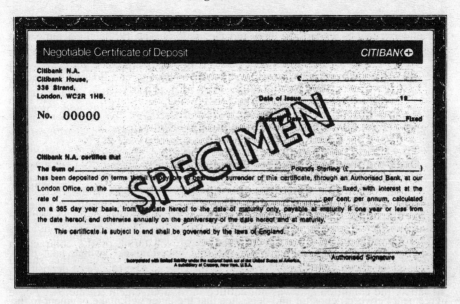

Fig 21.2 Negotiable certificate of deposit

As the result of exchange control restrictions (now abolished) affecting bearer securities, the bearer debenture went out of use, being replaced by the non-negotiable debenture or debenture stock, transferable (in the same way as shares) by entry in the company's register. But since the 1950s a number of new negotiable investment securities have evolved in both the short-term money market and the longer-term capital market. They include, in the former, the negotiable certificate of deposit (Figure 21.2) and Treasury and commercial bills and, in the latter, Eurodollar bonds (a much more complex and sophisticated animal than the old-style domestic bearer bond) and floating rate notes.[29] Each of these instruments contains or evidences an express or implied undertaking by the issuing company to pay a stated amount at maturity, with interest at a fixed or floating rate. As with leasing, hire and rental agreements, discussed elsewhere in this book, the different labels reflect functional, rather than legal, distinctions,[30] each instrument being governed by a distinctive issue procedure and being tailored to a particular market requirement as to maturity, frequency and rate of interest etc. Such instruments feature prominently in the Euromoney market, the development of which has been powerfully assisted by the substantial degree of immunity it enjoys from controls ordinarily imposed by national law.

The methods of issue of these investment securities are not dissimilar to those used in the marketing of unsecured loan stock. The terms of the issue are set out in a trust

---

29 See Terence Prime, *International Bonds and Certificates of Deposit* (1990); Ravi Tennekoon, *The Law and Regulation of International Finance* (1991).

30 There are, however, certain differences in the legal character of the three types of instrument, discussed below.

deed, a detailed prospectus is issued, managers are appointed to organize the issue and underwriters to underwrite it,[31] and the issue is usually listed on the Stock Exchange in order to enhance the marketability of the instruments.

The legal characterization of bonds, certificates of deposit and floating rate notes may be material for two distinct purposes. First, there is the question of their status, if any, under the Bills of Exchange Act; secondly, their negotiability under general law; and, thirdly, their subjection to securities regulation.

(i)   Does the Bills of Exchange Act apply?

It seems reasonably clear that none of the above instruments falls within the Bills of Exchange Act. They are not bills of exchange since they do not embody an order to pay but merely contain or evidence a promise of payment. They are equally not promissory notes, for they are not treated as such by the financial community[32] and the terms of their issue import conditions and uncertainties[33] which take them outside the statutory definition. Moreover, in the case of a certificate of deposit the instrument is not even an implied promise of payment, merely evidence of a prior agreement between depositor and depositee that the latter will make payment to the holder of the certificate on the stated terms.

(ii)   Are the instruments negotiable?

Despite the conditions attaching to their issue, and the fact that the amount of the obligation may in some respects be uncertain at the time of issue, there is little doubt that the negotiability of Eurobonds and other bearer bonds, certificates of deposit and floating rate notes would be recognized by the courts as established by mercantile usage. They are issued as negotiable and are accepted as such by financial institutions the world over, and billions of pounds of business are transacted on this basis. The words of Bigham J in *Edelstein v Schuler & Co*[34] in relation to old-style bearer bonds are particularly pertinent:

> ... but it is to be remembered that in these days usage is established much more quickly than it was in days gone by; more depends on the number of the transactions which help to create it than on the time over which the transactions are spread; and it is probably no exaggeration to say that nowadays there are more business transactions in an hour than there were in a week a century ago. Therefore the comparatively recent origin of this class of security in my view creates no difficulty in the way of holding that they were negotiable by virtue of the law merchant; they were dealt in as negotiable instruments in every minute of a working day ... Thus it has been found convenient to treat securities like those in question as negotiable ... It would be a great misfortune if it were otherwise, for it is well known that such bonds are treated in all foreign markets as deliverable from hand to hand; the attribute not only enhances their value by making them easy of transfer, but it

---

31   Ie, to take up the issue to the extent to which it is undersubscribed.
32   A relevant factor, as shown by *Bechuanaland Exploration Co v London Trading Bank* [1898] 2 QB 658 and *Edelstein v Schuler & Co* [1902] 2 KB 144.
33   Eg, in the case of a floating rate note, the interest payable.
34   See n 32, following *Bechuanaland Exploration Co v London Trading Bank*, n 32.

qualifies them to serve as a kind of international currency; and it would be very odd and a great injury to our trade if these advantages were not accorded to them in this country.[35]

All the instruments described have been recognized in the market for many years as negotiable and it is highly unlikely that the court would take a different view, particularly if proper expert evidence were adduced as to market practice and understanding. Nevertheless, this view has not passed unchallenged in the case of bonds and other instruments which are subject to the terms of a trust deed entered into between the issuer and trustees for bondholders. There are those who contend that instruments of the kind described do not satisfy the criteria of negotiability. Three main grounds are advanced for this view. The first is that the payment undertaking is subject to conditions imposed by the trust deed. But only instruments within the Bills of Exchange Act are required to embody an unconditional payment order or undertaking. The second is that title to the bonds is vested not in the bondholders but in the trustees, and all that the bondholders have is the equitable interest enjoyed by a beneficiary under a trust. So far as the normal form of bond is concerned this view is misconceived. The amount of the bond is expressed to be payable to the holder of the bond, and there can really be no doubt that the debt embodied in the bond is vested in the bondholder. The 'trust' created by the trust deed is not a trust in the property sense[36] but rather an irrevocable authority given by the issuer to the trustees, and assented to by the bondholder, to act on behalf of the bondholders collectively in monitoring performance by the issuer and taking enforcement measures in the event of default. If the bondholders were merely holders of an equitable interest under a true trust, the bonds would not, of course, be negotiable, thus depriving them of one of the key ingredients of their marketability. The third reason why such bonds are said not to be negotiable is that the right to sue upon them is vested in the trustees, not in the individual bondholders. This assumes that the right of a holder to sue on an instrument in his own name is an essential characteristic of its negotiability, an assumption which appears to be attributable to a passage in *Smith's Leading Cases*.[37] However, what the passage in question was seeking to emphasize was that an instrument is not negotiable if after its transfer the holder is obliged to sue in the name of the transferor. This is obviously correct, for clearly in that situation the holder would be merely an equitable assignee and the assignment would have to be in writing.[38] The essential point is not that the holder must himself have an immediate right of suit but that any right he has must be an original right derived from delivery of the instrument to him, not a derivative right exercisable in virtue of the title of the original holder or an intermediate transferor. As against the issuer the bondholder has a right of suit in his own name, but in procedural terms the exercise of this is subordinated to the right of the trustees to sue pursuant to the terms of the trust deed.

35 Ibid, at pp 154–155.
36 Except that if the bonds are secured the trustees hold title to the security.
37 13th edn (1929), vol 1, pp 533–534.
38 Law of Property Act 1925, s 53(1)(c).

(iii) Regulation as securities

Prior to the Financial Services Act 1986 there was considerable doubt how far some of the above instruments, in particular certificates of deposit, were securities for the purpose of legislation governing the issues of securities and the prevention of fraud in their marketing. Regulations under what is now section 22 of the Financial Services and Markets Act 2000 leave no doubt that all these instruments are securities and as such are regulated by the Act and by the regulatory regime it establishes.[39]

(iv) Dematerialization and immobilization

The issue and movement of paper-based investment securities has in recent years been significantly reduced by two developments: the issue and transfer of securities in dematerialized form through CREST and the shift from direct holdings of investments from the issuer to indirect holdings through a securities intermediary.[40] It is quite common for a single global note to represent an entire issue of securities and to be permanently immobilized by deposit with a national or international central securities depository, investors acquiring their interests through accounts with the depository and, in turn, holding for customers of their own. A permanent global note may be expressed to be negotiable but in view of the fact that it is rarely, if ever, intended to be moved its negotiable status must be a matter of doubt.

---

39 See Financial Services and Markets Act 2000 (Regulated Activities) Order 2001 (SI 2001/544), art 77(1).

40 See generally Joanna Benjamin, *Interests in Securities* (2000); A.O. Austen-Peters, *Custody of Investments: Law and Practice* (2000); Roy Goode, *Legal Problems of Credit and Security* (3rd edn, 2003), ch VI. See also p 653.

PART FOUR
Secured Financing

22　The Classification and Characteristics of Credit and Security

Enterprises live (and sometimes die) by credit. In any developed economy an essential feature of commerce is the provision of suitable media for the extension of credit. The running of a business involves staff, premises, equipment and the consumption of goods and services. To earn income, an enterprise must first spend money on various factors of production, and, unless the capital of its proprietors is sufficient for the purpose, it must look to lenders to bridge the interval between the outlay of funds and receipts of the fruits of trade. Moreover, as the enterprise expands, the amount of credit it needs tends to increase and the growth in its borrowing facilitates further expansion, the borrowed funds providing leverage for the enhancement of profits.

The question which any lender has to consider is whether he can be sure that his loan will be repaid on the due date. The proven quality of the debtor company's management over a number of years may be sufficient assurance without the need for any special safeguards, but even well-run companies can be seriously affected by events over which they have little control: international incidents which affect supplies; adverse exchange rates; a trade recession; prolonged or repeated industrial action; the unexpected financial collapse of the borrower's own customers; and unforeseen reduction in demand for the borrower's product. Where these misfortunes occur, the borrowed funds may prove a burden rather than a support, for the lender expects his interest, come what may, and if the return on the borrowed money, instead of being greater than the interest paid, falls below it, the servicing of the loan represents a steady drain on the borrower's resources. If the borrower is unable to trade out of his difficulties and is forced into liquidation with liabilities substantially in excess of assets, how is the lender to ensure that he or it will nevertheless be paid in full?

It is precisely to that end that security is taken. The general rule in bankruptcy or winding up[1] is that all creditors are treated *pari passu*, that is, on an equal footing, sharing in the proceeds of realized assets in proportion to the amount of their respective claims. Thus if the sale of the assets by the trustee in bankruptcy or liquidator produces, after deduction of expenses, £25,000 when liabilities are £100,000, each unsecured creditor will receive a dividend of 25p in the

---

1 Bankruptcy is the formal proceeding resulting from insolvency of an individual, winding up (or liquidation) the outcome of insolvency of a company. Partnerships of individuals are subject to the regime of bankruptcy but in certain cases may also be wound up under the Companies Acts. See generally, ch 31.

pound.[2] The principal reason why a lender takes a security is to avoid the effects of this *pari passu* distribution and to ensure for himself a privileged status, either by establishing real rights over one, some or all of the debtor's assets, which will thus have priority over the claims of unsecured creditors,[3] or by having recourse to a third party who has undertaken responsibility to the lender for payment if the debtor defaults. Other reasons for taking security include the fact that certain categories of collateral (particularly financial collateral) reduce or extinguish the risk-weighting of assets for capital adequacy purposes under the Basel Accord of 1988[4] and the EC Capital Adequacy Directive[5] and, in the case of all-assets security under fixed and floating charges, the influence the chargee enjoys vis-à-vis the debtor company and other creditors, over enforcement, reorganization, and the like.

Security over assets is known as real security, that is, security in or over a res or asset; security of the latter type is known as personal security, ie a personal claim against a third party, for example, under a guarantee, or against the debtor himself on a collateral undertaking given by way of security, such as a bill of exchange. Not infrequently, the latter is itself reinforced by a real security, as where A guarantees B's indebtedness to C and charges his house to C as security for performance of the guarantee.[6] Real security may be either consensual or legal, that is, it may be created by agreement between the parties or be conferred by law automatically when given conditions exist. The present chapter is concerned essentially with real security, and the term 'security' will hereafter be used in this restricted sense unless otherwise indicated. But first we must say a few words about credit.

I.   THE NATURE AND FORMS OF CREDIT

(i)   Loan, sale and lease

The word 'credit' has many meanings. It may signify no more than a person's financial standing ('his credit is good', 'he is a good credit risk') or may on the other hand be used in a legal sense, when its meaning will depend on the context in which it appears. For our purposes it will be employed to denote financial accommodation of some kind,[7] that is, the provision of a benefit (cash, land,

---

2   There are, however, numerous statutory exceptions to the general rule. Certain classes of creditor (eg employees for unpaid wages and certain other employment claims) enjoy preferential status, while others (eg shareholders of a company in winding up, a spouse in the other spouse's bankruptcy) are deferred, with no dividend entitlement until other creditors have been paid in full.

3   As the reader will recall, it is a characteristic of real rights that they survive the debtor's bankruptcy or liquidation, whereas personal rights against the debtor become converted into a right to prove for dividend in competition with other holders of personal rights.

4   In course of being revised. Basel II is intended to provide greater accuracy and flexibility but will also be undeniably more complex.

5   Directive 93/6 as amended.

6   It is also possible for a person to charge his property by way of guarantee without undertaking any personal liability for payment (*Re Conley* [1938] 2 All ER 127).

7   Cf the Consumer Credit Act 1974, s 9(1), which defines credit as including 'a cash loan, and any other form of financial accommodation'.

goods, services or facilities) for which payment is to be made by the recipient in money at a later date.[8] From a commercial viewpoint all credit takes one of three forms: loan, sale or lease. A loan is a payment of money to the debtor, or to a third party at the debtor's request, by way of financial accommodation upon terms that the sum advanced, with any stipulated interest, is to be repaid by the debtor in due course. Into this category fall such transactions as building society mortgage advances, bank loans and overdrafts, payments to suppliers under credit card or check trading arrangements, and the like.[9] Sale credit is price-deferment. Price-deferment agreements involve sales on open account, instalment sale and hire-purchase agreements, revolving charge accounts[10] and the sale or supply of land, services or facilities at a deferred price, as opposed to lease or hire at a rent.[11] To these two forms of credit we must add a third, finance leasing, that is, the leasing of equipment to a single lessee for all or most of its estimated working life, and without an option to purchase, at a rental which, instead of representing the use-value of equipment intended to be leased to a series of hirers, as would be the case for an operating lease, is calculated so as to ensure the return to the lessor of its capital outlay and desired return on capital. The finance lease is thus a financing tool by which legal title remains in the lessor but the economic benefits of ownership belong to the lessee.[12] From a legal viewpoint, leases without an option to purchase are not considered to involve the extension of credit at all, whether they are operating leases or finance leases. The distinction between the two other forms, loan credit and sale credit, is still very significant, though less than it was before the enactment of the Consumer Credit Act.[13] The courts have always regarded price-deferment as essentially different from loan, so that legislation regulating the lending of money has never[14] applied to instalment sales and hire-purchase, finance charges under sale and hire-purchase agreements have been immune from attack under usury legislation and the two forms of financial accommodation have been subjected to entirely different common law rules.[15] Similarly, the reservation of title under a sale or hire-purchase agreement is still considered to be no more than a stipulation as to whether and when property is to pass, and is not to be confused with a chattel mortgage, despite the fact that the two devices are intended to fulfil the same security function. So a document reserving title is outside the Bills of Sale Acts and is exempt from registration as a charge under s 395 of the Companies Act 1985.

8   For a detailed analysis of the concept of credit in the context of the Consumer Credit Act, see Roy *Goode: Consumer Credit Law and Practice* (looseleaf), ch 24.

9   See *Goode: Consumer Credit*, chs 3–10. A transaction may be a loan even though repayment is to be made exclusively from a designated fund or security, so that the borrower incurs no personal liability. See p 609.

10   Eg, budget and option accounts. See *Goode: Consumer Credit*, paras [3.25], [3.26].

11   See*Goode: Consumer Credit*, ch 40.

12   See p 721

13   Which largely obliterates the distinction in relation to transactions within the Act. See *Goode: Consumer Credit*, ch 25.

14   Prior to the Consumer Credit Act.

15   *Goode: Consumer Credit*, chs 11–20; *Report of the Committee on Consumer Credit* (Cmnd 4596, 1971), para 4.2.4.

There are many situations in which A would like to lend money to B, and B to borrow money from A, yet the parties are obstructed by legal difficulties. Suppose, for example, that A and B are both companies. A's ability to lend money may be restricted by legislation[16] or by its Memorandum or Articles of Association. B's powers of borrowing may be similarly restricted; or B may have undertaken, eg as a term of a debenture given to its bankers, to keep its external borrowing within defined limits, and the loan by A would take B's borrowing beyond those limits and thus put it into default under the debenture deed, with potentially disastrous consequences.[17] Now, with a little ingenuity A and B can bypass these difficulties by selecting a price-deferment form of accommodation or by utilizing a mechanism which in legal terms does not involve the grant of credit at all.

> *Example 1*: B Ltd wishes to borrow from A Ltd on the security of B's receivables[18] but is precluded from so doing by the terms of a debenture given to its bank.[19] So it is agreed that B will sell the receivables to A outright at a discount, B guaranteeing payment by the debtors concerned. The end result is the same as on a loan: A pays cash now and gets it back later. But a sale at a discount is not a loan at interest[20] even where recourse is given.[21]

Typical transactions of this kind are block discounting agreements between dealers and finance houses[22] and factoring agreements between trade suppliers and factoring companies.[23]

> *Example 2*: B Ltd wants to buy equipment from S but has insufficient funds for the purpose. S is not prepared to extend credit. A Ltd is willing to help but, as in example 1, B is debarred from taking a loan. The problem can be solved in at least two ways. S can agree to accept payment of the price by instalments with interest and immediately discount the agreement to A. The effect of this is that S gets his money[24] while B obtains the necessary financial accommodation. Alternatively, S can sell the goods to A, who can resell to B on instalment terms.

There may, however, be cases in which B Ltd wishes to receive short-term renewable finance as working capital for its day-to-day operations, rather than for any specific purchases, and does not have receivables which A is willing to buy. In this situation the cooperation of a third party may be needed.

> *Example 3*: A Ltd agrees to accept 180-day bills of exchange drawn upon it by B Ltd, up to an agreed limit, B putting A in funds to meet each bill as it falls due.

16 This will not usually be a problem for the commercial company incorporated under the Companies Act 1985, but statutory corporations may be subject to lending and borrowing restrictions.

17 Not the least of which is likely to be that under the terms of the deed the exceeding of the limits would constitute a default event making the full outstanding balance of the loan become due immediately and possibly triggering cross-default clauses in loan agreements with other lenders.

18 Ie, debts and other money obligations owed to B by third parties, typically under sale, hire-purchase, lease or loan contracts. See generally ch 30 as to financing against receivables.

19 Alternatively, B does not wish to have a charge on book debts registered against it under s 395 of the Companies Act 1985.

20 *Olds Discount Co Ltd v John Playfair Ltd* [1938] 3 All ER 275; *Chow Yoong Hong v Choong Fah Rubber Manufactory* [1962] AC 209. Indeed, such a sale is not a credit transaction at all.

21 See cases cited in n 20.

22 See p 702.

23 See p 720.

24 Since he is selling the right to receive interest as well as the cash price, he should be able to obtain from A a sum at least sufficient to leave him with that price after deduction of the discount.

B discounts the bills to C.[25] Alternatively, the bills are drawn on C and discounted to A.

Similarly, equipment financing may be arranged by way of instalment sale (with or without reservation of title in favour of the seller), hire-purchase or finance lease, each of which possesses characteristics that may influence the choice of instrument.[26] Retention of title sales, hire-purchase agreements and finance leases may therefore be regarded as quasi-security devices, forms of agreement intended to fulfil a security function even though not security in law. A slightly less obvious quasi-security device is the repo, a transaction involving the sale and repurchase of investment securities. In the case of the repo, and of similar transactions such as sell/buy-back, the seller transfers full ownership and the buyer agrees to sell the securities back to the transferor at a later date. But the economic effect is similar to that of a mortgage because of close-out provisions in the repo agreement by which, in the event of default by either party, the non-defaulting party may accelerate the repurchase date, whereupon any transfer or retransfer obligations are converted into obligations to pay the then value of the securities and the resulting money obligations are netted out, leaving a balance to be paid by one party to the other. Thus the seller is protected against failure of the buyer to perform its retransfer obligation, while the buyer is protected against failure of the seller to pay the repurchase price.

The point of these examples is not merely to illustrate the legal differences between sale credit and loan credit but to show the versatility of the commercial world in adapting its techniques to accommodate legal requirements and restrictions. In other words, there are more ways than one of killing a cat!

(ii) Fixed-sum credit and revolving credit

A distinction must also be drawn between fixed-sum credit[27] and revolving[28] credit. Under the former the debtor agrees to take a fixed amount of credit and to repay this with interest or charges, the transaction coming to an end on completion of the payments. Examples are the non-instalment loan, the (instalment) personal loan, the hire-purchase or instalment sale agreement. The characteristic of fixed-sum credit is that the amount of credit to be taken by the debtor is predetermined and the contract relationship is of finite duration, lasting only so long as there are sums outstanding from the debtor. By contrast, revolving credit is a *facility*. The debtor is given not a fixed amount of credit, but a credit limit or line of credit, which he can draw on as

---

25 This form of financing is known as acceptance credit. It is not in law a loan, for no money is being lent either by A Ltd (who will meet the bills with funds provided by B) or by C, who is a purchaser of bills, not a lender (*I. R. C. v Rowntree & Co Ltd* [1948] 1 All ER 482; *Re Securitibank (No 2)* [1978] 2 NZLR 136; *Begley Industries Ltd v Cramp* [1978] 2 NZLR 207). This type of acceptance must not be confused with that arising from the acceptance of bills under a documentary letter of credit given in connection with a sale transaction, as to which see pp 959 ff.

26 See p 000.

27 The term is taken from the Consumer Credit Act 1974, s 10(1)(b).

28 Termed in the Consumer Credit Act 'running-account credit' (s 10(1)(a)). The term 'revolving credit' is used here, since it is the usual business expression, and not all credit involving a running account between the parties is revolving credit.

and when he chooses,[29] each drawing reducing the amount of credit remaining available while each repayment *pro tanto* restores it. So the debtor can go on drawing on the credit indefinitely so long as his debit balance, after taking account of repayments he makes, does not at any time exceed the credit limit. The credit is said to be revolving because what comes off at the top by drawings is restored at the bottom by repayments. The relationship between the parties is thus of indefinite duration. Revolving credit may be either purchase-money or non-purchase money. Examples of the former are the trading check, the credit card (where used to buy goods or services) and the budget account.[30]

Among the latter are the credit card (where used to draw cash) and the overdraft. The distinction between fixed-sum credit and revolving credit is of legal as well as commercial significance. The contract providing for fixed-sum credit is bilateral in nature, consisting of an exchange of promises, whereas the terms of a revolving credit are usually no more than a standing offer, each drawing on the credit representing a separate acceptance, so that a series of unilateral contracts comes into existence, each governed by the standard terms of offer.[31] It is also possible to have a combination of fixed-sum and revolving credit, as where the parties enter into a master revolving credit agreement which sets a limit on total outstandings at any one time but within that limit permits a continuing series of fixed-sum credit agreements.

2.   THE SECURED CREDITOR VERSUS THE UNSECURED CREDITOR

The possession of a real right over one or more of the debtor's assets is what distinguishes the secured from the unsecured creditor. Until the debtor's bankruptcy or winding up, the unsecured creditor lacks even a vestigial interest in the debtor's property.[32] He has no claim either to a specific asset or to a fund, merely the right to sue for his money and to invoke the processes of the law to enforce a judgment against the defendant. As a corollary, the unsecured creditor has no *locus standi* to complain of the way in which the debtor deals with his assets,[33] the manner in which a secured creditor realizes his security,[34] the failure of a secured creditor to register or otherwise perfect his interest,[35] the enforcement of an unperfected

---

29 He may, indeed, decide not to use the facility at all.

30 For descriptions of these forms of credit, see *Goode: Consumer Credit*, ch 10.

31 See p 73 as to unilateral contracts.

32 *Re Ehrmann Bros Ltd* [1906] 2 Ch 697.

33 Ibid; *Re Cardiff Workmen's Cottage Co Ltd* [1906] 2 Ch 627, per Buckley J at 630. It is true that where the debtor is bankrupt or in liquidation or administration an individual creditor can apply to set aside, under ss 423–425 of the Insolvency Act 1986, a transaction at an undervalue designed to put assets out of the reach of, or otherwise prejudice, a creditor or potential creditor, but such an action is brought for the benefit of all victims of the transaction (s 424(2)) and the claimant need only show an intention to prejudice creditors at large, not necessarily himself.

34 See *Re Ehrmann Bros Ltd*, n 32, per Romer LJ at 708, where the learned Lord Justice makes the point that outside winding up, an unsecured creditor has no right to intervene to prevent a company from applying part of its property in payment of debentures even where these have not been registered.

35 Ibid.

security by the secured creditor[36] or the payment by the debtor in or towards discharge of an unperfected security interest.[37] Nor is the unsecured creditor protected by an order preserving the rights of intervening third parties where leave is given to register a secured interest out of time.[38]

These are simply illustrations of the general principle that while a business is solvent, it is for the proprietors, and for them alone, to decide how to use their unencumbered assets;[39] and even an unperfected security interest is good against the debtor himself, unless otherwise provided by statute. But if the debtor becomes bankrupt or goes into liquidation, the position changes dramatically. The proprietors cease to be masters in their own house;[40] their management functions are assumed by the trustee or liquidator, who, as the representative of the general body of unsecured creditors, has the right to impeach a security which is unperfected or is otherwise void or voidable under the insolvency statutes.[41] So a secured creditor has to be alert, for a security interest which is valid and enforceable outside insolvency may suddenly be deprived of effect by the onset of the debtor's bankruptcy or liquidation.

3.   CONSENSUAL SECURITY[42]

(i)   The forms of security

Real security[43] is a right in another's asset to secure performance of an obligation. The creditor acquires real rights over one or more of the debtor's assets in order to secure payment of the debt. In principle, security in an asset carries through automatically to its products and proceeds except where the agreement indicates a

36 Ibid; *Re Row Dal Constructions Pty Ltd* [1966] VR 249.
37 *Re Row Dal Constructions Pty Ltd*, n 36.
38 Ibid; *Re M.I.G. Trust Ltd* [1933] Ch 542.
39 Subject only to the qualification that if there is clear evidence of an intent to defraud creditors by wrongful payment or transfers of assets, the court can in its discretion grant an injunction to restrain those managing the business from committing the intended fraud.
40 In the case of a company this is true to a limited extent even before formal liquidation proceedings, in that where a company becomes or, *semble*, is likely to become unable to pay its debts, its members cease to be able to ratify transactions entered into by the directors in breach of duty, for at that stage it is the creditors, not the members, who have the primary interest in the proper application of the company's assets (*Winkworth v Edward Baron Development Co Ltd* [1986] 1 WLR 1512, per Lord Templeman at 1516; *Brady v Brady* [1988] 2 All ER 617; *Kinsela v Russell Kinsela Pty Ltd* (1986) 10 ACLR 395).
41 See pp 838 ff.
42 See generally Roy Goode, *Legal Problems of Credit and Security* (3rd edn, 2003); Iwan Davies, *Security Interests in Mobile Equipment* (2002).
43 The term 'security' is not ideal, since it is used in so many senses, being applied indifferently to describe the interest acquired in the asset, the instrument creating that interest and the asset which is the subject matter of the interest. It is also unhappily contiguous to 'securities', that is, investment securities, such as shares and bonds. There would be much to be said for substituting the word 'collateral' – despite our distaste for converting English adjectives into American nouns – but for the fact that in the securities industry the term is also used to include interests acquired by outright transfer under sale and repurchase ('repo') and similar sell/buy-back arrangements.

contrary intention.[44] Only four forms of consensual security *stricto sensu* are known to English law: the pledge, the contractual lien, the mortgage and the equitable charge. Reservation of title to goods until payment of the price – eg by the seller under a conditional sale agreement or the owner under a hire-purchase agreement – is intended as a security device, yet it does not constitute security as a matter of law, for what is reserved is merely a right *in re sua*. The seller/owner does not take security in the buyer's asset; he merely stipulates that ownership is not to pass until the full price has been paid.[45] This distinction between security *stricto sensu* and reservation of title, which was abandoned many years ago in America,[46] has important consequences[47] and is one of the principal incidents of the still more fundamental distinction between sale credit and loan credit to which reference has previously been made.[48]

The trust not uncommonly features in security transactions, as where an asset is transferred to trustees to secure an obligation or the owner of the asset declares himself a trustee for the creditors by way of security. But the trust is not a separate security device, merely a particular form of equitable mortgage or charge.[49]

(ii) The evolution of the security devices

1. The pledge

The earliest form of security was the pledge, in which the creditor took possession of the debtor's asset as security until payment of the debt. The common law understandably attached great significance to possession, for this was the principal *indicium* of ownership, and to allow the debtor to grant security over his assets while remaining in possession was the surest way to facilitate a fraud on his other creditor, who might be led to lend money on the strength of the debtor's apparent

---

44 See p 618, as to security in proceeds.

45 See pp 606, 720.

46 Under art 9 of the Uniform Commercial Code the buyer is treated as the economic owner and the seller's reservation of title is limited to a security interest, so that such a sale gives rise to a security agreement (ss 1–201(37), 9–102). This has the advantage of reflecting the security function of title reservation and of allowing a unified concept of security which makes it unnecessary to distinguish between one form of financing and another. It has now been adopted throughout Canada, and more recently in New Zealand, in the form of Personal Property Security Acts. A similar approach for this country was long ago recommended by the Crowther Committee in its report *Consumer Credit* (Cmnd 4596, 1971), ch 5 and Appendix III, which was later endorsed both by the Insolvency Law Review Committee, *Insolvency Law and Practice* (Cmnd 8558, 1982), paras 1620–1623 and by the report of Professor Aubrey Diamond, *A Review of Security Interests in Property* (1989). Following the Company Law Review and a consequent reference to the Law Commission on company charges there is now a real prospect of a move towards a functional approach to security. See the Law Commission's major consultation paper, *Registration of Security Interests: Company Charges and Property other than Land* (Cons Paper No 164, July 2002).

47 In particular, reservation of title is not registrable as a mortgage or charge and the buyer/hirer does not in principle have any equity of redemption. See generally Gerard McCormack, *Reservation of Title* (2nd edn, 1995).

48 See p 579.

49 A contractual right of set-off is not a real security at all, though its effects are not dissimilar. See p 610.

continued ownership of the assets in question. Hence in the early days of the common law the taking of possession by the creditor was almost[50] a *sine qua non* of a valid security interest. Even the mortgage of land was originally in the nature of a pledge, the mortgagee taking possession until payment, and it was not until the sixteenth century that the practice developed of leaving the mortgagor of land in possession. A further two centuries were to elapse before this could safely be done by the mortgagee of goods.[51]

With the development of documentary intangibles,[52] the scope of the pledge increased. It could now be applied not only to goods but also to documents of title to goods and to instruments embodying a money obligation. Further, it was not necessary for the creditor to take or retain *physical* possession; it sufficed that he had constructive possession through a third party or even through the debtor himself,[53] a particularly useful rule for banks financing the import of goods against a pledge of the shipping documents, for these could safely be released to the buyer against a trust receipt.[54]

To this day the pledge remains the most powerful form of security interest known to English law, for though the pledgee's interest is a limited one, his possession gives him a legal title to that interest, with an implied power of sale in the event of default; and the very fact of possession suffices both to evidence the transaction and to put third parties on notice of the pledgee's rights without any need for registration. But with the expansion of credit facilities, the limitations of the pledge as a security device long ago became apparent. It was often as inconvenient to the creditor to hold the asset as to the debtor to lose it; and if the asset was needed by the debtor in his business, as it frequently was, for the purpose of generating the income from which to pay the debt, a pledge to the creditor was out of the question. Finally, the pledge was by its very nature confined to physical assets, including documents; the pure intangible[55] could not be reached by this device and could be accommodated only by a valid non-possessory security interest.

2.   The contractual lien

A contractual lien is a right given to a creditor by contract to detain goods of the debtor to secure payment or performance of some other obligation, the goods having been delivered to the creditor for some purpose other than security, such as storage or repair. It is this last element that distinguishes the contractual lien from the pledge. The legal effect of a contractual lien differs from that of a pledge in that the latter carries with it an implied power of sale upon the debtor's default, whereas

---

50 An exception was the Jewish mortgage, a non-possessory security interest perfected by local registration under a system established by King Richard I. For descriptions of this, see J. M. Rigg, *Select Pleas, Starrs and Other Records from the Rolls of the Exchequer of the Jews* (1902), Selden Society, vol 15, pp xviii ff; Pollock and Maitland, *History of English Law* (2nd edn, 1898), vol I, pp 469 ff.
51 See p 581.
52 See p 48.
53 See p 649.
54 See p 1015.
55 See p 47.

a lien is in principle a right of detention only, so that a power of sale would have to be agreed.

3.   The mortgage

A mortgage is a transfer of ownership to the creditor by way of security, upon the express or implied condition that the asset shall be reconveyed to the debtor when the sum secured has been paid.[56] The delivery of possession is not now essential to a mortgage, nor, indeed, is it usual for possession to be given, in the absence of default, except by delivery of title deeds. On the other hand, the delivery of possession is in no way incompatible with a mortgage, though whether possession was given by way of mortgage or of pledge will depend on the intention of the parties.

Whereas the non-possessory mortgage of land had become established by the sixteenth century, it was some time before this form of security became readily available for other classes of asset. Until 1854 the non-possessory chattel mortgage was almost invariably doomed to failure, for the debtor's continuance in possession after granting a security bill of sale was regarded as nearly conclusive evidence of an intent to defraud creditors within the Fraudulent Conveyances Act 1571.[57] All this changed with the enactment of the Bills of Sale Act 1854, which for the first time provided a public registration system for non-possessory chattel mortgages in writing.[58] This Act and its successors enabled the courts to take a more relaxed attitude towards mortgages of chattels, for if the statute were not complied with, the unregistered bill would become void as to the chattels comprised in it,[59] while if for some reason the Act did not apply, then Parliament must be taken to have considered that in the case in point public notice was not required. However, there was a further peril for the non-possessory chattel mortgage in the shape of the so-called order and disposition clause,[60] first introduced by the Bankruptcy Act 1623 and eventually embodied in s 38(c) of the Bankruptcy Act 1914, which invalidated transfers of goods where they remained in the possession, order or disposition of the transferor in his trade or business in such circumstances that he was the reputed owner and he became bankrupt. The order and disposition clause, which never applied to charges by companies, was not displaced by registration of a security (as opposed to an absolute) bill of sale. It disappeared with the repeal of the 1914 Act by the Insolvency Act 1985.

---

56 A mortgage of land no longer takes this form, since by statute this is required to be effected either as a charge by way of legal mortgage or as a demise for a term of years absolute, the latter now being confined to unregistered land. See p 34.

57 Where the transfer was absolute, the creditor's failure to take possession was considered conclusive evidence of fraud, so that as a matter of law the transfer was invalidated as a fraudulent conveyance (*Edwards v Harben* (1788) 2 Term Rep 587). In the case of a transfer by way of security, the debtor's continuance in possession was very strong evidence of fraud (*Twyne's Case* (1602) 3 Co Rep 80b) but was not conclusive so as to render the security void in point of law (*Reeves v Capper* (1838) 5 Bing NC 136; *Martindale v Booth* (1832) 3 B & Ad 498).

58 The Act was amended in 1866 and ultimately repealed by the Bills of Sale Act 1878, which, with the amending Acts of 1882, 1890 and 1891, is still in force.

59 Bills of Sale Act (1878) Amendment Act 1882, s 8.

60 Also known as the reputed ownership clause.

The great merit of the mortgage was its flexibility. Since it did not depend upon possession, it could be applied to all classes of asset, tangible and intangible; and though at common law the scope for its development was severely limited because of the unwillingness of the common law to recognize assignments of future property or of contract rights, these obstacles were brushed aside by the courts of equity, which were perfectly happy to accord recognition both to transfers of after-acquired property[61] and to assignments of debts and other contract rights.[62] The mortgage thus became an instrument of great power. Not only could it be taken over any type of asset, whether currently owned by the debtor or to be acquired by him subsequently,[63] but it could be utilized to secure future as well as existing indebtedness. It is a form of security widely used at the present time.

4. The equitable charge

An equitable charge does not involve the transfer either of possession or of ownership but constitutes the right of the creditor, created either by trust or by contract, to have a designated asset of the debtor appropriated to the discharge of the indebtedness. The right is satisfied out of the proceeds of sale of the asset, whether sale results from the debtor's voluntary act or takes place under a court order for sale or the appointment of a receiver made on application of the chargee.[64] Since a charge is a mere encumbrance and does not involve any conveyance or assignment at law, it can exist only in equity or by statute. An agreement for a charge is itself a charge.

Equitable charges may be fixed or floating.[65] A fixed charge is one which attaches as soon as the charge has been created or the debtor has acquired rights in the asset to be charged, whichever is the later. The effect of this is that the debtor cannot dispose of the asset free from the charge without the chargee's consent except by satisfying the indebtedness secured by the charge. The floating charge, by contrast, is one which hovers over a designated class of assets in which the debtor has or will in the future acquire an interest, the debtor having a liberty to deal with any of the assets free from the charge so long as it remains floating. The chargee's interest is thus in a changing fund of assets, not in any asset *in specie*,[66] but when an event occurs which causes the charge to crystallize, it attaches as a fixed security to all the assets then comprised in the fund and to any assets of the specified description subsequently acquired by the debtor.[67] A creditor can take a fixed and floating charge over the same asset to secure different liabilities but not the same liability. Typically, a debenture will contain both a fixed and a floating charge, the former covering fixed assets and debts, the latter covering the remaining types of asset (see fig 22.1).

---

61 See p 626.

62 See pp 47, 744.

63 But s 5 of the Bills of Sale Act (1878) Amendment Act 1882 outlawed security bills of sale over after-acquired property.

64 *Swiss Bank Corp v Lloyds Bank Ltd* [1980] 2 All ER 419, per Buckley LJ at 425. The terms 'charge' and 'mortgage' are often used interchangeably. It is necessary to distinguish a *mere* charge from a charge which embodies an agreement for a mortgage and is treated in equity as a mortgage.

65 The same is true of the mortgage, but floating mortgages, though not unknown, are much less common.

66 As to interests in funds, see p 61.

67 For a fuller description, see ch 25.

588

Case Reference No.
5558

Debenture
by a company – own liabilities

This debenture is made on ....200... by you:

Comment: Full Regi
Name of Company. D
include registered ad

Registered Number:

in favour of us, **Barclays Bank PLC**, as security for your liabilities to us.

By executing this debenture, you enter into the agreements and covenants and create the charges set out in this document.

Index of Clauses

1. Definitions
2. Your covenant to pay
3. The charges you create
4. Collecting Receivables
5. Negative pledge and other restrictions
6. Further assurance
7. Continuing security
8. Insurance
9. Property obligations
10. Leases, possession, consolidation of mortgages
11. Powers of sale, leasing and accepting surrenders
12. Opening new accounts
13. Appointment of a Receiver or an administrator
14. Power of attorney
15. Costs, charges and liabilities
16. Set-off
17. Foreign currencies
18. Transfer and disclosure
19. Forbearance
20. Service of demands and notices

5558 (BLSC 06/03
©Barclays Bank PLC 2003
All rights reserved

BARCLAYS

Fig. 22.1. Fixed and floating charge

1. Definitions

In this debenture, unless the context otherwise requires:

'**Assets**' means all your undertaking, property, assets, rights and revenues, whatever and wherever in the world, present and future, and includes each or any of them;

'**Floating Charge Assets**' means those of the Assets that are for the time being comprised in the floating charge created by clause 3.1.3 but only insofar as concerns that floating charge;

'**Intellectual Property**' means all patents (including supplementary protection certificates), utility models, registered and unregistered trade marks (including service marks), rights in passing off, copyright, database rights, registered and unregistered rights in designs (including in relation to semiconductor products) and, in each case, any extensions and renewals of, and any applications for, these rights;

'**Intellectual Property Rights**' means all and any of your Intellectual Property and all other intellectual property rights and other rights, causes of action, interests and assets comprised in clause 3.1.2(h);

'**Land**' includes freehold and leasehold, and any other estate in, land and (outside England and Wales) immovable property and in each case all buildings and structures upon and all things affixed to Land (including trade and tenant's fixtures);

'**Receivables**' means all sums of money receivable by you now or in the future consisting of or payable under or derived from any Assets referred to in clause 3.1.2;

'**Receiver**' means every person we appoint as a receiver and manager under clause 13, including any substituted receiver and manager;

'**Secured Sums**' means all money and liabilities covenanted to be paid or discharged by you to us under clause 2;

3

'Securities' means all stocks, shares, debentures, debenture stock, loan stock, bonds and securities issued by any company or person (other than you) and all other investments (as listed in Part II of Schedule 2 to the Financial Services and Markets Act 2000):

- which now or in the future represent a holding in a subsidiary undertaking (as defined in section 258 of the Companies Act 1985) or an undertaking which would be a subsidiary undertaking if in sub-section (2)(a) of that section "30 per cent or more" were substituted for "a majority"; or
- the certificates for which are now or in the future deposited by you with us or which, if uncertificated, are held in an escrow or other account in our favour or held in our name or that of our nominee or to our order;

including in each case all rights and benefits arising and all money payable in respect of any of them, whether by way of conversion, redemption, bonus, option, dividend, interest or otherwise;

'we', 'our', and 'us' refer to Barclays Bank PLC and any transferee or successor whether immediate or derivative;

'you' and 'your' refer to the company shown as 'you' on the front page of this debenture.

Any reference to any statute or any section of any statute is deemed to include reference to any statutory modification or re-enactment of it for the time being in force.

2. Your covenant to pay

You covenant to pay or discharge to us on our demand in writing:

2.1 all money and liabilities now or in the future due, owing or incurred (before or after that demand) by you to us in any manner. This applies whether the money and liabilities are due, owing or incurred actually or contingently; whether by you alone or by you jointly with any other person; and whether you are a principal or a surety; and includes any liability (secured or unsecured) of yours to a third party which subsequently becomes payable to us by assignment or otherwise; and

4

2.2 all interest, commission, fees, charges, costs and expenses which we may charge to you in the course of our business or incur in respect of you or your affairs. The interest will be calculated and compounded in accordance with our usual practice, before and also after any demand or judgment.

3.   The charges you create

3.1 By executing this debenture you charge to us with full title guarantee with the payment or discharge of all Secured Sums:

3.1.1 by way of legal mortgage, all Land in England and Wales now vested in you and not registered at H.M. Land Registry;

3.1.2 by way of fixed charge:

- (a) all Land in England and Wales now vested in you and registered at H.M. Land Registry;

- (b) all other Land which is now, or in the future becomes, your property;

- (c) all plant and machinery now or in the future attached to any Land;

- (d) all rental and other income and all debts and claims which are due or owing to you now or in the future under or in connection with any lease, agreement or licence relating to Land;

- (e) all your Securities;

- (f) all insurance and assurance contracts and policies now or in the future held by or otherwise benefiting you:

  - which relate to Assets themselves subject to a fixed charge in our favour; or
  - which are now or in the future deposited by you with us;

  together with all your rights and interests in these contracts and policies (including the benefit of all claims arising and all money payable under them);

5

(g)   all your goodwill and uncalled share capital for the time being;

(h)
- all your Intellectual Property, present and future, including any Intellectual Property to which you are not absolutely entitled or to which you are entitled together with others;
- the benefit of all agreements and licences now or in the future entered into or enjoyed by you relating to the use or exploitation of any Intellectual Property in any part of the world;
- all trade secrets, confidential information and knowhow owned or enjoyed by you now or in the future in any part of the world;

(i)
- all trade debts now or in the future owing to you;
- all other debts now or in the future owing to you save for those arising on fluctuating accounts with associates (as defined in section 52(3) of the Companies Act 1989);

(j)   the benefit of all instruments, guarantees, charges, pledges and other rights now or in the future available to you as security in respect of any Asset itself subject to a fixed charge in our favour;

3.1.3   by way of floating charge:

(a)   all your Assets which are not effectively charged by the fixed charges detailed above; and

(b)   without exception all your Assets insofar as they are situated for the time being in Scotland;

but in each case so that you shall not without our prior written consent:

6

- create any mortgage or any fixed or floating charge or other security over any of the Floating Charge Assets (whether having priority over, or ranking *pari passu* with or subject to, this floating charge);
- take any other step referred to in clause 5.1 with respect to any of the Floating Charge Assets;
- sell, transfer, part with or dispose of any of the Floating Charge Assets except by way of sale in the ordinary course of business.

3.2   We may at any time crystallise the floating charge created in clause 3.1.3 into a fixed charge, or subsequently reconvert it into a floating charge, by notice in writing given at any time by us to you in relation to any or all Floating Charge Assets, as we specify in the notice.

3.3   Subject to the rights of any prior mortgagee, you must:

3.3.1   deposit with us for our retention all title deeds and documents relating to all Assets charged by way of fixed charge under clause 3.1 including insurance and assurance policies;

3.3.2   execute and deliver to us any documents and transfers we require at any time to constitute or perfect an equitable or legal charge or a pledge (at our option) over any Securities, including uncertificated Securities within any clearing, transfer, settlement and/or depositary system, and give any instructions and take any actions we may require to achieve this.

3.4   Unless and until this debenture becomes enforceable or we direct otherwise:

3.4.1   you may continue to exercise all voting and other rights attaching to Securities as long as you remain their registered owner;

3.4.2   if Securities are registered in our nominee's name, all voting and other rights attached to them will be exercised by the nominee in accordance with the instructions you issue from time to time. In the absence of instructions, the nominee will refrain from exercising any of these rights.

7

3.5 Any mortgage, fixed charge or other fixed security you create in our favour will have priority over the floating charge created by clause 3.1.3 unless we state otherwise on or after its creation.

3.6 Any debentures, mortgages or charges (fixed or floating) which you create in the future (except those in our favour) shall be expressed to be subject to this debenture and shall rank in order of priority behind the charges created by this debenture.

4. Collecting Receivables

4.1 You must collect and realise all Receivables and immediately on receipt pay all money which you receive in respect of them into your bank account with us, or into any other account designated by us, in each case on such terms as we may direct. Pending that payment, you will hold all money so received upon trust for us. You may not, without our prior written consent, charge, factor, discount, assign, postpone, subordinate or waive your rights in respect of any Receivable in favour of any other person or purport to do so.

4.2 If a credit balance on any account of yours with us includes proceeds of Receivables credited or transferred to that account, we shall have an absolute discretion whether to permit or refuse to permit you to utilise or withdraw that credit balance and we may in our sole discretion at any time transfer all or any part of that credit balance to any other account of yours with us or to an account in our own name.

4.3 If we release, waive or postpone our rights in respect of any Receivables for the purpose of enabling you to factor, discount or otherwise sell them to us or to a third party, the charges created by this debenture will in all other respects remain in full force and effect. In particular, all amounts due to you from us or the third party and any Receivables re-assigned or due to be re-assigned to you will be subject to the relevant fixed charge detailed in clause 3.1.2, subject only to any defences or rights of retention or set-off which we or the third party may have against you.

8

5. Negative pledge and other restrictions

You must not, except with our prior written consent:

5.1 create or attempt to create any fixed or floating security of any kind or any trust over any of the Assets, or permit any lien (other than a lien arising by operation of law in the ordinary course of your business) to arise or subsist over any of the Assets;

5.2 sell, assign, lease, license or sub-license, or grant any interest in, your Intellectual Property Rights, or purport to do so, or part with possession or ownership of them, or allow any third party access to them or the right to use any copy of them.

6. Further assurance

You must on our demand in writing execute and deliver to us at your cost any document that we may require further to secure the payment of the Secured Sums, or to create, enhance or perfect any fixed security over any of the Assets, or to give full effect to this debenture, or to vest title to any of the Assets in us or our nominee or any purchaser.

7. Continuing security

This debenture will remain a continuing security in our favour, regardless of any settlement of account or any other matter whatever, and shall be without prejudice and in addition to every other right, remedy or security which we may have now or in the future in respect of any of the Assets for the payment of any Secured Sums.

8. Insurance

8.1 You must insure all insurable Assets with an insurance office or underwriter acceptable to us against loss or damage by fire and such other risks as we specify from time to time. This insurance cover must be for the full replacement value and be index-linked. You must also maintain all other insurances normally maintained by prudent companies with similar activities to yours or as we may require.

8.2 You must punctually make all premium and other payments necessary to effect or maintain these insurances and produce receipts for these payments on our request. If, at any time, you fail to have the required insurance cover in place or to produce any receipt on request or to deposit any policy with us under clause 3.3 or on request, we may take out or renew any insurance in any sum and on any terms we think appropriate.

9. Property obligations

9.1 You must at all times keep all buildings, plant, machinery, fixtures, fittings and other effects charged under this debenture in good repair and in good working order and condition.

9.2 You must notify us promptly of any indication given to you that any of the Assets is or may be listed in a register of contaminated land or contaminative use, or similar register. You must also notify us if any environmental or other condition exists which could have a material adverse effect on the value of the Assets or your business.

9.3 You will fully indemnify us, and our employees and agents, at all times against every claim, liability, loss or expense incurred directly or indirectly as a result of your failure to comply with any of your obligations, whether statutory or contractual, relating to the Assets.

10. Leases, possession, consolidation of mortgages

10.1 You may not, without our prior written consent, exercise any power of leasing, or accepting surrenders of leases, of any Land, or (unless obliged to do so by law) extend, renew or vary any lease or tenancy agreement or give any licence to assign or underlet.

10.2 You must not part with possession (otherwise than on the determination of any lease, tenancy or licence granted to you) of any Land or share the occupation of it with any other person, or agree to do so, without our prior written consent.

10.3 Section 93 of the Law of Property Act 1925, dealing with the consolidation of mortgages, will not apply to this debenture.

11. Powers of sale, leasing and accepting surrenders

11.1 Section 103 of the Law of Property Act 1925 will not apply to this debenture, but the statutory power of sale (as between us and a purchaser from us) will arise on and be exercisable at any time after the execution of this debenture. However, we will not exercise this power of sale until this debenture has become enforceable. This provision will not affect any purchaser or require him to ask whether it has become enforceable.

11.2 Our statutory powers of sale, leasing and accepting surrenders are extended to allow us (whether in your name or in ours) to grant a lease or leases of any Land vested in you or in which you have an interest with such rights relating to other Land and containing any covenants on your part and any terms and conditions that we think fit.

11.3 Our statutory power of sale is extended to allow us to sever any fixtures from Land and sell them separately.

11.4 All powers of a Receiver under this debenture may be exercised by us to the full extent permitted by law after it has become enforceable, whether as your attorney or otherwise, and whether or not a Receiver or administrator has been appointed.

12. Opening new accounts

12.1 On receiving notice that you have encumbered or disposed of any of the Assets in breach of this debenture, we have the right to rule off your account or accounts and open a new account or accounts with you.

12.2 If we do not open a new account or accounts immediately on receipt of notice to that effect, as from that time all payments made by you to us will be treated as if we had credited them to a new account and will not reduce the amount owing from you to us at the time when we received the notice.

11

13. Appointment of a Receiver or an administrator

13.1 Paragraph 14 of Schedule B1 to the Insolvency Act 1986 shall apply to this debenture. At any time after we have demanded payment of any of the Secured Sums, or any step or proceeding has been taken for the appointment of an administrator, liquidator or provisional liquidator, or with a view to seeking a moratorium or a voluntary arrangement, in respect of you, or if requested by you, we may appoint by writing, insofar as permitted by law, any person or persons to be a receiver and manager of all or any of the Assets or an administrator or administrators; and this debenture shall in any of such events become immediately enforceable.

13.2 Where we appoint more than one person as Receiver or administrator, they shall have power to act separately unless we specify to the contrary in the appointment.

13.3 We may from time to time determine the remuneration of the Receiver.

13.4 Once a Receiver is appointed, we will not be precluded from making any subsequent appointment of a Receiver over any Assets, whether or not any Receiver previously appointed continues to act.

13.5 The Receiver will be your agent and you will be solely liable for his acts, defaults and remuneration unless you go into liquidation, after which he shall act as principal and not become our agent.

13.6 The Receiver will be entitled to exercise all the powers set out in Schedules 1 and 2 to the Insolvency Act 1986. In addition, but without limiting these powers (and without prejudice to our own powers), the Receiver will have power with or without the concurrence of others:

- a) to sell, let, lease or grant licences of, or vary the terms or terminate or accept surrenders of leases, tenancies or licences of, all or any of the Assets, or grant options over them, on any terms the Receiver thinks fit in his absolute discretion; and any sale or disposition may be for cash, payable in a lump sum or by instalments, or other valuable consideration;

b   to sever any fixtures from Land and/or sell them separately;

c   to promote a company to purchase all or any Assets or any interest in them;

d   to make and effect all repairs, renewals and improvements to the Assets and effect, renew or increase insurances on the terms and against the risks that he thinks fit;

e   to exercise all voting and other rights attaching to Securities and investments generally;

f   to redeem any prior encumbrance and settle and pass the accounts of the encumbrancer so that all accounts so settled and passed will (except for any manifest error) be conclusive and binding on you and the money so paid will be deemed to be an expense properly incurred by the Receiver;

g   to pay our proper charges for time spent by our employees and agents in dealing with matters raised by the Receiver or relating to the receivership;

h   to do all other acts and things which he may consider incidental or conducive to any of the above matters or powers or to the preservation, improvement or realisation of the Assets.

13.7   Neither we nor the Receiver will be liable to account as mortgagee in possession or otherwise for any money not actually received by us or him.

13.8   Subject to section 45 of the Insolvency Act 1986, we may at any time remove a Receiver from all or any of the Assets of which he is the Receiver.

14. Power of attorney

You, by way of security, irrevocably appoint us (whether or not a Receiver or administrator has been appointed) and any Receiver separately as your attorney (with full power to appoint substitutes and to delegate) with power in your name or on your behalf and as your act and deed or otherwise:

- to execute and deliver and otherwise perfect any agreement, assurance, deed, instrument or document; and

- to perform any act;

which may be required of you or may be deemed by the attorney necessary or desirable for any purpose of this debenture, or to create, enhance or perfect any fixed security over any of the Assets or to convey or transfer legal ownership of any Assets.

15. Costs, charges and liabilities

15.1 You will be responsible for all costs, charges and liabilities (including all professional fees and disbursements and Value Added Tax and/or any similar tax) and all other sums paid or incurred by us and/or any Receiver under or in connection with this debenture or your affairs. We may recover them from you (on a full indemnity basis) as a debt payable on demand and debit them without notice to any of your accounts. They will attract interest and be charged on the Assets.

15.2 The costs which may be recovered from you by us and/or any Receiver under this debenture include without limitation:

- a all costs incurred by us in preparing and administering this debenture or perfecting the security created by it;

- b all costs (whether or not allowable on a taxation by the Court) of all proceedings to enforce this debenture or to recover or attempt to recover the Secured Sums;

- c all money spent and all costs arising out of the exercise of any power, right or discretion conferred by this debenture;

- d all costs and losses arising from any default by you in the payment when due of any of the Secured Sums or the performance of your obligations under this debenture; and all our charges based on time spent by our employees and agents in connection with your affairs.

16. Set-off

We may retain any money standing to your credit with us (in any currency, in any country and whether or not in your name) as cover for the Secured Sums. We may apply all or any of that money in satisfaction of all or part of the Secured Sums as we may select (whether presently payable or not). We may also use that money to purchase any other currency required for this purpose.

17. Foreign currencies

If, for any reason, any amount payable by you is paid or recovered in a currency other than that in which it is required to be paid ('the contractual currency') and, when converted into the contractual currency at our exchange rate applicable at the time, leaves us with less than the amount payable in the contractual currency, you must make good the amount of the shortfall on demand.

18. Transfer and disclosure

18.1 We may at any time transfer all or any part of our rights under this debenture and the Secured Sums to any person or otherwise grant an interest in them to any person.

18.2 We may also at any time disclose any information about you, this debenture and the Secured Sums to:

- any of our associated companies;
- any prospective or actual transferee or grantee referred to in clause 18.1; and
- any other person considered by us to be concerned in the relevant or prospective transaction.

15

19. Forbearance

No delay or omission on our part in exercising any right, power or privilege under this debenture will impair it or be construed as a waiver of it. A single or partial exercise of any right, power or privilege will not in any circumstances preclude any other or further exercise of it or the exercise of any other right, power or privilege.

20. Service of demands and notices

20.1 A demand or notice under this debenture may be given by any of our managers or officers in writing addressed to you and served at any of the following:

- your registered office;
- any of your existing places of business;
- your last known place of business.

Alternatively, a demand or notice may be delivered by facsimile transmission to the facsimile number last known to us or by e-mail to the e-mail address last known to us or by any other form of electronic communication which may be available.

20.2 A notice or demand shall be deemed to have been served on you:

- at noon on the day after the day of posting, if sent by post, even if it is misdelivered or returned undelivered;
- at the time of transmission, if given or made by facsimile, e-mail or other electronic communication.

This debenture is executed by you as a deed and signed by us and it will take effect on the date shown on the front page.

16

Signed by

for and on behalf of Barclays Bank PLC   _____

Either

The Common Seal of   Limited

was hereunto affixed in pursuance of a Resolution of its

Board of Directors in the presence of

_____Director

_____Director/Secretary

Company's Registered Number

Or

Executed as a deed by   Limited

_____Director

_____Director/Secretary

Company's Registered Number

CERTIFICATE OF THE REGISTRATION
OF A MORTGAGE OR CHARGE
Pursuant to Section 401(2) of the Companies Act 1985

COMPANY NO. ....

THE REGISTRAR OF COMPANIES FOR ENGLAND AND WALES HEREBY CERTIFIES THAT A DEBENTURE DATED THE .... 200.. AND CREATED BY
....

FOR SECURING ALL MONIES DUE OR TO BECOME DUE FROM THE COMPANY TO BARCLAYS BANK PLC ON ANY ACCOUNT WHATSOEVER WAS REGISTERED PURSUANT TO CHAPTER I PART XII OF THE COMPANIES ACT 1985 ON THE ....
.... 200..

GIVEN AT COMPANIES HOUSE, CARDIFF THE .... 200..

for the Registrar of Companies

N.B. *The above copy of the Registrar's Certificate must be completed and the Certificate itself attached to this debenture*

5558 (BLSC 5/03)

This Release made this .... day of .... between ....

(1) **Barclays Bank PLC** ('the Bank') and (2) the company named in the attached debenture witnesses that the Bank releases from the charges created by the attached debenture all the Assets comprised in it.

Executed by Barclays Bank PLC the day and year first above written.

Signed as a deed by ....

as attorney of

Barclays Bank PLC

in the presence of: ....

(iii) Some problems of characterization

Whether a written agreement between creditor and debtor creates a security interest is usually apparent from even the most cursory reading of its terms. But some types of agreement, which fulfil a security function in that they are designed to promote the creditor's claim to a rank higher than it would otherwise enjoy, are not easy to characterize and may or may not constitute security in the strict sense. A further problem of characterization may arise where the creditor takes possession of tangible movables (goods, documents, instruments) pursuant to a security agreement. Is the transaction a pledge, a mortgage, a charge or a lien? On the answer to these questions may turn the registrability of the interest (eg under s 395 of the Companies Act 1985) and the extent of its validity and priority in the event of the debtor's insolvency.

1.   Purchase or loan on security?

An agreement which is in substance a loan on security may readily be disguised as a purchase. This has usually been done to evade either the Moneylenders Acts (now repealed) or the Bills of Sale Acts[68] or, where the 'seller' is a company, the registration requirements embodied in what is now s 395 of the Companies Act 1985.[69] Where an allegation is made that an apparent purchase is in reality a loan on security, the court has to inquire into the facts, where necessary looking behind the label which the parties have given the transaction.[70] The question to be decided is not whether the transaction would have the effect of avoiding the application of the relevant statute – for parties are free to organize their affairs in such a way as to ensure that they escape legislation they consider burdensome – but what is its legal nature. There are two distinct routes by which a transaction relied on as a sale may be struck down as a security for a loan.[71] These have conveniently been described as the external and internal routes.[72] The external route is to show that the document does not record the real agreement between the parties – in other words, that the document is a sham and is designed to conceal the true nature of the transaction. Most of the cases in which an agreement has been held a security rather than a sale have been decided on this basis. But even where the document is a true record of the parties' agreement, the court may conclude from an examination of its terms that its legal character is that of a security, not a sale. This is the internal route.[73] In short, the nature of the rights intended by the parties is to be ascertained from the terms of their agreement, while the characterization of such rights is a matter of law and is to

---

68 See, for example, *Re Watson* (1890) 25 QBD 27; *Polsky v S. & A. Services* [1951] 1 All ER 185, affirmed [1951] 1 All ER 1062n. For a more detailed discussion of the principal evasion techniques, see R. M. Goode, *Hire-Purchase Law and Practice* (2nd edn, 1970), pp 81 ff.

69 See p 660.

70 *Re Watson*, n 68; *Kingsley v Sterling Industrial Securities Ltd* [1967] 2 QB 747; *Welsh Development Agency v Export Finance Co Ltd* [1992] BCC 270.

71 *Curtain Dreams plc v Churchill Merchanting Ltd* [1990] BCC 341, per Knox J at 349; *Welsh Development Agency v Export Finance Co Ltd*, n 70.

72 *Welsh Development Agency v Export Finance Co Ltd*, n 70, per Staughton LJ at 301.

73 See the judgments of Dillon and Staughton LJJ in *Welsh Development Agency v Export Finance Co Ltd*, ibid, for a general discussion of the two routes.

be determined by the court.[74] But in each case it is the *legal* substance to which the court has regard, not the *economic* effect of the transaction.[75]

Typical cases in which the characterization of the agreement comes into consideration are the following:

(a) SALE AND LEASE-BACK A normal hire-purchase transaction, in which goods are sold by a dealer to a finance house and let on hire-purchase to a hirer who had no prior interest in them, does not embody a loan or create a security interest.[76] But sometimes, with a view to raising funds, the owner of goods sells them to a finance house and takes a lease back, eg under a hire-purchase agreement. The net effect is very much the same as if he had mortgaged the goods to secure a loan. He receives a cash sum and then has to pay instalments under the hire-purchase agreement which recoup to the other party its purchase outlay and give it finance charges in the same way as if interest had been levied. The reservation of title under the hire-purchase agreement produces an effect equivalent to security over the goods. There is nothing wrong with a genuine sale and lease-back, which is very common in property transactions[77] and is also encountered in equipment leasing in those cases where the intended lessee buys the equipment from the supplier himself.[78] But where goods are involved, the courts are likely to scrutinize the transaction with particular care to ensure that the transfer of ownership was genuinely intended as a sale and was not a mortgage in disguise.

The theme has a number of variants.[79] To add a little camouflage, the goods may be let back on hire-purchase not to the original owner but to his nominee.[80] Alternatively, instead of selling directly to the finance house the owner may find a dealer willing to collude with him in his search for funds, allowing the dealer to represent himself as the owner. The dealer will then sell the goods to the finance house to be let back on hire-purchase to the original owner or his nominee. If the finance house bought in good faith, the court will uphold the sale and hiring back despite the mala fides of the other parties.[81] Where, however, the finance house was itself a party to the simulation, the transaction will be treated as a disguised bill of sale and will almost invariably be void for want of compliance with the Bills of Sale Acts[82] or for non-registration under the Companies Act 1985.[83] A further variant is the so-called refinancing transaction, where

---

74 *Agnew v Commissioners of Inland Revenue* [2001] 2 AC 710, *per* Lord Millett at 725–726; *Lavin v Johnson* [2002] EWCA Civ 1138.
75 Ibid. For a wide-ranging discussion of the characterization question, see Alan Berg, 'Recharacterisation after Enron' [2003] JBL 205.
76 *Re Robertson* (1878) 9 Ch D 419; *McEntire v Crossley Bros Ltd* [1895] AC 457.
77 See, for example, *Lavin v Johnson* [2002] All ER (D) 501.
78 See p 733.
79 See Goode, *Hire Purchase Law and Practice*, pp 81 ff.
80 Ibid, at p 88.
81 *Eastern Distributors Ltd v Goldring* [1957] 2 QB 600; *Snook v London & West Riding Investments Ltd* [1967] 2 QB 786.
82 *North Central Wagon Finance Co Ltd v Brailsford* [1962] 1 All ER 502. However, the creditor will be entitled to recover his money, with reasonable interest, in a claim for money had and received (ibid).
83 Section 395. See p 660.

the owner of the goods genuinely sells them to a dealer who resells them to the finance house to be let back on hire-purchase to the original owner. Again, the question is whether the finance house was genuinely buying the goods or merely intending to lend on the security of them.[84]

(b) SALE AND REPURCHASE. A sells goods to B under an agreement providing for payment of the price by instalments. The agreement contains a stipulation that in the event of B's default, A may repurchase the goods from B, setting off the amount outstanding against the repurchase price. Does the grant of the right of repurchase constitute an agreement for a mortgage? In general, no, for reasons already given.[85] But if the right is coupled with an obligation, the transaction as a whole is more likely to be held a mortgage rather than a sale and repurchase.[86] Sale and repurchase agreements (repos) and similar arrangements such as sell/buy-back are a common form of dealing in securities and in English law will not normally be characterized as security transactions since the sale is intended as an outright transfer. But the securities industry equates this with secured lending because of the repurchase provisions and the ability of the parties to close-out their transactions, converting them into money obligations, and to net the amounts payable.[87] Concern over recharacterization risk in relation to title transfer, and consequential systemic risk, has led to a provision in the EC financial collateral directive requiring member states to ensure that a title transfer financial collateral arrangement can take effect in accordance with its terms.[88]

(c) CONSOLIDATION CLAUSE. A not uncommon provision in a hire-purchase agreement or equipment lease is that if, by reason of default by the hirer, the owner becomes entitled to terminate the agreement at a time when the hirer holds other goods from the owner under another agreement, the owner shall not be obliged to accept a tender of the balance due under the former agreement unless the hirer at the same time pays the balance due under the latter. Such a consolidation clause is intended to give the owner of goods let on hire or hire-purchase rights similar to those enjoyed in equity by a mortgagee against a defaulting mortgagor even where there is no express provision for consolidation.[89] A consolidation clause does not in itself convert a hire-purchase agreement into a security.[90]

(d) EXTENDED RESERVATION OF TITLE.[91] We have seen[92] that the simple reservation of title clause by which the seller retains title until payment by the buyer of the price

---

84 *Stoneleigh Finance Ltd v Phillips* [1965] 2 QB 537.

85 See p 414. See also *Orion Finance Ltd v Crown Financial Management Ltd* [1996] 2 BCLC 78

86 *Curtain Dreams plc v Churchill Merchanting Ltd*, n 71.

87 See Goode, *Legal Problems*, para 1-37.

88 Directive on financial collateral arrangements (2002/47/EC), art 6(1), implemented in the UK by the Financial Collateral Arrangements (No 2) Regulations 2003 (SI 2003/3226), reg 4(4) and 8, the former of which disapplies s 395 of the Companies Act 1985 in relation to charges over financial collateral, while the latter disapplies certain provisions of the Insolvency Act 1986.

89 See Fisher and Lightwood's *Law of Mortgage* (11th edn, 2002), ch 27; R. E. Megarry and W. Wade, *Law of Real Property* (6th edn, 2000), para 19–096 ff.

90 This follows from the decision of the House of Lords in *Armour v Thyssen Edelstahlwerke AG* [1991] 2 AC 339, referred to below.

91 See Gerard McCormack, *Reservation of Title* (2nd edn, 1995); Sally Wheeler, *Retention of Title Clauses* (1992).

92 See pp 579, 584.

of the goods agreed to be sold does not make the agreement a security agreement. This is because the buyer is not giving security rights over goods he owns but is simply agreeing with the seller as to the condition on which the property in the goods is to pass to him. However, the form of sale agreement examined in the *Romalpa* case[93] showed at least three ways in which the title reservation could be extended. In the first, the seller retains title until the buyer has paid not merely the price of the goods agreed to be sold but all other sums owing to the seller under prior or subsequent transactions. No argument was advanced in *Romalpa* that this made the agreement a charge. But in *Armour v Thyssen Edelstahlwerke AG*[94] the House of Lords, in a Scottish appeal, held that an 'all moneys' title retention clause did not create a charge, for the parties were entitled to agree on any conditions they chose for the transfer of the property.

A second extension of the title reservation clause is to pick up the proceeds of authorized sub-sales by the buyer and require these to be made over to the seller. In *Romalpa* the Court of Appeal held that the terms of the agreement showed an intention to secure the plaintiffs for all sums owing to them and established a fiduciary relationship between seller and buyer which conferred on the former an equitable proprietary right to the proceeds. However, the decision is unsatisfactory in a number of respects. The argument before the court focused on the construction of the contract rather than on the legal characterization of the agreement. Thus it was conceded that the buyer was a bailee of the goods, and it was not argued that the seller was in reality taking a registrable but unregistered charge over the book debts. It could no doubt have been argued that the seller's right to the proceeds was an equitable right to trace arising by operation of law rather than by way of contractual security. But such an argument would have enabled the seller to hoist itself up by its own legal bootstraps, in that the equitable duty to account was derived from the terms of the agreement itself. Relying on the fact that certain crucial points in the *Romalpa* case were either conceded or not argued, lower courts have consistently bypassed the decision, holding that the right to the proceeds derived from the agreement of the parties, not from some independent equitable tracing right, and that since the seller's only interest in the proceeds was to recover sums owing to it by the buyer the parties must be assumed to have intended that such interest should be by way of security only and not by way of outright transfer. On this basis the effect of the agreement was to create a charge on the book debts arising from the sub-sales, and, in the absence of registration, this was void against the liquidator and creditors.[95]

The third form of extended reservation of title is that which covers products made from the goods and other materials belonging to the buyer or a third party. Here the test is whether the product is intended to belong to the seller absolutely, in which case it vests in him automatically under the reservation of title clause without any

---

93 *Aluminium Industrie Vaassen B.V. v Romalpa Aluminium Ltd* [1976] 1 WLR 676.
94 See n 90.
95 *E. Pfeiffer Weinkellerei-Weineinkauf GmbH v Arbuthnot Factors Ltd* [1988] 1 WLR 150; *Tatung (UK) Ltd v Galex Telesure Ltd* (1988) 5 BCC 325; *Compaq Computer Ltd v Abercorn Group Ltd* [1991] BCC 484.

grant by the buyer,[96] or whether the seller's interest is to be limited to a security interest, as will almost invariably be the case, for otherwise the seller would receive a windfall.[97] Where, however, the processing of the original goods has resulted in their destruction and replacement by a wholly new product, there is no longer any asset susceptible to title retention and the seller's rights over the new product derive from a grant by the buyer, which if by way of security will constitute a charge and will be void if unregistered.[98]

(e)/DISCOUNTING OF RECEIVABLES/ Where book debts and other receivables are discounted by A to B under arrangements by which A is made responsible for collecting the debts on behalf of B and guarantees payment, the distinction between a purchase of the debts by B and a loan by him on the security of the debt becomes a fine one, for in both cases the accounting mechanism is such as to involve an exchange of money for money. Once again, the test is whether it was intended that outright ownership of the receivables should pass to B or whether the reality of the transaction was that he was to be a mere mortgagee.[99]

(f) /NON-RECOURSE FINANCING AGAINST RECEIVABLES/ Under certain forms of loan contract the borrower does not undertake any personal obligation to repay the advance, the lender looking solely to underlying security, typically in the form of receivables which the borrower undertakes to collect and hold for the lender's account. For example, in leveraged leasing transactions (common in the United States and regularly encountered in the United Kingdom), most of the capital required to purchase the equipment that is to be let on lease is advanced by a third party to the intending lessor, who assigns the future rentals to the third party by way of security, undertaking to collect these and account for them to the third party. The transaction is customarily described as a non-recourse loan, the rentals are treated as security for the loan and the parties are described as lender and borrower. Non-recourse lending is common in project finance and is a well-established concept in other forms of international financial transaction. It may seem odd to characterize a transaction as a loan when there is no personal liability for repayment, and to speak of security for a loan when there is no obligation to be secured, other than a duty to account for the 'security' itself and its proceeds. Nevertheless, the courts have held that it is for the parties themselves to decide how a loan is to be repaid, and the mere fact that repayment is to come exclusively from a designated fund or class of assets,

96 *Clough Mill Ltd v Martin* [1985] 1 WLR 111.
97 Ibid; *Re Peachdart Ltd* [1984] Ch 131; *Specialist Plant Services Ltd v Braithwaite Ltd* (1987) 3 BCC 119; *Kruppstahl A.G. v Quittman Products Ltd* [1982] 1 ILRM 551.
98 *Modelboard Ltd v Outer Box Ltd* [1992] BCC 945. See also *Borden (UK) Ltd v Scottish Timber Products Ltd* [1981] Ch 25, where the agreement contained no provision as to products and the Court of Appeal held that the reservation of title to the original goods could not survive their destruction in the course of processing.
    The head of registration of a charge over products is Companies Act 1985, s 396(1)(e), namely, a charge created or evidenced by an instrument which, if executed by an individual, would require registration as a bill of sale.
99 See the cases cited n 20, *and* the decision of the House of Lords in *Lloyds & Scottish Finance Ltd v Cyril Lord Carpets Ltd* (1979), belatedly reported in [1992] BCLC 609, affirming the decision of the Court of Appeal *sub nom Lloyds & Scottish Finance Ltd v Prentice* (1977) 121 Sol Jo 847. See also *Welsh Development Agency v Export Finance Co Ltd*, n 70.

without any personal liability on the part of the borrower, does not prevent the transaction from constituting a loan in law, as in colloquial usage.[100] The transaction also differs in commercial effect from a sale, in that the borrower retains an equity in the charged asset. Accordingly, the agreement is a security agreement and is registrable as such where the asset in question falls within s 396 of the Companies Act 1985, as where it consists of the borrower's book debts.[101]

2.   *Set-off agreement*[102]

A common provision in a commercial contract involving the payment of money by one person to another is that the former may set off against any sum for which he is liable under the agreement the amount of any cross-claim against the latter on some other account. For example, a bank may stipulate that it shall have the right to set off a sum due from a surety under a contract of guarantee against that surety's credit balance. Rights of set-off also exist in equity and to a limited extent under the Statutes of Set-Off,[103] but in either case only where given conditions are fulfilled,[104] and the purpose of a contractual set-off is usually to extend the right beyond that which would be given at law or in equity.

A contractual set-off, though fulfilling a security function, is not in point of law a security interest. It gives no right over the creditor's asset (ie the debt), merely an entitlement to set off one personal obligation against another. It is thus not registrable as a security interest.[105] So long as the creditor is not insolvent, a contractual set-off is considered unobjectionable even though it goes beyond the right of set-off in equity, as by entitling the debtor to set off a purely contingent claim against a sum due to the creditor; and such an agreement will in principle bind an assignee of the creditor's claim, for he cannot acquire rights greater than those of his assignor and he therefore takes the debt subject to the debtor's right of set-off.

But the matter is quite different where the debtor seeks to assert a contractual right of set-off against the creditor's trustee in bankruptcy or liquidator. To the extent to which the contractual right goes beyond the right of set-off allowed on insolvency,[106] it offends against the principle of *pari passu* distribution, for its effect would be to use a purely personal cross-claim to diminish an asset that would otherwise be available for the general body of creditors; and as we have seen, the feature which particularly distinguishes a personal right from a real right is that the former ceases to be available against the obligor's assets in bankruptcy or winding up and is converted into a right to prove in competition with other creditors. Instructive on this

---

100 *De Vigier v I.R.C.* [1964] 2 All ER 907, applying *Mathew v Blackmore* (1857) 1 H & N 762.
101 Companies Act 1985, s 396(1)(e).
102 See, generally, S.R. Derham, *Law of Set-Off* (3rd edn, 2003); Philip Wood, *English and International Set-Off* (1989); Shelagh McCracken, *The Bankers' Remedy of Set-Off* (2nd edn, 1998); Roy Goode, *Legal Problems of Credit and Security* (3rd edn, 2003), ch VII.
103 Though the Statutes of Set-Off were long ago repealed their effect is preserved by what is now s 49(2) of the Supreme Court Act 1981.
104 See Goode, *Legal Problems*, ch VII.
105 *Re Charge Card Services Ltd* [1987] Ch 150. The case was appealed, but not on this point.
106 Insolvency Rules 1986, r 4.90. See Goode, *Legal Problems*, paras 7–29 ff.; Wood, *English and International Set-Off*, ch 7.

point is the decision of the House of Lords in *British Eagle International Airlines Ltd v Compagnie Nationale Air France*.[107]

> The International Air Transport Association (IATA) provided a clearing-house scheme for settlement of debts between member airlines, and each member agreed to be bound by the clearing regulations. These provided that sums due from a member to other member airlines would be debited to that member's account with IATA, and sums due to the member from other airlines would be credited to the member's account with IATA, a balance being struck monthly, so that an airline in overall credit vis-à-vis other airlines would receive a remittance from IATA and an airline in overall debit would send a remittance to IATA.

> British Eagle, a member airline, went into liquidation and was owed money by Air France. The latter contended that the true creditor was IATA and that under the clearing-house rules IATA was entitled to set off sums due from British Eagle to other airlines so that there was no credit balance in favour of British Eagle.

> The House of Lords held by a majority that it would be contrary to public policy to allow a party to contract out of s 302 of the Companies Act (which provides for *pari passu* distribution among creditors) so as to give unsecured creditors, through the medium of set-off, the same rights as if they had taken a charge on the debts, and that accordingly the liquidator of British Eagle was entitled to recover the net balance due from Air France to British Eagle without being subject to set-off in respect of sums due from British Eagle to other airlines.

The crucial question, and that on which the majority differed from the minority, was whether the real creditors and debtors of British Eagle were the other airlines or IATA. On the minority view, no member airline could sue another member airline directly, the true creditor and debtor was IATA, and therefore the set-off was unobjectionable.[108] But the majority of their Lordships considered that IATA was in essence a clearing-house agent and on this basis British Eagle's claim was properly made against Air France and could not be reduced by sums owing from British Eagle to other airlines.

3.   Charge-backs and pledge-backs

Faced with the weakness of contractual set-off in the event of a customer's insolvency, banks now tend to play safe by taking and, where necessary, registering[109] a charge over the customer's credit balance. Can this be done? In *Re Charge Card Services Ltd*[110] Millett J held that such a charge is conceptually impossible,[111] for, it was said, the debtor cannot become his own creditor and sue

---

107   [1975] 1 WLR 758. See further p 474, n 136.

108   In setting up the now superseded Talisman, the London Stock Exchange was quick to draw the moral from this. See Charles Abrams, 'Talisman: A Legal Analysis' (1980) 1 Co Law 17 at p 19.

109   Where the customer is an individual or partnership, there is no registration requirement. Moreover, money on deposit with a bank is not usually a book debt, for the term 'book debt' means a debt due to a trader in the course of his trade, and which in the ordinary course of business would be entered in his books (*Shipley v Marshall* (1863) 14 CBNS 566), while a trader's right to repayment of surplus funds deposited with his bank is not a debt due to him in the course of his trade (*Re Brightlife Ltd* [1986] 3 All ER 673). The position would no doubt be otherwise where the depositor carries on the business of investment or money market operations and the deposit is made in pursuance of that business. See also W. J. Gough, *Company Charges* (2nd edn, 1996), pp 684–685.

110   See n 105.

111   The view put forward in the first edition of this book at p 721.

himself; his remedy is to withhold payment. In short, a purported charge over the customer's credit balance was in substance a contractual right to withhold payment and set off the bank's claim against its liability in respect of the deposit. But this view, on which both judicial and academic opinion were divided, did not find favour with Lord Hoffmann in the House of Lords decision in *Re Bank of Credit and Commerce International SA (No 8)*,[112] and while Lord Hoffmann's observations were obiter they clearly have great persuasive force, particularly since despite the theoretical difficulties[113] they respond to banking practice both in Britain and in other countries.[114] It is therefore likely that in future cases courts will uphold the charge-back as an effective security, and presumably the same is true of pledge-backs – for example, the pledge of a negotiable instrument or a negotiable security back to the issuer.

4.   Restrictions on right to withdraw deposit

Even assuming – in light of what has been stated above – that such a security is possible, a corporate customer may be unwilling to give a charge over its credit balance at the bank, eg because of restrictions on its right to give security over its assets or for fear that the bank will register the charge, adversely affecting the company's credit. So in recent years a new arrangement has evolved by which the bank, instead of taking a charge or letter of set-off, imposes restrictions on the company's right to withdraw sums on deposit with the bank. Deposits made subject to such restrictions have become known as 'flawed assets'. For example, the bank may stipulate that sums deposited by Company A shall not become repayable to A so long as money is due to the bank from A's associated company, B. At first sight this looks like a charge under another name, but there is an important difference. Security over a credit balance is intended, when enforcement becomes necessary, to result in the credit balance being applied in or towards discharge of the indebtedness which it secures. In effect, the bank takes over the credit balance to the extent necessary to satisfy the secured indebtedness and in so doing reduces or extinguishes its liability to the company in whose name the credit balance had been held. By contrast, a restriction on the right to withdraw money on deposit merely qualifies the bank's repayment obligation without giving it rights over the credit balance. The customer's claim against the bank remains at all times intact. The bank does not, as in the case of an enforced charge, take over the credit balance, nor does its withholding of repayment in any way reduce the liability of the third party the discharge of whose indebtedness is made a condition precedent to the depositor's right to withdraw its money.[115] Equally, the restriction on withdrawal does not constitute a contractual set-off, for the bank's countervailing claim is not against its creditor, A, but against a third party, B, and in any event the credit balance is not reduced by any cross-claim, it is merely frozen until the cross-claim has been discharged.

---

112 [1998] AC 214.
113 See the second edition of this book at p 659 and Roy Goode *Commercial Law in the Next Millennium* (1998), pp 69–71.
114 See Goode, *Legal Problems*, para 3–12.
115 For a perceptive analysis along similar lines, see F. W. Neate, 'Set Off' (1981) International Bus Lawyer 247.

As a second stage, the bank may reach an agreement with Company A and Company B whereby B is to take over responsibility for repayment of A's deposit, the bank being released from liability to A. The net effect is to put the bank in much the same position as if it had enforced a charge on A's credit balance to reduce or extinguish the indebtedness of B, but the agreement does not create a charge in law for it requires the assent of B to assume responsibility for the obligation to repay A and amounts simply to a novation of the contract established by A's deposit.

5. Negative pledge clause[116]

Under the typical negative pledge clause a company giving a floating charge undertakes that it will not, without the consent of the chargee, grant any other mortgage or charge ranking in priority to or *pari passu* with the floating charge. Such a clause is of particular significance vis-à-vis a subsequent fixed chargee having notice of it, for its effect is then to displace the priority which that charge would ordinarily have over the floating charge. No problem of classification arises in this situation, since a floating charge creates a security interest effective as from the time of its creation, the charge is registrable and the negative pledge is thus part and parcel of the security agreement.

More difficult is the case where the covenant not to encumber is given in favour of a creditor who does not take a security on the asset to which the covenant relates. For example, A Bank agrees to lend B Co Ltd £100,000 on an unsecured debenture, B Co Ltd undertaking not to charge any of its assets to any third party without the consent of the bank. Is this covenant a mere personal obligation or does it create a security interest? It might be supposed that the answer depended on whether the covenant would be binding on a third party to whom B Co Ltd wrongfully charged its property. But this does not necessarily follow. The critical question is whether a negative pledge gives the creditor, A Bank, a real right over the asset or whether it merely exposes the chargor to personal liability (including the possibility of an injunction) for breach of contract, with a possible claim against the chargee for knowingly inducing or facilitating a breach of contract.[117] There seems no good policy reason for allowing a creditor who has not chosen to take security expressly to elevate a purely personal covenant into a security interest, to the detriment of other creditors; and even the now very long reach of the constructive trust would not, it is thought, be extended so as to confer proprietary rights on A Bank merely by virtue of the covenant not to encumber.

---

116 For a description of the negative pledge in international loan finance, see Philip Wood, *International Loans, Bonds and Securities Regulation* (1995), paras 3-10 ff. A comprehensive analysis of the status of the negative pledge in American law will be found in Grant Gilmore, *Security Interests in Personal Property* (1965), ch 38. It should, however, be borne in mind that the exclusion of the negative pledge from art 9 of the Uniform Commercial Code is for reasons of policy and for the avoidance of doubt and does not necessarily indicate that a negative pledge would not be treated as creating a security interest at common law.

117 On the principle enunciated in *De Mattos v Gibson* (1858) 4 De G & J 276, and unsuccessfully invoked in *Swiss Bank Corporation v Lloyds Bank Ltd* [1979] 2 All ER 853, reversed on other grounds by the Court of Appeal [1980] 2 All ER 419, an appeal to the House of Lords [1981] 2 All ER 449, being dismissed.

6. *Agreement for further security if required*

The debtor may undertake to give security, or further security, if and when required by the creditor at a later date. For example, it is not uncommon for bank consortium loan agreements to provide that any charge of his property by the borrower in favour of a third party shall be matched by a charge on another asset of comparable value in favour of the consortium or of the lead bank on its behalf. Such an agreement is a mere contract and does not constitute a present equitable charge of the property, as not only is the undertaking for security contingent but the asset is not identifiable without a subsequent act of appropriation by the debtor. A variant of such an agreement is one by which the debtor undertakes that if any of his assets are charged to another borrower, a charge on the *same* asset shall automatically come into existence in favour of the original creditor equally and rateably with the charge in favour of the subsequent financier. This form of clause removes the problem of identification, but the agreement is still a purely contingent agreement, not an agreement for present security in an existing or future asset, and it therefore takes effect purely as a contract. Under both types of agreement, the occurrence of the contingency does not by itself create a security interest. The debtor must either give a completed mortgage or pledge of the asset or make a new agreement for security over it, and in the latter case the agreement will require to be supported by new value (ie an actual advance) in order to constitute an equitable security.[118]

7. *Subordination agreement*[119]

The subordination agreement is in a sense the obverse of the negative pledge. Instead of trying to obtain priority over other parties, the creditor voluntarily agrees to subordinate his prior right to that of another. As in the case of the negative pledge, the subordination agreement can arise in the context of both a secured and an unsecured transaction. For example, Debtor grants a fixed mortgage of Blackacre to A Bank and a second mortgage to B Bank. To facilitate the provision of further funds by the latter, A Bank agrees that to the extent to which its advances to Debtor exceed £100,000, its security shall rank behind B Bank's mortgage as regards loans by B Bank up to £40,000. The effect of such an agreement is simply to modify priorities as between the competing security interests.[120]

118 See pp 626, 628, and Goode, *Legal Problems*, paras 1–76, 2–15.
119 See Philip Wood, *The Law of Subordinated Debt* (1990); Bruce Johnston, 'Contractual Debt Subordination or Legislative Reform' [1991] JBL 325; John R. Powell, 'Rethinking subordinated debt' [1993] LMCLQ 357; Goode, *Legal Problems*, paras 1–79 ff; Gilmore, *Security Interests*, ch 27.
120 There is an alternative view that a legal mortgagee who agrees to postpone himself in priority to the holder of a second equitable charge in effect necessitates or brings about an exchange of proprietary interests. There are serious objections to this argument. First, it is a highly artificial way of viewing what is intended as a mere adjustment of priorities by agreement, an adjustment that the Privy Council has confirmed binds the debtor whether or not he was asked for and gave his consent (*Cheah Theam Swee v Equiticorp Finance Group Ltd* [1992] 1 AC 472). Secondly, if the exchange theory were correct, it would be necessary to register a transfer of each of the exchanged security interests. It has never been suggested that a subordination agreement attracts such a requirement. See also *Re Portbase (Clothing) Ltd* [1993] BCC 96, where Chadwick J (at 109) rejected the argument that the subordination agreement in that case had the effect of producing an exchange of security interests.

But two financiers may also agree on the subordination of unsecured claims. For example, B Bank agrees to lend Debtor £100,000 against an undertaking by a prior financier, A Bank, that the latter will not seek to enforce repayment of its advances to Debtor until B Bank has been paid in full. By this contractual arrangement the loan by B Bank becomes the senior debt while A Bank's claim is relegated to the status of the junior debt. The agreement may further provide that any repayments received by A Bank while a subordinated creditor, and any dividends received from the liquidator of Debtor in the event of Debtor going into winding up, shall be made over to B Bank and meanwhile be held on trust for B Bank. Alternatively, A Bank may simply undertake not to prove in Debtor's liquidation in competition with B Bank until B Bank has been paid in full.

So long as the junior creditor, A Bank, remains solvent, the question whether the subordination agreement creates a security interest is largely academic except in relation to accounting requirements for disclosure of security interests in A Bank's balance sheet. But if A Bank were itself to go into liquidation, the matter would become most material, for if the subordination agreement were held to be an unregistered charge over book debts, it would be void against the liquidator,[121] and any book debts vested in A Bank at the time of liquidation or arising thereafter would (subject to the claims of any other party having real rights over the debts) form part of the assets available for the general body of creditors in the winding up.

In analysing this problem it is necessary to split it up into its constituent parts and to consider separately a subordination *simpliciter*; an undertaking to account for receipts prior to Debtor's liquidation; and an undertaking as to proof and application of dividends in the winding up.

(a) SUBORDINATION SIMPLICITER. If the agreement between A Bank and B Bank goes no further than obliging A Bank to refrain from collecting payments from Debtor until B Bank has been paid in full, no question of security arises. A Bank's undertaking is purely personal, giving B Bank no rights over sums received by A Bank in breach of the undertaking, merely a claim for breach of contract, which would no doubt carry with it a right *in personam* to require A Bank to account for the monies so received.

(b) UNDERTAKING TO ACCOUNT. Suppose that the subordination agreement goes a stage further and requires A Bank to account to B Bank for sums paid to it by Debtor while A Bank is still the junior creditor. It is then a question of construction whether the undertaking is to be construed as creating a proprietary right in B Bank to sums received by A Bank or whether it gives rise merely to a personal obligation on A Bank to make over such sums, ie a *ius ad rem*.[122] In the latter case the subordination agreement creates no security interest and is not registrable. Where, however, the undertaking is intended to create a charge or trust in favour of B Bank, it will be registrable as a charge on A Bank's book debts (the obligation secured by the charge being the indebtedness of a third party, namely Debtor) and will be void

---

121 Under s 395 of the Companies Act 1985. See p 667.
122 See p 26.

against the liquidator if not registered. This will not, however, affect B Bank's right to retain sums paid over by A Bank prior to the commencement of its liquidation or, indeed, sums received from Debtor by A Bank before winding up and not yet paid over to B Bank, for on payment a book debt ceases to exist and the subsequent invalidity of the charge over it is without significance.[123]

(c) UNDERTAKING NOT TO PROVE IN DEBTOR'S WINDING UP. In so far as the subordination agreement is merely a contractual variation of the *pari passu* rights of senior and junior creditor *inter se*, there is no reason why the liquidator of Debtor should object (since the rights of the remaining creditors are not adversely affected), nor is there any ground for treating the agreement as a security agreement that would be void (if unregistered) in the event of A Bank's liquidation. By undertaking not to prove in Debtor's liquidation until B Bank has been paid in full, A Bank does not transfer any of its own rights of proof or dividend to B Bank but merely disables itself from participating in any distributions until such time as B Bank has received l00p in the pound. It has recently been held that an agreement of this kind does not contravene any principle of insolvency law.[124] Such an agreement, though common in bank mortgages and guarantees, is not very sensible from B Bank's point of view, since the effect of A Bank forbearing to prove is to benefit all the unsecured creditors, not merely B Bank. Hence B Bank loses the right of double dividend that it would obtain by allowing or obliging A Bank to prove but requiring it to hand over its dividends to B Bank.

(d) UNDERTAKING TO ACCOUNT FOR DIVIDENDS RECEIVED IN DEBTOR'S WINDING UP. If A Bank undertakes to account to B Bank for dividends received in Debtor's liquidation, then it is again a question of construction as to whether that agreement creates a purely personal obligation to transfer or whether it is intended to make A Bank a trustee-chargor for B Bank. In the latter event, dividends received by A Bank will not be available for its own creditors but will belong in equity to B Bank, subject to the fulfilment of any registration requirement if applicable. Whether such an agreement is registrable depends on whether a creditor's entitlement to dividend in a debtor's winding up is a book debt. It seems clear that it is not, for the book debt is that which produced the dividend rather than the dividend itself. Moreover a dividend entitlement is not a debt. The liquidator has statutory duties to perform but is not a debtor in respect of a dividend declared by him, and no action lies against him for payment of the dividend.[125]

(e) ASSIGNMENT OF RIGHT TO DIVIDEND. A Bank, having become entitled to a dividend, can assign its right to B Bank, in which case the liquidator must pay the dividend to B Bank.[126]

123   *Re Row Dal Constructions Pty Ltd*, n 36, in which the principle is admirably elucidated by Herring CJ.
124   *Re Maxwell Communications Corp. plc (No 3)* [1993] BCC 369, in which Vinelott J conducted an extensive review of the authorities both in England and elsewhere.
125   *Spence v Coleman* [1901] 2 KB 199, applying to winding up a similar rule enunciated in bankruptcy in *Prout v Gregory* (1889) 24 QBD 281. The rule is now enshrined in s 325(2) of the Insolvency Act 1986.
126   Insolvency Rules 1986, r 11.11(1).

8. Waiver of security rights

A creditor may agree not merely to subordinate his security interest but to waive it altogether, as regards a specified asset or class of assets, in favour of a third party. So a bank holding a floating charge from its customer covering book debts may agree to waive the charge in favour of a factoring company to enable its customer to factor the debts.[127] The effect of the waiver is that the factor acquires the debts free from the charge. The effect of a waiver on an assignee of the charge who takes in good faith and without notice of the waiver agreement is unclear. Probably it is a mere equity and as such is not binding on a chargee or purchaser for value, whether acquiring his interest at law or only in equity.[128]

9. Sub-participation in loan assets

A sub-participation, by which a lender 'sells' to another (the sub-participant) the right to receive a stated percentage of loan repayments received by the lender does not create a security interest, for the sub-participant does not acquire any beneficial interest either in the loan contract or in any assets securing repayment.[129]

10. Lien on sub-freights

Decisions holding that a lien on sub-freights was registrable as a charge on book debts or a floating charge[130] have now been doubted by Lord Millett, who in a decision of the Privy Council has expressed the view that it is not a charge at all, merely a personal right to intercept freight before it is paid to the owner and thus a right analogous to a stoppage in transit.[131] This seems the historically correct approach.

11. Provision for possession and use under a construction contract

A standard provision in construction contracts enabling the employer, on default by the contractor, to take possession of plant and machinery on site and to use them to complete the contract works does not create a security interest, since its purpose is not to provide security for payment but to enable the employer to complete the construction.[132]

12. Pledge, mortgage, charge or lien?

A pledge, as mentioned earlier, involves the transfer of possession of the security, actual or constructive, to the creditor. But the delivery of possession does not

---

127 See p 750. Usually the bank reserves the right to give notice terminating the waiver agreement as to future receivables.

128 See Goode, *Legal* Problems, para 5–56. One of the many weaknesses of s 395 of the Companies Act 1985 is that it provides no machinery for registration of waiver or subordination agreements.

129 *Lloyds TSB Bank plc v Clarke* [2002] 2 All ER (Comm) 992.

130 The latest was *The Annangel Glory* [1988] 1 Lloyd's Rep 45.

131 *Agnew v Inland Revenue Commissioners* [2001] 2 AC 710, supporting the position taken by Fidelis Oditah, 'The Juridical Nature of a Lien on Sub-Freights' [1989] LMCLQ 191.

132 *Re Cosslett (Contractors) Ltd* [1998] Ch 495, which, however, also held that a separate power to sell the plant and machinery and apply the proceeds towards discharge of the contractor's obligations constituted an equitable charge.

necessarily signify the existence of a pledge; it may equally be referable to an intention to create an equitable mortgage or charge. The capacity in which the creditor holds possession depends on the agreement of the parties. Is he intended merely to have possession, with a right of sale in the event of the debtor's default, or is he to be a security owner (mortgagee) or chargee? It seems clear that the three types of security are mutually exclusive and that it is not possible, for example, for the creditor to be both a pledgee and a mortgagee of the same asset at the same time. Similarly, a common law or legal lien cannot co-exist with an equitable mortgage or charge by deposit of title deeds, for the creditor's right to retain the deeds derives from the implied contract between the parties for the giving of the mortgage and does not subsist independently by operation of law.[133]

(iv) Security in an asset and security in its proceeds[134]

Unless otherwise agreed, security in an identifiable asset carries through to its products and proceeds as a matter of property law.[135] It is quite possible for the creditor to have rights in the same item of property both as proceeds and as original security, as where he takes a charge over the debtor's stock in trade and receivables and the debtor then sells items of stock, producing receivables.[136] The strength and quality of a security interest in an asset is not necessarily the same as in its proceeds. The debtor who gives a charge over his stock and receivables may be allowed full freedom to dispose of the stock in the ordinary course of business free from the charge without reference to the creditor but be required to hold the proceeds separate from his own monies and pay them to the creditor or to an account which the creditor controls. Such a charge will be a floating charge as regards the stock[137] but a fixed charge as regards the receivables.[138] The security interest in proceeds, unless separately created, is not a distinct security interest but is part of a single and continuous security interest which changes its character as it moves from asset to proceeds. Moreover, a security interest in a debt cannot co-exist with a security interest in its proceeds, for upon collection the debt ceases to exist.[139]

There are dicta which on a superficial reading suggest that an obligation on the debtor to apply the proceeds of his asset towards discharge of the debt, and not for any other purpose, creates an equitable charge not merely over the proceeds but

---

133 *Re Molton Finance Ltd* [1968] Ch 325. The presumption is in favour of a charge rather than a lien (*Re Wallis & Simmonds Builders Ltd* [1974] 1 WLR 391).

134 For a more detailed discussion, see Goode, *Legal Problems*, paras 1–59 ff.

135 See p 52. It is necessary for the security to be specific. A floating charge covering assets of a particular description will not carry through to proceeds of a different description, for this would be inconsistent with the power of disposition inherent in the floating charge.

136 See p 697.

137 See p 741.

138 Ibid.

139 This point appears to have been overlooked by the Court of Appeal in its controversial decision in *Re New Bullas Trading Ltd* [1993] BCC 251. See Roy Goode, 'Charges over Book Debts: A Missed Opportunity' (1994) 110 LQR 592 at p 603. See further as to floating charges pp 676 ff.

over the asset itself.[140] But the dicta must be taken in context and are not, it is submitted, intended to lay down any such rule, which would lead to great confusion. A security interest in an asset carries forward to proceeds; a security interest in proceeds does not run backwards to the asset from which they derive. If it did, a creditor taking charge over book debts would automatically acquire a security interest in the trading stock the sale of which produced the book debts. A debtor who agrees to keep a class of assets separate from his other property and to account for the proceeds of those assets as and when these arise may well be held to have created an equitable charge over the assets, not, however, because of the duty to account for proceeds as such but because of the obligation to keep the assets themselves segregated for the benefit and protection of the creditor. The duty to account for proceeds is significant in relation to the asset only to the extent that it is a necessary concomitant of a fixed security in the asset itself, as in the case of a charge over book debts.[141]

4.   LEGAL SECURITY

There are many forms of security which are created not by agreement between the parties but by operation of law. No useful purpose would be served by trying to catalogue all these (legal) securities, but they may be divided into five principal categories: the lien, the statutory charge, the equitable right of set-off, the equitable right to trace and, finally, a group of what may be conveniently termed procedural securities.

(i)   The lien

There are four main categories of lien: the common law (or possessory) lien, the equitable lien, the maritime lien and the statutory lien.

1.   The common law (or possessory) lien

This is the most important class. It entitles a person who has done work for another to detain[142] goods in his possession belonging to that other until the charges for the work have been paid. In a limited number of cases the lien is exercisable over all goods in the lienee's possession, whether the charge is related to work done on those goods or to other work. Such liens are termed general liens and are enjoyed by solicitors,[143] bankers,[144] factors[145] and stockbrokers.[146] In most other cases the lien

---

140 See, for example, the judgment of Browne-Wilkinson J in *Swiss Bank Corporation v Lloyds Bank Ltd* [1979] 2 All ER 853 at 866. The decision was subsequently reversed on the ground that as a matter of construction there was no agreement for a charge.

141 See *Re Brightlife Ltd* [1987] Ch 200, and Goode, (1994) 110 LQR 592.

142 The lienee has no right to sell the asset unless authorized by statute (eg, under the Torts (Interference with Goods) Act 1977, ss 12, 13, in respect of uncollected goods) or by an order of the court.

143 *Stevenson v Blakelock* (1813) 1 M & S 535. Whether the lien of an accountant is a general or a particular lien is unsettled. See *Woodworth v Conroy* [1976] QB 884, where the Court of Appeal found it unnecessary to decide the point, ruling that accountants had at least a particular lien.

144 *Brandao v Barnett* (1846) 3 CB 519.

145 *Baring v Corrie* (1818) 2 B & Ald 137.

146 *Re London & Globe Finance Corporation* [1902] 2 Ch 416.

is only a particular lien, that is to say, it entitles the lienee to hold the debtor's goods pending payment of charges incurred in relation to the goods detained. Thus a warehouseman has a lien on goods in his possession to secure payment of warehouse charges for those goods;[147] a repairer, to secure his charges for repairs.[148] There are well-established rules as to the circumstances in which and the persons against whom a lien can be asserted.[149] In certain conditions the lien is available not merely against the debtor but against a third party to whom the goods deposited by the debtor belong.[150] Even where these conditions do not apply, the party to whom the charges are due may be able to secure comparable benefits by invoking the court's discretion to impose terms when ordering goods to be returned to their owner.[151]

2.   The equitable lien

The common lien is dependent on possession. By contrast, the equitable lien subsists independently of possession. Typical examples are the lien of the vendor of land to secure the purchase price[152] and the lien of the purchaser to secure repayment of his deposit if the transaction falls through.[153] The scope of the equitable lien is a matter of some obscurity;[154] it is exercisable in relation to personal property as well as real property but would seem inapplicable to a contract of sale of goods, under which the general rule is that even the prepaying buyer acquires no real rights until the property in the goods passes to him under the agreement.[155]

147   A warehouseman may be able to establish a general lien by contract or usage, and the typical warehousing contract provides for a general lien. This will be effective even against a stranger to the contract if he was aware of it (*K. Chellaram & Sons (London) Ltd v Butlers Warehousing and Distribution Ltd* [1977] 2 Lloyd's Rep 192, reversed on the evidence [1978] 2 Lloyd's Rep 412).

148   *Albemarle Supply Co Ltd v Hind & Co* [1928] 1 KB 307; *Tappenden v Artus* [1964] 2 QB 185.

149   See 28 Halsbury's Laws (4th edn, 1997 reissue), vol 28, title *Lien*.

150   For the circumstances in which a lien on goods deposited for repair by one holding them on hire-purchase can be asserted against the owner, see Goode, *Hire-Purchase Law and Practice*, pp 693–704.

151   Under the Torts (Interference with Goods) Act 1977, ss 3, 6.

152   Which arises upon the making of the contract of sale and becomes enforceable by action if there is default in payment after completion (*Re Birmingham* [1959] Ch 523). However, no lien arises where it is clear that the vendor intended to rely on other security, eg a charge. See *Capital Finance Co Ltd v Stokes* [1969] 1 Ch 261; *London & Cheshire Insurance Co Ltd v Laplagrene Property Co Ltd* [1971] Ch 499; and see n 153.

153   *Rose v Watson* (1864) 10 HL Cas 672. A lien which is followed by a mortgage or charge of the property is impliedly extinguished even if the mortgage or charge is or becomes unenforceable (*Orakpo v Manson Investments Ltd* [1978] AC 95; *Capital Finance Co Ltd v Stokes*, n 152; *London & Cheshire Insurance Co Ltd v Laplagrene Property Co Ltd*, n 152). The position is otherwise where the charge is void *ab initio*, for the inference is that the lien is intended to be given up only against a charge which is for some moment of time effective (*Nottinghamshire Permanent Benefit Building Society v Thurstan* [1903] AC 6, as explained in *Orakpo v Manson Investments Ltd*, above).

154   See generally John Phillips, 'Equitable Liens – A Search for a Unifying Principle' in *Interests in Goods* (2nd edn, eds Norman Palmer and Ewan McKendrick, 1998), ch 39; Ian Hardingham, 'Equitable Liens for the Recovery of Purchase Money' (1985) 18 MULR 65; and the decision of the High Court of Australia in *Hewett v Court* (1983) 149 CLR 639.

155   See p 216. If the buyer were to be accorded an equitable lien much of the case law on the position of the buyer prior to the passing of the property would be negated.

3. The maritime lien

This is a claim given by law over a ship and her cargo for salvage, seamen's wages, damage caused by the ship and the like.[156]

4. The statutory lien

This is a right of attachment given by statute, eg to the unpaid seller of goods to secure the price.

(ii) The statutory charge

Whereas a statutory lien merely confers on the lienee a right to detain the debtor's asset until the debt is satisfied, a statutory charge is an encumbrance and if the debt is not paid, the chargee can apply to the court for an order for sale.[157] An example is the first charge in favour of the Legal Services Commission on money and property recovered in proceedings by a litigant given aid under the Community Legal Service to secure payment of costs incurred by the Commission.[158]

(iii) The non-contractual right of set-off

Like contractual set-off,[159] this is not a security in the strict sense but a right which the law gives in certain conditions to set off one monetary obligation against another. There are two sources of non-contractual set-off outside insolvency, namely independent set-off and transaction set-off.[160] Independent set-off itself embraces two distinct forms, namely statutory (or legal) set-off[161] and that form of set-off which equity applied by analogy to the Statutes of Set-Off. These two forms of set-off are purely procedural and are designed to avoid circuity of action. They are independent in the sense that it is not necessary for the two claims to be connected. They are not substantive defences but may be set up only as procedural defences which operate to reduce the balance for which the claimant is entitled to judgment.[162] They are available where both claim and cross-claim are for liquidated money sums or for relief based on the non-payment of liquidated sums, are mutual (that is, due from the same parties in the same right) and have become due. Transaction set-off is that form of equitable set-off which arises where claim and cross-claim are closely connected and there is mutuality between the parties, and it

---

156 See D. R. Thomas, *Maritime Liens*; William Tetley, *Maritime Liens and Claims*; David Jackson, *Enforcement of Maritime Claims* (3rd edn, 2000), ch 18. A ship repairer does not have a maritime lien for the cost of repairs, merely a possessory lien. The nature of a maritime lien is a matter of controversy. See *The Halcyon Isle* [1980] 2 Lloyd's Rep 325, criticized by Professor D. C. Jackson in 'Foreign Maritime Liens in English Courts – Principle and Policy' [1981] 3 LMCLQ 335.

157 Sale is not a weapon normally available to a lienee. See n 142.

158 Access to Justice Act 1999, s 10(7).

159 See p 610.

160 See the works cited in n 102.

161 That is, set-off under rules carried over from the former Statutes of Set-Off and preserved by s 49(2) of the Supreme Court Act 1981.

162 For the significance of this, see Goode, *Legal Problems*, para 7–37.

operates as a substantive, not merely procedural, defence. Transaction set-off is allowed where both claims are for money, are mutual and are so closely connected that the defendant's cross-claim impeaches the claimant's claim. It is not necessary, however, that either the claim or the cross-claim must be for a liquidated amount. The time and manner at which transaction set-off is required to be exercised is unclear.[163] It is particularly difficult for a person liable on a bill of exchange to invoke a right of set-off, because of the character of a bill of exchange as near-cash and the fact that it generates a contract distinct from the underlying contract in respect of which it was given.[164]

(iv) Tracing in equity

This has been discussed earlier.[165]

(v) Procedural securities

A party whose claim is purely personal may nevertheless be able to invoke court procedures by which moneys or other assets of his opponent are taken into the custody of the law, either to abide the outcome of the action or for the purpose of enforcing a judgment or order in favour of the claimant. The effect of the attachment is to make the assets in question a security for the claimant to which he can have recourse for satisfaction of his judgment even if the other party has meanwhile become bankrupt or gone into liquidation.

Among the acts giving rise to a procedural security are: the issue of an Admiralty writ *in rem*;[166] the payment of money into court, whether in fulfilment of a condition of leave to defend[167] or in satisfaction of the claimant's claim[168] or in compliance with an order for security for costs;[169] the payment into court of a fund, or surrender into legal custody of other property, the subject of the action pursuant

---

163 See ibid, paras 7–54, 7–55.

164 See p 523.

165 See pp 52, 456 ff.

166 *Re Aro Co Ltd* [1980] Ch 196.

167 Under CPR 1998, PD 24, para 5.2. If after the payment, in the defendant becomes bankrupt and the claimant either succeeds in the action or has his claim admitted to proof in the bankruptcy, he can obtain an order for payment out of the money to him to the extent necessary to satisfy the amount due to him (*Re Ford* [1900] 2 QB 211) and prove in the bankruptcy for any deficiency.

168 Under CPR 36.2, 36.3. If the defendant becomes bankrupt after making a payment into court in satisfaction of the claimant's claim, the claimant may (subject to any leave necessary if the time for acceptance of the money in court has expired) take out such amount as he is entitled to do and prove in the bankruptcy for any remaining deficiency (*Re Gordon, ex p Navalchand* [1897] 2 QB 516).

169 Under CPR 25.12 ff or by statute, eg Companies Act 1985, s 726(1) (reason to believe claimant company would be unable to pay costs of successful defendant). Where the defendant obtains an order for costs in his favour at the trial or as the result of the action being discontinued or struck out for want of prosecution, he may resort to the fund in court for payment of his costs even if the claimant has meanwhile become bankrupt. Again, the defendant may prove in the bankruptcy for any deficiency. If it is the defendant who becomes bankrupt and the claimant's claim succeeds or is conceded by the defendant's trustee, the claimant is entitled to an order for payment to him of the sum he paid in (*Re Gordon*, n 168).

to an interim order for detention, custody or preservation of the fund or property;[170] the appointment of a receiver of property by the court at the behest of the claimant;[171] and the attachment of an asset by way of execution.[172]

By contrast, an order which merely restrains the defendant from dealing with his assets without attaching them in any way operates purely *in personam* and gives the claimant no preferential rights vis-à-vis other creditors. So the grant of a freezing order (previously termed a *Mareva* injunction), which is designed to prevent the defendant from rendering a judgment against him abortive by removing his assets from the jurisdiction, does not confer on the claimant a preferential claim to the frozen assets (in which he has no interest of any kind) as against other creditors of the defendant.[173]

5.   THE INCIDENTS OF REAL SECURITY

All forms of real security, whether consensual or legal, confer on the secured creditor at least two basic real rights: the right of pursuit and the right of preference. The secured party can follow his asset, and its products and proceeds, into the hands of any third party other than one acquiring an overriding title by virtue of some exception to the *nemo dat* rule; and the secured party is entitled to look to the proceeds of the asset to satisfy the debt due to him in priority to the claims of other creditors.[174]

Other real rights are available for the enforcement of the security, depending on the nature of the security interest. These are: the retention or recovery of possession of the asset; sale of the asset; foreclosure; and an order vesting legal title in the secured creditor.[175] They are discussed in the next chapter. In addition, of course, the secured creditor remains entitled (except where he has obtained foreclosure) to sue on the debtor's covenant for payment and on any other personal covenants and undertakings given by the debtor. These rights are considered in chapter 23.

---

170 Under CPR 25.1(1)(c)(i) or the inherent power of the court.

171 Under CPR 69.

172 Against goods, by issue of a writ of *fi. fa.* under CPR Sch 1, RSC Ords 46 and 47 (High Court) or warrant of execution under CPR Sch 2, CCR Ord 26 (county court), the writ binding the goods when delivered to the sheriff (Supreme Court Act 1981, s 138 and Sch 7, repealing and re-enacting Sale of Goods Act 1893, s 26) and the warrant when applied for (County Courts Act 1959, s 133A, added by the Supreme Court Act 1981, Sch 3, para.17); against land, security or funds in court, by a charging order (see Charging Orders Act 1979); against debts due to the defendant, by a third party debt order (previously styled garnishee order) under CPR 72 requiring the debtor to make payment direct to the claimant to the amount of the judgment debt and costs. But the claimant cannot retain the benefit of the execution or attachment (ie the 'charge' arising in his favour by virtue of the execution or attachment – *Re Andrews* [1937] Ch 122) unless he completes it before the commencement of the bankruptcy (Insolvency Act 1986, s 346(1)) or, in the case of a debtor company, before commencement of the winding up (ibid, ss 183(3), 346(5)). As to when execution is deemed to have been completed, see ibid, as amended by Charging Orders Act 1979, s 4.

173 *Cretanor Maritime Co Ltd v Irish Marine Management Ltd* [1978] 3 All ER 164; *Flightline Ltd v Edwards* [2003] 3 All ER 1200.

174 Except, of course, a creditor who himself has a security or other real right ranking in priority to that of the secured party in question.

175 See pp 637 ff.

6. ATTACHMENT, PERFECTION AND PRIORITIES

The process by which a security interest is made to fasten on an asset so as to be enforceable against the debtor as respects that asset is conveniently termed *attachment*.[176] Attachment is concerned only with relations between creditor and debtor and their respective representatives. It is to be contrasted with *perfection*, that is, the taking of any additional steps prescribed by law for giving public notice of the security interest so as to bind third parties. Perfection requirements are in turn to be distinguished from *priority* rules, ie rules declaring the ranking of the security interest in relation to rival claims to the asset, eg by a prior or subsequent encumbrancer. Perfection does not guarantee priority over *all* parties subsequently acquiring an interest in the asset; policy may require that certain parties (for example, buyers in ordinary course of business) be allowed to take free of even a perfected security interest. Attachment is discussed in chapter 23, and perfection and priorities in chapter 24.

7. THE TRANSFER OF SECURITY RIGHTS

A security interest may be voluntarily transferred, either absolutely or by way of sub-security, in the same way as any other interest, and may also be transferred or transmitted by operation of law, eg on death or bankruptcy or through marshalling or other rights of subrogation.[177]

---

176 The term is taken from art 9 of the American Uniform Commercial Code. See also *Report of the Committee on Consumer Credit* (Cmnd 4596, 1971), para 5.6.4 and Appendix III. It is beginning to come into use in England.

177 See pp 642 ff.

23 The Creation, Enforcement and Transfer of Security Rights

Our concern in the present chapter is with the steps necessary to create a security interest valid and enforceable against the debtor, the various methods of enforcement open to the secured creditor in the event of the debtor's default and modes of transfer of a security interest by act of parties or by operation of law.

I. THE GRANT OF SECURITY: CONTRACT AND CONVEYANCE

At law, the creation of a security interest involved a completed transfer of ownership (mortgage) or a delivery of possession (pledge), as opposed to a mere agreement for a mortgage or an agreement for a pledge. An agreement to give a mortgage was at best a contract, ineffective to confer on the intended mortgagee any real rights in the asset offered as security. For this reason, the common law courts were not prepared to recognize the efficacy of a mortgage of after-acquired property.[1] Since the debtor did not own the property at the time of the mortgage, it clearly could not operate as a present transfer and was merely an agreement to mortgage the property as and when acquired. The subsequent acquisition of the property by the debtor was not sufficient to give legal effect to the prior agreement as a mortgage: after acquisition the debtor had to execute the mortgage pursuant to the agreement or perform some new dispositive act prescribed by the agreement.[2] Similarly, an agreement that an article should be delivered to the creditor by way of pledge gave him no rights in the asset. Delivery was the essence of pledge; an unperfected undertaking to deliver counted for nothing, though the common law courts were surprisingly liberal as regards constructive delivery.[3] Again, the charge (or hypothecation) of assets was not within the armoury of the common law security devices, for it did not involve either the transfer of ownership or the delivery of possession but was merely a right created by contract, deed or trust to look to a particular asset for satisfaction of the debt.

---

1 See p 37. It is still the case that security over future assets has no proprietary effect at law, even after acquisition of the assets in question, without some new act of transfer. There are, however, exceptions. In particular, the principle does not apply to (a) potential property (see below); (b) contracts for the sale of goods (see p 219); (c) assignments of future copyright (Copyright, Designs and Patents Act 1988, s 91). For the distinction between present and after-acquired property, see p 631. For restrictions imposed by the Bills of Sale Acts 1878–1882, see p 681.

2 See p 37.

3 See p 648.

Equity, treating as done that which ought to be done, considered that an agreement to give a mortgage was itself a mortgage provided that certain conditions were satisfied, and on this basis saw no difficulty in treating a mortgage or charge of after-acquired property as constituting a present, albeit inchoate, security which fastened on the asset at the moment of its acquisition by the debtor, without the necessity for any separate *novus actus*.[4] Temporary confusion was caused by Lord Westbury's repeated assertion in *Holroyd v Marshall*[5] that to be effective for this purpose the contract by which the debtor undertook to mortgage or charge after-acquired property had to be of a kind susceptible to a degree of specific performance. But in later cases[6] the judges went to some pains to emphasize that Lord Westbury's admittedly infelicitous phraseology had been misunderstood. The creditor had to show that the consideration moving from him was 'executed', ie that he had actually advanced the money, not merely agreed to advance it, for equity would not decree specific performance of a contract to borrow and lend money.[7] But once this condition had been met, the criteria to be satisfied for the specific enforceability of *executory* contracts became irrelevant, for *ex hypothesi* the mortgage agreement was no longer executory, and equity thereupon recognized the mortgage as perfected provided that the requisite formalities had been complied with and that the existence of a security interest in the asset was consistent with the agreement that the parties themselves had made.[8] By this last requirement was meant that

(a)   the agreement should manifest an intention to confer a security interest on the creditor, and not merely to give him a contractual right to have the asset made over to him;[9]

(b)   the agreement should show an intention that the security interest was to attach to the property immediately or on subsequent acquisition by the debtor,[10] and was not to be dependent on some further act, eg execution of a mortgage or charge if so requested by the creditor;[11] and

4 The equitable rule allowing the creation of fixed security in future property, which was authoritatively restated in *Holroyd v Marshall* (1862) 10 HL Cas 191, went back several centuries before that case. See Roger Gregory and Peter Walton, 'Fixed and floating charges – a revelation' [2001] LMCLQ 123.

5 See n 4.

6 See, for example, *Tailby v Official Receiver* (1888) 13 App Cas 523, per Lord Watson at 535, and Lord Macnaghten at 547; *Western Wagon & Property Co v West* [1892] 1 Ch 271, per Chitty J at 275; *R v Greig* [1931] VLR 413.

7 *Rogers v Challis* (1859) 27 Beav 175.

8 See *Tailby v Official Receiver*, n 6, per Lord Macnaghten at 347. See also the discussion in Meagher, Gummow and Lehane's *Equity* (4th edn, 2002), p 652 ff. and J F. Keeler, 'Some Reflections on *Holroyd v Marshall*' (1969) 3 Adelaide L Rev 360.

9 *Palmer v Carey* [1926] AC 703; and see *Swiss Bank Corporation v Lloyds Bank Ltd* [1981] 2 All ER 449.

10 Even if he was thereafter to execute some other security instrument by way of further assurance (*Metcalfe v Archbishop of York* (1835) 4 LJ Ch 154, affirmed (1836) 6 LJ Ch 65). An agreement for an equitable charge will be treated as creating an equitable charge, for this form of security does not involve a transfer of ownership or possession, so that 'a contract for value for an equitable charge is as good an equitable charge as can be. It could not be made any better, though the aid of the Court might be required to protect or to give effect to it' (*Tailby v Official Receiver*, n 6, per Lord Macnaghten at 549).

11 See further p 629, text and n 28.

(c) the description of the property to be given as security should be such as to enable the court to find that the asset acquired by the debtor fell within the terms of the security.[12]

The property did not have to be precisely described, merely identifiable as covered by the security agreement. There was nothing to stop a debtor from charging a class of assets, if sufficiently defined, or indeed *all* his assets[13] (a still clearer definition, for then everything was brought into the net). The one possible qualification was that an assignment of all future property would be held contrary to public policy if its effect was to deprive the debtor of all means of support.[14] Equity would also treat a declaration of trust as effective to transfer the beneficial ownership of property, whether outright or by way of security, and in this case consideration was not required.[15] But equity confined itself to agreements for a mortgage or a charge. Possession was a matter exclusively for the common law. Equitable ownership could and did exist, but there was no such thing as equitable possession. Hence an agreement for a pledge could not be elevated to the status of an equitable pledge. Such a device, though featuring faintly in American jurisprudence,[16] never took root in English soil, perhaps because it was felt that commercial requirements were adequately catered for by the various forms of constructive possession established at law.

The differences between contract and conveyance remain of some importance in English security law. So long as the security is uncompleted and rests in contract, the agreement must satisfy the conditions for a valid and enforceable[17] contract as well as being capable of specific performance in the loose sense described above. In particular, no effective security interest is created by a mere charge, or a mere undertaking to give a mortgage, unless and until new value (in the case of money, an actual advance) is made. For this purpose, it makes no difference that the charge or undertaking is by deed, for equity will not enforce an uncompleted agreement for gift, or a charge by way of gift,[18] and the intended donee will be left to his common law remedy of damages.

Where a binding agreement for security, duly supported by consideration, is concluded, the real rights created by the agreement are equitable only, and though for the purposes of attachment an equitable right is as strong as a legal right, the perfection rules for the one differ from those of the other, in addition to which an equitable right or interest is usually displaced by transfer of the asset to a bona fide purchaser of the legal title or interest without notice.

2. THE INGREDIENTS OF ATTACHMENT

In order for a consensual security interest to attach to an asset, six conditions must be fulfilled:

---

12 *Tailby v Official Receiver*, n 6, per Lord Watson at 533.

13 *Re Kelcey* [1899] 2 Ch 530; *Syrett v Egerton* [1957] 3 All ER 331.

14 The point was adverted to but left open in *Syrett v Egerton*, n 13.

15 *Richards v Delbridge* (1874) LR 18 Eq 11. An agreement for a gift will not by itself be treated as a declaration of trust (ibid).

16 See Grant Gilmore, *Security Interests in Personal Property* (1965), para 14.4.

17 See p 629.

18 *Re Earl of Lucan* (1890) 45 Ch D 470.

(a)   There must be an agreement for security conforming to statutory formalities, if any.

(b)   The asset to be given in security must be identifiable as falling within the scope of the agreement.

(c)   The debtor must have power to give the asset in security.

(d)   There must be some current obligation of debtor to creditor which the asset is designed to secure.[19]

(e)   Any contractual conditions for attachment must have been fulfilled.

(f)   In the case of pledge, actual or constructive possession must be given to the creditor.

Attachment occurs when all the above conditions are satisfied and thereupon, unless otherwise agreed, *takes effect as from the date of the security agreement, regardless of the order in which the conditions were fulfilled.* This last point is worth emphasizing. If the making of the security agreement is the first step taken by the parties, then, while no security interest can attach until there is some asset on which it can fasten and an obligation which it can secure, the agreement is nevertheless effective to create an inchoate security interest which, when the other ingredients of attachment are furnished, will be deemed to have had continuous existence since the making of the security agreement.[20] Should any condition of attachment cease to be satisfied (ie because at a given time there is no current indebtedness or asset within the security), attachment ceases and the security interest again becomes inchoate, reviving *ab initio* as soon as the missing element is once more supplied.

It is now necessary to look at the ingredients of attachment more closely before going on to consider the significance of attachment.

(i)   The security agreement and transfer

1.   The agreement

The creditor cannot, of course, rely on his own unilateral act (eg wrongful seizure) to bring a security interest into existence. Except where the security is a legal security[21] there must be an agreement on the part of the debtor that the asset shall stand as security for the debt or other obligation.[22] If the security agreement is to be relied on as itself producing attachment, without the transfer of ownership or

---

19   However, for the purpose of what is now s 395 of the Companies Act 1985 a charge is treated as created on the date of execution of the charge instrument, whether or not any money has been advanced, and the twenty-one days allowed for registration runs from that date (*Esberger & Son Ltd v Capital & Counties Bank* [1913] 2 Ch 366; *Independent Automatic Sales Ltd v Knowles & Foster* [1962] 3 All ER 27).

20   The significance of this is discussed, p 634.

21   See pp 619 ff.

22   For ease of exposition it will be assumed in the following pages that the obligation is to repay money. Security can, of course, be taken for non-monetary obligations (eg a covenant to repair) but, ultimately, the liability has to be expressed in monetary terms (damages for breach of covenant) if it is desired to enforce the security.

possession required for a security at law, two conditions must be fulfilled. First, the agreement must be valid and enforceable as a contract.[23] To be valid it must be supported by consideration[24] and, if the intended security interest is an interest in land, it must be made in writing and signed by or on behalf of both parties, otherwise it is void.[25] Secondly, the prerequisites for recognition of a security interest by a court of equity[26] must be satisfied; that is to say, the agreement must manifest an intention to create a present security, as opposed to one which is merely contingent; the creditor must have advanced his money; the property must be sufficiently identifiable; and the conditions of attachment prescribed by the agreement itself, expressly or by implication, must be fulfilled. So a floating charge, though a present security, will not attach to an asset until crystallization,[27] and an agreement framed not as a present assignment or charge of future property but as an agreement to assign or charge it after acquisition if and when called upon to do so or on the occurrence of some other uncertain event is a mere contract which does not create a security interest.[28] It follows that the subsequent demand for security or the occurrence of the specified contingency does not by itself bring a security interest into existence. The creditor must either take a completed security (ie a mortgage or pledge) or furnish new value pursuant to the original agreement or under a new agreement; and in the latter case (ie agreement as opposed to completed transfer) his security interest will be limited to the value so furnished.

23 It is, of course, possible to have a valid but unenforceable contract (see p 78) and thus a valid but unenforceable security interest. However, we include enforceability as an element in attachment, for a security interest which cannot be enforced in any manner whatsoever is a theoretical abstraction.

24 The requirement of consideration for the creation of the contract will automatically be satisfied by the more stringent requirement of equity that the consideration should be not only promised but executed. This requirement is not dispensed with by the fact that the agreement for security is by deed (*Meek v Kettlewell* (1842) 1 Hare 464, affirmed (1843) 1 Ph 342; *Re Earl of Lucan*, n 18). The same applies to a purported mortgage of after-acquired property, for this cannot constitute a transfer at law (see n 1) but rests in contract. Accordingly, such a mortgage, like an agreement for a mortgage or charge of present property, requires to be supported by executed consideration, even if by deed (*Re Ellenborough* [1903] 1 Ch 697), otherwise the intended transferee will have, at best, a right to damages at common law for breach of the promise in the deed.

25 Law of Property (Miscellaneous Provisions) Act 1989, s 2(1). The Act repealed s 40 of the Law of Property Act 1925 and with it the equitable doctrine of part performance.

26 See p 626, and *Rogers v Challis*, n 7.

27 See p 678.

28 *Re Jackson & Bassford Ltd* [1906] 2 Ch 467; *Re Gregory Love & Co* [1916] 1 Ch 203, per Sargant J at 211; *Williams v Burlington Investments Ltd* (1977) 121 Sol Jo 424. But the agreement may nevertheless constitute an estate contract for the purpose of the Land Charges Act 1972, and if registered as such, will, in the event of security being given later, be effective to give it priority over an intervening encumbrance (*Williams v Burlington Investments Ltd*, above). This is one of the exceptional cases in which a mere personal contractual right can produce a security effect by virtue of the statutory registration provisions.

2.   The transfer

Where, on the other hand, the agreement between the parties has crystallized into a mortgage or pledge,[29] questions of consideration and formalities of contract do not arise, for the real rights of the creditor now rest not on the original agreement but on the transfer of ownership or possession.[30] However, if the security is a written mortgage of goods by an individual, it must conform to the requirements of the Bills of Sale Acts unless falling within one of the exemptions from the Acts,[31] while if the security is a mortgage of land or an interest in land, it is void for the purpose of creating or conveying a legal estate unless it is by deed,[32] and even to take effect as an equitable mortgage it must be in writing and signed by or on behalf of the parties.[33] Moreover, even a valid mortgage or pledge will not give the creditor an attached security interest unless and until money is advanced.[34]

(ii) Identifiability

English law, in contrast to that of a number of other states,[35] does not require specificity of assets for the purpose of security except where the Bills of Sale Acts apply.[36] Accordingly, in the case of transactions outside those Acts, the security agreement may be expressed to cover a specific asset, a class of assets, or, indeed, all the debtor's assets, present and future, without description. The absence of any requirement of particularity greatly facilitates charges on after-acquired property in general and floating charges in particular.[37]

---

29 A mere equitable charge (hypothecation), as opposed to a charge which includes an agreement for a mortgage, does not involve a transfer either of ownership or of possession. It may be created by contract or as a term of a settlement or other transfer or of a declaration of trust, as where A transfers property to B, or declares himself a trustee for B, but stipulates that the property is to stand charged with payment of a given sum or periodic payment to C. A mere voluntary undertaking to charge property does not suffice, even if by deed (see n 24).

30 As to what constitutes delivery of possession for this purpose, see p 648.

31 See Halsbury's Laws (4th edn, 1998 reissue), vol 4(1), title *Bills Of Sale*. By a curious legislative anomaly, registration of a bill of sale is made obligatory not only to perfect it against third parties but even to preserve its validity as against the grantor in relation to the chattels comprised in the bill (Bills of Sale Act (1878) Amendment Act 1882, s 8). See further, p 651. A security bill of sale cannot in general be taken over after-acquired property (Bills of Sale Act (1878) Amendment Act 1882, s 5).

32 Law of Property Act 1925, s 52(1).

33 Under s 2(1) of the Law of Property (Miscellaneous Provisions) Act 1989 if it is an agreement for a mortgage or an attempted legal mortgage which is imperfect, or s 53(1)(c) of the Law of Property Act 1925 where it is a mortgage of an equitable interest. The effect of the 1989 Act is that an equitable mortgage can no longer be created solely by deposit of the title deeds; it is necessary to have an agreement in writing signed by or on behalf of both borrower and lender (*United Bank of Kuwait v Sahib* [1995] 2 All ER 973). It seems pointless to require the signature of the lender when the agreement is purely unilateral and the lender is neither making promises nor giving undertakings – particularly since the purpose of the Act was to facilitate transactions, not make them more complicated!

34 See p 632.

35 Eg, France, Germany, Italy.

36 See Bills of Sale Act (1878) Amendment Act 1882, s 4.

37 See further pp 50, 207 ff, as to identifiability.

(iii) The debtor's power to give the asset in security

This requirement has two facets. First, the asset must be one which is capable of being given in security. We have already seen that a pledge cannot be taken over pure intangibles because it involves the delivery of possession.[38] Subject to this, security can be given over any kind of property, tangible or intangible, except where the asset is of a kind which, because of its personal nature, considerations of public policy or a contractual prohibition against assignment, is incapable of transfer.[39] Second, the debtor must have an interest in the asset or a legal power to dispose of it. A security interest cannot attach to an asset in which the debtor has no current interest[40] except where he is authorized by the holder of such an interest to enter into the security agreement or transfer, or has power to do so by virtue of some exception to the *nemo dat* rule.[41] A security agreement expressed to cover future property creates merely an inchoate security interest, but upon the debtor acquiring an asset within the after-acquired property clause, the security interest attaches to that asset with effect from the date of the agreement[42] unless the agreement itself evinces a contrary intention.[43]

The distinction between an existing and a future asset is not quite as clear-cut as one might suppose. This is because present property is considered to include what is commonly termed *potential* property, that is, property not yet in existence but growing out of that which is in existence and is owned by the debtor. The concept of potential property applies both to tangibles and to intangibles. Examples of potential tangibles are progeny of livestock, milk from cows, wool growing on sheep, growing crops. Provided that the security agreement identifies the asset (ie the particular livestock, cows, sheep, land) from which the potential property is to grow[44] and that the debtor has an interest in that asset at the time of making the security agreement, the grant of security over the potential property will be treated as a present assignment of existing property, not an agreement to assign after-acquired property,[45] though the security interest cannot, of course, be asserted until the potential property actually comes into existence. The same rule applies to rights growing out of existing contracts. So an assignment of the right to receive sums payable in the future under an existing hire-purchase agreement or building contract constitutes a present assignment of an existing chose in action, not an assignment of future property, even though (as in the case of the building contract) the assignor has to carry out work to earn the sums payable

---

38 See p 584. See also p 648.

39 See Roy Goode, *Legal Problems of Credit and Security* (3rd edn, 2003), para 1–55.

40 For this purpose the debtor's possession of a tangible or documentary intangible constitutes a sufficient interest even if unlawful vis-à-vis the absolute owner. See p 31.

41 See pp 55, 424 ff.

42 See *Tailby v Official Receiver*, n 6; *Re Lind* [1915] 2 Ch 345; and pp 633–634.

43 As in the case of a floating charge. See ch 25. A charge on an agreement for a lease also constitutes a charge on any lease created pursuant to the agreement, even without an express undertaking to execute a charge on the lease when this comes into existence (*Property Discount Corp Ltd v Lyon Group Ltd* [1980] 1 All ER 334, affirmed [1981] 1 All ER 379).

44 See p 229.

45 See pp 229–230.

under the contract.[46] The position is otherwise, however, as regards the assignment of sums payable under future contracts, for the prospective entitlement to such sums is a mere expectancy and is thus assignable only in equity, taking effect when the debts come into existence.[47]

(iv) The subsistence of an obligation

Until the creditor has made his advance, so as to impose on the debtor an obligation of repayment, no security interest can be said to attach, even if all other requirements for attachment have been met. We are not here speaking of what is necessary to render an agreement for security effective as a security in equity.[48] Even if the debtor has executed a mortgage of property he currently owns, so that reliance on a contract for security is unnecessary, no security interest attaches to the mortgaged property until there is an obligation to be secured.[49] If there is no current indebtedness, there can be no attachment; and if an advance is made and then repaid, attachment ceases, though it will revive with effect from the date of the security instrument if a new advance is made pursuant to that instrument. This is the true analysis of so-called continuing security of the kind exemplified by a charge in favour of a bank to secure a current account. So long as there is a debit balance on the account there is a security interest with continuous existence as from the date of the security agreement. But at those times when the account is in credit or has a nil balance, the security reverts to the inchoate status it possessed before the first drawing was made on the account.

Consider the case of A Bank which takes a legal charge over B's factory premises to secure present and future advances to B. Let us suppose that B does not draw on the account at all in the week following the execution of the charge. Then during this period A Bank, though it may have the equivalent of a legal estate in the premises,[50] has no attached security interest, for it has not made any advance. Unless the parties have otherwise agreed, B is free to terminate the current account facility and ask for the return of its title deeds or land certificate and the surrender of the charge instrument. If B, without doing this, were to grant a second charge to C to secure a contemporaneous advance of £20,000, C would *at that stage* be the only secured creditor in the field. A Bank would, indeed, still have its charge but, in the absence of any drawing on the account, the interest created by the charge would have no quantum, merely a position in time. However, B now draws a cheque for £12,000 on its account with A Bank. The requirement of a subsisting obligation is

---

46 *G. &. T. Earle Ltd v Hemsworth R. D. C.* (1928) 140 LT 69. See also *Norman v Federal Commissioner of Taxation* (1963) 109 CLR 9; *Hughes v Pump House Hotel Co Ltd* [1902] 2 KB 190.

47 See *Chitty on Contracts* (29th edn, 2004), vol I, paras 20–028 ff.

48 See p 626.

49 A past indebtedness suffices for this purpose. A mortgage granted to secure a debt previously incurred is perfectly valid – for the contract law requirement of consideration applies only to the contract, not to the conveyance – but the want of new value may render the mortgage vulnerable in certain circumstances. See pp 636, 838–839.

50 Law of Property Act 1925, s 87(1). Even this is not free from doubt.

now satisfied and the legal charge in favour of A Bank fastens on the asset with effect from the date of the charge.[51] If B were subsequently to pay £12,000 into its account, extinguishing the debit balance, A's security interest would again go into limbo, giving C's interest exclusivity once more until B drew again on his account with A Bank.

Attachment requires that there be an existing obligation, even if falling to be discharged in the future (*debitum in praesenti, solvendum in futuro*). A mere contingent obligation, such as that given by a surety in respect of the indebtedness of another which has not yet matured, is insufficient. So if S Ltd gives a guarantee to A Bank for advances to S's parent, P Ltd, and secures its guarantee obligations by a charge over its assets, no security interest attaches to those assets until P has made default or some other event has occurred which makes the debt payable by P become due. Nevertheless, A Bank having made its advance to P, S is contractually committed to leaving the assets in A's hands as inchoate security so that A can have recourse to them if P defaults.

(v) Fulfilment of contractual conditions for attachment

Even if all other conditions are satisfied, a security interest will not attach until any contractual conditions for attachment have been fulfilled. Even then there will be no attachment if there was merely a contingent agreement for security. For this purpose an agreement for security over after-acquired property is treated as creating a present, not a contingent, security interest, though of course it cannot take effect until the property has been acquired.[52] An agreement is also not contingent if the stipulated event is one that is bound to occur, such as the arrival of a given date, the expiry of a specified period of time or the death of a party. But an agreement that a security interest will arise on the occurrence of a future uncertain event does not suffice to create security even in equity and even if the event occurs.[53]

(vi) In the case of pledge, delivery of possession

What satisfies this requirement is discussed later.[54]

3.   EFFECT OF ATTACHMENT

The attachment of the security interest gives the creditor real rights over the asset vis-à-vis the debtor.[55] Moreover, in a few cases attachment suffices to perfect the

---

51 This means that A's interest is first in time. Whether this suffices to give it priority is a separate question. See p 657.

52 See p 634.

53 See p 629.

54 See p 648.

55 The rights will be legal if conforming to the common law requirements for transfers (p 630) or if so provided by statute, eg a legal charge of land (Law of Property Act, s 87(1)) or an assignment of future copyright (Copyright, Designs and Patents Act 1988, s 91), otherwise they will be equitable.

security interest against third parties,[56] including the debtor's trustee or the liquidator. This seems clear enough. There are, however, certain conceptual problems involved in the concept of attachment to which we must now turn our attention.

(i)   The time factor

We have remarked earlier that when all the ingredients of attachment come together then, unless otherwise agreed, the security interest attaches as from the date of the security agreement. In other words, the security agreement creates an inchoate security which is treated by the law in very much the same way as it treats an unborn child. Until birth, a child has no legal existence and cannot be the claimant in an action. After birth, it acquires legal status and can sue even for injuries it sustained before birth. The birth gives it rights in law which run back to the time of conception. So also with the inchoate security interest. It exists by virtue of the security agreement but requires the added components of interest and obligation to give it substance. Thus, after some judicial hesitation, the courts have come down firmly in favour of the somewhat abstract notion of an existing security over a non-existing asset.

> Choses in action do not come within the scope of the Bills of Sale Acts, and though not yet existing, may nevertheless be the subject of present assignment.

Thus Lord Watson in *Tailby v Official Receiver*,[57] echoing the words of Lord Chelmsford a quarter of a century earlier in *Holroyd v Marshall*:

> At law property, non-existing, but to be acquired at a future time, is not assignable; in equity it is so.[58]

Similarly in *Re Lind*:

> It is true that the security was not enforceable until the property came into existence, but nevertheless the security was there, the assignor was the bare trustee of the assignee to receive and hold the property for him when it came into existence.[59]

The retroactive effect of attachment greatly enhances the value of the security interest. It means that where priority falls to be determined by the date of creation of competing interests, an attached security interest in favour of A is considered to have effect as from the date of the security agreement and will thus have priority over an interest granted to B and attaching after the date of A's security agreement and before attachment of A's interest.[60] Further, the after-acquired property clause binds the debtor's trustee in bankruptcy as regards moneys or other assets falling

---

56 See p 647, n 1.

57 See n 6.

58 See n 4 at 220.

59 See n 42, per Bankes LJ at 374. See to the like effect *Re Reis* [1904] 2 KB 769, and cases on the floating charge, discussed at p 000. For a spirited attack on *Re Lind*, see Paul Matthews, 'The Effect of Bankruptcy upon Mortgages of Future Property' [1981] 11 LMCLQ 40.

60 However, (1) A will not have priority as regards advances made after notice of B's interest (see p 655) and (2) crystallization of a floating charge is not retrospective, so that it is only *qua* floating security that this will relate back to the date of the security instrument (see p 679, n 18, where other consequences of the floating charge's relative weakness compared with a fixed charge are discussed).

into possession after the commencement of the bankruptcy,[61] unless, of course, the monies or assets were earned by the activities of the debtor's trustee himself;[62] and even assets coming to the bankrupt after his discharge from bankruptcy will be claimable by the secured party under the charge over after-acquired property, in priority to the claims of an assignee under an assignment made by the debtor after discharge.[63] It follows that where a company, having given a charge over its future property, goes into compulsory liquidation, s 127 of the Insolvency Act 1986, which renders void dispositions of the company's property made after the commencement of the winding up,[64] does not affect the chargee's rights over property acquired by the company after the presentation of the petition, for the date when the company is to be taken to have disposed of the property to the chargee is not the date the company acquired the property but the date of the charge.

(ii) One security interest or several?

The next question is one that greatly occupied American commercial lawyers but has received little or no attention in England. If A takes security over B's future property, does a new security interest spring up in favour of A each time B acquires an additional asset or is there but a single security interest which expands as assets come in under the after-acquired property clause? Again, if A takes security over an asset for future advances, does each advance generate a separate security interest or is there merely one security interest which varies in quantum according to the amount from time to time outstanding?[65]

Though the answer to this question has never been articulated so far as English law is concerned, the inchoate security principle just discussed compels us to support the single-interest theory, for how else are we to explain the retroactive effect of attachment?[66]

(iii) Value

Value, in the sense of an actual advance, is a prerequisite of attachment. However, where the agreement has crystallized into a transfer of ownership or delivery of

---

61 *Re Lind*, n 42; *Re Reis*, n 59.

62 *Re Jones, ex p Nichols* (1883) 22 Ch D 782 (distinguished in *Re Davis & Co, ex p Rawlings* (1888) 22 QBD 193); *Wilmot v Alton* [1897] 1 QB 17; *Re Collins* [1925] Ch 556. In particular, where what is charged is a right to future monies payable under contracts, there is a distinction between cases where the consideration for the payments is wholly executed by the debtor and those where the consideration is merely executory and is executed after the commencement of the bankruptcy by the debtor's trustee (*Re Collins*, above, per Astbury J at 562–563).

63 *Re Lind*, n 42.

64 See p 843.

65 A similar question arises in relation to security interests in proceeds. See Goode, *Legal Problems*, paras 1–64, 1–65.

66 It is true that the law restricts the ability of a secured creditor to tack further advances ranking in priority to the rights of an intervening encumbrancer, but the protection of the latter results from a priority rule and does not necessitate treatment of the further advances as creating fresh security interests. See, as to tacking, p 656.

possession, the security is perfectly valid even if given for a past consideration, as when a creditor who originally lends on an unsecured basis subsequently desires to strengthen his position by taking security. Nevertheless, security taken for new value is inherently stronger than security taken for past value. Under the former, the creditor does not remove from the debtor's estate, in cash or in kind, a penny more than he puts in; the giving of the security leaves the debtor's net asset position entirely unchanged. But where security is taken for past value, the debtor's estate is *pro tanto* diminished, to the potential disadvantage of his other creditors. It is for this reason that statute provides for the avoidance of security taken during the run-up to bankruptcy or winding up[67] if no new value was given for it.

What constitutes new value for this purpose? In general, money or money's worth given by the creditor at the time of or subsequent to the security agreement and in consideration of the security.[68] It is not necessary that the amount of the advance should match the value of the asset taken as security, for the security interest cannot in any event be greater in quantum than the amount of the debtor's indebtedness. It follows that where an advance is made on the security of after-acquired property, value is taken to be given in relation to every asset subsequently coming in under the after-acquired property clause. In effect, the secured creditor is permitted to rely on the clause to increase his security margin almost *ad infinitum*, even to the extent of picking up assets which accrue to the debtor's estate after he has become bankrupt[69] and, indeed, assets acquired after his discharge.[70] Having bargained for an elastic security before making his advance, the creditor is entitled to the benefit of his bargain.

Where the creditor provides financial accommodation in the form of an overdraft facility on a current account and there is continuing movement on the account, what starts as past indebtedness may become converted into new value through the operation of the rule in *Clayton's Case*.[71] This very important rule says that unless otherwise agreed between the parties, and in the absence of a contrary appropriation by either at the time of payment, sums paid to the credit of a current account are to be applied in discharge of the indebtedness in the order in which this was incurred, so that the earliest debit item is to be deemed settled first. The 'washing' of the account with new money may thus result in the discharge of all the indebtedness advanced before the grant of the security, leaving the security entirely for new value. For example:

> Auric Acceptance lends Beta Ltd £20,000 unsecured. Later, Auric takes a charge over Beta's factory to secure the repayment of the £20,000. Beta draws a cheque on its account for £10,000 and subsequently pays into the account two cheques received from customers, for £5,000 each. It then goes into liquidation, two months after executing the charge. The ultimate debit balance is still £20,000 but the two cheques paid into the account are applied, under the rule in *Clayton's* case, in reduction of the pre-charge indebtedness, bringing this down to £10,000, while the fresh drawing of £10,000

---

67   As to the run-up period, see pp 840 ff.
68   For the particular provisions of s 245 of the Insolvency Act 1985, see p 842.
69   *Tailby v Official Receiver*, n 6; *Re Clarke* (1887) 36 Ch D 348.
70   *Re Lind*, n 42.
71   *Devaynes v Noble, Clayton's Case* (1816) 1 Mer 572.

constitutes new value. Thus half of what was previously a past consideration has become converted into new value, and the charge is vulnerable to attack by the liquidator only in relation to the other half.[72]

New value is typically furnished by the advance of money, but benefit in kind – eg through the supply of land, goods, services or facilities – is, in general, equally effective. However, a floating charge taken from an insolvent company which goes into liquidation within twelve months (or in the case of a charge in favour of a connected person, two years) is void except to the extent that the new value falls within one of the statutory categories.[73]

(iv) Cross-over security

The most flexible form of security agreement is that by which all the debtor's present and after-acquired property is made to secure existing and future in-debtedness. Under this form of 'cross-over' security no particular asset stands as security for any particular indebtedness but the entire block of assets is made to secure a global indebtedness. For example, a finance house may agree to make advances from time to time to a motor dealer to enable the dealer to purchase stock, the finance house taking a charge over all the stock from time to time acquired and held by the dealer. The global character of the security and the indebtedness secured makes it unnecessary to consider which particular advances for which particular vehicles have been repaid. Each unit is, in effect, securing not only the advance of the purchase price of that unit but the advances for the purchase of all the other units. Provided the security agreement preceded or was contemporaneous with all the advances, the charge on stock will be treated as given entirely for new value.

4.   ENFORCEMENT OF THE SECURITY

The primary remedies of the secured creditor, apart from an action on the debtor's personal covenant for payment (if any[74]) are possession, sale, the appointment of a receiver, foreclosure and, in the case of financial collateral, appropriation towards discharge of the debt.[75]

(i)   Possession

A pledgee is, of course, in possession from the start, this being the essential ingredient of pledge. But the typical modern security interest is non-possessory. The debtor needs the asset for immediate use or enjoyment, the creditor lacks the facilities to store it (and with accommodation at a premium, the rental value of space occupied by the asset given in security would be substantial) and possession

---

72   As a preference. See p 841.
73   Insolvency Act 1986, s 245(2). See p 842.
74   A person sometimes gives his property as security for another's debt without himself undertaking personal liability as surety, as in *Re Conley* [1938] 2 All ER 127.
75   He may also have a claim against a surety.

is also burdensome in that the asset has to be looked after and, as a matter of prudence, insured.

The creditor will, however, wish to have the right to take possession in given events, notably the debtor's default. The right to take possession[76] can be (and in practice almost invariably is) expressly reserved in the security instrument, and is then exercisable regardless of the nature of the security interest, so that it is equally available, whether the creditor is the holder of a legal mortgage, an equitable mortgage[77] or a charge. Quite apart from any express right to possession, a legal mortgagee is, by virtue of his security ownership, entitled to possession the moment the mortgage is executed, irrespective of whether there has been any default by the mortgagor.[78] Whether the equitable mortgagee can take possession in the absence of an express provision to that effect is not settled.[79] It is clear that a mere equitable chargee, who has no proprietary interest in the asset but only an encumbrance over it, cannot take possession without a contractual right to do so or an order of the court.[80]

If the security comprises goods which can be seized without entry on to the premises of the debtor, the creditor may use self-help, taking the goods without an order of the court; but where the asset given as security is land, the creditor will usually either appoint a receiver to take possession for him or apply for a possession order so as to avoid the possibility of a breach of the peace, as well as liability to prosecution[81] if he were to make a violent entry.

The mortgagee's right to possession without a court order is in some circumstances restricted by statute. For example, a court order is necessary to enforce a right to possession of land under a mortgage securing a regulated agreement[82] within the Consumer Credit Act;[83] and the court has statutory power to adjourn any proceedings for recovery of a dwelling house and to stay an order for possession and postpone the date of delivery of possession.[84] No security for a regulated agreement within the Consumer Credit Act can be enforced without service of a seven-day notice on the debtor;[85] and the grantee of a bill of sale can seize the goods comprised in the bill of sale only on one of the grounds specified in s 7 of the Bills of Sale Act (1878) Amendment Act 1882.

---

76 Where the property is not in the physical possession of the debtor but is lawfully occupied by a third party, eg under a lease or rental agreement, the creditor's right to possession is exercised by directing the lessee or hirer to pay the rent to him.

77 *Ocean Accident & Guarantee Corp Ltd v Ilford Gas Co* [1905] 2 KB 493.

78 *Four-Maids Ltd v Dudley Marshall (Properties) Ltd* [1957] Ch 317. But the right to possession may be excluded by the express or implied terms of the mortgage.

79 See H. W. R. Wade (1955) 71 LQR 204; R. E. Megarry and W. Wade, *Law of Real Property* (6th edn, 2000), para 19–087.

80 *Garfitt v Allen* (1887) 37 Ch D 48. But a chargee of land by way of legal mortgage has the same rights and remedies as a legal mortgagee (Law of Property Act 1925, s 87(1)).

81 Under the Criminal Law Act 1977, s 6(1).

82 As defined by the Consumer Credit Act 1974, ss 8(3), 15(2) and 189(1).

83 Section 126.

84 Administration of Justice Act 1970, s 36.

85 Consumer Credit Act, ss 76(1), 87(1).

(ii) Sale

Possession is usually sought as a precursor to sale so that the creditor will be able to give possession to the purchaser. As in the case of possession, every class of secured creditor can sell the security if so agreed by the security instrument, and subject to any applicable statutory restrictions.[86] Even in the absence of an express provision, a mortgagee or chargee under a mortgage or charge by deed (whether legal or equitable) has a power of sale under the Law of Property Act 1925[87] except where the mortgage is a mortgage of goods within the Bills of Sale Acts, in which case the goods can be sold only after they have been held for five days or (if the mortgage secures money payable under a regulated agreement within the Consumer Credit Act) if the requisite seven-day notice has been served and has expired without the default being made good.[88] The Law of Property Act itself imposes restrictions on exercise of the statutory powers of sale,[89] but these are almost invariably excluded by the mortgage deed. In addition to his right of sale under the Law of Property Act a legal mortgagee of goods who is in possession has an implied right of sale[90] in the event of the mortgagor's default, and this power is exercisable even if the mortgage is not by deed.[91] Whether an equitable mortgagee of goods has a similar right of sale if in possession is unclear. It is thought that he would need the assistance of the court to pass a good title to the purchaser. A pledgee has an implied right of sale at common law where the pledgor defaults.[92] An equitable charge which is not by deed confers no right of sale out of court, and if the chargee wishes to sell he must apply for an order for sale.

Where there are several mortgagees, any mortgagee may sell but the effect depends on his priority. Sale by a first mortgagee extinguishes the debtor's equity of redemption and overrides the second mortgage, which then attaches to any surplus proceeds of sale remaining after the first mortgagee has taken what is due to him. Sale by a second mortgagee takes effect subject to the first mortgage unless that is discharged from the proceeds of sale.

---

86 See below. The secured creditor owes a duty to act in good faith and to take reasonable care to obtain a proper price (*Downsview Nominees Ltd v First City Corp Ltd* [1993] AC 295; *Cuckmere Brick Co Ltd v Mutual Finance Ltd* [1971] Ch 949), but apart from this he owes no general duty of care in dealing with the assets of the company (*Downsview Nominees Ltd v First City Ltd*, above). This is somewhat surprising; the mortgagee would be adequately protected by a rule that he is entitled to put his own interests first. For a criticism of the decision, see G. Lightman and G. S. Moss, *The Law of Receivers and Administrators of Companies* (3rd edn, 2000), para 7-013. See also p 852, n 174.

87 Law of Property Act 1925, s 101.

88 Consumer Credit Act 1974, s 87(1); Bills of Sale Act (1878) Amendment Act 1882, s 7A, inserted by Consumer Credit Act, Sch 4, para.1.

89 Section 103.

90 At common law and, *semble*, if the charge is within the Bills of Sale Act (1878) Amendment Act 1882, then under s 7 of that Act (*Re Morritt* (1886) 18 QBD 222, per Lopes LJ at p 241–242).

91 *Re Morritt*, n 90; *Deverges v Sandeman, Clark & Co* [1902] 1 Ch 579. But if no date was fixed for repayment, the notice must give the debtor a reasonable opportunity to pay (*Deverges v Sandeman, Clark & Co.*).

92 *Deverges v Sandeman, Clark & Co*, n 91; *Re Morritt*, n 90.

The court has power to order a sale of mortgaged property.[93] The remedy is primarily designed for cases where there is no power of sale out of court, but even where there is such a power the court is willing to make an order for sale in an appropriate case.[94]

If the proceeds of sale of the mortgaged property produce a surplus, the mortgagee is accountable for it to the next ranking incumbrancer, if there is one, or, if not, then, to the debtor. Where the sale leaves a deficiency this remains governed by the express covenant for payment, which the mortgagee is entitled to enforce.[95]

(iii) Appointment of receiver

A receiver may be appointed either pursuant to the provisions of the Law of Property Act 1925[96] or under an express power in the security instrument. The statutory power is exercisable in the same circumstances as the statutory power of sale, and is subject to the same restrictions. For this reason most receivers are appointed under express powers in the mortgage or charge.

Originally, the function of the receiver appointed by a mortgagee was to collect the income arising from the mortgaged property and apply it in keeping down interest and the expenses of the receivership, and it is this type of receiver which is envisaged by the statutory provisions[97] making the receiver the deemed agent of the mortgagor.[98] But with the growth of the modern corporation it was found necessary to confer much more extensive powers on receivers so as to enable them to utilize the charged assets to the best advantage of the appointing creditor. So the modern debenture deed will normally empower the debenture holder to appoint an administrative receiver,[99] with power to run the business of the debtor company, enter into contracts on its behalf, realize assets and ultimately dispose of the business altogether, if possible on a going concern basis. The deed will usually

---

93 Law of Property Act 1925, s 91(2).

94 As where the buyer is a special purchaser who is concerned that he may not get a good title on a sale out of court (*Arab Bank plc v Merchantile Holdings Ltd* [1994] 2 All ER 74). Another case where a party may wish to obtain a court order is to secure recognition of the validity of his acts in a foreign court, particularly in a jurisdiction which does not accept the idea of self-help remedies.

95 *Bristol and West plc v Bartlett* [2003] 1 WLR 284.

96 Law of Property Act 1925, ss 109, 101.

97 Ibid, s 109(2).

98 *Deyes v Wood* [1911] 1 KB 806; *Re Vimbos Ltd* [1900] 1 Ch 470. Originally the receiver was appointed by the mortgagor at the direction of the mortgagee; later, it was found more convenient to empower the mortgagee to make the appointment directly. One of the principal benefits of appointing a receiver and making him the agent of the mortgagor was, and is, that the mortgagee avoids the obligation imposed on a mortgagee in possession of being liable to account on the footing of wilful default. A mortgagee who takes possession has always been held strictly accountable not only for rents and profits actually received but for those he would have received if he had not been guilty of wilful neglect or default. See *Chaplin v Young* (1864) 33 Beav 330; *White v City of London Brewery Co* (1889) 42 Ch D 237.

99 Prior to the Insolvency Act 1985 he was called a receiver and manager, the two offices being invariably combined. See generally Lightman and Moss, *Law of Receivers and Administrators of Companies*.

provide that the receiver is to be the agent of the debtor company, which is to be solely responsible for his acts, omissions and remuneration.[100] Save in certain excepted categories of case, the Enterprise Act 2002 has abolished administrative receivership[101] and replaced this with the power to appoint an administrator.[102] But this power is of diminished value in that the administrator so appointed may not perform his functions with a view to realizing assets for the benefit of his debenture holder unless (a) he thinks that it is not reasonably practicable to fulfil objectives having priority, namely rescue of the debtor company or achieving a better result for creditors than would be achieved on a winding up without administration, and (b) he does not unnecessarily harm the interests of the creditors as a whole.[103]

(iv) Foreclosure

A mortgagor has the right to redeem the mortgaged property at any time by tender of the amount due, with accrued interest. This right exists even if the tender is made after the due date for repayment, and it cannot be excluded by contract between the parties.[104] Only three events can extinguish the right to redeem: sale, foreclosure and the expiry of the prescribed limitation period. Sale by the mortgagee under a court order or in exercise of his power of sale overrides the mortgagor's equity of redemption, and his rights in any surplus over and above the mortgage debt attached to the proceeds of sale. Foreclosure is the termination by court order of the right to redeem. Its effect is to vest the mortgaged property in the mortgagee absolutely free from the equity of redemption. Foreclosure also extinguishes the residue of the debt, for by obtaining foreclosure the mortgagee is deemed to have elected to take the property in satisfaction. Since the effect of foreclosure is to give the mortgagee a windfall where the value of the mortgaged asset exceeds the outstanding balance of the debt, the court is naturally reluctant to make a foreclosure order without giving the mortgagor every opportunity to redeem.[105] This means that foreclosure proceedings tend to be protracted, and in consequence have become very rare.[106] The right to recover land becomes barred by statute if the mortgagee has been in possession for twelve years without proceedings for redemption being brought.[107]

---

100 Such a provision is no longer necessary, since s 44(1) of the Insolvency Act 1986 provides that the administrative receiver is deemed to be the agent of the company unless and until it goes into liquidation. See further p 845.

101 Enterprise Act 2002, s 250, inserting ss 72A–72H into the Insolvency Act 1986.

102 Insolvency Act 1986, Sch B1, para 14. Sch B1 was inserted into the Act by s 248 of the Enterprise Act.

103 Insolvency Act, Sch B1, para 3(4). See further p 852

104 See generally *Snell's Equity* (30th edn, 2000), pp 455 ff.

105 The almost invariable practice is to make an order *nisi* in the first instance, allowing the debtor an opportunity to redeem within a specified period, after which the creditor can apply to have the order made absolute if the debtor has not then paid the amount due.

106 *Palk v Mortgage Services Funding plc* [1993] Ch 330, per Sir Donald Nicholls V-C at 336.

107 Limitation Act 1980, s 16. There is no comparable provision relating to chattels, though the claim may become barred by the equitable doctrine of *laches*; and see Limitation Act 1980, s 36.

(v)   Appropriation of financial collateral

An entirely new remedy has recently been introduced by the Financial Collateral Arrangements (No 2) Order 2003[108] in relation to cash and financial instruments given in security. This, too, allows the collateral taker, where so empowered by the security financial collateral arrangement, to appropriate the collateral in or towards satisfaction of the debt. Its effect is nevertheless different from that of foreclosure in that the collateral taker is required to value the collateral in accordance with the terms of the arrangement and in any event in a commercially reasonable manner and to account to the debtor for any excess of value over debt, while being entitled to recover any deficiency.[109] No order of the court is required.

5.   TRANSFER OF THE SECURITY

A security interest, like any other right, may be charged or disposed of by a consensual dealing or transmitted by operation of law.

(i)   Consensual dealings in security

A secured creditor may freely assign his security interest without the debtor's consent. The rules for consensual assignment of a security interest, whether outright or by way of mortgage, depend on the nature of the asset constituting the security.

1.   Goods

The transfer of a chattel mortgage entails an assignment of title to the goods comprised in the mortgage and must therefore comply with the statutory provisions applicable to such an assignment. If the assignment is by way of sale and is in writing, it must be registered as an absolute bill of sale[110] except where the mortgage is itself registered as a bill of sale, in which event the transfer is exempt from registration.[111] Where the assignment is by way of security (eg is a submortgage), it must be registered as a security bill of sale[112] unless the mortgage is registered as a bill of sale[113] or the transferor is a company.[114] In the latter case, it must be registered under the Companies Act 1985.[115]

---

108   SI 2003/3226, implementing art 4 of the 2002 EC Directive on financial collateral arrangements (2002/47/EC).

109   Regulation 18.

110   Under the Bills of Sale Act 1878, s 8.

111   Ibid, s 10.

112   Ibid, s 8 and Bills of Sale Act (1878) Amendment Act 1882, s 8. See *Jarvis v Jarvis* (1893) 63 LJ Ch 10

113   Bills of Sale Act 1878, s 10.

114   Bills of Sale Act (1878) Amendment Act 1882, s 17; *Re Standard Manufacturing Co* [1891] 1 Ch 627; *Slavenburg's Bank NV v Intercontinental Natural Resources Ltd* [1980] 1 All ER 955.

115   Section 395.

2. Land

Again, the transfer of a mortgage of land may be by outright sale or by sub-mortgage. If the transfer of a legal mortgage of land is to pass a legal title or the equivalent[116] to the transferee, it must be by deed[117] or by receipt indorsed on the mortgage and showing payment by the transferee;[118] and if the mortgage is of an equitable interest, the transfer must be in writing.[119] Writing is also necessary if the transferee is to have a legal right to sue for the mortgage debt, and must be followed by written notice of assignment to the mortgagor.[120] The transfer of a registered charge over registered land[121] is effected by a registered subcharge.[122] A legal submortgage of unregistered land may be effected either by sub-demise[123] or by legal charge.[124]

3. Life policy

A life policy assigned by way of security may be subassigned either by written assignment under the hand of the assignor followed by notice in writing to the assurance company[125] or by indorsement of the policy under the Policies of Assurance Act 1867 or assignment in the form prescribed by the schedule to that Act.[126]

4. Debts and other choses in action

A debt the subject of a legal mortgage may be submortgaged by written assignment under the hand of the mortgagee and written notice to the debtor.[127] A debt may be submortgaged or subcharged in equity in the same ways as on the creation of an equitable mortgage of a debt.[128]

5. Contractual subrogation

A person may succeed to security rights by virtue of the principle of subrogation;[129] and subrogation may arise either by contract or by operation of law.[130] The typical case of implied contractual subrogation is where moneys are advanced by lender A

---

116 See Law of Property Act 1925, s 87(1).

117 Ibid, s 114.

118 Ibid, s 115(2).

119 Ibid, s 53(1)(c).

120 Ibid, s 136. The transferee can resort to the security only for the assigned debt; he is not entitled to tack his own advances to the secured sum (*OBG Ltd v Allan* [2001] Lloyd's Rep Bank 365).

121 It is no longer possible to create a mortgage of registered land by lease or sub-lease, the sole method available being the registered charge (Land Registration Act 2002, s 23(1)(a)).

122 Land Registration Act 2002, s 23(2)(b).

123 Law of Property Act, s 86. This must, as in the case of an ordinary lease, be for a term shorter than that of the head mortgage, otherwise it will take effect as an assignment. It is no longer possible to create a legal submortgage of registered land (Land Registration Act 2002, s 23(2)(a)).

124 Ibid.

125 Law of Property Act, s 136.

126 Section 1.

127 Law of Property Act, s 136.

128 Ie by a formal or informal assignment or charge or agreement for the same.

129 See Robert Goff and Gareth Jones, *Law of Restitution* (6th edn, 2000), ch 3.

130 As to subrogation by operation of law, see below.

to discharge a mortgage previously granted by the debtor to lender B. The contract may provide expressly that on making the advance A shall become subrogated to B's rights, including all securities held by him for repayment of his loan, but an express stipulation to that effect is not essential. It suffices that it is a term of the contract between A and the debtor that the advance is to be utilized to discharge the prior indebtedness; in such a case, it is an implied term of the new loan contract that A shall stand in the shoes of B,[131] though if a fresh legal charge is executed by the debtor over the property in favour of A, then prima facie the equitable charge by subrogation merges in the higher security interest.[132] However, the mere fact that the debtor chooses to use A's money to pay off B's loan does not of itself entitle A to claim subrogation to B's charge. A must go further and show that it was an express or implied term of the agreement between himself and the debtor that the advance should be utilized in this way.[133] On the other hand, since contractual subrogation is based on the presumed intention of the parties,[134] the fact that it may result in A acquiring security for a loan for which he had not specifically stipulated security is not an objection to allowing subrogation.

(ii)   Transfer by operation of law

1.   Bankruptcy

If a creditor holding security becomes bankrupt, the debt and security pass automatically to his trustee in bankruptcy.[135]

2.   Death

In the event of the creditor's death, debts due to him and security for such debts vest in his personal representatives.[136]

3.   Subrogation by operation of law[137]

Though subrogation to a security may arise as a matter of contract,[138] this is not the sole source of the remedy of subrogation to another's security, for subrogation may also arise by operation of law. It has been said of subrogation that

> this expression embraces more than a single concept in English law. It is a convenient way of describing a transfer of rights from one person to another, without assignment or

---

131   *Orakpo v Manson Investments Ltd* [1978] AC 95, per Lord Diplock at 104; per Lord Keith at 120. For comments on the case, see Jack Beatson (1978) 41 MLR 330.
132   *Orakpo v Manson Investments Ltd*, n 131, per Lord Diplock at 105.
133   Ibid.
134   *Paul v Speirway Ltd* [1976] Ch 220.
135   Insolvency Act 1986, ss 306, 287. For the somewhat different position in the case of companies, see p 836.
136   Ie his executors, if he left a will appointing executors, or, if not, then the President of the Family Division until the grant of letters of administration (Administration of Estates Act 1925, s 55(1)(xv); Administration of Justice Act 1970, s 1(6) and Sch 2, para.5).
137   See Charles Mitchell, *Law of Subrogation* (1994); Goff and Jones, *Law of Restitution*, ch 3; Meagher, Gummow and Lehane's *Equity*, ch 9.
138   See above.

assent of the person from whom the rights are transferred and which takes place by operation of law in a whole variety of widely differing circumstances.[139]

Subrogation is a restitutionary remedy given to prevent unjust enrichment and is not dependent on the intention of the parties.[140] Subrogation to security arises by operation of law where, inter alia, a surety pays off the principal indebtedness[141] and where a creditor is entitled to invoke the equitable doctrine of marshalling.[142] This doctrine is designed to ensure that where creditor A has a charge over assets *x* and *y* and creditor B takes a second charge over asset *y*, B does not suffer, and the debtor is not unjustly enriched, as the result of A resorting to asset *y* before he resorts to asset *x*. While equity does not restrict A's right to enforce his securities in any order he chooses, B will become subrogated to A's rights over asset *x* to the extent to which A has recouped himself from asset *y*.[143] For example:

> A lends D £10,000 secured by first charges on Whiteacre, worth £8,000, and Blackacre, worth £6,000. B then lends D £5,000 secured by a second charge on Blackacre. Upon D defaulting in his payments under A's charge, A, who could have recovered all but £2,000 of his debt from the sale of Whiteacre, proceeds instead to sell Blackacre for £6,000, taking the remaining £4,000 out of the proceeds of sale of Whiteacre. Since B has thereby been prejudiced to the extent of £4,000, he is subrogated to A's charge over Whiteacre to that amount.

But for the marshalling principle B would have suffered through A's resorting to Blackacre in the first instance instead of to Whiteacre, while D would have been unjustly enriched in that the value of his equity in Whiteacre would have been *pro tanto* increased.

Subrogation is not normally allowed where the plaintiff acted officiously in discharging the debtor's liability or otherwise conferring a benefit on him.[144]

6.   ASSIGNMENT OF SECURITY WITHOUT DEBT, AND VICE VERSA

A transfer of a mortgage which contains no reference to the debt or other obligation secured by it nevertheless carries with it by necessary implication of law a transfer

---

139   *Orakpo v Manson Investments Ltd*, n 131, per Lord Diplock at 104. See also *Re T. H. Knitwear (Wholesale) Ltd* [1988] 1 Ch 275; *Lord Napier and Ettrick Ltd v R. F. Kershaw Ltd* [1993] 1 All ER 385.

140   *Banque Financière de la Cité v Parc (Battersea) Ltd* [1999] 1 AC 221.

141   *Craythorne v Swinburne* (1807) 14 Ves 160; *Mayhew v Crickett* (1818) 2 Swan 185. This applies to a mortgage as to any other security; and although the mortgage debt is satisfied by the payment, the mortgage is notionally kept alive for the benefit of the surety, who becomes in effect an assignee by operation of law. This rule of equity is now embodied in s 5 of the Mercantile Law Amendment Act 1856. See also *Ghana Commercial Bank v Chandiram* [1960] AC 732.

142   See Paul A.U. Ali, *Marshalling of Securities*, who makes a powerful case (paras 4.20 ff) for saying that whether or not marshalling is a category of subrogation, it works in an entirely different way from ordinary forms of subrogation. See also *Fisher & Lightwood's Law of Mortgage*, paras 26.8 ff.

143   *Wallis v Woodyear* (1855) 2 Jur NS 179.

144   *Owen v Tate* [1976] 1 QB 402; *Esso Petroleum Co Ltd v Hall Russell & Co Ltd* [1989] AC 643. This means that to be able to invoke the remedy of subrogation, the party discharging the liability must usually have done so either under legal compulsion (eg pursuant to a guarantee) or at the request of the debtor.

of the debt or other obligation in question,[145] and presumably the same is true of transfer of a charge. In the converse case, where the debt is transferred without mention of the mortgage, the transferor holds the mortgage as trustee for the transferee, who thus becomes entitled to it in equity;[146] but it is the transferor as legal estate owner who has the power to enforce the mortgage and is the proper party to proceedings for foreclosure or redemption.[147]

145 *Jones v Gibbons* (1804) 9 Ves 407. In the case of transfer of a mortgage of land by deed, this is expressly provided by the Law of Property Act 1925, s 114.
146 *Morley v Morley* (1858) 25 Beav 253.
147 Ibid.

24 Principles of Perfection and Priorities

This chapter is concerned with the general theory of perfection and priorities. The chapters following are designed to show the relevance of the theory to everyday business life by examining the way in which the priority rules impact on different classes of typical financing transaction.

I. THE NEED TO PERFECT

The steps necessary to create a security interest enforceable against the debtor were discussed in chapter 23. But in order to perfect the interest so as to make it effective against third parties, the law usually[1] requires a further step, namely the performance of some act which puts third parties on notice of the security interest. The effect of perfection varies according to the mode of perfection and the interest of the claimant against whom the perfected security interest is asserted. There are similar variations as regards the consequences of failure to perfect.[2] Reservation of title under a hire-purchase or conditional sale agreement[3] or a leasing transaction[4] is not regarded by English law as a form of security interest and is thus wholly immune from perfection requirements.

2. METHODS OF PERFECTION

Methods of perfection requiring a step additional to attachment[5] fall into one of two categories: those designed to give notice to the world of the existence of the security interest and those designed merely to enable an intending purchaser or incumbrancer of the asset given in security to discover the existence of the security interest. The rationale of the perfection requirement is broader for the former than for the latter.[6] Notice to the world may be given in one of two ways: by taking

---

1 There are, however, cases where mere attachment suffices. One is a charge by a company over an item of personal property outside the categories prescribed by s 396 of the Companies Act 1985, eg a fixed mortgage or charge on goods to be imported, other than a ship or aircraft. Another is the oral mortgage or charge on goods by an individual, which takes effect at law without formality of any kind (see p 629). One of the more curious aspects of the Bills of Sale Acts is that while they require a written chattel mortgage to be registered as a bill of sale, they do not prescribe writing, nor, indeed, do they apply at all if the mortgage is not reduced to writing.
2 See pp 650 ff.
3 See p 713.
4 See p 721.
5 See n 1.
6 See Roy Goode, *Principles of Corporate Insolvency Law* (2nd edn, 1997), pp 419–421.

actual or constructive possession and by registration or filing. Either of these forms of notice perfects the security interest as against third persons generally without proof of specific notice to any particular claimant or any actual knowledge on his part of the prior interest. Possession is a mode of perfection developed at common law,[7] though receiving implicit recognition in legislation relating to fraudulent conveyances[8] and bills of sale.[9] By contrast, registration/filing is purely statutory. Registration is not (indeed, under EU law cannot be) required to perfect a security interest in financial collateral already perfected by possession or control,[10] though it remains a permissible form of perfection in other cases.

In addition, a security interest which is otherwise unperfected may, in the absence of a statutory provision to the contrary,[11] be perfected vis-à-vis a particular third party by notice to that party[12] or by knowledge *aliunde* on his part or, in the case of registered securities, by novation, or of a securities entitlement held through an intermediary or a deposit account, by novation or attornment. Novation and attornment may be subsumed under the general label 'control'.[13]

(i)   Possession of the security

This is the oldest and safest method. Divesting the debtor of possession puts anyone dealing with him on inquiry and is thus equivalent to notice to the world at large. A pledge of the documents of title to goods is a pledge of the goods themselves. There are, it is true, dicta suggesting otherwise – for example, the speech of Lord Wright in *Official Assignee of Madras v Mercantile Bank of India* that 'a pledge of documents is not in general to be deemed a pledge of the goods; a pledge of the documents (always excepting a bill of lading) is merely a pledge of the *ipsa corpora* of them …'.[14] But the true explanation is that the bill of lading remains the only document recognized by the common law as a document of title to goods.[15] Given, however, that a document *is* a document of title (whether because it is a bill of lading or because it is made a document of title by statute), a pledge of the document is a pledge of the goods if so intended. The strongest form of possession is, of course, physical possession by the creditor himself with intent to assert his security interest, but the law also recognizes various forms of constructive possession, any of which suffices to perfect the creditor's security interest, save in

---

7   Even before the Fraudulent Conveyances Act 1571, the courts viewed non-possessory security with great suspicion, and after that Act the failure to take possession was regarded as almost conclusive evidence of fraud (see p 586). Notice to the debtor of an assignment of the debt by the creditor, a requirement established in what became known as the rule in *Dearle v Hall* (1828) 3 Russ 1, was conceived as the nearest one could get to possession of an intangible.

8   Fraudulent Conveyances Act 1571.

9   Bills of Sale Acts 1878–1891.

10   Financial Collateral Arrangements (No 2) Regulations 2003, reg 4(4), implementing the 2002 EC financial collateral Directive, art 3(1).

11   As will be seen, most statutes provide that failure to register shall invalidate a security interest even as against a party taking the asset with knowledge of the unregistered interest. See pp 659, 668.

12   *Dearle v Hall*, n 7.

13   A concept developed in art 8 of the Uniform Commercial Code and defined by §8–106.

14   [1935] AC 53 at 59.

15   See p 265.

those unusual cases where statute imposes a registration requirement even in relation to possessory security.[16]

Among the various forms of constructive possession is attornment, by which a third party previously holding identified goods for the debtor intimates to the creditor that those goods will now be held to the creditor's order.[17] Moreover, the debtor may himself attorn to the creditor while retaining physical possession;[18] and a creditor who as pledgee takes possession of the goods or of documents of title to them may release the goods or documents to the debtor to hold as the creditor's trustee-agent without destroying the pledge.[19]

But an attornment by the debtor must be distinguished from an executory agreement to give a pledge. The distinction may seem a fine one but it is necessary to insist upon it. A mere agreement for a pledge leaves the debtor in possession and free to deal with the asset as he chooses. Such an agreement does not of itself constitute a pledge,[20] for as we have seen[21] English law does not recognize the concept of an equitable pledge, though the debtor may be exposed to a personal liability for breach of contract if he fails to surrender the asset at the appointed time. An attornment is an immediate transfer of constructive possession to the creditor, which forthwith divests the debtor of the right to use or deal with the asset except as authorized by the creditor. Attornment thus fulfils the dual rule of attachment and perfection of the security interest. An agreement for a pledge, if in writing, is caught by the Bills of Sale Acts[22] and will inevitably be void, since it is impossible to reduce an agreement of this kind to the statutory form.[23] The same applies to constructive delivery effected by the debtor's written attornment to the creditor.[24]

(ii) Registration or filing

Some types of security interest are perfectible by registration or filing. The terms tend to be used interchangeably, but it is more accurate to speak of registration as the lodgement of particulars relating to the security, and filing as the lodgement of

---

16 As in the case of s 395 of the Companies Act 1985. See p 65.

17 There may also be attornment in respect of a fund of money or securities, but this is different in character, being simply a mode of perfection of a security interest previously created by agreement between the parties. See pp 653–654.

18 *Martin v Reid* (1862) 11 CBNS 730; *Meyerstein v Barber* (1866) LR 2 CP 38; *Dublin City Distillery Co Ltd v Doherty* [1914] AC 823, per Lord Parker of Waddington at 852. Cf the speech of Lord Sumner at 865 commenting on the different position under Scots law, which required a third independent person. In *Meyerstein v Barber*, Willes J cited *Reeves v Capper* (1838) 5 Bing NC 136 in support of the proposition that the debtor may attorn to the creditor. However, the case is not directly on the point, for it involved the momentary delivery of the pledged article, a chronometer, by the debtor to a third party, who, having received it on behalf of the creditor-pledgee, then returned it to the debtor temporarily for use on a forthcoming voyage.

19 See p 1015.

20 *Dublin City Distillery Co Ltd v Doherty*, n 18.

21 *See* p 627.

22 *Re Townsend* (1886) 16 QBD 532.

23 Which requires a transfer of ownership by way of security. See Halsbury's Laws (4th edn, 2002 reissue), vol 4(1) para 621.

24 *Dublin City Distillery Co Ltd v Doherty*, n 18.

the security instrument itself or a copy of it.[25] Two systems of registration are possible for the protection of a security interest: registration against the asset and registration against the debtor. The former is, of course, more efficacious, since anyone proposing to acquire an interest in the asset can, by making a search against the asset, discover the existence of an adverse title or security interest, whether created by the prospective debtor or by one of his predecessors in title. In other words, an assets register gives a complete picture of registered rights, whether granted by the particular debtor with whom the creditor is dealing or by anyone else. Such a register is feasible only as regards assets that are relatively substantial and uniquely identifiable – land, aircraft, ships etc. By contrast, a register of debtors will not throw up security rights granted by someone other than the debtor himself unless that other party is also on the register and his existence as a possible secured party is known to the person making the search. On the other hand, registration by name of debtor is capable of accommodating any class of asset, and after-acquired as well existing property, without the need for individual specification.[26] The searcher does not need to have a detailed description of the asset before making his search; he simply looks under the name of the debtor. No current English register relating to movables is indexed by asset.[27]

The present position with respect to registration/filing as a method of perfection is profoundly unsatisfactory on account of the multiplicity of registers,[28] the varying, and sometimes uncertain, effects of registration[29] and the lack of a rational policy underlying the sanctions for non-registration.[30] Several of the registers attract their own priority rules;[31] and certain types of security interest are registrable in more than one register.[32]

---

25 *Report of the Committee on Consumer Credit* (Cmnd 4596, 1971), para 5.7.13. The distinction is one of substance, for the filing of a security instrument or copy is public notice of its contents, whereas according to the orthodox view registration of particulars of the security interest constitutes notice only of the existence of the security and of the other particulars registered (see further, p 664). For convenience, the ensuing pages will be devoted to registration, but the distinction should be borne in mind.

26 Debtor registration is thus responsive to the general cover. See p 630.

27 In respect of all registered land, the Land Registry maintains a property register, a proprietorship register and a charges register, while an index map enables a person making a search to discover whether a particular property has been registered and, if so, its title number. All entries in the Register are open to public inspection, as are documents (other than leases or charges) referred to in the Register. As to the international register for mobile equipment, see p 1107.

28 There are currently at least eleven different registers for different types of consensual security. Written chattel mortgages are required to be filed in the bills of sale register; certain charges by companies, in the Companies Registry; charges over registered land, in the Land Registry; agricultural charges, in a separate register in the Land Registry; charges over unregistered land not protected by deposit of the title deeds, in the Land Charges Registry; mortgages of ships, in the register of shipping mortgages; mortgages of aircraft, in the register of aircraft mortgages; and charges over assets of societies regulated by the Industrial and Provident Societies Acts, in the register maintained for that purpose. In addition, there are registers of patents, trade marks and designs, and registration in the appropriate register is required for a mortgage or charge over them.

29 Discussed in relation to priorities, pp 658 ff.

30 See pp 667, 669.

31 See pp 659; 661, nn 105, 106.

32 Eg, charges by companies over land, which in addition to being registrable under the Land Registration Act or the Land Charges Act must also be registered in the Companies Registry. See below.

Since the object of registration is to give notice of the security interest to third parties, failure to register ought not in principle affect the enforceability of the security as against the debtor himself. Most registration rules reflect this approach, recognizing that registration is a requirement of perfection, not of attachment. Once again, the bill of sale is exceptional. Non-registration invalidates the security even as against the debtor himself.[33]

As will be seen, the range of third parties affected by registration, or entitled to disregard an unregistered interest, varies with the particular registration requirement.[34]

Particularly unsuitable as a perfection requirement in its present form is registration in the Companies Registry. The statutory requirements are designed to fulfil two entirely separate objectives: the provision of a company file giving prospective lenders and investors information as to the company's proprietors, management and general financial position; and the notification of a specific security interest so as to bind third parties acquiring rights over the assets given as security, and thereby preserve the secured creditor's priority. Reflecting these disparate functions, the Companies Act provides a default fine for failure to register a security interest,[35] and the civil sanction of invalidity of an unregistered interest as against subsequent secured creditors and the liquidator and creditors in a winding up.[36] Unhappily, the criteria for registrability of an interest and the sanctions for non-registration fail to distinguish between the two objectives of registration. The result is that in order to preserve the validity of his security vis-à-vis third parties the creditor is required to register it in the Companies Registry even where it is a possessory security (eg a mortgage protected by deposit of the title deeds) or is registrable in some other, specialist, register, such as the Land Registry[37] or the Land Charges Registry.[38] There have been many instances of a hapless creditor giving full public notice of his charge on land through possession of the deeds or registration in the Land Registry or Land Charges Registry only to find that he has lost his priority through failure to register the same charge in the Companies Registry. The proper penalty for such failure is the criminal penalty provided, not avoidance of the security against creditors who have in no way been misled. Again, while a criminal sanction is appropriate for failure to file within 21 days, the imposition of this period is unsatisfactory as a requirement of validity. It would be much better to make the date of registration a priority point[39] with a facility to a prospective chargee to file a priority notice or an art 9-type financing statement.[40] A further problem with the

33 Bills of Sale Act (1878) Amendment Act 1882, s 8.
34 See p 669.
35 Companies Act 1985, s 399(3).
36 Section 395(1).
37 Land Registration Act 2002, ss 27(2)(f), 29(1).
38 Land Charges Act 1972, re-enacting with amendments the Land Charges Act 1925. Conversely, registration of a charge under the Companies Act does not now dispense with the necessity for registration under the Land Charges Act except where the charge is a floating charge (Law of Property Act 1969, s 26; Land Charges Act 1972, s 3(7)).
39 Cf *Report of the Committee on Consumer Credit*, paras 5.7.4 ff.; Diamond Report, *Security Interests in Property* (1989), para 24.2.6.
40 See pp 674–675. The creditor who deliberately defers registration until the debtor is on the verge of insolvency is adequately dealt with under the rules as to fraudulent preference. See p 661, n 110.

existing system is that it is transaction-based: each charge from the same debtor has to be separately registered. This may work reasonably well for security as currently defined but would be extremely difficult if registration were to be extended to reservation of title agreements. A notice-filing system of the kind embodied in 9 of the Uniform Commercial Code is what is required. On the other hand, the registration requirements, which go too far in one direction, are too limited in another, in that they provide a *numerus clausus* of registrable interests instead of starting from the position that, for the purpose of giving protection against third parties, all security interests not perfected in some other manner should be registered, with such exceptions as are expedient.

Recent proposals by the Law Commission would remove these defects. Charges registrable in a specialist registry would not be registrable in the Companies Registry,[41] while registration would become a priority point, not merely a perfection requirement;[42] transaction-filing would be replaced by notice-filing, which would allow filing in advance of the grant of a security interest;[43] and all charges would be registrable unless exempted.[44]

(iii) Notice to the debtor or fundholder

A special mode of perfection is available as regards security in a debt or other chose in action, namely notice to the party owing the debt or holding the fund. This is the well-known rule in *Dearle v Hall*.[45] For example, A, who is owed money by X, mortgages the debt to B as security for a loan and then fraudulently mortgages the same debt to C. If C gave value and is the first to give notice of his interest to X, he gets priority, even though his mortgage is last in time, provided that when he made his advance[46] he had no notice of B's mortgage. This mode of perfection encompasses two distinct but related ideas. The first is that in the case of a chose in action notice to the debtor is the nearest equivalent to taking possession. The debt is removed from the apparent possession of the original creditor and taken into the possession of the assignee. The second is that a prospective mortgagee or purchaser of the debt can, by inquiring of the debtor, ascertain whether the debtor has had notice of a prior assignment. The rule thus provides a method of searching for a previous disposition of the debt.

It is high time that the rule in *Dearle v Hall* was abolished. No doubt it works well enough when a single debt is assigned, so that it is not unduly burdensome on the creditor to inquire of the debtor as to previous notices of assignment, but this procedure is quite impracticable when applied to a continuous flow of dealings in

---

41   *Registration of Security Interests: Company Charges and Property other than Land* (Law Com Cons Paper No 164, 2002), paras 4.199 ff, 5.55.

42   Ibid, paras 3.25 ff.

43   Ibid, Pt IV.

44   Ibid, Pt V.

45   See n 7. See John de Lacy, 'Reflections on the Ambit of the Rule in *Dearle v Hall*' (1999) 28 Anglo-Am L Rev 87, 197.

46   It is the date of the advance, not the date of the mortgage, that is relevant for this purpose. See *Bailey v Barnes* [1894] 1 Ch 25.

receivables involving a substantial number of debtors, and unnecessarily impairs the efficacy of transactions such as invoice discounting[47] and block discounting.[48] The rule is effectively displaced where the previous security or assignment is registrable and is duly registered, for the second assignee is then fixed with notice of the previous assignment,[49] and if registration were to be extended to cover all assignments of pure intangibles, whether outright or by way of security, *Dearle v Hall* would de facto become obsolete.[50] The rule is, in any event, inapplicable in cases where the debtor is under no duty to receive the notice of assignment, as where the agreement under which the debt arises prohibits assignment[51] or the chose in action is a negotiable instrument[52] or corporate security;[53] nor is a person who has not yet become a debtor affected by notice of assignment of the future debt.[54]

(iv) Control

Two further forms of perfection, which are confined to pure intangibles, are based on the idea of control, that is, the replacement of the debtor by the creditor as the person entitled to give instructions for the disposal of the asset given in security.[55] Control is obtained either by novation or by attornment. A security interest in directly held investment securities is perfected by novation, through registration of the creditor as holder in place of the debtor.[56] A security interest in securities held through an account with a securities intermediary or in a bank deposit or

---

47   See p 745.

48   See p 719.

49   See p 659.

50   The present rules governing registrability of an assignment of a chose in action do not indicate any uniform policy. A charge on book debts by a company is registrable under s 395 of the Companies Act 1985, but the section does not apply to a sale of book debts nor to a charge or other disposition of other kinds of debt. A general assignment of book debts to a sole trader or partnership firm is registrable as if it were a bill of sale, but this does not apply to an assignment of book debts due at the date of the assignment from specified debtors or of debts due under specified contracts, nor to an assignment of book debts included in a transfer of business made bona fide and for value or any assignment for the benefit of creditors generally (Insolvency Act 1986, s 344).

51   See p 749.

52   See *Chalmers & Guest on Bills of Exchange* (15th edn, 1998), pp 331–332.

53   See Companies Act 1985, s 360, which precludes a company from entering any notice of a trust on the register, and *Société Générale de Paris v Tramways Union Co Ltd* (1884) 14 QBD 424.

54   *Re Dallas* [1904] 2 Ch 385; *Johnstone v Cox* (1881) 19 Ch D 101.

55   The concept of control in English law is thus somewhat narrower than under UCC §8–106, which involves the taking of 'whatever steps are necessary, given the manner in which the securities are held, to place itself in a position where it can have the securities sold, without further action by the owner' (Official Comment, para 1). Under this formulation the secured creditor has control if he has the right to intervene in relation to the security, whether or not he has exercised that right, so that the debtor's own continued power of disposal is not considered inconsistent with control by the creditor. Under English law, by contrast, this would result in the security interest being characterized as a floating charge. See p 683, n 41.

56   Control by attornment is not legally possible in the case of shares, since s 360 of the Companies Act 1985 precludes the company from entering any notice of trust on the register or, indeed, from validly accepting such a notice (*Société Générale de Paris v Walker* (1885) 11 App Cas 20, per Earl of Selborne at 30–31).

other fund may be perfected either by novation – that is, transfer of the holding to an account in the name of the creditor – or by attornment, the intermediary, bank or other fundholder undertaking to act only on instructions from the creditor.[57] In the case of a deposit or other fund this mode of perfection is alternative to notice of assignment.

3.   PRIORITIES: SOME GENERAL POINTS

(i)   Types of priority conflict

A creditor taking a security interest will wish to satisfy himself on two points: that no prior interest subsists which will prevail over his security, and that his security will not be overridden by a subsequent disposition by the debtor. Hence any prospective secured creditor must look both backwards and forwards to safeguard his position. He looks backwards by search or inquiry, forwards by registering or otherwise perfecting his interest. Where the competing interest is a security interest only, the subordination of the creditor's rights is not necessarily fatal, for any surplus value after discharging the competing interest enures for his benefit. Where, on the other hand, the superior opposing interest is absolute, the question ceases to be one of more priorities, since the security interest is extinguished altogether.[58]

(ii)   Basic priority rules

The most important priority rules established at common law and in equity prior to 1925 have been set out in an earlier chapter.[59] They have not been fundamentally changed by the 1925 property legislation, though their significance has been reduced by the registration machinery which that legislation set up.[60] To recapitulate:

(a)   a person cannot, in general, transfer a better title than he himself possesses, so that, in general, priority among competing interests is determined by the order of their creation;[61] but

(b)   a legal estate or interest is preferred to an equitable interest; accordingly,

(c)   while as between competing equitable interests the first in time prevails, if the holder of the second interest, having advanced his money without notice of the first, gets in the legal title, he obtains priority;

(d)   the priority of successive assignees of a debt or other chose in action is determined by the order in which the assignments are made except that

---

57 A mechanism commonly used in the case of investment securities is to transfer the debtor's holding to another account in his name but designated as a pledge or escrow account and under the control of the creditor or his escrow agent.

58 See further, p 51.

59 See pp 51 ff.

60 See pp 658–659.

61 See p 55.

an assignee who takes without notice of an earlier assignment and is the first to give notice of assignment to the debtor has priority over the earlier assignee;

(e)   both legal and equitable interests acquired for value and without notice prevail over mere equities; and

(f)   one whose interest derives from the holder of an indefeasible title can shelter behind that title, even if taking with notice of an earlier title or if taking otherwise than for value, unless he committed or assisted in the wrongdoing by which that earlier title was lost.

These principles are supplemented by the following subsidiary, but none the less important, rules:

(a)   Even the holder of a legal estate or interest will lose his priority where:

   (i)   he has connived at or participated in a fraud as the result of which the later interest was acquired without notice of the prior legal title;[62] or

   (ii)   he has held out the debtor, or permitted the debtor to hold himself out, as the unencumbered owner of the asset or as authorized to deal with it free from the security interest;[63] or

   (iii) he has by his gross negligence in failing to obtain or, possibly, to retain, the title deeds enabled the debtor to deal with the asset as if it were not encumbered by the security interest.[64]

(b)   The holder of a floating charge is postponed to the grantee of a subsequent fixed charge unless this is taken with notice of a negative pledge clause in the floating charge.[65]

(c)   Normal priority rules may be displaced by agreement between the competing interests. So a first mortgagee may agree to have his interest subordinated to that of a second mortgagee. Such subordination agreements are not uncommon[66] and do not require the consent of the debtor.[67]

(d)   There are special rules governing the ability of a secured party, after the grant of a subsequent encumbrance, to tack advances or further advances ranking in priority to the later encumbrance.[68]

(e)   Discharge of a security interest automatically promotes junior security interests. So if Blackacre is mortgaged first to A, then to B, then to C, and

---

62   *Peter v Russell* (1716) 1 Eq Cas Abr 321.
63   *Brocklesby v Temperance Building Society* [1895] AC 173; and see p 666.
64   *Walker v Linom* [1907] 2 Ch 104; *Oliver v Hinton* [1899] 2 Ch 264. This last exception is a rule of equity only, to resolve competing claims between the holder of a legal title and the holder of a subsequent equitable interest. At law, the owner of property owes no duty to be careful in preventing fraudulent dealings by another. See p 000. Despite authority to the contrary there seems no logical reason to distinguish negligent failure to retain the deeds from negligent failure to obtain them in the first place.
65   See pp 686–687
66   See p 614.
67   *Cheah v Equiticorp Finance Group Ltd* [1992] 1 AC 472.
68   See below.

the mortgage in favour of A is discharged,[69] B becomes the first mortgagee, C the second mortgagee.[70]

(iii) Tacking of further advances

The superiority of the legal estate gave rise to two recognized forms of 'tacking'. Under the first, a legal mortgagee[71] making a further advance without notice that the debtor had granted a second mortgage was entitled to tack that further advance to his original loan, in priority to the later mortgage. But under the rule in *Hopkinson v Rolt*[72] tacking was not permitted without the consent of the second mortgagee as regards an advance made after notice of the second mortgage, even if the prior legal mortgagee was contractually obliged to make the further advance. In relation to voluntary further advances this restriction on tacking was sound, for otherwise, as was pointed out in *Hopkinson v Rolt*, the first mortgagee would secure a complete monopoly of the debtor's financing, even where not obliged to make further advances. Under the second form of tacking, if a legal mortgage was granted to A, followed by a mortgage to B and a mortgage to C, C could, by buying out A's interest, squeeze out B. In other words, C could use A's legal estate as a *tabula in naufragio* on which to latch C's mortgage advance and thus promote this over B's head.

Section 94 of the Law of Property Act 1925 (which apparently applies to personalty as well as to realty) abolished this form of the *tabula in naufragio*[73] and modified the rule in *Hopkinson v Rolt*. The effect of the statutory changes is that any mortgagee, whether legal or equitable,[74] can make further advances ranking in priority to a subsequent mortgage (whether legal or equitable):

(a)   if an arrangement has been made to that effect with the subsequent mortgagee; or

(b)   if he had no notice of the subsequent mortgage at the time he made the further advance; or

(c)   whether or not he had such notice, where the mortgage imposes on him the obligation to make such further advances.[75]

---

69 Discharge must be distinguished from assignment. If A transfers his mortgage to C, C steps into A's shoes as first mortgagee.

70 To English lawyers this rule of promotion seems axiomatic. German law, however, views the matter quite differently. The junior encumbrancer has no right to promotion, for he did not bargain for it and does not deserve it. The rate of interest he charges will have been fixed after taking account of his subordinate status. Hence German law provides that if the debtor discharges the mortgage in favour of A, the debtor himself can register a security interest (*Grundschuld*) over his own property, having the rank of the discharged mortgage. This is not, of course, an interest which the debtor can assert against his own unsecured creditors but it enables him to transfer the *Grundschuld* as a first charge if he wishes to obtain further funds. Seé E. J Cohn, *Manual of German Law* (2nd edn, 1968), paras 379, 461.

71 But not an equitable mortgage.

72 (1861) 9 HL Cas 514.

73 It did not, however, abolish the rule by which the holder of an equitable interest, having advanced for value and without notice of a prior equitable interest, can secure priority by getting in the legal title. See *Bailey v Barnes*, n 46.

74 In contrast with the previous position. See above.

75 A typical case is the construction mortgage, where the lender financing the construction of a building undertakes to advance stage payments as the building proceeds.

The above provisions apply even if the mortgage is not expressly taken to secure further advances, but in this case registration of the subsequent mortgage constitutes actual notice to the prior encumbrancer[76] and puts an end to his right to tack. Where, however, the prior mortgage is made expressly for securing a current account or other further advances, the prior mortgagee is not fixed with notice of a subsequent mortgage merely by reason of its registration.[77] Section 94 does not apply to registered land, but a somewhat similar set of rules is provided by s 49(1) of the Land Registration Act 2002, which does, however, introduce the somewhat surprising modification that where the mortgage is taken to secure sums up to a stated maximum, the mortgagee may tack further advances to the extent that the maximum is not exceeded,[78] even if the mortgagee has notice of the later mortgage and is under no obligation to make the further advance.

(iv) Initial advance made after notice of second mortgage

Section 94 of the Law of Property Act and s 49 of the Land Registration Act are concerned only with the tacking of further advances, not with priorities as to the first mortgagee's initial advance. But the policy underlying *Hopkinson v Rolt* would appear to apply with equal force to the initial advance,[79] for it would be unfair to the second mortgagee (M2) to subordinate his interest to that of the first mortgagee (M1) as regards even an initial advance made after notice of the second mortgage. So in relation to such an advance M1 is bound by the rule in *Hopkinson v Rolt* but without the benefit of the statutory exceptions. The rule in *Hopkinson v Rolt* seems harsh on M1 in not allowing priority even for advances made pursuant to a binding commitment to the mortgagor, and this aspect of the rule could usefully be reviewed by the House of Lords. It would also be reasonable for the common law to follow by analogy the statutory rule as to actual notice, for where the mortgagor is given a current account facility, M1 can no more control the timing of the first drawing on the account than he can subsequent drawings.

Once M2 has given notice of his second mortgage to M1, he secures priority for all subsequent advances he makes to the debtor, whether before or after fresh advances by M1.[80] It follows that if at the time of receipt of such notice M1 has not yet made any advance, the ranking of the two mortgages is effectively reversed and M1 becomes the junior encumbrancer, under the rule in *Hopkinson v*

---

76 Law of Property Act 1925, s 198; Land Charges Act 1972, s 18(5).
77 Law of Property Act 1925, s 94(2). Without this dispensation, a bank would have to make a search every time a cheque drawn by its customer was presented for payment. *Quaere* whether, in the case of a company debtor, the protection given by s 94(2) is destroyed by the entirely separate constructive notice arising from registration of the second mortgage in the Companies Registry under s 395 of the Companies Act. It is thought that the court would not apply the doctrine of constructive notice in this situation, for no banker or other person making advances on current account could reasonably be expected to search the register *de die in diem*.
78 Land Registration Act 2002, s 49(4).
79 Though that case concerned the tacking of further advances, it is clear from the speeches that no distinction is to be drawn between a further advance made after notice of the second mortgage and a first advance so made.
80 Except where M1 is allowed to tack by virtue of an obligation to make the fresh advances in question.

Rolt. The only way in which M1 can halt M2's continuing priority, short of agreement between them, is by taking a third mortgage and giving notice of it to M2, who will then be postponed to M1 as regards advances by M2 subsequent to such notice. M1 and M2 can go on playing such games indefinitely, with an endless series of further mortgages. In practice, they would get together and conclude a priority agreement.

Where M1, having taken a charge to secure a current account, receives notice of M2's second charge, he should immediately rule off the debtor's account and open a new account to record new moneys received from or for the debtor. This is necessitated by the all-pervasive impact of the rule in *Clayton's Case* previously referred to.[81] If the existing account is not ruled off or *Clayton's Case* excluded in some other manner,[82] sums received into the account after notice of the second mortgage will go to reduce the earliest indebtedness first, that is, the indebtedness ranking in priority to M2's mortgage, while as regards new drawings, M1 will be subordinated to M2. The crediting of fresh moneys to a new account ensures that there is no reduction in the debit balance existing on the debtor's account with M1 at the time M2 gave notice of the second charge.

4.   REGISTRATION REQUIREMENTS AND THEIR IMPACT ON PRIORITIES

(i)   Under the 1925 property legislation

The 1925 property statutes made no fundamental alterations to the priority rules. What they did was to provide a system of registration of mortgages and charges of unregistered land[83] not protected by deposit of the title deeds,[84] making registration equivalent to actual notice.[85] The result, however, is largely to obliterate the previously superior status of the legal title, for where registrable but unregistered,

---

81   See p 636.
82   Eg, by a contrary appropriation made in pursuance of a power conferred by the agreement or in the absence of an appropriation by the debtor himself.
83   Ie, land the *title* to which is unregistered. There remains a fundamental division between registered land and unregistered land conveyancing, the former being governed primarily by what is now the Land Registration Act 2002, the latter by the Law of Property Act 1925. Since 1 December 1990 all conveyances on sale must be registered in the Land Registry under the Land Registration Act 1925, so that unregistered titles will gradually disappear. An unexpected by-product of the registration system for charges over unregistered land was to elevate the status of a contract for purely contingent security over land, so that such a contract, though not itself creating an equitable security, is registrable as an estate contract, and, if so registered, gives priority over a later encumbrancer to any security subsequently executed pursuant to the agreement. See *Williams v Burlington Investments Ltd* (1977) 121 Sol Jo 424, and p 629, n 28.
84   If possession of the title deeds is taken, registration is not available, being considered unnecessary in that a third party dealing with the debtor is put on inquiry by the absence of the deeds. But the protection given by possession of the title deeds is not absolute. If the third party is given a reasonable explanation for the absence of the deeds and takes a legal title for value and without notice, he will obtain priority, the pre-1925 rules continuing to apply. See, for example, *Hewitt v Loosemore* (1851) 9 Hare 449.
85   Law of Property Act 1925, s 198; Land Charges Act 1972, s 18(5).

this will be postponed to a subsequent limited interest and overridden by a subsequent absolute interest,[86] while registration of an equitable interest constitutes notice to the world and thus prevents that interest from becoming overreached by a later transfer of the legal title. The distinction between legal and equitable estates and interests is now of little significance in a priority situation,[87] save in the few cases where registration of a non-possessory security interest[88] is not available, eg on a mortgage or charge of an equitable interest in land.[89]

Whether registration constitutes a priority point or is merely a perfection requirement has never been conclusively settled. The doubt arises because of a conflict between s 97 of the Law of Property Act 1925 and what is now s 4(5) of the Land Charges Act 1972.[90] The former provides priority in the order of registration, the latter preserves the common law rule of priority by date of creation of the interest, subject to displacement of the earlier interest if this is not registered before creation of the later interest. The preponderant opinion is that s 4(5) prevails.[91]

Failure to register a registrable security interest has the result that the secured creditor is postponed to a subsequent encumbrancer and loses out altogether to an outright purchaser. This is so even if the subsequent encumbrancer or purchaser was aware of the prior unregistered security.[92] This may seem odd but has a sound policy base, in that it avoids factual disputes, endemic in the pre-1925 law, as to whether the later party did or did not have notice. This principle of conclusiveness of the register applies also in the other registration systems to which reference has previously been made, including registration of charges under the Companies Act 1985.[93]

Similar principles govern security interests in registered land, but the position is here more complex, in that the registered/unregistered classification cuts across the traditional legal/equitable dichotomy.[94]

---

86 See below.
87 However, the holder of an equitable interest may need the assistance of the court to perfect his remedy against the debtor himself, eg where he wishes to sell.
88 In this context a mortgage or charge not protected by deposit of the title deeds.
89 Priority as between such charges remains governed by the rule in *Dearle v Hall*; see n 7.
90 Previously s 13(2) of the Land Charges Act 1925.
91 There is an extensive literature on this question, which has not, however, been the subject of a single reported case. See the discussion in Megarry's *Manual of the Law of Real Property* (8th edn, 2002). pp 538 ff; *Cheshire and Burn's Modern Law of Real Property* (16th edn, 2000), pp 667 ff.
92 Law of Property Act 1925, s 199(1)(i); *Coventry Permanent Economic Building Society v Jones* [1951] 1 All ER 901.
93 See p 662.
94 The standard work is Theodore B. F. Ruoff and Robert B. Roper, *Registered Conveyancing* (looseleaf, 2003).

(ii) Under the Companies Act 1985[95]

1. The registration requirement

Section 396(1) of the Companies Act 1985 gives a list of security interests requiring registration in the Companies Registry under s 395. In contrast to the Bills of Sale Acts, s 395 is aimed at transactions, not merely at documents, and may thus embrace even oral securities. Whether s 395 applies depends on the nature of the asset over which the security is taken. The following charges[96] created by the company[97] are registrable:

(a)   a charge for the purpose of securing any issue of debentures;[98]

(b)   a charge on uncalled share capital of the company;

(c)   a charge created or evidenced by an instrument which, if executed by an individual, would require registration as a bill of sale. This head covers written chattel mortgages, but only so far as not exempted from the Bills of Sale Acts. So registration is not required under this head for a mortgage or charge on goods which is not in writing[99] or which covers identified goods to be imported,[100] nor for a charge on a chose in action;[101]

(d)   a charge on land[102] (wherever situated) or any interest in it, but not including a charge for any rent or other periodical sum issuing out of the land;

---

95   Part IV of the Companies Act 1989 prospectively introduced numerous changes to the registration provisions of Part XII of the Companies Act 1985, including certain interim changes recommended by Professor Aubrey Diamond in his report *A Review of Security Interests* (1989). However, the drafting is generally considered to have been seriously flawed and the provisions are unlikely ever to be brought into force, particularly in view of the more fundamental changes that have been proposed by the Law Commission in its paper *Registration of Security Interests: Company Charges and Property other than Land Law* (Cons Paper No 164, June 2002), to which reference has been made earlier (p 652) The text which follows is based on the current provisions of the 1985 Act. See generally Gerard McCormack, *Registration of Company Charges*.

96   In this context 'charge' includes a mortgage (s 396(4)) and, *semble*, an agreement for a pledge (*Dublin City Distillery Ltd v Doherty*, n 18, per Lord Parker of Waddington at 854).

97   Section 395(1). Thus only consensual charges are registrable, not charges or liens created by operation of law (*Capital Finance Co Ltd v Stokes* [1969] 1 Ch 261; *London & Cheshire Insurance Co Ltd v Laplagrene Property Co Ltd* [1971] Ch 499).

98   'Issue' implies a series of debentures, as opposed to a single debenture or two or more debentures issued separately. As to the permitted procedure for registration of a series of debentures, see Companies Act, s 397(1).

99   Eg, an oral mortgage or a charge created by deposit of documents of title without an instrument of charge. This is because the Bills of Sale Acts bite on documents, not transactions. However, a floating charge is registrable under head (f) and a charge on a ship or aircraft under head (h).

100   Exempt from the Bills of Sale Acts by s 1 of the Bills of Sale Act 1890 as amended by s 1 of the Bills of Sale Act 1891. As to 'identified' see *Slavenburg's Bank N.V. v Intercontinental Natural Resources Ltd* [1980] 1 All ER 955, citing with approval 4 Halsbury's Laws (4th edn, 1974), para 636, n 1. (See now Halsbury's Laws, vol 4(1) (2002 reissue), para 642.) For other exceptions to the Bills of Sale Acts, see ibid.

101   To which the Bills of Sale Acts do not apply. But a charge on book debts is registrable under head (e) and a floating charge on receivables (or on any other asset) under head (f).

102   This is also required to be protected, in the case of unregistered land, by deposit of the title deeds or registration as a land charge under the Land Charges Act 1972 or, in the case of registered land, in one of the ways prescribed by the Land Registration Act 1925.

(e)   a charge on book debts of the company;[103]

(f)   a floating charge on the company's undertaking or property;[104]

(g)   a charge on calls made but not paid;

(h)   a charge on a ship[105] or aircraft[106] or any share in a ship;

(i)   a charge on goodwill or on any intellectual property.[107]

An unconditional agreement to execute a charge constitutes a charge[108] and is registrable.[109] By contrast, an agreement to give a charge at a later date if called upon by the creditor to do so does not constitute an existing charge[110] and is thus not registrable under s 395.[111]

The position in relation to charges over investment securities and other financial collateral is a little complex. Financial collateral does not as such fall within the categories of asset to which the registration requirement applies. A floating charge over financial collateral is, however, registrable unless it has crystallized and become perfected by possession or control, in which case the registration requirement ceases to apply.[112] Registration is thus alternative to possession or control as a means of perfection. The only other possible head of registration is a charge on book debts, which in the view of some might apply to charges over future dividends, but this seems unlikely.

---

103   As to what constitutes a book debt, see *Shipley v Marshall* (1863) 14 CBNS 566; *Independent Automatic Sales Ltd v Knowles & Foster* [1962] 3 All ER 27; *Paul & Frank Ltd v Discount Bank (Overseas) Ltd* [1967] Ch 348; and W. J. Gough, *Company Charges* (1996), ch 26.

104   See ch 25.

105   A mortgage of a registered ship must also be registered in the ship's port of registry under Sch 1 to the Merchant Shipping Act 1995 if it is to retain priority over a subsequent mortgage, but failure to register does not affect any status of the mortgage as a legal mortgage (*The Shizelle* [1992] Lloyd's Rep 444).

106   A mortgage of a registered aircraft must also be registered in the register of aircraft mortgages under the Mortgaging of Aircraft Order 1972 if it is to retain priority over a subsequent mortgage but failure to register does not affect its status as a legal mortgage.

107   Defined as a patent, trade mark, registered design, copyright or design right and any licence under or in respect of any such right (s 396(3A)). To preserve priority it is also necessary to register with the Patent Office a charge over a patent (Patents Act 1977, s 33(1)(a), (3)(b)), a trade mark (Trade Marks Act 1994, s 25(3)) and a registered design (Registered Designs Act 1949, s 19(1)).

108   See p 587.

109   It is not necessary that the instrument of charge subsequently executed pursuant to the agreement should also be registered (*Cunard S.S. Co Ltd v Hopwood* [1908] 2 Ch 564; *Re William Hall (Contractors) Ltd* [1967] 2 All ER 1150). Conversely, registration of the subsequent charge is effective even if the antecedent agreement for charge was not registered (*Re Columbian Fireproofing Co Ltd* [1910] 2 Ch 120). But see n 110. The whole topic is admirably dealt with in Gough, *Company Charges*, ch 27.

110   *Williams v Burlington Investments Ltd*, n 83; *Re Gregory Love & Co* [1916] 1 Ch 203. However, a creditor who deliberately refrains from asking for execution of the charge in order to avoid damaging the debtor's credit by reason of registration runs the risk of having the charge struck down as a preference if taken from the debtor when insolvent and during the six months (or in the case of a chargee connected with a company debtor, two years) prior to bankruptcy or winding up (*Re Jackson & Bassford Ltd* [1906] 2 Ch 467; *Re Eric Holmes (Property) Ltd* [1965] Ch 1052; and see p 841, as to preferences).

111   See n 110.

112   Financial Collateral Arrangements (No 2) Regulations 2003 (SI 2003/3226), regs 3 (definition of 'security financial collateral arrangement') and 4(4). See also p 843.

To comply with s 395 application for registration, accompanied by the prescribed particulars of charge together with the instrument, if any, creating or evidencing the charge, must be delivered to or received by the Registrar of Companies within 21 days after the date of creation of the charge.[113] If this is done, the charge is perfected under s 395 even if there is a delay in the registration process itself, or, indeed, even if through inadvertence or loss of the documents the particulars delivered are never placed on the register at all.

The issue of a certificate of registration is conclusive evidence that the registration requirements of the Act have been satisfied,[114] even if it is later found that the filed particulars omitted a class of asset covered by the security,[115] misstated the date of creation of the charge[116] or the amount secured[117] or contained some other inaccuracy, and even if the charge should never have been accepted for registration in the first place.[118]

2.   The effect of registration

Registration of the security interest is merely a perfection requirement. It does not validate an ineffective security, nor does it constitute a priority point. Provided that the interest is registered within 21 days, it has priority according to the date of its creation, and thus prevails over a later interest registered first, despite the fact that the grantee of the latter interest had no means of discovering from the register the existence of the prior charge.[119]

Conversely, registration does not guarantee priority; it merely serves negatively to prevent avoidance of the security as against a subsequent encumbrancer.[120] Whether a security interest perfected by registration has priority in any given conflict is to be determined by the normal priority rules established at common law and by any special rules prescribed by other legislation for the particular type of asset in question.[121] Since notice of the security interest is usually a relevant factor under any priority rule, the first question to consider is the extent to which registration of a charge given by a company constitutes notice of the existence of the terms of the charge. It should, however, be borne in mind that

---

113   Section 395(1). The 21 days runs from the date of execution of the charge even if no money has then been advanced or the advance was made before execution of the charge (*Re Columbian Fireproofing Co Ltd*, n 109).

114   Section 401(2).

115   *National Provincial and Union Bank of England v Charnley* [1924] 1 KB 431.

116   *Re Eric Holmes (Property) Ltd*, n 110; *Re C. L. Nye Ltd* [1971] Ch 442. Hence if as the result of misstatement of the date the Registrar of Companies was led to believe that the application had been lodged in due time, the certificate of registration is conclusive, even if more than 21 days had in fact elapsed since the date of creation of the charge (*Re C. L. Nye Ltd*, above; see also *R. v Registrar of Companies, ex p Central Bank of India* [1986] QB 1114).

117   *Re Mechanisations (Eaglescliffe) Ltd* [1966] Ch 20.

118   *R v Registrar of Companies, ex p Central Bank of India*, n 116; *Exeter Trust Ltd v Screenways Ltd* [1991] BCLC 888.

119   So the security obtained by a clear search is by no means as complete as is commonly supposed.

120   See p 667.

121   As to land, see p 659; as to ships and aircraft, p 669.

not all third parties taking with notice of the security interest are necessarily affected by it.[122]

As respects those filed particulars for which filing is prescribed, registration constitutes notice to all persons dealing with the charged asset who could reasonably be expected to search the register. So much at least is certain. Beyond this, the extent to which registration constitutes notice is a matter of conjecture. The problem can be broken down into segments.

(a) PARTICULARS FILED VOLUNTARILY. It is commonly supposed that all particulars of security featuring on the company file are matters of public record. On this basis it is usual practice to include in the filed particulars relating to a charge or debenture reference to any provision prohibiting or restricting the creation of subsequent charges, the assumption being that the inclusion of these restrictions in the filed particulars constitutes notice of them. But as Professor Farrar has rightly pointed out, confidence in this device is misplaced.[123] If it be the case that registration of a security agreement is notice only of the existence of the agreement, not of its contents, so that discovery of the former does not impose on the discoverer the duty to inquire for the latter, a person who does not choose to search cannot be fixed with notice of any facts which are not *required* to be included in the filed particulars, for he has no reason to expect that they will be on file. It is no answer to say that had he searched for the prescribed particulars, he would also have come across the further details voluntarily filed, for he is entitled to take his chance in not searching for the former without having his risk increased by a filing not prescribed by statute.

(b) INFORMATION OMITTED FROM THE FILED PARTICULARS. As a corollary of (a), a third party should not be affected by notice of information which should have been included in the filed particulars and was not.[124] If a class of assets comprised in the security is omitted from the particulars or if these erroneously describe the amount secured as limited to a particular figure when in fact it covers other indebtedness, why should the secured creditor be allowed to assert the security over the undisclosed assets or additional indebtedness as against innocent third parties? Are they not entitled to rely on the particulars filed? A contrary conclusion would be wholly inconsistent with the proposition (which we shall for the moment assume to be correct) that registration of an instrument of charge is not notice of its contents; for if, by reason of an omission in the filed particulars, the true coverage of the security is ascertainable only from an examination of the charge instrument, the omitted information cannot be a matter of public record solely by reason of the registration.

---

122 See p 666.

123 'Floating Charges and Priorities' (1974) 38 Conv 315 at p 325. The device is, in any event, necessary only on the assumption, which Professor Farrar challenges, that registration of the charge does not constitute notice either of its terms generally or of the restriction on creation of subsequent charges. See further below.

124 The particulars prescribed by s 401(1)(b) are the date of creation of the charge, the amount it secures, short particulars of the property charged and the persons entitled to the charge. It is generally assumed that the reference to 'the amount secured by the charge' does not preclude a charge to secure 'all moneys due and to become due', though the point is not free from doubt.

It is unfortunate that none of the cases in which the question of erroneous particulars arose[125] involved a priority dispute. The issue before the court was thus a different one, viz whether the omission vitiated the registration, a point readily disposed of by reference to the conclusive nature of the registrar's certificate of registration. Thus in *National Provincial and Union Bank of England v Charnley*,[126] where in the same instrument a company granted to its bank a mortgage over its leasehold premises and an equitable charge over its movable plant[127] but the filed particulars omitted reference to the plant, it was held that the charge on the plant was nevertheless valid against an execution creditor, since registration had been duly effected. Notice was here irrelevant, for a charge on chattels binds an execution creditor[128] whether or not he has notice of it. But suppose that the claimant, instead of being an execution creditor, had acquired a legal title to plant within the bank's equitable charge,[129] whether by purchase from the company or by taking a legal mortgage for value. Then he could surely have claimed that despite the validity of the registration of the bank's charge he had obtained priority, under the normal rule that a bona fide purchaser of the legal title for value and without notice has priority over a previous equitable encumbrance.[130]

(c) NOTICE OF CONTENTS OF SECURITY AGREEMENT. It has been said in a number of cases that registration of an instrument of charge constitutes notice of the existence of the charge but not notice of the contents of the charge instrument.[131] Practitioners regard the principle as well established, and this is why the filed particulars relating to a floating charge usually record restrictions imposed on subsequent dealings with the asset, though, as we have seen, this technique may well not be effective.

However, Professor Farrar, while apparently accepting the soundness of the principle that registration of a charge instrument is not, as such, notice of its contents, argues that once a person has notice of the existence of the instrument he also has, at common law, inferred knowledge of all matters as regards which he could reasonably have been expected to make inquiry.[132] Professor Farrar contends that one such matter is the existence of clauses restricting the grant of subsequent charges ranking in priority to or *pari passu* with a floating charge. He deals with the cases by saying that most of these were decided before the introduction of registration of charges and at a time when such restrictive clauses were less universally used than now, making the additional point that the courts addressed

---

125 See nn 115, 118.

126 See n 115.

127 The instrument was framed as a 'demise' of the plant but, as it covered further chattels brought on the premises, the court treated it as creating an equitable floating charge in relation to the further assets.

128 Even if it is a floating charge, provided that (as in this case) the charge crystallizes before completion of the execution (*Robson v Smith* [1895] 2 Ch 118; *Cairney v Back* [1906] 2 KB 746).

129 Ie, plant acquired after the date of that charge.

130 See p 656.

131 *English & Scottish Mercantile Investment Co v Brunton* [1892] 2 QB 700; *Re Standard Rotary Machine Co* (1906) 95 LT 829; *Wilson v Kelland* [1910] 2 Ch 306; *G. & T. Earle Ltd v Hemsworth R. D. C.* (1928) 44 TLR 605; *Siebe Gorman & Co Ltd v Barclays Bank Ltd* [1979] 2 Lloyd's Rep 142. The cases prior to *Siebe Gorman* are reviewed by Farrar (1974) 38 Conv 315 at 320 ff.

132 Farrar (1974) 38 Conv 315 at p 322.

themselves only to the question of constructive notice arising from registration, not factually inferred knowledge at common law.[133]

Before we consider these arguments, it is worth making the point that the issue will normally be of relevance only in relation to a floating charge. A fixed charge, being a specific security, does not allow the debtor freedom to deal with the charged assets in the ordinary course of business. So, in principle, a fixed chargee has priority over all subsequent encumbrancers except a bona fide purchaser for value of the legal estate or title without notice; and notice of the existence of the prior fixed charge suffices to subordinate the purchaser of the legal estate or title, whether or not he has notice of the contents of the charge instrument. The peculiarity of the floating charge is that, by virtue of the powers of disposition left to the debtor company, it is in principle subordinated to a subsequent fixed charge, whether legal or equitable.

Is Professor Farrar right in saying that because restrictive clauses are now so common, a subsequent purchaser or encumbrancer, though not having constructive notice of them by reason of the registration, has at least a duty to inquire further and will be bound by restrictions which reasonable inquiry would have revealed? The argument is an attractive one, particularly since a creditor has a statutory right to inspect a copy of the charge instrument at the company's registered office[134] and to take a copy of it.[135] Nevertheless, there are compelling reasons for upholding the traditional view. In the first place, it is the approach adopted in all the cases, even at a time when restrictive clauses had become quite common, and it is difficult to accept that the courts did not have in mind inferred knowledge as well as constructive notice in the narrow sense. Secondly, it is important to avoid undue restraints on dealings with assets in the ordinary course of business. The courts have always been reluctant to apply the doctrine of notice to commercial transactions,[136] and the policy is a sound one. The mere fact that a particular contractual provision is in common use has never been regarded as sufficient in commercial law to put a party on notice of its existence in relation to an individual transaction. Knowledge of facts specific to that transaction is required.[137] If the position were otherwise, most buyers of goods would now be considered to have notice of the fact that their sellers had bought under reservation of title. Thirdly, a person does not have inferred knowledge of facts at common law merely because a reasonable man would have been put on inquiry. It must be shown that he deliberately turned a blind eye.

133 Ibid.
134 Companies Act 1985, s 408.
135 *Nelson v Anglo-American Land Mortgage Agency Co* [1897] 1 Ch 130.
136 See n 138, and *Eagle Star Insurance Co Ltd v Spratt* [1971] 2 Lloyd's Rep 116, per Lord Denning MR at 128.
137 We can here pray in aid the various property cases which say that an intending purchaser or mortgagee has no duty to investigate documents the existence of which is disclosed or discovered unless from the information given it is apparent that those documents will necessarily affect the title (*Jones v Smith* (1841) 1 Hare 43, affirmed (1843) 1 Ph 244; *English & Scottish Mercantile Investment Co v Brunton*, n 131). See also the judgment of Deputy Judge Susan Kwan in *ABN Amro Bank NV v Chiyu Banking Corp Ltd* [2001] 2 HKLRD 175.

(d) LIMITATIONS ON THE DOCTRINE OF CONSTRUCTIVE NOTICE. The equitable doctrine of constructive notice was pushed to its limits, if not beyond them, in the nineteenth century, and towards the end of that century the courts were beginning to react against its excesses. In several cases we find judges saying that the constructive notice doctrine ought not to be extended, and in particular that it should not be applied in relation to chattels or commercial transactions.[138] But these statements must be read in the context of the facts of the particular case before the court. It is, indeed, important that commercial dealings in goods and receivables should not be equated with dealings in land, for there is not the time to pursue the types of inquiry that are commonly pursued in land transactions, and commercial dealings would be seriously hampered if subject to the full rigour of the doctrine of constructive notice. There is, however, a distinction to be drawn between traders and consumers buying goods sold in the ordinary course of business and creditors taking security for advances. A buyer in the ordinary course of business cannot be expected to search against his seller in the Companies Registry before consummating his purchase, and he does not, by reason only of registration of a security interest, have constructive notice of that interest.[139] On the other hand, there is no reason why a bank or other financier taking commercial security over the movable plant and other chattels of an enterprise should not be expected to search for prior charges. To try to define the limits of the constructive notice doctrine by reference to types of asset or classes of transaction is an exercise in futility. The court must be free to adopt a flexible approach, and consider the circumstances of the particular facts before it. With respect to the effect of registration we would reformulate the principle as follows: *registration fixes a party with notice, within the limits previously described, if and only if the dealing between him and the debtor with respect to the asset is of such a kind that it would be reasonable to expect the party in question to search*. So registration of a charge in the Companies Registry will not by itself constitute constructive notice to a buyer in ordinary course of business or to a bank which, having taken a prior charge to secure a current account, continues to make advances after registration of the later charge.

(e) NOTICE DOES NOT ALWAYS GIVE PRIORITY. Not all parties taking with notice of a security interest are bound by it. It will be recalled that even the holder of a legal estate or a title may lose his priority where he has held out the debtor, or allowed the debtor to hold himself out, as entitled to deal with the asset free from the security interest. So if a creditor takes a floating charge over the debtor's trading stock, and thereby holds the debtor out as free to dispose of his stock in the ordinary course of business, restrictions on the debtor's power of sale will not bind a buyer in ordinary course of business, even if he is aware of the existence of the floating charge, unless he bought with notice of the fact that the sale to him was in breach of the seller's obligations under the charge.[140]

---

138 *Manchester Trust v Furness* [1895] 2 QB 539; *By Appointment (Sales) Ltd v Harrods Ltd* (1977) unreported, CA (Bar Library transcript No 465); *Feuer Leather Corp v Frank Johnstone & Sons* [1981] Com LR 251; *Ashburner's Principles of Equity* (2nd edn, 1933), p 69.

139 And in this case he would not necessarily be bound by the security interest even if he had actual notice of it. See (e).

140 See p 686.

3.   Effect of failure to register

Failure to register a charge in compliance with s 395 of the Companies Act renders the charge void against the liquidator or administrator and any creditor of the company.[141] It does not invalidate the charge as against the company itself,[142] unless it is in liquidation or administration,[143] or against a purchaser or any other third party who is not a creditor,[144] nor does it extinguish the company's personal obligation for repayment;[145] indeed, on the expiry of the 21-day period allowed for registration, the money secured by the charge becomes immediately payable,[146] so that the invalidity of the charge accelerates the debtor company's liability.[147] It is not generally appreciated that this acceleration occurs automatically under s 395(2) not only where the debtor company goes into liquidation or administration but also where it grants a subsequent charge.

It has been held that 'creditor' means a creditor who has acquired real rights over the property comprised in the charge and who thus has a *locus standi* to restrain the company from dealing with the property – eg a subsequent encumbrancer and an execution creditor whose execution has been completed[148] – and does not include an unsecured creditor except where the company has gone into liquidation.[149] This limitation on the meaning of 'creditor' is consistent with the continued enforceability of the charge against the company, which would be meaningless if the charge were open to attack by any creditor. If, at a time when there is no party entitled to impeach the charge, the chargee sells the security or obtains a foreclosure order absolute[150] or perfects the charge by seizure[151] or procures payment in satisfaction of it,[152] the charge becomes exhausted and its invalidity as against subsequent secured creditors or a liquidator does not affect the chargee's right to retain the property or proceeds of sale.

For some curious reason a purchaser, as opposed to a creditor, is not protected by s 395[153] and is thus bound by an unregistered charge, unless he acquires an overriding legal title or can invoke an estoppel, eg by holding out.[154]

---

141   Section 395(1). But there is nothing to stop the company from giving the creditor a fresh charge, though this may, of course, be subordinate to an intervening charge and may also be vulnerable to attack as a preference if the company goes into liquidation.

142   Accordingly, the company is not a proper party to proceedings to declare the charge void (*Independent Automatic Sales Ltd v Knowles & Foster*, n 103).

143   *Smith (Administrator of Cosslett (Contractors) Ltd v Bridgend County Borough Council* [2002] 1 AC 336.

144   *Stroud Architectural Systems Ltd v John Laing Construction Ltd* [1994] BCC 18.

145   Section 395(1).

146   Ibid.

147   Presumably the effect of registration out of time pursuant to an order giving leave for such registration is to restore the payment provisions contained in the charge.

148   See p 623, n 172.

149   See pp 582–583. This now applies to administration as well as liquidation.

150   See p 641.

151   See p 637 as to the chargee's right to possession.

152   *Re Row Dal Constructions Pty Ltd* [1966] VR 249.

153   See n 144.

154   The failure to register would not by itself, it is thought, create an estoppel, for s 395 lays down the classes of third party intended to be protected by the registration provisions, and common law principles ought not to be invoked to expand the ambit of the statute.

Non-registration avoids the charge against a subsequent encumbrancer, whether or not he had actual notice of it,[155] so that he obtains priority, and this is so even if the later charge was expressed to be subordinate to or to rank *pari passu* with the unregistered charge.[156] But failure to register appears to have no significance in relation to a prior encumbrancer.[157] Registration serves no purpose in relation to prior parties, for their interests have already been acquired. If the previous encumbrancer's charge is valid, he will usually have priority as the first in time.[158] If it is itself void for want of registration, the order of ranking is reversed and the later unregistered charge has priority. Moreover, the later chargee would, it is thought, continue to enjoy priority under the usual terms of an order giving the first chargee leave to register out of time.[159]

4.   Registration out of time

Where the court is satisfied that the omission to register a charge in due time was accidental, or due to inadvertence or to some other sufficient cause or[160] is not of a nature to prejudice the position of creditors or shareholders of the company, or that on other grounds it is just and equitable to grant relief, it may extend the time for registration on such terms and conditions as it considers just and expedient.[161] The power to extend time is liberally exercised and will usually be granted even where the company is in default under the security or has had judgment entered against it by other creditors unless a winding-up petition has been presented or a meeting to pass a resolution for voluntary winding up has been or is about to be convened. Where liquidation is imminent, the order extending time should contain liberty for the company to apply to discharge it if the company does in fact go into liquidation within a time specified in the order.[162]

The order giving leave to register out of time does not itself perfect the charge; this comes about only when registration has been effected in accordance with the order, so that if the company goes into liquidation before registration,[163] the charge will become void against the liquidator and creditors notwithstanding the order.[164]

155 Section 395 thus embodies the same principle as to the exclusive notice-giving character of the register as the registration provisions of the property statutes.

156 *Re S Abrahams & Sons* [1902] 1 Ch 695; *Bank of Scotland v T A Neilson & Co* 1991 SLT 8. The position is otherwise if the prior chargee obtains leave to register out of time and the proviso preserving rights of intervening secured creditors is expressed not to affect any agreement for subordination. See below.

157 There is no English authority on the point but the statement in the text is supported by an old American case. See *United States v New Orleans and Ohio Railroad Co* 79 US (12 Wall) 362, 365, 20 L Ed 434, 436 (1870). For the similar position arising in a conflict between two unregistered charges of land, see Megarry and Wade, *Law of Real Property* (6th edn, 2000), para 19-224, which states the point succinctly: 'Indeed, if there are several successive registrable mortgages, none of which has been registered, the maxim "qui prior est tempore, potior est jure" is now reversed, for the last will rank first and so on.' The contrary view would require s 395 to be read as if, in the phrase 'void against the liquidator and any creditor of the company', the word 'registered' appeared before 'creditor'.

158 In addition, he will be entitled to tack further advances until he has notice of the later charge.

159 See below.

160 Not 'and'; but despite this the court invariably imposes a condition that the order extending time is to be without prejudice to the rights of intervening creditors with real rights. See below.

161 Companies Act 1985, s 404.

162 *Re Braemar Investments Ltd* [1989] Ch 54; *Exeter Trust Ltd v Screenways Ltd*, n 118. The form of the order is that made in *Re L. H. Charles & Co Ltd* [1935] WN 15. See also *Re Ashpurton Estates Ltd* [1983] Ch 110, where the authorities are reviewed, and *Barclays Bank plc v Stuart Landon Ltd* [2001] 2 BCLC 316.

163 It should be borne in mind that a compulsory winding up is deemed to commence on the date of presentation of the petition (s 129(2)).

164 *Re Anglo-Oriental Carpet Manufacturing Co* [1903] 1 Ch 914.

The standard condition now imposed by an order extending time for registration is that the order is to be without prejudice to the rights of the parties acquired during the period between the date of creation of the charge and the date of its registration. So a subsequent encumbrancer whose interest is acquired before registration of the earlier encumbrance gets priority, even if he takes with actual notice, and, indeed, even if his interest was acquired before the 21 days allowed for registration of the earlier encumbrance had expired.[165] However, the proviso will not be used to override an agreement between the two encumbrancers that the earlier (unregistered) charge is to have priority.[166] The proviso protects only third parties acquiring real rights over the property given in security, and cannot be invoked by unsecured creditors except on a winding up or administration.[167]

(iii) Under other legislation

The various statutory provisions affecting other types of register previously referred to[168] do not disclose any uniform policy approach either to the effect of registration or to the categories of third party whom the registration requirements are designed to protect. Under some, registration is a priority point, so that the palm goes to the first to file, irrespective of the date of creation of the security agreement;[169] under others, registration is necessary merely to perfect the security interest but otherwise does not alter the ranking of the competing rights.[170] Some registration provisions say that failure to register avoids the security as regards any third party acquiring an interest in the asset for value, whether as purchaser or as mortgagee;[171] others protect only a mortgagee or chargee except in the event of winding up.[172] The Bills of Sale Acts are unique in avoiding an unregistered bill of sale, with respect to the chattels comprised in it, even as against the debtor himself.[173]

5. THE AFTER-ACQUIRED PROPERTY CLAUSE AND THE PURCHASE-MONEY SECURITY INTEREST

A question which has occasioned much difficulty is the resolution of a conflict between a charge over after-acquired property and a purchase-money security

---

165 The previous form of order did not protect a subsequent encumbrancer taking during this period (*Watson v Duff Morgan (Holdings) Ltd* [1974] 1 WLR 450).

166 *Barclays Bank plc v Stuart Landon Ltd*, n 162.

167 *Re Ehrmann Bros Ltd* [1906] 2 Ch 697. The position is otherwise if a winding-up order supervenes before registration, see above.

168 See n 28.

169 Eg, aircraft mortgages (Mortgaging of Aircraft Order 1972, art 14(1)) and shipping mortgages (Merchant Shipping Act 1894, s 33). This, of course, necessitates a priority notice system in order that an intending mortgagee can protect his security in advance of the transaction.

170 Eg, land charges and charges by companies.

171 Land Charges Act 1972, ss 4–7 (but non-registration of an estate contract as a Class C(iv) land charge invalidates it only as against a purchaser of a *legal* estate for money or money's worth); Land Registration Act 2002, s 30(1).

172 Companies Act 1985, s 395. See p 667.

173 Bills of Sale Act (1878) Amendment Act 1882, s 8.

interest[174] taken to secure the price of an asset falling within the class covered by the after-acquired property clause. For example, A Bank lends D £50,000 secured on D's factory premises and all land and premises which D may thereafter acquire. Subsequently, D purchases additional land for £20,000, the whole of which is advanced by B Bank against a charge of the land. Who has priority in relation to that land, A or B?

The instinctive reaction of the reasonable man is that B wins. He has put up the whole of the finance required to purchase the additional asset; it would surely be unfair if this could now be scooped up by A in disregard of B's own security interest. Until recently English law appeared to take a highly technical approach to the treatment of the purchase-money security interest. If D had agreed to give a charge to B prior to acquiring the property,[175] then it was considered at all times encumbered by the charge, so that the after-acquired property clause in A's mortgage would attach to the property only in its encumbered state, thus giving B priority.[176] In such a case the fact that B may have had constructive notice of the earlier interest was irrelevant.[177] But in *Church of England Building Society v Piskor*[178] the Court of Appeal held that, in the absence of such an agreement, the charge in favour of B, even if executed at the same time as the conveyance to D, was postponed to A's earlier charge, for it was a necessary concomitant of the *nemo dat* rule that D could not give B an effective charge before D had himself acquired the legal estate, so that there was a *scintilla temporis* (moment of time) between the conveyance and the purchase-money charge during which A's prior charge fastened on the property, thus giving A priority.

The decision in *Piskor* was overruled by the House of Lords in *Abbey National Building Society v Cann*[179] but in terms which fall well short of a full recognition of the priority of a purchase-money security interest. The reason why the ruling in *Piskor* was rejected was not that a conveyance and purchase-money charge executed simultaneously constituted a single, indivisible transaction without the

---

174   The term is borrowed from an earlier, and much simpler, version of what is now §9–103(b) of the American Uniform Commercial Code: 'A security interest is a "purchase money security interest" to the extent that it is (a) taken or retained by the seller of the collateral to secure all or part of its price; or (b) taken by a person who by making advances or incurring an obligation gives value to enable the debtor to acquire rights in or the use of collateral if such value is in fact so used.' This definition, with minor modifications, was used by the Crowther Committee in its *Report on Consumer Credit* (see Appendix III, para 3) and has been adopted in the Canadian Personal Property Security Acts, which are modelled on art 9. The element the formulation lacks, but which is assumed in the present discussion, is an agreement at or before the acquisition of the collateral that it is to be given in security, thus excluding the case where a purchase-money loan is initially advanced on an unsecured basis but after it has been used for the purchase the parties agree that the purchased asset is to be given in security.

175   Whether the relevant time for this purpose was the time of conveyance or the earlier exchange of contracts was uncertain.

176   *Re Connolly Bros. Ltd (No 2)* [1912] 2 Ch 25; *Security Trust Co v Royal Bank of Scotland* [1976] AC 507.

177   *Re Connolly Bros. Ltd (No 2)*, n 176; *Security Trust Co v Royal Bank of Scotland*, n 176; *Wilson v Kelland*, n 131.

178   [1954] Ch 553.

179   [1991] 1 AC 56.

need for any prior agreement for the charge but that the finding that there was no evidence in that case to support the existence of such a prior agreement flew in the face of reality. In the words of Lord Jauncey, 'It would be quite unrealistic to assume that the money was made available unconditionally and that only at or immediately after the moment of completion did the question of the execution of a charge in their favour arise.'[180] Both Lord Jauncey and Lord Oliver seemed to be in no doubt that the priority of the purchase-money charge resulted from the pre-completion agreement for a charge, which fettered the property at the moment of its acquisition.[181]

On this view of the case *Cann* does not appear to change the law at all, it merely rejects the inference of fact drawn in *Piskor* as to the absence of a pre-completion agreement for a purchase-money charge. If this is as far as the decision goes, then this is indeed unfortunate, for although at the time of *Cann* it was possible to enter into an agreement for a charge very informally, the effect of s 2(1) of the Law of Property (Miscellaneous Provisions) Act 1989, as we have seen, is to render an agreement for a charge wholly void unless it is in writing and signed by or on behalf of both lender and borrower. Accordingly, there may well be cases in which the intending purchaser agrees to give a charge upon acquiring the property, but the agreement is devoid of legal effect for want of compliance with the statutory formalities. In that situation will the purchase-money charge still prevail over the earlier security? It is submitted that it should. *Cann* addressed one factual reality, the near-inevitability of a pre-completion agreement for a charge, but failed to focus on the much more significant reality that even without such an agreement the conveyance and the simultaneously executed charge constituted a single, indivisible transaction without any *scintilla temporis* to separate the latter from the former. Such an approach would give substance to the priority of the purchase-money security interest, reflecting what the House of Lords appears to have intended but failed to state.

6. CIRCULARITY PROBLEMS

Lest the reader be tempted to conclude that all priority problems are readily soluble, we must draw attention briefly to the existence of a vicious circle that can be broken not on any logical basis but only by the selection of some arbitrary starting point. In its most common form, circularity arises where three security interests are granted, to A, B and C respectively; the circumstances are such that A has priority over B, B over C, and C over A; and the security is insufficient in value to meet all three claims. The problem will be familiar to students of real property law,[182] and Professor Grant Gilmore, in his superb work on security interests, devotes an entire chapter to it.[183] Let us look at a corporate finance situation which is by no means untypical.

---

180 Ibid, at 101.
181 Ibid, per Lord Jauncey at 102; per Lord Oliver at 92.
182 See Megarry and Wade, *Law of Real Property*, para 9–227; *Cheshire and Burn's Modern Law of Real Property*, pp 668 ff.
183 Grant Gilmore *Security Interests in Personal Property* (1965), ch 39.

Debtor Ltd grants a fixed charge of its factory to A and a subsequent floating charge of its other assets to B. A agrees that his fixed charge is to be subordinated to B's floating charge. Debtor Ltd then goes into liquidation, owing £60,000 to A, £40,000 to B and £50,000 to unsecured preferential creditors.[184] All interested parties agree to the sale of the company's one asset, its factory premises, for £100,000. How should these proceeds be distributed?

The liquidator points out to A, correctly, that the preferential debts rank in priority to B's floating charge.[185] He says that since A has agreed to subordinate his charge to that of B, A ranks behind the preferential creditors. A protests that this cannot be right, since a fixed charge has priority over preferential claims, and preferential creditors should not have their position improved solely because of his priority agreement with B. On this basis A argues that the order of distribution should be as follows:

A	£60,000
Preferential creditors	£40,000
B	Nil
	£100,000

B objects to this solution: A has agreed to his charge being subordinate to B's, so how can A have a right to be paid first? B contends that the proper approach is to apply the principle of subrogation. Since A's charge ranks behind B's by virtue of their agreement, B should be subrogated to A to the extent necessary to preserve B's priority over A. On this basis the order of distribution becomes as follows:

B (by partial subrogation to A's claim)	£40,000
A	£20,000
Preferential creditors	£40,000
	£100,000

This distribution modifies the positions of A and B, in conformity with the priority agreement, while leaving the position of the preferential creditors unchanged. So this type of circularity problem is soluble and in a manner which fairly balances the conflicting interests.

However, though the correctness of this approach was conceded in *Re Woodroffes (Musical Instruments) Ltd,* [186] it was considered by Chadwick J in *Re Portbase Clothing Ltd* to face insuperable difficulties.[187] First, it was said, the subject matter of the floating charge is not merely the debtor's equity of redemption remaining in the debtor after the grant of the fixed charge but the whole of the debtor's interest in the property. So by subordinating itself to the holder of the floating charge, the fixed chargee was, in effect, swelling the assets subject to the fixed charge and thereby increasing the amount available to secured creditors. Secondly, if it were assumed in our example that B was entitled to collect in right of A, B could assert his rights

---

184   Eg, for wages. See p 888.
185   Companies Act 1948, s 319(5).
186   [1986] Ch 366, referring to the first edition of the author's *Legal Problems of Credit and Security* advancing this solution. See now the 3rd edn (2003), pp 188–189.
187   [1993] Ch 388.

even if his floating charge were invalid, eg under s 245 of the Insolvency Act 1986[188] or for want of registration. The effect would be to put B in the same position as if A had assigned his security to B or declared a trust of the proceeds in favour of B. But this was not what had been done in the case before him. Accordingly, Chadwick J held that by subordinating his fixed charge to B's floating charge, A had also subordinated it to the claims of preferential creditors, for A was not entitled to receive payment until B's floating charge has been satisfied, and this could occur only after payment of the preferential debts in full. In reaching this result Chadwick J followed the decision of Nicholson J in the Victorian case *Waters v Widdows*[189] in which it was held that this outcome was dictated by the statutory policy of protecting preferential creditors. Thus on the basis of the ruling in *Re Portbase* the assets would be distributed as follows:

Preferential creditors	£50,000
B	£40,000
A	£10,000
	£100,000

Under this solution the preferential creditors are paid in full, so that they are better off by £10,000 than if A and B had never entered into their priority agreement. A can avoid this unfortunate outcome by assigning his secured debt or its proceeds to B to the extent of B's claim against Debtor Ltd, so that B can prove as A's assignee without having to rely on his floating charge.

Nevertheless, it is submitted that the decision in *Portbase* produces results not intended by the legislature and that the reasoning cannot be sustained. The statutory provisions are designed to provide for payment to preferential creditors from assets which would be free assets of the company but for the floating charge. But the additional assets that become available to the floating chargee as the result of the subordination do not come from the company and would not form part of its free assets if there were no floating charge; they result from the turnover subordination given by the fixed chargee to the floating chargee, a subordination intended for the benefit of the floating chargee and no one else. Nor is the fact that the floating charge might be invalid a reason for denying effect to the subordination,[190] which makes the fixed chargee a trustee for the floating chargee of receipts to which the fixed chargee would otherwise be entitled. As to the point that recourse to the doctrine of subrogation would place the floating chargee in the position of an assignee when there had been no assignment, it is in the nature of subrogation to proprietary rights that the subrogee is indeed placed in much the same position as an assignee. Nor is it easy to see why the outcome of *Portbase* or of *Waters v Widdows* is dictated by statutory policy. Surely the purpose of the legislation is to give preferential debts priority over those secured by a floating charge, not over debts secured by a fixed charge, and it cannot have been intended that an inter-creditor agreement should give the preferential creditors a windfall at the expense of the floating chargee.

188   See p 842.
189   [1984] VR 503.
190   See Philip R. Wood, *The Law of Subordinated Debt* (1990), para 9.8.

Greater difficulties arise where all claimants are equally meritorious, or all are equally at fault, and the *circulus inextricabilis* is set up by a clash of inconsistent priority rules. An example is the clash between s 97 of the Law of Property Act 1925, which fixes priority according to the date of registration, and s 4(5) of the Land Charges Act 1972, which gives priority to a mortgage or charge *completed before registration* of an earlier charge, even though not registered until after the registration of the earlier charge.[191] This type of circularity problem does not lend itself to any one solution that is demonstrably superior to all others.[192]

7.   GENERAL CONCLUSIONS ON PERFECTION AND PRIORITIES UNDER ENGLISH LAW

It will be apparent from what has gone before that the rules of English law as to perfection and priorities are seriously defective.[193] Perhaps the most fundamental weakness is the lack of any uniform policy or set of rules. Each type of security has evolved separately and is governed by its own particular rules. Reservation of title, which in the case of sale and hire-purchase at least is intended as a security device, is not recognized as such, with the result that in the absence of some applicable exception to the *nemo dat* rule innocent third parties are affected by rights the existence of which they have no official[194] means of discovering. Some types of security interest require to be registered, even though the creditor is in possession.[195] Many non-possessory security interests are exempt from registration.[196] The treatment of the purchase-money security interest remains highly unsatisfactory, despite the decision of the House of Lords in *Abbey National Building Society v Cann*.[197] Some statutes insist on the integrity of the register, others only half solve the notice problem in that they allow the secured creditor who has failed to register to assert that the third party had notice in some other form.

The Crowther Committee, having highlighted these deficiencies, proposed a system of registration of non-possessory security interests, modelled on art 9 of the American Uniform Commercial Code.[198] Reservation of title under a hire-purchase or conditional sale agreement or finance lease[199] would be equated with a purchase-money chattel mortgage. There would be an official and comprehensive register, with a simple and efficient filing system. The creditor would be able to perfect his security in any order he chose and would thus be at liberty to file a financing

191   See n 182.
192   The most sophisticated treatment of the problem is to be found in American literature. See Gilmore, *Security Interests in Personal Property*, ch 39 and literature there cited.
193   See further R. M. Goode, *Credit*, March 1973, p 12.
194   For the private register of hire-purchase and related agreements maintained by H. P. Information Ltd, see p 423, n 41.
195   Eg, charges by companies created by deposit of title deeds are registrable under s 395 of the Companies Act 1985.
196   Eg, oral mortgages, charges on pure personalty by a company which do not fall within any of the categories listed in s 396.
197   See p 670.
198   See *Report of the Committee on Consumer Credit*, paras 5.7.20 ff.
199   See ch 28.

statement, giving details of his intended security even before the making of the security agreement.[200] Attachment and perfection would not occur until all the ingredients (value, interest etc) had been fulfilled. Priority would then date from the time of filing. The financing statement would not have to itemize security but could, as now, describe it by class or even cover 'all assets'. The priority rules, instead of deriving from technical doctrines such as the superiority of the legal title, would be designed to produce a result that would generally be considered fair in typical situations.[201]

These recommendations were endorsed by the Insolvency Law Review Committee[202] and a very similar set of proposals was made in the Diamond Report.[203] Despite this, and despite the fact art 9 of the Uniform Commercial Code has been working well in the United States for well over forty years and has been taken up in the Personal Property Security Acts of several Canadian provinces, until recently no steps had been taken to implement this part of the Crowther Report. Happily, there now seems a reasonable prospect that progress will be made, consequent upon the provisional recommendations of the Law Commission in its consultation paper on registration of company charges to which reference has already been made.[204]

200 A technique well established in English law through the system of priority notices and pre-completion searches. The defect in both of these is that they are very short in duration.

201 This is the most priority rules can accomplish. There is no way in which justice in the individual case can be guaranteed; the function of priority rules is to secure the greatest satisfaction for the greatest number.

202 *Insolvency Law and Practice* (Cmnd 8558, 1982), paras 1620–1623.

203 *Review of Security Interests in Property* (1989).

204 See p 652.

25   The Floating Charge[1]

1.   EVOLUTION OF THE CHARGE

The growth of the limited liability company in the nineteenth century was accompanied by an increasing reluctance on the part of lenders to advance money to such companies without security. But then, as now, the most valuable asset of the company was in many cases not the land or buildings it occupied (which it might not own) but its equipment, trading stock and receivables. Equipment was, of course, susceptible to a security interest by way of mortgage or charge, but from time to time required replacement; and as the common law insisted that real rights could be created only by present transfer, not by a purported assignment of future property, a lender who wished to extend his security to cover new equipment brought on to the premises in substitution for that given as security would, under the common law rule, be obliged to take a fresh instrument of transfer or to rely on some new dispositive act by the debtor, after acquisition of the property, pursuant to the original security agreement.[2] The first breakthrough came with the decisions of courts of equity, authoritatively restated in *Holroyd v Marshall*,[3] that equity would recognize a charge over after-acquired property as effective to create a security interest attaching automatically on acquisition without the need for a new act. *Holroyd v Marshall* concerned an equitable mortgage of machinery in a mill,[4] which the mortgagor was required to hold for the mortgagee, with liberty to substitute new machinery that would then itself become subject to the charge, together with any additional machinery brought on to the premises. It was held that the mortgage took effect over the after-acquired machinery, purchased in substitution for the original equipment, in priority to the claims of an execution creditor.

This provided effectively for security over machinery and other equipment. The creditor could get his security; the debtor could not dispose of it except as permitted by the mortgage or with the creditor's subsequent consent. That, however, left the problem of security over shifting classes of asset – stock and receivables – which

---

1 See generally Roy Goode, *Legal Problems of Credit and Security* (3rd edn, 2003), chs IV and V; W. J. Gough, *Company Charges* (2nd edn, 1996), Pt 2.
2 See pp 37, 625.
3 (1862) 10 HL Cas 191. See pp 634, 676.
4 The case is sometimes regarded as one concerning an early form of floating charge, even though not so described (see, for example, R. R. Pennington, 'The Genesis of the Floating Charge' (1960) 23 MLR 630 at p 634), but the writer agrees with Dr Gough (*Company Charges*, p 82) that the security was a fixed equitable mortgage. In his speech Lord Westbury LC made it clear that if the mortgagor had attempted to remove any of the machinery except for the purpose of substitution, the mortgagee would have been entitled to an injunction restraining such removal.

did not lend themselves so readily to such treatment. It was quite impracticable to expect a trading company to ask permission of its mortgagee every time it wanted to sell an item of stock; and while there was not quite the same difficulty with receivables, the debtor company would want, in the normal course of things, to pay the proceeds of sale into its own bank account and treat the moneys as its own, without need to segregate the receivables and the proceeds for the benefit of the mortgagee. How was the security required by the creditor to be reconciled with the need of the debtor to deal with its circulating assets freely in the ordinary course of business?

The answer was the floating charge, a further manifestation of the English genius for harnessing the most abstract conceptions to the service of commerce.[5] The creditor would take security over the debtor's present and future property but would contract to allow the debtor liberty to manage the assets and dispose of them in the ordinary course of business, free from the charge, until such time as the company ceased to carry on the business as a going concern or some other event occurred which, by the terms of the security agreement, entitled the creditor to enforce his security and put an end to the company's powers of disposition. The first case in which the floating security device was tested and upheld came eight years after *Holroyd v Marshall* with the decision of the Court of Appeal in Chancery in *Re Panama, New Zealand and Australian Royal Mail Company*.[6] In that case the debtor company charged its 'undertaking and all sums of money arising therefrom' with repayment of the amount payable under its debenture. It was held that the word 'undertaking' signified not merely the income from the business but also present and future property of the company, and that while by the terms of the charge the debenture holder could not interfere in the running of the company and its dealing with its assets until the winding up of the company, the occurrence of that event entitled the debenture holder to realize its security over the assets, and to assert its charge in priority to the general creditors.

2. THE NATURE OF THE CHARGE[7]

Since *Re Panama*, the nature of the floating charge has been described in some detail in a number of cases, though the judges have been careful to avoid offering exhaustive definitions. Thus, in a much-quoted judgment, Romer LJ described the floating charge in the following terms:

> I certainly do not intend to attempt to give an exact definition of the term 'floating charge', nor am I prepared to say that there will not be a floating charge within the meaning of the Act which does not contain all the three characteristics that I am about

---

5 Compare the doctrine of estates in real property law, p 34.

6 (1870) 5 Ch App 318.

7 The term 'floating charge' is used generally to cover any floating security, whether it takes the form of an assignment of future property or a charge upon it. The wide powers usually given to the creditor by the present-day security instrument mean that he will normally have all the powers of an equitable mortgagee, including the power to get in the legal estate or title, even if the security takes the form of a charge. Whether a floating security is in fact a charge or a mortgage depends on the terms of the security agreement.

to mention, but I certainly think that if a charge has the three characteristics that I am about to mention it is a floating charge. (1) If it is a charge on a class of assets of a company present and future; (2) if that class is one which, in the ordinary course of the business of the company, would be changing from time to time; and (3) if you find that by the charge it is contemplated that, until some future step is taken by or on behalf of those interested in the charge, the company may carry on its business in the ordinary way as far as concerns the particular class of assets I am dealing with.[8]

This language was echoed by Lord Macnaghten on appeal:

I should have thought there was not much difficulty in defining what a floating charge is in contrast to what is called a specific charge. A specific charge, I think, is one that without more fastens on ascertained and definite property or property capable of being ascertained and defined; a floating charge, on the other hand, is ambulatory and shifting in its nature, hovering over and so to speak floating with the property which it is intended to affect until some event occurs or some act is done which causes it to settle and fasten on the subject of the charge within its reach and grasp.[9]

So the underlying concept is that of a class of revolving assets which the company is to be free to manage and deal with in the ordinary course of business[10] until an event occurs which entitles the creditor to intervene and assert his security rights over the assets then held or subsequently acquired by the company. The occurrence of such an event is said to cause the charge to 'crystallize'. Until crystallization, the security interest does not attach and the chargee has no rights *in specie*, merely an interest in a fluid fund of assets. It is unfortunate that the concept of a fund[11] was not more clearly articulated in relation to the floating charge, for it might have avoided a great deal of confusion as to the nature of the chargee's interest before crystallization. That interest is closely analogous to the interest of a beneficiary in a trust fund under an active trust. The fund is considered to have an existence distinct from the particular assets from time to time comprised in it, and the beneficiary's interest does not fasten on to any particular asset until the trustee's management powers come to an end and the beneficiary becomes entitled to a distribution *in specie*.[12] Failure to appreciate this fact led some courts, in the earlier days of the floating charge, to apply fixed charge concepts, so that in certain cases it was erroneously concluded that the chargee had an immediate interest not merely in the fund but in the individual assets comprised in it,[13] while in others the judges went to the opposite extreme and decided that until crystallization the chargee had no real

---

8   *Re Yorkshire Woolcombers Association Ltd* [1903] 2 Ch 284, at 295.
9   *Sub nom Illingworth v Houldsworth* [1904] AC 355, at 358.
10   See text to n 68.
11   See p 61. The fund need not be open-ended. Even a closed fund, which can only reduce, suffices as an object of a floating charge (*Re Bond Worth Ltd* [1979] 3 All ER 919).
12   See p 61.
13   *Driver v Broad* [1893] 1 QB 744; *Wallace v Evershed* [1899] 1 Ch 891; *Re Dawson* [1915] 1 Ch 626. In all three cases a debenture giving a floating charge over land was held to create an interest in the land even before crystallization. Of course, where there are statutory provisions relating to land, the meaning of 'interest in land' in those provisions is a matter of interpretation of the statute and does not necessarily coincide with principles of property law. The cases could, perhaps, be justified on this ground, though it would have been easier to do so if the decisions had been based more explicitly on the language and terms of the statute rather than on the nature of the floating charge.

rights of any kind, merely a personal claim against the chargor.[14] Both these notions were firmly put down by Buckley LJ in *Evans v Rival Granite Quarries Ltd*:

> A floating charge is not a future security; it is a present security, which presently affects all the assets of the company expressed to be included in it … A floating security is not a specific mortgage of the assets, plus a licence to the mortgagor to dispose of them in the course of his business, but is a floating mortgage applying to every item comprised in the security but not specifically affecting any item until some event occurs or some act on the part of the mortgagee is done which causes it to crystallize into a fixed security.[15]

So a floating charge creates an immediate security interest but, until crystallization, no specific asset is appropriated to the security and the debtor company is therefore free to deal with the asset in the ordinary course of its business. In contrast to a fixed charge, the debtor company's present ownership or subsequent acquisition of property covered by the floating charge is not sufficient to cause the security interest to attach; a further act is needed to cause the charge to crystallize. As Dr Gough perceptively observes in his admirable work on company charges:

> Appropriation under a floating charge is a two-fold process. Neither the ownership of present property nor the acquisition of future property of itself constitutes a specific identification or ascertainment such as to permit an equitable proprietary interest without more to vest in the floating chargee. Under a floating security, there is no qualitative difference between present and future property for the purposes of appropriation and passage of title. There is also no equitable interest that arises in present property for the time being, which subsequently disappears or is displaced upon disposal by the charger in the course of its business.[16]

Upon crystallization, the fund of assets comprised in the charge solidifies, terminating the debtor company's powers to manage the assets and converting the creditor's security interest into a fixed interest[17] as regards the property covered by the charge in which the company then has or subsequently acquires an interest.[18]

Though the floating charge is typically taken over property not readily susceptible to a fixed charge,[19] it is not confined to circulating assets but can be made to cover any description of property, including land. Conversely, a fixed charge may be taken over revolving assets. In practice, because of the advantages of a fixed charge

---

14 See *King v Marshall* (1864) 33 Beav 565; *British Provident Life and Fire Assurance Society, Stanley's Case* (1864) 4 De GJ & Sm 407.

15 [1910] 2 KB 979 at 999. The fact that the security is a present security gives the debenture holder a number of rights which he would not possess under a mere contract to assign assets in the future. These include priority, on crystallization, over a subsequent charge taken with notice of a negative pledge clause in the floating charge instrument, and efficacy of the crystallized charge as a real right on winding up of the company.

16 *Company Charges*, p 365.

17 As to the strength of this compared with a security taken as a fixed mortgage or charge from the outset, see pp 684 ff.

18 *N. W. Robbie & Co Ltd v Witney Warehouse Co Ltd* [1963] 3 All ER 613. Of course, as regards the company's future property, the usual rule applicable to fixed charges applies, viz that until acquisition, the security interest is inchoate, or dormant, but on acquisition it relates back to the date of the security agreement. However, it will rank as a fixed security only as from the date of crystallization. See p 634, n 60.

19 Eg stock in trade, receivables.

in the event of the debtor's liquidation or receivership,[20] creditors tend to take a fixed charge over fixed assets and a floating charge merely over circulating assets. Indeed, the present trend is to extend the ambit of the fixed charge still further to cover book debts and other receivables. As was well brought out in *Siebe Gorman & Co Ltd v Barclays Bank Ltd*,[21] the acid test for distinguishing between a fixed and a floating charge is not whether the assets comprising the security are fixed or circulating but whether the creditor has or has not excluded the debtor's right to continue to manage the assets and dispose of them in the ordinary course of business free from charge. However, a charge over circulating assets is presumptively intended as a floating charge, so that restrictions on the debtor company's ordinary dealing powers need to be specifically agreed, whereas a charge over fixed assets is assumed to be intended as a fixed charge, so that if the company wished to dispose of the asset free from the charge, it would need to obtain the chargee's assent.[22]

3.   CREATION OF THE CHARGE

Though a floating charge is usually created by an instrument expressed to cover the debtor company's 'undertaking' or its 'present and future property', no particular form of words is necessary; it suffices that the agreement manifests an intention to charge the company's present and future assets, or a designated class of assets, with freedom to deal with them in the ordinary course of business so long as the company is a going concern and the creditor does not exercise any contractual right to intervene.

Moreover, the fact that an instrument of charge is described as a fixed charge, and purports to create a fixed security, is not conclusive as to its character. The court looks at the overall tenor of the document and beyond the document to the substance of the transaction. So if it is clear that the debtor is, in fact, to be left free to manage the charged assets as if they were its own, the court will treat the charge as a floating charge over those assets, whatever label the parties themselves may have given the charge.[23] Similarly, if a charge is taken over moneys or over cash proceeds of other assets and the debtor is allowed freedom to mingle the moneys and proceeds with its own moneys, the court will regard this as incompatible with the concept of a fixed charge and will treat the security as a floating security.[24] On the other hand, the mere existence of a right of substitution on a unit-by-unit basis ought not to be considered incompatible with the existence of a fixed security

---

20 See pp 688, 837.

21 [1979] 2 Lloyd's Rep 142. See ch 29 as to receivables financing.

22 See Goode, *Legal Problems*, para 4–12, and *Re Cimex Tissues Ltd* [1994] BCC 626, per S. J. Burnton QC at 635.

23 The same rule applies in determining whether the agreement is to be characterized as a charge of any kind. See *Re Bond Worth Ltd*, n 11, referred to, at 43, and other cases on disguised security, pp 000 ff.

24 *Re Bond Worth Ltd*, n 11. If this freedom is tacitly given from the outset, the charge will be a floating charge *ab initio*. If it is given later, the charge will become converted, by contract or estoppel, into a floating charge. For the difficult decision in *Re New Bullas Trading Ltd* [1994] BCC 36, since disapproved by the Privy Council but held binding by the Court of Appeal, see n 41.

interest, particularly where the assets are not circulating assets.[25] Similarly, where a security interest is created in investment securities under an agreement empowering the debtor to substitute new securities or to withdraw securities to the extent of any excess over the value agreed to be maintained at any one time with the creditor, this should not by itself have the effect of converting the security interest into a floating charge or of negating the crystallization of a floating charge.[26] A more difficult case is that which arose in *Arthur D Little Ltd v Ableco Finance LLC*,[27] where the debenture created a charge over shares and separately charged dividends and other distribution rights. The debtor was not at liberty to dispose of the former, but distributions were at the free disposal of the charger. It was held that the charge over the shares was a fixed charge and that the distribution rights were not to be regarded as separate property, even though separately mentioned, but were ancillary to the shares themselves and were, therefore, part of the assets subject to the fixed charge. With respect, this does not seem correct. If the charges had not been extended to distributions, these would ordinarily have been regarded as the unencumbered property of the debtor. It was therefore necessary to provide specifically for these to be charged, and since the debtor was left free to deal with them, the charge should, it is thought, have been treated as a floating charge over the distribution rights.

4. CRYSTALLIZATION OF THE CHARGE

(i) Events causing crystallization

The subsistence of the security as a floating charge presupposes the continuance of the debtor company's business as a going concern under the management of the directors.[28] The charge will accordingly crystallize upon the occurrence of an event falling within one of the heads set out below. As a preliminary point, the position will here be taken that crystallization comes about through the withdrawal of the authority of the company to continue management of the assets comprised in the security, and that the termination of the company's actual (as opposed to its apparent) authority to manage the assets is purely a matter between the chargee and the company. The effect of crystallization on third parties should be seen as an entirely distinct question which, as will be argued hereafter, involves consideration of the company's *apparent* authority to continue management of the assets notwithstanding the termination of its actual authority. The failure to distinguish the two has caused much misunderstanding in the literature on crystallization, particularly in relation to the effect of automatic crystallization clauses.[29]

---

25 For an example, see *Holroyd v Marshall*, above, n 3.

26 This approach is in line with the general thrust of the EC directive on financial collateral arrangements (2002/47/EC, art 2(2)) to preserve the efficacy of substitution and withdrawal clause. See the Financial Collateral Arrangements (No 2) Regulations 2003 (SI 2003/3226), reg 1, definition of 'security financial collateral arrangement', para (c) and definition of 'security interest', para (d).

27 [2003] Ch 217.

28 As opposed, for example, to management by a receiver appointed by debenture holders.

29 See p 684.

1.   *De facto cessation of business*

The charge will crystallize if the company ceases to trade,[30] whether it does so voluntarily[31] or in response to a winding-up petition[32] or other external cause. The fact that the directors retain theoretical powers of management does not prevent crystallization.

2.   *Termination of management powers*

Even if the company is still trading, termination of the power of the directors to run the company as a going concern will cause the charge to crystallize, whether such power is terminated generally or merely with respect to the particular debenture holder whose charge is in issue. So crystallization will result from the passing of a resolution for voluntary winding up,[33] the making of a winding-up order[34] or the appointment of a receiver by the chargee or by the court on the chargee's application.[35] However, if the directors' powers of management come to an end only as regards part of the assets comprised in the floating charge, as where the chargee exercises a power given by the debenture to effect a selective crystallization, the charge continues to float as regards the remainder of such assets.[36] The charge is not, however, crystallized by the appointment of a receiver by a chargee under another charge, whether later[37] or earlier, because, vis-à-vis the non-intervening debenture holder, the company's powers of management continue and there is no reason why the debenture holder should be compelled to treat its charge as crystallized when it might consider this contrary to its interests.[38] The appointment of an administrator by the debenture holder[39] plainly has the same crystallizing

---

30   *National Westminster Bank plc v Jones* [2002] 1 BCLC 55.

31   *Re Woodroffe's Musical Instruments Ltd* [1986] 2 All ER 908, per Nourse LJ at 913–914; *Edward Nelson & Co Ltd v Faber & Co* [1903] 2 KB 367, per Joyce J at 376–377. Cessation of trade may be indicated by a transfer of the company's undertaking or a sale of its assets, as in *Hubbuck v Helms* (1887) 56 LJ Ch 536; but this is not necessarily the case (*Re Borax Co* [1901] 1 Ch 326).

32   *Re Victoria Steamboats Ltd* [1897] 1 Ch 158, per Kekewich J. But the debenture holder must adduce evidence showing that the company has ceased to trade. The presentation of a winding-up petition does not as a matter of course cause a floating charge to crystallize (ibid).

33   *Re Colonial Trusts Corporation* (1879) 15 Ch D 465, per Jessel MR at 472; *Re Crompton & Co Ltd* [1914] 1 Ch 954. The former case also decided that where, before the passing of the resolution, a provisional liquidator is appointed, that marks the date of crystallization of the charge.

34   *Re Panama, New Zealand & Australian Royal Mail Co*, n 6. On the other hand, the mere presentation of a petition does not by itself have this effect, for it may be unfounded and in any event will not necessarily indicate that the company has ceased trading (see also n 32).

35   *Evans v Rival Granite Quarries Ltd*, n 15. This is so whether he is an ordinary receiver (ie without powers of management) or an administrative receiver, though the ability of a debenture holder to appoint an administrative receiver has now been severely curtailed (see p 849). The appointment of a receiver also crystallizes the charge under head (3) below. Unless otherwise ordered, the appointment of a receiver by the court does not take effect until he has furnished security. Crystallization does not depend upon the receiver's taking possession of the charged assets. An entirely separate question, however, is the extent to which a competing third party is bound by a crystallizing event of which he has no notice. See pp 686, 687.

36   See Gough, *Company Charges*, pp 401 ff and para 5 below.

37   As in *Re Woodroffes (Musical Instruments) Ltd* [1986] Ch 366.

38   Ibid.

39   Under the Insolvency Act 1986, Sch B1, paras 2(b), 14.

effect as its appointment of a receiver. By parity of reasoning, the appointment of an administrator by another creditor or by the company would not appear to have this effect.[40]

3.   Chargee's exercise of power of intervention

If the chargee has become entitled, under the terms of the charge, to intervene in the management of the company's assets and exercises that power,[41] so divesting the directors of their own management powers in relation to the charged assets, the charge will crystallize,[42] though in the case of an authorized partial crystallization only in relation to the assets in respect of which the debenture holder intervenes.[43] The typical mode of intervention is by the appointment of an administrative receiver.[44] Other events of intervention include exercise of a power to take possession of the assets[45] or to sell them[46] and crystallization of the charge by notice pursuant to a provision in the debenture.[47] Indeed, any acts of intervention permitted by the agreement between the parties would be sufficient, as between the chargee and the company, to terminate the company's management powers. On the other hand, mere demand for payment to the company or its bankers does not of itself produce crystallization,[48] unless so provided by the terms of the charge.

4.   Automatic crystallization

Over the years there has been an increasing tendency to expand crystallization clauses in floating charges to cover not merely acts of intervention by the chargee but a variety of other events, not all of which constitute public acts of which third

---

40 See Goode, *Legal Problems*, para 4–38; G. Lightman and G. S. Moss, *The Law of Receivers of Companies* (3rd edn, 2000), para 3–067.

41 The mere fact that the power has become exercisable is not sufficient. The chargee must actually have exercised it (*Governments Stock and Other Securities Investment Co Ltd v Manila Rly Co* [1897] AC 81; *Evans v Rival Granite Quarries Ltd*, n 15, per Vaughan Williams LJ at 986–987; Fletcher Moulton LJ at 993). It is not easy to reconcile the decision of the Court of Appeal in *Re New Bullas Trading Ltd*, n 24, with this long-established principle (see Roy Goode, 'Charges over Book Debts: A Missed Opportunity' (1994) 110 LQR 592 at p 600) and in *Agnew v Commissioners of Inland Revenue* [2001] 2 AC 710 the Privy Council considered it to have been wrongly decided. Doubt also attaches to the decision in *Siebe Gorman & Co Ltd v Barclays Bank International Ltd* [1979] 2 Lloyd's Rep 142. But in *National Westminster Bank plc v Spectrum Plus Ltd* [2004] EWCA Civ 670 the Court of Appeal, reversing the decision of the Vice-Chancellor, declined to follow *Agnew v IRC* on the ground that, in the light of *Young v Bristol Aeroplane Co* [1944] KB 718, it was bound by *Re New Bullas*. The Court of Appeal also supported the conclusions of Slade J in *Siebe Gorman*. The difficulty with *Siebe Gorman* is the way it treated the bank's *power* to assert control as equivalent to control itself.

42 *Governments Stock and Other Securities Investments Co Ltd v Manila Rly Co*, n 41; *Evans v Rival Granite Quarries Ltd*, n 15.

43 See above.

44 See pp 640, 846.

45 As to seizure of part only of the charged assets under a partial crystallization clause, see para 5 below.

46 For the creditor's power of sale, see p 639. Usually, extensive powers are conferred by the debenture.

47 As in *Re Brightlife Ltd* [1987] Ch 200.

48 Ibid.

parties would be on notice. For example, the charge may provide for automatic crystallization if the debtor company allows its external borrowing to exceed a stated figure, fails to pay a sum due under the charge within a specified period of the due date, allows a judgment against it by some other creditor to remain unsatisfied for more than a stated period or has distress or execution levied against any of its property. To what extent are the parties free to agree on any act they choose as causing crystallization, even if involving no active step by the chargee? The English authorities on automatic crystallization support its validity,[49] and the same is true of most other Commonwealth decisions,[50] though it has been contended that the views expressed by the judges do not go all one way.[51]

Much of the concern expressed about the adverse effects of automatic crystallization results from a failure to distinguish questions of attachment, which concern only the creditor and the debtor, from questions of priorities, which involve third parties. Crystallization of a floating charge causes the charge to become fixed; it is thus assumed that the charge thereafter operates in all respects as if it had been expressly created as a fixed charge at the time of crystallization. Herein lies the fallacy. The grantor of a fixed charge is circumscribed from the outset. He has no authority to deal with the asset as his own in the ordinary course of business; nor does he have even apparent authority to do so, for if he were held out by the chargee as having such authority, this would be incompatible with the status of the charge as a fixed charge.

By contrast, the chargor under a floating charge has a contractual right to manage the fund of assets comprised in the security, and to change the composition of the fund by acquisitions and disposals in the ordinary course of business. His actual authority may be terminated on any ground prescribed by the security agreement[52] and such termination will be fully effective as between the parties, but it does not follow that third parties continuing to deal with the company will be bound, for they may be able to invoke the well-established rule of agency law that entitles a party having prior dealings with an agent to assume continuance of the agent's authority until the party in question has notice of its termination.[53]

49 Ibid; *Re Horne & Hellard* (1885) 29 Ch D 736; *Davey & Co v Williamson* [1898] 2 QB 194; *Illingworth v Houldsworth*, n 9.

50 The fullest treatment of automatic crystallization clauses and of the policy issues arising in connection with them is to be found in Gough, *Company Charges*, chs 11 and 16.

51 See, for example, A. J. Boyle, 'The Validity of Automatic Crystallisation Clauses' [1979] JBL 231; J.H. Farrar, 'The Crystallisation of a Floating Charge' (1976) 40 Conv 397, and 'World Economic Stagnation Puts the Floating Charge on Trial' (1980) 1 Co Law 83 at pp 87–88. Farrar (1980) 1 Co Law 83, at p 88. These writers interpret the judgments of Vaughan Williams LJ and Fletcher Moulton LJ in *Evans v Rival Granite Quarries Ltd*, n 15, as requiring active intervention by the debenture holder and as disapproving the notion of automatic crystallization. This appears to be a misreading of the judgments, which were concerned to show only that a mere *right to intervene*, unaccompanied by any steps to put an end to the company's management powers, did not suffice. The judgments were not dealing with automatic cessation of such powers by virtue of a provision in the debenture deed itself.

52 For the dangers of overkill in the use of automatic crystallization clauses, see R. M. Goode , 'Some Aspects of Receivership Law – III' [1981] JBL 473 at p 474, and Goode, *Legal Problems*, paras 4–54, 4–55.

53 See *Bowstead and Reynolds on Agency* (17th edn, 2001), art 123. See p 687.

5. *Partial crystallization*

Most floating charges provide for crystallization over the whole of the charged assets in stated events. But there seems no reason why the charge cannot provide for crystallization over part of the assets, leaving the charge floating as to the remainder, so long as the property which is to be the subject of the partial crystallization is clearly identifiable from the description in the security agreement.[54] Provided that the intention of the parties can be sufficiently ascertained, there is no reason why the court should not give effect to it, thus enabling the chargee to take possession of particular assets only, leaving the charge floating as to the remaining assets.

5. EFFECT OF CRYSTALLIZATION AS BETWEEN CHARGOR AND CHARGEE

As previously mentioned, crystallization results in the charge becoming a specific charge over any property covered by the security agreement in which the company has or subsequently acquires an interest. As against the company, the chargee has all the rights of the holder of a specific equitable charge,[55] and the company's actual[56] authority to deal with the charged assets free from the charge comes to an end. Usually the remedies given at law or by statute[57] are extended in the debenture creating the charge, so that in the ordinary way the chargee will be able to appoint a receiver,[58] to take possession,[59] to sell[60] or to apply for foreclosure.[61] Where crystallization occurs by reason of the appointment of a receiver or because the company goes into liquidation, the receivership or liquidation creates a priority point for the computation of preferential claims, which usually rank above the floating charge.[62] In addition, liquidation may trigger statutory provisions rendering the charge void or voidable if taken at a time when the company was insolvent.[63]

6. EFFECT OF CRYSTALLIZATION AS BETWEEN CHARGEE AND THIRD PARTIES

This is a question of priorities, discussed below.

---

54 See Gough, *Company Charges*, pp 401 ff. In the absence of a provision in the debenture for partial crystallization, the chargee has no right to crystallize the charge as to some assets only. If he purports to do so, the charge will be treated as continuing to float. See *R v Consolidated Churchill Copper Corporation Ltd* [1978] 5 WWR 652.

55 Or equitable mortgage, if the 'charge' takes the form of an assignment (n 7). As to the enforcement remedies of chargees and mortgagees, see pp 637 ff.

56 As opposed to its apparent authority. See below.

57 See p 637.

58 In most cases, however, it will be the receiver's appointment that has caused the charge to crystallize in the first place.

59 See p 637.

60 Getting in the legal title either by exercise of a power of attorney contained in the debenture or by application to the court.

61 See p 641.

62 Insolvency Act 1985, ss 40(2), 175(2)(b). See pp 688, 838, text and n 54.

63 Ibid, s 245. See p 842.

7.   PRIORITIES

(i)   As regards competing interests arising prior to crystallization

1.   *General*

Since a floating charge leaves the company free to deal with its assets in the ordinary course of business, a subsequent disposition by the company will in principle take effect free from the charge, while the grant of a subsequent fixed charge or mortgage will take priority over the floating charge.[64] The ability to grant a fixed charge ranking in priority to the floating charge arises by implication from the nature of the floating charge, in the absence of a term of the charge to the contrary,[65] and does not require to be provided expressly in the charge. By contrast, the grant of a subsequent floating charge ranking in priority to the first floating charge is prima facie against the intention of the earlier charge and, even if the later charge is the first to crystallize, it is ineffective vis-à-vis the holder of the earlier charge except in so far as thereby authorized.[66]

The company's implied authority to deal with its assets is limited to dealings in the ordinary course of business,[67] though this is liberally interpreted.[68] Not infrequently, the instrument of charge narrows the normal meaning of 'ordinary course of business' by excluding designated classes of transaction, eg the factoring of the company's receivables. Whether a third party who purchases or takes a charge of assets from the company outside the company's ordinary business as so defined is governed by such a restriction depends on ordinary principles of agency law. If the transaction was within the company's apparent authority, the third party gets priority, otherwise he does not.[69]

Since no specific asset is affected by the floating charge until crystallization, it follows that an execution creditor who completes his execution[70] before crystallization gets priority.[71] However, crystallization of a charge covering goods on

---

64 *Wheatley v Silkstone & Haigh Moor Coal Co* (1885) 29 Ch D 715.

65 See below.

66 *Re Benjamin Cope and Sons Ltd* [1914] 1 Ch 800; *Re Household Products Co Ltd* (1981) 124 DLR (3d) 325. These decisions, which do not depend on the existence of a negative pledge clause in the first floating charge, were, unfortunately, not drawn to the attention of Morritt J in *Griffiths v Yorkshire Bank* [1994] 1 WLR 1427, as to which, see n 74. It has been held that the grant of a second floating charge over part of the assets comprised in the first floating charge is permissible (*Re Automatic Bottle Makers Ltd* [1926] Ch 412), though the true ratio of the decision is based not on a distinction between a floating charge over all the assets and a floating charge over part of them but simply on a construction of the charge instrument.

67 *Re Florence Land & Public Works Co* (1878) 10 Ch D 530; *Wallace v Universal Automatic Machines Co* [1894] 2 Ch 547, per Kay LJ at 554; *Fire Nymph Products Ltd v The Heating Centre Pty Ltd* (1992) 7 ACSR 365.

68 See *Re Modern Terrazzo Ltd* [1998] NZLR 160, approved by the Privy Council in *Countrywide Banking Corp Ltd v Dean* [1998] AC 338; Gough, *Company Charges*, ch 9.

69 See p 168.

70 See p 623, n 172.

71 *Evans v Rival Granite Quarries Ltd*, n 15; *Robson v Smith* [1895] 2 Ch 118.

premises held by the chargor or lessee does not preclude a subsequent distress by the landlord,[72] though it may prevent a distress for rates.[73]

2. Restrictions on dealings

The company's liberty to dispose of assets free from the floating charge and to grant subsequent fixed charges ranking in priority to the floating charge may be, and usually is, restricted by the terms of the instrument of charge. Such restrictions are fully effective as between the chargee and the company but will not bind a subsequent purchaser or encumbrancer unless he has notice of them.[74]

(ii) As regards competing interests arising after crystallization

Once the charge has crystallized, the company's authority to deal with the assets comes to an end and the charge fastens on them as a fixed charge. For this purpose the parties are free to agree on any event they choose as constituting a crystallizing event, whether or not it is visible to the outside world, for we are here speaking only of the effect of crystallization as between them.

But while crystallization puts an end to the company's *right* to dispose of the asset, it does not follow that its *power* to do so is fully terminated. This depends on the extent to which its apparent authority continues. In principle, a person who dealt with the company prior to crystallization should be entitled to assume the continuance of its authority to deal until he has had notice of the termination of that authority.[75] Similarly, one who dealt with the company for the first time after crystallization and was aware of the existence of the floating charge[76] but not of its crystallization can reasonably contend that the company was held out to him as continuing to have authority to deal. It is one of the mysteries of the development of this branch of law that priority conflicts between the holder of a crystallized charge and a third party claiming rights over the charged property have always been viewed in purely property law terms, without reference to agency principles, and the issue has thus been expressed in the form: whose interest was first, that of the

---

72 *Re New City Constitutional Club Co* (1886) 34 Ch D 646. This is because at common law a landlord has a right to distrain for rent on all goods on the demised premises, whether belonging to the tenant or not. *Quaere* whether the receiver is a party entitled to serve a notice of claim under s 1 of the Law of Distress Amendment Act 1908.

73 *Re ELS Ltd* [1995] Ch 11.

74 *English & Scottish Mercantile Investment Co Ltd v Brunton* [1892] 2 QB 700. As to whether he has notice by virtue of registration of the charge, see p 662. The effect of notice is to subject the subsequent purchaser or encumbrancer to a personal equity in favour of the floating chargee, so that the latter has priority even though his security interest has not yet attached. See Gough, *Company Charges*, p 228. The decision of Morritt J in *Griffiths v Yorkshire Bank Ltd*, n 66, that the restriction is purely a matter of contract and does not affect subsequent encumbrances even if taking with notice of it is inconsistent with the underlying assumption in *English & Scottish Mercantile Investment Co Ltd v Brunton*, and with *Cox v Dublin City Distillers Co* [1906] 1 IR 446.

75 See to the same effect Lightman and Moss, *Law of Receivers of Companies*, paras 3–080 ff; *Fire Nymph Products Ltd v The Heating Centre Pty Ltd*, n 67, per Gleeson J at 373.

76 Constructive notice through registration would not be sufficient for this purpose. It is necessary that the party in question shall have acted in reliance on the company's continued apparent authority to deal with its assets.

holder of the charge or that of the rival claimant? But the priority of the first in time is not absolute. He may lose it if he allows the debtor to hold himself out as at liberty to deal with the asset free from the security. Where the crystallizing event is itself a public act, the termination of apparent authority will coincide with the time of crystallization, so that the holder of the crystallized charge will have priority over a subsequently created interest. Such is the case where the crystallizing event is the winding up of the company or the cessation of its trading activity.[77] But not all crystallizing events are of this character. The appointment of a receiver is usually effected by a document in writing under the hand of the chargor, coupled with the receiver's express or implied acceptance of the appointment.[78] Some further act is necessary to give public notice of the receiver's intervention, as by filing notice of his appointment[79] or taking possession of the security.[80] A fortiori, a crystallizing event such as default in payment or failure to satisfy a judgment does not of itself constitute notice to third parties of the termination of the company's management powers and will not, it is submitted, bind a bona fide purchaser for value[81] without notice.

On the other hand, unsecured creditors (including execution creditors who have not completed the execution) have no *locus standi* to complain of want of notice, for they have no real rights in the company's assets and are therefore not regarded as concerned with the company's ability to deal with its property, and to circumscribe its own powers of disposition, as it thinks fit.[82]

(iii) Statutory subordination of the floating charge

A floating charge will be subordinate to the claims of preferential creditors where the chargee takes possession of the security,[83] a receiver is appointed[84] or the debtor company goes into winding up,[85] and this is so even where the charge has crystallized before the right of the preferential creditor accrued.[86] In addition, where the company goes into liquidation, administration or receivership or a provisional liquidator is appointed, a prescribed part of the net property comprised in the floating charge must be made available for the satisfaction of unsecured debts.[87] Winding up or administration will in certain circumstances invalidate the charge.[88]

77　See pp 681–682.

78　The appointment is not effective until accepted within the prescribed time (Insolvency Act 1986, s 33).

79　As required by the Companies Act 1985, s 405(1). But even such filing will not of itself bind a bona fide buyer in ordinary course of business. See p 666. An administrative receiver is also required to give notice of his appointment in the prescribed form to the company and creditors (Insolvency Act 1986, s 46; Insolvency Rules 1986, r 3.2) and to include a statement of the appointment on invoices, orders and business letters (Insolvency Act 1986, s 39).

80　Relevant for this purpose, but not for crystallization of the charge. See n 35.

81　Including an encumbrancer.

82　See p 582.

83　Companies Act 1985, s 196(1),(2).

84　Insolvency Act 1986, s 40.

85　Ibid, s 175(2)(b). There is no subordination as to liquidation expenses. See p 838, n 71.

86　This is because 'floating charge' in s 251 of the Insolvency Act 1986 means a charge which *as created*, was a floating charge.

87　Insolvency Act 1986, s 176A; Insolvency Act (Prescribed Part) Order 2003 (SI 2003/2097).

88　Insolvency Act 1986, s 245.

8.   THE FUTURE OF THE FLOATING CHARGE

The floating charge has proved a brilliantly successful device in many ways, yet the fundamental concept continues to cause difficulty and the huge volume of case law that has built up around it presents a serious obstacle to the modernization of English personal property security law. The floating charge was never adopted in the United States, while in the various Canadian provinces and in New Zealand it has ceased to be a distinct form of security and is treated as a form of fixed security under which the debtor continues to have dealing powers. The purpose of the floating charge has always been to provide the creditor with some form of security interest, despite the debtor's dealing powers, while ensuring that third parties acquiring rights in the subject matter of the charge obtain a title free from the floating charge. But the case law has thrown up recurrent difficulties: the characterization of the charge, particularly where it relates to receivables, and the impact of that characterization on the rights of preferential creditors; the adverse position of execution creditors who have no means of knowing that a prior floating charge has crystallized; and the events that are sufficient to cause crystallization. These problems are now best dealt with by legislation along the lines of art 9 of the American Uniform Commercial Code and comparable legislation since enacted in Canada and New Zealand, which provide that the debtor's continued power to dispose of its assets in the ordinary course of business is not inconsistent with the existence of the creditor's (fixed) security interest in the debtor's present and future property, and which balance the competing interests by a set of clear priority rules, rather than leaving these to be inferred by the courts from the characterization of the security interest. This was recommended more than 30 years ago by the Crowther Committee[89] and later by the Cork Committee[90] and Professor Aubrey Diamond,[91] but there was no legislative action. Now the prospects look brighter with the issue of the Law Commission's consultation paper *Registration of Security Interests: Company Charges and Property other than Land*,[92] which paves the way for a major reform of the existing system, and a sea change in the attitude of financiers, who now see many positive benefits from the proposed new approach. The floating charge as a distinct form of security has served us well but has now had its day.[93]

---

89   In its report on Consumer Credit (Cmnd 4596, 1971).

90   In its report *Insolvency Law and Practice* (Cmnd 8558, 1982)

91   *A Review of Security Interests in Property* (1989).

92   Cons Paper No 164, July 2002.

93   See Roy Goode, 'The Exodus of the Floating Charge' in *Corporate and Commercial Law: Modern Developments* (eds David Feldman and Frank Meisel), ch 10; Rizwan Jameel Mokal, 'The Floating Charge – An Elegy', in Sarah Worthington (ed) *Commercial Law and Commercial Practice* (2003) p 479.

PART FIVE
Specific Forms of Secured Business Finance

26 General Financing Considerations

I. SELECTING THE SECURITY INSTRUMENT

In Part Four we examined the structure of English security law and explored some of the conceptual subtleties inherent in security over future property under fixed and floating charges. We also noted that reservation of title, though serving a security function, is not considered as security *stricto sensu* and is governed by a quite different set of principles.

These theoretical abstractions may seem far removed from the practical world of business finance. Nothing could be further from the truth. The in-house lawyers employed by banks and finance houses, and their outside legal advisers, are constantly driven to examine fundamentals in devising new and untested credit instruments and security devices. The ground covered by reported cases may seem well trodden, but all too often the case law reflects the atypical or obsolete transaction and fails to furnish a reliable guide to the validity and effectiveness of a proposed new form of agreement. This is why we have devoted so much print to fundamental principle, for it is to principle that the practitioner must turn when there is no decisional law precisely in point. Where the loss or recovery of millions of pounds may turn on the soundness of his advice and the precision of his documents, the mind of the practising commercial lawyer becomes concentrated wondrously.

Now, the financier and his legal adviser approach security law from a standpoint rather different from that of the theoretician. The latter is concerned to discuss and evaluate the principles, the rules and the underlying policies. The financier and his lawyer want to arrive at a particular result, using the most appropriate legal tool available. The floating charge, the hire-purchase agreement and the loan are important not for what they are but for what they do in meeting the business objectives. The financier's concern is to provide his customers with what they need while at the same time ensuring as far as possible that he will be repaid.

The businessman who needs finance for the purchase of equipment has four basic mechanisms at his disposal: instalment sale, hire-purchase, lease and loan. The legal character of any particular credit instrument is of no great concern to him so long as that instrument serves his purpose. He needs equipment now but wants to pay for it later. In terms of pure cash flow, and ignoring taxation and accounting considerations, it matters little whether he buys the equipment and pays the price by instalments, takes it on hire-purchase, leases it and pays a similar amount by way of rental, or purchases it outright for cash with a loan which he repays by instalments. The sale by instalments or hire-purchase will attract a finance charge, the lease a hidden ingredient in the rental to provide the lessor with the desired return on capital, and the loan a levy of interest. If the creditor is to be given security over the equipment, it is largely a matter of indifference whether this takes the form of reservation of title (under a sale, hire-purchase or leasing agreement) or a purchase-money mortgage. Again, if a trading company wants to improve its liquidity by getting in money against outstanding receivables, it can, in cash-flow terms, achieve the same results whether it sells the receivables outright for cash, giving a guarantee of payment by the debtors, or charges them to secure a loan. Cash is cash, and what's in a name?

But in so far as the legal differences between sale, lease and loan affect the businessman's ability to achieve his objectives, he is liable to become profoundly interested So, too, is the financier when he learns that one form of security gives him greater protection, or more flexibility, than another. This part of the book is thus devoted to what may be termed the applied law of credit and security – the application of the principles and rules in Part Four to specific forms of financial transaction. The factors influencing selection of a particular security device (including reservation of title as a security for this purpose) vary in nature and importance and often pull against each other, so that the parties have to balance the pros and cons and decide whether the advantages of a particular form of agreement are so significant compared with the others as to outweigh the disadvantages from which the other types of agreement might be free. It is impossible to give an exhaustive list of criteria influencing the choice of security, but the following are among the more important.

(i)   From the viewpoint of the creditor

1.   The legal ability to enter into the transaction

This has been adverted to earlier. A financier may be precluded from lending money[1] but entitled to buy and resell on credit. He may need official authorization for one type of transaction but not for the other.

2.   The strength of the security interest

How easily is the security enforceable against the debtor? How effective is it against subsequent purchasers, encumbrancers and unsecured creditors? Will it stand up against a receiver or liquidator? Does it enjoy priority or is it deferred to other real rights or to preferential creditors in a winding up? The answers to some of these questions may depend on whether the security is fixed or floating and whether it is required to be registered in some public register.

3.   The enforceability of the personal covenants

Are there restrictions imposed by law on the enforceability of covenants in one form of agreement (eg hire-purchase) which do not apply to another (eg loans) as regards the amount recoverable from the debtor? [2]

---

1 See p 580. Financiers have sometimes sought to dress up a loan on security as a purchase. See p 605.
2 Of particular relevance (a) where the rule against penalties is involved (pp 123, 713–714), or (b) if legislation limits the amount recoverable under one form of agreement (eg hire-purchase or conditional sale within the Consumer Credit Act 1974) but not another (eg credit sale or loan).

4. The nature of the formalities involved

The more stringent the legal requirements for validity and perfection, the more expensive the transaction is to set up and administer and the greater the risk of something going wrong. For example, those lending to individuals and partnerships are reluctant to take written chattel mortgages, because of the complexities of the Bills of Sale Acts, which are wholly avoided if the credit takes the form of price deferment and the price is secured by reservation of title to the seller. Again, a charge given by a company may need to be registered under the Companies Act 1985,[3] whereas there are currently no provisions for registration of reservation of title.[4]

5. Freedom to deal with the asset

A creditor advancing funds against a mortgage, charge or pledge of investment securities may grant a sub-mortgage, sub-charge or sub-pledge, but is not entitled to dispose of the securities in the absence of a default or other event entitling the creditor to do so. That is why the preferred mode of finance is the sale and repurchase transaction ('repo'), by which the party providing the finance does so by way of outright sale with a provision for repurchase by the seller at a later date. Since the financier acquires outright ownership, it is free to dispose of the securities by way of sale or stock loan and thus take advantage of market conditions in the case of sale and of an additional return in the case of a stock loan. Repayment is 'secured' by the seller's repurchase obligation and a provision for close-out and netting in the event of default.

6. Freedom from equities

This is particularly relevant to receivables financing. For example, if a mortgage of a bank deposit is effected by assignment, the mortgagee takes subject to the bank's right of set-off and other equities, whereas if it is effected by transfer of the deposit to an account in the name of the mortgagee, the question of equities affecting the mortgagor does not arise.

7. The liabilities incurred

The advantage of a purchase-money loan over a sale or hire-purchase agreement[5] is that, except where s 75 of the Consumer Credit Act applies,[6] the creditor is not legally involved in the supply transaction, is not liable for breach of the supply contract and is entitled to enforce the covenants in the loan agreement, and the security for the loan, whether or not the purchased asset is delivered by the buyer or is of the contract description and of proper quality. If, for some reason, the debtor wants to have the goods on instalment sale or hire-purchase terms, the

---

3 See p 660.
4 But this will change if the proposals put forward by the Law Commission relating to registration of company charges are adopted (see pp 652, 675, 689). Extension of the retention of title to cover products and proceeds will usually be treated as a registrable charge.
5 See ch 27.
6 See *Goode: Consumer Credit Law and Practice* (looseleaf), paras [33.1] ff., [33.141] ff.

creditor may prefer to come in as assignee of the supplier's rights rather than acting as seller himself, in order to avoid the legal liabilities falling upon a supplier.[7]

8.   Taxation

The impact of tax is all-pervasive in commercial transactions. If an intending finance lessor finds that the expenditure he is proposing to incur in buying the asset to let on lease will not qualify for capital allowances,[8] he may feel driven to offer an entirely different form of instrument, eg conditional sale, under which the debtor will pick up the allowances and the financial terms of the agreement will be adjusted accordingly. Again, it may be material to the financier whether his profit comes to him in the form of interest on the one hand or a finance charge ('time-price differential') on the other, in that interest payments must normally be made under deduction of tax,[9] substantially reducing the financier's cash flow compared with what he would receive from other types of charge payable gross.

9.   Accounting

Business concerns are often preoccupied with the impression given by the accounts as to the financial stability of the business. The choice of financing instruments may determine to what extent money comes in as income rather than as capital, and whether the subject matter of the transaction is to appear as an asset, and the future instalments payable as a liability, in the balance sheet.[10] A financier also has to bear in mind that accounting conventions do not always match legal rules[11] and that for tax purposes the income, profits and expenditure of the taxpayer may have to be computed somewhat differently than for general accounting purposes.

(ii)   From the viewpoint of the debtor

Considerations relevant to the selection of the credit instrument from the debtor's viewpoint include the following.

1.   Ability to enter into the transaction

This was discussed in an earlier chapter. The debtor may, for example, be free to buy on credit or acquire equipment on lease but his borrowing powers may be restricted [12]

---

7   See p 709.
8   See Capital Allowances Act 2001; and generally *Simon's Direct Tax Service* (looseleaf), Pt B2.
9   See Income and Corporation Taxes Act 1988, s 349(2). But there are various exemptions, eg in respect of interest paid to or by a bank (s 349(3)).
10 However, the modern accounting approach of substance over form has to a considerable extent reduced the accounting significance of choice of instrument. See further, p 695.
11 For example, it is still the accounting convention to show goods supplied on hire-purchase or conditional sale as an asset in the balance sheet of the hirer or buyer, not of the owner or seller, even before they have been paid for.
12 Eg, in the case of a company, by its Memorandum of Association or by the terms of a debenture it has given.

2. Cash flow

Will one form of agreement meet his cash-flow requirements more fully than another? This may depend on complex calculations as to the amount and timing of tax allowances, the manner in which repayments are structured,[13] the treatment of residual value of the asset at the end of the financing period, and so on.

3. Publicity

Though registration of charges against companies is commonplace, a particular debtor company may nevertheless want a form of finance which does not involve the registration of a charge against it in the Companies Registry. Thus it may prefer to factor its receivables by outright sale[14] rather than charge them as security for a loan.

4. Taxation

This is perhaps even more important for the debtor than for the creditor. Typically, the choice is between buying the asset and paying by instalments (on the basis that the purchase price will qualify for capital allowances and the finance charge for deduction as revenue expenditure) or taking a lease and paying rentals (deductible as revenue expenditure).

5. Accounts

The treatment of particular types of transaction in annual accounts has traditionally been a relevant factor in making a choice between one form of agreement and another. For example, sales of debts traditionally removed them from the seller's balance sheet, while rentals under a finance lease were treated as revenue expenditure, so that rentals falling due in future accounting periods did not feature as balance sheet liabilities. But accounting practice has changed to reflect the economic reality of transactions, and, in particular, which party is in substance the owner of the asset and upon which party the risk primarily falls. So a sale of debts will not take them off the balance sheet where the sale is with recourse, and rentals payable under finance leases are now required to be capitalized in much the same way as on an instalment purchase.[15]

6. Flexibility or certainty

This is a major consideration for borrowers. For example, an overdraft is both cheaper and more flexible than a loan. The debtor can choose his own time for

---

13 It is a common, if curious, phenomenon that while there may be nothing in theory to prevent repayments from being structured in the same way under, eg, a loan as under a hire-purchase agreement, the separate evolution of the two forms of finance, coupled with the fact that the personnel engaged on the lending side of a business tend to be separate from those occupied with hire-purchase or conditional sale, means that the financial package offered under the one facility may be significantly different from that presented under the other, both as to the spread of payments and as to the degree of flexibility available.

14 See pp 746 ff.

15 See pp 722–723.

drawing on the facility and (apart from any commitment fee) incurs no interest charges until he draws, whereas on a loan he is obliged to take it at the outset and pay interest on the full amount outstanding. As against that, a term loan gives him the assurance of the agreed contract period, whereas overdrafts are, in theory at least, repayable on demand. Again, charges in some types of transaction are precomputed and fixed (eg finance charges under a conditional sale or hire-purchase agreement) and are thus not liable to increase or decrease with variations in market rates,[16] while others fluctuate eg by being tied to a given base rate. So the assurance of fixed terms must be set against the advantages of flexibility.

2.   THE ASSETS CYCLE

(i)   From raw materials to cash

A manufacturer buys raw materials and component parts and makes them up into finished products. He then sells his stock to distributors or retailers, generating receivables which in due course crystallize into cash. Part of this is then reinvested in the purchase of further raw materials, beginning the cycle all over again.

The character of the asset changes with each phase in the cycle. The raw materials and components are doomed to a short life, for they will quickly lose their identity in the process of manufacture. The resultant stock (or inventory) is not intended to remain long on the premises but will be constantly turned over. So its useful life may be long but its possession by the manufacturer (and in turn by intermediate parties between him and the end user) will be short. By sale of the stock, the tangible chattel is converted into the intangible debt (chose in action, receivable), an asset having no physical substance but valuable for all that.[17] When payment falls due, the buyer sends a cheque. The pure intangible has now changed into a documentary intangible, a debt locked up in an instrument, and thus equated with a chattel to the extent of being susceptible to the common law of possessory rights and remedies.[18] The cheque is paid into the manufacturer's bank account and is collected for him through the clearing system,[19] an equivalent amount being credited to his account, so that his so-called 'cash at bank' is in reality another pure intangible, namely a claim against the bank, reduced to possession only where he draws cash from his account.

Purchase-money finance may be made available to any party in the distribution chain and may be secured by a purchase-money or non-purchase-money security interest.[20] The security may be extended to cover products and proceeds, and the nature and strength of purchase-money security will to some extent depend on the

---

16 However, this is not an inevitable feature of term loans and other fixed-term credit such as hire-purchase or instalment sale. There is nothing to stop the creditor from inserting a clause providing for adjustments in the sum payable to take account of fluctuations in interest and tax rates, and this is not uncommon in commercial financing.

17 See further as to proceeds, p 697.

18 See p 47.

19 See p 535.

20 See p 670, n 174.

purpose for which the asset is being acquired. The broad division is between assets bought for sale and assets bought for use in the business, including use by letting them out on lease or rental. Assets bought for sale, ie stock, represent a tenuous form of security, in that the creditor is on notice from the outset that it is from the sale of the stock that his advance will be repaid, so that he necessarily allows the debtor to hold himself out as entitled to sell and will find it almost impossible to assert his security interest against a bona fide purchaser in ordinary course of business.[21] It is because stock is manufactured and acquired for resale, and because it is impracticable to make the debtor seek advance permission for each sale of an item of stock, that a charge on stock will almost inevitably be a floating charge.[22] Hence, as an object of security, stock is inherently different from other assets. It is true that receivables share the characteristic of stock in constantly being turned over, new receivables coming into existence while old ones crystallize into payment, but there is nothing in the nature of receivables which compels the debtor to dispose of them to a third party instead of holding them to maturity. They are, therefore, as susceptible to a fixed charge as tangible assets in the hands of the end user. These will usually, in the nature of things, be held for their working life or until part-exchanged for new equipment, so that the debtor's ownership is likely to be enduring and continuous.

(ii) Proceeds

Purchase-money security may be made to cover (and in given conditions will as a matter of law cover) not only the purchased asset but its products and proceeds. Indeed, in the case of stock, security over the proceeds is in some respects a stronger interest, in that it can be taken as a fixed security, whereas for stock this is normally possible only where security is by reservation of title.

Proceeds are likely to increase in variety as one moves down the distribution chain. For example, a retailer engaged in the sale of both new and second-hand goods and accepting credit cards while also offering instalment credit facilities on his own may, on making a cash sale, receive currency, a cheque or a right to payment from the issuer of the credit card, or may take payment of part of the price by acceptance of other goods in part-exchange. Alternatively, he may sell on open or revolving account or by way of fixed-sum credit sale, or may supply the item under a hire-purchase or conditional sale agreement, generating what the Americans conveniently label chattel paper.[23]

All these forms of proceed are capable of being given as security (or collateral[24]) though it does not need much imagination to perceive that security over cash (coins and notes) is not as strong as security over equipment. Cash can be made to disappear very rapidly indeed! Proceeds in the form of accounts or chattel paper are regularly charged or sold outright under factoring or block discounting agreements.[25]

21 See p 743.
22 *Re Bond Worth Ltd* [1979] 3 All ER 919.
23 Uniform Commercial Code, §9–102(a)(11).
24 As to the use of the word 'collateral', see p 583, n 43.
25 See ch 29.

The distinction between original security and proceeds becomes blurred where, as not infrequently occurs, the secured creditor acquires rights over an asset both as proceeds and as original security. For example Creditor supplies Debtor, a car dealer, with motor vehicles under conditional sale agreements and also lends money to Debtor against a fixed charge over Debtor's receivables. Eventually, Debtor gets into difficulties and defaults in payment under the conditional sale agreements, which are in consequence terminated by Creditor. Despite this, Debtor makes an unauthorized sale of a car on terms of payment by the buyer within twenty-eight days. Creditor's security attaches to the resultant receivable (ie the money due from the buyer) both as proceeds of an unauthorized disposition of Creditor's vehicle, traceable in equity,[26] and as a receivable within the scope of the fixed charge.

At every stage the secured creditor faces the prospect of challenge from a competing security interest or other real right. For example, if he takes a charge over the manufacturer's stock, he may find himself subject to a claim by a components supplier that the components incorporated into the finished product were supplied under reservation of title. A more likely conflict is between a stock financier who claims a security interest in receivables arising from the sale of stock as being proceeds of his security and a bank or finance house laying claim to the same receivables as original collateral by virtue of a charge on the manufacturer's book debts.[27]

3.   TYPES OF FINANCE REQUIRED

The form of credit offered to an enterprise, the duration of the credit and the manner in which it is secured depend to a large extent on the purpose for which the financial accommodation is required. Let us take the case of a motor dealer engaged in the sale and repair of cars. He may need at least four different kinds of finance: funds to purchase new premises or extend his existing building; advances to enable him to purchase his stock; credit for the acquisition of new machinery and equipment; and working capital. Finance of the first type is likely to take the form of a fixed medium- or long-term loan secured by a legal charge on the premises. Advances in the second category are short term, since the stock is being constantly turned over and new stock purchased. A variety of forms of stocking finance is available, and in selecting these, regard will no doubt be had to some of the factors mentioned earlier as well as to such additional matters as value added tax.[28] If security is to be taken on the stock itself, then much will depend on whether this takes the form of title reservation or charge, and the shifting character of the security makes for particular problems.[29]

---

26 See pp 443, 720.

27 Or the rival claimant may be a factor who asserts rights as a purchaser of the receivables under a factoring agreement. Competing claims to receivables by inventory financiers and receivables financiers have been much more common in the United States, where they have given rise to considerable litigation and literature. This has occurred less frequently in England, presumably because it is only since *Romalpa* that creditors have given thought to proceeds as security. See pp 608, 720.

28 See p 742.

29 See pp 740 ff.

The creditor is unlikely to be interested in stock finance as such, since this does not generate a very high level of profit. The main reason for offering stocking finance is to capture the dealer's retail credit business by getting him to introduce to the financier customers wishing to acquire the dealer's goods on credit terms. The purchase of equipment may be financed by a purchase-money fixed-term loan or through hire-purchase or instalment sale. The working capital is conveniently provided by an overdraft, which may or may not be secured by a fixed and/or floating charge.

4. THE FUNCTIONAL CLASSIFICATION OF COLLATERAL

It will be apparent from the foregoing that the nature and strength of a security interest depend very much on whether it is tangible or intangible and whether, in the latter case, it is held by the debtor for use or for sale. The chapters which follow reflect this functional classification of collateral. Chapter 27 looks at the situation of the financier who supplies business equipment under a conditional sale or hire-purchase agreement. Chapter 28 examines a further title reservation alternative, the finance lease. In Chapter 29 we move up the distribution chain to the dealer requiring stocking finance and the trader who wishes to convert his receivables into cash under factoring arrangements. The position of the manufacturer is very similar to that of the dealer and is not dealt with separately. The writer has dealt elsewhere with security interests in investment securities[30] and only the conflict of laws aspects are discussed in the present work.[31]

---

30 *Legal Problems of Credit and Security* (3rd edn, 2003), paras 6–23 ff.
31 See p 1111.

27 Conditional Sale and Hire-Purchase

In this chapter we outline the procedures adopted, and some of the legal problems involved, where business equipment is supplied on conditional sale or hire-purchase and a finance house is either itself the legal supplier or comes in subsequently as assignee of the legal supplier's contracts.

I. THE FINANCING TECHNIQUE

Where a supplier of business equipment[1] (hereafter termed 'the dealer') wishes to meet his customers' demands for instalment credit facilities but lacks the capital to bear the burden of the credit extension himself, there are two primary methods by which he can involve a cooperative finance house. The first is to sell the equipment to the finance house and arrange for the latter to supply it to the customer on conditional sale or hire-purchase. From the viewpoint of the finance house this is known as 'direct' or 'direct collection' business, since the finance company is placed in direct and overt contractual relations with the customer and collects the instalments directly from the customer. The second is for the dealer to conclude the conditional sale or hire-purchase agreement with the customer himself as principal and then sell the contract to the finance house. In this situation the finance house is not a party to the conditional sale or hire-purchase agreement, merely a purchaser of the receivables resulting from it and (if so agreed with the dealer) of the title to the underlying goods; and usually, though not invariably, it is arranged that the dealer shall continue to collect the instalments, ostensibly on his own behalf[2] but in reality as agent for the finance house. The agreements are commonly sold to the finance house at a discount in batches at a time and the transaction is termed 'block discounting'.

The legal relationships set up by direct collection business are rather different from those involved in block discounting, as will become apparent, and it is necessary to describe the two systems separately. In the paragraphs that follow, D is the dealer, F is the finance house and B the business buyer or hirer on hire-purchase.

---

1 This work is concerned essentially with commercial transactions, so that consumer credit agreements will not be discussed in this chapter, though the common law rules apply to the latter in almost the same way. For a treatment of the law relating to consumer credit, see *Goode: Consumer Credit Law and Practice* (looseleaf); A. G. Guest and M. G. Lloyd, *Encyclopaedia of Consumer Credit Law* (1975); *Chitty on Contracts* (29th edn, 2004), ch 38.

2 It is customary not to give notice to customers of the assignment of the debtor's rights to the finance house, in order to avoid disturbing business relations between the dealer and his customers, who in the ordinary course will never get to know of the finance house's involvement in the transactions. If, however, the dealer gets into financial difficulty, the finance house will usually take over the collection of instalments, giving formal notice of assignment to the customers.

(i) Direct collection[3]

D concludes an arrangement with F to introduce to F customers of D wishing to acquire his equipment on instalment terms. The arrangements may be recorded in a formal master agreement or more informally by an exchange of letters. D is remunerated for his introductions by a commission, calculated as a percentage of the finance charge made by F under the conditional sale or hire-purchase agreement. F installs a point of sale computer system on the dealer's premises, which generates the agreement document. D then signs up the customer to an agreement, collects any down payment required by F and sends the agreement to F for its approval, together with D's pro forma invoice incorporating a request to F to purchase the equipment. If F accepts the transaction, it signs the agreement itself,[4] dispatches a copy to the customer and pays D the cash price of the equipment, as stated in his invoice, less the down payment made by B. D then delivers the equipment to B. Expressed diagrammatically the relationship is as shown in figure 27.1.

In figure 27.1 transaction 1 is the sale by D to F, transaction 2 the conditional sale/hire-purchase agreement between F and B. It will be observed that in this form of transaction, in contrast to block discounting, B has no contractual relationship with D at all.[5] D is the physical supplier, but B's contract is with F.[6] If the transaction is a conditional sale agreement, F is the seller for the purpose of the Sale of Goods Act 1979 and of any other legislation affecting sale transactions.[7] It follows that by using this method F places itself directly in the firing line if the equipment proves to be unfit for its purpose or not of merchantable quality. Since F's role is intended to be financial, it may seem odd that it should choose this form of doing business, but that is

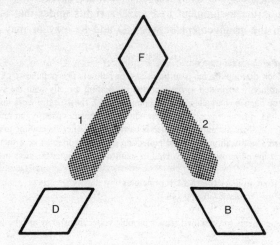

Fig 27.1 The parties to a direct collection transaction

3 See R. M. Goode, *Hire-Purchase Law and Practice* (2nd edn, 1970), pp 644 ff.
4 Sometimes the procedure is reversed, with the finance house signing first and the customer afterwards.
5 Except where D gives a collateral warranty of some kind. See p 720.
6 The problems created by this kind of triangular relationship are discussed in relation to finance leasing, p 729.
7 Eg, the Consumer Credit Act 1974.

how hire-purchase developed historically[8] and, despite the legal drawbacks, it remains the preferred method except for small-unit business.[9]

A word should be said about the formation of the contract between B and F. The submission of the agreement signed by B represents an offer by B to take the equipment under the terms of the agreement. It does not crystallize into a contract until F has accepted the offer (usually by signing the agreement) and has intimated his acceptance to B.[10] Until that point is reached, B is free to withdraw his offer.[11]

(ii) Block discounting[12]

F and D conclude a master agreement (fig 27.2) by which D agrees to offer for sale to F batches of conditional sale and/or hire-purchase agreements[13] made directly between D as seller/owner and the buyers/hirers. The agreement will provide that if F accepts the agreements offered, it will pay D the collection value[14] of the purchased agreements less a security retention (later released if the instalments payable by the debtors are duly paid) and a discount calculated by reference to the period or average period for which F will be out of its money.[15] D undertakes to collect the instalments as agent for F and to guarantee payment by the debtors under the agreements.[16] Though the block discounting agreement is often printed and signed by both parties, it is essentially facultative in nature (since D is not obliged to sell any receivables or F to purchase them) and, indeed, is not a true contract at all at the time of signature, merely an agreed standard set of terms regulating specific transactions as and when concluded.[17] Figure 27.3 shows the relationship of D, F and B.

Transaction 1 is the conditional sale/hire-purchase agreement between D and B. Transaction 2 is the assignment to F of D's rights under that agreement, which (depending on the arrangement between D and F) may or may not include D's

8   Goode, *Hire-Purchase Law*, pp 6 ff.
9   For which block discounting tends to be used (see below). The popularity of the direct collection method is commonly attributed to the fact that by dealing directly with the customer, F has more control, and the finance charge levied on B compensates F for the extra work involved, whereas non-notification block discounting places a premium on D's business sense and integrity, and generates less income for F, since the ultimate burden is carried by D. There is nothing to prevent F from block discounting on a notification basis and collecting payments direct, like a factor under a factoring agreement, but the administration involved in small-unit consumer business makes direct collection less attractive.
10   This follows from ordinary contract law principles.
11   See Goode, *Hire-Purchase Law*, pp 144 ff.
12   Ibid, pp 657 ff.
13   Pure rental agreements (or specified rentals payable under them) may also be included. See ibid, pp 667 ff.
14   Ie, the balance outstanding.
15   Ie, because it is paying D in a lump but receives the amounts due under the agreements by instalments.
16   Since this 'recourse' provision means that D is responsible for getting the instalments to F come what may, even if the debtors themselves default, it is usually found convenient for D to give instalment bills of exchange, or to make a standing order or direct debit in favour of F, rather than accounting for instalments as and when received from the debtors. This practice has been accepted by the courts as consistent with a purchase of the receivables and does not convert the transaction between D and F into a loan transaction. See *Olds Discount Ltd v John Playfair Ltd* [1938] 3 All ER 275; *Chow Yoong Hong v Choong Fah Rubber Manufactory* [1962] AC 209.
17   See p 73.

MA 4
Block Discounting
Agreement types as in paragraph 1.1.1 below.

THIS MASTER BLOCK DISCOUNTING AGREEMENT is made the   day of

BETWEEN: LIMITED
whose registered office is at

(hereafter called 'the Purchaser' which shall include the Purchaser's successors and assigns)

AND:

of (being the registered office, if a company)

(hereafter called 'the Vendor')

WHEREBY IT IS AGREED as follows:

1.   **Definitions**
1.1. The following expressions shall, unless the context otherwise requires, have the following meanings:

Agreements	agreements entered into between the Vendor and hirers or debtors which are hire or leasing agreements and credit agreements including conditional sale agreements, hire purchase agreements, credit sale agreements and any other credit agreements;
HP Agreements	Agreements which are hire purchase agreements or conditional sale agreements as defined in the Consumer Credit Act 1974;
Customer	a person who is a debtor or hirer, as appropriate, under an Agreement;
clause	a clause in this agreement;
Hire Agreements	hire and lease agreements being agreements which are for the bailment or hire of goods and which are not HP Agreements;
Guarantee	a guarantee or an indemnity or both given in relation to an Agreement;
Guarantor	a person who gives a Guarantee;
Purchased Agreement	an Agreement listed in an Offer for Sale which the Purchaser agrees to purchase as set out in clause 2.3;
Offer for Sale	has the meaning set out in clause 2.1;
purchase	in respect of an Agreement, means the purchase of those rights set out in clause 2.2.
purchase price	the price referred to in clause 2.2.

1.2 In this agreement unless the context otherwise requires, the singular shall include the plural, and vice versa, and the masculine shall include the feminine and the neuter and the headings are for convenience only and do not affect the construction of this agreement.

2.   **Offers for sale**
2.1 The Vendor shall from time to time submit an Offer for Sale to the Purchaser in such form and containing such details as the Purchaser may from time to time require listing those Agreements which the Vendor requests that the Purchaser shall purchase. Together with the Offer for Sale, the Vendor shall submit to the Purchaser all the Agreements listed in the Offer for Sale and all proposal forms, Guarantees and all other documents in the Vendor's possession which relate to each Agreement so listed together with an Assignment (in the form prescribed by the Purchaser). Until notification by the Purchaser under clause 2.3 the Purchaser shall hold such documents in trust for the Vendor.
2.2 The purchase price payable to the Vendor by the Purchaser shall in each instance be a sum representing the total of the outstanding balances payable under Agreements (other than Hire Agreements) and the total of the minimum sums required to be paid by hirers under Hire Agreements (hereafter called 'The Outstanding Balance') less in each case such proportion thereof as may from time to time be agreed between the parties in respect of each type of agreement.
2.3 The Purchaser will, on receipt of an Offer for Sale in accordance with clause 2.1 and if the Purchaser thinks fit, purchase upon the terms and conditions set out in this agreement the contractual rights of the Vendor in such Agreements (together with the goods the subject matter of such Agreements as are HP Agreements or Hire Agreements) and in Guarantees relating to such Agreements.
2.4 On or about the seventh day after receiving any Offer for Sale, the Purchaser (who shall be entitled without disclosing any reason to decline to purchase any or all Agreements listed in the Offer for Sale) shall notify the Vendor of its agreement to purchase any or all of the Agreements so listed together with the purchase price to be paid. Immediately upon the Purchaser giving notice of its agreement the relevant Assignment shall become absolute and effective for all purposes. If the Purchaser rejects an Offer for Sale the relevant Assignment shall cease to be of any force or effect and the Purchaser shall return it and all other documents relating to that Offer for Sale to the Vendor.

3.   **Warranties**
3.1 With each Offer for Sale the Vendor shall be deemed to warrant as follows:
    3.1.1. that in respect of each Agreement listed in the Offer for Sale there has been compliance with all applicable statutes and statutory instruments for the time being in force and the goods the subject matter thereof (if any) comply in all respect with every applicable warranty and condition both express and implied;
    3.1.2 that each such Agreement and Guarantee is and shall remain in all respects valid and effective and fully enforceable against the respective Customer and Guarantor as the case may be and that in relation to each Agreement the outstanding balance is the sum shown in the Offer for Sale;
    3.1.3 that, in respect of each such Agreement, neither the Customer nor the Guarantor has in any way disputed liability nor may either of them acquire (or have acquired) any right of counterclaim or set off;
    3.1.4 that any initial payment specified in each such Agreement has been duly paid either in cash or by proper and lawful allowance by way of part exchange and that all subsequent payments which have fallen due have been received;

Fig 27.2 Block discounting agreement

3.1.5   that none of such Agreements has been submitted to any other person, firm or company otherwise than in such manner (if any) as shall already have been fully disclosed by the Vendor to the Purchaser;

3.1.6   that with reference to the goods comprised in a HP Agreement or Hire Agreement:

    3.1.6.1 the Vendor has a good title to the goods and that they are the absolute property of the Vendor free of any charges and encumbrances of whatsoever nature save and except, in the case of HP Agreements, the option to purchase contained in each Agreement;

    3.1.6.2 they have not been the subject of any previous transaction with the respective Customers;

3.1.7   that the Vendor is unaware of any matter which, if disclosed, might affect the judgement of the Purchaser as to the advisability of purchasing any such Agreement; and

3.1.8   that the details of the Customer, the particulars of any goods, and any other information set out in any Agreement are correct in every respect.

4.   Collection

4.1   The Vendor shall be deemed to be appointed the agent of the Purchaser to collect and shall diligently collect on behalf of the Purchaser all sums payable under Purchased Agreements and any relevant Guarantees. All such sums of money should immediately upon receipt by the Vendor be impressed with and shall be held by the Vendor subject to a trust in favour of the Purchaser and each and every such sum of money shall be deemed to be payable to the Purchaser on demand.

4.2   The Vendor shall notify the Purchaser of any exercise of any right of cancellation or termination or upon the early settlement of any Purchased Agreement by a Customer immediately upon its occurrence.

4.3   The Vendor shall keep separate and accurate records of account in respect of all monies collected by the Vendor on behalf of the Purchaser and shall permit the Purchaser or its representatives at all reasonable times on demand to inspect and or audit such records and such records shall be kept in a form which clearly identifies each Purchased Agreement and each payment in relation to each Purchased Agreement and each such record shall be easily legible or, in the case of computer records, easily accessible in the event of an inspection or audit. The Vendor shall give such assistance as is requested by the Purchaser or its representative for the purpose of the audit or inspection.

4.4   The Vendor shall, in the case of a manual or printed accounting system, endorse upon the record relating to each Purchased Agreement that it has been purchased hereunder and shall do likewise to the extent that it is reasonably practicable in the case of a computerised accounting system and the Purchaser shall have the right to enter such endorsement upon such records should the Vendor fail so to do.

4.5   The Vendor shall at the request of the Purchaser supply the Purchaser with a copy of the Vendor's latest Balance Sheet and Profit and Loss Account as certified by his auditors.

5.   Payment Over

Without prejudice to the obligations of the Vendor, set out in clause 4, but for the purposes of facilitating the operation of this agreement, the Vendor shall complete and forward to the Purchaser herewith or with the first Offer for Sale (and thereafter as and when requested to do so) a duly completed variable direct debit or, if the Purchaser shall agree or require, the Vendor shall submit a duly completed standing order or series of bills of exchange with each Offer for Sale in such form as the Purchaser shall require. The payment to the Purchaser of all sums collected hereunder from Customers shall be made by equal or approximately equal monthly payments of a number and in such amount as the parties shall agree in respect of all the Purchased Agreements listed in each Offer for Sale, the first payment to become due one month after the payment by the Purchaser of the purchase price.

6.   Termination

6.1   The Purchaser may, by written notice, forthwith determine the Vendor's agency and authority to collect payments on the Purchaser's behalf set out in this agreement if:

  6.1.1   the Vendor is in default of any payment of any sum due to the Purchaser or upon the rejection by a bank or the failure of a direct debit or of a standing order payment or the debiting back by a bank of any sum paid under the direct debit or standing order or if any bill of exchange is dishonoured;

  6.1.2   the Vendor commits a breach of any other of the terms and conditions herein contained to be performed and observed by the Vendor.

6.2   The Vendor's agency and authority to collect payments on the Purchaser's behalf set out in this agreement shall forthwith automatically determine and end if;

  6.2.1   the Vendor has an interim or bankruptcy order made against him or is in receipt of a creditor's demand under the Insolvency Act 1986 or the Bankruptcy (Scotland) Act 1985;

  6.2.2   the Vendor makes or proposes a formal composition, scheme of arrangement or trust deed with or on behalf of his creditors or calls a meeting of them;

  6.2.3   the Vendor, being a company, allows a receiver, manager or administrator to be appointed over all or part of its assets or a winding up petition to be presented or a resolution to be passed for its winding up (other than for the purpose of reconstruction or amalgamation);

  6.2.4   the Vendor permits execution to be levied against or, in Scotland, permits a poinding or arrestment, over any of his assets or income; or

  6.2.5   any step is taken or threatened to levy distress or distraint or if there is executed any legal diligence upon the property in the possession of the Vendor for rent or taxes.

6.3   This agreement may be terminated at any time by either party giving to the other 30 days written notice to that effect but such notice shall not prejudice the rights of the Purchaser or affect the liabilities of the Vendor in respect of any transactions effected prior to the expiration of the notice.

6.4   The termination of this agreement by whatever means shall not prejudice or otherwise affect the rights and liabilities of the parties hereto in respect of transactions effected hereunder prior to the date of such termination and in particular shall not affect the rights of the Purchaser under clause 7.

7.   Repurchase

7.1   Upon any Purchased Agreement or where relevant the hiring thereby created becoming determined otherwise than by the due payment to the Purchaser of the full outstanding balance under such Agreement (either by the Vendor or the Customer) or upon the Customer becoming in default of any instalment or rental for a period exceeding two months, the Vendor:

  7.1.1   shall, if so required by the Purchaser; or

  7.1.2   may, if the Purchaser shall so agree:

exchange for the relevant Purchased Agreement referred to in this clause as 'the Existing Agreement' an Agreement of a similar kind to the Existing Agreement in respect of which Agreement the outstanding balance due under the Agreement shall be not less than that outstanding balance under the Existing Agreement prior to the deduction of any rebate to which the Customer shall be entitled at law and in respect of which the Customer shall not have committed any breach of any of its terms.

7.2 As an alternative to such exchange the Purchaser may require the Vendor to pay to the Purchaser the outstanding balance under the said Purchased Agreement and any other monies as may have become payable by the Customer in respect of that Agreement.

7.3 Upon such payment being made together with such other moneys as may have become payable by the Customer in respect of that agreement the Purchaser shall transfer to the Vendor the contractual rights of the Purchaser in the Purchased Agreement together with the goods comprised in the agreement if it is an HP Agreement or a Hire Agreement and any Guarantee relating to it.

7.4 Any payment made by the Vendor pursuant to this clause shall be treated as being in satisfaction of the obligation on the Vendor set out in clause 4 and such payment shall be deducted from the final payment or, if in excess of the final payment, payments to be made by the Vendor to the Purchaser under the direct debits or, as the case may be, the standing orders referred to in clause 5 in relation to the purchase of Agreements set out in the same Offer for Sale as the relevant Purchased Agreement to which this clause relates.

8. Satisfaction

If each of the payments payable under the direct debit, or as the case may be, the standing order or bills of exchange in respect of Purchased Agreements listed in the same Offer for Sale shall be made on the due date, the Purchaser shall accept the total amount thereof in satisfaction of all moneys payable by the Vendor under this agreement in respect of those Purchased Agreements and the Vendor shall be entitled to retain for the Vendor's own benefit and by way of renumeration for the Vendor's services in having collected payments for the Purchaser hereunder all further moneys payable by the Customer under the Purchased Agreements and, if applicable, in respect of clause 9.

9. Maintenance Clause

Where the Purchaser purchases an Agreement and where that Agreement provides that the owner of the goods shall have an obligation to maintain the goods, howsoever expressed, the Vendor hereby undertakes to the Purchaser to carry out without undue delay, free of cost other than under clause 8, and in accordance with the provisions of the Agreement the obligation to repair or maintain the goods and the Vendor shall indemnify and keep indemnified the Purchaser against and shall pay the Purchaser on demand all claims, damages, losses or expenses arising out of a breach by the Vendor or any of the obligations of the Vendor under this clause.

10. Power of Attorney

The Vendor hereby irrevocably appoints the Purchaser the Vendor's attorney for the execution of any assignment to be required to be executed by the Vendor in favour of the Purchaser under the provisions of this agreement and for the purpose of executing all other documents necessary to vest title in the Purchaser to any of the Purchased Agreements including any Guarantees relating thereto and to any goods the subject matter of the Agreements. The Vendor hereby further irrevocably appoints the Purchaser the attorney of the Vendor for the purpose of commencing actions in any court of law whether in the name of the Vendor alone or in the joint names of the Vendor and the Purchaser in order to prosecute or defend the Purchaser's rights under this agreement and any under any Purchased Agreement.

11. Miscellaneous

11.1 Where any sum is payable by the Purchaser hereunder and at the same time moneys are due and payable to the Purchaser by the Vendor, the Purchaser may set off the amount so due from the Vendor against the amount payable by the Purchaser.

11.2 Except as provided in this agreement or as may be expressly notified by the Purchaser in writing, the Vendor shall not be nor hold the Vendor out to be the agent of the Purchaser for any purpose whatsoever.

11.3 Subject to the provisions of clause 7, any goods which may be returned to the Vendor by a Customer under an agreement shall be held by the Vendor in trust for the Purchaser and within three days of such goods being so returned the Vendor shall notify the Purchaser and the Purchaser shall within seven days of receipt of such notification give the Vendor written disposal instructions. The Vendor shall immediately comply with any such disposal instructions and the Vendor shall pay to the Purchaser the amount required by the Purchaser for the repurchase of the Purchased Agreement pursuant to clause 7.

11.4 No relaxation or indulgence which the Purchaser may from time to time or at any time extend to the Vendor hereunder or to a Customer or Guarantor in respect of any Purchased Agreement or Guarantee shall prejudice or act as a waiver of the Purchaser's strict rights against the Vendor under this agreement.

11.5 The Vendor must notify the Purchaser immediately in writing of any change of the Vendor's address.

11.6 Where two or more persons are named as the Vendor, their liabilities under this agreement shall be joint and several.

11.7 This agreement shall be governed by the laws of the country in which is situated the address of the Purchaser shown above. In Scotland any word or phrase in this agreement not in current use there shall be given the meaning and effect of the nearest equivalent word or phrase in use in Scotland. The Vendor submits to the non-exclusive jurisdiction of the English Courts.

11.8 The Vendor shall pay to the Purchaser interest at the rate of four per cent per annum above the Finance House Base Rate for the time being in force on any sum payable to the Purchaser from the Vendor from its due date until actual payment whether before or after judgment.

11.9 Any notice or demand to be given under this agreement may be served by delivering the same or sending the same by first class post by telex or by electronic facsimile transmission:

11.9.1 to the Vendor at the Vendor's address or telex number set out above (or such other address or telex number as the Vendor notifies the Purchaser) or at the Vendor's last address telex number or electronic facsimile transmission telephone number known to the Purchaser; or .

11.9.2 to the Purchaser at the address referred to above or such other address as the Purchaser notifies the Vendor.

11.10 Any notice or demand shall be deemed to have been received, in the case of a letter, on the second day following the date of posting and in respect of telex or electronic facsimile transmission on the date of transmission. In proving the service it shall be sufficient, in the case of a letter, to show that the envelope was properly stamped, addressed and posted or, in the case of a telex or electronic facsimile transmission, that the message was properly transmitted.

706

AS WITNESS the hands of persons duly authorised on behalf of the Vendor and the Purchaser

SIGNED on behalf of

LIMITED (the Purchaser)
in the presence of:

SIGNED by
on behalf of

in the presence of: (the Vendor)

ASSIGNMENT MA4

THIS ASSIGNMENT is made the   day of   **20**

between..

(1) of/whose Registered Office is situate at †(2) ....
(hereafter called "the Assignor")
of the one part ....

and (3)   ....

of/whose Registered Office is situate at †(4) ....

....
(hereafter called "the Assignee" which shall include the Assignee's successors and assigns) of the other part.

WHEREAS:—

(1)   The Assignor has entered into Agreements with Customers particulars whereof are set but in the Schedule †[overleaf] [annexed hereto marked "A"].
(hereafter called "Purchased Agreements").

(2)   Pursuant to a Master Block Discounting Agreement between the parties hereto dated the
day of   **20**
(hereafter called "the Master Agreement") the Assignor has agreed with the Assignee for the sale to the Assignee of (inter alia) the Purchased Agreements and the Assignor's contractual rights therein together with the goods the subject matter of such Agreements as are HP Agreements or Hire Agreements and the Assignor's rights in Guarantees relating to such Agreements at the purchase price hereinafter specified.

NOW THIS DEED WITNESSETH as follows:—

1.   In pursuance of the said recited agreement and in consideration of the sum of £   †now paid by the Assignee to the Assignor (receipt whereof the Assignor hereby acknowledges) the Assignor as beneficial owner hereby sells and assigns unto the Assignee ALL THOSE the said Purchased Agreements TOGETHER WITH the contractual rights of the Assignor therein and in all Guarantees relating thereto and all monies now and hereafter payable thereunder and TOGETHER ALSO where relevant the goods comprised therein TO HOLD the same unto the Assignee absolutely.

2.   This Assignment is supplemental to and shall be subject in all respects to the provisions of the Master Agreement and in particular (but without prejudice to the generality of the foregoing) each and every warranty on the part of the Assignor contained in the Master Agreement shall be deemed to be imported into this Assignment and ratified and confirmed by the Assignor accordingly.

3.   Unless the context otherwise require words and expressions defined in the Master Agreement shall bear the same meanings in this Agreement.

4.   IT IS HEREBY CERTIFIED that the transaction hereby effected does not form part of a larger transaction or of a series of transactions in respect of which the amount or value or the aggregate amount or value of the consideration exceeds £   †

IN WITNESS whereof the Assignor [has hereunto set his hand and seal]* [has caused its Common Seal to be hereunto affixed]† the day and year first above written.

*SIGNED and DELIVERED   (All partners in a firm to sign)

by the said

in the presence of:

†THE COMMON SEAL of

                                    LIMITED

was hereunto affixed in the presence of:

                                    Director

                                    Secretary

†Insert/delete as appropriate

*(If an individual or firm)

(1) and (2) Name and Address of Vendor as in Master Block Discounting Agreement.

(3) and (4) Name and Address of Purchaser as in Master Block Discounting Agreement.

708

MA 4 (Indemnity)
    (Block Discounting)

† *To* ....

....

....

WE hereby request you to enter into a Master Block Discounting Agreement or Agreements in your present
standard form or such other form as you may require with
†

(hereinafter called "the
Vendor") in respect of the proposed purchase by you from the Vendor of the Vendor's contractual rights under
hire, leasing and/or credit agreements (including conditional sale, hire purchase and credit sale agreements)
together with goods the subject matter of such agreements as are hire, leasing, conditional sale or hire purchase
agreements and in consideration of your so doing we (namely):

† ....

of ....

AND

† ....

of ....

AND

† ....

of ....

hereby jointly and severally guarantee the due and prompt performance and observance of all the terms and
conditions of the said Master Block Discounting Agreements on the part of the Vendor to be so performed and
observed and if the Vendor shall in any respect commit any breach of the Vendor's obligations or of any
warranties or representations thereunder then we will jointly and severally keep you and your successors and
assigns indemnified against and will on demand pay to you all losses damages costs and expenses which may be
suffered or incurred by you in any way arising out of such breach AND we further agree that no relaxation or
indulgence which you may from time to time or any time extend either to the Vendor or to a customer of the
Vendor or to us or any of us shall in any way prejudice or act as a waiver of your strict rights against us or any of us
hereunder.

DATED the   day of

†SIGNED by the said   ⎫
                                           ⎬
in the presence of: ⎭

†SIGNED by the said   ⎫
                                           ⎬
in the presence of: ⎭

†SIGNED by the said   ⎫
                                           ⎬
in the presence of: ⎭

† Insert full names and addresses

**This Indemnity is the copyright of the Consumer Credit Trade Association and may not be reproduced without
express permission in writing.**

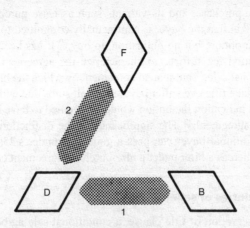

Fig 27.3 Block discounting

underlying title to the equipment. D's interest in the equipment, encumbered as it is by the conditional sale agreement in favour of B, is of no intrinsic value except in the event of B's default. What F is paying for is the receivables generated by the conditional sale/hire-purchase agreement, not the title to the equipment itself.

It will be observed that, in contrast to the position shown in figure 27.1, there is no contractual nexus between F and B. The latter's contract is with D, and D alone. F is merely a purchaser of the rights vested in D under the conditional sale/hire-purchase agreement. F does not assume any of D's liabilities and cannot be sued by B if, for example, the equipment proves defective. On the other hand, F as assignee cannot stand in a better position than D himself. F takes subject to 'equities', that is, to all rights and defences available to B against the original creditor, D.[18] Of course, so long as the assignment is not notified, B may know nothing of F's existence and will continue making payment to D. But if F gives notice of the assignment to B and calls upon B to pay future rentals to F, then subject to any defences or rights of set-off he may have, B is obliged to respect F's title to the receivables and pay F direct. A payment to D after notice of assignment would not be a good discharge of B's liability for the instalment paid and he could be made to pay again, to F.

2.   CONDITIONAL SALE

We now turn to look at the incidents of the relationship between the parties to a conditional sale agreement. The position here is the same whether the seller is F (direct collection) or D (block discounting).

(i)   Distinguished from hire-purchase

A conditional sale agreement is an agreement for sale under which title remains in the seller until the purchase price has been paid in full or the buyer has complied with any other conditions prescribed by the agreement for the transfer of title to him.

---

18 For the circumstances in which set-off is available, see pp 610, 621.

It differs from hire-purchase, and its variants such as lease purchase and personal contract purchase,[19] in that the buyer is contractually committed to buying while the hirer has merely an option, but no obligation, to buy.[20] It has been held that even a purely nominal option fee suffices to characterize the agreement as hire-purchase rather than conditional sale,[21] but that an agreement by which the hirer could indicate he did not wish to take title even after payment of all sums due under the agreement, in default of which indication the option would be deemed to have been exercised, is a conditional sale agreement.[22] The significance of the distinction lies primarily in the fact that a conditional buyer can pass a good title under s 25(1) of the Sale of Goods Act 1979 whereas a hirer under a hire-purchase agreement cannot.[23]

(ii)   Rights and duties of seller and buyer

Apart from the reservation of title clause, a conditional sale agreement has all the normal incidents of a contract of sale, and the provisions of the Sale of Goods Act apply save in so far as effectively excluded.[24] The typical agreement[25] will require the buyer to maintain punctual payment of the instalments, to keep the equipment in his possession, comprehensively insured and in good repair and condition, not to sell or otherwise dispose of it and not to allow any lien to be created on it, eg for repairs. The agreement will contain a provision entitling the seller to terminate the agreement and repossess the equipment in various events, including breach of the buyer's obligations, levy of distress or execution against his goods by another creditor, bankruptcy etc. In addition, the buyer will usually be required, in the event of termination of the agreement by the seller, to compensate the seller for any loss remaining after repossession and sale of the equipment, eg by paying the unpaid balance of the purchase price less the proceeds of sale of the equipment and a discount to allow for the acceleration of the buyer's payment liability. As an alternative, the seller may rely on the rights given him by the Sale of Goods Act.[26]

Exercise of a right of repossession rescinds[27] the contract of sale and bars an action for recovery of the price as such,[28] and the same consequences flow from exercise of the statutory power of resale.[29]

The seller's right of repossession may be enforced by application to the court or by physical seizure (recaption). But recaption of business equipment is not always as easy as one might think. The seller cannot enter on the buyer's premises to recover the equipment without the buyer's consent unless authorized to do so by the

---

19 See below.
20 *Helby v Matthews* [1895] AC 471.
21 *Close Asset Finance Ltd v Care Graphics Machinery Ltd* [2001] GCCR 2617.
22 *Forthright Finance Ltd v Carlyle Finance Ltd* [1997] 4 All ER 90.
23 See the decision in n 20 and p 435.
24 For the restrictions imposed by legislation on the exclusion or limitation of liability for breach, see pp 97, 100 ff.
25 See fig 27.4.
26 See pp 407 ff.
27 Ie, in this context terminates, as opposed to cancelling from the beginning. See p 362.
28 Goode, *Hire-Purchase Law*, p 858.
29 Ibid. The seller will, of course, be entitled to damages.

Citibank Savings

VAT Reg No. 242803285

Part Two: The Schedule

Please use BLOCK CAPITALS with black pen (or type) to ensure clarity

Conditional Sale Agreement

No. |__|__|__|__|__|__|__|__|

Section H: The Buyer(s)
Name(s) in full

Address

Postcode

Section I: Description of Goods
Make
Model   New/used*
Year of manufacture
Date first registered
Registration No.
Chassis/frame No.
Rating (cc)
Type of body
Engine No.

Insurance details
Goods insured with
                                    (Insurance Company name)
Address of Branch Office (or Brokers)

Policy/Cover Note No.
Renewal date

Section J: Financial details   £   p
Price of the Goods (excluding VAT)
VAT @   %
Insurance and/or Licence
Total cash price

Less Initial Payment   £   p
Cash/Cheque
Part exchange allowance
Total   A

Balance of total cash price
Add Cr'safe Ins. Prem. (if applic.)
Amount financed

Add total charges

Documentation fee (to be paid with first instalment)   7   00

Balance of total purchase price   B

Balance of total purchase price payable by £
due on   followed by   monthly
instalments of £   commencing on   19
and thereafter on the same day of each succeeding month.
Total Purchase Price equals the total of **A + B**

---

* Delete as appropriate

Declaration by Buyer and signature of Parties

The Buyer in signing this Agreement acknowledges that before he did so:

(a) he had seen and examined the Goods and satisfied himself that they are in good condition and suitable for the purpose for which he requires them;

(b) he had seen and read the terms and conditions of this Agreement and fully understood them.

The Buyer realises that Citibank Savings have not seen or examined the Goods and invites them to rely on his assurances given above and to purchase the Goods and sell them to him on the terms of this Agreement.

If a Company:
For and on behalf of Buyer

Signature
Director/Secretary who is duly authorised to sign

If not a Company

Signature

Signature

Sales note To be completed by the Dealer
To: Citibank Savings

We offer to sell to you at the price stated below the goods set out in the schedule to this conditional sale agreement with the under-mentioned buyer and briefly described below. We warrant that all the particulars in the schedule and customer details are correct, that the goods are our unencumbered property, that they are of merchantable quality and fit for the purpose requied by the buyer and that there has been no act or omission by ourselves or third parties which would affect the validity and enforceability of the conditional sale agreement or give the buyer any claim against you. We agree to indemnify you against any such claim and against any costs incurred in connection therewith.

Buyer ....
Goods ....
Price ....
Dealer's name ....
Signature ....
Address ....
....
Date .... Credit Brok. Lic. No. ....

Signature of witness
Name BLOCK CAPITALS
Address BLOCK CAPITALS

Two witnesses required in Scotland only

Signature of witness
Name BLOCK CAPITALS
Address BLOCK CAPITALS

Date of Agreement
Signature for and on behalf of Owners

Fig 27.4 Conditional sale agreement outside the Consumer Credit Act 1974

Terms and Conditions

The Conditional Sale Agreement is made BETWEEN Citibank Savings ('the Sellers' which expression shall include their successors and assigns) of the one part and the Buyer described in the Schedule of the other part whereby the Sellers agree to sell and the Buyer agrees to buy the goods specified in the Schedule ('the Goods').

1. Payment

(a) The Buyer, having made the initial payment specified in the Schedule, shall promptly pay the balance of the total purchase price in the manner and by the instalments therein stated. All payments shall be at the Buyer's risk until received by the Sellers.

(b) Punctual payment shall be of the essence of this Agreement. Without prejudice to the Seller's right to treat a default in payment as a repudiation of this Agreement the Sellers shall be entitled to charge interest on any instalment or part thereof in arrear at a rate not exceeding Finance House Base rate for the time being plus 4 per cent, such interest to accrue from day to day after as well as before any judgment.

2. Credentials Insurance

Where the total purchase price includes a Credentials Insurance premium, the Buyer enjoys the benefit of insurance policies under which the insurance company pays instalments becoming due while the Buyer is off work through accident, sickness or unemployment and also, in the event of his death, pays the full balance outstanding under this Agreement. This protection is subject to the limits and conditions contained in the Creditsafe group policies Nos. 7703 and GC-26 of which particulars will be supplied to the Buyer.

3. Possession and Care of Goods

(a) The Buyer shall keep the Goods in good working order and repair, indemnifying the Seller against loss resulting from loss or deterioration of or damage to the Goods from whatever causes, promptly notifying the Sellers of such loss, deterioration or damage and comply with any directions fo the Sellers as to the nature and place of repairs to the Goods.

(b) The Buyer shall not encumber, sell or otherwise dispose of the Goods or any of the Buyer's rights under this Agreement without the Sellers' prior written consent and shall use the Goods only in the manner and circumstances for which they are designed and for which their use is permitted by law.

4. Insurance

(a) The Buyer shall throughout the period of this Agreement keep the Goods comprehensively insured to their full replacement value under a policy which notes the Sellers' int4erest in the Goods. The Buyer's rights under the policy and any policy monies the Buyer may receive shall be made over to the Sellers on demand and shall meanwhile be held on trust for them.

(b) Sums paid by the insurers will atg the Seller's option be applied in repairing or replacing the Goods or in reducing the balance of the total purchase price and other sums remaining outstanding under this Agreement. Where the Sellers exercise the last option, they shall pay to the Buyer any surplus of policy monies over the balance outstanding or the Buyer any shortfall, and when such payment has been made this Agreement will come to an end in all other cases, thisAgreement and the Buyer's duties under it will continue even if the Goods are lost, damaged, stolen or destroyed. The Buyer hereby authorises the Sellers to negotiate with the insurers and to accept any payment they may make and conclude any compromise with them that the Sellers may consider appropriate.

5. Us of Goods

The Buyer shall give all notices and obtain or effect all licences or registrations necessary for th elawful use of the Goods and pay all taxes, duties, fees and charges which are or may be payable in respect of the Goods whilst the Agreement is in force and in the event of such taxes, duties, fees or charges being paid by the Sellers shall repay the same on demand.

6. Title to the Goods

Title to the Goods shall pass to the Buyer upon payment by the Buyer to the Sellers of the total purchase price and all other sums payable by the Buyer under this Agreement.

7. Termination by Sellers

(a) Upon the occurrence of a default event the Sellers may, without prejudice to their other rights and remedies under this Agrement, forthwith and without notice determine this Agreement, whereupon the Buyer shall cease to be in possession of the goods with the consent of the Sellers, who may retake possession of the Goods. In Scotland the buyer's sequestration or liquidation shall have the like effect.

(b) For the purpose of this clause, a default event is one of the following, namely a breach by the Buyer of any of his obligations under this Agreement, the levy of distress of execution against or the appointment of a receiver of any of the Buyer's assets or income, the dissolution of the buyer where a partnership, the presentation of a bankruptcy or winding up petition or making of a sequestration order against the Buyer or the convening of a meeting to pass a resolution for voluntary winding up of the Buyer or to conclude an arrangement with the Buyer's creditors.

8. Sums payable by the Buyer upon determination

In the event of the Sellers determining this Agrement under Clause 7 hereof the buyer shall upon demand pay to the Sellers:

(a) all payments due and unpaid as at the date of termination,

(b) any other sums which shall have become payable by the Buyer to the Sellers under this Agreement,

(c) any expenses incurred by the Sellers in tracing and recovering possession of the Goods and the costs of such repairs and replacements as are required to put the Goods in the good order, condition and repair and to the standard provided in Clause 3(a) hereof together with any value added tax payable by the Sellers in respect of any of the above costs,

(d) the balance of the Sellers' loss which is hereby agreed to be the amount by which the total purchase price exceeds the aggregate of:

(i) the net proceeds of sale of the Goods by the Sellers after deducting the cost of repairs (so far as not recovered under paragraph (c), storage, insurance, sale and any other costs, including legal costs, reasonably incurred in connection therewith, or due and unpaid at the date of termination.

(ii) the Buyer's total payments made under this Agreement,

(iii) a discount for the acceleration of payment computed according to the 'rule of 78' method.

9. Exclusion

The Sellers do not sell the Goods subject to any express warranty condition or stipulation whether as to correspondence with description, fitness, quality or otherwise and all warranties, conditions or stipulations of any nature whatsoever which might be implied either at Common Law or by Statute are excluded, save that the Buyer is entitled:

(a) in all cases to the Buyer's statutory rights under Section 12 of the Sale of Goods Act 1979 ('the 1979 Act'),

(b) where the transaction recorded by this Agreement is with a consumer and constitutes a consumer transaction as defined in The Consumer Transactions (Restrictions on Statements) Order 1976 (as amended) or the Buyer is dealing as a consumer as defined by the Unfair Contract Terms Act 1977 ('the 1977 Act'), to the Buyer's statutory rights and in particular those referred to in Section 6(2) of the 1977 Act (namely Sections 113, 14 and 15 of the 1979 Act).

It is expressly recorded that where the transaction is of the nature set out in (b) above this Clause does not and will not affect the Buyer's statutory rights referred to in the above Order.

10. Consolidation

(a) I(f at any time there is any other agreement subsisting between the Sellers and the Buyer a termination of this Agreement for any reason whatsoever shall entitle the Sellers in their discretion to terminate without notice such other agreement or agreements. Thereupon the sum payable by the Buyer to the Sellers shall be the aggregate of all the sums which become payable to the Sellers upon such termination under the provisions of this Agreement and the other agreement or agreements so terminated and the Sellers shall be entitled to set off any sum which might otherwise be due to the Buyer against any sum then outstanding by the Buyer to the Sellers.

(b) It is expressly agreed that this Clause constitutes a distinct and severable clause from the remainder of this Agreement.

11. Contents of this Agreement

All the terms and conditions agreed between the Sellers and the Buyer are contained in this Agreement and no person has authority to vary or alter such terms or conditions or to introduce other terms.

12. Two or more Buyers

Where the Buyer is more than one person, their rights hereunder shall be joint and their obligations joint and several and the expression 'the Buyer' shall mean all or any one or more of the Buyers and the giving or serving of any notice or communication upon any one of them shall effectively bind them all.

13. Notices

Any notice demand or communication from the Sellers to the Buyer shall be deemed to have been received by the Buyer 48 horus after posting if it is despatched in the ordinary course of first class post to the Buyer's last known address and at the date of delivery if delivery otherwise than by post to the Buyer's last known address.

14. Commencement of Agreement

This Agreement shall not take effect until it has been signed by or on behalf of the Sellers and any deposit prescribed by law has been paid.

Citibank Savings is the trading style of Citibank Trust Limited which is registered in England No. 853179. Registered office is at 336 Strand London WC2R 1HB. it is ultimately controlled by Citicorp, New York USA.

agreement.[30] Where the equipment has become incorporated into the fabric of the building as a fixture, it becomes part of the freehold (*quicquid plantatur solo, solo cedit*) and while such incorporation would be actionable as a conversion if not expressly or impliedly assented to by the seller, he would have no right to sever the equipment from the premises unless empowered to do so by the conditional sale agreement and would be restricted to a personal claim for damages. Even a contractual right of entry and severance will in certain cases be unavailing if the premises are vested in a third party.

The seller is entitled to trace proceeds of unauthorized dispositions.[31]

(iii) Rights of the seller vis-à-vis third parties

In principle, the seller can assert his title against any third party into whose hands the equipment may pass as the result of an unauthorized disposition by the buyer. There are, however, certain exceptions to the *nemo dat* rule which, if applicable, will lead to the loss of title or the subordination of the seller's rights to a subsequent limited interest.[32] Title may also be lost as the result of incorporation of the equipment into a building as a fixture[33] or into other chattels as an accession.[34]

3. HIRE-PURCHASE

Much of what has been said in relation to conditional sale applies with equal force to hire-purchase. But the distinction between the two forms of agreement is not wholly without significance. The typical hire-purchase agreement[35] allows the hirer to terminate at any time by notice in writing, in which event he is required to return the equipment to the owner in good order and to compensate the owner for the loss resulting from termination. It is at this point that hire-purchase begins to part company from conditional sale. Under a conditional sale agreement, the buyer is committed to payment of the full price; accordingly, any contractual provision for agreed compensation to the seller upon termination of the agreement by reason of the buyer's default can properly be predicated on the assumption that but for the default the seller would have received the full price. So a clause in the conditional sale agreement designed to ensure that the seller receives the full price, after giving credit for the value of the repossessed equipment and allowing a proper discount for accelerated payment, is in principle a reasonable pre-estimate of liquidated damages, and as such is enforceable.[36] By contrast the hirer under a hire-purchase agreement is entitled to put an end to his future rental liability by exercising his contractual right to terminate. So a clause designed to ensure that upon such

---

30 If he enters without authority, he commits an actionable trespass, while if his entry is violent he may be prosecuted under the Criminal Law Act 1977, s 6, replacing the offence of forcible entry under the Forcible Entry Acts 1381–1623.

31 As to proceeds of authorized dispositions, see p 720.

32 See pp 417 ff.

33 Goode, *Hire-Purchase Law*, ch 32.

34 Ibid, ch 33.

35 Figure 27.5.

36 After deducting the proceeds of sale of the repossessed equipment and a discount for acceleration of payment.

termination the owner recovers the full price is likely to be struck down as a penalty,[37] on the ground that it seeks to impose on the defaulting hirer a liability greater than that which he would have incurred if he had not broken the agreement but simply exercised his contractual power of termination. The rule against penalties, as developed by the cases,[38] is not strong on logic[39] but it does indicate a feeling on the part of the courts that a hire-purchase agreement should be taken at face value and should not be treated as merely another form of conditional sale. If the owner wants the advantages of hire-purchase, he must also put up with the disadvantages. The Consumer Credit Act 1974 limits the liability of the debtor under a hire-purchase agreement who exercises his statutory right of termination.[40] There is no corresponding provision relating to termination by the creditor but the writer has submitted elsewhere[41] that a contractual provision seeking to impose a greater liability than would arise on termination by the debtor would be struck down as a penalty, a view which has now been endorsed in a county court decision.[42]

And there is indeed a compensating advantage to hire-purchase. Since it is not a contract of sale, it is unaffected by the provisions of the Sale of Goods Act and of every other statutory provision relating to contracts of sale.[43] It follows that the hirer under a hire-purchase agreement cannot give a good title to a bona fide purchaser under s 9 of the Factors Act 1889 or s 25 of the Sale of Goods Act. But where the agreement relates to a motor vehicle which is disposed of by the hirer to a bona fide private purchaser, the provisions of Part III of the Hire-Purchase Act 1964[44] apply in just the same way as they do on a wrongful disposition by a conditional buyer.

So in relation to business equipment the choice between hire-purchase and conditional sale is marginal. If the financier is not worried about the extra risk of loss of title under s 9 of the Factors Act or s 25 of the Sale of Goods Act and is more concerned to ensure that he can recover a sum equal to the full price on default, he will opt for conditional sale. If the feature that troubles him is the chance of losing title on an unauthorized disposition, he will be minded to choose hire-purchase. Since most business transactions are carried through without a hitch, the distinction between the two forms of agreement is in practice much smaller than the legal differences would suggest.

37 But the consequences of this are less draconian than had at one time been thought, in that the liquidated damages clause is enforceable up to the amount of the actual loss (*Jobson v Johnson* [1989] 1 WLR 1026).
38 See, for example, *Bridge v Campbell Discount Co Ltd* [1962] AC 600; *Anglo-Auto Finance Co Ltd v James* [1963] 3 All ER 566; and generally Goode, *Hire-Purchase Law*, ch 18.
39 But as Oliver Wendell Holmes remarked: 'The life of the law has not been logic; it has been experience' (*The Common Law*, 1881 (reissued 1991), p 1).
40 Consumer Credit Act 1974, s 100, which provides that the debtor's liability is to be limited to the excess of one-half of the total price over the aggregate of the sums paid and the sum due immediately before the termination, together with any installation charge specified in the agreement as part of the total price.
41 *Goode: Consumer Credit Law and Practice,*, para [45.56].
42 *Rover Finance Ltd v Peter Siddons* (2002) 9 July, Leicester County Court (District Judge Eaton).
43 However, while the provisions of the Sale of Goods Act – as amended by the Sale and Supply of Goods Act 1994 and the Sale and Supply of Goods to Consumers Regulations 2002 (SI 2002/3045) – as to implied terms in favour of the buyer do not apply to hire-purchase agreements, comparable provisions are contained in the Supply of Goods (Implied Terms) Act 1973 as so amended.
44 See p 438.

(VR)
OSG
10/01

For agreements outside the scope of the Consumer Credit Act and for business use only.

Agreement No. _____

Original – White
Copy – Pink

This Hire Purchase Agreement is made between _____ (Owners' name)

Address _____

_____ VAT Reg. No. _____

Telephone No. _____ Co. Reg. No. _____

Fax No. _____

('the Owners' which expression includes their successors and assigns) and the Hirer whose particulars are set out in the Schedule below whereby the Owners agree to let and the Hirer agrees to hire the goods specified in the Schedule on the hire purchase terms set out in the Schedule and overleaf.

SCHEDULE

1. PARTICULARS OF HIRER

Full Name _____ Title _____
(Mr, Mrs, Miss, Ms, PLC, Ltd, etc.)

Address _____ Date of birth _____

*Fax No. _____ Tel. No. _____ Co. Reg. No. _____

Nature of business _____ Year established _____

Name and address of bankers _____ *E-mail: _____

*This information will be used for marketing purposes only

2. DESCRIPTION OF GOODS

	Net Price		VAT		
	£	p	%	£	p
Serial/Identification/Registration Nos:					
Total					

3. FINANCIAL DETAILS

	£	p
Total Amount Repayable (F) is payable by: a first instalment (including documentation fee) of		
followed by:		
_____ instalments each of		
a final instalment of		

each instalment payable on the same day of each successive *month/quarter commencing on _____
*delete where not applicable

Total VAT-inclusive Cash Price	A	
Less: Cash £		
Part Exch. £	= Deposit	
Balance of Cash Price	B	
Add Hire Purchase Charges¹	C	
Add Documentation Fee	D	
Add Option to Purchase Fee² (payable with final instalment)	E	
Total Amount Repayable	F	
= B + C + D + E		

1. See Section 4 below and Clause 2 overleaf if charges are variable.

2. VAT Exempt within current limit (£10), otherwise show VAT-inclusive amount.

4. HIRE PURCHASE CHARGES – VARIABLE RATE (delete this section if not applicable)

The Hirer hereby opts to pay variable rate charges at _____% above Finance House Base Rate from time to time in accordance with Clause 2 overleaf or _____% per annum whichever is greater.
The assumed constant Finance House Base Rate for the initial calculation of the Hire Purchase Charges shown above is _____%

Signature of Hirer _____

DECLARATION BY HIRER
I/we declare and warrant that
(a) the goods are required for the purpose of a business carried on by me/us, that I/we have carefully examined and selected the goods and in my/our judgement they are satisfactory and suitable for the purpose for which they are required;
(b) my/our attention was drawn to Clause 4 overleaf;
(c) the information contained in Sections 1, 2 and 3 of the Schedule is correct and I/we understand that in considering whether or not to accept this Agreement the Owners will have relied on the truth of that information.

Signature of Hirer _____

Position _____
(Director, Proprietor, Partner, etc.)

Acceptance by Owners

Signature _____ Date _____

NOTE: The Hirer's attention is drawn to Clause 4 overleaf.

IMPORTANT USE OF YOUR INFORMATION

You have a right to know how we will use your personal information. It is important that you read the **"Use of Your Information"** Notice (overleaf) **before** you sign since by signing you are agreeing to this use and disclosure of your information. We may:
• send you useful information about ours and other businesses products and services;
• pass your details to other selected businesses and to anyone who introduced you to us, to send you information about their products and services;
You may at any time stop us doing so. **To stop us, tick this box ☐ or write to us.**
We and other businesses may contact you by telephone or e-mail to offer you other products and services. **To stop us, tick this box ☐ or write to us.**
If you are willing to be contacted by automated calling system or personal fax, tick this box ☐
Information held about you by credit reference agencies may be linked to records relating to any person with whom you are linked financially. Read the **"Use of Associated Records" before** you sign.

Fig 27.5 Hire-purchase agreement outside the Consumer Credit Act 1974

TERMS OF AGREEMENT

1 Payment

The Hirer, having paid the deposit specified in the Schedule on signing this Agreement, shall punctually pay the instalments set out in the Schedule at the times and in the manner specified in the Schedule. Each payment by the Hirer shall be appropriated first in discharge of the Hire Purchase Charges accrued and due and secondly in reduction of the Balance of Cash Price. Payments shall only be made to the Owners or to such persons as the Owners may nominate in writing. Payments sent by post shall be at the Hirer's risk. The Hirer shall pay interest on all instalments in arrears at a rate equal to the annual percentage rate represented by the Hire Purchase Charges or, where the Hirer opts to pay Variable Rate Charges by those charges as adjusted in accordance with Clause 2, such interest to accrue from day to day and to run after as well as before any judgment.

2 Variable Rate Charges

Where the Hirer has opted to pay Variable Rate Charges then, following each twelve month period of this Agreement and upon expiry or termination of this Agreement or exercise of the Hirer's option to purchase, the Owners shall recalculate the Hire Purchase Charges for the preceding period by substituting for the assumed constant Finance House Base Rate stated in the Schedule the level of such rate prevailing from day to day during the period in question. If this results in a sum for Hire Purchase Charges and interest on overdue instalments higher or lower than that specified in the Schedule such increase or reduction shall be paid by the Hirer within seven days of demand or credited to the Hirer, as the case may be.

3 Option to Purchase

Upon payment of the sum specified in the Schedule as the Total Amount Repayable, all other sums payable under this Agreement and the Option to Purchase Fee, ownership of the Goods shall pass to the Hirer. Until such time the Goods shall remain the sole property of the Owners and the Hirer shall be a mere bailee or, in Scotland a hirer, of the Goods.

4 Hirer's Acknowledgement and Indemnity

a) The Hirer acknowledges that:
   i) the Goods are required for the purpose of a business carried on by the Hirer, were selected by the Hirer and acquired by the Owners at the Hirer's request for the purposes of this Agreement;
   ii) the Hirer relied on his own skill and judgement in selecting the Goods;
   iii) acceptance by the Hirer of delivery of the Goods is proof that the Goods are of satisfactory quality, in good working order and condition and conform to the Hirer's requirements;
   iv) the Owners do not accept responsibility for the Goods corresponding with any description or for their quality, condition or suitability for the Hirer's purposes; and
   v) except where expressly authorised by the Owners, no dealer in or supplier of the Goods is or shall be deemed to be the Owner's agent.

b) The Hirer indemnifies the Owners against all claims, damages, loss, costs and expenses (including legal costs on a full indemnity basis) arising out of possession or use of the Goods, except for injury or death caused by the Owner's negligence.

5. Possession and Use

a) The Hirer shall not make or attempt any sale or other disposition of the Goods or part with possession of them otherwise than for the purpose of repair, and shall promptly inform the Owners in writing of any change in the address where the Goods are customarily kept.

b) The Hirer shall observe all the manufacturer's and/or the suppliers instructions regarding the use and operation of Goods.

c) The Hirer shall not permit the Goods to become affixed to any premises and shall keep them free from any mortgage, charge, lien, pledge, hypothec or other encumbrance and free from distress, execution, or in Scotland poinding or arrestment or other legal process.

6 Repair and Inspection

a) The Hirer shall maintain the Goods in good order and condition and shall be liable for all loss of or damage to the Goods however caused (fair wear and tear only excepted). The Hirer shall give immediate notice in writing of any loss or damage to the Owners who may in their absolute discretion require the Hirer to have any necessary repairs effected by repairers approved in writing by them. The Hirer shall not pledge the Owners credit or create or allow to be created a lien upon the Goods or any of them.

b) The Hirer shall ensure that any tests or inspections required by law or by the insurers are duly carried out.

c) The Hirer shall not without the previous written consent of the Owners make any alteration or addition to the Goods, and any addition shall immediately become the property of the Owners.

9 Default

If it should transpire that any part of the information given by the Hirer in the schedule of this Agreement is in any material respect inaccurate or if the Hirer shall:
a) default in the performance of any of the Hirer's obligations under this Agreement;
b) make or propose any composition or scheme of arrangement or trust deed with his creditors or call a meeting of them;
c) permit execution to be levied against, or in Scotland permit execution of a poinding or arrestment of, any of his assets or income;
d) have an interim or bankruptcy or sequestration order made against him or receive a statutory demand under the Insolvency Act 1986, or, in Scotland, the Bankruptcy (Scotland) Act 1985;
e) cease to carry on business or, being a partnership, be dissolved or if proceedings for its dissolution be commenced;
f) suffer a receiver, administrative receiver or administrator to be appointed over its assets or a petition too be presented or pass a resolution for its winding up (otherwise than for the purposes of reorganisation);
g) do or suffer to be done any act or thing which in the opinion of the Owners may prejudice the Owner's rights of ownership of the Goods;
then the Owners shall be entitled;
   i) immediately with or without notice to terminate the hiring under this Agreement by repossessing the Goods and for that purpose to enter any premises where the Goods are believed to be : or to terminate this Agreement by notice in writing, whereupon the Hirer shall no longer be in possession of the Goods with the Owner's consent and shall forthwith return them to the Owners; and
   ii) to recover all sums due under this Agreement at the date of termination of the hiring or this Agreement, as the case may be and damages for all loss sustained by the Owners, including loss of profit resulting from such termination.

10 Automatic Termination

a) This Agreement and the consent of the Owners to the Hirer continuing in possession of the Goods shall terminate automatically and without notice upon any steps being taken by any person for the levying of distress on the Goods. No payment subsequently accepted by the Owners without knowledge of such event shall prejudice or affect the operation of this clause.

b) Upon termination under this clause the Owners shall be entitled to exercise the rights conferred on them by Clause 9.

11 Expenses

The Hirer shall repay on demand the Owner's expenses and all legal costs on a full indemnity basis for;
a) finding the Hirer's address if the Hirer changes address without notifying the Owner in writing within 7 days of a change of address; and/or
b) finding the Goods if it is not at the address notified by the Hirer; and/or
c) takings steps including court action to recover the Goods or to obtain payment for it.
The Hirer shall pay on demand the Owner's reasonable expenses in relation to any letter that the Owners might send to the Hirer and any reasonable expenses incurred by the Owners where the standing order or direct debit payment is not made by its due date, for whatever reason.

12 General Provisions

a) The complete and punctual performance of the obligations of the Hirer under Clauses 1, 2, 5, 6 and 7 of this Agreement including the payment of all sums payable on their due date is of the essence of this Agreement. A breach of any such obligations shall constitute a repudiation of this Agreement.

b) In Scotland any word or phrase not in current use in that country shall be given the nearest equivalent meaning.

c) In this Agreement 'Goods' includes all replacements or renewals and all additions and accessions to them made with the consent of the Owners or by the Insurer.

d) No relaxation or indulgence which the Owners may extend to the Hirer shall prejudice the Owner's strict rights under this Agreement.

e) The expression the Hirer shall include a company or two or more persons constituting the Hirer and the liability of such two or more persons shall be joint and several.

f) The rights conferred on the Hirer under this Agreement shall be personal to the Hirer, who shall not attempt to assign or otherwise deal with any of those rights.

g) Notice to the Hirer may be communicated to the Hirer orally and notices required to be given in writing may be given by delivery, post or facsimile to the Hirer at the Hirer's address stated in this

717

7 Insurance

The Hirer shall keep the Goods insured under a fully comprehensive policy to their full replacement value against all risks and third party liability and shall punctually pay all premiums under the policy and produce receipts for such payments to the Owners on demand. In the event of a claim being made against the insurers the Owners may in their absolute discretion conduct any negotiations and effect any settlement with the insurers and the Hirer agrees to abide by such settlement. The Hirer shall hold on trust for the Owners all monies payable under the policy and hereby irrevocably authorise the Owners to receive such monies which:

a) where the Goods are lost or stolen or damaged beyond repair shall be applied in payments to the Owners of any sums previously accrued due to them and of any sum necessary to make up the unpaid balance of the Total Amount Repayable less any rebate in respect of accelerated payment as the Owners in their discretion may allow, any surplus being payable forthwith by the Hirer.

b) In any other case shall be retained by the Owners until the Goods have been repaired to their satisfaction and then shall be released to the repairer or (if the cost of the repairs has been paid by the Hirer) to the Hirer.

Payment of the surplus or deficiency under sub-clause (a) above shall bring this Agreement and the liability of the parties hereunder to an end. Until then, the loss or destruction of or damage to the Goods (for which the Hirer shall remain fully liable) shall not affect the continuance of this Agreement and the Hirer's liability for any sums payable under this Agreement.

8 Hirer's Right to Terminate

The Hirer may terminate this Agreement by giving notice to the Owners and returning the Goods together with, in the case of a vehicle, the registration document, licence and, if applicable, test certificate. The Hirer shall then be liable to pay to the Owners the unpaid balance of the Total Amount Payable adjusted where the Hirer has opted to pay Variable Rate Charges for any net shortfall or overpayment calculated under Clause 2 of this Agreement, less the aggregate of (a) the net proceeds of sale of the Goods after deduction of expenses or charges incurred by the Owners in respect of repair or storage or which may be due under Clause 11, (b) the sum stated in the schedule as the Option to Purchase Fee and (c) such rebate for accelerated payment as the Owners in their discretion may allow.

Agreement or the Hirer's private or last known address and to the Owners at the Owner's address stated in this Agreement or other address notified by the Owners to the Hirer. Notices sent by first class post shall be deemed to have been received within forty-eight hours of posting.

h) If this Agreement (or the hiring hereunder) is terminated by the Owners or terminated automatically then the Owners may by 24 hours written notice to the Hirer, terminate any other Agreement between the Owners and the Hirer. Similarly, if any other Agreement (or the hiring thereunder) is terminated by the Owners or terminated automatically, then the Owners may terminate this Agreement. The Owners may then exercise their rights under this Agreement (or any other Agreement referred to in this Clause) as if they had terminated the same by reason of a repudiatory breach thereof. This clause will not apply to any regulated agreement.

i) Words and expressions to which meanings have been assigned in the Schedule overleaf shall those meanings in these terms. Words in the masculine gender shall include the feminine and neuter genders. Headings are for convenience only and shall not affect the interpretation of any provision.

j) No variation of this Agreement shall be valid unless it is in writing and signed by the Owners.

k) This Agreement, and the documents referred to in it, constitutes the entire Agreement and understanding of the parties and supersedes any previous Agreement between the parties relating to the subject matter of this Agreement.

l) If any provision of this Agreement shall be found to be invalid, illegal or unenforceable, such invalidity, illegality or unenforceability shall not affect the remaining provisions which shall remain in full force and effect.

13 Commencement of Agreement

This Agreement shall only come into force if and when it is signed by or on behalf of the Owners and on the date when it is so signed.

14 Exclusion of Third Party Rights

Nothing in this Agreement shall be construed as creating a right which is enforceable by any person who is not a party or a permitted assignee or transferee of such a party to this Agreement .

USE OF YOUR INFORMATION

In considering whether to enter into this Agreement we will search your record at credit reference agencies. They will add, to their record about you, details of our search and your application and this will be seen by other organisations that make searches. This and other information about you and those with whom you are linked financially may be used to make credit decisions about you and other members of your household.

We may use a credit scoring or other automated decision making system.

We will also add to your record with the credit reference agencies details of your Agreement with us, any payments you make under it and any default or failure to keep to its terms. These records will be shared with other organisations and may be used and searched by us and them to:

• consider applications for credit and credit related services, such as insurance, for you and any associated person;

• trace debtors, recover debts, prevent or detect money laundering and fraud, and to manage your account(s).

It is important that you provide us with accurate information. We may check your details with fraud prevention agencies and if you provide false or inaccurate information or we suspect fraud, this information may be recorded.

Fraud prevention agency records will be shared with other organisations to help make decisions on credit, motor, household, life and other insurance proposals or claims, for you and members of your household. We will use personal information about you which we acquire in connection with any application you make to us, or any agreement you enter into with us, to manage your agreement and for statistical or market research purposes.

Please telephone or write to us at the telephone number / address stated overleaf if you want to have details of the credit reference agencies or any other agencies from whom we obtain, and to whom we pass, information about you. You have a legal right to these details. You have a right to receive a copy of the information we hold about you. A fee may be payable.

USE OF ASSOCIATED RECORDS

We may before entering into this Agreement search records at credit reference agencies which may be linked to your spouse/partner or other persons with whom you are linked financially and other members of your household. For the purposes of any application or this agreement you may be treated as financially linked and you will be assessed with reference to "associated" records.

Where any search or application is completed or agreement entered into involving joint parties, you both consent to us recording details, at credit reference agencies. As a result an "association" will be created which will link your financial records and your associate's information may be taken into account when a future search is made by us or another lender unless you file a "disassociation" at the credit reference agency.

718

(VR)
OSG
10/01

SUPPLIER'S OFFER AND WARRANTY

To _____
Name of Finance Company

We offer to sell to you the Goods at the price as shown alongside and in respect of such offer we hereby DECLARE and WARRANT as follows:

1 That the deposit as shown has been received by us in cash or by way of a proper and lawful allowance in part-exchange.

2 That the Agreement was correctly completed in respect of all details before it was signed by the Hirer named in the Agreement and that we have complied with the provisions of all Statutes and Statutory instruments affecting this transaction.

3 That we are not aware of any matter not fully disclosed herein which might affect your judgement in respect of this transaction.

4 That the goods are our absolute property free from any lien or encumbrance and has not been the subject of any previous transaction with the Hirer.

5 That the goods conform in all respects to any representations, warranties, descriptions, conditions or stipulations which may have been made by our servants or agents to you or to the Hirer or which may be implied, and that, where applicable they comply with the provisions of the Road Traffic Acts

6 That the goods have been insured by the Hirer to their full value as shown below.

7 That any indemnity in respect of this agreement has been signed by the person whose name and address appears in it.
AND we agree that on your accepting this transaction the property in the goods shall immediately pass to you and we will be responsible for the delivery of the goods to the Hirer.

Details of Goods – New/Used	Price	
	£	p
Serial/Identification/Registration Nos.		
Pre-VAT price		
VAT at _____ %		
Total Price		
Deposit received from Hirer		
Balance due		

Name of Supplier _____   Date _____

Address _____   VAT Registration No. _____

_____   Signature of Supplier _____

INSURANCE OF THE GOODS (Hirer to complete)

Name of Insurance Company _____ Type of Policy _____

Address of Branch _____

Name and address of Agent _____

Date of Policy or Cover Note _____ Policy or Cover Note No. _____

BANKER'S ORDER FORM

I/We authorise you to debit my/our account with you by Standing Order the undermentioned payments for the credit of:

_____ at _____ Bank Plc
(Name of Owners)

Account No. [ ][ ][ ][ ][ ][ ][ ]   Branch: Title _____ Sort Code No. ___ – ___ – ___
(not Address)

	No. of Payments	Frequency	Amount		Commencing Date
			£		
Followed by		Monthly/Quarterly*	£		
Followed by			£		

* Delete as necessar

To _____ Bank Plc

Bank Account No. _____

Name(s) _____
(Block Capitals)

Address _____

_____

Postcode _____ Date _____

Signature(s) _____

When paying please quote Agreement No.

Hire-purchase agreements come in a variety of forms and with different labels. Lease purchase is hire-purchase, frequently with a facility to pay reduced rentals and a balloon payment of the end of the lease period if the lessee elects to buy the goods. Somewhat similar is personal contract purchase: a lease of a motor vehicle, such as a company car, for a set period with a reduced down payment and rentals, and a balloon payment at the end of the lease, the lessee having the option to buy the vehicle, to refinance it, to part-exchange it or simply to return it. The various forms of hire-purchase are differentiated by the different ways in which they are structured, but in law they are all hire-purchase agreements and are subject to the same legal rules.

4. RELATIONS BETWEEN FINANCE HOUSE AND DEALER

(i) Direct collection

It will be recalled that in a direct collection transaction D sells the equipment to F. The sale contract is governed by the normal statutory provisions and common law rules relating to contracts of sale, but is usually buttressed by express warranties on the part of D, eg as to the quality and condition of the equipment and its conformity with the requirements of the hire-purchase or conditional sale agreement. Breach of any terms of the agreement entitles F to pursue the usual remedies of a buyer whose seller commits a breach of contract.[45] D is sometimes required to give recourse, by guaranteeing B's performance or by undertaking to repurchase the equipment if B defaults. F's rights under the guarantee are governed by the general principles of the common law relating to guarantees[46] except so far as the parties otherwise agree in their contract.

Prima facie D is not the agent of F or of B but conducts on his own account the negotiations leading up to the conditional sale or hire-purchase agreement.[47] So except where otherwise agreed or provided by statute,[48] F is not liable for misrepresentations by D in relation to the equipment;[49] nor is D considered to have actual or ostensible authority to accept on F's behalf notice of termination of a hire-purchase agreement.[50] Equally, D is not the agent of F to receive the pre-contract down payment; but if B's offer to take the equipment on conditional sale or hire-purchase is accepted and F agrees to buy the equipment from D, F is treated as having received the down payment in a balance of account with D and can, therefore, be required to return it in a restitutionary claim if the agreement is rescinded or otherwise becomes ineffective.[51]

(ii) Block discounting

If D, when discounting the hire-purchase or conditional sale agreements, transfers to F title to the underlying equipment, the transaction is to that extent a sale and as regards the equipment the normal Sale of Goods Act rules apply. The assignment of

---

45 See ch 14.
46 See ch 30.
47 *Branwhite v Worcester Works Finance Ltd* [1969] 1 AC 552. The same is true of leasing agreements. See *J. D. Williams & Co v McAuley, Parsons & Jones* [1999] GCCR 1375, [1994] CCLR 78; *Woodchester Equipment (Leasing) Ltd v British Association of Canned and Preserved Fruit Importers and Distributors* [1999] GCCR 1923.
48 Eg, Consumer Credit Act 1974, s 56.
49 See Goode, *Hire-Purchase Law*, p 289.
50 Ibid, p 293.
51 *Branwhite v Worcester Works Finance Ltd*, n 47.

the contract rights does, it is thought, imply a condition that D has not disposed of or encumbered them. Beyond this it is doubtful whether the law implies any conditions or warranties in relation to the contract rights, eg that the discounted agreements are valid and enforceable. In practice, express warranties are almost invariably set out in the block discounting agreement, and the circumstances may be such as to imply warranties *in fact*. If F chooses not to exact warranties and none are implied in fact, F presumably has no legal ground for complaint if a particular debt assigned proves irrecoverable, eg because of non-compliance with legal requirements.[52] This is subject to the qualification that if all the agreements were wholly invalid, F would presumably have a right to recover the price as paid on a total failure of consideration.

5.   RELATIONS BETWEEN DEALER AND BUYER OR HIRER IN DIRECT COLLECTION TRANSACTIONS

In direct collection business there is in principle no privity of contract between D and B: B is not a party to the contract of sale between D and F, while D is equally a stranger to the contract between F and B. If the equipment is defective, it is to F as seller or owner that B must turn. However, if B was induced to enter into the agreement with F by a false statement of fact on the part of D which was intended to be promissory in character, this will constitute a collateral warranty by D the consideration for which is B's entry into the agreement with F. In this event B can recover damages against D for breach of the collateral contract.[53] But B must be able to show that D's statement was intended to have contractual force, otherwise his claim will fail.[54]

6.   TRACING PROCEEDS OF AUTHORIZED RESALES

The owner's equitable right to trace proceeds of an *unauthorized* disposition of his asset[55] was carried a stage further in the *Romalpa* case,[56] in which the Court of Appeal, affirming the decision of the trial judge, held that where, under a contract of sale, the seller reserved title until payment but authorized the buyer to resell the goods meanwhile, and the language of the contract indicated that he was to be accountable to the seller for the proceeds of resale, such proceeds vested in the seller in equity when they came into existence and did not form part of the buyer's assets. The relationship between seller and buyer as regards the proceeds was that of principal and fiduciary agent, not of creditor and debtor, in the case in question.

The decision is not free from difficulty, and in subsequent cases the courts have shown a marked inclination to confine *Romalpa* within close limits.[57]

---

52 This would be most likely to occur in relation to agreements within the Consumer Credit Act 1974.

53 *Andrews v Hopkinson* [1957] 1 QB 229; *Brown v Sheen & Richmond Car Sales Ltd* [1950] 1 All ER 1102.

54 *United Dominions Trust (Commercial) Ltd v Pidgeon* (14 November 1963, unreported), 14 No, CA (Bar Library transcript No 289).

55 See p 52.

56 *Aluminium Industrie Vaassen B V v Romalpa Aluminium Ltd* [1976] 1 Lloyd's Rep 443. For the facts of this case, see R. M. Goode, 'The Right to Trace in Commercial Transactions' (1976) 92 LQR 528 at p 548. For other analyses, see the literature cited, p 52, n 176.

57 See p 608.

28 The Finance Lease

In the eyes of English law a lease of goods is a hire contract, by whatever name it is called. Its essential characteristic is that goods are bailed by one party, A, to another party, B, for B's use[1] or enjoyment in exchange for payment of rent. It is distinguished from hire-purchase and conditional sale in that B has neither the option nor the obligation to purchase the goods but is required to return them to A, or deal with them as A directs, when the bailment comes to an end.

The leasing industry has become increasingly sophisticated over the years, and various forms of lease or hire have evolved, each designed to cater for a particular need.[2] Leasing periods may range from fifteen years at one end to one day (car hire) at the other, and may encompass equipment ranging from 'big ticket' items such as oil tankers and aircraft to relatively small items of business equipment such as typewriters and photocopiers. A considerable proportion of business is extended to the public sector, including local authorities and nationalized industries.

I.   THE NATURE OF THE FINANCE LEASE

Lessors have coined a variety of labels to describe different leasing schemes. These have no *legal* significance, but are used to market particular leasing products,[3] and reflect functional distinctions between one type of lease and another. While there is no universally agreed labelling system, one classification is fundamental, namely that which divides the *operating lease* from the *finance lease*. An operating lease is typically one under which equipment is let out on lease to a series of different lessees in sequence, each taking the equipment for the period for which he needs it and paying a rent reflecting its use-value. By contrast, a finance lease is, as its name implies, essentially a financial tool, in which the lessor's retention of ownership is little more than nominal. The characteristics of the finance lease are that the minimum period of the lease[4] approximates to the estimated working life of the equipment, so that there is only one lessee, responsibility for maintaining the equipment rests on the lessee and the rentals are calculated not on the use-value of

---

1 Including derivation of income through sub-hire.
2 See generally *Tolley's Leasing in the UK* (4th edn, 2002).
3 'Product' here refers to the leasing agreement, or package, offered to potential lessees.
4 This is the period (usually termed the 'primary period') over which the lessor expects to recoup his capital outlay and most of his desired return on capital. The lessee is usually, though not invariably, able to extend the lease for a secondary period at a rate substantially below the then use-value of the equipment.

the equipment but on the basis of producing for the lessor a total amount which, taking account of the rental cash flows and capital allowances to which he is entitled, will recoup his capital expenditure in acquiring the equipment and give him the desired return on capital. That is to say, the rentals are so structured as to amortize the capital cost over the period, or primary period,[5] of the lease and give the lessor his required addition for profit, so that, if one ignores the influence of taxation, the end result is that the lessor receives and the lessee pays a total sum not dissimilar to that which would be received and paid under a conditional sale agreement providing for payment by instalments. The assumption is that at the end of the lease the equipment will have a relatively small residual value,[6] and the usual practice is for the lessor to return the greater part of this to the lessee by paying him, or crediting to him against a future transaction, most of the proceeds arising from sale of the equipment by the lessor (or by the lessee as his agent) upon termination of the lease. The lessee must not be given the ability to acquire the equipment himself, for this would convert the transaction into a hire-purchase agreement.

A finance lease has been defined for accounting purposes as one that transfers substantially all the risks and rewards of ownership of an asset to the Lessee.[7]

2.   REASONS FOR USE

The huge growth in finance leasing illustrates how little importance is attached by the businessman to the legal concept of ownership. To him what matters is the substance, not the form. For practical purposes the lessee *is* the owner. But if he is to be committed to payment of the full capital cost of the equipment, why does he not choose to take title and purchase the equipment under a conditional sale agreement? There are many reasons, some more cogent than others. The lessee's tax position in general, and the likely flow of his income and profits in particular,

---

5   See n 4.

6   In the late 1970s this assumption was confounded by high rates of inflation, in consequence of which residual values rose sharply and in some cases resulted in the lessee receiving a 'rebate' in excess of the total rentals he had paid!

7   Statements of Standard Accounting Practice, SSAP 21 (1984), *Accounting for Leases and Hire Purchase Contracts*, paras 15, 16. SSAP 21 is issued by the Accounting Standards Committee of the Institute of Chartered Accountants in England and Wales and is to be interpreted in such a way as to reflect the substance of the transaction in accordance with Financial Reporting Standard 5, *Reporting the substance of transactions*, issued by the Accounting Standards Board, and the Finance & Leasing Association's Statement of Recommended Account Practice (SORP) *Accounting issues in the finance and leasing industry*. For listed companies for accounting periods beginning on or after 1 January 2005 compliance with International Accounting Standards (IAS) and International Financial Reporting Standards (IFRS) (and applicable interpretations) issued by the International Accounting Standards Board is *mandatory*. Non-listed companies can adopt IAS and IFRS if they wish. The definition of finance lease in IAS 17 is similar to that in SSAP 21: 'a finance lease is a lease that transfers substantially all the risks and rewards incident to ownership of an asset. Title may or may not eventually be transferred.' Again, the classification depends on the substance of the transaction rather than the form. The Capital Allowances Act 2001, s 219, defines a finance lease in terms which defer to normal accounting practice. In regard to the adoption of IASs and IFRS, the Inland Revenue have announced that legislation will ensure that accounts prepared in accordance with IAS/IFRS or UK generally accepted accounting practice will equally be an acceptable starting point for computing taxable profits.

may make it more advantageous for him to leave the capital allowances[8] to be claimed by the lessor and secure in exchange a reduction in rentals,[9] these being deductible in computing his profits assessable to tax. A second reason advanced for selecting finance leasing is that the lessor provides 100% of the finance required, whereas on hire-purchase or conditional sale the hirer or buyer is expected to make a down payment. This is one of the less compelling arguments. There are many finance leases which do require a down payment; conversely, there is no reason why hire-purchase business should not be underwritten on the basis of a 100% advance by the finance house. Another attraction of leasing at one time was that it was a form of off-balance-sheet financing[10] and enabled the lessee to present accounts showing a greater degree of liquidity than for conditional sale, when the future instalments would have to be capitalized as a liability in the balance sheet. But future rentals under finance leases are now required to be capitalized in the balance sheet for accounting purposes.[11] There are various other factors to which the popularity of leasing is ascribed; but one of the most important, ranking with taxation, is that it is seen as a flexible financing tool that can be tailored to the lessee's particular cash-flow requirements.

3.   SETTING UP THE TRANSACTION

The initiative for a leasing transaction comes from the lessee. It is he who selects the equipment and the supplier, and the finance house is often not brought into the picture until a very late stage – sometimes, indeed, after the customer has gone so far as to place an order with the supplier.[12] These features are often put forward as being peculiar to leasing, but of course they are not. Even a domestic hire-purchase agreement relating to, say, a dishwasher or a motor car involves initial selection of the goods and of the supplier by the intending hirer. The particular characteristic of business leasing in general and finance leasing in particular is the level of the prospective lessee's involvement and expertise. In many cases the lessee has a very precise picture of its requirements and, indeed, may negotiate detailed specifications with the supplier to meet the particular needs of its business. The finance house is very much the pig in the middle. It will never see the equipment, its knowledge of the technical aspects of the equipment is likely to be no more than the general

8   Ie, annual writing-down allowances in respect of so much of the capital cost as has not been the subject of the first-year allowance. See *Simon's Direct Tax Service* (1995), Pt B2. The old first-year allowance has largely been abolished. As to fixtures, see p 197, n 55.

9   For the tax treatment of finance lease rental payments, see the Inland Revenue Statements of Practice, SP3/91. The mere fact that leasing arrangements are made for the purpose of securing a tax advantage to the lessor in the form of capital allowances is not a ground of objection to them (*Barclays Mercantile Business Finance Ltd v Mawson* [2003] STC 66) although the Inland Revenue have appealed to the House of Lords. The hearing is expected in October 2004.

10   See p 695. The significance of this should not be overrated. Most bankers and financiers of any sophistication would readily have picked up a leasing commitment from a perusal of the lessee's accounts.

11   SSAP 21 (under IAS 17 the lessee recognizes at the inception of the lease a liability equal to the fair value of the leased property or, if lower, the present value of the minimum lease payments).

12   A complication which necessitates either a rescission of the sale contract or at least a variation of it to provide for the transfer of title to the lessor instead of the lessee and for payment by the lessor.

understanding which a good financier seeks to acquire of the nature and working of its client's business, and it has perforce to rely on its client's expertise and on the skill and integrity of the supplier. As we shall see, these factors are none too well accommodated by the law.

The straightforward method of setting up a leasing transaction is for the intending lessee, having found the equipment it wants, to request the finance house to purchase it from the supplier and let it to him on lease. The lessee will usually sign the lease at that time. The finance house places the order with the supplier and is in turn invoiced by the supplier, who later delivers the equipment direct to the lessee. Upon receipt of a certificate by the lessee that the equipment has been delivered in satisfactory condition, the finance house pays the price to the supplier, and signs the leasing contract, notifying its acceptance to the lessee, whereupon the leasing agreement becomes operative.

Where the lessee expects to use the finance house for a regular series of transactions, the two may enter into a master agreement (fig 28.1) setting out the standard terms by which specific leasing transactions subsequently entered into are to be governed. Like the block discounting agreement, the master agreement is facultative. There is no obligation on either party to enter into future leasing transactions. Despite signature by both parties, the master agreement does not as a rule have the status of a binding contract at the time that it is made. It is merely a set of terms subsequently incorporated into specific transactions, sometimes by signature of leasing schedules identifying the equipment to be purchased, the price and the rentals.

Some lessees (eg local authorities) do not want it brought to the notice of their suppliers that they are utilizing a leasing facility. They can be accommodated in various ways. For example, the lessor may authorize the lessee to purchase the equipment in its own name as apparent principal but in reality as agent for the lessor, who will reimburse the price paid by the lessee to the supplier.[13] Alternatively, it may be agreed that the intending lessee shall buy the equipment on its own account in the first instance and then sell it to the lessor and take it back on lease.[14] Sale and lease-back is not uncommon, though there are certain tax pitfalls which have to be avoided.[15]

The lessor will not necessarily want to use its own money to purchase the equipment. It may conclude an agreement with a bank or another funder[16] to advance the whole or part of the price by way of loan, repayable with interest either on an unsecured basis or secured on the rental income.[17] Leasing of this kind is known as leveraged leasing, because the capital put up by the lender gives leverage to the lessor's purchasing power and thus increases the volume of business it can undertake, so long as it can ensure that the interest on the loan is less than the net

13   See p 733.
14   See p 733.
15   See, for example, Capital Allowances Act 2001, ss 221–226.
16   Or, in the case of 'big ticket' lessees (eg aircraft, oil tankers), a syndicate.
17   See p 736.

LA1 09/03

LEASING AGREEMENT
for EQUIPMENT INCLUDING MOTOR VEHICLES

These Documents must not be used for transactions governed by the Consumer Credit Act 1974.
Includes provision for an administration fee.

The document is constructed as a basic leasing agreement. The user should read carefully through the agreement and in particular the "Terms of Agreement" on the reverse to be satisfied that it is suitable for the individual circumstances and addresses all of the requirements of the user.

Fig 28.1 Leasing agreement outside the Consumer Credit Act 1974

LA1 SUPPLIER'S OFFER AND WARRANTY

To _____
Name of Lessor

Details of Equipment	Equipment Price	
	£	p
For a motor vehicle give Make, Type, Registration No. and date first registered		
Pre-VAT price		
VAT at _____ %		
Total Price		
Advance Rental received from Lessee		

We offer to sell to you the equipment described alongside at the total price as shown and in respect of such offer we hereby DECLARE and WARRANT that:

1 The Advance Rental shown has been received by us in cash or by way of a proper and lawful allowance in part-exchange.

2 The Agreement was correctly completed in respect of all details before it was signed by the Lessee named in it and that we have complied with the provisions of all Statutes and Statutory instruments affecting this transaction.

3 We are not aware of any matter not fully disclosed herein which might affect your judgement in respect of this transaction.

4 The equipment is our absolute property free from any lien or encumbrance and has not been the subject of any previous transaction with the Lessee.

5 The equipment conforms in all respects to any representations, warranties, descriptions, conditions or stipulations which may have been made by us or our servants or agents to you or to the Lessee or which may be implied except as may be properly excluded in the Terms of the Agreement.

6 Where the equipment comprises a motor vehicle, that vehicle is in a road-worthy condition and complies with all relevant statutory provisions.

7. The equipment has been insured by the Lessee as shown in the Agreement.

AND we agree that on your accepting this transaction the property in the equipment shall immediately pass to you and we will be responsible for the delivery of the equipment to the Lessee.

Name of Supplier _____

Address _____

_____

Name of Lessee _____

Date _____

VAT Registration No. _____

Signature of Supplier _____

BANKER'S ORDER FORM

I/We authorise you to debit my/our account with you by Standing Order the undermentioned payments for the credit of:

_____ at _____ Bank Plc
(Name of Lessor)

Account No. ☐☐☐☐☐☐☐☐

Branch Title _____
(not Address)

Sorting Code ____ – ____ – ____

	No. of Payments	Frequency	Amount		Commencing Date
		Monthly/Quarterly/Annual	£		
Followed by		Monthly/Quarterly/Annual	£		
Followed by		Monthly/Quarterly/Annual	£		

To _____ Bank Plc

_____

_____

_____

Signature(s) _____

Bank Account No. _____

Name(s) _____
(Block Capitals)

Address _____

_____

Postcode _____ Date _____

When paying will Bank please quote Agreement No.

To (Lessor's Name) _____

CERTIFICATE OF ACCEPTANCE

Agreement No. _____

To be signed by the Lessee only upon the delivery of the equipment

The Lessee hereby acknowledges having taken delivery in good order and condition of the equipment set out in detail in the above numbered Lease and that it is in conformity with the Lessee's specification and requirements. The Lessor is hereby authorised to pay the supplier.

The leased equipment is located at _____

_____

Name of Lessee _____

Signature of (or on behalf of) Lessee _____

Date _____

Original – White
Copy – Pink

LA1 LEASING AGREEMENT
For use outside the scope of the Consumer Credit Act.

Agreement No. _____

The Lessor _____ VAT Reg. No. _____
Name and Address
_____

Telephone No. _____ Fax. No. _____ Co. Reg. No. _____

The Lessee _____ Co. Reg. No. _____
Full name in block letters
Address _____ VAT Reg. No. _____

_____ Tel. No. _____

*E-mail _____ *Fax No. _____
* This information will be used for marketing purposes

Nature of Business _____ Year Established _____

Name and address of bankers _____

Details of Operator's Licence (if any) held under the Goods Vehicles (Licensing of Operators) Regulations 1995

Licence Number _____ Date of Issue _____

Name of Licensee _____

Particulars of Equipment

Description _____

Maker's Name _____ Model _____ Year _____ NEW/USED

Registration No. _____ VIN or Serial No. _____

Accessories _____

Period of Lease

(1) _____ months ('the Primary Period') commencing _____

*(2) and thereafter until ended by either party by not less than three months' notice in writing given to expire not earlier than the end of the Primary Period.
*Delete if no secondary period is envisaged

Rentals	Net £	p	VAT at £	% p	Total £	p
Advance Rental Rent for the first/last* _____ months/quarters* of the primary period						
Primary Period Rentals A first primary rental, including £ _____ + VAT* as an administration fee payable on _____						
For each of the remaining _____ successive months/quarters* of the primary period						
Final Primary Rental (if different) Final primary rental payable on* _____						
Secondary rentals After completion of the Primary Period monthly/quarterly/annual* rentals commencing _____						

Residual Value
£ _____ + VAT
(Complete only when applicable – see Clause 6(c)(ii))

Subsequent rentals are payable on the same day of the month/quarter or year as the first of the series.
*Delete as appropriate

DETAILS OF INSURANCE OF EQUIPMENT: fully comprehensive cover required

Insurance Co. _____ Name and address of Agent _____

Address of Branch _____

_____ Type of Policy _____

Date of Policy or Cover Note _____ Policy or Cover Note No. _____

LESSEE'S REQUEST TO ENTER INTO LEASING AGREEMENT FOR BUSINESS USE
I/We, the Lessee named above request you, the Lessor named above, to purchase the Equipment described above for business use by me/us.
I/We offer to take on lease the Equipment and agree to be bound by the terms set out in this agreement above and overleaf.
If before conclusion of the agreement but after purchase of the Equipment by the Lessor I/we withdraw this offer I/we will indemnify the Lessor against all claims, losses, costs and expenses incurred by the Lessor by entering into a commitment to purchase the Equipment from the supplier of the Equipment in anticipation of conclusion of the agreement.

IMPORTANT – USE OF YOUR INFORMATION

You have a right to know how we will use your personal information. It is important that you read the **"Use of Your Information"** Notice (overleaf) **before** you sign, since by signing you are agreeing to this use and disclosure of your information. We may:
• send you useful information about our products and services and those of other businesses;
• pass your details to other selected businesses and to anyone who introduced you to us, to send you information about their products and services;

To stop us doing this write to us or tick this box ☐

To stop us or other businesses contacting you by telephone to offer you other products or services write to us or tick this box ☐

If you are willing to be contacted by e-mail, automated calling system or personal fax, tick this box ☐
Information held about you by Credit Reference Agencies may be linked to records relating to any person with whom you are linked financially. Read the **"Use of Associated Records"** overleaf **before** you sign.

Signed on behalf of Lessee _____

Position _____
(Director, Proprietor, Partner, etc.)

NOTE: The Lessee's particular attention is drawn to Clauses 8 and 12(b) overleaf.

Acceptance by Lessor.

Signature _____

Date _____

LA1

TERMS OF AGREEMENT

1. Period of Lease
This agreement shall commence if and when signed by both the Lessor and the Lessee and, (subject to Clauses 5 and 6), shall continue for the Period of Lease specified overleaf

2. Payment
a) Upon the Lessor's acceptance of this Agreement the Lessee shall forthwith pay to the Lessor the advance rental specified overleaf (if he has not already done so).
b) The Lessee shall pay all rentals set out overleaf, by their specified dates to the Lessor at the address stated overleaf or to any person or address notified by the Lessor in writing.
c) The Lessee shall punctually pay all rent, rates, taxes, licence duties, fees and other sums payable in respect of the use of the Equipment and in respect of any land or premises where the Equipment is for the time being situated, and shall produce receipts for such payments to the Lessor on demand.
d) Any payment sent by post to the Lessor shall be at the Lessee's risk.
e) The Lessor has the right to charge interest at the rate of 5% over the Finance House Base Rate from time to time on all overdue amounts. This interest will accrue on a daily basis from the date the amount falls due until it is received and will run both before and after any judgment or decree.

3 Care of the Equipment
The Lessee:
a) shall keep the Equipment safe at the address stated overleaf or at that stated in the Certificate of Acceptance if different and may not move it elsewhere without the Lessor's prior written consent.
b) is responsible for all loss or damage to the Equipment (except fair wear and tear) even if caused by acts or events outside his control.
c) shall:
(i) keep the Equipment properly protected and in good working order;
(ii) not allow a repairer or any other person to obtain a lien on or right to retain the Equipment;
(iii) comply strictly with all legal requirements relating to the Equipment and the written instructions of the manufacturer or other supplier and ensure that the Equipment is maintained and operated in a manner which is safe and without risk to health;
(iv) permit the Lessor or its authorised representative at all reasonable times to inspect and test the Equipment, to affix nameplates to it and to enter upon any land or premises for this purpose.
d) shall not:
(i) sell or attempt to sell or dispose of the Equipment or part with possession of it, except for the purpose of repair;
(ii) make any material alteration or addition to the Equipment or permit it to become affixed to any land or building.

4 Insurance
a) The Lessee shall keep the Equipment continuously insured under a fully comprehensive policy of insurance, free from restriction or excess, covering the Equipment to its full replacement value against fire, theft accidental damage and other risks against which it is commercially prudent to insure or against which the Lessor shall require the Lessee to insure, and shall punctually pay all premiums and produce premium receipts to the Lessor on demand.
b) The Lessee shall hold on trust for the Lessor all money ("the insurance moneys") payable under the policy and irrevocably authorises the Lessor to receive such money from the insurance company and to agree the amount of any claim with the insurance company or any other person and receive payment from them.
c) Where the Equipment is lost or destroyed, or the Lessor notifies the Lessee in writing that in its opinion it is incapable of economic repair, the insurance moneys shall be applied in payment to the Lessor of any sums previously accrued due to the Lessor (whether for debt or damages) and of a sum equal to what would have been payable under Clause 6(c) if this Agreement had been terminated following the happening of an event referred to in Clause 5. Any deficiency shall forthwith be payable by the Lessee and any surplus by the Lessor. Upon payment of the insurance moneys (and any deficiency) this Agreement shall come to an end.
d) In every other case of damage this Agreement shall continue and the insurance moneys shall be retained by the Lessor until the Equipment has been repaired to the Lessor's satisfaction, when they shall be released to the repairer or (if the cost of repairs has been paid by the Lessee) to the Lessee.
e) The Lessee shall effect and maintain a policy or policies of insurance to cover any claim, action or demand for injury, death or damage caused by the Equipment, its condition or use (except for any injury or death caused by the Lessor's negligence) and such policy shall have a limit of liability no lower than is reasonable having regard to the nature of the Equipment and its intended and actual use or such other sum as the Lessor shall require. The Lessee shall punctually pay all premiums under the policy or policies and shall produce receipts for such payments to the Lessor on demand.

5 Default
The Lessor shall have the rights stated in Clause 6 if:-
a) the Lessee commits any breach of the clauses referred to in Clause 12(b); or
b) a meeting is called of the Leesee's creditors or any scheme or arrangement, composition or trust deed is made or proposed with or for the benefit of his creditors; or
c) a petition is presented for the making of an administration, winding-up, bankruptcy or sequestration order in respect of the Lessee or a resolution is passed for the presentation of any such petition; or
d) a receiver, administrator or administrative receiver is appointed over, or takes possession of all or any part of the assets of the Lessee; or
e) the Lessee is deemed unable to pay his debts or becomes apparently insolvent within the meaning of the Insolvency Act 1986 or the Bankruptcy (Scotland) Act 1985 respectively; or
f) the Lessee ceases to carry on business or, being a pertnership, is dissolved or proceedings for the Lessee's dissolution are commenced; or
g) execution or, in Scotland, any attachment is levied or attempted, or an auction is held of any of the assets or income of the Lessee; or
h) the landlord of the premises where the Equipment is kept threatens or takes any step to distrain on or, in Scotland, exercise any right of hypothec over the Equipment or any other goods of the Lessee.

6 Default Remedies
Upon the occurrence of any of the events described in Clause 5 the Lessor shall be entitled (without prejudice to any previously accrued rights and remedies it may have), immediately to end this agreement and to:-
a) repossess the Equipment and for that purpose to enter upon any land or premises where the Equipment is or is reasonably believed to be in order to remove the Equipment;
b) sell the Equipment; and
c) recover from the Lessee (together with VAT):
(i) all sums already accrued due to the Lessor plus;
(ii) a sum equal to the present value of the rentals, as at the date of termination of this agreement (including the Final Primary Rental) that would, but for such termination, have accrued due between the date of termination and the expiry of the Primary Period plus, where there is no Final Primary Rental, any Residual Value shown overleaf, discounted at the rate referred to in Clause 13(d) from the date of termination to the end of the Primary Period; less
(iii) the net proceeds of sale of the Equipment if repossessed and sold (or its value as determined by the Lessor, if not sold).

7 Responsibility for the Equipment after termination
Upon termination of this Agreement, the Lessee shall at the request of the Lessor;
a) return the Equipment at the Lessee's expense to any address in the United Kingdom reasonably specified by the Lessor; or
b) keep the Equipment insured under Clause 4 and store it for the Lessor at the Lessee's expense for 30 days or until the return of the Equipment to the Lessor, whichever is the earlier.

8 Lessee's acknowledgement and indemnity
a) The Lessee acknowledges and warrants that;
(i) the Equipment is required for the purpose of a business carried on by the Lessee, and was acquired at the Lessee's request, by the Lessor from the supplier of the Equipment for the purpose of this agreement;
(ii) in selecting the Equipment the Lessee relied on its own skill or judgement;
(iii) acceptance by the Lessee of delivery of the Equipment is conclusive proof that the Lessee is satisfied that it is in all respects in good working order and in conformity with the Lessee's requirements;
(iv) the Lessor does not accept responsibility for the Equipment's correspondence with description, quality, condition or suitability; and
(v) except as provided by statute or where expressly authorised by the Lessor, the supplier of the Equipment is not the agent of the Lessor.
b) The Lessee indemnifies the Lessor against all claims, damage, loss, costs and expenses (including all legal costs on a full indemnity basis) arising out of the possession or use of the Equipment, except in respect of injury or death caused by the Lessor's negligence.
c) Without limiting the above, the Lessor's liability for any breach of this agreement shall not exceed the total Primary Period Rentals paid at the time such liability arises.

9 Operator's Licence
a) Where the Equipment is a goods vehicle subject to the Goods Vehicles (Licensing of Operators) Regulations 1995 ('the Goods Vehicles Regulations') the Lessee warrants that the Lessee holds the licence ('the Licence') issued under the Goods Vehicles Regulations specified overleaf and that the Licence is in full force and effect.
b) The Lessee shall ensure that the Licence will not be revoked or the Equipment impounded under the Goods Vehicle (Enforcement Powers) Regulations 2001.
c) The Lessee shall produce the Licence for inspection and copying by the Lessor within seven days of the date of this agreement and at such reasonable intervals (at least annually) thereafter as the Lessor shall require.

10 Variation of rentals
If, during the period of this agreement there is any alteration in the corporation tax or capital or writing down allowances, the Lessor may, by written notice to the Lessee, vary the rentals by such amount or require payment of such additional rental as the Lessor considers necessary to leave it in the same position as if such event had not taken place.

11 Expenses
The Lessee shall repay on demand the Lessor's expenses and legal costs on a full indemnity basis for:
a) finding the Lessee's address if the Lessee changes address without notifying the Lessor in writing within 7 days of such change of address; and/or
b) finding the Equipment if it is not at the address notified by the Lessee; and/or
c) takings steps, including court action, to recover the Equipment or to obtain payment for it.
The Lessee shall pay on demand the Lessor's reasonable expenses in relation to any letter that the Lessor might send to the Lessee and any reasonable expenses incurred by the Lessor when any direct debit or standing order payment is not made by its due date, for whatever reason.

12 Miscellaneous
a) Any relaxation or indulgence which the Lessor may grant to the Lessee shall not affect the Lessor's strict rights under this agreement.
b) The complete and prompt performance by the Lessee of his obligations under Clauses 2, 3(a), 3(c), 3(d), 4(a), 4(e) and 9 is of the essence of this agreement. A breach of any of these obligations shall constitute a repudiation of this agreement entitling the Lessor to end this agreement under Clause 6.
c) The Equipment shall at all times remain the property of the Lessor and the Lessee shall have no right or interest otherwise than as a bailee or, in Scotland a hirer.
d) If the Lessee fails to perform any of the Lessee's obligations under this agreement the Lessor shall be entitled to perform the same on behalf of the Lessee at the Lessee's cost and the Lessee shall reimburse the Lessor on demand.
e) Where two or more persons are named as the Lessee their liability shall be joint and several.
f) Payment of VAT at the prevailing rate must accompany all rentals.
g) The Lessee's rights under this agreement cannot be transferred.
h) The Lessor may at anytime assign, transfer, charge or deal in any other manner with this agreement or any of the Lessor's rights under this agreement.
i) If this agreement is ended under Clause 6, the Lessor may, by written notice to the Lessee, end any other agreements between the Lessor and the Lessee. Likewise, if any other agreement between the Lessor and the Lessee is ended by the Lessor or terminates automatically as a result of any breach, the Lessor may end this agreement. The Lessor may then exercise its rights under this agreement (or under any other relevant agreement referred to in this clause) as if the Lessor had ended the same by reason of a repudiatory breach thereof.
j) This agreement, and the documents referred to in it, constitutes the entire agreement and understanding of the parties and supersedes any previous agreement between the parties relating to the subject matter of this agreement.

13 Definitions
In this agreement:
a) 'Lessor' includes the Lessor's successors and assigns;
b) 'Equipment' means the equipment described overleaf together with replacements, renewals, additions and accessions made to it by, or with the consent of, the Lessor or by the insurer;
c) 'net proceeds of sale' means the proceeds of sale after deducting all expenses (including all legal costs) of ascertaining the whereabouts of the Equipment and of its repossession, valuation, insurance, storage, repair and sale and net of any Value Added Tax;
d) 'present value of the rentals' in Clause 6 means the aggregate of such rentals net of Value Added Tax after discounting each rental at 4% from the date of termination to the date on which such rental would have fallen due but for termination

14 Exclusion of Third Party Rights
Nothing in this agreement shall be construed as creating a right which is enforceable by any person who is not a party or a permitted assignee or transferee of a party to this agreement.

15. General Provisions
(i) This agreement shall be governed by, and construed in accordance with, English law and shall be subject to the non-exclusive jurisdiction of the English courts. If the Lessee is situated in Scotland any expression not in current use in Scotland shall bear its nearest equivalent meaning.
(ii) No variation of this agreement or of any documents referred to in it shall be valid unless in writing and signed by or on behalf of the Lessor and the Lessee.
(iii) If any provision of this agreement shall be found to be illegal, invalid or unenforceable, it shall be severable from, and shall not affect, the other provisions of this agreement which shall remain in full force and effect.
(iv) Any notice to the Lessee may be communicated to the Lessee orally and notices required to be given in writing may be given by delivery, post or facsimile to the Lessee at the Lessee's address stated in this agreement or the Lessee's private or last known address and to the Lessor at the Lessor's address stated in this agreement or other address notified by the Lessor to the Lessee. Notices sent by first class post shall be deemed to have been received within forty-eight hours of posting.

USE OF YOUR INFORMATION
In considering whether to enter into this agreement, we may search your record at credit reference agencies. If we do they will add, to their record about you, details of our search and your application and this will be seen by other organisations that make searches. This and other information about you and those with whom you are linked financially may be used to make credit decisions about you and those with whom you are financially linked.
We may use a credit scoring or other automated decision making system.
We may also add to your record with the credit reference agencies details of your agreement with us, any payments you make under it and any default or failure to keep to its terms. These records will be shared with other organisations and may be used and searched by us and them to:
- consider applications for credit and credit related services, such as insurance, for you and any associated person;
- trace debtors, recover debts, prevent or detect money laundering and fraud, and to manage your account(s).

It is important that you provide us with accurate information. We may check your details with fraud prevention agencies and if you provide false or inaccurate information or we suspect fraud, this information may be recorded.
Fraud prevention agency records will be shared with other organisations to help make decisions on credit, motor, household, life and other insurance proposals or claims.
We will use personal information about you which we acquire in connection with any application you make to us, or any agreement you enter into with us, to manage your agreement and for statistical or market research purposes. If we transfer, charge or assign your agreement to a third party or if we employ a third party to manage any aspect of your account we will pass relevant information about you to them.
Please telephone or write to us if you want to have details of the credit reference agencies or any other agencies from whom we obtain, and to whom we pass, information about you. You have a legal right to these details. You have a right to receive a copy of the information we hold about you if you apply to us in writing. A fee may be payable.

USE OF ASSOCIATED RECORDS
We may before entering into this Agreement search records at Credit Reference Agencies which may be linked to your spouse/partner or other persons with whom you are linked financially. For the purposes of any application or this agreement you may be treated as financially linked and you will be assessed with reference to "associated" records.

Where any search or application is completed or agreement entered into involving joint parties, you both consent to us recording details at credit reference agencies. As a result an "association" will be created which will link your financial records and your associate's information may be taken into account when a future search is made by us or another lender unless you file a "disassociation" at the credit reference agency.

return on capital derived from the lease. Leveraged leasing is common in the United States, where it is promoted with sophisticated techniques involving trust deeds and the issue of non-recourse loan notes secured against rentals,[18] but the use of these has never caught on in England.

Sometimes a lessor with insufficient profits to absorb its capital allowances will bring in another party with surplus profits to act as head lessor, and take the equipment from such party under a hire-purchase agreement with authority to sub-lease to the business user. But the ability to utilize this procedure as a tax shelter is now severely circumscribed in that the sub-lessor's entitlement to capital allowances is restricted to the rentals due in the relevant accounting period[19] and, in the case of rentals payable during the year of acquisition, to that proportion of such rentals as the period from the time of acquisition to the end of the accounting period bears to the length of the accounting period.[20]

4.   THE TRIANGULAR RELATIONSHIP

The sets of legal relations set up by a simple finance lease transaction in which the lease is granted by a separate leasing company rather than by the manufacturer correspond exactly to those of the traditional hire-purchase or conditional sale agreement.[21] For convenience, we repeat these in figure 28.2, substituting Lessor for F (finance house), Lessee for B (buyer) and Supplier for D (dealer).

The reader is reminded that (apart from any express collateral warranty[22]) there is no contractual nexus between Supplier and Lessee, and so far as Lessee is concerned, his supplier is Lessor. English law regards transaction 1, the sale from Supplier to Lessor, as entirely distinct from transaction 2, the lease by Lessor to Lessee. This principle of separation has unfortunate consequences. It means that, unless otherwise agreed, Lessor is committed to Supplier on placing the order for the equipment even if Lessee wrongfully rejects a subsequent tender of delivery or withdraws his offer to take the equipment on lease. A more serious problem, in practical terms, used to exist at common law, namely that if the equipment was not in accordance with the sale contract[23] or was delivered late, the remedy against Supplier was vested in Lessor, whereas it was Lessee who principally suffered the loss, while Lessee's redress was against the hapless Lessor when the real culprit was Supplier. Most finance leases exclude any liability on the part of Lessor for defects in the equipment. This is understandable enough, for Lessor is not involved in the selection or delivery of the equipment, claims no expertise and relies on L to use his own judgment. But an effective exemption clause[24] used to bear heavily on Lessee, for he was then deprived of all remedy unless he could establish some collateral warranty on the part

18 For the characterization of such a transaction so far as English law is concerned, see p 609.
19 See Capital Allowances Act 2001, s 229(3).
20 Ibid, s 220.
21 See p 701.
22 See pp 83, 93, 720.
23 Which will incorporate the lessee's specifications.
24 The court has power to strike this down under s 7 of the Unfair Contract Terms Act 1977 if not satisfying the requirement of reasonableness. See p 732.

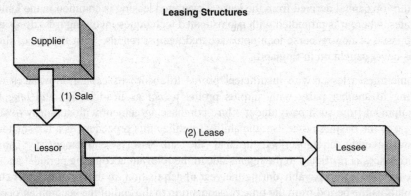

Fig 28.2 Simple triangular leasing structure. Lessor buys equipment and lets it on lease. Two contracts, no contractual relationship between supplier and lessee (except by collateral contract).

of Supplier. Attempts to deal with this problem either by Lessor agreeing to enforce the sale agreement for the benefit of Lessee or by Supplier assigning its rights to Lessee walked into the problems concerning the question whether an assignee could recover for its own loss, as opposed to that of the assignor, or whether a party enforcing a contract for the benefit of another could recover more than its own loss,[25] questions on which there was much complex case law.[26]

An elegant solution to these problems at the international level had been provided by the 1988 UNIDROIT Convention on International Financial Leasing. Under art 8 of the Convention the lessor is, for the most part, rendered immune from liability to the lessee for nonconforming equipment accepted by the lessee, while under art 10 the duties of the supplier under the supply agreement are owed to the lessee as if it were a party to the supply agreement and as if the equipment were to be supplied directly to the lessee. The Convention did not help lessees in the United Kingdom, since it does not apply to domestic transactions and anyway has yet to be ratified by the United Kingdom. Happily, a solution is now provided by the Contracts (Rights of Third Parties) Act 1999, since where the sale contract expressly provides that the lessee may enforce the contract or the Act otherwise applies,[27] the lessee is entitled to any remedy, including damages, that would have been available to him in an action for breach of contract if he had been a party to the contract.[28]

5.   THE RIGHTS AND DUTIES OF LESSOR AND LESSEE *INTER SE*

Relations between Lessor and Lessee are governed by the terms of the agreement between them.[29] In general, the parties are free to agree such terms as they choose,

---

25   See the second edition of this book at pp 783–785.

26   See *Chitty on Contracts* (29th edn, ed H. G. Beale, 2004), paras 18–042 ff.

27   See p 103.

28   Contracts (Rights of Third Parties) Act 1999, s 1(5).

29   The range of terms implied in favour of a lessee or hirer under the Supply of Goods and Services Act 1982 is similar to that of a buyer under a contract of sale.

and leasing agreements frequently specify a series of default events the occurrence of any one of which will entitle the lessor to terminate the agreement, subject to the lessee's right to apply for relief against forfeiture.[30] There are, however, two types of contractual provision that may attract judicial scrutiny.

The first is the clause invariably found in leasing agreements by which Lessor seeks to ensure that if he has to terminate the agreement because of Lessee's default, he, Lessor, will not suffer a loss. It is necessary to ensure that a minimum payment clause designed to give Lessor the value of his defeated contractual expectation is not struck down as a penalty.[31] This is less difficult than in the typical hire-purchase transaction, for a finance lease commits Lessee to payment of the rentals for the primary period without power to terminate the agreement,[32] so that a minimum payment clause can properly be framed on the assumption that but for the breach Lessee would have been liable for the primary rentals in full. The difficulty is to know what discount to allow for the acceleration of Lessee's payment liability. In the case of hire-purchase or conditional sale this is relatively straightforward, for the finance charge is separately expressed and can be rebated according to an appropriate formula. In a finance lease, on the other hand, there is no distinct interest or finance charge; the return on capital is subsumed within the rental payments. None the less, these are calculated by reference to Lessor's desired internal rate of return, and though this may not be furnished to Lessee, he will usually be quoted a rental in terms of £x per mille of capital cost.

If all Lessor's income were pure interest or profit, the calculation of the discount would largely be a matter of mathematics. The 'interest' represented by the difference between the total rentals payable and the capital cost would be notionally spread on an actuarial basis and the discount for acceleration of Lessee's liability would be represented by the part of the 'interest' unearned at the date of termination plus the amount by which the value of the repossessed equipment exceeded the value it would have had, discounted to the date of expiry of the primary period, if the lease had run its full minimum course.[33]

But mathematics is not everything. Lessor's income is not pure income. In an ideal world Lessor would first be allowed to recover the full costs attributable to the

---

30 *On Demand Information Ltd v Gerson (Finance) plc* [2003] 1 AC 368.

31 See *Lombard plc v Butterworth* [1987] QB 527, where the Court of Appeal held that the stipulated minimum payment would have been a penalty if the breach had not been made repudiatory by the terms of the agreement. But the penalty clause remains enforceable up to the amount of the loss suffered (*Jobson v Johnson* [1989] 1 All ER 621).

32 However, some agreements allow termination in cases where Lessor is protected by a buy-back arrangement with Supplier.

33 This is subject to the qualification that loss of future rentals resulting from the lessor's exercise of a right to terminate the lease for default will not be recoverable either under a liquidated damages clause or as unliquidated damages unless the lessee's breach was repudiatory. See *Financings Ltd v Baldock* [1963] 2 QB 104, applied to a leasing contract by the Manitoba Court of Appeal in *Canadian Acceptance Corp Ltd v Regent Park Butcher Shop Ltd* (1969) 3 DLR (3d) 304, and n 29. By contrast, a clause providing for acceleration of rentals on the basis that the lessee continues in possession of the equipment appears unobjectionable. See R. M. Goode, 'Acceleration Clauses' [1982] JBL 148 at p 152.

transaction up to the date of termination and only the remainder of the 'interest' would be discounted. But since no one has devised a method of matching costs against income, the court should, it is submitted, be prepared to recognize any stipulated loss value formula that, as seen at the time when the agreement was made, is likely to do substantial justice between the parties,[34] taking account also of the fact that early termination deprives Lessor of part of its tax deferral, a loss which it is entitled to have reflected in the stipulated loss value.

The other type of clause that may come under particular consideration is that by which Lessor seeks to exempt himself from liability for defects in the equipment. Such a clause is effective to exclude the common law implied terms[35] only so far as it satisfies the test of reasonableness.[36] In the context of a transaction in which Lessee relies essentially on his own skill and judgment and/or that of Supplier such an exemption clause would seem to be prima facie reasonable. On the other hand, if the effect of upholding it would be to deprive Lessee of all remedy, owing to the lack of privity with Supplier, this may induce the court to take a more jaundiced view of the clause. So the prudent Lessor will do what he can to protect Lessee by incorporating undertakings, imperfect though their effect may be,[37] to assign his rights as buyer to Lessee or to enforce them for Lessee's benefit.

6.   THE LESSOR AND THE SUPPLIER

The relationship of supplier and lessor is that of seller and buyer and as such calls for no special comment. Where Lessor authorizes Lessee to purchase equipment in his own name, though in reality as agent for Lessor, Supplier may either treat Lessee as the purchaser or, on discovering the existence of Lessor as undisclosed principal, hold Lessor liable on the sale contract. Once having made his election with knowledge of Lessor's status as undisclosed principal, Supplier is bound by it.[38]

The difficulty that may arise from Lessor's inability to prove that he has suffered loss as the result of breach of the supply contract has been adverted to earlier. The damages recoverable are in any event limited by the rule in *Hadley v Baxendale*.[39] Since Supplier knows from the outset that Lessor is buying the equipment to supply to Lessee on lease, Supplier will be aware that his failure to tender equipment in accordance with the supply contract is likely to cause loss to Lessor under the leasing agreement, so that Supplier will usually be liable for all such loss in so far as it is of an order that would normally flow from the breach and does not derive from the fact that Lessor concluded the leasing contract on unusually favourable terms.[40]

---

34 See R. M. Goode, *Hire-Purchase Law and Practice* (2nd edn, 1970), pp 887 ff and Supplement.

35 See n 29.

36 Unfair Contract Terms Act 1977, s 7(3). As against a person dealing as consumer, liability in respect of correspondence with description or sample, quality or fitness for purpose cannot be excluded at all.

37 See p 730.

38 See *Bowstead and Reynolds on Agency* (17th edn, 2001), art 84.

39 (1854) 9 Exch 341. See p 121.

40 See p 376, n 127.

7. MORE DEVELOPED STRUCTURES

We have already drawn attention to the fact that leasing structures are frequently more developed than the simple triangular relationship identified in figure 28.2. Sometimes they can be very complex indeed, particularly in cross-border leasing transactions. We shall briefly depict some of these structures and say a few words about their legal implications.

(i) Purchase by intending lessee as disclosed agent

Where a flow of transactions is envisaged, the leasing company may authorize the lessee to buy equipment as disclosed agent of the lessor (fig 28.3). Title passes directly to the lessor, the lessee being merely an intermediary so far as the sale is concerned. The lessor loses a measure of control in that if the lessee exceeds its authority in making a purchase, the lessor may be bound in accordance with the principle of apparent authority described earlier.[41]

(ii) Purchase by intending lessee as apparent principal

Where, for business reasons, the parties do not wish it to be known to the supplier that the leasing company is involved, the lessor may authorize the lessee to buy in its own name, the lessor being the undisclosed principal (fig 28.4). This is still more risky for the lessor, for there is no apparent limit to the lessee's purchasing powers. Moreover, legal title to the equipment passes in the first instance to the lessee, who will therefore have the power (though not the right) to dispose of it. Title becomes vested in the lessor as the result of an act of appropriation by the lessee.[42] Signature of the leasing agreement identifying the equipment would seem to be sufficient for this purpose.

(iii) Novation

Sometimes the intending lessee concludes the purchase before putting the leasing arrangement in place, so that the parties may decide to unscramble the transaction by a novation, the supplier, lessor and lessee agreeing that the sale to the lessee shall be cancelled (at least as regards transfer of title and the payment provisions) and replaced by a sale to the lessor, which then leases the equipment to the lessee (fig 28.5). This calls for no special comment.

(iv) Purchase by lessee, and sale with lease-back

The lessee may decide on a leasing facility after it has purchased the equipment. Alternatively, the lessor may for some reason not wish to be involved in the purchase, even as undisclosed principal. Accordingly, the lessee buys the equipment as the real principal, sells it to the leasing company and takes it back on lease (fig 28.6). Such a sale and lease-back may give rise to questions whether the transaction

---

41 See p 168.
42 See R. M. Goode, *Proprietary Rights and Insolvency in Sales Transactions* (2nd edn, 1989), ch III.

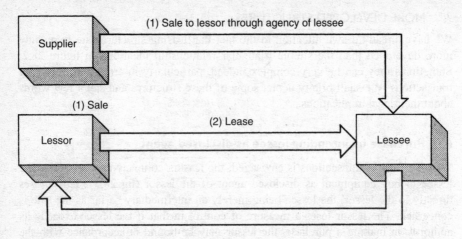

Fig 28.3 Purchase by intending lessee as disclosed agent. Lessee buys equipment as disclosed agent of lessor and takes it on lease. Contractual relationships are as in figure 28.2

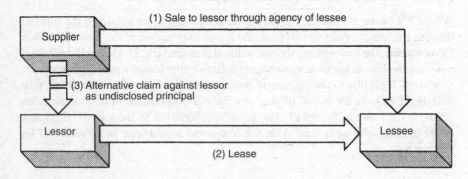

Fig 28.4 Purchase by intending lessee as apparent principal. Lessee buys equipment as apparent principal, but in reality as agent for lessor, and takes lease. Two contracts, but supplier has alternative claim against lessor as undisclosed principal.

is a disguised chattel mortgage (in which event it would be void for want of registration against the lessee's liquidator and creditors), but it is a well-established and legitimate practice, and so long as the parties intend an outright transfer of title to the lessor, so that the documents truly record the nature of their agreement, it will not be treated as a security.[43]

(v) Leveraged lease; sublease

The lessor may, both for financial and for tax reasons, wish to bring in a third party as funder to finance the purchase. The funding may be provided in one of two ways. The first involves the funder becoming the owner of the equipment, purchasing it

---

43 See p 606 and text and n 15.

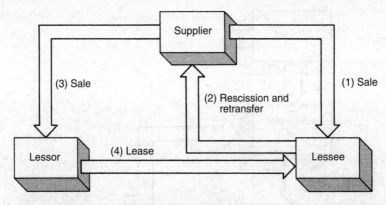

Fig 28.5 Novation. Sale by supplier to lessee, followed by novation, involving cancellation of original sale (at least as regards transfer of title and payment obligation), resale to lessor and lease.

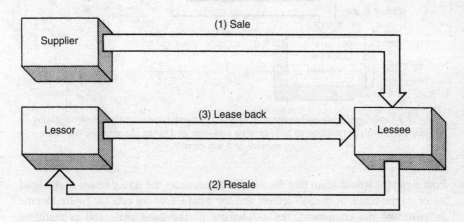

Fig 28.6 Purchase by lessee, sale and lease-back. Sale by supplier to lessee, who resells to lessor and takes lease back. Three contracts, no contractual relationship between supplier and lessor.

from the supplier and letting it on lease or hire-purchase to the leasing company with permission to grant sub-leases (fig 28.7). The arrangements will usually be governed by a master hire-purchase or leasing agreement. This does not constitute a security agreement and is not registrable as a charge. Typically, the funder reinforces its rights by taking a charge over the sub-leases and sub-rentals. Such a charge is registrable under s 395 of the Companies Act 1985 as a charge on book debts[44] and if not registered, is void against the liquidator and creditors of the intermediate lessor, though this will not affect the head lessor as regards sub-rentals it collects before commencement of the winding up. But if the head lessor exercises a power to terminate the head lease or this otherwise comes to an end, the intermediate lessor loses all interest in the equipment and all right to receive income

44 And if a floating charge, it is separately registrable under that head.

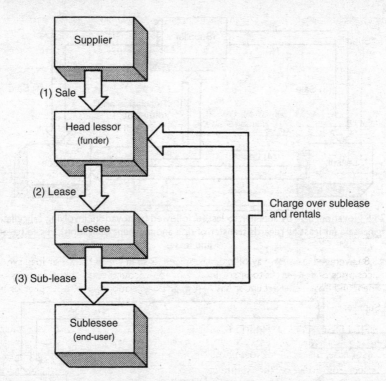

Fig 28.7 Leveraged lease by funder acquiring equipment. Funder grants lease to leasing company with permission to sub-lease to end-user and takes charge over sub-lease agreement and sub-rentals.

from it, and it would seem that the sub-lessee becomes the direct lessee of the head lessor on the terms of the sub-lease[45] and the head lessor collects the future income as owner of the equipment, not as chargee of the sub-rentals and is therefore unaffected by the invalidity of the charge as regards that income.

An alternative method of funding is by loan to enable the leasing company to buy the equipment with permission to lease it out to end-users, the lender taking a charge over the equipment and leases and lease rentals (fig 28.8). This charge is registrable under two distinct heads[46] and failure to register will be fatal in the event of the lessor's winding up, since the lender's only interest in the equipment and income from it is as chargee.

---

45 The sub-lease will continue to be binding on the head lessor if, in giving it, the intermediate lessor acted within the scope of its actual or apparent authority and the sub-lease is not expressed to be dependent on the continuance of the head lease. The doctrine of estates does not apply to chattels (see p 34), so that the sub-lease does not automatically come to an end with the cessation of the head lease, for the sub-lessee's interest in the equipment is not carved out of the head lease but is an independent interest derived from possession (see p 34).

46 As a charge on goods which, if executed by an individual, would be registrable as a bill of sale, and as a charge on book debts.

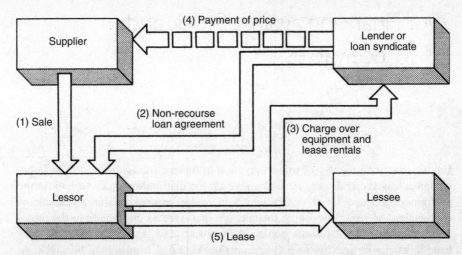

Fig 28.8 Leveraged lease by way of loan. Leveraged lease in which lender or loan syndicate advances price of equipment to lessor by way of non-recourse loan on the security of the equipment and lease rentals. Lender has no contractual relationship with supplier or lessee.

8. THE LESSOR AND THIRD PARTIES

The lessor runs little risk of losing his title in the event of a wrongful disposition by the lessee, for none of the statutory exceptions to the *nemo dat* rule[47] rule is applicable.[48] A greater hazard is the prospect of the equipment losing its identity as a chattel by incorporation into the premises occupied by the lessee.[49]

---

47 See pp 417 ff.
48 The market overt exception has been abolished. See p 425.
49 See p 38, and Goode, *Hire-Purchase Law*, ch 32.

29 Financing against Stock and Receivables

Having examined the use of title reservation to finance the acquisition of business equipment by the end-user, we now move up the distribution chain to look at the position of finance for a dealer which is to be secured on his stock and/or receivables. As regards stocking finance, we shall take as our paradigm the motor dealer supported by a finance house. In theory at least, security over stock goes hand in hand with security over the receivables resulting from sale of the stock. At first blush it makes little sense to take rights over assets that are by their nature destined to be turned over rapidly and pass into the hands of third parties while leaving the dealer-seller free to retain and apply the proceeds as if they were his own unencumbered moneys. But theory is not always matched by practice. The obvious method of taking security over trading stock and receivables is by a floating charge,[1] which in one instrument can cover both forms of collateral and, indeed, can be extended to embrace all the dealer's assets. But some finance houses feel safer if title itself passes to or through them, while some dealers are said to be reluctant to give a floating charge because of the fact that (in contrast to reservation of title) this is registrable in the Companies Registry. Further, the motor dealer has become used to a regime under which he is left free to treat the proceeds of stock as belonging to him, and to mingle cash proceeds with his own moneys, even though they result from a sale of stock to which title was held by the finance house. So, in practice, the finance house may not in fact take security over proceeds even though this would be the logical thing to do. For this reason, the discussion of finance against receivables in the second half of this chapter will move away from the motor dealer to other types of supplier.

---

1 See ch 25. Following the decision in *Siebe Gorman & Co Ltd v Barclays Bank Ltd* [1979] 2 Lloyd's Rep 142 that there is no legal impediment to a fixed charge on receivables, such charges became more common. A fixed charge has certain advantages. See pp 679–680, 689. However, it is usually not practicable for the chargee to control the application of the proceeds, and, in the absence of a contractual provision reserving such control, the charge will be held a floating charge (see p 683). The finding in *Siebe Gorman* that such a contractual provision was implicit in the agreement has been supported by the Court of Appeal in *National Westminster Bank plc v Spectrum Plus Ltd* [2004] EWCA Civ 670 (see p 673, n 41). The floating charge has, however, lost much of its attractiveness following the Enterprise Act 2002, which, by s 252, inserts a new section, 176A, in the Insolvency Act 1986, allocating a share of the assets of a company in liquidation or receivership to unsecured creditors. Note also that it is no longer possible to appoint an administrative receiver pursuant to a floating charge (Insolvency Act 1986, s 72A, inserted by the Enterprise Act 2002, s 250).

I.   STOCKING FINANCE[2]

(i)   Its purpose

Stocking finance, often referred to as 'wholesale finance' because it is furnished to the dealer-purchaser as opposed to the retail purchaser, arises from the need of dealers for funds to acquire and maintain stock. Stock financing, which is extended both by finance houses independent of the manufacturer and, increasingly, by the manufacturer itself or its associated finance company, is provided almost exclusively to motor dealers, who need to maintain adequate supplies of stock not only to be able to satisfy orders promptly but also to attract custom by display. The capital outlay required for the maintenance of a reasonable level of stock of motor vehicles is such that few dealers have the cash flow to provide it from their own resources, and car manufacturers are notoriously reluctant to extend credit to their distributors. The role of the finance house is thus to furnish accommodation to the dealer which will tide him over for the period between acquisition and sale of stock. But since the dealer will certainly need to replenish his stock, such accommodation tends to be of a revolving character, generating a continuous flow of acquisitions and disposals of stock and, in consequence, of advances and repayments.

The primary objective of finance houses in furnishing stocking finance to motor dealers is to capture the dealers' lucrative retail paper. The relative insensitivity of consumer buyers to interest rates is well known. Hence the income which a finance house can derive from consumer hire-purchase and instalment sale contracts is, in terms of a percentage rate of charge, considerably higher than it could expect to obtain from loans to business; and while the administrative costs involved in servicing a large volume of small- or medium-cost transactions are obviously greater than those of controlling a small number of large transactions, the risk of default is much more widely spread.

While one might have thought that the finance house, as controller of the purse strings, would hold the whip hand in negotiations, bargaining power has in practice lain with the dealer, by reason of the strong competition among finance houses for the dealer's retail contracts. Finance houses vie with one another in offering attractive inducements to dealers to secure their business. These inducements may take various forms, the two most convenient being the provision of stocking finance at low cost (the rate being sometimes geared directly to the volume of retail business introduced) and the payment of commission on retail business introduced, the commission being calculated as a percentage of the finance charge payable under the hire-purchase or instalment sale contract.

From time to time finance houses have come together to consider whether, by collective action, they can control the level of commission and thus avoid engaging in an economic war which, if carried beyond a certain point, would make business unprofitable, to the detriment of them all. The Finance Houses Association for

---

2 See Vic Lock, 'Stocking finance – a special report', *Leasing Life* 2003, p 24; J. S. Ziegel, 'Legal Impediments to the Financing of Dealers' Stock and Accounts Receivable' in *Instalment Credit* (ed A. L. Diamond, 1970), pp 117 ff.; John R. Peden, *Stock-in-Trade Financing* (1974).

many years operated a Code of Practice for Motor Vehicle Business by which members of the Association bound themselves not to impose finance charges on hirers or buyers, nor to pay commission to dealers, exceeding the rates prescribed by the Code. However, in 1965 the Code (which in practice was not always scrupulously observed) was struck down by the Restrictive Practices Court as against the public interest and therefore void under the Restrictive Trade Practices Act 1956.[3] Since then, finance houses in the United Kingdom cannot lawfully arrange to control the level of dealers' commissions, so that the era of the economic war has returned and still exists at the present day.

Not all stocking finance is provided on a secured basis. At one time it was common to give the dealer unsecured purchase money finance against a 90-day renewable bill of exchange. But in business, as in other walks of life, fashions change. There is always a period when some procedures are out and others in. The history of stocking finance shows fluctuations between secured and unsecured credit and between one form of secured credit and another.

(ii) Security over financed stock

A finance house desiring security for its stocking finance can, of course, avail itself of all the forms of security which the law allows over different classes of asset owned by the dealer or in which he has or will acquire an interest. But we are here concerned with interests in the stock itself. Such an interest may take various forms, but these divide broadly into two groups: a charge to secure a loan and title reservation under a bailment, or floor plan. Each has its advantages and disadvantages. The charge is more flexible in that it can secure a revolving facility enabling the dealer to draw on its account at any time up to a stated maximum and can legitimately cover products and proceeds, while the extension of reservation of title to products and proceeds may render it vulnerable as a disguised charge.[4] On the other hand, title reservation is inherently stronger, since it is not a floating security (or, indeed, security at all in the legal sense), whereas a charge on stock will usually be a mere floating charge.[5]

(iii) Charge on stock

It is theoretically possible to have a fixed charge on stock, but this is far from easy in practice. The essence of a fixed charge is that it gives the creditor an attached security interest. It is incompatible with the nature of a fixed charge that the debtor should have unfettered liberty to dispose of the asset free from the charge in the ordinary course of his business. No matter what language is employed, the court will construe a charge giving such liberty as a floating charge.[6] This is clear from the judgment of Vaughan Williams LJ in *Re Yorkshire Woolcombers Association Ltd*:

3   *Re Finance Houses Association Ltd's Agreement* [1965] 3 All ER 509. The Restrictive Trade Practices Acts were repealed by the Competition Act 1998, s 1, and replaced by Pt III of the latter Act.
4   See pp 607, 769.
5   See below.
6   See p 680.

I do not think that for a 'specific security' you need have a security of a subject matter which is then in existence. I mean by 'then' at the time of the execution of the security; but what you do require to make a specific security is that the security whenever it has once come into existence, and been identified or appropriated as a security, shall never thereafter at the will of the mortgagor cease to be a security. If at the will of the mortgagor he can dispose of it and prevent its being any longer a security, although something else may be substituted more or less for it, that is not a 'specific security'.[7]

This was followed in *National Provincial Bank of England Ltd v United Electric Theatres Ltd*,[8] a still stronger case in that the movables charged, though referred to as 'stock' in the judgment, did not appear to be stock in trade in the normal sense, since the chargor was not a trader but a theatre company. If, therefore, security on stock is to qualify as a fixed security, it must give the financier such control over the disposal of the stock as is sufficient to manifest an intention to appropriate it to an existing security interest. Failing this, the charge will be considered a floating charge, a form of security which suffers a number of disadvantages.[9] The most effective method, of course, is to take a pledge rather than a charge. A pledge device which became highly developed in the United States is field warehousing. The dealer's stock is required to be stored in a warehouse under the control of a custodian appointed by the financier. Alternatively, and less expensively, the dealer leases a warehouse or segregated area in his own premises to the financier at a nominal rent, and arranges that one of his own employees shall act as the financier's warehouseman, controlling and releasing stock in accordance with the financier's directions.[10]

Field warehousing has never taken root in England[11] and there is no indication that it will ever do so. A non-possessory fixed charge could be obtained by requiring the dealer to secure the prior assent of the finance house to every sale transaction, but the time and administrative effort involved are considered to render this impractical. What relaxation could be allowed without converting the charge into a floating charge has never been fully tested What does seem necessary is either that there should be some form of express assent to dispositions which is given by the creditor *after* acquisition of the stock (whether given in relation to one item of stock or a batch of items) or that any licence to deal given in advance of acquisition should be limited.[12]

7 [1903] 2 Ch 284, at 294.
8 [1916] 1 Ch 132.
9 See pp 680, 683.
10 See Grant Gilmore, *Security Interests in Personal Property* (1965), ch 6; James J. White and Robert S. Summers, *Uniform Commercial Code* (4th edn, 1995), vol 3, pp 262 ff.
11 However, imported goods the purchase of which is financed by a bank or confirming house are often stored in its name in an independent warehouse or released to the buyer to be held under a trust receipt in the buyer's own premises. The development of field warehousing in America was powered by the refusal of American courts to recognize the validity of a non-possessory mortgage of inventory on the ground that this was a fraudulent conveyance, since the debtor retained dominion over the property. This 'dominion' rule was extended to security over receivables in the famous case of *Benedict v Ratner* 268 US 353 (1925). American law never adopted the English floating charge; either the security was a valid *specific* charge, albeit over shifting security (and this is the meaning of the American 'floating lien'); or it was invalid and conferred no real rights on the creditor. The rule in *Benedict v Ratner* was jettisoned in s 9–205 of the United Commercial Code.
12 See *Re Cimex Tissues Ltd* [1994] BCC 626; William J. Gough, *Company Charges* (2nd edn, 2000), pp 630–632.

The fact that the stock held by the dealer at the date of the charge is itemized and scheduled to the charge would not seem to strengthen the case for treating the charge as fixed, except in so far as it may negate the inference that the dealer is to be entitled to deal with the stock freely in the ordinary course of business. Nor is the character of the charge altered by a provision requiring the dealer to account for the proceeds of stock and meanwhile to keep those proceeds separate from his own moneys. Such a provision, if genuinely intended and not negated by a subsequent implied assent to use of the proceeds by the dealer as its own moneys, may be effective to create a fixed charge over the proceeds of the stock but would not, it is thought, be relevant to the character of the charge over the stock itself.[13] Conversely, if the creditor does reserve proper control over stock disposals, the absence of a proceeds clause will not convert the charge of the stock from a fixed charge into a floating charge, though if the dealer is allowed freedom to use the proceeds as its own moneys, the charge will be floating as to the proceeds.[14] In short, a proceeds clause is relevant to the characterization of a charge on the proceeds, but not to the characterization of a charge on the stock.[15]

(iv) Bailment

There are many forms of bailment plan but they have a common characteristic: the dealer does not purchase the equipment from the supplier and charge it to the finance house but derives his interest from the finance house itself, whether as buyer under a conditional sale agreement, hirer under a hire-purchase agreement or consignee under a consignment or subconsignment. The finance house is either the owner or is itself a buyer, hirer or consignee from the manufacturer.

While car manufacturers are reluctant to give extended credit, an immediate sale to the dealer attracts value added tax, which would have to be accounted for to the Customs and Excise. So the normal procedure is for the manufacturer to consign each vehicle or batch of vehicles to the dealer on a sale-or-return basis, collecting from the dealer a consignment deposit equal to the tax-exclusive price. The dealer is deemed to appropriate the vehicle (inter alia) by resale or by retaining it for more than a specified period. In that event, the price becomes payable, the manufacturer looks to the consignment deposit in its hands and the dealer is simply left with the tax to pay. If the dealer returns the car to the manufacturer before a deemed appropriation, his consignment deposit is refunded to him and value added tax will be avoided, provided the dealer has not held the vehicle for more than a year.[16]

The finance house supports the dealer by providing the consignment deposit, where consignment is used, or by advancing the price and value added tax where the transfer of title is not deferred by use of a consignment plan. The provision of the consignment deposit can be effected in various ways. One is for the finance house to advance this by way of loan, secured by a floating charge on the stock and receivables and/or on other assets of the dealer, which might include the

---

13 See p 618.
14 *Agnew v Commissioners of Inland Revenue* [2001] 2 AC 710.
15 See p 619.
16 Value Added Tax Act 1994, s 6(2)(c).

consignment deposit itself. An advance by way of loan secured by a charge has the advantage that the finance house does not have to interpose itself between manufacturer and dealer in relation to the supply of the vehicles, while the tax deferment obtained by the consignment method is preserved

But some finance houses prefer that title to the vehicle shall pass to or through them. Thus the finance house may, by agreement of the manufacturer, interpose itself as consignee and subconsign the vehicles to the dealer on similar terms, resale by the dealer constituting an appropriation of the vehicle by the finance house as against the manufacturer and by the dealer as against the finance house, so that title notionally passes through both of them to the retail buyer. This arrangement makes the finance house to some extent dependent on the manufacturer's cooperation for enforcement of the finance house's remedies, the latter, as a consignee, never getting title beyond that which flows through it on sale or other appropriation by the dealer. The subconsignment agreement will give the finance house a right to repossess the subconsigned vehicles upon the dealer's default, but these must be held to the order of the manufacturer unless the finance house itself decides to appropriate them by retention or sale. Because of this, certain finance houses prefer to purchase the vehicles outright from the manufacturer through the agency of the dealer and resell them to the dealer on conditional sale, reserving title until payment, which falls due on appropriation. The sale/conditional sale technique has the disadvantage that value added tax becomes payable on sale by the manufacturer, instead of being deferred until the making of the retail sale, so that the finance house may be called upon to finance the dealer's tax liability as well as the price. In addition, the detailed contract between manufacturer and dealer, which covers many other aspects of the relationship between them (eg levels of stock to be held, sales promotion etc.) has to be varied by excluding or modifying the financial provisions.

The advantage of these unit-stocking plans,[17] compared with a loan secured by a charge, is that they tailor the finance provided at any given time to the amount of units actually held in stock (in contrast to the rough-and-ready loan method, which may result in the dealer being either overfinanced or underfinanced at any particular moment) and give the finance house greater stock control, since it can monitor daily the stock holdings and disposals. There are, however, some disadvantages. First, the unit-by-unit facility is expensive to administer and tends to lead to overstocking by the dealer. Secondly, the intervention of the finance house between manufacturer and dealer to some extent interferes with the manufacturer–dealer contract, which will need to be modified to accommodate the altered method of financing.

Whether the interest of the finance house in the dealer's stock is as conditional seller, subconsignor or chargee, one thing is clear, and that is that the finance house will not be allowed to assert its security interest against a buyer in the ordinary course of business.[18] It is submitted that this is so even where the security is a

17 So called because the finance house provides finance on a unit-by-unit basis as each item comes into stock. For a specimen vehicle stocking plan, see fig 29.1.

18 See *St Margaret's Trusts Ltd v Castle* [1964] CLY 1685, CA, 30 July (Bar Library transcript No 247); R. M. Goode, *Hire-Purchase Law and Practice* (2nd edn, 1970), pp 599, 616.

registered charge of which the buyer has actual knowledge, for he is entitled to assume, unless put on notice to the contrary, that the dealer is authorized to dispose of the stock in the ordinary course of business. Only notice that the disposition to him is in breach of the dealer's obligations to the finance house will suffice to subordinate the buyer to the finance house's rights.[19]

2.   RECEIVABLES FINANCING[20]

(i)   Sale and loan

A trader who wishes to convert his receivables into cash may do so in one of two ways: by selling them or by charging them as security for a loan. Sales may be made with or without recourse, that is to say, the sales agreement may or may not provide for the trader to guarantee the purchaser against default by the debtors. In economic terms, a sale of receivables with recourse is virtually indistinguishable from a loan on the security of the receivables, for in both cases the trader receives money now and has to repay it himself, or ensure payment by debtors, later. But the two types of transaction are treated quite differently in law. A loan to a company on the security of book debts is registrable under s 395 of the Companies Act 1985 as a charge on book debts,[21] a purchase of book debts is not. Legal restrictions on the ability to borrow or lend do not apply to sale and purchase. The chargor of receivables has an equity in them, the seller does not. The chargee is precluded from enforcing his security pending the hearing of a petition for an administration order against the chargor company or during the currency of such an order,[22] while a purchaser of debts is entitled to collect them, since this does not involve any interference with any proprietary or possessory rights of the seller of the debts or any proceedings against the seller.

Where the sale form of receivables financing is used, difficulties sometimes arise because of the fact that while the lawyers draft the document in terms of sale and purchase, the staff of the finance house are more realistic in their characterization of the transaction and, despite all instructions to the contrary, tend to use words such as 'loan', 'advance', 'interest', in their internal documents and in correspondence, so casting doubt on the genuineness of the transaction as a sale transaction. Fortunately, the courts have usually recognized the right of the businessman to use the business language he understands without having this interpreted as if it were in a legal dictionary. So documents drawn up by the lawyers to record a sale transaction have almost always been accepted as such where the court has been satisfied that they genuinely reflected the intention of the parties, even though the terms subsequently used in operating the agreement were such as would ordinarily

---

19 See p 666.
20 For an excellent treatment of the whole subject, see Fidelis Oditah, *Legal Aspects of Receivables Financing* (1991).
21 And separately as a floating charge if it leaves the debtor free to collect in the debts for its own account. See pp 680, 683.
22 Insolvency Act 1986, ss 10(1)(b), 11(3)(c).

suggest a loan on security rather than a purchase.[23] Nevertheless, a party seeking to show that an assignment was absolute may face formidable difficulties if it was expressed to be by way of security[24] and the language of security should be avoided wherever possible if what is intended is an outright transfer. Thus the standard form of block discounting agreement by which hire-purchase receivables are expressed to be sold to a finance house by the trader will almost always be upheld as a true sale – that being the intention of the parties – not as a disguised charge.[25]

Where a purported purchase of receivables is held to be a disguised loan on the security of the receivables, it will be void against a liquidator and creditors except in the unlikely event of its having been registered as a charge on book debts, if the assignor is a company,[26] or as if it were a bill of sale, if the assignor is an individual and the assignment is a general assignment rather than assignment of debts due from specified debtors or becoming due under specified contracts.[27]

(ii) Notification and non-notification financing

Receivables financing may be conducted either on a notification or on a non-notification basis. In the former, the debtor is given notice of the assignment whereas in the latter the assignor is left in apparent ownership, no notice of assignment being given to the debtor, so that the assignor continues to collect the debt, ostensibly on his own behalf but in reality as agent for the assignee, to whom he is accountable.

Non-notification financing, as exemplified by block discounting[28] and invoice discounting,[29] is inherently more risky for the financier. The debtor gets a good discharge by payment to the assignor, even if the latter subsequently fails to account to the assignee;[30] while if the assignor fraudulently assigns the same debts to a third party who is the first to give notice to the debtors, he gets priority.[31] Moreover, if

---

23 See *Lloyd's and Scottish Finance Ltd v Cyril Lord Carpets Ltd* (1979), a previously unreported decision of the House of Lords now reported in [1992] BCLC 609.

24 See, for example, *Orion Crown Finance Ltd v Crown Financial Management Ltd* [1996] 2 BCLC 78.

25 See pp 580, 702 and *Anglo-Irish Asset Finance Co v DSG Financial Services* [1995] CLY 4491.

26 Companies Act 1985, s 396(1)(e).

27 Insolvency Act 1986, s 344. So a whole turnover agreement (see p 747) may be vulnerable if not followed by specific assignments, whereas a facultative agreement is not.

28 See p 719, and Goode, *Hire-Purchase Law*, pp 657 ff.

29 The sale of receivables due from trade debtors where the assignor continues to be responsible for collections as agent for its undisclosed principal, the assignee, whose services are limited to the provision of finance (by purchase, with or without an arrangement for prepayment and/or acceptance of the credit risk).

30 Thus, by contrast with the notification financier whose risk of non-payment is distributed among a number of debtors, the non-notification financier puts all his eggs in one basket as regards debts collected in by the assignor, for if the latter becomes insolvent and the sums he has collected are no longer traceable, the assignee is without remedy.

31 Under the rule in *Dearle v Hall* (1828) 3 Russ 1. See p 56. However, the debtor is not obliged to recognize or act on a notice of assignment given to him before the debt comes into existence (as opposed to a notice of assignment of a present debt payable in the future). See *Re Dallas* [1904] 2 Ch 385; *Johnstone v Cox* (1881) 19 Ch D 17. Such a notice is a nullity and is therefore ineffective to give priority.

the assignee does ultimately find it necessary to get in the receivables himself, he may discover that his delay in giving notice has subjected his claim to defences and rights of set-off that would not have been available against him had notice been given promptly, for the debtor is entitled to set up equities arising under all dealings between him and the assignor, whether before or after the assignment, up to the time when the debtor has received notice of assignment.[32] Despite these disadvantages, commercial pressure from suppliers has led to non-notification financing becoming the dominant form of receivables financing, since suppliers are reluctant to have their arrangements with factors disclosed to their customers with consequent disturbance to their relations.

(iii) Factoring: the mechanism

The vehicle we shall use to illustrate typical security procedures in notification receivables financing goes by the name of *factoring*.[33] A factor in the sense here discussed[34] is one who, pursuant to a continuing relationship with a supplier of goods or services to trade customers,[35] purchases debts from time to time arising in respect of supplies to those customers. The assignor is commonly called the client or supplier, the account debtor is the customer. The factor offers three main types of service: the acceptance of risk of non-payment by customers, the provision of finance by prepayment of part of the purchase price of the debts, and the administration of the sales ledgers. A client may opt for all or any of these services. A client who is not concerned about risk will sell on a recourse basis, that is, giving the factor the right to require debts that go into default to be repurchased. A client who does not need finance will opt for maturity factoring, where payment can be taken as and when the factor collects from the customer or on expiry of an agreed numbers of days after invoice date.[36] Where the client is happy to keep the ledger administration and only requires finance, the arrangement is customarily referred to as invoice discounting. This is typically on a recourse basis, customers are not notified of the assignment except in stated events and the client collects the debts as agent for the factor, its undisclosed principal.[37]

Relations between the factor and the trader ('client') are governed by a detailed master agreement, the factoring agreement (fig 29.1), which regulates the terms upon which the factor will purchase receivables due to the client from those to whom he supplies goods or services ('customers'). Receivables which the factor is prepared to purchase on a non-recourse basis[38] are termed 'approved receivables'.

---

32 *Roxburghe v Cox* (1881) 17 Ch D 520; *Re Pinto Leite & Nephews* [1929] 1 Ch 221.

33 For an admirable treatment of this subject, see F. R. Salinger, *Factoring Law and Practice* (3rd edn, 1999).

34 As opposed to the mercantile agent referred to in the Factors Acts. The receivables factor has his origins in the mercantile factor.

35 As opposed to consumers.

36 Or, if the factoring is non-recourse, when the customer becomes insolvent.

37 Invoice discounting on a notification basis is usually known as agency factoring; invoice discounting without recourse, as undisclosed factoring; but the terminology is not uniform. See generally Salinger, *Factoring Law*, paras 1–42 ff.

38 That is, without the right to require unpaid debts to be bought back.

These denote receivables arising from transactions specifically approved by the factor or falling within an overall funding limit authorized by the factor in respect of a particular customer. Unapproved receivables, in so far as purchased by the factor, are taken with recourse to the client if the relevant customers default.

Factoring agreements are either facultative agreements or whole turnover agreements. In a facultative agreement, as with block discounting,[39] the specific transaction concluded under the umbrella of the factoring agreement takes the form of an offer of batches of receivables for sale, the client being under no obligation to offer or the factor to purchase any particular batch of receivables.[40] In a whole turnover agreement, all receivables not specifically excluded by the agreement are agreed to be sold to and purchased by the factor and are to vest in the factor automatically on coming into existence.[41] Unless the receivables are to be assigned on a non-notification basis the factoring agreement will require the client to stamp on his invoices to customers notice of the fact that the invoiced account has been assigned to the factor and that payment should be made direct to the factor at the latter's stated address. In the case of maturity factoring, the client is not paid the price of a receivable until it matures or the customer becomes insolvent, whichever first occurs. In the case of advance factoring, the client is given the facility of drawing on the account with the factor against the receivables prior to maturity, paying a discount charge for the privilege.

(iv) The factor and the client

Once a receivable has become vested in the factor in equity pursuant to the factoring agreement and notice of assignment has been given to the customer, it is the customer's duty to pay the factor, not the client. But mistakes occur in the best-regulated circles, and it is not uncommon for the customer's accounts department to overlook the notice of assignment and send a cheque to the client. Most factoring agreements provide for this eventuality by stipulating that cheques and money received from customers are to be made over to the factor and are meanwhile to be held on trust for the factor; even without such a provision, it is clear that the client is a trustee for the factor as to cheques and money so received.[42] If the client

---

39 See p 719.

40 The client may, however, be placed under obligation not to factor his receivables elsewhere without consent.

41 This cannot happen by virtue of the factoring agreement unless the terms are such as to impose on the factor an obligation to purchase the receivables. In the absence of such an obligation, the agreement for transfer of the receivables to the factor lacks the consideration which is necessary to create a valid assignment of future rights even where the agreement is by deed (see p 629, n 24). The further requirement for the creation of an equitable interest in future property, viz that the consideration be executed, is satisfied in respect of each batch of receivables by payments or credits by the factor to the client in respect of earlier receivables, for the agreement has to be considered as a whole and such payments or credits are made in reliance on the vesting clause covering receivables generally. Where there is no commitment to purchase, receivables will normally vest not by virtue of the factoring agreement but pursuant to a subsequent equitable assignment made after they have come into existence and resulting from an offer of sale of the receivables by the client and its acceptance by the factor.

42 *International Factors Ltd v Rodriguez* [1979] QB 351.

wrongfully retains or deals with cheques in defiance of the factor's title, it commits a conversion and is liable for the face value of any cheque so converted.[43] So too is a director of the client company who causes it to commit the act of conversion, for he is then guilty of conversion himself.[44]

The typical case is where the client pays the cheque into its overdrawn bank account. The bank can retain the proceeds of the cheque to the extent to which it gives value for them without notice of the factor's rights.[45] Subject to this, the factor can trace the proceeds into the account, and through it into the hands of volunteers and third parties taking with notice of the factor's rights, in accordance with the ordinary rules of tracing.[46]

(v) The factor and the customer

As assignee of the debt, the factor incurs no positive liability to the customer for breaches of duty by the client under the supply agreement,[47] but the factor takes subject to all defences of which the customer could have availed itself against the client and also to all equities arising up to the time when the customer has notice of the assignment or otherwise closely connected with the assigned debt. So if the goods or services supplied by the client to the customer are not in conformity with the contract, the customer may assert against the factor the same defences as he would have been entitled to assert against the client, whether these arose before or after the customer's receipt of notice of assignment. Where there are mutual dealings between client and customer, the latter is entitled to set off against the factor's claim on one transaction a cross-claim which is closely connected to that claim,[48] whether arising before or after the customer's receipt of notice of assignment. Under a separate rule, in proceedings by the factor, a customer is also entitled to set off an independent cross-claim which it has against the client on another transaction where the cross-claim is a liquidated claim for money that has become due at the time of commencement of the proceedings.[49] A few examples serve to illustrate these points.

Example 1: substantive defence

Client sells factory equipment to Customer for £10,000, and assigns the debt to Factor. Notice of the assignment is given to Customer. Subsequently, Customer exercises a

---

43 Ibid.

44 Ibid.

45 This will be the case where the bank receives the cheque without notice of the factor's rights and (a) applies it in reduction of the client's overdraft, or (b), when still without notice, allows the client to draw against the cheque. In this latter case, value is given by the bank to the extent to which the drawing exceeds any credit balance existing at the time the cheque was collected

46 See p 52.

47 Since an assignee does not, as such, become a party to the contract.

48 That form of equitable set-off which has become known as transaction set-off. See generally Philip R. Wood, *English and International Set-Off* (1989); S. R. Derham, *Law of Set-Off* (3rd edn, (2003)); Roy Goode, *Legal Problems of Credit and Security* (3rd edn, 2003), ch VII.

49 This appears still to be the rule, though it has been criticized by several writers, who consider it is too strict and that it should suffice if the cross-claim has matured by the time of judgment. See, for example, Derham, *Law of Set-Off*, paras 2–09 ff.

right to return the equipment because it is not of satisfactory quality and to terminate the sale contract. When Factor claims payment of the £10,000, Customer is entitled to rely on Client's repudiatory breach as a defence to the claim, though he is not entitled to recover damages from Factor for any additional loss.

Example 2: transaction set-off

Client sells manufacturing equipment to Customer for £100,000 and by a separate contract agrees to provide maintenance services for a specified period. Client then assigns the debt to Factor and gives notice of the assignment to Customer. Subsequently, the equipment's manufacturing capacity is reduced because of faulty servicing by Client. Customer is entitled to set off its claim for unliquidated damages for breach of the maintenance agreement against the £100,000 due to Factor even though that claim did not arise until after Customer received the notice of assignment.

Example 3: independent set-off

Client buys timber from Customer for £10,000, to be made up into furniture which Client sells back to Customer for £15,000. The £15,000 receivable is assigned by Client to Factor and notice of the assignment is given to Customer. At a later date Customer makes a loan of £5,000 to Client, repayable in two years' time. When Factor calls for payment of the £15,000, Customer is entitled to set off the £10,000 owing to him for the timber but not the sum owed to him under the loan agreement unless this has become payable by the time of commencement of proceedings by Factor or, possibly, the time when judgment on Factor's claim comes to be given.[50]

Where the assigned contract contains a provision prohibiting Client from assigning, Customer is not obliged to recognize Factor's title and will get a good discharge on paying Client.[51] But the prohibition will rarely be construed as intending to render the assignment void as between Client and Factor so as to preclude Factor from asserting a proprietary right to the proceeds of the debt in the hands of Client as assignor.[52] Indeed, any attempt by Customer to fetter the ability of Client to deal with the proceeds of the collected debt would, it is thought, be void as repugnant to Client's ownership of the sum paid and as serving no legitimate interest of Customer.[53]

(vi) Priority conflicts between the factor and third parties[54]

The after-acquired property clause in a factoring agreement may come into conflict with a competing security interest or other real right in various ways. One, of course, results from the fraudulent double assignment of receivables by the client, a

---

50 See n 49.

51 *Helstan Securities Ltd v Hertfordshire County Council* [1978] 3 All ER 262; *Linden Garden Trust Ltd v Lenesta Sludge Disposals Ltd* and *St Martin's Property Corp Ltd v Sir Robert McAlpine Ltd* [1994] 1 AC 85. The effect of such a prohibition is to limit the factor's title to the proceeds of the assigned debt in the hands of the assignor.

52 See R. M. Goode, 'Inalienable Rights?' (1979) 42 MLR 553, in an analysis approved by Lord Browne-Wilkinson in the *Lenesta Sludge case*, n 51. To the extent that *Helstan Securities* held that the assignment was wholly void, it went beyond what was necessary to decide the case and it is submitted that it is wrong; see Goode, ibid, at p 556.

53 See ibid, pp 556–557. In the *Lenesta Sludge* case, n 51, Lord Browne-Wilkinson expressed no final view on the public policy point but thought it might well be the case that such an extension of the prohibition against assignment was contrary to public policy.

54 See Oditah, *Legal Aspects of Receivables*, ch Six; Salinger, *Factoring Law*, ch 8.

relatively infrequent event, where priorities are regulated by the rule in *Dearle v Hall*.[55] The factor wins unless the subsequent assignee advanced without notice of the factoring agreement and was the first to give notice of assignment to the debtor concerned. What is more likely is that a conflict results through inadvertence on the part of the client (eg in failing to mention the existence of a floating charge in favour of his bank) or external events such as receivership or liquidation of the client company. The rule in *Dearle v Hall* does not apply in cases where the debtor is entitled to refuse to recognize the notice of assignment.[56]

I.   *Factor versus holder of floating charge*

If the floating charge precedes the factoring agreement and contains no relevant restrictions against dealings of which the factor has notice, the factor's rights prevail as regards receivables vesting in the factor before it has notice of crystallization of the charge,[57] for the client has liberty under the floating charge to dispose of its receivables in the ordinary course of business. However, the modern floating charge often excludes the chargor's right to factor its receivables, and if the factor is on notice of such prohibition,[58] it is bound by it and will acquire the receivables as encumbered by the charge, with a consequent duty to pay over the proceeds to the extent necessary to satisfy the charge. Because of this danger, the prudent factor exacts a waiver from the chargee before commencing the factoring operation.[59]

Where the factoring agreement comes first, the outcome of the conflict depends on its effect. If the agreement is one under which receivables vest automatically in the factor pursuant to a binding agreement for sale and purchase embodied in the factoring agreement and a sum has been paid or credited to the client under the agreement, the factor's equitable title attaches to a receivable at the moment of its birth and the client thus has no interest in it, so that there is nothing on which the floating charge can fasten. In this situation the fact that the factor may have acquired notice of the floating charge is irrelevant.[60] Where, on the other hand, the factoring agreement provides for receivables to be offered to the factor, no real rights, even of an inchoate character, vest in the factor until a binding agreement for sale and purchase has been concluded by acceptance of the client's offer for sale, and while the factor will still prevail as regards receivables purchased before notice of the crystallization of the charge, or of a prohibition contained in it against the factoring of the receivables, the factor will be postponed to the chargee as regards receivables purchased after such notice.

Failure to register a floating charge does not, as such ,invalidate it as against a factor, for it is a buyer, not a secured creditor, and s 395 protects only creditors.[61]

55 See n 31.
56 See pp 648, 653.
57 It is submitted that, for reasons already advanced, crystallization does not by itself affect the factor unless and until he has notice of it. See p 686.
58 As to what constitutes notice, see pp 662 ff.
59 As to whether it binds an assignee of the floating charge, see p 617.
60 See p 670.
61 See p 667.

But if the effect of non-registration is that the factor does not become aware of the restrictions imposed by the charge on the factoring of receivables, the factor will obtain priority, regardless of whether it is the first to give notice to the debtor.[62]

2. Factor versus holder of fixed charge

A prior fixed charge of the receivables binds the factor, whether or not it has notice of it, except that if the factor, having put out its money without notice of the charge, is subsequently the first to give notice to the debtors, it wins.[63]

3. Factor versus receiver

The appointment of a receiver crystallizes a floating charge, if it had not crystallized earlier, but the only effect on the factor is that the charge becomes a fixed charge as regards all receivables within its scope that subsequently come into existence,[64] and the priority rules given above in relation to fixed charges apply.

4. Factor versus liquidator or administrator

The winding up or administration of the client company has no impact on the factor's position except, of course, that, unless the liquidator or administrator chooses to continue the factoring agreement, the factor cannot assert rights over receivables coming into existence after the winding up or administration as the result of the continuance of business by the liquidator on behalf of the company.[65] Subject to this, an automatic vesting clause in a factoring agreement will continue to operate even in relation to receivables coming into existence after presentation of a winding-up petition and falling due for payment after the making of the winding-up order.[66]

5. Factor versus execution creditor

A creditor can attach moneys due to the judgment debtor only so far as the right to such moneys is still vested in the debtor. If these have become vested in the factor prior to completion of the attachment,[67] the factor wins; otherwise the execution creditor prevails.

6. Factor versus conditional seller

What is the outcome of a contest between a factor as purchaser of receivables and a supplier claiming the same receivables as proceeds of the sale of goods to which he had reserved the title under a *Romalpa* clause? Assuming that the seller does, in fact, have an equitable right to trace, is this superior or subordinate to the factor's

---

62 *Ward v Royal Exchange Shipping Co Ltd* (1887) 58 LT 174; *Re Ind Coope & Co Ltd* [1911] 2 Ch 223. If the charge does not contain such restrictions, the factor will obtain priority anyway, as stated above.
63 See p 749.
64 For the distinction between a present and a future receivable, see p 631.
65 See p 635.
66 See p 635.
67 See p 623, n 172.

own equitable title? And can the factor obtain priority by taking a statutory assignment, thus getting in the legal title?

Where both titles are equitable, the seller has an initial priority as the first in time, but this is displaced under the rule in *Dearle v Hall*[68] if (as will almost invariably be the case) the factor is the first to give notice of its interest to the customer and advances its money without notice of the seller's equitable rights.[69] But where the factor is for some reason unable to invoke the rule in *Dearle v Hall*, it will be postponed, even where getting in the legal title, for even as a statutory assignee, it takes subject to equities, including the seller's prior equitable interest.[70]

7.   Factor versus (mercantile agent) factor

If the client sells his goods through a factor (in the sense of a mercantile agent, as opposed to a factor of receivables), the factor has a lien on the goods and their proceeds to secure payment of his commission; and the better view is that this is so whether the factor sells in his own name or in the name of his principal.[71] The lien has priority over the equitable title of the receivables factor.[72] Such a situation is particularly likely to arise in export factoring, where the client sells the goods to an overseas buyer through a (mercantile agent) factor and then factors the receivables to a United Kingdom factor ('the export factor'), who re-factors them to a factor in the buyer's own country ('the import factor').[73]

---

68 See n 31.

69 *Compaq Computer Ltd v Abercorn Group Ltd* [1991] BCC 484. This conclusion had earlier been disputed by D. W. McLauchlan, who contended that the rule in *Dearle v Hall* was restricted to competing assignments and did not apply in a situation where one of the interests was an equitable tracing right arising by operation of law. See (1980) 96 LQR 90, at 95 ff.). But there is no good policy reason for distinguishing a conflict between competing assignees and one between a beneficiary under a trust of a receivable and an assignee of the receivable. The case for applying *Dearle v Hall* to the priority conflict raised in the text is even stronger in that while the equitable tracing right of the original supplier does in a sense arise as a matter of law rather than of contract, it is the supplier himself who chose the form of his interest, by imposing the accounting obligation in the sale contract, and if he chooses to leave himself with an equitable interest in receivables knowing that they may very well be disposed of to a purchaser for value without notice and in the ordinary course of business, he can hardly complain if the rule in *Dearle v Hall* is applied against him. See further the excellent discussion in Meagher, Gummow and Lehane's *Equity* (4th edn, 2002), paras [8–095] ff.

70 *Compaq Computer Ltd v Abercorn Group Ltd*, n 69; *E. Pfeiffer Weinkellerei-Weineinkauf GmbH & Co v Arbuthnot Factors Ltd* [1988] 1 WLR 150. For an argument to the contrary, see Fidelis Oditah, 'Priorities: Equitable versus Legal Assignments of Book Debts' (1989) 9 OJLS 521.

71 See Peter M. Biscoe, *Credit Factoring* (1975), p 143, citing the dictum of Lord Denning MR in *Rolls Razor Ltd v Cox* [1967] 1 QB 552 at 568 that a person could not be a common law factor unless he sold in his own name.

72 Biscoe, *Credit Factoring*, p 143; Salinger, *Factoring Law*, para 8–62.

73 For a discussion of international factoring, see Salinger, *Factoring Law*, ch 12. The 1988 UNIDROIT Convention on International Factoring is designed to remove impediments to international factoring. The Acts and Proceedings of the Diplomatic Conference at Ottawa, at which the Convention was signed, have been published in two volumes by UNIDROIT.

Dated   2001

FIRST NATIONAL MOTOR PLC
of
3 Princess Way
Redhill
Surrey
RH1 1UR
("the Company")

- and -

("the Dealer")

NEW AND USED
VEHICLE PURCHASE AGENCY AND SALES
AGREEMENT

Fig 29.1 Vehicle stocking plan

754

CONTENTS

AGREEMENT dated the   day of   2003

BETWEEN:-

(1)   **FIRST NATIONAL MOTOR PLC**, company number 2248924, the address of which is confirmed on the front cover of this agreement; and

(2)   **THE DEALER,** the name and address of whom is confirmed on the front cover of this agreement.

WHEREAS:-

(A)   The Company has agreed with the Dealer to appoint the Dealer its agent to enter into Purchase Contracts on behalf of the Company for the purchase of Vehicles and to make payments in respect thereof on the Company's behalf subject to and on the terms and conditions of this Agreement.

(B)   The Company has agreed that the Dealer may display Purchased Vehicles (as defined below) in its premises for the purpose of making them available for sale and in return the Dealer has agreed to pay certain charges to the Company.

(C)   The Company has agreed to make a standing offer to sell to the Dealer Purchased Vehicles and the Dealer has agreed to make a standing offer to the Company to purchase from the Company Purchased Vehicles subject to the terms of this Agreement. The Dealer has also agreed to purchase any Purchased Vehicles which are Demonstrators.

IT IS AGREED as follows:-

1.   **DEFINITIONS AND INTERPRETATION**

1.1   In this Agreement:-

"APAK" means the computer software interface systems which have been selected by the Company for giving effect to the purchase of Vehicles by the Dealer as agent for the Company and their subsequent offer for sale by the Company to the Dealer and purchase by the Dealer as hereafter provided;

"Bank Account" means the bank account of the Dealer nominated by the Dealer as the bank account to be credited with payments by the Company and direct debited by the Company under the terms of this Agreement;

"Base Rate" means the Finance House Base Rate from time to time quoted by or on behalf of the Finance and Leasing Association Limited as its base rate, or, if no rate of interest is quoted as such, the rate of interest from time to time certified by the Company as being the rate which members of the Finance and Leasing Association use in London as the base for determining rates of interest charged to customers;

"Business Day" means a day (not being a Saturday or Sunday) on which banks are open in London for the transaction of business;

"Clean Guide Value" means the clean condition trade guide price for a used Vehicle in the Price Guide Book current at the date of purchase of the Vehicle by the Dealer as agent of the Company;

"Corporation Tax" means corporation tax chargeable in the context of a scheme of taxation applied to UK resident companies generally at the rate applicable to such companies or Tax of a similar nature enacted in addition to or in substitution for corporation tax;

"Defective Vehicle" means any vehicle which does not comply with the Road Vehicles (Construction and Use) Regulations 1986 (as amended) or which otherwise is unsafe or suffers from any design or manufacturing defect which makes it potentially unsafe;

"Demonstrator" means a used Vehicle to be purchased by the Company which in addition to being available for sale on the Dealer's premises is also to be used as a demonstrator and/or courtesy and/or business support vehicle by the Dealer in the ordinary course of its business and which is designated as such by the Dealer to the Company via APAK pursuant to Clause 3.3;

"Demonstrator Vehicle Purchase Available Amount" means at any time the sum of the financial limit in respect of Demonstrators notified to the Dealer by the Company in the Offer Letter minus the aggregate of all Demonstrator Payments;

"Demonstrator Payments" means at any time, the aggregate of:

(a)   all amounts paid or payable by the Company to the Dealer under Clause 5.1 of this Agreement by way of reimbursement of the purchase price in respect of Demonstrators which the Dealer has purchased pursuant to Clause 4 where the purchase price has been paid by the Dealer on the Company's behalf (but which have not at that time been sold by the Company to, and paid for by, the Dealer pursuant to this Agreement); and

(b)   any payments made by the Company to the Dealer in respect of a Defective Vehicle which is a Demonstrator which have not at that time been repaid to the Company pursuant to Clause 4.9 of this Agreement or Clause 4.8 of the Stock Purchase Agreement (as the case may be); and

(c)   any payments for display charges payable by the Dealer under this Agreement or the Stock Purchase Agreement in respect of Demonstrators which were dishonoured or otherwise returned when first presented and which remain outstanding; and

(d)   Demonstrator Stock Purchase Payments.

"Deposit" means the deposit paid or to be paid by the Dealer to the Company in respect of a Purchased Vehicle in accordance with Clauses 10.1 and 10.2;

"Instalments" means, in respect of a Sale Contract for a Demonstrator, the instalments of the purchase price paid or payable by the Dealer for the Demonstrator under the Sale Contract and "Instalment" shall be construed accordingly;

"Irrecoverable VAT" means any amount paid or payable by or on behalf of the Company in respect of Value Added Tax under this Agreement to the extent that the Company does not or will not receive and retain a credit (whether by way of set-off or repayment) for that amount as "input tax" (as that expression is defined in Section 24(1) of VATA) under Sections 24, 25 and 26 of VATA nor receives and retains a credit for it under any similar or equivalent legislation;

"Margin" means such percentage as notified to the Dealer by the Company in the Offer Letter;

"New Stock Purchase Payments" means at any time the aggregate of all amounts paid or payable by the Company to the Dealer under Clause 5.1 of the Stock Purchase Agreement in respect of the purchase price of the Dealer's stock of new Vehicles purchased by the Company under the Stock Purchase Agreement (but which have not at that time been sold by the Company to, and paid for by, the Dealer under the Stock Purchase Agreement).

"New Vehicle Purchase Available Amount" means at any time the sum of the financial limit in respect of new Vehicles notified to the Dealer by the Company in the Offer Letter minus the aggregate of all New Vehicle Payments.

"New Vehicle Payments" means at any time, the aggregate of:-

(a)   all amounts paid or payable by the Company to the Dealer under Clause 5.1 of this Agreement by way of reimbursement of the purchase price in respect of new Vehicles which the Dealer has purchased pursuant to Clause 4 where the purchase price has been paid by the Dealer on the Company's behalf (but which have not at that time been sold by the Company to, and paid for by, the Dealer pursuant to this Agreement); and

(b)   any payments made by the Company to the Dealer in respect of a new Defective Vehicle which have not at that time been repaid to the Company pursuant to Clause 4.9 of this Agreement or Clause 4.8 of the Stock Purchase Agreement (as the case may be); and

(c)   any payments for display charges payable by the Dealer under this Agreement or the Stock Purchase Agreement in respect of new Vehicles which were dishonoured or otherwise returned when first presented and which remain outstanding; and

(d)   New Stock Purchase Payments.

"Offer Letter" means the letter issued by the Company offering the arrangements described in this Agreement (as may be amended, varied or supplemented from time to time);

"Price Guide Book" means the book of used car guide prices compiled monthly by CAP Nationwide Motor Research Limited or such other appropriate book of used car guide prices as the Company may choose from time to time;

"Purchase Contract" means a contract for the purchase of a Vehicle entered into after the date hereof by the Dealer as agent on behalf of the Company as purchaser and a third party selected by the Dealer as seller being in conformity with the Stipulated Purchase Terms;

"Purchased Vehicles" means at any time each and every Vehicle which the Dealer has on behalf of the Company purchased pursuant to Clause 4 and which has not then been sold by the Company to, and paid for by, the Dealer pursuant to this Agreement and shall for the avoidance of doubt include any Demonstrator;

"Records" means all log books, registration documents, test certificates, manuals, technical and maintenance records and handbooks relating to a Vehicle;

"Sale Contract" means a contract for the sale of a Purchased Vehicle entered into after the date hereof pursuant to Clauses 8, 9 or 15.4 by the Company as seller and the Dealer as buyer being in conformity with the Stipulated Sale Terms;

"Stipulated Purchase Terms" means the terms set out in Schedule 1 upon which Purchase Contracts are required to be made;

"Stipulated Sale Terms" means the terms set out in Schedule 2;

"Stock Purchase Agreement" means the Stock Purchase and Sales Agreement of today's date between the Dealer and the Company;

"Tax" means all present and future taxes, charges, imposts, duties or levies of any kind whatsoever, or any amount payable on account of or as security for any of the foregoing, payable at the instance of or imposed by any statutory, governmental, international, state, federal, provincial, local or municipal authority, agency, body or department whatsoever or any European Community institution, in each case whether in the United Kingdom or elsewhere, together with any penalties, additions, fines, surcharges or interest relating thereto and "Taxes" shall be construed accordingly;

"Tax Liability" means in respect of the Company:-

(a)   any liability or any increase in the liability of that person to make any payment or payments of or in respect of Tax;

(b)   the loss or setting-off against income profits or gains or against any liability to make a payment or payments of or in respect of Tax of any relief, allowance, deduction or credit ("a Relief") which would otherwise have been available to that person; and

(c)   the loss or setting-off against any Tax Liability of a right to repayment of Tax which would otherwise have been available to that person;

and in a case falling within (b) or (c) above the amount that is to be treated as a Tax Liability ("the Deemed Tax Liability") shall be determined as follows:-

(i)   in a case which falls within (b) above and where the Relief that was the subject of the loss or setting-off was or would have been a deduction from or offset against the Tax the Deemed Tax Liability shall be the amount of that Relief;

(ii)   in a case which falls within (b) above and which involves the loss of a Relief which would otherwise have been available as a deduction from or offset against gross income profits or gains the Deemed Tax Liability shall be the amount of Tax which would (on the basis of the Tax rates current at the date of the loss and assuming that the person has sufficient gross income profits or gains to utilise the Relief) have been saved but for the loss of the Relief;

(iii)   in a case which falls within (b) above and which involves the setting off of a Relief which would otherwise have been available as a deduction from or offset against gross income profits or gains the Deemed Tax Liability shall be the amount of Tax which has been or will be saved in consequence of the setting-off;

(iv)   in a case which falls within (c) above the Deemed Tax Liability shall be the amount of the repayment that would have been obtained but for the loss or setting-off.

For the purposes of this definition any question of whether any relief, allowance, deduction, credit or right to repayment of tax has been lost or set-off and if so the date on which that loss or set-off took place shall be conclusively determined by the Company;

"Used Stock Purchase Payments" means at any time the aggregate of all amounts paid or payable by the Company to the Dealer under Clause 5.1 of the Stock Purchase Agreement in respect of the purchase price of the Dealer's stock of used Vehicles purchased by the Company under the Stock Purchase Agreement (but which have not at that time been sold by the Company to, and paid for by, the Dealer under the Stock Purchase Agreement).

"Used Vehicle Purchase Available Amount" means at any time the sum of the financial limit in respect of used Vehicles notified to the Dealer by the Company in the Offer Letter minus the aggregate of all Used Vehicle Payments.

"Used Vehicle Payments" means at any time the aggregate of:

(a)   all amounts paid or payable by the Company to the Dealer under Clause 5.1 of this Agreement by way of reimbursement of the purchase price in respect of used Vehicles which the Dealer has purchased pursuant to Clause 4 where the purchase price has been paid by the Dealer on the Company's behalf (but which have not at that time been sold by the Company to, and paid for by, the Dealer pursuant to this Agreement); and

(b)   any payments made by the Company to the Dealer in respect of a used Defective Vehicle which have not at that time been repaid to the Company pursuant to Clause 4.9 of this Agreement or Clause 4.8 of the Stock Purchase Agreement (as the case may be); and

(c)   any payments for display charges payable by the Dealer under this Agreement or the Stock Purchase Agreement in respect of used Vehicles which were dishonoured or otherwise returned when first presented and which remain outstanding; and

(d)   Used Stock Purchase Payments.

"Value Added Tax" means value added tax as provided for in VATA and any tax similar or equivalent to value added tax imposed by any country other than the United Kingdom and any similar or turnover tax replacing or introduced in addition to any of the same;

"VATA" means the Value Added Tax Act 1994 and legislation (or purported legislation and whether delegated or otherwise) supplemental thereto;

"Vehicle" means any motor vehicle of a kind normally used on public roads (other than a Defective Vehicle) which has at least four wheels and includes any vehicles (other than a Defective Vehicle) in respect of which the Company makes a reimbursement payment to the Dealer pursuant to Clause 5 and any reference to a Vehicle includes a reference to the Records relating thereto.

1.2   Any reference in this Agreement to:-

      (a)   an "encumbrance" shall be construed as a reference to a mortgage, charge, pledge, lien, retention of title Clause, right of tracing or other encumbrance securing any obligation of any person;

      (b)   a "person" shall be construed as a reference to any person, firm, company or corporation or any association or partnership (whether or not having separate legal personality) of two or more of the foregoing;

      (c)   words importing the singular shall include the plural and vice versa;

      (d)   a statutory provision shall include a reference to any modification or re-enactment of that provision for the time being in force;

      (e)   a sub-Clause is, unless otherwise stated, a reference to a sub-Clause of the Clause in which the reference appears; and

      (f)   a new Vehicle means a Vehicle which is unregistered and has a recorded mileage of less than 100 miles at the time purchased by the Company pursuant to this Agreement and, for the avoidance of doubt, any Vehicle which is not a new Vehicle shall be and shall be deemed to be a used Vehicle.

1.3   Clause headings are for convenience only and shall not affect the interpretation of the terms contained in the Clause concerned.

1.4   References in this Agreement to any provision of any statute shall be construed as including a reference to any statutory modification or re-enactment thereof for the time being in force.

1.5 References in this Agreement to Clauses and to Schedules are to Clauses of, and Schedules to this Agreement.

2. **CONDITIONS PRECEDENT**

2.1 The Company's agreement to appoint the Dealer as its agent for purchasing Vehicles and to make a standing offer to sell Purchased Vehicles to the Dealer upon and subject to the terms of this Agreement is subject to the prior receipt by the Company of the following in the form and substance acceptable to the Company:-

   (a) an original of this Agreement duly executed by the Dealer;

   (b) the security documents (if any) which the Company may require the Dealer to complete to secure the Dealer's obligations and liabilities under this Agreement;

   (c) if the Dealer is a limited company, a certified copy of a resolution of the Board of Directors of the Dealer authorising acceptance of the terms and conditions of this Agreement and the execution by the Dealer of this Agreement and, as may be required, authorising the execution of the security documents (and any related documents) referred to in paragraph (b) above (if any);

   (d) if the Dealer is a limited company, the Memorandum and Articles of Association of the Dealer, certified as up to date by the Secretary or a Director of the Dealer (including if relevant copies of all amending resolutions) and if the Dealer is a partnership, a copy of the Deed of Partnership of the Dealer certified as up to date by one of the partners of the Dealer (including if relevant copies of all amendments); and

   (e) a copy of the Dealer's Consumer Credit Licence in form and substance satisfactory to the Company.

2.2 The conditions precedent detailed in Clause 2.1 must be satisfied by no later than:

   (a) the date falling 14 days after the date of this Agreement where the Company does not require security as specified in Clause 2.1(b); or

   (b) the date falling 3 months after the date of this Agreement where the Company does require security as specified in Clause 2.1(b);

   or in either case, such later date as the Company may agree.

3. **AGENCY PURCHASES AND REIMBURSEMENT, OFFERS FOR SALE AND ACCEPTANCE - APAK**

3.1 The Dealer will operate APAK for giving effect to the arrangements set out in this Clause 3 and Clauses 4, 7 and 8 of this Agreement at all times in accordance with instructions issued by the Company from time to time.

3.2 The Dealer and the Company will use APAK for the purposes of recording details and the purchase price of each Vehicle purchased by the Dealer as agent for the Company, claiming the reimbursement required by the Dealer of the expenditure disbursed in such purchases and issuing the Dealer's composite invoice to the Company in respect of such purchases. Details will be recorded by the Dealer on the purchase of each Vehicle as agent in accordance with Clause 4.

3.3 The Dealer shall when first recording details of the vehicle on APAK pursuant to Clause 3.2 designate as a Demonstrator any Vehicle which in addition to being available for sale on the Dealer's premises is or is to be used as a demonstration and/or courtesy and/or business support vehicle by the Dealer in the ordinary course of its business, and the Company and the Dealer will also respectively use APAK for the purposes of recording details of the Deposit paid by the Dealer in respect of each Purchased Vehicle and acceptances under Clauses 8 and 9 hereof in respect of Purchased Vehicles for which a standing offer of sale or purchase (as the case may be) by the other applies under each of such Clauses.

3.4   In the event that APAK shall cease to function or shall not function to the satisfaction of the Company all recordings, claims, notifications, invoices and other operations required to be effected through APAK under this Agreement shall be effected in such manner as the Company shall notify to the Dealer.

4.   **APPOINTMENT OF THE DEALER AS AGENT OF THE COMPANY TO PURCHASE VEHICLES**

4.1   With effect from the satisfaction of the condition precedent detailed in Clause 2 and in full reliance upon each of the representations and warranties set out in Clause 17 the Company authorises the Dealer upon and subject to the terms of this Agreement on behalf of and as the Company's agent:-

(a)   to bind the Company under and to cause the Company as purchaser to enter into Purchase Contracts with third parties (selected by the Dealer) as seller;

(b)   to arrange all matters relating to the transfer of title to, and delivery of Purchased Vehicles;

(c)   to accept delivery of Vehicles under Purchase Contracts;

(d)   to sign in its own name, as undisclosed agent of the Company, all contracts, delivery receipts and certificates relating to the purchase and delivery of Vehicles under Purchase Contracts; and

(e)   to be responsible to the sellers under all Purchase Contracts for settling sums due thereunder.

4.2   The agency given by the Company to the Dealer pursuant to Clause 4.1 shall be undisclosed and the Dealer undertakes not to disclose the said agency to any third party.

4.3   The Dealer represents and warrants that it will not pursuant to this Agreement cause the Company to enter into any Purchase Contract (or to incur any liability or additional liability under any Purchase Contract) if:-

(a)   in the case of a new Vehicle, used Vehicle or Demonstrator the monetary liability of the Company under the Purchase Contract (or such liability or additional liability) would cause the then current New Vehicle Purchase Available Amount, the Used Vehicle Purchase Available Amount or Demonstrator Vehicle Purchase Available Amount to be exceeded;

(b)   the terms of the Purchase Contract would not be in accordance with the Stipulated Purchase Terms;

(c)   any of the events specified in Clauses 15.1 or 15.2(a)-(e) inclusive shall have occurred;

(d)   the purchase price of the Vehicle (being a used Vehicle) exceeds such percentage of the Clean Guide Value for the Vehicle as notified to the Dealer by the Company in the Offer Letter;

(e)   the purchase price of the Vehicle (being a new Vehicle) is not the actual wholesale price paid by the Dealer; or

(f)   the purchase price of the Vehicle (being a new Vehicle) is more than the percentage notified to the Dealer by the Company in the Offer Letter of the manufacturer's recommended retail price (including any factory fitted options) of the Vehicle.

4.4   The Dealer further represents and warrants that it will not cause the Company to enter into any Purchase Contract in respect of any of the following:-

(a)   vehicles capable of accommodating only one person or suitable for carrying twelve or more persons;

(b)   vehicles of more than three and a half tonnes gross vehicle weight;

(c)   caravans, ambulances and prison vans;

(d)   vehicles of a type approved by the Assistant Commissioner of Police of the Metropolis as conforming to the conditions of fitness for the time being laid down by him for the purposes of the London Cab Order 1934;

(e)   vehicles constructed for a special purpose other than the carriage of persons except for light commercial vehicles;

(f)   vehicles that are more than an age notified to the Dealer by the Company in the Offer Letter at the date of the prospective agency purchase by the Dealer;

(g)   vehicles which have been previously treated as a total loss by an insurance company and which have been registered as such with the Department of Vehicle Licensing and Registration and/or with H.P. Information PLC;

(h)   vehicles with a Clean Guide Value exceeding the maximum amount, or less than the minimum amount, in each case as notified to the Dealer by the Company in the Offer Letter; or

(i)   vehicles with a recorded mileage exceeding the mileage as notified to the Dealer by the Company in the Offer Letter;

4.5   The Dealer agrees to perform on behalf of the Company each and every obligation, direct or indirect, of the Company and to discharge each and every liability or responsibility of the Company resulting directly or indirectly to the Company as a result of, pursuant to or in connection with the Purchase Contracts and each of them, including, but not limited to, making all payments (together with any Value Added Tax) on behalf of the Company upon the due date and in all respects in accordance with the relevant Purchase Contract. The Dealer agrees that upon causing the Company to enter into any Purchase Contract, it will act as the Company's agent in carrying out all the actions referred to in Clause 4.1(b) to (e) inclusive.

4.6   As soon as practicable after (but in any event within 5 Business Days of) causing the Company to enter into any Purchase Contract pursuant to Clause 4.1, the Dealer shall use APAK to enter details of that Purchase Contract, including details of the Vehicle and the purchase price.

4.7   In addition to the Dealer's obligations under Clause 4.6 the Dealer shall keep and make available to the Company (and its auditors) on request copies of all sales and purchase invoices of any Vehicles purchased by the Dealer under this Agreement and the Dealer shall keep the Company informed of all material matters in relation to Purchase Contracts and on

"Used Vehicle Payments" means at any time the aggregate of "Used

request report as to all matters arising thereunder. The Dealer shall take all steps as the Company may request to enforce all Purchase Contracts.

4.8 If the Dealer enters into a contract to buy a Vehicle on behalf of the Company in breach of any representation or warranty made by the Dealer to the Company under this Agreement, title to such Vehicle shall nevertheless vest in the Company in accordance with the relevant Purchase Contract and, notwithstanding anything to the contrary, any reimbursement payment made to the Dealer pursuant to Clause 5 in respect of such Vehicle shall be without prejudice to any claim the Company may have against the Dealer in respect of such breach.

4.9 For the avoidance of doubt, if the Dealer purchases a Defective Vehicle, such purchase shall be a purchase by the Dealer on its own account and not on behalf of the Company. If, however, the Company has made or makes any payment to the Dealer in respect of a Defective Vehicle, the Dealer shall repay such amount to the Company immediately on demand together with interest at the aggregate of Base Rate plus Margin calculated on a daily basis on the outstanding amount from the date of payment by the Company to the Dealer to the date of repayment (as well after as before judgment).

5. **REIMBURSEMENT PAYMENTS**

5.1 Provided that:-

(a) the Dealer has recorded details of its purchase as agent of each Purchased Vehicle (including the identity of the seller) and has notified the Company of its claim for reimbursement by operating APAK in accordance with Clause 4.6 and the instructions issued by the Company under Clause 3.1 of this Agreement;

(b) the amount claimed by way of reimbursement in respect of a new Vehicle, used Vehicle or Demonstrator does not exceed the New Vehicle Purchase Available Amount, the Used Vehicle Purchase Available Amount or the Demonstrator Vehicle Purchase Available Amount and would not cause the New Vehicle Purchase Available Amount, the Used Vehicle Purchase Available Amount or the Demonstrator Vehicle Purchase Available Amount to be exceeded;

(c) none of the events specified in Clauses 15.1 or 15.2(a)-(e) inclusive have occurred;

(d) the Dealer shall have paid all sums which it is required to pay under this Agreement; and

(e) the Dealer shall have provided evidence satisfactory to the Company of compliance with the insurance requirements under Clause 6.3 in respect of the relevant Vehicle

the Company shall pay to the Dealer by way of reimbursement in accordance with Clause 5.2 for each such Purchased Vehicle the amount invoiced to the Company in the composite invoice issued via APAK together with any Value Added Tax payable thereon less an amount equal to any Deposit (or in the case of a Demonstrator the initial Instalment) payable by the Dealer for each such Purchased Vehicle which shall be deducted from the full amount otherwise payable by the Company.

5.2 Each payment by way of reimbursement to be made by the Company under Clause 5.1 shall be made in sterling by Bankers Automated Clearing Services (BACS) and will be credited to the Bank Account by the third Business Day following issue of the composite invoice.

5.3 Each claim for reimbursement notified via APAK by the Dealer in respect of the purchase of a Vehicle under Clause 4 shall constitute a representation and warranty by the Dealer to the Company that:-

(a) the relevant Purchase Contract is in conformity with the Stipulated Purchase Terms, and constitutes the legal valid binding and enforceable obligations of the relevant seller;

(b) the relevant Purchase Contract is a bona fide contract for the sale of goods and that the relevant seller owned the relevant Vehicle free from encumbrances of any nature and passed good title thereto to the Company free of all encumbrances;

(c) the Dealer is not aware of and has no reason to suspect that there may arise any dispute or claim of any kind in respect of the relevant Vehicle or Purchase Contract;

(d) the relevant Vehicle is not a Defective Vehicle and is in good order, repair and condition and complies in all respect with the provisions of the law and this Agreement; and

(e) the Dealer has complied with Clause 4.6 in respect of that Vehicle.

6. STORAGE MAINTENANCE DISPLAY AND INSURANCE ARRANGEMENTS

6.1 Storage and Maintenance

From the time any Purchased Vehicle is delivered to the Dealer as the Company's agent under a Purchase Contract the Dealer shall comply with the following obligations in relation to such Purchased Vehicle:-

(a) safely store and keep secure Purchased Vehicles and all Records relating thereto on the Dealer's own premises and, if the Company shall so request, deliver any specified Purchased Vehicles to premises specified by the Company and make them available to the Company for inspection save that the Dealer shall be entitled to use Demonstrators in the ordinary course of its business for demonstration purposes and/or as a courtesy Vehicle and/or as a business support Vehicle;

(b) comply with the Company's directions from time to time in making arrangements with all appropriate authorities (including H.P. Information PLC) to ensure that the Company is registered as the owner of Purchased Vehicles and that all steps are taken to identify Purchased Vehicles as being the Company's property which are necessary or desirable in the Company's opinion;

(c) ensure that Purchased Vehicles are operated only in a skilful and proper manner and in accordance with all laws and all operating instructions and recommendations of the manufacturers and suppliers, and ensure that Purchased Vehicles are operated only by properly qualified skilled and trained personnel;

(d) maintain each Purchased Vehicle at all times in good roadworthy condition and in working order properly serviced and in compliance with manufacturer's and suppliers' recommendations, legal requirements and with all policies of insurance required pursuant to this Agreement and in particular but without limitation ensure that each Purchased Vehicle is in compliance with the Road Vehicles (Construction and Use) Regulations l986 (as amended);

(e) repair all damage to Purchased Vehicles at the Dealer's own cost (not being damage constituting destruction or total loss);

(f) not remove any parts from Purchased Vehicles unless the parts are as soon as practicable replaced by an appropriate replacement part;

(g) not alter Purchased Vehicles except in compliance with paragraphs (d), (e) and (f) above;

(h)   keep accurate complete and current records of all use, operation, maintenance, servicing, repairs and replacements in relation to Purchased Vehicles and make such records available to the Company on request;

(i)   not remove Purchased Vehicles from the Dealer's own premises in the United Kingdom except to the extent necessary for demonstration purposes in the United Kingdom to enable them to be offered for sale and except in accordance with arrangements approved by the Company from time to time and in any event the Dealer shall ensure that the mileage of a Purchased Vehicle does not increase by more than 100 miles in the case of new Vehicles 1000 miles in the case of used Vehicles or 15,000 miles in the case of Demonstrators (or such other mileage as may be notified by the Company from time to time) from the Purchased Vehicle's mileage at the date it was purchased by the Company;

(j)   obtain and maintain all permissions, licences and permits from time to time required in connection with the Dealer's business or Purchased Vehicles or the purchase, ownership, delivery, possession, operation, maintenance, import, sale or export of Purchased Vehicles and to comply with all statutory and other obligations in relation to Purchased Vehicles and their use;

(k)   protect Purchased Vehicles against distress, execution or seizure and on all occasions when ownership of Purchased Vehicles is relevant to make it clear that they are the Company's property (but subject to Clause 4.2); and

(l)   clean and valet Purchased Vehicles at frequent intervals for the purposes of display in accordance with Clause 6.2.

6.2   Display

The Company agrees that the Dealer may display each Purchased Vehicle as available for sale on the Dealer's premises, and that Purchased Vehicles shall be displayed in the same manner as vehicles owned by the Dealer and displayed as available for sale save that in addition the Dealer shall be entitled to use Demonstrators in the ordinary course of its business for demonstration purposes and/or as a courtesy Vehicle and/or as a business support Vehicle. In consideration of the Company so agreeing, the Dealer agrees to pay the display charges plus Value Added Tax set out in Clause 7.

6.3   Insurance

From the time a Vehicle becomes a Purchased Vehicle, the Dealer shall:-

(a)   be fully responsible for all loss or damage to the whole or any part of any of the Purchased Vehicles for whatever reason including loss or damage caused by third parties and the Dealer shall indemnify the Company in respect thereof;

(b)   obtain and maintain from such insurance company as the Company may approve ("the Insurer") a fully comprehensive motor insurance policy which meets with the Company's prior approval ("the Policy") in respect of Purchased Vehicles, such Policy to insure each Purchased Vehicle to the Company's reasonable satisfaction and to its full purchase price against all risks covered. The Policy shall:-

    (i)   by means of endorsement, note the Company's interest; and

    (ii)   provide, by means of endorsement in a form and manner satisfactory to the Company, that in respect of the Company's interest in the Policy, the Policy shall not be invalidated by any action, inaction, misrepresentation or non-disclosure of the Dealer or any other person.

(c)   pay all insurance premiums on time in respect of the above insurance and will show the certificate of insurance and premium receipt to the Company when requested to do so.

6.4   The Company and the Dealer hereby agree that:-

(a)   in the event of a claim against the Insurer in respect of a Purchased Vehicle, the Dealer shall not commit any act or omission that would prejudice any entitlement the Company may have in respect of a Purchased Vehicle and the Company reserves the right to assume conduct of all negotiations with the Insurer in the assessment and settlement of liability and/or quantum; and

(b)   in the event of a dispute with the Insurer of any matter arising out of or in connection with the Policy, the Company reserves the right to assume the conduct of the dispute on its own and the Dealer's behalf and to direct appointment of any legal or professional adviser whose fees shall be paid by the Dealer.

6.5   The Dealer agrees that at no expense to the Company it will keep on the Company's behalf all such records and accounts which the Company may be required to keep for the purposes of the Value Added Tax (Cars) Order l992 and Value Added Tax Notice No. 718.

7.   **DISPLAY CHARGES**

7.1   The display charges payable by the Dealer to the Company as referred to in Clause 6.2 shall be calculated in accordance with this Clause 7.

7.2   Display charges in respect of each Purchased Vehicle shall accrue on a daily basis commencing on the date on which the Company makes payment to the Dealer under Clause 5.1 by way of reimbursement of the purchase price for that Purchased Vehicle and ending on the date the Company receives payment in full from the Dealer of all sums due under Clause 10 and under and pursuant to Clauses 15.3(e) and 15.4 in respect of that Purchased Vehicle.

7.3   The amount of the daily display charge in respect of each Purchased Vehicle on any day shall be:-

$$\frac{BR + M}{365} \times P$$

where:-

BR is the Base Rate on that day (subject to a minimum Base Rate to be notified to the Dealer by the Company in the Offer Letter)

M is the Margin, and

P has the meaning given to it in the Offer Letter.

7.4   The Company will submit monthly invoices for the display charges to the Dealer and the Dealer shall pay display charges plus Value Added Tax in arrears on the tenth day of each calendar month by the Company debiting from the Bank Account the amount shown on the relevant invoice.

8.   **THE COMPANY'S STANDING OFFER TO SELL PURCHASED VEHICLES TO THE DEALER**

8.1   Subject to Clause 2, the Company hereby offers to sell to the Dealer any Purchased Vehicle (other than a Demonstrator) in respect of which the Dealer (as seller acting on its own account) may from time to time have entered into a sale contract with a third party as buyer. Such offer is made on the terms set out in the following provisions of this Clause 8 and subject to the payment of the Deposit for such relevant Purchased Vehicle as specified in Clause 10. The Dealer shall notify the Company promptly upon entering into any such sale contract with a third party as buyer.

8.2 This offer is a standing offer which may be accepted by the Dealer in relation to any Purchased Vehicle (other than a Demonstrator) by notifying the Company via APAK (or by such other means as the Company directs) of the Dealer's acceptance and identifying the relevant Purchased Vehicle through the appropriate input to APAK in such form as the Company may from time to time stipulate giving full details of the Purchased Vehicle to which it relates, together with such additional documentation and information as the Company may from time to time stipulate.

8.3 Receipt by the Company of an acceptance under Clause 8.2 together with such documentation referred to therein shall constitute an agreement by the Company to sell and by the Dealer to purchase the Purchased Vehicles specified therein on the Stipulated Sale Terms and the Company and the Dealer shall be deemed to have entered into a Sale Contract for such Purchased Vehicles.

8.4 The purchase price (excluding Value Added Tax) of any Purchased Vehicle sold by the Company to the Dealer pursuant to this Clause 8 shall be equal to the purchase price (excluding Value Added Tax) of that Purchased Vehicle paid (or payable) by the Company under the Purchase Contract relating to that Purchased Vehicle. The Dealer shall make payment of the purchase price in accordance with Clause 10.

8.5 Save in relation to any Purchased Vehicle in respect of which this offer may have previously been accepted, the Company may at any time by written notice forthwith withdraw or vary this offer as it thinks fit.

8.6 Upon entering into any Sale Contract with the Company the Dealer shall use APAK to record the fact that the relevant Purchased Vehicle has been sold.

9. **THE DEALER'S AGREEMENT TO PURCHASE DEMONSTRATORS AND STANDING OFFER TO PURCHASE OTHER PURCHASED VEHICLES FROM THE COMPANY**

9.1 With effect from the Dealer designating a Vehicle as a Demonstrator via APAK in accordance with Clause 3.3, the Dealer agrees to purchase and the Company agrees to sell such Vehicle to the Dealer on and subject to the Stipulated Sale Terms (as they apply to Demonstrators).

9.2 The Dealer hereby offers to purchase from the Company any Purchased Vehicles in respect of which no Sale Contract has been concluded pursuant to Clause 8 within 180 days or such other period as notified to the Dealer by the Company in the Offer Letter in the case of new Vehicles or within 120 days in the case of used Vehicles (or in either case such other period as notified in writing by the Company to the Dealer) after the date such Purchased Vehicle was purchased by the Company and the Dealer further hereby offers to purchase from the Company at any time any Purchased Vehicles which were Vehicles the Dealer contracted to buy on behalf of the Company either in breach of any representation or warranty made by the Dealer to the Company under this Agreement or otherwise in breach of this Agreement.

9.3 Each offer referred to in Clause 9.2 is a standing offer which may be accepted in relation to any Purchased Vehicle by the Company notifying the Dealer via APAK of the Company's acceptance and identifying the relevant Purchased Vehicle through the appropriate input to APAK.

9.4 The notification via APAK by the Company of such acceptance shall constitute an agreement by the Dealer to purchase and by the Company to sell the Purchased Vehicles specified therein on the Stipulated Sale Terms and the Dealer and the Company shall be deemed to have entered into a Sale Contract for such Purchased Vehicles.

9.5 The purchase price (excluding Value Added Tax) of any Purchased Vehicle sold by the Company to the Dealer pursuant to Clause 9 shall be equal to the purchase price (excluding Value Added Tax) of that Purchased Vehicle paid (or payable) by the Company under the Purchase Contract relating to that Purchased Vehicle. The Dealer shall make payment of the purchase price in accordance with Clause 10.

9.6 Each offer referred to in Clause 9.2 is irrevocable and may not be withdrawn by the Dealer at any time.

10. **PAYMENT OF DEPOSIT/INSTALMENTS AND BALANCE OF THE PURCHASE PRICE BY THE DEALER**

10.1 The Dealer shall be obliged to pay to the Company, at the time specified in Clause 10.2, a Deposit for each Purchased Vehicle (other than a Demonstrator) which is a used Vehicle in an amount (if any) calculated as notified to the Dealer by the Company in the Offer Letter, such Deposit representing a down payment by the Dealer towards the anticipated future acquisition of the relevant Purchased Vehicle by the Dealer from the Company on an acceptance by the Dealer of the Company's standing offer under Clause 8 or on an acceptance by the Company of the Dealer's standing offer under Clause 9. The Company may also apply such Deposit towards an acquisition of a Purchased Vehicle by the Dealer pursuant to Clause 15.4. Unless the Company notifies the Dealer to the contrary, no Deposit shall be payable in respect of Purchased Vehicles which are new Vehicles.

10.2 The Deposit payable for each Purchased Vehicle (other than a Demonstrator) shall be paid by the Dealer on the day the Dealer is paid by the Company in respect of the relevant Purchased Vehicles under Clause 5.2 and the Dealer hereby authorises the Company to deduct the amount of the relevant Deposit from the amount to be paid to the Dealer for a Purchased Vehicle as specified in Clause 5.1.

10.3 The Dealer shall pay the Instalments for each Demonstrator to the Company (together with any Value Added Tax) as notified from time to time by payment being made from the Bank Account by direct debit initiated by the Company through APAK.

10.4 The Dealer shall pay to the Company the balance of the purchase price (taking account of any Deposit already paid and which has not already been set off (in whole or in part) in respect of any other amount due from the Dealer) of each Purchased Vehicle (other than a Demonstrator) and taking account of any Instalments already paid and which has not already been set off (in whole or in part) in respect of any other amount due from the Dealer) of each Demonstrator in respect of which a Sale Contract has been entered into (together with any Value Added Tax) by payment being made from the Bank Account by direct debit initiated by the Company through APAK on or before the third Business Day following the recording of the Company's acceptance under Clause 9.2 above or the Dealer's acceptance under Clause 8.2 above, as the case may be.

11. **INDEMNITY TO THE COMPANY**

11.1 The Dealer will at all times indemnify the Company and keep it indemnified from and against any action, proceedings, claims and demands which may be brought or made against it and any costs, claims, damages, demands, charges, expenses, liabilities or loss which the Company may suffer, incur or sustain:-

(a)   as a direct or indirect result of any failure by the Dealer fully to comply with the terms of this Agreement; or

(b)   without prejudice to the Company's obligations under this Agreement, as a direct or indirect result of or arising in any way out of the Company becoming a party to any Purchase Contract or Sale Contract; or

(c)   without prejudice to the Company's obligations under this Agreement, as a direct or indirect result of or arising in any way out of the Dealer acting as agent of the Company under this Agreement; or

(d)   as a direct or indirect result of the Dealer exceeding its authority hereunder or disclosing to any third party the agency hereby granted; or

(e)   in connection with the delivery, possession, operation, maintenance, import or export of Purchased Vehicles or by reason of any loss or damage thereto; or

(f)   in respect of or in connection with any Defective Vehicle; or

(g)   without prejudice to the Company's obligations under this Agreement, as a direct or indirect result of any dispute with or claim by or against any seller under any Purchase Contract or any buyer under any Sale Contract.

11.2   The Dealer shall pay and discharge or cause to be paid and discharged, as soon as the same arise or become payable (and shall, if requested by the Company, produce to the Company evidence of the payment and discharge thereof) and indemnify the Company and keep the Company fully indemnified against:-

(a)   any Tax Liabilities; or

(b)   any licence, duties, registration, recording, filing or other fees, charges or levies and any interest or penalties payable in connection with any of the same

which arise or become payable at any time in respect of:-

(A)   the Purchased Vehicles or any interest therein; or

(B)   any document, payment, matter, circumstance or transaction contemplated by this Agreement or by any Purchase Contract or any Sale Contract including (without limitation) the purchase, ownership, possession, operation, storage, maintenance, protection, sale, attempted sale or other disposition of the Vehicles or any interest therein;

or which arise or become payable as a result (whether alone or in connection with any other matter or circumstance) of anything done in response to any request by the Dealer, provided that the Dealer shall not be obliged to indemnify the Company pursuant to this Clause 11.2 against Corporation Tax attributable to any amount actually paid by the Dealer under Clause 7 by way of display charges.

11.3   The indemnities set forth in Clauses 11.1 and 11.2 shall continue in force notwithstanding any termination of the Dealer's agency under this Agreement.

12.   **THE DEALER'S AUTHORITY**

The Dealer shall not have and shall not hold itself out as having authority on behalf of the Company other than as expressly provided in and subject to the terms of this Agreement and the Dealer shall not be entitled to sub-delegate its authority hereunder without the prior written consent of the Company.

13. **LIABILITY OF THE COMPANY**

The Company shall not be liable for any loss or damage (whether direct, indirect or consequential) howsoever arising which may be suffered by the Dealer other than that arising through the Company's wilful default or, in respect of death or personal injury, caused by the Company's negligence and the Dealer shall be liable for and indemnify the Company against any claims, demands or actions made or brought by any third party (including any employee of the Dealer) in respect of any injury or damage occurring as a result of the use of or presence of any Vehicle (and any Defective Vehicle) and for the purpose of this provision, indirect and consequential loss shall include any loss or damage in respect of any loss of profits or income or business of whatever kind.

14. **FURTHER ASSURANCE**

14.1 The Dealer shall from time to time, at the request of the Company and at the Dealer's cost, execute in favour of the Company, or as it may direct, such security or additional security, as the case may be (including assignments, transfers, mortgages, charges or other similar documents) as the Company shall stipulate over the Dealer's estate or interest in any property or assets of whatsoever nature or tenure and wheresoever situate, for the purpose of providing security to the Company for the payment or discharge of any obligations of the Dealer under or in connection with this Agreement.

14.2 The Dealer shall not create or permit to subsist any encumbrance affecting any of its assets or undertaking without the prior written consent of the Company (which shall not be unreasonably withheld).

15. **TERMINATION**

15.1 Either the Dealer or the Company may at any time by notice in writing to the other terminate the authority of the Dealer to act as the Company's agent hereunder. The Company may also give notice of termination to the Dealer at any time by precluding the Dealer from entering details of any further Purchase Contracts or Vehicles on APAK.

15.2 The Company may with immediate effect terminate the Dealer's authority to act as the Company's agent under this Agreement, and the standing offer made by the Company in Clause 8 shall automatically terminate, if:-

(a) the Dealer becomes insolvent or is or is deemed to be unable to pay its debts within the meaning of Section 123 of the Insolvency Act 1986 or an administrative receiver or other receiver or manager is appointed over the whole or any part of its undertaking, business or assets; or

(b) a petition is presented applying to the Court for the winding up of the Dealer or for an administration order to be made in relation to the Dealer or a resolution is passed for its winding up or dissolution or the Dealer enters into any voluntary arrangement with its creditors or ceases or threatens to cease to carry on its business; or

(c) where the Dealer is an individual, an application is made to the court for an interim order to be made in relation to the Dealer or a petition is presented for a bankruptcy order to be made against the Dealer or the Dealer enters into a voluntary arrangement with the Dealer's creditors; or

(d) where the Dealer is a partnership, a petition is presented for its winding up or a petition is presented for a bankruptcy order to be made against one or more of the partners for non-payment of a partnership debt or any one or more of the partners enters into a voluntary arrangement with creditors of the partnership; or

(e)   there occurs a material change in the ownership, control or management of the Dealer from that subsisting at the date of this Agreement or, without prejudice to the generality of the foregoing, the Dealer ceases to be a subsidiary of the company or corporation of which it is a subsidiary at the date of this Agreement and for the purpose of this provision "subsidiary" shall bear the meaning assigned to it by Section 736 of the Companies Act 1985.

15.3   Upon any termination specified in Clauses 15.1 or 15.2 or on withdrawal of the Company's standing offer detailed in Clause 8:-

(a)   the authority of the Dealer to cause the Company to enter into Purchase Contracts and Sale Contracts shall terminate forthwith;

(b)   the Company shall be entitled to take immediate possession of all Purchased Vehicles and to enter into any premises of the Dealer in order to do so;

(c)   the Dealer shall on request redeliver any Purchased Vehicles to a location specified by the Company;

(d)   the Company shall be obliged to repay to the Dealer any Deposit paid provided that the Company shall firstly be entitled to set-off and apply any Deposits it has received against any amount which the Dealer may owe to the Company whether in respect of Purchased Vehicles sold by the Company to the Dealer or otherwise;

(e)   the Company shall be entitled by notice in writing to require the Dealer forthwith to purchase from the Company any one or more Purchased Vehicles in accordance with Clause 15.4;

(f)   the Company shall be entitled to require the Dealer on demand to pay all display charges accrued under Clauses 6.2 and 7; and

(g)   all Instalments in respect of each Demonstrator shall become and be immediately due and payable.

15.4   Forthwith upon receiving a notice from the Company under Clause 15.3(e), the Company and the Dealer shall be deemed to have entered into a Sale Contract for the relevant Purchased Vehicles and the Dealer shall immediately purchase from the Company all Purchased Vehicles specified in the notice for a price equal to the price (exclusive of Value Added Tax) paid by the Company for such Purchased Vehicles under the Purchase Contracts relating thereto (together with Value Added Tax thereon) and otherwise on the terms of the Stipulated Sale Terms provided that the Dealer shall only be obliged to pay the balance of the purchase price for each Purchased Vehicle taking into account the relevant Deposit (if any) already paid by it and which has not already been set-off (in whole or in part) by the Company in respect of any other amount due from the Dealer.

16.   **PAYMENTS AND TAXES**

16.1   Payments Gross

All sums payable by the Dealer hereunder or pursuant hereto (including, for the avoidance of doubt, any sums payable by the Dealer to the Company pursuant to its obligations to account for monies received by it as the Company's agent) whether in respect of commission, fees or otherwise, shall be paid in full without any set-off or counterclaim whatsoever and free and clear of and without any deduction or withholding whatsoever save only as may be required by law and in the event of any such requirement the Dealer will ensure that such deduction or withholding is made and that it does not exceed the minimum legal requirement therefore and contemporaneously with the payment which is subject to such deduction or withholding the Dealer shall pay to the Company such additional amount as will result in the receipt by the Company of the full amount which would otherwise have been received hereunder or pursuant hereto had no such deduction or withholding been required to be made.

16.2   Taxes due on Deductions and Withholdings

If the Dealer makes any payment hereunder in respect of which it is required to make any deduction or withholding and to account for the same to the relevant taxation or other authority, it shall pay the full amount to be deducted or withheld to the relevant taxation or other authority within the time allowed for such payment under applicable law and shall deliver to the Company within thirty (30) days after receipt thereof, the original receipt (or a certified copy thereof) issued by such authority evidencing the payment to such authority of all amounts so required to be deducted or withheld in respect of such payment.

16.3   Value Added Tax

If the Company makes any supply for Value Added Tax purposes pursuant to or in connection with this Agreement or any transaction or document contemplated herein the Dealer shall (save to the extent that the Company is entitled to be indemnified in respect of that Value Added Tax by an increased payment under sub-Clause 16.4 below) pay on demand to the Company an amount equal to any Value Added Tax which is payable in respect of that supply.

16.4   All payments to be made by the Dealer under and pursuant to this Agreement are calculated without regard to Value Added Tax. If any such payment constitutes the whole or any part of the consideration for a taxable or deemed taxable supply for the purposes of Value Added Tax (whether that supply is taxable pursuant to the exercise of an option or otherwise) by the Company, the amount of that payment shall be increased by an amount equal to the amount of Value Added Tax which is chargeable in respect of the taxable supply in question.

16.5   No payment or other consideration to be made or furnished by the Company to the Dealer pursuant to or in connection with this Agreement or any transaction or document contemplated herein may be increased or added to by reference to (or as a result of any increase in the rate of) any Value Added Tax which shall be or may become chargeable in respect of the taxable supply in question and accordingly the provisions of Section 89 of VATA shall not apply in respect of any such payment or other consideration.

16.6   If and to the extent that any payment or other consideration to be made or furnished by the Company to any person (other than the Dealer) pursuant to or in connection with this Agreement or any transaction or document contemplated herein may be increased or added to by reference to (or as a result of any increase in the rate of) any Value Added Tax, the Dealer shall pay to the Company on demand an amount equal to that increase or the value of that addition.

16.7   In the event that there shall be any delay in the recovery by the Company of input tax (as the expression is defined in Section 24(1) of VATA) paid by the Company caused solely by the failure of the Commissioners of Customs and Excise to treat any supply by a seller under a Purchase Contract or by the Company under a Sale Contract in accordance with Section 47(3) VATA or any provision introduced in addition to or as a replacement for the same both as a supply to the Dealer and as a supply by the Dealer beyond the normal payment date (being the date on which the Company or the VAT group representative member should have received and retained a credit or repayment in respect of such input tax) for the relevant prescribed accounting period for the purposes of Value Added Tax, the Dealer shall indemnify the Company in respect thereof by payment to the Company of any amount equal to interest at two per cent (2%) above Base Rate on the amount of the input tax in respect of which the delay has occurred from the relevant normal payment date to but excluding the date upon which a credit is given or a repayment is actually received in respect of such input tax.

16.8 If the Company makes a payment of Value Added Tax under this Agreement and, as at the date falling three (3) calendar months after such payment, neither the Company nor a VAT Group Member has received and retained a credit (whether by way of set off or repayment) for that payment as input tax under Sections 24, 25 and 26 of VATA, nor received and retained a credit for it under any similar or equivalent legislation, such payment shall be deemed to be irrecoverable VAT and the Dealer shall (subject to the adjustment provisions of Clause 16.1) pay to the Company on demand an amount equal to such payment together with interest thereon at Base Rate from the date of payment by the Company to the date of demand and thereafter to the date of reimbursement by the Dealer at the rate equal to the aggregate of Base Rate and four per cent (4%) per annum.

16.9 If, after a particular payment has been made under this Agreement, it transpires that Value Added Tax has not been charged when it was chargeable, or that the amount of Value Added Tax (if any) that has been charged is not correct, the person making the relevant supply shall (subject to the provisions of Clause 16.5 above) submit an invoice or a supplementary invoice to recover any shortfall (as the case may be), or a credit note in respect of any overpayment, and the necessary payments or adjustment payments (as the case may be) shall be made on or within ten (10) Business Days thereafter. In respect of any such overpayment by the Company, the Company shall be entitled to charge the Dealer interest on the sum overpaid at Base Rate from and including the date of such overpayment to but excluding the date the necessary adjustment payment is made.

16.10 The Dealer shall notify the Company immediately if the Dealer's VAT registration number changes or the Dealer becomes de-registered for Value Added Tax purposes or the Dealer changes business address.

16.11 <u>Documentary and other Taxes</u>

All stamp, documentary, registration or other like duties or taxes, including any penalties, additions, fines, surcharges or interest relating thereto, which are imposed or chargeable on or in connection with this Agreement or any other document connected with or contemplated by this Agreement shall be paid by the Dealer **PROVIDED THAT** the Company shall be entitled but not obliged to pay any such duties or taxes (whether or not they are its primary responsibility), whereupon the Dealer shall on demand indemnify the Company against those duties or taxes.

17. **REPRESENTATIONS AND WARRANTIES**

The Dealer represents and warrants to the Company that:-

(a) it has power to enter into this Agreement and to exercise its rights and perform its obligations hereunder and all corporate or other action required to authorise the execution of this Agreement by it and the performance by it of its obligations hereunder has been duly taken;

(b) the execution of this Agreement and its exercise of its rights and performance of its obligations hereunder (i) will not result in the existence of nor oblige it to create any encumbrance over all or any of its present or future revenues or assets and (ii) will not result in any breach by it of any provision of its memorandum of association or its articles of association, any provisions of law or any agreement or other instrument binding on it; and

(c)   it has not taken any corporate action nor have any other steps been taken or legal proceedings been started or, to the best of its knowledge and belief, threatened against it for its winding-up dissolution or reorganisation or for the appointment of an administrator, administrative receiver, receiver, trustee or similar officer of it or of any or all of its assets; and

(d)   it is registered for Value Added Tax purposes.

18. LOSS AND DESTRUCTION

The Dealer shall notify the Company promptly of any loss or destruction (including constructive loss) of any Purchased Vehicle. Within seven Business Days following any such loss or destruction of any Purchased Vehicle the Dealer shall make a payment to the Company by way of indemnity equal to the purchase price paid by the Company for that Purchased Vehicle under the relevant Purchase Contract but having regard to any Instalment already paid in the case of a Demonstrator and any Deposit already paid by the Dealer in respect of any other Purchased Vehicle and which has not already been set-off (in whole or in part) by the Company in respect of any other amount due from the Dealer.

19. FEES COSTS AND EXPENSES

19.1   The Dealer agrees to pay the Company an administration fee in respect of each Purchased Vehicle in an amount specified by the Company in the Offer Letter to cover the Company's costs of administering this scheme. Such sum is payable after entry into the Purchase Contract in respect of the relevant Purchased Vehicle. The Company shall within 10 days of the end of each calendar month submit a monthly invoice for the administration fees which became payable in the immediately preceding month and the Company will debit from the Bank Account the amount shown on the relevant invoice (including any Value Added Tax).

19.2   The Dealer shall pay on demand all costs and expenses and Value Added Tax thereon incurred by the Company in connection with:

(a)   the negotiation preparation and execution of this Agreement;

(b)   the granting of any waiver or consent or any variation of this Agreement or any documents contemplated hereby; and

(c)   the perfection, protection, preservation or enforcement (whether attempted or successful) of any of the Company's rights under this Agreement, any Purchase Contract and any Sale Contract.

19.3   The Dealer shall be liable to pay to the Company on demand an additional administration fee of £50 (plus any Value Added Tax thereon) on each occasion that there is a failure by the Dealer either to notify the Company of a sale contract with a third party as buyer pursuant to Clause 8.1 or a failure by the Dealer to comply with any of its obligations under Clause 6.1 as a contribution towards the additional administrative costs of and monitoring undertaken by the Company as a result of such failures.

20. FORCE MAJEURE

20.1   Except for the obligation to pay money properly due and owing, a party shall be excused from any delay or failure in performance hereunder caused by reason of Force Majeure. For the purposes of this Clause 20 "Force Majeure" means any occurrence or contingency beyond the reasonable control of the relevant party, including, but not limited to, failure of performance by the other party, acts of God, earthquake, labour disputes (including those with employees of the relevant party), riots, governmental requirements, any failure of computer or telecommunications equipment, failures or delays of sources from which information or data is obtained and transportation difficulties.

"Used Vehicle Payments" means at any time the aggregate of:

20.2 The parties shall be relieved from the obligations under this Agreement during the period and to the extent only that they are prevented from complying with this Agreement by reason of Force Majeure.

21. **GENERAL**

21.1 Interest on late payment

Interest will be charged on all amounts due from the Dealer to the Company hereunder and not paid on the due date; such interest will be charged on a daily basis at the rate which is the aggregate of four per cent (4%) per annum and the Base Rate for the time being.

21.2 Notices

Each communication to be made hereunder or pursuant hereto shall be in writing. Any communication to be made hereunder or pursuant hereto shall be addressed to the recipient at the address identified herein or such other address in England as it may for this purpose notify to the other and shall be deemed to have been given upon delivery, or when sent (if by telex or facsimile) or three (3) days after posting if sent by mail.

21.3 Assignment

The Dealer may not assign its rights or obligations under this Agreement or any agreement which may be made pursuant hereto or in connection herewith without the prior written consent of the Company.

21.4 Severability

If at any time any provision of this Agreement or any agreement which may be made pursuant hereto or in connection herewith is or becomes illegal, invalid or unenforceable in any respect under the law of any jurisdiction neither the legality, validity or enforceability of the remaining provisions hereof nor the legality, validity or enforceability of such provision under the law of any other jurisdiction shall in any way be affected or impaired thereby.

21.5 Title to Purchased Vehicles

The Dealer and the Company confirm and agree that the payment of any Instalment or Deposit by the Dealer will not give any rights or interest to the Dealer (or pass any legal or equitable title to the Dealer) in any Purchased Vehicle.

21.6 Waiver, Remedies Cumulative

No failure to exercise, nor any delay in exercising, on the part of the Company of any right, remedy, power or privilege under this Agreement or any agreement which may be made pursuant thereto or in connection herewith shall operate as a waiver thereof, nor shall any single or partial exercise of any such right, remedy, power or privilege prevent any further or other exercise thereof or the exercise of any other right or remedy. The rights and remedies herein provided are cumulative and not exclusive of any rights or remedies provided by law.

21.7 Rights of set-off

Without prejudice to any of its other rights and remedies the Company shall be entitled to set off all or any of its liabilities to the Dealer against all or any of the Dealer's liabilities to the Company under or pursuant to this or any other agreement or account.

21.8   Bank Account

The Dealer agrees to keep sufficient funds available in the Bank Account in order to meet its obligations to the Company under the Agreement (and any security documents as the case may be) from time to time. The Company is hereby authorised to debit from the Bank Account payments due to it under and in accordance with this Agreement.

21.9   Audit

(a)   the Dealer will permit the Company without notice at any time during the business hours of the Dealer to carry out a check of stocks of Purchased Vehicles held by the Dealer under the terms of this Agreement and for this purpose to enter on any premises of the Dealer where such stock is held.

(b)   the Dealer will permit the Company without notice at any time during the business hours of the Dealer to carry out an audit of the Dealer's relevant books and records relating to the operation of the agency granted by this Agreement and the Purchase Contracts and Sales Contracts and payments due or made thereunder and for this purpose to enter on any premises of the Dealer where such books, records and stocks are held.

21.10   Offer Letter

The Offer Letter may be amended, varied and/or supplemented by the Company at any time giving notice to the Dealer of such amendment, variation and/or supplemental provisions.

21.11   Information

The Dealer shall provide each year to the Company no later than the date referred to in the Offer Letter, if the Dealer is a company, a copy of its audited annual accounts and the audited annual accounts of its holding company (as such term is defined in the Companies Act 1985), if any, and if the Dealer is a partnership or sole trader, a copy of his annual certified accounts. In addition the Dealer shall submit to the Company any information of an accounting, financial or statistical nature in such form as the Company may reasonably require.

21.12   Governing Law

This Agreement and any agreement which may be made pursuant hereto or in connection herewith shall be governed by and construed in all respects in accordance with the laws of England.

22.   **RETAIL FINANCE**

The Dealer will at all times during this Agreement in good faith give to the Company the right of first refusal to provide on the terms available from the Company from time to time finance for hire purchase, conditional sale, loan, lease purchase, hire, leasing contract hire and any other instalment credit facilities ("Retail Facilities") required by customers of the Dealer for the acquisition from the Dealer of used motor vehicles and the Dealer shall give to the Company such right of first refusal in relation to each and every proposal. Accordingly, without prejudice to the above, the Dealer shall not recommend, introduce, offer or otherwise make available to a customer Retail Facilities in relation to any motor vehicle supplied under the terms of this

777

Agreement unless the Company has first been given the opportunity to provide such Retail Facilities on the same terms to that customer.

AS WITNESS the hands of the parties hereto the day and year before written.

SCHEDULE 1

STIPULATED PURCHASE TERMS

The following terms and conditions shall apply to each Purchase Contract in respect of any Vehicles purchased by the Company pursuant thereto:-

(1)   title to each Vehicle shall pass to the Company free of all encumbrances immediately on payment of the purchase price for such Vehicle;

(2)   the Dealer represents and warrants that:

    (a)   in respect of each used Vehicle, the purchase price does not exceed such percentage specified in the Offer Letter of the Clean Guide Value for the Vehicle in the Price Guide Book current at the date of purchase of that Vehicle; and

    (b)   in respect of each new Vehicle, the purchase price is the actual wholesale price paid by the Dealer being not more than the percentage notified to the Dealer by the Company in the Offer Letter of the manufacturer's recommended retail price (including any factory fitted options) for that Vehicle;

(3)   the purchase price is payable in Sterling in one single instalment in immediately available funds upon the making of the Purchase Contract;

(4)   each Vehicle shall have the benefit of the unexpired period of the manufacturer's standard new car warranty which shall be transferable to subsequent purchasers of the Vehicle;

(5)   risk in each Vehicle shall be with the Dealer at all times;

(6)   the Dealer represents and warrants that each Vehicle is in good working order and repair and of merchantable quality and roadworthy in all respects;

(7)   the Company shall have no obligations under the Purchase Contract other than to pay the purchase price;

(8)   the Purchase Contract shall be governed by English law;

(9)   the Dealer shall have no right of cancellation or rescission;

(10)   the Dealer represents and warrants that in respect of each used Vehicle, the Vehicle complies with the trade clean condition as described in the Price Guide Book; and

SCHEDULE 2

STIPULATED SALE TERMS

The following terms and conditions shall apply on all sales of Vehicles from the Company to the Dealer:-

(1)   Vehicles which are supplied by the Company to a Dealer, shall remain the property of the Company until full payment of the Vehicles supplied to the Dealer and all other payments due from the Dealer to the Company have been made;

(2)   in the case of a Demonstrator, the Dealer shall pay the purchase price for the Vehicle in Instalments in the amounts or percentages set out in the Offer Letter (except for a Demonstrator in respect of which a Sale Contract has been entered into when the balance of the purchase price (following payment of any Instalment) shall be paid in sterling in one single instalment in immediately available funds as specified in Clause 10.4 of this Agreement) and in the case of all other Vehicles the balance of the purchase price (following payment of any Deposit) shall be paid in Sterling in one single instalment in immediately available funds as specified in Clause 10.4 of this Agreement;

(3)   risk in each Vehicle shall be with the Dealer at all times;

(4)   the Company will transfer such title to the Dealer as was acquired by it through the agency of the Dealer;

(5)   Each Vehicle shall have the benefit of the unexpired period of the manufacturer's standard new car warranty which shall be transferable to subsequent purchasers of the Vehicle;

(6)   the Vehicle being at the time of purchase in the possession and control of the Dealer, the Dealer hereby acknowledges and agrees that it inspected the Vehicle itself upon taking physical delivery of the Vehicle. Accordingly the Dealer shall acquire each Vehicle from the Company as and where it lies and in the condition it is in and the Company sells each Vehicle to the Dealer only upon the express agreement of the Dealer that all warranties, conditions, guarantees or representations express or implied, statutory or otherwise, relating to each Vehicle are excluded and the Company shall not be liable for any loss, damage, expense or injury of any kind whatsoever, consequential or otherwise, arising out of or due to or caused by any defect or deficiencies of any sort in each Vehicle;

(7)   the Consumer Credit Act 1974 does not regulate such a sale and does not confer any rights of cancellation or rescission on the Dealer;

(8)   the Sale Contracts shall be governed by English law;

(9)   each Sale Contract is validly entered into and authorised by the Dealer.

780

SIGNATURES

1.   Signed by or on behalf of the **DEALER**:

IF THE DEALER IS A SOLE PROPRIETOR, HE OR SHE MUST SIGN. IF THE DEALER
IS A PARTNERSHIP, ALL PARTNERS MUST SIGN AND THEIR NAMES MUST BE
PRINTED IN THE SPACE BELOW. IF THE DEALER IS A LIMITED COMPANY, A
DIRECTOR MUST SIGN AND HIS OR HER NAME MUST BE PRINTED IN THE SPACE
BELOW.

Signature ....   Signature ....

Name   ....   Name ....

Signature ....   Signature ....

Name   ....   Name ....

Position: Director/Partner/Sole Trader   Position: Partner
(Delete as appropriate)

2.   Signed for and on behalf of **THE COMPANY** ....

Name ....

Position: Senior Appraisal Manager

FORTIS COMMERCIAL FINANCE LIMITED

AGREEMENT FOR THE FACTORING OR DISCOUNTING OF DEBTS

SCHEDULE OF PARTICULARS

These Particulars form part of an agreement for factoring or discounting of debts between you, the company whose name and address appears in section 1 below, and Fortis Commercial Finance Limited ("this Agreement").

You have chosen the following service:

Confidential Invoice Discounting with Recourse for domestic sales
Disclosed Invoice Discounting with Recourse for export sales

The explanatory notes attached to (but not forming part of) this Agreement outline certain of these Particulars which apply to the service chosen by you.

Section
number

1.	**Your Name and Address**	XXXX Limited [address]
	Registered Number	[ ]
2.	**Starting Date** (clause 2)	
3.	**States and Territories for Inclusion** (clause 5)	United Kingdom and European Economic Community
4.	**Debts within Credit Limits that are Unapproved** (clauses 9.2.5, 10.3.1 and 19.1.5)	
5.	**Prepayment Percentage** (definition of Prepayment)	70%
6.	**Maximum Funds in Use** (clause 10.5.3 and definition)	£3,000,000
7.	**Concentration Percentage** (clause 10.5.3.2)	15% except Makro @ 25%
8.	**Discounting Charge Rate** (clause 13.4)	1.5%

Fig 29.2 Extract from factoring agreement

9.	**Administration Charge** (clause 14.1.1.)	0.2% (to be reviewed 6 months after start date)
10.	**Minimum Administration Charge** (clause 14.2 and definition of Shortfall)	£2,000 per month
11.	**Assignment Notices to Debtors** (clauses 15.4 and 15.11)`	Export sales only
12.	**Your Agency to Collect Debts** (clauses 15.8 to 15.10)	Yes
13.	**Nature of your Business** (clause 16.1)	Wholesale of machine tools
14.	**Currencies of Payment** (clause 16.1.1.)	Great Britain Pounds, Euros and United States Dollars
15.	**Terms of Payment** (clause 16.1.1.)	30 days from the date of the invoice
16.	**Laws Governing Contracts of Sale** (clauses 16.1.2)	England and Wales
17.	**Recourse Period** (clauses 17.3 and 19.1.5 and definition)	120 days from date of invoice
18.	**Credit Periods** (definition of "Collection Date")	Not applicable
19.	**Electronic Exchange of Information**	Included
20.	**Security Documentation** (clause 10.5.1)	
21.	**Other Conditions Precedent** (clause 10.5.2)	

AGREEMENT FOR THE FACTORING OR DISCOUNTING OF DEBTS

1. Parties

This Agreement is made between Fortis Commercial Finance Limited (incorporated in England with the number 2713317) of Westcombe House, 2-4 Mount Ephraim, Tunbridge Wells, Kent, TN4 8AS, ("we" or "us") and the client ("you") named in section 1 of the particular terms attached to and forming part of this Agreement ("the Particulars")

2. Date

This Agreement is made on the date on which the party, last to sign it, does so.

3. Definitions and Interpretation

...

4. Period of this Agreement and its End

4.1 This Agreement will start on the date shown in section 2 and, unless it is ended by us under clause 21.1, it will continue until it is ended on the expiry of not less than three month's written notice to end it given by either you or us to the other.

4.2 Except as provided, the ending of this Agreement (including the ending of it under clause 21.1) will not affect the rights and obligations of you and us under this Agreement in relation to any transaction started before the end of this Agreement or any Debt in existence at that time and such rights and obligations will remain in full force and effect until duly satisfied.

4.3 All licences and authorities given to us by you in this Agreement are irrevocable and will continue after the end of this Agreement until all your Obligations have been fully discharged.

4.4 All the provisions of this Agreement will remain in effect in spite of any change of your name or your constitution.

5. Debts for Inclusion

The Debts included within the scope of this Agreement are all those, and only those, that arise from your Contracts of Sale under which the invoices are to be addressed to places in the states or territories listed in section 3. Any reference to Debt in this Agreement is to a Debt included in it.

6. Sale and Purchase of Debts

6.1 Immediately after the Starting Date (or as soon as the Goods have been Delivered if that is later) you will offer to sell to us every Debt in existence on that date by sending to us a schedule of all such Debts in a form acceptable to us.

6.2 We may accept or decline any Debt included in a schedule under clause 6.1. Our acceptance of any Debt will be evidenced by our crediting the Purchase Price of it to the Current Account.

6.3 You will sell to us and we shall purchase all Debts coming into existence during the period of this Agreement described in clause 4.1 so that those Debts will belong to us automatically as soon as they come into existence without the need for any other act of transfer.

6.4 All Debts purchased by us will be sold by you with full title guarantee.

7. Notification of Debts

7.1 At least once in each week you will notify us, in the way we require, of every Debt relating to Goods Delivered other than any Debt previously notified to us or offered to us under clause 6.1.

7.2 You will furnish us with such documents evidencing the Debts included in a Notification as we may require.

7.3 All Debts included in any one Notification are to be expressed in the same currency.

7.4 You will notify us separately of every Debt in respect of which you are unable to give us every warranty and undertaking included in this Agreement and on that separate Notification you will mark clearly the nature of the warranty or undertaking that you cannot give.

8. Ownership of Debts and Goods

8.1 If we ask you at any time to complete, sign and deliver to us a written assignment of any Debt and give written notice of that assignment to the Debtor then you will do so at your expense (including any applicable stamp duty) in the form that we require.

8.2 If, for any reason, the ownership of any Debt fails to be transferred to us then you will hold that Debt in trust for us.

8.3 You will hold in trust for us and keep separate from your own property any Goods in your possession at any time which are included in the Related Rights. You will mark all such Goods plainly with our name as owner and deal with any such Goods as we may require.

8.4 We shall have the right by oral or written notice to you to have transferred to us the ownership of any Goods (other than those referred to in clause 8.3) which are the subject of a Contract of Sale and of which the ownership has not passed to the Debtor. You will deal with those Goods as required by us.

9. Approved and Unapproved Debts and Eligible Debts

9.1   We may, without giving any reason, by written notice to you establish a Credit Limit and/or a Funding Limit in relation to any Debtor or increase any established Credit Limit or Funding Limit.

9.2   A Debt (but excluding any interest included in the Related Rights pertaining to that Debt) will rank as an Approved Debt at any time if:

    9.2.1   at that time, when added to the total of all other Debts owing by the same Debtor, it is within a Credit Limit relating to that Debtor; and

    9.2.2   it is not a Debt in respect of which you are at that time in breach of any representation, warranty or undertaking given by you in this Agreement; and

    9.2.3   it was not notified under clause 7.4; and

    9.2.4   it is not a Debt which the Debtor will be unable (or claims to be unable) to pay owing to the law or rules or regulations of any government (except those relating solely to the insolvency of the Debtor) or war or civil commotion or the circumstances in the territory in which the Debtor is situated; and

    9.2.5   it is not a Debt described in section 4.

For the purposes of this clause Debts will be deemed to fall into a Credit Limit in the order in which they are notified.

9.3   We may by oral or written notice to you reduce or cancel any established Credit Limit or Funding Limit to take effect immediately except in respect of any Approved Debt arising from Goods sold and Delivered before your receipt of that notice.

    ...

10.   Purchase Price of Debts and our Payments to you

10.1   The Purchase Price payable by us for each Debt will be equivalent to the amount to be paid for it by the Debtor according to the Contract of Sale for that Debt less:

    10.1.1   any discount or other allowance taken or claimed by the Debtor; and

    10.1.2 the discount charge provided for in clause 13.4 so far as attributable to that Debt.

10.2   We shall credit the Purchase Price of every Debt to the Current Account upon Notification of the Debt. We may do so before making any deductions and debit any amount to be deducted as soon as it is known.

10.3   Except where any of the provisions of clauses 10.4, 10.5 or 21.2.2 apply you may draw against the credit balance on your Current Account and we shall pay to you:

    10.3.1   at your request a Prepayment in respect of any Eligible Debt at any time after Notification;

    10.3.2   the Purchase Price of any Debt (less any Prepayment made in respect of it) on its Collection Date.

We may, if we see fit, pay to you a Prepayment in respect of any Debt even if you have not asked for it.

10.4 We may pay to you other amounts on account of the Purchase Price of Debts on terms (including an arrangement fee if we require it) to be agreed between you and us.

10.5 We shall not be obliged to make any Prepayment:
10.5.1 before all the security documentation specified in section 20 has been completed to our satisfaction; or
10.5.2 while any other condition contained in section 21 remains unsatisfied; or
10.5.3 at any time if the effect of that payment would be that:
10.5.3.1 the debit balance on the Funds in Use Statement would exceed the Maximum Funds in Use at that time; or
10.5.3.2 the total of Prepayments made in respect of Outstanding Debts owing by any one Debtor would exceed the percentage shown in section 7 of the total amount of all Approved Debts Outstanding at the time of the payment.
...

11. Purchase Price payable in a Currency other than that of the Invoice

11.1 If, at your request, we agree to pay the Purchase Price of a Debt in a currency other than that of its invoice then:
11.1.1 we shall calculate the Purchase Price of that Debt by using the spot selling rate quoted in London by our Bankers on the Collection Date; and

11.1.2 for the purpose of crediting its Purchase Price to the Current Account we may apply such rate as we may determine on the date of the Notification of the Debt and make any adjustment to that credit that may be required after the Collection Date.

11.2 You undertake to indemnify us against any additional loss and expense incurred by us in the collection or attempted collection of any such Debt and of the conversion of the currency of the amount received by us in payment of the Debt (including bank charges and commissions) and we may debit the Current Account for such loss or expense so incurred by us.

12. Your Obligations to us and Group Companies

12.1 The amount of any of the monetary liabilities included in your Obligations or any liability of you to any Group Company of ours may be debited to the Current Account or applied in the discharge of any amount payable by us to you. For this purpose we may make a reasonable estimate of any of your Obligations the amount of which cannot be immediately ascertained.

12.2 At any time we may combine any two or more accounts held by us in your name and, if we so decide, we may combine any such account held by us with any such account held by any Group Company of ours.

12.3 Where (i) any monetary liability is in a currency other than that of the account to which it is to be debited or (ii) accounts held in different currencies are to be combined, then we may apply the middle spot rate of exchange quoted by our bankers in London at the time of the debit or combination.

12.4 You will pay to us upon our demand:

  12.4.1 any Prepayment made in respect of an Eligible Debt upon its ceasing to be Eligible;

  12.4.2 any debit balance owing to us on the Current Account at any time; and

  12.4.3 the equivalent of any amount by which a debit balance on the Funds in Use Statement (or if more than one a combination of them) at any time exceeds the Maximum Funds in Use at that time.

  Such payments will be made by you in the currency of such of the Current Accounts as we require.

12.5 You undertake to indemnify us against all claims made against us by any Debtor (save any claim arising solely from our own default) and against all losses, costs, charges, interest and expenses (including legal costs and applicable taxes and duties) incurred by us at any time and arising from or in any way connected with any of the following:

  12.5.1 our entering into or enforcing, exercising or protecting our rights under this Agreement or any guarantee or indemnity or security given to us in respect of your Obligations;

  12.5.2 enforcing or attempting to enforce payment of any Unapproved Debt or settling or compromising any dispute with or claim by a Debtor or any other person in relation to any Debt;

  12.5.3 the securing by us of any release of any Debt from any trust charge or other encumbrance;

  12.5.4 any indemnity which we may be required to give to our bankers in connection with the collection on our behalf of any cheque or other instrument made payable to you;

  12.5.5 any agreement by us under clause 26 to provide you with the EDI Services (including any corruption of our data or systems by or through any Intermediary);

  12.5.6 any breach by you of any of the terms of this Agreement or any other of your Obligations;

  12.5.7 any bank charges incurred by us for the collection of cheques from Debtors including the maintenance of any trust account in your name for our benefit for that purpose;

  12.5.8 our dealing with cheques and other instruments of payment returned unpaid;

  and we may debit to the Current Account the amount of any such losses, costs, charges, interest and expenses.

12.6 You will repay to us on our demand any amount paid to you by us in respect of any Unapproved Debt to the extent that payment by the Debtor or any guarantor of the Debt is subsequently recalled under the law of the country of the payer or by reason of any decision of a court or tribunal of competent authority in that country.

13. Current Accounts, Funds in Use Statements and Discounting Charge

13.1 We shall send to you once in every month or at such other intervals as may be agreed:

13.1.1 a statement of the Current Account and Funds in Use Statement in respect of each currency of your invoices; and

13.1.2 (except while you are our agent under clause 15.8) an analysis of the Outstanding Debts.

...

14. Administration Charges

14.1 You will pay to us (or we may in our discretion deduct from any payment to be made by us to you at any time):

14.1.1 an administration charge equal to the percentage shown in section 9 of the notified amount of each Debt (before deduction of any discount, credit note or other allowance) when the Debt is due to be notified; and

14.1.2 an arrangement fee for any variation of this Agreement requested by you or any services for you which we agree to provide outside the scope of this Agreement.

Every administration and other charge under this clause 14 which is calculated in a currency other than sterling will be converted into sterling at the selling rate for that currency notified to us by our Bankers on the date when the charge is due to be paid.

14.2 You will be liable to us for any administration charge Shortfall which:

14.2.1 where based on a monthly amount stated in section 10 will be payable by you at the end of each month; and

14.2.2 where based on an annual amount stated in section 10 will accrue monthly during any year with any requisite adjustment at the end of each subsequent month and will be so payable by you at the end of each month.

...

14.3 All our charges are quoted in this Agreement exclusive of applicable taxes or duties.

15. Sales Ledger Administration and Collection of Debts

15.1 We shall have the sole right to enforce payment of and collect any Debt so long as we are the owner of it or it is held by you in trust for us. We have the right to start, carry on, defend or compromise proceedings in respect of any Debt in such manner and upon such terms as we may choose and to use your name for those purposes if we think fit. However, nothing obliges us to take any such proceedings.

15.2 Whether or not you are our agent under clause 15.8 you will, at your expense, co-operate with us in any enforcement collection or proceedings in respect of any Debt including the production of such documents and the giving of such evidence as may be necessary for such enforcement or collection or proceedings.

15.3 Except where we appoint you as our agent under clause 15.8 you will not collect or attempt to collect any Debt.

...

15.5 You will deliver promptly upon its receipt to us or, if we so require, direct to our bank account (and meanwhile hold in trust for us) all the identical remittances received by you in or on account of payment of any Debt.

15.6 We may apply any payment or other benefit received from or credit granted to a Debtor in or on account of payment of any Approved Debt owing by that Debtor in priority to any Unapproved Debt in spite of any different allocation made by the Debtor.

...

16. Your Warranties and Undertakings in respect of Notified Debts

16. By notifying us of any Debt (except to the extent that clause 7.4 applies) you warrant or undertake (as applicable) in respect of that Debt that:

16.1 the Goods and the invoice for them have been Delivered and the Debt has arisen from a Contract of Sale entered into by you in the normal course of your business as described in section 13 and that the Contract of Sale:

16.1.1 provides for payment to be made in a currency of a state or territory shown in section 14 on terms not more liberal than those described in section 15;

16.1.2 is governed by the law of a state or territory shown in section 16;

16.1.3 is otherwise as approved by us in writing; and

you will not vary that Contract of Sale except with our written consent;

16.2 you have performed all your obligations to the Debtor and the Debtor is obliged to accept the Debt and the invoice for it as a legally binding obligation of the Debtor to pay the full amount as notified of the Debt;

16.3 the Debtor has no right to prohibit the assignment nor any right of set-off nor any other right by which we may be prevented from collecting the full amount of the Debt as notified except only the right to any settlement discount approved by us;

16.4 in the insolvency of the Debtor, the person having the duty to administer the estate will accept proof of debt for the amount as notified;

16.5 the Debt is free from all trusts, charges, liens and other encumbrances and no other person, including any of your suppliers, has any right or interest to or in the Debt or the Goods to which it relates;

16.6 you have no obligations to the Debtor other than under any Contract of Sale and you have no agreement or arrangement with the Debtor for retrospective discounts or otherwise whereby the amount of the Debt may be reduced except in accordance with the Contract of Sale;

16.7   the Debtor has an established place of business in the country to which the invoice is addressed and is not an Associate of yours;

16.8   the Debtor has complied with all formalities required by law or rules or regulations having the force of law necessary for the receipt and acceptance of the Goods and for payment to us on the due date in the currency in which the invoice is expressed according to the Contract of Sale; and

16.9   if the Goods are to be exported you have complied with all such formalities (if any) for the export of the Goods.

17.   Other Undertakings by you

17.   In addition to all other undertakings given by you in this Agreement you undertake:

17.1   to keep proper books and records of account and to make appropriate entries in them to show the sale to us of the Debts;

17.2   promptly to pay all taxes and carriage and freight charges and effect any insurance and to pay the premium and make any claim under it in every case in which you are liable to do so under the Contract of Sale;

17.3   to pay to us the amount of any Unapproved Debt which remains unpaid after the end of its Recourse Period so that your liability under this undertaking may be enforced against you as principal debtor without the need for us to make any prior demand on the Debtor by whom such Debt is payable;

17.4   without our prior written consent not to assign or create any charge over any of your rights or benefits under this Agreement nor to delegate any of your responsibilities under it;

17.5   not to enter into any agreement for the factoring or discounting or otherwise for the sale of any Debt except with us (and entry into any such agreement by any Associate of yours will be deemed to be a breach of this provision);

17.6   not to create any mortgage, charge or other encumbrance or any trust which affects or may affect any of your assets or rights or your undertaking;

17.7   if we require you to do so by written notice to you, to procure that any company which you control, or make your best endeavours to procure that any other Group Company of yours, enters into an agreement with us on terms and conditions similar to those of this Agreement;

17.8   for the purpose of procuring for our benefit a refund of any value added tax included in any Approved Debt which becomes bad or doubtful in any case in which the regulations of H M Customs and Excise for the recovery of such value added tax apply, to accept a transfer back to you of that Debt for the consideration of:

     17.8.1   your immediate payment to us of the amount of value added tax recoverable; and

     17.8.2   your payment to us of any recovery or dividend received by you in respect of that Debt and meanwhile to hold that recovery or dividend in trust for us; and

17.9   to comply with all procedures for the operation of this Agreement which we may make known to you from time to time.

18.   Disagreements with Debtors, Credit Notes and Credit Balances:

18.1   You undertake that if, in spite of the warranties given by you in clause 16, a Debtor fails to accept its liability to pay to us the full amount of any Debt as notified (less only any discount for prompt payment in accordance with the Contract of Sale) on its due date then you will;

18.1.1 immediately inform us of all the circumstances of the case; and

18.1.2 use your best endeavours promptly to obtain the Debtor's acceptance of that liability; and

18.1.3 promptly perform any obligations under the Contract of Sale giving rise to the Debt that have not been performed.

18.2   On or at any time after any of the events specified in clause 21.1 or at any other time if you fail to perform your obligations under clause 18.1 then we may, at your expense, settle or compromise any such dispute on such terms as we may think fit and/or to perform any such remaining obligations but shall not be bound to do so.

18.3   You will be bound by anything done or omitted to be done by us under clause 18.2 including any reduction in the Purchase Price of any Debt.

18.4   On the Starting Date you will furnish us with a copy of every credit note already then issued relating to any Debt then Outstanding. After that, on the Business Day next following the issue of any credit note by you, you will deliver to us a copy of that credit note. The amount of every credit note will be debited to the Current Account.

18.5   We may make payment in settlement of or on account of any credit balance appearing on a Debtor's account in our records at any time however it may have arisen.

19.   Recourse:

19.1   We shall be entitled to exercise Recourse as follows:

19.1.1 in respect of any Debt included in a separate Notification under Clause 7.4, at any time after its Notification;

19.1.2 in respect of any Debt which is at any time the subject of a breach of any representation, warranty or undertaking given by you to us or which consists entirely of a deduction wrongly claimed or deducted by the Debtor, at any time after such breach or claim or deduction occurs;

19.1.3 in respect of any Unapproved Debt owing by a Debtor the subject of Insolvency Proceedings, at any time after the start of the Insolvency Proceedings;

19.1.4 in respect of any Debt which the Debtor claims to be unable to pay owing to rules or regulations of any Government or war or civil commotion or the circumstances in the territory in which the Debtor is situated, at any time after the event giving rise to the claim;

19.1.5 in respect of every other Unapproved Debt, at the end of the Recourse Period relating to that Debt.

19.2 We may exercise Recourse by written notice to you or by debiting the repurchase price to the Client Account. We shall remain the owner of every Debt in respect of which we shall exercise Recourse until the repurchase price has been fully discharged.

19.3 We shall account to you for any payment made to us in or on account of settlement of any Debt the ownership of which has been transferred back to you by reason of Recourse.

...

21. Termination Events

21.1 On or at any time after the occurrence of any of the following events we shall have the right to bring this Agreement to an end immediately by notice to you:
    21.1.1 any Insolvency Proceedings relating to you;
    21.1.2 a resolution of your members for your winding up;
    21.1.3 the seizure of the whole or any part of your income or assets under any execution, legal process or distress for rent or the making or the threat of any attachment on any Debt owing to you;
    21.1.4 the occurrence of any of the events referred to in clauses 21.1.1, 21.1.2 or 21.1.3 in relation to any person who has given or may at any time give a guarantee or indemnity in respect of your Obligations or the death of that person or the end of any such guarantee or indemnity;
    21.1.5 any breach or the ending of any covenant or undertaking given by any person in reliance on which we entered into or continued this Agreement;
    21.1.6 the withdrawal or attempted withdrawal of any waiver or release or agreement as to priorities in our favour in respect of any security right over any of your assets;
    21.1.7 the cessation of your business or your threat to cease business;
    21.1.8 any adverse change in your financial position or your performance which we consider may increase the risk to us of the recovery of the Funds in Use;
    21.1.9 any alteration in your ownership, control or constitution which we consider material;
    21.1.10 the making of a statutory demand on you under the Act by any of your creditors or your failure to satisfy any judgment against you within seven days of its entry;
    21.1.11 any borrowing by you becoming due for repayment before its stated maturity date owing to your breach of any of the conditions of that borrowing;
    21.1.12 the absence of any Notification for a consecutive period of 28 days;
    21.1.13 any breach of any of your Obligations (or of any obligation of you to a Group Company of us) considered by us to be material or not redressed by you within two Business Days of our request to you to do so.

21.2 At any time after any event listed in clause 21.1 (whether or not we bring this Agreement to an end) we shall be entitled to any one or more of the following:

21.2.1 Recourse in respect of all Debts then Outstanding (including all Approved Debts) but so that they will all continue to belong to us until the repurchase price of all of them has been fully discharged by you;

21.2.2 the withholding of all payments to you until the full discharge of all your Obligations;

21.2.3 a reduction in the Prepayment percentage shown in section 5 to such percentage as we may think fit;

21.2.4 on our demand the immediate repayment by you of all Prepayments previously made;

21.2.5 payment by you of the full cost and expense of any exercise of our rights under clause 20.2;

21.2.6 to appoint at your expense accountants or other professional experts to verify the Outstanding Debts and to obtain such information regarding your financial position as we may require;

21.2.7 as compensation for the additional expense of our collecting the Outstanding Debts, a service charge, additional to the administration charges under clause 14, equivalent to 7.5% of the notified amount of any Debt then Outstanding and of every Debt subsequently becoming Outstanding;

21.2.8 to require that no credit note be issued by you without our prior consent;

21.2.9 to change the status of any or all of the Approved Debts to Unapproved.

21.3 If you should see fit to issue any credit note at any time after we have exercised our rights under clause 21.2.8 you will promptly advise us of that credit note in such manner and with such documents (including the original of the credit note) as we may require. Upon our giving consent to the issue of any credit note of which the original is in our possession we shall despatch it (at your expense) to the Debtor.

21.4 Upon the occurrence of any Insolvency Proceedings in relation to you without any notice or other formality:

21.4.1 notice under clause 8.4 will be deemed to have been given to you to be effective on the day before such occurrence in respect of all Goods then ready for delivery and remaining in your possession; and

21.4.2 all accounts held by us in your name (other than any memorandum account) will be deemed to have been combined.

...

27. Meanings of Words and Expressions

27.1 ...

27.2 In this Agreement the following expressions have the meanings assigned to them below:

"the Act":
the Insolvency Act 1986;

"Approved":
in relation to any Debt, Approved in accordance with clause 9 and not subject to a change in status to Unapproved under clause 21.2.9;

...

"Collection Date":
in relation to any Debt, the date on which our Bankers receive for our account cleared funds in payment of it and in relation to any unpaid Approved Debt the earlier of:
(i)   the date on which we are informed of Insolvency Proceedings in relation to the Debtor by whom the Debt is payable; or
(ii)   the last day of the credit period stated in section 18.

"Contract of Sale":
a contract for the supply of goods or services or for hiring by you;

"Credit Limit":
a limit established, increased or reduced under clause 9 in relation to any Debtor for the purpose of determining which Debts owing by that Debtor may be Approved;

"Current Account":
the accounts maintained by us in your name and in the currencies in which we make payments to you for the purpose of recording transactions between you and us;

"Debt":
a debt (including any tax or duty payable) and any other obligation incurred by a Debtor under a Contract of Sale together with its Related Rights (and, where the context requires, a Debt means part of a Debt);

"Debtor":
any person who has incurred or may incur an obligation to you under a Contract of Sale;

"Delivered":
in the case of any goods or any invoice, despatched to the Debtor from a place in the United Kingdom and, in the case of services or hiring, completed (and the word "delivery" is to be construed accordingly);

"Domestic Debt"
a Debt which is not an Export Debt;

...

"Eligible Debt"

any Debt which is eligible for a Prepayment being a Debt which either:

(i)   is Approved or would be Approved but for an entry in section 4; or

(ii)   is Outstanding and within a Funding Limit when aggregated to all other Outstanding debts then owing by the same Debtor and is not a Debt in respect of which we may exercise recourse under clause 19.1;

"Export Debt"
A Debt arising from any Contract of Sale under which the invoice is to be addressed to a place outside the United Kingdom (and where the name of a state or territory appears after this expression then it means that the Debt arises from a Contract of Sale under which the invoice is to be addressed to a place in that state or territory);

"Funding Limit"
a limit established, increased or reduced under clause 9 in relation to any Debtor for the purpose of determining which Debts owing by that Debtor may be Eligible;

"Funds in Use Statement":
the statement described in clause 13.1;

"Goods":
any goods or services or hiring the subject of a Contract of Sale;

"Group Company":
any company whose relation to you or us (as the case may be) is that of:

(i)   a parent undertaking;

(ii)   a subsidiary undertaking; or

(iii)   any subsidiary undertaking of that parent undertaking;

(in accordance with the meanings given to those expressions in section 258 of the Companies Act 1985) or any partnership or joint venture of which you or we (as the case may be) or any of the above is a member;

"Insolvency Proceedings":

(i)   the issue of a petition for winding up or bankruptcy or for an administration order under the Act; or

(ii)   a proposal for a voluntary arrangement under the Act; or

(iii)   the calling of any meeting of creditors; or

(iv)   the appointment of a receiver in respect of any part or the whole of the undertaking or property of any firm or company;

…

"Maximum Funds in Use":
the smaller of the amount shown in section 6 or an amount at any time equal to the percentage shown in section 5 of the total of all Approved Debts (or all those that would be Approved Debts but for an entry in section 4) which are Outstanding at that time;

…

"your Obligations":
all your monetary and other actual or contingent or prospective obligations incurred at any time to us whether arising under this Agreement or otherwise and whether arising in or by contract, tort, restitution or assignment;

"Outstanding":
in relation to any Debt, remaining unpaid and not reassigned to you and for this purpose a Debt is deemed to be paid on its Collection Date;

"Prepayment":
a payment by us to you on account of the Purchase Price of any Debt before its Collection Date up to the percentage specified in section 5 of the amount of the Debt as notified;

"Purchase Price":
the price payable by us for a Debt calculated as in clause 10.1;

"Recourse":
our right to require that you repurchase any Outstanding Debt at a repurchase price equivalent to the amount of that Debt as notified;

"Recourse Period":
in relation to any Debt, a period of the length specified in section 17 starting on the date when that Debt is due for payment in accordance with the Contract of Sale;

"Related Rights":
in respect of any Debt all of the following:
(i)   all your rights under the Contract of Sale other than your rights to any Goods;
(ii)   the benefit of all guarantees, indemnities, insurances and securities given to or held by you;
(iii)   all cheques, bills of exchange and other instruments held by or available to you;
(iv)   the right to possession of all ledgers, computer data records and documents on or by which any Debt is recorded or evidenced;
(v)   any Goods the subject of a Contract of Sale returned or rejected by the Debtor or repossessed by you;
(vi)   our right to any other Goods under clause 8.4;
(vii)   any interest to which you become entitled in relation to the Debt as a result of any law or any rule or regulation of government;

"Shortfall":
the amount by which the total of the administration charges under clause 14.1.1 in respect of Debts notified:
(i)   in any year starting on the Starting Date or any anniversary of it; or
(ii)   in any month starting during the period of this Agreement (as specified in clause 4.1);

is less than respectively the annual amount or the monthly amount shown in section 10;

...

"Unapproved":
in relation to any Debt, not Approved;

"Writing":
any form of communication that is accessible so that it may be recorded in a permanent form and used at any time after it has been made and "written" is to be construed accordingly.

30   Guarantees[1]

Vast sums of money are lent every year on the security of a guarantee furnished by a third party.[2] The directors of a private limited company applying to its bank for a loan are likely to be asked by the bank to demonstrate their confidence in their own management by guaranteeing the company's overdraft. A company may be asked to guarantee the obligations of its parent or subsidiary. Not infrequently, a number of companies in a group enter into arrangements with the group's bankers by which each member of the group guarantees the liabilities of every other member, each guarantee being reinforced by security over the guarantor's assets.

Much of our export trade is stimulated by institutional guarantees. In common with most other countries, the United Kingdom offers government credit insurance to its exporters, through the Export Credits Guarantee Department, giving cover to sellers of goods against the default of their overseas buyers by guaranteeing bills of exchange on the buyer purchased by banks.[3] Banks themselves play a prominent part in the furnishing of guarantees and analogous instruments such as bid bonds and performance bonds.[4] States are frequently called upon to guarantee the obligations of their trading enterprises.

At a much humbler level, guarantees are often exacted in connection with consumer credit. For example, a dealer block discounting hire-purchase agreements may be asked to guarantee the obligations of the hirers; an intending hirer may himself be required to put forward the name of a third party as a surety.

The law has always adopted a protective attitude towards guarantors, taking the view that any act of the creditor which increases the guarantor's risk without his consent entitles him to be discharged from liability, wholly or in part. So for those advising banks and finance houses who intend to provide funds on the security of a guarantee, a knowledge of the legal principles involved is of first importance.

---

1   The most comprehensive treatment of this subject is by James O'Donovan and John C. Phillips, *The Modern Contract of Guarantee* (3rd edn, 2003). The other principal English textbooks are Geraldine Andrews and Richard Millett, *Law of Guarantees* (3rd edn, 2001) and *Rowlatt on the Law of Principal and Surety* (5th edn, 2001). See also *Chitty on Contracts* (29th edn, 2004), ch 44. For a concise treatment, see Roy Goode, *Legal Problems of Credit and Security* (3rd edn, 2003), ch VIII.
2   Termed a guarantor or surety. The terms are treated by modern writers as interchangeable. The former is used throughout this chapter.
3   The system of state guarantees was anticipated some 4,000 years ago in the Code of Hammurabi. See Willis D. Morgan, 'The History and Economics of Suretyship', 12 Corn LQ 153, 487 (1927). See also O'Donovan and Phillips, *Modern Contract of Guarantee*, paras 1–01 ff.
4   See pp 1015 ff.

I.   THE LEGAL NATURE OF A GUARANTEE

(i)   Characteristics of a suretyship guarantee

In the sense used in this chapter[5] a guarantee is an undertaking to answer for another's default. It is thus both a secondary and an accessory engagement. It is secondary in that the guarantor can be sued only after default by the principal debtor; and it is accessory in that, in principle, the guarantor's obligation is coterminous with the obligation of the principal debtor and is enforceable only where and to the extent that the principal contract is enforceable.[6] Just as a loan contract may limit the lender's rights to a specific fund or security, imposing no personal repayment obligation on the borrower, so also a guarantee may take the form of real security furnished by the guarantor without personal commitment on his part. For example, in consideration of A lending money to B, B's friend C may deposit the deeds of his house with A by way of equitable mortgage without personal obligation for repayment of the loan in the event of B's default.[7] In such a case the rights conferred by the guarantee are restricted to the enforcement of the security, and if this proves inadequate, that is A's misfortune; he cannot look to C for the deficiency.

The typical guarantee is an undertaking to meet the money liability of the principal debtor arising from his default, whether the default itself relates to the payment of money or the performance of some other obligation, for example, to execute building works. But there is nothing to prevent a guarantor from assuming a secondary liability for performance of the principal debtor's non-money obligations, and it is not uncommon for suretyship bonds given in connection with construction contracts to empower the issuer of the bond to take over the contract upon default by the contractor, as an alternative to payment of damages. There has been much case law as to the circumstances in which a woman who gives a bank a guarantee for her husband's debts can have the guarantee set aside on the ground of misrepresentation or undue influence. This is not discussed in the present chapter, which focuses on guarantees by commercial parties.

(ii)   Suretyship guarantee distinguished from primary undertaking

A guarantee is to be distinguished from a contract involving a primary obligation to the creditor, eg an indemnity. The classic exposition of the difference is the example given in *Birkmyr v Darnell*.[8] A says to B: 'Supply goods to C and, if he does not pay you, I will.' That is a contract of guarantee. But if A says to B: 'Supply goods to C and I will see that you are paid', that is a contract of indemnity. The illustration is neat, but the usual explanation of it tends to obscure rather than to illumine the principle. It is said that in the first case A's liability is dependent on B's default, while in the second it is not. This by itself tells us little in a situation where

---

5   Demand guarantees, performance bonds and standby credits are not suretyship guarantees but undertakings which are primary in form, though secondary in intent. See p 1015.

6   See p 814, and Johan Steyn, 'Guarantees: The Co-Extensiveness Principle' (1974) 90 LQR 246.

7   *Re Conley* [1938] 2 All ER 127. As to non-recourse loans, see p 609.

8   (1704) 1 Salk 27.

the obligations of the indemnifier have the same content as those of the principal debtor and both fall due at the same time, for the indemnifier will then be called upon to pay only where payment has not already been made by the principal debtor. The essential point of an indemnity, or other primary undertaking, is that it is a distinct, autonomous undertaking which is in no way dependent for its content or enforceability on the terms or validity of the undertaking given by the debtor.[9] Into this category fall undertakings by A:

(a) to be answerable for any loss suffered by B as a result of contracting with C;
(b) as issuer of a letter of credit;[10]
(c) as acceptor of a bill of exchange where the acceptance is given for C's accommodation;[11]
(d) as issuer of a demand guarantee or performance bond for performance of C's obligations.[12]

In each of these four cases A's payment undertaking is a primary obligation that exists independently of the contract between B and C, which is governed by its own terms and which B can in principle enforce against A whether or not B has an enforceable claim against C. The distinction between a guarantee, a parallel primary obligation and an obligation as co-contractor can be expressed diagrammatically as shown in figure 30.1.

It is not uncommon to find contracts of a hybrid character in which the obligations of A to B are in principle made dependent on C's default, but which differ in some measure from C's obligations, whether as to amount or as to the time of performance, so that they have an independent force of their own. Indeed, there is nothing to stop a guarantee and an indemnity from being combined in the same document; and it is always open to A and B, when concluding a guarantee, to agree on terms which qualify the correlation between A's liability to B and C's liability to B.

Two parties who contract with the creditor as principals may nevertheless agree between themselves that one is to be a mere surety and the whole burden is to fall on the other. Such an agreement, to which the creditor is a stranger, does not affect him until he has notice of it, after which he is obliged to treat the first co-debtor as a surety.[13]

(iii) Analogous transactions

Some undertakings, though not strictly guarantees, are analogous in character and have similar incidents. For example, the primary party liable on a bill of exchange is the acceptor, and vis-à-vis the holder, the drawer and indorsers stand in the position

---

9 *Yeoman Credit Ltd v Latter* [1961] 2 All ER 294; *Argo Caribbean Group Ltd v Lewis* [1976] 2 Lloyd's Rep 289.
10 See pp 971, 980.
11 See p 499.
12 See p 1015.
13 *Rouse v Bradford Banking Co* [1894] AC 586. The equity of allowing a creditor's position to be adversely changed in this way after the making of the principal contract and without his prior knowledge or consent is not self-evident.

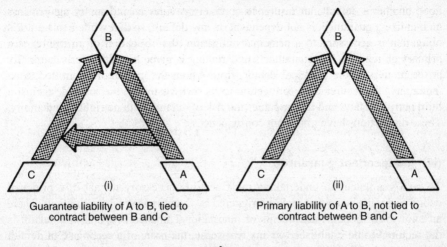

(i)
Guarantee liability of A to B, tied to
contract between B and C

(ii)
Primary liability of A to B, not tied to
contract between B and C

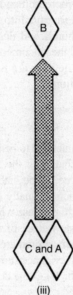

(iii)

Primary liability of C and A to B as
principals under the same contract

Fig 30.1 Structure of guarantee and primary liability relationships

of sureties for the acceptor, so that, in principle, their liability is dependent on that
of the acceptor, they cannot be sued before the bill falls due for payment by the
acceptor and they are discharged if the liability of the acceptor is extinguished.[14]

A guarantee at first sight looks similar to a contract of insurance by which the
insurer undertakes to make a payment to the insured on default by a third party. But
the similarity is more apparent than real. A guarantee is an undertaking to make

14 *Byles on Bills of Exchange* (27th edn, 2002), pp 464–465.

good another's default; an insurance contract provides an indemnity against loss and, unlike a guarantee, is not dependent on any default, so that while a guarantor's obligation is accessory to a principal obligation, the obligation of an insurer is a primary obligation. The guarantor's undertaking is given to a third party, normally at the request of the principal debtor, from whom the guarantor is entitled to an indemnity; the insurer gives protection to its own customer, the insured, against a third party's default and thus assumes the risk of default, with no right of indemnity. These distinctions have important consequences.[15]

(iv) Independent guarantee

To be a guarantee, an undertaking must be truly accessory to that of a principal debtor and must be an undertaking triggered by the principal debtor's default. There are, however, modern instruments of international finance in which the default is not required to be established in any real sense, the issue of a certificate of default by the creditor himself, or even his mere demand for payment, being sufficient to impose on the 'guarantor' the duty to pay. Into this category fall many standby credits, unconditional performance bonds and demand guarantees.[16] Undertakings of this kind, in which production of the document is specified as the condition of payment, not merely as evidence of default, are not suretyship guarantees but take effect as independent primary obligations.

(v) Letter of comfort

A document is not a guarantee unless intended to be legally binding. A letter of comfort – for example, a letter confirming that it is the issuer's policy to ensure that its subsidiaries are at all times able to meet their liabilities – may be so framed as to indicate an assumption of liability[17] but is usually designed to provide no more than moral reassurance.[18] This is particularly the case where the party issuing the letter has refused to give a guarantee. The same is true of letters of awareness.[19] There is a presumption that an undertaking given in a commercial context is intended to be legally binding but this is readily rebuttable by evidence showing that this was not the intention of the parties, and it is that intention which it is the task of the court to ascertain.[20]

---

15 See generally R. M. Goode 'Surety and On-Demand Performance Bonds' [1988] JBL 87 at pp 88–89; O'Donovan and Phillips, *Modern Contract of Guarantee*, paras 1–111 ff; Andrews and Millett, *Law of Guarantees*, para 1.08; *Rowlatt on The Law of Principal and Surety*, pp 7 ff.

16 See p 1015. The position is otherwise for guarantees that require default but permit this to be proved by a certificate, as under the ICC Uniform Rules for Contract Bonds, art 7(j).

17 As in *Chemco Leasing SpA v Rediffusion plc* [1987] FTLR 201.

18 See *Kleinwort Benson Ltd v Malaysian Mining Corp.* [1989] 1 All ER 785, in which the letter of comfort was held not to be contractual in character, a conclusion which was hardly surprising in view of the fact that it would have given the plaintiffs stronger rights than under a guarantee which the defendants had already declined to provide.

19 *Hongkong and Shanghai Banking Corp Ltd v Jurong Engineering Ltd* [2000] 2 SLR 54. A letter of awareness fulfils the same role as a letter of comfort and is so called because it contains a statement by the party issuing it that it is aware of the addressee's offer to make a loan facility available to the prospective borrower. A letter of intent is similar.

20 See *Edwards v Skyways Ltd* [1964] 1 All ER 494; *Hongkong and Shanghai Banking Corp Ltd v Jurong Engineering Ltd*, n 19.

2. TYPES OF GUARANTEE

There are various ways in which guarantees may be classified, but the two divisions of most importance are discrete (or fixed) versus continuing guarantees, and guarantees given at the debtor's request as opposed to those given solely at the request of the creditor.

(i) Discrete and continuing guarantees

We have seen that a credit transaction may take one of two forms: fixed-sum credit, in which the amount of financial accommodation to be provided is determined at the outset, the transaction is a discrete transaction and the debtor's payments are intended to lead to the ultimate discharge of his indebtedness and termination of the debtor– creditor relationship; and revolving (or running-account) credit, in which the debtor is given a *facility* on which he can draw at leisure, the relationship between the parties is intended to be of indeterminate duration and the agreement contemplates a flow of dealings between the parties in which the debtor's primary obligation is to keep within the agreed credit limit.

The contract of guarantee, true to its accessory nature, divides on similar lines. A may guarantee C's liability to B on a specific transaction or transactions,[21] or may give a continuing guarantee covering a flow of transactions between B and C pursuant to a facility or master agreement agreed between them, in which event A's liability is not fixed but varies according to C's outstanding indebtedness to B at any one time.[22] The characteristic of a continuing guarantee is that it endures for as long as the debtor–creditor relationship between B and C continues or until such earlier time as A chooses to withdraw his guarantee as regards future transactions. Thus in the case of a continuing guarantee there is no specific amount of credit the repayment of which is guaranteed; there is merely a fluctuating *balance*, which rises as B utilizes the credit and falls as he makes payment in reduction of his indebtedness, and it is the ultimate debit balance for which A is responsible in the event of C's default. This is why a bank guarantee of a customer's overdraft commonly provides that the guarantee is not to be treated as discharged by an intermediate satisfaction of the customer's indebtedness. The customer may clear his overdraft by a payment to the credit of his account, reducing the debit balance to nil, but if a week later his account goes into debit again as the result of fresh drawings, the guarantor under a continuing guarantee is not out of the wood, for his undertaking relates to the customer's indebtedness from time to time, and the extinction of the debit balance at any particular time does not bring an end to the debtor–creditor relationship nor, in consequence, to his guarantee of defaults arising from that relationship.

21 As in fig 30.2.
22 See fig 30.3.

804

Guarantee

To _____ , Registered in England number _____
whose registered office is at

Account
number

In consideration of your agreeing at my request to enter into a hire purchase agreement ('the Agreement') with the hirer named in Part 1 of the Schedule

hereto (hereinafter called 'the Hirer') for ————————————————————————————————

I the undersigned Guarantor named in Part 2 of the schedule hereto hereby agree:

1 To guarantee the due observance and performance by the Hirer of all terms contained in the Agreement

2 To pay upon written demand being made to me by you any sum due to you from the Hirer and unpaid by him

3 My liability under this guarantee shall be computed on the footing that the Agreement is fully binding and enforceable against the Hirer and that my said liability shall not in any way be discharged diminished or affected by the invalidity or unenforceability of the Agreement or by:

   i   The granting of time or indulgence to me or to the Hirer;
   ii The effecting of any release or compromise with the Hirer or any agreement not to sue the Hirer;
   iii The impairment of any security taken from the Hirewr or the failure to realise or enforce such security;
   iv The variation of any term or terms of the Agreement or the substitution of any new goods for goods comprised in the Agreement which are damaged lost stolen or destroyed; but so that i shall not be liable by reason of such variation or substitution for payment of any sum greater than the total amount for which I would have been liable if such variation or substitution had not been made

4 In the interpretation of this guarantee words in the singular shall include the plural and ther masculine the feminine and vice versa and where this guarantee ios made by two or more persons all such persons shall be jointly and severally liable for the due performance and observance of all the terms and conditions herein contained and neither the release of nor granting of time or any other indulgence to any one of such persons shall release or discharge the other or others of such persons from his or their obligations hereunder neither shall bankruptcy insolvency winding-up; or death of one or more of such persons discharge the other or others

5 Any demand made by you hereunder shall be validly made if served upon me personally or sent to me by pre-paid post to or left at my address stated below or to or at my current business or private address or that last known to you and if sent by first clasee pre-paid post shall be conclusively deemed to have been received by me within forty-eight hours after the time of posting   *delete as appropriate*

Part 1 Full name of Hirer *Mr/Mrs/Miss		Period at residence years
Full address of Hirer *Number and road*	*Town*	*County and postcode*
Part 2 Full name of Guarantor *Mr/Mrs/Miss	Telephone number	Period at residence years
Full address of Guarantor *Number and road*	*Town*	*County and postcode*
Previous address *if less than 2 years at present address*		Period at previous residence years
Name and address of bankers		Bank sorting code — —
Date of birth *Married/Single	Number of dependants (i.e. spouse, if not employed, & children under 18)	Type of resident *Owner/Council tenant/Other (R)	is property jointly owned *Yes/No
Occupation *(describe fully)*	Present employer's name *(trading name is self-employed)*		
Present employer's address *(trading address is self-employed)*		How long in present employment years
Name and address of previous employer *(if less than 2 years in above employment)*		How long in present employment years
Name and address of finance companies with whom you have, or have had transactions *(please give details)*		

If this guarantee is not to be entered into by a limited company it must be signed by a Director or another authorised person or if by a partnership or firm it must be signed by all partners

Signature of Guarantor ————————————————————   Date ————————————————

Signature of
independent witness ————————————————————   Name of witness ————————————
                                                       Capital letters please

Address ————————————————————   Occupation ————————————
A second witness is required if the guarantor is signed in Scotland

Signature of
independent witness ————————————————————   Name of witness ————————————
                                                       Capital letters please

Address ————————————————————   Occupation ————————————

2500   8.80

Fig 30.2 Specific guarantee

Guarantee

To **Barclays Bank PLC**

1. In consideration of your giving time credit and/or banking facilities and accommodation to

("the Principal") I/we the undersigned hereby guarantee the payment or discharge to you and undertake that the undersigned will on demand in writing made on the undersigned pay or discharge to you all moneys and liabilities which shall for the time being be due owing or incurred by the Principal to you whether actually or contingently and whether solely or jointly with any other person and whether as principal or surety including interest commission or other lawful charges and expenses which you may in the course of your business charge in respect of any of the matters aforesaid or for keeping the Principal's account (including any further advances made by you to the Principal and any other liabilities of the Principal to you arising during the three months period of notice hereinafter referred to) together also with:-

(i) such further sum for interest (whether or not the same shall have been compounded) and banking charges accruing due to you from the Principal before or after the date of demand or expiration of the said notice as the case may be and not debited to the Principal's account at such date, and

(ii) all costs and expenses recoverable by you from the Principal

Provided always that the total amount recoverable hereunder shall not exceed the sum of   pounds and in addition the interest (on that amount or on such less sum as may be due and owing) charges costs and expenses referred to in sub-paragraphs (i) and (ii) above and in Clause 2 below.

2. The undersigned hereby agree to pay you all costs and expenses (on a full indemnity basis) arising out of or in connection with the recovery by you of the moneys due to you under this Guarantee.

3. This Guarantee is to be a continuing security to you notwithstanding any settlement of account or other matter or thing whatsoever but may and shall be determined (save as below provided) and the liability hereunder

305 (BLSC 4/02)

Fig 30.3 'All-moneys' continuing guarantee and indemnity

crystallised (except as regards unascertained or contingent liabilities and the interest charges costs and expenses hereinbefore referred to) at the expiration of three months after the receipt by you from the undersigned of notice in writing to determine it but notwithstanding determination as to one or more of the undersigned this Guarantee is to remain a continuing security as to the other or others.

4. A demand for payment or any other demand or notice under this Guarantee may be made or given by any manager officer or agent of yours or of any branch of yours by letter addressed to the undersigned and sent by post to or left at the last known place of business or abode of the undersigned or at your option in the case of a company its registered office and if sent by post shall be deemed to have been made or given at noon on the day following the day the letter was posted.

5. For all purposes of the liability of the undersigned to you under this Guarantee (including in particular but without prejudice to the generality of the foregoing for all purposes the liability of the undersigned for interest) every sum of money which may now be or which hereafter may from time to time become due or owing to you as aforesaid by the Principal (or would have become so due or owing were it not for the bankruptcy or winding up of the Principal) shall be deemed to continue due and owing to you by the Principal until the same shall be actually repaid to you notwithstanding the bankruptcy or winding up of the Principal or any other event whatever and in case of the death of the Principal all sums which would have been due or owing as aforesaid to you by the Principal if the Principal had lived until the time at which you shall receive actual notice of his death shall for all purposes of this Guarantee be deemed included in the moneys due and owing to you by the Principal.

6. This Guarantee is to be in addition to and is not to prejudice or be prejudiced by any other securities or guarantees (including any guarantee signed by the undersigned) which you may now or hereafter hold from or on account of the Principal and is to be binding on the undersigned as a continuing security notwithstanding any payments from time to time made to you or any settlement of account or disability or incapacity affecting the undersigned or the death of the undersigned or any other thing whatsoever.

7. This Guarantee is to be applicable to the ultimate balance that may become due to you from the Principal and until payment of such balance the undersigned shall not be entitled to participate in any security held or money received by you on account of such balance or to stand in your place in respect of any such security or money.

8. You are to be at liberty in the event of this Guarantee ceasing from any cause whatsoever to be binding as a continuing security on the undersigned to open a fresh account and to continue any then existing account with the Principal and no moneys paid into any such fresh account by or on behalf of the Principal shall on a settlement of any claim

3

under this Guarantee be appropriated towards or have the effect of payment of any part of the moneys due from the Principal at the time of this Guarantee ceasing to be so binding as aforesaid unless the person (other than the undersigned) paying in such moneys shall at the time direct you in writing specially to appropriate the same for that purpose.

9. In the event of this Guarantee being determined either by notice by the undersigned or by demand in writing by you, or in the event of your receiving notice of any disability or incapacity of the undersigned, it shall be lawful for you to continue the account with the Principal notwithstanding such determination or notice of disability or incapacity and the liability of the undersigned for the amount due from the Principal at the date upon which such determination of this Guarantee shall become operative and of effect or when you shall receive notice of any disability or incapacity of the undersigned shall remain, notwithstanding any subsequent payment into or out of the account by or on behalf of the Principal.

10. Any admission or acknowledgement in writing by the Principal or any person on behalf of the Principal of the amount of the indebtedness of the Principal or otherwise in relation to the subject matter of this Guarantee or any judgment or award obtained by you against the Principal or proof by you in Bankruptcy or Companies Winding Up which is admitted or any statement of account furnished by you the correctness of which is certified by any one of your Directors, Assistant Directors, Regional Directors or Managers shall be binding and conclusive on the undersigned.

11. You are to be at liberty without thereby affecting your rights hereunder at any time and from time to time (whether before or after any demand for payment made by you under or any notice of determination of this Guarantee or receipt by you of any notice of any disability or incapacity of the undersigned) to refuse or grant (as the case may be) further credit to the Principal to renew any bills of exchange or promissory notes for any period and to compound with give time for payment or grant other indulgence to the Principal or to any obligant on bills of exchange or promissory notes or otherwise or to accept compositions from and make any other arrangements with the Principal or any persons liable to you in respect of securities held or to be held by you to give up modify exchange or abstain from perfecting or taking advantage of or enforcing any securities guarantees or other contracts or the proceeds of any of the foregoing and to discharge any parties thereto and to realise any securities in such manner as you may think expedient.

12. In the event of the bankruptcy or insolvency of the Principal or of his entering into a composition or arrangement with his creditors or if the Principal is a company society or corporation in the event of the Principal going into liquidation or being wound up or reconstructed or making any arrangement with their creditors any dividends or payments which you may receive from the Principal or his estate or any other person shall be taken and applied as payments in gross and shall not prejudice your right

4

to recover from the undersigned to the full extent of this Guarantee the ultimate balance which after the receipt of such dividends or payments may remain owing to you by the Principal.

13. You are also to be at liberty without thereby affecting your rights hereunder at any time and from time to time at your absolute discretion to release discharge compound with or otherwise vary or agree to vary the liability under this Guarantee of or make any other arrangements with any one or more of the undersigned and no such release discharge composition variation agreement or arrangement shall prejudice or in any way affect your rights and remedies against the other or others of the undersigned.

14. You are also to be at liberty, without prejudice to any other rights you may have, at any time and from time to time to place and keep for such time as you may think prudent any moneys received recovered or realised under or by virtue of this Guarantee to or at a separate or suspense account to the credit either of the undersigned or of you as you shall think fit without any intermediate obligation on your part to apply the same or any part thereof in or towards the discharge of the moneys due or owing to you as aforesaid by the Principal.

15. In the event of the bankruptcy or winding up of the Principal you are to be at liberty (notwithstanding payment to you by the undersigned or any other person of the whole or any part of the amount hereby guaranteed or any release settlement discharge or arrangement made or given by you) to rank as creditors and prove against the Principal's estate or in the Principal's liquidation for the full amount of your claim and you may and shall receive and retain the whole of the dividends to the exclusion of the rights (if any) of the undersigned as guarantor in competition with you until your claim is fully satisfied.

16. No assurance security or payment which may be avoided under any enactment relating to bankruptcy or under section 127, 238 to 245 (inclusive) of the Insolvency Act 1986 or any of such sections and no release settlement discharge or arrangement which may have been given or made on the faith of any such assurance security or payment shall prejudice or affect your right to recover from the undersigned to the full extent of this Guarantee as if such assurance security payment release settlement discharge or arrangement (as the case may be) had never been granted given or made And any such release settlement discharge or arrangement shall as between you and the undersigned be deemed to have been given or made upon the express condition that it shall become and be wholly void and of no effect if the assurance security or payment on the faith of which it was made or given shall be void or (as the case may be) shall at any time thereafter be avoided under any of the before-mentioned statutory provisions to the intent and so that you shall become and be entitled at any time after any such avoidance to exercise all or any of the rights in this Guarantee expressly conferred upon you and/or all or any other rights which by virtue and as a consequence of this Guarantee you would have been entitled to exercise but for such release

settlement discharge or arrangement And where any security is held by you for the liability of the undersigned hereunder you shall be at liberty at your absolute discretion to retain such security for a period of twenty five months after the repayment of all sums that are or may become due to you from the Principal notwithstanding any release settlement discharge or arrangement given or made by you on or as a consequence of such repayments and if at any time within the period of two years after such repayment either a bankruptcy petition shall be presented against the Principal or a petition shall be presented to a competent Court for an order for the winding up of the Principal or the appointment of an administrator in respect of the Principal or the Principal (being a company) shall commence to be wound-up voluntarily you shall be at liberty and notwithstanding as before mentioned to continue to retain such security or any part thereof for and during such further period as you in your absolute discretion shall determine and the undersigned agree that such security shall be deemed to have been and to have remained held by you as and by way of security for the payment to you of all or any sums which shall or may become due and owing to you from and by the undersigned either under and by virtue of the terms and conditions of this Guarantee in the event of and upon or after any avoidance of any assurance security or payment under the said enactment relating to bankruptcy or the said sections of the Insolvency Act 1986 or any of such sections or under or as a consequence of an Order (if any) made under section 241 of the Insolvency Act 1986.

17. In the event of any Order being made under section 241 of the Insolvency Act 1986 then, unless you in your absolute discretion shall otherwise determine, any sum (other than any sum for or representing costs) which shall be paid to you by the undersigned with the object of complying with the requirements of such Order or which upon a realisation of any security deposited with you by the undersigned shall be retained and applied by you in or towards the payment or discharge of any sum (other than costs) payable to you by the undersigned pursuant to any such Order shall for all or any of the purposes of this Guarantee and notwithstanding that it shall have been so paid with the aforesaid object or so retained and applied in manner before stated be treated as between you on the one hand and the undersigned on the other hand as having been paid by the undersigned pursuant to a demand for payment made by you or on your behalf under this Guarantee.

18. As a separate and independent stipulation (but without increasing the before-mentioned total amount recoverable hereon) the undersigned agree that all sums of money which may not be recoverable from the undersigned on the footing of a guarantee whether by reason of any legal limitation disability or incapacity on or of the Principal or any other fact or circumstance and whether known to you or not shall nevertheless be recoverable from the undersigned as sole or principal debtor(s) in respect thereof and shall be repaid by the undersigned on demand in writing made by you or on your behalf.

6

19. When the Principal is or are an unincorporated body committee partnership trustees or debtors on a joint account this Guarantee shall not be affected by any change, whether by death retirement or addition or by any other means, or, the Principal being a partnership firm, by any change in respect of the style of the firm, but shall remain valid continuing and effective as fully and in all respects as if the person or persons constituting such body committee partnership trustees or debtors on joint account at the date of any demand for payment made by you under or any notice of determination of this Guarantee or at any time previously was or were the same as at the date hereof.

20. This Guarantee shall continue to bind the undersigned notwithstanding any amalgamation that may be effected by you with any other company or person whether the new company thus formed shall or shall not differ in its name objects character and constitution from you the above named Bankers it being the intent that this Guarantee shall remain valid and effectual in all respects and for all purposes in favour of and with reference to any such new company when formed and may be proceeded on and enforced in the same manner to all intents and purposes as if such new company had been expressly named in and referred to herein instead of you Barclays Bank PLC.

21. In case of the death of the undersigned any demand made or given as aforesaid and addressed to him shall for all purposes of this Guarantee be deemed a sufficient demand by you upon him and his executors or administrators and shall be as effectual as if he were still living.

22. Where this Guarantee is signed by more than one party the liability of each of them hereunder to you shall be joint and several and every agreement and undertaking on their part shall be construed accordingly.

23. The liability hereunder of the undersigned and each of them if more than one shall not be avoided or invalidated by reason of any guarantee or any charge by any co-surety being invalid or unenforceable.

24. Throughout this Guarantee wherever the context admits, the singular shall include the plural and vice versa, the expression "the undersigned" shall mean and include every person liable hereunder (including all partners in a firm) or any one or more of them and his/their executors and administrators and (in addition) the committee receiver or other person lawfully acting on behalf of every such person but no personal liability shall attach to any duly authorised agent or attorney signing as such, the expression "person" shall mean and include a company, society, corporation, firm or an individual, and in the case of an individual his executors administrators committee receiver or other person lawfully acting on behalf of every such person and the expression "this Guarantee" shall be construed as including and extending to any separate or independent stipulation or agreement hereinbefore contained.

7

25. Any reference herein to any section in any Statute shall be deemed to include a reference to any statutory modification or re-enactment thereof for the time being in force.

26. The paper upon which this Guarantee is printed is, and at all time shall remain, your property.

Execution of Guarantee

Executed by us this   day of   20

Either

The Common Seal of   Limited
was hereunto affixed in pursuance of a Resolution of its
Board of Directors in the presence of

_____Director

_____Director/Secretary

Company's Registered Number

Or

Executed as a deed by   Limited

_____Director

_____Director/Secretary

Company's Registered Number

I/Each of us hereby acknowledge(s) receipt of a copy of the above Guarantee.

(ii) Guarantees given at request of debtor and guarantees given solely at request of creditor

It is important to distinguish guarantees given at the express or implied request of the debtor from those given without reference to the debtor at all. The world of hire-purchase finance provides a neat example of the distinction. Where a finance house supplies goods on hire-purchase to a debtor introduced by a dealer, the finance house may require a relative or a friend of the debtor to join in as a guarantor. The debtor will then ask the intended guarantor to assist him in this way in order that the debtor may obtain the hire-purchase facility. In addition, the finance house may have an arrangement with the dealer by which the latter guarantees payment by all the debtors he has introduced. Such a guarantee is fixed solely as the result of negotiation between finance house and dealer, and the debtors concerned are never consulted. The difference between the two forms of guarantee is significant in that in the former case the guarantor has an implied right of indemnity from the debtor, whereas in the latter, as we shall see later, his only rights against the debtor are those acquired by subrogation or assignment.

3.   UNILATERAL NATURE OF THE CONTRACT

The typical guarantee (and particularly the continuing guarantee) is unilateral in character. The bank gives no promise to the guarantor to extend credit to its customer; the consideration for the guarantor's undertaking is the bank's conduct in making the loan or honouring a drawing on the customer's account. In other words, the guarantor in effect says to the bank: 'If you lend C £100, I will repay you if he does not', or, in the case of a continuing guarantee: 'In consideration of your making advances to C from time to time, I will repay you if he does not.' So in the normal case[23] the guarantor's promise is an offer which the bank accepts by making the advance; and in the case of a continuing guarantee, the guarantor's undertaking is in the nature of a continuing offer generating a distinct act of acceptance, and thus a distinct contractual commitment, each time the bank honours a drawing on the account. So unless the guarantor receives consideration for making his offer irrevocable, he is entitled to withdraw it at any time before the advance to which it relates has been made, and this is so even if the creditor is contractually committed to the debtor to make the advance. This is why a guarantor under a continuing guarantee is always entitled to terminate it as to future advances, for as to these his offer has not yet been accepted.[24] But if the consideration for the guarantee is indivisible, the guarantor is committed for the whole of it where the creditor has begun performance by advancing part.[25]

---

23 There are, of course, many transactions in which the creditor does commit himself to the guarantor to make the advance to the principal debtor, and the contract of guarantee comes into force as an ordinary bilateral agreement through an exchange of promises. But such a transaction is atypical.

24 *Offord v Davies* (1862) 12 CBNS 748; *Coulthard v Clementson* (1879) 5 QBD 42. See also p 73.

25 See *Errington v Errington* [1952] 1 KB 290, per Denning LJ at 295. The case did not concern a guarantee but the judgment of Denning LJ reaffirmed the general principle that once the stipulated performance under a unilateral contract has begun, the promisor cannot revoke his promise, though of course he does not have to fulfil it until performance has been completed.

4.   RELATIONS BETWEEN CREDITOR AND GUARANTOR

(i)   Validity and enforceability

1.   Formalities

To bind the guarantor, a guarantee must either be by deed or be supported by consideration. Many guarantees are executed as deeds; where they are not, the consideration usually takes the form not of a counter-promise by the intending creditor to enter into the transaction with the prospective debtor but the actual conclusion of that transaction by the making of the advance.[26] Even if it is a valid contract, a guarantee constituting a 'special promise to answer for the debt, default or miscarriage of another' is unenforceable under the Statute of Frauds unless evidenced by a note or memorandum in writing signed by the guarantor or by some other person authorized to sign it on his behalf.[27] The note or memorandum must identify the parties and set out all the material terms but need not specify the consideration.[28] However, not all guarantees are within the statute, only those which require the guarantor to pay from his own resources. So if the guarantor agrees to pay from funds he owes the principal debtor and the latter agrees to their use for that purpose, the guarantor is not paying from his own funds and the guarantee is outside the statute. By contrast, if the debtor did not so agree, so that the payment was an officious payment not going towards extinguishment of the debt, the guarantor's obligation remains to pay from his own funds and the guarantee is unenforceable if not evidenced by the requisite note or memorandum in writing.[29]

2.   Creditor's duty of disclosure

When procuring the guarantee the creditor owes no general duty of disclosure to the prospective guarantor, but he is obliged to disclose any unusual feature of his contract with the debtor which the prospective guarantor would not otherwise have expected, failing which any resulting guarantee may become voidable.[30]

---

26   See above.
27   Statute of Frauds 1677, s 4. A guarantee securing a regulated agreement within the Consumer Credit Act 1974 must be in writing, not merely evidenced by writing (s.105(1)).
28   Mercantile Law Amendment Act 1856, s 3.
29   *Actionstrength Ltd v International Glass Engineering IN.GLEN Spa* [2002] 1 WLR 566. An appeal to the House of Lords [2003] 2 WLR 1060 on a separate ground, namely that the debtor was estopped from relying on the statute, was dismissed, there being no evidence of any representation by the guarantor that it would honour the guarantee despite the lack of writing or that it would confirm the guarantee in writing. It is, however, clear from this and earlier cases that where the necessary elements are present, a party may be estopped from invoking a statute that would otherwise shield him from liability.
30   *Royal Bank of Scotland v Etridge (No 2)* [2002] 2 AC 773, per Lord Nicholls at para 81; *Far Eastern Shipping Co Public Ltd v Scales Trading Ltd* [2001] 1 All ER (Comm) 319 (failure to disclose dishonest inflation of invoices).

(ii) Nature and extent of guarantor's liability

1.   Nature of the undertaking

What the guarantor undertakes is a matter of construction of the contract; but, in the absence of a contrary intention, the guarantor's responsibility is not merely[31] to pay £x to the creditor if the debtor fails to do so, but to procure the debtor's performance of his own obligations to the creditor. So if the debtor repudiates the contract and the creditor accepts the repudiation, thus converting a future right to payment of a debt into a right to damages, the guarantor is not discharged from liability. On the contrary, this, like the liability of the principal debtor, becomes transmuted from debt to damages. The creditor's election to accept the debtor's repudiation is not a variation of the contract, discharging the guarantor if made without his consent; it is an enforcement of it. This is well brought out by the decision of the House of Lords in *Moschi v Lep Air Services Ltd*:[32]

> A company which owed a substantial sum of money agreed to discharge its indebtedness by weekly instalments, and performance of its obligations was guaranteed by the appellant. The company failed to carry out the terms of the agreement, and the respondents treated the failure as a repudiation and elected to terminate the contract. The company having gone into liquidation, the respondents sued the appellant for the full unpaid balance of the debt with interest. The appellant contended that by terminating the contract with the principal debtor, the respondents had released him from liability, since the termination was to be regarded as the equivalent of a variation which he had not authorized.

> The House of Lords, affirming the decision of the Court of Appeal, rejected the appellant's contention, holding that his undertaking as guarantor was not to pay the instalments as such in default of payment by the company but to procure performance by the company of its obligations under the agreement. Accordingly, the claim against the guarantor was in reality for damages, not debt, the measure of damages being the amount of the debtor company's liability, whether the primary liability in respect of the instalments or the secondary liability to pay damages into which the company's primary liability was transmuted when the contract came to an end by acceptance of its repudiation.

In rejecting the appellant's contention, the House came to the only possible decision. As Lord Simon pointed out, the result of the appellant's argument would be to lose the guarantor at the very moment the creditor most needed him, namely at the moment of fundamental breach by the principal promisor.[33]

Less convincing is the proposition advanced by several of their Lordships that a claim against a guarantor on a guarantee of a debt sounds not in debt but in damages, the measure of damages being the amount of the debt. In support of this proposition Lord Diplock pointed out that in the old days the form of action against a guarantor was in special *assumpsit* not *indebitatus assumpsit*. There are, however,

---

31 See below for a comment on the statement in *Moschi v Lep Air Services Ltd* [1973] AC 331 that the guarantor's liability does not sound in debt at all but is for damages even where the guaranteed obligation is itself a debt.

32 Ibid.

33 Ibid at 355. For a later decision of the House of Lords to the same effect, see *Hyundai Heavy Industries Co Ltd v Papadopoulos* [1980] 2 All ER 29; cf *Chatterton v Maclean* [1951] 1 All ER 761.

dangers in relying on the old forms of action to demonstrate the basis of a monetary claim in present-day procedure. The fact is that *all* forms of *assumpsit*, even those in respect of what we should now call debt, such as a claim for the price of goods sold and delivered, were, in theory, claims to damages. The difference between *indebitatus assumpsit* and special *assumpsit* was not between debt and damages (both were in form a claim for damages for non-payment of debt) but between a mere allegation of indebtedness and a detailed pleading of the underlying transaction. Nowadays, however, a claim in contract for the price of goods or for repayment of money is characterized as a debt claim, and the same is true of a claim against a guarantor for the amount of the guaranteed debt. It is, no doubt, correct to say that the guarantor does not *merely* undertake payment of the guaranteed sum, he also undertakes to be answerable for performance of the contract by the debtor and pay any damages resulting from the principal debtor's repudiation of his contract. But that is not a good reason for characterizing the claim against the guarantor in respect of the debt itself as a claim for damages. The claim is never pleaded in this way, and the effect of characterizing it as damages would be to attract the normal incidents of a damages claim, including the duty to mitigate. But it is well established that the creditor is entitled to payment of the guaranteed sum as of right; he does not need to show that he has first exhausted his remedies against the principal debtor or taken any other steps to mitigate his loss. If B lends C £1,000 repayable by ten instalments, payment being guaranteed by A, then by implication A gives two undertakings: first, that if an instalment or part of it is not paid by C, A himself will pay it; secondly, that if C breaks his contract in such a way as to attract a liability in damages, A will be responsible in damages for an equivalent amount. The first part of A's undertaking sounds in debt, the second in damages. In other words, true to its accessory nature, the guarantee embodies undertakings having the same character as those of the obligations guaranteed. [34]

2. Correlation with debtor's liability

Except so far as otherwise provided by the terms of the guarantee, the liability of the guarantor is coterminous with that of the principal debtor. The guarantor therefore incurs no liability until the principal debtor has made default, is not liable for any amount in excess of that recoverable from the principal debtor and is discharged by an event which extinguishes the principal debtor's liability.[35] Moreover, if the contract with the principal debtor is void or unenforceable, the contract of guarantee is likewise void or unenforceable [36] except to the extent to which the parties have otherwise expressly or impliedly agreed. In each case it is a question of construction of the guarantee whether the risk assumed by the guarantor is only the default of the principal debtor or whether it extends to the invalidity or

---

34 See in this connection *Hampton v Minns* [2002] 1 WLR 1 and Goode, *Legal Problems*, para 8–10.
35 *Bechervaise v Lewis* (1872) LR 7 CP 372. As to the effect of receipts from the guarantor on the amount for which the creditor can prove it the principal debtor's liquidation, see p 837. As to the effect of a 'principal debtor' clause, see *M. S. Fashions Ltd v Bank of Credit and Commerce International SA (No.2)* [1993] 3 All ER 769.
36 *Coutts & Co v Browne-Lecky* [1947] KB 104; *Stadium Finance Co Ltd v Helm* (1965) 109 Sol Jo 471.

unenforceability of the principal contract itself.[37] The giving of the guarantee may itself be void, eg as ultra vires the guarantor.[38] The guarantor is entitled to invoke not only defences available to the principal debtor but also rights of transaction (or equitable) set-off arising from the close connection between claim and cross-claim, but not, it is thought, a right of independent (or statutory) set-off.[39]

3.   *Liabilities covered by the guarantee*

The scope of a guarantee's undertaking depends upon a proper interpretation of the guarantee itself. Many guarantees are 'all moneys' guarantees by which the guarantor accepts a secondary obligation for all sums previously advanced or to be advanced in the future to the principal debtor, for whatever reason. Nevertheless, the courts will not construe the wide terms of such a guarantee as covering liabilities outside those which the parties could reasonably have contemplated. So it has been held that an all moneys guarantee will not readily be construed as covering the debtor's obligations to the creditor in the creditor's capacity as assignee of a debt previously owed by the principal debtor to a third party.[40]

5.   RIGHTS OF THE GUARANTOR AGAINST THE DEBTOR

(i)   Indemnity

Where the guarantee was given at the request of the debtor, the guarantor has an implied contractual right to be indemnified by the debtor against all liabilities he incurs.[41] This is a specific application of the general principle that one who incurs expenditure or liabilities at another's request or with his authority is entitled to reimbursement or indemnity, since the request or authority implies an undertaking to reimburse or indemnify.[42]

At law the guarantor cannot enforce his right of indemnity by an action in debt except as regards payments he has actually made to the creditor; the mere fact that he has incurred a liability to pay is not sufficient.[43] However, in equity the guarantor may seek an order for indemnity as soon as he has incurred a liability for payment as the result of the principal debtor's default.[44] Such an order, however, is quite different from a judgment in debt. The debtor will not be directed to pay the amount of the debt

---

37 *Garrard v James* [1925] Ch 616. The effect of the difficult decision in *Coutts & Co v Browne-Lecky*, n 36 (guarantee of unenforceable contract with minor held unenforceable) has been reversed by s 2 of the Minors' Contracts Act 1987.

38 *Crédit Suisse v Allerdale Borough Council* [1995] 1 Lloyd's Rep 315 (guarantee by local authority).

39 See John Phillips, 'When should the guarantor be permitted to reply on the principal's set-off?' [2001] LMCLQ 383; Goode, *Legal Problems*, para 8–02.

40 *Kova Establishment v Sasco Investments Ltd* [1998] 2 BCLC 83, adopting a passage from the judgment of Brooking J in *Re Clark's Refrigerated Transport Pty Ltd* [1982] VR 989 at 995–996.

41 *Toussaint v Martinnant* (1787) 2 Term Rep 100; *Re a Debtor* (No. 627 of 1936) [1937] 1 All ER 1, per Greene LJ at 7–8. Frequently a right of indemnity is expressly stipulated eg under a counter-guarantee.

42 *Re a Debtor*, n 41, per Greene LJ at 8

43 *Re Mitchell* [1913] 1 Ch 201; *Re Richardson* [1911] 2 KB 705.

44 *Re Mitchell*, n 43; *Ascheson v Tredegar Dry Dock and Wharf Co Ltd* [1909] 2 Ch 401.

to the guarantor, for this would not exonerate the debtor's liability to the creditor, and the guarantor might apply the sum paid to some other purpose.[45] The normal order in equity is a declaration of a right to indemnity, coupled with a direction to the principal debtor to pay or secure the debt.[46] The declaration itself may be obtained in a *quia timet* action even before the principal debtor has made default, where there is evidence that he will do so,[47] and the plaintiff may be given liberty to apply for an order directing the debtor to pay or to secure the debt when the time for payment has accrued due and the amount of indebtedness has been ascertained.[48]

It is no defence to the guarantor's indemnity claim that he could not have been successfully sued by the creditor, eg because the guarantee was not evidenced by a note or memorandum in writing.[49]

No right of indemnity is given where the guarantor neither entered into the guarantee at the request of the debtor nor did so under legal compulsion or as an agent of necessity, for it is well established that one who officiously assumes responsibility for payment of another's debt cannot invoke an implied undertaking for indemnity and has no claim on the conscience of the debtor, who has had the benefit of the guarantee thrust upon him.[50] Again, the guarantee may qualify his right of indemnity by contract. A typical case is where the guarantor undertakes to the creditor not to prove in competition with the creditor in the bankruptcy of the principal debtor until the creditor has received payment in full.[51]

(ii) Subrogation

A guarantor who discharges the debt he has guaranteed is entitled to step into the shoes of the creditor and take over by subrogation all the creditor's rights against the debtor in respect of the debt and all the securities held by the creditor for payment of the debt, whether taken before or after the giving of the guarantee and whether or not their existence was known to the guarantor.[52] Even though the payment extinguishes the debt for which the security was given, the security is notionally kept alive for the benefit of the guarantor, who is entitled to have it transferred to him, together with the benefit of any judgment obtained by the creditor.[53] The guarantor acquires the same measure of priority as the creditor previously held, so that, for example, a guarantor who pays a preferential debt becomes himself a preferential creditor.[54]

45 *Wolmershausen v Gullick* [1893] 2 Ch 514; *Re Fenton* [1931] 1 Ch 85.
46 Ibid.
47 *Tate v Crewdson* [1938] Ch 869; *Watt v Mortlock* [1964] Ch 84.
48 Ibid; *Thomas v Nottingham Incorporated Football Club Ltd* [1972] Ch 596.
49 *Alexander v Vane* (1836) 1 M & W 511; *Re Chetwynd's Estate* [1938] Ch 13; *Argo Caribbean Group Ltd v Lewis*, n 9.
50 *Owen v Tate* [1976] QB 402, which contains a valuable exposition by Scarman LJ of the principles involved. The claim in that case was only for an indemnity. Had the plaintiff invoked the principle of subrogation he might have been successful. See on this Robert Goff and Gareth Jones, *Law of Restitution* (6th edn, 2002), pp 431–432. See also *The Zuhal K and Selin* [1987] 1 Lloyd's Rep 151.
51 As to this form of subordination agreement, see p 616.
52 *Forbes v Jackson* (1882) 19 Ch D 615; *Lake v Brutton* (1856) De GM & G 440.
53 Mercantile Law Amendment Act 1856, s 5; and see *Re McMyn* (1886) 33 Ch D 575, where it was said that the Act produced an implied assignment of the security.
54 *Re Lamplugh Iron Ore Co Ltd* [1927] 1 Ch 308.

Subrogation does not depend on any implied contract with the debtor or even on his consent. It is a right given by law to prevent unjust enrichment of the debtor, who would otherwise obtain the release of his securities without payment.[55] The right is limited to what is necessary to recoup to the guarantor the money actually paid by him in discharging his liability; any surplus obtained by the guarantor as a result of enforcing the rights acquired by subrogation must be accounted for to the principal debtor.[56] Unless he takes a statutory assignment, the guarantor cannot sue in his own name; he must bring proceedings in the name of the debtor.[57]

The guarantor cannot claim subrogation to securities or other rights of the creditor until he has paid the full amount of the indebtedness to which his guarantee relates.[58] He does not, on paying part of the guaranteed debt, acquire a proportionate interest in securities[59] or a proportionate right to prove in the principal debtor's bankruptcy.[60] On the other hand, a guarantor who guarantees only part of the debt (as opposed to one who guarantees the full indebtedness with a limit of liability[61]) does acquire a pro rata interest in the securities and a right to prove in the debtor's bankruptcy upon payment of the part of the debt which he guaranteed. [62] In effect, that part is treated as if it were a separate debt.

(iii) Rights as assignee

There is nothing to prevent the guarantor from purchasing the debt from the creditor and taking an assignment of the creditor's rights and securities. In such a case the guarantor is not limited to the sum necessary to recoup his outlay, for his payment is by way of purchase, not in discharge of his liability as surety.[63]

6.   DISCHARGE OF THE GUARANTOR

(i)   Failure of consideration for guarantee

In accordance with general principles of contract law a guarantor is discharged from liability where the creditor commits a repudiatory breach of the contract of guarantee[64] or where a non-promissory condition of the guarantee is not fulfilled.

55 *Yonge v Reynell* (1852) 9 Hare 809.
56 *Reed v Norris* (1837) 2 My & Cr 361; and cf *L. Lucas Ltd v Export Credits Guarantee Department* [1973] 2 All ER 984.
57 *Swire v Redman* (1876) 1 QBD 536.
58 *Re Howe* (1871) 6 Ch App 838, per Mellish LJ at 841; *Ewart v Latta* (1865) 4 Macq 983.
59 *Re Sass* [1896] 2 QB 12.
60 Ibid.
61 Ibid. This is why banks are always careful to ensure that a guarantor whose liability is to be limited to, say, £1,000 gives a guarantee of the whole indebtedness but with a limit of liability of £1,000, as opposed to a guarantee of the first £1,000 of the indebtedness.
62 *Goodwin v Gray* (1874) 22 WR 312.
63 Such liability is extinguished by merger, the debt becoming vested in the same person as the party liable for its payment in the event of the debtor's default.
64 *Ankar Pty Ltd v Westminster Finance (Australia) Ltd* (1987) 70 ALR 641; *Scott v Forster Patoral Co Pty Ltd* (2000) 35 ACSR 294.

(ii) Acts prejudicial to guarantor's rights

In any guarantee which does not otherwise provide it is implicit that the guarantor is to have the benefit and protection given by his implied rights of indemnity and subrogation against the principal debtor. Accordingly, any act or omission by the creditor which has the effect of altering or extinguishing any part of the guarantor's rights against the debtor operates to discharge the guarantor from liability except so far as the guarantee itself otherwise provides or the guarantor assents to the act or omission in question.[65] So protective is the law towards the guarantor that it does not require him to prove that he has suffered loss as a result of the creditor's conduct, prejudice being assumed except where it is self-evident that the act or omission is to the guarantor's benefit or that the effect of the act or omission is insignificant.[66] Nor is the relief given to the guarantor limited to the amount of loss he has suffered Once the guarantor's rights against the principal debtor are adversely affected by the creditor's conduct, the guarantor is in general entitled to a full discharge.[67] This may seem draconian, but appears to be founded on two distinct principles: first, that the preservation of the guarantor's rights against the principal debtor is by implication of law an essential part of his bargain with the creditor, a condition of the guarantor's engagement, the breach of which, like that of any other condition, entitles him to be discharged;[68] secondly, that in many cases it is hard to establish whether the creditor's act is prejudicial or not, and to assess the damage the guarantor will suffer, so that to avoid controversy on the question it is considered preferable to have a simple rule by which the guarantor is discharged.[69]

Whatever the basis for the rule, it is well established that, unless otherwise provided by the terms of his guarantee, the guarantor is released altogether if, without his consent, his rights of indemnity and subrogation are varied or extinguished by the deliberate act of the creditor, as where the creditor binds himself to give time to the debtor without reserving his rights against the guarantor[70] or otherwise varies the terms of the principal contract in a manner which is not self-evidently non-prejudicial,[71] or releases

---

65 In general, this total or partial discharge is sufficient to protect the guarantor, and it is interesting that there appears to have been no case to date in which it was necessary to establish a positive duty to the guarantor a breach of which would be actionable in damages. But one could imagine such a case. For example, as the result of the creditor's negligent handling of a sale following the principal debtor's default, there is a deficiency which the guarantor, not knowing of the breach of duty, then pays. There seems no reason why, on discovering the facts, he should not be able to recover such part of his payment as would have been unnecessary if the creditor had not been negligent.

66 *Smith v Wood* [1929] 1 Ch 14.

67 *Samuell v Howarth* (1817) 3 Mer 272, per Lord Eldon LC at 279; *Polak v Everett* (1876) 1 QBD 669, per Blackburn J at 674.

68 *Rees v Berrington* (1795) 2 Ves 540.

69 Ibid; *Polak v Everett*, n 67, per Blackburn J at 674.

70 *Webb v Hewett* (1857) 3 K & J 438; *Swire v Redman*, n 57. The effect of a stipulation by the creditor that in granting time to the debtor he reserves his rights against the guarantor is that (whether the reservation be communicated to the guarantor or not) he is entitled, on paying the creditor, to enforce his indemnity against the debtor without regard to the extension of time (*Webb v Hewett*). A mere indulgence by the creditor, as opposed to a binding agreement to give time, does not release the guarantor (*Rouse v Bradford Banking Co Ltd* [1894] AC 586).

71 *Holme v Brunskill* (1878) 3 QBD 495; *Smith v Wood*, n 66.

the principal debtor [72] or a co-guarantor, [73] or varies or surrenders a security taken from the principal debtor.[74]

However, in determining whether the creditor's act discharges the guarantor wholly or *pro tanto*, a distinction must, it seems, be drawn between an act which affects the guarantor's legal rights against the principal debtor or a co-guarantor or his legal ability to enforce his security and one which merely diminishes de facto the value of his rights of indemnity or subrogation without altering the content of his legal entitlement. So the intentional release of a security discharges the guarantor, whether the security was taken before the guarantee or after it, and the guarantor is wholly discharged even if it is clear that the security released could not have produced as much as the guaranteed debt in any event;[75] whereas if the guarantor's legal rights over the security are left untouched but its value to him is diminished or extinguished, eg by the creditor's failure to take legal steps to perfect the security by registration or the failure to take proper care to obtain a reasonable price when realizing the security,[76] the guarantor is discharged only to the extent to which the value of the security has been reduced or lost.[77] The principle underlying the distinction seems to be that in the latter class of case the creditor has not been guilty of unilaterally altering the terms of the bargain to which the guarantor assented in entering into the guarantee but has merely caused the guarantor loss through carelessness. So it is not a case of a breach of a condition of the guarantor's engagement, but simply a failure to have regard to his interests, which is considered adequately dealt with by releasing the guarantor to the extent of his resultant loss. The same applies where the creditor fails to exercise reasonable care to obtain a proper price on realization of the security.[78]

A mortgagee owes no duty to his mortgage to exercise a power of sale vested in him; it follows that the surety is not discharged merely by a reason of a reduction in the value of the security through the creditor's delay in selling.[79]

The creditor is not obliged to sue the principal debtor, or even make demand on him[80] before proceeding against the guarantor, for it was the guarantor's duty to

---

72   *Commercial Bank of Tasmania v Jones* [1893] AC 313. This is so even if the creditor purports to reserve his rights against the guarantor, since a guarantee depends for its existence on the continuance of the principal indebtedness, such a reservation is meaningless (*Webb v Hewett*, n 70). The position is otherwise, however, if the creditor reserves his rights against the guarantor as part of a mere agreement not to sue the principal debtor (*Green v Wynn* (1868) LR 7 Eq 28).

73   *Mercantile Bank of Sydney v Taylor* [1893] AC 317.

74   *Pledge v Buss* (1860) John 663.

75   *Polak v Everett*, n 67. Loss of the security through realization by the creditor in exercise of his rights does not, of course, affect the guarantor's liability, for the whole object of the security is to safeguard the creditor's position, and, in any event, the proceeds of the realization reduce the guaranteed debt, so that the guarantor suffers no loss.

76   See p 000, as to the extent of a creditor's duty of care on realization.

77   *Skipton Building Society v Stott* [2001] QB 261; *Wulff v Jay* (1872) LR 7 QB 756.

78   *Skipton Building Society v Stott*, n 77; *Wulff v Jay*, n 77.

79   *China and South Sea Bank Ltd v Tan Soon Gin* [1990] 1 AC 536. See also *Downsview Nominees Ltd v First City Corp Ltd* [1993] AC 295. But an administrator of a company in administration is now under a duty to avoid steps which do not unnecessarily harm the interests of the creditors as a whole. See Insolvency Act 1986, Sch B1, para 3(4)(b), and at p 852, n 174.

80   Unless such demand is a condition precedent to his right to be paid.

procure the debtor's performance of his obligations.[81] For the same reason the creditor is not obliged to give the guarantor notice of the debtor's default.[82]

(iii) Extinction of principal indebtedness

Since the guarantor's liability is limited to that of the principal indebtedness, it follows that he is discharged if the guaranteed debt is paid, or released or if the liability to pay it is extinguished by operation of law.[83] But the creditor's acceptance of the debtor's repudiation, which converts the debtor's primary liability in debt into a secondary liability to pay damages, does not discharge the guarantor, for this secondary liability is encompassed by his undertaking.[84]

(iv) Determination of guarantee

The guarantor under a continuing guarantee can always terminate the guarantee as to future advances, for such a guarantee is a standing offer which is separately accepted each time the creditor makes an advance and can therefore be withdrawn as to advances not yet made.[85] Such termination may be by express unilateral declaration of the guarantor or by inference from the fact that the continuing relationship between creditor and principal debtor which the guarantee supports has come to an end.[86] Care should be taken to avoid ambiguity as to the indebtedness covered by the guarantee at the time of its termination.[87]

7. CONTRIBUTION BETWEEN GUARANTORS[88]

Where there are two or more guarantors of the same obligation who are liable for the same amount, then, unless otherwise agreed between them, their burden is to be

---

81 *Moschi v Lep Air Services Ltd*, n 31, per Lord Diplock at 348.

82 *Hitchcock v Humfrey* (1843) 5 Man & G 559. The position is different if the agreement otherwise provides (*Re Brown's Estate* [1893] 2 Ch 300).

83 *Stacey v Hill* [1901] 1 KB 660; *Unity Finance Ltd v Woodcock* [1963] 1 WLR 455.

84 *Moschi v Lep Air Services Ltd*, n 31. See p 814.

85 *Silverburn Finance (UK) Ltd v Salt* [2001] 2 All ER (Comm) 438.

86 Ibid, where the Court of Appeal, affirming the decision of the trial judge, held that a guarantee supporting the obligations of the supplier under a factoring agreement impliedly came to an end with the termination of the factoring agreement so as to be inapplicable to future invoices and was not revived by the entry of the supplier and factor to a new agreement on the same terms.

87 See *National Westminster Bank plc v Hardman* [1988] FLR 302, CA (continuing guarantee providing for payment on demand; guarantor not liable for sums not demanded prior to expiration of guarantee). See R. M. Goode, 'Guarantees – rights, rites and rewrites' [1988] JBL 264.

88 See generally O'Donovan and Phillips, *Modern Contract of Guarantee*, paras 12–116 ff; Andrews and Millett, *Law of Guarantees*, ch 12; *Rowlatt on the Law of Principal and Surety*, pp 164 ff; Goff and Jones, *Law of Restitution*, pp 381 ff; Glanville Williams, *Joint Obligations* (1949), ch 9.

shared equally, and if one pays more than his share,[89] he is entitled to recover the excess in an equitable action for contribution.[90] This is so whether the guarantors are joined in the same instrument or have given quite separate guarantees;[91] but the right to contribution is confined to cases where the same obligation is guaranteed, and does not extend to a situation in which, for example, A guarantees X's indebtedness to Y, and B guarantees X's indebtedness to Z, or A guarantees X's indebtedness to Y for the price of goods sold to X while B guarantees X's indebtedness to Y on a separate loan transaction[92] or A and B guarantee different parts of the same debt.[93] Similarly, it is necessary to distinguish co-suretyship from sub-suretyship. Co-sureties are those who undertake a common liability in the same degree. By contrast, a sub-surety is one who guarantees the performance of the surety's obligations and his position vis-à-vis the surety is analogous to that of the surety vis-à-vis the principal debtor, so that the sub-surety is entitled to a full indemnity from the surety, not merely a contribution.[94]

Given that the same obligation is guaranteed, the fact that each guarantor was unaware of the other's existence does not affect his right to contribution,[95] for this is grounded in equity and not on an implied contract between the guarantors. So a dealer giving recourse to a finance house in respect of the liabilities of a debtor under a hire-purchase agreement[96] and paying more than half the guaranteed indebtedness is entitled to recover the excess from another guarantor who, unknown to him, gave his guarantee at the request of the debtor.

The principle of equality of contributions does not apply where the guarantees given in respect of the common indebtedness are of different amounts, as where A guarantees X's overdraft up to a limit of £10,000 and B gives a guarantee without limit. In such a case, A and B must contribute to the common indebtedness in proportion to their respective liabilities, so that if the total claim is £30,000 A's share of the guaranteed liability is one-third, and B's, two-thirds.[97]

---

89 By this is meant payment of more than his share of the entire liability to which his guarantee relates, not merely that part of the debt due at the time he makes his payment (*Stirling v Burdett* [1911] 2 Ch 418).

90 *Dering v Earl of Winchelsea* (1787) 2 Bos & P 270. The fact that the creditor has not yet made demand in accordance with the guarantee is not by itself a barrier to recovery, for it is open to a guarantor to waive a procedural requirement designed for his protection (*Stimpson v Smith* [1999] Ch 340). If a guarantor has become insolvent, the share of the burden he would have carried is to be borne equally by the solvent guarantors or, if their liability *inter se* is for unequal proportions (see below), then pro rata (*Lowe v Dixon* (1885) 16 QBD 455).

91 *Dering v Earl of Winchelsea*, n 90; *Re Ennis* [1893] 3 Ch 238.

92 *Dering v Earl of Winchelsea*, n 90; *Coope v Twynam* (1823) 1 Turn & R 426.

93 *Pendlebury v Walker* (1841) 4 Y & C Ex 424.

94 *Craythorne v Swinburne* (1807) 14 Ves 160; *Scholefield Goodman & Sons Ltd v Zyngier* [1985] 3 All ER 105. Similarly, the indorser of a bill of exchange who is sued on the bill is entitled to a full indemnity from prior parties (Bills of Exchange Act 1882, ss 55(1)(a), 55(2)(a)), for, in relation to them, his position is analogous to that of a sub-surety, not a co-surety.

95 *Dering v Earl of Winchelsea*, n 90; *Craythorne v Swinburne*, n 94.

96 See p 719.

97 *Ellesmere Brewery Co v Cooper* [1896] 1 QB 75; *Naumann v Northcote* (1978), unreported, CA (Bar Library transcript No 7835).

To avoid multiplicity of actions, a guarantor claiming contribution must join the principal debtor and all other guarantors to the proceedings, except where this would be pointless, eg because a party who would otherwise be joined is insolvent.[98]

A guarantor cannot claim contribution unless he brings into hotchpot securities or other benefits obtained by him from the debtor.[99]

---

98 *Hay v Carter* [1935] Ch 397; *Naumann v Northcote*, n 97.
99 *Berridge v Berridge* (1890) 44 Ch D 168; *Steel v Dixon* (1881) 17 Ch D 825.

Part Six
Corporate Insolvency

31   Principles of Corporate Insolvency Law

1.   HISTORICAL BACKGROUND

The principal concern of the creditor is, of course, to obtain payment of his money with stipulated interest; and his one overriding fear is that his debtor will become insolvent without the creditor holding adequate security. This chapter is concerned primarily with the insolvency of companies, not of individuals, though the regimes of personal bankruptcy and corporate winding up are to a considerable extent governed by common principles and will be briefly compared.

(i)   The development of insolvency law

Life for the medieval debtor was likely to be nasty, brutish and short. Just as the charging of usury by moneylenders was regarded as contrary to the laws of God, and was punished accordingly both by the Church and by the powers temporal,[1] so also falling into debt was considered mortal sin. Two years after the Statute of Acton Burnell,[2] an Act was passed[3] by which receivers who fell into arrears with their accounts were to be imprisoned in irons, and if they were unable to make restitution, they were left to rot, if necessary for the rest of their lives. But these were measures designed for the protection of the individual creditor; more than 250 years were to elapse before the notion took hold of official collection and realization of a debtor's estate for the purpose of distribution among his creditors generally. This was introduced by a statute of Henry VIII,[4] the first bankruptcy statute to be enacted. As its preamble indicates, it was not a measure designed for the relief of debtors.

> Where diverse and sundry persons, craftily obtaining into their hands great substance of other men's goods, do suddenly flee to parts unknown, or keep their houses, not minding to pay or restore to any of their creditors their debts and duties, but at their own wills and pleasures consume the substance obtained by credit of other men, for their own pleasure and delicate living, against all reason, equity and good conscience. Be it therefore enacted …

---

1 The Church excommunicated the usurer until he repented of his evil ways; the king forfeited his goods and chattels, though he usually found it expedient to wait until after the offender had died, when he was no longer present to refute the charges against him and the profits of the forfeiture were likely to be maximized.

2 See p 4, n 8.

3 Statute of Westminster II, 13 Edw 1, c 11 (1285).

4 34 & 35 Hen VIII, c 4 (1542).

The Act of 1542 empowered the Lord Chancellor and other designated officials to seize the body and assets of the debtor, to realize the assets and to distribute the proceeds to his creditors 'rate and rate alike, according to the quantity of their debts'. Thus was enshrined the principle of *pari passu* distribution, which remains a cardinal principle of bankruptcy law to this very day, though, as we shall see, things turn out somewhat differently in practice.

For several hundred years bankruptcy was confined to traders. As the list of bankruptcy offences multiplied, so the severity of the laws increased. Perjury was initially made punishable by two hours in the pillory, to which one of the debtor's ears was to be nailed and then cut off.[5] In later statutes,[6] debtors committing perjury, embezzlement or concealment of property were to be adjudged guilty of felony and to suffer as felons without benefit of clergy – a euphemistic way of describing their translation into a better world. On the other hand, those who made full disclosure and conformed to the requirements of the statutes were entitled to a certificate of discharge from their debts. In time, the severity of the penalties was mitigated, and bankruptcy began to be seen not merely as a process for examining the conduct of the bankrupt and organizing the realization of his estate and the distribution of dividends among creditors but also as a means by which an insolvent debtor could be relieved of the burden of his debts which he had no prospect of repaying. Eventually, bankruptcy was extended to non-traders by the Bankruptcy Act 1861, later repealed and replaced by a series of bankruptcy statutes culminating in the Bankruptcy Act 1914. That Act continued in force until 1986, when it was replaced by the Insolvency Act 1985, itself repealed, on the very day it was due to come into force, by the Insolvency Act 1986.

(ii) Corporate insolvency law[7]

The Bankruptcy Acts never applied to companies, for which an entirely distinct regime was created, albeit one which incorporated many of the bankruptcy rules. The history of corporate insolvency law begins with the enactment of the Joint Stock Companies Act 1844, the first statute to provide for the incorporation of a company as a distinct legal entity. However, it was not until the Companies Act 1862 that a detailed set of winding-up rules was enacted Thereafter corporate insolvency law remained governed primarily by successive Companies Acts up to the Companies Act 1985. Though laying down a distinct regime for the winding up of companies, those Acts incorporated by reference the provisions of the bankruptcy legislation relating to provable debts and fraudulent preferences.

---

5 1 Jac 1, c 15 (1604); 21 Jac 1, c 19 (1623). Women were not exempt from this punishment.

6 See, for example, 4 & 5 Anne, c 17 (1705); 5 Anne, c 22 (1706); 3 Geo I, c 12 (1716); 5 Geo II, c 30 (1732).

7 See Ian Fletcher, *Law of Insolvency* (3rd edn, 2002); R. M. Goode, *Principles of Corporate Insolvency Law* (2nd edn, 1997) Vanessa Finch, *Corporate Insolvency Law: Perspectives and Principles* (2002); Peter Totty and Gabriel Moss, *Insolvency* (looseleaf); Bailey, Groves and Smith, *Corporate Insolvency Law and Practice* (2nd edn, 2001).

(iii) The reform of insolvency law

Following a wide-ranging review by the Insolvency Law Review Committee under the chairmanship of Mr (later Sir) Kenneth Cork,[8] sweeping changes were made to UK insolvency law. The Bankruptcy Act 1914 and the winding-up provisions of the Companies Act 1985 were repealed and replaced by the Insolvency Act 1985, which was altogether broader in scope, covering all forms of insolvency, individual and corporate, and introducing major revisions both to substantive law and to insolvency procedures. That Act was re-enacted by the Insolvency Act 1986, which is now the principal insolvency enactment. It is supplemented by the Company Directors Disqualification Act 1986, which includes certain provisions for the disqualification of unfit directors of insolvent companies, and the Insolvency Rules 1986, which combine rules of procedure with a number of substantive law provisions relating, for example, to proof and priority of debts and rules of insolvency set-off. There are also numerous subsidiary statutory instruments with which we need not be concerned

Among the many new measures introduced by what is now the Insolvency Act 1986 is the regime of company administration, seen as a potentially powerful mechanism for rehabilitating companies in difficulty. The legislation also lays down rules for the qualification of those acting as insolvency practitioners. The 1986 Act has been amended by the Insolvency Act 1994,[9] the Insolvency (No 2) Act 1994,[10] the Insolvency Act 2000,[11] and the Enterprise Act 2002.[12] The Insolvency Act is supplemented by the Insolvency Rules 1986,[13] which have been extensively revised since they were first issued [14]

2. WINDING UP DISTINGUISHED FROM BANKRUPTCY

Bankruptcy and liquidation law have many features in common. Under both regimes an insolvency practitioner is appointed – a trustee of a bankrupt and a liquidator of a company – to collect and realize the insolvent's assets and distribute dividends according to a statutory order of priority. Both regimes have common underlying principles as to preferential debts, *pari passu* distribution among

---

8 *Insolvency Law and Practice* (Cmnd 8558, 1982).

9 Dealing with the position of administrators and administrative receivers in relation to contracts of employment.

10 Which amends some of the avoidance provisions.

11 Dealing with company voluntary arrangements and resulting moratoria.

12 Which, with certain exceptions, abolished the institution of administrative receivership and substituted complex provisions concerning administration, and dispensed with the need to obtain an administration order.

13 SI 1986/1925.

14 For details, see Len Sealy and David Milman, *Annotated Guide to the Insolvency Legislation* (7th edn, 2004), pp 674 ff. The rules on insolvency set-off are currently in course of revision in order to align the provisions on administration and winding up and also to apply them to a claim *by* the insolvent company *against* the solvent party, which would have the effect of changing the present law as described by Hoffmann LJ in *MS Fashions Ltd v Bank of Credit and Commerce International SA (No 2)* [1993] Ch 425 and, in the case of a contingent claim, accelerating the solvent party's liability to the extent of the set-off.

ordinary unsecured creditors and the avoidance of transactions as preferences or transactions at an undervalue. But there the resemblance ends. The ultimate objective of the bankruptcy process is to discharge the bankrupt from his liabilities, so that he can begin again with a clean slate, free from the burden of his debts, and thus rehabilitate himself into the community. The ultimate fate of a company in winding up is not discharge but dissolution, that is, the termination of its existence.

3. THE REGIMES OF CORPORATE INSOLVENCY

Four distinct corporate insolvency regimes are now recognized by statute: administrative receivership, administration, winding up (liquidation) and arrangements with creditors. Each has its distinctive purposes and characteristics.[15] In addition, major creditors of a company in financial difficulty may adopt informal arrangements ('workouts') for its reorganization. Bank-led workouts have been strongly promoted by the Bank of England, which has issued guidelines collectively known as the London Approach.[16] But administrative receivership, for long widely used as an enforcement tool by banks holding debentures, has now been abolished as regards new charges except for certain exempt categories.[17]

4. THE OBJECTIVES OF CORPORATE INSOLVENCY LAW[18]

Corporate insolvency law embodies a number of distinct objectives, some of which are mutually exclusive while others are not. For example, placing a company in administration or administrative receivership may be seen as a prelude to its return to profitable trading (though in practice, such an outcome is relatively infrequent), whereas on liquidation it must cease to trade except so far as may be required for its beneficial winding up.[19] Most corporate insolvency regimes are collective procedures intended to benefit all unsecured creditors; administrative receivership, though collective in character for certain limited purposes, is primarily an enforcement remedy for a debenture holder. The focus at the present day is very much on restoration of the business of the company[20] or, if this is not possible, on achieving through administration a better result for creditors than would be achieved on an immediate winding up. But whatever insolvency regime is adopted in the first instance, the eventual outcome for the company as a legal entity is almost always winding up, followed by dissolution. Accordingly, in looking at the objectives of corporate insolvency law we shall take winding up as the paradigm case and begin with this before examining other collective insolvency procedures.

---

15 See pp 836 ff.
16 See Nick Segal, 'Rehabilitation and Approaches Other than Formal Insolvency Procedures' in *Banks and Remedies* (ed Ross Cranston, 1999), ch 8; 'An Overview of Recent Developments and Future Prospects in the United Kingdom' in *Current Developments in International and Comparative Corporate Insolvency Law* (ed Jacob S. Ziegel, 1994), ch I at pp 8–9.
17 See p 849.
18 See, generally, Goode, *Corporate Insolvency Law*, pp 25 ff.
19 Insolvency Act 1986, ss 87(1), 167(1)(a), Sch 4, para 5.
20 Which does not necessarily, or even usually, mean the continuance of the company itself.

The principal purposes of corporate insolvency law in the context of winding up are:

(a) to transfer the management of the company to an outside independent insolvency practitioner who is duly authorized to act as such;

(b) to provide for the orderly realization of assets and meeting of claims,[21] and for that purpose to suspend the individual pursuit of claims by creditors;

(c) to prescribe an equitable ranking of claims among different classes of (primarily unsecured) creditor, and distribution of the proceeds of realizations among creditors according to a statutory order of priorities;

(d) to set aside transactions made by the company in the run-up to winding up which are prejudicial to the interests of the general body of creditors or which unfairly give a preference to one creditor over others; and

(e) to investigate the causes of failure and the conduct of those concerned in the management of the company with a view to the institution of criminal or civil proceedings, including disqualification, for culpable behaviour causing loss to the creditors.

5. THE CARDINAL PRINCIPLES OF CORPORATE INSOLVENCY LAW

Corporate insolvency law is underpinned by five cardinal principles.[22]

(i) Pre-liquidation rights are respected

Insolvency law respects rights acquired against the company before winding up except so far as policy requires that these be displaced, eg as a transaction at an undervalue or an improper preference of a creditor. Personal rights do, it is true, undergo some change in that a right to sue for debt or damages is converted into a right to prove in the winding up in competition with other creditors, but the quantum of the right is unaffected, though the assets are usually insufficient to meet claims in full and sometimes are inadequate to enable any payment to be made to the general creditors. Of especial importance is the recognition of pre-liquidation real rights. In particular, winding up does not affect the rights and remedies of those who own property in the possession of the company or who hold a security interest over all or any of its assets.

---

21 See generally Fidelis Oditah, 'Assets and the treatment of claims in insolvency' (1992) 108 LQR 459.

22 For others, see Goode, *Corporate Insolvency*, pp 55 ff.

(ii) Only assets in which the debtor has an interest are available for its creditors

1. The general rule

As a corollary of the principle just stated, assets are available for distribution among creditors[23] only to the extent that the debtor company has or acquires a beneficial interest in them. Property in the possession of the company but belonging to another is returnable to its owner, subject to any right which the company may have to remain in possession (eg under a lease) and is not an asset available for distribution to creditors. Similarly, the liquidator takes the debtor's property as he finds it, and thus has a duty to respect the interest of a secured creditor, such as a mortgagee, and other real rights to which the property is subject, such as a reservation of title in favour of a supplier of goods to the company, so that only the equity of redemption or other residual interest constitutes a distributable asset.

Moreover, while control of the company's assets passes to its liquidator, the latter for most purposes stands in the shoes of the company itself and is not treated as a purchaser for value without notice. Two things follow from this. First, the liquidator takes subject to equities, so that if, for example, the company has acquired property under a contract which is voidable by the other party, eg for misrepresentation, that party's right to rescind remains exercisable despite the winding up.[24] Secondly, no question can arise of a priority dispute between the holder of a real right and the liquidator, so that, vis-à-vis the liquidator, equitable ownership is for all practical purposes as effective as legal and beneficial ownership.

In general, then, we can say that at common law an attached security interest or other real right is enforceable against the liquidator whether or not it has been perfected.[25] Perfection is relevant only where expressly made so by statute, as in the case of a requirement to register a charge by the company falling within s 396 of the Companies Act 1985.[26] Subject to this, liquidation is of little concern to secured creditors except to the extent to which they are owed an amount in excess of the value of the security. A fully secured creditor is able largely to ignore the liquidation process[27] and to go his own way, enforcing his security very much as if the debtor were still solvent.[28] Nevertheless, the rules of insolvency law are of great

---

23 The phrase 'distribution among creditors' is here used as a shorthand to indicate the distribution of realizations of assets. On the winding up of an insolvent company assets are rarely distributed among creditors *in specie.*

24 *Re Eastgate* [1905] 1 KB 465; *Tilley v Bowman* Ltd [1910] 1 KB 745. See p 27. As to set-off in insolvency, see p 610.

25 So an equitable assignee of a debt due to the company can assert his title against the liquidator even if he has not given notice of assignment to the company prior to the winding up. See *Re Wallis* [1902] 1 KB 719; *Re Anderson* [1911] 1 KB 896.

26 See p 667.

27 This applies in general even to property falling within an after-acquired property clause in a security agreement which is acquired by the debtor after the commencement of the winding up. In principle this is just as much claimable under the after-acquired property clause in the security agreement as property acquired before such commencement. See pp 634–635.

28 This is true of all insolvency procedures except administration, which freezes the enforcement of all security and title retention rights. See p 852.

importance to a secured creditor, for they provide the supreme test of the strength of the security interest. So long as the debtor is solvent, the validity of a security interest is largely academic; it is only where there is not enough money to go round that the enforceability and ranking of his security become matters of moment.

2. Exceptions

To the rule that the liquidator can take only assets belonging to the company at the date of commencement of the winding up or acquired by the company thereafter, there are three principal statutory exceptions. First, the assets available to the general body of creditors may be swelled by the amount of payments or transfers made by the debtor before winding up under a transaction which is void or voidable at the instance of the liquidator.[29] Secondly, in a compulsory winding up all dispositions of the company's property made after the presentation of the winding-up petition are void unless authorized or ratified by the court.[30] Thirdly, the assets may be augmented by payments to the company ordered by the court in proceedings for fraudulent or wrongful trading.[31]

(iii) Personal rights are converted into rights of proof

It is a cardinal principle of corporate insolvency law (and the same is true of bankruptcy) that purely personal rights against the debtor, whether to money, property or the performance of services, cease to be exercisable by action[32] and become converted into rights to prove[33] in competition with other unsecured creditors. It is this characteristic which in the last resort marks off real from personal rights. The former are, in principle, unaffected by the insolvency process, for the liquidator takes subject to them; by contrast, liquidation puts an end to a creditor's ability to enforce purely personal rights and *iura ad rem*[34] and limits the rights of an individual unsecured creditor to a share in realizations of assets.

The right of proof extends to future and contingent debts.[35] So liquidation has the effect of accelerating the debt, which is discounted according to the degree of futurity or contingency involved

(iv) Unsecured creditors rank *pari passu*

The underlying principle of distribution is that unsecured creditors rank *pari passu* and are thus entitled to a dividend proportionate to their respective claims. However, the principle of *pari passu* distribution,[36] which has been a feature of

---

29 But where the transaction is void, as opposed to voidable, the liquidator takes the assets to which it relates subject to any prior charge or assignment. See further, p 838.

30 Insolvency Act 1986, s 127.

31 See p 854.

32 But self-help remedies may be available. See p 835.

33 A proof is simply a formal intimation to the liquidator of the amount and nature of the creditor's claim, which, if accepted, qualifies the creditor to share in any distribution of dividends.

34 See p 26.

35 Insolvency Rules 1986, r 12.3.

36 See generally Goode, *Corporate Insolvency Law*, ch 7.

bankruptcy law since the first bankruptcy statute in 1542, has been gravely diminished, first by the extensive range of security rights and analogous devices[37] that have evolved over the years, and, secondly, by a massive expansion of the range of debts made preferential by statute.[38] In the result, the amount left over for ordinary unsecured creditors after the rights of real creditors have been satisfied, the costs of the liquidation paid and the preferential creditors discharged is usually small and in the majority of cases ordinary unsecured creditors receive no dividend at all. Various attempts have been made in recent times to alleviate their lot, in particular by abolishing administrative receivership, thus leaving debenture holders to appoint an administrator in a collective proceeding designed primarily for the benefit of general creditors;[39] by providing for a portion of assets subject to a floating charge to be surrendered for the benefit of unsecured creditors;[40] and by abolishing Crown preference.[41] Though these are welcome measures, it may be doubted whether they will significantly improve the lot of ordinary unsecured creditors. To summarize the position as regards unsecured creditors: first in the queue are the expenses of the liquidation,[42] which are payable in a prescribed order of priority;[43] next come preferential creditors, who have priority over claims secured by a floating charge[44] but are not organized in any priority ranking among themselves, sharing *pari passu*;[45] then follow the ordinary unsecured creditors; and at the end of the queue are certain classes of creditor whose claims are deferred under the provisions of various statutes.

It has been objected that the *pari passu* principle is not, in fact, a central principle at all and that what insolvency law really seeks to ensure is that creditors do not make private arrangements that would have the effect of disturbing the principle of collectivity which the insolvency proceedings are designed to impose, a principle which in itself says nothing about the priority of claims in insolvency.[46] There is some force in this contention. It is clear that insolvency law does not treat all unsecured creditors alike. In particular, preferential creditors and creditors enjoying a right of set-off rank higher in the distribution stakes,[47] as do post-liquidation

---

37   Eg (1) reservation of title on the sale of goods, which became a widespread feature of non-instalment sales after the *Romalpa* case (see p 608) and (2) rights of insolvency set-off (see p 837, n 67). The priority given to security and quasi-security rights is not a true exception to the *pari passu* principle, for to the extent of such rights the assets are not the property of the company at all. By contrast insolvency set-off is a true exception.

38   A modest move in the other direction was initially the exclusion of assessed taxes (as opposed to 'collected' taxes such as value added tax and PAYE) from the list of preferential debts and subsequently the abolition of Crown preference altogether. See p 838.

39   See p 849.

40   See p 838.

41   See p 838.

42   Which now include expenses incurred by the liquidator in the conduct of legal proceedings to get in assets of the company, eg proceedings for wrongful trading or to recover a voidable preference.

43   Insolvency Rules 1986, r 4.218. But the court may vary the priority (Insolvency Act 1986, s 156).

44   Insolvency Act 1986, s 175(2)(b). But such claims are not subordinate to liquidation expenses, because these are payable only out of assets of the company and to the extent that assets are subject to a floating charge they are not assets of the company. See n 71 .

45   Insolvency Act 1986, s 175(2)(a).

46   See Rizwaan Jameel Mokal, 'Priority as Pathology: The *Pari Passu* Myth' [2001] CLJ 581.

47   Though among themselves they rank *pari passu*.

creditors and even pre-liquidation creditors who are in a position to require payment as a condition of continuing to provide goods or services on credit. But these are exceptions to the general rule, which is that all unsecured creditors should be treated equally. So it is not the *principle* of *pari passu* distribution that is in question but rather the fact that, because of carve-outs in favour of creditors holding security and quasi-security interests and rights of set-off, the quantum of the company's assets in the typical winding up is insufficient to leave much, if anything, to general creditors after the preferential debts have been paid.

The *pari passu* principle applies only to pre-liquidation creditors. Those who become creditors as the result of contracts entered into by the liquidator are entitled to have their claims treated as expenses of the liquidation and paid out of the assets in priority even to the claims of preferential creditors.[48] Such a priority is necessary, for otherwise the liquidator would be unable to obtain goods or services for the company during the winding-up process. Even pre-liquidation creditors will be able to jump the queue where the liquidator is dependent on their continuing to supply goods or services and they make it a condition that existing debts must first be paid. In such a case the liquidator is entitled to pay the pre-liquidation claims in question as being expenses of the liquidation necessary to preserve the company's business or its other assets.[49]

(v) Winding up accelerates personal rights

This results from the fact that debts provable in the winding up include future and contingent debts.[50]

6. SUBSIDIARY PRINCIPLES

The four cardinal principles stated above are buttressed by three subsidiary principles. Contracts entered into by the company before liquidation remain in force until disclaimed;[51] on liquidation the company ceases to be the beneficial owner of its assets;[52] and no unsecured creditor has any interest *in specie* in the company's assets or realizations.[53]

---

48 Insolvency Act 1986, s 115; Insolvency Rules 1986, r 4.180(1).

49 Such a stipulation can no longer be lawfully imposed by public utility suppliers (Insolvency Act 1986, s 233), who are entitled merely to require the liquidator personally to guarantee payment for future supplies (ibid, s 233(2)(a)).

50 See p 837.

51 See Goode, *Corporate Insolvency Law*, pp 127–128. The liquidator's failure to disclaim does not commit him to performance of the contract, it merely deprives him of the right to terminate it unilaterally by notice (*Re Sneezum, ex p Davis* (1876) 3 Ch D 463; *Stead, Hazel & Co v Cooper* [1933] 1 KB 840). On a compulsory winding up all directors' appointments and contracts of employees come to an end automatically (*Measures Ltd v Measures* [1910] 2 Ch 248; *Re General Rolling Stock Co, Chapman's Case* (1866) LR 1 Eq 346; *Re Oriental Bank Corp, ex p McDowall* (1886) 32 Ch D 366).

52 See Goode, *Corporate Insolvency Law*, p 58.

53 Ibid, p 21.

7.   THE WINDING-UP PROCESS

The winding up of a company on the ground of insolvency may be effected either by resolution of the members of the company[54] or by a winding-up order on a petition by a creditor or other party having a *locus standi* to present a petition.[55] The former is termed a creditors' voluntary winding up,[56] the latter a compulsory winding up. The usual ground on which a winding-up order is made is that the company is unable to pay its debts.[57] But whatever the ground, the petitioning creditor must show that he has a legitimate interest in having the company wound up,[58] which he will not have if there is a bona fide dispute as to the existence of the debt[59] or if there are no assets from which the petitioner could benefit and no other legitimate reason (eg a desirable investigation into the company's affairs) to have the company wound up.[60] Even where the debt is undisputed, the court will have regard to the wishes of the majority in value of creditors, though the views of creditors who are associated with the company itself and its directors will be discounted.[61] Winding up does not divest the company of title to its assets but makes it notionally a statutory trustee of the assets for its creditors.[62] Control of the company passes to the liquidator, who may be either the Official Receiver or an outside liquidator appointed by the company itself or by the creditors.[63] The liquidator is usually assisted by a liquidation committee, and certain of his powers may be exercised only with the sanction of that committee or of the court.[64] The liquidator is responsible for getting in and realizing the assets, ascertaining the debts and distributing dividends. After the costs of administration, the liquidator must pay preferential creditors, then ordinary unsecured creditors, then deferred creditors, any surplus being paid out to the members of the company. When all the assets have been got in, the liabilities established and the distribution

---

54 Insolvency Act 1985, ss 73(1), 84(1)(c).

55 Ibid, ss 73(1), 122–125.

56 'Creditors' voluntary winding up' because the conduct of the winding up is under the general control of the creditors, through a liquidation committee they appoint, rather than of the court. But it is only the members who have the power to put the company into voluntary winding up. The fact that a company is in voluntary winding up does not debar a petition for it to be wound up by the court (Insolvency Act 1986, s 116).

57 Inability to pay debts is defined by s 123 of the Insolvency Act 1986. Leaving aside the particular forms of deemed inability prescribed by this section, a company is insolvent either where it is unable to pay its debts as they fall due (known as commercial insolvency, or the cash-flow test of insolvency) or where its liabilities exceed its assets (the balance-sheet test of insolvency). See generally Goode, *Corporate Insolvency Law*, ch 4. Not infrequently the petition is based alternatively on the Companies Act 1985, s 459.

58 In which case he is prima facie entitled to a winding-up order *ex debito justitiae*.

59 *Re MCI WorldCom Ltd, WorldCom Ltd v Primus Telecommunications Ltd* [2003] 1 BCLC 330; *Re LHF Wools Ltd* [1970] Ch 27.

60 *Bell Group Finance (Pte) Ltd v Bell Group (UK Holdings) Ltd* [1996] BCC 505.

61 *Re Lummus Agricultural Services Ltd* [1999] BCC 953.

62 *Ayerst v C. & K. (Construction) Ltd* [1976] AC 167. However, 'trust' is here used in a broad sense, not in its technical meaning.

63 An outside liquidator will be appointed only where the assets are considered sufficient to cover the costs of the liquidation. The company's nomination is effective only where the creditors fail to make a nomination or the court accedes to an application to appoint the company's nominee instead of the creditor's nominee (Insolvency Act 1986, s 100).

64 Insolvency Act 1986, ss 165, 167.

completed, the winding-up process is at an end. The final act is dissolution of the company, which terminates its legal existence.

8. PROOF AND RANKING OF CLAIMS IN WINDING UP

(i) Proof

Winding up was formerly the only collective procedure involving the statutory distribution of assets among creditors. It was therefore only on winding up that there was a requirement to lodge proofs of debt. That has changed in that the court may now give leave to an administrator to make a distribution to ordinary unsecured creditors.[65] Where a distribution is to be made in an administration, proofs are lodged in the same way as in a winding up.[66] In general, all claims by creditors are provable as debts against the company, whether they are present and future, certain or contingent, ascertained or sounding only in damages.[67]

A creditor may maintain his proof for the full amount of the debtor's indebtedness as it stands at the date of the winding-up resolution or order, without giving credit for partial payments subsequently made by a guarantor, whether before or after the creditor has lodged his proof,[68] though the creditor cannot, of course, receive in total more than 100p in the pound.

(ii) Priority of debts

In principle, a secured creditor is not a contender in the priority stakes. Assuming his security to be valid against the liquidator and creditors,[69] he is entitled to have recourse to it before anyone. Even the costs of the liquidation cannot be taken out of an asset given as security before the secured creditor has realized what is necessary to pay his debt.[70] To this principle there are now two exceptions. First, the holder of a floating charge given by a company is postponed to preferential creditors where the chargee takes possession of any of the charged property, a receiver is appointed

---

65 Ibid, Sch B1, para 65(1),(3). Leave is not necessary to make a distribution to a creditor who is secured or preferential.

66 Insolvency Rules 1986, r 2.72.

67 Ibid, r 12.3(1). Prior to 1986 claims for unliquidated damages in tort were not provable. Now the only non-provable debts are those specified in r 12.3(2). As to insolvency set-off, see r 4.90; *Stein v Blake* [1995] 2 All ER 961; Philip Wood, *English and International Set-Off*, ch 7.

68 *Re Rees* (1881) 17 Ch D 98; *Re Sass* [1896] 2 QB 12. See Roy Goode, *Legal Problems of Credit and Security* (3rd edn, 2003), para 8–18.

69 As to the circumstances in which a security is vulnerable, see p 838.

70 The secured creditor has a quadruple choice: to rest on his security without proving at all; to surrender it and prove for the full amount of the debt (Insolvency Rules, r 4.88(2)) – a course which can rarely be to his advantage; to realize his security and prove for the deficiency (Insolvency Rules, r 4.88(1)); and to state the value of the security in his proof and prove for any deficiency.

or the company goes into liquidation[71] or into an administration in which a distribution is made.[72] Presumably it was felt that the ease with which the whole of a company's assets can be picked up in a floating charge would largely destroy the status of preferential creditors if provision were not made for them. Secondly, the amendments made to the Insolvency Act 1986 by the Enterprise Act 2002 provide for a proportion of assets subject to a floating charge to be made available for the claims of unsecured creditors,[73] reviving an idea first floated by the Insolvency Law Review Committee in its 1982 Report.[74]

The order of application of assets among unsecured creditors has been touched on earlier.[75] We need not dwell on this further, except to repeat that the range of preferential debts has now been sharply reduced with the abolition of Crown preference, leaving only unpaid contributions to occupational pension schemes and the state pension scheme within Sch 4 to the Pension Schemes Act 1993, up to four months' unpaid wages with a maximum of £800,[76] unpaid holiday remuneration for employees whose employment has been terminated and sums advanced to pay the above sums due to employees.[77]

9.   VULNERABLE TRANSACTIONS[78]

Though insolvency law takes as its starting point the recognition of rights acquired from or against the company prior to liquidation, there are certain circumstances in which a transaction entered into by the company before winding up will be either wholly void or voidable at the instance of the liquidator.

The avoidance provisions of the Insolvency Act 1986 are designed to fulfil one or other of four broad objectives. The first is to ensure that a company which has

71 Insolvency Act 1986, s 175(2)(b). It had been previously thought to follow from this that his claim was also postponed to the costs and expenses of liquidation, which rank ahead of preferential debts (*Re Barleycorn Enterprises Ltd* [1970] Ch 465). But the decision has recently been overruled by the House of Lords in *Buchler v Talbot* [2004] 1 All ER 1289, in which Lord Millett pointed out that the floating chargee was not competing for the same fund as the liquidator but for the separate fund of assets covered by the floating charge. If the chargee is able to realize his security without taking possession or appointing a receiver and the company is not in winding up, the floating charge retains its priority over unsecured creditors (*Griffith v Yorkshire Bank plc* [1994] 1 WLR 1427). However, it would seem that the proceeds of sale would fall within the statutory provisions. See Goode, *Legal Problems*, p 196, n 13.

72 Insolvency Act 1986, Sch B1, para 65(2), applying s 175 of the Act.

73 Insolvency Act 1986, s 176A. The prescribed proportion is nil for net property not exceeding £10,000 in value, and for property exceeding £10,000 50% of the first £10,000 plus 20% of the excess over £10,000 up to a maximum of prescribed part of £600,000 (Insolvency Act 1986 (Prescribed Part) Order 2003 (SI 2003/2097), art 3.

74 For this and the genesis of the idea, see Goode, *Legal Problems*, p 120, n 62.

75 See p 834.

76 Insolvency Act 1986, Sch 6, para 9; Insolvency Proceedings (Monetary Limits) Order 1986, art 4. Remuneration includes guarantee payments, remuneration on suspension on medical grounds, payment for time off and remuneration under a protective award (ibid, para 13(1),(2)).

77 Insolvency Act 1986, Sch 6, paras 8–12.

78 See generally Goode, *Corporate Insolvency Law*, ch 11; A.R. Keay, *Avoidance Provisions in Insolvency Law* (1997).

become insolvent does not do anything outside the ordinary course of business to diminish still further the value of the assets available to unsecured creditors. Hence the provisions enabling the liquidator to avoid transactions at an undervalue. The second is to maintain the integrity of the *pari passu* principle by disabling an insolvent company from giving preferential treatment to one of its creditors at the expense of others and by restricting the types of consideration for which a floating charge given by an insolvent company will be valid. The Act thus provides for the avoidance of transactions which have the effect of giving such a preference. The third is to deter secured creditors from ignoring statutory provisions requiring their charges to be registered so that outsiders, including unsecured creditors, have notice of their existence. This objective is achieved by making registrable but unregistered charges void against the liquidator and creditors. The fourth is to prevent transfers in fraud of creditors.

At least four conditions must be satisfied before a transaction entered into by the company can be set aside under insolvency law. The company must be in winding up or administration; the transaction must have resulted in a diminution of the assets available to the general body of creditors; the company must have been unable to pay its debts at the time of or in consequence of the transaction; and the transaction must have been entered into within a specified time prior to the onset of insolvency.

(i)   Transactions at an undervalue

Where a company which has at a relevant time entered into a transaction at an undervalue subsequently goes into liquidation,[79] the liquidator may apply to the court to make an order restoring the position to what it would have been if the company had not entered into the transaction.[80] A company enters into a transaction with a person at an undervalue if (a) it makes a gift to that person or otherwise enters into a transaction with that person on terms that provide for the company to receive no consideration, or (b) the company enters into a transaction with that person for a consideration the value of which, in money or money's worth, is significantly less than the value, in money or money's worth, of the consideration provided by the company.[81] The section is thus directed to transactions which diminish the company's net asset value, as where it makes a gift of money or property, or sells an asset for significantly less, or buys an asset for significantly more, than its true value. In determining the value of the consideration the court looks not only to the transaction between the parties but also to the value to the company of any transaction it enters into with a third party as part of the deal;[82] and

---

79   Or administration.

80   Insolvency Act 1986, s 238. The types of order the court can make for this purpose are set out in s 241.

81   Ibid, s 238(4).

82   *Phillips v Brewin Dolphin Bell Lawne Ltd* [2001] 1 WLR 143, where Lord Scott observed (at para 20) that the question is not whether the arrangement formed part of the transaction but whether the benefit derived from it by the company formed part of the consideration. For a detailed comment on the case see Rizwaan Jameel Mokal and Look Chan Ho, 'Consideration, Characterisation, Evaluation: Transactions at an Undervalue after *Phillips v Brewin*' [2001] Journal of Corporate Law Studies 359.

though the value of the consideration is to be measured as at the date of the transaction, the court is entitled to look at post-transaction events which help to establish that value.[83]

The statutory provisions do not bite unless the transaction was made at a relevant time, that is, within two years ending with the onset of insolvency[84] and at a time when the company was insolvent or became so in consequence of the transaction.[85] It is only transactions by an insolvent company which are caught; if the company is solvent when entering into the transaction, creditors are not adversely affected. If the company, though insolvent, manages to avoid liquidation[86] for two years, the transaction ceases to be vulnerable. This is a sensible limitation, for the purpose of the avoidance provisions is to strike at disadvantageous transactions entered into by the company in the run-up to liquidation, and after two years the causal link between the transaction and loss to creditors becomes tenuous. In any event, it is necessary to have some cut-off point, however arbitrary, in order to allow finality for business transactions.

It is important to appreciate that s 238 is concerned solely with transactions that reduce a company's net asset value. It does not touch transactions which simply give one creditor an advantage over others; that is the province of s 239, dealing with preferences. So payment by the company in discharge of an existing debt is not a transaction at an undervalue, for the reduction in assets resulting from the payment is exactly matched by the disappearance of the debt from the liabilities side of the balance sheet. Similarly, if the company borrowed money on an unsecured basis and later gave security for the previous loan, this may be a preference of the creditor to whom the security was given but it is not a transaction at an undervalue, for the company's net asset position remains unchanged.[87] Realization of the security removes an asset from the company to the extent of the debt or the value of the asset (if lower), but at the same time *pro tanto* extinguishes the debt itself. All that has happened is that an asset previously available for the general body of creditors has been given in security to a particular creditor. The position would, of course, be otherwise if the company's security were given for a debt owed to the creditor by a third party, for in that situation the company would suffer a reduction in the net value of its assets.

The court cannot make an order under s 238 if satisfied that the company entered into the transaction in good faith and for the purpose of carrying on its business and that at the time it did so there were reasonable grounds for believing that the transaction would benefit the company.[88] It is, of course, necessary to protect bona fide business transactions but it is remarkable that the party of whom good faith is required is the company itself, not the party with whom it deals.

---

83   *Phillips v Brewin Dolphin Bell Lawne Ltd*, n 82. For an earlier decision of the Court of Appeal to the effect that the totality of the benefits to be received on either side has to be looked at, see *Agricultural Mortgage Corp plc v Woodward* [1994] BCC 688.

84   'Onset of insolvency' is defined in Insolvency Act 1986, s 240(3).

85   Section 240(1),(2).

86   Or administration.

87   *Re M. C. Bacon Ltd* [1990] BCC 78.

88   Section s 238(5).

(ii) Preferences

Section 239 provides for the avoidance of acts by which an insolvent company gives a preference to a creditor or surety at a relevant time.[89] The test of a preference is whether, assuming the company were to go into liquidation immediately afterwards,[90] the creditor or surety would be put in a better position as the result of the act the company has done or suffered to be done than if the act in question had not been done.[91] Though this definition does not use the language of preference, it is obvious that an improvement in the creditor's position compared to what it would have been without the act has the effect of preferring him to other creditors. The most common forms of preference are payment to a particular creditor and the giving of security to a creditor for a past advance.

However, the fact of preference is not by itself sufficient to enable the effect of the transaction to be undone. It is necessary to show that in giving the preference the company was influenced by a desire to improve the creditor's position as described above.[92] In policy terms this statutory requirement is doubly unfortunate. It looks to the company's desire when the mere fact of preference should be sufficient; and it gives no protection to a creditor who has acted in good faith and dealt with the company in the ordinary course of business.

Desire is subjective but its existence can be inferred from the circumstances of the case.[93] In order for the statutory provisions to apply, it has to be shown that the desire to improve the creditor's position was one of the factors (though not necessarily the only factor or even the decisive factor) operating on the minds of those who made the decision to do the act alleged to be a preference.[94] It is not a preference if the company pays a creditor, not with a desire to improve his position but simply for proper commercial considerations such as a wish to avoid the creditor calling in an overdraft[95] or to induce him to extend further credit.[96]

The statutory provisions apply not only to the preference of a creditor but to the preference of a surety. The typical case is where the directors of a company who have given a creditor a guarantee for an advance to the company cause the company to pay off the debt with a view to extinguishing their liability under the guarantee.

Where a payment, transfer or other act is held to be a preference, the court has the same wide powers to make orders restoring the status quo as it has in relation to transactions at an undervalue.[97] These include the making of an order which provides

---

89 For this purpose relevant time is within the period of six months (or in the case of preference of a person who is connected with the company, two years) ending with the onset of insolvency and at a time when the company is insolvent or becomes so in consequence of the preference (s 240(1),(2)).
90 See Goode, *Corporate Insolvency Law*, p 394.
91 Insolvency Act 1986, s 239(4).
92 Ibid, s 239(5).
93 *Re M. C. Bacon Ltd*, n 87.
94 Ibid.
95 Ibid.
96 *Re Fairway Magazines Ltd* [1992] BCC 924.
97 Insolvency Act 1986, s 241.

for a discharged surety to be under such new or revived obligation to the creditor as the court thinks fit.[98]

The application of the preference rules raises particular difficulties in relation to running accounts, which have been discussed by the writer elsewhere.[99]

(iii) Floating charges given otherwise than for prescribed new value

Section 245 provides for the avoidance of a floating charge given by an insolvent company in the period of 12 months ending with the onset of insolvency[100] (two years, in the case of a charge in favour of a person connected with the company) except to the extent of new value for the charge of a kind falling within s 245(2). This section is significantly less stringent than its predecessor, s 617 of the Companies Act 1985, which limited the permissible new value to cash paid at or after and in consideration of the charge. The current statutory provisions allow new value in the form of money paid, or goods or services supplied, to the company at the same time as, or after, the creation of the charge; the discharge or reduction of any debt of the company[101] at the same time as, or after, creation of the charge; and interest on the above in pursuance of any agreement under which the money was so paid, the goods or services were so supplied or the debt so discharged or reduced. But not all forms of new value will save a floating charge. The intention seems to be to restrict permissible new value to those forms of benefit to the company which arise from day-to-day trading and have a readily ascertainable value, and thus to exclude assets such as land and buildings, intellectual property rights, debts and other receivables and rights under contracts.[102] Also excluded, of course, are money paid or goods or services supplied prior to the creation of the charge.

(iv) Failure to register

A charge by a company which is not registered in conformity with the provisions of the Companies Act 1985[103] is void against the liquidator and creditors. The rationale of such avoidance has never been clearly articulated but there would seem to be a good policy justification for it.[104]

---

98 Ibid, s 241(1)(c).

99 Goode, *Corporate Insolvency Law*, pp 397–398. See also the decision of the Federal Court of Australia in *Ferrier and Knight (as liquidators of Compass Airlines Pty Ltd) v Civil Aviation Authority* (1994) 55 FCR 28 containing a detailed and illuminating analysis of the question in the context of the Australian rules of preference; A. R. Keay, *Avoidance Provisions in Insolvency Law* (1997), pp 175–177.

100 As defined by s 245(5). See *Re Shoe Lace Ltd* [1993] BCC 609.

101 Ie to the creditor himself while he is refinancing or to a third party.

102 See Goode, *Corporate Insolvency Law*, pp 414–415.

103 See pp 660, 667.

104 See Goode, *Corporate Insolvency Law*, pp 420–421.

(v)   Other grounds of avoidance

Other types of vulnerable transaction are extortionate credit bargains, to which the provisions of s 238 are applied,[105] dispositions made by the company after the commencement of a compulsory winding up and not authorized or validated by the court[106] and transactions defrauding creditors.[107]

(vi) Special protection for transactions involving financial assets

Central bankers have been concerned for some time about the impact of insolvency laws in invalidating transactions involving investment securities and other financial assets, with consequent systemic risk. To that end two EC directives have been issued designed to remove from attack under insolvency law netting and close-out arrangements under the rules of designated systems[108] and, more broadly, contractual arrangements to similar effect relating to financial collateral.[109] Working on the efficacy of contractual arrangements in insolvency is also being carried out at international level by a Contact Group set up by the Bank for International Settlements.[110]

10.   ADMINISTRATIVE RECEIVERSHIP[111]

(i)   The development of administrative receivership

One of the long-standing remedies available to a mortgagee is the appointment of a receiver to collect the rents and profits of the mortgaged property and apply them towards payment of the mortgage interest. Originally the mortgagee applied to the court to appoint a receiver; later, the practice developed of having the appointment made by the mortgagor at the request of the mortgagee; later still, mortgage deeds began to incorporate a power for the mortgagee to make the appointment directly, the receiver nevertheless remaining agent of the mortgagor. This type of

---

105 Insolvency Act 1986, s 244.

106 Ibid, s 127. The section has caused difficulties in relation to the payment of moneys into or from the company's bank account without court approval. See in that connection the helpful decision of the Court of Appeal in *Hollicourt (Contracts) Ltd v Bank of Ireland* [2001] Ch 555, holding that a payment made from an account in credit was recoverable from the payee but that no liability was incurred by the bank.

107 Ibid, ss 423–425, which are not confined to cases where the company is in winding up and which cover not only transactions in fraud of creditors generally but those designed to put assets beyond the reach of a particular creditor or potential creditor.

108 Directive on Settlement Finality in Payment and Securities Systems, 98/26/EC, implemented in the UK by what are now the Financial Markets and Services (Settlement Finality) Regulations 2001, SI 2001/1349.

109 Directive on Financial Collateral Arrangements, 2002/47/EC, implemented in the UK by the Financial Collateral Arrangements (No 2) Regulations 2003, SI 2003/3226.

110 See *Insolvency Arrangements and Contract Enforceability*, prepared by the Contact Group on the legal and institutional underpinnings of the international financial system (December 2002).

111 See generally Gavin Lightman and Gabriel S Moss, *The Law of Receivers and Administrators of Companies* (3rd edn, 2000); Goode, *Corporate Insolvency Law*, ch 9.

receivership, confined to income, is governed by the Law of Property Act 1925[112] as modified by the terms of the mortgage deed.

But creditors financing the debtor company's undertaking began to feel the need for stronger powers to protect their investment, and began to take debentures reserving the right to appoint a receiver who would not only collect in income but manage the business, with power to sell off the whole undertaking or particular assets and use the proceeds to pay off his debenture holders. Though it was possible to appoint a manager who was not the receiver, the two posts were almost invariably combined. The receiver and manager thus acquired extensive powers to continue trading, and for that purpose commit the company to new contracts, to collect in debts and other assets, to sell the whole undertaking or to dispose of the assets or transfer them by a 'hive-down' to a new company, formed as a wholly owned subsidiary of the debtor company, the new company then being traded profitably free of the debts of the parent and sold off to an outside buyer. In order for the receiver and manager to be able to run the business effectively it was obviously necessary for the debenture to give a charge covering the whole or substantially the whole of its assets and undertaking, for without the proprietary base given by the security interest, the receiver and manager would be seriously inhibited in dealing with the company's assets.

The Insolvency Act 1986 uses the term 'administrative receiver' to denote the office previously labelled receiver and manager. The underlying concept is the same but the administrative receiver's status and powers have been given statutory definition. As will be seen, the institution of administrative receivership is now considered so inimical to the rescue culture that, apart from a set of eight exceptions, the holder of a floating charge may no longer appoint an administrative receiver where the charge was created on or after 15 September 2003,[113] and instead has to appoint an administrator. But the fact that this prohibition on the appointment of an administrative receiver is not retrospective means that, quite apart from the excepted cases where it remains permissible to make an appointment, administrative receiverships will be with us for several years and therefore continue to merit attention.

(ii)   The administrative receiver defined

By s 29(2) an administrative receiver means:

(a)   a receiver or manager of the whole (or substantially the whole) of a company's property appointed by or on behalf of the holders of any debenture secured by a charge which as created was a floating charge, or by such a charge and one or more other securities; or

(b)   a person who would be such a receiver or manager but for the appointment of some other person as the receiver of part of the company's property.

It will be seen from this definition that for a receiver[114] to qualify as an administrative receiver, with all the powers that flow from this, three conditions must be satisfied

---

112   Sections 101, 109.

113   Sections 72A(1),(4); Insolvency Act 1986, s 72A (Appointed Date) Order 2003 (SI 2003/2095).

114   In what follows the term 'receiver' refers solely to an administrative receiver except where otherwise indicated

First, the receivership must cover the whole or substantially the whole of the company's property, apart from property the subject of a prior receivership. Secondly, the debenture under which the receiver is appointed must provide or include a floating charge. It is not necessary that this should cover a substantial part of the company's property or, indeed, that at the time the debenture is given the company should have any property at all falling within the scope of the floating charge, so long as there is the potential for at least some class of assets to fall within it.[115] But if the debenture contains no floating charge at all, not be an administrative receiver.[116] Hence the importance of ensuring that the debenture includes at least a residual floating charge. Thirdly, the receiver must be appointed by the debenture holder; a court-appointed receiver cannot be an administrative receiver. In practice, the appointment of a receiver of property the subject of a debenture is almost invariably made by the debenture holder.

(iii) The nature of administrative receivership

The peculiar feature of administrative receivership is that it is an enforcement remedy for a debenture holder rather than a true collective insolvency proceeding. It is true that the global control of the debtor's assets or business which is given to a receiver by the modern debenture tends to inhibit pursuit of proceedings by unsecured creditors and in this respect produces a de facto moratorium not dissimilar to the freeze on actions imposed by law in the event of a compulsory winding up, but this is simply a practical effect, not a legal consequence, of the receiver's appointment. By statute, the receiver is required to see that preferential creditors are paid ahead of the holders of a floating charge[117] and to file accounts and present a report to creditors.[118] Apart from this and the fact that on winding up the receiver's agency powers come to an end,[119] he is largely unaffected by the liquidation process. His primary duty is to the debenture holder who appointed him and his primary function is to ensure that, through the disposal of assets or of the business as a going concern, he raises such money as he can to pay off the amount due to the debenture holder. Though he is deemed the agent of the debtor company,[120] his duty to the company is subordinate to the interests of the debenture holder, so that while he must refrain from conduct which needlessly damages the company's business or goodwill, and on realizing assets must exercise reasonable

---

115 *Re Croftbell Ltd* [1990] BCC 781.

116 However, the fact that a charge has been given to another creditor over the same property is irrelevant; s 29(2)(a) is concerned solely with relations between the appointing chargee and the company, not with competing security interests. See Goode, *Corporate Insolvency Law*, p 209.

117 Insolvency Act 1986, ss 40, 175(2)(b). 'Floating charge' means a charge which, as created, was a floating charge (s 251). Accordingly, the fact that the charge has crystallized before the winding up does not now give the chargee priority over preferential creditors, though it did prior to the legislation. Where (as will normally be the case) the appointment of the receiver precedes the winding up, it is the date of that appointment which is the reference point for computing the preferential debts.

118 Ibid, ss 38, 48; Insolvency Rules 1986, r 3.32.

119 See below.

120 See below.

care to obtain a proper price, he is entitled to give priority to the need to procure discharge of what is owed to his debenture holder and is not obliged to consider the interests of general creditors in the timing of the realization.[121] Subject to this, he owes a duty of care, though in equity, not in tort,[122] and this has now been held to cover not only the way in which assets are realized but also the management of the company's business if the receiver decides to continue this,[123] which he is not bound to do.[124]

Although he owes duties both to the company and to his debenture holder, the receiver is not the servant of either. Rather he is an independent contractor who is not obliged to accept instruction from either party as to the manner in which he conducts his receivership. His independence is buttressed by the fact that he cannot be removed without a court order.[125]

The receiver's objective will usually be to sell the business as a going concern rather than dispose of it on a break-up basis. So the present-day receiver has to have the skills of a business manager and to be able to identify and close down or sell off loss-making parts of the business while striving to move what is left on to a profitable basis. Once he has realized sufficient to discharge the preferential claims (for which he may resort only to the company's free assets and to assets comprised in a floating charge[126]) and the sums due to his debenture holders and any subsequent[127] encumbrancer of whose rights he has notice, he is required to surrender any surplus assets to the company and to hand back control to its directors. Occasionally this happens as the result of successful operations by the receiver in trading the company out of its difficulties. In most cases this happy result is not achieved and the company goes into liquidation.

(iv) Appointment of receiver

The debenture holder can appoint an administrative receiver only where so empowered by the terms of the debenture. There are no restrictions on the events that may be specified in the debenture as entitling the debenture holder to make the appointment, but a receiver cannot be appointed once an administration order has

---

121 See p 639. The position is otherwise in the case of an administrator. See p 852, n 174.

122 *Downsview Nominees Ltd v First City Corp Ltd* [1993] AC 295. For an extensive discussion see Lightman and Moss, *Law of Receivers*, paras 7–019 ff.

123 *Medforth v Blake* [2000] Ch 86, in which the Court of Appeal declined to adopt the more restrictive view of the receiver's duties taken by Lord Templeman in the *Downsview* case.

124 *Downsview Nominees Ltd v First City Corp Ltd*, n 122; *Medforth v Blake*, n 123.

125 See below.

126 See Insolvency Act 1986, s 40, the net effect of which is that to the extent to which the free assets are insufficient to cover the preferential debts these must be paid from assets coming into the hands of the receiver in priority to the claims of the debenture holder.

127 He must, of course, respect the claims of a prior chargee, and on sale of the asset must either pay the claims of the prior chargee from the proceeds or sell subject to the prior charge. However, the court may empower the receiver to dispose of property free from a prior security interest, subject to discharging that interest out of the proceeds and making good any deficiency (Insolvency Act 1986, s 43(3)).

been made.[128] Only a qualified insolvency practitioner can be appointed a receiver.[129] Normally, the debenture empowers the debenture holder to appoint a receiver by an appointment in writing. The appointment is of no effect unless accepted by the appointee before the end of the business day next following that on which he receives the instrument of appointment, but, subject to this, is deemed to be made at the time of such receipt.[130] At one time the debenture holder was free to remove a receiver and appoint a new receiver in his place, but now a receiver can be removed only by order of the court.[131]

(v) Powers of receiver

The receiver's powers are determined primarily by the provisions of the debenture. However, to avoid the need for these to be set out *in extenso* Sch 1 to the Insolvency Act contains a long list of powers which are deemed to be included in the debenture except so far as inconsistent with its provisions.[132]

The receiver's powers are broadly of two kinds. First, there are what may be described as *in rem* powers, that is, powers held in right of the debenture holder and derived from the security created by the debenture. These include power to collect, hold and dispose of the assets comprised in the security. The exercise of such powers is unaffected by the winding up of the company, which, as we have seen, has little impact on the enforcement of security interests. Secondly, there are personal, or agency, powers, that is, powers vested in the receiver as deemed agent of the company.[133] To the extent that these embrace the power to deal with the assets comprising the security they overlap with the *in rem* powers. But they also include powers not, or not necessarily, connected with the security, in particular, the power to carry on the business, hire and fire staff, commit the company to new contracts and decline to allow it to perform existing contracts.[134] These agency powers come to an end on winding up,[135] after which the receiver will not only be personally liable on contracts entered into in the name of the company[136] but have no right to be indemnified out of the assets of the company save to the extent to which the liquidator authorized the contracts for the purpose of beneficial winding up of the company or procures the company freely to accept the benefit of the contracts in question.[137]

---

128 Insolvency Act 1986, s 11(2),(3). But the presentation of a petition for an administration does not bar the appointment of a receiver (s 10(2)), and if a receiver is appointed, an administration order cannot subsequently be made except where the debenture holder consents or the security under which the receiver was appointed is vulnerable under the statutory provisions (s 9(3)).

129 Section 230(2).

130 Section 33(1).

131 Section 45(1).

132 Section 42(1).

133 Section 44(1).

134 See below.

135 Insolvency Act 1986, s 44(1). An administration order displaces the receiver altogether (s 41(1)).

136 As he is even before winding up except in so far as the contract otherwise provides (ibid, s 44(1)(b)).

137 See Goode, *Corporate Insolvency Law*, p 256.

(vi) Receiver's liability on contracts

In general the receiver is personally liable on contracts entered into by him, except so far as the contract otherwise provides,[138] but incurs no liability on existing contracts, even as regards continuing obligations they impose on the company.[139] Only by a novation can he incur personal liability on a continuing pre-existing contract. This immunity from liability for causing or allowing the company to break its contracts results partly from the fact that the receiver holds the company's assets in right of the debenture holder, and is thus entitled to prevent those assets, which constitute the security, from being applied to meet the claims of unsecured creditors,[140] and partly from the general principle of agency law that an agent (as the receiver is deemed to be) cannot be sued for interfering with contractual relationships between his principal and the other contracting party.[141] However, special provision is made for contracts of employment, where the starting position is that the receiver is liable on contracts of employment which he 'adopts', that is, causes or permits to continue. The receiver is not taken to adopt a contract of employment by reason of anything done or omitted to be done within 14 days after his appointment[142] but, under s 44 as originally enacted, adoption thereafter was thought to commit him to the whole liability of the company, including liability incurred prior to the adoption.[143] This exposed receivers to potentially huge personal liability. In consequence, s 44 of the Insolvency Act was amended to restrict his liability to a 'qualifying liability', namely a liability for wages, salary or contribution to an occupational pension scheme incurred while the receiver is in office and in respect of services rendered after the adoption of the contract.[144] The receiver cannot escape this liability by writing a letter to employees saying that he is not adopting their contracts, for mere words of this kind cannot displace the reality;[145] indeed, having adopted the contract, he cannot exclude liability at all for services rendered to him.[146]

(vii) Receiver's liability under leases

The receiver incurs no liability under a lease held by the company even where he takes possession of the leased premises,[147] for he is merely the manager, not the company itself, and is no more liable for rent than a director would be. As a corollary,

---

138 Ibid.

139 *Re Newdigate Colliery Ltd* [1912] 1 Ch 468; *Parsons v Sovereign Bank of Canada* [1913] AC 160.

140 There are, however, certain limits to this principle. In particular, the receiver will be expected to make payments where default would place the company in breach of the criminal law, as on a failure to pay value added tax (*Re John Willment (Ashford) Ltd* [1980] 1 WLR 73).

141 This principle, established in *Said v Butt* [1920] 3 KB 497, was applied by the Court of Appeal in *Welsh Development Agency v Export Finance Co Ltd* [1992] BCC 270 in dismissing a claim for wrongful interference with contract.

142 Insolvency Act 1986, s 44(2).

143 *Powdrill v Watson* [1994] 2 All ER 513, reversed on this point by the House of Lords [1995] 2 All ER 65 after s 44 had been changed

144 Insolvency Act 1986, s 44(2A), (2B).

145 *Powdrill v Watson* [1995] 2 All ER 65.

146 Ibid; Goode, *Principles of Corporate Insolvency Law*, p 102.

147 *Hand v Blow* [1901] 2 Ch 721.

whereas rent accruing due under a lease of premises occupied by the liquidator for the benefit of the company's business becomes a first charge on the assets as an expense of the liquidation, there is no equivalent position in receivership.[148] If the receiver fails to pay the rent, the lessor has no claim against him personally but must pursue other remedies, eg forfeiture of the lease, distress on goods on the leased premises,[149] or service of a notice on sub-lessees requiring rent to be paid direct to the lessor to the extent necessary to discharge the arrears under the head lease.[150] Until such notice is served, the receiver is, it seems, free to collect the rentals under the sub-leases without accounting for them to the lessor or paying rent under the head lease.[151] Once the notice has been served, the lessor can collect the sub-rentals direct except where the debenture holder can establish a prior right to them, eg under a charge or assignment of the sub-rentals.[152]

(viii) Partial abolition of administrative receivership

A review committee set up by the Treasury and the Department of Trade and Industry published a report in 2003 recommending that the power of veto given to the holder of a floating charge to block an administration by appointing an administrative receiver should be abolished.[153] But under the influence of the Treasury, which considered that the whole institution of administrative receivership was inimical to corporate rescue through a collective insolvency proceeding, the Enterprise Act 2002 went much further by prohibiting the appointment of an administrative receiver altogether except under charges created before 15 September 2003 or, as regards charges created on or after that date, in cases falling within specified exempt categories.[154] Save in these cases, the debenture holder's remedy is to appoint an administrator, which is less efficacious in that while an administrative receiver's primary task was to safeguard the interests of his debenture holder, an administrator is required to give priority to other objectives, where reasonably practicable.[155] There are eight categories of exemption, which are designed to safeguard large capital market financings, step-in rights in public–private partnership projects or large financed projects, utility projects, urban regeneration projects,

---

148   See *Re Atlantic Computer Systems plc* [1992] Ch 505 at 524–525.

149   Which at common law are subject to distress even if not owned by the tenant. By s 1 of the Law of Distress Amendment Act 1908 the true owner (not being the tenant) may preserve his goods from distress by serving a declaration and inventory on the lessor. It is not clear whether a receiver can invoke the section, though in principle he should be able to do so, acting in right of his debenture holder.

150   Law of Distress Amendment Act 1908, s 6.

151   *Contra, Kerr on Receivers* (17th edn, 1989), p 188, citing *Re Levi* [1919] 1 Ch 416. But that case involved a liquidator, not a receiver. Given that the latter holds in right of the debenture holder, there is no good reason to require him to account for rents received under sub-leases. It is for the lessor to serve a notice under s 6 of the Law of Distress Amendment Act 1908.

152   In *Rhodes v Allied Dunbar Pension Services Ltd* [1989] 1 WLR 800 the Court of Appeal held that as a matter of construction the charges on book debts did not extend to the sub-rentals. If it had, the priority issue would then have had to be determined

153   *Review of Company and Business Reconstruction Mechanisms* (May 2000), para 73.

154   Enterprise Act 2002, s 250, inserting s 72A into the Insolvency Act 1986.

155   See p 852.

financial market charges, registered social landlords and protected railway companies.[156]

II. ADMINISTRATION[157]

(i) The nature of administration

Administrative receivership, as we have seen, is essentially a default remedy for a particular debenture holder. Prior to 1986 there was no collective procedure for the appointment of an external manager to run a company and hold and dispose of its assets for the benefit of the company itself and the general body of creditors. Moreover, it was all too easy for attempts at reorganization of a company in financial difficulty to be frustrated by enforcement action by individual creditors, for even the appointment of a receiver did not preclude a company from being put into winding up. It was to resolve these weaknesses in insolvency law that the administration procedure was devised

Administration is thus similar to administrative receivership in relation to the management function and the power to dispose of assets; it differs from it primarily in being designed for the benefit of the company and the general body of creditors, who must therefore be consulted on the administrator's proposals. It is normally an interim and temporary regime intended to provide a breathing space for the company by way of a moratorium on the enforcement of proprietary and personal rights.[158] Administration also differs from liquidation in that the liquidator's task is to wind up the company, distribute dividends and then have the company dissolved, while the task of the administrator is to restore the company's fortunes or improve the realization of its assets and put proposals before the creditors, including any proposals for a voluntary arrangement under Pt I of the Act where he is the nominee for the office of supervisor of the arrangements.[159] It is not in general the function of the administrator to receive proofs of debt or distribute dividends except in the capacity of supervisor of a voluntary arrangement where this takes place and he is appointed supervisor.

However, sweeping changes have been made to the administration regime by Sch B1 to the Insolvency Act 1986.[160] These are designed to streamline the administration procedure, and thereby reduce cost and speed the process, by (1) dispensing with the need to obtain an administration order and the concomitant requirement to prepare a report for the court, and (2) providing for the appointment of an administrator by the holder of a floating charge, consequent upon the abolition of

---

156 Insolvency Act 1986, ss 72A–72G and Sch 2A. The exceptions relating to urban regeneration and protected railway companies were inserted by the Insolvency Act 1986 (Amendment) (Administrative Receivership and Urban Regeneration etc) Order 2003 (SI 2003/1832).

157 See also Goode, *Corporate Insolvency Law*, ch 10.

158 *Re Atlantic Computer Systems plc*, n 148 at 528.

159 Where he is not, he must put the proposals to the nominee.

160 Inserted by the Enterprise Act 2002, s 248. For certain purposes the original regime prescribed by Part II of the Insolvency Act 1986 continues to apply. What follows is confined to the new regime contained in Sch B1 to the Act.

administrative receivership, thus replacing a mode of individual enforcement of a security by a collective insolvency procedure for the benefit of creditors generally. The new provisions reflect three underlying objectives: transparency, accountability and collectivity. They are designed to promote the rescue culture, with a shift from saving the business to saving the company itself, and to increase the choice of exit routes.[161] Moreover, the new power given to the administrator, with leave of the court, to make distributions to ordinary unsecured creditors[162] means that administration is no longer solely an interim regime but may be the sole insolvency procedure with the eventual outcome of dissolution, as in the case of winding up.[163] Administration under the new regime may therefore take one of two forms, rescue or realization and distribution of assets.

(ii) Initiating an administration

Prior to the changes made by the Enterprise Act 2002 a company could be put into administration only by a petition followed by an order of the court. This procedure remains available,[164] but usually only when the company is insolvent, which is not a requirement for an out-of-court appointment. It is to be expected that in the normal case, administration will be initiated by the appointment of an administrator[165] by the holder of a qualifying floating charge, the debtor company[166] or its directors, followed by the filing with the court of a notice of appointment and such other documents as may be prescribed, the company entering into administration when the appointment takes effect.[167] A qualifying floating charge is one created by an instrument which states that paragraph 14 of Sch B1 to the Insolvency Act applies to the floating charge and which purports to empower the holder of the floating charge to appoint an administrator or an administrative receiver.[168] But to be the holder of a qualifying floating charge in respect of a company's property it is necessary for the creditor to have a charge or charges over the whole or substantially the whole of the company's property and for at least one of the charges to be a qualifying floating charge.[169] The holder of a qualifying floating charge has first choice in appointing an administrator.[170]

The alternative route to administration is the appointment of an administrator by the court on application by the company, the directors, one or more creditors or a magistrates' court chief executive under s 87A of the Magistrates' Courts Act

---

161 Steve Leinster, 'Policy Aims of the Enterprise Act', *Recovery*, Autumn 2003, 27 at 28.
162 Insolvency Act 1986, Sch B1, para 65.
163 Ibid, para 84.
164 Ibid, paras 10–13. What was formerly described as a petition is now termed an application.
165 Who must be a qualified insolvency practitioner (ibid, para 6).
166 By shareholders' resolution or agreement.
167 That is, when the requirements as to filing, etc, have been fulfilled
168 Insolvency Act 1986, Sch B1, para 14(2).
169 Ibid, para 14(3).
170 This is not directly stated but is implicit in the requirement that the company or directors proposing to appoint an administrator must first give notice to any person entitled to appoint an administrative receiver or administrator under a floating charge (ibid, para 26). See also para 36 dealing with cases where there is an application for an administration order.

1980.[171] The court may make an order only if satisfied that the company is or is likely to become unable to pay its debts and that the administration order is likely to achieve the purpose of administration.[172] One of the options open to the court is to treat the application as a winding-up petition and make a winding-up order.[173]

(iii) The purpose of administration

The administrator must perform his functions with the objective of:

(a)   rescuing the company as a going concern, or

(b)   achieving a better result for the company's creditors as a whole than would be likely if the company were wound up without first being in administration, or

(c)   realizing property in order to make a distribution to one or more secured or preferential creditors.

These objectives are arranged hierarchically, so that the administrator cannot perform his functions with the second objective unless he thinks either that it is not reasonably practicable to achieve the first objective or that the second objective would achieve a better result, and he may perform his functions with the third objective only if he thinks that it is not reasonably practicable to adopt either of the first two objectives and he does not unnecessarily harm the interests of the creditors as a whole.[174] There is therefore little incentive for the holder of a floating charge to make an appointment except where it is not reasonably practical for either of the first two objectives to be achieved, as where the company has reached the point of no return and the debts secured by the floating charge, with any fixed charges, are such that there will be no benefit to the creditors as a whole.

(iv) The effect of administration

The effect of administration, whether out of court or by court order, is to place an almost total freeze on the enforcement of real and personal rights, including enforcement of security rights, rights of repossession under hire-purchase agreements, a landlord's right of forfeiture, or any legal process, including proceedings, execution or distress, except with the consent of the administrator or the approval of the court.[175] This freeze, which even precludes the making of a winding-up resolution or order, is peculiar to administration and is one of its most valuable features, for it means that the administrator can get on with the job of reorganizing the company free from the burden of fending off attacks on the company and its assets by individual creditors. Prior to the administration there is an interim moratorium where an application has been made for an administration order or

---

171   Insolvency Act 1986, Sch B1, para 12(1).

172   As to which, see (iii) below.

173   Insolvency Act 1986, Sch B1, para 13(1). However, the converse is not true: the court cannot make an administration order on the hearing of a winding-up petition.

174   Insolvency Act 1986, Sch B1, para 3. So an administrator, unlike a mortgagee (see p 820), no longer has unfettered discretion as to whether and when to sell. 'Harm' appears to mean the same as the previous term 'prejudice'.

175   Ibid, paras 40–43.

notice of intention to appoint an administrator has been filed.[176] The interim moratorium imposes a slightly less wide-ranging freeze in that it does not prevent the presentation of a winding-up petition, the appointment of an administrator by the holder of a floating charge under paragraph 14, the appointment of an administrative receiver or the carrying out by the latter of his functions.[177]

The statutory provisions for avoidance of transactions on winding up[178] also apply to an administration.

(v) Powers of the administrator

Except that he is concerned for the interests of the company and the general body of creditors and not for those of a particular creditor, the position of an administrator is not dissimilar to that of a receiver. The administrator may do anything necessary or expedient for the management of the affairs, business and property of the company.[179] In addition, he may remove or appoint directors and call any meeting of the members or creditors of the company.[180] Like the receiver, he is deemed to act as the company's agent.[181]

(vi) Conduct of the administration

The essential function of the administrator is to seek to achieve the objective of the administration as previously described and to lay before the creditors proposals to that end. Meanwhile he has the task of managing the company consistently with the objective in question, and obtaining and assembling the financial and other information needed to assess the company's position and prospects, deciding how far the desired objectives are achievable and annexing to his proposals the statement prescribed.[182] The creditors may approve the administrator's proposals or reject them but they may not modify them without his consent to each modification.[183] If the proposals are not accepted, with any agreed modification, the court may discharge the administrator, adjourn the hearing, or make an interim order or a winding-up order on any suspended petition or any other order it thinks appropriate.[184]

A creditor or member may apply to the court for relief where the administrator is acting or has acted or proposes to act so as unfairly to harm the interests of the

---

176   Ibid, para 44(1)–(5).
177   Ibid, para 44(7).
178   See pp 838 ff.
179   Insolvency Act 1986, Sch B1, para 59(1).
180   Ibid, s 14(2).
181   Ibid, s 14(5). The termination of the agency power on liquidation cannot arise in relation to an administrator, for during the currency of the administration the company cannot be put into winding up.
182   Ie by the Insolvency Act 1986, Sch B1, para 49, and para 2.33 of the new Pt 2 of the Insolvency Rules 1986 governing the new regime.
183   Schedule B1, para 53(1).
184   Ibid, para 55(2).

applicant (whether alone or in common with some or all other members or creditors).[185]

(vii) Exits from the administration

The administrator's proposals must state how it is envisaged the purpose of the administration will be achieved and how it is proposed that the administration shall end.[186] There are a number of possibilities. The administration could, with any necessary leave of the court, come to an end by distribution of realizations without any further proceedings. Alternatively, the administration could be converted into a voluntary winding up or could be followed by a winding-up petition and order. Further alternatives are a voluntary arrangement under Pt I of the Insolvency Act 1986, a compromise or scheme of arrangement under s 425 of the Companies Act 1985 or the transfer of all realizations to the holder of one or more security interests pursuant to leave of the court. A novel feature of the new regime is the provision for automatic ending of the administrator's appointment after one year unless extended by the court on his application.[187] The administrator may also apply to the court for the ending of his appointment.[188] The administrator's remuneration and expenses are payable in priority to claims secured by a floating charge[189] and of preferential and other unsecured creditors to whom any distribution is to be made,[190] after which come preferential claims *pari passu*, who rank ahead of claims secured by a floating charge,[191] followed by floating charge claims and then by the claims of ordinary unsecured creditors *pari passu*.[192]

12. LIABILITY OF DIRECTORS FOR IMPROPER TRADING

The directors of a company owe a duty to creditors to trade responsibly. They are subject to both criminal and civil penalties for fraudulent trading and to civil sanctions for wrongful trading.

(i) Fraudulent trading

If in the course of winding up of a company it appears that any business of the company has been carried on with intent to defraud creditors of the company or creditors of any other person or for any fraudulent purpose, the court may, on the application of the liquidator, declare that any persons knowingly party to the fraudulent trading are to be liable to make such contributions (if any) to the company's assets as the court thinks proper.[193] Fraudulent trading is also a criminal

---

185 Ibid, para 74(1).
186 Insolvency Rules 1986, r 2.33(2)(m).
187 Insolvency Act 1986, Sch B1, para 76.
188 Ibid, para 79.
189 Insolvency Act 1986, s 99(3).
190 Insolvency Rules 1986, r 2.68(3).
191 Insolvency Act 1986, Sch B1, para 65(2), applying s 175 of the Act.
192 Insolvency Rules 1986, r 2.69.
193 Ibid, s 213.

offence.[194] Directors are guilty of fraudulent trading if they cause the company to incur further credit in the knowledge that it would not be able to pay its debts as they fall due or shortly thereafter; it is not a defence that they had some expectation that at some indeterminate time in the future all debts would be paid.[195] Knowledge includes deliberately shutting one's eyes to the obvious and reckless indifference to the fraudulent nature of the transaction.[196] The fact that a transaction has been entered into fraudulently is not by itself sufficient to attract the operation of s 113; it must be shown that the company *carried on business* with intent to defraud. And while it is possible for a single transaction in fraud of a single creditor to constitute the carrying on of a business,[197] it is not every fraudulent transaction that makes the business a business carried on with intent to defraud.[198]

(ii) Wrongful trading

Though civil and criminal proceedings for fraudulent trading are from time to time pursued successfully, the standard of proof required and the time and expense involved have greatly inhibited proceedings of this kind. It was because of this that the Cork Committee recommended the introduction of new statutory provisions enabling contribution orders to be made for wrongful trading, for which proof of dishonesty would not be required. These provisions are now contained in s 214 of the Insolvency Act 1986. Their effect is that a person can be found guilty of wrongful trading, and ordered to make a contribution to the company's assets, where the following conditions are satisfied:

(a)   The company has gone into insolvent liquidation.[199]
(b)   At some time before the commencement of the winding up the person in question knew or ought to have concluded that there was no reasonable prospect that the company would avoid going into insolvent liquidation.
(c)   That person was a director at that time.
(d)   The director fails to establish the statutory defence of taking every step he ought to have taken with a view to minimizing the potential loss to creditors.[200]

194   Companies Act 1985, s 458. This does not depend on the company being in winding up.
195   *R. v Grantham* [1984] 3 All ER 166, disapproving of the statement of Buckley LJ in *Re White & Osmond (Parkstone) Ltd* (30 June 1960, unreported) that it was sufficient if the directors genuinely believed the clouds would roll away and the sunshine of prosperity shine upon them again (the so-called 'clouds and sunshine' test).
196   *Re Bank of Credit and Commerce International SA* (2003) BCC 735.
197   *Re Gerald Cooper (Chemicals) Ltd* [1978] Ch 262. However, in such a case payment under s 213 is made not to the defrauded creditor but to the company, the creditor's remedy being a claim under the general law.
198   *Morphitis v Bernasconi* [2003] 2 BCLC 53.
199   The provisions cannot be invoked by an administrator.
200   For this purpose the standard applied is that of a reasonably diligent person having both the general knowledge, skill and experience reasonably expected of a person carrying out the same functions and the general knowledge, skill and experience that the director has (Insolvency Act 1986, s 214(4), (5)). In other words, the director is held to the standard of the reasonable person and such higher standard as is to be expected of a person having his particular general knowledge, skill and experience.

Wrongful trading is to be distinguished from fraudulent trading in a number of respects. First, fraud or dishonesty is not a necessary ingredient; want of care suffices. Secondly, the onus of showing the exercise of reasonable care is on the director concerned, whereas the onus of showing dishonesty is on the prosecution or the liquidator. Thirdly, only a director or shadow director[201] can be made liable for wrongful trading. Fourthly, proceedings for wrongful trading are purely civil, the sanctions being the making of a contribution order, subordination of any debt owed by the company to the director to all other debts of the company and disqualification.[202] Finally, whereas in the case of fraudulent trading the whole period of trading is potentially relevant, the wrongful trading provisions are confined to culpable conduct after the time when the director knew or ought to have known that there was no reasonable prospect of the company avoiding insolvent liquidation. The duty to minimize potential loss to creditors is owed to the creditors at large, so that the director would not be entitled to continue trading for the benefit of existing creditors by incurring fresh credit at the expense of the new creditors when there was no reasonable prospect of their being paid.[203]

The purpose of the statutory provisions is to recoup loss to the company so as to benefit creditors as a class. The court has no power to order the director to pay creditors or to require sums paid to the company to be applied in payment to one class of creditor in preference to another; indeed, creditors whose debts are incurred after the critical date have no stronger claim than those whose debts were incurred before that date.[204] It is also the better view that sums recovered from a defaulting director under s 214 do not enure for the benefit of the holder of a floating charge or a charge over future assets, for the policy of the section is that recoveries should be treated as held for the general body of creditors, not as a free asset of the company.[205]

13. CROSS-BORDER INSOLVENCIES[206]

National corporate insolvency laws are ill-equipped for cross-border, or international, insolvencies in which a company trades, has assets, and may be the subject of concurrent insolvency proceedings, in two or more jurisdictions. What is required is an international regime, but this has raised singularly intractable

---

201 Insolvency Act 1986, s 214(7).
202 Ibid, ss 214, 215; Company Directors Disqualification Act 1986, ss 4(1)(a), 10.
203 Indeed, to do this knowingly would be fraudulent trading.
204 *Re Purpoint Ltd* [1991] BCC 121.
205 In *Re Produce Marketing Consortium Ltd (No.2)* [1989] BCLC 520 Knox J appears to have assumed the recoveries would go to the debenture holders, but there are powerful arguments to the contrary. See Fidelis Oditah, 'Wrongful Trading' [1990] LMCLQ 205; D. D. Prentice, 'Creditor's Interests and Director's Duties' (1990) OJLS 265; Sally Wheeler, 'Swelling the Assets for Distribution in Corporate Insolvency' [1993] JBL 256.
206 There is now a prodigious amount of literature on this subject. See in particular Ian F. Fletcher, *Insolvency in Private International Law*, 1999; Jay Lawrence Westbrook, 'A Global Solution to Multinational Default' 98 Mich L Rev 2276 (2000); and for earlier but still relevant analyses, Jacob S. Ziegel (ed), *Current Developments in International and Comparative Corporate Insolvency Law*, 1994.

problems, partly because of the difficulties involved in organizing judicial cooperation and a coordinated approach to the collection and distribution of assets located
in different jurisdictions and partly because of the different legal approaches to
certain fundamental concepts.[207] Two opposing pairs of principles are of particular
significance, namely unity versus plurality, and universality versus territoriality.
The principle of unity ascribes exclusive jurisdiction over winding up to the courts
of a particular state (eg the state of incorporation, the centre of the company's main
interests), to which all other courts defer. It has been found impossible to apply this
concept fully, because states are reluctant to give up jurisdiction over local assets
where there are local creditors. What has, however, developed is the concept of
limited plurality in the shape of a main insolvency proceeding covering all the
debtor's assets and a secondary insolvency proceeding in a jurisdiction where the
debtor has an establishment and confined to assets within that jurisdiction. The
second opposing pair of principles relates to the assets covered by the insolvency
proceeding. In some jurisdictions, including England, the principle of universality is
adopted by which all assets of the debtor company, wherever situated, are brought
within the insolvency,[208] while other countries adopt the principle of territoriality,
limiting the impact of the insolvency proceeding in their jurisdiction to local assets.
A number of countries that themselves adopt the principle of universality are
reluctant to concede exclusivity of asset control to other countries that also adopt
the principle.

Two instruments are of particular significance, the EC Regulation on Insolvency
Proceedings[209] and the 1997 UNCITRAL Model Law on Cross-Border Insolvency.

(i) The EC Insolvency Regulation[210]

Apart from a few peripheral rules the EC Insolvency Regulation, which has direct
effect without need for implementation by domestic legislation, is a conflict of laws
regulation which deals with insolvency jurisdiction, the applicable law, the effects
of insolvency proceedings and recognition across the EU of judgments by a court in
a member state having jurisdiction. The regulation does not, however, deal with
substantive insolvency law, which remains within the exclusive competence of

---

207 See Ian F. Fletcher, 'The quest for a global insolvency law: a challenge for our time' [2002]
Current Legal Problems 427.
208 Though obviously the ability of the insolvency administrator to gain control of assets situated
outside the insolvency jurisdiction may depend on authorization by the courts of the country
concerned
209 Council Regulation (EC) No 1346/2000 of 29 May 2000 on insolvency proceedings, which has
effectively superseded the 1990 Istanbul Convention on Certain International Aspects of
Bankruptcy, a European convention which lapsed because of the refusal of the UK, alone of the 15
member states, to sign, partly because of failure to obtain a clear statement that the convention
applied to Gibraltar and partly because of a wholly unconnected spat over continuing restrictions
on the exportation of British beef at the time of the BSE crisis!
210 See Gabriel Moss, Ian F. Fletcher and Stuart Isaacs, *The EC Regulation on Insolvency Proceedings*
(2002), and the Virgos-Schmit *Report on the Convention on Insolvency Proceedings*, 1996, a report
on the failed Istanbul Convention which remains relevant to the very similar provisions of the
Insolvency Regulation.

member states.[211] The regulation covers both winding up and collective reorganization proceedings. In order for the regulation to apply, the centre of the debtor's main interests must be situated within the territory of an EC member state.[212] Insolvency proceedings opened in that state ('main insolvency proceedings') cover all the debtor's assets.[213] The opening of such proceedings normally precludes the opening of insolvency proceedings in any other member state, but the courts of another member state in the territory of which the debtor possesses an establishment[214] have jurisdiction to open proceedings ('secondary proceedings') the effects of which are restricted to assets situated in the territory of that member state.[215] Thus the regulation allows the possibility of different sets of secondary proceedings. In restricted cases proceedings in a State of establishment may be opened prior to the opening of the main insolvency proceedings.[216] 'Centre of main interests', a crucial phrase, is not defined, though recital (13) of the Preamble states that it 'should correspond to the place where the debtor conducts the administration of his interests on a regular basis and is therefore ascertainable by third parties' and art 3(1) provides that in the case of a company, the place of the registered office is to be presumed to be the centre of its main interests in the absence of evidence to the contrary. Where the company trades from one place only, the centre of main interests will be that place, and the fact that it is incorporated in a state which is not a EU state does not affect the court's jurisdiction;[217] where it carries on activities in different countries the presumption in favour of the place of the registered office is readily displaced if it can be shown that the company's head office or chief executive office is located elsewhere.

The general principle is that the law applicable to insolvency proceedings and their effects is that of the member state within the territory of which the proceedings are opened.[218] This determines the range of issues listed in art 4(2), including determination of the assets forming part of the debtor's estate, the conditions in which set-off may be invoked and the ranking of claims. As regards the last of these, it is necessary to distinguish the law applicable to pre-insolvency entitlements and the rules of insolvency law which may affect those entitlements. For example, in considering the validity, perfection and priority of a security interest, the insolvency court should, as a starting point, apply the law determined by its own conflict of laws rules, typically the *lex situs* (*lex rei sitae*),[219] which may well be

---

211 That has not, however, prevented the EC Commission from insisting that art XI of the Aircraft Equipment Protocol to the 2001 Convention on International Interests in Mobile Equipment is capable of affecting the Insolvency Regulation even though the provisions of art XI deal exclusively with the substantive law rights of a creditor on the debtor's insolvency. Member states have agreed a compromise on this issue which is designed to ensure that it does not lead to the assertion of EC competence over substantive insolvency law.

212 Article 3.

213 This is implicit in the Preamble, para 11, and art 3(2).

214 That is, any place of operations where the debtor carries out a non-transitory economic activity with human means and goods (art 2(h)).

215 Article 3(2).

216 Article 3(3).

217 *Re BRAC Rent-A-Car International Inc* [2003] 2 All ER 201.

218 Article 4(1).

219 See p 1090.

that of another member state or of a non-member state. The application of such law may lead to the conclusion that a security interest has been validly created and perfected and has priority over unsecured claims. Where the law in question is that of another member state in which assets belonging to the debtor were situated at the time of opening of the insolvency proceedings, then, under art 5, the opening of the proceedings is not to affect the rights *in rem* of creditors or third parties. In such a case the insolvency court must respect those rights and cannot, for example, alter priorities by reference to its domestic rules of insolvency ranking, though it remains entitled to apply such rules so far as they invalidate or render unenforceable transactions, eg as preferences or transactions in fraud of creditors.[220] But the principle of universality applies to such assets so far as consistent with the preservation of the *in rem* rights, so that, subject to the *in rem* rights, they form part of the insolvency estate and any surplus remaining after discharge of such rights will go to the estate. In cases outside art 5 – for example, where at the relevant time the assets are situated in the territory of a non-member state – the starting position of the insolvency court is to respect rights acquired under the law determined by its own conflict of laws rules – typically the *lex situs* (*lex rei sitae*) – but it may then apply any special rules of insolvency law to determine not only whether the rights are vulnerable as preferences, etc, but also whether, inter alia, any pre-insolvency priority is displaced by the ranking rules of the insolvency law, which may, for instance, give priority to certain types of unsecured claim over a perfected security interest.

(ii) The UNCITRAL Model Law

The UNCITRAL Model Law is designed to promote cooperation between the courts and other competent authorities of the enacting state and foreign states. It authorizes a foreign representative (typically an insolvency administrator) to apply directly to the courts of the enacting state[221] and to institute or participate in insolvency proceedings in that State.[222] It also contains provisions for the recognition of foreign proceedings[223] and, where proceedings ('main proceedings') have been instituted in the state where the debtor has its centre of main interests, the stay of proceedings in another enacting state except as to assets in that state.[224] The Secretary of State may by regulations make any provision he considers necessary or expedient for the purpose of giving effect to the Model Law, with or without modifications.[225]

---

220 Article 5(4).
221 Article 9.
222 Articles 11 and 12.
223 Articles 15 and 16.
224 Article 28.
225 Insolvency Act 2000, s 14. Regulations are now being prepared.

PART SEVEN
International Trade and Finance

32 The Characteristics and Organization of International Sales Transactions

1. CHARACTERISTICS

There are various ways in which the law might identify a sale transaction as international in character. The first is where the transaction involves the movement of goods from one state to another. This may seem a quite sensible yardstick, for the goods are moving from one legal regime to another, even if the seller and the buyer have their places of business in the same state. For example, to satisfy an order placed by his New York customer, C, a London merchant, B, may order goods from a trader in Liverpool, S, and stipulate that the goods are to be delivered to C in New York. Though B and S have their places of business in England, an international movement of goods is concerned, and in that sense we are involved with an international transaction. On the other hand, since B and S both trade in England, many of the usual risks associated with dealings with a foreigner are eliminated If litigation results, it is almost certain that the proceedings will be brought in England, that English law will be applied as the proper law of the contract and that the successful party will look to the other party's assets in England to satisfy the judgment.

So another approach is to look at the places of business of the parties and to designate the transaction as international where the place of business of the seller is in one state and that of the buyer in another. Here the two parties are governed by different legal systems, enforcement steps by one party will usually have to be taken in the other's jurisdiction and, as a rule, performance of the contract will involve at least some steps by one party to bring about a result (eg delivery or payment) that will occur outside his own jurisdiction. This test of the international character of a transaction has now gained general acceptance. Under the United Nations Convention on Contracts for the International Sale of Goods[1] it will be sufficient by itself.[2] Pursuant to this test, it is quite possible to have an international contract of sale which does not involve the movement of goods outside the territory of a single state.

In this and the ensuing chapter we shall be primarily concerned with export sales, in the sense of sale transactions between an English seller and a foreign buyer involving the movement of goods from England to an overseas country, usually that in which the buyer carries on business. Such a transaction is international in the

1 See ch 33.
2 Article 1.

fullest sense and is the most convenient for purposes of exposition.[3] When dealing with the finance of international trade we shall also look at the position of the English buyer who wishes to raise finance against imported goods.

2.   TRENDS IN EXPORT PROCEDURES

There have been significant changes in export procedures and documentation since the 1970s. At least three major trends can be identified. First, the traditional emphasis on shipment as the contractual delivery point has given way increasingly to multimodal transport under a contract of carriage covering all stages of the journey, starting with delivery to an inland terminal or collection of a full container load from the seller's premises. Nevertheless, the contract remains a dispatch contract, not an arrival contract;[4] all that changes is the dispatch point and the stages of the transit covered by the transport document. Secondly, the delays associated with bills of lading, coupled with a growing recognition that a document of title to shipped goods serves no useful purpose if they are not intended to be dealt with in transit, has led to growing use of the non-negotiable sea waybill.[5] Thirdly, systems have rapidly developed for electronic data interchange (EDI), and with them the evolution of the so-called electronic bill of lading[6] and the steady replacement or supplementation of other paper documents (eg ship's delivery orders and manifests) by electronic communications.

Despite these developments the documentary sale, in which goods are shipped under a bill of lading enabling them to be pledged or sold in transit by delivery of the bill of lading with any necessary endorsement, remains of great importance because of the sheer volume and value of bulk cargo shipped under f.o.b., c.i.f. and related contracts, and it is the documentary sale that will be the focus of this and the following chapters. Carriage of goods by air does not necessitate the use of a document of title, the period of the transit being too short for such a document to be useful.

3.   PROBLEMS PECULIAR TO EXPORT SALES

Why does an export sale to a foreigner pose special legal problems for the seller? There are several reasons.

(a)   It is generally less easy for the seller to check on the credit standing of an overseas buyer than of a buyer in his own country.

(b)   Export and import licences may be required, quotas imposed and the transfer of funds restricted by exchange control regulations.

---

3 See generally *Schmitthoff's Export Trade* (10th edn, ed Leo D'Arcy, Carole Murray and Barbara Cleave, 1106.

2000,); and for a useful practical manual, the P & O Nedlloyd *The Merchants Guide* (ed J. W. Richardson, 2003).

4 See p 867.

5 See the CMI Uniform Rules for Sea Waybills (1990) and p 906.

6 See the CMI Rules for Electronic Bills of Lading (1990).

(c)   Some aspects of the transaction may, so far as not effectively excluded by the contract of sale, be governed by the buyer's own law, with which the seller may not be familiar, and vice versa.

(d)   Claims against the buyer may need to be enforced in the courts of the buyer's own country, whose procedure may be unknown, slow or more expensive than in the seller's country.

(e)   In certain foreign countries, additional risks arise from the political stance or instability of the government.

(f)   The seller may be adversely affected by fluctuations in exchange rates.

(g)   The mechanism for executing the sale contract is likely to be considerably more complex than for a domestic sale, involving different forms of transportation, a range of ancillary contracts (warehousing, insurance, finance etc) and customs clearance at both ends.

The buyer for his part faces a comparable range of problems when purchasing from an overseas supplier.

The international sale transaction, with its central contract of sale and ancillary arrangements for insurance, storage, transportation and finance, epitomizes the commercial operation. It is in the international sale that the importance of documents as a means of harmonizing the security interests of seller and buyer becomes most evident; it is here that the ingenuity of financier and businessperson in developing instruments that will answer emerging commercial needs reaches its highest point. The international sale is thus for the lawyer, as well as for the businessperson, a fascinating area of study, and one of which we can, necessarily, give only a brief glimpse in the pages that follow.

4.   THE SINGLE EUROPEAN MARKET

The creation of the Single European Market has to some extent led to a redefinition of the words 'international', 'export' and 'import'. The concept of the Single Market predicates that the movement of goods from one EU state to another is not an export/import operation at all but a purely internal one in which there are no customs barriers and there is a EU-wide liberalization of transport, telecommunications and financial services, and European product standards, the observance of which displaces the need for separate compliance with individual national standards.[7] But though the concept is of great importance as regards the free movement of goods, services and capital within the Single Market, it remains the case that each member state has its own laws regulating sales transactions, its own courts, its own need of information for statistical and revenue purposes. Accordingly, we have not yet reached the stage where we can treat contracts of sale between parties in different member states as if they were transacting business in the same state. This is particularly true of the United Kingdom, which alone of the major European countries has not ratified the Vienna Convention on Contracts for the International Sale of Goods.[8]

7 See generally Alan E. Branch, *Export Practice and Management* (4th edn, 2000), ch 18.
8 See ch 33.

5.   SOURCES OF LAW

The primary source of the rights and duties of the parties to a contract of sale is, of course, the contract itself. This encompasses not only the express terms spelled out in the contract document but usages of trade and any codification of trade terms incorporated into the contract and thereby adopted by the parties as their contractual dictionary. The most widely adopted of these are Incoterms, published by the International Chamber of Commerce.[9]

The rights of the parties to an international sale transaction will normally be governed by a particular national law. Where the contract expressly designates the law to which it is to be subject, the court will usually give effect to that choice; where it does not, the court must determine the applicable law by reference to the conflict of law rules of the forum, including, in courts of member states of the European Union, the rules embodied in the Rome Convention.[10] Of particular interest as a source of law, so far as not excluded or varied by the contract, is the Convention on Contracts for the International Sale of Goods, to which the next chapter is devoted.[11]

6.   THE DELIVERY POINT ON SALE TO AN OVERSEAS BUYER

It will be apparent that exporting involves not only a series of expensive and time-consuming procedures but also a measure of risk for both parties. Where the parties do not have an established relationship involving open account payment terms, the seller will want to be sure that he will be paid, while the buyer may not wish to part with money unless he is reasonably satisfied that he will receive the goods punctually and in proper condition. But these considerations will affect the arrangements for payment rather than the delivery point. This is influenced by a range of factors. The more services the seller provides, the greater the price he can charge, so that he maximizes his profit by delivering to the buyer's premises. By the same token, the exporting country's export earnings are likewise enhanced. The buyer, however, may find it cheaper to collect the goods ex works and make his own transportation arrangements than pay the seller a price which includes the seller's transportation costs; and the buyer's government may be keen to maximize its own revenues by requiring shipment on the ships of its nationals. At the end of the day much depends on the bargaining power of the parties and the seller's need to attract business by meeting his customer's requirements.

(i)   Price and delivery terms

The delivery point on which the contract price is based is usually expressed in the form of an abbreviation established by trade usage, eg f.a.s., f.o.b.[12] The term used

---

9   The current edition is Incoterms 2000 (ICC Publication No 560). See below.

10   See ch 37.

11   As stated earlier, the convention has not been ratified by the United Kingdom and does not have the force of law in this country.

12   For a table of such terms, see p 869. For a detailed treatment of f.o.b. and c.i.f. contracts, see ch 34.

is thus a price term, ie it signifies the extent to which the transportation of the goods is covered by the contract price and is thus at the seller's expense. The quoted term may also be a delivery term, that is, it may be intended to show that the buyer is, in fact, to take delivery at the point stipulated. But this is not necessarily the case. For example, in quoting a contract price of £100 ex warehouse, the seller is indicating that the sum of £100 covers only delivery at his own premises, but he may nevertheless be willing to effect delivery of the goods elsewhere (eg to the docks or on board a vessel or to a designated port in the buyer's country) so long as the costs are met by the buyer.[13] If an agreement to this effect is concluded, '£100 ex works' is merely a price term stating what is covered by the quoted price and does not denote the intended delivery point, which must be found elsewhere in the contract. But if the contract is silent, the quoted term will be both a price term and a term establishing the contractual delivery point.

(ii) Dispatch and arrival contracts

In an export sale, as in a domestic sale, the range of possible delivery points runs from the seller's premises at one end to the buyer's at the other. But, unless the buyer is to collect the goods from the seller's premises, the main choice is between a *dispatch* contract and an *arrival*, or destination, contract. In the case of a dispatch contract the seller must either ship the goods from his own country or deliver them into the charge of a carrier or other party alongside the ship or at some inland delivery point prior to shipment. Thereafter the seller has no responsibility for them; in particular, he is not liable for their loss or damage in transit and does not undertake that they will arrive at the destination to which they have been dispatched. In the case of an arrival contract the seller's duty is to deliver the goods to the buyer at an agreed destination point in the buyer's country, and the seller is responsible for them up to that point.

(iii) Incoterms 2000

The great variety of modern transportation and handling arrangements has made it even more necessary than formerly to secure consistency in the use of price and delivery terms, so that each party has a clear picture of what the price does or does not cover and of the point at which the seller's delivery obligation is to be considered fulfilled. The widespread adoption of Incoterms greatly facilitates this objective, though, as we shall see, the parties often find it necessary to qualify these by additional words. Incoterms take effect by incorporation into the sale contract.

(iv) Degrees of localization

Under Incoterms 1990 trade terms are divided into four groups:

(a) a single E-term (ex works), in which the seller has no responsibility for delivery to a carrier or even for loading the goods on to the buyer's vehicle;

---

13 Usually these would be advanced by the forwarding agent and recovered from the consignee via the carrier with an additional profit element.

(b)   F-terms, in which the seller's duty is to deliver to the carrier but the freight is payable by the buyer and is not included in the price;

(c)   C-terms, in which the seller is responsible for arranging the carriage of the goods from his country at his own expense, so that the freight is included in the price; and

(d)   D-terms, under which the contract is an arrival contract, requiring the seller to deliver the goods to an agreed delivery point in the buyer's country.

Only four terms are specific to shipment: f.a.s., f.o.b., c.f.r. and c.i.f. One or other of these terms, or variants of them, should be used whenever the contract requires the seller to have the goods shipped. All other terms are general delivery terms applicable to any mode of transport and to multimodal transport.

Table 32.1, based on Incoterms 2000, shows in relation to each stated price term the delivery point up to which expenses are borne by the seller; the expenses of any subsequent movement or handling of the goods are for the buyer's account.[14] The seller is not responsible for arranging the shipment except in the case of a c.i.f. contract and its variants and of the extended f.o.b. contract.[15] Hence these are the only cases in which the duty to deliver shipping documents is superimposed on the seller's physical delivery obligation. The table is arranged in descending order of localization. The first column shows the abbreviation of the term; the second, its full expression; the third, the delivery point to be specified after the trade term; and the fourth, the point up to which expenses are borne by the seller, which is normally the delivery point shown in the third column, but in the case of c.i.f. contracts covers the cost of shipment to the port of destination.

Certain additions are common. These may affect the delivery point, and thus usually the risk, or merely what is covered in the price. Thus EXW loaded requires the seller to load on to the buyer's vehicle at the seller's premises; FCA undischarged, to deliver to the stated terminal ready for unloading but not to unload; FOB stowed, to arrange and bear the costs of stowage as well as placement on board;[16] CIF landed, to arrange and pay for unloading at the port of destination; DDU cleared, to clear for import but not to pay the import duties.

It is important that as far as possible terms contained in all the relevant contracts – in particular, the contract of sale, the contract of carriage and the engagement generated by the issue of a letter if credit – should be consistent with each other, but this does not always happen, nor do expressions used in the one necessarily have the same meaning as those used in the other. The International Chamber of Commerce, which produces both Incoterms and the Uniform Customs and Practice for Documentary Credits, has done much valuable work in helping to ensure that the two are aligned. Nevertheless, exporters using Incoterms continue to make arrangements which are not fully consistent with them, as by procuring a combined

---

14 Reference should be made to Incoterms 2000 for a full description of each price and delivery term and of the duties of the respective parties.

15 See, pp 870–871.

16 Extensions such as f.o.b.s. (f.o.b. stowed), f.o.b.t. (f.o.b. trimmed) and f.o.b.s.t. (f.o.b. stowed and trimmed) are normally used only where the goods are to be shipped on a vessel chartered by one of the parties.

Table 32.1 Price and delivery terms

(1) Term	(2) Meaning	(3) Delivery point to be stated	(4) Point to which delivery made and risk and expenses borne by seller
E-term: departure			
EXW	Ex works	Seller's premises (works, factory, warehouse etc)	Seller's premises (no duty to load)
F-terms: main carriage unpaid			
FCA	Free carrier	Named place in country of departure	Into custody of carrier or other person at named place in country of departure
FAS	Free alongside ship	Vessel at named port of shipment	Alongside vessel (in tug, barge, lighter etc), at named port of shipment
FOB	Free on board	Vessel at named port of shipment	Over ship's rail at port of shipment, carriage unpaid
C-terms: main carriage paid			
CFR	Cost and freight	Vessel at port of shipment	Over ship's rail at port of shipment, carriage paid to port of destination
CIF	Cost, insurance and	Vessel at port of shipment freight	Over ship's rail at port of shipment, carriage and insurance paid to port of destination
CPT	Carriage paid to	Named place in country of departure	Into custody of carrier, carriage paid to named place in country of destination
CIP	Carriage and insurance	Named place in country of departure paid	Into custody of carrier, carriage and insurance paid to named place in country of destination
D-terms: arrival			
DAF	Delivered at frontier	Named place at frontier	Named place at frontier
DES	Delivered ex ship	Named port of destination	On board vessel at usual unloading point at port of destination
DEQ	Delivered ex quay	Named port of destination	On quay or wharf at named port of destination
DDU	Delivered duty unpaid	Named place of destination	Named place of destination, duty unpaid
DDP	Delivered duty paid	Named place of destination	Named place of destination, duty paid

SUMMARY

Inland point in country of departure			Ship at named point in country of departure			Named point in country of destination
EXW	FCA	CPT CIP	FAS	FOB	CFR CIF	DAF DES DEQ DDU DDP

Note: unless otherwise agreed, risk passes at the delivery point stated in column (4).

transport bill of lading with a shipped on board indorsement for f.o.b. and c.i.f. contracts, which strictly require that the seller himself shall have shipped on board rather than having the goods delivered to an internal collection or delivery point.[17]

(v) Nature of the delivery obligation when the goods are to be carried by ship

Suppose that S in Southampton contracts to sell goods to B in New York, and that B wishes to collect the goods on their arrival by ship in New York. There are at least four alternative ways in which S's delivery obligation may be framed in the contract. Arranged in ascending order of obligation they are as follows.

1.   Delivery to ship procured by buyer (strict f.o.b.)[18]

In this, the narrowest, form of f.o.b. contract, it is B who acts as shipper and is responsible for procuring space in a vessel under a contract of carriage between himself and the shipowner providing for transportation of the goods to New York. S's duty is limited to putting the goods on board the ship nominated by B and procuring and delivering to B a mate's receipt[19] or other receipt document, leaving B to collect the bill of lading. S has to pay all expenses involved up to delivery of the goods over the ship's rail. These include customs entry but not port dues. Though an f.o.b. contract is prima facie of this type, the presumption is slight and is readily displaced by the language of the contract or by custom, course of dealing or other circumstances.[20] The f.o.b. contract is a very flexible instrument and though it possesses certain central features, the ancillary obligations may be divided between the parties in a wide variety of ways, particularly in the case of shipment under a charterparty.[21]

2.   Delivery to ship procured by seller (extended f.o.b.)

Here, S acts as shipper, so that instead of waiting for a vessel to be nominated by B[22] he must himself book space on a vessel and deliver the goods on board that vessel.[23] Whether in booking space S acts as principal or as B's agent depends on the contract. In neither case is S responsible for the freight, nor is he obliged to advance it on behalf of the buyer, so that if the shipping company refuses to accept the goods on a 'freight collect' basis,[24] the seller need not proceed to load the goods

---

17 Where Incoterms are not used, the problem is perhaps less acute under English law, since the courts, which already recognize the right of the c.i.f. seller to buy goods afloat that have previously been shipped by someone else, could be expected to accept the practice of tendering a combined transport bill of lading indorsed to show shipment on board and thus giving the buyer the requisite rights against the sea carrier. See p 938.

18 See, in more detail, pp 929 ff.

19 Normally used only in the case of delivery alongside the vessel. Where the goods are loaded on board, the standard shipping note is used as a receipt.

20 See 2 below.

21 As to additions such as 'f.o.b.s.', 'f.o.b.t.' etc, see p 936.

22 See further, p 930.

23 The duty to deliver at this point is a crucial element in an f.o.b. contract and is one of the factors distinguishing it from a c.i.f. contract. See below.

24 Ie under an agreement to collect freight from the buyer at the other end.

unless he is put in funds by B. The capacity in which S acts in booking space may bear on the strictness of S's obligation to procure a bill of lading,[25] and is relevant to the incidence of charges. If by the terms of the contract (express or implied) the f.o.b. price includes the making of arrangements for shipment, then in organizing the shipment S acts as principal and at his own expense and will normally be responsible for customs entry and port charges. Where, on the other hand, the f.o.b. price does not cover the procurement of the bill of lading but S agrees to do this for B's convenience and at B's expense, then the charges involved in obtaining the bill of lading, and other charges falling upon the shipper as such (including port dues and customs entry), will be for B's account, and in addition he will usually incur an extra charge to S by way of commission for S's trouble.

Since it is usually more convenient for S to arrange shipment than for B, the duty on S to procure the bill of lading will readily be inferred and may, indeed, be apparent from the language of the contract, as where payment is to be made against shipping documents.

S does not undertake that the goods will arrive safely or, indeed, at all. He is not concerned with their fate after they have been put on board. If they are lost or damaged in transit, through the negligence of the master or crew or other breach of contract by the shipping company, B will have a claim under the contract of carriage; and if the loss or damage is due to some other event covered by a contract of marine insurance taken out by B (or by S for B's account), he will recoup his loss by making a claim on the insurance policy.

3. Transfer to B of contracts of carriage and insurance concluded by S (c.i.f.)[26]

The third method is for S to undertake to ship the goods to New York at his own expense, duly insured under a policy of marine insurance covering the sea voyage, or to buy afloat goods so shipped and insured, and to transfer to B S's rights under the contract of carriage and insurance by delivering to B, with any necessary indorsement, the bill of lading, insurance policy or certificate and other shipping documents. This is the c.i.f. contract. It resembles the extended f.o.b. contract in that S does not undertake that the goods will arrive,[27] merely that B will be given the benefit of contractual claims against the carrier and insurers, together with the property in the goods if they are in existence at the time of tender of the documents.[28] But there are important differences between a c.i.f. contract and an

---

25 See p 872.

26 See further, pp 937 ff. If insurance is not included, the contract is a c.f.r. (formerly called c. & f.) contract. The shipment obligation is the same as for c.i.f.

27 However, the contract may provide for payment 'on arrival'. These words may show that the contract is not intended as a true c.i.f. contract; but if the court is satisfied that the parties intended the duty of payment to come into existence on tender of documents in the usual way, the provision for payment 'on arrival' will usually be considered as an indication of the time of payment rather than as making arrival a condition precedent to payment, so that if the ship fails to arrive, payment will be treated as due at the time it would normally have arrived. See *Fragano v Long* (1825) 4 B & C 219 and David Sassoon, *C.i.f. and F.o.b. Contracts* (3rd edn, 1984), para 15. For a case where the terms of the contract were held to show an intention to make arrival a condition of payment, so that the contract was not a true c.i.f. contract despite its reference to c.i.f. terms, see *The Julia* [1949] AC 293.

28 See p 937.

extended f.o.b. contract. In an f.o.b. contract where S ships as B's agent, B is responsible for the freight and insurance; in a c.i.f. contract these are included in the price. The extended f.o.b. seller is usually required merely to use his best endeavours to procure a bill of lading, while in a c.i.f. contract this is a strict obligation. Even where S is responsible as principal for arranging the shipment, bringing the contract much closer to a c.i.f. contract, there remains the significant difference that an f.o.b. contract requires delivery by or on behalf of S on board a vessel at the contractual port of departure, whereas in a c.i.f. contract S is not obliged to act as shipper but may perform the contract by buying goods afloat.[29] The distinctive feature common to c.i.f. and extended f.o.b. contracts in which S ships as principal is that the price includes the cost of carriage beyond the agreed delivery point, so that the delivery and price obligations are not coterminous.

4.   Delivery ex ship (DES)

S may undertake not merely to dispatch the goods, as in the previous two cases, but to deliver them, say, ex ship New York, in which case the contract is a destination or 'arrival' contract, that is, it is S's responsibility to ensure that the goods arrive safely and in proper condition in New York, ready for collection by B from the ship, all expenses up to this point being paid by S.[30] If the goods are lost or damaged in transit, then subject to rules of risk and frustration the loss falls on S, for the contractual delivery point is from the ship in New York.

7.   A TYPICAL EXPORT TRANSACTION[31]

(i)   Procedural steps

Export procedure takes a variety of forms, but there are certain basic stages in a typical transaction, which will briefly be described. In the illustration that follows it will be assumed that under the contract of sale it is the exporter's responsibility to arrange for shipment of the goods. This, of course, will not necessarily be the case.

1.   The purchase order

The first step, of course, is for the foreign buyer to place the order. The contract of sale is the core of the operation, and all subsequent ancillary contracts must be in

---

29 This is not to say that the port of departure is irrelevant in a c.i.f. contract (on the contrary, it is frequently made a contractual term), merely that the shipment need not be by or on behalf of S but is effective if made by a predecessor. However, under the Incoterms a c.i.f. term involves shipment by the seller himself; if he wishes to be able to buy afloat, an addition should be made to that effect, eg 'c.i.f. afloat'.

30 However, not all 'arrival' contracts are ex ship in this sense. The words 'arrival' or 'to arrive' may mean that the seller's obligation to deliver ex ship and the buyer's obligation to pay are dependent on the safe arrival of the ship and/or the goods at the stated destination, and that if this does not occur, the contract is discharged, neither party having any claim against the other. See *Benjamin's Sale of Goods* (6th edn, 2002), paras 21–022 ff.

31 See generally Clive Schmitthoff, *The Export Trade* (10th edn, 2000); Branch, *Export Practice and Management*.

conformity with it, a point to which we shall return when considering the documents for which the buyer can call and which the seller is entitled to tender. Usually the contract will be a standard-term contract, on the buyer's terms (see fig 3.1), the seller's (see fig 3.2) or a combination of the two. Whose terms are made to prevail will, in large measure, depend on the respective bargaining positions of the parties, a matter influenced as much by supply and demand for the goods as by the relative size and substance of the parties themselves.[32] A well-drawn contract will stipulate by which law it is to be governed (in practice, it will usually be that of the seller), and in most cases the choice-of-law clause will be upheld and applied in the courts of both seller and buyer. In the absence of an express choice of law by the parties, or the application of the CISG to the contract, an English court will have to apply the law determined by English conflict of laws rules.[33]

2. Assurance of payment

Where the contract provides for payment in advance, or for some advance assurance of payment such as an irrevocable letter of credit,[34] the seller will wish to have this in his hands before proceeding further.

3. Procurement of the goods

Unless he is able to supply the goods from stock, the exporter must proceed to manufacture or acquire them. The goods must, of course, conform to the requirements of the contract of sale and, assuming that the sale transaction is governed by English law, the normal rules contained in the Sale of Goods Act will apply.

4. Export licence

Where an export licence is required, it is usually for the seller to obtain this.[35] Most exports do not require a licence, but for those categories listed in the Export Control Act 2002, and regulations made thereunder,[36] as from time to time amended, a licence from the Department of Trade and Industry is necessary except so far as the order otherwise provides. Exports of specified classes of controlled goods are covered by an open general export licence which may be utilized without application, provided that the exporter registers its intention to use the licence. In other cases the exporter must apply for a standard individual licence to export specified goods to a specified consignee or an open individual export licence covering multiple shipments.

---

32 As to the battle of the forms, see p 87.
33 See pp 1104 ff.
34 See pp 949 ff.
35 See p 933.
36 See in particular the Export of Goods, Transfer of Technology and Provision of Technical Assistance (Control) Order 2003 (SI 2003/2764) and the Trade in Goods (Control) Order 2003 (SI 2003/2765). An EU general export authorization for dual-use items (ie those than be used for both civil and military purposes) may also be obtained pursuant to Council Regulation (EC) 1334/2000 of 22 June 2000 on setting up an EU regime for control of exports of dual-use items and technology.

874

The delivery point on sale to an overseas buyer   887

MASTER DOCUMENT

(c) SITPRO 1992

Exporter VAT no.	Invoice no. MD-2	Customs reference/status [DUCR]

SITPRO®
The Simpler Trade Procedures Board
29 Glasshouse Street   London W1R 5RG
VAT Reg. No. 241 8235 77

Invoice date 24.5.04	Carrier's bkg. no.	Exporter's reference MD-2

U N I C

Buyer's reference PO 4123	Forwarders reference JP-24

Consignee   VAT no.

Aikashinko Shibakhoen Inc
6-1 Honcho
Kanamatsu Cno, Naka-Ku
Kyoto
Japan

Buyer   VAT no.

Freight forwarder   VAT no.

Dolphin Freight Ltd
Selvey Road
Ashford, Kent

Country of despatch UK	Carrier	Country of destination code JP
Country of origin UK (EU)	Country of final destination Japan	

Other UK transport details

Terms of delivery and payment

DDP - Delivered Duty Paid Kyoto
Incoterms 2000

Payment via: Bank of Foreign Trade

Vessel/flight no. and date Gala Del Mar	Port/airport of loading Liverpool	
Port/airport of discharge Osaka	Place of delivery Kyoto	Insured value 440.00	EUR1 or C. of O. remarks

Shipping marks: container number

Aiashinko
PO 4123
Kyoto
via Osaka
Japan

Number and kind of packages: description of goods *

1 Case
Electric Table Lamps

Item No.	Commodity code 940520 19 0
	Quantity 2	Gross weight (Kg) 85.50	Cube (m3)
	Procedure	Net weight (kg) 78.50	Value(£) 440
	Summary declaration/previous document		

DANGEROUS GOODS:
Refer to IMDG, ADR, IATA, CIM and UK regulations
as appropriate for proper shipping name; hazard class; UN no; flashpoint deg C.

LIMIT OF SAD BOX 31

Commodity code		
Quantity 2	Gross weight (Kg)	Cube (m3)
Procedure	Net weight (kg)	Value(£)
Summary declaration/previous document		

Commodity code		
Quantity 2	Gross weight (Kg)	Cube (m3)
Procedure	Net weight (kg)	Value(£)
Summary declaration/previous document		

Identification of warehouse	FREE DISPOSAL	Invoice total (state currency) GBP 515.00
		Total gross wt (kg) 85.50 Total cube (m3)

Freight payable at Pre Paid	Signatory's company and telephone number SITPRO 020 7222 2222
Number of bills of lading original copy	Name of signatory A D Smith
	Place and date London 24.5.04
	Signature

SITPRO Licensee No. 000.

Fig 32.1 SITPRO master document

A typical export transaction   893

EXPORT CARGO SHIPPING INSTRUCTIONS

(c) SITPRO 1992

Approved by BIFA

A Exporter/shipper	VAT no.	Customs reference/status
		[DUCR]

SITPRO®
The Simpler Trade Procedures Board
29 Glasshouse Street   London W1R 5RG
VAT Reg. No. 241 8235 77

Booking number	Exporter's reference	U
ACL-418964	MD-2	N
	Forwarder's reference	I
	JP-24	C

To ►

B Consignee	VAT no.	D Other address	VAT no.
Aikashinko Shibakhoen Inc			
6-1 Honcho			
Kanamatsu Cho, Naka-Ku			
Kyoto			
Japan			

C Freight forwarder	VAT no.
Dolphin Freight Ltd	
Selvey Road	
Ashford, Kent	

If required, this space may be used for other addresses, e.g. buyer, place of acceptance/ delivery, additional notify party.

Country of origin of goods	Country of final destination
UK (EU)	Japan

Other UK transport details

E If required this space may be used for extra addresses or other information

A D Smith
Mideco Ltd London
Tel: +020 7222 2222

Vessel/flight no. and date	Port/airport of loading
Gala Del Mar	Liverpool

Port/airport of discharge	Place of delivery
Osaka	Kyoto

Please insure for

Unless otherwise instructed cover will be for ILU clauses "A" and will be charged to A

Shipping marks: container number	Number and kind of packages: description of goods *	Item No.
	1 Case	
Aiashinko	Electric Table Lamps	
PO 4123		
Kyoto		
via Osaka		
Japan		

Commodity code		
940520	19	0

Quantity 2	Gross weight (Kg)	Cube (m3)
	85.50	

Procedure	Net weight (kg)	Value(£)
	78.50	440

Summary declaration/previous document

Commodity code		

Quantity 2	Gross weight (Kg)	Cube (m3)

Procedure	Net weight (kg)	Value(£)

Summary declaration/previous document

Commodity code		

Quantity 2	Gross weight (Kg)	Cube (m3)

Procedure	Net weight (kg)	Value(£)

Summary declaration/previous document

Commodity code		

Quantity 2	Gross weight (Kg)	Cube (m3)

Procedure	Net weight (kg)	Value(£)

Summary declaration/previous document

* DANGEROUS GOODS: Refer to IMDG, ADR, IATA, CIM and UK regulations as appropriate and specify: proper shipping name, hazard class; UN no; flashpoint deg C.

Identification of warehouse

FREIGHT ►

Inland carriage to	Groupage depot/ICD	A
	UK port/airport	A

Trade Term	Invoice price
DDP	GBP 515.00

Certificate of shipment	A
Air, sea or other waybill	A
Bill of lading	A
Consular formalities/certs. of origin	A
Other documentation charges	A
Customs formalities Export	A
Transit	A
Import	A

◄ DOCUMENTATION

Indicate services required, and to whom charges should be debited, by entering

A,B,C,D or **E**

in check box

Depot/ICD or port charges including unloading	A

Freight to:

Depot/ICD or port charges at destination	A

Oncarriage at destination to	Depot/ICD	A
	Place of delivery	A

Special Instructions	Total gross wt (kg)	Total Cube (m3)
	85.50	

STATUS Enter T1/T2/MIX or T2L (as applicable)	►	T1

Indicate who post ► enters if SCP

Make out documents as indicated and dispose of as follows:

Ocean Freight Payable at	Name of contact and telephone number
Pre Paid	SITPRO 020 7222 2222

No. of bills of lading required	
Original Copy	A D Smith

I/we hereby declare that the above particulars are correct and agree to your published Regulations and Conditions, including those as to liability.

Date
24.5.04
Signature

SITPRO Licensee No. 000.

Fig 32.2 Shipping instructions

5.   Transportation arrangements generally[37]

At this stage the exporter has a variety of choices. If his contract requires him merely to ship the goods, without further responsibility for them, he may reserve space on a suitable vessel and attend to all the shipping arrangements himself [38] or have this done for him, wholly or in part, by a freight forwarder, an organization specializing in the handling of all aspects of exportation,[39] including booking of space, transportation to the docks, customs clearance,[40] packaging, insurance, consolidation of cargo, warehousing, and the like. But suppose the exporter's contract requires him not merely to ship the goods to the contract port of destination but to deliver them to the buyer's premises at the other end. The journey may here involve combined, or multimodal, transport,[41] eg by road from the exporter's warehouse to the docks, by ship to an intermediate country, followed by transhipment to the buyer's country and then by rail to an inland terminus and by road to the buyer's premises. The exporter could arrange separate contracts with each carrier for each stage of the journey. If he wishes to avoid this cumbrous and time-consuming process, he may take out a through bill of lading by which the shipping company, having received the goods at the dock or on board the vessel, undertakes not merely to carry the goods for the first sea leg of the journey but to attend to all stages of the transit, either as principal or by arranging contracts with the oncarriers as agent of the exporter.

The through bill of lading has obvious advantages compared with the traditional port-to-port shipment. Nevertheless, it does not solve all the exporter's problems. In the first place, it functions as an acceptable combined transport document only if issued by a shipping company, and thus does not cover earlier stages of the transit or journeys not involving a sea leg at all. Secondly, the shipping company issuing a through bill of lading almost invariably limits its responsibility to its own stage of the transit and disclaims liability for the goods after these have been delivered to the oncarrier. Happily, there developed, by a logical progression, the combined (or multimodal) transport document, pursuant to which a combined (multimodal) transport operator undertakes responsibility as principal for the entire transit, from the time he takes the goods in his charge (which may be at the exporter's own premises) to the time of their delivery to the buyer. Such an arrangement has been greatly facilitated by the development of containerization. Instead of warehouses and carriers having to handle individual items of merchandise, these are packed into containers of standard sizes that are kept sealed throughout the journey, and can be

---

37 See further, ch 36.

38 See below.

39 And, of course, importation, which will not be discussed here.

40 A large freight forwarder or consortium may now arrange customs clearance at its own inland clearance depot (ICD) under a system called ERTS (enhanced remote transit shed).

41 Ie 'the carriage of goods by at least two different modes of transport from a place at which the goods are taken in charge situated in one country to a place designated for delivery situated in a different country' (Uniform Rules for a Combined Transport Document (1975 Revision), published by the International Chamber of Commerce (ICC Publication No 298). The term used by the ICC is 'combined transport'. Other expressions used as equivalents are 'inter-modal transport' and 'multimodal transport'. See pp 1061 ff.

rapidly transferred from one recipient to the next without intermediate handling of the separate items, each recipient having premises, equipment or transport vehicles or vessels specially equipped to receive and hold containers.

6. Booking space on the vessel

Whether the exporter acts directly or through a freight forwarder, he will have to decide by what shipping line and vessel he intends to ship the goods, and then book space on the vessel. This may be done with the shipping company direct or through a forwarding agent, and is usually done verbally. The shipping line makes available its sailing schedules showing the dates between which cargo will be received for loading and the estimated sailing date, and deals with the calculation and payment of freight and the issue of bills of lading.

7. Packaging, marking and dispatch

Next, the goods must be packaged and got down to the docks. Packaging of products has been of major importance in trade, and the exporter may well wish to use a specialist firm for this task. The outside of the package must also carry the shipping marks and numbers by which the consignment is to be identified and the route and certain other information specified.[42] Again, the exporter may make his own arrangements for dispatch to the docks or may use a forwarding agent, to whom he will give shipping instructions (fig 32.2). Where the goods are being sent by container, they will be collected from the exporter's premises by the freight forwarder if comprising a full container-load (FCL) or, if not, will be sent by the exporter to the forwarder's container depot as a less than container load (LCL) to be consolidated with other goods by the groupage agent.[43] The goods must be accompanied by a standard shipping note (fig 32.3) setting out details of the exporter/shipper, the ship, the ports of departure and destination, the descriptions, dimensions and weights of the packages and other relevant details of the consignment.[44] The standard shipping note is prepared in multi-part sets and serves as a receipt by the forwarding agent (or if the exporter is shipping direct to the port, by the terminal operator) and an approved customs document for pre-entry presentation, with copies for the shipping line, terminal operators, customs and any other parties involved. When the container has been loaded the exporter will issue its bill of lading instructions to the shipping line, from which the manifest and bills of lading can be completed, the bills being released to the exporter or the forwarding agent once the goods have been shipped on board.

---

42 Packaging and marking as appropriate are expressly included as duties of the seller in Incoterms 1990.
43 Alternatively, they will be delivered to an ICD. The goods will be deconsolidated by a groupage agent at the port of destination.
44 The standard shipping note has largely replaced the mate's receipt formerly issued as a receipt for the goods on board prior to issue of the bill of lading. Where issued, a mate's receipt is prima facie evidence of receipt of the goods in good order and condition (*The Nogar Marin* [1988] 1 Lloyd's Rep 412).

© SITPRO 1999

STANDARD SHIPPING NOTE - FOR NON - DANGEROUS GOODS ONLY

IMPORTANT
USE THE
DANGEROUS
GOODS NOTE
IF THE
GOODS ARE
CLASSIFIED AS
DANGEROUS
ACCORDING TO
APPLICABLE
REGULATIONS
SEE BOX 10A

Exporter	1	Customs reference/status	2
		Booking number	3	Exporters reference	4
		Forwarder's reference	5
Consignee	6		
Freight forwarder	7	International carrier	8
		For use of receiving authority only	
Other UK transport details (e.g. ICD, terminal, vehicle bkg. ref. receiving dates)	9		

The Company preparing this note declares that, to the best of their belief, the goods have been accurately described, their quantities, weights and measurements are correct and at the time of despatch they were in good order and condition; that the goods are not classified as being hazardous by reference to relevant national and international regulations applicable to the intended modes of transport. **10A**

| Vessel/flight no. and date | Port/airport of loading | 10 |
| Port/airport of discharge | Destination | 11 |

TO THE RECEIVING AUTHORITY- Please receive for shipment the goods described below subject to your published regulations and conditions (including those as to liability)

| Shipping marks | Number and kind of packages; description of goods; non-hazardous special stowage requirements | 12 | Gross wieght (kg) of goods | 13A | Cube (m³) of goods | 14 |

TATE FREIGHT FORMS (01908) 221162
SITPRO APPROVED Licensee No. 20

| For use of Shipping company only | | Total gross wieght of goods | Total cube of goods |

| Container identification number/ vehicle registration number | 16 | Seal number(s) | 16A | Container/ vehicle size and type | 16B | Tare (kg) | 16C | Total gross wieght (including tare) (kg) | 18D |

HAULIER DETAILS	**DOCK/TERMINAL RECIEPT** RECEIVING AUTHORITY REMARKS		Name and telephone number of company preparing this note	17
Hauliers name	Received the above number of packages/containers/trailers in apparent good order and condition unless stated hereon.			
Vehicle reg. no.		Name/status of declarant	
Drivers signature	Receiving authority signature and date	Place and date	
		Signature of declarant	

630 Non-completion of any boxes is a subject for resolution by the contracting parties.

Fig 32.3 Standard shipping note

8. Preparation of the bill of lading

The exporter must obtain and complete the shipping line's form of bill of lading (fig 32.4 or fig 32.5) showing details of the goods, shipper, consignee etc,[45] and forward the bill of lading, with the requisite number of copies, to the shipping company or loading broker.

9. Preshipment inspection

In principle, the buyer under a documentary sale is not entitled to inspect the goods before shipment.[46] But it is not uncommon for buyers to stipulate in the contract of sale that the goods are to be inspected prior to shipment, whether at the manufacturer's premises or some other place, by an independent inspection organization, which will issue a certificate as to the sampling, quality and analysis of the goods, suitability of the packaging, or as may be required, after laboratory testing, sampling or other quality evaluation method. The inspection certificate will normally be specified in the contract of sale as one of the required shipping documents and may be made conclusive evidence of the quality and condition of the goods.[47]

10. Loading

In due course the cargo is loaded on or pumped into the vessel, the process depending on the type of cargo. This may be broadly divided into liquid bulk cargo (eg crude oil, chemicals, spirits) pumped directly into the holds of tankers, dry bulk cargo (eg grain, flour, rice, sand) loaded directly into the hold of a bulk carrying vessel from the terminal, container cargo loaded into cellular container vessels and general (ie loose, or break-bulk) cargo. Oil is pumped into tanks in specially designed tankers, either from the terminal or off-shore. Much cargo, both dry and liquid, that is not of high tonnage is now shipped in containers, which in the case of perishables are refrigerated ('reefers'). Cargo is loaded by crane or fork-lift truck from the docks or ship or from a roll-on/roll-off vehicle (such as a trailer or lorry driven directly on to the vessel) or a barge alongside. Uncontainerized goods are checked by the shipping company's tally clerks to ensure correspondence with the bill of lading, particulars of any apparent defects in the condition of the goods or their packaging being noted on the bill of lading, and the goods are then entered on the ship's manifest, after which, if all is in order, the bill will be signed on behalf of the shipping company and given to the shipper. In the case of cargo shipped in containers, each container is sealed to ensure its security, details of the seal being entered on the ship's manifest, and every container is allocated an identified cell on the vessel. Obviously, sealed containers cannot be checked for their contents; the carrier merely acknowledges receipt of identified containers in apparent good order and condition and sealed. But where several LCL items are to be consolidated into a groupage container, the contents are first checked by tally clerks for their apparent

---

45 For a description of the functions of a bill of lading, see p 886.
46 Prior to this the seller will not normally have made an unconditional appropriation.
47 As an alternative to preshipment inspection the buyer may stipulate inspection after discharge of the goods.

good order and condition and details recorded showing which cargo has been loaded into which container.

11. Customs clearance[48]

The customs procedure for export is designed to fulfil two distinct functions. The first is to ensure that certain categories of goods are not exported without prior clearance, termed 'pre-entry'. These include goods from bonded warehouses on which duty has not been paid and goods the exportation of which requires a licence. The second is to provide the customs with details of the export for record and statistical purposes. For goods not requiring pre-entry, this information need not be supplied in advance but may be furnished after shipment, a procedure known as 'entry'.

12. Remaining stages

On arrival at the port of destination the goods will be unloaded by stevedores or terminal operators (and in the case of groupage containers, deconsolidated by a deconsolidating agent), passed through customs in the buyer's country, inspected by an inspection agency where this is required by the sale contract, and released or delivered to the buyer at the port or at his premises or other agreed contractual delivery point. Possession of goods shipped under a bill of lading is given up by the shipping company itself only on presentation of the requisite bill of lading.[49] In the case of goods shipped under a sea waybill it is not necessary for the consignee to produce the sea waybill; all its representative has to do is to furnish evidence of identity if required

8.   DOCUMENTS IN EXPORT SALES[50]

(i)   The importance of documents

It will have become apparent from the preceding discussion that the export of goods involves the contract of sale as the core of the operation; a range of ancillary contracts (transport, insurance, finance), which may entail a number of intermediaries; the physical movement of goods; and the physical movement of documents.

As mentioned earlier in this chapter, the distance between exporter and importer creates several problems. In particular, the buyer may not want to pay until he has

---

48 See generally Schmitthoff, *The Export Trade*, ch 26; Branch, *Export Practice and Management*, ch 9.

49 Not infrequently there are lengthy delays in the preparation and dispatch of bills of lading, which, in consequence, may arrive after the goods themselves, thus defeating the object of a bill of lading as a document of title and causing serious difficulties for both carrier and consignee. To deal with this, an elaborate system of guarantees and warranties has developed to enable the goods to be released by the carrier without production of the bill of lading. See generally R. M. Goode, *Proprietary Rights and Insolvency in Sales Transactions* (2nd edn, 1989), pp 72 ff.

50 See the UNCTAD publication *The Use of Transport Documents in International Trade*, UNCTAD/SDTE/TLB/2003/3 26 November 2003.

Bill of Lading for Combined Transport shipment or Port to Port shipment

| Shipper | | B/L No.: |
| | | Reference: |

Consignee or Order (for U.S. Trade only: Not Negotiable unless consigned 'To Order')

P&O Nedlloyd

www.ponl.com

Notify Party/Address (It is agreed that no responsibility shall attach to the Carrier or his Agents for failure to notify (see clause 20 on reverse))

Place of Receipt (Applicable only when this document is used as a Combined Transport Bill of Lading)

Vessel and Voy. No.

Place of Delivery (Applicable only when this document is used as a Combined Transport Bill of Lading)

| Port of Loading | Port of Discharge |

Undermentioned particulars as declared by Shipper, but not acknowledged by the Carrier (see clause 11)

Marks and Nos; Container Nos;	Number and kind of Packages; Description of Goods	Gross Weight (kg)	Measurement (cbm)

* Total No. of Containers/Packages received by the Carrier

Movement

Freight payable at

Received by the Carrier from the Shipper in apparent good order and condition (unless otherwise noted herein) the total number or quantity of Containers or other packages or units indicated in the box above entitled "Total No. of Containers/Packages received by the Carrier" for Carriage subject to all the terms and conditions hereof (INCLUDING THE TERMS AND CONDITIONS ON THE REVERSE HEREOF AND THE TERMS AND CONDITIONS OF THE CARRIER'S APPLICABLE TARIFF) from the Place of Receipt or the Port of Loading, whichever is applicable, to the Port of Discharge or the Place of Delivery, whichever is applicable. If the acknowledged tally is of Containers, this indicates that the Container has been packed and sealed by the Merchant at his premises without the Carrier being represented and able to check or verify either the tally of Goods or the stowage, which are consequently unknown to him (See Clause 8). The Merchant accepts that, except by special arrangement or pursuant to Clause 9 hereof, Containers are not weighed by the Carrier at any time. If the Carrier so requires, before he arranges delivery of the Goods one original Bill of Lading, duly endorsed, must be surrendered by the Merchant to the Carrier at the Port of Discharge or at some other location acceptable to the Carrier. In accepting this Bill of Lading the Merchant expressly accepts and agrees to all its terms and conditions whether printed, stamped or written, or otherwise incorporated, notwithstanding the non-signing of this Bill of Lading by the Merchant. Without prejudice to the generality of this reference, attention is drawn, inter-alia, to Clauses 12 (Shipper's/Merchant's Responsibility), 19 (Dangerous Goods) and 24 (Law & Jurisdiction).

| Number of Original Bills of Lading | Place and Date of Issue | IN WITNESS of the contract herein contained the number of originals stated opposite has been issued, one of which being accomplished the other(s) to be void |

EXCESS VALUATION: REFER TO CLAUSE 7 (3) ON REVERSE SIDE (U.S. TRADE ONLY). . . . . .

5422308

1/DRS B/L5 8/00

Fig 32.4 Received for shipment bill of lading

TERMS AND CONDITIONS

(Enlarged print available from the Carrier or his agents.)

1. DEFINITIONS

In this Bill of Lading the word—

"Carrier" means the party named in the Signature box on the face hereof.

"Merchant" includes the Shipper, Holder, Consignee, Receiver of the Goods, any Person who owns or is entitled to the possession of the Goods or of this Bill of Lading and any Person acting on behalf of any such Person.

"Person" includes an individual, group, company or other entity.

"Sub-Contractor" includes, but is not limited to, owners and operators of any Vessels (other than the Carrier), stevedores, terminal and groupage operators, road, rail and air transport operators and any independent contractors employed by the Carrier in performance of the Carriage and any sub-sub-contractors thereof.

"Goods" means the whole or any part of the cargo received from the Shipper and includes the packing and any equipment or Container not supplied by or on behalf of the Carrier.

"Container" includes any container, trailer, transportable tank, flat pallet, or any similar article used to consolidate goods and any ancillary equipment.

"Carriage" means the whole or any part of the operations and services undertaken by the Carrier in respect of the Goods covered by this Bill of Lading.

"Port of Loading" means any port at which the Goods are loaded on board any Vessel (which may not necessarily be the Vessel named overleaf) for Carriage under this Bill of Lading.

"Vessel" means any waterborne craft used in the Carriage under this Bill of Lading, which may be a feeder vessel or an ocean-going vessel.

"Combined Transport" arises if the Place of Receipt and/or the Place of Delivery are indicated on the face hereof in the relevant spaces.

"Port to Port" arises if the Carriage is not Combined Transport.

"Shipped on Board" means that the Goods have been loaded on board the Vessel.

"Freight" includes all charges payable to the Carrier in accordance with the applicable Tariff and this Bill of Lading.

"Hague Rules" means the provisions of the International Convention for the Unification of Certain Rules relating to Bills of Lading signed at Brussels on 25th August 1924 as amended by the Protocol signed at Brussels on 23rd February, 1968, but only if such amendments are compulsorily applicable to this Bill of Lading.

2. CARRIER'S TARIFF

The terms and conditions of the Carrier's applicable Tariff are incorporated herein. Particular attention is drawn to the terms and conditions therein relating to container and vehicle demurrage. Copies of the relevant provisions of the applicable Tariff are obtainable from the Carrier or his agents upon request. In the case of inconsistency between this Bill of Lading and the applicable Tariff, this Bill of Lading shall prevail.

3. WARRANTY

The Merchant warrants that in agreeing to the terms and conditions herein he is, or has the authority of the Person owning or entitled to the possession of the Goods and this Bill of Lading.

4. SUB-CONTRACTING AND INDEMNITY

(1) The Carrier shall be entitled to sub-contract the Carriage on any terms whatsoever.

5. CARRIER'S RESPONSIBILITY FOR LOSS OR DAMAGE

7. SUNDRY LIABILITY PROVISIONS

8. SHIPPER-PACKED CONTAINERS

13. FREIGHT

14. LIEN

15. OPTIONAL STOWAGE AND DECK CARGO

16. LIVE ANIMALS

17. METHODS AND ROUTES OF CARRIAGE

21. FCL MULTIPLE BILLS OF LADING

22. GENERAL AVERAGE & SALVAGE

18. MATTERS AFFECTING PERFORMANCE

9. INSPECTION OF GOODS

6. CARRIER'S RESPONSIBILITY COMBINED TRANSPORT

10. CARRIAGE AFFECTED BY CONDITION OF GOODS

11. DESCRIPTION OF GOODS

12. SHIPPER'S/MERCHANT'S RESPONSIBILITY

19. DANGEROUS GOODS

20. NOTIFICATION AND DELIVERY

23. VARIATION OF THE CONTRACT

24. LAW AND JURISDICTION

25. VALIDITY

26. LIMITATION OF LIABILITY

27. USA CLAUSE PARAMOUNT (if applicable)

BEAGLE HOUSE, BRAHAM STREET, LONDON E1 8EP

1/DRS B/L5 8/00

control of the goods, while the seller may be unwilling to deliver the goods until he is assured of payment. The buyer may wish either to dispose of the goods or raise finance against them before their arrival; and the seller, if giving credit, may himself wish to raise money against the payment due to him from the buyer.

How are these conflicting desires to be satisfied? The answer is, through the use of documents: in the case of the buyer, documents giving control of the goods; in the case of the seller, documents embodying a payment obligation. Simultaneous exchange of delivery documents against payment documents means that the buyer can safely pay before physical delivery, since he gets his hands on the means of control which enable him to deal with the goods before their arrival, while the seller obtains a payment instrument which either entitles him to immediate payment or, if a time bill, can be converted into cash before maturity by way of discount or pledge.

It is worth emphasizing here that neither party is obliged or entitled to furnish documents in performance of his obligations unless the contract of sale so provides. In the absence of agreement to the contrary, the seller's duty is to make delivery of the goods at the contractual delivery point,[51] while the duty of the buyer is to pay the price in legal tender[52] in exchange for delivery. Deviation from these methods of performance can be only by mutual agreement.

The multiplicity of documents used in export and import transactions can be an obstacle to the efficient operation of the system. Valuable work has been done by the Simpler Trade Procedures Board (SITPRO) in rationalizing and simplifying documents and procedures, particularly through the development of an aligned documentation system based on a master document containing all the relevant information from which separate documents can be run off. Moreover, there have been considerable efforts to reduce the volume and movement of paper through the electronic transmission of bills of lading data and images and ship manifests, the issue of electronic bills of lading (though the legal status of these as bills of lading for the purposes of the Hague and Hague-Visby Rules has yet to be established),[53] a shift from bills of lading to non-negotiable sea waybills and, in the case of container cargoes intended for different importers at a particular destination, the use of electronically communicated PIN numbers instead of ship's or merchant's delivery orders.

If documentary procedures are to work properly, it is essential that the various rules governing the documentary requirements of each of the different contracts should be consistent. For example, the rules determining what constitutes an acceptable transport document should, in principle, be the same for the contract of sale, the contract of carriage and the Uniform Customs and Practice for Documentary Credits (UCP), a goal not easily achieved.[54]

---

51 See pp 866 ff.
52 See Coinage Act 1971, s 2, as amended by the Currency Act 1983, s 1(3).
53 See p 895.
54 At first sight it would seem possible to avoid the problem as regards letters of credit by requiring the applicant for the credit to set out the requirements for an acceptable transport document in detail. But this would make letters of credit very much longer and more complex, and, in practice, it is found much more satisfactory to set out the requirements in the UCP themselves and then incorporate the UCP by reference. See further, p 985.

(ii) The principal delivery documents

The documents tendered to the buyer must be such as will, inter alia, enable the buyer:

(a) to procure delivery from the carrier;

(b) to assert rights against the carrier if the goods have been lost or damaged in transit through breach of the carrier's obligations;

(c) where the contract is a c.i.f. contract or a variant of it, to recover from an insurer for loss of or damage to the goods in transit so far as resulting from perils normally covered by marine insurance;

(d) to calculate the freight;

(e) to clear the goods through the customs in the country of import.

The documents which confer these rights in the highest degree[55] are the bill of lading, the policy of marine insurance covering the goods in their sea transit and the commercial invoice. To these may be added other documents particular to the buyer's requirements as specified in the contract of sale, eg a certificate of origin, a certificate of quality, a consular invoice.

(iii) The key features of a transport document

The late Mr Bernard Wheble, a leading banking expert, listed five features required of a transport document if it is to have maximum efficacy. It must:

(a) give control of the goods vis-à-vis both the carrier and third parties;

(b) constitute a receipt for identified goods by the party undertaking responsibility for their carriage;

(c) establish the apparent condition of the goods when received by the carrier;

(d) show that the goods are in movement rather than static;

(e) establish privity of contract between the holder of the document and the carrier.

Only the bill of lading meets all these requirements. The exclusivity of the bill of lading is attributable partly to the reluctance of the courts to recognize new forms of negotiable document and partly to the Carriage of Goods by Sea Act 1971, which embodies the Hague-Visby Rules[56] and imposes on the carrier the obligation, inter alia, to furnish to the shipper on demand a bill of lading setting out identification marks and other details of the goods. Moreover, under the Bills of Lading Act 1855, only the transfer of a bill of lading operated to transfer the holder's contractual rights against the carrier to the transferee, but that Act has been repealed by the Carriage of Goods by Sea Act 1992, which extends the statutory transfer of contractual rights to persons entitled to receive the goods under a sea waybill or ship's delivery order.[57] Despite these attributes of a bill of lading, there has been a

55 Though, as we shall see, there are lesser documents often used instead, for example, a ship's delivery order or, in the case of multimodal transport, a freight forwarder's certificate of receipt or transport.

56 Ie, the Hague Rules 1924 as amended by the Protocol of 23 February 1968. See further, p 1031.

57 See pp 1055 ff.

significant shift in favour of the non-negotiable sea waybill in cases where the importer does not wish to sell or pledge the goods in transit and production of a document of title is not required under the terms of a letter of credit, for the sea waybill has the great advantage that, since it does not have to be produced in order to obtain delivery, the delays associated with the physical transfer of a bill of lading along what may sometimes be a long chain are avoided, while most of the advantages of a bill can be incorporated by the terms of the waybill.[58] Its is, however, clear from a recent UNCTAD study[59] that a significant obstacle both to the use of sea waybills and to the issue of electronic bills of lading is the concern that these may not be acceptable under letters of credit covering shipments.

(iv) The characteristics of a shipped bill of lading

A shipped bill of lading (see fig 32.5) possesses five main characteristics.

1.   It is a document of title

At common law a bill of lading is a document of title (indeed, the only document of title) to goods.[60] What does this mean? Right up to the latter part of the nineteenth century the term 'document of title' was used by the courts in a literal sense to denote that delivery of the document, with any necessary indorsement, transferred ownership of the goods where so intended; It may be that this emphasis on the transfer of title reflected the normal purpose for which a bill of lading was transferred; certainly that seems to have been the assumption underlying s 1 of the Bills of Lading Act 1855.[61] But where goods are agreed to be sold under a contract of sale, it is the terms of that contract which govern the transfer of the property of the goods. Under s 17 of the Sale of Goods Act 1979 the property passes when the parties intend it to pass, and they may, of course, agree expressly or by implication that the act which is to produce this result is the transfer of the bill of lading, but it is the contract of sale, not the transfer of the bill of lading as such, which operates to transfer the property.

The focus on title is therefore misleading, for the transfer of title is an aspect of the relationship between seller and buyer, whereas the bill of lading concerns the relationship between holder and carrier. We have seen that where a bailee holds goods for another, the bailor has constructive possession[62] and that this may be changed by the bailee intimating that he is now holding the goods for a new bailor, an intimation known as attornment.[63] The bill of lading constitutes an acknowledgement by the carrier that the goods will be held for whoever is the current holder of the bill of lading. The holder thus has constructive possession and can

---

58 See pp 905 ff.
59 See p 1069.
60 For a comprehensive analysis of the history and proprietary and possessory effects of a bill of lading, see Michael D. Bools, *The Bill of Lading* (1997).
61 Which referred to consignees or indorsees 'to whom the property in the goods therein mentioned shall pass upon or by reason of such consignment or indorsement'.
62 See p 43.
63 See p 44.

Bill of Lading for Combined Transport shipment or Port to Port shipment

Shipper R T & SONS 27 NEW NORTH ROAD EPPING IG24 6ES	B/L No.: PONLBHX22045997 Reference:
	P&O NedLloyd www.ponl.com
Consignee or Order (for U.S. Trade only: Not Negotiable unless consigned 'To Order') TO ORDER OF NATIONAL BANK OF AUSTRALIA	

Notify Party/Address (It is agreed that no responsibility shall attach to the Carrier or his Agents for failure to notify (see clause 20 on reverse)) ROUNDABOUT LOGISTICS 24 NEWBURY ROAD STAFFORD QLD 4120 AUSTRALIA	Place of Receipt (Applicable only when this document is used as a Combined Transport Bill of Lading) R T & SONS 27 NEW NORTH ROAD EPPING IG24 6ES
Vessel and Voy. No. P&O NEDLLOYD PALLISER PLE4004	Place of Delivery (Applicable only when this document is used as a Combined Transport Bill of Lading) BRISBANE CONTAINER FACILITY
Port of Loading TILBURY	Port of Discharge BRISBANE

Undermentioned particulars as declared by Shipper, but not acknowledged by the Carrier (see clause 11)

Marks and Nos; Container Nos;	Number and kind of Packages; Description of Goods	Gross Weight (kg)	Measurement (cbm)

PONU2881057
SEAL: 10B2955
 	
ROUNDABOUT
LOGISTICS
NOS 1-500
	1x20'RE CONTAINER SAID TO CONTAIN
	
	500 CARTON(S) FCL/FCL
	       CHOCOLATE BISCUITS
	
	       FREIGHT COLLECT
	
	       GOODS CARRIED UNDER
	       TEMPERATURE CONTROL.
	       REFRIGERATION MACHINERY
	       SET TO A TEMPERATURE OF
	       +5 DEGREES CELCIUS WHILST
	       ON BOARD THE VESSEL.
	
	       SHIPPED ON BOARD PER
	       OCEAN VESSEL
	       P&O NEDLLOYD PALLISER
	       AT TILBURY
	       ON 20/01/2004
	       FOR P&O NEDLLOYD LIMITED
	
	TOTAL: 1x20' CONTAINER(S) ONLY
		2528	18.500

FREIGHT AND CHARGES:

ORIGIN INLAND HAULAGE CHARGE	P HAI
ORIGIN TERMINAL HANDLING/LCL SERVICE CHARGE	P HAI
OCEAN FREIGHT	C BNE
DESTINATION TERMINAL HANDLING/LCL SERVICE CHARGE	C BNE
DESTINATION INLAND HAULAGE CHARGE	C BNE

* Total No. of Containers/Packages received by the Carrier 1	Movement FCL/FCL	Freight payable at PONL BRISBANE

Received by the Carrier from the Shipper in apparent good order and condition (unless otherwise noted herein) the total number or quantity of Containers or other packages or units indicated in the box above entitled "Total No. of Containers/Packages received by the Carrier" for Carriage subject to all the terms and conditions hereof (INCLUDING THE TERMS AND CONDITIONS ON THE REVERSE HEREOF AND THE TERMS AND CONDITIONS OF THE CARRIER'S APPLICABLE TARIFF) from the Place of Receipt or the Port of Loading, whichever is applicable, to the Port of Discharge or the Place of Delivery, whichever is applicable. If the acknowledged tally is of Containers, this indicates that the Container has been packed and sealed by the Merchant at his premises without the Carrier being represented and able to check or verify either the tally of Goods or the stowage, which are consequently unknown to him (See Clause 8). The Merchant accepts that, except by special arrangement or pursuant to Clause 9 hereof, Containers are not weighed by the Carrier at any time. If the Carrier so requires, before he arranges delivery of the Goods one original Bill of Lading, duly endorsed, must be surrendered by the Merchant to the Carrier at the Port of Discharge or at some other location acceptable to the Carrier. In accepting this Bill of Lading the Merchant expressly accepts and agrees to all its terms and conditions whether printed, stamped or written, or otherwise incorporated, notwithstanding the non-signing of this Bill of Lading by the Merchant. Without prejudice to the generality of this reference, attention is drawn, inter-alia, to Clauses 12 (Shipper's/Merchant's Responsibility), 19 (Dangerous Goods) and 24 (Law & Jurisdiction).

Number of Original Bills of Lading 3/THREE	Place and Date of Issue PONL HAINAULT 20/01/04	IN WITNESS of the contract herein contained the number of originals stated opposite has been issued, one of which being accomplished the other(s) to be void FOR P&O NEDLLOYD LTD, AS CARRIER.*

EXCESS VALUATION: REFER TO CLAUSE 7 (3) ON REVERSE SIDE (U.S. TRADE ONLY)......

DRAFT - COPY ONLY

1706511

1/DRS B/L 10/03   *OPERATING IN PARTNERSHIP WITH P&O NEDLLOYD BV*

Fig 32.5 Shipped bill of lading. For terms and conditions, see fig. 32.4.

TERMS AND CONDITIONS

(Enlarged print available from the Carrier or his agents.)

1. DEFINITIONS

In this Bill of Lading the word—

"Carrier" means the Party on whose behalf this Bill of Lading has been signed.

"Merchant" includes any Person who at any time has been or becomes the Shipper, Holder, Consignee, Receiver of the Goods, any Person who owns or is entitled to the possession of the Goods or of this Bill of Lading, and any Person acting on behalf of any such Person.

"Holder" means any Person for the time being in possession of (or entitled to the possession of) this Bill of Lading.

"Person" includes an individual, group, company or other entity.

"Sub-Contractor" includes (but is not limited to) owners and operators of any Vessels (other than the Carrier), stevedores, terminal and groupage operators, road, rail and air transport operators and any direct or indirect sub-contractor of any such Person.

"Goods" means the whole or any part of the cargo received from the Merchant and includes any packing and any equipment or Container not supplied by or on behalf of the Carrier.

"Container" includes any container, trailer, transportable tank, flat or pallet, or any similar article used to consolidate goods and any ancillary equipment.

"Carriage" means the whole or any part of the operations and services undertaken by the Carrier in respect of the Goods covered by this Bill of Lading.

2. CARRIER'S TARIFF

The terms and conditions of the Carrier's applicable Tariff are incorporated herein.

3. WARRANTY

The Merchant warrants that in agreeing to the terms and conditions hereof he is, or has the authority of the Person owning or entitled to the possession of the Goods and this Bill of Lading.

4. SUB-CONTRACTING AND INDEMNITY

5. CARRIER'S RESPONSIBILITY PORT-TO-PORT SHIPMENT

7. SUNDRY LIABILITY PROVISIONS

13. FREIGHT

14. LIEN

15. OPTIONAL STOWAGE AND DECK CARGO

16. LIVE ANIMALS

17. METHODS AND ROUTES OF CARRIAGE

18. SHIPPER-PACKED CONTAINERS

21. FCL MULTIPLE BILLS OF LADING

22. GENERAL AVERAGE & SALVAGE

6. CARRIER'S RESPONSIBILITY COMBINED TRANSPORT

9. INSPECTION OF GOODS

10. CARRIAGE AFFECTED BY CONDITION OF GOODS

11. DESCRIPTION OF GOODS

12. SHIPPER'S/MERCHANT'S RESPONSIBILITY

18. MATTERS AFFECTING PERFORMANCE

19. DANGEROUS GOODS

20. NOTIFICATION AND DELIVERY

23. VARIATION OF THE CONTRACT

24. LAW AND JURISDICTION

25. VALIDITY

26. LIMITATION OF LIABILITY

27. USA CLAUSE PARAMOUNT (if applicable)

BEAGLE HOUSE, BRAHAM STREET, LONDON E1 8EP

J/DRS B/LS 8/00

transfer this by delivery of the bill of lading with any necessary indorsement. The bill of lading should therefore be seen as a control document by which constructive possession is transferred rather than as a document by which title is passed.[64] Its particular characteristic is that, where the parties to the transfer of the bill of lading so intend, it imposes on the carrier a duty to the transferee without the need for any separate act of attornment. It may thus be described in a loose sense as embodying an attornment in advance. But it is not a true attornment, for the mere transfer of the document does not confer rights against the carrier unless the parties to the transfer so intend.[65] Plainly the parties cannot intend the transfer to operate as a transfer of constructive delivery where to their knowledge the goods have already left the control of the carrier;[66] and, in any event, while this may not exhaust the bill of lading to the extent of any personal rights it gives against the carrier, its function as a document of title obviously comes to an end when the carrier no longer has control of the goods.

The bill of lading fulfils in relation to the goods specified in it much the same functions, and is transferred in much the same way, as a negotiable instrument in relation to a stated money obligation. Thus the consignee named in a bill of lading corresponds to the payee of a bill of exchange and the indorsee of a bill of lading to the indorsee of a bill of exchange. A bill of lading may be negotiable or non-negotiable. It is negotiable if it is expressed to be transferable, either by the manner in which the consignee is designated or by the other terms of the bill. Where the consignee is designated 'order', this means that it is transferable by indorsement of the shipper and delivery. Where the bill is made out in favour of a named consignee 'or order', it is transferable by indorsement of the named consignee. If the consignee is shown as 'bearer' or 'holder' or is left blank, the bill is transferable by delivery without indorsement. Where, on the other hand, the bill is consigned to a named consignee without the addition of the words 'or order', the bill is a non-negotiable ('straight' or 'straight consigned') bill unless the terms of the bill provide for its transfer, in which event it will be transferable by the consignee's indorsement and delivery as if the words 'or order' had been added. [67] Like a bill of exchange, a bill of lading may be indorsed to a named indorsee or in blank, and in the latter case becomes a bearer document transferable by delivery without indorsement.

Thus the essence of an ordinary bill of lading is that it is transferable to different people in succession by delivery with any necessary indorsement. By contrast, a straight bill of lading may be transferred once only, to the named consignee, and then only by delivery without indorsement, the transferee being identified in the bill

---

64 See *The Delfini* [1990] 1 Lloyd's Rep 252, per Mustill LJ at 268.

65 See *The Future Express* [1992] 2 Lloyd's Rep 79, per His Honour Judge Diamond QC at 94, affirmed by the Court of Appeal [1993] 2 Lloyd's Rep 542.

66 Ibid.

67 Bills of lading also contain a space for entry of 'notify party', ie the name and address of the party whom the shipper requires to be notified of arrival of the shipment – for example, the consignee, his bank or other intended indorsee of the bill of lading, or a freight forwarder who is to collect the goods on their arrival. A 'notify party' entry imposes a contractual duty on the carrier to notify the party stated, unless otherwise provided by the terms of the contract (*E. Clemens Horst & Co v Norfolk & North American Steam Shipping Co Ltd* (1906) 22 TLR 403).

itself. Until recently the status of a straight bill of lading was unclear in English law; in particular it was unsettled whether it was to be treated as a true bill of lading within the Carriage of Goods by Sea Act 1971 or whether on the other hand it was to be equated with a sea waybill. The issue has now been authoritatively determined by the Court of Appeal, in a ruling that a straight bill of lading (1) is both a bill of lading for the purposes of the 1971 Act and a document of title, since rights are transferred by its delivery, albeit only once,[68] and in contrast to a sea waybill its production is required in order to obtain delivery, and it is drawn in the traditional form of a classic bill of lading, but (2) is a sea waybill under s 1 of the Carriage of Goods by Sea Act 1992 for the purposes of that Act,[69] though this does not affect the transferability of the holder's rights.[70]

A negotiable bill of lading possesses in relation to goods most of the features of negotiability accorded to instruments in respect of money. Thus

(a)   in the conditions previously mentioned it gives the holder control of the goods and entitles him to collect them from the carrier on surrender of the bill;

(b)   it is transferable by delivery with any necessary indorsement, no separate assignment or notice of assignment being needed;[71]

(c)   by virtue of (a) and (b) its possession enables the holder to deal with the goods before delivery.

But in two respects the negotiability of a bill of lading differs from that of a bill of exchange. First, negotiability denotes no more than transferability by delivery with any necessary indorsement. The transferee does not, by virtue of the character of the document, acquire any better title than his transferor.[72] There is thus no equivalent to the holder in due course status which is available for instruments. Secondly, negotiability is not presumed, as in the case of instruments; it is necessary for the bill to be made negotiable, in one of the ways indicated above.

2.   It is a receipt by the carrier

The bill of lading also serves as a receipt by the carrier. It is prima facie evidence in favour of the shipper, and conclusive evidence in favour of the consignee or indorsee, that the goods were received on board in the number or quantity or of the weight stated.[73]

---

68   In this respect it differs from the straight bill of lading under s 29 of the US Pomerene Act 1916, which is transferable to different holders in succession but lacks the feature of full negotiability of an ordinary bill of lading under US law enabling a holder to pass a better title than he himself possesses. By contrast English law treats a bill of lading as transferable but not fully negotiable. See below.

69   *The 'Rafaela S'* [2003] 2 Lloyd's Rep 113, which followed the decision of the Singapore Court of Appeal in *Peer Voss v APL Co Pte Ltd* [2002] 2 Lloyd's Rep 707 in holding that, in contrast to the position with a sea waybill, production of a straight bill of lading is necessary in order to obtain delivery. The judgment of Rix LJ, which reviewed the history of debates on the issue, is particularly instructive.

70   See below.

71   Cf the position in relation to bills of exchange, p 527.

72   He may, however, do so by virtue of some exception to the *nemo dat* rule, eg estoppel or statute (see, for example, the Factors Act 1889, ss 2, 8, 9 and the Sale of Goods Act 1979, ss 24, 25).

73   See pp 1051 ff.

3.   *It evidences the apparent condition of the goods*

Statements in a bill of lading as to the condition of the goods when taken on board – eg 'shipped in apparent good order and condition' – are not contractual (since the contract of carriage will have been concluded before shipment) but, at most, constitute evidence of the stated condition, which in certain circumstances will be treated as conclusive and thus constitute an estoppel.[74]

4.   *It evidences the terms of the contract of carriage*

The bill of lading is not itself the contract of carriage – for this is concluded before the goods are taken on board – but is the best evidence of its terms.[75] However, the documentation system developed by SITPRO, which is based on uniformity of documentation, has led to the availability of a short-form bill of lading which incorporates the carrier's standard terms by reference, the name of the carrier being typed on the front of the form.

The bill of lading should indicate whether the freight is prepaid or 'freight collect', that is, payable on arrival of the ship at the port of destination. In the latter case the seller must deduct the freight from the amount of his invoice.

5.   *It is a vehicle for transferring the contract rights it embodies*

By statute, though not at common law, the transfer of a bill of lading also operates, in certain conditions, to transfer to a consignee or indorsee the rights and liabilities of the original shipper under the contract of carriage contained in or evidenced by the bill of lading, and this transfer is no longer dependent upon the property in the goods having passed to the consignee or indorsee at the relevant time.[76]

(v)   Seller's duties as to the quality of the bill of lading

1.   *In general*

Unless the contract of sale otherwise provides, a bill of lading tendered to a buyer must conform to the following requirements, in default of which the buyer is entitled to reject it.[77]

(a)   It must be a shipped bill of lading, not a received for shipment bill. That is, it must show the carrier's receipt of the goods on board the vessel, not merely receipt alongside or at a dock or warehouse for the purpose of shipment. The point here is that the buyer is entitled to a document showing that the sea transit has begun. It is a common practice nevertheless for sellers to tender and buyers under f.o.b. and c.i.f. contracts to accept a combined transport bill

---

74   See pp 1051 ff.
75   See p 1051.
76   Carriage of Goods by Sea Act 1992, repealing the Bills of Lading Act 1855. See pp 1055 ff. In consequence of s 2 of the Act rights of suit against the carrier are not confined to a holder of a bill of lading. See p 1056.
77   As to the effect of rejection, see pp 936, 944.

of lading showing initial receipt by the carrier at the seller's premises or at an inland delivery point but bearing an indorsement showing shipment on board. But f.o.b. and c.i.f. contracts are not suitable where the parties to the sale contract incorporate Incoterms, and instead the FCA term should be used.[78]

(b)   It must be a clean bill, not a claused (or foul) bill.[79]

(c)   It must not be issued under a charterparty (for its terms would then be qualified by the charterparty, so adversely affecting the buyer's rights).[80]

(d)   It must record a date and place of shipment that indicates compliance with the contract of sale.[81]

(e)   It must cover the whole of the agreed transit, and not, for example, be a bill of lading issued by an intermediate carrier holding the goods at the time when they are purchased afloat, for the buyer will then have no direct claim against the first carrier for the first part of the voyage.[82]

(f)   Where transhipment is prohibited, the bill must be one which indicates continuous carriage by the same vessel to the port of destination, as opposed to a through bill of lading or a combined transport bill of lading.[83]

(g)   It must sufficiently identify the goods.[84] If it does not do this, the property will not pass to the buyer as the result of the transfer of the bill of lading to him.[85] However, the requirement of identification may be excluded by the express terms of the contract or by course of dealing or usage, a common occurrence in the case of bulk cargo such as oil, grain etc, which are not packed, boxed or crated but are poured as an undivided mass into the ship's hold and where a single shipment may be covered by a large number of bills of lading in favour of different buyers and segregation of each buyer's entitlement would be impracticable.[86]

---

78   See pp 868–869.

79   See para 2.

80   However, a mere reference to the charterparty does not render the bill of lading defective if it is clear that the terms of the charterparty are not incorporated into the bill of lading and do not affect the buyer's rights (*S.I.A.T. Di Del Ferro v Tradax Overseas SA* [1978] 2 Lloyd's Rep 470, *per* Donaldson J at 492).

81   *Hansson v Hamel & Horley Ltd* [1922] 2 AC 36; *S.I.A.T. Di Del Ferro v Tradax Overseas SA*, n 80. If it does not, the buyer will usually be entitled to reject it, since prima facie shipment within the contractual shipping period is a condition which must be strictly complied with.

82   *Hansson v Hamel & Horley Ltd*, n 81. But the fact that the bill of lading allows transhipment would not by itself entitle the buyer to reject it, so long as it was clear from the terms of the bill that the carrier at the port of shipment was undertaking responsibility for the entire sea transit (ibid).

83   See p 0000. Even if by the terms of the bill of lading the carrier reserves the right of transhipment, banks issuing letters of credit will refuse to accept such a bill unless the relevant cargo is shipped in containers or otherwise satisfies the requirements of UCP 500, art 23d.

84   See *Re Reinhold & Co* (1896) 12 TLR 422; *Benjamin's Sale of Goods*, para 18–180; Andrew G. L. Nicol, 'The Passing of Property in a Bulk' (1979) 42 MLR 129 at pp 141–142. Sellers usually take steps to facilitate identification by the use of shipping marks and numbers on the packages, details of the marks being given in the bill of lading and commercial invoice.

85   Sale of Goods Act, s 16.

86   See Goode, *Proprietary Rights and Insolvency*, pp 70 ff, for a discussion of some of the problems arising from this. For the prepaying buyer these are alleviated by the Sale of Goods Act 1979, ss 20A and 20B, discussed at p 220.

(h)   It must be confined to the buyer's goods and must not include goods consigned to another purchaser,[87] for obviously the buyer cannot then deal with the bill of lading without committing a conversion of the other purchaser's goods. But this requirement obviously does not apply where the parties have agreed, expressly or impliedly, that the seller may furnish a bill of lading covering an undivided part of a bulk cargo.

(i)   It must be signed on shipment or within a reasonable period thereafter.[88] Traditionally, bills of lading were signed by the master on the vessel after checking against the mate's receipt or other document; now, with electronic communication between ship and shore, it is usually signed by the carrier or its agent after shipment.

(j)   It must, like the other shipping documents, be 'reasonably and readily fit to pass current in commerce',[89] a requirement not satisfied if the bill of lading is altered, unless the alteration is a correction of a minor clerical error and is duly authenticated by signature or initials before the bill is issued. [90]

Of course, any of these requirements may be varied or displaced by the terms of the contract or by usage. The gradual displacement of port-to-port contracts by multimodal transport documents,[91] coupled with extension of the statutory assignment of contractual rights against the carrier to those entitled to delivery under a ship's delivery order or sea waybill,[92] is making insistence on a shipped bill of lading, and indeed the whole concept of 'shipment' as delivery on board a vessel, increasingly out of date. It is to be anticipated that in due course the courts will recognize this shift in transport practice and will give a more extended meaning to the words 'shipment' and 'shipping documents'.

2.   The problem of 'clean' bills of lading

The Uniform Customs and Practice for Documentary Credits,[93] dealing with transport documents generally, defines a clean transport document as one which bears no clause or notation which expressly declares a defective condition of the goods and/or the packaging. The issue of a clean bill of lading does not constitute a statement by the carrier that the goods are in fact sound, merely that they are in apparent good order and condition. Hence a clean bill vouches for the external appearance of the goods and/or packaging. If apparent good condition is qualified by a statement of defects – eg that the goods are damaged or that the packaging is inadequate, damaged, stained or wet – the bill is a foul, or claused, bill and unacceptable. However, in *The Galatia*[94] it was held that this is so only where the

---

87   *Re Keighley Maxted & Co and Bryan, Durant & Co (No.2)* (1894) 70 LT 155.

88   *S.I.A.T. Di Del Ferro v Tradax Overseas SA*, n 80.

89   *Hansson v Hamel & Horley Ltd*, n 81, per Lord Sumner at 46; *The Galatia* [1979] 2 All ER 726, affirmed [1980] 1 All ER 501.

90   *S.I.A.T. Di Del Ferro v Tradax Overseas SA*, n 80.

91   See pp 1061 ff.

92   Carriage of Goods by Sea Act 1992, s 2(1). But only a signed bill of lading is conclusive evidence of shipment, or receipt for shipment, in favour of a transferee under s 4 of the Act.

93   1993 revision (UCP 500), art 32.

94   See n 89.

notation refers to a defective condition existing at the time of shipment. Thus where, subsequent to shipment, a fire broke out and the goods were damaged by the fire and by water used to extinguish it and were discharged from the ship, a notation on the bill recording these facts was held not to preclude the bill from constituting a clean bill of lading, since it did not cast doubt on the condition of the goods at the time of shipment.[95] In the same case two further propositions were laid down. First, a bill is not rendered unclean by the inclusion of the common provision 'weight, measure, quantity, condition, contents and value unknown', since, even assuming that a standard term in the body of the bill, as opposed to a notation in the margin, could constitute a clausing of the bill, such a statement does not qualify the acknowledgement of receipt in *apparent* good order and condition. Secondly, whether a bill is clean is to be determined by the so-called 'legal' test, that is, the requirement that nothing on the bill should qualify the statement as to apparent good order and condition of the goods at the time of shipment, and not by the 'practical' test of whether the bill has in fact proved acceptable to a banker or other party to whom it was presented. Moreover, the contractual duty imposed on the carrier to issue a bill of lading stating whether the goods are in apparent good order and condition is satisfied if the master honestly believes, in the exercise of his own judgment, that the facts are as stated and that view could properly be held by a reasonably observant master, even if not all or even most other masters would agree with him.[96] The mere fact that a notation is unusual does not, it was held, render the bill unclean.[97]

When clausing a bill of lading because of apparent defects such as discoloration affecting only a small proportion of the cargo, the master must be careful not to use words conveying that the whole or substantial part of the cargo is affected, which would render the statement of apparent good order and condition an untrue statement.[98]

3. The electronic bill of lading

The delay and expense associated with the physical movement of paper-based bills of lading have led to various initiatives to replicate their effects by electronic means. Under the SeaDocs scheme[99] a bill of lading was issued in paper form but immobilized in a central registry, transfers being effected by an instruction to the registry, which would then indorse the bill of lading as agent of the shipper.[100] However, the scheme was abandoned for lack of support. More recently, the idea has been revived, but with the modification that the bill of lading is itself communicated electronically to the registry, the transfers being effected by attornment and novation, as in the Bolero system.[101] Though the Bolero bill of lading is in current use and the Bolero rule book seeks to give effect by contract to the

---

95 Which is, of course, the relevant time.
96 *The 'David Agmashenebeli'* [2003] 1 Lloyd's Rep 92.
97 For a criticism of this decision, see Clive Schmitthoff 'Export Trade' [1979] JBL 164.
98 *The 'David Agmashenebeli'*, n 96.
99 Seaborne Trade Documentation Scheme.
100 For a description, see Goode, *Proprietary Rights and Insolvency*, p 80.
101 An acronym for the **B**ill **of** **L**ading **E**lectronic **R**egistration **O**rganization.

established rules governing the carriage of goods, the fact that it is a system which is confined to members and entails not insignificant expense has meant that the take-up has so far been limited. Moreover, it remains doubtful that an electronic bill of lading falls within the Carriage of Goods by Sea Act 1971,[102] though its provisions would as between the parties be capable of taking effect as contractual terms[103] and the proprietary effects can be achieved, as in the Bolero system, by attornment of the registry to each transferee.

(vi) The insurance policy

Where the seller is required to insure the goods for their sea voyage, the buyer is, unless otherwise agreed, entitled to a policy of marine insurance covering the goods against the usual marine risks and such others as may be specified in the contract.[104] The buyer is entitled to reject a policy which covers goods beyond those comprised in the bill of lading.[105] In practice, the delivery of the policy itself may not be feasible, eg because it is a policy covering other goods or is a floating policy or open cover.[106] In such cases, the seller should stipulate in the contract for delivery of a cover note or certificate of insurance (fig 32.6) instead of a policy. In the absence of such a stipulation the buyer is not obliged to accept a cover note or certificate, for just as the transfer of a ship's delivery order does not operate to convey to the buyer the shipper's rights under the contract of carriage, so also the transfer of a certificate of insurance does not give the buyer a direct right of action against the insurer.[107] By contrast, a marine insurance policy (unlike most other policies of indemnity insurance) is, unless its terms otherwise provide, assignable without the consent of the insurer[108] by indorsement or in any other customary manner.[109]

(vii) The commercial invoice

The third basic shipping document is the commercial invoice (fig 32.7), that is, an invoice prepared on shipment of the goods and thus evidencing the start of the transit, as opposed to a pro forma invoice, which is, in effect, a quotation in invoice

---

102 Under s 1(5) of the Carriage of Goods by Sea Act 1992 the Secretary of State may make regulations extending the Act to, inter alia, electronic bills of lading but no such regulations have so far been made. For discussions, see Malcom Clarke, 'Transport documents: their transferability as documents of title; electronic documents' [2002] LMCLQ 356; Paul Todd, *Cases and Materials on International Trade Law* (2003), ch 16, especially at pp 819 ff; Hugh Beale and Lowri Griffiths, 'Electronic commerce: formal requirements in commercial transactions' [2002] LMCLQ 467 at 477; Diana Faber, 'Electronic bills of lading' [1996] LMCLQ 232.

103 The BOLERO rules preclude the parties from invoking the absence of a paper writing.

104 Under Incoterms the seller's duty, unless otherwise agreed, is to insure for minimum cover only, under Institute of Cargo Clauses (C) of the Institute of London Underwriters.

105 *Manbré Saccharine Co v Corn Products Co* [1919] 1 KB 198; *Hickox v Adams* (1876) 34 LT 404.

106 For an explanation, see Schmitthoff, *The Export Trade*, pp 34–36, 182 ff.

107 *Wilson, Holgate & Co Ltd v Belgian Grain & Produce Co Ltd* [1920] 2 KB 1.

108 Marine Insurance Act 1906, s 50(1).

109 Ibid, s 50(3).

ORIGINAL

THIS CERTIFICATE
REQUIRES ENDORSEMENT IN
THE EVENT OF ASSIGNMENT

CLAIMS SETTLEMENT
INSTRUCTIONS

1. Lloyd's Settling Agent nearest destination is
authorised to adjust and settle on behalf of the
Underwriters, and to purchase on behalf of the
Corporation of Lloyd's, in accordance with Lloyd's
Standing Regulations for the Settlement of Claims
Abroad, any claim which may arise on this
Certificate.

2. If Lloyd's Agents are not to deal with claims, it
should be clearly marked by an 'X' in the adjacent
box and claim papers sent to :- A. Short & Co. Ltd.,
1 London Road, London EC9 1OC.

Certificate of Insurance No. C 0000/

This is to Certify that there has been deposited with the Council of Lloyd's a Contract effected by *A. Short & Co. Ltd.*, of Lloyd's, acting on behalf of *Bodgit and Scarpa Ltd.*, with Underwriters at Lloyd's, for insurances attaching thereto during the period commencing the *First day of March, 1997*, and ending the *Twenty-eighth day of February, 1998*, both days inclusive, and that the said Underwriters have undertaken to issue to *A. Short & Co. Ltd.*, Policy/Policies of Insurance at Lloyd's to cover, up to *US$5,000,000 (or equivalent in other currencies)*, in all by any one *steamer and/or conveyances, or sending by air and/or post, General Merchandise and/or Goods and/or Equipment of any nature whatsoever including but not limited to Rice, Sugar, Motor Spare Parts, Bicycles, Generator Sets, Raw Jute, Jute Goods, from any port or ports, place or places in the World, to any port or ports, place or places in the World, including all transhipments as and when occurring*, and that *Bodgit and Scarpa Ltd.*, are entitled to declare against the said Contract insurances attaching thereto.

for the Council of Lloyd's.
Dated at Lloyd's, London, 4th March, 1997.

Conveyance	From	
Via/To	To	INSURED VALUE/Currency
Marks and Numbers		Interest

© Lloyd's, 2001.

We hereby declare for Insurance under the said Contract interest as specified above so valued subject to the special conditions stated below and on the back hereof.

Institute Cargo Clauses (A) or Institute Cargo Clauses (Air) (excluding sendings by Post) as applicable. Excluding rust, oxidisation, discolouration, twisting and bending.
Institute War Clauses (Cargo) or Institute War Clauses (Air Cargo) (excluding sendings by Post) or Institute War Clauses (sendings by Post) as applicable.
Institute Strikes Clauses (Cargo) or Institute Strikes Clauses (Air Cargo) as applicable.
Institute Classification Clause.
Institute Radioactive Contamination Exclusion Clause.
Institute Replacement Clause.

Underwriters agree losses, if any, shall be payable to the order of BODGIT AND SCARPA LTD., on surrender of this Certificate.

In the event of loss or damage which may result in a claim under this Insurance, immediate notice must be given to the Lloyd's Agent at the port or place where the loss or damage is discovered in order that he may examine the goods and issue a survey report. The survey agent will normally be the Agent authorised to adjust and settle claims in accordance with the terms and conditions set forth herein, but where such Agent does not hold the requisite authority, he will be able to supply the name and address of the appropriate Settling Agent.
A full list of Lloyd's Agents can be found at www.lloydsagency.com
(Survey fee is customarily paid by claimant and included in valid claim against Underwriters.)

SEE IMPORTANT INSTRUCTIONS BELOW

This Certificate not valid unless the Declaration be signed by
BODGIT AND SCARPA LTD.

Dated

Brokers : A. Short & Co. Ltd.,
1 London Road, London EC9 1OC.

Signed

Authorised Signatory
7489CM

Fig 32.6 Certificate of marine insurance

898

IMPORTANT INSTRUCTIONS IN EVENT OF CLAIM

DOCUMENTATION OF CLAIMS

To enable claims to be dealt with promptly, the Assured or their Agents are advised to submit all available supporting documents without delay, including when applicable:-

1. Original policy or certificate of insurance.

2. Original or copy shipping invoices, together with shipping specification and/or weight notes.

3. Original Bill of Lading and/or other contract of carriage.

4. Survey report or other documentary evidence to show the extent of the loss or damage.

5. Landing account and weight notes at final destination.

6. Correspondence exchanged with the Carriers and other parties regarding their liability for the loss or damage.

IMPORTANT
LIABILITY OF CARRIERS, BAILEES OR OTHER THIRD PARTIES

It is the duty of the Assured and their Agents, in all cases, to take such measures as may be reasonable for the purpose of averting or minimising a loss and to ensure that all rights against Carriers, Bailees or other third parties are properly preserved and exercised. In particular, the Assured or their Agents are required:-

1. To claim immediately on the Carriers, Port Authorities or other Bailees for any missing packages.

2. In no circumstances, except under written protest, to give clean receipts where goods are in doubtful condition.

3. When delivery is made by Container, to ensure that the Container and its seals are examined immediately by their responsible official. If the Container is delivered damaged or with seals broken or missing or with seals other than as stated in the shipping documents, to clause the delivery receipt accordingly and retain all defective or irregular seals for subsequent identification.

4. To apply immediately for survey by Carriers' or other Bailees' Representatives if any loss or damage be apparent and claim on the Carriers or other Bailees for any actual loss or damage found at such survey.

5. To give notice in writing to the Carriers or other Bailees within 3 days of delivery if the loss or damage was not apparent at the time of taking delivery.

Note.- The Consignees or their Agents are recommended to make themselves familiar with the Regulations of the Port Authorities at the port of discharge.

NOTE.- The Institute Clauses incorporated herein are deemed to be those current at the time of commencement of the risk.
It is necessary for the Assured when they become aware of an event which is "held covered" under this Insurance to give prompt notice to Underwriters and the right to such cover is dependent upon compliance with this obligation.
Lloyd's Agents referred to herein are not insurers and are not liable for claims arising on this Certificate. The service of legal proceedings upon Lloyd's Agents is not effective service for the purpose of starting legal proceedings against Underwriters.
This insurance shall be subject to the exclusive jurisdiction of the English Courts.

7489CM

form.[110] The commercial invoice is a document of commercial importance to the buyer. Quite apart from the normal purposes served by an invoice (eg in setting out details of the goods, the price, and the mode and time of dispatch), it will be required by the buyer in order to clear the goods through customs (since it is on the basis of the invoice that customs duty is assessed) and may also be needed for presentation to other authorities, eg to identify the goods as covered by an import licence or foreign exchange approval. The commercial invoice also fulfils an important role in documentary credits, since it is this document, rather than the bill of lading, which is required to record the full description of the goods as set out in the letter of credit.[111]

To fulfil its required functions, the commercial invoice should identify the buyer's order and should set out full details of the parties, the goods, the price and payment terms, shipping marks and numbers, and the shipment itself, including port of loading, route and port of discharge.

(viii) Other documents

Among the other documents commonly called for in a contract of sale are the following.

1.   Certificate of origin

This is a certificate issued by the exporter[112] or a third party of suitable standing (eg a Chamber of Commerce) as to the place of growth, production or manufacture of the goods. Arab countries in particular usually require the production of a certificate of origin (fig 32.8).

2.   Certificate of quality/quantity

This is a certificate issued by the exporter or a recognized third party (eg a government or other quality evaluation agency) that the goods are of a stated quality, grade or quantity (fig 32.9). Where the contract provides that such a certificate is to be final and conclusive as to the quality or condition of the goods, the certificate is binding in the absence of fraud and cannot be called into question[113] even if the certifier acted negligently.[114]

---

110 Buyers frequently require pro forma invoices in order to obtain an import licence or arrange finance. Since the invoice is merely a quotation, it is not passed through the books of either seller or buyer and, indeed, has no legal significance at all unless the buyer decides to accept the quotation. In that event, it will be followed by the commercial invoice on shipment. Figure 32.7 shows a certified commercial invoice, as to which see p 900.

111 See p 985.

112 Either as a separate form or by certification on the commercial invoice.

113 *Gill & Duffus SA v Berger & Co Inc* [1983] 1 Lloyd's Rep 622, affirmed on this point by the House of Lords [1984] AC 382.

114 *Alfred C. Toepfer v Continental Grain Co* [1973] 1 Lloyd's Rep 289; *Focke & Co Ltd v Thomas Robinson, Sons & Co Ltd* (1935) 52 Ll L Rep 334. Though the Unfair Contract Terms Act 1977 brings 'evidence' clauses within its provisions, export transactions will usually be excluded from the Act under s 26.

900

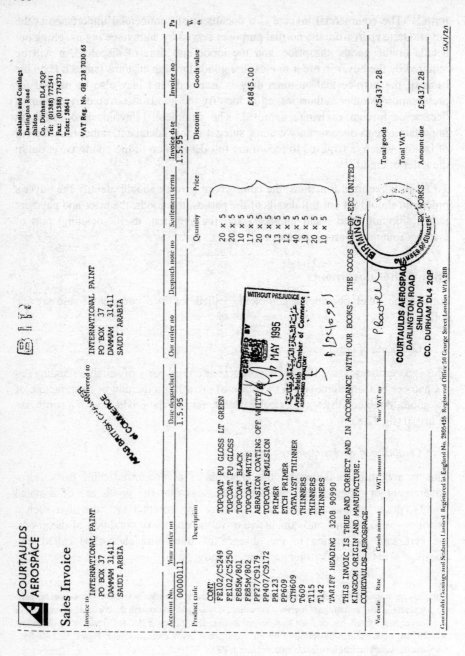

Fig 32.7 Certified commercial invoice

901

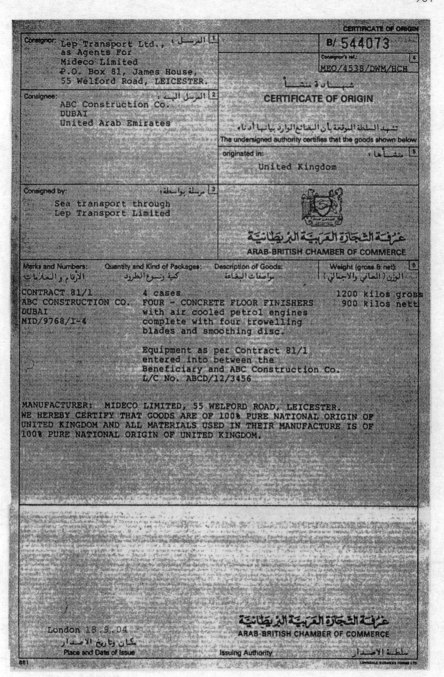

Fig 32.8 Certificate of origin

Supplier

SITPRO Export Ltd
High Street
Burton-on-Trent   DE15 1YZ
England   VAT No.   214 8235 77

Our Ref.
682-12345   CD

Buyer's Ref.
SME4784

Agent's Ref.
ST348   J48478912

Consignee
SITPRO Mid East
First Avenue
Jeddah
Saudi Arabia

Buyer (if not Consignee)
SITPRO Buying
Second Road
Rivadh   Saudi Arabia

CERTIFICATE OF QUALITY/QUANTITY
CERTIFICAT DE QUALITÉ/QUANTITÉ
QUALITATE/QUANTITATS BESCHEINIGUNG
CERTIFICADO DE CALIDAD/CANTIDAD

Import Licence No. & Date
SA BPB   2   9 GB ELL

Country of Origin
United Kingdom

Country to which consigned
Saudi Arabia

| Vessel. Aircraft etc.
City of Burton | Sea/Air Port of Loading
Ellesmere Port |
| Sea/A. Port of Discharge
Jeddah | Place of Delivery by On Carrier
Jeddah |

Marks. Nos. & Containers	Packages & Description of Goods	Quantity
	1 x 20ft Container Holding	
1) 4784 1/4	4 Cases Machine tools Automatic Lathes	
2) 4784 5/6	2 Cartons Machine tool parts	
3) 4734 7/11	5 Unpacked pipe joints	
4) 4784 10/17	6 Drums Cutting Oil	

We certify that the quality and quantity of the above-mentioned goods correspond to the relevant specification and contracted standard.

Nous certifions par la présente que la quantité et la qualité de la marchandise indiquée ci-dessus sont conformes aux spécifications correspondantes et aux normes accordées.

Wir bestätigen, dass die Qualität und Menge der oben angegebenen Waren der entsprechenden Spezifikation und der Vertragsnorm entsprechen.

Certificamos que la calidad y la cantidad de las mercancias arriba mencionadas corresponden a la especificacion pertinente y a la norma contratada.

SIRPRO Export Ltd/0283 41835

| Name of Signatory
H J Helliar, Chief Clerk |
| Place & Date
Burton 2 Oct 1996 |
| Signature
H J Helliar |

Fig 32.9 Certificate of quality/quantity

3.   Certified invoice

This is a commercial invoice certified by the exporter or an independent third party (eg a Chamber of Commerce) as correct (see fig 32.7). Frequently, the certificate relates to the origin of the goods as well as their value.

4.   Consular invoice

This is an invoice on an official consulate form which gives details of the goods, the price, the shipment etc, and is signed by a consular official of the country to which the goods are being consigned after verification against the shipping documents. Nowadays consular invoices are not often called for. If, which is not usually the case, a consular certificate is specified, this is normally given on the commercial invoice itself.

5.   Movement certificate

A movement certificate may be required to attract the benefit of preferential tariffs or duty exemptions on the movement of goods between or among states who are parties to the relevant convention.

6.   Packing list

This gives particulars of the consignee, the vessel and port of departure, the terms of delivery and payment, the contents and weight of each package, with shipping marks but without prices and the port of discharge (see fig 32.10). The packing list is used for various purposes, eg as the basis for freight calculations and to satisfy the requirements of customs and of banks making payment for the goods under a documentary credit.

7.   Inspection certificate

Reference has already been made to the practice of preshipment inspection and the inclusion of the inspection certificate as a shipping document.[115] Where inspection is not to take place until after shipment, the inspection certificate cannot, of course, be a shipping document and its absence does not entitle the buyer to reject a tender of the shipping documents.[116]

8.   Health certificate

This certifies that health regulations have been complied with in relation to agricultural and animal products that are being exported.

---

115   See p 879.
116   *Gill & Duffus SA v Berger & Co Inc*, n 113.

PACKING LIST
LISTE DE COLISAGE   VERSANDLISTE
ESPECIFICACION DE EMBALAJE

Seller (name, address)			
SITPRO® The Simpler Trade Procedures Board 29 Glasshouse Street London W1R 5RG VAT Reg. No. 241 8235 77	Invoice number MD-2		UNIC

(c) SITPRO 1992

Invoice date (tax point) 24.5.04	Seller's reference MD-2
Buyer's reference PO 4123	Other reference

Consignee	Buyer (if not consignee)
Aikashinko Shibakhoen Inc 6-1 Honcho Kanamatsu Cho, Naka-Ku Kyoto Japan	

Country of origin of goods	Country of destination
UK (EU)	Japan

Terms of delivery and payment
DDP - Delivered Duty Paid Kyoto   Incoterms 2000

Vessel/flight no. and date	Port/airport of loading	Payment via: Bank of Foreign Trade 18-22 Valentine Place, London WC2 Account No: 123 456 78
Gala Del Mar	Liverpool	
Port/airport of discharge	Place of delivery	
Osaka	Kyoto	

Shipping marks: container number	No. and kind of packages: description of goods	Commodity code	Total gross wt (kg)	Total cube (m3)
Aiashinko PO 4123 Kyoto via Osaka Japan	1 Electric Table Lamps		KG 85.50 Total net wt (kg) 78.50	

Item/packages	Gross/net/cube	Description	Other details
	85.50 78.50	1 Case 100 Electric Table Lamps	UK
TOTAL GROSS & NET WT & CUBE	-------- 85.50 78.50		

Additional packing information

	Name of signatory A D Smith
	Place and date of issue London 24.5.04
	Signature

SITPRO Licensee No. 000.

V5

Fig 32.10 Packing list

(ix) Substitutes for a bill of lading

1. *Documents to be produced by consignee to obtain the goods*

Despite the legal superiority of the bill of lading, it is often neither practicable nor necessary for a shipper to be issued with his own bill. Thus, one of the services performed by a freight forwarder is to consolidate consignments by different shippers, or by the same shipper acquiring goods from different suppliers which are destined for the same port, and thus to secure for his client the benefit of preferential freight rates, as well as reducing the risk of damage and pilferage. Obviously, the bill of lading cannot in such a case be issued to any one shipper. Instead, the bill (termed a groupage bill) is taken by the forwarder in his own name, and he will then split the groupage consignment among his respective clients either by procuring the issue of separate ship's delivery orders (fig 32.11),[117] by which the ship undertakes to release designated goods to the consignee or other holder of the relevant delivery order, or by issuing his own 'house' bill of lading, or certificate of shipment, or a forwarder's certificate of transport (FCT) enabling the holder to collect the goods from the forwarder's agent or other consignee at the port of destination on production of the document.[118] A more recent alternative is for the forwarder to issue no document at all but simply release goods to each consignee upon electronic communication of the consignee's PIN.

2. *Documents of which production by consignee is not required*

Where the buyer does not wish to have the facility of reselling or pledging the goods afloat, he should not specify a bill of lading, with all its attendant delays, in the contract of sale but should ask for a non-negotiable (ie non-transferable) sea waybill (fig 32.12) or forwarder's certificate of receipt (FCR) (fig 32.13). Such a document constitutes a receipt for the goods and incorporates by reference the standard conditions of contract of the carrier or forwarder, but it is not transferable, so that the goods will be collected at their destination by the consignee himself, who will not have to produce the document, merely evidence of identity. A non-negotiable sea waybill has several advantages. Much of the detailed checking at both ends that is

---

117 Which to be effective must be either issued or assented to by the ship (see p 44, n 128; and see the Carriage of Goods by Sea Act 1992, s 1(4)). The buyer is not obliged to accept a delivery order unless the contract of sale so provides. A delivery order is not as valuable to him as a bill of lading since it does not identify the goods sufficiently to make them ascertained. Until recently it also suffered the disadvantage that it did not attract the provisions of the Bills of Lading Act 1855 passing the property and contract rights to the consignee or indorsee, but this disadvantage has been removed by the repeal of that Act by the Carriage of Goods by Sea Act 1992 and the extension of the statutory assignment of the contract rights to the holder of a ship's delivery order (s 2(1)).

118 A house bill of lading, not being issued by the sea carrier, is not technically a bill of lading at all; and though forwarders may claim negotiable status for such documents, the general view is that this is not supportable in law, though de facto the house bill expressed to be negotiable operates well enough as such in the sense that the forwarders agent at the port of destination will recognize the right of an indorsee to possession of the goods. It was with a view to securing international recognition of a freight forwarders document as a negotiable transport document that FIATA introduced the FCT, which is now widely used (see below). Again, however, it would probably not be treated by an English court as a document of title.

(c) SITPRO 1992

COLLECTION/DELIVERY ORDER

Exporter	A

Exporter's reference

Forwarder's reference

U N I C

Collection address if different from A	B

Other UK transport details e.g. delivery address	C

Haulier	D

Vessel/flight no. and date	Port/airport of loading

Port/airport of discharge

Shipping marks: container number	Number and kind of packages description of goods	Gross weight (kg)	Cube (m3)

DANGEROUS GOODS

Specify proper shipping name: hazard class: UN No.: flashpoint deg C
Shipper must provide the appropriate dangerous goods declaration

IMPORTANT - DOCUMENTS TO BE COLLECTED

Collect documents from **A B**

Deliver documents to **C D** or:-

Total gross weight of goods	Total cube of goods

Prefix and container/trailer number(s)	Seal number(s0	Container/trailer size(s) and type(s)	Tare wt(kg) as marked on CSC plate	Weight of container and goods (kg)

Received the above packages/containers/trailers in apparent good order unless stated hereon

For and on behalf of

Haulier's name

Vehicle reg no.

Date

Driver's signature	Signature and date

SITPRO Licensee No. 000.

Fig 32.11 Ship's delivery order

associated with the preparation and dispatch of a bill of lading is avoided. The document can be made available to the shipper as soon as the forwarder has taken the goods into his charge, so that if acceptable to the relevant bank it can be immediately furnished by the shipper to obtain payment under a letter of credit or to procure an advance from his bank. The other documents can be sent to the consignee without having to await the issue of a bill of lading. Finally, the fact that the consignee can collect the goods on arrival without the need to produce the document means that he avoids the delay in collection, and consequent storage charges, that may occur due to late arrival of the documents. By contrast, a bill of lading cannot be issued until shipment, and not infrequently does not reach the consignee until some time after the goods themselves have arrived, causing serious problems.[119]

A sea waybill is, in principle, a 'received for shipment' document but can be converted into a 'shipped' or 'loaded on board' document (or even into a negotiable bill of lading) by an appropriate notation by the carrier, so long as the goods are still in his hands. The disadvantage of carriers' sea waybills and of forwarders' documents, whether or not expressed to be negotiable, is that they may not be acceptable to banks[120] and do not confer the protection of the Hague-Visby Rules[121] unless expressly incorporated.

3.   Multimodal transport documents

A further development has been the increasing involvement of the freight forwarder as a carrier himself, not necessarily in a physical sense but as a multimodal operator (MTO)[122] contracting as principal to perform or procure performance of a multimodal transport (MT) from door to door under an MT bill of lading governed by the UNCTAD Multimodal Transport Convention of 1980 or by the Uniform Rules for a Combined Transport Document issued by the International Chamber of Commerce.[123] Multimodal/combined transport bills of lading may be either negotiable[124] (fig 32.5) or non-negotiable. The efficacy of multimodal transport is to some extent weakened by the fact that there is no international convention covering all stages of the transit. Instead, there are different conventions applicable to the different types of transport and, where loss, damage or delay occurs, this may involve complex questions as to the incidence of liability. UNCITRAL is currently engaged on an ambitious project to prepare an international instrument dealing with the responsibilities of parties involved in the carriage of goods wholly or partly by sea.[125]

---

119   See p 864. See the CMI Uniform Rules for Sea Waybills, n 5.
120   This is not, of course, a problem in the field of documentary credits where the credit calls for a sea waybill, multimodal transport document or freight forwarder's transport document, all of which are covered in detail in arts 24, 26 and 30 of the UCP.
121   See p 1045.
122   Also termed a combined transport operator.
123   See pp 1056 ff. See also the UNCTAD/ICC Rules for Multimodal Transport Documents, published in 1990.
124   There is as yet no reported decision recognizing the negotiability of a multimodal transport document, but if this is established by trade usage, there seems no reason why the courts should not give it recognition. See further, p 1064.
125   See p 1069.

Non-Negotiable Waybill for Combined Transport shipment or Port to Port shipment

Shipper		
R T & SONS 27 NEW NORTH ROAD EPPING IG24 6ES	Waybill No.: PONLBHX22045997 Reference:	

P&O NedLloyd

www.ponl.com

Consignee (If the name shown in this space is a Bank, the Bank named is specifically excluded from the list of parties coming within the definition of Merchant in the Carrier's contract of carriage and incurs no liability to the Carrier under said contract unless applying for delivery in its own name.)
ROUNDABOUT LOGISTICS 24 NEWBURY ROAD STAFFORD QLD 4120 AUSTRALIA

Notify Party/Address (It is agreed that no responsibility shall attach to the Carrier or his Agents for failure to notify)	Place of Receipt (Applicable only when this document is used as a Combined Transport Waybill)
ROUNDABOUT LOGISTICS 24 NEWBURY ROAD STAFFORD QLD 4120 AUSTRALIA	R T & SONS 27 NEW NORTH ROAD EPPING IG24 6ES

Vessel and Voy. No.	Place of Delivery (Applicable only when this document is used as a Combined Transport Waybill)
P&O NEDLLOYD PALLISER PLE4004	BRISBANE CONTAINER FACILITY

Port of Loading	Port of Discharge
TILBURY	BRISBANE

Undermentioned particulars as declared by Shipper, but not acknowledged by the Carrier

Marks and Nos; Container Nos;	Number and kind of Packages; description of Goods	Gross Weight (kg)	Measurement (cbm)
PONU2881057 SEAL: 1082955 ROUNDABOUT LOGISTICS NOS 1-500	1×20'RE CONTAINER SAID TO CONTAIN 500 CARTON(S) FCL/FCL CHOCOLATE BISCUITS FREIGHT COLLECT SHIPPED ON BOARD PER OCEAN VESSEL P&O NEDLLOYD PALLISER AT TILBURY ON 20/01/2004 FOR P&O NEDLLOYD LIMITED TOTAL: 1×20' CONTAINER(S) ONLY	2528	18.500

FREIGHT AND CHARGES:

ORIGIN INLAND HAULAGE CHARGE	P	HAI
ORIGIN TERMINAL HANDLING/LCL SERVICE CHARGE	P	HAI
OCEAN FREIGHT	C	BNE
DESTINATION TERMINAL HANDLING/LCL SERVICE CHARGE	C	BNE
DESTINATION INLAND HAULAGE CHARGE	C	BNE

* Total No. of Containers/Packages received by the Carrier	Movement	Freight payable at
1	FCL/FCL	PONL BRISBANE

Received by the Carrier from the Shipper in apparent good order and condition (unless otherwise noted herein) the total number or quantity of Containers or other packages or units indicated in the box above entitled "Total No. of Containers/Packages received by the Carrier" for Carriage from the Place of Receipt or the Port of Loading, whichever applicable, to the Port of Discharge or the Place of Delivery, whichever applicable, SUBJECT TO THE TERMS OF THE CARRIER'S STANDARD BILL OF LADING TERMS AND CONDITIONS AND TARIFF FOR THE RELEVANT TRADE, WHICH ARE MUTATIS MUTANDIS APPLICABLE TO THIS WAYBILL (copies of which may be obtained from the Carrier or his agents). Except for live animals and Goods which are stated herein to be carried on deck and are so carried, these terms and conditions are warranted by the Carrier in respect of the sea portion of the Carriage to apply the Hague Rules or Hague Visby Rules, whichever would have been applicable if this Waybill were a Bill of Lading. In either case the provisions of Article III Rule 4 of the Hague Visby Rules are deemed to be incorporated herein. The contract evidenced by this Waybill is deemed to be a contract of carriage as defined in Article 1 (b) of the Hague Rules and Hague Visby Rules. However this Waybill is not a document of title to the Goods. Delivery will be made to the Consignee named, or to authorised agent, on production of proof of identity at the Port of Discharge or the Place of Delivery, whichever applicable. Should the Consignee require delivery to a party and/or premises other than as shown above in the "Consignee" box, then written instructions must be given by the Consignee to the Carrier or his agents. Unless the Shipper expressly waives the right to control the Goods and to give the Carrier, and/or receives, such instructions from the Consignee will be subject to any instruction to the contrary by the Shipper. Unless instructed to the contrary by the Shipper prior to the commencement of Carriage and noted accordingly on the face hereof, the Carrier will, subject to the aforesaid terms and conditions, process cargo claims with the Consignee. Claims settlement, if any, shall be a complete discharge of the Carrier's liability to the Shipper. The Shipper accepts the said standard terms and conditions on his own behalf, on behalf of the Consignee and the Owner of the Goods, and authorises the Consignee to bring suit against the Carrier in his own name but as agent of the Shipper, and warrants that he has authority so to accept and authorise. The Shipper further undertakes that no claim or allegation in respect of the Goods shall be made against the Carrier by any person other than in accordance with the terms and conditions of this Waybill.

This Waybill is issued subject to the CMI Uniform Rules For Sea Waybills	Place and Date of Issue PONL HAINAULT 20/01/04	IN WITNESS whereof this Waybill is signed.

FOR P&O NEDLLOYD LTD, AS CARRIER:*

DRAFT - COPY ONLY

0409060

Beagle House, Braham Street, London E1 8EP

3/DRS W/B 10/03

*OPERATING IN PARTNERSHIP WITH P&O NEDLLOYD BV

Fig 32.12 Non-negotiable sea waybill

Suppliers or Forwarders Principals

BIFA

FIATA FCR

Forwarders
Certificate of Receipt

No.

Country Code
GB

ORIGINAL

Forw. Ref

Consignee

Marks and numbers;   Number and kind of packages   Description of Goods   Gross Weight   Measurement

COPY FOR
INFORMATION ONLY

according to the declaration of the consignor

The goods and instructions are accepted and dealt with subject to the General Conditions printed overleaf

We certify having assumed control of the above mentioned consignment in external apparent good order and condition

☐   at the disposal of the consignee

with irrevocable instructions*

☐   to be forwarded to the consignee

Remarks

Instructions as to freight and charges

*   Forwarding instructions can only be cancelled or altered if the original Certificate is surrendered to us, and then only provided we are still in a position to comply with such cancellation or alteration.

Instructions authorizing disposal by a third party can only be cancelled or altered if the original Certificate of Receipt is surrendered to us, and then only provided we have not yet received instructions under the original authority.

Place and date of issue

Stamp and signature

Fig 32.13 Forwarder's certificate of receipt

BRITISH INTERNATIONAL FREIGHT ASSOCIATION (BIFA) - STANDARD TRADING CONDITIONS 2000 EDITION

The Customer's attention is drawn to the Clauses hereof which exclude or limit the Company's liability and those which require the Customer to indemnify the Company in certain circumstances.

DEFINITIONS AND APPLICATION

1 In these Conditions:-

"Company" Is the BIFA Member trading under these Conditions.

"Person" Includes persons or any Body or Bodies Corporate.

"The Owner" Means the Owner of the goods (including any packaging, containers or equipment) to which any business concluded under these Conditions relates and any other person who is or may become interested in them

"Customer" Means any person at whose request or on whose behalf the Company undertakes any business or provides advice, information or services.

2(A) Subject to Sub-Paragraph (B) below, all and any activities of the Company in the course of business whether gratuitous or not are undertaken subject to these Conditions.

(B) If any legislation is compulsorily applicable to any business undertaken, these Conditions shall, as regards such business, be read as subject to such legislation and nothing in these Conditions shall be construed as a surrender by the Company of any of its rights or immunities or as an increase of any of its responsibilities or liabilities under such legislation and if any part of these Conditions be repugnant to such legislation to any extent such part shall as regards such business be overridden to that extent and no further.

3 The Customer warrants that he is either the Owner or the authorised Agent of the Owner and also that he is accepting these Conditions not only for himself but also as Agent for and on behalf of the Owner.

THE COMPANY

4(A) Subject to Clauses 11 and 12 below, the Company shall be entitled to procure any or all of its services as an Agent or to provide those services as a Principal.

(B) The Company shall on demand by the Customer provide evidence of any Contract entered into as Agent for the Customer. Insofar as the Company may be in default of this obligation, it shall be deemed to have contracted with the Customer as a Principal for the performance of the Customer's instructions.

5 When the Company contracts as a Principal for any services, it shall have full liberty a) to perform such services itself or b) to subcontract the whole or any part of such services to third parties (including the Company's own parent, subsidiary, or associated companies).

6 When the Company acts as an Agent on behalf of the Customer, the Company shall be entitled (and the Customer hereby expressly authorises the Company) to enter into all such Contracts on behalf of the Customer as may be necessary or desirable to fulfil the Customer's instructions and subject to the trading conditions of the parties with whom such contracts are made.

7 The Company reserves to itself a reasonable liberty as to the means, route and procedure to be followed in the handling, storage and transportation of goods.

8(A) Subject to Sub-Clause (B) hereof, the Company shall have a general lien on all goods and documents relating to goods in its possession, custody or control for all sums due at any time from the Customer or Owner, and shall be entitled to sell or dispose of such goods or documents as Agent for and at the expense of the Customer and apply the proceeds in or towards the payment of such sums on 28 days notice in writing to the Customer. Upon accounting to the Customer for any balance remaining after payment of any sum due to the Company, and the costs of sale or disposal the Company shall be discharged of any liability whatsoever in respect of the goods or documents.

(B) When the goods are liable to perish or deteriorate, the Company's right to sell or dispose of the goods shall arise immediately upon any sum becoming due to the Company subject only to the Company taking reasonable steps to bring to the Customer's attention its intention of selling or disposing of the goods before doing so.

9 The Company shall be entitled to retain and be paid all brokerages, commissions, allowances and other remunerations customarily retained by or paid to Freight Forwarders.

THE CUSTOMER

17 The Customer warrants:

(A) that the description and particulars of any goods furnished by or on behalf of the Customer are full and accurate.

(B) that all goods have been properly and sufficiently prepared, packed, stowed, labelled and/or marked, and that the preparation, packing, stowage, labelling and marking are appropriate to any operations or transactions affecting the goods and the characteristics of the goods.

(C) that where the Company receives the goods from the Customer already stowed in or on a container, trailer, tanker, or any other device specifically constructed for the carriage of goods by land, sea or air (each, hereafter individually referred to as "the transport unit"), the transport unit is in good condition, and is suitable for the carriage to the intended destination of the goods loaded therein or thereon.

18 Should the Customer otherwise than under special arrangements previously made in writing as set out in Clause 15 above deliver to the Company or cause the Company to deal with or handle goods of a dangerous or damaging nature, or goods likely to harbour or encourage vermin or other pests, or goods liable to taint or affect other goods, he shall be liable for all loss or damage arising in connection with such goods and shall indemnify the Company against all penalties, claims, damages, costs and expenses whatsoever arising in connection therewith, and the goods may be dealt with in such manner as the Company or any other person in whose custody they may be at any relevant time shall think fit.

19 The Customer undertakes that no claim shall be made against any Director, Servant, or Employee of the Company which imposes or attempts to impose upon them any liability in connection with any services which are the subject of these Conditions and if any such claim should nevertheless be made, to indemnify the Company against all consequences thereof.

20 The Customer shall save harmless and keep the Company indemnified from and against:-

(A) All liability, loss, damage, costs and expenses whatsoever (including without prejudice to the generality of the foregoing, all duties, taxes, imposts, levies, deposits and outlays of whatsoever nature levied by any authority in relation to the goods) arising out of the Company acting in accordance with the Customer's instructions or arising from any breach by the Customer of any Warranty contained in these Conditions or from the negligence of the Customer,

(B) Without derogation from Sub-Clause (A) above, any liability assumed or incurred by the Company when by reason of carrying out the Customer's instructions the Company has reasonably become liable or may become liable to any other party, and

(C) All claims, costs and demands whatsoever and by whomsoever made or preferred in excess of the liability of the Company under the terms of these Conditions regardless whether such claims, costs and demands arise from or in connection with the negligence or breach of duty of the Company, its Servants, Sub-Contractors or Agents, and

(D) Any claims of a General Average nature which may be made on the Company.

21(A) The Customer shall pay to the Company in cash or as otherwise agreed all sums immediately when due without reduction or deferment on account of any claim, counterclaim or set-off.

(B) In respect of all sums which are overdue, the Customer shall be liable to pay to the Company interest calculated at 8% above the prevailing base rate of the London clearing banks.

22 Despite the acceptance by the Company of instructions to collect freight, duties, charges or other expenses from the Consignee or any other person, the Customer shall remain responsible for such freight, duties, charges or expenses on receipt of evidence of proper demand and in the absence of evidence of payment (for whatever reason) by such Consignee or other person when due.

23 Where liability for General Average arises in connection with the goods, the Customer shall promptly provide security to the Company or to any other party designated by the Company in a form acceptable to the Company.

Company shall be entitled to store the goods or any part thereof at the sole risk of the Customer, whereupon the liability of the Company in respect of the goods or that part thereof stored as aforesaid shall wholly cease and the cost of such storage if paid for or payable by the Company or any Agent or Sub-Contractor of the Company shall forthwith upon demand be paid by the Customer to the Company.

(B) The Company shall be entitled at the expense of the Customer to dispose of (by sale or otherwise as may be reasonable in all the circumstances):-

(i) on 28 days notice in writing to the Customer, or (where the Customer cannot be traced and reasonable efforts have been made to contact any parties who may reasonably be supposed by the Company to have any interest in the goods) without notice, any goods which have been held by the Company for 90 days and which cannot be delivered as instructed; and

(iii) without prior notice, goods which have perished, deteriorated or altered or are in immediate prospect of doing so in a manner which has caused or may reasonably be expected to cause loss or damage to the Company or Third Parties or to contravene any applicable laws or regulations.

11(A) No insurance will be effected except upon express instructions given in writing by the Customer and all insurances effected by the Company are subject to the usual exceptions and conditions of the Policies and the Insurance Company or Underwriters taking the risk. Unless otherwise agreed in writing the Company shall not be under any obligation to effect a separate insurance on each consignment but may declare it on any open or general Policy held by the Company.

(B) Insofar as the Company agrees to effect insurance, the Company acts solely as Agent for the Customer. The limits of liability under Clause 27(A)(ii) of these Conditions shall not apply to the Company's obligations under Clauses 11(A) and (B).

12(A) Except under special arrangements previously made in writing or under the terms of a printed document signed by the Company, any instructions relating to the delivery or release of goods in specified circumstances only, such as (but without prejudice to the generality of this Clause) against payment or against surrender of a particular document, are accepted by the Company where the Company has to engage third parties to effect compliance with the instructions, only as Agents for the Customer.

(B) The Company shall not be under any liability in respect of such arrangements as are referred to under Sub-Clause (A) hereof save where such arrangements are made in writing.

(C) In any event, the Company's liability in respect of the performance or arranging the performance of such instructions shall not exceed the limits set out in Clause 27(A) (ii) of these Conditions.

13 Advice and information, in whatever form it may be given, is provided by the Company for the Customer only and the Customer shall not pass such advice or information to any Third Party without the Company's written agreement. The Customer shall indemnify the Company against all loss and damage suffered as a consequence of any breach of this Condition by the Customer.

14(A) Except under special arrangement previously made in writing the Company will not accept or deal with bullion, coin, precious stones, jewellery, valuables, antiques, pictures, human remains, livestock, pets or plants. Should any Customer nevertheless deliver any such goods to the Company or cause the Company to handle or deal with any such goods otherwise than under special arrangements previously made in writing the Company shall be under no liability whatsoever for or in connection with such goods howsoever arising.

(B) The Company may at any time waive its rights and exemptions from liability under Sub-Clause (A) above in respect of any one or more of the categories of goods mentioned herein or of any part of any category. If such waiver is not in writing, the onus of proving such waiver shall be on the Customer.

15 Except following instructions previously received in writing and accepted by the Company, the Company will not accept or deal with goods of a dangerous or damaging nature, nor with goods likely to harbour or encourage vermin or other pests, nor with goods liable to taint or affect other goods. If such goods are accepted pursuant to a special arrangement and then in the opinion of the Company they constitute a risk to other goods, property, life or health, the Company shall where reasonably practicable contact the Customer, but reserves the right at the expense of the Customer to remove or otherwise deal with the goods.

16 Where there is a choice of rates according to the extent or degree of the liability assumed by carriers, warehousemen or others, no declaration of value where optional will be made except under special arrangements previously made in writing.

24 The Company shall perform its duties with a reasonable degree of care, diligence, skill and judgement.

25 The Company shall be relieved of liability for any loss or damage if and to the extent that such loss or damage is caused by:-

(A) strike, lock-out, stoppage or restraint of labour, the consequences of which the Company is unable to avoid by the exercise of reasonable diligence;

(B) any cause or event which the Company is unable to avoid and the consequences whereof the Company is unable to prevent by the exercise of reasonable diligence.

26 Except under special arrangements previously made in writing the Company accepts no responsibility for departure or arrival dates of goods.

27(A) Subject to clause 2(B) and 11(B) above and sub-clause (D) below the Company's liability howsoever arising and notwithstanding that the cause of loss or damage be unexplained shall not exceed

(i) in the case of claims for loss or damage to goods: (a) the value of any goods lost or damaged or (b) a sum at the rate of two SDR's per kilo of the gross weight of the goods the subject of the said transaction, or (c) 75,000 SDR's in respect of any one transaction whichever shall be the least.

(ii) in the case of all other claims:
(a) the value of the goods the subject of the relevant transaction between the Company and the Customer, or (b) a sum at the rate of two SDR's per kilo of the gross weight of the goods the subject of the said transaction, or (c) 75,000 SDR's in respect of any one transaction whichever shall be the least.

For the purposes of Clause 27(A) the value of the goods shall be their value when they were or should have been shipped. The value of SDR's shall be calculated as at the date when the claim is received by the Company in writing.

(B) Subject to Clause 2(B) above, and Sub-Clause (D) below, the Company's liability for loss or damage as a result of failure to deliver or arrange delivery of goods in a reasonable time or where there is a special arrangement under Clause 26) to adhere to agreed departure or arrival dates shall not in any circumstances whatever exceed a sum equal to twice the amount of the Company's charges in respect of the relevant transaction.

(C) Save in respect of such loss or damage as is referred to at Sub-Clause (B) and subject to Clause 2(B) above and Sub-Clause (D) below, the Company shall not in any circumstances whatsoever be liable for indirect or consequential loss such as (but not limited to) loss of profit, loss of market or the consequences of delay or deviation however caused.

By special arrangement agreed in writing, the Company may accept liability in excess of the limits set out in Sub-Clauses (A) to (C) above upon the Customer agreeing to pay the Company's additional charges for accepting such increased liability. Details of the Company's additional charges will be provided upon request.

28(A) Any claim by the Customer against the Company arising in respect of any service provided for the Customer or which the Company has undertaken to provide shall be made in writing and notified to the Company within 14 days of the date upon which the Customer became or should have become aware of any event or occurrence alleged to give rise to such claim and any claim not made and notified as aforesaid shall be deemed to be waived and absolutely barred except where the Customer can show that it was impossible for him to comply with this Time Limit and that he has made the claim as soon as it was reasonably possible for him to do so.

(B) Notwithstanding the provisions of Sub-Paragraph (A) above the Company shall in any event be discharged of all liability whatsoever howsoever arising in respect of any service provided for the Customer or which the Company has undertaken to provide unless suit be brought and written notice thereof given to the Company within nine months from the date of the event or occurrence alleged to give rise to a cause of action against the Company.

JURISDICTION AND LAW

29 These Conditions and any act or contract to which they apply shall be governed by English Law and any dispute arising out of any act or contract to which these Conditions apply shall be subject to the exclusive jurisdiction of the English Courts.

(x) Time of dispatch of documents

Since one of the main functions of shipping documents is to enable the buyer to deal in the goods while they are afloat, he will naturally expect to receive them before the goods arrive at the port of destination. But the increased speed of modern vessels, coupled with delays in the processing of documents, not infrequently results in the documents arriving after the goods. Inconvenient though this may be from the buyer's viewpoint, it does not necessarily give him a right of action against the seller, for the latter is not an insurer so far as arrival of the documents is concerned; his duty is merely to forward the documents with reasonable dispatch,[126] and in so far as delays are outside his control he is not responsible for them.

Where the documents arrive late through the seller's default, the buyer is entitled to damages for any loss resulting from the delay. One of the advantages that the buyer may lose as the result of late arrival of the documents is the ability to sub-sell the goods while afloat and thus pass on to the sub-buyer the risk of loss or damage in transit, leaving the sub-buyer to claim over against the carrier or insurer. Thus if the goods arrive damaged through some neglect on the part of the carrier and before the documents themselves, so that the buyer has to sub-sell the goods on the basis of physical delivery and not on the basis of delivery of documents, and is accordingly faced with rejection of the goods by his sub-purchaser, there seems no reason why the buyer should not be able to claim his resulting loss from the seller, even if the goods have been loaded in sound condition. However, there appears to be no authority directly on the point.

9. BREACH OF DUTY TO TENDER DOCUMENTS

As in the case of the goods themselves, the duty to deliver the shipping documents may be broken in one of three ways: by failure to tender at all; by tender of nonconforming documents; and by a late tender. The buyer's remedies will depend, first, on which form the breach takes, secondly, the manner in which the buyer exercises his option (if he has one) to accept or reject the tender, and thirdly, the manner in which he deals with the tender of the goods if and when they arrive. The question of a late tender has already been referred to. The remaining matters are discussed in chapter 34.

126 *Sanders Bros v Maclean & Co* (1883) 11 QBD 327.

33 The Vienna Convention on International Sales[1]

The harmonization of national laws may be effected, or encouraged, in various ways: by a convention or uniform law which is binding on contracting states, subject to reservation and denunciation; by an EC directive, binding on member states, as to the result to be achieved;[2] or by a model law, which states are free to adopt, with such variations as they choose. A uniform law regulating contracts may be designed to cover both internal and international transactions or it may be confined to the latter. Its rules may be mandatory, that is, applicable irrespective of the agreement between the parties, or permissive, becoming operative only to the extent consistent with the expressed intention of the parties. Where the harmonization of the substantive laws of contracting states in the field of law would be too complex, the convention may instead lay down a set of conflict of laws rules. A convention embodying uniform rules of substantive law is designed to obviate the necessity of referring to national law and, as a consequence, the need to invoke conflict of laws rules. A conflict of laws convention, though not providing a substantive rule itself, prescribes the state whose law is to apply to a given problem and thereby relieves the forum of the task of applying its own conflict of laws rules. Sometimes the two types of harmonization are embodied in one convention, so that in a convention which for the most part lays down uniform rules of substantive law, certain issues upon which the contracting states cannot agree a solution are instead referred to a designated state law by a conflicts rule.

The 1955 Hague Convention governing international sales transactions was a conflicts convention.[3] In 1964 substantive uniform rules were agreed in the shape of

---

1 There is now a massive volume of literature on the convention. See generally Peter Schlechtriem, *Commentary on the Convention on the International Sale of Goods* (2nd edn, in translation, 1998); Michael Bridge, *The International Sale of Goods: Law and Practice* (1999); John Honnold, *Uniform Law for International Sales* (3rd edn, 1999); C. M. Bianca and M. J. Bonell, *Commentary on the International Sales Law* (1987); Franco Ferrari (ed), *The 1980 Uniform Sales Law: Old Issues Revisited in the Light of Recent Experience* (2003); Franco Ferrari, Harry Flechtner and Ronald Brand (eds), *The Draft UNCITRAL Digest and Beyond* (2003); Barry Nicholas, 'The Vienna Convention on International Sales Law' (1989) 105 LQR 201. For details of decisions and articles on the Convention, see the Unilex database edited by Professor M. J Bonell and others and the UNCITRAL database, Case Law on UNCITRAL Texts (CLOUT). There are numerous other web sites containing details of cases on CISG, of which the more prominent is that developed by the Institute of International Commercial Law of the Pace University Law School.

2 EEC Treaty, art 189(3).

3 Convention on the Law Applicable to International Sales of Movable Corporeal Objects. This is prospectively replaced by the 1986 Hague Convention on the Law Applicable to Contracts for the International Sale of Goods, which has not, however, been brought into force.

the Uniform Law on the International Sales of Goods (ULIS), with a separate Uniform Law on the Formation of Contracts for the International Sale of Goods (ULFIS). ULIS, adopted by a number of states,[4] was essentially suppletory in character, the parties being free to exclude its application, wholly or in part.[5] Though a major step towards the unification of international sales law, ULIS suffered serious deficiencies which limited its utility,[6] and substantial changes were made by its successor, the United Nations Convention on Contracts for the International Sale of Goods (CISG) concluded at Vienna in 1980. It is CISG which is referred to hereafter unless otherwise indicated. The convention came into force on 1 January 1988 and has been ratified by 65 states.[7] Unhappily, the United Kingdom is not one of them. The reluctance of the United Kingdom to ratify the convention despite the overwhelming advantages of doing so reflects this country's penchant for making major contributions to the work of harmonization and then walking away from the finished product without any adequate explanation.[8] In the case of CISG the United Kingdom's refusal to adopt the convention appears to be based on a naive belief in the superiority of a Sale of Goods Act which has remained largely unchanged for over 100 years, coupled with a failure to appreciate that for every international sales contract governed by English law there will be another one governed by a foreign law with which the English party may not be familiar and which may be in a language he does not understand. Moreover, the convention is essentially gap-filling in character, since the parties are almost entirely free to vary or exclude its provisions,[9] so that English parties who favour English domestic law can so provide in their contracts. A further consequence of our non-participation is that English courts are largely[10] deprived of the opportunity to contribute to the jurisprudence of the convention.

The convention incorporates rules as to formation of international contracts of sale which have previously been the subject of ULFIS. A protocol of the same date makes certain amendments to the 1974 Vienna Convention on the Limitation Period in the International Sale of Goods.

---

4 Including the United Kingdom, but only where the parties have chosen to adopt it (Uniform Law on International Sales Act 1967, s 1(3)). Since they could have incorporated the ULIS rules anyway without legislation, the Act represents a purely political gesture.

5 Article 3.

6 In particular, (a) it allowed contracting states to restrict the Uniform Laws to contracts in which it was selected by the parties (a provision of which the United Kingdom took advantage – see n 4); (b) its attempt to exclude conflict of laws rules, and to impose itself on international transactions not involving contracting states, was overambitious; (c) its definition of fundamental breach (based not on detriment actually caused by the breach but on whether the reasonable man would have entered into the contract had he foreseen the breach and its effects) was unpopular in that it generated too much uncertainty to satisfy commercial requirements; (d) the provision for ipso facto avoidance (see n 00) was highly inconvenient.

7 As at 19 April 2004.

8 However, the Department of Trade and Industry is again considering the enactment of the convention.

9 Indeed, the convention is regularly excluded in contracts for the sale of commodities, for which it is considered less suitable than for manufactured goods. See below.

10 Not entirely, for an English court may find itself applying the convention as part of the law of a contracting state applicable under English conflict of laws rules. So far this has not happened.

CISG has become a reference point for subsequent international commercial law instruments, including the UNIDROIT Principles of International Commercial Contracts and the Principles of European Contract Law prepared by the Commission on European Contract Law, which can, in turn, be used to supplement some of the less detailed rules in CISG, for example, art 78 on the entitlement to interest.

The purpose of the present chapter is not to give a detailed analysis of CISG but rather to show the sphere of its application, the approach to its interpretation, the general principles underlying it, and the more significant differences between its provisions and those of the English Sale of Goods Act.

It will be apparent that, though a substantial improvement on ULIS, CISG possesses a number of ambiguities, inconsistencies and other shortcomings. This is inevitable in any convention in a major field of law involving a number of contracting states. Criticism of the text should not necessarily be taken to imply criticism of the draftsmen. The convention seeks to maintain a delicate balance between the contrasting attitudes and concepts of the civil law and of the common law, and very often rules have to be blurred or omitted altogether in order to produce an acceptable compromise. CISG, like its predecessor, should be read with this in mind.[11] That said, it is undoubtedly the case that the very restricted view of fundamental breach in art 25, coupled with the vagueness of its provisions, is widely considered to make the convention unsuitable for use in documentary sales, where the doctrine of strict compliance – particularly in relation to letters of credit – holds sway, or in the sale of commodities, which typically involve rapidly fluctuating markets, long chains of parties and potential exposure to huge amounts of damages, all of which necessitate a high degree of legal predictability.[12]

I. SPHERE OF APPLICATION OF CISG

(i) CISG rules on sphere of application

Under art 1(1) of CISG three distinct criteria must be satisfied before the convention can apply. These relate to the nature and subject matter of the contract, the internationality of the contract and the connection with one or more contracting states. First, the contract must be a contract for the sale of goods.[13] Contracts for the

---

11 CISG provides a good example of the way in which the focal point of interest in legislation or a convention is often quite different from what was expected. Who could have foreseen that of all the articles in CISG that which has attracted the most litigation is also one of the shortest, art 78, dealing with interest?

12 See Michael Bridge, 'Uniformity and Diversity in the Law of International Sale' 15 Pace Int Law Rev 55, 69 (Spring 2003); F. M. B. Reynolds, 'Some Reservations About CISG' in *New Trends in International Trade Law* (eds G. Ajani and G. Porro, 2000) 287; and to similar effect, Koji Takahashi, 'Right to Terminate (Avoid) International Sales of Commodities' [2003] JBL 102 at pp 103–104.

13 The Koblenz Oberlandesgericht has held that CISG does not apply to a distribution agreement but it does apply to each separate contract of sale concluded under the agreement (Case No 2 U 1230/91 [1995] Unilex D 93–21). For the problems involved in applying the convention to futures contracts, see Simon Fisher and Michael Hains, 'Futures market law and the Vienna Sales Convention' [1993] LMCLQ 531.

supply of goods to be manufactured or produced are to be considered sales unless the party ordering the goods undertakes to supply a substantial part of the materials, or a preponderant part of the obligations of the party furnishing the goods is the supply of labour and other services.[14] Secondly, the parties to the contract must have their places of business in different states.[15] Thirdly, CISG applies only when (a) both those states are contracting states, or (b) the rules of private international law lead to the application of the law of a contracting state.[16]

The new art 1 is much simpler than the old. It is no longer necessary to show an additional international element (intended movement of goods from one state to the other, or acts constituting offer and acceptance in different states etc), while on the other hand there must be some point of contact with a *contracting* state. So if S, whose place of business is in England, contracts to sell goods to B, with a place of business in Ruritania, CISG will apply if both the United Kingdom and Ruritania are contracting states or if the law applicable to the contract is that of a contracting state. The location or intended place of delivery of the goods is irrelevant. It is also not open to a contracting state (as it was under ULIS) to limit the application of the convention to cases where the parties incorporate it in their contract. So far as the United Kingdom is concerned this means that, when the convention has been implemented by legislation, it will apply except so far as excluded by the parties. In cases within art 1(1)(a) the courts of a contracting state must apply CISG even if their conflict of laws rules lead to the application of the law of a non-contracting state, though the position is otherwise if the parties expressly choose the law of a non-contracting state.[17]

The addition of limb (b) of art 1(1) proved controversial, and some states have exercised their right under art 95 to make a declaration that they will not apply it,[18] taking the view that it unduly narrows the sphere of application of their domestic law and, further, that reference to rules of private international law, which vary from state to state, creates uncertainty. But there is no question that art 1(1)(b) has achieved its objective in substantially accelerating the application of CISG, as well as expanding its scope, since the early cases under the convention applied art 1(1)(b) rather than art 1(1)(a), usually because the transaction took place before

---

14 Article 3.

15 If a party has more than one place of business, the place of business for the purpose of the convention is that which has the closest relationship to the contract and its performance, having regard to the circumstances known to or contemplated by the parties at any time before or at the conclusion of the contract (art 10). By art 1(2), the fact that the parties have their places of business in different states is to be disregarded whenever this fact does not appear either from the contract or from any dealings between, or from information disclosed by, the parties at any time before or at the conclusion of the contract.

16 Some courts have concluded that limb (b) of art 1(1) applies only where the parties have not chosen the applicable law expressly, but this cannot be correct, for recognition of party selection of the applicable law is itself a rule (indeed, the primary rule) of private international law relating to contracts. In the case of proceedings in the courts of a member state of the European Community the rules of private international law laid down in the 1980 Rome Convention on the law applicable to contractual obligations will determine the applicable law.

17 See p 919.

18 Namely China, the Czech Republic, Singapore, the Slovak Republic and the United States.

ratification of the convention by the two states. With the substantial number of ratifications now achieved, art 1(1)(a) now commonly applies, reducing the need for reliance on art 1(1)(b).

CISG empowers a contracting state to exclude certain of its provision by declaration.[19] Thus under art 92 a contracting state may declare that it will not be bound by Pt II of the convention (formation of the contract) or by Pt III (sales), and reference has already been made to the power of a contracting state to exclude art 1(1)(b) by a declaration under art 95, discussed below.

(ii) The effect of a declaration under Article 95   S1(1)(b)

The effect of a declaration under art 95 disapplying art 1(1)(b) depends on whether it is made by the forum state or by another state whose law is applicable under the rules of private international law of the forum, and there is much controversy about some aspects. On the assumption that in each case the parties carry on business in different states,[20] the following questions arise:

(a) Where proceedings are brought in a non-reserving contracting state whose rules of private international law lead to the application of the law of a reserving contracting state, should the court apply CISG? The view of the government of the Federal Republic of Germany is that a state which makes such a declaration is not a contracting state for the purpose of art 1(1)(a), so that where the rules of private international law lead to the application of the law of such a state, there is no obligation on Germany to apply the convention, and German legislation commits German courts to this approach, which is also shared by a number of scholars.[21] But whereas art 92 expressly provides that a contracting state making a declaration under that article is not to be considered a contracting state within art 1(1), there is no such provision in art 95, and the better view is that only the courts of the reserving state are bound by that state's declaration, and that the courts of non-reserving contracting states should treat CISG as applicable if their rules of private international law apply to the law of the reserving state, regardless of the latter's reservation.

(b) Where the rules of private international law of the forum state lead to the application of the law of a non-reserving contracting state but the forum state has made a declaration under art 95, should its courts apply CISG? The answer is yes, but they will do so not by virtue of art 1(1)(b) but in pursuance of their own conflict rules, and it is for the court concerned to determine the application of these. However, the position is otherwise if the forum state's conflict rules lead to the application of the *lex fori* itself, for by making its declaration under art 95 the forum state has manifested its policy decision not to apply CISG via a conflict rule.

(c) Where proceedings are brought in a non-contracting state whose rules of private international law lead to the application of the law of a contracting

---

19 The declaration is in substance a reservation.
20 A condition which has to be satisfied whether art 1(1)(a) or art 1(1)(b) applies.
21 See, for example, Honnold, *Uniform Law for International Sales*, para 47.5.

state, should CISG be applied? Where the law referred to is that of a non-reserving state, the court will apply CISG, but, again, under its own conflict rules, not under art 1(1)(b). Where the law referred to is that of a reserving state, the better view is that CISG should be applied, for the same reason as in (a) above.[22]

(iii) Other bases of application

The provisions of CISG as to the sphere of its application are exhaustive only so far as the convention rules are relied on as treaty provisions. There are at least three other ways in which courts and arbitral tribunals have succeeded in holding the convention rules applicable despite the absence of the necessary link with a contracting state.[23]

1.   Contractual incorporation

It is open to the parties to incorporate CISG provisions by reference in their contract. In the United Kingdom the sole effect of such incorporation is that the convention rules are applied as if they had been set out as terms of the contract. Accordingly, an English court would have no duty to apply the convention as such, but would do so only to the extent that it would apply any other terms of the contract.

2.   Trade usage

In an arbitration under the Rules of Conciliation and Arbitration of the International Chamber of Commerce the arbitral tribunal, relying on what is now art 13(5) of the ICC Rules, which requires account to be taken of relevant trade usages, held that there was no better source for determining those usages than CISG.[24] That is itself a large assumption, but even if it were justified, it is harder to support the application of CISG in a case where neither the country of the seller nor that of the buyer was a contracting state, the contract had been made before CISG had even been concluded and the tribunal applied its provisions in the teeth of the law which it had determined was applicable but considered unreasonable. A potentially more fruitful source for identifying trade usage is the ICC's Incoterms 2000, which could be resorted to as evidence of usage even where, under national law, they would not have been considered incorporated into the contract.

---

22 See Franco Ferrari, 'The CISG's sphere of application: Articles 1–3 and 10' in *The Draft UNCITRAL Digest and Beyond*, 53.

23 See further Louis F. Del Duca and Patrick Del Duca, 'Practice under the Convention on International Sale of Goods (CISG): A Primer for Attorneys and International Traders' 27 UCC LJ 331, 343–344 (1995).

24 ICC Case No 5713/1989, summarized in (1990) XV Yearbook of Commercial Arbitration 70 and [1989] Unilex D 89–1, and discussed Roy Goode, 'Usage and its Reception in Transnational Commercial Law' (1997) 46 ICLQ 1 at pp 20 ff, 29.

3. *Lex mercatoria*

There is a body of opinion which holds that there exists a corpus of uncodified international trade law and usage, the *lex mercatoria*, which subsists independently of any national legal system. In line with this view the Iran–United States Claims Tribunal applied CISG rules as part of the *lex mercatoria*.[25] English law does not, it is thought, subscribe to this concept of *lex mercatoria*, but would, of course, be free to apply any trade usage by reference to which the parties expressly or impliedly contracted and to look to the convention for best evidence of such usage where appropriate.

(iv) Transactions excluded by CISG

The convention does not apply to consumer sales[26] or· sales by auction or under execution, nor to sales of securities, negotiable instruments or money, ships, vessels, hovercraft or aircraft[27] or electricity.[28] It also does not apply to the liability of the seller for death or personal injury caused by the goods to any person.[29]

(v) Exclusion or variation by the parties

The parties may exclude the application of CISG or, subject to art 12,[30] derogate from or vary the effect of any of its provisions.[31] Exclusion of the convention may be express or implied. Choice of the law of a contracting state is not an implied exclusion (since CISG is part of the law of the selected state) unless the parties have shown an intention to apply the domestic sales law of the state concerned or otherwise to exclude CISG.[32] By contrast selection of the law of a non-contracting state is an implied exclusion of CISG, though this would not be so where the parties have made no choice of law and it is only through the conflict rules of the forum that the law of the non-contracting state is applicable.[33] There will also be an implied exclusion where the parties have entered into a contract the provisions of which are so detailed

---

25 *Watkins-Johnson Co and Watkins-Johnson Ltd v Islamic Republic of Iran* (1990) XV Yearbook of Commercial Arbitration 220.

26 More precisely, sales 'of goods bought for personal, family or household use, unless the seller, at any time before or at the conclusion of the contract, neither knew nor ought to have known that the goods were bought for any such use' (art 2).

27 However, the Hungarian Supreme Court has held that although the convention does not apply to the sale of aircraft, it does apply to the sale of individual components of an aircraft (*MALEV Hungarian Airlines v United Technologies International Inc* (1993) 13 Journal of Law and Commerce 1, [1992] Unilex D 92–20).

28 Article 2.

29 An exclusion designed to avoid conflict with any applicable products liability convention.

30 Which preserves the power of a contracting state, by declaration under art 96, to preserve its legislative requirements as to writing. Although this is the only provision expressed to be of a mandatory nature, art 28 is also mandatory. See Schlechtriem, *International Sale of Goods*, p 208.

31 Article 6.

32 This is disputed by some authorities but is supported by Ferrari, *The Draft UNCITRAL Digest*, pp 124 ff and decisions there cited.

33 It will be recalled that the courts of a contracting state must apply the convention where art 1(1)(a) is satisfied even if the governing law is that of a non-contracting state.

and wide-ranging that either the CISG rules cannot sensibly be applied or the provisions indicate an intention to rely on purely domestic law or other non-CISG rules. In all cases where CISG is excluded, the law to be applied under the conflict rules of the forum is the domestic law of the state referred to excluding CISG.

(vi) Ambit of CISG

The convention governs only the formation of the contract and the rights and obligations of the seller arising from it. CISG is not concerned with the validity of the contract or any of its provisions or of any usage, nor with the effect the contract may have on the property in the goods sold.[34] In other words, the rules as to formation are devoted exclusively to questions of offer and acceptance, extrinsic grounds of invalidity (mistake, fraud etc) being a matter for the applicable law under conflict of laws rules;[35] and it is only the personal rights of seller and buyer *inter se* that are regulated. The convention is not concerned with the proprietary effects of the contract, nor with title conflicts between seller or buyer and a third party. Add to this the fact that CISG, like its predecessor, has nothing to say about f.o.b., c.i.f. and combined transport transactions, and it will be apparent that the scope of the convention remains limited. Since the parties are free to exclude or vary its provisions, and the seller will usually want to impose his own standard terms, the provisions of the convention are likely in practice to be confined to cases where the parties either omit to exclude it through inadvertence or choose to allow it to govern the contract because they are unable to agree on any national law as the governing law.

The convention does not purport to be a comprehensive code. Gaps in its provisions are to be filled in the first instance by reference to the general principles on which it is based. [36] Only in the absence of such general principles may resort be made to the law applicable by virtue of the rules of private international law.[37]

(vii) Interpretation of CISG

Article 7(1) is of some significance in view of the absence of any general requirement of good faith in English law as regards the exercise of legal rights and remedies:

> In the interpretation of this Convention, regard is to be had to its international character and to the need to promote uniformity in its application and the observance of good faith in international trade.

This is an exhortation to national courts to beware of rigidity in interpreting the provisions, since rules of interpretation suitable for internal contracts are not necessarily appropriate for transactions of an international character. In particular, especial care has to be taken not to assume that words or phrases in the convention

---

34 Article 4. Accordingly, the Koblenz Oberlandesgericht has held that the convention does not apply to the validity of a retention of title clause (Case No 5 U 534/91, [1992] Unilex D 92–4).

35 See pp 1089 ff.

36 Article 7(2).

37 Ibid.

which are terms of art in a given national legal system bear the same meaning as they do under the national law; instead, the provisions of CISG should be given an autonomous interpretation, a process assisted by the sound practice of reviewing decisions on the convention in other jurisdictions so far as these are available, a practice mandated by the need to have regard to uniformity in the application of the convention.[38]

There has been much debate about the role of good faith in CISG. On one view, and that likely to be adopted by English courts, neither art 7(1) nor the other provisions of CISG impose a general duty of good faith on parties to a contract of sale governed by the convention, and art 7(1) means exactly what it says, namely that regard must be had to the observance of good faith in the *interpretation* of the convention. But even on this view it is not easy to determine the effect of art 7(1). The underlying idea seems to be that the convention rules are intended to be used, not abused, and must be read down accordingly. Quite apart from the difficulty of disentangling interpretation from substance, the problem is to know what constitutes an abuse. For example, where CISG provides a default remedy, is the provision to be interpreted as inapplicable where the innocent party has suffered no loss and is simply seeking to escape from what has become a bad bargain through a fall or rise in the market?[39] Others consider that CISG embodies a general duty of good faith, which is to be applied in accordance with art 7(2). However, there is no common understanding of the meaning and content of good faith, and this militates against a uniform interpretation of the convention in relation to good faith. All we can do is to search for a common core, such as the avoidance of behaviour which to right-thinking members of the commercial community would be considered either dishonest or unethical, contravening generally accepted standards of fair dealing.

(viii) Gap-filling

Article 7(2) embodies what has become a standard provision in international private law conventions:

> Questions concerning matters governed by this Convention which are not expressly settled in it are to be settled in conformity with the general principles upon which it is based or, in the absence of such principles, in conformity with the law applicable by virtue of the rules of private international law.

The first point to note is that art 7(2) comes into play only where the matter in issue falls within the scope of the convention. In some cases that question is readily determined. For example, an issue concerning the transfer of property is not merely not dealt with by the convention, it is outside its scope altogether. But it may

---

38 The CISG Advisory Council (CISG-AC), consisting of leading international experts supported by the Centre for Commercial Law Studies, Queen Mary, University of London, and Pace Law School Institute of International Commercial Law, was established to issue advisory opinions of the interpretation of CISG provisions. Opinion No 1, *Electronic Communications under CISG*, prepared in response to an informal invitation by the International Chamber of Commerce, was issued on 15 August 2003, and Opinion No 2, on C156, arts 38 and 39 was issued on 7 June 2004.

39 See the example given by Michael Bridge, ''A Commentary on Articles 1–13 and 78', in *The Draft UNCITRAL Digest and Beyond* at p 251.

sometimes be difficult to know at what point the line is crossed between an unsettled matter governed by CISG and one that is outside it. Secondly, where art 7(2) does apply the matter in question is to be settled in conformity with the general principles of the convention, so far as these can be identified. This generally requires that the asserted principle be common to several provisions, though there is at least one exception to this in that art 6 suffices by itself to establish the principle of party autonomy. Principles common to a number of provisions include estoppel,[40] a duty to act reasonably,[41] and strict liability in the performance of the seller's obligations.[42] Only where there is no relevant general principle is there to be recourse to the applicable law as determined by the rules of private international law of the forum, a last resort which is to be avoided wherever possible because it substitutes a conflict rule for a uniform substantive law rule to be extracted from the convention.

2.   FORMATION OF THE CONTRACT

Under art 11 a contract of sale need not be concluded in or evidenced by writing and it is not subject to any other requirements as to form. It may be proved by any means, including witnesses. So, as under English law, a contract made on the telephone or by electronic communication is fully enforceable so long as it can be proved. But this is subject to the right of a contracting state to make a declaration under art 96 excluding art 11 where its law requires contracts of sale to be concluded in or evidenced by writing and any party has a place of business in that state.

USSR & Eastern bloc countries

The rules as to offer and acceptance follow the civil law rather than the common law, and in many respects are much more closely attuned to commercial requirements. An acceptance does not become effective until it reaches the offeror,[43] and may be withdrawn if the withdrawal reaches the offeror before or at the same time as the acceptance would have become effective.[44] So *mere* dispatch of an acceptance does not bind the offeree; on the other hand, it suffices to prevent the offeror from subsequently revoking his offer.[45] Revocation is also excluded where the offeror indicates (whether by stating a time for acceptance or otherwise) that it is irrevocable[46] or where it was reasonable for the offeree to rely on the offer as being irrevocable and he has acted in reliance on the offer.[47] A purported

---

40 See, for example, arts 35(3), 40, 43(2), 68.

41 See, for example, arts 25, 34, 37, 49.

42 See, for example, arts 35, 36, 44. For other, more specific, illustrations, see Schlechtriem, *International Sale of Goods*, p 67.

43 Article 18(2). The acceptance 'reaches' the offeror when it is made orally to him or delivered by any other means to him personally, to his place of business or mailing address or, if he does not have a place of business or mailing address, to his habitual residence (art 24). But where acceptance by conduct is permitted by the terms of the offer or by course of dealing or usage, acceptance becomes effective when the stipulated act is performed, if within the time fixed or, where none, within a reasonable time (art 18(3)).

44 Article 22.

45 Article 16(1).

46 Article 16(2)(a).

47 Article 16(2)(b).

acceptance containing additions, limitations or other modifications is a rejection of the offer and constitutes a counter-offer.[48] But where the additional or different terms do not materially alter the offer, the acceptance is effective on the terms of the offer as added or varied unless the offeror objects to them without undue delay.[49]

3. RIGHTS AND DUTIES OF THE PARTIES

The rights and duties of the parties *inter se* correspond in many respects to those provided by the Sale of Goods Act, though with differences in language and detail. Among the more important comparisons and contrasts between CISG and English law are the following.

(i) Seller's obligations

As under English law, the two principal duties of the seller are to effect delivery in accordance with the contract terms and to tender goods that conform to the contract. The requirement of conformity embraces, in provisions closely following those of the Sale of Goods Act, the duty to supply goods for their ordinary purposes and for any particular purposes expressly or impliedly made known to the seller,[50] with an additional requirement that the goods be contained or packaged in the manner usual for such goods.[51]

(ii) 'Breach' and 'fundamental breach'

fundamental breach = sub standard deprivation

Certain remedies for failure in performance are given only where the failure constitutes a 'fundamental breach'. The word 'breach' is not defined, but it is apparent from art 79 that it denotes any failure to perform, whether or not excused, and is not limited to breach of contract in the English law sense of an unexcused failure in performance.[52] 'Fundamental breach' is defined by art 25 as a breach which 'results in such detriment to the other party as substantially to deprive him of what he is entitled to expect under the contract, unless the party in breach did not foresee and a reasonable person of the same kind in the same circumstances would not have foreseen such a result'.[53] The application of a foreseeability test to determine whether a breach is fundamental is novel to English lawyers and may produce some problems. Equally, the 'substantial deprivation' requirement, though now coming into vogue in contracts where the law has not previously classified the terms as conditions and warranties, does not find a place in English law as regards a breach of one of the statutory implied conditions in a contract of sale. The rule here

---

48 Article 19(1).
49 Article 19(2). However, the impact of this article in preserving the efficacy of qualified acceptances is limited, since additional or different terms relating, among other things, to the price, payment, quality and quantity of the goods, place and time of delivery, extent of one party's liability to the other or the settlement of disputes are considered to alter the terms of the offer materially (art 19(3)).
50 Article 35(2).
51 Article 35(2)(d).
52 See p 927.
53 Expectation and foreseeability are to be determined as at the date of conclusion of the agreement, not as at the date of breach.

is that any breach, however small, can be treated as fundamental in the sense of allowing the buyer to regard the contract as repudiated The CISG definition looks to the consequences of the breach rather than the nature of the term broken.

Remedies not exercisable except where the breach is fundamental are:

(a)   the buyer's right to require substitute goods in replacement of nonconforming goods;[54]

(b)   the right of one party to avoid the contract[55] for non-performance by the other;[56]

(c)   the buyer's right to avoid the contract for partial delivery.[57]

(iii) Rejection or avoidance by the buyer

As under English law, rejection is not synonymous with avoidance of the contract. Avoidance for nonconformity is permitted only where the breach is fundamental,[58] whereas the buyer may reject the goods and ask for the nonconformity to be remedied by repair,[59] whether or not the breach is fundamental, unless this request is unreasonable in the circumstances.[60] Another option open to the rejecting buyer, though only if the nonconformity is a fundamental breach, is to require the delivery of substitute goods.[61]

The buyer's right to avoid the contract is given in two cases: where the seller's breach is fundamental and where the buyer has fixed an additional time for delivery which the seller has failed to observe or has declared he will not observe.[62] This last corresponds to the English contract law entitling a party to give notice making time of the essence. A frequently invoked basis for avoidance is the tender of

---

54 Article 46(2).

55 'Avoid' appears to denote rescission ab initio, followed by restitution on both sides but without prejudice to a right to damages (art 81). Under art 36(1) of ULIS, the contract is ipso facto avoided for non-delivery amounting to fundamental breach unless the buyer informs the seller within a reasonable time of his decision to perform. This provision has proved most troublesome (see Jan Hellner, 'Ipso Facto Avoidance', in Jan Hellner (ed), *Julskrift* (1980), p 73) and has been abandoned in the CISG.

56 Articles 49(1)(a), 64(1)(a), 73. But in the case of non-delivery, non-payment or failure to take delivery, the innocent party may also exercise this right if the other does not perform within an additional period of reasonable notice fixed by the innocent party under arts 47 or 63 (arts 49(1)(b), 64(1)(b)). It has been held by the Frankfurt am Main Oberlandesgericht that the buyer need not give express notice; it suffices that he does so by implication, as by giving the seller notice to discontinue the relationship (Case No 5 U 164/90, (1993) Journal of Law and Commerce 261, [1991] Unilex D 91–10).

57 Article 51.

58 Article 49(1)(a). English law regards any breach of condition as fundamental, but for the purpose of CISG the definition of 'fundamental breach' in art 25 (p 932) is to be applied and the test of 'substantial deprivation' would clearly produce a different result if applied, eg, to the facts of *Arcos Ltd v. E. A. Ronaasen & Son* [1933] AC 470. Even a fundamental breach may not entitle the buyer to avoid the contract if he is unable to give restitution of goods he has received substantially in the condition in which he received them (art 82(1)).

59 Article 46(3).

60 Ibid. The request must be made either in conjunction with notice given under art 39 or within a reasonable time thereafter.

61 Article 46(2).

62 Article 49(1).

nonconforming goods, and here the case law indicates a greater reluctance under CISG than under English law to allow the buyer to treat the tender of nonconforming goods as repudiatory, the general approach being that the breach is not fundamental if the goods are capable of use, resale or repair. On the other hand, instead of the rather stringent conditions laid down by s 35 of the Sale of Goods Act,[63] art 39(1) of CISG adopts an approach more consistent with general principles of contract law, stating that the buyer loses his right to reject the goods for nonconformity with the contract if he does not give notice to the seller specifying the lack of conformity within a reasonable time after he has discovered it or ought to have discovered it.[64] In a number of cases the buyer has been held to have lost the right to reject because of failure to give notice within a reasonable time and has been ordered to pay the price of the goods. An outside time-limit of two years from physical delivery is also prescribed. [65] Moreover, art 39(1) must be read in the light of the obligation imposed on the buyer to examine the goods, or cause them to be examined, within as short a period as is practicable in the circumstances.[66]

(iv) Buyer's remedies on acceptance of nonconforming goods

If the buyer does not have, or loses or chooses not to exercise, a right to reject, he may instead claim a reduction in the price and/or damages. The price-reduction remedy,[67] which is exercisable either by withholding the sum to be deducted or by recovering it if the price has already been paid, is calculated by adjusting the price in the same proportion as the value of the goods at the time of delivery bears to the value they would have had at that time if they had conformed to the contract.[68]

(v) Seller's right to cure

The seller is given the right to cure a defective or incomplete delivery of documents or goods up to the due delivery date,[69] and even thereafter if he can do so without

---

63 See pp 348 ff.

64 Article 39(1). By art 39(2) the buyer must specify the nature of the defect in his notice of lack of conformity, and the Munich Landgericht has consistently held that his failure to do so extinguishes his right to reject under art 39(1) (Case No 10 HKO 2375/94; 17 HKO 3726/89). For a detailed discussion of the notice requirements, see S. A. Kruisinga, *(Non-) conformity in the 1980 UN Convention on Contracts for the International Sale of Goods: a uniform concept* (2004), ch III, and the CISG AC Opinion No 2 *Examination of the Goods and Notice of Non-Conformity Articles 38 and 39.*

65 Article 39(2).

66 Article 38(1).

67 A well-known remedy in civil law systems and distinguished from damages by (inter alia) the fact that whereas damages are usually given only against a party who is at fault, price reduction for nonconformity is allowed irrespective of fault. The distinction is less significant in CISG, which adopts the common law approach that damages do not depend on fault. The remedy of price reduction is given by the Sale of Goods Act in relation to short delivery (s 30(1)) but not as regards nonconformity with description or lack of satisfactory quality of goods which the buyer chooses to accept, where his claim is in damages for breach of warranty, which can be set up in diminution or extinction of the price (s 53(1)(a)).

68 Article 50.

69 Articles 34, 37 (but only if the exercise of the right does not cause the buyer unreasonable inconvenience or unreasonable expense, and without prejudice to the buyer's right to damages).

unreasonable delay and without causing the buyer unreasonable inconvenience or uncertainty of reimbursement by the seller of expenses advanced by the buyer.[70] However, the right to cure is lost once the buyer has exercised a right to avoid the contract.[71]

(vi) Anticipatory breach

A party may suspend the performance of his obligations if, after the conclusion of the contract, it becomes apparent that the other party will not perform a substantial part of his obligations as a result of (a) a serious deficiency in his ability to perform or in his creditworthiness, or (b) his conduct in preparing to perform or in performing the contract.[72] A reputiatory breach by a party before the due date for performance entitles the other to avoid the contract.[73]

(vii) Measure of damages

CISG, though providing a current-price rule for assessing damages, avoids the rigidity (or, if you prefer, the certainty) of the English market-price rule by stipulating that where the innocent party deals with the breach by making a substitute transaction (as where on non-delivery a buyer purchases other goods and on non-acceptance the seller resells to another buyer), the actual loss on the substitute transaction replaces the current price loss as the basis of damages. So (assuming that in either case the seller or the buyer acted reasonably) the damages will, in the case of a claimant seller, be the excess of the original contract price over the resale price and, if the claimant is the buyer, the excess of the purchase price of the substitute goods over the original contract price.

(viii) Risk

This is linked not to property but to control. If the contract involves the carriage of goods and the seller is not bound to hand them over to the carrier at a particular place, risk passes to the buyer when the goods are handed over[74] to the first carrier for transmission to the buyer. If a place is fixed for delivery to the carrier, risk passes when the goods are handed over to the carrier at that place.[75] The risk of goods sold in transit passes on the conclusion of the contract.[76] In other cases risk passes to the buyer when he takes over the goods or, if he does not do so in due time, from the time when they are placed at his disposal and he commits a breach of contract by failing to take delivery.[77] As in English law, difficult questions arise

---

70 Article 48. Again, this is without prejudice to the buyer's right to damages.
71 Since the right to cure under art 48(1) is expressly made subject to art 49, which provides the grounds of avoidance by the buyer.
72 Article 71(1).
73 Article 72(1).
74 This means delivery in the physical, not the legal, sense (P. M. Roth, 'The Passing of Risk', 27 Am J Comp L 291 at p 296).
75 Article 67.
76 Article 68.
77 Article 69.

where at the time of loss or damage the goods did not conform to the contract. In that situation, the incidence of risk appears to depend on whether the buyer exercises a right given to him to avoid the contract,[78] in which case the risk is transferred back to the seller. But art 70 makes it clear that the passing of risk does not affect the buyer's remedies for fundamental breach.

(ix) Force majeure

Under art 79(1) a party is not liable in damages for a failure to perform any of his obligations if he proves that the failure was due to an impediment beyond his control and that he could not reasonably be expected to have taken the impediment into account at the time of the conclusion of the contract or to have avoided or overcome it or its consequences.[79] As under English law, the fact that the event was reasonably foreseeable is not necessarily a bar to the application of art 79. Most events can be foreseen as taking place at some time, but not necessarily during the life of the contract, and, moreover, their impact on the contract may not have been foreseeable. In any event, the circumstances may be such that the party concerned could not reasonably have been expected to take the impediment into account even if it was foreseeable. 'Impediment' is wide enough to cover both physical impediment and supervening legal impediment, but not initial illegality, which goes to the validity of the contract and is therefore outside the scope of the convention.[80] Nothing in art 79 prevents either party from exercising any right other than to claim damages under the convention.[81] So where the impediment results in a failure to perform constituting a fundamental breach under art 25, the other party can avoid the contract under art 49(1); and where the impediment results in delay in delivery, the buyer may fix an additional period for delivery of reasonable length under art 49(1) and avoid the contract if the seller does not deliver within the additional period. This represents a markedly different approach from English law, where non-performance due to an impediment, which, under the rules of frustration, relieves a party of any liability in damages, is not a breach of contract at all. It is therefore apparent that 'breach' in the convention covers any failure in performance, whether or not excused under art 79.

Article 79 is more akin to the French law of *force majeure* than to the English law of frustration. The effect of the event of *force majeure* is purely suspensory; once the impediment is removed, the duty to perform is restored [82] Hence the continued availability of the remedy of specific performance even in cases within art 79. Even if the impediment is incapable of removal the contract does not come to an end by force of law, as it would under the English doctrine of frustration; it is for the other

---

78 See Roth, 27 Am J Comp L 291 at 300 ff, contrasting the solutions offered by ULIS and CISG.

79 Article 79 is one of the most difficult and controversial articles in the whole convention. For a discussion see A. H. Hudson, 'Exceptions and Impossibility under the Vienna Convention' in Ewan McKendrick (ed) *Force Majeure and Frustration of Contract* (2nd edn, 1995), ch 14. See also Bianca and Bonell, *International Sales Law*, pp 572–595; Honnold, *Uniform Law for International Sales*, paras 423–435.5; Schlechtriem, *International Sale of Goods*, pp 600–626.

80 Article 4.

81 Article 79(5).

82 Article 79(3).

party to invoke his right to avoid the contract. Moreover, the party prevented from performing must give notice of the impediment and its effect on his ability to perform. If the other party does not receive this within a reasonable time after the non-performing party knew or ought to have known of the impediment, the latter is liable for damages resulting from such non-receipt.[83]

Since art 79 excludes only liability for damages, leaving other rights unimpaired, it is open to the other party to sue for price reduction[84] or for specific performance, which under the convention is a primary remedy and remains available where the impediment was purely temporary and has ceased to exist.

Article 79 may be varied or excluded by agreement of the parties,[85] and many contracts contain *force majeure* clauses in which the parties themselves prescribe the effect of impediments to performance, though it is a question of construction whether in any given case a *force majeure* clause was intended to cover the particular facts so as to displace Article 79 or whether that article is applicable despite the clause.

83 Article 79(4).
84 Article 50.
85 Article 6.

34 Documentary Sales

1. STRICT F.O.B.

The f.o.b. contract has many variants, and though the basic concepts as to delivery, property and risk are common to them all, other incidents of the relationship between the parties are not susceptible to rigid rules but depend very much on the language of the contract and the surrounding circumstances.[1] In the strict f.o.b. contract, the seller's duty is to ensure that goods conforming to the contract are put on board the ship[2] nominated by the buyer at the port of shipment[3] by the date or within the shipment period stipulated in or under the contract, and that the buyer is furnished with such documents as will enable him to obtain possession from the carrier. The buyer for his part must procure space on the vessel and nominate it to the seller in sufficient time to enable the seller to dispatch the goods to the docks and have them put on board[4] the vessel.[5] Though the f.o.b. Incoterm defines 'free on board' as requiring that the goods pass the ship's rail, the statement of the duties of the seller in paragraph A4 sensibly makes no reference to the ship's rail, which for many types of cargo is no longer relevant, and instead requires that the seller deliver the goods 'in the manner customary at the port on board the vessel nominated by the buyer'. This flexible approach, which would almost certainly be adopted by English courts even where the Incoterms were not incorporated into the contract, accommodates all modes of shipment, including Ro-Ro vessels driven up a ramp and the pumping of liquid cargo into the ship's hold.

(i) Identification of the port of shipment

Since the due delivery point is the port of shipment designated in the contract of sale, it is obviously important that the contract be as specific as possible in naming

---

1 See generally *Benjamin's Sale of Goods* (6th edn 2002), ch 20; David M. Sassoon and H.O. Merrens, *C.i.f. and f.o.b. contracts* (4th edn, 1995).

2 English law has so far continued to treat 'f.o.b.' as a shipment term in the literal sense of placement on board a vessel. But there is a growing trend in business to use 'f.o.b.' as a general delivery term capable of being applied to any designated mode of transport. Despite this, Incoterms 2000 wisely retains the f.o.b. label even though delivery on board could be accommodated within the more general FCA term. As to multimodal transport operations, see ch 36.

3 Frequently, the desired delivery point is more precisely specified, identifying the particular dock or wharf at which the ship is to load. The phrase 'port of shipment' should be read in this extended sense throughout.

4 Ie, over the rail. See below.

5 Incoterms 2000 contain a comprehensive statement of the duties of the parties to an f.o.b. contract where they are incorporated into the contract. See p 867.

that port. Where the designation is ambiguous, three alternative situations are possible: that the choice of nomination is the seller's; that the choice lies with the buyer; or that the contract is void for uncertainty.[6] In *Cumming & Co Ltd v Hasell*[7] the High Court of Australia held that where the only evidence as to the delivery term under an alleged contract of sale was a telegram referring to 'f.o.b.' without qualification, the contract was too uncertain to be enforceable. The ground for the decision is not entirely clear. Want of compliance with the Statute of Frauds was certainly mentioned, but the court may also have considered the alleged agreement to be vitiated by uncertainty at common law. Indeed, the evidence as to the existence of a contract was decidedly tenuous. By contrast, in *David T. Boyd & Co Ltd v Louis Louca*,[8] where the phrase 'f.o.b. stowed good Danish port' was used, it was held that in the absence of any express or implied agreement or any custom or other circumstances from which the particular port intended might be inferred, the contract was to be construed as giving the buyer both the option and the duty to nominate the port of shipment, and that since he had failed to do so, he had committed a breach of contract for which the seller was entitled to damages.

The two decisions are not irreconcilable. There are many contracts in which a party is given a measure of choice, and if in the circumstances it is reasonable to infer an intention to give the buyer the right to select one of a limited number of alternative ports, the question of uncertainty does not arise. The matter is otherwise, however, if the stipulation is so vague, and the range of alternatives so wide, that it cannot reasonably be supposed that the matter was to be left to the buyer's choice. The word 'f.o.b.' without qualification clearly comes within this category, for it cannot be imagined that this was intended to allow the buyer to designate any port in the world, and since the 'contract' thus affords no machinery for ascertainment of the delivery point it must fail for uncertainty.[9]

(ii) Nomination of vessel

Given that the contractual port of loading is or has become identified, the first step towards performance of the contract must usually be taken by the buyer.[10] Prima facie it is he who has the option of deciding on what date, within the permitted shipping period, the goods are to be loaded[11] and it is thus for him to procure space on a vessel at the relevant port and to give the appropriate shipping instructions, notifying the seller as to the vessel selected and the place at which and the date on which it will be ready to load, in sufficient time to enable the seller to arrange for the goods to be got down to the docks and loaded. [12] If, contrary to the prima facie rule, the parties agree that it is the seller who is to have the right to decide on the

---

6   See *David T. Boyd & Co Ltd v Louis Louca* [1973] 1 Lloyd's Rep 209 at 211.

7   (1920) 28 CLR 508.

8   See n 6.

9   Cf *Bushwall Properties Ltd v Vortex Properties Ltd* [1976] 2 All ER 283.

10   *J & J Cunningham Ltd v Robert A. Munro & Co Ltd* (1922) 28 Com Cas 42.

11   The position is otherwise in the case of the extended f.o.b. contract. See p 870.

12   *J & J Cunningham Ltd v Robert A. Munro & Co Ltd*, n 10; *Bremer Handelsgesellschaft mbH v J H. Rayner & Co Ltd* [1978] 2 Lloyd's Rep 73.

loading date, within the shipment period, then it is his duty to advise the buyer of the date on which loading is to be expected to take place, and until this information has been communicated to the buyer, his duty to nominate a vessel does not arise.[13]

Time of nomination is usually of the essence, and failure to nominate in due time entitles the seller to treat the contract as repudiated and claim damages.[14] The nomination must not only be made but must be effective, that is, it must be made in sufficient time to enable the goods to be loaded within the shipping period and the nominated vessel must in fact be made available for loading by the seller within that period.[15] It follows that the nomination must be capable of proving effective and must not be one which is manifestly false or wholly artificial.[16] *Texaco Ltd*

Unless the contract otherwise provides,[17] the buyer is entitled to make a substitute nomination if he is able to do so in due time and the substitute vessel proves to be an effective vessel.[18] But the substitute nomination must itself be contractually valid.[19] Moreover, the original nomination remains contractually binding if the substitute nomination proves ineffective; the buyer cannot in that situation treat the original nomination as if it had never been made at all so as to rely on events of frustration or *force majeure*[20] affecting the substitute vessel as discharging him from liability where the substitution was not itself occasioned by an event of frustration or *force majeure*.[21] The ambit and limits of the right to make a substitute nomination are not altogether clear. The typical case is where the vessel originally nominated will not be able to receive the goods by the contractual loading date, because of breakdown, diversion or other cause of delay. But the buyer's right to make a substitute nomination is not restricted to events of frustration or *force majeure* affecting the original nomination; he would seem to be entitled to substitute a new vessel on any ground he chooses, for example, because he has decided to use the original vessel for another contract;[22] and if the initial nomination is invalid, the buyer may cure the

---

13 *Harlow & Jones Ltd v Panex (International) Ltd* [1967] 2 Lloyd's Rep 509.

14 *Bunge Corporation v Tradax Export SA* [1981] 2 All ER 513. But he cannot recover the price as such, for prima facie this is payable only where the property has passed (Sale of Goods Act, s 49(1)), which in an f.o.b. contract is normally when the goods are placed on board (see below). The fact that it is the buyer's breach that has prevented the goods from being loaded and the property passing does not alter the situation (*Colley v Overseas Exporters* [1921] 3 KB 302), for it is a general rule of contract law that the contract price can be recovered only where it has been earned by performance, and if this is obstructed, the innocent party's remedy is in damages (see p 114). The case of *Mackay v Dick* (1881) 6 App Cas 251 is distinguishable in that there the property had passed, the contract being subject to a resolutive condition, not a condition precedent to the vesting of the property in the buyer.

15 *Bunge & Co Ltd v Tradax England Ltd* [1975] 2 Lloyd's Rep 235; *The New Prosper* [1991] 2 Lloyd's Rep 93.

16 *Texaco Ltd v Eurogulf Shipping Ltd* [1987] 2 Lloyd's Rep 541.

17 As it was held to have done by implication in *Cargill U.K. Ltd v Continental U.K. Ltd* [1989] 2 Lloyd's Rep 290.

18 *Agricultores Federados Argentinos Sociedad Cooperativa Limitada v Ampro SA Commerciale Industrielle et Financière* [1965] 2 Lloyd's Rep 157.

19 Ibid.

20 *Force majeure* here denotes events short of frustration which fall within the scope of a *force majeure* clause in the contract discharging or suspending the buyer's duty to nominate.

21 *The Marine Star* [1993] 1 Lloyd's Rep 329.

22 As in *The Marine Star*, ibid.

default by a valid nomination.[23] It would seem that the mere fact that the seller has incurred abortive expenditure in reliance on the first nomination, as by bringing the goods down to the docks in readiness for the intended shipment, will not by itself preclude the buyer from making a substitute nomination or entitle the seller to compensation. A seller who relies on the first nomination knowing that the buyer has a right of substitution acts at his peril. The buyer will normally be estopped from making a substitution only where he has made some representation, express or implied, that he would not exercise his right of substitution and the seller has acted in reliance on that representation.[24]

(iii) Notice enabling buyer to insure

Section 32(3) of the Sale of Goods Act, requiring a seller who sends goods by sea to give such notice to the buyer as may enable him to insure them during their sea transit,[25] has rather surprisingly, been held to apply even to a strict f.o.b. contract, despite the fact that since it is the buyer's responsibility to fix the loading date and furnish the vessel, he ought normally to possess all the information necessary to enable him to arrange insurance.[26] In holding s 32(3) applicable to f.o.b. contracts, the Court of Appeal obviously felt unable to escape from the language of the section. However, the court effectively minimized the impact of the subsection by ruling that it was satisfied if the buyer already had sufficient information to take out insurance. Consequently, in most cases involving strict f.o.b. contracts 32(3) would be deemed complied with despite the absence of any notice by the seller.[27]

(iv) Loading

The seller must arrange for the goods to be available and loaded on the nominated vessel at or within the notified loading time.[28] A term of the contract requiring the buyer to give a specified period of notice of the ship's readiness to load is a condition, breach of which entitles the seller to treat the contract as discharged.[29] Traditionally, the duty to load was generally considered to be discharged when the goods had been passed over the ship's rail, even if they were still in mid-air when some untoward event occurred. [30] That is still the position where the goods are indeed carried over the

---

23 *Modern Transport Co Ltd v Ternstrom & Roos* (1924) Ll L Rep 345.

24 *Erg Petroli SpA v Vitol SA (The 'Ballenita' and 'BP Energy')* [1992] 2 Lloyd's Rep 455, per Judge Diamond QC at 460. The case concerned a c.i.f. contract in which the nomination was to be made by the seller and it was the buyer who relied on estoppel, but the same principle applies to an f.o.b. contract where the nomination is to be made by the buyer. See also Howard Bennett, 'F.O.B. Contracts: Substitution of Vessels' [1990] LMCLQ 466 at pp 470–472, supporting the view expressed in the text, and *Benjamin's Sale of Goods* (6th edn, 2002), para 20–051, taking a contrary position.

25 See p 255.

26 *Wimble, Sons & Co Ltd v Rosenberg & Sons* [1913] 3 KB 743 (Hamilton LJ dissenting), followed, somewhat reluctantly, by the Court of Appeal in *Northern Steel & Hardware Co Ltd v John Batt & Co (London) Ltd* (1917) 33 TLR 516.

27 The position is otherwise, of course, in the extended f.o.b. contract. See p 870.

28 *Compagnie Commerciale Sucres et Denrees v C Czarnikow Ltd (The 'Naxos')* [1990] 1 WLR 1337.

29 *Bunge & Co Ltd v Tradax England Ltd*, n 15.

30 *Pyrene Co Ltd v Scindia Navigation Co Ltd* [1954] 2 QB 402, per Devlin, J at 414.

ship's rail, but in other cases it suffices that they are considered to have been shipped in accordance with the customary practice of the port of loading.[31] In f.o.b. contracts the contractual delivery month forms part of the contract description, so that, for example, if the contract provides for goods to be shipped in August and the shipment is not made until September, the goods will not conform to the contract description, for a September shipment is not the same as an August shipment.[32] In a strict f.o.b. contract payment of the freight is the buyer's responsibility. Accordingly, the buyer is not entitled to require the handing over of a bill of lading marked 'freight prepaid', this being incompatible with the nature of an f.o.b. contract.[33]

Delivery on board is a term for the benefit of both parties, so that unless otherwise agreed the buyer is not entitled to collect the goods beforehand, even at the port of shipment itself.[34]

(v) Duty to procure export licence

Where an export licence is required, two questions may arise: whose duty is it to procure the licence, and is the duty absolute or merely to use the parties' best endeavours to obtain it?

In determining on whom the duty lies it is necessary to distinguish the internal, or 'supply', f.o.b. transaction from the export transaction. For example, a London merchant, for the purpose of satisfying an order from a New York buyer, may order goods from a Liverpool merchant, to be shipped to London f.o.b. Liverpool. So far as the Liverpool merchant is concerned, the transaction is a purely domestic transaction and he is not concerned with the exportation of the goods. Hence there will ordinarily be no question of his becoming involved in the obtaining of the export licence.[35] But as between the London seller and the New York buyer the usual inference is that the duty to obtain an export licence is on the seller, for he is in the better position to do so.[36] Prima facie the seller discharges his duty by using his best endeavours to obtain the licence.[37] If, despite those endeavours, he is

---

31 See p 879 as to loading generally.

32 *Bowes v Shand* (1877) 2 App Cas 455; *The Golden Rio* [1990] 2 Lloyd's Rep 273.

33 *Glencore Grain Rotterdam BV v Lebanese Organisation for International Commerce (Lorico)* [1997] 2 Lloyd's Rep 386.

34 *Maine Spinning Co v Sutcliffe & Co* (1917) 23 Com Cas 216.

35 *H. O. Brandt & Co v H. N. Morris & Co* [1917] 2 KB 784.

36 *A. V. Pound & Co Ltd v M. W. Hardy & Co Inc* [1956] AC 588.

37 Generally the contract itself provides that the sale is to be 'subject to licence', in which event there is an implied term that the seller will use his best endeavours to procure a licence, and battle is usually joined on the factual question whether he has done so. See, for example, *Overseas Buyers Ltd v Granadex SA* [1980] 2 Lloyd's Rep 608, and cases there cited. A seller who has not made reasonable attempts to obtain a licence will be in breach unless he can show that nothing he could have done would have enabled him to ship the goods; and the burden of proving this is a heavy one (ibid; *Windschuegl v Alexander Pickering & Co* (1950) 84 Ll L Rep 89; *Vidler & Co (London) Ltd v R. Silcock & Sons Ltd* [1960] 1 Lloyd's Rep 509). It would seem that even in the absence of a 'subject to licence' clause the seller's obligation is presumptively to use best endeavours only, not to guarantee his ability to ship. See *Peter Cassidy Seed Co Ltd v Osuustukkukauppa I.L.* [1957] 1 WLR 273, per Devlin J at 279. See also Basil Eckersley, 'International Sale of Goods – Licences and Export Prohibitions' [1975] LMCLQ 265 at pp 267–268.

unable to do so, the contract will normally be discharged by frustration.[38] But the language of the contract or the surrounding circumstances may indicate that the seller was intended to assume an absolute duty, in which case his inability to obtain the licence is no defence to the buyer's claim for breach of contract.[39] For example, it may appear that the parties were alive to the possibility of the licence being refused and that the seller, confident that he could obtain it, chose to take a calculated risk.

Since the seller must at the very least use his best endeavours, it follows a fortiori that if he neglects to do so and cannot show that such endeavours would have been doomed to failure[40] he cannot rely on his self-induced frustration to treat the contract as at an end.[41]

(vi) Delivery of documents and payment

Unless otherwise agreed, it is the seller's duty to furnish to the buyer such document or documents as will enable the latter to obtain possession of the goods from the carrier. Typically, the document to be handed over will be a bill of lading, but in a strict f.o.b. contract the seller does not contract to arrange for transportation by sea, and he fulfils his contractual obligation if he furnishes some other document entitling the buyer to obtain possession, or to procure a bill of lading, eg a mate's receipt, shipping certificate or standard shipping note. Unless otherwise agreed, the documents need be handed over only in exchange for payment, for prima facie payment and delivery are concurrent conditions[42] and here the delivery obligation is satisfied by the furnishing of the documents.

(vii) Transfer of property[43]

In general, the property in the goods passes to the buyer when they are placed on board the nominated vessel pursuant to the contract.[44] This results from the presumed intention of the parties, as formulated in r 5(1) and (2) of s 18 of the Sale of Goods Act.[45] However, problems may arise where the bill of lading is made out

---

38 *Re Anglo-Russian Merchant Traders Ltd and John Batt & Co (London) Ltd* [1917] 2 KB 679.

39 *Peter Cassidy Seed Co Ltd v Osuustukkukauppa I.L.*, n 37; *Partabmuli Rameshwar v K. C. Sethia (1914) Ltd* [1951] 2 Lloyd's Rep 89 (quota); and see *Pagnan SpA v Tradax Ocean Transportation SA* [1986] 2 Lloyd's Rep 646.

40 See n 37.

41 See cases referred to n 37, and *Agroexport State Enterprise for Foreign Trade v Compagnie Européenne de Céréales* [1974] 1 Lloyd's Rep 499. As to the seller's position where he has concluded several export contracts, each requiring a licence, but is unable to obtain sufficient licences to fulfil all the contracts, see p 000.

42 Sale of Goods Act, s 28.

43 See generally ch 8.

44 *Carlos Federspiel & Co SA v Charles Twigg & Co Ltd* [1957] 1 Lloyd's Rep 240; *Colley v Overseas Exporters Ltd*, n 14. This, of course, assumes that the goods have by then become identified to the contract, instead of being merely an unidentified part of a bulk shipment. See Sale of Goods Act, s 16.

45 See p 233.

to the order of the seller[46] or, though made out to the buyer, is retained by the seller, eg pending payment of the price. The question is then whether the seller is to be taken to have reserved a right of disposal, thereby negating an unconditional appropriation of the goods to the contract and preventing the passing of the property under the Sale of Goods Act.[47]

The matter is entirely one of intention. Did the seller, by taking possession of the bill of lading or by having it made out in his own favour, intend to leave himself free to allocate the goods to another contract, or did he intend merely to retain constructive possession of the goods, allowing property to pass to the buyer but subject to the seller's rights of lien and stoppage in transit?[48] Prima facie the seller who procures a bill of lading by which the goods are deliverable to the order of himself or his agent is deemed to reserve the right of disposal.[49] It is now established that s 19(2) applies to f.o.b. contracts.[50]

In practice, the problem of determining whether the seller intended to reserve a right of disposal is often avoided as the result of the seller sending the buyer a notice of appropriation pursuant to the contract. This has the effect of making the appropriation unconditional.[51] In the absence of such a notice, the presumption in s 19(2) is not readily displaced where the seller has not been paid, for the assumption is that he will wish to reserve the right of disposal until payment in full.[52] Section 19(2) does not apply where the bill of lading is made out in favour of the buyer. But where the seller retains possession of the bill of lading or delivers it to his bank or other agent for release against payment, there is a presumption that the seller intends to reserve the right of disposal until payment,[53] and this is not displaced merely by the fact that the seller, having received part of the price, is to be paid the balance under a letter of credit, for 'even the most copper-bottomed letter of credit sometimes fails to produce payment'.[54]

---

46 This usually arises in the context of the extended f.o.b. contract.

47 Ie, s 18, r 5.

48 There is a third possibility, viz that the seller intended to appropriate the goods to the contract unconditionally but to retain ownership until payment. In such a case, the presumption raised by r 5(1) of s 18 is displaced.

49 Section 19(2).

50 *The Ciudad de Pasto* [1989] 1 All ER 951. For a discussion and rejection of the argument to the contrary, see the first edition of this work at p 588.

51 The precise effect of the notice depends on whether it fully identifies the goods or merely refers to an unidentified part of a designated bulk shipment. In the former case, the seller becomes contractually committed to delivery of the specified goods and no other. In the latter, his commitment is to supply goods of the contract description and quantity from the identified bulk. The appropriation necessary for the passing of the property in goods within s 18, r 5(1), is, of course, of the former kind, and the buyer is prima facie entitled to shipping documents which fully identify the goods. See pp 939, 941. But under s 18, r 5(3), inserted by the Sale of Goods (Amendment) Act 1995, the prepaying buyer becomes owner in common of the bulk instead of having a mere personal right as now; see p 220.

52 *The Ciudad de Pasto*, n 50. The earlier decisions in *The Sorfareren* (1916) 114 LT 46 and *The Parchim* [1918] AC 157 indicating the contrary should be regarded as decided on their own special facts and in the light of practice then prevailing (*The Kronprinsessan Margareta* [1921] 1 AC 486, per Lord Sumner at 516–517; *The Ciudad de Pasto*, per Staughton LJ at 957).

53 *The Ciudad de Pasto*, n 50.

54 Ibid, per Staughton LJ at 957.

(viii) Risk

Whereas the normal rule for domestic sales is that risk passes with the property,[55] in export transactions that presumption is usually rebutted. In an f.o.b. contract, therefore, the risk passes to the buyer on shipment even though the seller has retained the bill of lading, or has had it made out to his own order to secure the price,[56] and even if he intended to reserve a right of disposal.[57] Again, if (which he is not obliged to do[58]) the buyer accepts shipping documents relating to goods that are only quasi-specific (eg as part of a larger consignment on board the vessel), the risk may pass to him even though the property does not,[59] though if only part of the whole is lost or damaged, nice questions may arise as to the incidence of the risk.[60]

(ix) Rejection of documents and goods

The buyer is entitled to expect both documents and goods to be in conformity with the contract. If the documents are not in order, he may reject them, leaving the seller to cure the nonconformity by a fresh and conforming tender if he still has time to do so. Even if the buyer accepts the documents, he may subsequently reject the goods for any nonconformity that was not apparent from the documents. The principles applicable to the exercise of the two rights to reject are the same as for c.i.f. contracts, discussed below.

2.   EXTENDED F.O.B.

In the case of an extended f.o.b. contract, one or more of the rules applicable to a strict f.o.b. contract will be displaced, depending on the nature of the seller's undertaking. A common variant is to add words such as 'stowed' ('f.o.b.s.'), 'trimmed' ('f.o.b.t.') or 'stowed and trimmed' ('f.o.b.s.t.').[61] These extend the seller's obligations beyond the point of putting the goods over the ship's rail but without involving him in procurement of the contract of carriage. Stowage involves arrangement of the goods in the ship's hold (or, where permitted, on deck) in such a way as to make effective use of the available space while ensuring that the safety of the vessel is not impaired by instability of the cargo and that where necessary the goods are segregated from other cargo to avoid contamination of one or the other. Trimming involves levelling of dry bulk cargo such as grain. Such terms are price terms in that the seller has to perform the additional duties at his own expense. Less clear is whether they extend the contractual delivery point or the point at which

---

55 Sale of Goods Act, s 20(1).

56 See *Stock v Inglis* (1884) 12 QBD 564, per Brett MR at 573, affirmed by the House of Lords (1885) 10 App Cas 263; *The Parchim*, n 52.

57 *Williams v Cohen* (1871) 25 LT 300, per Bramwell B at 303.

58 See p 246, n 21.

59 *Sterns Ltd v Vickers Ltd* [1923] 1 KB 78. But as to the property, see nn 51, 79.

60 The fairest solution would be for the parties interested in the bulk to suffer in the proportions of their respective interests, which now seems the case for prepaying buyers. See p 257.

61 See, generally, Barney Reynolds, 'Stowing, trimming and their effects on delivery, risk and property in sales "f.o.b.s.", "f.o.b.t." and "f.o.b.s.t." ' [1994] LMCLQ 119.

property and risk pass to the buyer. No general answer can be given to this question, for so much depends on the terms of the contract and in particular on how much control the seller has over the loading and trimming operations.[62]

In what we have described earlier as 'extended f.o.b.' the seller undertakes responsibility for procuring the contract of carriage itself at the buyer's expense. As we have seen,[63] this does not produce the same legal effect as a c.i.f. contract, for the seller acts as agent of the buyer, not as principal, and the freight is not included in the price. But what constitutes a sufficient contract of carriage for this purpose is the same as in c.i.f. contracts, though the seller's duty is not strict but is limited to the agent's duty to exercise reasonable care and skill.

3.   C.I.F.

The essential nature of a c.i.f. contract has already been described.[64] The seller does not undertake that the goods shall arrive, but agrees at his own expense:

(a)   to procure and tender to the buyer the requisite shipping documents,[65] which, unless otherwise agreed,[66] comprise:

  (i)   a bill of lading showing shipment at the contractual port of shipment (if any) of goods conforming to the contract;

  (ii)   a policy of insurance covering the goods for their sea transit; [67]

  (iii)   a commercial invoice relating to the goods;

(b)   to transfer the property in the goods to the buyer at the due time for such transfer, provided that the goods are then in existence.

If the goods, having been shipped sound,[68] are lost or damaged in transit, the buyer's remedy (if any) is not against the seller but against the carrier and/or insurer, pursuant to the contracts of carriage and insurance taken out by the seller and transferred or to be transferred to the buyer.[69] For this reason, the c.i.f. contract has sometimes been described[70] as being not a sale of goods but a sale of documents relating to goods, the buyer purchasing the documents rather than the goods themselves. But this is true only in the sense that the seller undertakes no obligation

---

62 See ibid. for an illuminating analysis of the problems.

63 See p 871.

64 See p 871.

65 For a full description, see pp 880 ff.

66 For common variants, see pp 899 ff.

67 For the position under Incoterms, see A. Odeke, 'The insurance element in Incoterms CIF and CIP contracts' (1995) 4 Insurance Law & Practice 86.

68 That is, in such condition that with a normal voyage they will arrive sound. See p 311.

69 The seller does not, however, contract that the buyer will have a remedy against the carrier or insurer. If the contracts of carriage and insurance taken out for the buyer's benefit are in conformity with the stipulations in the contract of sale (see p 255, as to what is implied), the fact that the particular loss or damage suffered is not of a kind for which the carrier or insurer is responsible does not invalidate the seller's tender (*Arnhold Karberg & Co v Blythe, Green, Jourdain & Co* [1915] 2 KB 379, per Scrutton J at 388, 392; [1916] 1 KB 495, per Bankes LJ at 510–511).

70 Eg, by Scrutton J in *Arnhold Karberg & Co v Blythe, Green, Jourdain & Co*, n 69, at 388, disapproved by Bankes LJ on appeal, n 69, at 510 and by Warrington LJ at 514.

as to physical delivery and remains free to tender the shipping documents even if the goods have been lost after the making of the contract of sale and before the tender.[71] In other respects the seller has the normal duties of the seller under a contract of sale. Thus the goods shipped must conform to the contract as to description and/or sample, quality and fitness, and the seller must be in a position to pass a good title to the buyer.

The duties of the parties must now be examined in a little more detail.

(i)   Shipment

The seller is not himself obliged to ship the goods unless the contract so requires. He may instead purchase goods afloat and appropriate them to the contract or appropriate to the contract goods already purchased by him afloat before he entered into the contract. In short, under a c.i.f. contract (in contrast to an f.o.b. contract) there is no obligation on the seller to deliver the goods themselves to any delivery point,[72] and provided that the seller is able to furnish the buyer with the requisite shipping documents in due time[73] it is immaterial who shipped them or at what point, prior to the tender of the documents, the seller obtained the property in the goods. But whether the shipment be by the seller or a predecessor in title, and whether it be effective before or after the making of the contract of sale, it must comply, as to time, place and manner, with any shipment terms of the contract. Further, shipment represents the temporal point by reference to which the validity of the seller's performance is required to be tested. The goods must be shipped in sound condition;[74] the bill of lading must evidence shipment in that condition, but is not to be treated as claused by reason of notations showing damage to the goods after the time of shipment;[75] and the insurance cover must be effective as from the time of shipment.

(ii)   Payment of freight

Under a c.i.f. contract freight is, of course, included in the price. The seller may either prepay the freight and invoice the full c.i.f. price to the buyer or leave the freight to be paid by the buyer at the other end, in which case he will procure the issue of a 'freight collect' bill of lading[76] and will deduct the freight from the amount of the invoice. In such a case the buyer's obligation to pay freight is conditional on

---

71 See p 942.
72 In this respect the normal construction of 'c.i.f.' by English courts differs from that of Incoterms, which require the seller himself to deliver the goods on board the vessel at the port of shipment unless otherwise indicated, eg by the addition of 'afloat'.
73 As to which, see p 912.
74 See n 68.
75 *The Galatia* [1980] 1 All ER 501.
76 Ie, a bill of lading which provides that freight is payable at destination. The carrier is not, of course, obliged to contract on those terms and may stipulate for prepayment of freight (see p 1054), or for an indemnity from the shipper. The carrier also enjoys the protection of a lien on the goods for the freight. See p 1055.

the arrival of the goods[77] unless the contract of carriage otherwise provides, as it usually does.

(iii) Appropriation to the contract

Since the buyer is not obliged to accept shipping documents comprising any goods other than those he is purchasing,[78] it is for the seller to ensure that, if they are not identified at the time of the contract, the goods become identified by an effective appropriation on or before the delivery of the shipping documents to the buyer.[79] That delivery may itself constitute the act of appropriation, or this may be some earlier act, eg dispatch of a notice of appropriation pursuant to the contract.[80]

(iv) Tender of shipping documents

The composition of the shipping documents and the responsibility for a valid tender of each of these have been discussed earlier.[81] If the documents are not in order, the buyer may reject them, even if there is a contrary custom, for this would be inconsistent with the fundamental nature of the contract; and the seller cannot require the buyer to accept a guarantee instrument to cover the discrepancy.[82] The seller may thereafter make a fresh and conforming tender if he still has time to do so;[83] if not, the buyer is entitled to treat the contract as repudiated. [84] Acceptance of the documents does not preclude a subsequent rejection of the goods themselves for nonconformity with the contract,[85] provided that this was not apparent on the face of the documents.[86]

(v) Transfer of property

1. Time of transfer

In contrast to f.o.b. sales, shipment does not usually produce a transfer of the property in the goods under a c.i.f. contract, for the seller is not obliged to ship the goods himself and may not have acquired them until they are afloat. Of course, the paramount consideration is the intention of the parties, and, where the seller is to act as shipper, it may well be that in a particular contract the parties intend that property

77 *The Pantanassa* [1970] 1 Lloyd's Rep 153; *Ireland v Livingston* (1861) LR 5 HL 395.
78 See p 893.
79 But such identification is dispensed with where there is a term or custom to the contrary, as, for example, in the shipment of bulk cargo, such as oil; see p 000. Under the Sale of Goods 1979, s 18, r 5(3), the prepaying buyer of an unidentified part of a bulk cargo becomes a co-owner of the bulk; see p 220.
80 See p 935. Such a notice, once given, cannot be withdrawn (*Grain Union SA Antwerp v Hans Larsen Aalborg A.S.* (1933) 150 LT 78).
81 See, pp 885 ff.
82 *Soules CAF v PT Transap of Indonesia* [1999] 1 Lloyd's Rep 917.
83 See p 342.
84 See further p 944 as to the buyer's rights of rejection.
85 See p 944.
86 See pp 944, 945 ff.

shall pass on shipment, in which case the court will give effect to that intention,[87] so long as the goods have become ascertained.[88] But the presumption is that the property is not intended to pass until delivery of the shipping documents to the buyer,[89] or posting of the documents to him where this is expressly or impliedly authorized by the contract;[90] and since, unless otherwise agreed, the condition of transfer of the documents is payment by the buyer, the property does not normally pass to him until the conjunction of delivery and payment. If, therefore, the seller hands over the documents without receiving payment in exchange, the presumption is that he intends to reserve the property until payment,[91] and this is not necessarily affected by the fact that payment is to be made under a letter of credit.[92] But the presumption will be displaced where the evidence indicates that the seller was intending to give credit[93] or was not concerned to secure himself by retaining ownership pending payment[94] or where, pursuant to the contract, the seller arranges for release of the goods by the carrier against a letter of indemnity without production of the bill of lading, so that it is clear that the property is intended to pass independently of the bill of lading.[95]

2.   Duty to transfer

As in other contracts of sale, the seller must have a right to dispose of the goods. If he does not, he is in breach of s 17 of the Sale of Goods Act and the buyer has a right to reject (or to accept and claim damages) even after taking delivery of the bill of lading. In this connection, it should be borne in mind that the bill of lading is not a fully negotiable document of title and that the transferor cannot pass a better title than he himself possesses, except under some common law or statutory exception to the *nemo dat* rule.[96]

The obligation to transfer ownership is subject to the qualification, not peculiar to c.i.f. contracts, that if the goods are destroyed after the risk has passed to the buyer, he cannot complain, and remains bound to pay the price.[97]

(vi) Risk

Though the property prima facie passes to the buyer when he makes payment against the documents, the presumption is that the risk passes as from the time of

---

87 See Sale of Goods Act, s 17(1).

88 Section 16.

89 *The Miramichi* [1915] P.71.

90 *The Albazero* [1977] AC 774.

91 *The Miramichi*, n 89; *Stein, Forbes & Co v County Tailoring Co* (1916) 86 LJKB 448; *Ginzberg v Barrow Haematite Steel Co Ltd* [1966] 1 Lloyd's Rep 343. Where the documents are accompanied by a draft on the buyer, the property does not pass until he accepts and returns the draft (Sale of Goods Act, s 19(3)).

92 *The Filiatra Legacy* [1991] 2 Lloyd's Rep 337.

93 See n 48.

94 See, for example, *The Albazero*, n 90, where the buyer and the seller were associated companies.

95 *The Delfini* [1990] 1 Lloyd's Rep 252; *The Filiatra Legacy*, n 92.

96 See pp 417 ff.

97 See pp 248, 260 and below.

shipment.[98] This is because, from the very nature of the contract, the parties contemplate the risk of loss or damage in transit and cover it by the contracts of carriage and insurance which the seller is required to take out and transfer to the buyer. Hence, in principle, provided that the goods were in good condition and otherwise in conformity with the sale contract at the time of shipment and the seller is in a position to furnish the shipping documents, he is not liable for loss, damage or deterioration of the goods in transit, nor is this a ground for the buyer to withhold payment or (in the case of damage or deterioration) to reject the goods on their arrival. The position is otherwise, of course, if the goods shipped were not in conformity with the contract. In that event, their subsequent loss does not deprive the buyer of his right to reject.[99]

We must now consider in a little more detail the rights and duties of the parties in the event of loss[100] of the goods at different stages. Our discussion does, of course, presuppose that the goods lost were or included the contract goods, that is, that the goods to be supplied by the seller, if not identified at the time of the contract, had become ascertained as the result of an effective appropriation or formed part of a specific or ascertained bulk which was lost.[101] If at the time of the loss occasioning the dispute the contract goods remained wholly unascertained, the question of risk does not arise, for it cannot be predicated that it is the contract goods that have been lost. The seller simply has to accept that what he may have intended as the source of supply is no longer available and he must fulfil his obligations by procuring goods from another source.[102]

1. Loss after acceptance of documents by buyer

If the goods are lost after the buyer has accepted the documents, the risk is on the buyer[103] and he must look to his rights against the carrier or insurer.

2. Loss after tender of documents but before acceptance

The position is the same where the goods are lost after the tender of the documents but before acceptance (eg after posting and before receipt[104]), unless the buyer has other grounds for rejecting the documents.[105] In this connection it will be borne in mind that the buyer is prima facie entitled to shipping documents relating

---

98 *Johnson v Taylor Bros* [1920] AC 144, per Lord Atkinson at 156.

99 See pp 248, n 35; 353, n 43.

100 Hereafter, unless otherwise indicated, 'loss' includes (a) damage and (b) deterioration which is not attributable to the goods being unfit at the time of shipment to withstand a normal voyage.

101 If the loss was only partial, nice problems arise as to whether, and if so to what extent, the part lost is to be considered to have included the contract goods. But as to prepaying buyers, see p 257.

102 See p 245.

103 Assuming the goods conformed to the contract or that any defect which would have entitled the buyer to reject was apparent on the face of the documents, so that he is to be taken to have accepted the goods as regards that defect.

104 *The Albazero*, n 90.

105 For the requisites of a valid tender of documents, see pp 885 ff.

exclusively to the goods he has contracted to buy,[106] so that if at the time of the loss the goods still formed an unidentified part of a larger bulk, the buyer will be entitled to reject the documents and thereby throw the risk of loss back on to the seller.[107]

3.   Loss after contract and shipment and before tender of documents

The position is the same as under (2). The fact that the goods have perished before tender of the documents does not preclude the seller from making a valid tender, even if he was aware of the loss at the time of tender.[108] Again, however, the tender will normally be valid only if the goods had been earmarked to the contract by the time of the loss.[109] The principle is clear, but difficulty is created by two decisions at first instance, *C. Groom Ltd v Barber*[110] and *Manbré Saccharine Co Ltd v Corn Products Co Ltd.*[111] In the first, Atkin J declined to accept the argument that loss of the goods[112] before appropriation to the contract invalidated a subsequent tender of the documents relating to them. However, he appears to have been concerned primarily to reject the proposition that a tender of the documents after loss would be valid only if the property had previously passed to the buyer. Having rightly held that the seller was under no obligation to transfer the property until the due tender of the bill of lading, and that such obligation was extinguished if the goods had meanwhile been lost, the learned judge went on to conclude that the absence of a pre-loss appropriation *by which the property would have been transferred* was irrelevant. This, however, misses the point. Appropriation is relevant not merely to property but to identification of the goods for the purpose of establishing that they, and they alone, were the goods comprised in the bill of lading and in the insurance policy. In the absence of appropriation it is not possible for the seller to perform his duty of tendering shipping documents relating exclusively to the goods the subject of the contract of sale.

In *Manbré Saccharine* McCardie J, citing with approval the decision in *C. Groom Ltd v Barber*, held that loss of the goods did not preclude a subsequent tender of the documents by the seller. However, he did not discuss the question of pre-loss appropriation as such, and he went on to hold that 'a purchaser under a c.i.f. contract is entitled to demand, as a matter of law, a policy of insurance which covers and covers only the goods mentioned in the bills of lading and invoices'.[113] But unless the goods are identified by the policy and the bill of lading, the buyer is not able to get that to which he is entitled.

---

106   See pp 893–894. The position is different, however, if the contract otherwise provides, expressly or by implication (eg by permitting the seller to tender a delivery order instead of a bill of lading) or if the normal rule is displaced by custom or by course of dealing between the parties.

107   But see n 106. It is not easy to reconcile with this principle the decisions in *C. Groom Ltd v Barber* [1915] 1 KB 316 and *Manbré Saccharine Co Ltd v Corn Products Co Ltd* [1919] 1 KB 198. See below.

108   *Manbré Saccharine Co Ltd v Corn Products Co Ltd*, n 107; *Arnhold Karberg & Co v Blythe, Green, Jourdain & Co* [1916] 1 KB 495.

109   But see n 106.

110   See n 107.

111   Ibid.

112   *Semble*, at a time when they were quasi-specific, ie an unidentified part of a shipped cargo.

113   [1919] 1 KB 198 at 205.

It is accordingly submitted that while the location of the property in the goods at the time of loss is irrelevant, the seller cannot make a valid tender of shipping documents after loss of the goods unless before loss they had become fully identified as the contract goods.[114]

4. Loss after shipment but before contract

This case is more difficult. The general rule is that if the goods, unknown to the parties,[115] have ceased to exist by the time the contract is made, the contract is either void or frustrated,[116] while if they were damaged or deteriorated before the contract, and were not sold as being in a damaged state, the buyer will have a right to reject for want of fitness and/or quality. The question is whether these rules become inapplicable if the seller, having procured shipping documents issued at a time when the goods were on board the vessel and in sound condition, is able to deliver them to the buyer, so enabling him to claim against the carrier or insurer. It is considered that this is not sufficient to displace the ordinary rules, and that the buyer is entitled to reject a tender of the documents in these circumstances, whether the goods are lost wholly or in part or are merely damaged or have deteriorated. [117] Quite apart from s 6 of the Sale of Goods Act, where applicable,[118] even the c.i.f. buyer is contracting primarily to buy goods, not claims. If, therefore, the goods had suffered loss, damage or deterioration before even the contract of sale was concluded, the buyer cannot be compelled to accept the tender of the documents, for there never was a moment when goods conforming to the contract were available to him. Moreover, if it be right that the seller cannot appropriate the goods to the contract after they have been lost,[119] it must equally be true that an appropriation of damaged or deteriorated goods is ineffective, at least if the damage or deterioration results in their not conforming to the contract description.

5. Loss before shipment

Prima facie this must be borne by the seller, since the risk passes to the buyer only as from shipment unless otherwise agreed.[120]

---

114 The same view is taken by *Benjamin's Sale of Goods*, para 19–095.
115 If the facts were known to the seller, then the buyer may be entitled to avoid the contract but the seller is liable upon it. See p 200.
116 Void under s 6 of the Sale of Goods Act if the contract was for the sale of specific goods; frustrated, if the goods lost had been appropriated to the contract or included all the goods so appropriated. If the goods remained wholly unascertained, the contract is unaffected, for the seller will be unable to contend that the lost merchandise constituted or included the contract goods.
117 *Contra, Benjamin's Sale of Goods*, para 19–074, where it is argued that the buyer is released only if there is a total loss.
118 See n 116.
119 See above, and *Benjamin's Sale of Goods*, paras 19–072–19–073.
120 See pp 940–941.

(vii) Rejection of documents

As noted earlier, the c.i.f. seller has two distinct sets of duties: the duty to ship goods conforming to the contract of sale, or to buy afloat goods so shipped, and the duty to tender shipping documents conforming to the contract. It follows that the buyer has two separate rights of rejection: the right to reject nonconforming documents and the right to reject nonconforming goods. If the documents are properly rejected and the defect in them is not cured by a fresh and conforming tender within the time allowed by the contract, the seller will be guilty of a repudiatory breach and the question of rejection of the goods will not arise, for *ex hypothesi* the buyer will not have the documents. If the defective documents are accepted or the defect is cured by a new and conforming tender, the buyer may still have the right to reject the goods themselves on their arrival if they are found not to conform to the contract and the nonconformity was not apparent on the face of the documents.[121]

Where the buyer rejects documents that are in fact in conformity with the contract, he thereby commits a repudiatory breach. The seller then has the option of accepting the repudiation, in which event the contract comes to an end and he is released from his delivery obligation and has a right to damages for non-acceptance, or of holding the contract open for performance. But what is the position if, the seller having elected to accept the repudiation, the buyer later discovers that the goods are nonconforming? Can he rely on this to justify retrospectively what was originally an improper rejection of the documents? The starting point is the general principle of contract law that a party to a contract who gives a bad reason for terminating it is entitled to rely subsequently on facts not known to him at the time which would have constituted a valid ground of termination, provided that the other party would not have been in a position to remedy the breach if the correct ground had been advanced at the time.[122] In *Henry Dean & Sons (Sydney) Ltd v O'Day Pty Ltd*[123] the High Court of Australia invoked this principle to uphold the c.i.f. buyer's right to refuse to pay for goods, on the basis that this was justified by the later discovery that the goods did not conform to the contract description. However, in *Gill & Duffus SA v Berger & Co Inc (No 2)*[124] Lord Diplock roundly declared that this was not the law of England. In that case:

> The sellers contracted to sell 500 tonnes of Argentina Bolita beans c.i.f. Le Havre, payment to be made against documents. The buyers rejected the documents on the ground that they did not include a quality certificate to be issued at the port of discharge. This rejection was wrongful since the certificate would not come into existence until after discharge and accordingly could not be one of the shipping documents. The sellers elected to affirm the contract and subsequently made a fresh tender of the documents together with the certificate. The buyers again rejected the documents despite the fact that these conformed to the contract and later sought to justify this rejection on the ground that a quantity of beans did not correspond with sample or description.

---

121   See p 946, n 132.
122   See *Chitty on Contracts* (29th edn, 2004), para 24-014.
123   (1927) 39 CLR 330.
124   [1984] AC 382.

The House of Lords held that the buyers were not entitled to do so. The duty to ship conforming goods and the duty to present conforming documents were separate and independent duties. The buyers had no right to reject the goods until their arrival. It followed that their earlier rejection of the documents was a repudiation of the sale contract which released the sellers from any further duty to perform, so that the buyers lost their putative right to reject the goods on arrival.[125]

The decision is not free from difficulty.[126] It is clear from the facts of the case that by the time of rejection of the second tender of documents the contract delivery date had nearly passed, so that the sellers could not have shipped new and conforming goods within the contract period. Why, then, were the buyers not entitled to treat the sellers as guilty of an anticipatory breach preceding the rejection of the second tender of documents, making this rejection lawful? In the Court of Appeal Goff LJ entertained no doubt that the buyers were indeed entitled to do this.[127] Lord Diplock's answer, in which he characterized this view as 'wrong', appears to be that the seller's undertaking to ship conforming goods and the buyer's undertaking to pay against conforming documents are independent covenants, so that the breach of the former does not excuse a failure to honour the latter. This analysis, which reflects the principle 'pay now, argue later', is open to serious objection. There is only one contract, the contract of sale, and while it is certainly possible to have independent undertakings in such a contract this surely cannot be the case where each of the two undertakings is a condition, the breach of which therefore goes to the root of the contract. Moreover, the proposition that the buyer's remedy is to pay against the documents and then reject the goods on arrival and sue for recovery of the price lacks commercial realism. What is the point of requiring the buyer to go through such an exercise? And why should he be put in the position of being out of both goods and money, and therefore entirely dependent on the seller's ability to repay the price? It is submitted that the view of Goff LJ is to be preferred as consistent both with principle and with commercial sense. Lord Diplock's analysis is open to the further objection that he considered it sufficient if the seller tendered *apparently* conforming documents,[128] whereas it must surely be the case that the documents must *in fact* be conforming documents.[129]

(viii) Rejection of goods

Even where the documents conform to the contract the buyer has the right to reject the goods themselves if on arrival it is found that they were not in conformity with

---

125 If the sellers had not accepted the buyers' repudiation but had elected to keep the contract on foot, this would have enured for the benefit of both parties, so that on arrival of the goods the buyers would have been entitled to exercise their right to reject them and the sellers would have been restricted to purely nominal damages for the earlier breach. The case also involved a number of other issues not discussed here.

126 For a penetrating analysis see G. H. Treitel, 'Rights of rejection under c.i.f. sales' [1984] LMCLQ 565.

127 [1983] 1 Lloyd's Rep 622 at 635.

128 Reflecting his view, which, it will be submitted later, is equally erroneous, that a bank is obliged to pay under a letter of credit on the presentation of apparently conforming documents. See p 995.

129 See Michael Bridge, 'Documents and Contractual Congruence in International Trade' in Sarah Worthington (ed), *Commercial Law and Commercial Practice* (2003) at pp 214 ff.

the contract[130] at the time of shipment.[131] The buyer usually has no opportunity to examine the goods before their arrival at the port of destination, and defects or nonconformity will not necessarily have been apparent on the face of the documents.[132]

The buyer need not, of course, exercise his right to reject the goods but may elect to accept them and sue for damages for breach of warranty, or may be compelled to do so by deemed acceptance.[133] In that event the normal measure of damages applies, ie the difference between the value of the goods as warranted and their value as delivered. There is, however, an exceptional case where, despite the fact that the claim is for breach of warranty, the buyer can recover damages on the same basis as if he had rejected the documents. This is where the documents were not, in fact, in accordance with the contract but the nonconformity was concealed, whether by the seller himself [134] or his predecessor in title. In such a case, the buyer is entitled to recover as damages the loss he would have avoided if he had been aware of the defect in the documents and exercised his right to reject them.[135] Moreover, the fact that he elects to accept the goods after becoming aware of the defect in the documents does not alter the position, for at that stage he will usually have paid the price against the documents and cannot reasonably be expected to reject the goods and thereby leave himself in the hazardous position of having neither money nor goods. The point is well illustrated by the decision of Devlin J in *Kwei Tek Chao v British Traders and Shippers Ltd.* [136]

> The plaintiffs contracted to purchase from the defendants twenty tons of chemicals at £95 a ton c.i.f. Hong Kong, shipment to be made on or before 31 October. By a fraud to which the defendants' own supplier was a party, the bill of lading, which had originally borne an indorsement showing that the goods had been received for shipment on 31 October and shipped subsequently, was altered to show shipment on 31 October. Accordingly, the shipped goods did not conform to the contract.[137] The plaintiffs, having lost a sub-sale as the result of their purchaser discovering the facts and claiming cancellation, took delivery of the goods on their arrival in Hong Kong, but were unable to resell them due to a fall in the market. They then sued the defendants for return of the price or for damages for fraud or, in the further alternative, damages for loss suffered by their inability to resell.

130 Whether through non-correspondence with description or sample, lack of merchantable quality or fitness, or otherwise.

131 *Kwei Tek Chao v British Traders & Shippers Ltd* [1954] 2 QB 459.

132 If they were, and the buyer nevertheless accepts the documents, he loses his right to reject as regards such defects or nonconformity. See *Panchaud Frères SA v Etablissements Général Grain Co* [1970] 1 Lloyd's Rep 53. But if the contract shipping documents appear to be in order, the buyer is not under a duty to investigate the possibility thrown up by statements in noncontractual documents that the bill of lading or other contract document was false (*The Manila* [1988] 3 All ER 843).

133 See pp 348 ff.

134 In this event, of course, the buyer has an alternative claim in tort for deceit.

135 For the measure of damages, see below.

136 See n 131.

137 Because the month of shipment is part of the contract description of the goods themselves, so that a November shipment is not of the same description as an October shipment.

Held that:
(a) the defendants were not responsible for the fraud;
(b) the plaintiffs must be taken to have affirmed the contract with knowledge of the breach and were thus restricted to a claim for damages for breach of warranty;
(c) the breach by the defendants in shipping goods not in conformity with the contract was entirely distinct from their breach in tendering incorrect documents, and the plaintiffs' election in regard to the former breach could not affect the measure of damages to which they were entitled in respect of the latter breach;
(d) the loss of the sub-sale contract was not recoverable as such, since there was no evidence that the defendants knew the plaintiffs were committed to sub-selling the identical goods or that there was a string contract of any kind;[138]
(e) following *James Finlay & Co Ltd v Kwik Hoo Tong*,[139] the correct measure of damages was that which would put the plaintiffs in the same position as if they had known of the defect in the bill of lading and exercised a right to reject, thus avoiding a fall in the market.

Damages were subsequently assessed as the excess of the contract price over the market price of the goods in Hong Kong on the date on which the plaintiffs ought reasonably to have resold the goods, which for this purpose was taken as the date on which they knew or ought to have known of their right to reject.

It is important to note that in the *Kwei Tek Chao* case both the goods and the documents were nonconforming, so that the buyer would have been entitled to reject the goods upon arrival and lost that right through the falsification of the bill of lading, without which the nonconformity of the goods would have been apparent. But there may be concealed defects in the bill of lading without any nonconformity in the goods themselves, as where the bill of lading gives a false date of shipment but the true date is still within the shipment period[140] or where the shipping marks are incorrectly stated but the goods arrive safely and in full conformity with the contract. In such cases the buyer's damages are restricted to such loss as he has suffered because of the defect in the documents, and where no loss is suffered, damages will be purely nominal.[141]

138 For a discussion of this point, see p 384.
139 [1929] 1 KB 400.
140 *Proctor & Gamble Philippine Manufacturing Corp v Kurt A. Becher* [1988] 2 Lloyd's Rep 21.
141 Ibid. See further G. H. Treitel, 'Damages for breach of a c.i.f. contract' [1988] LMCLQ 457.

35   The Financing of International Trade[1]

1.   PAYMENT ARRANGEMENTS GENERALLY

There are various ways in which the price of exported goods may be paid. If the seller is unsure of the creditworthiness of the buyer and is in a strong bargaining position, he may be able to stipulate payment wholly or partly in advance, or may have recourse to a float kept on deposit with him by the buyer. Alternatively, following the normal Sale of Goods Act rule,[2] the price may be payable on shipment. As a further alternative, the seller may agree to give the buyer credit, in one of the ways described below. Whether or not credit is to be given, the seller may want to reinforce his position by exacting payment undertakings from a third party (usually a bank), under a suretyship guarantee, a documentary credit, a demand guarantee (or performance bond) or a standby credit. In some cases (and invariably in the case of a documentary credit) the third party's payment obligation is a primary one and is not dependent on default by the buyer; in other cases, it is that of a surety, and it is the buyer to whom the seller must look for payment in the first instance.

Where credit is to be extended, this itself may take a variety of forms. The seller may simply supply on open account, allowing the buyer, say, 28 days from shipment, or the seller may specify payment by a term bill of exchange against documents or pursuant to a documentary credit. Other possibilities are payment by instalments, with or without reservation of title to the seller until payment, and supply on consignment, where the deliveree has no purchase obligation at the outset but holds the goods as bailee, with an obligation to purchase if he does not return them within a stated period or if he performs some other act of appropriation.[3]

The present chapter, after dealing briefly with the documentary bill, will be devoted principally to the topic of documentary credits. A concluding section will examine demand guarantees, performance bonds and standby credits, and will discuss the raising of funds, by the seller against bills or credits given by the buyer, and by the buyer on the security of the imported goods.

---

1 See, generally, Alasdair Watson, Paul Cowdell and Derek Hyde, *Finance of International Trade* (7th edn, 2000); Paul Todd, *Cases and Materials on International Trade Law* (2003), ch 8; Jan H. Dalhuisen, *Dalhuisen on International Commercial, Financial and Trade* Law (2000); and, in relation to documentary credits and demand guarantees, the publications cited in nn 11, 25, 312.

2 Section 28. See pp 393–394.

3 Consignment is widely used in domestic transactions on the supply of motor vehicles by car manufacturers to their distributors, since it has the advantage of deferring liability for value added tax.

2. THE DOCUMENTARY BILL

The term 'documentary bill' denotes a bill of exchange accompanied by shipping documents and intended to be accepted or paid in exchange for those documents, as opposed to a 'clean' bill, that is, a bill of exchange not accompanied by other documents.

The seller may send the bill of exchange and shipping documents direct to the buyer, who is then required to accept or pay the bill (depending on whether it is a sight or term bill) and return it to the seller. If the buyer fails to honour the bill of exchange, he is bound to return the bill of lading;[4] and if he wrongfully retains it, the property in the goods does not pass to him,[5] and his retention of the bill of lading constitutes a conversion. If thereafter the buyer proceeds to sell the goods, he commits a further act of conversion where the sale is effective to pass title or where delivery is made to the subpurchaser. The latter may acquire title under some exception to the *nemo dat* rule – typically, under s 9 of the Factors Act 1889 or s 25 of the Sale of Goods Act 1979.[6]

To avoid the risk of loss of title through the buyer's fraud in disposing of the goods without honouring the bill of exchange, the seller will usually arrange for collection through a bank. For example, the seller's own bank (the 'remitting bank') may dispatch the bill of exchange and shipping documents to its correspondent (the 'collecting bank'[7]) in the buyer's country with instructions not to part with the documents except against payment[8] or acceptance.[9] The collecting bank will then present the documents to the buyer, procuring his payment or acceptance of the bill of exchange. The relations between seller and remitting bank, and between remitting and collecting banks, are usually governed by the Uniform Rules for Collections;[10] and the SITPRO standard form of collection request (fig 35.1) is frequently used by sellers and banks.

3. THE DOCUMENTARY CREDIT: NATURE, MECHANISM AND RELATIONSHIPS[11]

Though the seller who stipulates for acceptance or payment against documents has some measure of security, he is not fully protected, for by that stage he has incurred the expense of manufacturing or acquiring the goods and shipping them to the buyer's country, and if the bill is dishonoured the seller will be left with the goods on his hands and will have the trouble and expense of disposing of them elsewhere.

---

4 Sale of Goods Act, s 19(3).

5 Ibid.

6 See pp 434 ff.

7 The term 'collecting bank' is applied to any bank involved in the collection process at the request of the remitting bank. Where the collecting bank is that which presents the documents, it is known as the presenting bank.

8 Known as 'D/P', ie documents against payment.

9 Known as 'D/A', ie documents against acceptance.

10 The latest revision is URC 522 (1995). The Rules depend for their application on incorporation into the contracts of the parties concerned, whether expressly or by course of dealing or usage.

950

(c) BBA/SITPRO 1976/1981/1987

FOREIGN BILL AND/OR DOCUMENTS FOR COLLECTION

AUTHORISED BY THE BRITISH BANKERS' ASSOCIATION

Drawer/exporter	Drawer's/exporter's reference(s) (to be quoted by bank in all correspondence)
Consignee	Drawee (if not consignee)
To (bank)	For bank use only

FORWARD DOCUMENTS ENUMERATED BELOW BY AIR MAIL. FOLLOW SPECIAL INSTRUCTIONS AND THOSE MARKED X

Bill of exchange	Commercial invoice	Certified/consular invoice	Certificate of origin	Insurance policy/ certificate	Bill of lading	Parcel post receipt	Air waybill
Combined transport document	Other documents and whereabouts of any missing original bill of lading						

	ACCEPTANCE	PAYMENT			protest	do not protest
RELEASE DOCUMENTS ON			If unaccepted ➡			
If documents are not taken up on arrival of goods	warehouse goods	do not warehouse	and advise reason by		telex/cable	airmail
	insure against fire	do not insure	If unpaid ➡		protest	do not protest
Collect ALL charges			and advise reason by		telex/cable	airmail
Collect correspondent's charges ONLY			Advise acceptance and due date by		telex/cable	airmail
Return accepted bill by airmail			Remit proceeds by		telex/cable	airmail
In case of need refer to					for guidance	accept their instructions

SPECIAL INSTRUCTIONS: 1. Represent on arrival of goods if not honoured on first presentation.

Date of bill of exchange	Bill of exchange value/amount of collection
Tenor of bill of exchange	
Bill of exchange claused	
	Please collect the above-mentioned bill and/or documents subject to the Uniform Rules for Collections (1978 Revision), International Chamber of Commerce, Publication No. 322. I/We agree that you shall not be liable for any loss, damage, or delay however caused which is not directly due to the negligence of your own officers or servants.
	Date and signature

SITPRO Licensee No. 000.

Fig 35.1 Request for collection of foreign bill of exchange and/or documents

What the seller needs when dealing with a buyer with whom he has not previously had a relationship is an assurance, before he makes the shipping arrangements, that he will be paid after shipment. It is this need that the documentary credit[12] is designed to satisfy.

(i) The Uniform Customs and Practice for Documentary Credits (UCP), the eUCP and the International Standard Banking Practice (ISBP)

In international trade almost all documentary credits are expressed to be subject to the UCP published by the International Chamber of Commerce.[13] The UCP were later supplemented by the eUCP for electronic presentation. Until 1983 the UCP were confined to documentary credits in their true sense, that is, credits under which the issuing or confirming bank is the party primarily liable and therefore the first port of call for payment.[14] But in the 1983 revision the UCP were extended to standby credits, in which the bank's payment undertaking, though primary in form, is not properly invoked unless the principal has defaulted. [15] This extension, maintained in UCP 500, was introduced primarily to assist American banks, most of which are not legally entitled to issue suretyship guarantees, by sending a signal to American courts and regulators that standby credits, unlike suretyship guarantees and suretyship bonds, do not depend on proof of actual default and can therefore lawfully be issued. The extension was therefore understandable but introduced a measure of conceptual confusion into the UCP, most of which are predicated on the assumption that the bank is the first port of call for payment, so that the majority of the provisions are simply inappropriate to standby credits.[16] Happily, the problem

---

11 The leading English textbooks on the subject are Raymond Jack, Ali Malek and David Quest, *Documentary Credits* (3rd edn, 2001); Richard King (ed), *Gutteridge and Megrah's Law of Bankers' Commercial Credits* (8th edn, 2001); William Hedley and Richard Hedley, *Bills of Exchange and Bankers' Documentary Credits* (4th edn, 2000); and *Benjamin's Sale of Goods* (6th edn, 2002), ch 23. Strongly recommended additional reading is John F. Dolan, *The Law of Letters of Credit* (2nd edn and supplement, 2003). For excellent early comparative studies, see Boris Kozolchyk, 'Letters of Credit' in IX *International Encyclopaedia of Comparative Law* (eds K Zweigert and Ulrich Drobnig, 1978), ch 5 and *Commercial Letters of Credit in the America, A Comparative Study of Contemporary Commercial Transactions* (1966).

12 Also termed 'banker's commercial credit' and 'commercial letter of credit'. Letters of credit are also used to cover payment obligations which do not arise from the supply of goods and therefore do not involve the presentation of shipping documents. These are known as 'clean' credits.

13 The UCP are an outstanding successful codification of banking practice in relation to documentary credits. First published in 1933, they were revised in 1951, 1962, 1974, 1983 and 1993. The last of these (UCP 500) is the current text but is in course of revision. For the legal status of the UCP, see p 968.

14 See p 980.

15 See p 1017.

16 The ICC later published its Uniform Rules for Demand Guarantees (URDG), which from a purely legal viewpoint are synonymous with standby credits and in concept are therefore more suited to them than the UCP. However, these were designed very much with the European-style demand guarantee in mind and lack the detail and comprehensiveness necessary to accommodate the much more diverse uses of standby credits. See further below and p 1019.

has since been resolved by the issue of two further sets of rules, the Uniform Rules for Demand Guarantees (ICC 458), published in 1992, and the International Standby Practices (ISP98), a set of rules tailored specifically to standby credits and published by the Institute of International Banking Law and Practice. Demand guarantees and standby credits are considered later.[17]

The eUCP are concerned not with the electronic issue of letters of credit, for which there is a well-established practice, but with presentation of electronic records, either alone or with paper-based records. When fully developed, a system of electronic presentation will have a number of advantages, allowing the beneficiary conveniently to present documents directly to the issuing bank instead of to an advising or confirming bank, and providing an automated system for the checking of documents, which is currently a laborious manual process, thus saving labour and reducing the currently high percentage of discrepancies. But it is likely to be many years before electronic presentation comes into general use.

The International Standard Banking Practice (ISBP) for the examination of documents under documentary credits[18] is a practical complement to UCP 500 designed to bring uniformity of standards into documentation examination.

(ii)   The documentary credit defined

A documentary credit is, in essence, a banker's assurance of payment against presentment of specified documents. It is defined by the UCP as:

> any arrangement, however named or described, whereby a bank (the 'Issuing Bank') acting at the request and on the instructions of a customer (the 'Applicant') or on its own behalf,
>
> i.   is to make a payment to or to the order of a third party (the 'Beneficiary'), or is to accept and pay bills of exchange (Draft(s)) drawn by the Beneficiary,
>
> or
>
> ii.   authorises another bank to effect such payment or to accept and pay such bills of exchange (Draft(s)),
>
> or
>
> iii.   authorises another bank to negotiate,
>
> against stipulated document(s), provided that the terms and conditions of the Credit are complied with.[19]

In the case of a documentary credit opened pursuant to a contract of sale, the buyer (B) will be the applicant for the credit and the seller (S) will be the beneficiary.[20]

---

17 See p 1015. The ICC provides a swift dispute resolution machinery for resolving disputes arising under the UCP, URDG and other ICC payment rules. These are governed by the 2002 ICC Rules for Documentary Instruments Dispute Resolution Expertise (DOCDEX) administered by the ICC's International Centre for Expertise. Decisions are made by a panel of three independent experts but are not binding unless otherwise agreed. The proceedings are conducted exclusively in writing.

18 ICC Publication No 645, 2003.

19 Article 2.

20 'Seller' is hereafter used for convenience to denote the beneficiary, though the letter of credit is not always issued to the seller himself but may, at his request, be opened in favour of a third party.

It will be seen from the above definition that a credit may take one of three forms. It may entitle S to collect payment on presentation of documents (sight payment credit), to present with the documents a draft for acceptance and payment at maturity (acceptance credit) or to negotiate (sell) a draft and/or documents to an authorized bank, which then becomes the beneficiary in place of S.[21] Despite the references to banks throughout the UCP, there is nothing to preclude a non-bank institution from issuing a documentary credit governed by the UCP. Several non-banking financial institutions do so, and even some corporates, though the Banking Commission has emphasized the importance of ensuring that the issuer is truly independent of the parties.

(iii) Factors influencing use of documentary credits

Documentary credits provide the seller with security (at any rate if irrevocable) but they also cost money. The banks involved in issuing, advising and confirming the credit make a charge for their services and the cost is passed back to the buyer. Hence the buyer may be reluctant to agree to payment under a letter of credit, and whether the seller will be in a position to insist on this without agreeing to bear the cost himself will depend on the relative bargaining position of the parties. In practice, the seller will usually require a letter of credit only where he has not developed a sufficient relationship with the buyer to enable him to adopt a cheaper payment method, such as payment against documents.

The popularity of letters of credit has fluctuated widely over the years. The demand for letters of credit varies not only according to whether it is a sellers' or a buyers' market and the degree of confidence felt by sellers in the creditworthiness of their customers but also with governmental controls. Where strict exchange controls are applied, the letter of credit tends to become more prominent, for it provides the exchange control authorities with a means of ensuring that payments due on exported goods are, in fact, received in the country of export.[22] Again, letters of credit tend to be used on the sale of goods overseas in countries with aid programmes. In recent years the letter of credit appears to have entered a period of gradual decline, and one leading authority, Professor James Byrne, has observed a dramatic decline in the willingness of banks to invest in this field,[23] while another, Professor John Dolan, has noted in the same volume that 'commercial letters of credit in general and the negotiation credit in particular arise in transactions at the margin of commerce. Financially sound enterprises with significant banking relationships do not need letters of credit.'[24]

---

21 See pp 961 ff.
22 This is a factor which ceased to be relevant in the United Kingdom in 1979, when exchange controls were abolished.
23 'Overview of Letter of Credit Law and Practice' in *2003 Annual Survey of Letter of Credit Law and Practice* (2003) at p 3.
24 'Negotiation Letters of Credit' in *2003 Annual Survey of Letter of Credit Law and Practice*, n 23, at p 25.

(iv) Stages in the opening of a credit[25]

The starting point, as always, is the contract of sale, for the seller is not entitled to require, nor the buyer to offer, payment by documentary credit unless the contract of sale so provides; and the credit opened in favour of the seller must comply in all respects with the terms of the contract, otherwise the seller will be entitled to reject it. Sometimes the contract of sale fails to indicate the type of credit required, this being left to the subsequent agreement of the parties. Such agreement impliedly varies or supplements the contract of sale.[26]

Let us suppose that S in London has agreed to sell a quantity of machinery to B in New York and that payment is to be made under an irrevocable credit issued by a New York bank and advised and confirmed by a London bank.[27] From the viewpoint of the London bank such a credit is an 'inward' credit, while to the New York bank it is an 'outward' credit. The procedure will be as follows.

1.   Application by B to his bank

The first step is taken by B, who must apply to his bank in New York, known as the issuing bank (IB), to open the credit in favour of S, that is, to issue a letter of credit to S undertaking payment of a sum equal to the contract price or payment, acceptance or negotiation of a bill of exchange drawn for that sum.[28] B will be asked to complete the bank's standard form of application to open a credit giving full details of his requirements (for a specimen, see fig 35.2). In completing the application B must ensure, first, that his instructions are clear[29] and capable of being complied with by his bank and, secondly, that they conform to the terms of the contract of sale. IB is not itself concerned with the contract of sale, and is unlikely to see this document. It will act on B's instructions, but if in accordance with those instructions the letter of credit issued to S calls for documents other than those specified in the contract of sale or is otherwise at variance with that contract, S will be entitled to reject the letter of credit as not in conformity with the contract of sale.

IB may require its customer, B, to put it in funds to cover IB's projected commitment to S, or it may be willing to rely on B's creditworthiness or the likelihood of funds coming in before the documents are due to be presented by S for

---

25 See generally Charles del Busto, *ICC Guide to Documentary Credit Operations for the UCP 500* (1994).

26 *Ficom SA v Sociedad Cadax Ltd* [1980] 2 Lloyd's Rep 118; *Shamsher Jute Mills Ltd v Sethia (London) Ltd* [1987] 1 Lloyd's Rep 388. If the parties do not conclude a later agreement identifying the type of credit, then, unless this can be inferred from the circumstances or a prior course of dealing, the contract of sale is likely to be held void for uncertainty or want of consensus (*Schijveshuurder v Canon (Export) Ltd* [1952] 2 Lloyd's Rep 196).

27 The terms 'irrevocable' and 'confirmed' are explained at pp 958–959.

28 Sometimes B's bank does not itself issue the credit but asks its correspondent in S's country to do so. In such a case there is no contractual relationship between B's bank and S.

29 If they are not, so that the credit is ambiguous, it will be construed against the issuer. See *Credit Agricole Indosuez v Muslim Commercial Bank Ltd* [2000] 1 Lloyd's Rep 275, where the terms of the credit left it unclear whether the presentation of certain specified documents was a condition of the credit, and the confirming bank was held entitled to conclude that they were not and to receive payment from the issuing bank.

To: HSBC Bank plc _____ International Branch

APPLICATION FOR IRREVOCABLE DOCUMENTARY CREDIT

Transferable? ☐ No ☐ Yes	D C Number	Date of application

Applicant (name and full address)	Beneficiary Name and Address (and telephone no, Fax no. Contact name within company, if known)

Applicant's reference

Expiry Date ....

Place of Expiry ....

Amount: Currency.......................... Figures ....

Words ....

Acceptable variance in quantity of goods*/DC amount*: +/-...........................% (*Delete as appropriate)

Partial Shipment ☐ allowed ☐ not allowed	**Transhipment** ☐ allowed ☐ not allowed

Latest Shipment Date...

Shipment/Despatch/Taking in charge

From...

To ....

Method of Advice: ☐ Full teletransmission ☐ Airmail ☐ Courier

☐ Drafts required drawn on Issuing Bank for full invoice value of the goods: ☐ At Sight: ☐ ....days after Sight

☐ ....days after B/L, AWB, CMR; ☐ ....days after Invoice Date: ☐ Other ....

Advising Bank/Routing Bank (if applicable)	Instruct Advising Bank to add their confirmation
	☐ Yes ☐ No
	If Yes, confirmation charges payable by
	☐ Applicant ☐ Beneficiary
(If left blank, DC will normally be advised through an HSBC Group Office)	

Documents to be presented within ....days after the date of ☐ Shipment ☐ Receipt but within validity of the documentary credit

Trade term .... Place ....

(e.g. FOB, FCA, CFR, CPT, CIF, CIP, EXW, DDU, DDP)

Goods (brief description including quantity without excessive detail)

1016-8 (01/99 - UOI = 1PK x 25)

Fig 35.2 Application to open documentary credit

Documents Required:

Original Invoice(s) signed plus.................................copies

☐ Full set of original clean "on board" marine bills of lading

    ☐ made out to the shipper's order, blank endorsed and marked   ☐ freight prepaid   ☐ freight collect

    and notify ....

    ☐ made out to order of...and marked   ☐ freight prepaid   ☐ freight collect

    and notify ....

☐ Air waybill, marked "for the consignor/shipper", marked   ☐ freight prepaid   ☐ freight collect
and notify...bearing reference to this documentary credit number, showing actual date of despatch of
goods including flight number and evidencing despatch of goods to ....

☐ Original CMR/Truck waybill marked   ☐ freight prepaid   ☐ freight collect   ☐ evidencing goods consigned to.................

☐ Other transport documents (please specify).................

☐ If CIF/CIP: Insurance policy/certificate for full CIF/CIP value plus   ☐ 10%   ☐ ....% blank endorsed, covering
institute cargo clauses 'A'/war/strike/other (please specify if required).................clauses

☐ If FOB etc: Insurance covered by applicant/buyer

Additional Documents

☐ Packing list in.................copies   ☐ Export licence/certificate in.................copies   ☐ Weight list in.................copies

☐ GSP certificate form A in.................copies   ☐ Certificate of.................origin in.................copies   ☐ Other (please specify)

Special Instructions

Documents to be delivered in one lot unless otherwise specified to the Issuing Bank by   ☐ Courier   ☐ Registered Airmail
☐ Other (please specify).................

DC charges	Applicant	Beneficiary *(see note 13 below)*	☐ On receipt of documents in order, please debit our
Within UK	☐	☐	Account number ....
			Sort code 40-.................-.................
Outside UK	☐	☐	Utilising Forward Contract No/Spot Rate.................

Please debit DC opening commission, advising expenses to our

    Account number ....

    Sort code   40-.................-.................

We request you to issue your irrevocable Documentary Credit
for our account in accordance with the above instructions and
subject to the conditions printed below:

Signature verified

....
signed on behalf of applicant in accordance with our mandate held by the Bank

In case of query, please telephone.................and ask for.................

Conditions

1. Except so far as otherwise expressly stated, this Documentary Credit is subject to Uniform Customs and Practice for Documentary Credits (1993 Revision), International Chamber of Commerce Publication No 500.
2. We agree to take out and to the extent required by the Bank all insurance necessary for the full protection of the Bank's interest in the goods shipped under this Credit, and on behalf of the Bank and subject to its instructions to prosecute or to ensure the prosecution of any claim that may arise under any insurance and to pay the proceeds thereof to the Bank and to provide evidence of insurance if called upon to do so.
3. If this Credit is to be advised through an agency or correspondent bank in USA, you are authorised to accept at your sole discretion and under our responsibility American Institute clauses insurance policies.
4. You are authorised to make any additions to the documents specified under this Credit which you may consider necessary to ensure compliance with government regulations but you are not obliged to do so.
5. We certify that the import of goods described above is not prohibited or restricted and that we hold and undertake to exhibit to you a valid import licence where such licence is required.
6. The words "we" and "our" shall be read as "I" and "my" if this application is signed by or on behalf of an individual.
7. You are authorised at your sole discretion and without obligation to do whenever you consider it advisable, customary or appropriate to waive or delete the following from the instructions contained on this form (whether completed by me/us or not), namely: "Drafts required at sight/at   days drawn on issuing bank for full invoice value of goods"
8. In the absence of any instructions to the contrary specified in "Special Conditions" above, you are authorised to instruct any bank or branch concerned to despatch any draft(s) and or any documents by one or more mails or other method of conveyance at your sole discretion.
9. We undertake on demand to reimburse you in respect of all payments and to indemnify you in respect of all liabilities, including legal costs, on a full indemnity basis and to discharge all liabilities which you may make or incur for us at our request or as a result of your allowing any drawer and or negotiating bank to

obtain reimbursement before you have had the opportunity to inspect any documents in connection with this Credit and to pay interest from the date of the same having been made or incurred until repayment both before and after any demand made at the stipulated rate by you.

10. We are aware of the implications of article 15 of UCP 500 and acknowledge that where a bank claims to have paid/accepted/negotiated under this Credit, its good faith and the fact of payment/acceptance/negotiation thereof shall be presumed in the absence of evidence to the contrary.
11. As continuing security for the payment of all sums for which we may from time to time actually or contingently indebted or liable to you for any reason and on any account:
  (a) we hereby pledge and agree to pledge to you with full title guarantee firstly all bills, documents or title, transportation documents, insurance policies and other documents representing or relating to the goods shipped under this credit which goods and/or documents are in or come into your or your agent's actual or constructive possession or control and secondly, the goods represented thereby, and we warrant that such documents and goods shall not be subject to any lien, charge or other encumbrance in favour of any other person; and
  (b) we agree to ensure that all such documents are properly endorsed and delivered to you and you are hereby authorised to demand the same from any party on your behalf.
12. We furthermore agree that this Credit and any drawing(s) or advance(s) relating thereto shall be subject to the terms of the separate pledge (being in addition to that contained in Condition 11 above) where given to you.
13. Where charges are for the account of the beneficiary and are unpaid for any reason we undertake to reimburse you in full.
14. We are aware and agree that, in connection with this Documentary Credit, such Credit will be subject to and the Bank will comply with the ICC Decision dated 6th April 1998 on "The impact of the European single currency (euro) on monetary obligations related to transactions involving ICC Rules."

payment. Usually the reverse side of the application for the credit, setting out the terms on which IB is prepared to issue the letter of credit and incorporating the provisions of the UCP, will contain a clause by which B gives IB a general charge or hypothecation over the goods to be supplied by S and over the shipping documents relating to them.

The credit to be issued by IB may be either revocable or irrevocable. The former, little used at the present time, can be withdrawn without notice and thus gives S little security;[30] the latter constitutes a binding undertaking which IB is not entitled to cancel, whether with or without notice.[31]

2. Notification of opening of credit

IB may issue the letter of credit directly to S, but almost invariably it will arrange for notification by another bank, known as the 'advising bank' (AB), in S's country. In our case IB will ask its correspondent bank or branch in London to advise S of the opening of the credit in his favour. The advice is almost always given in electronic form via SWIFT.[32] The notification by AB will then constitute the letter of credit. IB becomes bound to S immediately S receives the letter of credit.

3. Nomination of bank

Unless the credit stipulates that it is available only with IB, it must nominate the bank ('the nominated bank') which is authorized to pay, to issue a deferred payment undertaking, to accept drafts or to negotiate.[33] In a freely negotiable credit any bank is a nominated bank.[34] Unless the nominated bank is the confirming bank, neither the nomination by IB nor the nominated bank's receipt, examination or forwarding of the documents commits the nominated bank.[35] So AB does not itself incur any liability to S merely by advising the opening of the credit. However, if (as will often be the case) the contract of sale calls for a confirmed credit, IB will ask AB[36] to add its own undertaking to honour the credit on presentation of the documents. This undertaking is known as a 'confirmation' and the credit is then said to be a confirmed credit, that is, a credit under which the undertaking given by IB is reinforced by a separate payment undertaking by the confirming bank, AB. The advantages to S are obvious: instead of having to rely exclusively on a foreign bank, whose standing may not be known to him and who would have to be sued in New York, S has the benefit of a separate commitment by a London bank which can, he

---

30 See p 959.

31 See p 959.

32 The fast international payment system operated by the Society for Worldwide Interbank Financial Telecommunications. If B specifically requests it, IB may advise the issue of the credit through S's bank instead of its own correspondent bank.

33 UCP, art 10(b)(i). Most credits are payable at the counters of a bank other than the issuing bank.

34 Ibid.

35 Article 10(c).

36 But sometimes the confirmation is by a third bank and AB's role is simply to advise the opening of the credit by IB and the confirmation by the third bank and to examine the documents. Under UCP 500 it is now possible for an overseas branch of the issuing bank to confirm the credit. For the effect of this, see p 986, n 186.

assumes, be relied on to pay or procure payment and is subject to process in England. Where AB does not add its confirmation, the credit is known as an unconfirmed credit.

Armed with the letter of credit, S can now proceed to fulfil the order.

4.   Presentation of documents

After dispatch, S must arrange for the transport documents to be presented in accordance with the terms of the letter of credit. All credits must stipulate the place of presentation.[37] Usually, the letter of credit will provide for presentation of the documents to AB rather than IB, as it is obviously more convenient to S for the documents to be presented to a bank in his own country. Assuming the credit is a straight (or specially advised) credit, only S or his agent may present the documents.[38] The presentation will usually be made by S's bank, not by S himself, whose identity may not be known to the paying bank. S's bank thus acts as a collecting bank in much the same way as if collecting a cheque[39] and vis-à-vis the paying bank, it presents the documents as S's agent, not in its own right, even where it has made an advance to S on the strength of the credit, so that where S has been guilty of fraud,[40] his bank is not entitled to payment. If the documents are in order,[41] AB will pay, accept or negotiate the bill of exchange in accordance with the letter of credit.[42] AB will then pass the documents back to IB, who will release them to B, either unconditionally or in exchange for a trust receipt.[43]

(v) Types of credit

Credits may be classified in various ways, in particular by reference to the revocability or otherwise of the bank's undertaking, the presence or absence of a separate undertaking from a second bank, the time and mode of settlement, the range of parties entitled to enforce the undertaking, whether the credit is fixed or floating, the transferability of the benefit of the undertaking given to S by the bank, and so on.

1.   Revocable and irrevocable credits

As previously mentioned, a revocable credit is one which may be cancelled by IB without notice.[44] IB incurs no real commitment under such a credit, except that if AB or some other authorized bank has accepted, paid or negotiated the credit prior

---

37 Article 42(a).
38 The position is otherwise in the case of a negotiation credit. See p 987.
39 See p 542.
40 As to which, see p 991.
41 Which in many cases they are not. See p 977.
42 See p 987.
43 See p 1015.
44 UCP, art 2; *Cape Asbestos Co Ltd v Lloyds Bank Ltd* [1921] WN 274, where it was held that the right to refuse payment existed even if the beneficiary had already shipped the goods (the judgments speak throughout of a 'revocable' credit, though in modern terminology it would be an unconfirmed credit).

to receiving notice of its cancellation, it will be entitled to reimbursement from IB,[45] which, in turn, will recoup itself from B. Hence, revocable credits are of little value to a seller who requires security. They are, however, quite commonly used as a convenient payment mechanism where security for payment is not an objective, as where seller and buyer are associated companies or have a well-established relationship. The use of such credits may also be prompted by governmental desire to police the operation of exchange control regulations. Moreover, a buyer who is unwilling to incur the commitment attendant upon an irrevocable credit (which he has no power to cancel or countermand), may be quite happy to arrange for the issue of a revocable letter of credit, which leaves him free to instruct his bank to cancel the credit if there is a risk of default of performance by the seller, eg through insolvency, political interference or instability or the tender of a defective instalment of goods to be delivered by instalments.

By contrast, an irrevocable credit commits IB to honour the credit, notwithstanding instructions by its customer to the contrary, provided the terms of the credit are fulfilled by S.

Prior to the 1993 revision there was a presumption that credits were revocable. This was out of line with normal usage, and UCP 500 provides that a credit is deemed irrevocable unless it clearly indicates that it is revocable.[46]

2. Unconfirmed and confirmed credit

As previously explained, a confirmed credit is one under which IB's undertaking under an irrevocable credit is reinforced by that of another bank, usually AB. A credit may be irrevocable without being confirmed, but a confirmed credit is always irrevocable. A confirmed credit within the meaning of the UCP is one in which AB or some other bank is authorized by IB to add its confirmation, in which event it is entitled to reimbursement and commission from IB. But it is not uncommon for an advising bank to add its confirmation without authority from IB in return for a commission from S himself. This so-called 'silent confirmation' is outside the UCP, and the 'confirming' bank, though committed to S by virtue of its confirmation, is no more than an advising bank vis-à-vis IB.

3. Sight payment, acceptance and deferred payment credits

Classified by the time at which S is entitled to payment, letters of credit divide primarily into sight payment credits, acceptance credits and deferred payment credits.[47] A sight payment credit is one which provides for payment against documents. The credit calls for S to draw a sight bill of exchange[48] on IB, AB or

---

45 UCP, art 2.

46 Article 6(c).

47 The fourth type of credit mentioned in art 10(a), the negotiation credit, is not a truly distinct category but a particular form of acceptance credit in which the right to present the documents and collect payment is extended beyond the original beneficiary, S, to authorized purchasers of S's drafts and documents. See p 987. There are also specialized forms of credit, such as red clause and green clause credits, which are the antithesis of the deferred payment credit. See p 967.

48 See p 487.

another bank and present the documents with the bill for immediate payment.[49] Since no acceptance of the bill is involved,[50] the bank retains the bill with the documents after payment.[51] An acceptance credit (fig 35.3) requires S to present a term bill to IB, AB or another bank for acceptance against documents and payment by the accepting bank at maturity.[52] Payment of a sight payment or acceptance credit will usually be made by AB, which in our example will be a London bank. S then receives payment in London. If the credit is an acceptance credit, AB will accept it and will pay it at maturity and thereupon debit IB with the face value of the bill and AB's commission. Under a deferred payment credit (fig 35.4(3)), payment is made not on presentation of documents or by acceptance of a draft but after expiry of a stated period from shipment[53] or bill of lading date or from presentation (eg 60 days after sight), the documents being meanwhile released to B. Deferred payment credits came into vogue for the purpose of avoiding the high stamp duty payable on drafts in some countries. However, beneficiaries were not keen to have payment deferred, so that it became common for banks to negotiate deferred payment credits. But a bank which does this without first obtaining authority to negotiate from the issuing bank takes the risk of discovery of fraud by the issuing bank prior to the due payment date, and in that event the issuing bank is entitled to refuse to pay the credit.[54] In *Banco Santander SA v Bayern Ltd*[55] the facts were as follows:

> Banque Paribas issued a deferred payment credit in favour of Bayern payable at the counters of Banco Santander, which in accordance with instructions from Paribas confirmed the credit. Several months prior to maturity of the credit Paribas discounted its own obligation and took an assignment of Bayern's rights under the credit. No notice of the assignment was given to Paribas, to whom the documents were passed by Santander. Two weeks after the assignment Paribas notified Santander that some of the documents presented by Bayern were false or fraudulent. On maturity of the credit Paribas refused to pay on the ground that Santander, as assignee of Bayern, stood in no better position than Bayern itself. For Santander it was argued that Santander was entitled to be paid in its capacity of confirming bank, that there had been no assignment, since the effect of the transaction between Bayern and Santander was to extinguish Bayern's claim and that, even if there had been an assignment, Santander, as bona fide

---

49 This type of credit is used where the contract of sale between S and B does not provide for B to receive a period of credit. However, even where the contract and the ensuing letter of credit provide for immediate payment against documents, S may subsequently be willing to accommodate B by drawing a term bill if AB is willing to negotiate the bill and B is prepared to pay the discount. S will then receive from AB the full face value of the bill (which from S's viewpoint then achieves the same effect as a sight bill), and AB will debit IB for the account of B, who gets the credit he needs

50 See p 486.

51 Sometimes the bill is dispensed with, even where the credit provides for it, since it has no legal significance. But banks usually call for a bill in the letter of credit since (a) the bill shows at a glance the amount to be paid, and (b) after payment is retained by the paying bank, it is a useful record of payment which will identify the credit under which it was drawn and also, in many cases, the shipment of the goods to which it relates.

52 But S will not necessarily hold the bill until maturity. He may instead negotiate it. See below.

53 A provision for payment a stated number of days after shipment is interpreted as documentary in character and as referring to the date of shipment shown on the bill of lading.

54 *Banco Santander SA v Bayern Ltd* [2000] 1 All ER (Comm) 776.

55 See n 54.

purchaser for value, took free from defences available against Bayern as assignor. On the hearing of a preliminary issue the Court of Appeal, affirming the decision of Langley J, rejected the arguments advanced on behalf of Bayern, holding that there had been an assignment; that, as assignee, Santander took subject to defences and that it could not recover in its capacity of confirming bank because it had no authority to negotiate or pay prior to maturity of the credit, by which time its knowledge of established fraud on the part of Bayern would have given it a defence to a payment claim by Bayern and thus precluded it from obtaining reimbursement from Paribas. [56]

The position is otherwise in the United States under art 5 of the Uniform Commercial Code, which protects an assignee for value and without notice of the fraud[57] so that Santander would have succeeded.[58]

4.   Straight (or specially advised) credits and negotiation credits

Prima facie, IB's undertaking (and that of AB, if confirming the credit) is given in favour of S alone. The letter of credit itself is not a negotiable instrument, and while there is nothing to stop S from selling a draft drawn on IB or AB under the credit, the purchaser of the draft would have no claim against the drawee bank for refusal to honour the bill, since the undertaking in the letter of credit was not given to the purchaser. A credit of this kind is termed a 'straight' or 'specially advised' credit.

But the undertaking given in the letter of credit may be framed as an undertaking not merely to S but also to those negotiating S's drafts and/or documents. Such a credit is known as a negotiation credit[59] and its effect is that anyone who, pursuant to the authority in the credit, negotiates S's drafts in good faith and in reliance on the credit may call upon IB (and on AB if confirming) to honour the draft, provided that this is accompanied by documents presented in accordance with the credit and in apparent good order at the time the draft was purchased.

Under art 10(b)(ii) of the UCP negotiation means the giving of value for drafts and/or documents by the bank authorized to negotiate. Mere examination of the documents without giving of value does not constitute a negotiation, nor, it seems, does the mere promise to give value at a later date, eg on receipt of funds.[60] This is a new and useful definition, for banks often refer loosely to credits being 'available at our counters for negotiation' when all they mean is that the documents may be presented to them with a draft for payment or acceptance.

---

56 This is how it was put by Waller LJ in the Court of Appeal; but a more satisfactory basis for the decision is that Santander would have been not merely entitled to withhold payment but obliged to do so. In situations where the evidence presented to the confirming bank falls short of established fraud, the bank is not obliged to expose itself to a law suit by being compelled to take a position on the evidence but has a choice: to pay and obtain reimbursement or to refuse payment and take its chance on being able to show fraud when the case comes before the court for decision.

57 Uniform Commercial Code, §§ 5–109(a).

58 See *2001 Annual Survey of Letter of Credit Law and Practice* (eds James E. Byrne and Christopher S. Byrnes) at pp195–196.

59 A very useful analysis is provided by Dolan, *Law of Letters of Credit*, n 11.

60 For a discussion of the point, with relevant citations, see E. P. Ellinger, 'Documentary Dialogue' (1995) 1 *Documentary Credits Insight* 12. See also Alan Ward, 'The Nature of Negotiation under Documentary Credits' [1999] JIBL 292.

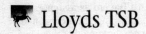

Lloyds TSB

Trade Services
Documentary Credits - Exports
Transmission Services
Lloyds TSB Bank plc
P O Box 63
Two Brindleyplace
Birmingham
B1 2AB

Direct Line	:	0121 625 5887
Switchboard	:	0121 643 9840
Facsimile	:	0121 625 6255

grptfgen@lloydstsb.co.uk

M. J. SMITH & CO LTD
168 WARKWORTH DRIVE,
CIRENCESTER
GLOS. GL7 1HU

6 May 2004

Dear Sir or Madam,

LETTER OF CREDIT NUMBER	:	**2BRXH2178**
AMOUNT	:	**USD 74,200.00**
ISSUING BANK	:	**SHANGHAI INTERNATIONAL BANK**
		YAUNLIN, TAIWAN
OUR REFERENCE	:	**XQS40037142**

We have been instructed to advise you that SHANGHAI INTERNATIONAL BANK,
YAUNLIN, TAIWAN has issued the above-mentioned Irrevocable Letter of Credit in your
favour.

The terms and conditions of the Letter of Credit are as follows:-

40A/FORM OF DOCUMENTARY CREDIT	: IRREVOCABLE

20 /DOCUMENTARY CREDIT NUMBER	: 2BRXH2178

31C/DATE OF ISSUE	: 6 May 2004

31D/DATE AND PLACE OF EXPIRY	: 15 July 2004 - ENGLAND

50 /APPLICANT :-	
JIN SHENG SUPPLY LTD 50 CHUNGSHAN CHANG HUA TAIWAN	

59 /BENEFICIARY :-	
M. J. SMITH & CO LTD 168 WARKWORTH DRIVE, CIRENCESTER GLOS. GL7 1HU	

SPECIMEN

This is page 1 of a 4 page advice

Lloyds TSB Bank plc Registered Office 25 Gresham Street, London EC2V 7HN.
Registered in England and Wales no. 2065. A signatory to the Banking Codes.
Certificate No. FS 22626

Fig 35.3 Acceptance credit advised by issuing bank direct

Lloyds TSB

32B/CURRENCY CODE, AMOUNT	:	USD 74,200.00

39A/PERCENTAGE CREDIT AMOUNT TOLERANCE (+/-)	:	5/5

41A/AVAILABLE WITH ... BY ...	:	LOYDGB2L LLOYDS TSB BANK PLC LONDON BY NEGOTIATION

42C/DRAFTS AT ...	:	SIGHT
42A/DRAWEE	:	SCSBTWTP016 SHANGHAI INTERNATIONAL BANK YUANLIN BRANCH 240 DAH AN YUANLIN, TAIWAN

43P/PARTIAL SHIPMENTS	:	PERMITTED
43T/TRANSSHIPMENT	:	PERMITTED

44A/LOADING ON BOARD/DISPATCH/TAKING IN CHARGE AT/FROM ...	:	U.K. PORT

44B/FOR TRANSPORTATION TO ...	:	TAICHUNG PORT TAIWAN

44C/LATEST DATE OF SHIPMENT	:	30 June 2004

45A/DESCRIPTION OF GOODS AND/OR SERVICES :-

DESCRIPTION OF GOODS	QUANTITY	UNIT PRICE	AMOUNT
ORIGINAL WHITE DUCK FEATHER QUALITY AS THE SAMPLE PROVIDED 2 CONTAINERS (40 FT)	28000 KGS	USD2.65/KG	USD74,200.-

TOTAL AMOUNT.......................................USD74,200.-
DETAILS AS PER PROFORMA INVOICE NO. MJS/218 DD APR 28 2004
CFR TAICHUNG PORT TAIWAN

46A/DOCUMENTS REQUIRED :-

1. COMMERCIAL INVOICE IN SEXTUPLICATE INDICATING THIS CREDIT
   NUMBER
2. PACKING LIST IN SEXTUPLICATE
3. FULL SET OF ORIGINAL CLEAN BOARD MARINE BILLS OF LADING
   MADE OUT TO ORDER OF THE SHANGHAI INTERNATIONAL BANK
   LTD. TAIWAN SHOWING ACCOUNTEE AS NOTIFY PARTY
   MARKED FREIGHT PREPAID AND THIS CREDIT NUMBER
4. BENEFICIARY'S CERTIFICATE CERTIFYING THAT ONE COMPLETE SET
   OF NON-NEGOTIABLE DOCUMNETS HAVE BEEN SENT TO ACCOUNTEE
   BY COURIER DIRECTLY
5. ONE ORIGINAL HEALTH CERTIFICATE

Certificate No: __FS 22626__

This is page 2 of a 4 page advice

Lloyds TSB Bank plc Registered Office 25 Gresham Street, London EC2V 7HN.
Registered in England and Wales no. 2065. A signatory to the Banking Codes.

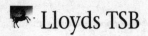 **Lloyds TSB**   \Continuation of our letter dated 6 May 2004 under our reference XQS40037142

---

6. ONE ORIGINAL CERTIFICATE OF ORIGIN

47A/ADDITIONAL CONDITIONS :-

1. A FEE OF USD50.- FOR EACH PRESENTATION OF DOCUMENTS WITH
   DISCREPANCIES UNDER THIS CREDIT IS FOR ACCOUNT OF BENEFICIARY
   AND WILL BE DEDUCTED FROM THE PROCEEDS
2. 5 PCT. MORE OR LESS IN QUANTITY AND AMOUNT ARE ALLOWED

71B/CHARGES   :   ALL BANKING CHARGES OUTSIDE TAIWAN ARE
                        FOR BENEFICIARY'S ACCOUNT

---

48 /PERIOD FOR PRESENTATION   :   **DOCUMENTS MUST BE PRESENTED WITHIN
                                        20 DAYS AFTER THE DATE OF SHIPMENT
                                        BUT WITHIN VALIDITY OF THE CREDIT**

---

49 /CONFIRMATION INSTRUCTIONS   :   WITHOUT

---

78 /INSTRUCTIONS TO THE PAYING / ACCEPTING / NEGOTIATING BANK :-

1. ALL DOCUMENTS MUST BE SENT TO OUR YUAN LIN BRANCH AT 240 DAH AN
   ROAD YUAN LIN CHANG HUA TAIWAN R.O.C.
2. UPON RECEIPT OF THE RELATIVE DOCUMENTS IN ORDER, WE SHALL
   REIMBURSE THE NEGOTIATING BANK IN ACCORDANCE WITH THEIR
   INSTRUCTIONS

---

72 /SENDER TO RECEIVER INFORMATION   :   NO MAIL CONFIRMATION WILL FOLLOW

Our comments regarding the above-mentioned Letter of Credit are as follows:-

This Letter of Credit is subject to the Uniform Customs and Practice for Documentary Credits,
1993 Revision, I.C.C. Publication No. 500 except as otherwise specifically stated in the Letter of
Credit.

This Letter of Credit is irrevocable on the part of the Issuing Bank but conveys no liability or
engagement on the part of Lloyds TSB Bank plc.

FS 22626

Lloyds TSB Bank plc Registered Office 25 Gresham Street, London EC2V 7HN.
Registered in England and Wales no. 2065. A signatory to the Banking Codes.

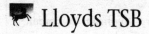 Lloyds TSB

\Continuation of our letter dated 6 May 2004 under our reference XQS40037142

Lloyds TSB Bank plc charge details under this Letter of Credit are as follows-

Our Commission and Charges relating to this Letter of Credit are for your account. Therefore, please remit the sum of GBP 40.00 to us in settlement of the following:-

Charge Description	Amount	
- Advising Commission	GBP	40.00
- **Total Charges**	GBP	40.00

The following further charges will be levied as appropriate:-

Payment Commission	:	0.125% (minimum £75) of presentation value applicable to all presentations per set of documents
Amendment Commission	:	£40
Cancellation Commission	:	£50

Miscellaneous

The cost of dispatching documents, any teletransmission costs and Reimbursing Bank charges will be deducted from the proceeds of each documentary presentation.

If you would like any further assistance or advice regarding the above, please contact CUSTOMER SUPPORT TEAM on telephone number 0121 625 5887.

Yours faithfully,

Authorised Signatory

SPECIMEN

Certificate No **FS 22626**

This is page 4 of a 4 page advice

Lloyds TSB Bank plc Registered Office 25 Gresham Street, London EC2V 7HN. Registered in England and Wales no. 2065. A signatory to the Banking Codes.

[Names of advising bank, issuing bank, beneficiary, applicant for credit, amount of credit, etc. Other details on separate attachment.]

(1) Unconfirmed restricted negotiation credit

We are pleased to advise you of an irrevocable credit opened in your favour by the above-mentioned issuing bank as stated above of which further details are attached This credit is available by negotiation of your drafts at sight drawn on the issuing bank accompanied by the documents specified in the credit and presented in conformity therewith. We are not instructed to add our confirmation and this advice is given without responsibility on our part This credit is subject to the Uniform Customs and Practice for Documentary Credits, 1993 Revision, ICC Publication No 500.

(2) Confirmed open negotiation credit

We are pleased to advise you of an irrevocable credit opened in your favour by the above-mentioned issuing bank as stated above of which further details are attached This credit is available with any bank by negotiation of your drafts at sight drawn on us accompanied by the documents specified in the credit and presented in conformity therewith. We are instructed to confirm this credit and hereby undertake to drawers and/or bona fide holders that drafts drawn and negotiated in conformity with the terms of this credit will be honoured on presentation. This credit is subject to the Uniform Customs and Practice for Documentary Credits, 1993 Revision, ICC Publication No 500.

(3) Confirmed deferred payment credit

We are pleased to advise you of an irrevocable credit opened in your favour by the above-mentioned issuing bank as stated above of which further details are attached This credit is available 30 days after presentation to us of the documents specified in the credit and presented in conformity therewith. We are instructed to confirm this credit and undertake to pay as above. This credit is subject to the Uniform Customs and Practice for Documentary Credits, 1993 Revision, ICC Publication No 500.

Figure 35.4 Forms of advice by advising bank to beneficiary of (1) unconfirmed restricted negotiation credit, (2) confirmed open negotiation credit, (3) confirmed deferred payment credit

It is important to distinguish negotiation of drafts and documents from payment of a credit. Negotiation involves the purchase by an authorized bank of the draft and documents,[61] and, with it, the entitlement to present the documents and collect payment in its own right at the due date. The original beneficiary, S, receives payment for the drafts[62] and documents, not payment under the credit,[63] and then drops out of the picture, being replaced as beneficiary by the negotiating bank. So the negotiation credit is a particular form of acceptance credit under which the right to present and collect payment is extended beyond the original beneficiary.

A negotiation credit may be open or restricted. That is, IB may, by the terms of the letter of credit, permit negotiation by any bank which cares to do so, or may restrict negotiation, eg to banks or to a designated bank (typically IB's own correspondent, AB). The effect of an open negotiation credit (fig 35.4(2)) is that IB undertakes to any bank negotiating the bill that it will be honoured on due presentment of the documents. A restricted negotiation credit (fig 35.4(1)) does not prevent S from negotiating the draft to a person other than one authorized by the credit, but the indorsee then negotiates at its own risk, in that he will have no claim against IB on the credit if the draft is dishonoured The matter is discussed in more detail later in this chapter.

The negotiation credit is a useful device for reconciling the interests of B, who wishes S's drafts to be payable in New York, and S, who needs to be able to cash them in London. It also enables S to sell his drafts in the foreign currency of his choice when he does not desire to be paid in sterling.

Where a negotiation credit is advised by AB, but not confirmed, AB incurs no commitment to S to negotiate,[64] and if it does negotiate the draft for S, it has the indorsee's usual right of recourse against S in the event of the bill being dishonoured.[65] Where, however, AB has confirmed the credit, it is under a duty to negotiate[66] and it will not have recourse, for this would be incompatible with its confirmation, by which it undertakes responsibility for ensuring payment of the bill in due course, so that to allow it to recover would produce circuity of action.

5. Red clause and green clause credits

Red clause credits (so called because such credits used to bear a notation in red) were found primarily in connection with the Australian wool trade and were designed to enable a shipper who is acting as a middleman, with limited resources, to obtain funds before shipment in order to pay the actual supplier. Nowadays red

---

61 There may not be a draft. Banks frequently purchase documents without asking for a draft. Note that the letter of credit itself is not a negotiable instrument.

62 If any. See n 61.

63 See the analogous distinction between purchase (negotiation) of a bill of exchange and payment of a bill in due course, discussed p 525.

64 The same is true of any other authorized bank which is not the confirming bank; mere nomination does not commit the nominated bank to negotiate (art 10(c)).

65 See p 503.

66 If it fails to do so, IB is in breach and must make payment under the credit without waiting for the draft to mature.

clause credits are used mainly to finance large orders for capital goods. The credit will provide for payment against specified preshipment documents (eg a receipt or warehouse warrant) or sometimes merely on presentation of a draft, and may allow the whole or a specified part of the price to be drawn, upon the terms that the sum so paid will be deducted from the amount payable on presentation of the full shipping documents under a letter of credit. A variant is the green clause credit, which operates in similar fashion except that the goods are required to be warehoused in the bank's name. Nowadays such credits are relatively infrequent, pre-presentation advances being made under an advance payment guarantee.[67]

6.   Revolving credits

Instead of a credit being for a fixed amount or for a fixed time, it may revolve around value or time. A credit revolving around value enables the beneficiary to present documents as often as he wishes during the credit period so long as the overall limit specified in the credit is not exceeded. Hence, as in the case of a bank overdraft, drawings reduce the available credit while payments by the buyer automatically replenish it, until the credit period expires. A credit revolving around time allows the beneficiary to draw up to, say, £x a month for the period of the credit, and may or may not permit the beneficiary to carry forward under-drawings from one month to the next.

7.   Transferable credits and back-to-back credits

These are described later.[68]

8.   Demand guarantees and standby credits

These are within the UCP but are of a different character from ordinary documentary credits and are discussed towards the end of this chapter.[69]

(vi) Fundamental concepts

1.   The legal status of the UCP

Almost invariably, the different contracts initiated by B's application to open a credit will be expressed to be subject to the UCP. The traditional view in England is that the UCP are simply a set of standard rules having no legal force except so far as incorporated by reference into the contract between the parties concerned This accords with the text of the UCP themselves.[70] Upon this basis, no contracting party is bound by the UCP unless the contract expressly or impliedly so provides. By contrast, certain writers in other countries have described the UCP in more elevated

---

67 See p 1021
68 See pp 1000, 1010.
69 See pp 1015 ff.
70 Article 1. However, where, as is now common, a credit is communicated through the SWIFT network, the SWIFT rules themselves provide for incorporation of the UCP if the party transmitting the message does not otherwise stipulate.

terms, as a code, a codification of usage or even a uniform law of an international character operative of its own force without dependence on incorporation by contract.[71] So far as English law is concerned, the status of the UCP probably lies somewhere between the two extreme positions. As Professor Kozolchyk has pointed out in his superb comparative study,[72] 'The text of the UCP is neither systematic nor comprehensive enough to warrant the legal characterization of "code".'

There are many facets of the relationships between the various parties on which the UCP are silent and which have to be answered by reference to the common law. It seems equally exaggerated to refer to the UCP as an international uniform law.[73] On the other hand, to regard the UCP as a set of model rules which have no significance for the parties unless adopted by their contract is to take too narrow a view of their standing.

In the first place the UCP embody, in considerable measure, usages which have gained international acceptance among bankers. Hence even where they have no contractual force they are strong evidence of banking custom and practice, which themselves will readily be treated by the court as impliedly incorporated into the various documentary credit contracts as established usage. Of course, the UCP are not, and are not intended to be, purely declaratory of existing practices, for these vary somewhat from one country to another and, indeed, from one locality to another, and a primary objective of the UCP is to produce consistency and to remove difficulties created by bad practice. Moreover, the UCP are revised from time to time in order to eliminate weaknesses and to accommodate new developments (such as combined transport) and are thus intended to be normative in some measure. But in so far as the UCP have gained near-universal acceptance, it can reasonably be assumed, in the absence of evidence to the contrary, that even if a rule in the UCP does not embody what was previously settled practice, the practice will have become broadly uniform as the result of the rule, so that if at the relevant time the rules have been in operation for a reasonable period, they will have become indicative of prevailing practice.

But we can reasonably go a stage further and, instead of treating the UCP merely as evidence of usage impliedly incorporated into the contract, regard them as directly incorporated by implication into the contract on the basis that their adoption is so much a matter of course that the parties must be taken to have intended to contract with reference to them even if the contract does not state this in terms and even if one of the parties (eg a non-banking party such as B or S) was not aware of the UCP.[74]

The place of the UCP in the hierarchy of binding sources is a complex question which cannot be examined in detail here.[75] Suffice it to say that so far as English

71 Frederic Eisemann, Charles Bontoux and Michael Rowe, *Le crédit documentaire dans le commerce extérieure* (1985), p 6.

72 See n 11 at para 23.

73 See *Royal Bank of Scotland v Cassa di Risparmio delle Provincie Lombard* [1992] 1 Bank LR 251, per Mustill LJ at 256.

74 The approach taken by Gatehouse J in *Harlow and Jones Ltd v American Express Bank Ltd* [1990] 2 Lloyd's Rep 343 in reference to the Uniform Rules for Collections.

75 See Kozolchyk, *Letters of Credit*, paras 25 ff.

law is concerned the UCP are contractual in nature, are subordinate to mandatory legislation, may be excluded or restricted by contract and, if incorporated into the contract, are, as a set of contractual terms, subject to the court's normal powers, at common law and by statute,[76] to adjudicate upon the enforceability of contractual provisions.

2.   The nature and enforceability of the bank's promise

In banking usage an irrevocable credit binds IB, and the confirmation of a credit binds AB, upon issue of the credit, that is, upon its release from the control of the issuer or confirmer, irrespective of the time it is delivered to or received by the beneficiary, S.[77] If the credit is rejected by S, eg because it does not conform to the contract of sale, it ceases to have effect.

Though there is no reported case since the adoption of the 'irrevocable' label[78] in which the point has directly arisen for determination, there are several dicta indicating judicial acceptance of the binding nature of the credit by virtue of the issue of the document. Similarly, it is accepted that IB and that AB, as confirming bank, become committed to the second beneficiary under a transferable credit upon issue of the new letter of credit to him. The problem is to reconcile the binding nature of the bank's undertaking with traditional concepts of general law, which deny legal effect to a simple promise unless consideration is furnished by the promisee, producing a contract,[79] or the promisee is induced to act in reliance on the promise, generating some form of estoppel.[80] The difficulty created by the undertaking embodied in an irrevocable letter of credit is that it appears to be binding on IB, and enforceable by S, despite the fact that S has furnished no consideration for IB's promise and, indeed, may not have taken steps to act upon it nor even have signified his assent to its terms. The same applies to AB's confirmation. How, then, can the bank concerned become bound to the beneficiary solely by virtue of the issue of the letter of credit to him?

Various ingenious theories have been advanced designed to accommodate the binding nature of the bank's undertaking within the framework of traditional contract

---

76 In particular, the Unfair Contract Terms Act 1977, so far as applicable. Thus the disclaimers in arts 16 and 18 of the UCP might well, as contract terms, fall to be tested by reference to the requirements of reasonableness. See pp 969, 983.

77 See del Busto, *Documentary Credits*, p 25, discussing the time of effectiveness of an amendment, to which the same principle applies. Cases indicating that the credit becomes binding only on receipt by the beneficiary (see, for example, *Dexters Ltd v Schenker & Co* (1923) 14 Ll L Rep 586, per Greer LJ at 588; *Bunge Corp v Vegetable Foods (Pte) Ltd* [1985] 1 Lloyd's Rep 613, per Hobhouse J at 617) are now out of line with banking practice and should not, it is thought, be followed

78 Prior to that, the House of Lords had held, in *Morgan v Larivière* (1875) LR 7 HL 423, that a letter issued to a seller stating that a special credit had been opened in the sum of £40,000 was merely a normal undertaking to pay against documents, not an equitable assignment or declaration of trust of funds deposited with the issuer of the letter. No claim was brought in contract, so that the case is not authority for the proposition that an undertaking in a letter of credit is unenforceable for want of consideration, though Lord Chelmsford expressed doubt (at 435) whether there was sufficient consideration to support the promise.

79 See p 67.

80 See p 69.

law.[81] All of these fall to the ground because, in an endeavour to produce an acceptable theoretical solution, they distort the character of the transaction and predicate facts and intentions at variance with what is in practice done and intended by the parties. The defects in these various theories show the undesirability of trying to force all commercial instruments and devices into a strait-jacket of traditional rules of law. Professor Ellinger has rightly argued[82] that the letter of credit should be treated as a *sui generis* instrument embodying a promise which by mercantile usage is enforceable without consideration. Professor Kozolchyk takes the description a stage further, treating a letter of credit as a new type of mercantile currency embodying an abstract promise of payment, which, like the bill of exchange, possesses a high, though not total, immunity from attack on the ground of breach of duty of S to B.[83]

3. The autonomy of the credit

One of the primary functions of the letter of credit is to create an abstract payment obligation independent of and detached from the underlying contract of sale between S and B and from the separate contract between B and IB. It is thus a cardinal rule of documentary credits that the conditions of the bank's duty to pay are to be found exclusively[84] in the terms of the letter of credit, and that the right and duty to make payment do not in any way depend on performance by S of his obligations under the contract of sale.[85] In general, therefore, a breach of those obligations by S, eg by shipment of goods which fail to correspond to the contract description, are of unsatisfactory quality or fall short of the contract quantity, does not entitle B to instruct the bank to withhold payment under the credit if the terms of the letter of credit have been fully complied with. This is brought out in art 3(a) of the UCP:

> Credits, by their nature, are separate transactions from the sales or other contract(s) on which they may be based and banks are in no way concerned with or bound by such contract(s) even if any reference whatsoever to such contract(s) is included in the Credit. Consequently, the undertaking of a bank to pay, accept and pay Draft(s) or negotiate and/or to fulfil any other obligation under the Credit, is not subject to claims or defences by the Applicant resulting from his relationships with the Issuing Bank or the Beneficiary.

Similarly, IB cannot, as a defence to a claim under the letter of credit, plead that it has a claim for damages or right of set-off against B or that it has not been put in funds by B to meet the credit. Conversely, S as beneficiary is not entitled to avail himself of the contract between B and IB.[86]

The autonomy of the credit closely resembles that of the bill of exchange, and the courts have shown an equal reluctance to allow the personal claims and defences of

---

81 See *Gutteridge and Megrah's Bankers' Commercial Credits*, ch 4; E. P. Ellinger, *Documentary Letters of Credit* (1970), ch IV.

82 Ellinger, *Documentary Letters of Credit*, at p 122.

83 Kozolchyk, 'Letters of Credit', ch 5 at pp 138–143. See also Roy Goode, 'Abstract Payment Undertakings', in *Essays for Patrick Atiyah* (ed Peter Cane and Jane Stapleton, 1991), and pp 972, 989.

84 Subject to the qualifications mentioned below.

85 See below and pp 989 ff.

86 Article 3(b).

the buyer under the underlying contract of sale to be set up by the bank as an answer to a claim by the seller on the letter of credit. Attempts by buyers to invoke breaches of the sale contract to prevent payment under a letter of credit have almost invariably been blocked by the courts, whether the buyer's line of attack has been an application for an injunction against the seller to restrain him from presenting the documents and collecting payment or against the bank to restrain it from making payment under the credit.[87] Even the illegality of the contract of sale does not affect the enforceability of the letter of credit.[88] This approach reflects the need of the business community for a high degree of certainty in relation to payment obligations contained in commercial instruments, and is applied equally to negotiable instruments, performance bonds and other commercial documents embodying an abstract promise of payment.

Of course it remains the case that the beneficiary must conform to the terms of the credit as a condition of his entitlement to be paid. Unfortunately, English courts have become so beguiled by the autonomy principle that they decline to allow refusal of payment in favour of a beneficiary acting in good faith even where the documents are forged or otherwise fraudulent, on the supposed principle that the beneficiary's duty is to tender documents which *appear* to conform to the credit, even if they are in fact fraudulent and worthless. Such an approach, far from enhancing the documentary credit system, does a disservice to its integrity, and it will be argued a little later that it is high time it was abandoned. [89]

As in the case of negotiable instruments, the autonomy rule is not absolute. Fraud by the beneficiary or his agent, whether in relation to the contract established by issue of the credit (eg fraud in the obtaining of the credit or the presentation of the documents) or in relation to the underlying contract of sale entitles, and indeed obliges, the bank, if on notice of it, to withhold payment,[90] whether the documents are tendered by the original beneficiary or by an innocent third party who has negotiated the seller's drafts.[91]

It is also a defence that the honouring of the credit would be illegal according to the law of the place where the bank's performance is due.[92] Moreover, the bank is

---

87 See p 984.

88 The position is otherwise so far as the illegality of the sale contract infects the letter of credit transaction, as where the sale constitutes (wholly or in part) an exchange transaction which contravenes the Bretton Woods Agreement. See *The American Accord* [1983] 1 AC 168, discussed further on a different point p 215; *Mahonia Ltd v J. P. Morgan Chase Bank* [2003] 2 Lloyd's Rep 911. Moreover, if the illegality renders the contract of sale not merely unenforceable but void, or if the contract is void on some other ground (eg want of consensus), the credit itself would seem to be void or voidable on the ground of mistake. See below and Goode, 'Abstract Payment Undertakings'.

89 See p 996.

90 But this is so only where the fraud is that of the beneficiary or his agent (see p 993). The bank has no duty to investigate a mere suspicion of fraud. See p 974.

91 But once the bank has accepted a draft presented by a holder in due course it must pay, for the instrument itself generates an autonomous contract independent of that created by the letter of credit. See p 988.

92 But illegality under some other law, eg the law of a foreign country in which B or IB is situated when payment is to be made by AB in England, is irrelevant (*Toprak Mahsulleri Ofisi v Finagrain Compagnie Commerciale Agricole et Financière SA* [1979] 2 Lloyd's Rep 98).

entitled to rescind a credit induced by a fraudulent conspiracy or a misrepresentation by S or his agent,[93] or to have the credit set aside for mistake, as where it has been issued to the wrong party who is aware that he has no right to it; and it has been held that the bank may set off against the amount due to the beneficiary, S, a liquidated sum due from S to the bank.[94]

However, if IB or AB has accepted S's drafts pursuant to the credit, then while IB is entitled to refuse payment to S himself or to a holder not in due course,[95] a holder in due course is in an almost unassailable position, for just as the credit itself creates an obligation independent of the underlying contract of sale, so also the autonomous contract generated by the acceptance of the drafts means that in the hands of a holder in due course these are enforceable despite the nullity or unenforceability of the credit. The holder is thus insulated both from the sale contract and from the letter of credit transaction.

4. Each bank's undertaking is as principal

Though IB opens the credit on the instructions of B, its undertaking to S is given as principal,[96] not as B's agent. B is not even an undisclosed principal. He is a complete stranger to the contract established by the letter of credit. IB's role is analogous to that of a commission agent,[97] authorized to conclude a contract with S but to do so on his own account, without bringing B into a contractual relationship with S. Several consequences flow from this. B is not entitled to give instructions to IB to refuse payment under the credit, or to vary the terms of the credit without S's consent, for IB is already committed to S under the letter of credit. B can, it is true, obtain an injunction to prevent IB from paying against nonconforming documents or with knowledge of fraud, but this is merely because in that situation IB has neither the right nor the duty to pay, and does not imply that B has any power to interpose himself directly into a separate contract generated by the letter of credit.[98] Again, B cannot be sued *under the letter of credit* if IB fails to honour its obligations to S. B will, of course, incur a liability for breach of the sale contract, but he can raise any defences that would ordinarily be available to him in an action brought by S for the price. In other words, the autonomy of the credit insulates S from the underlying contract of sale in his relations with IB but not in his relations with B himself. Thirdly, if IB, in breach of its mandate, accepts a tender of nonconforming documents, B has no *locus standi* to assert that, in the relation

---

93 *Solo Industries UK Ltd v Canara Bank* [2001] 1 WLR 1800 (a decision on a performance bond, but the principle is the same); *Rafsanjan Pistachio Producers Co-operative v Bank Leumi (UK) plc* [1992] 1 Lloyd's Rep 513, where it was held unnecessary to show the bank's reliance on the misrepresentation and that potential reliance suffices.

94 *Hongkong and Shanghai Banking Corp v Kloeckner & Co AG* [1989] 3 All ER 513.

95 *Bank Russo-Iran v Gordon Woodroffe & Co Ltd* (1972) 116 Sol Jo 921. If IB makes the payment, it can recover it as money paid under a mistake of fact.

96 This is true even if the credit is revocable, for even a revocable credit is a promise.

97 In civil law, a commissionaire, Kommissionär, etc. See Clive Schmitthoff, *Agency in International Trade: A Study in Comparative Law* (1970), pp 136 ff.

98 Conceptually, it would be better if the act prohibited by the injunction were not the honouring of the credit as such but the debiting of B's account.

between IB and S, such acceptance is ineffective. Put another way, B cannot himself reject the documents vis-à-vis S, but only vis-à-vis IB.[99]

Similar considerations apply as regards AB where AB is instructed to confirm the credit. Though the relationship between IB and AB is that of principal and agent, AB's undertaking to S is as principal, not as agent for IB or B.[100] AB's relationship to IB, like IB's relationship to B, is not an ordinary agency relationship[101] but is analogous to that of a commission agent, and the comments made above apply *mutatis mutandis*.[102] The position is otherwise, of course, if AB is instructed merely to advise the credit and/or receive and examine the documents, for in that situation AB is a mere agent having no contractual nexus with S at all, and IB is the principal.

5.   The bank's concern is with documents, not facts

Closely allied to the principle of the autonomy of the credit is the rule that the paying or negotiating bank is, in the absence of strong evidence of fraud or illegality,[103] concerned only to ensure that the documents presented to it conform on their face to the terms of the letter of credit, not to check the veracity of the statements contained in the documents, still less to examine the goods the subject of the contract of sale. In the words of the UCP:

> In Credit operations all parties concerned deal with documents, and not with goods, services and/or other performances to which the documents may relate.[104]

If the documents appear to be in order,[105] then, in general, the bank is both entitled and obliged to pay. Conversely, if the documents deviate from the language of the letter of credit, the bank is entitled to withhold payment even if the deviation is purely terminological and has no materiality in fact. This is well brought out in the leading case of *J H. Rayner & Co Ltd v Hambros Bank Ltd*,[106] in which the credit called for documents covering the shipment of coromandel groundnuts but the bill of lading tendered by S referred to machine-shelled groundnut kernels. Everyone in the trade knew that the latter description was a synonym for the former. Nevertheless, the bank's refusal to pay was upheld by the court on appeal.

> ... it is quite impossible to suggest that a banker is to be affected with knowledge of the customs and customary terms of every one of the thousands of trades for whose dealings he may issue letters of credit.[107]

---

 99 See pp 981, 985. As a corollary, B's right to reject defective or nonconforming goods is not affected by the fact that the defect or nonconformity was apparent on the face of the documents accepted by IB. See n 145.

100 *Bank of Baroda v Vysya Bank Ltd* [1994] 2 Lloyd's Rep 87.

101 *Credit Agricole Indosuez v Muslim Commercial Bank Ltd* [2000] 1 Lloyd's Rep 275, *per* Sir Christopher Staughton at 280. Nevertheless many of the incidents of an agency relationship as between AB and IB.

102 See R. M. Goode, 'Reflections on Letters of Credit – IV' [1981] JBL 73 at p 74.

103 See p 990.

104 Article 4.

105 Even if they are in fact fraudulent or forged, the bank is protected if it accepts them in good faith and without negligence. See p 976.

106 [1943] KB 37.

107 Per Mackinnon LJ at 41. The learned judge went on to give the 'homely illustration' of tender of a bill of lading showing shipment of copies of *The White Book* when the credit called for documents covering *The Annual Practice* (now *The Supreme Court Practice*), the former being a synonym in common use by practitioners.

The documentary character of letters of credit is not always understood by exporters or even their banks, so that it is quite common for credits to be issued which include non-documentary conditions, such as shipment on a Liner Conference vessel. The approach of the English courts under the 1983 revision and its predecessors has been to construe such stipulations as if they called for reasonable documentary evidence of the stated condition,[108] a sensible approach which accorded with banking practice. However, art 13(c) of UCP 500 starkly provides that if a credit contains conditions without stating the documents to be presented under them, banks will deem such conditions as not stated and will disregard them. Though art 13(c) reflects an understandable desire to introduce greater discipline into the issue of letters of credit, it has potentially serious consequences. It would seem to preclude the interpretative approach previously adopted by English courts and raises questions as to the possible liability of a bank which, at the request of its customer, incorporates non-documentary conditions which it knows or should know are entirely nugatory.

Unless otherwise stipulated in the credit, the beneficiary is required to present documents that are originals.[109] The quality of photocopies and other reprographic productions of documents sometimes makes it difficult for a bank to determine whether what is presented is an original document. The bank is protected if accepts as an original a document which appears to be such.[110] What constitutes an original has also been the subject of two Court of Appeal decisions, *Glencore International AG v Bank of China*[111] and *Kredietbank Antwerp v Midland Bank plc.*[112] In the former, the Court of Appeal, applying Article 20b of the UCP, held that a photocopy did not constitute an original, even if authenticated by signature, unless marked as an original. In the latter, the court held that the requirement to mark a document as an original did not apply if the document was in fact an original, though not marked as such. Subsequent to the events giving rise to those decisions, the Banking Commission of the ICC has produced a helpful policy statement explaining that the 'marked as original' proviso is satisfied by any mark on a document or any recital in the text of a document that indicates that the issuer of the document intends it to be treated as an original rather than a copy; and a document that is signed by hand or facsimile is treated as an original even if, as regards all the other elements, it is a photocopy or draft.[113] On this basis the result in *Glencore* would now be different. Given that banks rely heavily on opinions of the Banking Commission to interpret the UCP and that these are treated as the best evidence of what bankers are to understand by particular UCP provisions, it would not be inconsistent with the doctrine of *stare decisis* for future courts to take account of the policy statement in interpreting art 20b, and, indeed, David Steel J did just that in *Crédit Industriel et Commercial v China Merchants Bank.*[114]

---

108 *Banque de l'Indochine et de Suez SA v J. H. Rayner (Mincing Lane) Ltd* [1982] 2 Lloyd's Rep 476, per Parker J at 480; [1983] 1 Lloyd's Rep 228, per Sir John Donaldson MR at 230–231; *The Messiniaki Tolmi* [1986] 1 Lloyd's Rep 455, per Leggatt J at 462, affirmed [1988] 2 Lloyd's Rep 217.

109 ISBP, para 32.

110 See below.

111 [1996] 1 Lloyd's Rep 135.

112 [1999] Lloyd's Rep Bank 219.

113 ICC Banking Commission Policy Statement 12 July 1999, paras 2 and 3.

114 [2002] 2 All ER (Comm) 427.

6.   *Verification of documents limited to their apparent good order*

Just as the bank to whom the documents are presented has neither the facilities nor the responsibility for verifying the physical state of the goods or any other facts external to the documents, so also it is not responsible for ensuring the accuracy, genuineness or authenticity of the documents but must simply exercise reasonable care to ensure that these appear to be in order. This is made clear in art 13 of the UCP and in a series of other articles describing the documents which banks will accept. The principle that the bank's duty is limited to verifying the apparent good order of the documents has been upheld by the Privy Council in *Gian Singh & Co Ltd v Banque de l'Indochine*,[115] in which a bank that paid out against a document on which the signature was forged after comparing the signature with that contained in what purported to be the passport of the apparent signatory to the document was held to have complied with its mandate and to have been entitled to debit its customer's account.

> In business transactions financed by documentary credits banks must be able to act promptly on presentation of the documents. In the ordinary case visual inspection of the actual documents presented is all that is called for. The bank is under no duty to take any further steps to investigate the genuineness of a signature which, on the face of it, purports to be the signature of the person named or described in the letter of credit.[116]

Unhappily, what the courts have lost sight of is the fact that the rule as to the apparent conformity of documents was designed for the protection of bankers and was never intended to permit the beneficiary to tender nonconforming documents which appear on their face to be in order. We shall return to this question later.[117]

7.   *The doctrine of strict compliance*

The 'perfect tender' rule governing the tender of goods under a contract of sale applies with equal force to the tender of a letter of credit and the tender of documents by S under a letter of credit.

> There is no room for documents which are almost the same, or which will do just as well.[118]

The doctrine of strict compliance (which is to some extent cut down by the disclaimer provisions in the UCP[119]) applies to all the contracts involved in the credit operation. It must thus be observed by the buyer who procures the issue of the credit;[120] the seller wishing to claim payment under the credit; the paying bank that seeks reimbursement from the issuing bank; and the issuing bank that claims reimbursement from the buyer. The fact that the discrepancy is minor or that stipulations in the letter of credit might appear to the bank to serve no useful purpose is irrelevant.[121] Nevertheless, the degree of strictness varies according to

---

115 [1974] 2 All ER 754. See also *The American Accord*, n 88.

116 Per Lord Diplock at 758.

117 See pp 995 ff.

118 *Equitable Trust Co of New York v Dawson Partners Ltd* (1927) 27 Ll L Rep 49, at 52.

119 See p 983.

120 Ie the credit must strictly conform to the contract of sale.

121 *Seaconsar Far East Ltd v Bank Markazi Jambouri Islami Iran* [1993] 1 Lloyd's Rep 236, per Lloyd LJ at 239; *Commercial Banking Co of Sydney Ltd v Jalsard Pty Ltd* [1973] AC 279, per Lord Diplock at 286.

the particular circumstances and the parties involved in Professor Kozolchyk's survey of the application of the rule of strict compliance in different jurisdictions showed, in particular, that 'courts were inclined to take more seriously a banker's objection of noncompliance raised against a beneficiary's tender of documents than a customer's objection raised against the issuing bank's verification'.[122]

The rule of strict compliance is particularly important to bankers in that it is so widely neglected by sellers who tender documents, necessitating re-presentation in what has been estimated as 60% of all tenders.[123] But while it is not for the courts to condone lax standards, the problem confronting bankers who, with a limited time for perusal of the documents, wish to assure adherence to the credit while at the same time avoiding unnecessary impediments to the business transactions undertaken by their customers, needs to be borne in mind,[124] and, in deciding whether or not a tender conforms to the credit, a distinction should be drawn between deviations that are minor but apparently not insignificant and those that are trivial or insignificant.[125] Article 13(a) of the UCP contains a new provision which is designed to encourage courts not to be mechanistic in applying the doctrine of strict compliance:

> Compliance of the stipulated documents on their face with the terms and conditions of the Credit shall be determined by international standard banking practice as reflected in these Articles.

An additional and important reference point is the ISBP, which must be read consistently with the UCP but provides a useful elaboration of international standard banking practice. The UCP provides for certain built-in tolerances, eg by providing that unless a credit stipulates that the quantity of the goods specified must not be exceeded or reduced, a tolerance of 5% more or 5% less is permissible so long as the credit does not stipulate the quantity in terms of a stated number of packing units or individual items and the amount of the drawing does not exceed the amount of the credit.[126] Moreover, sellers can themselves help to reduce the likelihood of defective tenders by avoiding unnecessarily detailed stipulations and by providing for tolerances expressly in the application for the credit.[127]

---

122 *Letters of Credit*, p 82.
123 A major study by Professor Ronald Mann in the United States gave an even higher nonconforming rate, with only 27% of 500 presentations conforming to the credit but, astonishingly, only one case in which the buyer had not waived the discrepancy ('The Role of Letters of Credit in Payment Transactions', 98 Mich L Rev 2494 (2000)). A study by SITPRO of letter of credit practice in the UK would seem to indicate a much higher rejection rate, at an estimated cost to business of £113 million a year. Among the principal grounds of rejection were expiry of the credit, late presentation of documents (eg more than the specified period of time after shipment date – see UCP art 43), inconsistent data, incorrect data, absence of documents and failure to name the carrier or signing capacity (SITPRO, *Report on the Use of Export Letters of Credit 2001/2002*, Appendix 1).
124 A point made by the courts on more than one occasion. See, for example, *Hansson v Hamel & Horley Ltd* [1922] 2 AC 36, per Lord Sumner at 46: *British Imex Industries Ltd v Midland Bank Ltd* [1957] 2 Lloyd's Rep 591, per Salmon J at 597. In *Hing Yip Hing Fat Co Ltd v Daiwa Bank Ltd* [1991] 2 HKLR 35, which dealt with a number of interesting documentary credit points, Kaplan J held that the court would disregard obvious typographical errors.
125 *Kredietbank Antwerp v Midland Bank plc* [1999] All ER Comm 801.
126 Article 39(b).
127 Under art 39(a) of the UCP, the words 'about', 'approximately', 'circa' or similar expressions used in connection with the amount of the credit or the quantity or unit price of the goods are to be construed as allowing a difference not to exceed 10% more or 10% less.

In many cases, B is willing to disregard small nonconformities in a tender, and such nonconformity may in any event be waived by conduct.[128]

8.   Correlation of right to withhold payment and duty not to pay

In general, the circumstances which entitle a bank to withhold payment also impose on it a duty to its principal so to do. But this does not always follow. The bank sometimes has the choice to pay or not to pay.[129] Thus it is not the bank's duty to investigate allegations or suspicions of fraud. It is entitled to pay in the absence of compelling evidence of fraud, but is equally free to withhold payment on mere suspicion, provided that in any proceedings brought against it by the beneficiary, the bank is then able to establish fraud.[130]

(vii) The contractual relations set up by a confirmed credit

Leaving on one side the introduction of additional parties through negotiation of a draft or transfer of a credit, the issue of an irrevocable confirmed credit involves the consideration of no less than five different contractual relationships, namely: (1) between B and S (under the contract of sale); (2) between B and IB; (3) between IB and AB; (4) between IB and S; and (5) between AB and S. These are shown in diagrammatic form in figure 35.5. Contracts (2)–(5) will almost invariably be expressed to be governed by the UCP, and the principles examined in the previous section apply to all of them. In addition, each set of relationships attracts its own particular rules, which will now be discussed. Where drafts are accepted and/or negotiated pursuant to a letter of credit, further contractual relationships of the kind discussed in an earlier chapter[131] arise under the drafts themselves, and these are quite distinct from the contract generated by the letter of credit.[132] Consideration of the measure of damages to which S, as beneficiary under a credit, is entitled if IB or AB fails to honour the undertaking embodied in the credit will be deferred to a later stage.[133]

1.   The contract of sale

(a) GENERAL DUTY TO COMPLY WITH THE CONTRACT. The contract between B and S is, of course, the root contract from which all the others stem. S's right to demand a letter of credit, and the nature of the credit to which he is entitled, depend on the terms of the contract of sale. B, for his part, must ensure that the letter of credit issued to S is that prescribed by the contract.

Fulfilment of this obligation is a condition precedent to S's own duty to perform his delivery obligations.[134] For example, if the contract provides for a confirmed credit,

128   See p 982.
129   See p 993.
130   See p 993.
131   Chapter 19.
132   See p 988.
133   See p 998.
134   *Garcia v Page & Co Ltd* (1936) 55 Ll L Rep 391; *Etablissements Chainbaux SARL v Harbormaster Ltd* [1955] 1 Lloyd's Rep 303.

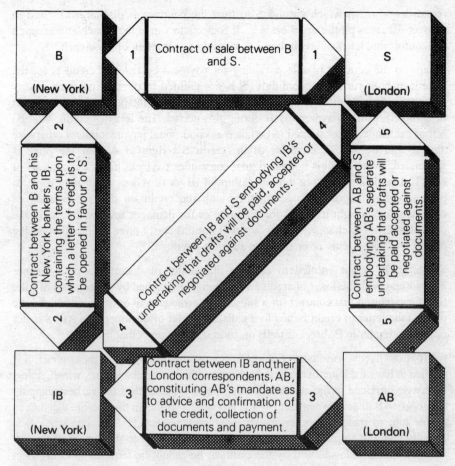

Note: Where no credit is to be given, drafts are sometimes dispensed with.

Fig 35.5 The parties to a confirmed credit

the seller is entitled to reject an unconfirmed credit; and if the letter of credit stipulates a bill of lading as one of the shipping documents when the contract permits S to tender a delivery order, the letter of credit will likewise be defective and can be rejected by S. If a nonconforming letter of credit is tendered and rejected, B may cure the defect by procuring the issue of a fresh and conforming credit if still in time,[135] but if he fails to do so or is out of time, he commits a

---

135 *Forbes, Forbes, Campbell & Co v Stanley & Co* (1921) 9 Ll L Rep 202. As to the time for issue of a credit, see below.

repudiatory breach which entitles S to treat the contract as discharged,[136] and to recover damages on the usual basis.[137] If S elects to waive the breach and accept a nonconforming letter of credit, he loses his right to complain of the breach.[138]

A term in the contract of sale providing for payment by letter of credit is for the benefit of both parties. Accordingly, S is not entitled to demand payment in any other way (eg by B direct) nor to sue for the price during the pendency of the credit or complain of non-payment by B during this period. The letter of credit, like the bill of exchange, is considered to be taken as conditional payment unless otherwise agreed, and during the currency of the credit S's right to sue for the price is suspended. If the credit is honoured, that constitutes payment under the contract of sale. If it is dishonoured (eg through failure of IB, or of AB as confirming bank, to pay, accept or negotiate in accordance with the credit on due presentation of documents), S's right to sue B for the price or for damages revives, for, as in the case of a bill of exchange,[139] the court will not ordinarily infer an intention on the part of S to take a letter of credit as an absolute payment.[140]

Similarly, B is not entitled to call for the tender of documents in a manner inconsistent with the letter of credit arrangements prescribed by the contract of sale. So, if pursuant to that contract (or a subsequent arrangement or acquiescence by the parties) the letter of credit issued to S calls for tender of documents to AB, S is not obliged to tender to B direct or to IB or, indeed, to anyone other than AB.

(b) TIME OF OPENING OF CREDIT. Subject to any express provisions in the contract, S is entitled to have the letter of credit in his hands within a reasonable time, which, unless otherwise provided in the contract of sale, means no later than the earliest shipping date open to S under the contract, [141] and probably a sufficient time before that date to enable him to make the necessary shipping arrangements.[142] The date when S is actually ready to ship is irrelevant; and since he is entitled to the benefit of the full shipment period allowed him by the contract, he cannot be required to notify B in advance of the date of shipment as a precondition of obtaining the letter of credit.[143]

---

136   *Dix v Grainger* (1922) 10 Ll L Rep 496; *Trans Trust SPRL v Danubian Trading Co Ltd* [1952] 1 Lloyd's Rep 348.

137   See pp 407 ff.

138   In this situation no question of damages as for breach of warranty arises; by waiving the breach S assents to the letter of credit in the form in which it is issued.

139   See p 526.

140   *E. D. & F. Man Ltd v Nigerian Sweets & Confectionery Co Ltd* [1977] 2 Lloyd's Rep 50; *W. J Alan & Co Ltd v El Nasr Export & Import Co* [1972] 1 Lloyd's Rep 313; *Maran Road Saw Mill v Austin Taylor & Co Ltd* [1975] 1 Lloyd's Rep 156; and see E. P. Ellinger, 'Does an Irrevocable Credit Constitute Payment' (1977) 40 MLR 91.

141   *Ian Stach Ltd v Baker Bosley Ltd* [1958] 2 QB 130; *Pavia & Co SpA v Thurmann-Nielsen* [1952] 2 QB 84.

142   See *Ian Stach Ltd v Baker Bosley Ltd*, n 141, per Diplock J at 142. This latter formulation, not expressly adopted by Diplock J but not dissented from by him when addressed by counsel, is to be preferred, for a shipper cannot make instantaneous shipping arrangements and if he does not receive the letter of credit until the day before the commencement of the shipping period, he will almost certainly be deprived of the benefit of at least the first few days of that period.

143   *Pavia & Co SpA v Thurmann-Nielsen*, n 141.

(c) DURATION OF CREDIT. The date of expiration of the credit is a vital statement in the letter of credit, for in the absence of such a statement the implication is merely that the credit endures for a reasonable time, a somewhat vague concept which leaves S in a state of uncertainty as to whether he is covered for the full shipment period and as to the latest date by which a tender of documents is acceptable. Article 42(a) of the UCP provides in terms that all credits must stipulate an expiry date for presentation of documents. Hence a statement of the latest date for shipment is not sufficient; if the credit contains no expiry date, S is entitled to reject it. Article 42(a) is reinforced by art 43, which provides that every credit calling for a transport document must also stipulate a specified period of time after the date of shipment during which presentation of documents must be made. If no such period is stipulated, banks will, under art 43, refuse documents presented to them later than 21 days after the date of shipment.[144]

(d) REJECTION OF GOODS. The acceptance of documents under a letter of credit does not preclude B from subsequently rejecting the goods themselves if on arrival they are found not to conform to the contract of sale.[145]

2. The contract between B and IB

The relationship between IB and B is that of banker and customer. In contrast to the relatively informal contract established in the opening of an ordinary loan account or overdraft facility, the terms of the contract are set out in detail in IB's standard form of application to open the credit which B is required to complete and sign, and which invariably incorporates the UCP.[146] In English practice the contract is usually a unilateral contract in which B's submission of the application constitutes an offer which IB accepts by conduct in issuing the letter of credit. That is to say, IB does not, as a rule, engage itself to issue the credit but either issues it or declines to do so. IB owes the usual duties of a banker strictly to observe the terms of the mandate, and to act in other respects with reasonable care and skill in relation to the credit, except so far as these duties are effectively qualified by the contract. In particular, IB is responsible for ensuring that the letter of credit issued to S complies strictly with the instructions contained in the application for the credit and that payment, acceptance or negotiation is effected only on presentation of documents which fully accord with the terms of the credit. Where payment etc is made not by IB but by AB, or by some other bank authorized to negotiate under an open negotiation credit, then subject to the effect of art 18 of the UCP, discussed below, IB is responsible for the errors and omissions of the bank in question, which is its agent.

144 The reference to 'the date of shipment', in contrast to the equivalent provision in UCP 400 referring to the date of issue of the transport document, is unfortunate, for it infringes one of the UCP's own fundamental tenets that all conditions should be documentary. Presumably, art 43 is to be construed as referring to the date shown on the shipping document. Contrary to appearances, art 43 is not confined to shipping documents but includes, for example, multimodal transport documents (art 46(a)).

145 And since, in accepting the documents, the paying or confirming bank acts as principal, not as B's agent, it would seem that B is entitled to reject even for a defect apparent on the face of the documents, which he would not be entitled to do if the documents had been accepted by him or his agent. See n 99.

146 See fig 35.2, p 955.

As we have seen, the letter of credit issued by IB to S constitutes an autonomous engagement in which IB acts as principal, not as agent for B. It follows that B is not entitled to give instructions to IB to withhold payment or to deviate from the terms of the credit. IB is both entitled and obliged to ignore any such instructions so long as the documents are presented within the period of the credit and conform to it.

If the credit is not honoured, IB is obliged to indemnify B against any liability he may incur to S. Where, on the other hand, payment etc is made by IB or AB without authority against nonconforming documents,[147] B, though not entitled to reject conforming goods vis-à-vis S,[148] may as between himself and IB decline to adopt the transaction, on account of the breach of mandate, in which event IB cannot debit B with the price paid or with remuneration for its services, while B for his part is taken to have 'abandoned' the goods to IB, in whom they will then vest.[149] In addition, B may claim damages for any loss reasonably foreseeable by IB as likely to flow from the breach.[150] In many cases it will be difficult for B to prove that he has suffered such loss. If, for example, IB's breach consisted of accepting a claused bill of lading showing the goods to be in damaged condition, B's loss through exercise of his right to abandon the goods to IB will normally be no greater than if IB had itself rejected the documents as it should have done.

As an alternative to rejecting the documents, B may either waive the breach altogether[151] or accept the documents without prejudice to his right to damages for any resulting loss. B will be deemed to have waived any nonconformity if he obtains delivery of the goods from the carrier without production of the bill of lading,[152] for where this is to be tendered under the credit, B has no right to take the goods from the carrier and it would be a fraud on S for B, having wrongfully procured the goods, to prevent payment under the credit. There is no English case law at all on the acceptance of documents under reservation of the right to damages[153] and thus no

---

147   If he moves in time, B may be able to obtain an injunction to restrain such payment. See p 990.

148   See p 974, n 99. The position is otherwise where the goods do not conform to the contract. See p 980.

149   See Kozolchyk, *Letters of Credit*, para 169. (If the unauthorized acceptance was by AB, IB has a similar right of abandonment as against AB – see p 0000.) The theory underlying abandonment has not been fully worked out even in countries where the courts have specifically adopted it. There appears to be no reported English case in which abandonment has been referred to, though it would seem to follow from general principles of restitution that B cannot have his cake and eat it by retaining the documents and goods without paying for them. *Semble*, if B abandons, he cannot claim any surplus arising from IB's disposal of the goods at a higher price. If B wants to preserve his interest in a surplus, he should accept the documents and resell himself or get IB to do so as his agent, reserving his rights of action against IB in the event of there being a deficiency.

150   Under the rule in *Hadley v Baxendale*. See p 121.

151   This is sometimes described as ratification, but the term is best avoided since it is customarily taken to denote retrospective authorization of a contract entered into by an agent on behalf of the ratifying party, whereas we are here concerned only with adoption of the transaction as between B and IB.

152   Nowadays it is not uncommon for carriers to agree to release goods without a bill of lading against guarantees and warranties. See p 880, n 49.

153   A reflection of the fact that, as in other jurisdictions, allegations of wrongful honour of a credit rarely come before the courts, whether because they seldom occur or because they are rarely complained of or are dealt with by an out of court settlement.

guide to the measure of damages. Where the defect in the document is unconnected to any defect in the goods and these conform in all respects to the contract, the damages will usually be nominal, though where B has, as a result of the defect in the documents, become prevented from transferring them under a resale contract and has suffered loss in consequence, this may be recoverable if it was within IB's contemplation. If the goods themselves do not conform to the contract of sale and in consequence are worth less than they would otherwise have been, B's loss through the bank's acceptance of the documents is nil, since he still has a right to reject the goods.[154]

Where the defective documents are accepted not by IB but by AB, IB is in principle responsible for AB as its agent[155] and B's remedy is not against AB (with whom he is not in privity[156]) but against IB. However, the first two paragraphs of art 18 of the UCP provide as follows:

(a)   Banks utilizing the services of another bank or other banks for the purpose of giving effect to the instructions of the Applicant do so for the account and at the risk of such Applicant.

(b)   Banks assume no liability or responsibility should the instructions they transmit not be carried out, even if they have themselves taken the initiative in the choice of such other bank(s).

The width of these provisions is deplorable. They amount to a disclaimer by IB of responsibility for the acts and omissions of its own agents, with the result that while IB would be liable for breach of the duty of care imposed by art 10 if it were itself to accept nonconforming documents, it can (if art 18 is effective) shuffle off all responsibility by delegation to AB, thereby depriving B of all remedy.[157] In no way can this result be described as reasonable, particularly since it is IB itself who normally selects the advising banker. It is submitted that if AB's breach is serious, either as regards the magnitude of the nonconformity or as regards the gravity of the consequences of AB's breach, the court should feel free to invoke the common law rule of construction as to fundamental breach[158] to limit the exempting terms, and/or to declare that such terms fail to satisfy the requirement of reasonableness for the purpose of the Unfair Contract Terms Act 1977 and are thus ineffective under s 3 of that Act.[159] The disclaimer embodied in art 18 has met with widespread hostility from courts and textbook writers abroad[160] and in practice tends not to be invoked by issuing banks.[161] It is not without significance that the ICC's Uniform Rules for Demand Guarantees, though containing similar provisions, preclude a bank from relying on them to excuse liability for failure to act in good faith and with reasonable care.[162]

154   See n 145.
155   Ie, responsible to B. But as against S the relevant bank acts as principal. See n 145.
156   See p 987.
157   B would have no claim against IB because of art 18, and no claim against AB on account of want of privity. His only possibility of redress is a doubtful claim against AB for negligence. See p 987.
158   See p 97.
159   See p 98.
160   See Kozolchyk, *Letters of Credit*, para 143.
161   Ibid, para 145.
162   Uniform Rules for Demand Guarantees, art 15.

3.   The contract between IB and AB

The relationship between IB as issuing bank and AB as confirming bank is that of principal and agent.[163] AB must comply strictly with the instructions in the letter of credit, failing which it cannot claim reimbursement or remuneration from IB,[164] and if the latter rejects the documents, AB will be left with the goods on its hands. If it complies with the credit, AB is entitled to payment by IB or other designated reimbursing bank[165] in accordance with the credit, as well as to its charges.

4.   The contract between IB and S

IB undertakes that payment etc will be made on due presentation of documents.[166] This undertaking must be honoured despite breach of the underlying contract of sale.[167] Though given in response to B's request, it is given by IB as principal and not as agent, disclosed or undisclosed, for B.[168] It follows that if IB accepts a tender of nonconforming documents, then, while this may be a breach of his duty to B under the agreement between them, B, as a stranger to the separate contract generated by the letter of credit, has no *locus standi* to complain that IB's acceptance of the tender was not valid and binding for the purpose of that contract. B must base any claim he wishes to make on breach of his contract with IB, and/or breach of the underlying contract of sale with S.[169] As with the other contracts, the doctrine of strict compliance applies. The documents normally called for in c.i.f. and f.o.b. contracts have been described in an earlier chapter,[170] where the prerequisites of acceptability under the contract of sale were discussed. In the case of a tender under a documentary credit, there is the additional requirement[171] that the documents as a whole should be commercially acceptable and should not be in such condition or contain such features as are calculated to put a reasonable banker on inquiry.[172] Further, the documents should not appear on their face to be inconsistent with one another.[173] This requires that the terms of each document should be consistent with

---

163 See p 974.

164 However, AB's wrongful acceptance of the documents will probably bind IB, vis-à-vis S, if within the scope of AB's apparent authority, and will certainly bind IB where AB had confirmed the credit.

165 Bank-to-bank reimbursement is covered by art 19. If the reimbursing bank fails to honour claims made on it, IB is itself liable to AB as the claiming bank (art 19(c), (d)). See also the Uniform Rules for Bank-to-Bank Reimbursements under Documentary Credits (ICC Publication No 525, 1996).

166 The exceptional cases in which payment may be refused despite the conformity of the documents with the credit are discussed at pp 990–991.

167 See p 971, and, as to grounds for withholding or blocking payment, p 989.

168 See p 973. Whether in the case of a confirmed credit S must look for payment to AB or to IB in the first instance before calling upon the other depends on the terms of the credit. Usually this will call for presentation of documents to AB and payment by AB, in which event recourse can be had to IB only if AB dishonours the credit. But the credit may call for presentation to and payment by IB, in which case the position is reversed. If the bank primarily liable to pay fails to do so, S is not obliged to seek payment from the other bank before proceeding against B.

169 See p 974.

170 See pp 885 ff.

171 If indeed it be an additional requirement. It is at least arguable that the rule applies to any tender of documents under a c.i.f. or f.o.b. contract, whether or not a documentary credit is involved.

172 See Jack, Malek and Quest, *Documentary Credits*, paras 8.39–8.45; *Gutteridge and Megrah's Bankers' Commercial Credits*, pp 190–191.

173 UCP, art 7.

those of the others and that all documents should appear on their face to relate to the same transaction. This, in turn, entails that they should be linked to each other either by direct reference or by the fact that they appear on their face to relate to the same goods.[174] However, the following points should be noted.

(a)   While the description of the goods in the commercial invoice must correspond with the description in the credit, in all other documents the goods may be described in general terms not inconsistent with the description of the goods in the credit.[175]

(b)   UCP 500 introduce substantial changes in the requirements for transport documents. These are designed to cater in particular for the steadily growing use of non-negotiable sea waybills and multimodal transport documents. In each case it is for the credit to specify the type of transport document to be furnished by S. The UCP then set out in detail for each such type the details it has to indicate in order for it to be accepted by banks.[176] Article 31 also deals specifically with deck cargo, stating that, unless otherwise indicated in the credit, banks will accept a transport document which contains a provision that the goods may be carried on deck provided that it does not specifically state that they are or will be loaded on deck.

(c)   Banks and importers have become much more relaxed about transhipment since containerization and the introduction of multimodal transport operations, because goods can safely be left at the intermediate port in sealed containers and thus protected from the elements. Accordingly, unless transhipment is prohibited by the terms of the credit, banks will accept a bill of lading indicating that the goods will be transhipped, provided that the entire ocean carriage is covered by one and the same bill of lading; even if the credit prohibits transhipment, banks will in certain conditions accept a bill of lading which indicates that the goods will be transhipped.[177]

(d)   The documents must be presented not only before the expiry date specified in the credit but also within such period of time after shipment as is provided by the credit or, if none, then within 21 days after shipment.[178]

If the documents do not conform to the credit, IB has various options open to it. It can consult its customer, B,[179] to see whether he is willing to waive the discrepancy,

---

174   See *Banque de l'Indochine et de Suez SA v J H. Rayner (Mincing Lane) Ltd* [1983] 1 Lloyd's Rep 228; Jack, Malek and Quest, *Documentary Credits*, paras 8.30–8.38.

175   UCP, art 37(c).

176   See Part D, arts 20–38. An important requirement regularly overlooked is that the name of the carrier must appear as such on the front of the bill of lading or non-negotiable sea waybill and if the document is signed by an agent for the carrier, the agent must be named and must indicate its principal. See UCP art 23 and the ICC's *Position Paper No 4* (1 September 1994).

177   UCP, art 23d.

178   Article 43(a). In the case of a negotiation credit the presentation that has to be made prior to expiry of the credit is presentation to the negotiating bank. The time when that bank, in turn, presents the documents to IB or AB as confirming bank (if AB is not itself the negotiating bank) is irrelevant to S's rights as beneficiary.

179   Where the documents are presented to AB as confirming bank, AB's consultation (if any) will be with IB, who, in turn, may consult B.

which in most cases he will, as the commercial objective is to obtain the goods, not to take technical points on the documents; it may reject the documents;[180] or it may pay 'under reserve', the effect of which is that if B refuses to ratify its action, whether legitimately or not, it will be entitled to recover the payment.[181] Where IB decides to reject the documents as not in conformity with the credit, it must so inform the party from whom it received them within a reasonable time, not exceeding seven banking days following receipt of the documents.[182] The notice must state all discrepancies in respect of which the bank refuses the documents[183] and that it is holding the documents at the disposal of or is returning them to the presenter.[184] If any of these requirements is not complied with or if the bank fails to hold the documents at the disposal of, or return them to, the presenter, it is precluded from claiming that they are not in compliance with the terms of the credit.[185]

IB's acceptance of S's drafts pursuant to the credit generates a distinct payment obligation independent of that arising under the credit itself. The fact that the documents are later found not to have conformed with the credit does not entitle IB to refuse payment to a holder in due course of the drafts. However, as mentioned earlier, IB is entitled to refuse payment to S or to a subsequent holder not in due course, and to recover any payment made to S or such holder against nonconforming documents.

5. The contract between AB and S

By adding its confirmation AB is giving its own undertaking that the credit will be honoured on due presentation. This undertaking is given by AB as principal, not as agent for IB, still less as agent for B, and is entirely distinct from that given by IB.[186] It is not a case of a joint and several liability on the part of IB and AB. IB's

---

180 It cannot rely on any consultation with B as extending its time for rejection (*Bankers Trust Co v State Bank of India* [1991] 2 Lloyd's Rep 443).

181 *Banque de l'Indochine et de Suez SA v J H. Rayner (Mincing Lane) Ltd*, n 108.

182 Articles 13(b), 14(d)(i). The setting of the seven-day maximum period for rejection is new and is intended to set a limit on the concept of reasonable time. What is reasonable will depend on the circumstances and, in particular, on the volume of documents to be examined. Seven days is the outside limit and should not be taken as reasonable in itself. In London, for example, it is generally considered that even a set of documents running to hundreds of pages can be examined within three days (*Bankers Trust Co v State Bank of India*, n 180).

183 Article 14(d)(ii). Prior to the UCP 500 English law did not consider a bank which rejected documents on one ground precluded from rejecting a fresh tender containing some other discrepancy featuring in the original documents (*The Lena* [1981] 1 Lloyd's Rep 68); but in Hong Kong Kaplan J took a different view in *Hing Yip Hing Fat Co Ltd v Daiwa Bank Ltd*, n 124, which art 14(d)(ii) adopts.

184 Article 14(d)(ii).

185 Article 14(e).

186 It is assumed here and in what follows that AB is a legal entity distinct from IB. However, art 2 of the UCP now provides that branches of a bank in different countries are considered another bank. This means that it is possible for a credit issued by IB's head office in B's country to be confirmed by IB's branch in S's country. Of course, it remains the case that there is only one legal entity, but the ability of a branch to confirm may be significant in fixing the place of presentation and payment as that of the branch rather than IB's head office, a fact which may be relevant, for example, where there are foreign exchange controls, embargoes or expropriatory measures in the country of the head office but not in that of the branch.

promise and AB's promise are separate and self-contained. So if the terms of the confirmation are more restricted than those of the credit as issued, AB's liability to S is limited accordingly.[187] Conversely, the fact that IB may have a defence to S's claim, or a right of set-off, does not entitle AB to withhold payment except where the same facts happen to constitute a defence to AB also.

In general, AB as confirming bank is obliged to honour the credit if the documents appear on their face to be in order, whether or not there has been a breach of the contract of sale.[188] AB's position when it accepts drafts against documents which are later found not to conform to the credit is the same as where IB accepts.[189]

6.   Does AB owe a duty to B?

It remains only to note that English law does not recognize any privity of contract between B and AB. If AB advises the letter of credit in erroneous terms or pays the credit against nonconforming documents, B's remedy is against IB, who, in principle, is responsible for the acts and omissions of its agent. However, IB could, in theory (though in practice usually does not), set up art 18 of the UCP by way of defence. If it did, B would have to fall back on the usual common law and statutory weapons available against exemption clauses.[190] A remaining possibility is an action against AB in tort for negligence, in accordance with the principle established in *Hedley Byrne & Co Ltd v Heller & Partners*[191] and developed in later cases, but while there is some judicial support for the existence of such a duty,[192] the better view is that there is no such duty.[193]

(viii) Negotiation and discount of S's drafts

So far we have assumed that the documents are presented by the original beneficiary, S, and that in the case of a term draft, the draft is still in S's hands and is presented by him for payment, at maturity. But S may wish to negotiate the draft before acceptance or discount it after acceptance. Where the credit is a negotiation credit, IB incurs a commitment either to procure negotiation, if S so wishes, by a bank authorized to negotiate by the terms of the credit or to make payment itself if such a bank declines to negotiate the draft and/or documents. As stated earlier, the purpose of the negotiation credit is to give S the facility of selling to an authorized bank his right to present the documents and collect payment, and a nominated bank which buys the documents then replaces S as the beneficiary and presents the documents and receives payment in its own right. A nominated bank which is not

---

187   Whether AB will thereby be in breach of its mandate from IB is a separate question.
188   See p 973. As to grounds for withholding or blocking payment, see p 989.
189   See above.
190   See pp 96 ff.
191   [1964] AC 465.
192   See *United Trading Corp SA v Allied Arab Bank* [1985] 2 Lloyd's Rep 554, where the Court of Appeal, in a case concerning a performance bond, held that a confirming bank arguably owed a duty of care to the applicant for the credit.
193   See *GKN Contractors Ltd v Lloyds Bank plc* (1985) 30 BLR 48, where doubt was cast upon the view expressed in the earlier decision, n 192.

the confirming bank has no obligation to negotiate, so that if AB is merely an advising bank, it may decline to negotiate, leaving S to collect payment from IB. But where AB or some other authorized bank has confirmed the credit, it is obliged to negotiate S's draft and to do so without recourse to S in the event of the draft being dishonoured. Of course, S need not avail himself of the negotiation facility but may, if he prefers, present the draft and documents direct to IB for acceptance of the draft.

We shall now consider the case where the credit is freely negotiable and AB is the confirming bank but the credit is negotiated by a third bank, N. In considering N's rights (and we shall assume throughout that he is a holder in due course) we must distinguish three alternative fact-situations. The first is where N has negotiated the draft (ie purchased it before acceptance) without authority in the letter of credit. The second is where the credit is a negotiation credit and N has negotiated pursuant to an authority in the letter of credit. The third is where the draft is a term bill which has been discounted by N (ie sold to N after acceptance by the drawee).

1. Negotiation without authority

We have seen earlier[194] that where N negotiates S's draft without authority in the letter of credit to do so,[195] N acquires no rights against IB or the confirming bank AB *under the letter of credit* (for *ex hypothesi* the letter of credit contains no undertaking to N), and N's rights will be limited to the ordinary rights of the holder of an indorsed bill of exchange. Thus if the bill is drawn on IB, there is no obligation on IB to accept it, though if IB does accept the bill, it must pay it on due presentation at maturity. If the bill is drawn on B,[196] N will have no rights against IB or AB at all. If the bill is a term bill which B declines to accept when it is presented, N will have recourse to S as his indorser.[197] If the bill is accepted by B but dishonoured on presentment for payment, N can sue B, S or both. In each case, the letter of credit is irrelevant so far as N is concerned. His rights stem solely from the instrument. As holder in due course, N can recover from B notwithstanding a breach of the underlying contract of sale, or nonconformity with the terms of the credit, and even if there has been a total failure of consideration or the contract of sale or letter of credit is tainted with illegality.[198]

2. Authorized negotiation

Here N buys the unaccepted draft pursuant to an authority to negotiate contained in the letter of credit. He thereby acquires two distinct and independent rights: the right to require IB and (if it confirmed the credit) AB to see that the credit is honoured upon due presentation of documents; and the right to hold his indorser, S,

---

194 See pp 960, 967.
195 This may be either because the letter of credit does not permit negotiation or because the negotiation credit restricts negotiation to a designated bank or banks and N is not such a bank.
196 Which the UCP discourages but does not prohibit (art 9(a)(iv)).
197 N will not have a claim against B, who cannot be made liable on the bill unless he accepts it, though his failure to accept will no doubt be a breach of his contract with S.
198 See p 523.

liable on the draft if this is dishonoured by non-acceptance or non-payment.[199] N cannot, of course, sue the drawee *on the bill* if the latter declines to accept it; but if the drawee is IB or AB, N has a claim against both of them for failure to honour the letter of credit,[200] and if the drawee is B himself, B's refusal to accept constitutes a breach by B of the sale contract, though it is not a breach by IB or AB.[201]

Once the draft has been accepted, N's position becomes almost unassailable, for the payment obligation of the acceptor and (if the acceptor is B) the responsibility of IB and AB under the letter of credit for ensuring payment by B at maturity become insulated not only from the underlying contract of sale but even from the conditions attaching to the letter of credit,[202] so that a belated discovery by IB or AB that the documents were not, after all, in order would constitute no defence to a claim by N for non-payment of the bill.[203] This is so whether the acceptor is B or IB. Unlike S, N is not deemed to warrant the genuineness of the documents or their conformity with the credit, and is not obliged to repay the sum received from the bank if the documents are later found to be forged or otherwise defective.[204]

3. Discount to N

In this case S procures the drawee's acceptance before discounting the bill to N. Hence from the outset N takes the bill as an accepted bill divorced from the documents and is thus at no time concerned with the terms of the credit but is entitled to payment at maturity.

4. DOCUMENTARY CREDITS: GROUNDS FOR WITHHOLDING OR BLOCKING PAYMENT

While under the principle of the autonomy of the credit the bank's duty to pay is not in general affected by matters relating to the underlying transaction, there are exceptional cases in which the bank is entitled to withhold payment, and in most of these it owes a duty to its customer, B, to do so. Where the bank is insufficiently certain of the facts to refuse payment or is concerned that its reputation may be adversely affected if it does so voluntarily, B may apply to the court for an injunction, either to restrain the bank from paying or to restrain the beneficiary, S,

---

199 But if N is itself the confirming bank, it has no right of recourse against S, for this would be inconsistent with the assurance of payment implicit in its confirmation. See p 967.

200 IB is liable for breach of its undertaking to accept the bill; AB is liable on its confirmation, which makes it responsible for acceptance (and subsequent payment on maturity) by IB. See UCP, art 9(a)(iii), (b)(iii).

201 This is because art 9(a)(iv) provides that credits should not be issued available by drafts on the applicant, so that neither IB by issuing the credit nor AB by confirming it undertakes to procure acceptance of a draft on the applicant. The sole effect is that the draft is to be considered an additional document to be presented under the credit.

202 *Gutteridge and Megrah's Law*, pp 106–107.

203 In this respect, the bona fide indorsee of S's draft stands in a better position than S himself, who is deemed to have warranted that the documents presented by him and upon which he secured the bank's acceptance were genuine and complied with the credit. See p 998.

204 See p 998.

from presenting the documents and/or collecting payment. Despite a view to the contrary by Staughton LJ in *Group Josi Re v Walbrook Insurance Co Ltd*,[205] there is a powerful argument that the considerations affecting the grant of an injunction against the bank are not quite the same as those influencing the grant of an injunction against S. This is because the bank is not a party to the underlying contract, so that, in the absence of fraud, its duty to pay is not affected by S's breach of that contract. The position is otherwise in the case of proceedings against S in that where B can show that S's right to present the documents and obtain payment is dependent on an unfulfilled condition precedent, so that S ceases to be entitled to the benefit of the credit, B may obtain an injunction to restrain presentation and payment.[206] Similarly, where the presentation of the documents and/or collection of payment by S would constitute a breach of the underlying contract (which would not necessarily be the case), there seems no reason why B should not be able to obtain an injunction to restrain the threatened breach in accordance with ordinary contract principles.

As a party to the contract established by the letter of credit the relevant bank (IB or AB, as the case may be) is entitled to invoke any ground open to it under the general law to refuse payment. What is distinctive about a letter of credit is that because it is opened pursuant to a mandate from its bank's customer, B, the bank is under a duty to observe its mandate and is thus not entitled to waive a right to refuse payment unless B consents to this. It follows that except where the ground of refusal is personal to the bank and of no interest to B, as where by coincidence the bank has an existing relationship with S under which it has acquired a right of set-off,[207] the bank has an obligation to its customer to refuse payment if it is, or ought from a reasonable examination of the documents to be aware of, its right to do so. So the bank is both entitled and obliged to refuse to honour a credit if:

(a)   the documents tendered do not on their face conform to the credit,[208]

(b)   the person presenting the documents is not the party entitled to payment,[209]

(c)   the issue of the letter of credit was induced by fraud or misrepresentation,[210]

(d)   there is other established fraud, whether in relation to the credit or the underlying sales transaction,[211]

(e)   by the governing law or the law of the place where the credit is due to be honoured, it would be illegal to do so,[212] or

---

205 [1996] 1 WLR 1152 at 1161.

206 *Sirius International Insurance Corp (Publ) v FAI General Insurance Co Ltd* [2004] 1 All ER 308; *Kvaerner Singapore Pte Ltd v UDL Shipbuilding (Singapore) Pte Ltd* [1993] SLR 352, a decision on a performance bond in favour of the buyer, which was dependent on the prior issue of a letter of credit in favour of the seller but that was never issued.

207 See p 610.

208 Since the tender of conforming documents is a condition of the beneficiary's right to be paid, a point that seems to have been ignored in some of the cases. See p 995.

209 *Cleveland Manufacturing Co Ltd v Muslim Commercial Bank Ltd* [1981] 2 Lloyd's Rep 646.

210 *Solo Industries UK Ltd v Canara Bank* [2001] 1 WLR 1800.

211 See p 991.

212 See Jack, Malek and Quest, *Documentary Credits*, paras 13.41 ff.

(f)   the credit was issued to support an underlying transaction which to the knowledge of the bank was either unlawful in itself or lawful in the making but entered into for an unlawful purpose.[213]

These defences to payment are not available against a holder in due course of S's drafts when these have been accepted by the bank. But this is not an exception to the above rule, merely a consequence of the fact that the acceptance of a bill of exchange creates an autonomous payment obligation which is divorced from the letter of credit transaction that gave it birth and, as against a holder in due course, is unaffected by defects in that transaction.

Three particular issues have generated much debate:

(a)   In what conditions is forgery or other fraud in the documents or the underlying transaction a defence to a claim for payment of the credit?

(b)   Is nullity of the documents an independent ground for refusal to pay?

(c)   Can payment be refused on the ground of unconscionability?

(i) Fraud as a defence to payment

Of all the defences to payment, fraud is the one least likely to succeed, partly because of the heavy standard of proof required to establish it and partly because the defence is limited to the fraud of the beneficiary himself or of others for whose acts he is legally responsible. The fraud defence has generated a series of questions which have occasioned differing degrees of difficulty.

1. What is fraud?

This question typically arises in the context of a false statement made in a document. It is not necessary that the maker of the statement should be dishonest in the sense used in the criminal law; it suffices that it constitutes the tort of deceit in that it is made knowingly and with intent that it should be acted upon by the person to whom it is addressed. So where the confirming bank sent a letter to the issuing bank falsely stating that the documents had been presented within the period limited by the credit and the statement was known to the confirming bank's checkers to be false and was intended by them to be acted upon by the issuing bank, this constituted fraud entitling the issuing bank to refuse payment and exposing the confirming bank to liability even though the checkers were not dishonest or fraudulent in the criminal law sense.[214]

---

213 *Mahonia Ltd v J P Morgan Chase Bank* [2003] 2 Lloyd's Rep 911; *Group Josi Re v Walbrook Insurance Co Ltd* [1996] 1 Lloyd's Rep 345. These decisions follow the general principles concerning illegality in relation to contracts (see p 130) and establish that the principle of the autonomy of the credit does not insulate the credit from the effects of illegality in the making or purpose of the underlying transaction, so that if it discovers the facts before payment, the bank is entitled, and indeed obliged, to refuse payment.

214 *Standard Chartered Bank v Pakistan National Shipping Corp (No 2)* [2000] 1 Lloyd's Rep 218. An unusual feature of the case was that the claim was brought by the confirming bank itself against the owners and charterers of the vessel concerned and one of the charterer's employees for loss suffered as the result of refusal of payment by the issuing bank, and the conduct of its employees was held not to be so egregious as to attract the defence *ex turpi causa non oritur action.*

2.   What is the juridical basis of the defence?

There are two alternative approaches. The first is that the injunction can be given only in support of a substantive cause of action, namely the bank's breach of its duty to its customer if it made payment. The difficulty with adopting this as the sole juridical basis is that if the bank was unaware of the fraud at the time of presentation, it would be entitled to pay, so that its refusal to make payment could not be justified by after-acquired knowledge. So the alternative approach is that the true basis of the defence is that the beneficiary cannot be allowed to benefit from his own fraud – in other words, 'fraud unravels all.'[215]

3.   Does fraud in the underlying transaction suffice?

There is no reason in principle why the fraud exception should be confined to fraud in relation to the issue of the letter of credit. Indeed, in *Themehelp Ltd v West*[216] the Court of Appeal held, in a majority decision, that it was equally available in the case of fraud in the underlying transaction, as where it was seriously arguable that the seller-beneficiary had been guilty of fraudulent misrepresentation. However, the decision is open to the objection that, as pointed out by Evans LJ in his dissenting judgment, the primary remedy sought by the buyers in respect of the alleged misrepresentation was not rescission but damages, leaving the contract on foot and the buyers still liable for the price, and there was equally no basis upon which the fraud exception could be made available to the bank if payment were demanded under the guarantee. It is therefore necessary in each case to examine the effect of the fraud on the beneficiary's rights under the underlying transaction.

4.   What is the standard of proof?

This depends on the stage of the proceedings at which the matter comes before the court. In proceedings for an interlocutory injunction the mere allegation of fraud is insufficient, nor is it enough that the bank has an 'arguable case'. But what does suffice has been formulated in different ways as the courts have struggled to set a standard which is high enough to safeguard the autonomy principle but not so high as be unattainable. This has led to differences of emphasis, ranging from 'established or obvious' fraud[217] to 'a good arguable case that on the material available the only realistic inference' is that the beneficiary was fraudulent[218] (a slightly difficult combination of a relatively low and a relatively high threshold) or simply a 'real prospect' of establishing fraud.[219] The result of these decisions, taken together, is that the evidence of fraud must be compelling but not irrefutable. As

---

215 *United City Merchants (Investments) Ltd v Royal Bank of Canada* [1983] 1 AC 168 (also *sub nom The American Accord*), per Lord Diplock at 184.

216 [1996] QB 84 (Evans LJ dissenting), a case on a performance guarantee given to secure the purchase price under the underlying contract of sale.

217 *Edward Owen Engineering Ltd v Barclays Bank International Ltd* [1978] QB 159, per Lord Denning MR at 169, a decision on a performance bond, but the principle is the same.

218 *United Trading Corp SA v Allied Arab Bank* [1985] 2 Lloyd's Rep 554n, per Ackner LJ at 561. The decision involved a performance guarantee, so that it was the seller who had to show fraud.

219 *Solo Industries UK Ltd v Canara Bank* [2001] 1 WLR 1800, per Mance LJ at 1815–1816.

Ackner LJ explained in the *United Trading* case, this does not mean that every possibility of an innocent explanation has to be excluded. It is enough that there is strong corroborative evidence of fraud and that the buyer has been given an opportunity to answer the allegation of fraud and has failed to provide any, or any adequate, answer.[220] But even if this test is satisfied, the balance of convenience must favour the grant of an injunction, otherwise it will be refused.[221] The position is otherwise at the trial itself, where the bank has to establish fraud only on a balance of probabilities, though in fraud cases this is at the high end of the scale.

5. Whose fraud is relevant?

Where the documents conform on their face to the terms of the credit, the bank's right to withhold payment on the ground of fraud is limited to cases where the fraud is that of the beneficiary himself or his agent. Thus in *The American Accord* [222] the House of Lords, reversing the decision of the Court of Appeal[223] and restoring that of the trial judge on this point,[224] held that a beneficiary who tendered a bill of lading in which a false date of shipment had been inserted by an employee of the ship's broker was entitled to be paid, since the beneficiary had acted in good faith and the broker was not his agent. We shall examine Lord Diplock's speech in more detail a little later in discussing whether forged or other fraudulent documents can truly be regarded as conforming documents.[225]

6. At what time is the party against whom injunctive relief is sought required to furnish clear evidence of fraud?

Suppose that the bank, though not having clear evidence of fraud at the time of presentation of the documents and therefore having a choice to pay, nevertheless declines to pay because it suspects fraud. Can it resist an application for summary judgment if by the time the application is heard it has obtained the evidence? The answer is yes. It would be absurd if the court were to be compelled to give summary judgment to the beneficiary in the face of clear evidence of fraud merely because that evidence was not available at the time of demand.[226] *A fortiori* the bank is not precluded from adducing such evidence at a trial.

---

220 *United Trading Corp SA*, n 218.

221 *Czarnikow-Rionda Sugar Trading Inc v Standard Bank London Ltd* [1999] 2 Lloyd's Rep 187, where it was pointed out that some of the parties may already have received the fruits of the credit in the form of discounted payments but were subject to a *Mareva* injunction, a protection to the claimant which had to be taken into account in weighing the balance of convenience.

222 [1983] 1 AC 168.

223 [1982] QB 208.

224 [1979] 1 Lloyd's Rep 267. In reaching its decision the Court of Appeal cited with approval the author's article in [1981] JBL 291 criticizing (at p 294) the basis of the decision at first instance on this point.

225 See p 995.

226 *Safa Ltd v Banque du Caire* [2000] 2 Lloyd's Rep 600, per Waller LJ at 606, citing *Balfour Beatty Civil Engineering Ltd v Technical & General Guarantee Co Ltd* (1999) 68 Con LR 180, CA.

7.   Who is immune from the effects of the beneficiary's fraud?

The fraud exception is not available against a bank which, in conformity with an authorization from the issuing bank, has confirmed or negotiated the credit prior to becoming aware of the fraud or against a bona fide transferee of a transferable credit or a holder in due course of a draft.[227] The position is otherwise as regards a party who acts without authorization, as where a confirming bank negotiates a deferred payment credit without having authority to do so[228] or a bank takes an assignment of a credit (as opposed to the proceeds of a credit[229]) which is not transferable.[230]

8.   The need to join the beneficiary in proceedings against the bank based on fraud

If fraud is to be alleged, it is important to join the beneficiary as the party against whom the allegation is made, since courts are reluctant to make such a serious finding against a person who has not been joined so as to be given the opportunity of rebutting the allegation. In *Discount Records Ltd v Barclays Bank Ltd*,[231] where B sought an injunction, against both the issuing bank and a confirming bank which had accepted a draft drawn by S to restrain payment, on the ground not only that there was a shortfall in delivery and that many of the goods delivered did not comply with the contract but also that the serial numbers on the boxes in which they had been dispatched had been fraudulently altered to comply with the order. As regards the confirming bank, Megarry J accepted the argument that the application was misconceived, for it was quite likely that the draft had come into the hands of a holder in due course. As regards the issuing bank, Megarry J held that a mere allegation of the fraud was not sufficient to justify the use of the injunctive power to restrain a bank from honouring a letter of credit. An even stronger argument would have been that the issuing bank had already become committed to reimbursing the confirming bank. But the really crucial point was that the beneficiary had not been joined, so that Megarry J was constrained to treat the case as one in which fraud had merely been alleged but not established

9.   The freezing injunction

The final question is whether the customer, B, can bypass the restrictions on the rules as to injunctive relief for fraud by applying for a freezing injunction[232] to restrain S from dealing with the benefit of the credit or its proceeds until trial of an action against S, the ground for the injunction being that S is likely to remove his assets (including the proceeds of the credit) from the jurisdiction, if not restrained, in order to render abortive any judgment against him.[233] The writer has argued

---

227 See Xiang Gao, 'Presenters immune from the fraud rule in the law of letters of credit' [2002] LMCLQ 10.

228 *Banco Santander SA v Bayern Ltd*, n 54, discussed p 960.

229 See p 1001.

230 So decided by the Vienna Commercial Court in *Singer & Friedlander Ltd v Creditanstalt-Bankverein* (1980). See n 278.

231 [1975] 1 All ER 1071.

232 Formerly called the Mareva injunction, so named after the decision of the Court of Appeal in *Mareva Compania Naviera SA v International Bulkcarriers SA* [1975] 2 Lloyd's Rep 509.

233 As to the principles on which such injunctions are granted, see p 1151. For a more detailed description, see F. D. Rose, 'The *Mareva* Injunction – Attachment *in personam*' [1981] LMCLQ 1, 177.

elsewhere[234] that while there is nothing objectionable in restraining the beneficiary of a credit from dealing with the proceeds of the credit after this has been honoured by the paying bank, the use of a freezing injunction to restrain the bank from honouring the credit in the first place would be extremely inadvisable save in the most exceptional circumstances, for this would interfere with the assurance of payment upon which the whole letter of credit mechanism depends.[235]

(ii) Is nullity of the documents an independent ground of refusal to pay?

We have seen that fraud is not a defence to a claim for payment under a credit unless it is the fraud of the beneficiary or his agent, and it was on that basis that the beneficiary's claim was upheld by the House of Lords in *The American Accord*.[236] The House of Lords also rejected the argument that the false statement in the bill of lading precluded it from being a document against which the bank had to make payment. The decision is supportable on the ground that the bill of lading was a genuine document in that it was issued by the party by whom it purported to be issued without unauthorized alteration of its terms, so that what was false was simply the information in it. What cannot be sustained is the process of reasoning which led Lord Diplock to allow the appeal and which was seriously flawed in a number of respects. In particular, Lord Diplock formulated the following propositions, all of which are, with respect, untenable.[237]

(a) That the UCP imposes a duty on the bank to pay against documents which appear on their face to conform to the credit even if they do not in fact conform. This is not so; the UCP *entitles* the bank to pay against apparently conforming documents, but the rule is for the protection of banks and does not oblige them to do so if they know that the documents are not in conformity, eg because they are forged. The undertaking to pay is contained in the letter of credit and is to pay against conforming documents, not those which appear to conform, and the bank's duty is expressed in similar terms in the UCP itself, referring to payment against 'the stipulated documents'.[238]

(b) That the contractual duty owed by the bank to *the buyer* to honour the credit on presentation of apparently conforming documents is matched by a corresponding duty to the seller. But the notion that the bank owes the buyer, its own customer, a duty to pay against forged or fraudulent documents, thus allowing the buyer to be defrauded, is surely bizarre!

(c) That the bank may not be entitled to withhold payment even if the documents presented are forged. This proposition is equally untenable and seems to conflate two distinct principles, that the documents must conform to the credit

---

234 'Reflections on Letters of Credit – II' [1980] JBL 378 at p 380. Strong support for this conclusion is provided by the decisions of the Court of Appeal in *Power Curber International Ltd v National Bank of Kuwait SAK* [1981] 3 All ER 607 and *The Bhoja Trader* [1981] 2 Lloyd's Rep 256.

235 Cf Rose [1981] LMCLQ 1, 177 at 184 and *The Bhoja Trader*, n 234 (demand guarantee).

236 See n 88.

237 See further Goode, 'Abstract Payment Undertakings', at pp 228–232.

238 See now arts 2, 9.

and that the bank may withhold payment in the event of fraud but only if the fraud is that of the beneficiary or his agent. But documents which are forged cannot conceivably be treated as conforming documents; the bank may be safe in paying them if it has examined them with reasonable care and they appear to be in order, but to say that the beneficiary has a right to payment against even forged documents if he is not party to the forgery finds no justification in the terms of the letter of credit or in the provisions of the UCP and has the effect of extending to beneficiaries the benefit of a rule designed exclusively to safeguard the banks.

(d)   That under the American Uniform Commercial Code a person who has taken a draft under circumstances such that he becomes a holder in due course is entitled to payment irrespective of the forgery, and there is nothing in the Code to suggest that the seller who has not negotiated the draft is in any worse position. This last proposition is equally remarkable. It is trite law (to use one of Lord Diplock's favourite phrases) that a holder in due course is in a favoured position and is insulated from defences not available even to other holders of the bill, let alone to a seller whose documents and draft have been rejected. Moreover, the Uniform Commercial Code, far from protecting the seller in this situation, provides no fewer than four exceptions to the autonomy principle, including forgery, the presentation of fraudulent documents and 'fraud in the transaction'.[239]

Unhappily, Lord Diplock's influence manifested itself in a subsequent decision of the Court of Appeal in *Montrod Ltd v Grundkötter Fleischvertriebs GmbH*,[240] where it was held that nullity of the documents was not an independent ground for refusal of payment and that a beneficiary who tendered documents in good faith was entitled to payment even if the documents were fraudulent or otherwise devoid of commercial value. Again, reliance was placed on the importance of certainty in international banking operations. This, with respect, is misconceived. The certainty that is required lies in the ability of banks to pay against apparently conforming documents. Nothing in the requirement to make a beneficiary tender genuine documents in any way impairs that ability, since the banks are protected by the express provisions of the UCP. It is a distortion of the autonomy principle to allow a beneficiary, so long as he acts in good faith, to tender documents which purport to be what they are not and to collect payment against worthless pieces of paper. Far from serving the purpose of the apparent conformity rule, which is to protect banks exercising reasonable care, such an approach undermines the security of transactions for banks where they advance funds to their customers on the security of the documents. The short point is that the UCP and the terms of every credit require the presentation of specified documents, that is, documents which are what they purport to be, and there is no warrant for the conclusion that this entitles the beneficiary to present, for example, any old piece of paper which purports to be a bill of lading issued by the named carrier or a certificate of insurance issued by a named insurer even if it is forged, unauthorized or otherwise fraudulent. The decision itself can be justified on the ground that the document in that case was not

239   Section 5–114(2).
240   [2002] 1 WLR 1975.

a nullity but unauthorized. There is thus no decision of an English court which has held a good faith beneficiary entitled to tender a document which was not a genuine document at all but forged. On this issue the Singapore Court of Appeal has robustly declared, in *Beam Technology (Manufacturing) Pte Ltd v Standard Chartered Bank*,[241] that a bank is not obliged to pay against a document which is forged and therefore null and void. The court added that it was not possible to generalize as to when a document is null and void, and that such a question could be answered only on the facts of each case. It is to be hoped that this decision, which sets a proper limit to the autonomy principle, will be followed in England if the case should arise. It is worth repeating that this places no burden of investigation on banks, who remain entitled to pay against apparently genuine and conforming documents; it merely precludes the beneficiary from taking advantage of a rule which was never designed to allow him to tender worthless pieces of paper.

In conclusion, reference may be made to the 1996 UN Convention on Independent Guarantees and Stand-By Letters of Credit, art 19(1) of which provides that the guarantor may withhold payment if it manifest and clear that any document is not genuine or has been falsified.

(iii) Can payment be refused on the ground of unconscionability?

In a series of cases the Singapore courts have fashioned a new independent ground for granting an injunction, namely that in the particular circumstances the beneficiary would be guilty of unconscionable conduct in presenting the documents and collecting payment. The root decision is *Bocotra Construction Pte Ltd v A-G (No 2)*,[242] a decision on a performance bond, where the beneficiary threatened to call the bond after a dispute, in which it was alleged that the beneficiary had itself impeded the work in respect of which the bond was given, had been referred to arbitration. The court granted an injunction. The case was followed in *GHE Pte Ltd v Unitrack Building Construction Pte Ltd*,[243] where there had been a substantial revision in the sum payable under the underlying contract and the beneficiary had never demanded or taken delivery of the bond; again, it was held that to call the bond was unconscionable and would be restrained. No such principle has yet evolved in English law but there is much to be said for its application in exceptional cases.

(iv) Recovery of money paid against nonconforming documents

We have seen that a bank which is led to make a payment under a credit through forgery of documents or other fraud is entitled to recover the payment as made under a mistake of fact. In other cases it remains an open question whether, and in what circumstances, a bank which inadvertently pays against nonconforming documents can recover the payment from the beneficiary.[244] There are three

---

241 [2003] 1 SLR 597. See L Y Chin and Y K Wong, [2004] LMCLQ 14.
242 [1995] 2 SLR 733.
243 [1994] 4 SLR 904.
244 See Jack, Malek and Quest, *Documentary Credits*, paras 9.37 ff; R. M. Goode 'Reflections on Letters of Credit – III' [1980] JBL 443.

possible grounds of recovery: negligence, mistake of fact and breach of warranty. The first seems insupportable, since S owes no duty of care to the paying bank, which itself is under an obligation to its principal to examine the documents with reasonable care; and if it does so, it is entitled to recoupment from the principal. Mistake of fact is the basis of recovery advocated by the courts[245] and by English writers,[246] and seems appropriate enough where the documents are totally valueless. In other cases this ground of recovery is open to serious objection, for it has always been considered inapplicable where the payment sought to be recovered was made pursuant to a contractual obligation. In such a case the rights of the parties are, in principle, to be determined by the contract,[247] though it is accepted that if S's performance is of no value at all, the restitutionary remedy of money paid on a total failure of consideration is available. To allow the bank to reject documents which it has accepted seems contrary to general principles of contract law; to allow full recovery of moneys paid where there is only a partial failure of consideration is again contrary to principle; and, as a matter of policy, rejection of documents after acceptance is to be discouraged, for it is economically wasteful, imposing on S far greater prejudice than would be suffered by the bank if its remedy were restricted to damages for breach of warranty, a remedy much more accurately tailored to the bank's actual loss.

It is therefore at once more consonant with principle and more sensible as a matter of policy that recovery of the money paid should be denied and that the law should imply a warranty by the beneficiary that the documents are genuine and that there is no latent[248] nonconformity with the terms of the credit.[249] There is no English authority either supporting or denying the existence of such a warranty,[250] but in America this has now been made the primary basis of recovery,[251] and seems to produce the best solution. The bank's claim will usually be nominal, since if the nonconformity is latent, the bank is entitled to debit its principal's account; the buyer will have his usual claim for damages for breach of warranty if the goods themselves are defective or if his position on a sub-sale on the documents is adversely affected in a manner which the seller could reasonably have foreseen; while if the goods conform to the contract and the buyer has not been prejudiced by any difficulty in using the documents to effect a sub-sale, the buyer suffers no loss.

There is, of course, no right to recover payments made to a purchaser of the seller's drafts who tendered the documents in good faith.

(v)   The measure of damages for dishonour of a credit

The issue of an irrevocable credit is designed to give S an assurance of payment whether on presentation of documents or subsequently through maturity of a draft

---

245   See, eg, *Bank Tejarat v Hong Kong and Shanghai Banking Corp CI) Ltd* [1995] 1 Lloyd's Rep 239, where it was common ground that there was this right of recovery.

246   Jack, Malek and Quest, *Documentary Credits*, para 9.37; and cf. R. R. Pennington, A. H. Hudson and J. E. Mann, *Commercial Banking Law* (1978), p 358.

247   Robert Goff and Gareth Jones, *The Law of Restitution* (6th edn, 2000), para 1–063.

accepted under an acceptance credit or at the date fixed by the terms of a deferred payment credit. If the bank responsible fails to honour the credit, the question arises as to the monetary relief to which S is entitled. [252]

If the contract established by the credit were to be viewed in isolation, the case would simply be one of failure to pay money, and damages would in general be restricted to interest.[253] In other words, English law begins with the assumption that any consequential loss that a person may suffer through not receiving a money payment at the due date (eg loss of an opportunity to use the money to make an advantageous purchase) is too remote, since quite apart from the fact that the intended application of the money will usually have been outside the defendant's reasonable contemplation, the direct cause of the plaintiff's loss is his lack of access to other funds to make the purchase pending recovery of the debt itself, and loss due to the plaintiff's own impecuniosity is not, it is said, recoverable.[254]

But it is now settled that loss due to impecuniosity may not be too remote if the loss might reasonably have been in the contemplation of the parties at the time of the contract[255] and the loss resulting from dishonour of a letter of credit is just such a case.[256] The bank is aware from the outset that the credit is opened for the purpose of providing for payment of the price of goods under an associated contract of sale, and that if the credit is dishonoured, the seller will be entitled to treat the contract of sale as repudiated, and may, on so doing, suffer substantial loss which he ought to be entitled to recover.

The damages recoverable by S will depend on a variety of factors: the time at which the bank repudiates its obligations under the letter of credit; the extent to which, through being deprived of the credit, S is unable to proceed with contracts with his own suppliers and incurs a liability to them; whether S elects to treat the underlying contract of sale as repudiated or to affirm it and seek payment from B; and, above

---

248 The beneficiary can reasonably expect the bank to take note of manifest defects in the documents, this being the bank's duty to its principal under art 13 of the UCP.

249 See Goode [1980] JBL 443, at pp 445–446,

250 In their book *Commercial Banking Law*, Pennington, Hudson and Mann deny the existence of such a warranty, ascribing its absence to the unilateral nature of the contract generated by the letter of credit. But this, with respect, is a non sequitur. Given that the beneficiary owes no duty to the bank to present the documents at all, the question remains whether, if he does so, he warrants their conformity. (See in this connection s 5–111(1) of the American Uniform Commercial Code, which expressly provides such a warranty.) The cases cited by Pennington, Hudson and Mann in support of the denial of warranty do not bear out the proposition advanced, for they all involved payment to a subsequent holder in due course, whose position is quite different from that of S himself.

251 UCC, s 5–111(1).

252 B's remedies against IB where payment is wrongly made under a credit have been considered at p 981.

253 *Fletcher v Tayleur* (1855) 17 CB 21. The sum itself would be recoverable as a debt only if payment had been caused by performance. See below.

254 Ibid; *The Liesbosch (Owners) v The Edison (Owners)* [1933] AC 449.

255 *President of India v La Pintada Compania Navegacion SA* [1985] AC 104; *Wadsworth v Lydall* [1981] 1 WLR 598; *President of India v Lips Maritime Corp* [1988] AC 395; *International Minerals and Chemical Corp v Karl O. Helm AG* [1986] 1 Lloyd's Rep 81; *Trans Trust SPRL v Danubian Trading Co* [1952] 2 QB 297.

256 *Trans Trust SPRL v Danubian Trading Co*, n 255.

all, the steps open to S to mitigate his loss and the extent to which any loss that he unavoidably suffers ought reasonably to have been in the contemplation of the parties at the time of issue of the letter of credit. The general principle that can be extracted from the various cases[257] is that the bank's refusal to honour a letter of credit is not a mere failure to pay money[258] but is an act which, in breaching the contract established by the letter of credit, also interferes with performance of the underlying contract of sale. Hence in appropriate cases – eg where S elects to treat the contract of sale as repudiated – the court will award damages against the bank assessed on the same basis as they would be in an action against the buyer himself for wrongful non-acceptance.[259]

Can S, instead of suing for damages, with a concomitant duty to take reasonable steps to mitigate his loss, sue instead for the face value of the credit and interest?[260] Yes, if he has kept the documentary credit contract open for performance and is still able to perform by tendering or retendering the documents.[261] Where, on the other hand, S has resold the goods or has taken any other step indicating acceptance of the bank's repudiation, the contract established by the documentary credit is at an end and S must sue for damages. This is simply an application of the general contract rule that a sum payable under a contract cannot be claimed unless it has been earned by performance, and this requirement is not dispensed with merely because performance was prevented by the wrongful act of the defendant himself.[262]

5   THE TRANSFER OF A CREDIT AND ITS PROCEEDS

(i)   Transfer of a credit

The transferable credit is typically used where the beneficiary wishes to pay his own supplier or is a middleman acting as agent for an undisclosed seller or buyer. Suppose, for example, that S, who has contracted to sell goods to B on terms that payment is to be made under an irrevocable confirmed credit, is not himself the physical supplier but is buying them from the manufacturer, M, who is to be paid under a similar letter of credit. In this situation S, instead of arranging for the opening of a separate letter of credit in favour of M, may find it convenient to

---

257 Ibid; *Ian Stach Ltd v Baker Bosley Ltd* [1958] 2 QB 130.

258 Where the bank makes a delayed payment, with the result that S suffers currency losses which could reasonably have been contemplated at the time of the contract as likely to result from the delay, these may be recoverable as damages (*President of India v Lips Maritime Corp* n 255; *International Minerals and Chemical Corp v Karl O. Helm AG*, n 255).

259 *Trans Trust SPRL v Danubian Trading Co Ltd*, n 255; *Urquhart Lindsay & Co Ltd v Eastern Bank Ltd* [1922] 1 KB 318.

260 We are not here concerned with S's rights against a bank which has accepted a draft and failed to pay. In such a case, S's claim would not be on the credit but on the bill itself, with a clear right of recovery under the Bills of Exchange Act.

261 *Belgian Grain & Produce Co Ltd v Cox & Co (France) Ltd* (1919) 1 Ll L Rep 256 (where judgment for the amount of the credit was given after an assurance by counsel for the sellers that the goods had not been resold, and on condition of the documents being given to the defendants in exchange); *British Imex Industries Ltd v Midland Bank Ltd* [1958] 1 QB 542.

262 *Colley v Overseas Exporters* [1921] 3 KB 302.

transfer to M, wholly or in part, the benefit of the credit that is being opened in S's favour at the request of B. Article 48 of the UCP contains detailed provisions governing such transferable credit.

A transferable credit is one under which the beneficiary (first beneficiary) may request the authorized bank to pay, incur a deferred payment undertaking, accept or negotiate (the 'transferring bank') or in the case of a freely negotiable credit, the bank specifically authorized in the credit as a transferring bank, to make the credit available in whole or in part to one or more other beneficiaries (second beneficiaries).[263] A credit is transferable only if expressly designated as such by the issuing bank.[264] S, as first beneficiary, has no right to demand a transfer; he can merely request it. This is reinforced by a separate provision that the transferring bank[265] is under no obligation to effect such transfer except to the extent and in the manner expressly consented to by such bank,[266] which reflects a principle of general contract law, applicable to other aspects of documentary credit operations such as confirmation and negotiation, that IB may commit itself by the terms of its credit but cannot commit other banks.

A letter of credit is not a negotiable instrument and cannot be transferred by indorsement and delivery. It could, with the consent of the issuing bank, be transferred by assignment, but this is not the practice.[267] What in fact happens is that when IB issues a transferable credit to S, who wishes to transfer this to M, S returns the letter of credit to the transferring bank, which at S's request (fig 35.6) issues a new letter of credit to M for the whole or part of the amount of the original credit.[268] In short, there is a novation by substitution of M for S to the extent of the transfer.[269]

Suppose that S in London has contracted to sell a quantity of widgets to B for £15,000 f.o.b. London, payment to be made under an irrevocable transferable letter of credit. S places an order for the widgets with his own supplier, M, in Liverpool at a price of £10,000 f.o.b. London, payment to be made under an irrevocable credit. Upon receiving the letter of credit for £15,000 from IB through the advising bank AB, S will ask AB to furnish a new letter of credit direct to M for £10,000 providing for payment against documents. This will be sent by AB to M. When M furnishes the documents to AB under the new letter of credit, M will be paid £10,000 and the remaining £5,000 will be paid to S. The documents will be remitted by AB to IB as received, except that AB must, when notifying S that it has received M's documents, give S the opportunity of substituting for M's £10,000 invoice S's

---

263 UCP, art 48(a).

264 Ibid, art 48(b).

265 Which in the case of a credit where no other bank is involved and the documents are to be presented to the issuing bank will be that bank.

266 Article 48(c). The Privy Council had previously concluded that this was true also of art 46 of the 1974 revision (*Bank Negara Indonesia 1946 v Lariza (Singapore) Ltd* [1988] AC 583).

267 Indeed, it would not usually be practicable. See n 271.

268 Obviously the amount of the second credit issued to M (who is known as the second beneficiary) cannot exceed the original figure. Usually it will be less, since S will naturally resell to B at a higher price than he is paying M. The only situation in which S is likely to transfer to M the whole of the credit is where S is M's agent and will be receiving commission direct from M himself.

269 See p 1009.

HSBC ◆X◆

Request for Transfer of Documentary Credit

To:
HSBC Bank plc
Trade Services
(Insert Branch Address:_____)

Date: _____200__

Documentary Credit No:_____

Issuing Bank:_____

As beneficiary of the above-mentioned transferable credit, we request that you make this credit available to:

(1) _____

upon the same terms and conditions as the original credit with the exception of the following:-

(2)   Amount: _____ (Words_____)

(3)   Quantity (if part shipments allowed): _____Unit price: _____

(4)   Valid in _____until: _____

(5)   Latest shipment date: _____

(6)   Period for presentation in accordance with UCP500 Article 43: _____Days.

(7)   The percentage of insurance cover required (if applicable) under the transferred credit is increased to_____%

(8)   We request you to notify the transferee by: ☐ Airmail   ☐ Courier   ☐ Teletransmission

(9)   We ☐ intend ☐ do not intend   to substitute our own invoices and drafts (if any) for those of the transferee.

(10) In accordance with UCP500 sub-article 48(d), amendments to the original credit ☐ require   ☐ do not require our consent before being advised to the above-mentioned second beneficiary.

11)   Any irregularities in documents presented ☐ must ☐ need not be referred to us before you take any action.

(12) Disclosure of the parties to this transaction ☐ must ☐ need not be avoided.

(13) Disclosure of our profit margin ☐ must ☐ need not be avoided.

☐ Delete not applicable

The transferred credit will be subject to the Uniform Customs and Practice for Documentary Credits (1993 Revision) International Chamber of Commerce Publication No.500.

For and on behalf of
(Insert customer name)

_____   _____
Authorised Signature(s)

Contact Name ....   Bank: _____

Telephone No. ....

Fax No. ....   Verified:_____

P:\qualityme\HTVforms\dctransferrequest VER1 RH   page 1 of 2

Fig 35.6 Request for transfer of a transferable credit

HSBC ⟨X⟩

Note: The following requirements must also be fulfilled before any advice of transfer is issued by HSBC Bank.
- All Requests for Transfer must be accompanied by the original L/C advice, together with any attachments and amendments.
- Receipt by the Bank of the company's remittance (cleared funds) in respect of our charges as follows:
  -Transfer commission calculated at the rate of 0.5% of the amount transferred (Minimum £125)
  -Transmission costs   -Teletransmission Minimum £30   -Courier £25
  -All other outstanding charges advised to you to date
- This form must be signed by an authorised official(s) of your company and the signature(s) verified by your Bankers.

NOTES ON COMPLETION OF TRANSFER FORM

(1)   Complete this area with the full name and address of the company to which you require the credit to be transferred; this information can include the contact point(s) within the company. If the transfer is to be in favour of a company outside the UK, provide details of their banker, if known.

(2)   This is the amount that you require to be transferred. The amount must be in the same currency as the original credit.

(3)   The goods description must remain the same as that in the original credit. The unit price(s) however, may be altered.

(4)   The expiry date must not be after the expiry date of the original credit.

(5)   The latest shipment date must not be after the latest shipment date of the original credit.

(6)   The period for presentation may be shorter than that quoted in the original credit.

(7)   Amount of insurance cover may be increased to cover the value of your invoice(s).

(8)   Signify the manner in which the transferred credit is to be advised.

(9)   Tick the appropriate box dependent upon whether your own invoices will be substituted or not. The name of the original applicant must appear in any documents (other than the invoice) if it is a specific requirement of the original credit. We will assume (unless informed otherwise) that you require your name to be substituted for that of the applicant.

(10)   Tick the appropriate box dependent upon whether you wish to provide separate   instructions to amend the transfer credit, or whether we are authorised to amend this credit simultaneously with the original.

(11)   Tick the appropriate box dependent upon whether you require notification of document discrepancies before we revert to the transferee.

(12)   Tick the appropriate box dependent upon whether disclosure of the identity of the original applicant and/or the transferee to the other party must be avoided.

(13)   Tick the appropriate box dependent upon whether disclosure of your profit margin to the original applicant and/or the transferee must be avoided.

We are obliged by the Uniform Customs and Practice for Documentary Credits ICC No500 to issue the transfer credit on the same terms and conditions as the original credit with the exception of those points made above; you should therefore consider very carefully the terms of the credit to ensure that any information that you do not wish to be passed on to either the Applicant or Transferee is handled by way of amendment prior to the transfer instruction being completed.

```
********************************************************************************
*  PRINT NUMBER SRBCONQ01141 PRINTED BY SRB OPR D18 ON 11SEP2003 AT 10:12:04  *
*                          PRINT CLASS CO CONSTRUCT                           *
*                                                                            *
*  IRN 254097864              SERVICE IN  TTY      HASH C9C3                  *
*  SRN SRB254                 SERVICE OUT SWF      ISN                        *
*                                                                            *
*  RECEIVER ADDRESS           HSBCHKHH                                        *
*  ROUTE CODE (HSBCHHO )      HK+SHANGHAI BANKING CORPORATION LTD             *
*                             HONG KONG                                       *
*                             HONG KONG                                       *
********************************************************************************
                     CONSTRUCT HEADER WITH TRANSLATED TEXT
--------------------------------------------------------------------------------
MSG TYPE: 720   PRIORITY: 02    PDM: N
ORIGINATOR: P/MDSRB        DESTINATION: S/HSBCHKHH (HSBCHHO)
DEFAULT ROUTE: SWF
COUNTRY CODE: HK
--------------------------------------------------------------------------------
TO: .
FROM: HSBC TRADE SERVICES HSBC BANK PLC LONDON
      LONDON INTL BRANCH TEAM 2
MT720 TRANSFER OF A DOCUMENTARY CREDIT
27  SEQ OF TOTAL
    SEQUENCE                     1/1
40B FORM OF DC
    FORM OF DC     .             IRREVOCABLE
    CONFIRMATION                 WITHOUT OUR CONFIRMATION
20  OUR REF                      .
21  DC NO                        . ,
31D EXPIRY DATE AND PLACE
    DATE OF EXPIRY               31DEC2001
    PLACE OF EXPIRY              AT OUR COUNTERS
52D DC ISSUING BK
    FULL N/A                     .
50  FIRST BENEF                  .
59  SECOND BENEF
    FULL N/A                     .
32B DC AMT
    CCY/AMT                      USD1.00
41D AVAILABLE WITH/BY
    AVAILABLE WITH               HSBC BANK PLC
                                 HSBC TRADE SERVICES
                                 LONDON INTERNATIONAL BRANCH
                                 LONDON
    BY                           BY NEGOTIATION
42C DRAFTS AT                    SIGHT
42D DRAWEE
    FULL N/A                     XYZ BANK
47A ADDITIONAL CONDITIONS
    FIRST BENEFICIARY ADVISES
    UNQUOTE
    ISSUING BANKS STATES
    QUOTE
    UNQUOE
    EXCEPT SO FAR AS OTHERWISE EXPRESSLY STATED THIS CREDIT IS
    SUBJECT TO UNIFORM CUSTOMS AND PRACTICE FOR DOCUMENTARY CREDITS
    1993 REVISION I.C.C.PUBLICATION NO.500
--------------------------------------------------------------------------------
                    PRINT NUMBER SRBCONQ01141 WILL CONTINUE ON PAGE 2
```

Fig 35.7 Transfer of a transferable credit

THIS ADVISE CONSTITUTES A TRANSFER UNDER OUR ABOVE NAMED
CORRESPONDENTS IRREVOCABLE LETTER OF CREDIT.
IN ACCORDANCE WITH ARTICLE 48D WE NOTIFY YOU THAT THE TRANSFEROR
HAS RETAINED THE RIGHT TO REFUSE TO ALLOW US TO PASS TO THE
TRANSFEREE ANY AMENDMENTS IN FAVOUR OF THE TRANSFEROR.
WE ALSO INFORM YOU THAT THE TRANSFEROR HAS INDICATED TO US THAT
THEY INTEND TO EXERCISE THEIR RIGHT TO SUBSITUTE THEIR INVOICES
FOR THOSE OF THE TRANSFEREE
WE HAVE NOT BEEN REQUESTED TO ADD OUR CONFIRMATION TO THIS
DOCUMENTARY CREDIT,CONSEQUENTLY THIS CREDIT CONVEYS NO ENGAGEMENT
/RESPONSIBILITY ON OUR PART.
WE WOULD BE WILLING TO CONSIDER NEGOTIATING DOCUMENTS SUBJECT TO
THEIR FULLY COMPYING WITH THE CREDIT TERMS AND CONDITIONS SUBJECT
TO A DEDUCTION OF INTEREST IN RESPECT OF THE KNOWN/ANTICIPATED
PERIOD DURING WHICH WE WILL BE AWAITING A REMITTANCE FROM THE
ISSUING BANK.ANY NEGOTIATION WHICH WE MAY EFFECT WILL BE ON A
WITH RECOURSE BASIS.IN THE EVENT THAT YOU DO NOT WISH US TO
NEGOTIATE OR,AT THE TIME OF PRESENTATION,WE ARE UNWILLING TO
NEGOTIATE,WE SHALL,WITHOUT ENGAGEMENT ON OUR PART AND IN THE
ABSENCE OF ANY INSTRUCTION TO THE CONTARY FROM THE PRESENTER,
FORWARD DOCUMENTS TO THE ISSUING BANK FOR SETTLEMENT.PAYMENT
THEREOF MAY ONLY BE MADE BY US UPON RECEIPT OF FUNDS FROM THE
ISSUING/REIMBURSING BANK.
OUR CHARGES ARE FOR THE ACCOUNT OF THE SECOND BENEFICIARY
INCLUDING PAYMENT COMMISSION OF 0.1 PER CENT MINIMUM GBP 50.00
WE SHALL DEDUCT PROM THE PROCEEDS THE SUM OF GBP 10.00 (OR
CURRENCY EQUIVALENT) FOR EACH TELEGRAPHIC TRANSFER EFFECTED.
WHERE DOCUMENTS ARE PRESENTED WITH DISCREPANCIES THE FOLLOWING
CHARGE WILL ALSO BE FOR THE SECOND BENEFICIARIES DISCREPANCY
HANDLING FEE GBP 30.00 PLUS CABLE CHARGES IF APPLICABLE.
ALL CHARGES IN   ARE FOR THE ACCOUNT OF THE SECOND
BENEFICIARY.

71B DETAILS OF CHARGES   ALL CHARGES IN   ARE FOR
                                  ACCOUNT OF THE SECOND BENEFICIARY.
48 PERIOD FOR PRESENTATION   DOCUMENTS MUST BE PRESENTED WITHIN
                                     DAYS AFTER DATE OF SHIPMENT BUT
                                  WITHIN VALIDITY OF THE CREDIT.
49 CONFIRMATION INSTRUCTIONS   WITHOUT
78 INFO TO PRESENTING BK
    NOTWITHSTANDING ANYTHING TO THE CONTARY THAT APPEAR IN THE
    FOREGOING CREDIT.IT IS ESSENTIAL THAT DOCUMENTS UNDER THIS CREDIT
    BE SENT TO US AT THE FOLLOWING ADDRESS FOR PROCESSING.
    HSBC BANK PLC
    TRADE SERVICES
    LONDON INTERNATIONAL BRANCH
    PO BOX 585
    6 ARTHUR STREET (ASO4)
    LONDON EC4R 9HR
    ATTENTION TEAM 2
72 BK TO BK INFO   ENSURE THAT THE FOLLOWING STATEMENT
                                  IS INCLUDED IN YOUR PRESENTATION
                                  SCHEDULE ALONGSIDE THE DC NUMBER
                                  ATTN LONDON TEAM 2 AS04
                                  AND OUR REFERENCE NUMBER WHICH
                                  INCLUDES THE SUFFIX -

                    PRINT NUMBER SRBCONQ01141 WILL CONTINUE ON PAGE 3

1006

PRINT NUMBER SRBCONQ01141 PRINTED BY SRB OPR D18 ON 11SEP2003 AT 10:12:04
END OF MESSAGE

own invoice for £15,000.[270] Figure 35.8 shows in diagrammatic form the flow of documents and money after S's return of the original letter of credit to AB.

In general, the new credit issued to M must match that originally issued to B, but certain deviations are authorized by art 48(h) to reflect the fact that two distinct contracts of sale are involved. In particular, when indicating in the letter of credit on whose instructions the credit is issued, AB can substitute S's name for that of B; the period of validity of the credit or period of shipment may be reduced (it usually is, to ensure a sufficient margin of time for S to comply with AB's request to furnish his own invoice in substitution for M's); and the amount of the credit and of any unit price stated in it may likewise be reduced. [271]

Where the letter of credit issued to the second beneficiary is for less than the full amount of the original credit, the latter remains in force in favour of S as to the balance,[272] though S will not have a document in his hands to that effect, the bank merely indorsing the original letter of credit with a note of the portion transferred. A transferable credit is transferable once only.[273] This does not preclude S from giving instructions to split the credit into fractions to be allocated separately to two or more beneficiaries,[274] but since this will result in B's order being satisfied by two or more shipments from different sources, the division of the credit in this way is allowed only where the original credit does not prohibit partial shipments.[275] The effect of the rule allowing only one transfer is that the second beneficiary cannot himself transfer the credit.

(ii) Legal effect of transfer

The transfer of a transferable credit not merely entitles the second beneficiary to have the credit honoured on presentation of documents but constitutes an authority to him to perform the conditions of the credit himself instead of performance having to be by S. That is to say, M is considered to fulfil the terms of the credit by furnishing his own documents.

The relationship between IB/AB and the first and second beneficiaries after transfer of a transferable credit remains curiously undefined. Is the transfer an assignment of the benefit of the contract or is it a novation, in which S ceases to be in contractual relations with IB/AB as regards the transferred part of the credit and the second beneficiary takes his place as a contracting party in relation to that part? As mentioned above, the transfer of a credit goes beyond a mere assignment in that the transferee becomes entitled to tender his own performance in place of that of the

---

270 S will usually want his own invoice, not M's, to go to B; but if he is dilatory, AB is entitled to send M's invoice to B, which would no doubt cause considerable confusion and, worse still, would reveal to B the identity of S's supplier and the size of the mark-up on the resale, creating the possibility for B to deal in future directly with M.

271 It is because of deviations of this kind, which will occur in the vast majority of transferable credits, that transfer by indorsement and delivery of the original letter of credit is rarely practicable.

272 S's application to transfer the credit in part will include a request to pay the difference to him.

273 Article 48(g).

274 Ibid.

275 Ibid.

1008

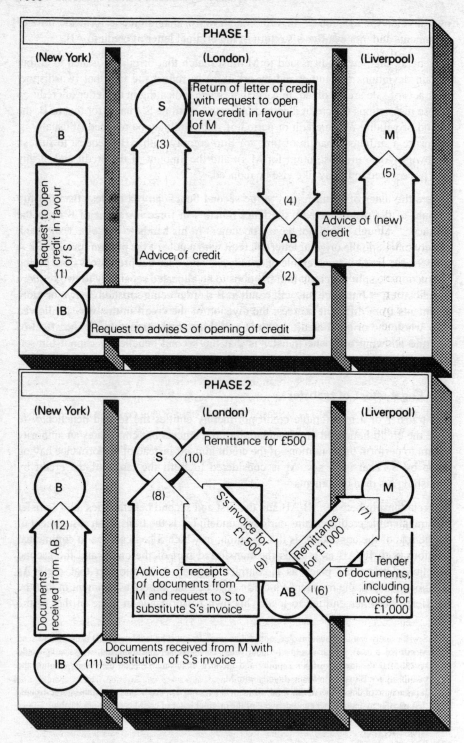

Fig 35.8 Flow of documents and money on transfer of a credit

first beneficiary, while the transfer itself cannot be effected by sole act of the transferor but entails the cooperation of IB/AB; and a novation involves not a transfer of rights but a change of parties. In view of the procedure adopted for transfer, by which the original letter of credit is taken back and a new credit or credits issued to one or more second beneficiaries, it would seem more accurate to treat the partial transfer of a credit as a new contract by novation in relation to the part transferred, and a variation of the original contract as regards the original beneficiary by reduction of the credit to the amount retained.[276] If this be the correct view, the partial transfer of an irrevocable credit from S to M extinguishes IB's liability to S as regards the part of the credit transferred and involves IB in a new commitment, to M, upon the terms of the new letter of credit furnished to M. M will also enjoy the benefit of AB's confirmation if, in advising the new letter of credit, AB adds its own confirmation, but not otherwise. That is to say, the confirmation given by AB to S does not as such enure for the benefit of M, who must, if he desires AB's confirmation, see that this is embodied in the new credit. M will assume the liability to IB/AB on implied warranties arising from the presentation of the documents and, consistently with the novation theory, S will incur no liability to IB/AB for repayment of sums paid out against forged or nonconforming documents presented by M. This seems right in policy terms, for S is not involved in procuring the documents and has no control over their presentation. If B agrees to a transferable credit, he accepts the concomitant risk.

Another unresolved question is S's liability to B under the contract of sale if M fails to make a valid and timely presentation of documents. It seems clear that B, in agreeing to procure the issue of a transferable credit, cannot thereby be taken to have intended that S shall be released from his obligations on transfer of the credit, for this would leave B without remedy if M failed to proceed, there being no privity between B and M. Accordingly, if M fails to comply with the terms of the credit, he places S in breach of the contract of sale, and S will be liable to B accordingly.

(iii) Transferable credit distinguished from negotiation credit

A transferable credit should not be confused with a negotiation credit. The former is a credit which the original beneficiary can require to be replaced, wholly or in part, by a new credit in favour of a second beneficiary. A negotiation credit does not involve the replacement of one credit by another. It is a mechanism by which S is enabled to sell to an authorized bank his right to present the documents and collect payment. The original credit remains in force throughout and the purchaser of S's drafts and/or documents becomes the new beneficiary under the terms of the credit itself.[277]

276 Novation is also the view taken by Pennington, Hudson and Mann, *Commercial Banking Law*, p 322. Banks tend to consider a transferable credit to be a single credit. But there are compelling arguments in favour of characterization of a transfer as a *pro tanto* novation. The mechanism used is not an assignment mechanism; the terms of the transferred credit are in some respects different (in particular, there is a different beneficiary and the amount may be less than that of the original credit); the documents may in certain respects be different; and if the credit were a single credit, the transferee would take subject to any right of set-off the bank might have against the original beneficiary, which is not what the parties intend.

277 See p 987.

(iv) Assignment of proceeds of credit

Article 49 of the UCP provides as follows:

> The fact that a Credit is not stated to be transferable shall not affect the beneficiary's right to assign any proceeds to which he may be, or may become, entitled under such Credit, in accordance with the provisions of the applicable law. This Article relates only to the assignment of proceeds and not to the assignment of the right to perform under the Credit itself.

Whereas the transfer of a credit involves the bank's acceptance of performance by the transferee instead of by the first beneficiary (for which reason the bank's consent to transfer is stipulated by the UCP as a necessary term of the credit if it is to be transferable), a beneficiary who assigns the proceeds is merely transferring the right to ask for payment as and when earned by his own performance. Hence, to claim under the credit the assignee must present the beneficiary's documents *as agent of the beneficiary*, or get the beneficiary to present them. The assignee of the proceeds cannot tender documents in his own right.[278]

It would, presumably, be open to a bank to exclude even assignability, thus avoiding art 49 of the UCP. This would not prevent an assignment from becoming effective as between beneficiary and assignee,[279] but it would entitle the bank to ignore any notice of assignment and to insist on making payment to the beneficiary himself and no one else.[280]

Assignments of proceeds are typically in favour of the advising or confirming bank itself where it has provided pre-shipment finance or has made an advance of funds payable under a deferred payment credit or in favour of the beneficiary's own supplier to cover the price payable to that supplier, in which case the bank notifies the supplier of the assignment, though usually without commitment.[281] In both cases the assignment of the proceeds is arranged prior to presentation of the documents. On maturity the beneficiary presents the documents in the usual way to the advising or confirming bank, which pays itself or the supplier, as the case may be, and credits any balance to the beneficiary.

6   BACK-TO-BACK CREDITS

A back-to-back credit is a credit which is issued at S's request to his supplier, M, against the letter of credit which S himself has received from B. Whereas a transferable credit is in concept a single credit, a back-to-back credit is entirely distinct from that issued at B's behest to S, and it does not concern B in any way. It is essentially a mechanism by which S's bank, relying on the prospect of receiving

---

278 *Singer & Friedlander v Creditanstalt-Bankverein* (1980) 13 August, a decision of the Vienna Commercial Court (the action was subsequently settled). The same position would, it is thought, be taken by an English court. See further R. M. Goode 'Reflections on Letters of Credit – V' [1981] JBL 150 at pp 152–154.

279 See pp 749–750, and R. M. Goode, 'Inalienable Rights?' (1979) 42 MLR 553, commenting on the decision in *Helstan Securities Ltd v Hertfordshire County Council* [1978] 3 All ER 262.

280 Goode (1979) 42 MLR 553.

281 This is because, among other things, the bank may wish to exercise a right of set-off against the beneficiary or may have a security interest in the proceeds.

on S's behalf payment under the letter of credit issued to him against presentation of documents, is prepared to issue a corresponding letter of credit to M in fulfilment of the obligation contained in the separate sales contract between M and S. Accordingly, the back-to-back credit, unlike the transferable credit, does not attract any special provisions of the UCP.

Where S's bank (SB) agrees to issue a back-to-back credit, it will take possession of the letter of credit issued to S and itself issue a countervailing letter of credit to M. The documents specified in this second credit must, of course, be such as can, when received by SB, be tendered on S's behalf in conformity with the requirements of the first credit. Thus the specification must be identical[282] and must, of course, relate to the same goods.[283] When the documents are tendered by M, SB will pay M under the back-to-back credit, will substitute S's invoice for that of M and will present the documents to IB or AB pursuant to the primary credit, collecting payment in exchange. SB will then retain the amount necessary to recoup the price paid to M and SB's own charges, and will release the balance of the sum received to S. In diagram form, the flow of documents and money is as shown in figure 35.9.

The back-to-back credit is relatively uncommon compared with the transferable credit. It is encountered mainly in connection with string contracts. Banks dislike issuing back-to-back credits, except for customers of first-class standing. The cover afforded by possession of the original letter of credit is weak, since apart from the risk of the issuing bank finding a flaw in the documents, S may become insolvent before SB has collected payment under the first letter of credit, in which case S's bank will have made or become committed to payment to M under the back-to-back credit, whereas any payment that falls to be made under the primary credit will (in the absence of the grant of an effective security interest over the credit or its proceeds by S to SB) be claimed by S's trustee in bankruptcy or liquidator.

7. RAISING OF FUNDS BY SELLER AGAINST DRAFTS OR CREDITS

There are various ways in which a bank may make funds available to its customer, S, in anticipation of the receipt of the price of the exported goods under S's contract with B. Thus, S's bank may:

(a)   negotiate S's draft on B, IB or AB,[284] such negotiation being on a recourse basis; [285]

(b)   advance the whole or part of the draft at interest, collecting the draft for S at maturity and recouping itself from the sum collected; [286]

---

282   Except that, as with a transferable credit, an earlier date for presentation will be stipulated and the amount will normally be less.

283   In addition, the credit should call for the document to be issued in a name that will not reveal M's identity to B.

284   See p 987.

285   Unless, coincidentally, S's bank is also the bank which has issued or confirmed the credit.

286   The difference between purchase with recourse and advance on security is that (apart from the distinction in the legal character of the two transactions) the loan may be repayable on demand and carries interest on the amount from time to time outstanding, whereas if it negotiates the draft, the bank must wait till maturity to receive its money (unless it discounts the bill), and its return will be the discount charged at the time of negotiation.

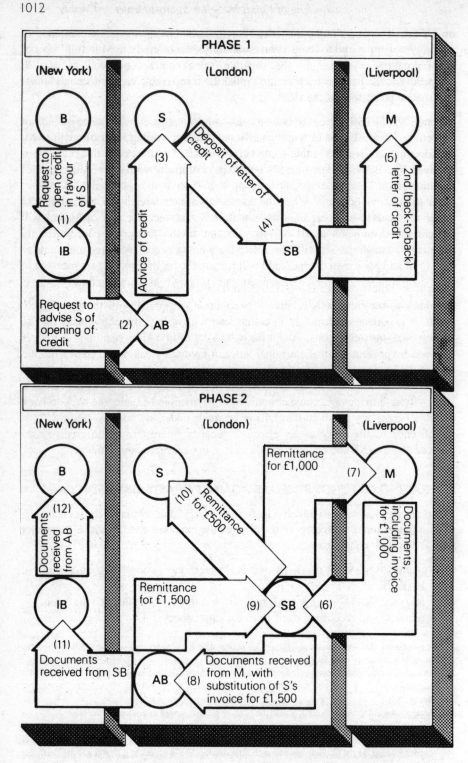

Fig 35.9 Flow of documents and money under a back-to-back credit

(c)   open an acceptance credit in favour of S, that is, undertake to accept drafts drawn on it by S up to the agreed amount, which S will then be able to discount; [287]

(d)   issue a back-to-back credit in favour of S's supplier, M, to enable S to fulfil his own payment obligation to M under his contract of sale with M.[288]

A form of bill discounting particularly designed for exporters is forfaiting. This is the provision of finance through the non-recourse negotiation of freely negotiable debt instruments, such as promissory notes made by or bills of exchange drawn on importers or of drafts drawn under letters of credit. Since the forfaiter buys the instruments without recourse to the exporter who draws or indorses them, he usually requires the obligations of the importer on the notes or bills to be supported by a bank guarantee or by a suretyship indorsement or 'aval' on the instruments themselves. The instruments can then be rediscounted by the forfaiter in the secondary market.

The use of bills of exchange drawn by the exporter on the importer creates difficulties where the Geneva Convention on Bills of Exchange applies in that the convention does not allow the drawer to exclude recourse. Indorsers are, however, permitted to do so, and it is therefore more usual for the exporter to take a promissory note in his favour and indorse it to the forfaiter.

8.   RAISING OF FINANCE BY BUYER ON SECURITY OF IMPORTED GOODS

Just as S may require to raise funds from his bank in anticipation of receipt of the price, so also B may need an advance from his own bank to pay for the goods, repaying this from the proceeds of sale after the goods have arrived and been disposed of. B's bank may, of course, be willing to give B facilities on an unsecured basis, but usually it will want to take security over the imported goods and documents relating to them pending resale by the buyer.

Where the bank contemplates providing finance for B's imports generally, and not merely for a specific transaction, it may take from B a general letter of charge or hypothecation, by which B charges to the bank all goods from time to time imported by him to secure all advances from time to time made by the bank. A general letter of charge of this character is outside the exemption from the Bills of Sale Acts given[289] in respect of charges over imported goods,[290] with the result that

---

287   In this case, the bill will be an accommodation bill and S's bank an accommodation party. The bank will, in effect, be lending money to S and will be entitled to repayment on whatever terms are agreed between them.

288   See p 1010.

289   By the Bills of Sale Act 1890, s 1, as replaced by the Bills of Sale Act 1891, s 1.

290   *NV Slavenburg's Bank v Intercontinental Natural Resources Ltd* [1980] 1 All ER 955, citing with approval the statement in *Halsbury's Laws of England* (4th edn), vol 4, para 636, n 1. Similarly, it is thought it would not be within the separate exemption conferred by s 4 of the Bills of Sale Act 1878 in relation to documents used in the ordinary course of business as proof of the possession of goods.

where B is not a company, the charge will be ineffective against third parties unless registered as a bill of sale in conformity with the Bills of Sale Acts, and, where B is a company, will be void against a liquidator and creditors unless registered under s 395 of the Companies Act 1985.[291]

Usually, however, the bank will not rely exclusively on a general letter of charge but will take a specific security over each shipment of goods imported by B.[292] The most common form of security is a pledge of the bill of lading and other shipping documents. This is treated in law as equivalent to a pledge of the goods themselves[293] and is thus effective to give the bank a legal possessory interest in the goods. The pledge is effected by delivery of the bill of lading (with other documents) to the bank, indorsed to the bank or in blank.[294] The bank will not, of course, want to be involved with the physical handling of the goods themselves (indeed, taking physical possession might expose it to a claim for any unpaid freight[295]) and will thus concern itself solely with the documents. Only a bill of lading will suffice as a pledgeable document. Delivery orders are not considered negotiable, and their deposit with the bank would, at best, be evidence of an agreement to give an equitable charge. The pledge of the bill of lading is effected by delivery to the bank (with any necessary indorsement) without further formality. In particular, registration is not required. [296]

However, B will need the documents in order to obtain possession of the goods from the shipping company for the purpose of selling them, for it is out of the proceeds of sale that he will repay the bank. If the bank were to part with possession of the documents unconditionally, its pledge rights would be extinguished, for a pledge depends on the continuance of possession. But this difficulty has been neatly surmounted by the ingenuity of the commercial lawyer. By way of exception to the general rule, redelivery of the goods or documents to the pledgor does not destroy the pledge if the redelivery is for some designated purpose of the pledgor himself (eg to hold for him in safe custody or to sell as his agent), for in taking possession

---

291 See p 660.
292 Provision for such security is often embodied in the bank's standard form of application to open the credit.
293 Assuming the goods are identified in the bill of lading. But see p 220.
294 Alternatively, the bank could ask B to arrange with S for the goods to be consigned directly to the bank. In practice, banks prefer not to become consignees, in order to avoid the risk of being held liable for unpaid freight (see p 1057). As a matter of law, the mere fact that a bank is named as consignee or becomes an indorsee of a bill of lading and takes possession of the documents does not make it the owner, for the transfer of ownership depends on the intention of the parties, and if the documents are taken by way of pledge, the law gives effect to this intention, leaving the general property in B (*Sewell v Burdick* (1884) 10 App Cas 74).
295 See p 1057.
296 A pledge, being a possessory security, is outside the registration requirements both of the Bills of Sale Acts and the Companies Act, provided that it does not take the form of constructive delivery through the debtor's written attornment (see *Halsbury's Laws of England*, vol.4(1), para 621). Moreover, there is no document of transfer to which the Bills of Sale Acts could relate. The bill of lading is exempt as a document used in the ordinary course of business as proof of possession or control of the goods (Bills of Sale Act 1878, s 4) and there is, in any event, a separate exemption in relation to charges over imported goods (Bills of Sale Act 1890, s 1, as amended by Bills of Sale Act 1891, s 1).

the pledgor receives the pledged articles not on his own behalf but for the pledgee, who thus continues in constructive possession. Accordingly, there emerged the letter of trust, or trust receipt (fig 35.10), by which B undertakes that, in consideration of the release of the documents to him, he will hold them on trust for the bank, will use them to sell the goods as the bank's agent and will hold the goods themselves until sale, and the proceeds after sale, on trust for the bank. The letter of trust thus establishes that delivery of the documents to B is for the bank's purposes, not for his own.[297] In this sense the letter of trust is to be regarded as a means of securing the continuance of the pledge rather than as an independent security device; and on this ground, as well as on others,[298] it has been held not to constitute a bill of sale for the purpose of the Bills of Sale Acts.[299] Nor does the letter of trust amount to a charge on book debts so as to attract registration under s 395 of the Companies Act 1985.[300]

When releasing the documents, the bank will usually insist that the goods are warehoused in the bank's name. This will enable the bank to retain the goods as against the purchaser until the sum secured by the goods has been paid.

Can the bank's pledge rights be defeated by B's rejection of the goods if these are not in conformity with the contract of sale? It is thought that they cannot and that, on the contrary, the pledge of the documents will prevent B from exercising his right to reject, at any rate if he is not able to secure the return of the documents to S at the time he gives notice of rejection.[301]

9.   DEMAND GUARANTEES, PERFORMANCE BONDS AND STANDBY CREDITS

We conclude this chapter with a brief discussion of payment undertakings in which the traditional legal distinction between a primary obligation of the type characterized by the undertaking embodied in an irrevocable credit and a secondary obligation, where the obligor's liability does not arise until default by the principal debtor (as in the case of the ordinary guarantee), has become decidedly blurred These forms of undertaking are variously known as demand guarantees, on-demand or first-demand performance bonds and standby letters of credit.[302] Many of the principles governing documentary credits apply equally to demand guarantees; indeed, several of the cases referred to earlier involved demand guarantees.

---

297 In *North Western Bank v Poynter* [1895] AC 56 it was unsuccessfully argued that the rule allowing redelivery for a purpose of the pledgee without destroying the pledge applied only where redelivery was to a stranger, not to the pledgor himself.
Possession under a letter of trust is deemed in law to be held by pledgor and pledgee together and is a further illustration of the concept of shared possession referred to p 42.

298 In particular, that it falls within the exemptions mentioned in n 296.

299 *Re David Allester Ltd* [1922] 2 Ch 211; *Re Hamilton Young & Co* [1905] 2 KB 772.

300 *Re David Allester Ltd*, n 299.

301 See p 352.

302 For an excellent comparative treatment, see Roeland F Bertrams, *Bank Guarantees in International Trade* (2nd revised edn, 1996).

TRUST LETTER

_____19___

To   **BANK LIMITED**

I/We acknowledge receipt from you of the undermentioned documents of title relating to the undermentioned goods which are now pledged to you upon the terms of a Memorandum of pledge dated the _____19___, which Memorandum we hereby confirm and declare to continue.

I/We acknowledge that I/we have received the said documents and will hold the same (and also the said goods and all and any proceeds thereof upon sale) as trustee(s) for you.

I/We hold the said documents and will deal with the same for the following purposes and on the following terms:

Whichever of these Clauses is applicable should be used and the other deleted.

(1) In order to obtain delivery of and to warehouse the goods. The goods will be warehoused in your name or otherwise as directed by you and the warrants will be handed to you as soon as they are received by me/us. The goods will be duly covered by insurance as provided by the said Memorandum.

(2) In order to deliver the goods to the buyers, Messrs._____
_____. The Proceeds (whether cash or acceptances) will be kept separate and will be handed by me/us to you specifically and immediately on receipt of the same.

I/We undertake to return to you forthwith on your request at any time (irrespective that the purpose set out above may not have been completed) the documents and/or any other documents received by me/us in exchange therefor and to comply promptly and fully with any instructions which you may give as to the manner of dealing with the goods or any of them or the removal of the same to any place or the storage of the same at any place.

I/We further undertake that this transaction shall be kept separate from all other transactions, and that the documents the goods and any proceeds thereof shall be kept separate and distinct from any other documents goods or proceeds relating to or arising from any other transaction.

DOCUMENTS

DESCRIPTION OF DOCUMENT. (Bill of Lading, Warrant, Delivery Order, etc., with particulars of date, identification, etc.)	DESCRIPTION AND QUANTITY OF GOODS.

Fig 35.10 Trust receipt

(i)   Terminology and nature

In describing the nature of these instruments it is necessary to clear up some terminological confusion arising from the lack of consistency in the use of labels. The words 'guarantee' and 'performance bond' are now used in two entirely different senses. In origin the word 'guarantee' denotes a suretyship contract in which the guarantor, or surety, assumes a liability to answer for the debt or default of another. The guarantor's liability is therefore secondary in character in that the guarantor's payment obligation does not arise until the principal debtor has defaulted and is in principle limited to the liability of the principal debtor.[303] Where the guarantee is by deed, it is commonly termed a bond; and where the bond is to secure the performance of non-monetary obligations, such as the execution of construction works under a building contract, it is labelled a performance bond. It is inherent in these suretyship guarantees and bonds that they are secondary in character.[304] They are commonly issued by insurance companies, rather than by banks, who prefer to confine themselves to documentary payment undertakings. But 'guarantee' and 'performance bond' are now also used to denote undertakings which are documentary in character. They partake of the character of documentary credits in that they are primary in form, being conditioned only by presentation of a written demand for payment and any other specified documents[305] without the issuing bank being concerned with whether there has been actual default by the principal. But unlike documentary credits, where it is intended that the bank shall be the first port of call for payment, demand guarantees and similar instruments are secondary in intent, their function being to provide the beneficiary with a rapid access to payment if the principal defaults. Put another way, in a true (suretyship) guarantee the secondary nature of the guarantor's obligation is not merely a matter internal to the agreement between the guarantor and the principal but is also inherent in the guarantee itself, whereas in the case of the demand guarantee the secondary character of the undertaking is confined to the guarantor–principal relationship and is not a term of the guarantee document, so that the bank is neither obliged nor entitled to go behind the specified documents and inquire whether the principal has, in fact, defaulted. For this type of instrument the labels 'bank guarantee' and 'performance bond' are synonymous; the bond is not by deed and is therefore not a bond in the traditional sense. As the result of the ICC Uniform Rules on Demand Guarantees (URDG),[306] the term 'demand guarantee' is now coming into use to describe what have previously been referred to as bank guarantees or performance bonds.

Demand guarantees,[307] which, in contrast to documentary credits are almost invariably issued in paper form, are used almost exclusively to underpin non-monetary

---

303   See p 814.

304   The International Chamber of Commerce has published a set of rules, *The Uniform Rules for Contract Bonds* (ICC Publication No 524), designed primarily for suretyship bonds issued in international transactions. They are not discussed here.

305   In most cases all that is called for is a written demand by the beneficiary. Hence such guarantees are often referred to as on-demand, or simple, guarantees.

306   See below.

307   For the different types of demand guarantee see p 1020.

obligations in international transactions, typically the obligations of the contractor under an international construction contract and those of the seller under an international contract of sale. By contrast the standby credit, developed in America because of sensitivity over the word 'guarantee',[308] is altogether more diverse in character. It has evolved into a general-purpose financial tool used to support financial as well as non-financial undertakings and domestic as well as international transactions, and to secure credit enhancement of public issues of securities, which, if underpinned by a standby credit issued by a first-class bank, may attract a higher credit rating from agencies such as Moody's and Standard and Poor's than would otherwise be the case. Standby credits are also used to support the issuer's own commitments, whereas demand guarantees are issued only for the account of third parties as principals; and while the confirmed credit is found in relation to standby credits as well as documentary credits, confirmation is unusual in the case of demand guarantees, where in the ordinary way the beneficiary is content to rely on the undertaking of the issuing bank alone but may stipulate that it is to be a local bank known to him, that bank, in turn, relying on the instructing party's counter-guarantee. Standby credits are governed by the International Standby Practices.[309] But it is important to appreciate that the differences between a standby credit and a demand guarantee lie in business practice, not in law, in much the same way as the labels, 'lease', 'rental', 'contract hire' are used by leasing companies to distinguish transactions which in a business sense are different from each other though legally they are the same.[310]

The rest of this chapter will be confined to demand guarantees, with particular reference to guarantees issued under the URDG.

(ii)   Rules of the International Chamber of Commerce

The ability of the beneficiary to invoke a demand guarantee by simple written demand without proof of default by the principal obviously renders it liable to abuse by fraudulent calling. With a view to redressing the balance between beneficiaries and principals, the International Chamber of Commerce published in 1978 a set of Uniform Rules for Contract Guarantees.[311] These provided that where the guarantee did not specify the documents to be produced in support of a claim or specified only a statement of claim by the beneficiary, then the beneficiary had to present a court decision, an arbitral award or the principal's written approval of the claim and its amount. This proved too far removed from market practice to be acceptable, for the demand guarantee was originally conceived as a near-cash substitute for a cash deposit by the contractor, and to require a judgment or arbitral award as a condition

---

308 See p 951 and, for a form of standby letter of credit, pp 1024–1025, and fig 35.15, pp 0000–0000.

309 See, p 000. For a detailed treatment see James E. Byrne (ed), *The Official Commentary on the International Standby Practices* (1998) and, for comparison of the two sets of rules, Byrne, *UCP 500 and ISP98 Compared.*

310 These remarks do not apply to the somewhat oddly named 'direct pay' standby credit, in which the issuing bank is intended as the first port of call for payment. It is not clear why the label 'standby' is applied to these credits at all; in essence they are virtually indistinguishable from conventional clean credits.

311 ICC Publication No 325.

of payment was to render the guarantee almost indistinguishable from the traditional suretyship guarantee.

Accordingly, in 1992 the ICC published a new set of rules, the URDG,[312] which accommodates the market need for the simple on-demand guarantee but build in certain forms of protection designed to provide some safeguard against unfair calling. The response to the URDG has been favourable and they are now increasingly being incorporated into demand guarantees. The URDG have been endorsed by UNCITRAL and recommended for the UK by SITPRO. The International Federation of Consulting Engineers (FIDIC) has incorporated the URDG into its model forms of guarantee for construction works and the rules have also been incorporated into the model unconditional guarantee forms issued by the World Bank and are now available as an option in SWIFT messages.

(iii) The UN Convention on Independent Guarantees and Stand-By Letters of Credit

The URDG, like the UCP, have effect by virtue of incorporation into contracts.[313] Like the UCP, they are necessarily confined to issues that can be dealt with by agreement and cannot, for example, deal with the power of courts to grant injunctions restraining presentation or payment. The 1995 UN Convention on Independent Guarantees and Stand-By Letters of Credit covers much the same ground as the URDG and adopts a very similar approach. The convention is limited to independent undertakings (standbys, demand guarantees and counter-guarantees) and does not apply to suretyship guarantees. In general, the convention leaves it to the parties to determine the terms of the guarantee, and, in practice, they are likely to incorporate either the URDG or the ISP. But the Convention imposes a duty of good faith and reasonable care,[314] as well as providing exceptions to the guarantor's payment obligation and as to provisional court measures, including the grant of injunctive relief.[315]

(iv) The demand guarantee defined

Article 2(a) of the URDG provides that for the purpose of the Rules:

> a demand guarantee (hereinafter referred to as 'Guarantee') means any guarantee, bond or other payment undertaking, however named or described, by a bank, insurance company or other body or person (hereinafter called 'the Guarantor') given in writing

---

312 Uniform Rules for Demand Guarantees, ICC Publication No 458. Model forms have also been published (ICC Publication No 503). The 1978 Rules have not been formally withdrawn and may still be used for the time being, though their use is likely to continue to be limited. For the history and analyses of the rules see Georges Affaki, *ICC Uniform Rules on Demand Guarantees: A User's Handbook to the* URDG (ICC Publication No 631, 2001); Roy Goode, *Guide to the ICC Uniform Rules for Demand Guarantees* (ICC Publication No 510, 1992) and 'The New ICC Uniform Rules for Demand Guarantees' [1992] LMCLQ 190; Anthony Pierce, *Demand Guarantees in International Trade* (1993); and Jack, Malek and Quest, *Documentary Credits*, ch 12.

313 Article 1.

314 Article 14.

315 Article 20.

for the payment of money on presentation in conformity with the terms of the undertaking of a written demand for payment and such other document(s) (for example, a certificate by an architect or engineer, a judgment or an arbitral award) as may be specified in the Guarantee, such undertaking being given

i)   at the request or on the instructions and under the liability of a party (hereinafter called 'the Principal'), or
ii)   at the request or on the instructions and under the liability of a bank, insurance company or any other body or person (hereinafter 'the Instructing Party') acting on the instructions of a Principal

to another party (hereinafter 'the Beneficiary').

(v) Structure of demand guarantee transactions

It will be seen from the above definition that every demand guarantee involves at least three parties, the principal, the beneficiary and the guarantor, and may involve a fourth, the instructing party. The principal is the contractor at whose request the guarantee is issued.[316] The beneficiary is the person in whose favour the guarantee is issued. The guarantor is the bank or other person issuing the guarantee. Almost invariably, the principal and the beneficiary will carry on business in different countries. In a direct (or three-party) guarantee the principal's bank, located in the country where the principal has his place of business, issues the guarantee direct to the beneficiary. Figure 35.11 shows the triangular relationship arising where P, an English contractor, enters into a contract with B in Saudi Arabia for the construction of a plant in Saudi Arabia and arranges for its bank, G Bank, to issue a guarantee direct to B.

But B may wish to have a guarantee from a bank he knows in his own country, and that bank, G Bank, will itself wish to be protected by a counter-guarantee from P's bank, who in this case is termed the instructing party (IP Bank). This is the indirect (four-party) guarantee. At P's request, IP Bank communicates with G Bank and requests it to issue a guarantee in favour of B against IP Bank's counter-guarantee. The counter-guarantee will follow the same pattern as the guarantee and will require IP Bank to pay G Bank on the latter's first written demand and any other specified documents. This four-party structure is shown in figure 35.12.

(vi) Types of demand guarantee

Guarantees may also be classified according to the stage or segment of performance they are designed to secure. It would be possible to have a single guarantee covering all stages from the bid for the contract to the expiry of the maintenance liability period. But in practice it is found convenient to have different types of guarantee for different stages so as to limit the liability for each phase to the amount of the guarantee relating to that phase. The main types of guarantee are:

---

316   The principal therefore corresponds to the applicant for the credit in a documentary credit.

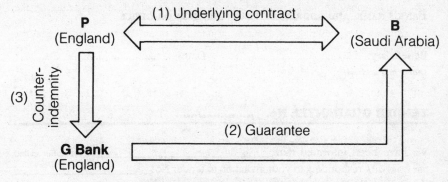

Fig 35.11 Structure of three-party demand guarantee

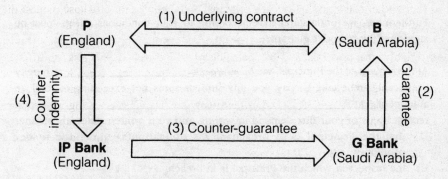

Fig 35.12 Structure of four-party demand guarantee

(a)   the tender (or bid) guarantee (fig 35.13), given for a percentage of the project value and providing for payment to the beneficiary if the principal, having tendered successfully for the contract, fails to sign it or to procure the issue of any main performance guarantee required by the tender conditions;

(b)   the performance guarantee, covering the main stage of performance (fig 35.14);

(c)   the advance payment (or repayment) guarantee, designed to provide repayment to the beneficiary of an advance payment made to the principal for work not later carried out;

(d)   the retention guarantee, furnished to the beneficiary in exchange for release of retention monies and available to be called up if the principal fails to complete the contract or the work is defective;

(e)   the maintenance (or warranty) guarantee, furnished to the beneficiary in exchange for release of retention moneys held to cover the cost of defects arising during the defects liability period.

BANK'S NAME, AND ADDRESS OF ISSUING BRANCH OR OFFICE

Beneficiary: .... Date: ....
(name and address)

TENDER GUARANTEE No. ....

We have been informed that _____, (hereinafter called
'the Principal'), responding to your invitation to tender No._____
dated _____ for the supply of _____
(description of goods and/or services), has submitted to you his offer No._____
dated _____.

Furthermore, we understand that, according to your conditions, offers must be
supported by a tender guarantee.

At the request of the Principal, we *(name of bank)* _____ hereby
irrevocably undertake to pay you any sum or sums not exceeding in total an
amount of _____ (say: _____) upon
receipt by us of your first demand in writing and your written statement stating:
i)   that the Principal is in breach of his obligation(s) under the tender
     conditions; and
ii) the respect in which the Principal is in breach.

Your demand for payment must also be accompanied by the following document(s):
(specify document(s) if any, or delete)

This guarantee shall expire on _____ at the latest.

Consequently, any demand for payment under it must be received by us at this
office on or before that date.

> **This guarantee is subject to the Uniform Rules for Demand Guarantees,
> ICC Publication No.458.**

Signature(s) :

Fig 35.13 Tender guarantee

BANK'S NAME, AND ADDRESS OF ISSUING BRANCH OR OFFICE

Beneficiary: ....   Date: ....
(name and address)

PERFORMANCE GUARANTEE No. ....

We have been informed that _____, (hereinafter called
"the Principal"), has entered into contract No. _____ dated
_____ with you, for the supply of *(description of goods and/
or services)*

Furthermore, we understand that, according to the conditions of the contract, a
performance guarantee is required.

At the request of the Principal, we *(name of bank)* _____ hereby
irrevocably undertake to pay you any sum or sums not exceeding in total an
amount of _____ (say:_____) upon
receipt by us of your first demand in writing and your written statement stating:
i)   that the Principal is in breach of his obligation(s) under the underlying contract;
      and
ii)   the respect in which the Principal is in breach.

Your demand for payment must also be accompanied by the following document(s):
(specify document(s) if any, or delete)

This guarantee shall expire on _____ at the latest.

Consequently, any demand for payment under it must be received by us at this
office on or before that date.

> **This guarantee is subject to the Uniform Rules for Demand Guarantees,
> ICC Publication No.458.**

Signature(s) :

Fig 35.14 Performance guarantee

standby letter of credit - *overdraft*

(issued to bank granting the facilities)

We hereby issue our irrevocable Standby Letter of Credit No. [*standby letter of credit number*] in your favour in the following terms:-

Applicant: [*name of applicant*]

Amount: Not exceeding [*currency and amount in figures and words*] inclusive of interest

Expiration/Expiry⁺ Date: [*expiry date*] subject to the **"Determination of Liability"** and **"Evergreen"** clauses set out below

Place of Expiration/Expiry⁺: Lloyds TSB Bank plc [*title and address of issuing office*] (or such other address as we may subsequently notify to you in writing)

Covering: Overdraft facilities to [*name of borrower*] [*address and/or account number"*]

Available by payment with: Lloyds TSB Bank plc against the following:-

Your written demand(s) for payment in the form of a signed letter or an authenticated teletransmission addressed to ourselves which must state:-

a) **our above Standby Letter of Credit number**
and
b) **the currency and amount demanded**
and
c) **that the amount demanded is now due to you under overdraft facilities granted to** [*name of borrower*] **and** [*name of borrower*] **has not repaid such amount to you**
and
d) **that, in the event that Lloyds TSB Bank plc has determined its liability in accordance with the terms of the Determination of Liability Clause, no further advances were granted under the overdraft facilities with recourse to us under this Standby Letter of Credit following receipt of our Notice of Determination and the demand does not include any amount in respect of any other advances granted thereafter.**

Settlement of demand(s) for payment made in compliance with the terms and conditions of this Standby Letter of Credit will be made to you in accordance with your instructions.

This Standby Letter of Credit shall not confer any benefit on or be enforceable by any third party.

Determination of Liability Clause

We shall have the right to determine our liability hereunder. Accordingly our liability hereunder shall be determined upon the date of receipt by you ("the date of determination") of our written (which includes teletransmitted) notice determining this Standby Letter of Credit. This Standby Letter of Credit will then expire on the earlier of the date which is 30 days after the date of determination and the then current expiration/expiry⁺ date.

Evergreen Clause

This Standby Letter of Credit expires on [*expiry date*]. However (but always subject to our right to determine our liability as provided for in the "Determination of Liability Clause" set out above) this Standby Letter of Credit shall be deemed to have been automatically extended for a further year and thereafter, annually, from the then current expiration/expiry⁺ date without express amendment to that effect unless we shall have notified you in writing (which includes teletransmission) at least 30 calendar days prior to the then current expiration/expiry⁺ date that this Standby Letter of Credit will not be extended.

Fig 35.15 Standby letter of credit

We hereby undertake that documents presented at this office on or before the expiration/expiry[+] date in compliance with the terms and conditions of this Standby Letter of Credit shall be honoured.

* This Standby Letter of Credit is subject to International Standby Practices (ISP98), International Chamber of Commerce Publication No. 590.

or

* This Standby Letter of Credit is subject to Uniform Customs and Practice for Documentary Credits (1993 Revision), International Chamber of Commerce Publication No. 500.

* DENOTES AN OPTION IN THE TEXT - SELECT APPLICABLE OPTION.
[+] USE 'EXPIRATION' IF SUBJECT TO ISP, 'EXPIRY' IF SUBJECT TO UCP

March 2000

(vii) Fundamental principles of demand guarantee law

Many of the fundamental concepts underlying documentary credits law apply equally in relation to demand guarantees[317] and counter-guarantees.[318] These include the abstract nature of the bank's payment undertaking, the independence of the guarantee from the underlying transaction and from the principal–guarantor relationship, its documentary character, the fact that each bank contracts as principal, the doctrine of strict compliance,[319] the bank's entitlement to pay against documents which appear on their face, after reasonable examination, to conform to the guarantee,[320] and the conditions of availability of injunctive relief.[321] The URDG also provide that all guarantees and counter-guarantees are irrevocable unless otherwise indicated, thereby anticipating the change introduced by UCP 500 in relation to documentary credits.

Even before the advent of the URDG, English courts had emphasized the essential purpose of the demand guarantee as an expeditious remedy conditioned only by presentation of the demand and any other specified documents. The courts took the view that if the guarantor and the principal place themselves at the mercy of the beneficiary in this way, they must accept the consequences. This is vividly illustrated by the decision of the Court of Appeal in *Edward Owen Engineering Ltd v Barclays Bank International Ltd*.[322]

> A contract between English suppliers and Libyan customers provided for the former to supply and erect glasshouses in Libya for the price of £502,030, payable by instalments under an irrevocable confirmed credit payable at Barclays Bank International. Prior to entering into the contract, the Libyan customers had exacted a performance guarantee from Umma Bank for 10% of the contract price payable 'upon first request' from the Libyan customers, and Umma Bank, in turn, had obtained an undertaking from Barclays Bank International to pay 'on demand without proof or conditions'.

> The Libyan customers committed a breach of the contract of sale in that the credit issued was not a confirmed credit. Nevertheless, they called upon Umma Bank to pay under the guarantee, and upon doing so Umma Bank claimed over against Barclays under the guarantee given by the latter. The plaintiffs sought an injunction to restrain Barclays from making the payment.

> It was held by Kerr J and affirmed on appeal, that notwithstanding the breach of the contract of sale, the undertaking given between the banks must be honoured, since the

---

317   See the decision of the Singapore Court of Appeal in *Bocotra Construction Pte Ltd v AG (No 2)* [1995] 2 SLR 733 at 744.

318   Some articles of the URDG refer to counter-guarantees but most do not. Nevertheless, the intention is that, with certain exceptions (eg art 20, which deals separately with guarantees and counter-guarantees), the rules apply equally to counter-guarantees, a point confirmed by the ICC Banking Commission in its opinion of 14 June 2000.

319   It has been said that this applies with less rigour to demand guarantees than to documentary credits (*Siporex Trade SA v Banque Indosuez* [1986] 2 Lloyd's Rep 146; *I. E. Contractors Ltd v Lloyds Bank plc* [1990] 2 Lloyd's Rep 496), but it seems more accurate to say that since in most cases the only document that has to be presented is the demand itself there is much less likelihood of noncompliance and therefore of the need to resort to the doctrine of strict compliance. See to the same effect Jack, Malek and Quest, *Documentary Credits*, para 12.45.

320   See generally Goode, *Guide to the ICC Uniform Rules for Demand Guarantees*, pp 18–20.

321   *Solo v Canara Bank* [2001] 1 WLR 1800.

322   [1978] QB 159.

payment obligation did not depend on compliance with the contract of sale, and, in the absence of fraud, the plaintiffs were not entitled to the injunction sought.[323]

The URDG make these principles explicit.[324]

A further consequence of the autonomy of the demand guarantee is that the beneficiary is entitled to be paid even if he has suffered no loss under the underlying contract,[325] though at some stage there will be an accounting between the parties, so that if the guarantee is insufficient to cover the beneficiary's loss, he is entitled to recover the deficiency under the underlying contract, while if he has collected under the guarantee a sum greater than that ultimately found due to him, he will have to pay it to the principal.[326]

But though for the most part demand guarantees are governed by the same principles as those applicable to documentary credits, there are certain considerations particular to demand guarantees. First, it is improper for the beneficiary to make a claim under the guarantee without at least an honest belief that the principal is in breach of the underlying contract, whereas in the case of a documentary credit the question of an abusive call on the paying bank does not arise, as the parties have agreed that the bank is to be the party primarily liable for payment. Secondly, the making of 'extend or pay' demands is a particular feature of demand guarantee practice necessitating special provisions in the URDG. Thirdly, in a four-party transaction the position of the parties to the counter-guarantee has to be covered. Broadly speaking, the same concepts apply to the counter-guarantee as to the guarantee, so that, for example, the instructing party's liability under the counter-guarantee is independent not only of the underlying transaction between principal and beneficiary but also of the guarantee itself and, indeed, of the separate mandate given by the instructing party to the guarantor, compliance with which is a condition of the latter's right to reimbursement as an agent but is not a prerequisite of its distinct right to payment under the autonomous counter-guarantee. Fourthly, the exemptions of the banks from liability for falsity or inaccuracy of documents, delay in transmission of messages, acts of intermediary banks, and the like,[327] though following the pattern of the UCP, are qualified by a provision that they do not apply to failure to act in good faith and with reasonable care.[328] Finally, there are special rules in art 20 as to the making of demands.[329]

(viii) Formalities for a valid demand

Article 20 of the URDG contains a very distinctive rule requiring the beneficiary to present with his demand a statement that the principal is in breach, and the respect

---

323 Similar decisions were given in *R. D. Harbottle (Mercantile) Ltd v National Westminster Bank Ltd* [1978] QB 146 and *Howe Richardson Scale Co Ltd v Polimex-Cekop* [1978] 1 Lloyd's Rep 161. It is clear that on-demand performance guarantees of this kind are not guarantees in the legal sense but undertakings embodying a primary obligation.

324 Article 2(b) and, in relation to counter-guarantees, 2(c).

325 *Cargill International SA v Bangladesh Sugar and Food Industries Corp* [1998] 2 All ER 406.

326 Ibid.

327 Articles 11, 12, 14.

328 Article 15.

329 See below.

in which he is in breach, even if on its face the only document specified is the demand itself.[330]

(a)   Any demand for payment under the Guarantee shall be in writing and shall (in addition to such other documents as may be specified in the Guarantee) be supported by a written statement (whether in the demand itself or in a separate document or documents accompanying the demand and referred to in it) stating:

    (i)   that the Principal is in breach of his obligation(s) under the underlying contract(s) or, in the case of a tender guarantee, the tender conditions; and

    (ii)   the respect in which the Principal is in breach.

(b)   Any demand under the Counter-Guarantee shall be supported by a written statement that the Guarantor has received a demand for payment under the Guarantee in accordance with its terms and with this Article.

(c)   Paragraph (a) of this Article applies except to the extent that it is expressly excluded by the terms of the Guarantee. Paragraph (b) of this Article applies except to the extent that it is expressly excluded by the terms of the Counter-Guarantee.

(d)   Nothing in this Article affects the application of Articles 2(b) and 2(c), 9 and 11.

The purpose of art 20 is to impose some constraint on unfair calling of the guarantee without undermining its efficacy as a swift remedy in the event of perceived default. The constraint is somewhat limited in that the statement of breach is required only from the beneficiary himself, not from an independent third party. Even so, a beneficiary who has little compunction in making a written demand where there has been no breach may feel somewhat inhibited from so doing where he has to commit himself to a statement that the principal is in breach, and in what respect.[331] The effect of incorporating the URDG is thus to impose an additional documentary credit that may not be apparent on the face of the guarantee itself. Misunderstanding can be avoided by setting out the requirements of art 20 in the guarantee, as in the ICC Model Forms. A demand by the guarantor under the counter-guarantee given by the instructing party must specify not only that the guarantor has itself received a demand from the beneficiary but that the demand conforms to art 20.

Article 20 may be excluded or varied by the terms of the guarantee or counter-guarantee, as the case may be, but is not excluded merely because the only document specified is the written demand.

---

330   Where the URDG do not apply it is not necessary for the demand to specify the nature of the breach or, indeed, go beyond a bare demand for payment unless the terms of the guarantee indicate otherwise, as they were held to do in *I. E. Contractors Ltd v Lloyds Bank plc*, n 319. In that case the guarantee embodied an undertaking to pay the amount of the guarantee on demand 'being your claim for damages brought about by the above named principal'. The Court of Appeal held that this wording imported a requirement that the demand should state that it was a claim for damages brought about by the contractors. See also *Esal Commodities Ltd v Oriental Credit Ltd* [1985] 2 Lloyd's Rep 546.

331   The phrase 'the respect in which' (as opposed to 'respects') is intended to require only a general statement of the nature of the breach (eg that the principal has been guilty of delay, defective workmanship, a shortfall in delivery of goods), not a detailed specification. See Goode, *Guide to the ICC Uniform Rules for Demand Guarantees*, pp 93–94.

(ix) 'Extend or pay' demands

It is not uncommon for a beneficiary to present an 'extend or pay' demand requiring the period of the guarantee to be extended, failing which payment is to be made forthwith. Demands of this kind are not necessarily fraudulent, for there may have been, or the beneficiary may honestly though mistakenly believe there has been, a breach, but the beneficiary may be willing to allow time for this to be rectified if the guaranteed is extended. Article 26 deals with demands of this kind in some detail. The first point to note is that if the demand is to be triggered automatically because of non-extension of the guarantee, it must be a demand which conforms to the rules, and in particular to the requirements of art 20. Upon receiving the extend or pay demand, the guarantor must without delay inform the party who gave him his instructions (in the case of a direct guarantee, the principal, and in the case of an indirect guarantee, the instructing party) and must suspend payment for as long as is reasonable to permit the principal and the beneficiary to reach agreement on the granting of the extension and for the principal to arrange for such extension to be issued. There are various possible outcomes. The principal may agree to the extension, wholly or in part, in which case it takes effect when issued by the guarantor. The guarantor is not obliged to issue it, and even if he has agreed with the principal to do so, that is not an agreement of which the beneficiary can take advantage. Alternatively, the principal may refuse the extension, in which case the guarantor must pay in the absence of fraud by the beneficiary. A third possibility is that the beneficiary withdraws the demand, which thereupon lapses. Finally, negotiations may still be uncompleted when a reasonable time has elapsed, in which event the guarantor must pay, even if by then the guarantee has expired.[332]

(x) Termination of guarantee

A demand guarantee comes to an end on expiry,[333] payment,[334] cancellation[335] or by force of law. Termination is not dependent on return of the guarantee[336] except where this act is itself relied on as the act of cancellation under art 23.

(xi) Demand guarantees and freezing injunctions

A freezing injunction will not be granted to restrain payment of a guarantee, as opposed to removal of the proceeds by the beneficiary after payment.[337]

---

332 This is because the rules require only that the documents be *presented* before expiry (arts 19, 22).

333 Articles 19, 22. A guarantee expires at the end of the expiry date or upon the occurrence of any specified expiry event. For example, a tender guarantee will normally expire when the contract has been awarded to another party or when the principal, having been awarded the contract, signs it and procures the issue of any stipulated performance guarantee.

334 Article 18.

335 Article 23.

336 Article 22.

337 *The Bhoja Trader*, n 234.

Hitherto the contract of carriage of goods has been discussed in relation to its function as an auxiliary to the central contract of sale. But the crucial role played by transport in both domestic and international commerce gives the law relating to carriage of goods a much wider significance. Indeed, it is no exaggeration to say that the transportation of goods is at once the most important and the most complex of all the fields of activity with which commercial law is concerned. The subject is vast, and only the barest outline can be given here. The present chapter is confined to contracts of carriage by sea (including contracts for combined transport involving a sea leg) which are governed by the Hague-Visby Rules.[1] The principal focus is on contracts evidenced by a bill of lading (other than a bill of lading issued to the charterer under a charterparty),[2] but reference will also be made to sea waybills and delivery orders, which acquired a new importance with the enactment of the Carriage of Goods by Sea Act 1992. Part of the complexity of the subject lies in the fact that in relation to export and import transactions the contract of carriage cannot be viewed in isolation from related contracts, in particular, the contract of sale and the provision of finance against documents.[3]

1. SOURCES OF LAW

Contracts of carriage are regulated partly by the common law of contract, tort and bailment, partly by statute.

---

1 See below.

2 A charterparty is an agreement by which the owner of a ship makes the vessel, or a specified part of it, available with or without crew to another, called the charterer. Charterparties fall broadly into two groups, those under which the owner parts with control of the vessel for the period of the charter, and thus has no responsibility for the carriage of goods on the vessel, and those under which the vessel remains in the control of the owner. The former are known as 'bareboat' charters, or charters by demise, and do not constitute contracts of carriage of goods at all. The latter divide primarily into time charters, where the ship is chartered for a specified period of time, and voyage charters, where it is chartered for a designated voyage. Under a time charter, the hire is fixed by reference to the period of the charter and may also be linked to the capacity of the vessel, irrespective of whether this is fully used by the charterer. Under a voyage charter, freight is calculated according to the tonnage actually shipped, unless the charterer agrees to load a full cargo, in which case he has to pay compensation (dead freight) for the space not used, or a lump sum freight is agreed. (For the significance of the distinction between hire under a time charter and freight under a voyage charter in relation to the charterer's right to make deductions for cross-claims, see n 190.) A charterparty under which two or more charterers take space in different parts of the vessel is known as a space charterparty. There are also hybrids which combine elements of voyage and time charterparties. See John Wilson, *Carriage of Goods by Sea* (4th edn, 2001), pp 3–6.

(i) Contract

The primary source of the rights of the parties to a contract of carriage is, of course, the contract itself. This is normally concluded prior to the issue of the bill of lading but on the carrier's standard bill of lading terms.[4] The common law imports certain terms into contracts of carriage of goods by sea, though, except as otherwise provided by statute, these may be varied or excluded by agreement of the parties.

(ii) Tort

Independently of the contract of carriage, which deals with the rights of the parties to that contract, the carrier owes a duty of care in tort to those having a proprietary or possessory interest in the goods he is carrying and is liable in damages for negligence if that duty is broken,[5] but any liability in tort may be excluded or limited by the operation of a *Himalaya* clause or an exclusion or limitation of liability in favour of the defendant under a contract between other parties made for his benefit.[6]

(iii) Bailment

While the law of bailment may not add much in situations involving parties to the contract of carriage, it continues to exert a significant influence in non-contractual relationships, typically in relation to the rights and duties of the carrier vis-à-vis a transferee of the original shipper's rights by or against whom a sub-bailment is alleged to exist.

(iv) The Hague, Hague-Visby and Hamburg Rules

The law relating to contracts of carriage by sea under bills of lading has evolved as a response to the imbalance of bargaining power between shipowners on the one hand and cargo owners on the other.[7] The nineteenth-century laissez-faire approach to contracts, coupled with the negotiating strength of the shipping companies, had enabled them to impose virtually any terms they chose on shippers, who had to take their contracts as they were presented and found themselves with minimal rights against the shipowners for loss of or damage to cargo.[8] Further, transferees of the bills of lading took on the same terms, over the negotiation of which they had no control at all.

---

3 A particular theme of Professor Charles Debattista's interesting work *The Sale of Goods Carried by Sea* (2nd edn, 1998).

4 See p 1039.

5 See p 1058.

6 See Contracts (Rights of Third Parties) Act 1999, ss 1, 6(5), and p 103.

7 Often referred to in depersonalized terms as 'ship' and 'cargo'. Thus the liability of 'the ship' (see, eg, art IV of the Hague Rules) denotes the liability of the person responsible for the vessel as owner or as charterer, depending on the circumstances. It may also refer to the susceptibility of the vessel itself to a claim *in rem*.

8 In addition to which the Merchant Shipping Act 1894 conferred further rights and immunities on shipowners. See p 1048, n 136.

Reaction against this state of affairs, coupled with serious disparities in the treatment of bills of lading by the laws of different states, led to the Brussels Convention of 1924, which adopted a set of uniform rules relating to bills of lading. These rules are known as the Hague Rules.[9] They regulated the rights, duties and immunities of the carrier, under a contract of carriage by sea covered by a bill of lading, in relation to the shipper, the consignee named in the bill of lading and the indorsee of the bill. The Brussels Convention was amended by the Brussels Protocol of 1968, which embodied a set of rules, known as the Visby Rules,[10] amending the Hague Rules. The Brussels Convention and the Protocol are to be read and interpreted as a single instrument,[11] and the original and amending rules thus form a single set of rules known as the Hague-Visby Rules.

Reference must also be made to the Hamburg Rules. These resulted from the United Nations Convention on the Carriage of Goods by Sea adopted in Hamburg in 1978. The Hamburg Rules, which differ in material respects from the Hague-Visby Rules,[12] are intended to replace the latter. Indeed, the Hamburg Convention requires a state which becomes a contracting state to denounce the Brussels Convention and Protocol with effect from the date when the Hamburg Rules come into force in respect of that state, subject to a right to defer the denunciation for up to five years.[13] The Rules came into effect on 1 November 1992 as regards contracting states, but none of the major maritime countries has yet ratified them, nor does there seem any likelihood of their doing so in the foreseeable future.

Dissatisfaction with the present situation has led a growing number of countries to introduce a hybrid Hague/Hague-Visby/Hamburg regime, which may represent an improvement for the countries concerned but does not advance the cause of uniformity. More recently, on the basis of a draft prepared by the CMI, UNITRAL has embarked on an ambitious project to create a new legal regime covering not only carriage by sea in isolation but multimodal contracts involving a sea leg.[14]

---

9 Having first been formulated at a meeting of the International Law Association at The Hague in 1921.

10 Since they resulted from the Conference of the Comité Maritime International (CMI) whose proposals were signed at Visby (the capital of the Swedish island of Gotland) in 1963.

11 Protocol, art 6. By a further protocol signed at Brussels in December 1979 the Rules were again amended by substituting special drawing rights for francs in the limitation provisions. See n 136.

12 In particular, they apply to contracts of carriage by sea generally, whether or not covered by a bill of lading, but not charterparties (see arts 2, 3) and they significantly increase the carrier's liability by imposing a general duty of care without the limits and exemptions provided by the Hague-Visby Rules, notably the exemption from liability for negligence in the navigation or management of the ship. For a detailed examination of the differences, see John O. Honnold, 'Ocean Carriers and Cargo: Clarity and fairness – Hague or Hamburg' [1993] 24 JMLC 75; William Tetley, 'The Hamburg Rules – A Commentary' [1979] LMCLQ 1.

13 Hamburg Convention, art 31.

14 See p 1061.

(v) The Carriage of Goods by Sea Acts 1924–1992

The Hague Rules were given statutory force in the United Kingdom by the Carriage of Goods by Sea Act 1924.[15] The Hague-Visby Rules were carried into effect in relation to the United Kingdom by the Carriage of Goods by Sea Act 1971, which did not come into force until 23 June 1977.[16] That Act repealed the Act of 1924, so that the unamended Hague Rules ceased to have legal effect in the United Kingdom. The Hague-Visby Rules (which have effect by force of law under the 1971 Act and do not require to be incorporated by a clause paramount[17]) expand the scope of application of the Hague Rules in various respects and make a number of changes in relation to the limits of liability, the limitation of actions and the evidential effect of a bill of lading vis-à-vis a bona fide transferee.[18] The Carriage of Goods by Sea Act 1992, which implements the recommendations of the Law Commissions,[19] is an important piece of legislation which is concerned not with the content of the carrier's duties but with title to sue and liability on the contract of carriage.

(vi) The London Convention and the Merchant Shipping Act 1979

The London Convention,[20] implemented in the United Kingdom by the Merchant Shipping Act 1979, sets out the conditions in which the carrier can limit his liability overall by reference to the tonnage of the vessel. It replaces the 1957 International Convention Relating to the Liability of Owners of Sea Going Ships, which had attracted strong criticism.

(vii) The Contracts (Rights of Third Parties) Act 1999

This Act provides that contracts made for the benefit of a third party may, subject to certain conditions, be enforceable by the third party in his own right.[21] Contracts for

---

15 Under s 1 of the Act, the Rules operated by force of the Act itself; but by s 3 the bill of lading was required to include a clause (commonly known as the paramount clause) stating that the bill of lading was subject to the provisions of the Rules. The result was that the carrier who pursuant to s 3 included a clause paramount in his bill of lading thus became bound by the Rules as a matter of contract even in relation to a dispute not governed by English law (see *Scrutton on Charterparties* (20th edn, 1996), p 414). The objective was to avoid conflict of laws problems. The Carriage of Goods by Sea Act 1971 does not require a clause paramount. See p 1035.

16 Carriage of Goods by Sea Act 1971 (Commencement) Order 1977, art 2. The Act has been amended by the Merchant Shipping Act 1979, Sch 5, para 5, and the Merchant Shipping Act 1981, s 2. See, nn 135, 136.

17 Section 1(2). This is in contrast to the position under the 1924 Act. See n 15. Section 1(2) of the 1971 Act, together with art X of the Rules, added by the Visby Amendments, closes the gap opened up by *Vita Food Products Inc v Unus Shipping Co* [1939] AC 277 and makes application of the Rules mandatory in an action before an English court for voyages to which they apply, irrespective of whether the bill of lading incorporates the Rules or the proper law of the contract is English (*The Hollandia* [1983] 1 AC 565; *The Antares* [1987] 1 Lloyd's Rep 424).

18 For an excellent discussion of the Hague-Visby Rules and the changes which they introduced, see Anthony Diamond, 'The Hague-Visby Rules' [1978] LMCLQ 225.

19 *Rights of Suit in Respect of Carriage of Goods by Sea* (Law Com No 196, Scot Law Com No 130, HC 250, 1991).

20 Convention on Limitation of Liability for Maritime Claims 1976.

21 Section 1. See p 103.

the carriage of goods by sea are excluded from the Act[22] in order to avoid overlap with the Carriage of Goods by Sea Act 1992, except that a third party may rely on an exclusion clause or limitation of liability in the contract.[23]

2.   APPLICATION OF THE HAGUE-VISBY RULES

The scope of the Hague-Visby Rules in the United Kingdom is determined partly by the Rules themselves in art X and partly by provisions of the Carriage of Goods by Sea Act 1971 extending their scope.

(i)   Scope of the Rules under Article X

The combined effect of arts I and X of the Hague-Visby Rules is that three requirements must be satisfied before the Rules can apply to a contract of carriage of goods.[24]

(a)   The contract of carriage must be covered by a bill of lading[25] or similar document of title.[26] The Rules are therefore inapplicable to contracts covered by a non-negotiable sea waybill or a non-negotiable multimodal transport document[27] unless incorporated by a clause paramount.[28]

(b)   The contract must satisfy an internationality test in that the bill of lading[29] must relate to the carriage of goods between ports in two different states. The Rules therefore do not apply to carriage between ports in the same country or through inland waterways.

(c)   The contract must either:

---

22   Section 6(5)(a).

23   Ibid.

24   'Goods' include goods, wares, merchandise and articles of every kind whatsoever except live animals and cargo which by the contract of carriage is stated as being carried on deck and is so carried (art I). As to deck cargo, see p 1040.

25   The phrase 'covered by a bill of lading' means that the contract of carriage provides, expressly or by implication, for the issue of a bill of lading evidencing the terms of the contract; whether or when it is issued is irrelevant (*Pyrene Co Ltd v Scindia Navigation Co Ltd* [1954] 2 QB 402). But the mere fact that the contract is entered into on the basis of a specimen bill of lading which, if issued at all, is not intended to embody the terms of the contract does not suffice to bring it within the Rules (*Parsons Corp v CV Scheepvaartonderneming 'Happy Ranger' (The 'Happy Ranger')* [2002] 2 Lloyd's Rep 357). As noted earlier, the Court of Appeal has held that a straight bill of lading (see p 891) is a bill of lading for the purpose of the Rules (see *J I McWilliam Co Inc v Mediterranean Shipping Co SA (The 'Rafaela S')* [2003] 2 Lloyd's Rep 113) and presumably the same is true of a combined transport bill of lading to the extent that it covers a sea leg of the transit.

26   Article I(b), which defines a contract of carriage for the purpose of the Rules and which is mirrored by s 1(4) of the Carriage of Goods by Sea Act 1971.

27   But there seems no reason why they should not apply to a multimodal transport document issued as in negotiable form.

28   See p 1033.

29   It is a curious feature of the Rules that while the definition of 'contract of carriage' in art I(b) covers not only bills of lading but 'similar documents of title', several of the subsequent articles, including art X, refer only to bills of lading.

(i) have a specified connection with a contracting state, by reason of the fact that the bill of lading is issued in a contracting state or the carriage is from a port in a contracting state, or

(ii) provide that the Rules or legislation giving effect to them are to govern the contract.[30]

(ii) Extension of scope in the United Kingdom

The Carriage of Goods by Sea Act 1971 extends the scope of the Hague-Visby Rules in three ways. First, so long as the port of shipment is in the United Kingdom it is not necessary that the port of destination shall be in another state.[31] Secondly, the ability of the parties to give the Rules the force of law by a provision to that effect in the contract is not confined to contracts contained in or evidenced by a bill of lading, as provided by art X, but is extended to contracts contained in or evidenced by a non-negotiable receipt (for example, a sea waybill) marked as such if the contract expressly states that the Rules are to govern it as if the receipt were a bill of lading.[32] Thirdly, if and so far as the contract contained in or evidenced by the bill of lading or receipt applies to deck cargo the Rules are extended to deck cargo,[33] which otherwise would be excluded.[34]

3. THE PARTIES TO THE CONTRACT OF CARRIAGE

The parties to a contract of carriage by sea are known respectively as the shipper and the carrier. The shipper is the person to whom the carrier undertakes the duty of transporting the goods. He may be the seller or buyer under a contract of sale, a freight forwarder or any other consignor.[35] His identity is prima facie established by the bill of lading, though it does not necessarily follow that the person named in the 'shipper' box is the true contracting party, for it may be shown that he acted as agent, as where the seller acts as agent of the buyer under an extended f.o.b. contract[36] or a freight forwarder as agent of the seller. By contrast, the identity of the carrier is often not stated in the bill of lading,[37] a fact which may pose serious

---

30 It is not sufficient that the parties select English law to govern the contract, whether expressly or impliedly by choosing England as the forum (*The Komninos S* [1991] 1 Lloyd's Rep 370).

31 Section 1(3).

32 Section 1(6). See *The European Enterprise* [1989] 2 Lloyd's Rep 185.

33 Section 1(7).

34 Article 1(1)(c).

35 The consignor and the shipper are not necessarily the same. For example, where a seller has goods shipped under a strict f.o.b. contract, the seller is the consignor while the buyer is the shipper.

36 See *Benjamin's Sale of Goods* (6th edn, 2002), para 18–045; *Carver on Bills of Lading* (2001), paras 4–003 ff.

37 The person signing the bill is rarely acting as principal but may sign as agent for a named or unnamed carrier or for the master, who himself is an agent, not a carrier (*International Milling Co v The Perseus* [1958] 2 Lloyd's Rep 272, a United States decision). The bill may contain an 'identity of carrier' clause making it clear that the contract is with the (unnamed) owner of the vessel, not with the signatory of the bill. This leaves the shipper the sometimes difficult task of ascertaining the identity of the owner. See, for example, *Homburg Houtimport BV v Agrosin Private Ltd (The Starsin)* [2003] 2 All ER 785; *The Venezuela* [1980] 1 Lloyd's Rep 393.

problems for the shipper.[38] The legal carrier (ie the party contracting with the shipper to carry the goods) may himself be the actual carrier or he may procure carriage by another.[39] In the former case, he may be the owner of the ship or a charterer.[40] In the latter, he may himself have no interest in the ship whatsoever but may simply arrange carriage by the owner or charterer. With the development of combined transport, many freight forwarders now contract as carriers,[41] though not in any way personally involved in the sea transit.

Where the ship has been let under a demise charter, difficult questions may arise as to whether the carrier is the owner, the charterer, or both, or is neither of these but some other party responsible for issuing the bill of lading, eg a charterer under a time or voyage charterparty or a freight forwarder undertaking to carry as principal. One of the causes of the problem is the practice of identifying one party as carrier on the face of the bill and a different and frequently unidentified party (eg 'the owner of the vessel') in small print on the reverse. The problems thus created for anyone wishing to sue on such a bill of lading were considerable. Happily, these have been considerably alleviated by the decision of the House of Lords in *The Starsin*,[42] which has robustly declared that the reasonable reader, versed in the shipping trade, looks to the identity of the carrier on the face of the bill and should not be expected to trawl through conditions in small print on the reverse. As pre-printed standard terms, these must, in accordance with normal rules of interpretation, give way to what the parties have specifically agreed on the face of the bill. A conclusion to the contrary would create an unacceptable trap.[43] In that case the facts were as follows:

> Proceedings were brought against the owner of a ship and against the demise charterers for damage caused by negligent stowage to cargo shipped under a bill of lading. The question was whether the bill of lading was an owner's or a charterer's bill of lading. The vessel had been let on a time charter to Continental Pacific Shipping (CPS), which at the time operated a liner service but subsequently became insolvent. The bill of lading on CPS's shipping form was drafted to express a contract of carriage between the shipper and the owner, but was signed on its face not by the master but by CPS's agent on behalf of CPS, which was described as the carrier. However, the reverse of the bill contained, as 'the Company's [ie CPS's] standard conditions', (a) a definition of 'carrier' as the party on whose behalf the bill of lading had been signed, (b) an identity of carrier clause stating that the contract of carriage was between the merchant and the

---

38   And is inconsistent with UCP art 23(a)(i). See below.

39   One of the virtues of the Hamburg Rules is that they distinguish the legal carrier from the actual carrier, making the former responsible for the acts and omissions of the latter.

40   Or sub-charterer.

41   Ie as between themselves and the shipper. But vis-à-vis the actual carrier, the forwarding agent will himself be the shipper if he ships in his own name. Whether, in the absence of a contractual provision to that effect, the Hague-Visby Rules will apply to the sea voyage is as yet undetermined. See p 1064.

42   *The Starsin*, n 37.

43   A further point made was that under art 23(a)(i) of the UCP, as clarified by the ICC's Position Paper No 4, UCP 500 – *Transport documents articles*, published 1 September 1994, the name of the carrier must appear on the front of the bill of lading in order to be acceptable to banks to whom the bill is presented under a documentary credit and that, failing this, banks will reject the document. The position paper also drew attention to UCP art 23(a)(v), which states that banks will not examine the contents of the terms and conditions of carriage.

owner of the vessel and (c) a demise clause[44] stating that if the vessel was not owned by or chartered by demise to the company or line by whom the bill was issued, the bill of lading should take effect only as a contract of carriage with the owners or demise charterer, as the case might be, made as principal through the agency of the company. The question was whether the bill was an owner's bill or a charterer's bill. The House of Lords, reversing the decision of the Court of Appeal and restoring the decision of Colman J at first instance, unanimously held that the bill was a charterer's bill and that the owner incurred no liability on it.[45]

We shall return to *The Starsin* in the context of *Himalaya* clauses and the applicability of art III, r 8, of the Hague/Hague-Visby Rules in relation to the exemption of third parties, including shipowners in relation to a charterer's bill of lading.[46]

Where the bill of lading is signed by the master (which was not the case in *The Starsin*), it may be necessary to determine for whom he acts in so doing. The main rules may be summarized as follows:

(a) The master of a ship has a usual authority to sign bills of lading on behalf of the owner.[47]

(b) A charterer by demise is for this purpose treated as the owner for the time being, with the result that when the master of a ship let under a demise charterparty signs a bill of lading, the presumption is that he does so on behalf of the charterer, not on behalf of the owner,[48] so that it is the former who will be the carrier. The fact that the shipper is unaware of the existence of the charterparty is irrelevant.[49]

(c) Where the charterparty is not by demise, the charterer is not treated as the owner for any purpose, possession and control remaining with the person letting the vehicle out under the charterparty. Accordingly, where the master of a vessel let out under a time or voyage charterparty signs a bill of lading, he will usually be treated as the agent of the owner, not of the charterer.[50] The charterparty may, it is true, exclude or restrict the master's actual authority to sign bills of lading on behalf of the owner, but under ordinary agency principles such an exclusion or restriction does not affect the shipper unless he had notice of it; and mere knowledge of the existence of the charterparty does not constitute constructive notice of its contents.[51] On the other hand, the fact that the owner is liable as a carrier does not necessarily absolve the charterer from liability, so that if, for example, he has been involved in loading, stowing and unloading operations, this may justify the inference that he and the owner together undertook the duties of carrier.[52]

44 See p 1038.
45 It was, however, liable in tort to one party who had obtained title before the voyage began.
46 See p 1060.
47 *The St Cloud* (1863) 8 LT 54.
48 *Baumwoll Manufaktur von Carl Scheibler v Furness* [1893] AC 8.
49 Ibid.
50 *Sandeman v Scurr* (1866) LR 2 QB 86; *Wehner v Dene Steamship Co* [1905] 2 KB 92, per Channell J at 98; *The Rewia* [1991] 2 Lloyd's Rep 325 (bill of lading signed by agents). But in each case it is a question of fact (*The Venezuela*, n 37).
51 *Manchester Trust v Furness* [1895] 2 QB 539.
52 See generally William Tetley, *Marine Cargo Claims* (3rd edn, 1988), pp 240 ff.

The person on whose behalf a bill of lading is issued may incur a liability as carrier even though he is neither the owner nor a demise charterer of the vessel.[53] To counter this possibility, it is common for bills of lading to contain a 'demise clause'[54] by which the issuer of the bill of lading stipulates that if the ship is not owned by or demised to the issuer, the bill of lading is to be treated as a contract[55] with the owner or charterer (as the case may be), not with the issuer.[56] The demise clause was also used by a charterer issuing a bill of lading in order to establish that the signatory of the bill was not his agent but that of the owner,[57] but in the light of *The Starsin* it will usually be disregarded if inconsistent with the statement of the carrier on the face of the bill.[58]

The validity of the demise clause is a matter of controversy.[59] It has been declared invalid in the United States[60] as contrary to the provisions of the Harter Act,[61] on the ground that a stipulation by a carrier that he was not to be treated as the carrier was an attempted exclusion of liability,[62] nullified by the Act. The clause has similarly been ruled invalid in Canada[63] as contrary to the Hague Rules, though more recently it seems to have been rehabilitated. [64] By contrast, the demise clause has been assumed to be valid in several cases in England,[65] its function being not to exclude liability but to identify the carrier.[66]

53 As in *Hiram Walker & Sons Ltd v Dover Navigation Co Ltd* (1949) 83 Ll L Rep 84 (time charter). Indeed, he may not even be a charterer at all.

54 For the history of the demise clause, see Lord Roskill, 'The Demise Clause' (1990) 106 LQR 403.

55 This is the usual wording. But the bill of lading is, strictly, not a contract itself but merely evidence of the previously concluded contract of carriage. See pp 1031, 1039.

56 'Identity of carrier' clauses are similar and are designed to achieve the same objective.

57 The charterer may be authorized by the charterparty to sign bills of lading on behalf of the master in the latter's capacity as agent of the owner, or to present bills of lading to the master for signature by him on behalf of the owner. See, for example, *Tillmans & Co v S. S. Knutsford Ltd* [1908] 1 KB 185; *The Berkshire* [1974] 1 Lloyd's Rep 185.

58 See above.

59 See Nicholas Gaskell, Regina Asariotos and Yvonne Baatz, *Bills of Lading* (2000), paras 3.66 ff; Tetley, *Marine Cargo Claims*, pp 248 ff.

60 *Thyssen Steel Co v M/V Kavo Yerakas* 50 F 3d 1349 (1995); *The Anthony II* [1966] 2 Lloyd's Rep 437. But not all US decisions have gone the same way. See generally Tetley, 'The Demise of the Demise Clause' (1999) 44 McGill LK 807; Russell W. Pritchett, 'The Demise Clause in American Courts' [1980] 4 LMCLQ 387.

61 Which nullifies clauses purporting to exculpate the carrier from liability or negligence. However, that Act does not apply in relation to bills of lading within the Carriage of Goods by Sea Act 1936.

62 Following *Bank of Kentucky v Adams Express Co,* 93 US 174 (1876).

63 *The Mica* [1973] 2 Lloyd's Rep 478, approving the statements in Tetley, *Marine Cargo Claims* (1st edn), pp 52–54 (see now the 3rd edn, pp 248 ff.). On appeal, [1975] 2 Lloyd's Rep 371, the decision was set aside by consent on terms of settlement agreed between the parties.

64 *Union Carbide v Fednav Ltd* (1997) 131 FTR 241, in which Nadon J declined to follow the earlier decision of Reed J in *Canastrand Industries Ltd v the Ship Lara S* [1993] 2 FC 553; *Jian Sheng Co v Great Tempo SA* [1998] 3 FC 418. See Tetley (1999) 44 McGill LK 807, who maintains his opposition to their validity.

65 The latest being *The Starsin*, n 37. See also Gaskell, Asariotis and Baatz, *Bills of Lading*, paras 3.66 ff.

66 Wilson, *Carriage of Goods by Sea*, pp 233–234.

4.   FORMATION AND EVIDENCE OF THE CONTRACT

As previously mentioned, the contract of carriage is concluded between carrier and shipper before the bill of lading is issued. Though the bill of lading is the strongest evidence of the terms of the contract, it is not itself the contract,[67] nor is it necessarily conclusive as against the original holder as to the terms or even the existence of the contract.[68] The terms must be ascertained after reference to all relevant facts and documents, including oral discussions between the parties or their respective agents, sailing advertisements, sailing cards, shipping notes, mates' receipts, and the like. If, therefore, the bill of lading is inconsistent with the terms of a prior warranty by the carrier, the shipper is entitled to adduce evidence of the true terms of the contract and the prior undertaking will prevail.[69] However, if a standard bill of lading is regularly used for transactions between shipper and carrier, its terms may be implied into future contracts as the result of their course of dealing, and thus govern their rights even in a transaction where no bill of lading is issued. [70]

Though the earlier contract may still have force as between shipper and carrier, in favour of a consignee or indorsee, the bill of lading is conclusive as to the terms of the carriage and the consignee or indorsee will not be bound by any prior agreement between the shipper and the carrier not reflected in the terms of the bill of lading. This was established long ago in *Leduc & Co v Ward*.[71] The primary ground of that decision was that under s 1 of the Bills of Lading Act 1855 the indorsee became the transferee of all rights of suit as if the contract 'contained in' the bill of lading had been made with him. A secondary ground, advanced by Lord Esher MR, was that reduction of the earlier contract of carriage to writing attracted the operation of the parol evidence rule,[72] making extrinsic evidence of those terms inadmissible. The difficulty with this second ground is that it is equally applicable to claims by the original shipper. Indeed, it is not clear why the parol evidence rule has not been invoked against the shipper. As to the first ground, the Act of 1855 has been repealed by the Carriage of Goods by Sea Act 1992. Section 2(1) of that Act refers to the transfer of rights of suit 'under the contract of carriage', which in relation to a bill of lading is defined as the contract contained in or evidenced by the bill of lading.[73] Accordingly, if the principle established in *Leduc & Co v Ward* is still good law, it is best explained on the basis that as against a transferee of the bill of lading without notice of any prior inconsistent contract the carrier is estopped from disputing that the terms of the contract of carriage (albeit concluded before issue of the bill of lading) are different from those set out in the bill of lading. By contrast,

---

67 *Sewell v Burdick* (1884) 10 App Cas 74, per Lord Bramwell at 105; *The Ardennes* [1951] 1 KB 55.

68 *Heskell v Continental Express Ltd* [1950] 1 All ER 1033.

69 *The Ardennes*, n 67 (undertaking to ship directly to London held to override a clause in the bill of lading permitting deviation).

70 Moreover, an agreement to ship the goods according to the carrier's regular practice incorporates by reference the terms of the carrier's bills of lading, even though in the particular transaction the bill was never issued (*Anticosti Shipping Co v St-Amand* [1959] SCR 372, [1959] 1 Lloyd's Rep 352).

71 (1888) 20 QBD 475. See Charles Debattista, 'The Bill of Lading as the Contract of Carriage – A Reassessment of *Leduc v Ward*' (1982) 45 MLR 652.

72 See p 91.

73 Carriage of Goods by Sea Act 1992, s 5(1).

the original holder of the bill of lading is entitled to treat the bill of lading as the exclusive embodiment of the terms of carriage.

5.   DUTIES AND LIABILITIES OF THE CARRIER UNDER OR BY VIRTUE OF THE CONTRACT OF CARRIAGE

The carrier's duties and liabilities under the contract of carriage[74] are governed primarily by the terms of the contract and the Hague-Visby Rules. Together these largely displace the common law rules as to the obligations of the sea carrier.

(i)   As to the ship

1.   *Availability*

If the shipper has booked space on a designated vessel in advance under a contractual arrangement,[75] then prima facie he has an action for damages for breach of contract if the goods are refused, or 'shut out', by the carrier.[76] But this is subject to the terms of the contract, and the carrier will usually make it clear that it undertakes no responsibility for shipment if the ship is already full at the time the goods are tendered. [77] In that event, any prepaid freight is almost invariably refunded.

2.   *Condition of the vessel*

The carrier is bound before and at the beginning of the voyage to exercise due diligence to make the ship seaworthy; to properly man, equip and supply the ship; and to make the holds, refrigerating and cool chambers, and all other parts of the ship in which goods are carried, fit and safe for their reception, carriage and preservation.[78] Thus the carrier's duty is not strict, as at common law,[79] but is limited to the exercise of due diligence, and if he fulfils this duty, he is not answerable for loss of or damage to the cargo resulting from unseaworthiness of the ship.[80]

(ii)   As to treatment of cargo on board

The carrier's obligation vis-à-vis the vessel is not the same as a requirement under the ordinary law of bailment that the goods be delivered in the same condition as

---

74   As to his liability in tort, see p 1058, and in bailment p 1059.

75   Not only bookings commit the carrier, who may be protected by a clause entitling it to shut out the cargo, eg if the vessel is already full.

76   This part of the carrier's obligation will not be reflected in the bill of lading, which is confined to his duties from the time of dispatch. Similarly, the Hague-Visby Rules apply only in relation to the period from loading to discharge (art I(e)).

77   This is commonly stated (inter alia) in the sailing card. Of course, such a stipulation is of no effect unless made as a term of the contract, so that if it is contained solely in a post-contract document it will be inoperative except, perhaps, to establish a usage or course of dealing for subsequent contracts.

78   Hague-Visby Rules, art III, r 1.

79   See *Scrutton on Charterparties*, pp 94 ff.

80   Hague-Visby Rules, art IV, r 1.

when received.[81] Subject to the provisio... properly and carefully load, handle, stov... goods carried. [83] This includes a duty, o... reasonable steps to ensure that the cargo is... cargo shipped by other shippers. What is rea... degree of knowledge which the carrier posses... nature and hazards of such other cargo.[84] Article... mandatory obligation on the carrier to load and stow; it... undertakes to do so, he must do it properly. So a provis... carriage that loading and stowage shall be effected by the ca... purported exclusion of art III, r 2,[85] which would be invalid under ar...

Something should here be said about deck cargo. The long-established ru... ...at unless so authorized by agreement or custom, the carrier is not entitled to stow the goods on deck.[86] The reason is that, by stowing on deck, the carrier impedes the safe navigation of the ship and exposes the cargo to a greater risk than that agreed, in particular to loss overboard, damage through seawater coming over the deck and an increased hazard of jettison.[87] To what extent this rule applies to the storage of containers on the deck of a vessel specifically constructed for on-deck container transportation is unclear. There are a number of American decisions to the effect that carriage on deck may be justified[88] by the nature of the cargo or the construction of the ship.[89] On the other hand, the definition of 'goods' in the Hague-Visby Rules excludes cargo which by the contract of carriage is stated as being carried on deck and is so carried,[90] and it is strongly arguable that the shipper ought not to be deprived of the protection of the Rules except with his consent or by established custom.[91] Moreover, it is significant that under the Hamburg Rules the carrier is entitled to carry goods on deck if this is in accordance with his contract with the shipper or with the usage of a particular trade or is required by statutory

81 *RPS Prodotti Siderurgici SRL v Owners and/or demise charterers of The Sea Maas (The Sea Maas)* [2000] 1 All ER 536, which held that if the goods arrive damaged, it does not follow that the carrier's obligation was breached at the port of discharge; it could be that it was on the high seas because of a lack of care during the voyage.

82 See p 1046.

83 Hague-Visby Rules, art III, r 2. These duties involve giving proper ventilation in the vessel.

84 For a full treatment of this complex topic, see Michael J. Mustill, 'Carriers' Liabilities and Insurance' in *Damage from Goods* (ed K. Grönfors, 1978), pp 71 ff.

85 *Pyrene Co Ltd v Scindia Navigation Co Ltd*, n 25, applied in *Jindal Iron & Steel Co Ltd v Islamic Solidarity Co Jordan Inc (The Jordan III)* [2003] 1 All ER (Comm) 747; *The Coral* [1993] 1 Lloyd's Rep 1.

86 *Royal Exchange Shipping Co v W. J. Dixon & Co* (1886) 12 App Cas 11.

87 *Strang, Steel & Co v A. Scott & Co* (1889) 14 App Cas 601, per Lord Watson at 609–610. There is the further point that since stowage on deck is not in the usual or proper place, the owner of deck cargo is not as a rule entitled to general average contribution (ibid). But see below.

88 In the sense of not constituting an unreasonable deviation for the purpose of the (US) Carriage of Goods by Sea Act.

89 See, for example, *The Mormacvega* [1974] 1 Lloyd's Rep 296 (US Court of Appeals, 2nd Circuit), affirming the decision at first instance [1973] 1 Lloyd's Rep 267.

90 Article III.

91 Cf Tetley, *Marine Cargo Claims*, ch 51.

...omitted that this represents the current state of English ...blished usage containers may be carried on deck where the ...pped for that purpose.[93]

...ggested that unauthorized stowage on deck is arguably akin to ...and that the effect is to disentitle the owner to rely on the exceptions and ...ons of liability in the bill of lading. But the view is gaining ground that ...iation clauses should be assimilated to the ordinary law of contract[94] and that in any event the concept of deviation should not be extended.[95] It is now considered inappropriate to apply principles of domestic law to interpret an international convention, even though effected by legislation, and it has been held that the mere fact that cargo is carried on deck does not affect the limitation of liability given by art IV, r 5, which in providing for the limitation of liability 'in any event', must be taken to mean exactly what it says and is not limited to events giving rise to the exemption under art IV.[96] Similarly, unauthorized shipment on deck does not entitle the shipper to ignore the one-year time bar under art III, r 6, for the institution of proceedings,[97] except where art VI applies,[98] in which case they are free to agree their own terms as to rights and immunities, and the normal rules of construction can be brought into play.

Where the goods are carried on deck but the bill of lading does not so state, the Hague-Visby Rules apply;[99] and a clause providing that the carrier is to be at liberty to carry the goods on deck is not, for the purpose of the Rules, a statement that they are in fact being so carried. [100]

---

92 Article 9, r 1.
93 This was the view of Kerr J at first instance in *J Evans & Son (Portsmouth) Ltd v Andrea Merzario Ltd* [1975] 1 Lloyd's Rep 162, but the point was left open by the Court of Appeal [1976] 1 WLR 1078 since it did not arise in that case.
94 *Kenya Rlys v Antares Co Pte Ltd, The Antares (Nos 1 & 2)* [1987] 1 Lloyd's Rep 424, per Lloyd LJ at 430.
95 Ibid, approved in *Daewoo Heavy Industries Ltd v Klipriver Shipping Ltd (The Kapitan Petko Voivoda)* [2003] 1 All ER (Comm) 801.
96 *The Kapitan Petko Voivoda*, n 95, approving *The 'Happy Ranger'*, n 25, where the obligation broken was of seaworthiness under art III, r 1, and overruling *The Chanda* [1989] 2 Lloyd's Rep 494. The decision concerned the Hague Rules.
97 This had been so held even before the abandonment of the deviation approach. See *The Antares*, n 17.
98 That is, in cases involving the shipment of particular goods which are not ordinary commercial shipments made in the ordinary course of trade but are other shipments where the character or condition of the property to be carried or the circumstances, terms and conditions under which the carriage is to be performed are such as reasonably to justify a special agreement.
99 Sound policy, for unless such a statement was required in order to exclude the Rules, a consignee or indorsee of the bill of lading would have no way of knowing that the goods were in fact being shipped on deck and that they were therefore outside the protection of the Rules.
100 *Svenska Traktor Aktiebolaget v Maritime Agencies (Southampton) Ltd* [1953] 2 All ER 570. It is for this reason that a permissive clause of this kind does not prevent the bill of lading from constituting a clean bill of lading for the purpose of the Uniform Customs and Practice for Documentary Credits. See p 985.

(iii) As to issue and contents of bill of lading

After receiving the goods into his charge, the carrier or the master or agent of the carrier is required, on demand of the shipper, to issue a bill of lading showing, among other things, the leading marks necessary for identification of the goods as furnished by the shipper before loading starts, together with either the number of the packages or pieces or the quantity or weight, as the case may be, as furnished in writing by the shipper.[101] The existence of this obligation is important to the shipper and consignees and indorsees, for it lays the foundation for statements in the bill of lading which may subsequently estop the carrier from disputing receipt of the designated articles in the apparent condition stated. However, marks, numbers, quantity or weight do not have to be stated where the carrier etc, has reasonable ground for suspecting that they do not accurately represent the goods actually received or where he has no reasonable means of checking the facts.[102] Similarly, the bill is required to state only the *apparent* condition of the goods. It is not the duty of the carrier to examine the contents of packages, nor has he the means of checking the condition of goods shipped in a container, though the external condition of the container itself is a matter to be stated. If the carrier honestly considers the cargo not to be in good order and that is a view that a reasonably observant carrier could hold, then he can qualify the statement as to the apparent condition of the cargo in the bill, as long as the words of qualification reflect reasonably closely the apparent condition of the cargo and the extent of any apparent defect.[103] Because of the lack of means of verification, it is common for bills of lading to carry statements such as 'shipper's load and count', 'weight, quality and condition unknown'. A carrier who fails to clause a bill of lading[104] when it should is estopped from disputing that the goods were shipped in apparent good order,[105] while on the other hand it is liable if, in clausing a bill on account of apparent defects affecting only a very small amount of the cargo, the master uses words implying that the whole or a substantial part of the cargo is affected.[106]

(iv) As to the voyage

The carrier is required to commence and complete the voyage contracted for with reasonable dispatch,[107] and to follow the contractual route or, if none is specified, then a usual and reasonable route, without unjustifiable deviation.[108] Breach of either of these obligations not only exposes the carrier to claims for any resulting loss or damage but may be held, as a matter of construction, to fall outside provisions in the

---

101 Hague-Visby Rules, art III, r 3(a),(b).
102 Ibid, art III, r 3, proviso.
103 *Owners of cargo lately laden on board the David Agmashenebeli v Owner of the David Agmashenebeli* [2003] 1 Lloyd's Rep 92.
104 See p 894.
105 For an example where the carrier's failure to clause the bill as required by the terms of a charterparty was accepted as rendering it liable to indemnify the shipowner, see *Transocean Liners Reederei GmbH v Euxine Shipping Co Ltd (The Imvros)* [1999] 1 Lloyd's Rep 848.
106 *The David Agmashenebeli*, n 103. See p 895.
107 See, generally *Scrutton on Charterparties*, pp 103 ff.
108 Ibid, pp 256 ff.

contract limiting his liability.[109] At common law, circumstances justifying deviation were severely limited. Deviation was permitted if necessary to save life, but not if made solely for the preservation of the property of another.

> The impulsive desire to save human life when in peril is one of the most beneficial instincts of humanity, and is nowhere more salutary in its results than in bringing help to those who, exposed to destruction from the fury of winds and waves, would perish if left without assistance. To all who have to trust themselves to the sea, it is of the utmost importance that the promptings of humanity in this respect should not be checked or interfered with by prudential considerations as to injurious consequences which may result to a ship or cargo from the rendering of the needed aid. Deviation for the purpose of saving property stands obviously on a totally different footing. There is here no moral duty to fulfil, which, though its fulfilment may have been attended with danger to life or property, remains unrewarded. [110]

Deviation in saving or attempting to save property is expressly permitted by the Rules, as is any other reasonable deviation.[111]

Under art IV of the Hague-Visby Rules neither the owner nor the ship is responsible for loss or damage arising or resulting from the act, neglect or default of the master in the navigation or management of the ship. But this exemption does not cover the case where, in breach of an instruction to proceed with the utmost dispatch and to take the shorter of alternative routes, the master proceeds by a different and longer route for reasons unconnected with sailing conditions or other navigational matters and without any rational justification, for this is a breach of a duty relating to the employment of the vessel, not its navigation or management.[112]

(v) As to delivery of cargo at destination

Upon arrival of the goods at the port of destination it is the carrier's duty to surrender them at the contractual place of discharge to the holder of the bill of lading, whether he be the original consignee or an indorsee. The bill is a document of title and its possession thus gives control of the goods to the holder. Conversely, the master cannot safely deliver the goods to a person not the holder of the bill of lading, unless he is satisfied that that person is entitled to possession of the goods and there is some reasonable explanation for the absence of the bill of lading.[113] Because of delays in the arrival of bills of lading it is now not uncommon for these to provide for release of the goods against a warranty of title and indemnity. But the charterer of a vessel is not entitled to give instructions to the carrier to release the goods without a bill of lading.[114] Where the master does release the goods against

---

109 At one time unjustified deviation was considered to go so much to the root of the contract as to disentitle the carrier as a matter of law to rely on exemption clauses. See *Joseph Thorley Ltd v Orchis Steamship Co Ltd* [1907] 1 KB 660; *James Morrison & Co Ltd v Shaw, Savill & Albion Co Ltd* [1916] 2 KB 783; *Stag Line Ltd v Foscolo, Mango & Co Ltd* [1932] AC 328; *Hain Steamship Co Ltd v Tate & Lyle Ltd* [1936] 2 All ER 597; *The Berkshire*, n 57.

110 *Scaramanga & Co v Stamp* (1880) 5 CPD 295, per Cockburn CJ at 304–305.

111 Article IV, r 4.

112 *Whistler International Ltd v Kawasaki Kisen Kaisha Ltd (The Hill Harmony)* [2001] 1 Lloyd's Rep 147.

113 *The Sormovskiy 3068* [1994] 2 Lloyd's Rep 266.

114 *The Houda* [1994] 2 Lloyd's Rep 541.

an indemnity without authorization, whether in the bill of lading or otherwise, he does so at his peril. Where the bill of lading has been lost, the remedy of the party entitled to the goods is to obtain a court order that, on his tendering a sufficient indemnity to the carrier, the loss of the bill is not to be set up as a defence.[115] The bill of lading must be genuine; a carrier who releases the goods against a forged bill of lading is liable even if acting in good faith.[116]

If the consignee or other holder of the bill fails to claim the goods within a reasonable time after arrival of the ship at its destination, the master is entitled at common law, and usually also by the express terms of the bill of lading, to warehouse the goods at the expense of their owner.[117] Such warehousing ends the transit and the carrier's responsibility for the goods. The shipowner who has a lien for unpaid freight or other charges may give notice of that fact to the warehouseman, who then becomes obliged to preserve the shipowner's lien.[118] The warehouseman is himself entitled to charge rent for the storage.[119]

Where a carrier receives a valid notice of stoppage in transit from an unpaid seller whose buyer has become insolvent, the carrier must surrender the goods to the unpaid seller, or as he directs, at the place of destination stated in the bill of lading.[120] However, by giving notice of stoppage, the unpaid seller becomes liable for freight, and the carrier has a lien on the goods until such freight is paid.[121] Having given notice of stoppage, the unpaid seller is not only entitled but bound to take delivery of the goods, or give directions for their delivery, at the place of destination, and if he fails to do so, he is liable to the carrier in damages.[122] The seller, in short, becomes liable to perform the buyer's obligations vis-à-vis the carrier.[123] On the other hand, his rights are limited to the delivery of possession. Stoppage in transit does not give the unpaid seller a *locus standi* to complain of damage to the goods in transit.[124]

(vi) Excepted perils

The common law admitted of certain exceptions to the otherwise strict liability of the carrier, and these were usually expanded by the terms of the contract of carriage.

---

115 Ibid.
116 *Motis Exports Ltd v Dampskibsselkabet AF 1912 Aktieselskab* [2000] 1 Lloyd's Rep 211.
117 In the case of goods imported into the United Kingdom a similar right was given by Merchant Shipping Act 1894, s 493, but that section was repealed by the Statute Law (Repeals) Act 1993, Sch, Pt XV, Group 6.
118 Ibid, s 494, giving effect to the common law rule, was repealed as above.
119 Ibid, s 499, giving effect to the common law rule, was repealed as above.
120 The seller is not entitled to require delivery at any other place, eg an intermediate port, and if the carrier accedes to an instruction to deliver at such other place, he is entitled to damages for any freight lost as the result of his not being allowed to complete the voyage (*Booth S.S. Co Ltd v Cargo Fleet Iron Co Ltd* [1916] 2 KB 570, in which there is a full analysis by Lord Reading CJ of the right of stoppage as well as its history).
121 Ibid.
122 Ibid.
123 Ibid.
124 *Berndston v Strang* (1868) 3 Ch App 588.

All of these are expressly provided by the Hague-Visby Rules, which also incorporate certain restrictions on the exclusion or limitation of liability.

Rule 2 of art IV of the Rules sets out a list of excepted perils, the loss or damage arising from which is not the responsibility of the carrier. In addition to the exclusions that one might expect (perils of the sea;[125] acts of God, of war, of public enemies; inherent vice of the goods; strikes, lock-outs etc), there is the surprising exclusion of liability for defects of the master or crew in the navigation or management of the ship.[126] This exception reflects the now outmoded view of a voyage as a joint venture between ship and cargo in which 'the crew of the ship were treated, in a sense, as though they were employed by both owner and cargo instead of being exclusively the shipowner's servants'.[127] The exception is generally considered to be an anachronism which tilts the burden unfairly against cargo,[128] and it does not feature in the Hamburg Rules. Nevertheless, errors in navigation and management remain an excepted peril as the law now stands. The exception was, however, capable of being bypassed in some measure when cargo was damaged through a collision between two vessels where both were at fault. In that situation, the owner of the cargo on board vessel A might sue the owner of vessel B for negligence; and he in turn would claim contribution from the owner of vessel A, whose immunity from a direct suit by the owner of the cargo would thus be undermined. Moreover, the right of vessel B to contribution from vessel A produced the anomalous consequence that the owner of vessel A incurred a liability to contribute to damages for loss of the cargo where vessel A was partially at fault, whereas if the negligence were solely that of vessel A, its owner would be immune from liability altogether. To counter this problem, it became common for bills of lading to include a 'both-to-blame' clause by which the shipper whose cargo was lost or damaged as the result of a collision between the ship on which the cargo was being carried and another vessel undertook to indemnify the carrier against liability incurred by the latter to the owner of the other vessel in respect of such loss or damage. The effect of the 'both-to-blame' clause was thus indirectly to require the shipper to indemnify the carrier against the shipper's own claim in so far as this resulted in the carrier incurring a liability to the other vessel. In this way the shipper's remedy for lost or damaged cargo ensuing from the collision was restricted to the proportion of the loss or damage commensurate with the degree of fault of the non-carrying vessel.

The 'both-to-blame' clause is now unnecessary where English law applies, since by statute the liability of the non-carrying vessel to the cargo owner is limited in proportion to the degree of its fault.[129] But the clause remains necessary for the protection

---

125 Where ship and cargo are exposed to a common danger which necessitates an extraordinary sacrifice by one or other for the common safety (as where cargo properly stowed is jettisoned in a storm to save the ship), the losses fall to be borne by all parties in proportion to their respective interests under rules relating to general average. Almost invariably, the bill of lading imports the York-Antwerp Rules, a set of model rules for general average formulated by the International Law Association, the latest version being produced in 1974.

126 As to which see Tetley, *Marine Cargo Claims*, ch 14.

127 Anthony Diamond, 'The Division of Liability as between Ship and Cargo' [1977] 1 LMCLQ 39, at p 48.

128 For a brief history of the way in which the carrier came to occupy this privileged position, see Lord Mustill, 'Ships are different – or are they?' [1993] LMCLQ 490.

129 Maritime Conventions Act 1911, s 1, which gives effect to the Collisions Convention of 1910.

of the carrier for those situations where the state whose law applies has not adopted the Collision Convention and the applicable law entitles the cargo owner to recover his loss in full from the non-carrying vessel if the latter was in the slightest degree at fault.[130]

The carrier may lose his right to rely on r 2 of art IV if he fails to exercise due diligence to provide a seaworthy ship as required by art III, r 1, of the Rules.[131]

(vii) Limitation of liability

It has been the tradition of shipowners to limit their liability for loss of or damage to cargo by the most detailed and widely drawn exemption clauses. The general principle of the Hague-Visby Rules is that any purported exclusion or limitation of a liability imposed by the Rules is null and void[132] except in relation to loss of or damage to the goods before loading or after discharge[133] or otherwise as permitted by the Rules themselves. In other words, the carrier can undertake liability in excess of that laid down by the Rules and in circumstances where under the Rules he would not incur a liability, and he can set a ceiling on liability which is above the ceiling laid down by the Rules, but he cannot specify a lower limit of liability than the Rules provide, nor can he in any other way contract out of the liabilities imposed on him by the Rules.[134] 'Benefit of insurance' clauses are within this prohibition, so that a clause purporting to give the carrier the benefit of insurance taken out by the shipper, in the sense of reducing the shipper's claim by the amount he is entitled to recover from his insurers, is void.

Limitation of liability is a complex topic on which there has been a considerable amount of litigation. We shall deal with it briefly under three main heads: the nature of the limitation of liability afforded by the Rules; the persons entitled to invoke the limitation provisions; and the circumstances in which the right to rely on the limitation provisions is lost.

1. Nature of limitations

Two separate conventions provide for limitation of liability, namely the London Convention[135] and the Hague-Visby Rules. Under the former (which applies even to

---

130 This is the position in the United States where, however, the 'both-to-blame' clause has been declared invalid as contrary to public policy. See *United States of America v Atlantic Mutual Insurance Co* [1952] 1 Lloyd's Rep 520.

131 *Standard Oil Co of New York v Clan Line Steamers* [1924] AC 100; *Maxine Footwear Co v Canadian Government Merchant Marine* [1959] AC 589, per Lord Somervell at 602–603.

132 Article III, r 8.

133 Article VII.

134 Article IV, r 8.

135 Ie the Convention on Limitation of Liability for Maritime Claims, 1976, implemented in the United Kingdom by the Merchant Shipping Act 1979, ss 17–19 and Sch 4, Pt I, which replaced Pt VIII of the Merchant Shipping Act 1894 and has itself been replaced by the Merchant Shipping Act 1995, s 185 and Sch 7. The limits of liability under the Convention were substantially increased by the 1996 Protocol, brought into force in the UK by the Merchant Shipping (Convention on Limitation of Liability for Maritime Claims) (Amendment) Order 1998 (SI 1998/1258) as amended by the Merchant Shipping (Convention on Limitation of Liability for Maritime Claims) (Amendment) Order 2004 (SI 2004/1273).

cases within the latter), limitation of liability is prescribed in terms of the unit of account and is tailored to the tonnage of the ship.[136] The limitation of liability provided by the Hague-Visby Rules is calculated on different lines. Rule 5(a) of art IV of the Rules provides that unless the nature and value of the goods have been declared by the shipper before shipment and inserted in the bill of lading, neither the carrier nor the ship shall 'in any event'[137] be or become liable for the loss or damage to or in connection with the goods exceeding the equivalent of 666.7 units of account[138] per package or unit, or 2 units of account per kilogramme of gross weight of the goods lost or damaged, whichever is the higher.[139] What, then, constitutes a 'package' or a 'unit'? The meaning of 'package' becomes critical in the context of goods shipped in a container or on a pallet or trailer or in a LASH[140] barge. Is the 'package' the container, pallet etc? Or is it each individual item stuffed into the container or loaded on the pallet? If the latter, the carrier's overall limit of liability will obviously be vastly greater than if the container or pallet is itself to be treated as a single package. In its original form, art IV of the Hague Rules offered no guidance on this point, the case law (mainly American[141]) was unclear and controversy raged between shipping interests on the one hand and cargo interests on the other. The former argued that to treat an item of contents as a package would be ruinous and that the shipper was seeking to combine the advantages of container freight rates with the benefit of a limitation by reference to individual contents. For the latter, it was contended that a limit of liability fixed by reference to the container

136   See arts 6 and 8. Under the Merchant Shipping Act 1894, s 503, as amended by the Merchant Shipping (Liability of Shipowners and Others) Act 1958, s 1, liability was limited by reference to the gold franc. The London Convention defines a unit of account as the Special Drawing Right (SDR) as defined by the International Monetary Fund, and provides for conversion into the national currency of the state in which limitation is sought (art 8). This reflects the decision of the International Monetary Fund to break with gold as a unit of value and substitute the SDR calculated by reference to a basket of currencies. It is intended to amend the various transport conventions in which limitations of liability are based on gold in order to give effect to this change. Thus in conformity with the Brussels Protocol of 1979 (see n 11) the Carriage of Goods by Sea Act 1971 has been amended by s 2 of the Merchant Shipping Act 1981 to substitute SDRs for the limitation provisions in the Hague-Visby Rules, with conversion to sterling as provided by s 3 of the 1981 Act. The conversion to sterling is now dealt with in s 1A of the Carriage of Goods by Sea Act 1971, inserted by the Merchant Shipping Act 1995, s 314(2) and Sch 13, para 45. The Hamburg Rules have adopted SDRs from the outset. For a general discussion of SDRs in relation to international transport, see L. Bristow, 'Gold Franc – Replacement of Unit of Account' [1978] LMCLQ 31 and Aleksander Tobolewski, 'The Special Drawing Right in Liability Conventions: An Acceptable Solution?' [1979] LMCLQ 169. See also below.

137   These words confer an exemption from liability notwithstanding deviation or other fundamental breach on the limitation of liability given by the Rules; see pp 1042, 1050.

138   See n 136. Prior to the adoption of SDRs as the basis of defining a unit of account, limitation of liability was expressed in francs, a franc meaning a unit consisting of 65.5 milligrammes of gold of millesimal fineness 900. This was commonly known as the Poincaré franc, after the French prime minister of that name in the Government of 1928.

139   This and other limitations and defences apply to claims in tort as well as in contract (art IV *bis*, rr 1, 2).

140   'Lighter aboard ship', ie a fully loaded barge which is carried on vessels specially constructed for that purpose.

141   Devoted to the construction of a comparable limitation of liability provision in the US Carriage of Goods by Sea Act.

itself was derisory and against the plain spirit and intention of the legislation, which was designed to protect cargo interests. From the American case law, at least two alternative tests emerged. The first turned on the intention of the parties as manifested in the description in the bill of lading, coupled with the presence or absence of the carrier's involvement in the selection of the container and/or the supervision of its stuffing. If the bill of lading described the container as a package and the container was selected by the shipper and packed under the supervision of himself or his agents without participation of the carrier, then the package was the container.[142] The second test, that of the 'functional package', was directed to the question whether the packaging of the individual items within the container would by itself be suitable for ocean transport. If not, the package was the container.[143] The Visby amendments to art IV have gone some way towards clarifying these issues. By r 5(c) of art IV:

> Where a container, pallet or similar article of transport is used to consolidate goods, the number of packages or units enumerated in the bill of lading as packed in such article of transport shall be deemed the number of packages or units for the purpose of this paragraph as far as these packages or units are concerned. Except as aforesaid such article of transport shall be considered the package or unit.

If, therefore, the bill of lading refers simply to 'one container', or 'one container said to contain shoes', the container is the package; if it refers to 'one container said to contain 500 cartons of shoes' each of the cartons is a package and will attract a separate limit of liability.[144] The meaning of 'unit' remains unclear.[145] It would seem to denote an unpacked shipping unit,[146] ie a specific article as shipped, as opposed to a freight unit[147] or bulk cargo.[148] It seems that a unit of goods is not determined merely by a physical test but incorporates the understanding of the parties as to the nature of the goods to be carried, so in a consignment of frozen fish loaded in cartons, each carton represented a unit.[149]

---

142 *Standard Electrica S. A. v Hamburg Sud* [1967] 2 Lloyd's Rep 193.

143 *Royal Typewriter Co v M/V Kulmerland* [1973] 2 Lloyd's Rep 428; *Cameco Inc v S.S. American Legion* [1975] 1 Lloyd's Rep 295 (US Court of Appeals, 2nd Circuit). However, the functional package test was criticized as unsatisfactory by a US District Court in *The Aegis Spirit* [1977] 1 Lloyd's Rep 93.

144 For the position under the Hague Rules, see *River Gurara (Owners of Cargo Lately Laden on Board) v Nigerian National Shipping Line Ltd* [1998] QB 610.

145 See M. Huybrechts, 'Limitations of liability and of actions' [2002] LMCLQ 370.

146 See Diamond [1978] 2 LMCLQ 225, at pp 240–241.

147 Ie, a unit selected not by reference to the physical state of the goods but as a basis for calculating the freight. Thus if the freight were charged at £10 per ton, the unit would be 1 ton and an article weighing 20 tons would constitute 20 units. A freight unit may be a contract freight unit or a 'customary' freight unit, ie, that normally used for cargo of the type in question, whether or not actually used in the particular case as the basis for calculating the freight.

148 Eg, oil, grain, sugar.

149 *Cook Islands National Line Agency v Yellow Fin Holdings* [2001] 2 NZLR 433.

2.   By whom the limitation provisions may be invoked

The question to what extent the limitation provisions may be invoked by the carrier's servants, agents[150] and independent contractors is discussed later in this chapter.[151]

3.   Loss of limitation of liability

The carrier loses his right to invoke the limitation provisions if it is proved that the damage resulted from an act or omission of the carrier done with intent to cause damage, or recklessly, or with knowledge that damage would probably result.[152] But deviation is no longer considered to affect the carrier's right to invoke the limitation of liability clause.[153]

(viii) Limitation of actions[154]

By r 6 of art III, the carrier and ship are discharged from liability in respect of the goods unless suit is brought[155] within one year of their delivery or of the date when they should have been delivered.[156] This period may be extended by agreement after[157] the cause of action has arisen. An action for an indemnity against a third person may, however, be brought after the expiration of the year if brought within the time allowed by the court seised of the case, being not less than three months from the date when the person bringing the action for indemnity has settled the claim or has been served with process in the action against himself.[158]

The one-year time limit, which does not apply to a pure defence, as opposed to a claim, counterclaim or set-off,[159] is very short. In the event of defective goods, for example, it may be some little while before the cargo owner discovers that the goods are not in proper condition;[160] he may then need to obtain expert evidence to establish that their defective state was due to conditions in transit and not, eg, to defects inherent at the time of loading; further time may elapse before he is able to discover the identity of the carrier; and when all this has been done, lawyers must be instructed, often in a foreign country and not infrequently through agents in the

---

150   If such an intermediate category exists.

151   See p 1060.

152   Hague-Visby Rules, art IV, r 5(e); and cf the Hamburg Rules, art 8, r 1; the London Convention, art 4.

153   See p 1042.

154   See, generally, Tetley, *Marine Cargo Claims*, ch 30.

155   An argument in *The Aries* [1977] 1 Lloyd's Rep 334 that it was sufficient to withhold the amount of the claim by deduction from the freight was unsuccessful.

156   As noted earlier (p 1032), the Rules have effect by force of law, not by virtue of contractual incorporation, so that art III, r 6, is not susceptible to a rule of construction of the contract rendering an exemption clause inapplicable in case of fundamental breach.

157   But not before, eg in the bill of lading itself.

158   Article III, r 6 *bis*.

159   *The Fiona* [1994] 2 Lloyd's Rep 506.

160   In which event he faces the additional hazard that unless notice of loss or damage and the general nature of the loss or damage are given to the carrier or his agent at the port of discharge before or at the time of removal of the goods into the custody of the person entitled to delivery of them under the contract of carriage, or, if the loss or damage is not apparent, within three days, such removal is prima facie evidence of the delivery by the carrier of the goods described in the bill of lading (art III, r 6).

intending plaintiff's own country, and they will require all the salient facts before proceeding.[161]

6. EVIDENCE AND BURDEN OF PROOF IN CONTRACTUAL CLAIMS AGAINST THE CARRIER

(i) Probative effect of bill of lading

Both at common law and under the Hague-Visby Rules signature of the bill of lading showing shipment or receipt for shipment constitutes prima facie evidence in favour of the shipper, and conclusive evidence in favour of a transferee, as to the fact, time and place of shipment, and as to the leading marks, the number, quantity or weight and the apparent order and condition of the goods as stated in the bill.[162] These provisions have been reinforced by s 6 of the Carriage of Goods by Sea Act 1992, which makes a representation of shipment or receipt for shipment in a bill of lading signed by the master, or by a person having the express, implied or apparent authority of the carrier to sign bills of lading, conclusive evidence against the carrier of shipment or receipt for shipment, in favour of a person who has become[163] the lawful holder of the bill.[164] Where an agent signed a bill of lading and backdated the bill without actual or implied authority, it was held to have ostensible authority of the shipowner who had placed its trust in the agent.[165]

(ii) Onus of proof[166]

'Apparent good order and condition' relates to the external appearance of the goods or their packaging, not to their internal condition.[167] Accordingly, if the shipper or a consignee or indorsee wishes to recover against the carrier for goods arriving internally damaged, it is for him to adduce evidence in the first instance that the damage occurred while they were in the carrier's charge.[168] The claimant does this either by leading evidence to indicate that the goods were internally sound when put on board or by showing that the damage to them is causally connected to some act

---

161 See, generally, ch 38 as to litigation and ch 39 as to arbitration.

162 *Silver v Ocean Steamship Co Ltd* [1930] 1 KB 416; Hague-Visby Rules, art III, r 4. At common law it is necessary for the transferee to give value and show that he acted in reliance on the bill, though the acceptance by a consignee or indorsee of a clean bill of lading without objection is prima facie evidence of reliance (*Silver v Ocean Steamship Co Ltd*, above; *The Dona Mari* [1973] 2 Lloyd's Rep 366).

163 This phrase appears to exclude the original shipper from the ambit of the section.

164 Thus abolishing the much-criticized rule in *Grant v Norway* (1851) 10 CB 665, in which it was held that the master has neither actual nor ostensible authority from the owner of the ship to sign a bill of lading for goods that had not in fact been shipped.

165 *Alimport v Soubert Shipping* [2000] 2 Lloyd's Rep 447.

166 See, generally, Regina Asariotis, 'Allocation of liability and burden of proof in the Draft Instrument on Transport Law' [2002] LMCLQ 382 at 385; Chinyere Ezeoke, 'Allocating onus of proof in sea cargo claims: the contest of conflicting principles' [2001] LMCLQ 261.

167 *The Peter der Grosse* (1875) 1 PD 414, affirmed (1876) 34 LT 749.

168 *J Kaufman Ltd v Cunard Steam-Ship Co Ltd* [1965] 2 Lloyd's Rep 564 (Canadian Exchequer Court).

or event for which the carrier is responsible.[169] It is then for the carrier either to rebut the evidence so adduced or to show that the damage resulted from one of the excepted perils.[170] Where, on the other hand, the damage complained of is external, the shipper discharges the initial onus on him by showing that the bill of lading recorded shipment in apparent good order and condition and that the goods were not in such condition at the time of discharge.

The carrier's right to rely on the excepted perils in art IV, r 2, is lost if the carrier has failed to exercise due diligence to render the ship seaworthy in accordance with r 1 of art III.[171] Whether it is for the carrier to show due diligence in the first instance in order to invoke one of the exceptions in art IV or whether this duty is cast upon him only if the claimant has first led evidence to indicate that the loss resulted from the unseaworthy condition of the vessel is unsettled. The former appears to represent the position in English law.[172] On this basis it is for the shipper to show in the first instance that the goods were lost or damaged while in the carrier's charge and for the carrier to show that one the exemptions applies and has not been lost by the failure to exercise due diligence.

7.   DUTIES AND LIABILITIES OF THE SHIPPER

(i)   As to the tender of cargo

It is the duty of the shipper to tender goods to the carrier at the time and place, and of the number, weight and quantity, appointed by the contract. If he fails to do so, he incurs a liability in damages for breach of contract.[173] Moreover, in certain conditions he may have to pay full freight despite not having delivered the quantity of goods contracted to be shipped.[174]

(ii)   As to supply of information

The shipper is deemed to have guaranteed to the carrier the accuracy at the time of shipment of the marks, number, quantity and weight as furnished by him, and the shipper must indemnify the carrier against all loss, damages and expenses arising or resulting from inaccuracies in such particulars.[175] Moreover, failure to declare the nature and value of the goods before shipment and to have these inserted in the bill of lading entitles the carrier to claim limitation of liability under the provisions of r 5 of art IV previously discussed.

---

169   Ibid.
170   *Gosse Millerd Ltd v Canadian Government Merchant Marine Ltd* [1929] AC 223.
171   See p 1040.
172   See citations in n 166.
173   For the measure of damages, see George Panagopoulos, 'Damages for a Charterer's Failure to Load: An Anglo-Australian Perspective' (1994) 25 JMLC 119.
174   *Casebourne v Avery & Houston* (1887) 3 TLR 795. This is an exception to the general rule of contract law that a party cannot claim the contract price if he does not perform, even where this is because performance is frustrated by the other party. See p 395.
175   Hague-Visby Rules, art III, r 5.

Where the goods are actually or potentially dangerous[176] and the fact is or ought to be known to the shipper, he has a common law duty to disclose this to the carrier. If he fails to do so, he will be liable to the carrier for any resulting loss or damage, except where the carrier knows or ought to have known of the danger.[177] The shipper may also incur a liability in tort to third parties, eg other cargo owners whose goods are damaged as the result of the shipment.[178]

(iii) As to dangerous and deleterious cargo

The circumstances in which cargo may cause loss or damage are extremely varied. Indeed, one authority, after identifying no less than ten different ways in which cargo may be potentially harmful,[179] has wisely suggested that it would be better to refer to dangerous situations resulting from cargo rather than to dangerous cargo as such.[180] This view receives support from *Effort Shipping Ltd v Linden Management SA*,[181] in which the House of Lords held that the words 'dangerous nature' were to be given a broad interpretation and that it was not necessary to show that the goods caused direct damage to other cargo; it sufficed that their condition resulted in other cargo having to be dumped at sea. The liability of the shipper to the carrier for damage caused by his cargo depends partly on the nature of the cargo and the adequacy of its protective casing or packaging and partly on the degree of knowledge imparted to the carrier or which he ought reasonably to have possessed.[182] The shipper impliedly warrants that the cargo is free from undisclosed dangers or potentially deleterious defects. Disclosure of potential hazards will usually safeguard the shipper against liability to the carrier, though not necessarily against the claims of third parties. In the absence of such disclosure the shipper will be liable for all damages or expenses directly or indirectly arising out of or resulting from the shipment, and in addition the carrier will have the right to land the goods at any place, or to destroy them or render them innocuous, if they are of an inflammable, explosive or dangerous nature to the cargo.[183] This is a strict liability and it is no defence that the shipper did not know or have the means of knowing that the cargo was dangerous.[184] There are various statutory provisions and regulations

---

176 'Dangerous' is here used to include goods that are potentially deleterious.
177 See below.
178 See below.
179 Eg, cargo dangerous however carried (such as nitroglycerine); cargo which can be carried safely if certain precautions are taken; cargo which, though not dangerous per se, can be injurious to other types of cargo; cargo which will be deleterious to marine life if discharged
180 See Mustill, 'Carriers' Liabilities and Insurance', pp 75 ff.
181 [1998] AC 605, also *sub nom The Giannis K*.
182 Ibid.
183 Article IV, r 6. However, the carrier's right to invoke art IV, r 6, is subject to performance of his obligations under art III, r 1, which is the overriding article, so that the shipper is not liable to the extent to which the loss was caused or contributed to by the carrier, eg by providing an unseaworthy vessel (*The Fiona*, n 159, where the court also applied the general principle that prima facie an indemnity is not to be construed as covering the consequences of the negligence of the person in whose favour it is given).
184 *Effort Shipping Co Ltd v Linden Management SA (The Giannis NK)* [1994] 2 Lloyd's Rep 171. The rule is the same at common law.

requiring the marking and written disclosure of dangerous goods. Noncompliance with these constitutes an offence.

(iv) As to receipt of cargo liable to cause delay

Article IV, r 6 of the Hague-Visby Rules is probably confined to goods that are physically dangerous.[185] There is, however, a distinct rule of the common law that the shipper undertakes not to ship goods which are liable to cause delay (eg contraband, goods shipped without the required export licence). The principle is unaffected by the Hague-Visby Rules.[186]

(v) As to freight[187]

By 'freight' is meant the carrier's charge for transporting the goods. Prima facie a contract of carriage is an entire contract and the carrier is not entitled to any payment unless and until he delivers the full cargo entrusted to him to the contractual destination.[188] If, therefore, the goods are lost on the voyage, the carrier cannot claim freight, even if the loss is not of a kind for which the carrier is legally responsible, eg where it results from an excepted peril. The same rule applies if the goods are so damaged that they cease to be merchantable under their contract description.[189] But damage falling short of this does not disentitle the carrier to freight if the goods are duly delivered at the port of destination; if the damage results from the fault of the carrier, the shipper's remedy is not to withhold the freight in whole or in part but to bring a separate action.[190] Similarly, where the agreement is for lump sum freight or for the intake quantity at the time of shipment and the carrier delivers less than the quantity of cargo shipped (short delivery), he is nevertheless entitled to payment of freight in full, without an allowance or set-off in respect of the short delivery, for such freight is considered to be calculated on the basis of the quantity of cargo taken on board, not the quantity discharged.[191] If, however, the carrier delivers to a point short of the contractual destination he is entitled to nothing – not even freight *pro rata itineris* – unless the shipper or consignee voluntarily accepts such delivery or there is an agreement for pro rata freight for it. In practice, the common law rules will almost invariably be modified by the terms of the contract. Thus the carrier may stipulate for advance freight, which is payable on shipment and in general is not

---

185 *The Fiona*, n 159.
186 So held by Longmore J at first instance in *Effort Shipping Co Ltd v Linden Management SA (The Giannis K)*, n 184, applying *Mitchell v Steel* [1916] 2 KB 610.
187 For a full treatment, see *Scrutton on Charterparties*, Ch XV.
188 *Hunter v Prinsep* (1808) 10 East 378.
189 *Asfar & Co v Blundell* [1896] 1 QB 123.
190 *The Aries*, n 155, which reaffirms the principle that freight is payable without deduction and is not subject to set-off in respect of a cross-claim against the carrier for breach of the contract of carriage. This is true even where the carrier's breach is repudiatory (*The Dominique* [1989] 1 All ER 545). But this principle has been held inapplicable to hire payable under a time charterparty where the charterer has been deprived of the use of the vessel for part of the contractual hire period (*The Nanfri* [1978] 2 Lloyd's Rep 132; *The Chrysovalandou-Dyo* [1981] 1 All ER 340).
191 *Shell International Petroleum Ltd v Seabridge Shipping Ltd (The Metula)* [1978] 2 Lloyd's Rep 5.

recoverable whatever the subsequent misfortunes of the voyage,[192] though if the loss results from an excepted peril the carrier would be liable and the damages would include the wasted freight. To make this clear the contract may provide that freight is payable 'ship and/or cargo lost or not lost'[193] and may require pro rata freight for delivery short of destination.

The carrier has a lien on the goods to secure payment of freight.[194]

(vi) As to shipment of cargo

If the shipper consigns the goods to his own order and retains the bill of lading, it is his duty to arrange for their collection from the vessel at the port of destination. If he fails to collect them within a reasonable time after arrival, the carrier may warehouse them at the shipper's expense.[195]

8. TRANSFER AND LOSS OF CONTRACTUAL RIGHTS AGAINST THE CARRIER

We have seen that at common law the contract evidenced by a bill of lading is a contract between shipper and carrier, and there is no privity of contract between carrier and consignee or indorsee.[196] In consequence, the consignee/indorsee does not at common law acquire rights under the contract of carriage.

Under s 1 of the Bills of Lading Act 1855, the consignee or indorsee became the statutory assignee of the shipper's rights under the contract of carriage but only where the property in the goods had passed to him 'upon or by reason of' the consignment or indorsement. This imposed severe limitations on transfer of the right of action.[197] In the first place, it was limited to bills of lading. Those who became entitled to delivery under a sea waybill or ship's delivery order did not qualify. Secondly, only a person who had acquired the property in the goods (by which was meant the general property) could sue. This eliminated a transferee of the bill of lading by way of pledge and a buyer taking goods to which the seller had reserved a right of disposal. Thirdly, even a buyer acquiring the property in the goods was not protected if the property did not pass 'upon or by reason of' the consignment or indorsement but only subsequently, as in the case of a bill of lading covering an unidentified part of a bulk cargo, or independently of the consignment or indorsement, as on delivery of the goods to the buyer against an indemnity without production of the bill of lading.[198] In all these cases the best the buyer could hope for, short of procuring an assignment to

---

192 *Colonial Bank v European Grain & Shipping Ltd (The Dominique)* [1987] 1 Lloyd's Rep 239, per Hobhouse J at 246.

193 *Compania Naviera General SA v Kerametal Ltd (The Lorna)* [1983] 1 Lloyd's Rep 373.

194 See generally *Scrutton on Charterparties*, Ch XVIII.

195 See p 1044.

196 Except where the shipper ships as agent of the consignee or indorsee.

197 For a full discussion of these, see the Law Commissions' Report *Rights of Suit in Respect of Carriage of Goods by Sea* (HC 250, 1991), Part II.

198 *The Delfini* [1990] 1 Lloyd's Rep 252.

himself of the shipper's claim, was to establish an implied new contract that might come into existence through presentation of the bill of lading and the tender and acceptance of freight[199] or a claim in tort based on a proprietary or possessory title at the time of the loss or damage complained of.[200]

It was to deal with these and associated problems that the Law Commissions recommended[201] and Parliament enacted legislation in the form of the Carriage of Goods by Sea Act 1992.[202] This Act, which repealed the Bills of Lading Act 1855, provides an altogether more liberal regime for the statutory assignment of the shipper's rights under the contract of carriage. Under s 2 of the Act a person who becomes the lawful holder of a bill of lading[203] or is a person to whom delivery is to be made under a sea waybill or ship's delivery order thereby has transferred to and vested in him all rights of suit under the contract of carriage[204] as if he had been a party to that contract. Where another person sustains loss or damage in consequence of the breach of the contract of carriage the lawful holder of the bill of lading etc, may sue on behalf of that person.[205] As a corollary of rights being transmitted to the current holder, all rights of action previously vested in the shipper or intermediate holders are extinguished,[206] except that in the case of a sea waybill the shipper retains his rights of action under the original contract of carriage,[207] which include his right to direct the carrier to deliver the goods to a person other than the named consignee.[208] However, it has been held that even if the statutory transfer carried with it more than contractual rights, as by giving the transferee a sufficient possessory interest to hold the carrier responsible for loss of or damage to the goods,[209] yet if the transferee holds the bill of lading not for an interest of its own but as agent of the transferor – eg as a bank for the purpose of collecting payment against the bill of lading – the transferor

---

199   *Brandt v Liverpool, Brazil and River Plate Steam Navigation Co Ltd* [1924] 1 KB 575. But the device of the *Brandt v Liverpool* contract, at one time widely used, had become more strictly controlled in recent years. See, for example, *The Aramis* [1989] 1 Lloyd's Rep 213.

200   See p 1058.

201   See n 197.

202   See F. M. B. Reynolds [1993] LMCLQ 436; J. Beatson and J. J. T. Cooper [1991] LMCLQ 196; Robert Bradgate and Fidelma White (1993) 56 MLR 188.

203   The Act does not define 'bill of lading', but s 1(2) provides that it does not include a document which is incapable of transfer, either by indorsement or, as a bearer bill, without indorsement, but subject to that does include a received for shipment bill of lading. A straight bill of lading is within the Act (see p 891) and there seems no reason why a multimodal transport document issued in negotiable form should not be a bill of lading for the purpose of the Act, subject to evidence that its negotiable status is accepted in mercantile usage. See pp 1064–1065.

204   As defined by s 5(1). In the case of a bill of lading it is the contract 'contained in or evidenced by the bill of lading', but the assumption is that in favour of a consignee or indorsee this means the bill of lading itself. See F. M. B. Reynolds, 'The Carriage of Goods by Sea Act 1992' [1993] LMCLQ 436, at p 441.

205   Section 2(4).

206   Section 2(5).

207   Ibid.

208   This is because the sea waybill provides for delivery to the named consignee or to such other person as the shipper may direct.

209   In *East West Corp v DKBS AF 1912 A/S* [2003] GB 1509, where Mance LJ was of the opinion that only the contractual rights were transferred under the Act, so that the banks did not acquire a sufficient possessory title to sue in bailment, but he held that it was unnecessary to decide the point.

retains a sufficient possessory interest to maintain an action in bailment against the carrier by virtue of his immediate right to possession even if the transferee has not indorsed the bill of lading back to the transferor.[210]

9.   CARRIER'S RIGHTS AGAINST TRANSFEREES

(i)   At common law

As mentioned earlier, there is no privity of contract between carrier and consignee or indorsee at common law, so that in principle the consignee is not liable on the contract of carriage and in particular is not responsible for freight. However, he may incur liability under a *Brandt v Liverpool* contract in appropriate cases.[211]

(ii)   By statute

The consignee or indorsee may incur certain duties and liabilities by statute. Though the transfer of rights to a consignee or indorsee under the Carriage of Goods by Sea Act 1992 does not by itself operate to transfer the liabilities, the transferee will incur those liabilities as if he had been a party to the contract of carriage where he

(a)   takes or demands delivery from the carrier of any of the goods to which the relevant document relates, or

(b)   makes a claim under the contract of carriage against the carrier in respect of any of those goods, or

(c)   is a person who, at a time before those rights were vested in him, took or demanded delivery from the carrier of any of those goods.[212]

In the *Berge Sisar*[213] the House of Lords held, first, that a buyer does not take or demand delivery merely because it cooperates in discharge of the cargo, as by directing the master to its import jetty, allowing the vessel to berth there and taking routine samples; and, secondly, that even if (contrary to the primary ruling) the buyers in that case had initially incurred a liability, this came to an end when they transferred the bills of lading and ceased to have any interest in the goods. This conclusion followed from the principle of mutuality embodied in the Act, which tied liabilities to the carrier to an existing interest in the goods.[214]

---

210   *East West Corp v DKBS AF 1912 A/S*, n 209, where Mance LJ, approving passages in Professor Norman Palmer's book *Bailment* (2nd edn, 1991 at pp 1285–1291), held that a person may be a bailee without any direct bailment or sub-bailment by virtue of holding possession by consent of the bailor and in the knowledge of the latter's interest in the goods, and that in the case before him the shipper had remained bailor of the carrier despite the fact that the bills of lading had been indorsed to banks and not indorsed back to the shipper.

211   See p 1056; *Swan v Barber* (1879) 5 Ex D 130; *Sanders v Vanzeller* (1843) 4 QB 260.

212   Carriage of Goods by Sea Act 1992, s 3(1).

213   *Borealis AB v Stargas Ltd (The Berge Sisar)* [2002] 2 AC 205, in which Lord Hobhouse discusses the variants of s 3 in some detail.

214   For a fuller discussion, see Guenter Treitel, 'Bills of Lading: Liabilities of Transferee' [2001] LMCLQ 344.

10. CLAIMS AGAINST THE CARRIER AND OTHERS IN TORT

(i) Types of claim available

Two main tort remedies are available for the protection of interests[215] in cargo shipped under a bill of lading: an action for negligence, if the cargo is lost or damaged through the negligence of the carrier or others; and an action for conversion or other unlawful interference with goods, if the carrier fails to deliver up the goods to the person entitled to possession of them or delivers them to one not so entitled.

There is nothing to prevent a claimant from proceeding against third parties exclusively in tort (negligence) or bailment in order to escape the limitations of the contract.[216]

(ii) Who can sue

It is now established that no action lies in tort against the carrier for negligent loss of or damage to the goods except at the suit of a person who at the time of the negligent act or omission was either the owner of the goods or the person in possession[217] or (probably) entitled to possession of them.[218] Thus, a buyer of the goods who did not acquire title or a right to possession prior to the negligence complained of has no right of action; and, as a corollary, if at the time of such negligence the goods had not been separated from the bulk of which they formed part, so that the plaintiff cannot show that at that time the goods he was acquiring had become ascertained, his claim will fail.[219] On the other hand, a party who can show that he had a proprietary or possessory right at the time of the loss or damage can recover damages for negligence even if he has not himself suffered loss because the risk is on another party. So charterers were held entitled to substantial damages for damage to the cargo caused by the defective condition of hatch coamings even though they had been able to collect the price from their sub-buyers.[220] In the case of a claim for conversion the principle is rather more restrictive. Even ownership of the goods at the time of the act of conversion complained of will not suffice unless it was accompanied by an immediate right to possession. Conversion is an interference with the right to possession rather than ownership as such; accordingly, it is only the person who had the right to possess at the time of the act of conversion who can sue; but this right suffices, and the claim is not barred by reason of the fact that ownership was then in another.[221]

---

215 As to the nature of the interest required to give a title to sue, see (ii) below.

216 S. Baughen, 'Bailment's continuing role in cargo claims' [1999] LMCLQ 393.

217 Almost invariably the possession in question will be constructive possession, since the carrier itself is the physical possessor.

218 *The Aliakmon* [1986] AC 785, approving the earlier decision of Roskill J in *The Wear Breeze* [1969] 1 QB 219; *Transcontainer Express Ltd v Custodian Security Ltd* [1988] 1 Lloyd's Rep 128.

219 *The Wear Breeze*, n 218. But see now the Sale of Goods Act, s 18 r 5(3) and p 220.

220 *The Sanix Ace* [1987] 1 Lloyd's Rep 465. The damages recovered must, however, be held on trust for the sub-buyers.

221 See p 62.

(iii) Who can be sued

Subject to any available defences and limitations of liability,[222] a claim for negligence lies against anyone through whose careless acts or omissions the goods are lost or damaged, whether he be the carrier, the carrier's servants,[223] or wholly independent contractors such as stevedores.[224] But a person not party to the contract of carriage who acts on instructions given by the carrier, within the carrier's actual or ostensible authority from the owner, owes no duty of care beyond adherence to those instructions, and if he fulfils that duty he cannot be guilty of negligence vis-à-vis the owner of the goods.[225]

A claim for conversion or other wrongful interference with the goods lies against anyone who delivers them to a party not entitled or acts in any other way inconsistent with the rights of the person entitled to possession; and this is so even if the defendant acted in good faith and without negligence.[226]

11. CLAIMS BASED ON BAILMENT AND SUB-BAILMENT

Quite independently of liability in tort for negligence, the carrier owes the ordinary duties of a bailee for reward. An action based on bailment has several advantages. Where it is shown that the goods were shipped in apparent good order and condition as recorded in the bill of lading but fail to arrive or are found to be damaged on arrival, the onus is on the carrier to show that it took reasonable care, whereas in a claim based on negligence the onus is on the claimant to show lack of care. A bailee is liable for the acts of independent contractors, whereas this is not generally true of a defendant in a negligence claim. Further, a bailee has to take reasonable steps to prevent theft, which is not usually a duty owed in tort.[227] The disadvantage of a bailment claim is that the claimant has to show either an attornment or at least possession by the bailee with the consent of a person having an interest in the goods and with knowledge of that interest.[228] This may also arise in the context of a sub-bailment, as where goods are delivered by the shipper to a time charterer as bailee and sub-bailed by the time charterer to the owner, who takes possession of them.[229] In such a case the sub-bailee owes duties of care both to its own sub-bailor and to the bailor, notwithstanding the absence of any contract with or an attornment to the bailor,[230] but is entitled to rely on any exemptions

---

222 See pp 1045 ff and below.
223 The carrier himself is, of course, responsible for the acts and omissions of his own employees on ordinary tort principles.
224 Stevedores have been held liable in a number of cases for negligence in unloading or for otherwise failing to take proper care of the goods. See, for example, *Scruttons Ltd v Midland Silicones Ltd* [1962] AC 446. See also below as to the ability of a stevedore to set up an exemption clause.
225 *Mayfair Photographic Supplies Ltd v Baxter Hoare & Co Ltd* [1972] 1 Lloyd's Rep 410.
226 See p 444.
227 See Simon Baughen, 'Bailment's continuing role in cargo claims' [1999] LMCLQ 393; John F. Wilson, 'A flexible contract of carriage – the third dimension?' [1996] LMCLQ 187.
228 As in *The Starsin*, n 37. See also pp 1056–1057.
229 Which Lord Hobhouse considered was the position in *The Starsin*, n 37, at para 133.
230 *Gilchrist Watt and Sanderson Pty Ltd v York Products Co Ltd* [1970] 1 WLR 1262; *The Starsin*, n 37, at para 136.

and limitations of liability available under the terms of the sub-bailment provided that the bailor had expressly or impliedly consented to the sub-bailment on those terms or ostensibly authorized them.[231]

12.   TO WHOM DEFENCES AND LIMITATIONS OF LIABILITY ARE AVAILABLE

It has been standard practice for many years for bills of lading to include what is known as a '*Himalaya* clause'[232] excluding any liability on the part of servants or agents of the carrier (including independent contractors) and providing that all exemptions, immunities and limitations of liability available to the carrier shall also be available to any servant or agent, including an independent contractor. The object of a *Himalaya* clause is, of course, to prevent a claimant from undermining the exemptions and limitations of liability available to the carrier under the contract and the rules by suing the carrier's servants and agents.[233] The problem that has exercised the courts is whether the privity rule precludes such servants or agents, as strangers to the contract of carriage, from invoking its provisions. In *Scruttons Ltd v Midland Silicones Ltd* [234] the House of Lords held by a majority (Lord Denning dissenting) that the provisions of a bill of lading purporting to extend to stevedores the same exemptions and limitations of liability as were conferred on the carrier could not be invoked by the stevedores as they were not parties to the contract of carriage evidenced by the bill of lading. Lord Reid did, however, consider that the agency argument had a prospect of success where

(a)   it was clear from the bill of lading that the stevedore was intended to be protected,

(b)   the bill of lading made it clear that the carrier, in addition to contracting on his own behalf, was stipulating limitation of liability on behalf of the carrier,

(c)   such stipulation by the carrier was authorized or, perhaps, ratified by the stevedore, and

(d)   difficulties about consideration moving from the stevedore were overcome.

The prospect thus held out was realized in *The Eurymedon*,[235] where a majority of the Privy Council (Viscount Dilhorne and Lord Simon of Glaisdale dissenting) held that the stevedores could avail themselves of the limitation given on the ground that in entering into the contract of carriage, the carriers were acting not only on their own behalf but also as agents of the stevedores; that the contract between the shipper (acting through the agency of the carrier) and the stevedores was a unilateral contract

---

231   *The Pioneer Container* [1994] 2 AC 324.

232   After *Adler v Dickson* [1955] 1 QB 158, involving a contract for the carriage of passengers on board the SS *Himalaya*. For an analysis of the authorities, see D. G. Powles, 'The Himalaya Clause' [1979] 3 LMCLQ 331.

233   An alternative mechanism for protecting the carrier against liability is the circular indemnity clause, by which the shipper promises not to make claims against servants, agents etc, of the carrier, and agrees that if he does make such a claim, he will indemnify the carrier against liability. See R. Halson, 'The scope of charterparty indemnity clauses' [1999] LMCLQ 9.

234   See n 224.

235   [1975] AC 154.

by which, in consideration of the stevedores unloading the goods, they were to enjoy the limitation of liability set out in the bill of lading; and that the acts of unloading brought that unilateral contract into existence and furnished the consideration for the shipper's agreement that the stevedores should enjoy the benefit of limitation of liability. This was followed in *The New York Star*[236] and *the Starsin*.[237]

The Hague-Visby Rules, where applicable, go some way towards answering the problem, by providing that a servant or agent of the carrier (not being an independent contractor) can avail himself of the same defences and limitations of liability prescribed by the Rules as the carrier himself,[238] those defences and limitations of liability being applicable both in contract and in tort.[239] But they cannot be invoked where the damage resulted from an act or omission of the servant or agent done with intent to cause damage, or recklessly and with knowledge that damage would probably result,[240] and in any case the people who would want to rely on this would normally be independent contractors.

The need to rely on the *Himalaya* clause is now reduced by the Contracts (Rights of Third Parties) Act 1999, which, though not in general applicable to contracts for the carriage of goods by sea,[241] contains an exception permitting a third party for whose benefit a contract is concluded to avail himself of an exclusion or limitation of liability in such a contract.[242]

13.   MULTIMODAL TRANSPORT OPERATIONS[243]

(i)   The unitization of cargo

A major preoccupation of shipping companies has been to reduce the time and expense involved in handling cargo. Bulk cargo[244] has long been susceptible to automatic handling. By contrast, the loading, stowage and unloading of general cargo[245] using traditional methods were extremely labour-intensive; and the more stages in the transit, the greater the number of operations to be performed, with not only an increase in the expense but also a higher risk of loss through damage or pilferage.

---

236   *Port Jackson Stevedoring Pty Ltd v Salmon & Spraggon (Australia) Pty Ltd (The New York Star)* [1980] 3 All ER 257.

237   See n 37.

238   Article IV *bis*, r 2.

239   Ibid, r 1.

240   Article IV *bis*, r 4.

241   Contracts (Rights of Third Parties) Act 1999, s 6(5).

242   Ibid.

243   See Clive Schmitthoff, *The Export Trade* (10th edn, 2000), ch 16; *Benjamin's Sale of Goods* (6th edn, 2002), paras 21–075 ff. The term 'multimodal' has tended to replace the original word 'combined', though it is still not uncommon for reference to be made to combined transport bills of lading.

244   Ie, cargo comprising raw materials, commodities and liquids (iron ore, coal, grain, timber, oil etc) shipped in bulk and stored loose in the ship's hold.

245   Ie, manufactured and other goods of various kinds separately packed into crates, cartons, boxes, and the like, which have to be individually handled and stored. Such cargo is often termed 'break-bulk' cargo.

The solution was seen to be the 'unitization' of cargo by shipping it in a standard unit which would not be opened or disturbed during the transit but would house its contents as a single unit-load carried from door to door. The most widely used units are containers,[246] pallets,[247] roll-on/roll-off (ro-ro) road vehicles (which may themselves carry containers) and barges,[248] all of which are transported in vessels specially designed to accommodate them.[249]

The development of containers and other forms of unit-load, coupled with the manufacture of carrying vessels and vehicles and terminal equipment specifically designed for the loading and storage of units, has dramatically reduced the time taken to handle cargo and, in consequence, the turn-around time of the carrying vessel. In addition, the use of containers has reduced packaging problems for exporters, pressure on warehouse space (since containers can be left in the open) and loss through damage or theft in transit.[250] The ro-ro vessel has tended to be used for short sea-routes, while the more expensive container transport, with its greater carrying capacity, is considered preferable for ocean voyages, though ro-ro is also used for these.

Containers are large metal boxes constructed to internationally prescribed standards.[251] They are purchased or leased by container operators to hold goods shipped by their customers. The container operator may be a shipping agency, a freight forwarder, a road haulier or some other organization or consortium. If the shipper has sufficient goods to make up a full container load (FCL), the container operator will supply the container on loan to the shipper, who will 'stuff' the container himself and deliver it[252] to the terminal to be loaded on board the ship. On arrival at the other end, it will be collected by or delivered to the consignee and unpacked by him. This door-to-door transportation represents the optimum use of the container and is known as FCL/FCL.[253] However, the shipper may not have enough goods to fill a complete container, in which case he will deliver the LCL[254] consignment to the container operator's depot or base, and the operator will consolidate this with other LCL consignments destined for the same port, issuing each consignor with the container operator's own bill of lading.[255] The container

246 Described below. For a comprehensive treatment of the law and practice governing the use of containers, see Mark D. Booker, *Containers* (1987).

247 Wood or metal rectangular platforms on which goods are placed and which are lifted on board by a fork-lift truck.

248 Eg the LASH (lighter aboard ship) barge. See n 140.

249 Ie container ships, ro-ro (roll-on/roll-off) vessels, pallet carriers, or combinations of these.

250 Nevertheless, a significant proportion of containers arrive in damaged condition through careless handling in the terminal, improper stowage, and other untoward acts.

251 Ie, those fixed by the International Standards Organization, an agency of the United Nations. For air transport, standards have also been formulated by IATA. Containers are usually made of steel or aluminium in standard lengths of 20ft and 40ft with a depth and height of 8ft.

252 Or have it delivered by the container operator or forwarder.

253 Ie, the container is to be both dispatched and delivered as a full container load and will thus be stuffed (packed) by the consignor and unstuffed by the consignee.

254 Less-than-container load.

255 Whether this is a bill of lading in the true sense depends on whether the container operator issues it as principal or merely as agent. In the latter case it is merely a 'house' bill of lading which enables the consignee to collect the goods from the forwarder or his agent at the other end. The form commonly used is the FIATA FBL Combined Transport Bill of Lading. See further p 887, fig 32.5.

operator will then arrange for the articles to be cleared by customs,[256] shipped and then collected at the other end and delivered to a depot where they will be unstuffed and the contents handed over to the respective consignees.

The carrier is not expected (or even entitled) to open a container to check for the apparent good order and condition of the goods. Accordingly, where a bill of lading records shipment of a container in apparent good order and condition, this estops the carrier from denying only the apparent good order and condition of the container itself at the time of shipment, not the apparent good order and condition of its contents[257] or the number of packages the container was said to contain,[258] assuming that 'said to contain' or words to similar effect were used.

(ii) The multimodal transport operator

The door-to-door concept embodied in container and railroad transportation has by a natural progression led to the evolution of the multimodal transport operator (MTO), that is, one who undertakes responsibility as principal[259] for the carriage of goods by different modes[260] from one country to another. Multimodal transport (MT) is in a sense an extension of the through-carriage concept, and the multimodal transport bill of lading may be likened to an extended through bill of lading. But the extension has produced a basic change in approach. The through bill of lading is issued by a sea carrier, and its use is that predominantly perceived in terms of sea transport. Though undertaking to arrange for transhipment by oncarriers, the sea carrier under a through bill of lading has always been careful to stipulate that he accepts no responsibility for oncarriers and that his liability is limited to the sea leg and delivery to the first oncarrier. Thus the shipper who arranges for shipment under a through bill of lading may find himself in the difficulty that this contract is with one principal only, namely the sea carrier,[261] but that the latter disclaims responsibility for subsequent legs of the transit, so that if the goods are lost or damaged, the shipper will have the burden of showing at what stage the loss or damage occurred, and, if it is not the sea leg, may have to proceed in tort rather than contract.

By contrast, the multimodal transport operation is not geared to any particular mode, and the MTO does not have to be a sea carrier. Indeed, there is no necessity for him to provide any transport himself. He may merely undertake the responsibility of a door-to-door carrier while arranging for all stages of the transportation to be undertaken by others. In short, he may if he wishes act merely as the main contractor, subcontracting all or any of the physical carriage arrangements to others. The important point is that the MTO, unlike the carrier issuing a through bill of lading, undertakes responsibility for the goods throughout

---

256 Facilities for this are provided at approved inland clearance depots (ICDs).

257 *Marbig Rexel Pty Ltd v ABC Container Line NV (The TNT Express)* [1992] 2 Lloyd's Rep 636.

258 *Ace Imports Pty Ltd v Companhia de Navagacao Lloyd Brasileiro (The Esmeralda)* [1988] 1 Lloyd's Rep 206.

259 In contrast to acting as forwarding agent.

260 See below and Booker, *Containers*, ch 6.

261 This is not necessarily the case, for the sea carrier may contract as agent for the oncarrier as regards the leg to be performed by the latter.

all the stages of the transit, so that in principal the shipper need not concern himself with anyone other than the MTO and, if his goods are lost or damaged, is relieved of the problem of identifying the party physically responsible.

(iii) The legal problems of multimodal transport operations

At first blush, then, the shipper contracting with the MTO appears to be in an entirely happy position. If anything goes wrong, it is the MTO who is primarily responsible as the contracting party, whether the loss or damage occurred during a sea transit, or on land in the hands of an oncarrier. But from the moment multimodal transport was conceived certain obvious difficulties presented themselves. First, different conventions and rules govern different modes. Carriage by sea is regulated by the Hague-Visby Rules; carriage by air by the Warsaw Convention;[262] carriage by road by the CMR Convention;[263] and carriage by rail by the CIM Convention.[264] If goods shipped through an MTO are lost or damaged in transit, which convention, and, accordingly, which set of duties, exemptions and limitations of liability will apply? Clearly, if this were to depend on the type of carrier having charge of the goods at the time of the loss or damage, the question of identifying the party responsible would remain, and much of the point of the MT contract would be lost. Secondly, only a bill of lading issued by a sea carrier has traditionally been recognized by the common law as a document of title to goods, for documents issued prior to shipment, such as 'received for shipment' bills of lading and multimodal transport documents, do not show shipment on board and therefore do not embody any acknowledgement of receipt by the sea carrier or any undertaking by the sea carrier to hold the goods for the current holder of the bill of lading so as to give the holder constructive possession. As a corollary, the buyer under an f.o.b. or c.i.f. contract cannot be compelled to accept such a document. However, the multimodal transport document is now commonly accepted by parties to contracts of sale, a practice recognized in art 26 of the UCP, and may be issued in either negotiable or non-negotiable form. Where it is issued in negotiable form there seems no reason why courts should not follow mercantile practice and recognize the status of the MT document as a document of title, for there is nowadays no particular magic in shipment as the delivery point, and both the ICC Rules for a Combined Transport Document[265] and the 1980 UNCTAD Multimodal Transport Convention[266] expressly recognize MT documents issued in negotiable form. Thirdly, only a bill of lading issued by a sea carrier was within the Bills of Lading Act 1855, so that even if an MT bill of lading

---

262 Implemented in the United Kingdom by the Carriage by Air Act 1961, the Carriage by Air (Supplementary Provisions) Act 1962 and, as regards amending protocols, the Carriage by Air and Road Act 1979.

263 Implemented by the Carriage of Goods by Road Act 1965, as amended by the Carriage by Air and Road Act 1979. See *Quantum Corp v Plane Trucking* [2002] 1 WLR 2678.

264 Not incorporated as such into English legislation but made effective by the Carriage by Railway Act 1972.

265 See p 1065.

266 See p 1066. See also *Kum v Wah Tat Bank* [1971] 1 Lloyd's Rep 439 and Jan Ramberg, 'The Multimodal Transport Document' in *International Carriage of Goods* (eds C. M. Schmitthoff and R. M. Goode, 1988), p 6.

were to be transferable, it would not operate to transfer to the consignee or indorsee the shipper's contractual rights against the MTO. That problem, however, has now probably disappeared with the repeal of the 1855 Act by the Carriage of Goods by Sea Act 1992, which in defining 'bill of lading' as including a received for shipment bill of lading[267] shows that receipt on board by the carrier is no longer considered a crucial element of a bill of lading.[268]

It was with a view to resolving these problems that the TCM Convention[269] was drafted for consideration at a diplomatic conference, but work on this was later abandoned. However, in 1973 the International Chamber of Commerce promulgated a set of Uniform Rules for a Combined Transport Document[270] based on the TCM Convention, while FIATA produced a combined transport bill of lading for issue by freight forwarders undertaking combined transport operations. Towards the end of the 1970s a growing interest by the developing countries in a multimodal transport convention led to a new initiative by the United Nations Conference on Trade and Development, and after intensive negotiations which very nearly came to naught, the UNCTAD Convention on International Multimodal Transport of Goods was signed in Geneva in 1980. But the Convention has never come into force, there being insufficient ratifications due to lack of interest on the part of the shipping industry and consequent want of government support, coupled with a sense that they were more closely aligned with the Hamburg Rules rather than the Hague-Visby Rules. In consequence, there are now proposals for a new international instrument, initially prepared by the CMI and later taken over by UNCTAD, to govern the carriage of goods wholly or partly by sea. However, the key features of the 1980 Convention will be briefly described and compared with the 1975 ICC Rules. The latter do not, of course, have the force of law but require to be incorporated into the combined transport (CT) contract in order to bind the parties.

(iv) The 1975 ICC Rules for a CT Document

Under the 1975 ICC Rules,[271] which apply to every contract concluded for the performance and/or procurement of performance of combined transport of goods which is evidenced by a CT document,[272] the CT document may be issued in either negotiable or non-negotiable form. By its issue the combined transport operator (CTO) undertakes to procure the performance of the combined transport from the time of taking the goods in charge to the time of delivery, and to accept responsibility not only for the acts and omissions of his own servants or agents acting within the

---

267 Section 1(2).
268 See the Law Commissions' Report *Rights of Suit in Respect of Carriage of Goods by Sea* (HC 250, 1991), para 2.49, indicating that multimodal transport documents are capable of falling within the ambit of the 1992 Act.
269 Convention sur le Transport International Combiné de Marchandise. The draft was prepared by UNIDROIT.
270 The current version is ICC No 298, published in 1975 and replacing ICC No 273 issued in 1973.
271 As to the 1992 UNCTAD/ICC Rules, see p 1069.
272 Rule 1(a). Combined transport is defined as the carriage of goods by at least two different modes (sea, inland waterway, air, rail, road), from a place at which the goods are taken in charge situated in one country to a place designated for delivery situated in a different country (r 2(a),(d)).

scope of their employment but also for those of other persons whose services he uses for the performance of the contract.[273] Hence the CTO, even if not physically involved in any transportation himself, accepts responsibility for the acts of the sea and land carriers he engages to transport the goods. The Rules contain some useful provisions governing the situation where loss or damage occurs to the goods but the stage of transport at which this occurs is not known. In such a case, compensation is to be calculated by reference to the value of the goods at the place and time they are delivered to the consignee or should, under the CT contract, have been so delivered,[274] with a limit of liability of 30 francs per kilogramme of gross weight unless the value of the goods has been declared with the consent of the CTO, in which case that value is the limit.[275]

Where the stage at which loss or damage occurred is known, the provisions of any international convention or national law applicable in relation to that stage are to govern the rights of the parties as if the claimant had made a direct and separate contract with the CTO in respect of that stage.[276] This is the so-called 'network liability' principle. Its effect is to diminish the force of the Rules as autonomous provisions, since instead of these applying across the board to all modes encompassed by the transport contract, the rights and duties of the parties are subjected to the applicable unimodal law or convention, in cases where the relevant mode is ascertainable.

The other great weakness of the Rules, so far as the cargo owner is concerned, is in the provisions for delay. Where goods are carried by successive carriers and delay occurs during one or more stages, complex questions of causation can arise.[277] One might have thought that in the case of a CT contract such questions would be avoided, since the CTO as the sole principal would be answerable for delay in delivery regardless of the stage at which this occurred. However, r 14 provides that the CTO is liable to pay compensation for delay only when the stage of transport where delay occurred is known, and to the extent that non-excludable liability for such delay is provided by any international convention or national law applicable to that stage.

(v) The UNCTAD Multimodal Transport Convention

The 1980 Multimodal Transport Convention[278] represents a compromise between the developing and the developed countries and reflects the influence of the Hamburg

---

273 Rule 5.
274 Rule 11(a).
275 Rule 11(c).
276 Rule 13.
277 For example, carrier A is late by three days in delivery to carrier B. In consequence the latter has no vehicle or vessel ready and performance of his stage of the transport is delayed by 28 days. The overall delay of 31 days is then reduced to 27 days by the expedition of the third carrier. How is responsibility for the 27 days' delay to be apportioned? For an analysis of these problems, see Max Ganado and Hugh M. Kindred, *Marine cargo delays: the law of delay in the carriage of general cargoes by sea* (1990).
278 See Wei Jia Ju, 'UN Multimodal Transport Convention' (1981) 15 Journal of World Trade Law 283.

Rules. The Convention applies to all contracts of MT[279] between places in two states, if (a) the place for the taking in charge of the goods by the MTO[280] as provided for in the applicable MT contract[281] is located in a contracting state, or (b) the place for the delivery of the goods by the MTO as provided for in the MT contract is located in a contracting state.[282] Where the MT contract falls within (a) or (b), the provisions of the Convention are mandatory;[283] but nothing in the Convention affects the right of the consignor to choose between MT transport and segmented transport.[284]

Article 5 requires the MTO, when taking the goods in charge, to issue an MT document, either in negotiable or in non-negotiable form, at the option of the consignor. The MT document must contain prescribed particulars[285] and, except to the extent to which it contains reservations specifying suspected inaccuracies in the particulars of the goods taken in charge, the document is prima facie evidence of the taking in charge of the goods by the MTO.[286] Further, except as above, proof to the contrary by the MTO is not admissible if the MT document is issued in negotiable form and has been transferred to a third party, including a consignee, who has acted in good faith in reliance on the description of the goods therein.[287] Intentional misstatements in or omissions from the MT document by the MTO deprive him of the benefit of limitation of liability provided by the Convention.[288]

The crucial provisions of the Convention are those dealing with the MTO's liability. Article 14(1) makes the MTO responsible for the goods from the time he takes them in his charge to the time of their delivery. The MTO is responsible not only for the acts and omissions of his servants and agents, when acting in the scope of their employment, but also for those of any other person of whose services he makes use for the performance of the MT contract, when such person is acting in the performance of the contract, as if the acts and omissions were those of the MTO himself.[289]

---

279 By virtue of the definition of 'multimodal transport contract' (see n 281), the Convention is confined to *international* multimodal transport, this being defined by art 1(1) as 'the carriage of goods by at least two different modes of transport on the basis of a multimodal transport contract from a place in one country at which the goods are taken in charge by the multimodal transport operator to a place designated for delivery situated in a different country'. The same paragraph adds that the operations of pick-up and delivery of goods carried out in the performance of a unimodal transport contract, as defined in such contract, are not to be considered as international multimodal transport.

280 Ie, 'any person who on his own behalf or through another person acting on his behalf concludes a multimodal transport contract and who acts as a principal, not as an agent or on behalf of the consignor or of the carriers participating in the multimodal transport operations, and who assumes responsibility for the performance of the contract' (art 2(2)).

281 'Multimodal transport contract' means a contract whereby a multimodal transport operator undertakes, against payment of freight, to perform or to procure the performance of international multimodal transport (art 1(3)).

282 Article 2.

283 Article 3(1).

284 Article 3(2).

285 Article 8. These follow the normal pattern for a transport document.

286 Article 10.

287 Ibid.

288 Article 11.

289 Article 15.

The MTO is made liable for loss resulting from loss of or damage to the goods, as well as for delay in delivery, if the occurrence which caused the loss, damage or delay in delivery took place while the goods were in his charge, unless he proves that he or those for whose acts or omissions he is responsible under art 15 took all measures that could reasonably be required to avoid the occurrence and its consequences.[290] As regards delay, this is a considerable improvement on the corresponding provisions in the ICC Rules, for the MTO is liable for delay regardless of the stage at which this occurred, so that it becomes unnecessary for the claimant to show on what leg of the transit delay ensued. However, the MTO is not an insurer. Where fault or neglect (whether by him or by others for whom he is responsible) combines with another cause to produce loss, damage or delay in delivery, he is liable only to the extent that the loss, damage or delay in delivery is attributable to such fault or neglect, provided that he proves the part of the loss, damage or delay in delivery not attributable thereto.[291]

In its provisions on limitation of liability the Convention largely, though not entirely, abandons the network liability approach and lays down its own rules, which apply even where the loss-making event can be localized. As regards loss of or damage to the goods, the Convention prescribes a limit of liability of 920 units of account[292] per package or other shipping unit[293] or 2.75 units of account per kilogramme of gross weight of the goods lost or damaged, whichever is the higher.[294] For delay in delivery, the limit of liability is two and a half times the freight payable for the goods delayed, but not exceeding the total freight payable under the MT contract.[295] The aggregate liability is not to exceed the limit of liability for total loss of the goods.[296] But where the loss or damage to the goods occurs during a particular stage in respect of which an applicable international convention or mandatory national law provides a *higher* limit of liability, then that limit applies.[297] To this extent the Convention adopts the network liability principle.

The Convention contains numerous other provisions – eg as to loss of the MTO's limitation of liability, dangerous goods, the intimation of claims, the time limit for initiating proceedings, rules of jurisdiction and the relationship of the Convention to other conventions – which space does not permit to be dealt with here. The Convention represents a major breakthrough in the regulation of multimodal transport contracts and, though by no means solving all the significant problems, it goes a long way towards removing those which have until now caused particular difficulty.

---

290 Article 16(1).
291 Article 17.
292 Ie, the Special Drawing Right as defined by the IMF (arts 18(7), 31). See n 136.
293 See art 18(2) as to what is to be deemed a package or shipping unit.
294 Article 18(1).
295 Article 18(4).
296 Article 18(5).
297 Article 19.

(vi) The UNCTAD/ICC Rules for Multimodal Transport Documents

In 1992 UNCTAD and the ICC joined forces to produce new Rules for Multimodal Transport Documents. These reflect a movement away from the liability regime of the Hague-Visby Rules towards that of the Hamburg Rules, which, as noted earlier, omit the tariff of exceptions provided by the Hague-Visby Rules. Given that there has been no support for the Hamburg Rules from the major seafaring states, it seems unlikely that the UNCTAD/ICC Rules will become widely used in the foreseeable future.

(vii) The UNCITRAL Draft Instrument on the Carriage of Goods [wholly or partly] [by sea]

In 2001 the Comiteé Maritime International (CMI) adopted a Final Draft Instrument on Issues of Transport Law and delivered this to UNCITRAL for action. The task of preparing a legislative instrument on issues relating to the international carriage of goods by sea was entrusted to Working Group III (Transport Law), which after many sessions presented a detailed report on the CMI draft, with proposals for change, in December 2003.[298] The UNCITRAL Secretariat then prepared a revised draft based on the deliberations and conclusions of the Working Group.[299] This was considered by the Working Group at its thirteenth session in May 2004, and its report was presented to the Commission in June 2004.[300] Work is continuing. The draft is extremely ambitious in scope, covering not only carriage of goods by sea but also, within limits, other modes of transport where used in conjunction with carriage by sea. There appears to be widespread support for a new international instrument covering multimodal transport as well as carriage of goods by sea, though doubts have been raised whether it is appropriate to take a unimodal instrument as the point of departure and there are many other controversial issues to be addressed. It remains to be seen whether this project will be brought to a successful conclusion.

---

298 A/CN.9WG.III/WP.32, 16 December 2003.
299 A/CN.9/WG.III/WP.36, 23 March 2004.
300 A/CN.9/552, 24 May 2004.

37   Conflict of Laws

Litigation in England between two Englishmen under a contract governed by English law can be complex enough, as the reader who has had the patience to reach this point will already have surmised. An entirely new cluster of problems may be introduced where the transaction is one involving a foreign element. Consider the following:

> S, a Liverpool manufacturer, contracts to sell to B, a multinational corporation with its head office in Copenhagen, armaments to be delivered to B's factory in Lyons, payment to be made in euros under a letter of credit to be issued by a German bank. The contract of sale is concluded by an exchange of letters through the post. Under English law an export licence is necessary, for which S has not applied. B's managing director later writes from his New York office stating that B wishes to renegotiate the price and is not prepared to arrange for the opening of the letter of credit.

Among the questions which now arise are the following:

(a)   Can S sue B in England?
(b)   If an English court has jurisdiction, must it be exercised?
(c)   If S obtains judgment against B in Denmark, France, Germany or the United States, will an English court be prepared to recognize the judgment? And how will the judgment be enforced in England?
(d)   By what law will S's rights be determined? Possible candidates are English, Danish, French, German and New York law. Does it necessarily follow that all aspects of the matter will be governed by the same law?
(e)   Assuming that the transaction as a whole is governed by a law other than English law, does this mean that an English court should disregard rules of public policy of English law or the mandatory provisions of an English statute or regulations, eg those requiring an export licence?
(f)   How should obligations expressed in a foreign currency be dealt with?

These questions fall to be determined in accordance with the principles developed in that branch of law known as the conflict of laws, or private international law. The latter term is somewhat misleading, for, in contrast to public international law, there is no such thing as a corpus of private international law common to nations. Each state has its own rules for resolving disputes possessing a foreign element and such conflict of laws rules form part of that state's law. A court trying a case will apply the conflict rules of its own legal system (*lex fori*) to answer the questions posed earlier, and, in particular, to decide whether it accepts jurisdiction and which law (*lex causae*) should govern the dispute.

The conflict of laws is a vast subject embracing all fields of law. We can do no more than give a vignette of the English conflict of laws rules applicable to contracts and commercial transactions. The subject is one in which many issues remain to be developed; and because of this and the relative paucity of reported case law, the influence of conflict of laws scholars is proportionately higher than in other areas of law.

1. JURISDICTION: THE TWO REGIMES

Since every state is master within its own boundaries and every court is the arbiter of its own jurisdiction, it is the *lex fori* which determines whether a case is triable by the forum. So if a claimant brings proceedings in England, it is English law and rules of procedure which determine whether the court has jurisdiction. However, in the case of proceedings in England against a defendant domiciled in another European Union state on a matter falling within the scope of the Council Regulation on jurisdiction and enforcement of judgments in civil and commercial matters[1] English domestic rules of jurisdiction are displaced by those of the Regulation. Where the defendant is domiciled in the United Kingdom or the proceedings fall within art 22 of the Regulation and the situation concerns the allocation of jurisdiction within the United Kingdom,[2] the Modification Regulation[3] applies; and where the defendant is domiciled in a state within the EFTA bloc (other than a state belonging to the EU), an English court is required to apply the provisions of the Lugano Convention, which is similar, though not identical, to the Regulation.[4] We shall first examine English domestic jurisdiction rules and then go on to consider the substantial changes resulting from our adherence to the Regulation where this applies.

2. ENGLISH DOMESTIC JURISDICTION RULES

It is always open to the defendant to submit to the jurisdiction of the court, either by express agreement or by acknowledging service of process without thereafter taking objection to the jurisdiction within the prescribed time.[5] Leaving aside this case of submission to the jurisdiction, English jurisdictional rules embody two distinct requirements: first, the defendant must not be a person immune from jurisdiction by virtue of status; secondly, the defendant or the matter in dispute must have some

---

1 See p 1076. Council Regulation (EC) No 44/2001 of 22 December 2000 (also known as Brussels I – to distinguish it from Brussels II which is concerned with matrimonial proceedings – and hereinafter referred to as 'the Regulation'). This has superseded the Brussels Convention on the Jurisdiction and Enforcement of Judgments in Civil and Commercial Matters 1968 (art 68 of the Regulation) except regarding Denmark, in relation to which the Brussels Convention 1968 still applies (Civil Jurisdiction and Judgments Act 1982 as amended by the Civil Jurisdiction and Judgments Order 2001 (SI. 2001/3929) s 1(3)). The terminology of 'Regulation state' rather than 'member state' has therefore been adopted, as member state correctly applies only to Denmark. Pursuant to the Regulation, SI 2001/3929 modifies the Civil Jurisdiction and Judgments Act 1982.

2 Ie, to courts in England and Wales, Scotland or Northern Ireland.

3 That is, ch II of the Regulation as modified by Sch 4 to the Civil Jurisdiction and Judgments Act 1982.

4 The present chapter is confined to the Regulation.

5 A defendant who wishes to object to the court having jurisdiction in a particular claim may make an application under the Civil Procedure Rules (CPR) Pt 11. He is nevertheless required to file an acknowledgment of service (under CPR Pt 10; CPR 11.2) and must make his application, objecting to jurisdiction, within 14 days of filing the acknowledgment of service (CPR 11.4). Whether an express jurisdiction clause is exclusive, in which event the court will usually stay proceedings brought in breach of it, or non-exclusive, leaving the parties free to resort to the courts of a state other than that designated, is a question of construction of the contract.

point of contact with this country. Both requirements must be satisfied before the court can entertain the action.

(i)   Immunity by status

This is now regulated primarily by the State Immunity Act 1978, which deals with state (or sovereign[6]) immunity, as opposed to diplomatic immunity.[7] The latter is of no interest in relation to commercial transactions. By contrast, state immunity, which derives from customary international law,[8] has assumed major importance because of the extent to which sovereign states now engage in commercial activity. The traditional rule of international law was that a sovereign state could not without its consent be impleaded in the courts of another sovereign state.[9] The doctrine of sovereign immunity was considered absolute, protecting the state in its commercial as well as in its governmental, legislative and diplomatic activities.[10] But as trading activity on the part of states began to develop, a reaction set in against a principle which gave states immunity from suit while leaving them free to invoke the law if they themselves wished to bring proceedings. Courts in other jurisdictions began to distinguish acts of sovereign activity (*acta jure imperii*) from trading activity (*acta jure gestionis*). In *The Philippine Admiral* [11] the Privy Council, though affirming in relation to actions *in personam* the doctrine of sovereign immunity even as regards state trading entities, held that a more restrictive approach was to be adopted to actions *in rem*, eg seizure of a ship, which did not involve impleading the person of the sovereign state, and as regards actions *in rem* the doctrine of sovereign immunity was to be confined to public activities of the state. Next came the *Trendtex* case,[12] one of the barrage of law suits initiated as the result of the extraordinary affair of the Nigerian cement.

6   Sovereign immunity is a wider concept than state immunity, covering the personal immunity of sovereigns as well as their sovereignty as the embodiment of their states. In their personal capacity, sovereigns are treated as heads of the diplomatic mission (albeit with some modifications); s 20 of the State Immunity Act. In *BCCI (Overseas) Ltd v Price Waterhouse* [1997] 4 All ER 108 it was held that the ruler of Abu Dhabi (also the President of the United Arab Emirates, of which Abu Dhabi is a part) was entitled to immunity as head of the diplomatic mission, rather than state immunity, because, although he was acting in his public capacity vis-à-vis Abu Dhabi, he was not acting in his public capacity vis-à-vis the UAE in general. For the treatment of former heads of state see *R v Bow Street Magistrates, ex p Pinochet (No 3)* [2000] 1 AC 147 (HL).

7   See Hazel Fox, *Law of State Immunity* (2002, paperback edn 2004 with updating preface and minor corrections); Dicey and Morris, *Conflict of Laws* (13th edn, 2000, and 3rd supplement, 2003), ch 10; Cheshire and North, *Private International Law* (13th edn, 1999), pp 388 ff; Malcolm N. Shaw, *International* Law (5th edn, 2003), ch 13. The principal statute regulating diplomatic immunity is the Diplomatic Privileges Act 1964.

8   And is further discussed at p 1195 in the context of arbitration.

9   *Compania Naviera Vascongada v S. S. Christina* [1938] AC 485, per Lord Atkin at 490. The European Union, though having legal personality, is not a state (see n 14). Moreover, art 288(1) EC provides that its contractual liability is to be governed by the law applicable to the contract in question, a matter to be determined by the conflict rules of the forum, which in the case of an EU member state will apply the Rome Convention. See p 1095.

10   The English cases consistently relied on for this proposition were *The Parlement Belge* (1880) 5 PD 197 and *The Porto Alexandre* [1920] P 30.

11   [1977] AC 373.

12   *Trendtex Trading Corporation v Central Bank of Nigeria* [1977] QB 529. The decision was not followed in *Uganda Co (Holdings) Ltd v Government of Uganda* [1979] 1 Lloyd's Rep 481 but was later approved in *I Congresi del Partido* [1983] AC 244. See below.

In 1975 some Nigerian officials, for reasons shrouded in obscurity, decided to order from some 80 different suppliers the equivalent of 10 years' normal supply of cement to Nigeria, amounting to 20 million tons to the value of well over US $8 billion. Over 400 ships, all loaded with cement, converged on Lagos, completely paralysing the port, which was in no way equipped to hold such quantities. The price of the shipments was covered by irrevocable letters of credit from the Central Bank of Nigeria, which, when sued, pleaded that as an arm of the Nigerian government it was protected by sovereign immunity.

The Court of Appeal rejected this contention, the majority on the ground that the defendants had not established that they were a department of state, while Lord Denning MR went further and held that even as to actions *in personam* the doctrine of sovereign immunity no longer applied in international law to states acting in their commercial capacity and that as English law incorporated international law in its changing concepts, the action should be allowed to proceed

Finally, there came *I Congreso del Partido*,[13] in which the restricted theory of state immunity espoused by Lord Denning was upheld. The State Immunity Act lays down a number of exceptions to the doctrine of sovereign immunity but does not confer jurisdiction *per se* on the English courts which they would otherwise not have. Alongside the other exceptions, s 3 now expressly provides that a state[14] is not immune as regards proceedings relating to a commercial transaction[15] entered into by the state or an obligation of the state which by virtue of a contract (whether a commercial transaction or not) falls to be performed wholly or partly in the United Kingdom. Most of the restrictions on state immunity apply not only where the state is directly impleaded by being named as defendant but where it is indirectly impleaded through intervention in proceedings between other parties or through the raising of an issue in those proceedings relevant to the state's property or sovereign power.[16]

A state may waive immunity from suit[17] by agreement[18] or by conduct, as by taking a step in the proceedings, but an application to dismiss or stay the proceedings on the

---

13 See n 12.

14 By s 14(2), references to a state include references to the sovereign or other head of state in his public capacity, the government of that state and any department of that government but not to any entity which is distinct from the executive organs of the government of the state and capable of suing or being sued. The EU is not a state and does not enjoy immunity in English law (*J. H. Rayner (Mincing Lane) Ltd v Department of Trade and Industry* [1989] Ch 72). Section 14(1) must be read as providing individual officers or employees of a foreign state with the same protection that is extended to the state: *Propend Finance Pty Ltd v Sing,* Times, 2 May 1997; 111 Int LR 611 (CA).

15 Defined by s 3(3) as (a) any contract for the supply of goods or services; (b) any loan or other transaction for the provision of finance and any guarantee or indemnity in respect of any such transaction or of any other financial obligation; and (c) any other transaction or activity (whether of a commercial, industrial, financial, professional or other similar character) into which a state enters or in which it engages otherwise than in the exercise of sovereign authority.

16 *Cheshire and North*, pp 393–394; *Dicey and Morris,* paras 10-010–10-014.

17 Which does not, however, constitute a waiver of immunity from enforcement of any judgment against it.

18 Eg *Sabah Shipyard (Pakistan) Ltd v Islamic Republic of Pakistan* [2003] 2 Lloyd's Rep 571.

ground of want of jurisdiction (as opposed, for example, to *forum non conveniens*) is not taking a step in the proceedings.[19] The enactment of the Human Rights Act 1998 has led to a spate of cases involving the doctrine of state immunity.[20]

(ii) The English connection

At present, the jurisdiction of the High Court[21] in an action *in personam*[22] in which the defendant does not voluntarily submit to the court's jurisdiction derives from valid service of process on the defendant, either within the jurisdiction[23] or outside it pursuant to permission granted to serve proceedings abroad. Under the CPR, the principles to be applied by the court in determining whether to grant permission to serve proceedings abroad are that: there must be a good arguable case that the court has jurisdiction within one of the grounds in CPR 6.20; there must be a serious issue to be tried;[24] and the court must be satisfied that England and Wales is the proper place in which to bring the claim.[25] The grounds in CPR 6.20 which are particularly

19 See *Kuwait Airways Corp v Iraqi Airways Corp* [1994] 1 Lloyd's Rep 276 (CA).

20 See, for example, *Holland v Lampen-Wolfe* [2000] 1 WLR 1573 (HL) where it was argued that giving the defendant immunity would deprive the claimant of the fundamental right of access to the English courts (under art 6 of the European Convention of Human Rights). The argument was rejected on the basis that state immunity is an attribute of a state under international law which all other states are required to respect. The European Court of Human Rights has held that granting immunity is not contrary to art 6 (*McElhinney v Ireland* (2003) 123 Int. LR 73; *Al-Adsani v UK* (2003) 123 Int. LR 24).

21 County court jurisdiction is limited by the County Courts Act 1984, the High Court and County Courts Jurisdiction Order 1991 (as amended) and special statutes, eg the Consumer Credit Act 1974.

22 The term '*in personam*' is here used to denote that the action is against a person, not a *res*. In general, actions are considered to be brought against persons even though relating to property. An exception is the Admiralty action *in rem*, brought against a ship by service on it within the jurisdiction, and it is primarily with this that the action *in personam* is contrasted.

23 Even if only here fleetingly. In *Maharanee of Baroda v Wildenstein* [1972] 2 QB 283 the writ was rather unsportingly served on the defendant, a resident of France, while he was at the Ascot races. See also *Colt Industries Inc v Sarlie* [1966] 1 All ER 673. Once assumed, jurisdiction continues despite the defendant's departure from England. A company registered in England may be served at its principal office or at any place of business within the jurisdiction which has a real connection with the claim (CPR 6.2(2)(a); 6.5(6)).

24 *Seaconsar Far East Ltd v Bank Markazi Jomhouri Islami Iran* [1994] 1 AC 428; and see Adrian Briggs and Peter Rees, *Civil Jurisdiction and Judgments* (3rd edn, 2002), para 4.57. CPR 6.19 sets out the cases where permission is not required.

25 CPR 6.21(2A). Since the matter is within the court's discretion, it can decline to entertain the action because of *forum non conveniens* (ie the appropriate court is not a court in England but a foreign court), *lis alibi pendens* (suit pending in a foreign court) or agreement of the parties to submit to the jurisdiction of a foreign court. The leading decision on the criterion to be applied in dealing with a plea of *forum non conveniens* is *The Spiliada* [1987] AC 460. In relation to cases falling within the scope of the Regulation the doctrine of *lis alibi pendens* is enshrined in art 27(2) (see pp 1083–1084), but in other cases it appears to be subsumed within the broader doctrine of *forum non conveniens*, so that the subsistence of the foreign *lis* is an additional factor to be taken into account in applying the tests laid down in *The Spiliada* (*de Dampierre v de Dampierre* [1988] AC 92). See Briggs, *Civil Jurisdiction*, para 4.16. The court also has a jurisdiction, which it has exercised in a number of cases, to grant an injunction restraining a party from instituting or continuing proceedings in a foreign jurisdiction. See, for example, *South Carolina Insurance Co v Assurantie NV* [1987] AC 24; *Midland Bank plc v Laker Airways Ltd* [1986] QB 689, and p 1076.

relevant to commercial disputes are actions for enforcement, rescission, dissolution or annulment of a contract or actions to recover damages or obtain other relief in respect of breach of contract being (in either case) a contract:

(a)   made within the jurisdiction, or
(b)   made by or through an agent trading or residing within the jurisdiction on behalf of a principal trading or residing out of the jurisdiction, or
(c)   by its terms or by implication governed by English law, or
(d)   containing a term that the High Court is to have jurisdiction, or[26]
(e)   in respect of a breach committed within the jurisdiction.[27]

A common ground of application of CPR Pt 6 is that the proposed defendant is a necessary or proper party to proceedings brought against a person duly served within or out of the jurisdiction.[28]

(iii) Declining jurisdiction

Even where the court has jurisdiction, it may decline to exercise it on the ground of *forum non conveniens* or *lis alibi pendens*.[29]

Brief reference has already been made to a stay on the ground of *forum non conveniens*.[30] Specific cases where justice requires that the court refuse a stay proceedings on the ground of *forum non conveniens* include the fact that the claimant would lack funding for representation and the fees of experts in the foreign court and would be unlikely to find lawyers willing to act on a contingency fee basis,[31] and that the foreign court lacked developed procedures for handling the type of litigation in question,[32] so that to stay proceedings in favour of the foreign court would violate the right given by art 6 of the European Convention on Human Rights to a fair trial on terms of litigious equality with the other party. It has also been held by the Federal Court of Australia that a stay should be refused where a cause of action given by statute would not be available in proceedings in the foreign court and that, in any event, the home court would be better placed to deal with it.[33]

A further ground for staying proceedings is *lis alibi pendens*.[34] Where there are already proceedings in a foreign court involving issues on the same facts, an English court will usually stay the English proceedings in order to avoid the additional inconvenience and expense of two sets of proceedings unless the would-be claimant can establish by cogent evidence that if he were not allowed to sue in England, he

---

26 CPR 6.20(5)(a)-(d).
27 CPR 6.20(6).
28 CPR 6.20(3), (3A).
29 See, generally, *Cheshire and North*, ch 13.
30 See p 1074, n 25. The doctrine is not free from criticism. See J. G. Collier, *Conflict of Laws* (3rd edn, 2001), p 99.
31 *Lubbe v Cape plc* [2000] 4 All ER 268.
32 Ibid, where the House of Lords held that South Africa was not a suitable forum for a major group action suit since it had no developed procedures.
33 *Reinsurance Australia Corp Ltd v HIH Casualty and General Insurance Ltd* [2003] FCA 56.
34 See Collier, *Conflict of Laws*, pp 159 ff.

would be deprived of some personal or juridical advantage available only in England and thereby suffer injustice.[35]

(iv) Anti-suit injunction

This is the converse of the stay of English proceedings. The court in England grants an injunction to restrain the institution or continuance of proceedings before a foreign court, for example, where the parties have agreed that the English courts shall have exclusive jurisdiction.[36] An anti-suit injunction will not normally be granted to restrain a claimant from pursuing proceedings in the jurisdiction designated by the parties in their agreement.[37]

3.   JURISDICTION UNDER THE REGULATION

The Regulation entered into force on 1 March 2002.[38] Where applicable it displaces English domestic jurisdiction rules, from which its provisions differ radically.

(i)   Relationship with the Rome Convention

The Regulation is concerned with questions of jurisdiction and the recognition and enforcement of judgments within the EU; the Rome Convention,[39] with determination of the applicable law in disputes concerning contracts. But though the two instruments are dealing with quite separate matters and their spheres of application are entirely different, they are nevertheless interrelated. For example, the formalities of an agreement on jurisdiction are governed by art 23 of the Regulation, but whether there is a contract at all is determined by the law applicable under the Rome Convention. Article 5 of the Regulation confers jurisdiction, in matters relating to a contract, on the courts of the place for performance of the obligation in question, but it is the Rome Convention which has to be applied to decide what law governs determination of the place for performance.[40] Conversely, determination of the state whose courts have jurisdiction under the Regulation will have a bearing on the application of mandatory rules and rules of public policy, which vary from state to state. Again, English law will usually infer that parties who have selected a jurisdiction but not the applicable law intend their contract to be governed by the law of the jurisdiction in question.[41] 'Contractual obligations' in the Rome Convention may be interpreted slightly more narrowly than 'matters relating to contract' in the Regulation.[42]

---

35 *The Abidin Daver* [1984] AC 398.
36 *Aggeliki Charis Compania Maritima SA v Pagnam SpA (The Angelic Grace)* [1995] 1 Lloyd's Rep 87; and as to anti-suit injunctions generally, see p 1148.
37 *Welex AG v Rosa Maritime Ltd (The Epsilon Rosa)* [2002] 2 Lloyd's Rep 701.
38 Article 76; the Civil Jurisdiction and Judgments Order 2001 (SI 2001/3929) came into force on the same date (with some exceptions): art 1.
39 Ie, the 1980 Convention on the Law Applicable to Contractual Obligations.
40 See below.
41 See p 1089, n 145.
42 *Agnew v Lansforsakringsbolagens AB* [2001] 1 AC 223; *Alfred Dunhill Ltd v Diffusion Internationale de Maroquinerie de Prestige SARL* [2002] 1 All ER (Comm) 950.

(ii) Interpretation of the Regulation

I. References to the European Court of Justice

English courts are required to observe the principles laid down by the European Court of Justice (ECJ).[43] To secure consistency in the interpretation of the Regulation, a reference can be made to the ECJ under art 234 of the EC Treaty. A court sitting in an appellate capacity may request, and the House of Lords must request, a preliminary ruling from the European Court on the interpretation of the Convention if it considers that a decision on the question is necessary to enable it to give judgment.[44]

2. The approach to interpretation

The European Court has laid down two important principles of interpretation, both of which are seen as essential to ensure uniformity across the EU.[45] Although these were established in relation to the Brussels Convention, they will continue to apply in interpreting the Regulation.[46] First, the Regulation is normally to be given an autonomous interpretation, so that national courts should not adopt the canons of interpretation applicable under their domestic law, nor should they apply their domestic law in categorizing claims, eg as contract or tort claims.[47] There have been limited deviations from this principle where national law concepts are so diverse that a uniform approach would be difficult to achieve. For example, the place for performance of a contractual obligation for the purpose of art 5(1) is, in general, to be determined by the applicable law,[48] though art 5(1) of the Regulation contains special rules for sales of goods and the provision of services,[49] and

---

43 Civil Jurisdiction and Judgments Act 1982, s 3.

44 For the procedure, see CPR Sch 1 (RSC Ord 114).

45 See, for example, Case 29/76 *LTU GmbH & Co v Eurocontrol* [1976] ECR 1541; Case 189/87 *Kalfelis v Bankhaus Schröder, Münchmeyer, Hengst & Co* [1988] ECR 5565; Case 34/82 *Peters v ZNAV* [1983] ECR 987.

46 The Preamble to the Regulation notes, at para 19, that 'Continuity between the Brussels Convention and this Regulation should be ensured, and transitional provisions should be laid down to that end. The same need for continuity applies as regards the interpretation of the Brussels Convention by the Court of Justice of the European Communities.'

47 *Jakob Handte & Co GmbH v Société Traitement Mécano-chimiques des Surfaces SA (TMCS)*, Case C-26/91, [1992] ECR 1–3967.

48 Case 12/76 *Industrie Tessili Italiana Como v Dunlop AG* [1976] ECR 1473; affirmed in Case C-288/92 *Custom Made Commercial Ltd v Stawa Metallbau GmbH* [1994] ECR I-2913. In Case C-440/97 *GIE Groupe Concorde v The Matter of the Vessel 'Suhadiwarno Panjani'* [1999] ECR I-6307 the ECJ confirmed that the place of performance of an obligation is to be determined by the applicable law and rejected the suggestion of the French Cour de Cassation that the place where the performance actually took place (or should have taken place) should instead be determined by undertaking an evaluation of the relationship creating the obligation and the circumstances of the case.

49 The ECJ's interpretation of art 5(1) had been criticised (for example Jonathan Hill, 'Jurisdiction in matters relating to a contract under the Brussels Convention' (1995) 44 ICLQ 591) for its bias towards giving the courts of the claimant's domicile jurisdiction rather than the courts of the place with the closest connection with the dispute. Under art 5(1)(b) unless otherwise agreed, the place of the obligation in question is, in the case of sale of goods, the place where the goods were delivered or should have been delivered and, in the case of provision of services, the place where the services were provided or should have been provided.

procedural issues are to be resolved by reference to the *lex fori*.[50] But such cases are the exception rather than the rule. Secondly, the provisions of the Regulation should be construed in the light of the objectives of the Regulation and should not be given either an excessively literal or an excessively liberal interpretation.[51]

3.   Aids to interpretation

In ascertaining the meaning or effect of any provision of the Regulation the court may (but is not obliged to) consider the various official reports on the Brussels and related conventions.[52] In addition, decisions of courts in other Regulation states are of persuasive value, though are not, of course, binding on English courts.[53]

(iii) Scope of the Regulation

The Regulation applies where the following conditions are satisfied:

(a)   The dispute is not purely domestic but involves a foreign element.[54]

(b)   The matter in dispute is a civil or commercial matter,[55] as opposed to a public law matter.[56] This is to be determined by the nature of the matter, not that of the tribunal,[57] so that an award of compensation by a criminal court could fall within the scope of the Regulation. One of the main problems has been to decide whether in any particular case a claim by or against a public body is to be considered to fall within its public law functions or within the realm of private law.[58]

---

50 Case 56/79 *Zelger v Salinitri (No.1)* [1980] ECR 89.

51 Case 133/81 *Ivenel v Schwab* [1982] ECR 1891; Case 220/88 *Dumez France SA v Hessische Landesbank* [1990] ECR I-49.

52 Civil Jurisdiction and Judgments Act 1982, s 3(3), which refers to the reports of P. Jenard on the 1968 Brussels Convention (OJ C59, 5.3.79, p 1) and 1971 Protocol on the interpretation of the convention by the ECJ (OJ C59, 5.3.79, p 60); the report of Peter Schlosser on the Accession Convention dealing with the accession to the convention and protocol by Denmark, Ireland and the United Kingdom (OJ C59, 5.3.79, p 71); the report by Demetrios I. Evrigenis and K. D. Kerameus on the 1982 Accession Convention dealing with the accession of Greece (OJ C298, 24.11.86, p 1); and the report of Martinho de Almeida Cruz, Manuel Desantes Real and P. Jenard on the 1989 Accession Convention dealing with the accession of Spain and Portugal (OJ C189, 28.7.90, p 35). All the above reports are reproduced in *Butterworths International Litigation Handbook* (eds Graham S. McBain, Roger Baggallay and Andrew Dickinson, 1999).

53 See Peter Kaye (ed), *European Case Law on the Judgments Convention* (1998).

54 Jenard Report, n 52, p 8.

55 Regulation, art 1.

56 Article 1 expressly excludes revenue, customs or administrative matters.

57 Ibid.

58 See, for example, Case 29/76, n 45; Case 814/79 *Netherlands State v Rüffer* [1980] ECR 3807. In *R v Harrow Crown Court ex p UNIC Centre SARL* [2000] 1 WLR 2112 it was held that proceedings against a French company by the trading standards services for the forfeiture of imported clothes were a civil, rather than criminal or administrative, matter. This was because the local authority had neither a duty nor any exclusive status to bring forfeiture proceedings and the relief obtained benefited the private interests of individuals.

(c)   The matter is not one which is excluded under art 1. Among matters excluded are insolvency proceedings and arbitration.[59]

(d)   The proceedings are commenced after the Regulation came into force in the state in which they were brought.[60]

Where the Regulation is applicable, service of process out of the jurisdiction may be undertaken without requiring the permission of the court.[61]

(iv) The primary jurisdiction rule: domicile of the defendant

If the defendant is domiciled in a Regulation state,[62] he must be sued in the courts of that state except where the Regulation itself permits him to be sued in the courts of another Regulation state.[63] This rule, which overrides other grounds of jurisdiction in national courts that are inconsistent with the Regulation,[64] is considered of cardinal importance, so that the exceptions to it contained in arts 5, 6 and 23[65] are to be restrictively construed.[66] If the defendant is not domiciled in a Regulation state, the

---

59   Cross-border insolvency is now the subject of EC regulation no 1346/2000, discussed pp 857 ff in the context of corporate insolvency. The exclusion of arbitration is to be interpreted in a broad sense so as to exclude also preliminary issues such as the appointment of the arbitrator and the existence and validity of the agreement to arbitrate (Case 190/89 *Marc Rich & Co AG v Società Italiana Impianti PA* [1991] ECR I-3855, [1992] 1 Lloyd's Rep 342). For a detailed discussion see Peter Kaye, 'The EEC and Arbitration: the Unsettled Wake of *The Atlantic Emperor*' (1993) Arbitration International 27. But note Case C-391/95 *Van Uden Maritime BV v Decoline* [1998] ECR I-7091 where the ECJ held that art 1(4) did not exclude proceedings to obtain provisional measures in support of arbitration. See further *Dicey and Morris*, paras 11-023–11-029.2.
60   See Kaye, (1993) Arbitration International 27.
61   CPR 6.19.
62   Domicile is not defined in the Regulation. Article 59 provides that in order to determine whether a party is domiciled in the Regulation state whose courts are seised of the matter, the court is to apply its internal law and if a party is not domiciled there then, to determine if the party is domiciled in another Regulation state, the court is to apply the law of that other state. Under s 41(2) of the Civil Jurisdiction and Judgments Act 1982 (as modified by SI 2001/3929, Sch 1, para 9(3)) an individual is domiciled in the United Kingdom if and only if he is resident in the United Kingdom and the nature and circumstances of his residence indicate a substantial connection with the United Kingdom. Article 60 of the Regulation provides that the domicile of a company will be ascertained by identifying its statutory seat/central administration/principal place of business and that this, in turn, will be determined by the private international rules of the Regulation state whose courts are seised of the matter. Section 42 of the 1982 Act provides that a company, legal person or association has its seat in the United Kingdom if, and only if, it was formed or incorporated under the law of a part of the United Kingdom or its central management and control is exercised in the United Kingdom. Section 42(6) applies a similar test to determine if the company has its seat in another Regulation state. Domicile is determined at the date the proceedings are issued: *Canada Trust Co v Stolzenberg (No. 2)* [2002] 1 AC 1 (HL).
63   See below.
64   Specifically, art 3 disapplies rules in the United Kingdom which enable jurisdiction to be founded on service of proceedings on the defendant during his temporary presence in the United Kingdom, the presence within the United Kingdom of property belonging to the defendant or the seizure by the claimant of property situated in the United Kingdom. More generally, jurisdiction cannot be taken under CPR 6.20 where this would be incompatible with the Regulation.
65   See below.
66   Case 220/88, n 51.

jurisdiction of the courts of each Regulation state is governed by the law of that state, subject to the provisions of arts 22–23.[67]

(v) Special jurisdiction *ratione materiae*

Article 5 sets out the types of claim for which courts of a Regulation state other than those of the defendant may exercise jurisdiction. The most important of these in a commercial context are claims in contract[68] and claims in tort.[69]

In matters relating to a contract a defendant domiciled in one Regulation state may be sued in the courts of another Regulation state of the place for performance of the obligation in question. Again, what constitutes a matter 'relating to a contract' is to be determined by the autonomous rules of interpretation of the Regulation, not by characterization under national law.[70] In *Effer SpA v Kantner*[71] the court held that a dispute as to the existence of a contract fell within art 5. It has been held in several English cases that the mere assertion of the existence of a contract does not suffice to attract the court's jurisdiction under art 5; the claimant must adduce evidence from which a conclusion can properly be drawn that a contract existed.[72] It follows from *Effer SpA v Kantner* that if he does this, then the court has jurisdiction under art 5, which is not retrospectively displaced if at the end of the day the court finds that no contract existed. Such a finding operates as *res judicata* and precludes the issue from being re-litigated in the courts of another Regulation state.[73] A restitutionary claim for recovery of money paid under a contract later held void does not fall within art 5(1) – the contract does not exist, so there is no 'matter relating to contract'.[74] Interestingly, a suit by a consumer association on behalf of consumers in relation to the consumers' contracts with the defendant is not a 'matter relating to contract';[75] rather, it appears, the contracting parties themselves have to be the parties to the proceeding.

Article 5(1), where it applies, confers jurisdiction on the courts of the 'place for performance of the obligation in question'. By this is meant the obligation on which

---

67 Article 4.

68 Article 5(1). See Ketilbjorn Hertz, *Jurisdiction in Contract and Tort under the Brussels Convention* (1998); Hill (1995) 44 ICLQ 591; W. Kennett, 'Place of Performance and Predictability' (1995) 15 Yb Eur L 193.

69 Article 5(3). See Hertz, *Jurisdiction in Contract and Tort*; Campbell McLachlan and Peter Nygh (eds), *Transnational Tort Litigation: Jurisdictional Principles* (1996).

70 *Jakob Handte & Co GmbH v Société Traitement Mecano-Chimiques*, n 47.

71 Case 38/81 [1982] ECR 825.

72 *Tesam Distribution Ltd v Schuh Mode Team GmbH* [1990] IL Pr 149, per Stocker LJ at 165; *Rank Film Distributors Ltd v Lanterna Editrice Srl* [1992] IL Pr 58; *New England Reinsurance Corp. v Messoghios Insurance Co SA* [1992] 2 Lloyd's Rep 251.

73 *Tesam Distribution Ltd v Schuh Mode Team GmbH*, n 72.

74 *Kleinwort Benson Ltd v Glasgow City Council* [1999] 1 AC 153. But a claim to set aside a contract for non-disclosure is a claim relating to a contract (*Agnew v Länsförsäkringsbolagens AB* [2001] 1 AC 223).

75 Case 167/00 *VKI v Henkel* [2002] ECR I-08111. Rather, it is a 'matter relating to tort, delict or quasi-delict'.

the action is based.[76] The phrase 'obligation in question' has been construed as determining not merely the court which is to have jurisdiction under art 5(1) but the very scope of art 5(1) itself, so that if the claim is based not on failure in performance of a contractual obligation but on breach of a pre-contractual duty of disclosure or good faith, art 5(1) does not apply.[77]

It seems that art 5(1) applies only where a single place of performance for the obligation in question can to be identified; where the obligation in question is an obligation not to do something, so that the potential number of places of performance and jurisdiction is indeterminate, art 5(1), the aim of which is to promote certainty, cannot apply, and the relevant article is art 2, which applies the domicile of the defendant.[78]

In matters relating to tort, proceedings may be brought in the courts of the place where the harmful event occurred.[79] What is a tort depends not on English law concepts but on the independent concept established by the Regulation, and the European Court has given it a very wide interpretation, covering any action, including a claim for unjust enrichment,[80] which seeks to establish the defendant's liability and is not one relating to a contract.[81] The harm is considered to have occurred both where the event giving rise to the damage occurred and where the damage itself occurred,[82] so that the defendant may be sued, at the claimant's option, in the courts of either place.[83]

(vi) Branches

As regards a dispute arising out of the operations of a branch, agency or other establishment, a person domiciled in a member state may be sued in the courts for the place in which the branch, agency or other establishment is situated.[84]

(vii) Special jurisdiction through procedural connection

Article 6 of the Regulation provides further exceptions to the rule based on other parties or claims having a procedural connection with a Regulation state. Thus

---

76 Case 14/76 *De Bloos Spril v Bouyer SA* [1976] ECR 1497. See also Case 266/85 *Shenavai v Kreischer* [1987] ECR 239 and Case 420/97 *Leathertex Divisione Sintetici SpA v Bodetex BVBA* [1999] ECR I-6747.
77 Case C-334/00 *Tacconi SpA v HWS* [2002] ECR I-0735.
78 Case C-256/00 *Besix SA v Wasserreiningungsbau Alfred Kretzschmar GmbH & Co KG (Wabag)* [2002] ECR I-01699.
79 Article 5(3).
80 Note the House of Lords interpretation of 'tort' (excluding a claim for restitution) in *Kleinwort Benson Ltd v Glasgow City Council* [1999] 1 AC 153, 167.
81 Case 189/87, n 45 and more recently Case C-51/97 *Réunion européenne SA v Spliethoffs Bevrachtings Kantoor BV* [1998] ECR I-6511.
82 Case 21/76 *Handelskwekerij G. J Bier B.V. v Mines de Potasse d'Alsace SA* [1978] QB 708, [1976] ECR 1735.
83 Case 220/88, n 51.
84 Regulation art 5(5). This requires such a nexus between the operations of the branch and the dispute as to render it natural to describe the dispute as one arising out of the operations of the branch (*Anton Durbeck GmbH v Den Norske Bak SA* [2003] 2 All ER (Comm) 411).

where the defendant is one of a number of defendants, proceedings may be brought in the courts for the place where any of them is domiciled;[85] where the defendant is joined as a third party in an action on a warranty or guarantee or in any other third party proceedings, he may be sued in the same court unless the proceedings were instituted solely with the object of removing them from the jurisdiction of the court which would be competent in his case;[86] and on a counterclaim arising from the same contract or facts on which the original claim was based, he may be sued in the court in which the original claim is pending.[87]

(viii) Exclusive jurisdiction under Article 22

Article 22 sets out various categories of proceeding in which courts have exclusive jurisdiction regardless of domicile. These include proceedings relating to immovables, the validity of the constitution, the nullity or the dissolution of companies and proceedings concerning stated forms of intellectual property right.

(ix) Prorogation of jurisdiction

Under art 23, where one or more of the parties is domiciled in a Regulation state, they may by agreement confer jurisdiction on a court or courts of a Regulation state over any dispute which has arisen or may arise in connection with a particular legal relationship. This 'prorogation of jurisdiction'[88] must comply with the formalities laid down by art 23 in order to be valid, but these are considerably more relaxed than under the original Brussels Convention and should not usually occasion difficulty.[89] Article 23(1), as it appears in the Regulation, provides that the jurisdiction so conferred is to be exclusive unless the parties have agreed otherwise. The ability of the parties to provide for the jurisdiction to be non-exclusive is thus made explicit, whereas under the Brussels and Lugano Conventions it was merely implicit.[90]

Where a party brings proceedings in breach of an exclusive jurisdiction clause, the defendant may apply for a stay. An alternative remedy recently developed is an action for damages for breach of the exclusive jurisdiction clause.[91]

---

85 Article 6(1), with domicile being determined at the date of issue of the proceedings and not at the time when it is sought to join the additional defendants: *Canada Trust Co v Stolzenberg (No. 2)* [2002] 1 AC 1 (HL); *Petrotrade Inc v Smith* [1999] 1 WLR 457. At least one defendant must be sued in his domicile: Case C-51/97 *Reunion europeenne SA v Spliethoff's Bevrachtingskantoor BV and the Master of the vessel Alblasgracht V002* [1998] ECR I-06511.

86 Article 6(2).

87 Article 6(3).

88 By which is meant the conferment of jurisdiction by agreement. The Hague Conference on Private International Law is in the final stages of work on an international convention on exclusive choice of court agreements. The current text was completed in April 2004 (Work Doc No 110 revised). The original project was a much larger one covering jurisdiction, recognition and enforcement of foreign judgments, but proved too ambitious to secure agreement. See further P. M. North, 'Rethinking jurisdiction and recognition of judgments' [2002] Current Legal Problems 395.

89 See, for example, Case C-214/89 *Powell Duffryn plc v Petereit* [1992] IL Pr 300; *I. P. Metal Ltd v Ruote O. Z. SpA* [1993] 2 Lloyd's Rep 60.

90 *Insured Financial Structures Ltd v Elektrocieplownia Tychy SA* [2003] GB 1260.

91 For an example, see *A/S D/S Svenborg D/S af 1912 A/S Bodies Corporate* [2003] EWHC 797. But the question is controversial. See Chee Ho Tham, 'Damages for breach of English jurisdiction clauses: more than meets the eye' [2004] LMCLQ 46.

(x) Voluntary submission

Article 24 confers exclusive jurisdiction on a court before whom the defendant enters an appearance otherwise than solely to contest the jurisdiction.

(xi) Exclusivity of jurisdiction

It will have been seen that several articles of the Regulation confer jurisdiction, so that it is necessary to establish an order in which these are to be applied. Articles 22 and 23 are the only articles under which the jurisdiction of the designated court is expressed to be exclusive. As between these two, art 22 has pre-eminence, so that the court second seised of a case under an exclusive jurisdiction agreement within art 23 must nevertheless stay proceedings until the court first seised of the case under art 22 has declared that it has no jurisdiction. [92] Article 23 also takes effect subject to the special rules in arts 13, 17 and 21 which restrict the validity of jurisdiction agreements in relation to, respectively, insurance and consumer contracts and individual contracts of employment.[93] The Regulation is designed to avoid, as far as possible, concurrent actions in different Regulation states between the same parties and relating to the same cause of action. A court not having exclusive jurisdiction must decline jurisdiction in favour of a court having exclusive jurisdiction, except in proceedings for provisional, including protective, measures.[94] Where two or more courts have exclusive jurisdiction, any court other than the court first seised must decline jurisdiction.[95] A court becomes seised of a case when the document instituting the proceedings (or an equivalent document) is lodged with the court (provided the plaintiff does not then fail to have service effected on the defendant) or, where a document has to be served before being lodged with the court, at the time the authority responsible for service receives it (provided the plaintiff does not then fail to have the document lodged with the court).[96] In England this is when the claim form is issued by the court at the request of the claimant, the date of issue being the date entered on the form by the court.[97] Where proceedings involving the same cause of action and between the same parties are

---

92 *Erich Gasser GmbH v Misat SARL,* Case C-116/02 [2004] 1 Lloyd's Rep 222, reversing the effect of the Court of Appeal decision in *Continental Bank NA v Aeakos Compania Naviera SA* [1994] 1 WLR 588. See Yvonne Baatz [2004] LMCLQ 25.

93 Article 23(5).

94 Article 31.

95 Article 29. Since the only articles expressed to confer exclusive jurisdiction are arts 22 and 23 and the latter cannot be used to derogate from art 22 (art 23(5)), exclusive jurisdiction under art 29 appears to refer only to art 22 and therefore there will be very few cases where art 29 can ever apply. One is where the defendant is a company whose domicile is determined differently under the laws of different states. Under art 60 a company's domicile is its seat, but in order to determine that seat the court is to apply its rules of private international law. It is therefore possible that a French court, for example, would entertain exclusive jurisdiction on the ground that a company had its central management and control in France while an English court would also claim exclusive jurisdiction on the ground that the company was incorporated in England (Civil Jurisdiction and Judgments Act 1982, s 42(3)).

96 Article 30.

97 CPR 7.2(1), (2). For the purpose of art 30 this is, of course, dependent on service being thereafter effected.

brought in the courts of different Regulation states, any court other than that first seised must decline jurisdiction.[98] Where related actions are brought in the courts of different Regulation states a court other than that first seised *may* decline jurisdiction but is not obliged to do so.[99] The European Court of Justice has held that what is now the Regulation precludes the grant of an anti-suit injunction.[100]

(xii) Declaration of non-liability

Where foreign proceedings have been commenced (or are about to be commenced) by Party B to impose liability on Party A, Party A may resist such proceedings by asking the English court to grant a declaration of Party A's non-liability to Party B.[101] This is becoming increasingly common for insurers or suppliers, who, for reasons of certainty, may wish to determine their liability (or lack of it) to an insured or a distributor, respectively. Such declarations are available regardless of whether the foreign proceedings take place in a member state or a non-member state, and despite their effect in pre-empting jurisdiction and thus depriving of jurisdiction courts that would otherwise have it the ECJ has held that they are not open to objection as inconsistent with the Brussels Regulation.[102]

(xiii) Refusal to take jurisdiction

Must a court which has jurisdiction under the Regulation accept it? Or can it decline the case, eg on the ground of *forum non conveniens*. Section 49 of the Civil Jurisdiction and Judgments Act 1982 preserves the court's right to stay an action, on the ground of *forum non conveniens* or otherwise, where this is not inconsistent with the Regulation. In England it has been held that while there is no power to decline jurisdiction in favour of the courts of another Regulation state, the power remains exercisable where the alternative forum is that of a non-Regulation state.[103]

---

98 Article 27. But where only some of the parties to the second action are parties to the first, art 27 applies only to the extent that the action involves the same parties and does not prevent the proceedings from continuing as regards the other parties (*The Maciej Rataj* [1995] 1 Lloyd's Rep 302).

99 Article 28.

100 Case C-159/02 *Turner v Grovit* (2004) April 27, adopting the views of the Advocate-General [2004] 1 Lloyd's Rep 216, and rejecting the approach of the House of Lords [2004] All ER (D) 259; [2002] 1 WLR 107.

101 *Messier Dowty Ltd v Sabena SA* [2000] 1 WLR 2040, 2049–51 (CA).

102 Case C-406/92 *The owners of the cargo lately laden on board the ship 'Tatry' v The owners of the ship 'Maciej Rataj'* [1994] ECR I-5439, 5455, 5474–6; *Boss Group Ltd v Boss France SA* [1997] 1 WLR 351, 358 (CA).

103 *Re Harrods (Buenos Aires) Ltd* [1992] Ch 72 (criticized in *Cheshire and North*, p 264 on the basis that the Brussels Convention (ie and therefore the Regulation) is not concerned simply with jurisdiction between Regulation states and that uniformity in the jurisdictional rules of the EU will be precluded by the use of a discretion to stay); *The Po* [1991] 2 Lloyd's Rep 206. See also *Re Polly Peck International plc (No 2)* [1998] 3 All ER 812, 830 (CA); *Eli Lilly & Co v Novo Nordisk AS* [2000] ILPr 73 (CA). Lord Bingham in *Lubbe v Cape plc* [2000] 1 WLR 1545, 1561–1562 stated that the answer to the question raised and decided in *Re Harrods* was not clear and that, had it been otherwise appropriate, he would have made a reference to the ECJ for a ruling on the application of art 2.

The Schlosser Report considered that the doctrine of *forum non conveniens*, which is not a feature of civil law systems, should not be available to courts having jurisdiction under the Regulation, and the distinction drawn by the English Court of Appeal between an alternative forum which is a Regulation state and one which is not has been heavily criticized by academic commentators.[104] It would seem unlikely to survive a reference on the point to the European Court.[105]

Where two or more courts have non-exclusive jurisdiction, the choice between them lies with the claimant. So a defendant sued in the courts of his own domicile under art 2 cannot obtain a stay of proceedings on the basis that he could have been sued in the courts of another state having non-exclusive jurisdiction, eg the courts of the place for performance under art 5(1).

4. RECOGNITION AND ENFORCEMENT OF FOREIGN JUDGMENTS: DOMESTIC RULES

Where the Regulation does not apply, a foreign judgment is treated quite differently from an English judgment. It is not directly enforceable but must either be sued upon in a fresh action[106] or (where so provided by statute) registered as an English judgment and then enforced as such in the ordinary way.[107] It will be recognized only where it is for a debt or definite sum of money and even then only where the foreign court had jurisdiction to give the judgment.[108] This will be the case (inter alia) where the defendant submitted to the jurisdiction (either by contract or by appearance[109]) or was present in the foreign country in question at the time of institution of the proceedings[110] or was served with process while in the jurisdiction, even if only fleetingly.[111] One might have thought that an English court would also recognize a foreign court as having jurisdiction in any circumstances in which the English court would have assumed jurisdiction had the action been brought in England, including cases within CPR 6.20, but this apparently is not the position in English law.[112] The problem in relation to jurisdiction under CPR 6.20 lies in part in the discretionary nature of orders made under that provision.

---

104 See in particular Adrian Briggs (1991) 107 LQR 180; *Cheshire and North*, pp 262–266; and H. Gaudemet-Tallon, 'Forum non conveniens, une menace pour la Convention de Bruxelles', Rev crit de droit international privé, 1991, 491.
105 The Court of Appeal made such a reference in *Owusu v Jackson* [2002] ILPr 45, and a decision from the ECJ is pending. See also the further appeal [2002] EWCA Civ 871.
106 Or pleaded by way of defence and/or counterclaim.
107 The claimant can no longer sue on the original cause of action (which anyway would rarely have been to his advantage) unless the foreign judgment is not enforceable or entitled to recognition in England (Civil Jurisdiction and Judgments Act 1982, s 34).
108 *Dicey and Morris*, paras 14R-018 ff.
109 Otherwise than to contest the jurisdiction or to ask for dismissal or stay of the proceedings on the ground that the dispute should be referred to arbitration or to the courts of another country (Civil Jurisdiction and Judgments Act 1982, s 33(1)).
110 *Dicey and Morris*, para 14R-048.
111 Ibid, paras 14054 ff; *Cheshire and North*, p 287.
112 *Dicey and Morris*, paras 14–080 ff; *Cheshire and North*, pp 420 ff.

Given that the foreign court had jurisdiction, then prima facie the judgment is conclusive as to the issues of fact and law decided by the foreign court and thus cannot be re-litigated in England.[113] So far as an English court is concerned, such issues have become *res judicata* in much the same way as if the judgment had been an English judgment.[114] So a claim on a foreign judgment, like a claim on a bill of exchange, is very much more powerful than a claim on the original cause of action.

There are, however, some limits to the conclusive nature of the foreign judgment. In the first place, it must be final and conclusive, according to the law of the state in which it was given. The fact that it is appealable, or even under appeal, does not prevent it from being final for this purpose.[115] What is meant is that the judgment should not be interim in character or subject to variation by the court which gave it.[116] Secondly, a foreign judgment is impeachable for fraud,[117] though where the defendant has already made an unsuccessful attempt in the court of origin to have the judgment set aside for fraud, he is estopped from invoking fraud in enforcement proceedings in England.[118] Thirdly, an English court may refuse to give recognition to the judgment if the proceedings in which it was obtained were conducted in a manner contrary to natural justice.[119] Fourthly, a foreign judgment will not be recognized where its enforcement would be contrary to English rules of public policy.[120] Fifthly, a judgment for multiple damages or based on a provision or rule of law specified by the Secretary of State as concerned with restrictive trade practices will not be enforced.[121]

Where the foreign judgment is not registrable as set out below, it is enforceable by action on the judgment.[122] The presumption in favour of enforceability of the foreign judgment, and its effect as grounding an estoppel *per rem judicatem*, will usually justify an application for summary judgment under CPR Pt 24.[123] If judgment is given, it is then enforced in the same way as any other English judgment. However, the foreign judgment may be registered automatically as an English judgment without the need for separate proceedings:[124]

---

113 *Dicey and Morris*, para 14R-109.

114 The party cannot seek a more favourable outcome in an English court (Civil Jurisdiction and Judgments Act 1982, s 34); *The Indian Grace (No 1)* [1993] AC 410; *(No 2)* [1998] AC 878.

115 *Colt Industries Inc v Sarlie* (No.2) [1966] 1 WLR 1287.

116 *Re Macartney* [1921] 1 Ch 522.

117 *Dicey and Morris*, 14R-127.

118 *House of Spring Gardens Ltd v Waite* [1991] 1 QB 241, where it was held that alternatively an attempt to raise fraud was an abuse of the process of the court. See, generally, Richard Garnett, 'Fraud and Foreign Judgments: The Defence that Refuses to Die' (2002) Journal of Int Com Law 161.

119 *Dicey and Morris*, para 14R-149.

120 Ibid, para 14R-141.

121 Protection of Trading Interests Act 1980, s 5. See p 1087.

122 An action cannot be brought on the judgment when it is capable of registration under Pt I of the Foreign Judgments (Reciprocal Enforcement) Act 1933 (ibid, s 6) or the Civil Jurisdiction and Judgments Act 1982 (Case 42/76, *de Wolf v Cox BV* [1976] ECR 1759).

123 As in *Colt Industries Ltd v Sarlie* (No.2), n 115.

124 For the procedure, see CPR Sch 1 (RSC Ord 71.

(a)   where it is a Scottish or Northern Ireland judgment;[125]

(b)   where it falls within the Administration of Justice Act 1920 as a judgment of a superior court in a Commonwealth country with which there are reciprocal registration arrangements, not being a country covered by the Foreign Judgments (Reciprocal Enforcement) Act 1933;[126]

(c)   where it falls within the Foreign Judgments (Reciprocal Enforcement) Act 1933 as a judgment of a superior court of a country, within or outside the Commonwealth, with which there is reciprocity, other than a country which is a contracting state under the Regulation or Lugano Convention;

(d)   where it is an EU judgment to which the Secretary of State has appended an order for enforcement.[127]

Each of the enactments referred to in (a)–(d) above lays down grounds on which recognition may be refused, corresponding broadly to the grounds for refusal of recognition at common law. Where there are two conflicting judgments on the same issue in two different jurisdictions and each is unimpeachable, it is the first in time that will be recognized and enforced.[128]

Special provisions are contained in the Protection of Trading Interests Act 1980 in relation to a foreign judgment awarding multiple damages.[129] Such a judgment is not to be registered and no court is to entertain proceedings at common law for the recovery of any sum payable under it.[130] Further, where the judgment is given against a qualifying defendant,[131] who has made a payment to the party in whose favour the judgment was given or to a party entitled to contribution, the excess of the payment over the compensatory amount is recoverable in the proportion which the compensatory sum assessed by the court giving the judgment bears to the total amount awarded.[132] The statutory provisions reflect a concern over the exposure of United Kingdom individuals and businesses to awards of treble damages by United States courts. The award of treble damages automatically under a statute such as the American RICO statute[133] does not infect the whole sum awarded but merely that part of it which exceeds the compensatory amount.[134]

---

125   Section 18, Civil Jurisdiction and Judgments Act 1982.

126   Below.

127   European Communities (Enforcement of Community Judgments) Order 1972 (SI 1972/1590).

128   *Showlag v Mansour* [1994] 2 WLR 615; [1995] 1 AC 341 (PC).

129   That is, a judgment for an amount arrived at by doubling, trebling or otherwise multiplying a sum assessed as compensation for the loss or damage sustained by the person in whose favour the judgment was given (s 5(3)).

130   Section 5(1).

131   Ie a citizen of the United Kingdom and Colonies, a body corporate incorporated in the United Kingdom or in a territory outside the United Kingdom for whose international relations the United Kingdom government is responsible or a person carrying on business in the United Kingdom

132   Section 6(2).

133   The Racketeer Influenced and Corrupt Organizations Act.

134   *Lewis v Eliades* [2004] 1 All ER (Comm) 545.

5.   RECOGNITION AND ENFORCEMENT OF JUDGMENTS UNDER THE REGULATION

A judgment given in a Regulation state in a case within the Regulation must be recognized in other Regulation states[135] except in cases within art 34 or art 35 or governed by another convention to which Regulation states are or will become parties.[136] In contrast to the common law rules of recognition, the Regulation rules do not limit recognition to money judgments or those that are final and conclusive.

Under art 34 a judgment is not to be recognized (inter alia):

(a)   where recognition is contrary to public policy in the Regulation state in which recognition is sought;[137]

(b)   where it was given in default of appearance, if the defendant was not duly served with the initiating process in sufficient time for him to arrange for his defence; or

(c)   if the judgment is irreconcilable with a judgment given in a dispute between the same parties in the state in which recognition is sought, or is irreconcilable with an earlier judgment given in a non-Regulation state involving the same cause of action and between the same parties where this latter judgment fulfils the conditions necessary for its recognition in the state addressed.

Under art 35 a judgment is not to be recognized, inter alia, where it conflicts with ss 3, 4 or 6 of Ch II of the Regulation, which deal respectively with jurisdiction in relation to insurance and consumer contracts and with exclusive jurisdiction. Subject to this, the jurisdiction of the court of origin may not be reviewed and the public policy exception may not be applied to the rules relating to jurisdiction. Under art 36 a foreign judgment may in no circumstances be reviewed as to its substance.

The registration procedure previously referred to does not apply to judgments within the Regulation, for which the sole permitted enforcement machinery is that

---

135   Article 33.

136   Article 71.

137   Clearly, reliance on this ground of refusal of recognition should be exercised extremely sparingly if the Regulation is not to be seriously weakened: as is illustrated by Case C-7/98 *Krombach v Bamberski* [2000] ECR I-1935 and Case C-38/98 *Regie Nationaledes Usines Renault SA v Maxicar Spa*, May 11, 2000. In *Maronier v Larmer* [2003] 1 All ER (Comm) 225, the Court of Appeal, while stressing the strong presumption that judgments of another Regulation state complied with art 6 of the 1950 European Convention on Human Rights, held that it would be contrary to public policy to enforce a judgment in The Netherlands against a defendant who was unaware that proceedings against him had been reactivated and was neither present nor represented at the trial. Similarly, in *Pordea v Times Newspapers Ltd* [2000] ILPr 763, M Lemontey (President), Cour de Cassation (Fr) a defamation action brought in England by the claimant, a French resident and national, was dismissed when he failed to comply with an order to provide security for costs. The defendant obtained an order for costs and sought to enforce it in France. Pordea eventually appealed to the Cour de Cassation, where his appeal was allowed on the basis that the right of access to courts under the European Convention of Human Rights art 6(1) is a matter of international public policy within the meaning of the Brussels Convention 1968 art 27(1); and that the enforcement of the costs order was contrary to public policy because the costs were disproportionately high and prevented Pordea obtaining access to justice contrary to art 6 of the European Convention of Human Rights.

specified in the Regulation itself.[138] For the United Kingdom, art 38 and s 4 of the Civil Jurisdiction and Judgments Act 1982[139] prescribe an application to register the judgment for enforcement. This application is made *ex parte*,[140] a procedure designed to ensure that the defendant does not remove his assets from the jurisdiction before the grant of a freezing injunction[141] or other protective measures to secure enforcement of the judgment. Once a judgment in the state of origin has been declared enforceable, it must be enforced there.[142] But the defendant has a right of appeal,[143] and there are various requirements and restrictions designed to safeguard his interests.[144]

6.   DETERMINING THE APPLICABLE LAW: SOME PRELIMINARY POINTS

The fact that the court of a particular country has jurisdiction to entertain a claim does not necessarily mean that its own law will govern the dispute. Jurisdiction and applicable law are entirely distinct questions.[145] It is for the forum to apply its own conflict of laws rules to determine by what law the matters in issue are to be decided, and such rules may lead to the application of its own law or that of one or more foreign states. Similarly, it is for the *lex fori* to determine the conditions in which, and the extent to which, a choice of law by the parties will be given effect. Where a state has adopted in its internal law a conflict of laws convention or a conflict rule in a substantive law convention, then its courts apply the convention or the rule, as the case may be, as part of its private international law, as in the case of the EEC contracts convention concluded in Rome in 1980.[146]

In contract and commercial matters the law determined by conflict of laws rules denotes the domestic law of the state in question, excluding its rules of private international law. In short, the doctrine of *renvoi* does not apply.

---

138   Case 42/76, n 122.
139   As modified by Sch 1, art 2 of SI 2001/3929.
140   Article 42. The procedure is prescribed by CPR Sch 1(RSC Ord 71, Pt III).
141   See p 1151.
142   Article 38.
143   Article 43; which also gives the claimant a right of appeal against refusal of an order for enforcement.
144   See *Cheshire and North*, pp 489–494.
145   Though the applicable law may influence jurisdiction. The link between the Regulation and the Rome Convention has already been mentioned (see p 1076). So far as English procedure is concerned, CPR 6.20 confers jurisdiction on an English court over disputes on a contract governed by English law. Moreover, a clause submitting disputes to the jurisdiction of the English courts or to arbitration in England is prima facie indicative of an intention to subject the contract itself to English law (*The Komninos S* [1990] 1 Lloyd's Rep 541; *Compagnie d'Armement Maritime SA v Compagnie Tunisienne de Navigation SA* [1971] AC 572), though this inference is less strong in cases within the Regulation. See the *Council Report on the law applicable to contractual obligations* by Mario Giuliano and Paul Lagarde (OJ C282, 31.1080, p 1), para 3; and generally J. J. Fawcett, 'The Interrelationships of jurisdiction and choice of law in private international law' *Current Legal Problems 1991* (1991) 39.
146   The convention on the law applicable to contractual obligations. See pp 1095 ff.

The conflict rule to be applied depends on the way in which the *lex fori* characterizes the issue, that is, determines the legal category to which the issue is to be assigned. Of particular importance is the distinction between a contractual issue, which in England was formerly determined by the proper law of the contract and is now governed by the Rome Convention, and a property issue, which is typically governed by the *lex situs* (or *lex rei sitae*). Upon this characterization depends the connecting factor, that is, the fact that links the issue to a particular legal system. In the case of a contractual question, the connecting factor is, as a starting position, the place of business of the party whose performance is characteristic of the contract. In the case of an issue relating to property, it is the location of the asset at the time of the relevant dealing or other event. In classifying the issue the court has regard to the international character of the matter rather than the classification adopted for purely domestic cases, so that, for example, where the case involves determining the law applicable to the rights of a party to whom a promise was made which would be binding under the law of the due place of performance though lacking the consideration required by English law, the court would treat the question as contractual even though under English law there would be no contract.[147] Not every classification under domestic law is relevant for conflict of laws purposes. Thus while the conflict rule varies according to whether, for example, the issue relates to contract or property, it is immaterial for conflicts purposes whether a transfer of property is classified by domestic law as an outright transfer or a transfer by way of security. In both cases the applicable law is the *lex situs*.

(i)   The various theories of choice of law in contract

In their ceaseless quest for the Holy Grail of certainty courts and scholars of different countries have over many years striven for rules of universal application which would lead ineluctably to the appropriate law governing contractual disputes. Most systems have agreed that within certain limits the parties themselves should be free to choose the law by which their rights are to be determined.[148] But where the intention of the parties has not been made manifest, the courts themselves have had to fashion rules of selection; and it is widely accepted that they cannot be deprived of the power to determine the applicable law by a provision of the agreement purporting to exclude the application of all law or rules of law. Even where the agreement contains an arbitration clause empowering the arbitral tribunal to act as *amiable compositeur* or to give a decision *ex aequo et bono*, thus freeing it from the obligation (though not the right) to apply rules which it considers would produce an unfair result, the tribunal remains bound by internationally mandatory rules or international public policy.

The range of options for determination of the applicable law in the absence of party choice is formidable: the nationality, the place of residence or place of business of one of the parties; the place where the contract was made; the contractual place of performance; the place having the closest connection with the contract; the location

---

147   *Re Bonacina, Le Brasseur v Bonacina* [1912] 2 Ch 394.
148   See, for England, *Vita Food Products Inc v Unus Shipping Co Ltd* [1939] AC 277.

of the subject matter of the contract; the place where the breach complained of was committed; the forum; the state having the most compelling interest in the dispute. The spectrum of theories runs from highly mechanical rules at one end to policy approaches at the other which are so generalized as to amount to little more than an exhortation to the courts to select whatever law seems appropriate in the particular case. Moreover, it was long ago seen that not all aspects of the transaction ought necessarily to be governed by the same law. For example, the formal validity of a contract has usually been regarded as governed by the place where the contract was made, whereas the connection of such place with performance of the contract might be too tenuous to make it appropriate for disputes as to the substantive effect of the contract. Further, the selection of the applicable law is influenced in no small measure by the way in which the issue before the court is classified.[149]

In order to reduce the problems created by the prevalence of different theories in different states there was a concerted effort over the last half of the twentieth century to harmonize conflict of laws rules in specific areas. This, indeed, is the *raison d'être* of the Hague Conference on Private International Law, the activities of which have resulted in a number of conflict of laws conventions, though few of these have been significantly concerned with contract or commercial law. In 1980 there came a breakthrough with the conclusion in Rome of the EEC Convention on the Law Applicable to Contractual Obligations. As stated earlier, the Rome Convention was given effect in the United Kingdom by the Contracts (Applicable Law) Act 1990, and, since it is universal in application,[150] it displaces the common law conflict rules relating to contracts except as regards matters excluded from the scope of the convention. Accordingly, the common law rules will not be considered further.

Like most harmonizing measures, the Rome Convention had a long gestation period, a full decade elapsing between the start of the work and the conclusion. It was intended to cover both contractual and non-contractual obligations, but at a later stage it was decided to leave non-contractual obligations to be dealt with in a separate convention, and the provisions relating to these were accordingly jettisoned.[151] Nevertheless, even in its reduced scope the Convention represents a major advance towards the resolution of problems arising from lack of uniformity in conflict rules affecting contracts. To understand the Convention it is first necessary to grapple with a few preliminary conflict of laws issues concerning contracts.

(ii) Selection and incorporation

In principle, the parties to a contract are free to subject its interpretation and effect to the law of their choice.[152] This may be done either by selection or by incorporation. The former involves the selection of a designated law as a whole to control the contract, the law then imposing itself on the parties *ab extra*. The latter entails the incorporation by reference of particular statutory provisions so as to make these

---

149 See p 1095.
150 See p 1096.
151 For detailed commentaries on the draft convention in the form in which it was prior to this point, see K. Lipstein (ed), *Harmonisation of Private International Law by the EEC* (1978).
152 See p 1097.

terms of the contract as if expressly set out in the contract document. For example, a contract of sale which provides that 'this contract shall be governed by English law' has the effect of applying English law not as terms of the contract but as a body of law operating externally on the contract in the same way as if it had been a domestic transaction. On the other hand, a provision that 'the Sale of Goods Act 1979 shall apply to this contract' is merely a shorthand form of reproducing the wording of the Act as express terms of the contract. The difference in effect between selection and incorporation is usually said to be that in the former case the governing law is that which exists from time to time, so that the parties by implication subject themselves to post-contract changes in the law, whereas in the latter case the designated statutory provisions operate as contract terms in the form in which they exist at the time of the contract.[153] It is questionable whether this is a necessary and inherent consequence of the distinction between selection and incorporation. What has been incorporated into the contract is a question of construction. No doubt the presumption is that the parties intended to be bound by the provisions of the Sale of Goods Act only in the form they took at the date of the agreement, but there is nothing to stop them, expressly or impliedly, from subjecting the contract to automatic variation through changes in the statute.[154] Equally, it is presumably open to the parties to decide that only those rules of a legal system that are in force at the time of the contract shall govern their rights. The real distinction between selection and incorporation is that selection involves subjection to the whole corpus of the chosen law, attracting even its mandatory rules[155] and displacing those of what would otherwise be the applicable law, whereas incorporation entails merely the transplanting of a specific part of the designated law into the contract as ordinary terms of the contract, leaving the rights and duties of the parties to be governed by the applicable law as determined by the conflict of laws rules of the forum.

Under English conflict of laws rules, selection of an applicable law is confined to the law of a state or public international law.[156] The adoption by the parties of rules which do not constitute a complete legal system operates only by way of incorporation as terms of the contract, not as an effective choice of law. This is the case whether the rules selected are the uncodified principles of the *lex mercatoria*, a codification of principles such as the UNIDROIT Principles of International Contracts or even a convention. So, in an action in England a purported selection of the Vienna Sales Convention as the applicable law will be treated as a contractual incorporation of the rules set out in the Convention, not as a choice of law. If the position were otherwise, an English court would find itself obliged to apply the Convention solely by reason of a private agreement between the parties despite the

---

153 *Dicey and Morris*, paras 32-086–32-088.

154 Moreover, as has been pointed out, the governing law may itself have something to say as to whether amendments to it are to apply to contracts previously concluded. See D. St. L. Kelly, 'Reference, Choice, Restriction and Prohibition' (1977) 26 ICLQ 857 at p 859.

155 Ole Lando, III *International Encyclopaedia of Comparative Law* (ed K Zweigert and Ulrich Drobnig), Chap 24, *Contracts* (1977), para 26. For the meaning of 'mandatory rules', see *below*.

156 But see *Deutsche Schachtbau- und Tiefbohrgesellschaft mbH v R'as Al Khaimah National Oil Co* [1990]1 AC 295 at 306 ff in the context of arbitration. The decision was partly reversed by the House of Lords on other grounds.

fact that under English conflict of laws rules the agreement was governed by English law and the United Kingdom has not ratified the Convention.

(iii) Dispositive and mandatory rules and rules of public policy

Rules of law, whether of the common law or prescribed by legislation, are of two kinds: dispositive (*ius dispotivum*) and mandatory (*ius cogens*). Dispositive (or suppletive) rules are those designed to regulate the rights and obligations of contracting parties on matters for which they have not provided in their agreement. Such rules may therefore be freely varied or excluded in their entirety by the terms of the contract. Examples are the provisions of the Sale of Goods Act 1979, which are for the most part (though not entirely) gap-filling provisions intended to provide a rule for situations not covered by the terms of the contract.[157] Mandatory rules are positive rules of law which the parties cannot vary or exclude by the terms of their agreement. Into this category fall certain common law rules (eg that a promise is not enforceable without consideration) and legislative provisions which are designed to override inconsistent contractual terms, such as the Consumer Credit Act 1974 and other consumer protection legislation.

Mandatory rules are to be distinguished from rules of public policy or morals rendering a contractual provision void or unenforceable. Whereas mandatory rules are rules of positive application, rules of public policy operate negatively, requiring the court to deny effect to an otherwise valid contract. In general, the effect of the two sets of rules is similar, though a contract which offends against public policy or morals is likely to be rendered wholly unenforceable, whereas a contract which is inconsistent with mandatory rules usually remains valid and enforceable except so far as inconsistent with those rules.

(iv) The spatial reach of mandatory rules and rules of public policy

Mandatory rules and rules of public policy are themselves of two kinds: those which are bounded only by the conflict of laws and those whose spatial reach is determined exclusively by the *lex fori* or the domestic law of some third state. Into the former category fall the many kinds of rule, both common law and statutory, which come into play as part of the applicable law under conflict of laws rules and which English public policy does not regard as necessary to impose on contracts governed by a foreign law. Though such rules cannot be excluded or varied by agreement where English law applies, the parties may avoid their application by choosing a foreign law to govern their contract. Examples are the rule of contract law requiring a promise not made by deed to be supported by consideration, the rule against penalties, and the statutory requirement for certain types of contract to be in or evidenced by writing. Rules of this kind do not have such a strong social or public interest content as to require them to apply to contracts which the parties have chosen to subject to a foreign law. Similarly, rules of public policy will be applied with less rigour to contracts governed by foreign law than to those governed by

---

157   Sale of Goods Act 1979, s 55(1).

English law. Again, there is a presumption that English legislation which does not embody some fundamental policy objective, such as the protection of consumers or employees, the safeguarding of the economy or the implementation of an international convention or treaty obligation, and which is silent as to its spatial reach, is bounded by conflict of laws rules and will thus apply only where the contract is governed by English law.[158]

But there are other rules which have such a strong social or economic imperative that they will be considered to apply, within their own terms, even to a contract which is otherwise governed by foreign law.[159] These rules, which for brevity we shall refer to as super-mandatory rules,[160] are themselves of two kinds, those which are spatially limited, that is, restricted to cases involving one or more connecting factors linking the issue to this country (eg the fact that the defendant carries on business in England or that England is the place for performance), and those which are universal, ie spatially unlimited. Whether mandatory rules are spatially limited or overriding is a matter for the internal law of the forum (or of a third state to whose law reference is being made), not of the conflict of laws.

Spatially limited rules which apply regardless of the applicable law under conflict of laws rules usually derive from statute. The connecting factors may be spelled out, but more often than not the legislation is silent and the court has to determine from the underlying policy whether the connections with this country are sufficiently strong and relevant to trigger the application of the statute. Most consumer protection statutes fall within this category, as do, for example, the Hague-Visby Rules.[161] By contrast, spatially unlimited rules are rules which are regarded as of such importance that they will be applied in every case coming before the court, even where it has no connections with England at all. For example, an English court will not enforce a contract to commit an act which would be a serious offence under the *lex actus*, whether English or foreign, even if the contract is expressed to be governed by a foreign law which would allow enforcement. Since such a rule of public policy is universal in scope, the question of a connecting factor does not arise.

(v)   Super-mandatory rules do not nullify the applicable law

Super-mandatory rules, even if universal in character, do not replace the applicable law; they simply override it within the scope of their provisions. So if a particular provision in a contract governed by French law is held to infringe a super-mandatory provision of an English statute, French law nevertheless remains the applicable law

---

158   *Dicey and Morris*, paras 32-227–32-238.2.

159   However, there is probably a presumption that such rules are intended only to override choice of law clauses designed to evade them and do not apply to a contract which objectively determined (ie disregarding any choice of law clause) is governed by a foreign law. This was the approach adopted by the Hong Kong High Court in *Hong Kong and Shanghai (Shipping) Ltd v Owners of Ships or Vessels 'Cavalry' (Panamanian flag)* [1987] HKLR 287, applying a dictum of Dixon J in *Wanganui Rangitikei Electric Power Board v Australian Mutual Provident Society* (1934) 50 CLR 581 at 601, and not following *English v Donnelly* 1958 SC 494.

160   Also termed 'overriding', or 'internationally mandatory'.

161   See p 1031.

and will be applied in a dispute before an English court, but on the basis that the contractual provision in question is unenforceable. What effect this has on the rest of the contract will be determined by French law, not by English law.

(vi) Adoption of mandatory rules by a choice of law

Where parties choose a particular law to govern their contract there is a presumption that they choose the whole of that law as it affects their contract, including the mandatory rules.[162] But they do not thereby adopt super-mandatory rules, for these apply by their own force, not by virtue of any rule of the conflict of laws, and their scope cannot be enlarged by the parties' choice of law. So parties cannot, for example, contract into the registration and other requirements of the Bills of Sale Acts by selecting English law as the applicable law of a contract that would otherwise be governed by a foreign law.[163]

7. THE ROME CONVENTION ON THE LAW APPLICABLE TO CONTRACTUAL OBLIGATIONS[164]

The Rome Convention lays down rules for determining what law is to be applied to determine contractual obligations. The Convention applies both to contracts containing a choice of law clause (which will usually, though not invariably, be given effect) and to those which do not. In each case the reference is to the internal law of the country specified, to the exclusion of its rules of private international law,[165] so that the doctrine of *renvoi* has no role to play.

(i) Interpretation

The principles and rules of interpretation governing the Rome Convention have much in common with those affecting the Regulation.[166] Their autonomous nature is apparent from art 18, which requires that in their interpretation and application regard is to be had to their international character and to the desirability of achieving uniformity in their interpretation and application. So in determining whether an obligation is contractual or tortious, an English court must not use characterizations under English law but must apply the autonomous interpretative rules to be derived from the Convention itself and, if not referred to the European Court of Justice in accordance with the Brussels Protocol,[167] from principles laid

---

162 However, the chosen law may have provisions excluding its own application in such a case. For example, under s 27(1) of the Unfair Contract Terms Act 1977 the Act does not apply where UK law applies only by choice of the parties and but for this the contract would be governed by a foreign law.

163 See *Halsbury's Laws of England*, vol.4(1) (4th edn, reissue 1992), para 618.

164 See Richard Plender, *The European Contracts Convention: the Rome Convention on the Choice of Law for Contracts* (2nd edn, 2001); Jonathan Hill, 'Choice of Law in Contract under the Rome Convention: the Approach of the UK Courts' (2004) ICLQ 325.

165 Article 15.

166 See p 1076.

167 However, the Protocol is not yet in force and is unlikely to be brought into force in view of the intention to convert the Rome Convention into a regulation.

down by decisions of the European Court.[168] The court may consider the Giuliano and Lagarde Report in ascertaining the meaning or effect of any provision of the Convention.[169] The House of Lords, and other courts when acting as appeal courts, may request the European Court to give a preliminary ruling on a question raised in a case before pending the appellate court as to interpretation of the Convention.[170]

(ii) Precedence of EU law

Provisions laying down choice of law rules which are contained in acts of the EU's institutions (directives, regulations etc) or in national laws harmonized in implementation of such acts have precedence over the rules in the Rome Convention.[171]

(iii) Scope of the Convention *ratione materiae*

The rules of the Convention apply to contractual obligations in any situation involving a choice between the laws of different countries,[172] other than those excluded under art 2(2) and (3). Decisions under the Brussels Convention, and now the Regulation, may be relevant in determining whether an obligation is a contractual obligation, though the phrase 'matters relating to a contract' therein is probably somewhat wider in scope.[173]

Article 1(2) lists the contractual obligations to which the Convention does not apply. These include questions involving the status or legal capacity of natural persons; obligations arising from negotiable instruments, arbitration agreements and agreements on the choice of court;[174] questions of company law; questions whether an agent is able to bind a principal, or an organ to bind a company or body corporate or unincorporate, to a third party; and contracts of insurance other than reinsurance. With these exceptions the Convention is universal in character, requiring any law which it specifies to be applied whether or not it is the law of a contracting state.[175] So, if the Convention rules lead to the application of the law of the State of New York, that law must be applied even though the United States is not a party to the Convention or, indeed, a member of the EU. The Convention itself

---

168   Contracts (Applicable Law) Act 1990, s 3(1).
169   Ibid, s 3(3).
170   First Protocol, arts 1, 2. These provisions differ from those of the Regulation in that a court acting as a court of first instance may not refer a case and the House of Lords, though able to refer a case, is not bound to do so.
171   Article 20.
172   Article 1(1).
173   There is a discussion of this, interestingly, in an Australian case: *Reinsurance Australia Corporation Limited v HIH Casualty and General Insurance Ltd (in liquidation)* [2003] FCA 56, paras 305–318.
174   So a jurisdiction clause, if valid under art 23 of the Regulation, is to be interpreted according to the applicable law under common law conflict of laws rules, not under the Rome Convention. However, the Convention rules may be expected to influence the future formulation of the common law rules.
175   Article 2.

has the force of law in England[176] and cannot be excluded or modified by agreement of the parties.[177]

(iv) Scope of the applicable law

The law applicable to a contract by virtue of arts 3 to 6 and 12 governs, in particular, interpretation, performance, the consequences of breach, including the assessment of damages,[178] the various ways of extinguishing obligations and the consequences of nullity of the contract.[179] However, in relation to the manner of performance and steps to be taken in the event of defective performance, regard is to be had to the law of the country in which performance takes place.[180] This embodies a principle well established in the English conflict of laws. One of its effects is that the court will not compel performance of a contract which would be unlawful under the *lex loci solutionis*.

(v) Party autonomy

1. The principle of party autonomy

The principle of party autonomy is everywhere recognized in the conflict of laws. Article 3(1) reflects this, providing that a contract shall be governed by the law chosen by the parties. The choice must be expressed or demonstrated with reasonable certainty by the terms of the contract or the circumstances of the case.[181] This emphasizes the point that art 3(1) is concerned with the intention of the parties, not with objective criteria. The rule that selection of England as the jurisdiction to entertain disputes in actions or arbitrations is considered strong evidence of an intention to choose English law[182] has been held applicable for the purposes of art 3.[183] By 'the law'[184] is meant the law of a state.[185] This is not to say that the incorporation of references to 'the *lex mercatoria*', 'general principles of law' or the UNIDROIT Principles of International

---

176 Contracts (Applicable Law) Act 1990, s 2(1).

177 With no disrespect to the late Dr Francis Mann, a distinguished jurist who was reluctant to envisage any convention as operative if not forming part of the applicable law despite its being given the force of law in England, and who considered that neither the Hague-Visby Rules nor the Rome Convention were applicable if excluded by contract. See *British Year Book of International Law 1972–73* 117 at pp 125–126; (1979) 95 LQR 346; and (1991) 107 LQR 353 at p 355.

178 But in these cases this is only within the limits of the powers conferred on the court by its procedural law.

179 Article 10(1).

180 Article 10(2).

181 Article 3(1). Despite the 'or', English courts have followed the Giuliano and Lagarde Report, n 145, in having regard to both. See, for example, *Marubeni Hong Kong and South China Ltd v Mongolian Government* [2002] 2 All ER (Comm) 873.

182 See p 1076.

183 *Egon Oldendorff v Libera Corp* [1996] 1 Lloyd's Rep 380.

184 Article 1(1).

185 *Dicey and Morris*, para 32–079; *Cheshire and North*, p 559. This conclusion is reinforced by the distinction now drawn in international commercial arbitration between 'law' and 'rules of law'. See p 1181.

Contracts is of no effect. The first two, so far as ascertainable, can be applied by the court, and the UNIDROIT Principles, being set out in a published text, can be resorted to without difficulty in many cases; indeed, in international arbitration arbitrators have resorted to all three of these sources of rights. But they can take effect only as terms of the contract incorporated by reference, not as part of the applicable law, and they are not within the scope of the Rome Convention. The same applies to the incorporation of provisions of the Vienna Sales Convention where this has not been adopted by the state whose law is applicable to the contract.[186]

What is not clear is whether selection of the applicable law falls within art 3(1) where the choice is made not by direct agreement between the parties but by one of them only or by a third party pursuant to a power conferred on him by the agreement. In other words, is a choice made *under* the agreement to be equated with a choice made *by* the agreement? This would seem to be the case.[187]

2.   Dépeçage

The parties can select the law applicable to the whole of their contract or only part of it.[188] So they are free to engage in dépeçage by subjecting different obligations to different laws, though this may not be possible for 'the general obligation'[189] or for rights or groups of rights so interconnected that to subject them to different laws would be unworkable. Another form of dépeçage which now seems to be sanctioned, in the light of the parties' freedom to change the applicable law,[190] is one under which the law of State A is made applicable as regards rights accrued up to a particular point in time or until the occurrence of a stated event while rights accrued subsequent to the time or event are determined by the law of State B.

3.   Changing the applicable law; 'floating law'

Article 3(2) allows the parties to agree at any time to subject the contract to a law other than that which previously governed it, whether that law resulted from an earlier choice or from the Convention provisions. This provision appears to permit a wide diversity of change of law clauses, including a change of the applicable law either prospectively or retrospectively, and a choice of alternative laws, depending on alternative specified events. However, it seems that art 3(2) envisages a change of law only by a new agreement, not by a provision for change in the original agreement, and that it does not cover the case of a 'floating law' under which the

---

186   See p 918. It would be surprising if it were not, given that even an implied choice of law is
        considered to fall within art 3(1).
187   *Egon Oldendorff v Libera Corp*, n 183, at 380, 387.
188   Article 3(1).
189   The undesirability of this has been endorsed by the Court of Appeal in *Centrax Ltd v Citibank*
        [1999] 1 All ER (Comm.) 557, 562 (CA) per Ward LJ, approving *Dicey and Morris*,
        para 32-049.22
190   See below.

choice of law is left to be determined by a party at a later date, leaving the applicable law up to that date to be determined by the provisions of the Convention.[191]

4. Restrictions on party autonomy

At common law the only restriction on the parties' freedom to choose their law was that the choice had to be 'bona fide and legal'; the courts saw no objection to parties selecting English law to govern their contract even where there was no point of contact with England.[192] The wisdom of this approach is shown by the fact that parties frequently choose English law, despite the fact that neither they nor the contract are connected with England, because they consider it to provide a sound basis for allocating rights and duties in commercial transactions; and what state could resist such flattery? The same freedom is given by the Rome Convention, but the restrictions on it are now provided by the Convention itself, not by the common law.

It goes without saying that, in general, parties to a contract, though able to choose the law which is to govern their own relationship, cannot impose that law (or any other) on third parties. A major exception to this principle is provided by the 2001 Hague Convention on the law applicable to certain rights in respect of securities held with an intermediary.[193]

5. Preservation of mandatory rules

Various provisions of the Convention, including art 3 on party autonomy, are expressed to be without prejudice to the relevant mandatory rules. Unfortunately, the phrase 'mandatory rules' is used in two different senses in the Convention. In art 7 it is employed in the narrow sense to denote what we have called super-mandatory rules, ie only those rules which the parties cannot exclude even by selecting a foreign law. Elsewhere in the Convention, for example in arts 3(3) and 5, the phrase is used in a broad sense to cover all rules incapable of exclusion by agreement, whether or not they are excludable by the choice of a foreign law. In the French text these two meanings are distinguished, mandatory rules in the broad sense being described as '*dispositions impératives*' and in the narrow, super-mandatory, sense as '*lois de police*'.

---

191 See M. N. Howard [1995] LMCLQ 1, at pp 7–8. English common law declined to recognize floating choice of law clauses on the grounds, first, that the governing law could not be changed retrospectively and, secondly, that the contract could not be left without a proper law pending the post-contract selection (*The Iran Vojdan* [1984] 2 Lloyd's Rep 380; *Armar Shipping Co Ltd v Caisse Algerienne d'Assurance et de Reassurance* [1981] 1 WLR 207). The second of these two propositions was directed against the view of Mustill J at first instance that, pending selection, the proper law was 'floating'. But this is not a necessary conclusion. The fact that the parties have deferred an express choice of law until a later date does not mean that until then the contract is without an applicable law, merely that the applicable law up to the time of selection has to be determined by conflict of laws rules without reference to any choice by the parties. So at the end of the day the only true objection at common law was to a contractual provision for change in the applicable law. This objection appears to survive art 3(3).

192 *Vita Food Products Inc v Unus Shipping Co Ltd*, n 148.

193 See p 1111.

6.   Purely domestic transactions

Where all the elements relevant to the situation, other than the selection of a foreign law with or without a foreign tribunal, are connected with one country only, the choice of law does not prejudice the application of that country's mandatory rules, that is, rules which cannot be derogated from by contract.[194] So if, for example, a contract is concluded in France between two French companies and provides for performance in France, the parties cannot, by selecting English law to govern what is essentially a French domestic contract, bypass the mandatory provisions of French law as to the formalities of contract. Article 3(3) is, in practical terms, significant only where the transaction is a domestic transaction of a foreign country; where the transaction is English and the parties choose a foreign law, an English court will typically resort to the wider provisions of art 7(2), which apply even if no elements, or only some elements, of the situation are connected with England. It would seem that despite the definition of 'mandatory rules' in art 3(3), it will apply only if it would have applied under the law of the foreign country concerned had it been the chosen law.[195]

7.   Consumer contracts

Where the making of a consumer contract involves points of contact, of a kind mentioned in art 5(2), with the country of the debtor's habitual residence, a choice of law does not deprive the consumer of the protection afforded to him by the mandatory rules of the country concerned.[196] Suppose, for example, that goods to the value of £1,000 are sold by an Italian company to a consumer buyer habitually resident in England, the contract is expressed to be governed by Italian law and provides for payment in Italy by twelve monthly instalments, and the Italian seller received the consumer's order in England. In such a case the choice of Italian law cannot override any applicable mandatory provisions of English law. Two points should be noted. First, in the example given, the choice of law clause is not displaced; the contract continues to be governed by Italian law but takes effect subject to any applicable mandatory rules of English law. Secondly, since the Consumer Credit Act is super-mandatory in character, the spatial reach of its provisions is determined by the Act itself, not by the applicable law under the Rome Convention. So the mere fact that art 5(2) routes the case to English mandatory rules does not enlarge the spatial application of the Act, which an English court might conclude does not as a matter of construction apply in view of the foreign elements involved.

8.   Third country with which situation has a close connection

Article 7(1) empowers the court to give effect to the mandatory rules of another country with which the situation has a close connection. However, the United Kingdom has exercised the right to disapply art 7(1), which, accordingly, has no effect in the United Kingdom.[197]

---

194 Article 3(3).
195 *Chitty on Contracts* (29th edn, 2004), para 31–060.
196 Article 5(2).
197 Contracts (Applicable Law) Act 1990, s 2(2).

9. Mandatory rules of the forum

Under art 7(2) nothing in the Convention is to restrict the application of the rules of the law of the forum in a situation where they are mandatory irrespective of the law otherwise applicable to the contract. It will be seen that art 7(2) is confined to what we have called super-mandatory rules, that is, rules which cannot be excluded even by choice of a foreign law. So where the contract is expressed to be governed by German law, art 7(2) does not enable an English court to decline to enforce the contract on the ground that it is not evidenced in writing as required by the Statute of Frauds,[198] or to enforce a liquidated damages provision on the ground that it infringes the rule against penalties, because these are not super-mandatory rules. By contrast, the court will apply the Hague-Visby Rules to a contract falling within its scope even if the parties have chosen to govern their contract the law of a country that has not adopted the Rules, because the Hague-Visby Rules have the status of super-mandatory rules in England.[199]

10. Public policy (ordre public) rules of the forum

Under art 16 the application of a rule of law of any country specified by the Convention may be refused only if such application is manifestly incompatible with the public policy (*ordre public*) of the forum. In contrast to the provisions of the Convention on mandatory rules, which are rules of positive application overriding the terms of the contract between the parties, art 16 sets out the circumstances in which the court can invoke a rule of rejection to refuse to apply a rule of foreign law that would otherwise be applicable. The court may invoke art 16 only where the application of the rules of foreign law would be 'manifestly incompatible' with the public policy of the forum. This sends a signal to national courts that art 16 should be used only in exceptional cases and that national courts should be slow to invoke purely domestic perceptions of public policy to deny efficacy to contractual provisions that would be valid under the applicable law as determined by the Convention. Into this category would fall, for example, a contract to commit an act which under English law would be a serious offence or would infringe Community public policy[200] or public international law.[201]

(vi) Applicable law in the absence of choice

To the extent that the law applicable to the contract has not been chosen by the parties in accordance with art 3 the contract is governed by the law of the country with which it is most closely connected.[202] This mirrors the common law rule. It applies in every case where there is no agreement on choice of law, save that a severable part of a contract which has a closer connection with another country may, by exception, be governed by the law of that other country.[203]

---

198 Eg, for a guarantee.
199 See p 1034.
200 Giuliano–Lagarde Report, n 145, commentary on art 16.
201 *Kuwait Airways Corp v Iraqi Airways* Co [2002] 2 AC 883; [2002] UKHL 19 (HL).
202 Article 4(1).
203 Ibid.

Article 4 lays down presumptions as to the country with which the contract is most closely connected. For this purpose we shall assume that both parties are acting in the course of business. The primary presumption is that the contract is most closely connected with the principal place of business of the party who is to effect the performance which is characteristic of the contract or, where the performance is to be effected through another place of business, the country in which that other place of business is situated.[204] In the case of unilateral contracts, where only one party makes a promise, it is obviously that party's performance which is characteristic of the contract. So in a unilateral contract of guarantee the characteristic performance is necessarily that of the guarantor, who is the sole party undertaking duties under the contract. In the case of bilateral contracts the general principle is that where the performance due on one side is payment of money and on the other a non-monetary obligation, it is the latter which is treated as characteristic of the contract. So in a contract of sale of goods it is delivery, not payment, which is the performance characteristic of the contract; in a construction contract, the performance of the construction works; in an agency contract, the performance due from the agent; in a letter of credit transaction, the place at which the beneficiary is entitled to be paid.[205]

But it is important to keep in mind that the place of closest connection is not where the characteristic performance is to take place but where the party who is to perform has his place of business. This marks a departure from the common law rule, which looked at the due place of performance of the obligation characteristic of the contract. The Convention rule, which had its origin in decisions of the Swiss and Dutch courts, has two important advantages. It avoids arguments as to the due place of performance, and it enables a party to have all the contracts of which he is the 'characteristic performer' presumptively governed by the same law instead of this being made to depend on the due place of performance under each separate contract.

It is, however, necessary to respect the autonomy of bank payment undertakings such as documentary credits and demand guarantees and counter-guarantees. In *Wahda Bank v Arab Bank plc*[206] Staughton LJ took issue with the statement in art 2(b) of the ICC's Uniform Rules for Demand Guarantees (URDG)[207] that counter-guarantees are separate from the guarantees in respect of which they have given, and expressed the view that bankers would find unattractive the rule in art 27 that the law governing the counter-guarantee is that of its issuer, and therefore will usually be different from the law governing the guarantee itself. However, the attention of the learned Lord Justice had evidently not been drawn to the fact that the URDG were prepared after

204   Article 4(2). See generally Hill (2004) ICLQ 325.
205   In the case of a confirmed credit this will usually be the branch of the confirming bank where payment is to be made; in the case of an unconfirmed credit, the branch of the issuing bank where payment is to be made. See *Bank of Baroda v Vysya Bank Ltd* [1994] 2 Lloyd's Rep 87 and C. G. J Morse, 'Letters of credit and the Rome Convention' [1994] LMCLQ 560. See also *Bank of Credit and Commerce Hong Kong Ltd v Somali Bank* [1995] 1 Lloyd's Rep 227, which, though not involving the Rome Convention, contains a useful analysis of the closest connection test in relation to letters of credit. In the case of a counter-guarantee, the applicable law will usually be that of the issuer of the counter-guarantee. See below.
206   [1996] 1 Lloyd's Rep 470.
207   See p 1019.

extensive consultation among experts over a long period and were approved both by the ICC's Commission on International Commercial Practice and by its Banking Commission, both of which drew their membership from bankers and others of long experience in jurisdictions around the world. The autonomy of the counter-guarantee expressed by the rules reflects banking practice and is essential for the smooth running of the system, since banks issuing counter-guarantees cannot be expected to concern themselves with issues concerning the validity or enforceability of the counter-guarantee, any more than banks issuing the primary guarantee can be required to consider the underlying transaction. Moreover, the rule that a counter-guarantee is governed by the law of its issuer follows the general rule of the Rome Convention in looking to the place of business of the party whose performance is characteristic of the contract.

Of course, there will be cases where it may be difficult, if not impossible, to identify performance on one side as more characteristic than performance on the other, as in the case of international loan agreements, barter transactions and distribution agreements. For such cases art 4(5) operates to exclude art 4(2) if the characteristic performance cannot be determined, and also provides that the presumptions in art 4(2) and (5) are, in any event, to be disregarded if it appears from the circumstances as a whole that the contract is more closely connected with another country.

Article 4(4) provides a special rule for contracts of carriage of goods.

(vii) Validity of the contract

The rules as to the law governing validity of the contract follow those of the common law. The existence and material validity of the contract or of any term of the contract are to be determined by the law which would govern it under the Convention if the contract or term were valid.[208] This reference to the putative applicable law does, of course, involve assuming the very question in issue, but one has to begin somewhere, and this *petitio principii* can be justified on the basis that, whether there be a valid contract or not, the putative applicable law has the closest connection with the contractual events contemplated by the contract. A contract is formally valid if it satisfies the formal requirements either of the law governing the contract under the Convention or of the law where it is concluded. [209]

(viii) Voluntary assignment of rights

The voluntary assignment of debts or other rights is discussed later in this chapter.[210.]

---

208   Article 8.
209   Article 9(1).
210   See pp 1107–1108.

8.   THE LAW APPLICABLE TO THE SALE OF GOODS

(i)   Sources of conflict rules

The Uniform Law on International Sales (ULIS),[211] consistent with its aims as a self-contained code of substantive law applicable even in relation to non-contracting states, purported to exclude rules of private international law,[212] a device of questionable merit and even more doubtful effect.[213] The United Nations Convention on Contracts for the International Sale of Goods (CISG)[214] wisely eschews this Canute-like stance before the sea of private international law, bows to the inevitable and provides that questions concerning matters governed by the Convention which are not expressly settled in it are to be settled in conformity with the general principles on which it is based, or, in the absence of such principles, in conformity with the law applicable by virtue of the rules of private international law.[215] The Hague Convention of 1955 on the Law Applicable to International Sales of Movable Corporeal Objects is in force but has not been ratified by the United Kingdom,[216] and two subsequent conflicts conventions, the 1958 convention on the law governing transfer of title in international sales of goods and the 1986 Hague Convention on the law applicable to contracts for the international sale of goods, have not entered into force. Accordingly, where in relation to a contract of sale of goods involving a foreign element issues arise which are not covered by ULIS (or when operative in the United Kingdom, by CISG), resort must be had, as regards the contractual aspects, to the more general rules embodied in the Contracts Convention[217] and, as regards the proprietary aspects, by English conflict of laws rules established at common law.

(ii)   Contractual aspects

In general, the contractual aspects of a contract of sale of goods will, in the absence of a choice of law by the parties, be governed by the law of the place of business of the seller, as the party whose performance is characteristic of the contract.[218]

(iii) Proprietary aspects

The proprietary aspects of a contract for the sale of goods, including the capacity to transfer, the formalities of a valid transfer, its essential validity, the time of the passing of the property, and the effect of a reservation of title in favour of the seller, are to be determined by the *lex situs*, that is, the law of the place where the goods

---

211   See p 914.
212   Article 2.
213   See Graveson, Cohn and Graveson, *Uniform Law on International Sales Act 1967* (1968), pp 11 ff.
214   See ch 33.
215   Article 7(2).
216   Nor has the 1958 Hague Convention on the law governing transfer of title in the international sale of goods.
217   See p 1095.
218   See p 1101.

are situated at the time of the contract.[219] It has now been held by Moore-Bick J that the *lex situs*, not the law applicable to the transfer, governs proprietary issues even where they arise solely between the parties to the contract and do not involve a third party.[220] This provides judicial confirmation of the views already expressed by the textbook writers.[221]

The starting point, then, is that the forum should recognize a title validly acquired under the *lex situs*, and should refuse to accept a claim to ownership not recognized by the *lex situs*, even if a different result would have been reached under the *lex fori*. The application of the principle is relatively straightforward where the *situs* of the goods remains unchanged at all relevant times. What, however, is the position where the goods move from State A to State B and while in State B are to be subjected to a new dealing? Here the position is that the law to be applied is that the law of the *situs* of the goods at the time of the last dealing or event. It is for that law to determine whether earlier law has any relevance. If under the law of the second *situs* the transferee acquired an overriding title, irrespective of any defect in title of his transferor, the transferee succeeds and it is unnecessary for reference to be made to the law of the first *situs*. If, on the other hand, the law of the second *situs* says that the transferee acquires only such title as the transferor had to convey, then a court applying the law of the second *situs* will refer to the law of the first *situs* to see whether the transferor was, in fact, the unencumbered owner at the time immediately before the goods left the first *situs*. A good illustration of acquisition of an overriding title under the law of the second *situs* is *Winkworth v Christie, Manson and Woods Ltd*.[222]

> Certain works of art belonging to the plaintiff were stolen from him in England and taken to Italy, where they were sold to the second defendant a bona fide purchaser without notice of the plaintiff's title. By the law of Italy, but not by English law, sale by a thief to a bona fide purchaser passed a good title. The second defendant subsequently returned the goods to England to be sold by the first defendant, a well-known firm of auctioneers. The plaintiff then brought proceedings against the defendants for detinue and conversion. The defendants contended that title had become vested in the second defendant as the result of the sale to him in Italy.

> On the trial of a preliminary issue as to whether English or Italian law governed the title dispute, Slade J, applying *Cammell v Sewell*,[223] held that the effect of the sale to the second defendant was governed by the *lex situs* at the time of that sale, ie Italian law, even though the goods had been removed to Italy without the plaintiff's consent and had subsequently returned to England.[224]

---

219 *Hardwick Game Farm v Suffolk Agricultural Poultry Producers' Association* [1966] 1 WLR 287, per Diplock LJ at 330. See also *Glencore International AG v Metro Trading International Inc* [2001] 1 Lloyd's Rep 286.

220 *Glencore International AG v Metro Trading International Inc*, n 219.

221 *Dicey and Morris*, para 24–005; *Cheshire and North*, pp 942 ff. Professor Cheshire had earlier advocated the proper law to govern the proprietary rights of the parties *inter se*. See Cheshire's *Private International Law* (7th edn, 1965), p 410.

222 [1980] Ch 496.

223 (1860) 5 H & N 728.

224 It may be noted that some of the goods the subject of the proceedings had been sold in England, so that English law would have determined the effect of that sale on the title acquired by the second defendant under Italian law, but, as Slade J noted (at 500) there was no suggestion in the agreed facts or on the pleadings that any person not a party to the proceedings ever acquired title to the goods, which would have destroyed the plaintiff's right to possession – or, one would add, the title of the second defendant.

Similarly, a purported transfer of title treated as invalid by the *lex situs* will be so treated by an English court. Let us suppose that S contracts to sell to B, under a contract governed by English law, goods situated in France, and the contract is void under French law. Suppose further that B brings the goods to England and then sells them to C. The starting point of the enquiry is the effect of English law. If under English law none of the exceptions to the *nemo dat* rule applies, S's continued ownership under French law will be upheld and C will not get a good title. But if the sale falls within one of the exceptions to the *nemo dat* rule,[225] it confers a good title on the purchaser, C, whether or not S himself had title, and no reference to French law is required. So a resale by B to C which falls within s 25 of the Sale of Goods Act[226] makes it unnecessary for the court to determine S's original ownership by reference to French law, for it would in any event be overruled by the sale to C.[227]

More complicated is the case where the original title claimed is not void but merely unperfected and thus void against third parties. For example, S supplies to B, on conditional sale, equipment situated in New York. Ownership is to remain in S until the full price has been paid. By the law of New York, the reservation of title in favour of S, though valid as between S and B, is of no effect against a subsequent purchaser unless filed in accordance with art 9 of the Uniform Commercial Code as adopted by the State of New York. S fails to file. If the equipment is sold by B to C while the goods are in New York and is then brought by C to London, an English court must uphold C's title as having been validly acquired under New York law.

Suppose, however, that the goods were brought to England by B and then sold to C while in England. Can C claim title on the ground that S had failed to perfect his security interest by filing in New York? No, because even if New York law purported to protect C in this situation, an English court would not consider New York law competent to govern the effect of a dealing in the goods after they had left the State of New York.[228] So the starting point for an English court would be that at the time of B's sale to C, S still had title to the equipment. Whether that title was overridden by the sale to C would be a matter for English law and would depend upon whether any of the exceptions to the *nemo dat* rule provided by English law[229] applied.

(iv) Goods in transit and mobile goods

The *lex situs* is not appropriate in relation to dealings in goods in transit, though as between the parties it can be made to work by giving the goods an artificial *situs*. In the case of goods transported by a means of carriage for which there is an internationally recognized system of national registration, as in the case of ships and aircraft, there is much to be said for subjecting the transaction to the law of the state of registration. In other cases it may be necessary to rely on the law applicable to the transfer agreement itself as regards formalities of transfer and proprietary rights

---

225 Eg, s 25(1) of the Sale of Goods Act 1979. See p 434.
226 See p 434.
227 *Cammell v Sewell*, n 223.
228 Ibid.
229 See pp 417 ff.

as between the parties themselves, though this is unsatisfactory where the dispute relates to the rights of third parties.

The problem is especially acute where the goods themselves are transport vehicles or other receptacles for goods, and are thus in transit for most of the time in the course of business of their owner or user. Examples are ships, aircraft, lorries and containers. No current conflicts rule works satisfactorily for mobile equipment of this kind. The question particularly affects those providing finance on the security of mobile equipment or supplying it on lease or conditional sale and wishing to ensure that their rights are not overridden by improper dealings between the bailee and third parties.

The Convention on International Interests in Mobile Equipment, prepared by UNIDROIT and concluded at Cape Town together with its Aircraft Equipment Protocol in 2001, is designed to resolve these problems in relation to three categories of high-value mobile equipment: railway rolling stock, aircraft objects and space assets.[230] These categories of mobile equipment have three characteristics as defined by the Convention: they are assets of high value; they move regularly across national borders; and each item is uniquely identifiable, typically by manufacturer's name, model and serial number. The Convention provides a set of uniform substantive law rules governing international interests in such equipment, that is, security interests, the rights of a person who is a conditional seller under a title reservation agreement and the rights of a person who is a lessor under a leasing agreement.[231] Compliance with relatively simple formalities suffices to establish the international interest.[232] Apart from prescribing default remedies for the creditor, with which we are not here concerned, the Convention establishes an international register for the registration of international interests and certain other kinds of interest, administered by a registrar under the supervision of a supervisory authority, and lays down a set of priority rules based on registration. The primary rule is that a registered interest has priority over a subsequently registered interest and an unregistered interest. The Convention and Protocol thus dispense with the need to resort to conflicts of laws rules as regards these three categories of object except where the Convention itself lays down a uniform conflicts rule.[233]

9. THE LAW APPLICABLE TO THE ASSIGNMENT OF DEBTS

Debts and other rights are very frequently the subject of transfer under contracts having a foreign element, whether by way of sale (as in the case of international

---

230 For a comprehensive analysis, see Roy Goode, *Convention on International Interests in Mobile Equipment and Protocol Thereto on Matters Specific to Aircraft Equipment: Official Commentary* (2002). The convention technically entered into force on 1 April 2004 but most of its provisions do not become operative until the relevant protocol enters into force, which in the case of the Aircraft Equipment Protocol requires adoption by eight States. To date, four have ratified but other ratifications are in train.

231 Article 2(2).

232 See arts 2, 7.

233 As it does in art 2(4), which leaves to the applicable law as determined by the rules of private international law of the forum the question whether the creditor's interest is to be characterized as a security interest, the interest of a conditional seller or the interest of a lessor. On a few other issues the Convention lays down no substantive rule but defers to the applicable law.

factoring) or by way of security. Article 12 of the Rome Convention deals with these in the following terms:

1. The mutual obligations of assignor and assignee under a voluntary assignment of a right against another person ('the debtor') shall be governed by the law which under this Convention applies to the contract between the assignor and assignee.

2. The law governing the right to which the assignment relates shall determine its assignability, the relationship between the assignee and the debtor, the conditions under which the assignment can be invoked against the debtor and any question whether the debtor's obligations have been discharged.

The first question to be considered is the scope of art 12. Here the position has been clarified by the Court of Appeal in *Raiffeisen Zentralbank Österreich AG v Five Star General Trading LLC,*[234] which concluded that art 12 governs, first, the contractual aspects of the relationship between the assignor and the assignee and, secondly, the effect of the assignment on the relations between assignee and debtor, on the basis that in that relationship what is involved is not an issue of property rights but rather a contractual issue to be determined by the law governing the obligation assigned. [235] So although the assignee's right of recovery against the debtor may be dependent on its having acquired title to the debt, the issue essentially concerns the conditions in which the assignee succeeds to the assignor's contractual rights against the debtor. The definitive judgment by Mance LJ to this effect accords with the principle underlying art 12, namely that a debtor's rights should not be affected by an assignment.[236] The judgment also provides implicit support for the view previously expressed by scholars[237] that art 12 is not concerned with the proprietary effects of an assignment against third parties other than the debtor, for example, a competing assignee or the assignor's liquidator.[238]

(i)   Assignor and assignee

1.   Contractual aspects

The core of every assignment is, of course, the transfer of the debt from creditor to assignee. However, the assignment may also incorporate undertakings and warranties by the assignor, eg that the assigned debt is valid and enforceable and that if the debtor disputes payment, the assignor will re-purchase the debt.[239] In its contractual aspects (if any), the assignment is like any other contract. Accordingly, the mutual obligations of assignor and assignee are governed by the applicable law under the Convention provisions, as is the formal validity of the assignment so far as its contractual aspects are concerned, except that, as with other contracts, the

---

234   [2001] QB 825.

235   Paras 26–57.

236   See p 1110.

237   See Mark Moshinsky, 'The Assignment of Debts in the Conflict of Laws' (1992) 108 LQR 591, and the second edn, of the present work at 1126 ff.

238   N 234. See paras 51, 52 of the judgment.

239   An assignment pursuant to a block discounting agreement is a typical example. The assignment transfers the debts upon the terms of the underlying master agreement between the parties incorporating a set of warranties, recourse provisions and the like.

assignment will also be formally valid as to its contractual aspects if in accordance with the *lex loci contractus* even if not fulfilling the formal requirements of the applicable law.[240]

On the other hand, except to the extent to which it affects the debtor, the proprietary effect of the assignment as between assignor and assignee is outside the scope of the Convention, for the reason previously stated, and in the case of assignment of a particular debt[241] should be governed, both in logic and as a matter of policy, by the law of the place where the debtor resides or has his place (or principal place) of business.[242] This is usually considered an application of the *lex situs*, though the value of ascribing an artificial *situs* to intangibles is questionable, given that the *situs* so attributed varies according to whether the intangible is a simple debt, a registered security or a bearer instrument, so that the *lex situs* does not constitute an organizing principle. It would make sense to dispense with this superfluous intermediate stage and simply formulate a direct rule, in this case, that the applicable law is that of the debtor's residence or place of business. However, the concept of control which underlies the *situs* theory in relation to the transfer of tangible movables applies with equal force to the transfer of intangibles. It is the courts of the debtor's residence which ultimately control the obligation of the debtor to make payment to B instead of to A. Accordingly, a transfer recognized as valid by those courts should be upheld elsewhere, and a transfer regarded as invalid by those courts should be refused recognition elsewhere.

Objection has been made that it is unsatisfactory to subject the transaction to the residential whims of a debtor of wandering disposition.[243] But is it likely that the debtor himself will be any more mobile than the chattels in his possession? If the *lex situs* is considered appropriate to regulate proprietary rights to the debtor's car, then *a fortiori* his country of residence, which is much less readily changeable than that of his car, should be accepted as providing the law applicable to the proprietary effects of the transfer of a debt he owes.

Somewhat different considerations apply where the assignor makes global assignments of existing and future debts, eg under factoring or invoice discounting agreements.[244] Here there is much to be said for applying the law of the assignor's place of business.[245] This avoids the problem that the *situs* of future debtors is unknown, and also has the advantage of subjecting the assignment to a single regime instead of the *situs* of each debt having to be determined separately. Moreover, it is the country of the assignor's place of business in which any public notice requirements for perfection of the assignment are likely to be imposed.

240　Article 9(1).
241　As to receivables financing, see below.
242　This is the *situs* of the debt even if it is payable elsewhere, eg in the creditor's country (*Re Helbert Wagg & Co Ltd's Claim* [1956] Ch 323).
243　A. E. Anton, *Private International Law* (2nd edn, 1990), p 409.
244　See Moshinsky (1992) 108 LQR 591, pp 609 ff.
245　Indeed, in order to have a uniform regime for debts generally even the assignment of specific debts could be subjected to the law of the assignor's place of business as regards their proprietary effects.

(ii) Assignee and debtor

When we consider the rights of the assignee against the debtor, the distinction between contractual and proprietary rights ceases to be relevant, for the cardinal rule, now embodied in art 12(2), is that the debtor's position should not be affected by the assignment. The terms on which the debt becomes payable, the defences and rights of set-off open to the debtor, the validity and effect of the contract under which the debt arises, are all matters for the 'law governing the right to which the assignment relates', which presumably means the law applicable to the contract under which that right arises. Similar considerations apply to the assignability of the debt vis-à-vis the assignee. If the contract under which the debt arises contains a prohibition against assignment which by the law applicable to that contract entitles the debtor to ignore the title of the assignee, the debtor should have a right to invoke the contractual prohibition, whether or not it would be effective under the law applicable to the assignment.[246] Conversely, if the law governing the right under which the debt arises makes a prohibition against assignment ineffective vis-à-vis the assignment,[247] the debtor cannot be allowed to improve his position by invoking the applicable law of the assignment effectuating such a prohibition.

(iii) Priorities

Conflicting claims to a debt (eg because the creditor has fraudulently assigned it to two assignees in succession or because one claimant asserts a right by virtue of assignment while the other claims the debt as proceeds of goods supplied by him on conditional sale) should be regulated by the situation of the debtor, this being the place where the courts have control over the debtor and thus recovery of the debt, and is also the place where an intending assignee would expect to make inquiry of the debtor as to a prior notice of assignment. The argument in favour of the law applicable to the debt has little to commend it, for this is concerned with relations between the parties *inter se* (including for this purpose the creditor's assignee and the debtor) and has little or no significance for third parties, who would expect to make their inquiries and searches in the country of the debtor's residence, not in the country of the law governing the debt, which will usually be that of the creditor by virtue of a choice of law clause. The law applicable to the debt would, in any event, be quite inappropriate where the asserted title of one of the competing claimants does not derive from an assignment but, eg, from a tracing right, for in that situation he is unlikely to be aware of the terms, or even the existence, of the contract under

---

246   Of course, if the assignment is void even *inter partes* according to the proper law of the assignment, it is unnecessary to go further. An assignee who has no title as against his assignor obviously has none against the debtor.

247   See, for example, s 2–210(3) of the American Uniform Commercial Code, which has the effect of giving the assignee the right to collect from the debtor notwithstanding any prohibition against assignment. The purpose of the provision is to avoid the serious obstacles that would be faced by receivables financiers if they had to check every contract purchased to see whether it prohibited an assignment. Where the UNIDROIT Convention on International Factoring applies, the assignment is effective despite the prohibition (art 6(1)) except in a state that has made a declaration under art 18 (art 6(2)).

which the debt arises. As stated earlier, it seems clear that art 12 of the Rome Convention has no application to priority disputes involving third parties.

10. THE LAW APPLICABLE TO SECURITIES HELD WITH AN INTERMEDIARY

Since the 1980s there has been a sharp move from the direct holding of investment securities by entry in the issuer's register or possession of certificates to bearer securities to indirect holdings through a securities account with a bank or other securities intermediary. Hand in hand with this shift has gone dematerialization of securities, which are now largely issued and transferred electronically[248] rather than in paper form. The substantive law governing the nature of an account-holder's rights, which are usually held in a pool with other account holders of the same intermediary having an interest in the same issue of securities, remains undeveloped, though it seems reasonably clear that under English law, in the absence of agreement to the contrary, the account holders are co-owners of the pool to the extent of their respective interests. But if the substantive law is not yet developed, this is even more true of the conflict of laws aspects of the indirect holding system. In the one case in which the question arose[249] the Court of Appeal equated the position with that applicable to directly held securities, leading to the law of the place of the issuer's incorporation. Though in the end this did not matter, since all routes led to New York law, this result has little to commend it. There is no relationship between the issuer and an account holder holding from an intermediary, nor, indeed, is there any between an intermediary and any account holder other than its own, and there is no way in which in the ordinary course of events an intermediary can be aware of lower-tier investors. Moreover, it is hard to see why the law of the issuer's incorporation in, say, France should be thought to have any relevance to the proprietary rights of a New York business in respect of a securities account held with a New York bank which itself holds through an account with a German bank.

This issue has now been addressed by the 2002 Hague Convention on the law applicable to certain rights in respect of securities held with an intermediary. The particular interest of this Convention for private international lawyers is the primary rule laid down in art 4(1) that the law selected by the parties to the account agreement to govern that agreement, or such other law as they choose to determine the various issues set out in art 2(1), applies not only to the rights of account holder and intermediary but to the rights of third parties, the requirements for perfecting a security and the priorities of competing claimants. Such a rule, which was not that originally envisaged,[250] is counter-intuitive and is contrary to a well-established

---

248 In England, through CREST. See Roy Goode, *Legal Problems of Credit and Security* (3rd edn, 2003), paras 6-04 ff, 6-29.

249 *Macmillan Inc v Bishopsgate Investment Trust plc (No 3)* [1996] 1 WLR 387.

250 The intended rule was based on the place of the relevant intermediary approach (PRIMA), that is, the office of the intermediary where the particular account in question is maintained. But industry experts pointed out that today the activities of maintaining accounts may be dispersed across offices in different countries, so that, for example, the account may be opened in State A and administered in State B, while statements may be sent from State C etc, and the location of the account may anyway be changed as the result of a decision to centralize accounting for administrative purposes and even to hold records in a 'virtual' office. So PRIMA was modified, retaining the concept of the relevant intermediary but dropping the place.

principle that two parties to a contract cannot by their agreement affect the rights of third parties, still less subject those rights to a given law. The great merit of the rule is that it leads to the application of a single law and thus to enhanced predictability. Any third party intended to buy or lend against an account holder's interest in securities will ask to see the account agreement and will thereby ascertain the applicable law. For the purposes of the Convention each account has to be looked at separately and is governed by its own law. The parties do not have complete freedom; they must select the law of a place where the intermediary is engaged in the business of maintaining securities accounts. There are three fall-back rules, arranged in a cascade, if the parties fail to make a choice, or an effective choice, of law. What this example shows is the importance of involving industry specialists in the preparatory work on a conflict of laws convention rather than simply leaving it to legal experts who are not necessarily familiar with the various methods by which businesses are organized and transactions conducted.

11. FOREIGN MONEY OBLIGATIONS[251]

(i) Money of account and money of payment

Where a contractual obligation is expressed in foreign currency, two questions arise: how much money does the debtor have to pay? And in what currency must payment be made? The former is termed the *money of account* and represents the substance of the obligation, the measurement of the debtor's liability. The latter is termed the *money of payment* and is concerned simply with the method by which the obligation is to be discharged. The distinction is well brought out in a judgment of Lord Denning MR in *Woodhouse AC Israel Cocoa Ltd S.A. v Nigerian Produce Marketing Co Ltd*:[252]

> Suppose an English merchant buys twenty tons of cocoa-beans from a Nigerian supplier for delivery in three months' time at the price of five Nigerian pounds a ton payable in pounds sterling in London. Then the *money of account* is Nigerian pounds. But the *money of payment* is sterling. Assume that, at the making of the contract, the exchange rate is one Nigerian pound for one pound sterling – 'pound for pound'. Then, so long as the exchange rate remains steady, no one worries. The buyer pays £100 sterling in London. It is transferred to Lagos, where the seller receives 100 Nigerian pounds. But suppose that, before the time for payment, sterling is devalued by 14 per cent while the Nigerian pound stands firm. The Nigerian seller is entitled to have the price *measured in* Nigerian pounds. He is entitled to have currency worth 100 Nigerian pounds because the Nigerian pound is the *money of account*. But the *money of payment* is sterling. So the buyer must provide enough sterling to make up 100 Nigerian pounds. To do this, after devaluation, he will have to provide £116 5s [£116.25] in pounds sterling. So the buyer in England, looking at it as he will in sterling, has to pay much

---

251 See R. M. Goode, *Payment Obligations in Commercial and Financial Transactions* (1983), ch V; F. A. Mann, *The Legal Aspect of Money* (5th edn, 1992); *Dicey and Morris*, ch 36; *Cheshire and North*, pp 90 ff.

252 [1971] 2 QB 23 at 54. For a comprehensive survey of the law, with provisional recommendations, see the Law Commission's Working Paper *Private International Law: Foreign Money Liabilities* (Law Com No 80, July1981), and subsequent Report (Law Com No 124, Cmnd 8318, October 1983).

more for his twenty tons of cocoa-beans than he had anticipated. He will have to pay £116 5s instead of £100. He will have to pass the increase on to his customers. But the seller in Nigeria, looking at it as he will in Nigerian pounds, will receive the same amount as he had anticipated. He will receive 100 Nigerian pounds just the same; and he will be able to pay his growers accordingly. But, now suppose that in the contract for purchase the price had been, not five Nigerian pounds, but five pounds *sterling* a ton, so that the *money of account* was sterling. After devaluation, the buyer in England would be able to discharge his obligation by paying £100 sterling; but the Nigerian seller would suffer. For, when he transferred the £100 sterling to Nigeria, it would only be worth 86 Nigerian pounds. So instead of getting 100 Nigerian pounds as he had anticipated, he would only get 86; and he would not have enough to pay his growers. So you see how vital it is to decide, in any contract, what is the *money of account* and what is the *money of payment*.

This passage also illustrates the principle of nominalism, which is universally adopted by states. Under this principle, it is the debtor's duty to pay the nominal amount, ie the face value, of the designated money of account, regardless of any changes in the internal or external value of the specified currency. So if a resident of the United States purchases goods from an English seller at the price of £10, the debt is discharged by payment of £10, even if the purchasing power of the pound in England at the due date of payment[253] is only half what it was at the date of contract (reduction in internal value) or the value of the pound in relation to the American dollar has halved or doubled in this time (change in external value). Whether a fall in the external value of the money of account prejudices the creditor depends upon whether he was intending to use that money to purchase the foreign currency in question.[254] If not, he suffers no loss, for the value of what he receives in relation to the foreign currency is of no concern to him.

Though English law does not provide for the revalorization of debts, if the applicable law is one which would allow revalorization in the particular case, then an English court seised of the matter must revalorize the debt in accordance with the applicable law.[255]

I.   Money of account

This is usually clear from the contract. If an Englishman sells goods to a Frenchman for £100, it is clear that the money of account is sterling; if a Frenchman sells goods to an Englishman for 100 euros, the money of account is obviously euros. Occasionally, problems arise because the designated currency has the same label but different values in different countries and it is not clear which state's currency is meant. For example, if an Englishman sold goods to a Frenchman for $1,000, it might not be clear whether this was a reference to US dollars, Canadian dollars, Australian dollars or the dollar currency of some other country. Here the rules of construction of the applicable law must normally be applied. [256]

---

253   For the position where the debtor does not pay the debt at the due date and there is a subsequent rise or fall in the value of the money of account, see below.
254   See below.
255   *Kornatzki v Oppenheimer* [1937] 4 All ER 133.
256   *Dicey and Morris*, paras 36R-001, 36R-031.22

2.   Money of payment

The debtor's obligation having been measured by the money of account, the next question is the currency in which the creditor is entitled to be paid. Where the contract does not specify any currency other than that of the due place for payment, there is, of course, no problem; payment is to be made in legal tender in the currency of that place. Where, however, the payment obligation is expressed in foreign currency, the matter is a little more complex. Suppose that an Englishman sells goods to a Frenchman for £100, the price to be paid in London in euros. There is nothing to stop the parties from providing for payment in a foreign currency; the question is whether there is an option for payment in sterling and, if so, who has that option. The presumption of English law is that the option lies with the debtor,[257] but this can be excluded by the terms of the contract, in which event the debtor would get a good discharge only by tendering euros or sterling as directed by the creditor.[258] Where the debtor has an option to convert his payment obligation into sterling, the rate of exchange at which the conversion is to be made is governed by the law applicable to the contract and is that applicable on the day payment is made.[259]

(ii)   Foreign currency judgments

Until 1975 it was considered settled law that an English court could give judgment only in sterling, even if the money of account and the money of payment were a foreign currency, and that the appropriate date for conversion of the foreign currency into sterling was not the date of judgment or the date of payment but the date of the breach. This long-standing principle was reaffirmed by the House of Lords in *Re United Railways of the Havanas and Regla Warehouses Ltd*,[260] and the rule was considered applicable not only to a claim for damages but also to a claim for debt in a foreign currency. But in *Miliangos v George Frank (Textiles) Ltd*[261] the House of Lords took the unusual step of reversing its earlier decision in *United Havana* and ruled that where the justice of the case so required, the court could give judgment in favour of the plaintiff for the amount of the foreign currency due to him or its sterling equivalent at the time of payment, which for this purpose is the date on which the court authorizes enforcement of the judgment in terms of sterling.[262] The House left

---

257   Ibid, para 36–053; Mann, *Legal Aspect of Money*, p 321. If payment in the foreign currency is impossible, the debt must be paid in sterling (*Libyan Arab Foreign Bank v Bankers Trust Co* [1989] QB 728). *Quaere* whether this is so where the law applicable to the contract is not English.
258   *Marrache v Ashton* [1943] AC 311.
259   *Dicey and Morris*, paras 36–053, 36–054.
260   [1961] AC 1007.
261   [1976] AC 443.
262   The amount of the judgment entered in a foreign currency must be converted into sterling when the judgment comes to be executed. Given this fact, there seems no reason why a judgment should not be entered in terms of any unit of account agreed between the parties, even if it is not reflected in a physical currency issued by a state. So if the contract provides for payment in SDRs (Special Drawing Rights), it should be open to the claimant to enter judgment accordingly and convert this into sterling at the official conversion rate. The procedure in England for claiming debts or damages in foreign currency is set out in CPR Pt 16 and PD 6, para 11. See also Steven Stern, 'The courts and foreign currency obligations' [1995] LMCLQ 494. Interest on foreign currency judgments may be awarded at such rate as the court thinks fit (s 44A of the Administration of Justice Act 1970, as added by the Private International Law (Miscellaneous Provisions) Act 1995 s 1).

open the question whether a similar rule should be adopted in claims for damages for breach of contract or in tort, but in subsequent cases it has been held that the power to give judgment in a foreign currency extends to these cases also,[263] and that a foreign currency credit balance in a bank is a debt due from the bank and can be attached in garnishee proceedings.[264]

There remains one question: in which foreign currency should judgment be given? Prima facie this should be the currency of the contract, but in a claim for damages there may be cases where this does not adequately compensate the claimant for his loss, eg because this is not the currency in which he has suffered his loss. In that event the court should award damages in the currency which most truly expresses the claimant's loss, which is not necessarily the currency in which the loss immediately occurs but may be a third currency, eg that which the claimant, because he normally trades in it, has to use to purchase the currency in which his loss was suffered.[265]

---

263 *The Despina R. and The Folias* [1979] AC 685; *Jean Kraut AG v Albany Ltd* [1977] QB 182.

264 *Choice Investments Ltd v Jeromnimon* [1981] QB 149.

265 *The Despina R. and The Folias*, n 263; *International Minerals & Chemical Corp v Karl O. Helm AG* [1986] 1 Lloyd's Rep 81. As a matter of principle, a third currency ought not to be selected unless the claimant can show that at the time of the contract the defendant knew or ought reasonably to have contemplated that such currency was likely to be that most truly expressing the claimant's loss. The question of what country's interest rates should be used to determine a claim for interest is the subject of conflicting authorities and of some interesting economic analysis. See the Law Commission's Working Paper No 80 (n 252), pp 120–133 and literature there cited.

PART EIGHT
The Resolution of Commercial Disputes

Most commercial contracts are carried through to completion without serious difficulty, and such differences as do from time to time arise are resolved by discussion between the parties. But sometimes they cannot agree, and it is necessary to resort to an outside individual or tribunal to settle the matter.

I.   LITIGATION AND ITS ALTERNATIVES

There are three principal methods by which contract disputes can be resolved: litigation, arbitration and alternative dispute resolution (ADR). By litigation is meant resort to a court established by law. In England this takes the form of trial by a single judge.[1] The subject of the present chapter is commercial litigation. Arbitration is the voluntary submission of disputes not to a court[2] but to a person or tribunal chosen by the parties or designated by a third party whom they have nominated to make the appointment.[3] In contrast to litigation, arbitration is a consensual process in that a person cannot be required to submit to arbitration without his agreement. But once he has agreed, typically through an arbitration clause in his contract with the other party, he can be compelled to accept arbitration, and any award against him is binding. Arbitration is dealt with in chapter 39. It is to be distinguished from decision by an expert appointed by the parties, whose role does not require him to decide on the basis of evidence and argument submitted by the parties but rather to make his own enquiries and to decide on the basis of his own expertise. Moreover, while arbitration presupposes the existence of a dispute, an expert may be appointed without any dispute having arisen, for example, where

---

1   Jury trials in civil cases are now unusual. A party against whom fraud, libel, slander, malicious prosecution or false imprisonment is alleged has a right to trial by jury except where the case involves prolonged examination of documents or accounts, or any scientific or local investigation which cannot conveniently be made with a jury (Supreme Court Act 1981, s 69(1)). The judge may also sit with the assistance of assessors; and an action can be ordered to be tried by a Master, an official referee or a special referee (Supreme Court Act 1981, s 70, Civil Procedure Rules 2.4 and Practice Direction 2B, para 6.1). For the purpose of this chapter, trial by judge only is assumed.

2   The arbitrator may be a judge, but then he acts qua arbitrator, not in a judicial capacity. If he is a judge of the Commercial Court an appeal against his award lies direct to the Court of Appeal (Arbitration Act 1996, s 93, Sch 2)

3   There are also procedures which partake of the characteristics of both litigation and arbitration, such as 'rent-a-judge', where the parties engage a lawyer, often a retired judge, to hear the case in private but otherwise in much the same way as an ordinary judge, his award being given effect to as an order of the court. This procedure, developed in the United States, does not yet exist in the United Kingdom.

the parties have agreed that the price of an asset is to be fixed by expert determination.

ADR is a process by which a third party, at the invitation of the contestants, is brought in with a view to the dispute being resolved amicably and without a legally binding award.[4] ADR itself takes a variety of forms, including mediation, conciliation and mini-trial.[5] The first two labels are often used interchangeably, but those working in the field tend to distinguish one from the other (though again not always consistently) according to the perceived role of the facilitator appointed to help the parties resolve the dispute. A broad division is made between 'facultative' mediation, in which the mediator's role is to help the parties to reach their own agreement without expressing views or judgments of his own, and 'evaluative' mediation, in which the mediator is asked to give an opinion which can guide the parties.[6] A mini-trial is a non-binding structured settlement process characterized by speed, limitation on disclosure of documents and relative brevity of the hearing. At the hearing lawyers for the two parties present their 'best case' to a panel consisting of a neutral adviser and senior representatives of the parties themselves with authority to negotiate a settlement. The neutral adviser may be asked to indicate his view of the likely outcome of litigation or arbitration if the parties fail to reach agreement.[7] Despite its label, ADR is not necessarily an *alternative* to arbitration but may be the first part of a two-stage process. 'Med-arb' is a procedure by which an ADR mediator or other designated third party is authorized to act as arbitrator[8] and give a binding decision if the mediation is unsuccessful. ADR is gaining popularity in international commercial disputes due to its relatively low cost, speed of resolution, confidentiality and privacy, flexibility, perceived fairness, effectiveness and the ability to allow the parties' business relationship to be continued,[9] this being facilitated by the ability of the process to produce non-legal

4 However, where the mediation results in an agreement, this will be binding if so intended by the parties. In *Cable & Wireless plc v IBM United Kingdom Ltd* [2002] 2 All ER (Comm) 1041 Colman J rejected an argument that an agreement to resort to ADR in accordance with the model procedure of the Centre for Effective Dispute Resolution was as uncertain as an agreement to negotiate and therefore void. See Karl Mackie, 'The Future for ADR Clauses after *Cable & Wireless v IBM*' (2003) 19 Arbitration International 345. See also Sir Anthony Colman, 'ADR: An Irreversible Tide?' (2003) 19 Arbitration International 303.

5 See, generally, Henry Brown and Arthur Marriott, *ADR Principles and Practice* (2nd edn, 1999); Karl Mackie, David Miles, William Marsh and Tony Allen (eds), *The ADR Practice Guide* (2002); Alan Redfern and Martin Hunter *Law and Practice of International Commercial Arbitration* (3rd edn, 1999) paras 1–49 ff. Because of the range and flexibility of ADR procedures a consistent terminology has not yet been developed. There is not even a wholly uniform usage as to what is encompassed within the term ADR, but in England it is generally used in contradistinction to both litigation and arbitration.

6 See, generally, Brown and Marriott, *ADR Principles and Practice,* ch 7 (pp 137 ff). A Practice Direction is shortly to be issued providing for a pilot mediation scheme to operate at the Central London Civil Justice Centre prescribing automatic reference, after the filing of the defence, to mediation of randomly selected cases meeting the necessary conditions.

7 See ibid, ch 15 (pp 349 ff).

8 The appointment of the mediator himself as arbitrator may occasion difficulty, not least because of his receipt of confidential information during the course of the mediation.

9 M. Wang, 'Are alternative dispute resolution methods superior to litigation in resolving disputes in international commerce?' (2000) 16 Arbitration International 189.

outcomes satisfactory to both parties which could not be awarded by a court. In the Commercial Court judges have for many years sought to identify cases suitable for ADR and either suggest ADR to the parties or order them to attempt it.[10] ADR, being non-binding, has relatively little legal content and is not further discussed.

However, the fact that parties resort to litigation or arbitration does not necessarily mean that their relationship is at an end or even that they are hostile to each other. Commercial people tend to take a robust view of life and to learn to live with each other to their mutual advantage, and not infrequently matters in issue are left to be resolved by a judge or an arbitrator precisely because the parties, being unable to agree, are content to have their differences settled by an outsider, and to abide by his decision, without disturbing the continuance of their good business relationship.

Mention should also be made of procedures for interim adjudication pursuant to which, by statute or agreement of the parties, disputes concerning performance of a contract while it is ongoing can be referred to an expert or expert panel for an interim decision as to how the contract should proceed, this being without prejudice to the rights of the parties to have the question finally determined on the merits by the court or an arbitral tribunal if either of them disagrees with the decision, which meanwhile is binding. Such a procedure, which has been found particularly useful in disputes arising during the course of a construction contract, was agreed in the contracts providing for the construction of the Channel tunnel[11] and also features in legislation.[12] It finds its international counterpart in the pre-arbitral referee procedure of the International Chamber of Commerce under the ICC Rules.[13]

2. THE NATURE OF LITIGATION

A contested action is in many respects like a civilized war. It involves not only law but evidence and persuasion, tactics and strategy. It entails detailed preparation of one's client's case so as to present it in the strongest light either to the court, if the action reaches trial, or to the other side, for the purpose of negotiating a favourable settlement. The game must be played according to the rules, both written and unwritten. Reputable lawyers do not engage in sharp tactics. They remember that while they have a duty to the client, they also have a paramount duty to the court to act in a proper fashion. This involves, inter alia, ensuring that all relevant documents for which privilege cannot be claimed are fully and frankly disclosed; that evidence is not put before the court, whether by witnesses or by documents, which is known to be false; and that no unfair advantage is taken of the opponent. But within the rules

---

10 A survey conducted by Professor Hazel Genn in 2002, *Court-Based ADR Initiatives for Non-Family Disputes: the Commercial Court and the Court of Appeal*, showed that ADR was attempted in a little over half the cases in which an ADR order had been issued and that of these a little over half were settled by ADR, while of the 63% of cases in which ADR was not attempted, about 20% were said to have been settled as the result of the ADR order. See also the Second Report of the Working Party on ADR of the Commercial Court Committee dated 14 July 1998.

11 See Redfern and Hunter, *International Commercial Arbitration*, paras 7-26–7-28.

12 See the Housing Grants , Construction and Regeneration Act 1996, s 108.

13 ICC Rules for a Pre-Arbitral Referee Procedure 1990. See Emmanuel Gaillard and Philippe Pinsolle, 'The ICC Pre-Arbitral Referee: First Practical Experiences' (2004) 20 Arbitration International 13.

the manner in which an action is handled can make or mar the client's case. Rules of court exist to ensure the proper conduct of the litigation, including the exchange of statements of case defining the issues and the disclosure and production of relevant documents. It is important that the rules should be thoroughly mastered and that the rights and benefits they confer should be fully utilized.

Civil litigation in England is based on the adversarial system. That is to say, the court adjudicates only on the issues which the parties present to it and upon the evidence which the parties choose to call. Apart from questions of illegality, the court cannot give a judgment on the basis of some issue not raised by the parties, nor has the court power to call witnesses of its own motion, other than experts. The adversarial system thus places a heavy burden on the lawyers on both sides, first, to ensure, by a proper selection of the issues, that they are litigating on the appropriate battleground and, secondly, that all the evidence which is available to establish the claims of their respective clients is properly collated and adduced at the trial. However, while the court cannot require parties to advance issues they do not wish to advance or adduce evidence they do not wish to adduce, the case management procedure does allow the court to curb the parties' enthusiasm by action of its own motion in excluding an issue from consideration[14] and excluding evidence that would otherwise be admissible.[15]

Litigation brings sharply into focus the difference between the theory and the practice of law. The client usually has no absorbing interest in the legal rules themselves; his concern is to secure a particular result. The problem he presents does not come neatly packaged as a tort, contract or property problem but will usually cover a number of traditional subject boundaries. The essence of successful practice in litigation is the art of persuasion. The client must be asked to state his objective and then be advised to consider whether this is either sensible or attainable, and must be encouraged to take alternatives that might be advantageous to him and to consider suitable opportunities for an out-of-court settlement.[16] The other side must be persuaded of the strength of the client's case, so that they will offer or accept terms of settlement favourable to him. The court must be persuaded to a decision favourable to the client if the action has not been previously settled. Persuasion has to be exercised at various stages: in correspondence and oral negotiations, in statements of case,[17] in interim applications[18] and at the trial itself.

In most actions questions of fact and practicality outweigh legal considerations. Is the client who proposes to bring an action eligible for state legal aid? If not, can he

---

14 CPR 3.1(2)(k). As to the CPR, see text and n 28.

15 CPR 32.1(2).

16 Almost all actions are settled without trial. One of the weaknesses of English civil procedure used to be that it was primarily concerned to ensure a fair trial when only a very small percentage of disputed cases reached a hearing. The Civil Justice Review and subsequent developments, which led to the replacement of most of the Rules of the Supreme Court by the Civil Procedure Rules, shifted the focus to procedures designed to encourage and facilitate negotiations for early settlement. See further below.

17 See below.

18 See below.

afford the costs of the proceedings?[19] Will the litigation promote or damage his reputation and his longer-term commercial interests? Is there sufficient evidence to prove his allegations?[20] Will the defendant be able to meet a judgment against him or is he a man of straw? The great majority of disputes involve questions of fact and of evidence rather than of law. But without a thorough knowledge of the law, the lawyer cannot know which facts are relevant.

Procedure is the handmaiden of the law. The two are inextricably entwined and the proper use of procedure plays a vital role in the establishment and enforcement of substantive rights. As we shall see, the courts have shown a remarkable degree of creativity in the development of procedural devices, the two most striking examples being freezing injunctions (formerly known as *Mareva* injunctions)[21] and search orders (formerly known as *Anton Piller* orders).[22]

Commercial litigation frequently involves multiple parties, and this complicates the procedure.[23]

3. THE CIVIL PROCEDURE RULES AND THE COURTS

(i)   The Civil Procedure Rules[24]

Civil procedure in England and Wales has undergone considerable change in the last few decades. Despite the numerous reforms resulting from the Civil Justice Review,[25] as well as the measures taken by the senior judiciary,[26] pressure for more radical change to reduce the cost and delay of litigation and shorten the length of trials continued. Following Lord Woolf's *Access to Justice* reports in 1995 and 1996,[27] comprehensive and far-reaching reforms, embodied in the Civil Procedure

---

19 Not infrequently the client decides to initiate proceedings on the basis that he can always bring them to an end if, contrary to expectations, the defendant fails to settle. But litigation has a momentum of its own, and it is all too easy for a claimant to reach the point of no return where the cost of discontinuance is perceived to outweigh the risk of going on. The client may be able to limit his risk by agreeing a contingency fee with his lawyers by which they agree to act on a no-win/no-fee basis and to charge a percentage of any recovery.

20 This can be a particularly difficult question for the lawyer when first instructed, for at that stage he has only one side of the story. Indeed, he may not know until the trial what witnesses the other side will call and the evidence they will give.

21 See p 1151.

22 See p 1154.

23 C. Hodges, *Multi-party actions* (2002).

24 SI 1998/3132 made by the Civil Procedure Rule Committee under the Civil Procedure Act 1997, ss 1, 2. See Adrian Zuckerman, *Civil Procedure* (2003), which is by far the best overall treatment of the subject.

25 *Report of the Review Body on Civil Justice* (Cm 394, 1988).

26 These reforms included a major expansion in county court jurisdiction and in the transfer of cases from the High Court to the county court; a more open approach to litigation through the exchange of witness statements and expert reports; the preparation of skeleton arguments for perusal by the opposing party and by the court prior to the hearing or appeal; the curtailing of opening speeches; and the abandonment of examination in chief.

27 *Access to Justice: Interim Report to the Lord Chancellor on the Civil Justice System in England and Wales* (1995); *Final Report to the Lord Chancellor on the Civil Justice System in England and Wales* (1996).

Rules (CPR),[28] made by statutory instrument, took effect from 26 April 1999. The CPR comprise the code governing civil procedure in county courts, the High Court, and the Court of Appeal (Civil Division).

The main concept underpinning the CPR is that of 'the overriding objective of enabling the court to deal with cases justly'.[29] This must be given effect to by the court when making decisions[30] and by actively managing cases,[31] and by the parties.[32] The CPR has introduced several changes in terminology. Most importantly, the parties to an action are now referred to as the claimant and the defendant, the former writ of summons has become a claim form pleadings are referred to as statements of case, and interlocutory applications are referred to as interim applications.

Statements of case include the claim form, particulars of claim, defence, counterclaim, Pt 20 claims, reply to defence and any further information in relation to the above. All statements of case must contain a statement of truth.[33] Obviously the parties cannot prepare for trial, or even negotiate effectively, unless each knows the nature of the case he has to meet. It is the function of statements of case to define the issues, so that the parties know what facts are disputed and will have to be proved, and what facts are admitted, making it unnecessary to call evidence about them. This laudable objective is not always achieved. Counsel settling statements of case are usually anxious to preserve the maximum amount of freedom to manoeuvre. This desire manifests itself in two ways: a reluctance to make admissions at an early stage in the proceedings, even where the allegation is unlikely to be seriously disputed at the trial; and the avoidance of particularity in the statements of fact set out in the statement of case, lest the party's case should be weakened if one of the details alleged is proved not to be correct. By contrast, counsel on the other side will endeavour to tie down his opponent to more precise contentions by requiring him to give further and better particulars of his statements of case.[34]

The drafting of statements of case is a task calling for considerable skill, judgment and legal knowledge. A statement of case is important for two reasons. First, a party

---

28 Referred to as the 'CPR'; all references in this chapter are to the CPR unless otherwise indicated. 'PD' indicates the Practice Directions supplementary to the rules. Very usefully, many of the materials, including regular updates of the CPR, are published on a government website: www.dca.gov.uk/civil/procrules.

29 CPR 1.1.

30 CPR 1.1(2): by ensuring that the parties are on an equal footing, saving expense, dealing with the case in a proportionate, expeditious and fair manner, and by allotting an appropriate share of court resources to it.

31 CPR 1.4: which includes encouraging the use of alternative dispute resolution proceedings (CPR 1.4(2)(e)).

32 CPR 1.3.

33 CPR 22.1; Commercial Court Guide (hereinafter 'CCG'; all references are to paragraph numbers, unless otherwise indicated) B3.7, C1.6, C1.7. A statement of case remains effective (unless it is struck out as a sanction) even where it is not verified by a statement of truth, although it may not then be relied on as evidence (PD 22, paras 4.1–4.3; CCG C1.10). Where a person makes, or causes to be made, a false statement in a document verified by a statement of truth, without an honest belief in its truth, he may be the subject of contempt proceedings (brought either by the Attorney-General or some other party with the permission of the court): CPR 32.14.

34 See p 1136.

will not be allowed to put forward at the trial grounds of claim or defence which he has not included in his statement of case. If he finds at the trial that he has omitted such a ground, he will have to seek permission to amend his statement of case and at this late stage permission may be refused. Secondly, a good statement of case is designed to convey an indication of the strength of the party's case and thus to induce the other party to discontinue the action (if he is the claimant) or settle on reasonable terms.

Pre-action protocols set out, in certain specific areas (while providing a general template), the steps that potential parties to litigation should explore prior to commencing proceedings in seeking and providing information to each other.[35] Penalties may be imposed where there is a failure to comply with pre-action protocols.[36] Currently pre-action protocols exist in several areas.[37]

(ii) The civil courts

Litigation involving a commercial dispute will almost invariably be brought in either the county court or the High Court,[38] either in the Queen's Bench Division or the Chancery Division. The Queen's Bench Division will usually be selected for actions involving breach of contract and common law rights, the Chancery Division for disputes involving equitable rights, the enforcement of mortgages, company matters and the administration of estates. Each of the divisions, in addition to its general work, has specialist courts within it for particular categories of business. The Patents Court and the Companies Court are part of the Chancery Division. The former deals with patent actions, the latter with company liquidations and receiverships and with reconstructions and schemes of arrangement and other matters arising under the Companies Acts. The Commercial Court and the Admiralty Court are part of the Queen's Bench Division. The latter deals with actions relating to ships and other Admiralty matters; the former is discussed in more detail below. Although the remainder of this chapter addresses the general rules relating to civil procedure, these rules apply equally to the Commercial Court, unless it is otherwise noted.

The need for adjudication of commercial disputes at a lower level[39] in London led to the creation of a Central London County Court Business List in 1994,[40] (now

35 PD-Protocols, para 1.3.
36 PD-Protocols, para 2.
37 These are: construction and engineering disputes, defamation, personal injury claims, resolution of clinical injury disputes, professional negligence, judicial review proceedings, disease and illness, and housing disrepair.
38 The High Court has always had unlimited jurisdiction except as provided by statute (eg the Consumer Credit Act 1974).
39 The main rule of thumb for allocating jurisdiction between the High Court and the county court, as set out in the High Court and County Courts Jurisdiction (Amendment) Order 1999 (SI 1999/1014) art 5 (inserting a new art 4A into the High Court and County Courts Jurisdiction Order 1991 (SI 1991/724)), is that claims for money in which county courts have jurisdiction may be started in the High Court only if the financial value is over £15,000.
40 The business list was established at the Central London County Court by Order 48C of the County Court Rules 1981 SI 1981/1687; Order 48C was inserted by SI 1994/1288. This jurisdiction was continued by Pt 49 of the CPR and its accompanying Practice Direction.

known as the Central London Civil Justice Centre). Furthermore, since 1990, disputes outside London have been heard in mercantile courts in Birmingham, Bristol, Cardiff, Leeds, Liverpool, Manchester and Newcastle. Circuit judges specializing in commercial work try cases in these courts.

(iii) The Commercial Court

1.   *The history and objectives of the Commercial Court*

The Commercial Court was first created as a formal court, as part of the Queen's Bench Division, in 1970.[41] Prior to this it existed as a Commercial List established by resolution of the judges of the Queen's Bench Division in 1895.[42] The court is manned by judges of the Queen's Bench Division with particular experience of commercial work, appointed to the court by the Lord Chancellor.

Many years ago Mr Justice Goff (now Lord Goff) described[43] two characteristics of the court's work: the large amounts involved (one case pending concerned a claim of over $3 billion, which even now is a huge sum) and the fact that in almost every action at least one of the parties was a foreigner. It would be fair to say that these are still characteristics of the court's work. The fact that the Commercial Court attracts such cases, (which is often, although not always, a reflection of other characteristics of the court's work: the complexity of the legal and factual issues involved) is no chicken and egg conundrum. As history shows,[44] the motivation behind the creation and maintenance of the Commercial Court was and has been the acknowledgement that, given the transactions conducted in and attracted by the commercial environment of London, there is a need to provide an equally commercial environment for the litigation of such disputes. It has also long been recognized that such an environment must be targeted and directed so that, against the backdrop of a general commercialism in the courts there is a honed expertise regarding cases of a particular commercial flavour, hence the separate existence of Commercial, Admiralty, Technology and Construction, Patents and Companies Courts.

This background highlights the key objectives of the Commercial Court's procedure: speed, simplicity, service. Various procedural aspects particular to the Commercial Court ensure that there is an inherent degree of flexibility, for example the provision for expedited applications, for trials without statements of case.[45] These aspects are juxtaposed against those which are more rigid than those under ordinary CPR. But that rigidity is traceable to the need to cater for the characteristic Commercial Court cases; for example, case management conferences are mandatory in the Commercial Court because of the size and complexity of the cases brought there and because there will often be an international element to the case, requiring a greater degree of

---

41 Supreme Court Act 1981, s 6(1) provides for an Admiralty Court and a Commercial Court as part of the Queen's Bench Division.

42 For the origins of the Commercial Court, see Anthony Colman, Victor Lyon and Philippa Hopkins, *The Practice and Procedure of the Commercial Court* (5th edn, 2000), ch 1.

43 'The Commercial Court – How It Works' (1981) 77 LS Gaz 1053.

44 Colman, Lyon and Hopkins, *Practice and Procedure of the Commercial Court*, ch 1.

45 See, eg, A. Hogan, *Fast track commercial claims* (1999).

trial preparation and organization. Likewise, there are a greater number of guidelines regarding the preparation of the trial bundles and a greater degree of supervision of the case development. This is underscored by ensuring that unlike ordinary Queen's Bench Division interim applications, those in the Commercial Court are heard before a commercial judge and not a Master. The expertise of the judiciary is buttressed by the accompanying administrative and developmental support particular to the Commercial Court (ie the Admiralty and Commercial Registry and the Commercial Court Committee).

The judge in charge of the Commercial List presides over the Commercial Court Committee, a body set up in 1977 to act as a link between the Commercial Court and its users. The committee consists of commercial judges, and representatives of the commercial Bar, City solicitors, leading City arbitrators' associations, commodity trade organizations, foreign individuals and organizations and others whose role is to discuss matters of mutual interest and concern relating to the practice of the court and the resolution of commercial disputes.[46] The Commercial Court Committee monitors the workings of the court and also produces reports on the state of the law in fields relevant to the work of the court, such as arbitration and carriage of goods by sea. It is expected to assist in synchronizing the procedure of the Commercial Court with the 'overriding objective'.[47]

The administrative office of the Commercial and Admiralty Courts is the Admiralty and Commercial Registry.

2. The CPR and the Commercial Court

The business of the Commercial Court is governed by CPR Pt 58, and the accompanying 'Practice Direction – Commercial Court'.[48] Part 58 provides that the CPR and Practice Directions apply to claims in the commercial list unless Pt 58 or a practice direction provides otherwise.[49]

A Commercial Court Guide[50] supplements Pt 58 and PD 58. The role of the Commercial Court Guide is that it

> is not intended to be a blueprint to which all litigation must unthinkingly conform: as in the past, it seeks to provide a modern and flexible framework within which litigation can be conducted efficiently and in the interests of justice…This Guide has been produced in order to set out in a convenient manner the practice which applies in the Admiralty and Commercial Courts. It should be read in conjunction with the Civil Procedure Rules and Practice Directions.[51]

The conduct of litigation in the Commercial Court is therefore to be understood by combining the general CPR and Practice Directions with Pt 58, PD 58 and the

---

46 For a detailed account of the role of the Committee, see Colman, Lyon and Hopkins, *Practice and Procedure of the Commercial Court*, ch 2.
47 CCG A3.2; on the overriding objective, see p 1124.
48 Hereinafter referred to as PD 58.
49 CPR 58.3.
50 Now in its 6th edition, issued in 2002.
51 CCG Introduction.

Commercial Court Guide.[52] The same terms apply to statements of case in the Commercial Court as elsewhere, although there are some forms that are exclusive to the Commercial Court. Appendix 4 of the CCG sets out specific requirements for the statements of case in the Commercial Court. There is a stipulation in the Commercial Court that where a statement of case extends beyond 20 pages, the party serving it must also prepare a case summary under 4 pages and include the summary, rather than the full statement of case, in the case management bundle.[53]

It is still technically possible to have a trial without statements of case in the Commercial Court[54] but it is questionable how often this is likely to be invoked in fact, given the practical difficulties which would ensue. Although there is no particular pre-action protocol for the Commercial Court, it is incumbent upon potential Commercial Court, and other, litigants to observe the spirit of the protocols and the overriding objective.[55]

3.   The jurisdiction of the Commercial Court[56]

Rather than providing a definition of 'commercial claim', Pt 58 describes the ambit of the term by *example*, by including possible issues which *may* fall within 'commercial claims'. It provides:[57]

> 58.1
>
> (2) In this Part and its practice direction, 'commercial claim' means any claim arising out of the transaction of trade and commerce and includes any claim relating to
>
> a   a business document or contract;
> b   the export or import of goods;
> c   the carriage of goods by land, sea, air or pipeline;
> d   the exploitation of oil and gar reserves or other natural resources;
> e   insurance and re-insurance;
> f   banking and financial services;
> g   the operation of markets and exchanges;
> h   the purchase and sale of commodities;
> i   the construction of ships;
> j   business agency; and
> k   arbitration proceedings.

52 Since 25 March 2002 the functions and procedures of the Mercantile Courts outside London have been governed by CPR Pt 59 and its accompanying Practice Direction. As stated in PD59 para 1.2(2), the Business List is now called the Mercantile List and is covered by the Commercial Court Guide, a separate guide having been discontinued.
53 CCG C1.4.
54 CPR 58.11; CCG B3.8.
55 For example, the court will expect parties to 'act reasonably in exchanging information and documents relevant to the claim and generally in trying to avoid the necessity for the start of proceedings.' (PD-Protocols, para 4).
56 Jurisdiction under the Brussels Convention and its successor, the Brussels Regulation, has already been considered in the previous chapter. See pp 1076 ff. State immunity from suit is considered in the context of commercial arbitration p 1195.
57 Where matters fall outside the specific examples set out in Pt 58, it appears that it is left to the practice (and possibly the discretion) of the commercial judges whether the Commercial Court is a suitable forum for a particular matter, and the best course, when in doubt, for ascertaining whether a matter will be treated as suitable is to consult (presumably for analogous cases) the index of *Lloyd's Law Reports* (Colman, Lyon and Hopkins, *Practice and Procedure of the Commercial Court*, pp 31–32).

A commercial claim can be started in the Commercial Court[58] or an application may be made, and which will be considered by a judge in the Commercial Court, to transfer a claim there from another list.[59] A commercial judge may order a claim started in the Commercial Court to be transferred elsewhere[60] (this is particularly true for cases which might more suitably be dealt with in one of the mercantile courts[61]). The procedure for transferring proceedings to or from the Commercial Court is set out in PD 58.[62]

It is theoretically open to a party to seek to challenge a commercial judge's discretion to treat a matter as either suitable or unsuitable for the Commercial Court by appealing to the Court of Appeal with the permission of the commercial judge or the Court of Appeal.

4.   The Future of the Commercial Court

The Lord Chancellor commissioned a study to 'examine the potential for establishing a new Commercial Court in London to handle a wide range of high value and international commercial litigation and to develop Britain's role as a global centre for dispute resolution.'[63] In this context, 'commercial court' was taken to encompass the work currently undertaken in the Commercial, Admiralty, Technology and Construction, Patents and Companies Courts. The CGEY Study[64] represented the most widespread survey to date of those involved in commercial courts. It was followed by a consultation paper issued by the Court Service.[65] The modernization programme remains ongoing.

4.   THE INTERIM STAGES

A great deal of work goes on between the start of a contested action and the trial, which may not take place for some considerable time, sometimes years after the commencement of the proceedings. The various interlocutory stages which occupy this interval have six primary objectives:

(a)   To define the issues. This is the function of the statements of case.[66]

(b)   To elicit relevant documents, through a process known as disclosure,[67] and advance details of evidence through the service of witness statements and an exchange of experts' reports.

(c)   To promote early settlement, through early formulations of the case and disclosure.

---

58 CPR 58.4(1).

59 CPR 58.4(2).

60 CPR 58.4(2).

61 CCG B12.5.

62 Paragraph 4.

63 Press release issued by the Lord Chancellor's Department's Press Office, 9 November 2000.

64 *Commercial Court Feasibility Study* (March 2001) produced by Cap Gemini Ernst and Young (CGEY Study).

65 *Modernisation of the Commercial Court* (10 December 2001).

66 Formerly called pleadings. See Zuckerman, *Civil Procedure*, ch 6.

67 Formerly called discovery. See p 1143.

(d)   Where necessary, to give one of the parties interim protection pending trial, eg by way of an interim injunction or a search order.[68]

(e)   To safeguard the fruits of success of the action, eg:

  (i)   by an order for payment into court as a condition of giving a defendant leave to defend[69] – a safeguard for the claimant;

  (ii)   by the grant of a freezing injunction restraining the defendant from transferring his assets abroad or otherwise dissipating them pending trial – a safeguard for the claimant;[70]

  (iii)   by an order requiring the claimant to give security for the costs he would have to pay if unsuccessful – a safeguard for the defendant.

(f)   To ensure that the action is in a proper state for trial.

5.   JUDGMENT WITHOUT TRIAL

The CPR prescribe a variety of situations in which a party[71] may obtain judgment without trial. The principal among these are the following.

(i)   Default judgment

If the defendant has not filed an acknowledgment of service or a defence and 14 days have expired since the particulars of claim were served or if the defendant has filed an acknowledgment of service but has not filed a defence and 28 days have expired,[72] then the claimant can apply to the court for a default judgment.[73] In such cases there is often no hearing, and obtaining the default judgment is simply an administrative act. Default judgments cannot be obtained in certain cases,[74] including Pt 8 proceedings, admiralty and arbitration proceedings. The claimant is also prevented from obtaining a default judgment where the defendant has taken particular steps, for example, applying for summary judgment or to have the claimant's case struck out.[75]

The most common types of case in which default judgments are sought are for the recovery of money or the delivery of goods. In these cases default judgments can be obtained by filing a standard form request; there will be no hearing and no need to persuade the court to enter judgment. An application to the court will often be necessary in other cases; usually where equitable relief is being sought. Judgment in money claims can be made either as a final judgment (requiring the defendant to

---

68   See p 1150.

69   This arises where the claimant applies for summary judgment. See p 1131.

70   See p 1151.

71   Not all of these are of general application, as is indicated below.

72   For the relevant rules governing the filing and serving of statements of case, see pp 1132 ff.

73   CPR 12.3. Pt 12 and PD 12 apply equally to the Commercial Court except that references to 'particulars of claim' should be read as reference to the claim form, because in the Commercial Court the period for filing the acknowledgement of service is taken from the service of the claim form (see p 1136): CPR 58.8(1), CCG B10.

74   PD 12, paras 1.2, 1.3.

75   CPR 12.3(3).

pay a particular amount within a specified period) or as an interlocutory judgment for damages (where, although liability has been determined, the amount payable has still to be determined).

It is possible for a default judgment to be set aside or varied.[76]

(ii) Summary judgment

The summary judgment procedure enables the court, on the application of either party or of its own initiative, to eliminate whole or parts of either a claim or a defence where the claim or defence does not have a real prospect of success. It is closely related to the court's power to strike out; both powers fulfil the overriding objective of active case management by the summary disposal of issues that do not require full trials.[77] The difference between the two procedures is that summary judgment is used where the facts of the claim seem so weak that it has little prospect of success whereas in a strike out the elimination is levied on the basis on which the statement of case is presented.[78]

Summary judgment can be applied for by either party but only after the defendant has filed either an acknowledgment of service or his defence.[79] As with other interim applications, it is necessary to complete an application notice and serve this together with all relevant evidence on the other party and the court, giving notice of 14 days before the hearing.[80] The respondent has to file and serve any evidence in reply seven days before the hearing.[81] If the applicant responds to the respondent's evidence, the reply evidence must be filed at least three days before the hearing.[82]

After the hearing the court may give judgment on the claim, dismiss the application, strike out or dismiss the claim, make a conditional order, or a combination thereof.

(iii) Striking out

Striking out of a statement of case, or a part thereof, can occur where it appears to the court that the statement of case discloses no reasonable grounds for bringing or defending the claim or is an abuse of the court's process or where there has been a failure to comply with a rule, practice direction or order.[83] Striking out can occur at the application of a party or on the court's initiative.[84] If the particulars of claim are struck out, an action will be stayed or dismissed, whereas if a defence is struck out, judgment will be entered for the claimant.

---

76 Part 13.
77 CPR 1.4(2)(c).
78 CPR 24.2(a).
79 Unless the court permits otherwise r 24.4(1).
80 CPR 24.4(3).
81 CPR 24.5(1).
82 CPR 24.5(2).
83 CPR 3.4(2).
84 PD 3, para 4.1.

6.   STAGES IN A CONTESTED QUEEN'S BENCH ACTION

The following are the principal stages in a typical contested action in the Queen's Bench Division.[85]

(i)   Commencing proceedings

1. The claim form and particulars of claim

A case is commenced by the issue of a claim form under Pt 7 or Pt 8.[86] Commercial Court claim forms must be marked with 'Queen's Bench Division, Commercial Court' in the top right corner.[87] Specific Commercial Court forms, corresponding to Pt 7 and Pt 8 claim forms, are available.[88] A Commercial Court claim form will be issued by the Admiralty and Commercial Registry.[89]

A claim form will include the names and addresses of the parties, a brief statement of the nature of the claim, the remedy sought and a statement of value where the claim is for money (although it may be that the amount cannot be stated). Particulars of claim, the formal written statement of the claimant's case, can be attached to the claim form or set out as a separate document.[90]

There is an insistence in the Commercial Court that the claim form (rather than, as is usual, only the particulars of claim) includes the basis for the claim of interest and the rate sought.[91] Furthermore, Commercial Court claim forms do not require a statement of value, as is generally needed under the CPR in the case of an ordinary Queen's Bench action.[92]

Service of the claim form must occur within four months of its being issued.[93] The claim form is served (either with or without the particulars of claim[94]) with a response pack, which contains forms relating to acknowledgment of service, admission, defence and counterclaim. Where the particulars of claim document is not served with the claim form, it must follow within 14 days of the service of the

---

85 We shall for the moment defer discussion of the more urgent forms of interim protection, for example freezing injunctions and search orders. See p 1151.

86 Part 8 proceedings are appropriate either where the claimant 'seeks the court's decision on a question which is unlikely to involve a substantial dispute of fact' (CPR 8.1(2)(a)) or where a rule or Practice Direction specifically requires or permits the use of Pt 8 (CPR 8.1(6)). PD 8B sets out a non-exhaustive list of situations in which proceedings must be commenced by a Pt 8 claim form (s A). A claimant must specifically state when using a Pt 8 claim form that Pt 8 applies and that he wishes or is required to proceed under it (CPR 8(2); CCG B4.2).

87 PD 58, para 2.3.

88 PD 58, para 2.4.

89 PD 58. para 2.1.

90 PD 16, para 3.1. Commercial Court practice does not require particulars of claim to be served with the claim form either (CCG B3.4).

91 CPR 58.5(3); CCG B3.9–3.10.

92 CPR 16.3, 16.5, 58.5(2), CCG B3.3.

93 CPR 7.5(2). This is extended to six months where the defendant is out of the jurisdiction: CPR 7.5(3).

94 For specimen particulars of claim, see fig 38.1.

claim form and within the period of validity of the claim form.[95] Rule 6.2 sets out possible methods of service but the most common is by the court.[96] After the claim form has been served, the claimant must file a certificate of service with the court within seven days.[97]

Where the particulars of claim are not served with the claim form, they must be served within 28 days after the filing of the acknowledgement of service,[98] rather than 14 days. The particulars of claim must be filed within seven days of the service, together with a certificate of service,[99] and service must be undertaken by the claimant rather than the court.[100]

2.   Acknowledgement of service and defences

When a defendant receives a claim form, he has three options:

(a)   He can admit the claim and file an admission (either of the whole claim or just a part).[101]

(b)   He can contest the claim by filing a defence and/or counterclaim.[102] A defence must address every statement of fact in the particulars of claim by either admitting it, denying it or requiring the claimant to prove it;[103] otherwise the defendant is typically deemed to accept the fact alleged.[104] Where the defendant has a claim against the claimant,[105] instead of going to the trouble and expense of bringing a separate action he can make a counterclaim in the same proceedings. The counterclaim is included in the same document as the defence, the document then being termed a defence and counterclaim. A counterclaim is treated in all respects as if it were a claim, so that the claimant must serve a defence to it (combining this with his reply to form a reply and defence to counterclaim[106]), failing which the defendant may enter judgment in default on the counterclaim in the same circumstances as the claimant could have done on his claim.[107] The defendant is also entitled to invoke Pt 24 to obtain summary judgment on a counterclaim to which there is no defence.

95 CPR 7.4(2).
96 CPR 6.3. Where the defendant is outside the jurisdiction but the Brussels Regulation, Brussels Convention or Lugano Convention is applicable, it is not necessary to obtain permission in order to issue proceedings in England and serve them abroad (CPR 6.19). Permission will be necessary where the defendant is outside the jurisdiction and where the Brussels Regulation, Brussels Convention and Lugano Convention are not applicable (CPR 6.20, discussed p 1074).
97 CPR 6.14(2); CCG para B6.6.
98 CCG C2.1a.
99 CCG C2.3.
100 PD 58 para 9; CCG B6.1.
101 This allows the claimant to apply for judgment on the admission (CPR 14.3).
102 For a specimen defence and counterclaim, see fig 38.2.
103 CPR 16.5(1).
104 CPR 16.5(5).
105 See pp 1141 for the situation where the defendant wants to claim against a third party under Pt 20.
106 For a specimen reply and defence to counterclaim, see fig 38.3.
107 CPR 12.3(2).

IN THE HIGH COURT OF JUSTICE   Claim No. CC/4566/04

QUEEN'S BENCH DIVISION

COMMERCIAL COURT

WHEATSHEAF LIMITED   Claimant

-and-

CORNWALL PLC   Defendant

PARTICULARS OF CLAIM

1. The Claimant is a company incorporated under the laws of England and Wales and carrying on business as a cattle farmer. The Defendant is a company incorporated under England and Wales and carrying on business as a manufacturer and supplier of cattle feed.

2. By an agreement in writing ('the Agreement') made between the Claimant and the Defendant on or about 15th January 2000 the Defendant agreed to make up and sell and the Claimant agreed to buy at the price of £5,000 a quantity of compound meal for feeding to the Claimant's cattle.

3. The following were, amongst others, express conditions of the Agreement:

   a. That the compound meal would be fit for the purpose of feeding to the Claimant's cattle.

   b. That the compound meal would be of satisfactory quality.

4. Further, or alternatively, the Agreement included the implied conditions that the compound meal would be fit for the purpose of feeding the Claimant's cattle and that it would be of satisfactory quality. These terms are implied as a matter of law and/or to give business efficacy to the agreement.

5. The compound meal was delivered to the Claimant in June 2000, but it was unfit for its purpose of being fed to the Claimant's cattle and was not of satisfactory quality.

Fig 38.1 Particulars of Claim

Particulars

The compound meal contained a toxin poisonous to cattle. In consequence, 50 head of cattle fed with the meal became ill and died at an average age of 5 months when they would otherwise have been sold at the age of 11 months.

6. In the premises, the Defendant breached the express and/or implied conditions of the Agreement.

7. By reason of the Defendant's said breaches of the Agreement, the Claimant has suffered loss and damage.

Particulars of loss and damage

Sale value of 50 head of cattle at £550 each	£27,500
Less credit for six months' feed saved, ie 1.5 tonnes per head at £150 a tonne	£11, 250

Net loss of profit	£16, 250
Veterinary fees	£ 250
	£16, 500

8. Further, the Claimant claims interest pursuant to section 35A of the Supreme Court Act 1981 at such rate and for such period as the court thinks fit.

And the Claimant Claims:

(1) Damages;
(2) Interest pursuant to section 35A of the Supreme Court Act 1981

JOHN DOUGHTY

I believe/ the claimant believes that the facts stated in these particulars of claim are true.

Served the 16th day of February 2004 by Messrs. Battle & Axe of Action House, Sloe Street, London, WC2R 2LS, solicitors for the Claimant.

(c)   He can simply file an acknowledgement of service. This can be used where he either lacks the time to put in a defence or where he wants to object to the court having jurisdiction.[108]

In a Pt 7 application, a defendant is not obliged to acknowledge service of the claim form. He can simply file his defence within 14 days of service of the particulars of claim.[109]

In comparison, the defendant in an action commenced in the Commercial Court is *required* to file acknowledgement of service in every case,[110] with the 14-day period running not from the date of service of the particulars of claim, as is the case under ordinary CPR,[111] but from the date of service of the claim form.[112] This specific Commercial Court requirement to serve an acknowledgement of service after receiving the claim form may cause defendants, incorrectly assuming that the ordinary CPR practice applies, to fail to serve an acknowledgement of service and therefore enable claimants to obtain default judgment.[113] The defendant who intends to defend a claim must file and serve his defence 28 days after the service of the particulars of claim.[114]

Where the Pt 8 procedure is used, there is a uniform rule under both the ordinary CPR and in the Commercial Court that an acknowledgement of service must always be filed.[115] A default judgment cannot be obtained where the Pt 8 procedure is deployed.[116]

3.   Subsequent statements of case: replies, further information and Part 20 proceedings

In an ordinary Queen's Bench action the claimant must file his reply at the same time that he files his allocation questionnaire.[117] Since no allocation questionnaire is necessary in the Commercial Court, the reply is to be served and filed 21 days after service of the defence.[118]

It may be that to prepare his own case, or understand the case he has to meet, a party needs information beyond that contained in the statements of case, witness statements or documents obtained via disclosure. The CPR provide a procedure for obtaining such further information, provided that the request for it is concise and restricted to matters which are reasonably necessary and proportionate to the purpose.[119]

---

108   Although he will be required to make an application under Pt 11, he is still required to acknowledge service.
109   CPR 15.4(1).
110   CPR 58.6(1).
111   CPR 9.1.
112   CCG B8.1b; B8.4a.
113   See p 1131.
114   CCG C3.2.
115   CPR 8.3, CCG B8.2.
116   CPR 8.1(5).
117   CPR 15.8, 26.3. See p 1142.
118   CPR 58.10(1); CCG C4.2.
119   PD 18, para 1.2.

IN THE HIGH COURT OF JUSTICE   Claim No. CC/4566/04

QUEEN'S BENCH DIVISION

COMMERCIAL COURT

WHEATSHEAF LIMITED   Claimant

-and-

CORNWALL PLC   Defendant

DEFENCE AND COUNTERCLAIM

DEFENCE

1.   Paragraph 1 of the Particulars of Claim is admitted.

2.   Paragraph 2 of the Particulars of Claim is admitted; that pursuant to a written agreement ('the Agreement') the Defendant agreed to make up and sell a compound meal to the Claimant for feeding to the Claimant's cattle.

3.   As to paragraph 3 and 4 of the Particulars of Claim:

   a.   It is denied that it was either an express or implied condition of the Agreement that the compound meal would be fit for the purpose for which the Claimant alleges it was required.

   b.   It is averred that the Claimant gave detailed instructions to the Defendant as to the required composition of the compound meal. The Claimant relied entirely on its own skill and expertise.

   c.   Further or alternatively, if, which is denied, the Claimant did rely on the Defendant's skill and judgment, such reliance was unreasonable in the above circumstances.

   d.   Further, it is denied that it was either an express or implied condition of the Agreement that the compound meal would be of satisfactory quality. As is noted in paragraphs 3b above, the Claimant specified the ingredients of the compound meal.

   e.   It is averred that the only implied term of the Agreement was that each ingredient in the compound meal should be of satisfactory quality.

Fig 38.2 Defence and Counterclaim

4. As to paragraphs 5–7 of the Particulars of Claim:

    a. It is denied that the compound meal contained a toxin poisonous to cows.

    b. Further or alternatively, if, which is denied, the compound meal did contain such a toxin, it could still have been safely fed to cattle if administered in accordance with the accompanying instructions. It is averred that the Claimant failed to feed its cattle in accordance with such instructions.

    c. In the premises, the Defendant denies that it breached the express and implied conditions of the Agreement as alleged in paragraph 6 of the Particulars of Claim.

    d. By reason of the matters aforesaid, it is denied that the Claimant has suffered loss or damage as alleged or at all, and it is further denied that such loss and damage as the Claimant may establish was caused by any breach of the Agreement on the part of the Defendant.

5. Further or alternatively, the Defendant relies on clause 3 of the Agreement, which provides that the Defendant "shall not be liable for any defects in any goods made up or supplied by them, whether or not due to negligence on their part, and all representations, conditions and warranties, express or implied, as to the quality of the goods or their suitability for any purpose are excluded".

COUNTERCLAIM

6. The Claimant has failed to pay the agreed price of the compound meal, namely £5,000 on the due date, 30th June 2000.

7. Further, the Defendant claims interest pursuant to section 35A of the Supreme Court Act 1981 from 30th June 2000 at the rate of X% above Barclays Bank base rate from time to time.

AND the Defendant counterclaims:

    (1) £5,000;

    (2) interest thereon pursuant to section 35A of the Supreme Court Act 1981 from 30th June 2000 at the rate of 4% above Barclays Bank base rate from time to time.

RICHARD ROBUST

I believe/ the defendant believes that the facts stated in this defence and counterclaim are true.

Served the 10th day of March 2004 by Messrs Helmut, Shield & Co. of Defence House, Barricade Street, London EC3 4RZ.

IN THE HIGH COURT OF JUSTICE   Claim No. CC/4566/04

QUEEN'S BENCH DIVISION

COMMERCIAL COURT

WHEATSHEAF LIMITED   <u>Claimant</u>

-and-

CORNWALL PLC   <u>Defendant</u>

REPLY AND DEFENCE
TO COUNTERCLAIM

<u>REPLY</u>

1. Paragraph 3b of the Defence, that the Defendant was supplied with instructions for the use of compound meal by the Claimant, is denied.

2. It is admitted that clause 3 of the agreement provides as set out in paragraph 5 of the Defence. It is averred that clause 3 fails to satisfy the test of reasonableness required by sections 3 and 6 of the Unfair Contract Terms Act 1977.

Particulars

Clause 3 fails to satisfy the test of reasonableness because:

a. the parties are not of equal bargaining power, the Claimant being a small private company while the Defendant is a large and powerful public company;

b. the Defendant is the leading specialist in the manufacture and supply of cattle feed whereas the Claimant is merely a farmer with no specialist knowledge;

c. the Defendant has, or alternatively could easily have, covered itself with insurance without significant cost;

d. the Agreement, including clause 3, was printed in miniscule print which the Claimant could not reasonably have been expected to read, and its attention was not drawn to the said clause, of which they were unaware at the time of entering the Agreement.

Fig 38.3 Reply and Defence to Counterclaim

1140

DEFENCE TO COUNTERCLAIM

3.   Paragraph 6 of the Defence is admitted, insofar as the Claimant has failed to pay the Defendant. It is averred that the compound meal supplied by the Defendant was of no value to the Claimant, and the consideration for the same has wholly failed.

4.   In the premises, it is denied that the Claimant is liable to pay the said agreed price or any part of it for the compound meal.

JOHN DOUGHTY

I believe/ the claimant believes that the facts stated in this reply and defence to counterclaim are true.

Served the 26th day of March 2004 by Messrs. Battle & Axe of Action House, Sloe Street, London, WC2R 2LS, solicitors for the Claimant.

Part 20 proceedings include counterclaims, claims for indemnity or contribution and other remedies.[120] They include situations where the defendant wants to claim against a person other than the claimant (but in a closely related matter) and where the defendant claims that if the claimant succeeds, then a third party should pay either the whole (an indemnity) or a part of the claim (a contribution). The court retains discretion on whether to allow Pt 20 proceedings.

Part 20 claim forms are issued and served in the same way as ordinary claim forms. A defendant will not need permission if the Pt 20 claim form is issued before the defence is filed but will do so thereafter.[121] The rules regarding time limits and case management are the same as for ordinary Pt 7 claims. Despite the fact that Pt 20 proceedings piggyback on an underlying claim, they do have a separate existence and the life of the underlying claim is not unequivocally bound to that of the Pt 20 claim. Special Pt 20 forms exist in the Commercial Court.

4. *Extensions of time and amendments*

The court may extend or shorten any time limit in the rules or a court order.[122] It is permissible for the parties to agree extensions of time (for example, in relation to the defence), provided this is evidenced in writing and notification is provided to the court.[123] Parties cannot agree to extend time limits relating to certain dates, for instance for case management conferences, trial dates or in relation to any step carrying a sanction in default.[124] In the Commercial Court extension by agreement of time between the parties is not permitted for the service and filing of the reply; and can be gained only via a court order.[125]

Amending a statement of case without permission is possible before the statement of case is served but otherwise either the consent of all parties or the permission of the court is needed.[126]

(ii) Case Management

Judicial case management is an integral part of the new system introduced by the CPR. The various aspects of case management, which are detailed in a non-exhaustive way in CPR 1.4(2), include encouraging the parties to cooperate with each other in the conduct of the proceedings. To comply with the overriding case management objective, the court will allocate every defended case to one of three case

---

120 CPR 20.2.
121 CPR 20.7(3).
122 CPR 3.1(2)(a).
123 CPR 15. 5(1); CCG C2.1, C3.2, C3.3, C3.4.
124 CPR 3.8(3).
125 Because of the practical impact this could have on the subsequent stages of a contested action in the Commercial Court, in particular the timing of the Case Management Conference and its preparatory stages: CCG C4.3. There appears to be no provision for parties to agree an extension of time for the service of a reply under the CPR although CPR 26.3(6A) provides that the date for filing the completed allocation questionnaire cannot be altered by the parties and, since this is the same as the date for filing of the reply under CPR 15.8(a), this would imply that parties cannot vary the date by which the reply must be filed.
126 CPR 17.1.

management tracks. This usually occurs after the defence has been filed, when the court will serve allocation questionnaires on the parties (although this is not an essential requirement). These questionnaires ask about, for example, compliance with any pre-action protocol, details of witnesses, contemplated applications, and the parties opinion on which track is most suitable. The allocation is made principally on the financial value of the claim, although other factors must also be considered.[127]

1.   Small Claims

With some exceptions (eg claims involving a disputed allegation of dishonesty), the small claims track accommodates simple claims with a value of less that £5,000.[128] Since they are easier to deal with than cases on other tracks, standard directions will usually be given. These typically provide that the parties are to serve documents on the other side no later than 14 days before the hearing, that the original documents must be brought to the hearing, that notice of the hearing date and the length of the hearing are given, and that the parties are to tell the court if they settle the case. There are various restrictions on the procedures that can be entertained in the small claims track; for example, most interim remedies, requests for further information and Pt 36 offers and payments are inappropriate, and a narrower than standard form of disclosure applies. Final hearings in small claims are usually before county court district judges.

2.   Fast Track

Claims of between £5,000 and £15,000 are generally allocated to the fast track.[129] The preparation involved in these will be more protracted and detailed than the small claims track. When the court determines that a case is to be put on the fast track, directions will be given for a schedule regarding the stages of the litigation, including the trial, with the trial window within 30 weeks after the track allocation decision. These directions will be made on the court's own initiative but the allocation questionnaires and statements of case will be taken into consideration. As well as the specific directions, the parties in a fast-track case will have to comply with other limits (for example, requirements relating to the preparation of trial bundles or the serving of hearsay notices under the Civil Evidence Act 1995). Listing questionnaires, to gauge whether the parties have been complying with the directions made at the allocation stage and whether the case is prepared for trial, must be returned to the court by the parties at least eight weeks before the trial date, and statements of costs also must be filed. Fast-track trials often take place in the county court before a district judge.

3. Multi-track

The most complex cases, often specialist proceedings and cases commenced under Pt 8, will be allocated to the multi-track.[130] The principal defining feature of this

---

127   CPR 26.8.
128   CPR 26.6(3).
129   CPR 26.6(4)–(5).
130   CPR 26.6(6) states that the multi-track is for those cases for which the small claims track or fast track are not the normal track.

track is that courts are given considerable flexibility to manage cases according to their specific requirements. When the case is allocated to the multi-track, the judge will decide whether to give directions, or arrange a case-management conference (CMC) or pre-trial review. The focus of CMCs is to ensure that the real issues between the parties are identified and the first CMC is the most suitable time for the consideration of any appropriate interim relief in a given case. Where pre-trial reviews are deemed necessary, they are usually timetabled for between 8 and 10 weeks before the trial and are before the actual trial judge. The aim of pre-trial reviews is to finalize the statement of issues to be tried as well as a programme and budget. The court will set a trial date or the period in which the trial will occur as soon as is practicable[131] and will give directions for when listing questionnaires should be filed. The trial date will be discussed at a listings hearing.

4. Case Management in the Commercial Court

Specialist courts have different procedures for dealing with case management. There is no allocation in the Commercial Court because all cases are automatically treated as multi-track.[132] The first CMC in a Commercial Court case is mandatory[133] and the responsibility of applying for it lies with the claimant,[134] although the court can arrange one on its own initiative.[135]

The CCG sets out the '10 key features' of case management in a normal Pt 7 claim form application.[136] These are noteworthy, as they highlight the role of the case memorandum and the list of issues,[137] the difference between the role of CMCs in non-Commercial Court and Commercial Court litigation, and that the progress monitoring date is distinct to the Commercial Court, giving the court a chance to revise case preparation and see whether it is ready for trial.[138]

(iii) Disclosure of documents and evidence

As previously stated, disclosure is the process by which parties to an action are required to reveal to each other the existence of all documents[139] which have been

---

131 CPR 29.2(2).
132 CPR 58.13(1).
133 CPR 58.13(3).
134 PD 58 para 10(2).
135 PD 58 para 10(6).
136 CCG D2.
137 These are not specifically noted either under the ordinary CPR or in other courts with a commercial jurisdiction. CCG D5 sets out the necessary content for a case memorandum. The case memorandum and the information sheet in the Commercial Court take the place of the allocation questionnaire under ordinary CPR (Pt 26), although they are not directly analogous as they have different functions, no allocation being necessary in the Commercial Court. CCG D7.2 sets out the content for the case management bundle; the preparation and updating for which the claimant is responsible (CCG D7.1). The case management bundle must be lodged with the Commercial Registry at least seven days before the first CMC.
138 The progress monitoring date does not involve a hearing, simply a review by the judge of the progress monitoring information sheet and case management bundle: CCG D12.
139 This includes anything on which evidence or information is recorded: CPR 31.4.

or are within their control and which are material to the issues in the action. The usual method is for lists of documents to be exchanged after a case has been allocated to either the fast or the multi-track and after directions regarding disclosure have been given. The list must note the documents which are privileged, and which cannot therefore be inspected or copied (for example, those protected by legal professional privilege[140] or requiring protection on grounds of public policy[141]), and those which are no longer available (indicating the reason for the unavailability). It is necessary for each party to provide a disclosure statement of the extent of the search that has been made and that the party understands the duty to disclose and has carried out the duty to the best of their knowledge. Each party can inspect and make copies of the documents disclosed by the other side.[142] Subject to some qualifications, documents provided in the course of disclosure can be used only for the proper conduct of the action.[143] It is the solicitor's responsibility to ensure that his client has effected full disclosure as required. An order compelling disclosure can be made where a party fails to make the appropriate disclosure, and penalties may be imposed on a party who fails to make full and proper disclosure.

Unless the court directs otherwise, an order for disclosure means standard disclosure.[144] Standard disclosure extends to documents upon which the party is relying, those which may adversely affect either *his own case* or that of another party, those which support another party's case and those required to be disclosed by a practice direction (cf small claims where the duty is simply to disclose documents that will be relied upon).[145]

Parties may apply for specific disclosure by making a particular request and providing evidence that in their belief the other party has or has had those documents, that they are disclosable under standard disclosure or on an application of the overriding objective. If made, an order for specific disclosure may require the disclosure of documents or classes of documents, a particular search, or disclosure of documents resulting from that search.[146]

In addition to the above, special disclosure orders can also be made. For example, *Norwich Pharmacal* orders can be made against a person who has facilitated a wrongdoing, requiring them to disclose to the prospective claimant the identity of the wrongdoer.[147] *Norwich Pharmacal* orders can also be sought to enable a prospective claimant to obtain documents necessary to bring a possible action in tort, even though, without the documents of which disclosure is sought, it could not be ascertained whether the alleged wrongdoer had actually committed a tort against the prospective

---

140 Zuckerman, *Civil Procedure*, ch 15.
141 Ibid, paras 14.50 ff. The fact that a party owes a duty of confidentiality in regard to a document is not by itself a sufficient justification for failing to disclose it in proceedings.
142 CPR 31.15.
143 CPR 31.22(1).
144 CPR 31.5.
145 CPR 31.6.
146 CPR 31.12.
147 *Norwich Pharmacal Co* v *Customs and Excise Commissioners* [1974] AC 133, HL.

claimant.[148] *Norwich Pharmacal* orders are not restricted to any particular type of case.[149] Furthermore, they are discretionary; therefore, even if the basic conditions are made out, they may be refused, for example on public interest grounds.

Another special disclosure order is that the court may order pre-action disclosure against a *likely* defendant. This can be ordered where it is likely that the applicant and defendant will be party to subsequent proceedings, and where the defendant appears likely to have had relevant documents in his possession, custody or power. Pre-action disclosure orders cater for the desirability in dealing with the anticipated proceedings fairly, to prevent the proceedings being commenced altogether or to save costs.[150]

It is possible for the court to order the inspection and examination of property which is relevant to proceedings. This can be done before the proceedings are issued, where property is in the possession of one of the parties,[151] or in the possession of a non party.[152] The Torts (Interference with Goods) Act 1977 s 4(2) provides that it is possible for the court to order the delivery up of goods which are or may become the subject matter of subsequent proceedings. Applications under this statute are included in the interim remedies available under r 25.1(1)(e).

Another aspect of the 'cards on the table' approach is the requirement to serve witness statements and exchange experts' reports.[153]

(iv) Negotiations for settlement: Part 36 offers and payments

Most cases are settled before trial, while the settlement of others may arise before the end of the trial[154] or prior to or during the hearing of an appeal.[155] Part 36 offers and payments are methods for exerting pressure on the other party to end the litigation. By a Pt 36 payment, the defendant pays money into court and serves a notice on the claimant informing him, with particulars, of the payment in.[156] The proceedings are stayed where the claimant decides to accept the payment, and he

---

148 *P v T* [1997] 4 All ER 200.
149 *British Steel Corporation* v *Granada Television Ltd* [1981] AC 1096, HL. This has been emphasized in *Ashworth Security Hospital* v *MGN Ltd* [2002] 1 WLR 2033, HL where the House of Lords disapproved the views of Sedley LJ in *Interbrew SA* v *Financial Times Ltd* [2002] EWCA Civ 274, that the detection of crime was not a proper object of the *Norwich Pharmacal* jurisdiction, as unduly restrictive and held that a *Norwich Pharmacal* order could be sought in cases where the wrongdoing was criminal, provided that the remedy was restricted to the victim of the wrongdoing.
150 Supreme Court Act 1981 s 33(2).
151 Ibid, s 33(1); CPR 25.1(1)(i), 25.5(1)(a).
152 Supreme Court Act 1981, s 34(3); CPR 25.1(1)(j), 25.5(1)(b).
153 CPR 32, 35; PD 35. See Zuckerman, *Civil Procedure*, chs 19 and 20. The expert's primary duty is to the court, not to the party from whom he receives instructions (CPR 35.3). As to expert evidence in arbitral proceedings, see p 1190.
154 The author was once involved in a case where, after closing speeches, the judge adjourned the case over the weekend, during which he prepared his judgment, only to be told when the court resumed on Monday that he would not be troubled, as the parties had settled – which had happened 10 minutes earlier!
155 See generally David Foskett, *The Law of Compromise* (5th edn, 2002).
156 CPR 36.3, 36.6. A Pt 36 offer to settle a money claim which is not followed by a payment into court does not usually produce the costs advantages provided by Pt 36 (CPR 36.3(1)).

will be entitled to his costs up to the date of serving the notice of acceptance.[157] If the claimant declines the payment, the case continues without the court being informed of the Pt 36 payment. At the conclusion of the case, if the claimant succeeds but judgment is lower than the payment in,[158] the claimant will be required to pay the costs of the defendant from the latest date on which the payment could have been accepted.[159] If judgment is for a higher sum, then the successful claimant recovers his costs in the usual manner. Part 36 payments can be made only after proceedings have started and in relation to money claims.[160] Permission of the court is needed if the person who made the payment in wants to withdraw it.

Part 36 offers (previously known as *Calderbank* offers[161]) can be made by either the defendant or the claimant, but must be in writing and stated in specific terms.[162] They are said to be 'without prejudice save as to costs'.[163] This means that the Pt 36 offer cannot be used against the offeror on the question of liability but that the court can have regard to the offer when resolving costs and interest. Part 36 offers can be made only if it is not possible to make a Pt 36 payment in; ie, before proceedings have been started and in relation to non-money claims.

The court must not be informed of either Pt 36 offers or payments in until all matters of liability and the quantum of damages have been decided.[164]

(v) Trial

Although it is preferable for a claim to be tried at once, it is sometimes necessary to deal with certain issues before others. In such cases three types of order can be made: there can be a trial of a preliminary issue on a question of law, a separate trial of preliminary issues on questions of fact or a separate trial of the issues of liability and damages. Parties can apply for a preliminary issue (via an application notice or at a CMC/pre-trial review) or the court can order one on its own initiative.

It is the claimant's responsibility to prepare trial bundles and these must be filed by the claimant with the court not more than seven and not less than three days before the start of the trial.[165] Trial bundles typically contain the claim form and all statements of case, case summaries/chronologies where appropriate, requests for further information and the response to those requests, witness statements (where they are to be relied on as evidence) and summaries, any notices of intention regarding evidence, any

---

157 CPR 36.13(1).
158 In calculating whether or not the judgment exceeds the payment in, interest must be considered: payment in will usually include interest until the last date for accepting payment in (CPR 36.22(1)) and therefore interest on the judgment amount will need to be calculated to this date to ensure comparable sums are being considered.
159 CPR 36.20(2); interest or costs sanctions may be imposed where the offeree is the defendant and where the claimant does better than he proposed in his Pt 36 offer: CPR 36.21.
160 CPR 36.3(2).
161 So named after the decision in *Calderbank v Calderbank* [1976] Fam 93; [1975] 3 All ER 333.
162 CPR 36.5.
163 CPR 36.19(1).
164 CPR 36.19(1)–(2).
165 CPR 39.5(2).

medical/expert reports and the responses thereto, and any orders giving case management directions. Skeleton arguments are compulsory in the High Court[166] and the Court of Appeal,[167] and should be lodged with the court and served on the other party three days before the hearing. They are intended to focus the judge on the relevant reading for the hearing and should summarize the parties' submissions on each issue, referring to and attaching the relevant authorities where appropriate.

All trials are in open court, unless, for example, publicity would defeat the point of the hearing.[168] Where witnesses are giving evidence, they will do so orally and in public,[169] although in certain cases, for instance where the witness is too ill to attend the trial, it is possible for evidence to be given in a deposition (ie, on oath before the trial).[170] The civil standard of proof is on a balance of probabilities (except contempt of court, which must be proved beyond reasonable doubt). The trial itself is generally conducted in the following order: the claimant will make an opening speech, which will be followed by the claimant's evidence.[171] The defendant may then make an opening speech and present his evidence. Thereafter, each party makes its closing speech, the defendant going before the claimant. Finally, judgment is given, either immediately (extempore judgment) or after an adjournment (reserved judgment), and costs are considered.

Proceedings may be stayed either on the application by a party or on the court's initiative.[172] There can be numerous reasons for staying proceedings, for example where the defendant raises *forum non conveniens*.[173] In contrast to a discontinuance,[174] staying proceedings does not terminate them; they are paused. It is also possible for proceedings to be tempered with court-imposed sanctions, where parties fail to comply with orders and directions.

7.   FORUM NON CONVENIENS[175]

The court has an inherent power to stay proceedings on the ground of *forum non conveniens* where it is satisfied that another forum has competent jurisdiction and is one in which the case may be more suitably tried for the interests of all the parties and the ends of justice.[176].

---

166 *Practice Direction (Civil Litigation: Case Management)* [1995] 1 WLR 262.
167 *Practice Direction: Court Of Appeal (Civil Division): Leave To Appeal And Skeleton Arguments* [1999] 1 WLR 2, Pt 2.
168 Supreme Court Act 1981, s 67; CPR 39.2(3). See also the European Convention on Human Rights, art 6.
169 CPR 32.2.
170 CPR 34.8–34.12.
171 Witnesses are no longer taken through their evidence by examination in chief; they are simply asked to verify their written witness statements and are then cross-examined.
172 Supreme Court Act 1981 s 49(3).
173 See below.
174 Which can generally occur without obtaining the court's permission, except for the situations noted in CPR 38.2(2).
175 See Adrian Briggs and Peter Rees, *Civil Jurisdiction and Judgments* (3rd edn, 2002), paras [5.34]–[5.50].
176 *Spiliada Maritime Corp v Cansulex Ltd (The Spiliada)* [1987] AC 460.

8.　ANTI-SUIT INJUNCTION

This is the antithesis of *forum non conveniens*. The court may grant an anti-suit injunction restraining the commencement or continuance of proceedings elsewhere if the English court has jurisdiction to grant it, England is the natural forum as having a sufficient interest in or connection with the matter in question, and the foreign proceedings are or would be vexatious and oppressive,[177] and the other party has been guilty of wrongful conduct of which the applicant is entitled to complain and which he has a legitimate interest to prevent.[178] Prima facie the applicant has a legitimate interest where he is relying on a contractual right not to be sued. In other cases he must show the existence of proceedings in England which he is entitled to have protected.[179] The English courts are sensitive to the need to promote international comity and will not lightly interfere with the pursuit of proceedings in another jurisdiction. Moreover, the European Court of Justice has held that it would be inconsistent with the Brussels Regulation to grant an injunction restraining proceedings in the courts of another member state of the European Union having jurisdiction under the regulation even if the purpose of such proceedings is unconscionably to frustrate the English proceedings.[180]

9.　INTERIM APPLICATIONS[181]

Interim applications are those which occur before the actual substantive hearing of the claim, ie they are pre-trial applications. They can be dealt with either in a hearing or without a hearing.[182]

(i)　General characteristics

Interim applications may be made either with or without notice. Applications with notice are the general rule.[183] They are made via an application notice with relevant evidence attached. The application must be served not less than three days before the application is to be heard.[184] The court responds with either specific details regarding a hearing or stating that the application will be disposed of without a hearing.

Applications without notice are made via an application notice and supported with written evidence, and are permitted only where there is sufficient reason, which includes where there is real urgency or where notice would defeat the purpose of the application.[185] A party making an application without notice is compelled to make

---

177　*British Airways Board v Laker Airways Ltd* [1985] AC 58.

178　*Turner v Grovit* [2002] 1 WLR 107; *Airbus Industrie GIE v Patel* [1999] 1 AC 119. See further Look Chan Ho, 'Anti-Suit Injunctions in Cross-Border Insolvency' (2003) 52 ICLQ 697; Edwin Peel (1998) 114 LQR 543.

179　Ibid, per Lord Hobhouse at para 27.

180　Case C-159/02 *Turner v Grovit*, ECJ 27 April 2004..

181　See Ian Goldrein (ed), *Commercial Litigation: Pre-Emptive Remedies* (looseleaf); David Bean, *Injunctions* (8th edn, 2003).

182　Where the parties agree to this or where the court considers that a hearing would be inappropriate: CPR 23.8.

183　CPR 23.4(1).

184　CPR 23.7(1).　　　　　　　　185　PD 23 para 3.

full and frank disclosure to the court of all material facts, including those which are *against* his own interests.

Where the matter is particularly urgent, it is possible for the court to waive the need for an application notice,[186] provided that informal notice, at least, is given to the other party (unless secrecy is necessary). Although such urgent applications can usually be brought only after a claim form has been issued, the court can dispense with this requirement too.[187]

The general rule is that any evidence necessary for the disposal of an interim application should be in writing rather than given as oral testimony. The CPR lay down specific stipulations for the provision of evidence in some cases.[188] In other cases, evidence is required so far as necessary to establish the merits of the application.[189]

(ii) Commercial Court characteristics

The Commercial Court is different from the remainder of the High Court (except in some respects the Admiralty Court) in that all interim and pre-trial applications are heard by the commercial judge and not by Masters of the Queen's Bench Division.[190] An applicant must file an application notice containing the reasons for making the application and attaching a draft order. As with other Commercial Court documents, it is served by the party and not the court.[191] The mandatory CMCs result in a considerable number of pre-trial applications.

The CCG, s F, deals with applications in four groups according to type: applications without notice, expedited, ordinary and heavy applications. Applications without notice are the exception in the Commercial Court rather than the rule, as they are in the High Court in general.[192] They can be made on paper where no undertakings are required (eg an application to serve a claim form out of the jurisdiction),[193] but otherwise the applicant must appear before the commercial judge.[194] Expedited applications are possible where the applicant applies, on notice, to the court, and the commercial judge deems that matter to be 'sufficient urgency and importance' to merit expedited status.[195] Ordinary applications constitute the majority of the applications before the Commercial Court and are classified as those that are predicted to last no more than half a day.[196] Heavy applications, in contrast, are those that are predicted to last longer than half a day.[197]

---

186 CPR 23.3.
187 CPR 25.2(2).
188 For example CPR 25.5(2) regarding the inspection of property.
189 PD 23 para 9.1.
190 PD 58 para 3.1.
191 PD 58 para 9, CCG F1.4.
192 CCG F2.1.
193 CCG F2.2.
194 CCG F2.3.
195 CCG F3.1.
196 CCG F5.1.
197 CCG F6.1.

(iii) Specific interim applications and relief

The principal specific kinds of interim applications and types of relief granted are as follows.

1. Interim Payments

Interim payments are payments on account of any damages, debt or other sum which one party to an action may be held liable to pay another party where that other party obtains final judgment. The court will order interim payment where it is likely that the claimant will be partly successful and where it would be unjust to delay the making of payment.[198] An interim payment will not include costs but may include interest and should not be for an amount greater than that ultimately awarded at trial. At the main trial the parties cannot reveal the interim payment until liability and quantum have been decided.[199]

Interim payment applications are made on notice and must be served 14 days before the hearing with all relevant evidence attached.[200] Applications for summary judgment are commonly combined with those for interim payments, the former being available where the defence has no prospect of success and the latter being available where the claimant can show liability will be established.

2. Interim injunctions

Interim injunctions are provisional measures to prevent continuing and irreparable harm to the claimant by the defendant's actions in the time before the trial date. Before an interim injunction will be granted, the claimant must show that there is a pre-existing cause of action against the defendant.[201] Thereafter the claimant must satisfy the requirements laid down in *American Cyanamid Co v Ethicon Ltd*:[202]

(a)   that there is a serious question to be tried;
(b)   that damages would not be an adequate remedy for the claimant, who would suffer irreparable harm if the injunction were not to be granted; and
(c)   that, should the defendant succeed at trial, he would be adequately compensated for any loss suffered by the undertaking in damages required to be given by the claimant as a condition of grant of the injunction.[203]

---

198   A full list of the circumstances where interim payments can be ordered is set out in CPR 25.7.
199   Unless the defendant agrees or there is a public interest in the disclosure, for example to prevent the creation of a false market where two private companies are involved and there is a large amount in issue: *British and Commonwealth Holdings plc* v *Quadrex Holdings Inc (No 2)* (1988) Times, 8 Dec.
200   CPR 25.3.
201   *The Siskina* [1979] AC 210 per Lord Diplock at 256.
202   [1975] AC 396.
203   The reasoning behind this is that where an interim injunction is obtained but no eventual order against the defendant is made, the defendant will have been unjustifiably restrained by the injunction while it was in force. The claimant is therefore usually required to give an undertaking in damages that he will pay the defendant compensation for any loss the defendant actually incurs as a result of the injunction.

Where these criteria are finely poised between the parties, a balance of convenience analysis should be undertaken. The difficulty with *American Cyanamid* is Lord Diplock's insistence that once the threshold of a serious question to be tried, or an arguable case, had been shown, it was not the function of the court to assess the strength of the parties' claims on the merits. This aspect of the decision has been heavily criticized, and subsequent cases have tended to erode its significance.[204]

Either party can apply for interim injunctions. Applications can even be made before the claim form has been issued, in urgent cases or where it is in the interests of justice to do so. Whether or not notice should be given to the other side depends on whether there is true impossibility in giving such notice.[205]

3. Freezing injunctions

In the mid-1970s an entirely new form of injunctive relief emerged, one of the most powerful ever to be devised by the courts, namely the *Mareva* injunction,[206] now known as the freezing injunction (or freezing order). The purpose of freezing injunctions is to prevent the defendant from rendering a judgment against him nugatory by transferring his assets abroad or otherwise dissipating them prior to the trial. This remedy, which had a curious history,[207] has now been put on a statutory basis.[208]

The grant of a freezing injunction is governed by principles quite distinct from those laid down for ordinary interim injunctions in *American Cyanamid Co.*[209] Before granting a freezing injunction the court will usually require to be satisfied that

(a)   the claimant has 'a good arguable case'[210] based on a pre-existing cause of action;211

(b)   the claim is one over which the court has jurisdiction;[212]

(c)   the defendant appears to have assets within the jurisdiction;[213]

---

204   For a good discussion, see Zuckerman, *Civil Procedure*, paras 9.19 ff.

205   *Bates v Lord Hailsham of St Marylebone* [1972] 1 WLR 1373.

206   So named after the injunction granted in *Mareva Compania Naviera SA v International Bulkcarriers SA* [1975] 2 Lloyd's Rep 509. See Colman, Lyon and Hopkins, *Practice and Procedure of the Commercial Court*, ch 7.

207   See the first edition of this work at pp 964–965.

208   CPR 25.1(1)(f); Supreme Court Act 1981 s 37(3). It should be noted that s 37(3) enables the court to grant freezing injunctions not only to restrain a party to any proceedings from removing assets located in the jurisdiction of the High Court but also to restrain the party from otherwise dealing with assets if that would prevent the other party, should they succeed, from getting satisfaction from the judgment.

209   See n 202.

210   *Rasu Maritima SA v Perusahaan* [1978] QB 644, per Lord Denning MR at 661; *The Niedersachen* [1984] 1 All ER 398; *Aiglon Ltd v Gau Shan Co Ltd* [1993] 1 Lloyd's Rep 164.

211   *The Niedersachen*, n 210; *The Veracruz* [1992] 1 Lloyd's Rep 353; *The P* [1992] 1 Lloyd's Rep 470.

212   See *The Siskina*, n 201.

213   *Third Chandris Shipping Corp v Unimarine SA* [1979] QB 645. But in certain circumstances the court may grant a world-wide freezing injunction. See p 1152.

(d)   there is a real risk that those assets will be removed from the jurisdiction or otherwise dissipated if the injunction is not granted;[214] and

(e)   there is a balance of convenience in favour of granting the injunction.[215]

The court can also order disclosure of documents or the administration of requests for further information to assist the claimant in ascertaining the location of the defendant's assets.[216]

In exceptional cases, typically where large sums of money are involved (and somewhat more freely where the application is made *after* the judgment or arbitral award than *before*), the court will be prepared to grant a world-wide freezing injunction covering foreign assets and addressed to third parties.[217] But the court is sensitive to the need to avoid exorbitant jurisdiction over foreign subjects, so that any such order will incorporate a provision that, so far as it purports to have extraterritorial effect, no person shall be affected by it or concerned with its terms until it has been declared enforceable or to be enforced by a foreign court and then (except as regards the defendant and persons subject to the jurisdiction of the English court)[218] only to the extent of such declaration or enforcement. Moreover, an order having extraterritorial effect will rarely be made for the purpose of enforcing judgments of courts of another state[219] except where it is a party to the Brussels Regulation, Brussels Convention or Lugano Convention.[220] The CCG Appendix 5 includes different forms of wording for freezing injunctions, depending

---

214   Ibid; *Montecchi v Shimco (UK) Ltd* [1979] 1 WLR 1180; *Z. Ltd v A.* [1982] 1 All ER 556.

215   *Barclay-Johnson v Yuill* [1980] 1 WLR 1259.

216   *A. v C.* [1981] QB 956.

217   This is known as the *Babanaft* proviso, so named after *Babanaft International Co SA* v *Bassatne* [1990] Ch 13; *Republic of Haiti* v *Duvalier* [1990] 1 QB 202; *Derby & Co Ltd* v *Weldon (No 1)* [1990] Ch 48. See also *Teo Siew Har v Lee Kuan Yew* [1999] 4 SLR 560, where the court held that a third party against whom the plaintiff has no cause of action may be joined as a defendant and a freezing injunction may be issued against him if a good arguable case could be shown that the third party was holding assets belonging to the original defendant.

218   This is known as the *Derby and Weldon* proviso, so named after *Derby & Co Ltd* v *Weldon (Nos 3 and 4)* [1990] Ch 65. The cumulated version of the *Babanaft* and *Derby and Weldon* provisos is incorporated in the standard form freezing injunction in CCG Appendix 5, p 14 at para 19(2). The *Baltic* proviso (ie that the person against whom the freezing injunction is obtained will not be prevented by the terms of the injunction from complying with his civil obligations under the laws of the country in which his assets are situated; so named after *Baltic Shipping v Translink* [1995] 1 Lloyd's Rep 673) is also now included as part of the standard form freezing injunction (CCG Appendix 5, p 14 at para 20). This presumably follows the recommendation by Tuckey LJ in *Bank of China v NBM LLC* [2002] 1 WLR 844, who, after considering the problems with the *Derby and Weldon* proviso suggested that the *Baltic* proviso, should be included in the standard form (para 22). See also CCG F15.10, F15.11 and *Gangway Ltd v Caledonian Park Investments (Jersey) Ltd* [2001] 2 Lloyd's Rep 715.

219   *Rosseel NV v Oriental Commercial Shipping (UK) Ltd* [1990] 1 WLR 1387.

220   Civil Jurisdiction and Judgments Act 1982, s 25(1). The approach to an application for interim relief under s 25 is to consider, first, if the facts would warrant the relief sought if the substantive proceedings were brought in England; and, secondly, if so, whether the fact that the court had no jurisdiction apart from s 25 made it inexpedient to grant the interim relief sought: *Refco v Eastern Trading Co* [1999] 1 Lloyd's Rep 159; *Credit Suisse Fides Trust v Cuoghi* [1998] QB 818. For a detailed consideration of the factors to be taken into account when making a freezing injunction under s 25, see *Ryan v Friction Dynamics Ltd* (2002) Times, 14 June.

on whether the injunction relates to assets solely within the jurisdiction or not.[221] A freezing injunction may also be granted in aid of foreign proceedings, though this raises special considerations.[222]

The relief granted by a freezing injunction is purely personal in character; it is not designed to give the claimant security in the frozen assets so as to place him in a preferential position compared with other creditors,[223] and the court will not usually refuse to allow the defendant to use his assets as he wishes in the running of his business and for ordinary daily living, or to discharge his ordinary business debts[224] or legal expenses.[225] Moreover, the rights of secured creditors are unaffected,[226] as are accrued rights of set-off;[227] and while an injunction binds those having notice of it and may be made directly against a bank or other third party,[228] it will rarely be granted to restrain a bank from honouring a letter of credit issued at the defendant's request and debiting the defendant's account.[229] Further, the fact that the assets are covered by a freezing injunction is not a ground for ordering the defendant to give security of the costs in respect of his counterclaim.[230]

As with interim injunctions in general, the High Court has a discretion over whether or not to grant a freezing injunction, ie provided it is just and convenient.[231] The purpose of freezing injunctions requires that they be made without notice. The evidence attached to the application notice must, exceptionally, be in the form of affidavits.[232] Freezing injunctions may be sought at any stage in the proceedings – even before a claim form is issued. The claimant must give an undertaking as to damages, must notify the defendant and affected third parties, and must indemnify any third parties for expense incurred in complying with the order.[233]

---

221 These standard forms of wording (which also include search orders) must be followed unless the judge in a particular hearing considers there is a good reason for adopting a different form: CCG F15.5.
222 *Motorola Credit Corp v Uzan (No 2)* [2004] 1 WLR 113.
223 *Flightline Ltd v Edwards* [2003] BCLC 427.
224 *Polly Peck International plc v Nadir (No 2)* [1992] 4 All ER 769; *The Cretan Harmony* [1978] 1 Lloyd's Rep 425; *The Angel Bell* [1981] QB 65; *Hitachi Shipbuilding & Engineering Co Ltd v Viafel Compania Naviera SA* [1981] 2 Lloyd's Rep 498.
225 *The Coral Rose (No 3)* [1991] 1 WLR 917; *Halifax plc v Chandler* [2001] EWCA Civ 1750.
226 *The Cretan Harmony*, n 224. However, the secured creditor (or his receiver, if he has appointed one) will need to apply to discharge the injunction as regards the assets comprising the security (ibid).
227 *The Theotokos* [1983] 2 All ER 65.
228 P. Devonshire, 'Mareva injunctions and third parties: exposing the subtext' (1999) 62 MLR 539.
229 *Bolivinter Oil SA v Chase Manhattan Bank* [1984] 1 All ER 351n.
230 *Hitachi Shipbuilding & Engineering Co Ltd v Viafel Compania Naviera SA*, n 224.
231 Supreme Court Act 1981 s 37(1).
232 PD 25, para 3.1. The principal difference between affidavits and witness statements (the more commonly used form of evidence) is that an affidavit is a sworn statement and a knowingly false statement in an affidavit is perjury, whereas a false statement of truth is a contempt of court.
233 Where the claimant seeks an order freezing moneys in the defendant's bank account or other assets held for the defendant by his bank, the claimant will usually be required to give an undertaking to indemnify the bank against liability and to pay any reasonable costs it incurs in complying with the injunction. See *Z Ltd v A*, [1982] 1 All ER 556, where detailed guidelines were laid down by the Court of Appeal.

It is possible for the defendant to apply to discharge the freezing injunction by undermining one of the basic conditions for the grant of the injunction or by offering security for the claimant's claim instead.

The freezing injunction has now become a much-used and highly flexible device for protecting a claimant against removal or dissipation of the defendant's assets pending trial. It is a striking illustration of the importance of procedural law and the creative role of the judiciary.

4.   Search orders

Equally striking is the *ex parte* search order (formerly known as the *Anton Piller* order),[234] which came into being at about the same time as the freezing injunction and is a further demonstration of the power of the court to create new procedural devices where the justice of the case so requires. Search orders are a response to the huge growth of piracy in the world of sound and video reproduction by illegal operators of little financial substance who obtain temporary possession of films, tapes and records made by another and proceed to reproduce them and market the reproductions illegally, making a substantial profit at the expense of the proprietors of the patents, trade marks and copyrights which are thereby infringed. The type of *inter partes* application for discovery and detention and preservation of property prescribed by the civil procedure rules as they stood prior to the innovation of the *Anton Piller* order did not avail against such operators, who would destroy or conceal the evidence of their wrongdoing.

Search orders allow the defendant's home and/or business to be searched. They are a form of relief to be resorted to only where other, less extreme, forms have failed (eg an application on notice to enter and inspect the defendant's premises, under CPR 25.1, or an order on notice for the defendant to deliver up documents to his solicitor).

The essence of the search order is its surprise. The application is made without notice and with affidavit evidence. While the court retains ultimate discretion on whether to make a search order, the applicant is nevertheless required to show that

(a)   there is an extremely strong prima facie case on the merits,
(b)   the defendant's actions will cause serious potential or actual harm to the claimant's interests,
(c)   there is clear evidence that the defendant possesses incriminating objects or papers, and
(d)   there is a real possibility that the defendant will destroy them before an application on notice is made.[235]

The applicant has to give various undertakings (for example not to use items seized other than for the purposes of the claim without the court's permission, and to serve the search order on the defendant) as does the claimant's solicitor (for example to keep the documents/objects seized in safe custody). The CCG requires the search

---

234   So named after the Court of Appeal decision in *Anton Piller KG v Manufacturing Processes Ltd* [1976] Ch 55. The jurisdiction to make search orders is in the Civil Procedure Act 1997, s 7.
235   *Anton Piller KG v Manufacturing Processes Limited* [1976] Ch 55.

order to include an undertaking by the applicant not to disclose the search order to any third parties until after a specified date.[236] Since 1992 it has been necessary to have a supervising solicitor to serve and execute the search order.[237]

Over time the orders have become increasingly detailed and stringent. The defendant is commonly required not only to permit entry to his premises and inspection and removal of the documents, but also to disclose on affidavit the names and addresses of all persons engaged in the production, distribution or sale of illicit copies, and to list all documents relating to illicit records and sales or offers for sale. Further, where the proceedings are for infringement of, or apprehended infringement of, intellectual property rights or for passing off, or for apprehended passing off, the defendant has no privilege against self-incrimination.[238] The House of Lords has held that even in other cases the defendant will not be able to plead self-incrimination as a ground for claiming privilege if he is adequately protected, eg by an undertaking by those empowered to give it that only material obtained independently of what is produced in the course of compliance with the order will be used in any criminal prosecution.[239]

In addition, the court will in appropriate cases grant an injunction restraining the defendant from warning third parties of the existence of the proceedings, except for the purpose of taking legal advice, and an injunction until trial to restrain him from continuing to make or supply illicit recordings.

The hardship caused to defendants by the excessively liberal grant of *Anton Piller* orders has led to a strong judicial reaction in recent years.

What is to be said of the *Anton Piller* procedure, which, on a regular and institutionalized basis, is depriving citizens of their property and closing down their businesses by orders made *ex parte*, on applications of which they know nothing and at which they cannot be heard, by orders which they are forced, on pain of committal, to obey, even if wrongly made?[240]

Refusal to comply with the search order can expose the defendant to contempt proceedings. Of course, it may also constitute damning evidence against the defendant at a subsequent trial.[241] A defendant may get the search order discharged if one or more of the basic conditions for its grant are not satisfied or where the claimant is guilty of material non-disclosure on the application.

5. Security for costs

It may be that a defendant considers that he had a good chance of successfully defending the claim brought against him but is concerned that in that event the claimant would not be able to meet the order for costs made at trial. In such a case

---

236 CCG F15.12; see the standard forms of search order in Appendix 5 of the CCG.
237 *Universal Thermosensors v Hibben* [1992] 1 WLR 840.
238 Supreme Court Act 1981, s 72.
239 *Istel Ltd v Tully* [1993] AC 45.
240 *Columbia Picture Industries Ltd v Robinson* [1987] Ch 38, per Scott LJ at 73–74, a line strongly endorsed by Hoffmann J in *Lock International plc v Beswick* [1989] 1 WLR 1268 at 1279.
241 Per Ormrod LJ in the *Anton Piller* [1976] Ch 55 at 62.

the defendant can apply[242] for the claimant[243] to provide security for costs, ie to pay a certain amount, at the court's discretion, into court by a particular date. Although it is possible to apply for security for costs at any stage of the case, it is advisable to do so at the earliest possible stage, as any unnecessary delay can be considered against the defendant. This is emphasized in the CCG, which states that delay will probably cause the application to fail and that first applications for security for costs should not be made later than the first CMC.[244]

The case will usually be stayed until the claimant has provided the security, although the preferred practice in the Commercial Court is to give the claimant a reasonable time to provide the security and if he defaults, the other party can apply to the court for a stay.[245] The CPR[246] set out conditions which must be satisfied before security for costs can be ordered, but even then the court retains a discretion over whether to grant the security for costs.[247] Claimants can also apply for security for costs against a defendant in relation to the costs of a counterclaim.

Non-compliance with an order to provide security for costs can result in the court dismissing the claim. At the end of the case, if the defendant succeeds, the money held as security can be used to pay his costs, whereas if the claimant is successful, the money will be returned.

Payment into court by way of security for costs constitutes a procedural security to which the claimant is entitled to resort on accepting the payment offer even if the defendant becomes insolvent.[248]

10.   COSTS

(i)   General principles

Generally, costs are a matter at the discretion of the court.[249] When exercising its discretion on costs, the court should particularly bear in mind:

(a)   the extent to which any pre-action protocol was followed,
(b)   whether the issues raised were reasonably raised and pursed,
(c)   whether the successful party exaggerated the claim,
(d)   whether a party was only partly successful, and
(e)   whether there was any payment into court or offer to settle.[250]

---

242   CPR 25.12.
243   An application can also be made against a person other than the claimant where the person either assigned the claim to the claimant in order to avoid a costs order being made against him or has contributed or agreed to contribute to the claimant's costs in return for a share of the money or property the claimant ultimately recovers.
244   CCG, Appendix 16, para 1.
245   Ibid, para 6.
246   CPR 25.13(2).
247   Factors the court should consider were set out in *Parkinson (Sir Lindsay) and Co Ltd v Triplan Ltd* [1973] QB 609.
248   See p 622.
249   CPR 44.3(1).
250   CPR 44.3(4).

Another general principle is that the unsuccessful party will pay the costs of the successful party (formerly referred to as the 'costs follow the event' rule). There are various exceptions to this rule, for example where a party is required to pay only a proportion of another party's costs or from a certain day or in relation only to certain parts of the proceedings.[251]

Costs are not generally ordered between the parties in small claims cases except regarding the fixed costs relating to issuing the claim, court and expert fees, witness expenses and a limited amount for legal advice and assistance in claims for injunctions or specific performance.

In fast-track cases, costs are normally dealt with at the end of the trial by the trial judge by way of summary assessment, ie the judge will decide how much the loser has to pay of the winner's costs. There are also fixed trial costs rules for fast-track cases.

In relation to orders made following interim applications, the order will typically set out who will pay the costs of the application. This will depend on the court exercising its discretion as to who it considered to have been successful.[252] If the order does not refer to costs, then none are payable in relation to the proceedings to which the order relates.[253]

(ii) Quantification

When an order as to costs has been made, the amount will need to be quantified. This can be agreed between the parties or may be referable, in relation to certain items, to fixed costs. The court can undertake summary assessment after a hearing on the basis of the statement of costs filed by the parties. Alternatively, and in contrast, a detailed assessment of costs may be undertaken. This is conducted by a costs officer at an assessment hearing after the parties have submitted the costs being claimed in the dispute.

Costs orders will set out the basis on which quantification will be undertaken: either on a standard or indemnity basis. The standard, commonly invoked, basis requires the court to allow only those costs which are proportional to the matter in issue and to resolve any doubt on whether costs were reasonably incurred in favour of the paying party.[254] The indemnity basis is used in particular situations, for example as a penalty for misconduct between parties to litigation or where a client is paying his own solicitor. It does not include a reference to proportionality and any doubt over whether costs were reasonably incurred is resolved in favour of the receiving party.[255]

251 CPR 44.3(6).
252 As well as the factors set out in CPR 44.3.
253 CPR 44.13(1) and PD 23 para 13.2.
254 CPR 44.4(2).
255 CPR 44.4(3).

11. ENFORCEMENT

If the defendant has no assets or income, then, needless to say, there is nothing the court can do to assist the judgment creditor. The point seems an obvious one, but many litigants appear quite unable to comprehend it. What is the use of the judgment if they cannot get their money? But where the debtor has income or assets capable of being reached, a whole range of enforcement measures is open to the judgment creditor. The selection depends on whether the judgment is a money judgment or a judgment requiring the debtor to perform some other act.

(i) Money judgments

Even before enforcement begins and in order to assist the judgment creditor[256] in identifying the assets of the judgment debtor[257] and, therefore, to ascertain the best method of enforcement, it is possible for the judgment creditor to apply to the court for an order to obtain information from the judgment debtor.[258] The most common method of actually enforcing a money judgment is to levy execution against the judgment debtor's goods by issue of a writ of *fieri facias*.[259] The bailiff or sheriff's officer will call at the judgment debtor's premises gain entry and seize goods to satisfy the judgment debt. The goods will be either taken away or left in the building where the officer enters into a 'walking possession' agreement. If the debtor fails to pay up then the goods are sold. There may, of course, be other judgment creditors in the queue who come ahead of our creditor,[260] and their claims will have to be met first. If the debtor has a beneficial interest in stocks or shares, funds in court or a trust, the judgment creditor can apply for a charging order.[261] The effect of such an order, when made absolute,[262] is the same as that of an equitable charge created by the debtor by writing under his hand.[263] If the debtor is himself owed money, a third party debt order may be obtained requiring the judgment debtor's debtor (traditionally known as a garnishee) to pay his debt direct to the judgment creditor to the extent necessary to satisfy the judgment.[264]

---

256   Defined as a person who has obtained or is entitled to enforce a judgment or order (CPR 70.1(2)(a)).

257   Defined as a person against whom a judgment or order was given or made (CPR 70.1(2)(b)).

258   CPR 71.2.

259   CPR Sch 1, RSC Order 47. The writ is abbreviated to *fi fa.*

260   Priority is governed by the date of delivery of the writ of *fieri facias* to the sheriff (Supreme Court Act 1981, s 138, repealing and re-enacting the Sale of Goods Act 1893, s 26).

261   Charging Orders Act 1979, ss.1, 2; CPR Pt 73.

262   The order is made nisi (ie unless the debtor shows cause to the contrary) in the first instance; if he fails to show why it should not be made, it is then made absolute.

263   Charging Orders Act 1979, s 3(4).

264   CPR Pt 72. Other remedies, used relatively infrequently, are the appointment of a receiver by way of equitable execution (CPR Sch 1, RSC Ord 51) and attachment of earnings; but the latter is available only in the county court (except in matrimonial causes), and the judgment would therefore have to be enforced in the county court to attract this enforcement method (ie the High Court judgment would have to be transferred to the county court, see CPR Sch 2, CCR Ord 27; r 70.3 provides that a judgment creditor wishing to enforce a High Court judgment or order in a county court must apply to the High Court for an order transferring the proceedings to that court).

All proceedings for the enforcement of any judgment or order for the payment of money either given or made in the Commercial Court will be automatically referred to a Master in the Queen's Bench Division or to a district judge unless the court orders otherwise.[265]

(ii) Other judgments

A judgment or order for possession of land is enforced by a writ of possession[266] executed by the sheriff. A judgment or order for the delivery of goods which does not give the debtor the option of paying their value is enforced by a writ of specific delivery.[267] Where the judgment or order gives the debtor the option of paying the value of the goods (as will usually be the case),[268] the judgment creditor must first get the value assessed by the Master, after which he may issue a writ of delivery to recover the goods or their assessed value.[269]

12. APPEALS

After a claim has been resolved, parties may wish to appeal from the judgment to a higher court. Although some appeals can be brought as a matter of right, most appeals can be brought only after permission has been obtained, either from the court that has given the judgment being appealed or, where this is refused, from the court to which an appeal is sought.[270] The threshold test for granting permission is whether the appeal has a real prospect of success.[271] It should be noted that embarking upon an appeal does not prevent the underlying judgment or order being executed[272] but a stay can be obtained, either from the court appealed from or the one appealed to.

An appellant must file an appeal notice setting out the grounds on which it is alleged the judge erred and must include a request for permission to appeal where this is necessary.[273] The appeal notice must usually be filed within 14 days after the date of the decision being appealed[274] and must be served on the respondent within seven days after being filed.[275] A respondent can oppose an appeal by arguing

(a)   that the decision being appealed is correct for the reasons given in the judgment (in which case there is no requirement to file a respondent's notice);

---

265   PD 58 para 1.2(2); CCG K3.1.
266   CPR Sch 1, RSC Ord 45, 3.1.
267   Order 45, r 4(1).
268   Ie where it is a writ (or warrant) to enforce the relief in s 3(2)(b) of the Torts (Interference with Goods) Act 1977, known as a writ (or warrant) of delivery, as opposed to a writ (or warrant) to enforce the relief in s 3(2)(a) of the 1977 Act, known as a writ (or warrant) of specific delivery.
269   Order 45, r 4(2).
270   CPR 52.3(1), (2).
271   CPR 52.3(6)(a).
272   CPR 52.7.
273   CPR 52.4(1).
274   CPR 52.4(2).
275   CPR 52.4(3).

(b)   that it is correct for reasons other than those given in the judgment (in which case a respondent's notice must be filed,[276] and a request for permission to cross-appeal must be included where necessary);[277] or

(c)   by cross-appealing that part of the judgment that went against the respondent (and also requiring a respondent's notice to be filed[278]).

Where a respondent's notice is required, it must be filed within 14 days after the respondent is served with the appellant's notice (where no permission to appeal is required) or 14 days after notification that the appellant has permission to appeal (where this is required); and served on the appellant within 7 days of being filed.[279]

13.   TRANSNATIONAL LITIGATION

Litigation in a foreign state or litigation in England which requires the assistance of a foreign court (eg in the examination of witnesses or the enforcement of judgments or orders) poses a range of problems for the practitioner over and above those he is likely to encounter in purely domestic litigation.

(i)   Forum shopping

Since conflict of laws rules differ from state to state, and since matters of procedure are in principle to be determined by the *lex fori*, the prospects of success in an action, the amount which the successful claimant can expect to recover and the interim remedies open to him may depend heavily on the choice of jurisdiction. There may, of course, be cases where the courts of only one state are prepared to accept jurisdiction, but the typical international contract is likely to involve points of contact with several states, and this gives considerable opportunity to the claimant and his advisers to engage in forum shopping and to select the state whose law and procedural rules are most favourable to the claim.[280] This may be highly satisfactory for an English claimant but is less so for an English defendant, especially where the litigation takes place in a country where liability is strict, awards of damages are high and the extraterritorial reach of its laws and rules of procedure excessive. Particular concern has been voiced in a number of European countries as to the size of damages awarded by American juries and as to the scope of certain United States statutes, executive orders and rules as to discovery and

---

276   CPR 52.5(2)(b).

277   CPR 52.5(3).

278   CPR 52.5(2)(a).

279   CPR 52.5(4)–(6).

280   See A. S. Bell, *Forum Shopping And Venue In Transnational Litigation* (2003). The scope for forum shopping within the European Union is now substantially reduced by the Brussels Regulation (see p 1076); and in contract cases the advantages of forum shopping are greatly attenuated as the result of the Rome Convention, which applies a set of largely uniform rules throughout the EU (see p 1095). See also the *ALI/UNIDROIT Principles of Transnational Civil Litigation* (2004) and The Future of Transnational Civil Litigation (ed Mads Andenas, Neil Andrews and Renato Nazzini, 2004).

evidence, which purport to apply to companies and individuals outside the United States.[281] The United States feels that such extraterritorial measures are necessary to prevent evasion of its laws by its nationals, while other countries consider that these represent an invasion of their sovereignty. It was problems of this kind that led to the abandonment of the proposed United Kingdom–United States Judgments Convention[282] and the passing of the Protection of Trading Interests Act 1980.

(ii) Practical problems

The English lawyer advising his client in England on overseas litigation has to face a number of practical problems: unfamiliarity with the intended overseas jurisdiction, its laws and procedures, its legal system and the structure of its legal profession; the selection of a lawyer who is competent, efficient and able to converse and correspond in English; the uncertainty of the level of costs his client will be incurring; the lack, in some cases, of procedural relief of a type available in England; and, of course, the question whether the intended court will assume jurisdiction and which law it will apply to determine the dispute.

(iii) Evidence

The taking of evidence abroad in an English action and the taking of evidence in England at the request of a foreign court are greatly facilitated by the 1970 Hague Convention,[283] where the other country concerned is a party to the Convention. In this and other cases, rules of court govern the procedure in England for securing the taking of evidence abroad [284] and the obtaining of evidence for foreign courts.[285]

---

281 Two examples of United States orders giving rise to disputed proceedings in England are the Westinghouse litigation, in which Westinghouse obtained letters rogatory in the United States addressed to the High Court in England requesting the latter to order the examination in London of present and former directors and employees of two British companies in the Rio Tinto Zinc group (*Rio Tinto Zinc Corporation* v *Westinghouse Electric Corp* [1978] AC 547), and the US Presidential Executive Order of 14 November 1979 purporting to block the dollar balances of the Iranian government and its nationals held by American banks and their branches overseas. The Westinghouse litigation, which involved a large number of actions against Westinghouse in different countries, was ultimately settled by a global compromise agreement which, though expensive for Westinghouse, was far below the amount of the liabilities it would have incurred if the claims had been successful. The outcome is interesting as showing a sensible appreciation by the commercial world that pursuing a claim to the point where it might put one's major supplier out of business will harm the claimant as well as the defendant.

282 Convention on the Reciprocal Recognition and Enforcement of Judgments in Civil Matters, Cmnd 6771, 1976; (1977) 16 ILM 71.

283 The Convention on the Taking of Evidence Abroad in Civil and Commercial Matters, ratified by the United Kingdom in 1976 and implemented by the Evidence (Proceedings in Other Jurisdictions) Act 1975.

284 CPR 34.13. The Commercial Court Guide provides that permission may be given for the taking of evidence abroad: CCG H4.1

285 CPR 34.16–34.21.

39   Commercial arbitration

I.   THE NATURE OF ARBITRATION[1]

Arbitration is a form of dispute resolution in which the parties agree to submit their differences to a third party or a tribunal for a binding decision.[2] It differs from litigation in that it is consensual in origin (though once parties have agreed on arbitration, whether in the substantive contract or after the dispute has arisen, they are bound by their agreement) and the person determining the dispute is appointed by the parties themselves, or by a third party or institution designated by them, not by the state. The fact that the parties agree to be legally bound by the arbitrator's award distinguishes arbitration from alternative dispute resolution. Arbitration is also to be distinguished from valuation, certification and other expert determination. A reference to arbitration presupposes the existence of a dispute, and the arbitrator's role is to determine the rights of the parties in a judicial manner in the light of the evidence and representations they submit to him, not by use of his own knowledge. By contrast, expert determination does not necessarily involve any dispute at all – the parties may agree, for example, that the price to be paid under their contract is to be determined by a valuation made by an appointed expert – and the task of the expert is not to exercise judicial functions by determining the parties' rights after hearing them and weighing their competing arguments but to make a determination based on the application of his specialist knowledge to the facts presented to or ascertained by him.[3]

---

1 The principal works on English arbitration generally include *Arbitration Law* (ed Robert Merkin, looseleaf); *Russell on Arbitration* (22nd edn, eds David St. John Sutton, John Kendall and Judith Gill, 2002); *Bernstein's Handbook of Arbitration and Dispute Resolution Practice* (4th edn, eds John Tackaberry and Arthur L Marriott, 2003); and Michael Mustill and Stewart Boyd, *Commercial Arbitration* (2nd edn, 1989 and *2001 Companion*). There are several excellent works on international commercial arbitration. See in particular Alan Redfern and Martin Hunter, *Law and Practice of International Commercial Arbitration* (3rd edn, 1999) and, for comparative studies, Julian D.M. Lew, Loukas A Mistelis and Stefan M Kröll, *Comparative International Commercial Arbitration* (2003); *Fouchard, Gaillard, Goldman on International Commercial Arbitration* (eds Emmanuel Gaillard and John Savage, 1999). For a fascinating insight into the culture of arbitration and arbitrators, see Yves Dezelay and Bryant E Garth, *Dealing in Virtue* (1996).
2 The agreement is nowadays usually concluded as part of the primary agreement between the parties and before the dispute has arisen. Parties may, alternatively, submit to arbitration after the dispute has arisen in what is known as a *compromis*, which in a number of countries was at one time the only form of agreement recognized by the courts.
3 See, for example, *Land Securities plc v Westminster City Council* [1993] 1 WLR 286; *Ipswich Borough Council v Fisons plc* [1990] Ch 709.

A contract may provide a two-stage approach in which the initial determination is to be by an expert and it is only after his determination that the parties may resort to arbitration.[4]

In any discussion of arbitration it is important to distinguish the agreement from which the substantive dispute arises (which for brevity will be called 'the primary agreement') from the agreement to arbitrate, which is now recognized as a separate agreement even if not physically distinct but merely an arbitration clause in the primary agreement.[5]

2.   ARBITRATION VERSUS LITIGATION

A great many commercial disputes are resolved not by litigation, but by arbitration. The relative merits of the two methods of determining disputes are a perennial topic of discussion and controversy.[6] Lawyers tend to prefer litigation, businessmen arbitration. Choice of the latter predominates in international contracts but is by no means universal. Neither system has any innate superiority over the other. Much depends on the nature of the dispute and the objectives of the parties. These may not be the same at the time of the dispute as they were at the date of the contract. In particular, the attitude of a claimant may be very different from that of a defendant.

That arbitration possesses certain advantages for the commercial man is undeniable. The parties can select an arbitrator or arbitrators in whom they have confidence (or can have the appointment made for them by a person or body whose judgment they respect) and who can be expected to be familiar with the kind of business in which the dispute arises. The proceedings are less formal and more flexible than litigation; the parties have greater control over them;[7] the arbitral tribunal is not bound by rules of evidence or procedure applicable to court proceedings, nor, in a case involving a foreign element, is it obliged to apply English conflict of laws rules; the venue can be fixed by agreement with the arbitrator and (a matter of considerable importance) the hearing is private; and the proceedings and award are relatively confidential.[8] Of particular importance in international commercial arbitration is the availability of enforcement of awards in other jurisdictions under the 1958 New York Convention. Arbitration may also be cheaper and speedier than litigation,[9] but this by no means necessarily follows. The court fees in an action are relatively

---

4 As in *Channel Tunnel Group Ltd v Balfour Beatty Construction Ltd* [1993] AC 334, where the House of Lords held that such an agreement was an arbitration agreement and could be stayed under the relevant arbitration legislation.
5 See p 1184.
6 For an instructive extrajudicial discussion of the question, see Kerr J, 'International Arbitration *v* Litigation' in [1980] JBL 164, and for a hilarious spoof account by the same judge, 'Arbitration v Litigation: the Macao Sardine Case' (1987) 3 Arbitration International 79, whose citation in a number of learned journals bestowed upon it, as he whimsically observed, a measure of undeserved authenticity!
7 This is one of the objects envisaged by the Arbitration Act 1996, s 1(b).
8 See p 1187.
9 This is one of the objects envisaged by the Arbitration Act 1996, s 1(a).

modest, whereas in an arbitration the parties are responsible for the arbitrator's remuneration and travel and accommodation expenses (which may be particularly heavy if there are several arbitrators coming from different countries), the hire of accommodation for the hearing and the payment of a stenographer if they wish to have a full record of the evidence.[10] In the case of an institutional arbitration the parties also have to pay the administrative charges of the arbitral institution. On the other hand, the arbitrator's greater familiarity with the practices of the industry or market may shorten the proceedings and thus save expense. Arbitration may be faster if the parties cooperate in bringing the case to a swift hearing, but allows more opportunity for delay to a defendant wishing to prolong the proceedings. Moreover, most of the advantages of arbitration, including finality and confidentiality, are lost if an award comes before the court for judicial review. Multi-party proceedings are best suited to litigation, not arbitration. A party cannot be brought before an arbitral tribunal without its prior consent, and procedures such as intervention or joinder of third parties or consolidation of proceedings to avoid multiplicity are not available.[11]

The atmosphere of arbitration is generally considered to be less hostile than that of litigation, and the arbitral award now has a greater degree of finality than a judgment.[12] As against this, the arbitrator's interlocutory powers, though recently reinforced by statute, are still not as extensive as those of a judge, a fact of particular importance if one of the parties wants interim or provisional relief or summary judgment and in multi-party disputes where it may be desirable to bring all parties before the court in a single or consolidated proceeding. Moreover, international commercial arbitration has in some ways become almost as formalized and protracted as litigation, so that over the past decade there has been increasing interest in commercial mediation. Finally, whereas judges are trained to think and act judicially and to treat the admissibility and weight of evidence with circumspection, some arbitrators without legal qualifications may be inclined to decide a case on their view of what is fair and without sufficient regard to the nature of the evidence or the appropriate rules of law.[13] To this the businessman will no doubt reply with conviction, and with some justification, that it is only natural for the lawyers to feel happier in their own habitat!

---

10 In an action the parties pay only for the transcript of the evidence, if they want it, not for the shorthand or machine recording itself.

11 See *Sacor Maritima v Repsol Petroleo* [1998] 1 Lloyd's Rep 518; B. Hanotiau, 'A New Development in Complex Multiparty-Multicontract Proceedings: Classwide Arbitration', (2004) 20 Arbitration International 39, and 'Problems raised by complex arbitrations involving multiple contracts – parties – issues: an analysis' (2001) 18 J International Arbitration 251. Some national laws provide a procedure for consolidation, for example, the Netherlands Arbitration Act 1986, constituting Book IV of its Code of Civil Procedure, prescribes a consolidation procedure (CCP art 1046), as does the Hong Kong Arbitration Ordinance 1997, s 6B.

12 See p 1191.

13 This, of course, may be what the parties want, the arbitrator being able to act as *amiable compositeur* and to decide the case *ex aequo et bono*. For a critical comment on the supposed value of the broad procedural discretion given to arbitrators, see William W. Park, 'The 2002 Freshfields Lecture – Arbitration's Protean Character: The Value of Rules and the Risks of Discretion' (2003) 19 Arbitration International 279.

3. TYPES OF COMMERCIAL ARBITRATION

There are three main classifications of arbitration, ad hoc versus institutional arbitration, domestic versus foreign and international arbitration, and private versus statutory and conventional arbitration.

(i) Ad hoc and institutional arbitration

In an ad hoc arbitration the parties themselves prescribe the mode of appointment of the arbitrator, who upon being appointed controls the proceedings himself, within the limits laid down by the parties and the law. The arbitration agreement may leave the procedure governing the arbitration to be determined by the parties themselves and the arbitrator or it may incorporate procedural rules promulgated by a trade association or a national or international organization, which may be an institution administering arbitrations[14] or a body having no arbitral functions of its own, such as the United Nations Commission on International Trade Law (UNCITRAL).[15] Ad hoc arbitration is regularly used for large arbitrations and has certain advantages.[16] It is likely to be quicker and also cheaper in that it avoids the administrative charges of the arbitral institution. It gives parties complete control over the appointment of an arbitrator who is willing to act, and the parties are less constrained procedurally. The arbitration agreement should provide that if the parties fail to agree on the appointment of an arbitrator, the appointment should be made by a designated appointing authority. The UNCITRAL Rules go on to provide that if no appointing authority has been agreed upon by the parties, or if the appointing authority agreed upon refuses to act or fails to make the appointment within 60 days of receipt of a request to do so, either party may request the Secretary-General of the Permanent Court of Arbitration at The Hague to designate an appointing authority.[17] Failing incorporation of rules such as the UNCITRAL Rules, the disadvantage of ad hoc arbitration is the ability of a party to slow the process by its refusal to cooperate in the appointment of an arbitrator and the progress of the arbitration proceedings.

An institutional arbitration is one in which the arbitrator is appointed, the proceedings conducted and the award issued in accordance with the rules of a national or international arbitral organization, and the arbitration is administered, wholly or in part, by that organization. Institutional arbitration has the advantage of possessing a clear framework of procedure outside that prescribed by law and, in many cases, of institutional facilities for the conduct of the arbitration as well as, in some cases, an internal appeal system. Administrative oversight helps to keep the arbitration on the move, to ensure that time limits are not overlooked and that the award is in a form that is likely to be enforceable. Where the rules of the arbitral institution require its approval to the appointment of arbitrators, this helps to ensure that an arbitrator known to be unsuitable is not appointed. In addition, the arbitral

---

14 See below. Usually parties adopting rules of an arbitral institution also agree to submit themselves to the supervisory function of that institution, but this is not necessarily the case. See below.

15 Which in 1976 issued its Arbitration Rules. These are now widely used.

16 For further detail, see Redfern and Hunter, *International Commercial Arbitration*, para 1–83.

17 Article 6(2).

institution may control the level of fees payable to the arbitrators.[18] Finally, the standing of the arbitral institution is likely to enhance respect for the award. These advantages necessarily involve some loss of flexibility but contribute greatly to consistency in the conduct of arbitrations within the system of business activity concerned. Among the London arbitral organizations are the London Court of International Arbitration (LCIA), the London Maritime Arbitrators' Association and the leading commodity associations, such as the Grain and Feed Trade Association (GAFTA)[19] and the Federation of Oils, Seeds and Fats Associations (FOSFA). Among the leading foreign national arbitral institutions are the American Arbitration Association, the Swedish Chamber of Commerce, the Netherlands Arbitration Institute and the Swiss Chamber of Commerce, each of which has its own arbitration rules.[20]

There is a profusion of foreign international organizations concerned with international commercial arbitration. Some of these are general and global in character, such as the International Chamber of Commerce (ICC)[21] and UNCITRAL. Others are specialist, such as the International Centre for Settlement of Investment Disputes (ICSID) and the Arbitration and Mediation Centre of the World Intellectual Property Organization (WIPO), or regional, such as the Inter-American Commercial Arbitration Commission. ICC arbitrations are closely controlled by the ICC's Court of Arbitration,[22] which exercises a high degree of procedural supervision with a view to ensuring that ICC awards are respected internationally and are, as far as possible, immune from challenge.[23]

An institutional arbitration operates at two levels, contractual and jurisdictional. The parties' adoption of institutional rules in their contract binds them *inter se* to observe the rules but does not in itself bring them into a relationship with the arbitral

---

18 There are two ways of fixing fees. The first, used by the International Chamber of Commerce, is *ad valorem*, the fees being set in bands geared to the amount of the claim; the second, adopted by the London Court of International Arbitration, is to fix fees by reference to a *per diem* rate. Each has its advantages and disadvantages. The fixing of a fee linked to the amount in issue may result in the payment of fees at a level having no relation to the work actually undertaken by the arbitrators. This problem is avoided by the use of a per diem rate, which, however, depends for its fairness on the arbitrators' self-discipline in the use of their time and their integrity in specifying the time spent.

19 The GAFTA contracts and arbitrations are the most widely known and have been the subject of numerous reported cases in the courts. See generally Derek Kirby Johnson, *International Commodity Arbitration* (1991) for a description of the arbitration rules and practices of the leading commodity associations.

20 The most recent being the Swiss Rules of International Arbitration (2004), which resulted from collaboration by the arbitral bodies of all the Swiss cantons. The rules are based on the UNCITRAL Arbitration Rules but with modifications to adapt them to institutional arbitration.

21 Whose Rules of Arbitration 1998 and Court of Arbitration are widely used.

22 Though the ICC Court has various powers, including the confirmation or appointment and removal of arbitrators, it is a largely administrative body, not a court in the judicial sense, and it exercises no adjudicatory functions, these being the prerogative of the appointed arbitrators. Nor are its orders considered to be arbitral awards. See Georgios Petrochilos, *Procedural Law in International Arbitration* (2004), paras 4.110–4.111.

23 See W. L. Craig, W. W. Park and J. Paulsson, *International Chamber of Commerce Arbitration* (3rd edn, 2000) and *Annotated Guide to the 1998 ICC Rules* (1998); Yves Derains and Eric A. Schwartz, *A Guide to the new ICC Rules of Arbitration* (1998).

institution. That occurs only when the institution receives the request for arbitration,[24] thereby generating a separate contract between the institution and the parties, by virtue of which the latter submit themselves to the institution's administrative regime and powers. It is possible for parties to select the rules without the administrative machinery, as where they decide not to refer the arbitration to the institution or where the latter declines to accept it.[25]

(ii) Domestic and international arbitration

Arbitration may be domestic or international. The Arbitration Act 1996[26] regards as 'domestic' an arbitration where the seat is in the United Kingdom, and where none of the parties to the arbitration agreement is a national of, habitually resides in, is incorporated in, or is controlled and managed from a state other than the United Kingdom, though for the purposes of the Act the distinction now has no significance.[27] The ICC Rules look to the international character of the business dispute,[28] while the 1985 UNCITRAL Model Law on International Commercial Arbitration treats an arbitration as international if

(a) the parties have their places of business in different states, or

(b) one of the following places is situated outside the state in which the parties have their places of business, namely the place of arbitration or any place where a substantial part of the obligations of the commercial relationship is to be performed or the place with which the subject matter of the dispute is most closely connected, or

(c) the parties have expressly agreed that the subject matter of the arbitration agreement relates to more than one country. [29]

Though not relevant under the provisions of the Arbitration Act 1996, the distinction between domestic and international arbitration, however defined, is of considerable practical and legal significance for other purposes. The international character of an arbitration may affect not only the approach to the applicable law but also the need to have regard to international usage and the fact that the parties or some of them may

---

24 This is the position under both the LCIA Rules (art 1) and the ICC Rules (art 4(1)). Submission of the request is thus to be considered an acceptance of the institution's offer to the world of its arbitration facilities, though it is subject to the willingness of the parties to observe those rules of the institution which it considers mandatory.

25 As in *Sumitomo Heavy Industries Ltd v Oil and Natural Gas Commission* [1994] 1 Lloyd's Rep 45. In that case the arbitration agreement incorporated the ICC Rules but the ICC declined jurisdiction because the contractual composition of the arbitral tribunal did not accord with the Rules. It was held that while this precluded the parties from using the administrative machinery of the ICC, including its scrutiny in relation to costs, this was not so fundamental as to frustrate the contract, since the parties remained free to use the ICC procedural rules so far as these did not depend upon actual participation by the ICC.

26 Section 85(2).

27 Because of a decision not to bring ss 85–87 into force, with the result that in relation to commercial arbitration the Act does not distinguish domestic from international arbitration. However, for other purposes there remain important differences between the two in that various considerations arise in international commercial arbitration which are not relevant to a domestic arbitration. See below.

28 ICC Rules of Arbitration 1998, art 1(1).

29 Article 1(3).

not be English. Arbitral tribunals in an international commercial arbitration have and exercise wide powers going well beyond those available to a judge of a national court – for example, as to the determination of the law applicable, the sources of law to which recourse may be made, the procedure to be adopted, and the admissible evidence – and the grounds for review of arbitral awards are much more restricted than for appeals from the decision of a judge. Moreover, where enforcement of an award is sought outside the United Kingdom, the law of the state of enforcement controls the extent to which the award and any decisions in the country of origin upholding or setting aside the award will be recognized, though in a state which is party to the 1958 New York Convention on the recognition and enforcement of foreign arbitral awards the grounds for refusal of recognition and enforcement are limited by art V of the Convention.

Except for a few provisions relating to consumer arbitration agreements,[30] the Arbitration Act draws no distinction between non-commercial and commercial arbitration. By contrast, the UNCITRAL Model Law is confined to international *commercial* arbitration, though a footnote indicates that the term 'commercial' is to be given a wide interpretation.

(iii) Private, statutory and conventional arbitration

The third classification relates to the source of the arbitrator's powers. Private arbitration derives from the agreement of the parties; statutory arbitration, from a special statute which imposes arbitration on the parties to the dispute;[31] and conventional arbitration from an international convention or other instrument, such as the Algiers Declarations of 19 January 1991, which established the Iran-United States Claims Tribunal as a semi-permanent body to deal with claims by US nationals arising from the dispute between Iran and the United States.

4.   THE DEVELOPMENT OF ENGLISH ARBITRATION LAW

Prior to the enactment of the Arbitration Act 1996 the principal statute governing arbitration was the Arbitration Act 1950. This suffered many deficiencies. Its rules on procedure were limited, it gave excessive powers of intervention to the courts[32] and there were several types of arbitral proceeding it did not cover. Accordingly, prior to the coming into force of the 1996 Act, it could confidently be asserted that 'by far the most important source of English arbitration law is the common law',[33] a fact which made it largely inaccessible to those not expert in the field. Growing dissatisfaction with this state of affairs and with what were seen as unnecessary

---

30 Sections 89–92.

31 For example, arbitration under the Agricultural Holdings Act 1986, s 84 and Sch 11. Statutory arbitrations are provided for in the Arbitration Act 1996, ss 94–98.

32 Including, until it was repealed by the Arbitration Act 1979, the notorious case stated procedure, by which the arbitrator, in the course of an arbitration, could be asked to state a special case on a point of law for the opinion of the court.

33 Mustill and Boyd, *Commercial Arbitration*, p 53.

restrictions on the power of arbitral tribunals led to pressure for reform and the setting up of the Departmental Advisory Committee (DAC) on Arbitration by the Department of Trade and Industry, which then took over a private initiative for new legislation. Having initially been somewhat hostile to the UNCITRAL Model Law in its Report of June 1989,[34] the DAC came to see the merits of it, and, while not recommending its wholesale adoption,[35] proposed legislation which sharply moved towards it. A Bill was drafted on which there was extensive consultation and a further report by the DAC,[36] culminating in what became the Arbitration Act 1996. It is no exaggeration to say that this completely changed the face of English[37] arbitration law, which for the first time set out in statutory form a clear and coherent framework of arbitration procedure, with stated underlying principles, in a logical sequence and in plain English,[38] and so comprehensive in its sweep that, though it does not provide a complete code of arbitration law, it does constitute a very detailed primary source.

5.   THE SOURCES OF ARBITRATION LAW

(i)   The arbitration agreement

In any analysis of arbitration it is necessary to distinguish the substantive law governing relations between the parties from the procedural law applicable to the arbitration. The sources of substantive law affecting commercial transactions have been discussed in an earlier chapter.[39] They include national and international trade usage, and principles and rules of transnational commercial law to be extracted from international instruments, comparative case law and 'soft law' in the form of international or regional restatements, model contracts, contractually adopted trade rules, and the like. We consider a little later in the context of international commercial arbitration the nature of the international *lex mercatoria* and the basis of its entitlement to recognition as normative in character. The primary source of the parties' procedural rights and duties in an arbitration is not the law as such but

---

34 *A New Arbitration Act for the United Kingdom? The response of the Departmental Advisory Committee to the UNCITRAL Model Law.* The report was later reproduced in (1990) 6 Arbitration International 3.

35 There were various reasons for this, including the fact that the Model Law, being designed exclusively for international arbitration, did not address various issues relevant to domestic legislation and, moreover, was considered to restrict unduly the judicial power to review awards. As to this last, see also Roy Goode, 'Arbitration: Should Courts Get Involved?' (2002) Judicial Studies Institute Journal 33 at pp 44–45.

36 *Report on the Arbitration Bill* (February 996), reproduced in Robert Merkin, *The Arbitration Act 1996: An Annotated Guide* (2000).

37 Scotland, whose arbitration law was much less developed, was happy to adopt the Model Law, so that the Act does not apply to Scottish arbitrations.

38 As witness the thunderous applause given to the parliamentary draftsman, Mr Geoffrey Sellers, at a conference on the Bill at Kings College London – an accolade surely without precedent in the annals of lawmaking!

39 See pp 11 ff.

the written agreement[40] of the parties as to the decision to arbitrate and the procedure to be adopted, for the Arbitration Act gives almost total supremacy to the wishes of the parties, with certain qualifications relating particularly to the right to challenge an award for lack of jurisdiction or serious irregularity. The express agreement of the parties may be supplemented by terms implied from the express terms or by usage or course of dealing or by law. In the case of an institutional arbitration the parties expressly or impliedly agree with each other and with the arbitral institution to observe the institutional rules laid down by the institution in question. So in an ICC or LCIA arbitration the parties agree to be bound by the 1998 ICC Arbitration Rules or the 1998 Rules of the LCIA, as the case may be, except so far as those rules may be varied or excluded by the parties or the tribunal. The effect of institutional rules not only in defining the procedures to be adopted but also in potentially enlarging or restricting the powers of the arbitrators is not always understood, and while many of these take effect subject to the agreement of the parties, it should be borne in mind that the parties do not have an entirely free hand in modifying them, because the arbitral institution is entitled to have regard to its own position and the standing of awards made under its aegis. So it is clear, for example, that in an ICC arbitration the parties cannot exclude the role of the ICC Court of Arbitration in supervising the arbitral process and in scrutinizing and approving the draft of the award,[41] a role designed to ensure the enforceability of ICC awards.

(ii)   The *lex arbitri*

So far as the law is concerned, the arbitral proceedings will be governed by the law of the place where the arbitration has its seat, otherwise known as the *lex arbitri* or curial law, and by such other laws as the parties may agree to the extent that the application of these is permitted by the curial law. By the seat is meant the juridical seat designated by the parties to the arbitration agreement or by any arbitral or other institution or person vested by the parties with powers in that regard or by the arbitral tribunal if so authorized by the parties.[42] The juridical seat is the place whose law is intended by the parties to govern the arbitral proceedings, not the place where the proceedings are actually held or the award given. The link establishing the seat is therefore legal, not territorial, a sound approach, for the place designated for a hearing or a pre-hearing meeting may have been chosen for convenience and not because of the relevance of its legal system.

---

40 Except in relation to consumer arbitration agreements, the statutory provisions are confined to agreements in writing, this being given an extended meaning by s 5. What constitutes writing continues to give trouble, both under the Act and under the New York Convention. Similarly, the 1958 New York Convention on the Recognition and Enforcement of Arbitral Awards applies only to written arbitration agreements. But an oral agreement is enforceable at common law as an agreement to submit to arbitration and to be bound by the arbitral award, and any such award can be enforced by action like any other contract.

41 Though without encroaching on the tribunal's right of decision on matters of substance.

42 Section 3. For detailed analyses, see Georgios Petrochilos, 'On the juridical character of the seat in the Arbitration Act 1996' [2002] LMCLQ 66 and *Procedural Law in International Arbitration*, paras 3.32 ff.

Identifying the seat of the arbitration is of great importance, as it is the law of the seat which determines the arbitrability of the issues referred to arbitration,[43] the constitution of the tribunal, the procedure for the arbitration, the duties, liabilities and immunities of the arbitrators and the procedure for challenges to an award. All these matters are dealt with by the Arbitration Act, and most of its provisions apply only where the seat is in England and Wales or Northern Ireland.[44] Thus the Act does not apply merely because England is designated as the place where the arbitration is to be conducted; the relevant law is the *lex arbitri*, though through the power of states to control all activity within their borders the choice by the parties of a *lex arbitri* which is not that of the place of arbitration depends for its effectiveness on the *lex loci arbitri*.[45] An award is deemed to be made at the seat, regardless of where it was actually signed, dispatched or delivered.[46] Moreover, as the place under the law of which the award is made, the seat plays a significant role under art V(1)(a) and (e) of the New York Convention, a point which tends to be ignored by those who argue in favour of the concept of a stateless award.[47]

(iii) Any different procedural law selected by the parties

There is a strong presumption, nevertheless, that the place designated by the parties for the conduct of the arbitration is intended to be the seat, the law of which will govern the proceedings. In theory, it is possible for the parties to choose a curial law other than that of the place where the arbitration is conducted. [48] But the disadvantages of selecting such a curial law when the physical control lies with the courts of the place of arbitration are potentially so serious that only in the most exceptional cases will the parties be taken to have intended to do so, and in general it will be assumed that where the arbitration is held in England, the reference to the foreign procedural law is intended purely to import the procedures there laid down into an arbitration governed by English law as the *lex arbitri*, so that the foreign procedural law takes effect only to the extent that it is not inconsistent with English arbitration law.[49]

(iv) Procedures agreed during the arbitral proceedings

There are certain stages of an arbitration which are common to many arbitrations, such as exchange of pleadings, disclosure and production of documents (discovery),

---

43 It is not, however, the only applicable law, for if the award comes before a foreign court for recognition and enforcement, it may apply its own rules of public policy to determine whether the award should be enforced (New York Convention 1958, art V(2)).

44 Section 2(1). Every statutory arbitration is to be taken to have its seat in England and Wales or, as the case may be, in Northern Ireland (s 95(2)).

45 See below and generally Roy Goode, 'The Role of the *Lex Loci Arbitri* in International Arbitration' (2001) 17 Arbitration International 19.

46 Section 53.

47 See p 1178.

48 *Channel Tunnel Group Ltd v. Balfour Beatty Construction Ltd*, n 4, per Lord Mustill at 357; *James Miller & Partners Ltd v. Whitworth Street Estates (Manchester) Ltd* [1970] AC 583, per Lord Wilberforce at 616–617; *Naviera Amazonica Peruana SA v. Compagnia Internacional de Seguros del Peru* [1988] 1 Lloyd's Rep 116, per Kerr LJ at 119).

49 *Union of India v McDonnell Douglas Corp* [1993] 2 Lloyd's Rep 48.

and the submission of written briefs where called for. But each arbitration, particularly at the international level, has its own distinctive features, and the parties will work with the arbitral tribunal to determine the most effective and efficient work of conducting the arbitration, the smooth progress of which greatly depends on cooperation by the parties and their lawyers. So much of what goes on is dictated less by rules than by party agreement and/or procedural orders of the tribunal.

6. THE ARBITRATION AGREEMENT

Reference has already been made to the importance attached to party autonomy, an underlying principle of the Arbitration Act. The parties control the form of the arbitration, the appointment of the arbitrators so far as not delegated to a third party and the procedure to be adopted for the arbitration itself, though the procedural stages are often developed by the tribunal in consultation with the parties. It is worth taking some care in drafting the arbitration clause, but all too often it features as a boilerplate provision without regard to the particular parties or their circumstances. Among the matters to be considered are the following:

(a)   *Is arbitration necessarily the best mode of dispute resolution?* Do the parties want to consider some prior step, such as a meeting of senior officers of both contestants, with a view to resolving issues amicably and, if not, deciding on the best method of proceeding?

(b)   *What should be the scope of the arbitration agreement?* In particular, should it be confined to specific issues or cover all disputes that may relate to or arise out of the contract, a wide sphere of application and one that would embrace not merely claims in contract but claims in tort or unjust enrichment arising from the contract?

(c)   *Is the arbitration to be institutional or ad hoc? And if institutional, what institution and under what rules?* The relative advantages and disadvantages of ad hoc and institutional arbitration have been discussed earlier.[50] It is an advantage to choose an arbitral institution located where the arbitration is to take place, though if this is the country of one of the parties, there may be a desire to choose another institution in the interests of neutrality. It goes without saying that in selecting the institution regard should be had to its standing, its reputation for care and efficiency and its ability to handle arbitrations of the type in question, as well as any facilities it offers for meeting and hearings. Finally, it is important to ensure that any selected institution still exists! In general, once the arbitral institution has been agreed, one would expect to choose the institution's own rules. But it may be willing to administer an arbitration under rules published by a non-administering body, such as the UNCITRAL Arbitration Rules 1976.

(d)   *How many arbitrators should be appointed?* Usually, the arbitration agreement provides either for a sole arbitrator or for three arbitrators, in order to avoid the risk of a deadlock. In international arbitrations the normal practice is to appoint three arbitrators, each party having an arbitrator of its choice, with an indepen-

50   See p 1165.

dent chairman, commonly appointed by the two party-appointed arbitrators and from a third country. There are several advantages to a three-person tribunal. Their combined knowledge and experience will be greater and more diverse than those of a single arbitrator. Each party is likely to feel more comfortable with having an arbitrator of its choice, usually one of its own nationals. The debate among arbitrators helps to ensure that each party's case is fully analysed, arguments focused and errors avoided. And a unanimous decision reduces the risk that the award will not be recognized or enforced. Inevitably there are disadvantages. Costs are considerably increased, meetings may be harder to arrange because of the number of diaries to be consulted and differences in time zones, and the duration of the arbitral process is likely to be longer.

(e) *What is to be the procedure for appointing or nominating arbitrators?* There are various possibilities, including appointment by the parties and appointment by a third party or institution designated for the purpose.

(f) *What is to happen if the designated machinery for the appointment (eg appointment by a third person or institution designated for the purpose) breaks down?* This actually happened in *Soleh Boneh v Uganda*,[51] where the person designated to make the appointment under an agreement for arbitration under the ICC rules declined to do so, and the ICC Court made an appointment which was later subjected to a sustained challenge, both unsuccessfully in the arbitral proceedings and later in the Swedish courts, where the proceedings dragged on for many years before the case was finally settled following enforcement proceedings in England. In an English arbitration the Arbitration Act empowers the court to appoint an arbitrator if the agreed mechanism fails and the parties have made no provision as to what is to happen in that event.[52]

(g) *Where is the arbitration to have its seat?* The first golden rule is to choose a New York Convention state so as to be sure of enforcement in other convention states. The second is to avoid a jurisdiction where there is too great a readiness to subject arbitral proceedings and awards to judicial intervention. The third is to choose a location where all the necessary administrative, secretarial and stenographic skills are available, together with suitable accommodation. Finally, avoid a location which is likely to be involved in a civil war!

(h) *Are the arbitrators to be given power to decide* ex aequo et bono *or as* amiables compositeurs *rather than according to legal rules?* This would be unusual because of the uncertainties generated, though it is now permitted by agreement of the parties under s 46(1)(b) of the Arbitration Act 1996.

(i) *What should be the language of the arbitration?* It is normally convenient to choose the language of the contract.

(j) *Should the arbitration clause be drafted to exclude judicial review, so far as this is possible?* Yes, if finality is desired. Section 69(1) of the Arbitration Act

---

51 ICC Case No 2321/1974, '*Two Israeli Companies v Government of an African State*', (1976) YB CA 133, where in a preliminary award the arbitrator rejected the challenge to his appointment, holding that the parties must have intended to allow an effective machinery for the settlement of disputes covered by the arbitration clause.

52 Arbitration Act 1996, s 18.

1996 allows the parties to exclude appeal on a point of law, though not a challenge as to substantive jurisdiction or serious irregularity.

(k) *How far should the arbitration clause seek to regulate the procedure of the arbitration?* In practice, it may be wise to avoid any detailed rules, which may fail to take account of the particular circumstances.

7.   PRINCIPLES OF ENGLISH ARBITRATION LAW

The general principles underpinning the Arbitration Act and in accordance with which Pt I is to be construed, are stated succinctly in the following terms in s 1:

(a)   the object of arbitration is to obtain the fair resolution of disputes by an impartial tribunal without unnecessary delay or expense;

(b)   the parties should be free to agree how their disputes are resolved, subject only to such safeguards as are necessary in the public interest;

(c)   in matters governed by this Part the court should not intervene except as provided by this Part .

Thus the three pillars are set up: fairness, party autonomy and very limited judicial intervention. These are supplemented by the following subsidiary principles:

(a)   There must be a dispute.

(b)   The question must be arbitrable.

(c)   The arbitration procedure operates within the confines of the law.

(d)   The issues referred to arbitration must be determined in accordance with the applicable law except as otherwise agreed by the parties.

(e)   The arbitrator must be impartial and, to that extent, independent.

(f)   The arbitrator must act within his remit.

(g)   The arbitrator cannot conclusively determine his own jurisdiction.

(h)   The agreement to arbitrate is notionally separate from the primary agreement of which it forms part.

8.   THE PRINCIPLES EXAMINED

(i)   The consensual nature of arbitration

The powers of the arbitrator derive from the agreement under which he is appointed. This fundamental principle of arbitration law pervades every aspect of arbitration. It means that the arbitrator cannot act at all in the absence of a valid agreement to arbitrate[53] or appointment by the court where it has power to do so,[54] nor can he adopt procedures inconsistent with those agreed by the parties, inquire into matters beyond his remit or exercise coercive powers for default in compliance with his orders except with the support of the court or as otherwise authorized by law.[55] Arbitration sets up a trilateral relationship based on the contract between the

---

53 Whether in advance of the dispute or by a voluntary submission (*compromis*) after it has arisen.

54 See Arbitration Act 1996, s 18.

55 See p 1189.

parties themselves and the separate contract between them and the arbitrator.[56] One should note, however, that after the enactment of the Contracts (Rights of Third Parties) Act 1999 it may be possible in some cases for a third party to enforce an arbitration agreement.[57]

But the agreement of the parties is not the sole source of the arbitrator's powers. These are supported and controlled by law and by such jurisdictional and procedural rules of any arbitral body or appointing authority as the parties have accepted as between themselves and vis-à-vis the body or authority in question. So the arbitrator's position has been described as partly a matter of contract and partly one of status.[58]

(ii) Fairness[59]

This entails, among other things, that the parties should be given, and be seen to be given, equality of treatment;[60] a reasonable opportunity to know the case they have to meet, to state their own case and to appear or be represented at all hearings; and an assurance of competence and impartiality on the part of the arbitrators. This principle is crystallized in s 33(1) of the Act. Failure to observe it may lead to an award being remitted or set aside or even in extreme cases, to removal of the arbitrator. Arbitrators also have a general duty to act in good faith.

(iii) The avoidance of unnecessary delay or expense

This again is embodied in s 33(1). The avoidance of delay is not always easy, particularly with a panel of three from three different countries, whose diaries have to be consulted with those of the lawyers for the parties as well as witnesses. Advance planning is the key to expedition, and a good arbitrator or chair will try to ensure this. Rather less thought tends to be given to the reduction of expense as the arbitration machine grinds on, but it is important for the parties.

(iv) A high degree of party autonomy

Party autonomy is central to arbitration, which principle involves a private dispute to be resolved by a private tribunal. It would not be wise to remove all legal controls from arbitration and there has to be some mechanism for recourse to the court to prevent an arbitrator from acting unfairly or with bias, exceeding his jurisdiction or

---

56 *K/S Norjarl A/S v. Hyundai Heavy Industries Co Ltd* [1991] 1 Lloyd's Rep 524; *Compagnie Européene De Céréals SA v. Tradax Export SA* [1986] 2 Lloyd's Rep 301.

57 See in particular s 8(1); *Nisshin Shipping Co Ltd v Cleaves & Co Ltd* [2004] 1 Lloyd's Rep 38; C. Ambrose 'When can a third party enforce an arbitration clause?' [2001] JBL 415.

58 *K/S Norjarl A/S v. Hyundai Heavy Industries Co Ltd*, n 56, per Sir Nicolas Browne-Wilkinson V-C at 536–537. See generally Mustill and Boyd, *Commercial Arbitration*, pp 220–221; Murray Smith, 'Contractual Obligations Owed by and to Arbitrators: Model Terms of Appointment' (1992) 8 Arbitration International 17.

59 For a detailed discussion, see Petrochilos, *Procedural Law in International Arbitration*, paras 4.50ff.

60 It would be a breach of this principle for an arbitrator to have communications with one of the parties without the knowledge of the others.

committing serious procedural irregularities. There is less agreement about the circumstances in which appeals should be possible on a point of law. We return later to challenges to an award.

There is an apparent tension between the overriding right of the parties to agree on all procedural and evidential matters[61] and the general duty of the tribunal under s 33, which is mandatory and thus cannot be excluded by agreement,[62] to avoid unnecessary delay or expense in conducting the arbitral proceedings. But this tension is more apparent than real. It is clear that if the parties choose to agree on a procedure which is extravagantly expensive or unnecessarily protracted, they cannot make complaint against the arbitral tribunal, though the arbitrators themselves, if they made protests which went unheard, might well be entitled to resign if burdens were being imposed on them substantially beyond what they could reasonably have expected. But if the arbitral tribunal is guilty of excessive delay or extravagance, its members will not be able to shield behind the terms of their appointment.

(v)   The existence of a dispute

An agreement which provides for determination of matters other than disputes or differences, such as determination by an expert, is not an arbitration agreement.[63] Likewise, the court will not stay an action and refer the matter to arbitration if liability is not disputed or if the contention advanced had never been put to the claimant, so that there is no dispute,[64] or the right to dispute liability has been lost under the contract or by law.[65] Under the previous law the court could also refuse a stay if it considered the claim was not disputable and could give the claimant summary judgment. That approach is no longer open and so long as the claim is disputed, it must be referred to arbitration (in the absence of an applicable exception) even if the court considers that the defendant does not have an arguable defence.[66]

(vi)   Arbitrability

In general, an issue is arbitrable if it is competent to the parties to determine it by agreement or if it involves the existence, validity or enforceability of the agreement from which the dispute arises.[67] But it is clear that an arbitrator cannot determine questions of legal status, such as marriage and divorce, or of matters exclusively within the public domain, such as the validity of a patent, nor can he make awards affecting the rights of those who are not parties to the arbitration. On the other hand, there is a growing international consensus that arbitrators are entitled to rule on the validity of the primary agreement itself even if this involves consideration of issues of public policy or of public law, such as restrictive trade practices legislation,

---

61 Section 34(1).
62 Sections 4(1), 110.
63 See p 1162.
64 *Edmund Nuttall Ltd v RG Carter Ltd* [2002] BLR 312, a decision on adjudication.
65 *Watkins Jones & Sons Ltd v Lidl UK GmbH* (2002) 86 Con LR 155.
66 *Halki Shipping Corp v Sopex Oils Ltd* [1998] 1 WLR 726.
67 As to the latter, see p 1184.

intellectual property rights or the antitrust legislation of the United States.[68] Maritime cargo disputes have long been held to be arbitrable in England, and recently the US has taken a similar approach.[69]

The European Community dimension deserves separate mention.[70] The European Court of Justice has held that arbitrators are obliged to respect EU competition law.[71] Several questions arise. First, in what circumstances is EU law to be applied? In proceedings before a court in a member state of the EU the court has a duty to apply mandatory rules of EU competition law, where applicable,[72] even if the governing law is not that of a member state. What is the position of an arbitrator where the seat of the arbitration is in England? There are two ways in which it would be open to the tribunal to apply EU competition law. The first is through the conflict of laws route, the second by the application of EU competition law as mandatory law in England. It seems clear that the parties can contract into EU law, either directly or by choosing the law of a member state. Where there is no choice of law clause, so that determination of the applicable law is left to the arbitral tribunal, this may lead it to apply the law of a member state. It seems that in most cases the tribunal examines the application of EU law not of its own motion but because one of the parties invokes it by way of defence.[73] This is unsurprising in that it is for one of the parties to raise the issue of non-compatibility with EU law in the first instance, as this will typically involve questions of fact, and it is not the task of the tribunal to investigate facts not

68 See the landmark decision of the US Supreme Court in *Mitsubishi Motors Corp. v. Soler Chrysler-Plymouth Inc* 473 US 614, 105 S Ct. 3346, 87 L Ed.444 (1985) holding that there was nothing to preclude arbitrators in a Japanese arbitration from considering whether a contract contravened US antitrust legislation, though the US courts retained the right to review this aspect of the award at the enforcement stage. Similarly, in *Scherk v Alberto-Culver Co* 417 US 506 (1974) the Illinois Supreme Court held that a claim based on a seller's fraudulent representations about its trade marks in violation of s 10(b) of the Securities Exchange Act of 1934 was nevertheless arbitrable. See, generally, Karl-Heinz Böckstiegel, 'Public Policy and Arbitrability' in Comparative Arbitration Practice and Public Policy in Arbitration (ICCA Congress series no 3, ed Pieter Sanders, 1987), at 177 ff; Redfern and Hunter, International Commercial Arbitration, paras 3-21–3-30; Julian D. M. Lew, 'Determination of arbitrators' jurisdiction and the public policy limitations on that jurisdiction' in Contemporary Problems in International Arbitration (ed Julian D. M. Lew, 1986), ch 7, at pp 78 ff; Mark Blessing 'Mandatory rules of law versus party autonomy in international arbitration' (1997) 14 Journal of International Arbitration 23; and International Law Association, Final Report on Public Policy as a Bar to Enforcement of Arbitral Awards, April 2002.

69 The controversy in the United States turned on whether the waiver of judicial remedies in an arbitration agreement was void under s 1303(8) of the Federal Arbitration Act 1925 as lessening the carrier's liability or was contrary to the underlying purposes of the Carriage of Goods by Sea Act 1992. See Kenneth-Michael Curtin, 'Arbitrating maritime cargo disputes – future problems and considerations' [1997] LMCLQ 31.

70 For an exhaustive treatment of this complex subject, see Natalya Shelkoplyas, *The Application of EC Law in Arbitration Proceedings* (2003). See also Lew, Mistelis and Kröll, *Comparative International Commercial Arbitration*, ch 19.

71 *Nordsee Deutsche Hochseefischerei GmbH v Reederei Mond Hochseefischerei Nordstern AG & Co KG* Case 102/81 [1982] ECR 1095.

72 Article 81 deals with anti-competitive acts which may affect trade between Member States and which have as their object or effect the prevention, restriction or distortion of competition within the common market. Article 82 deals with an abuse of a dominant position in so far as it may affect trade between Member States.

73 Shelkoplyas, *The Application of EC Law in Arbitration Proceedings*, p 160.

pleaded by either party. Where, however, the evidence put before the tribunal plainly indicates a breach of EU law, the tribunal does, it is thought, have an obligation to take notice of this and to address it even if it has not been put in issue by a party. In proceedings before an English court the Rome Convention on the law applicable to contractual obligations, enacted by the Contracts (Applicable Law) Act 1990, would be applied. But even though sitting in England, the tribunal has no obligation to apply English conflict of laws rules, so that it is left to the arbitral tribunal to determine whether it is appropriate to apply the conflict rules of the Rome Convention. In any event, in an arbitration having its seat in England the tribunal should apply EU competition law not (or not necessarily) as the applicable law but as rules of public policy of the *lex arbitri*,which operate regardless of the otherwise applicable law,[74] and failure of the tribunal to do so justifies annulment of the award.[75]

Arbitral tribunals face the additional difficulty that, unlike national courts of member states, an arbitral tribunal has no power to refer issues of the EU to the European Court of Justice for an advisory opinion, since it is a private body, not a 'court or tribunal' of the state.[76] Finally, if a tribunal decides not to apply EU law in cases where the contract between the parties produces effects within the EU, what is the consequence? It cannot, it is thought, be faulted for applying its own conflict rule to determine, in the absence of a choice of law by the parties, that the applicable law is not that of a member state. On the other hand, if the resulting award is sought to be enforced in a member state, it would be open to the courts of that state to invoke public policy, in the sense of a duty to respect the EU's mandatory laws, as a ground for refusing to allow enforcement of the award. Indeed, in the *Nordsee* case the ECJ hinted that it was the duty of national courts to uphold EU law in this way.[77] Accordingly, since arbitral tribunals will wish to ensure as far as possible that their awards are enforceable,[78] an arbitral tribunal should have regard to EU law wherever the contract between the parties produces effects within the EU and there is a prospect of enforcement being sought in a member state, even if the applicable law is not that of a member state and the seat of the arbitration is outside the EU.

(vii) The stateless award?

A question which has occasioned much debate in overseas literature is the source and content of the arbitrator's powers. Various theories have been propounded: that the source of the arbitrator's authority and the enforceability of his awards, though immediately deriving from the agreement of the parties, are ultimately determined by national law; that the arbitration agreement constitutes an autonomous source of authority wholly independent of any national legal system; that the arbitration

---

74 See the Rome Convention, art 7(1), and Mustill and Boyd, *2001 Companion*, p 80.

75 See the decision of the European Court of Justice in *ECO Swiss China Time Ltd v Benetton International NV*, Case C-126/97 [1999] ECR 1-3055, [1999] 2 All ER (Comm) 44.

76 *Nordsee Deutsch Hochseefischerei GmbH v Reederei Mond Hochseefischerei AG & Co KG* C-102/81 [1982] ECR 1095.

77 Ibid, at 1111, para 14.

78 In the case of an ICC arbitration art 35 of the ICC Rules imposes an obligation on the arbitrators to make every effort to ensure that the award is enforceable in law.

agreement brings into play an autonomous arbitral order derived from the institutional character of arbitration and based on principles common to civilized states. The view of the proponents of arbitral autonomy, who include among their number several internationally respected scholars, has been forcefully expressed by a leading authority in the following terms:

> Perhaps the largest proportion of international commercial arbitrations are conducted outside both national and legal boundaries. They are totally detached from every national system of law and are independent of the State in which they are held. The proceedings are consequently governed by and in accordance with international or at least non-national arbitration rules.[79]

The difficulty is that the total freedom from municipal law thus claimed for international arbitral procedure cannot exist except with the assent of the law of the place of arbitration, which in England entails application of the *lex arbitri*. This dependence on the *lex loci arbitri*, and through it the *lex arbitri*, coupled with the fact that all over the world states have enacted legislation governing international as well as domestic arbitrations, is wholly inconsistent with the autonomy claimed for international commercial arbitration. It is also inconsistent with the will of those parties whose arbitration agreement designates the seat of the arbitration with the specific purpose of subjecting themselves to the *lex arbitri*. Moreover, even if the *lex loci arbitri* permits the parties to exclude its application, the result is potentially dangerous, for it leaves the parties with nowhere to go if the arbitrators need judicial assistance to enforce their orders and may create problems at the point of enforcement.[80] The object of arbitration is to secure an enforceable award, and national laws as well as the New York Convention confer considerable privileges on the successful party to an arbitration. Enforcement involves access to the machinery of the state in which the enforcement proceedings are to be taken, or in some other state, and this in turn presupposes that the award is recognized by the law of the state in question. Since most states impose at least some curbs on the power of arbitrators, and in most states arbitral proceedings and awards are in some measure subject to judicial review, it is scarcely possible to divorce arbitration proceedings from the law of the place where they are conducted. Indeed, if one can predicate an arbitral procedural law detached from any municipal law, it cannot not be regarded as a closed system, for in so far as it is alleged to answer all queries of whatever character capable of arising in arbitration proceedings, it is uncodified and incapable of ascertainment, and in so far as it does not answer such questions, resort must be had to another source of authority. The law of the forum may, of course, permit reference to the law of another state (eg that selected by the parties in their contract) to govern

---

79 J. D. M. Lew, *Applicable Law in International Commercial Arbitration* (1978). For a discussion of English law on this point, see Mustill and Boyd, *Commercial Arbitration*, pp 66–68.

80 Belgium, with a view to attracting more international arbitration, once introduced a provision into its law excluding the power of Belgian courts to entertain an application for annulment of an award unless at least one of the parties to the dispute was Belgian (Judicial Code, art 1717(4)). This ingenious measure backfired because the arbitration community saw it as leaving parties having legitimate grounds for challenge to an award with no recourse anywhere (it is widely accepted that only courts of the state of origin have power to set aside an award), and the provision was changed in 1998.

their rights, but that other law will be allowed to operate only in the conditions and to the extent permitted by the *lex fori*.[81]

The proponents of the concept of the stateless award do, of course, recognize the power of courts to control what goes on in their own jurisdiction. Their point is that if it comes to enforcement in another jurisdiction the only relevant law is the law of the state of enforcement. French courts in particular have developed and applied the theory that an international award is not integrated into the national legal system of the state of origin of the award, so that in the state in which enforcement is sought the courts are free to allow enforcement of an award even if it has been set aside in the state of origin.[82] It is true that the courts of the state of enforcement necessarily have the last word, as expressly provided by art VII of the New York Convention. Nevertheless, the concept that the only relevant law is the law of state of enforcement is hard to reconcile with the freedom of parties to subject themselves to a designated *lex arbitri* and with the significance given to the *lex arbitri* by art V(1)(a) and (e) of the New York Convention, does little to promote international comity (which involves mutual respect between the courts of different states), and has the severe practical disadvantage of exposing the party against whom an award is made to the application of a different law in every country in which enforcement is sought, thus undermining the internationality of arbitration and destroying the finality which the arbitral process seeks to ensure and producing a multiplicity of potentially conflicting judgments in different jurisdictions.[83]

This is not to deny the importance of the role of the courts in the state of enforcement. It is clear, first, that under art VII of the New York Convention the courts of the enforcing state may allow the beneficiary of an award which is open to challenge under the *lex* arbitri to avail itself of any wider rights given by the law of the enforcement state, and, secondly, that such courts may refuse recognition of an award on any of the grounds provided by art V of the Convention even if the award is upheld by courts of the country of origin. Subject to this, enforcing courts should have a strong inclination to respect decisions of courts of origin, particularly decisions setting aside or varying an award.[84] English law does not recognize the concept of an a-national (or delocalized) arbitration 'floating in the transnational firmament, unconnected with any municipal system of law',[85] in which the procedure is left entirely within the control of the parties and the arbitrators. But there is no objection to a 'floating' curial law[86] in which the place of arbitration (and thus, by inference, the curial law) is to be determined by the parties or one of them at a later date.[87]

---

81 *Union of India v McDonnell Douglas Corp* [1993] 2 Lloyd's Rep 48. See also p 1197.

82 *Hilmarton Ltd v Omnium de Traitement et de Valorisation (OTV)* Cass le civ 23 March 1994, (1994) Rev de l'Arb 327,

83 For a fuller deployment of these arguments, see Goode, (2001) 17 Arbitration International 19.

84 See ibid at p 37.

85 *Bank Mellat v Helleniki Techniki SA* [1984] QB 291, per Kerr J at 301. But the delocalization theory has gained ground steadily in international arbitration. See Redfern and Hunter, *International Commercial Arbitration*, para 2–16 ff.

86 As opposed to a floating substantive law. See p 1098.

87 *The Star Texas* [1993] 2 Lloyd's Rep 445. See M. N. Howard QC [1995] LMCLQ 1.

(viii) Decision according to law

At one time English law appeared to take the position that every contract the subject of arbitration proceedings had to be governed by some municipal law and that it was not open to the parties to choose to have their rights governed by some system of 'law' other than English law or that of a foreign country or perhaps the principles of international law.[88] But the Arbitration Act 1996 makes it is clear that the parties are not limited to choosing a legal system. They may agree that the tribunal should decide the dispute in accordance with other considerations.[89] This would include a decision in accordance with 'internationally accepted principles of law governing contractual relations'[90] or 'rules of law'.[91] It would also seem to include decisions by the tribunal acting *ex aequo et bono* or as *amiable compositeur*,[92] which English law had not recognized previously. But the tribunal can do this only if authorized by the parties. Where they have chosen a law to govern the dispute,[93] it is the duty of the tribunal to apply that law, though, in so far as its provisions are dispositive rather than mandatory, the tribunal is, of course, free to determine that they have been modified or excluded by agreement, including any applicable trade usage or '*lex mercatoria*'. In addition, arbitral tribunals regularly have resort to other sources where the applicable law is undeveloped or does not explicitly cover the point, and there have been many awards in which arbitrators have drawn on the UNIDROIT Principles of International Commercial Contracts and on the Principles of European Contract Law prepared by the Commission on European Contract Law. Section 46(2) of the Arbitration Act makes it clear that where the parties have not chosen the law to govern the substance of the dispute, the tribunal does not have to apply English conflict of laws rules in order to determine the applicable law by the conflict of laws rules it considers applicable. It must, however, select the governing law by some conflict of laws route rather than directly, as is provided in the legislation of some countries,[94] though it is free to apply a conflict rule which is not that of a particular national legal system but is to be found in general principles of private international law.[95]

88 See *Maritime Insurance Co Ltd v. Assecurancz-Union von 1865* (1935) 52 Ll L Rep 16, per Goddard J at 20, cited by Megaw J in *Orion Compania Espanola de Seguros v Belfort Maatschappij voor Algemene Verzekgringeen* [1962] 2 Lloyd's Rep 257 at 264.
89 Section 46(1).
90 *Deutsche Schachtbau-und Tiefbohrgesellschaft mbH v Ras Al Khaimah National Oil Co* [1990] 1 AC 295.
91 It is interesting to see the progression of ideas. Article 33(1) of the UNCITRAL Arbitration Rules 1976 requires the tribunal to apply the *law* designated by the parties or, failing this, the *law* determined by the conflict of laws rules which it considers appropriate. By contrast art 28(1) of the UNCITRAL Model Law on International Commercial Arbitration refers to the *rules of law* chosen by the parties, but if they have not designated the applicable law the tribunal is then required by art 28(2) to apply the *law* determined by the conflict rules it considers applicable.
92 These two phrases are often used interchangeably but are thought by some to mean different things. Either way, their effect would be to dispense with the need to use rules of law to arrive at the result and to empower the arbitrator to act in accordance with notions of equity and fairness.
93 Which is to be understood as the substantive laws of the country in question, not its conflict of laws rules (s 46(2)).
94 See *Fouchard, Gaillard, Goldman on International Commercial Arbitration*, paras 1552 ff.
95 Ibid, paras 1548 ff.

(ix) Independence and impartiality

There are two connected principles concerning the suitability of an arbitrator: independence and impartiality.[96] The ICC Arbitration Rules require that the arbitrator be independent of the parties involved in the arbitration,[97] but independence is not defined and the meaning of the requirement has given rise to much controversy.[98] The underlying idea is that the arbitrator should not have had a personal, social or financial relationship with one of the parties which is either reasonably liable to lead to bias or creates a reasonable apprehension of bias. It was not thought appropriate to provide expressly for independence in the Arbitration Act for fear of unnecessarily excluding perfectly suitable arbitrators but rather to pick it up through the requirement of impartiality, a requirement not found in the ICC Rules. Thus the existence of a prior relationship with one of the parties is a ground for removal of an arbitrator by the court only where it gives rise to reasonable doubts as to his impartiality.[99] It is open to the party potentially affected by the lack of impartiality to waive this requirement by failing to object to the arbitrator's continuance in post after full disclosure.

By impartiality is meant that the arbitrator must not be biased towards one of the parties or have a predisposition as to the outcome of the disputed issue,[100] though the mere fact that the arbitrator has, prior to the initiation of the arbitration, indicated a view on a question of law that later arises in the arbitration is not a ground for impeaching his impartiality. Bias or the appearance of bias may, of course, result from a pre-existing relationship,[101] but there are many other grounds for inferring bias, including the fact that the arbitrator has a personal interest in the subject matter or outcome of the dispute or has indicated a concluded view before completion of the hearing or shown a predisposition to favour one party at the expense of the other. Impartiality is vital to the integrity of arbitration. So in a tribunal of three arbitrators, where each party appoints one arbitrator and appoints a neutral party as chairman, each arbitrator must avoid bias towards the party who appointed him. On the other hand, it is perfectly legitimate for a party-appointed arbitrator to ensure that the evidence and arguments advanced on behalf of the party who appointed him are fully considered by the arbitral tribunal.

(x) The arbitrator to act within his remit

The arbitrator must limit his inquiries and decision to the matters referred to him by the parties, whether in the arbitration agreement or by conduct amounting to submission to his jurisdiction over the issues in question.[102] To the extent that the

---

96 For a comparative treatment, see Lew, Mistel and Kröll, *Comparative International Commercial Arbitration*, paras 11–11 ff.

97 Article 7(1).

98 Derains and Schwartz, *A Guide to the new ICC Rules of Arbitration*, pp 108 ff.

99 Arbitration Act 1996, s 24(1)a); *Russell on Aritration*, para 7–077.

100 The term 'neutrality' is often treated as synonymous with impartiality but is also used in other senses, eg to distinguish an arbitrator appointed by an arbitral institution, or by the other arbitrators as chairman, from one appointed by the parties.

101 As in *Tracomin SA v Gibbs Nathaniel (Canada) Ltd* [1985] 1 Lloyd's Rep 586.

102 See *Westminster Chemicals & Produce Ltd v Eichholz & Loeser* [1954] 1 Lloyd's Rep 99.

arbitrator goes beyond his remit, his award is liable to be set aside for want of substantive jurisdiction.[103]

(xi) The arbitrator's competence to determine his own jurisdiction

The question whether an arbitrator has power to determine his own jurisdiction – commonly described under the German law label *Kompetenz–Kompetenz* – has been much debated over the years. It is sometimes used to refer to the problem arising where there is a dispute as to the very existence or validity of the agreement under which the arbitrator was appointed, but this is a distinct issue of separability of the agreement to arbitrate, not a true example of *Kompetenz–Kompetenz*.

It is obvious that a party cannot deprive an arbitrator of power to continue with the case merely by challenging his jurisdiction, for otherwise parties could readily frustrate the agreement to arbitrate. However, the statement that the arbitrator has power to determine his own jurisdiction is used in at least three senses.

1. The arbitrator has exclusive power to determine his own jurisdiction

In its full sense as formerly used in German arbitration law, *Kompetenz–Kompetenz* means not only that the arbitrator can determine his own jurisdiction but that where the parties have by their agreement given exclusive competence to the arbitrator, his ruling on his jurisdiction is binding and cannot in general be challenged before the court. In this sense the doctrine forms no part of English law, which insists that the ultimate decision on whether an arbitrator acted within his jurisdiction lies with the court

2. The arbitrator's ruling in favour of his jurisdiction is binding until after issue of the award

An intermediate position on the jurisdictional question is that the arbitrator's ruling that he has jurisdiction is susceptible to judicial challenge but only after issue of the award. This is the position taken in some jurisdictions but does not reflect English law, which allows a court challenge to the jurisdiction while the arbitration is proceeding, and the same is now true of German law.[104]

3. The court and the arbitrator have concurrent control over jurisdictional issues

The third position is that during the proceedings the court and the arbitrator have concurrent jurisdiction. This is the position in English law. The arbitrator can rule on his jurisdiction[105] but this does not affect a party's right to apply to the court while the arbitration is pending for a ruling that the arbitrator lacks jurisdiction.[106] This concurrency of control has the advantage that it helps to avoid the risk that the parties will engage in a long and expensive arbitration only to find after the award

---

103   See p 1192.
104   Arbitration Law 1998 (embodied in the German Code of Civil Procedure, Book 10), art 1040(3).
105   Arbitration Act 1996, s 30.
106   Ibid, s 32.

that the arbitrator never had jurisdiction in the first place. However, there is also concern that recourse may be made to the court as a tactic to delay the arbitration proceedings. English law[107] here follows the UNCITRAL Model Law [108] in allowing the arbitration to continue despite a pending application to the court challenging the arbitrator's jurisdiction.

The arbitrator's ruling on jurisdiction may be given either by way of an interim award, if a party so requests and the issue is capable of being dealt with in this way,[109] or in the (final) award. A party who does not accept that the arbitrator has jurisdiction has a choice of methods open to him for dealing with the matter. He can decline to participate in the arbitration proceedings and challenge the award when made, a risky procedure in that if the arbitrator is found to have had jurisdiction and the award is adverse to the party, he may have no other ground of challenge; he can contest the jurisdiction before the arbitrator and challenge the award when made; or he can apply to the court during the arbitration proceedings for a declaration that the arbitrator lacks jurisdiction and/or an injunction to restrain the continuance of the proceedings. What he cannot do is to take part in the arbitration proceedings without raising the jurisdiction issue and then rely on it after the award, for by participating in the arbitration without objection to the jurisdiction he waives the right to challenge it. He must have raised his objection to the jurisdiction not later than the time he takes the first step in the proceedings to contest the merits of any matter in relation to which he challenges the jurisdiction,[110] but the mere fact that he has appointed or participated in the appointment of an arbitrator does not preclude him from raising an objection to the arbitrator's jurisdiction.[111]

(xii) The agreement to arbitrate is considered separate from the primary agreement

In Europe and North America it has long been accepted that an agreement to arbitrate, even if not physically distinct but embodied as an arbitration clause in the primary agreement, is legally separate from the primary agreement, so that the arbitrator's jurisdiction is not affected by the invalidity, non-existence or unenforceability of the primary agreement,[112] still less by its termination, whether for breach or otherwise. English law finally came round to this position as the result of a landmark decision of the Court of Appeal in *Harbour Assurance Co UK v Kansas General Insurance Co Ltd*,[113] and it is now enshrined in statute.[114] It follows that an arbitrator can rule on the validity and legality of the primary agreement without thereby impinging on the validity of his own appointment.[115]

---

107   Ibid, s 30.
108   Article 16(3).
109   It may not be possible to do this before a finding on facts in dispute.
110   Arbitration Act 1996, s 31(1).
111   Ibid.
112   See the UNCITRAL Model Law, art 16(1).
113   [1993] QB 701.
114   Arbitration Act 1996, s 7.
115   See, for example, *Westacre Investments Inc v Jugoimport-SPDR Holding Co Ltd* [1990] QB 740.

But if it is the notionally separate agreement to arbitrate that is found to be non-existent or void, the arbitrator's appointment is necessarily invalid.

9. EFFECTIVENESS OF THE AGREEMENT TO ARBITRATE

Prior to the Arbitration Act 1996 the court would usually stay proceedings brought by a party under an agreement containing an arbitration clause, but, in the case of a domestic arbitration agreement, the grant of stay was a matter of discretion.[116] By contrast, in the case of a non-domestic arbitration agreement the grant of a stay was in given conditions compulsory under s 1 of the Arbitration Act 1975 unless the agreement was null and void or inoperative or incapable of being performed[117] or the court was satisfied that there was not in fact any dispute between the parties with regard to the matters agreed to be referred, which was taken to include cases where, though the defendant disputed the claim, the court consider that it was not reasonably disputable.[118] Under s 9 of the Arbitration Act 1996 a stay is compulsory unless the court is satisfied that the arbitration agreement is null and void, inoperative or incapable of being performed,[119] and there is no longer power to refuse a stay on the ground that in the opinion of the court the defendant does not have an arguable defence.[120] There must, however, be a dispute.[121]

10. THE CONDUCT OF THE ARBITRATION

(i) The arbitration proceedings in outline

The arbitration is usually initiated by one party writing to the other requesting him to concur in the appointment of an arbitrator or arbitrators. Depending on the terms of the arbitration agreement, the appointment may be made by agreement of the parties, by each party appointing an arbitrator (and in the case of a panel of three, the two arbitrators appointing a neutral third person as chairman), by an arbitral institution in accordance with its rules[122] or by a third party designated in the arbitration agreement.[123]

---

116 Arbitration Act 1950, s 4(1).
117 Reproducing verbatim a phrase in art II(3) of the New York Convention.
118 See p 1176.
119 It has been held that among such cases is the termination of the arbitration agreement as the result of a party's repudiatory breach in bringing an action despite the arbitration clause (*Downing v Al Tameer Establishment* [2002] 2 All ER (Comm) 545). However, it cannot be the case that the institution of proceedings is necessarily a repudiation of the arbitration agreement. A party may, for example, be doing no more than exercising his statutory right under s 30(2) of the Arbitration Act 1996 to challenge an interim award by the tribunal that it has jurisdiction.
120 See p 1176.
121 See p 1176.
122 So in disputes governed by the Rules of the London Court of International Arbitration or the International Chamber of Commerce the appointment must be confirmed by the LCIA or the ICC, as the case may be.
123 Eg, the President of the Law Society.

In international arbitrations it is also necessary to determine the place where the arbitration is to take place, a matter of considerable importance because almost invariably this will be the legal 'seat' of the arbitration and its law will be the curial law, which will determine the degree of judicial assistance available and the measure of judicial control and review exercisable before and after the award. Moreover, if the place of the arbitration is a country which has not adopted the New York Convention the successful party may be unable to avail itself of that Convention for the purposes of recognition and enforcement of any award elsewhere. The place may be fixed by the terms of the arbitration, by subsequent agreement of the parties, by the arbitral tribunal or, in the case of an institutional arbitration, by that institution.

When the arbitrator has been appointed, it is usual to hold a preliminary meeting with the parties to discuss the procedural steps and a timetable, and to agree on directions as to pleadings etc. A practice unique to ICC arbitrations is the settlement of terms of reference by the arbitrators in conjunction with the parties. The issues are then defined in pleadings – points of claim, points of defence, reply – in much the same way as in litigation, and disclosure and production of documents usually follow the exchange of pleadings. Except where the arbitration is on the basis of documents alone, a hearing is then fixed at which the parties and their witnesses give evidence and submissions are made by their lawyers. The final stage is the drawing up and issue of the award.

(ii)   The arbitrator and the parties

The appointment of the arbitrator creates a contract between him and the parties, and, except as subsequently agreed by the parties, the arbitrator must work within the confines of that contract. This applies not only to the extent of his remit but also to the procedure to be adopted. In the case of institutional arbitration the rules of the arbitral institution concerned will usually prescribe the procedure to be followed, and the parties are free to derogate from this only to the extent permitted, expressly or impliedly, by the rules themselves. In the case of an ad hoc arbitration the procedure will be agreed by the parties themselves, failing which it will be laid down by the arbitrator.

However, even in an ad hoc arbitration the autonomy of the parties is not complete. First, the arbitration must conform to the requirements and restrictions of the *lex arbitri*, though in an arbitration under the Arbitration Act 1996 these are relatively few. Secondly, having entered into a contractual engagement with the arbitrator involving a commitment on his part to conduct the arbitration with due diligence and at a reasonable fee,[124] the parties are not entitled to require him to implement a wider remit than, or perform his duties in a different way from, that originally agreed with him. This is a matter of simple contract law. What is unclear is the extent to which the arbitrator is obliged to implement agreements between the parties on procedural matters after the arbitration has commenced. No doubt, as a general rule, he should do so, but if the agreement is one which in his view is inimical to the proper and efficient conduct of the arbitration, he must surely have a right to indicate a line

---

124   *K/S Norjarl A/S v Hyundai Heavy Industries Co Ltd*, n 56.

beyond which he will not go.[125] There is, indeed, a good deal to be said for greater management of arbitrations by the arbitrators, a process assisted by institutional rules to which the parties have agreed to submit. In practice, a good arbitral tribunal will usually have no great difficulty in ensuring a sensible approach to the arbitration, since neither party will wish to risk upsetting the arbitrators!

The parties themselves are required to do all things necessary for the proper and expeditious conduct of the arbitral proceedings. This includes complying with any determination of the tribunal as to procedural or evidential matters or with any order or direction of the tribunal.[126] Both the parties and their lawyers owe a general duty to conduct the arbitral proceedings in good faith.[127]

It has been held to be an implied contractual term that arbitral proceedings are not merely private but confidential,[128] though the duty of confidentiality is not absolute.[129] The opposite had been decided by a bare majority of the High Court of Australia in *Esso Australia Resources Ltd v Plowman*,[130] a decision which attracted huge interest.[131] An interesting new aspect of confidentiality arises from the recent practice by which a judge orders the hearing of an arbitration claim[132] to be heard in private, and any order made to be furnished only to the parties and their lawyers, pursuant to the power conferred on the court by CPR 62.10. In *Department of Economic Policy and Development of the City of Moscow v Bankers Trust Co*[133] the Court of Appeal held that the consideration that the parties had elected for confidentiality and privacy was only the starting point and was not in itself determinative of the question whether the hearing should be in public or private, and that the public interest militated in favour of a public judgment,[134] although in the case in question the decision of the judge at first instance that his judgment under s 68 of the Arbitration Act should remain private was upheld because of the confidentiality and sensitivity of the subject matter.[135]

125 See p 1176.
126 Arbitration Act 1996, 40, which also refers to taking any necessary steps to obtain a decision of the court on a preliminary question of jurisdiction or law, where appropriate.
127 See V. V. Veeder, 'The Lawyer's Duty to Arbitrate in Good Faith' (2002) 18 Arbitration International 431.
128 *Ali Shipping Co v Shipyard Trogir* [1999] 1 WLR 314.
129 One exception is that a party cannot be injuncted from invoking the award to enforce his rights, eg to raise an issue estoppel (*Associated Electric and Gas Insurance Services Ltd v European Reinsurance Company of Zurich* [2003] 1 All ER (Comm) 253).
130 (1995) 183 CLR 10.
131 An entire issue of the *Journal of Internationmal Arbitration* was devoted to the decision and a reproduction of the various expert reports. See (1995) 11 Arbitration International and, for an update on developments, Leon E Trakman, 'Confidentiality in International Commercial Transactions' (2002) 18 International Arbitration 1.
132 As defined by CPR 62.2(1), which in essence covers the various forms of judicial review that can arise in the context of an arbitration, such as the validity of an arbitration agreement or a challenge to an award.
133 [2004] All ER (D) 476 (Mar).
134 Which is the general rule prescribed by CPR 39.2.
135 The leading judgment, given by Mance LJ, provides a detailed history and analysis of the various considerations, including art 6 of the European Convention on Human Rights.

(iii) Must the arbitrator observe rules of evidence?

The traditional view has been that, unless otherwise agreed by the parties, arbitrators are bound by the same rules of evidence as courts.[136] This approach, which in policy terms has absolutely nothing to commend it[137] and was widely disregarded in practice, was later shown to be without foundation.[138] The Arbitration Act 1996 makes it clear that, subject to the right of the parties to agree any matter, it is for the tribunal to decide all procedural and evidential matters, including whether to apply strict rules of evidence (or any other rules) as to the admissibility, relevance or weight of any material (oral, written or other) sought to be tendered on any matters of fact or opinion, and the time, manner and form in which such material should be exchanged and presented.[139] So there is no reason why the arbitrator should not admit hearsay evidence,[140] secondary evidence even where the best evidence is available and extrinsic evidence to explain or interpret a contract even if this would be inadmissible under the parol evidence rule. These are matters which should go to relevance and weight, not to admissibility, with which English procedural law (in theory, at least) has an excessive preoccupation. But underlying these technical rules is a fundamental concern for the principles of fairness and natural justice, which the arbitrator must observe in every case. So each party has a right to know in good time the case he has to meet and to be given a proper opportunity to put his case and answer that of his opponent.

(iv) Must the proceedings be adversarial?

In common law jurisdictions, in contrast to civil law jurisdictions, proceedings are adversarial in character, the judge acting as a referee to see fair play rather than taking the lead in examining witnesses. Whether in an English arbitration the arbitrator is bound to conduct the reference in an adversarial way in the absence of a contrary agreement by the parties was formerly a matter of uncertainty.[141] It is now clear that, either with or subject to the agreement of the parties, the tribunal is not obliged to adopt an adversarial system.[142] In practice, the question is usually disposed of by express or tacit agreement of the parties as to the procedure to be used or the individual style of the arbitrator.

---

136 Mustill and Boyd, *Commercial Arbitration*, p 352; *Russell on Arbitration*, para 5–155.
137 See Goode (1992) 8 Arbitration International 1 at pp 6–7.
138 Richard Buxton, 'The Rules of Evidence as Applied to Arbitrations' (1992) 58 Journal of the Institute of Arbitrators 229, approved extrajudicially by Steyn LJ (1994) 10 Arbitration International 1 at p 7.
139 Section 34.
140 In any event, the hearsay rule has been abolished in civil proceedings: Civil Evidence Act 1995, s 1.
141 Johan Steyn, 'England's Reponse to the UNCITRAL Model Law' (1994) 10 Arbitration International 1, pp 8–10.
142 See Arbitration Act 1996, s 34 and in particular s 34(2)(e): 'whether any and if so what questions should be put to and answered by the respective parties and in what form this should be done'.

(v) Provisional and conservatory measures

Section 38(4) of the Arbitration Act 1996 empowers the tribunal to give directions for the inspection, photographing, preservation, custody or detention by the tribunal, an expert or a party, of property owned by or in the possession of a party. But the tribunal has no power to make provisional awards unless the parties agree,[143] though such agreement may result from submission to arbitral institutional rules.[144]

(vi) Procedural orders

It is necessary to distinguish procedural orders from interim awards. The latter dispose of a part of the issues referred for arbitration and are, in substance, final as to those issues. Procedural orders are concerned with the conduct of the arbitration, not with the substantive rights of the parties. Subject to any agreement between the parties, the arbitrator has wide power to make orders for the conduct of the arbitration, including orders for delivery of pleadings and particulars, disclosure of documents, exchange of experts' reports, security for costs, and the like. The Arbitration Act 1996 gives the arbitrator greater coercive powers in the event of default in compliance with his orders. Security for costs can be ordered.[145] If the tribunal is satisfied that there has been inordinate and inexcusable delay on the part of the claimant in pursuing his claim and that the delay gives rise to, or is likely to give rise to, a substantial risk that it is not possible to have a fair resolution of the issues in that claim or has caused, or is likely to cause, serious prejudice to the respondent, the tribunal may make an award dismissing the claim.[146] In practice, such a power is exercised extremely sparingly. The tribunal may also make an award against a party who, without cause, fails to attend or be represented at an oral hearing of which due notice was given or, where matters are to be dealt with in writing, fails after due notice to submit written evidence or make written submissions.[147] This could happen where the failure is by the claimant, but in the case of non-attendance by the respondent most arbitral tribunals would be reluctant simply to make an award and would prefer to hear the claimant's evidence and submissions. The arbitrator may make peremptory orders against a party that has failed to comply with any order or directions, and contravention of such peremptory orders may lead to an award against the party,[148] though again such a power is likely to be exercised sparingly. The court may also exercise its supportive powers to secure compliance with the arbitrator's orders.[149] In practice arbitrators rarely resort to the courts, taking the sensible view that arbitration should, as far as possible, be conducted on consensual lines. Similarly, though it is open to a party to issue a subpoena in the High Court to compel the attendance of witnesses or the production of documents at the hearing,[150] this is rarely done.

---

143 Arbitration Act 1996, s 39(4).
144 See, for example, the LCIA Rules, art 25.1(c).
145 Arbitration Act 1996, s 38(3).
146 Section 41(3).
147 Sections 41(3), 41(4).
148 Sections 41(5), 41(6), 41(7).
149 Section 42.
150 Section 43.

The arbitrator may be asked to make a partial or interim award,[151] but has no power to do so unless the parties agree to confer such power.[152] Such an award is binding on the parties.

It is for the tribunal to decide whether to admit expert evidence. Such evidence, whether technical or legal, is commonly admitted. In the preparation of a legal opinion it is important for the expert to appreciate that his role is not that of an advocate but of an expert whose primary duty, as in the case of court proceedings, is to the tribunal, not to the party engaging his services. He must therefore state his honest belief as to what is the relevant law, whereas no such duty is imposed on the advocate, whose role is to advance arguments to support his client's case. There can be no objection to discussions between the expert and those instructing him with a view to clarifying the arguments, consideration of issues the expert may not have considered, and elucidating relevant facts. What is not proper is to seek to influence the expert to give an opinion he does not genuinely hold. An expert opinion should set out the qualifications of the witness as an expert and should define the issues in the case to which the opinion is directed, state the assumptions of fact on which the opinion is based and list the documents or bundles of documents with which the expert has been supplied. Where the expert is in agreement with propositions of law advanced by the expert instructed by the other party, he should state this openly, both to reduce the range of issues, with consequent saving of time and cost, and to fulfil his duty as an independent expert. The expert should be careful not to trespass beyond his remit and, in particular, should confine his opinion to the issues of law involved in the case and avoid stating the conclusions to which the tribunal should come, this being a matter for the tribunal.

(vii) The arbitrator and the court

The court has a threefold role to play in the arbitral process. During the course of the arbitration its function is primarily supportive, as by directing compliance with peremptory orders made by the tribunal preliminary[153] or ruling on points of law referred to it,[154] procedural orders as to the taking of evidence, preservation of evidence, inspection and preservation of property, sale of goods, interim relief such as an injunction (including a *Mareva* injunction) and appointment of a receiver.[155]

The court also has limited powers of control prior to the award, eg through a declaration that the arbitrator has no jurisdiction or an injunction restraining continuance of the arbitration,[156] but it has no general supervisory jurisdiction,[157] so that, short of an

---

151   The two terms are often used interchangeably, but it is helpful to distinguish an award covering part of the amount claimed from an award on some preliminary issue, eg jurisdiction, the applicable law, and liability.

152   Section 39(4).

153   Section 42.

154   Section 45. This can be done by a party only with the consent of the arbitrator or all the other parties.

155   Section 44.

156   Section 32.

157   *Bremer Vulkan Schiffbau und Maschinenfabrik v South India Shipping Corp Ltd* [1981] AC 909; and see Arbitration Act 1996, s 1.

application[158] to remove the arbitrator or revoke his authority, the conduct of the arbitration cannot in general be challenged until after issue of the award.

The third function of the court is to review awards and, where necessary, remit them to the arbitrator for further consideration and decision or set them aside altogether.[159]

(viii) The final award

The award must be in writing and signed by the arbitrators.[160] An award of a tribunal whose seat is in England is treated as made in England, regardless of where it was signed, delivered or dispatched to the parties.[161] The same rule applies for the purposes of the provisions of the Act relating to the New York Convention in the case of an award of a tribunal whose seat is elsewhere.[162] The award must contain the reasons for the award unless it is an agreed award or the parties have agreed to dispense with reasons.[163]

Within the limits set by his terms of reference, the arbitrator can, in principle, give any relief of a non-coercive nature that would be available against a party in private litigation, including payment of moneys due under the contract, damages, interest and costs. He can also grant injunctions, specific performance and rectification,[164] though he cannot, of course, impose penal sanctions for breach of such an order. But the arbitrator has no power to make an order affecting the rights of third parties.

11. JUDICIAL REVIEW OF ARBITRAL AWARDS

The extent to which arbitral awards should be subject to judicial review is a question of some delicacy. On the one hand parties select arbitration for its privacy, its finality and the ability to have adjudication by a person of their own choice. On the other, there is the perceived need for some form of judicial control of the arbitral system to ensure that proceedings are conducted fairly and that arbitrators do not go wildly wrong.

Until the enactment of the Arbitration Act 1979, English law allowed far too much judicial intrusion into the arbitral process, both during the reference through the special stated procedure, and after the award by way of appeal to the court to remit the award to the arbitrator for reconsideration or to set it aside for his 'misconduct', an unfortunate and rather offensive term conveying an implication of moral turpitude but, in fact, embracing such matters as error in procedure and errors of fact or law apparent on the face of the award.

---

158 Under ss 23 and 24.
159 See below.
160 Arbitration Act 1996, s 52(3).
161 Section 53.
162 Section 100(2)(b), reversing the effect of the controversial decision of the House of Lords in *Hiscox v Outhwaite* [1992] 1 AC 562.
163 Arbitration Act 1996, s 52(4).
164 Section 48(5).

The readiness of English courts to intervene in arbitral proceedings ran increasingly counter to opinion in other countries, particularly in relation to international commercial arbitration. The general view was that since the parties had entrusted their dispute to the adjudicator of their choice on issues of both fact and law, they took the chance of error and should not be allowed further bites at the cherry. In consequence, London began to lose a substantial amount of arbitration work which had previously come to it from overseas; and in order to recapture this lost business, and to strengthen London as world arbitration centre, the Arbitration Act 1979, implementing the recommendations of the Donaldson Report,[165] introduced major changes.

Further changes were made by the Arbitration Act 1996. Prior to an award, the court's role is limited to the determination of a preliminary point as to the substantive jurisdiction of the tribunal,[166] making orders in support of the arbitral proceedings,[167] a step which in practice is rarely necessary, and to determining preliminary points of law.[168] Once the award has been made, a party seeking to impeach it has three possible grounds of attack: an erroneous assumption or rejection of jurisdiction, serious irregularity, and, in restricted circumstances, error of law. Outside these cases the court has no power to disturb an arbitral award either because of mistakes of fact or because of errors of law.

(i)   Challenge as to jurisdiction

Section 67 sets out the provisions for challenges to an award as to the tribunal's substantive jurisdiction.[169] A challenge to the jurisdiction could be on a number of grounds, for example, that the arbitrator was not validly appointed; the award was against or in favour of a person not a party to the arbitration agreement;[170] the issue referred to the arbitral tribunal is outside the scope of the arbitration agreement or the respondent is entitled to state immunity from process.[171]

Two situations are dealt with in s 67: an award of the tribunal as to its substantive jurisdiction and an award on the merits in which the tribunal has assumed jurisdiction, whether or not the jurisdiction issue was before it.[172] In the first situation the award may be challenged not only where the arbitral tribunal rules that it has jurisdiction but also where it decides that it lacks jurisdiction. In the former case a successful challenge will result either in the award being set aside altogether if the lack of jurisdiction goes to the whole of it or in the varying of the award so as to

---

165 *Report on Arbitration* (Cmnd 7284, 1978).

166 Arbitration Act 1996, s 32.

167 Section 44.

168 Section 45(1).

169 Defined in s 30(1) as jurisdiction on the question whether there is a valid arbitration agreement, whether the tribunal is properly constituted and what matters have been submitted to arbitration in accordance with the arbitration agreement. Procedural irregularity, if serious, falls under s 68.

170 *Hussman (Europe) Ltd v Al Ameen Development Trade Co* [2000] 2 Lloyd's Rep 83 (award in favour of a person not party to the arbitration agreement).

171 See as to this p 1195.

172 This can occur because a person affected by the award is entitled to challenge the jurisdiction if he took no part in the arbitral proceedings. His right of challenge under s 67 of the Act does not depend on his having challenged the jurisdiction before the arbitral tribunal.

expunge that part which was in excess of jurisdiction; in the latter, the setting aside of the no-jurisdiction award results from a ruling that the tribunal did, after all, have jurisdiction, so that it should proceed with the reference. Where the challenge to the jurisdiction is on the basis that the tribunal has made an award on the merits which it had no jurisdiction to make, the award will be set aside or varied to the extent that it is held that the tribunal exceeded its jurisdiction. Where the tribunal's jurisdiction is upheld, the award will be confirmed

The provisions of s 67 are mandatory, so that the right of challenge cannot be excluded by agreement. But a right of challenge based on want of jurisdiction[173] by a person who took part in the proceedings[174] will be lost in three cases. The first is where the challenger takes part or continues to take part in the arbitral proceedings without objecting to the jurisdiction forthwith or within such time as is allowed by the arbitration agreement or the rules.[175] The second is where there was an internal right of appeal under the applicable arbitration rules – for example, in a GAFTA or FOSFA arbitration, where the rules of the association provide for a two-tier arbitration system in which a right of appeal lies to an appeal panel – and the party concerned fails to exercise that right or to exercise it in proper time.[176] The third is where the tribunal gives an award that it has jurisdiction and the party concerned fails to challenge the award or to do so in proper time.[177] Where the party's contention is that the tribunal lacks jurisdiction at the outset, he must raise his objection not later than the time he takes the first step to contest the merits of any matter in relation to which he challenges the tribunal's jurisdiction.[178] Where the objection arises in the course of proceedings – as where the tribunal indicates its intention to deal with an additional matter which is alleged to be beyond its jurisdiction – the challenge must be made as soon as possible after the matter is raised.[179]

(ii) Challenge based on serious irregularity

This is provided by s 68, serious irregularity being defined in s 68(2) and replacing the former, rather offensive, term 'misconduct'. Like s 67, it is mandatory and cannot be excluded by agreement. Section 68 sets out the kinds of irregularity to which it applies. These include the tribunal exceeding its powers otherwise than by exceeding its substantive jurisdiction,[180] ie exceeding its procedural powers. Where serious irregularity is established, the court may remit the award to the tribunal, in whole or in part, for reconsideration or set it aside, wholly or in part, or declare it to be of no effect, in whole or in part, but the power to set aside the award or declare it to be of no

---

173 As opposed to a declining of jurisdiction.
174 Referred to in the Act as a 'party' to the proceedings, in contrast to one electing to take no part, described in s 72(1) as a person 'alleged to be a party', to whom ss 70(2) (dealing with exhaustion of an available arbitral process of appeal or review) and 73 do not apply.
175 Section 73(1)(a).
176 Section 73(2)(a).
177 Section 73(2)(b).
178 Section 31(1).
179 Section 31(2).
180 Section 68(2)(b).
181 Section 68(3).

effect must not be exercised unless the court is satisfied that it would be inappropriate to remit the award.[181] So the primary remedy envisaged is remission. But it is not every irregularity that will justify the grant of a remedy; a serious irregularity means one that has caused or will cause substantial injustice to the applicant.[182]

(iii) Appeal on a point of law

The third form of challenge is an appeal on a point of law.[183] The starting position of the statutory provisions is that the parties, having entrusted the determination of their dispute to the arbitral tribunal, cannot complain if the tribunal gets things wrong, whether the error is of fact or law. In case of errors of fact there is no right of appeal, though where the error in question arises through a serious irregularity, there is a right of challenge on that ground under s 68. As regards errors of law, the right of appeal is closely circumscribed and reflects the guidelines laid down previously by the House of Lords in *The Nema*[184] and *The Antaios*,[185] possibly with a slight expansion.[186] Leave to appeal can be given only by agreement of all the parties or with leave of the court[187] and if the four further conditions specified in s 69(3) are satisfied, and not even then if the parties have agreed to exclude the right of appeal.[188] These four conditions are:

(a)   that the determination of the question will substantially affect the rights of one or more of the parties;

(b)   that the question is one which the tribunal was asked to determine;

(c)   that on the basis of the findings of fact in the award -
   (i)   the decision of the tribunal on the question is obviously wrong, or
   (ii) the question is one of general public importance and the decision of the tribunal is at least open to serious doubt; and

(d)   that, despite the agreement of the parties to resolve the matter by arbitration, it is just and proper in all the circumstances for the court to determine the question.

Even with all these restrictions, it remains difficult to predict with any reasonable degree of assurance in what circumstances the court will entertain an appeal that has not been the subject of an exclusion agreement, particularly if the point of law

---

182   Section 68(2); *Warborough Investments Ltd v S Robinson & Sons (Holdings) Ltd* [2003] All ER (D) 108.

183   Ie for a court in England and Wales, a question of the law of England and Wales (s 82(1)), not a foreign law. See *Reliance Industries Ltd v Enron Oil and Gas India Ltd* [2002] 1 All ER (Comm) 59.

184   *Pioneer Shipping Ltd v BTP Tioxide Ltd* [1982] AC 724

185   *Antaios Compania Naviera SA v Salen Rederierna AB* [1985] AC 191.

186   *CMA CGM SA Beteilungs-Kommanditgesellschaft (The Northern Pioneer)* [2003] 1 Lloyd's Rep 212, per Lord Phillips MR at 216.

187   There is no appeal to the Court of Appeal against a decision on an application for leave to appeal (*Henry Boot Construction (UK) Ltd v Malmaison Hotel (Manchester) Ltd* [2001] QB 388).

188   Section 69(1). An agreement to dispense with reasons for the tribunal's award is to be considered an exclusion agreement (s 69(1)).

involved is one which interests the court or is felt to require clarification.[189] It is therefore not a sufficient answer that leave to appeal is given in relatively few cases; the problem for parties to arbitration is that they have no means of predicting whether their case will be one of the few. There is a case for further restricting the availability of appeals on points of law.

12. THE ENFORCEMENT OF AN ENGLISH ARBITRAL AWARD

An English arbitral award may be enforced in this country by an action on the award, but such a procedure is rarely used. Instead, parties use the speedier procedure prescribed by s 66 of the Arbitration Act 1996, namely an application to the High Court for leave to enforce the award in the same manner as a judgment. An English award will be recognized and enforced abroad in any state which is a party to the New York Convention.[190]

13. INTERNATIONAL COMMERCIAL ARBITRATION

A number of issues relevant to international commercial arbitration have already been discussed. We have seen that it is not necessary to adopt the theory of the stateless award[191] to recognize that in international commercial arbitration the arbitrators enjoy wide powers derived from the international character of the dispute and the parties, and from the fact that their award can be refused recognition only on very restricted grounds. But three matters particular to international arbitration can briefly be mentioned.

(i) States and state entities as parties[192]

The traditional sovereignty of states and the immunity flowing from it[193] has many facets which may impinge on the ability of a private contracting party to pursue arbitration (or litigation) against a state. In particular:

(a) each state is considered sovereign in its own territory, so that as a general principle of international law the courts of a foreign state will regard as outside their competence and non-justiciable issues concerning 'acts of state' performed by the first state within its own jurisdiction (the act of state doctrine);

---

189 A salutary illustration of this is provided by the protracted *Panatown* saga previously mentioned (see p 117), which should surely be regarded as an affront to a modern arbitration process. See also Roy Goode, 'The Adaptation of English Law to International Commercial Arbitration' (1992) 8 Arbitration International 1, drawing attention to the nine pages of *Mustill and Boyd* analysing in detail the variety of phrases used to denote the requisite threshold for an appeal, only to conclude that, as all these were only guidelines, they were not exhaustive!

190 Under art V of the Convention recognition and enforcement may be refused only on one or more of the grounds set out in that article.

191 See pp 1178–1180.

192 See Lew, Mistelis and Kröll, *Comparative International Commercial Arbitration*, ch 27.

193 See generally Hazel Fox, *Law of State Immunity* (2002, paperback 2004 with updating preface and minor corrections and additions).

(b)   a state may not in principle be impleaded before the courts of a foreign state without the first state's consent (the doctrine of state, or sovereign,[194] immunity);

(c)   the constitution of a state may contain limitations on the power of the state or its entities to enter into commercial contracts or to submit to arbitration;

(d)   the law of a state may contain provisions limiting the range of persons having power to bind the state to contracts.

Act of state, non-justiciability and state immunity are separate concepts, though there is considerable uncertainty about where the line is to be drawn between them. An exploration of these complex issues is outside the scope of this work.[195] In regard to state immunity, which rests both on international and on municipal law, it is necessary to distinguish acts done in the exercise of sovereign or governmental power (*acta jure imperii*) from acts of a private law nature, such as entry into contracts (*acta jure gestionis*). States and state entities that are parties to commercial contracts at one time enjoyed absolute immunity from suit, no distinction being drawn between *acta jure imperii* and *acta jure gestionis*. But more recently there was a sharp shift in attitude, and the view came to prevail that if a state wished to engage in trading, thereby bringing itself within the area of private law, it should not be entitled to avail itself of immunity; in other words, state immunity should be confined to *acta jure imperii*. Thus in England, as stated earlier in connection with court proceedings,[196] immunity is no longer accorded to a foreign state[197] acting in a commercial capacity rather than in exercise of its sovereign powers.[198] In the case of a separate entity there is no immunity unless the proceedings relate to something done by the state entity in the exercise of sovereign authority and the circumstances are such that the state itself would have been immune.[199] Quite apart from this, a state which has entered into an agreement containing an arbitration clause thereby waives any right it might otherwise have had to claim state immunity from the arbitral proceedings[200] or from

194   The two terms are not fully interchangeable in that sovereign immunity encompasses the personal immunity of the sovereign.

195   For a masterly treatment, see Fox, *State Immunity*, especially chs 7 and 11.

196   See p 1072.

197   Which includes the the sovereign or other head of State in his public capacity, the government of that state and any department of that government but not any entity (a separate entity) which is distinct from the executive organs of government and capable of suing or being sued (State Immunity Act 1978, s 14(1)).

198   State Immunity Act 1978, s 3(1)(a). But this does not apply where the parties are states or have otherwise agreed in writing (ibid).

199   Section 14(1), (2). For an example, see *Kuwait Airways Corp v Iraqi Airways Co* [1995] 1 WLR 1147.

200   This is a general principle of international commercial arbitration and is based on the idea that submission to arbitration is not inconsistent with state immunity but, on the contrary, that the ability to submit to arbitration is an incident of sovereignty. See, for example, the notable award of the arbitrator in *Libyan American Oil Co (LIAMCO) v Government of the Libyan Arab Republic* (1981) 20 ILM 151, (1981) VI YBCA 89. The point is not covered by s 9 of the State Immunity Act 1978, which provides only that a state's agreement in writing to submit a dispute to arbitration removes its immunity to proceedings *in the courts* of the United Kingdom which relate to the arbitration and is silent on the effect of the agreement as a waiver of immunity from the jurisdiction of the arbitral tribunal.

proceedings relating to the arbitration,[201] and this is also the case where it takes a step in the arbitral proceedings without raising the defence of state immunity.[202] But the mere participation of a state entity in arbitration proceedings does not constitute a waiver by the state itself, even if the state entity is an instrumentality of the state.[203] A waiver of immunity from jurisdiction does not extend to any immunity the state might enjoy against enforcement of the award,[204] but such immunity is not available in respect of process to which the state has given its written consent or in relation to funds for the time being in use or intended to be used for commercial purposes.[205]

It is a widely accepted principle of international commercial arbitration that a state on whose behalf an arbitration agreement has been concluded cannot set up as a bar to jurisdiction its internal law restricting the capacity of the state to enter into the arbitration agreement or the authority of the person entering into it on behalf of the state.[206]

(ii) The applicable law

An international arbitration raises issues of conflict of laws which are not present in a purely domestic dispute. It is necessary to distinguish the agreement to arbitrate, the reference to arbitration, the arbitrability of the dispute, the arbitral procedure and the law applicable to the primary, or substantive, agreement between the parties to which the dispute relates. Each of these has its own applicable law under English conflict of laws rules,[207] and, in theory, they could all be different.[208] In practice, they are often the same. The main divide likely to occur is between procedural issues, which will be governed by the curial law (almost always the law of the place of the arbitration); and issues of substantive law affecting the primary agreement, which will be governed by the Rome Convention; and the agreement to arbitrate, which will be governed by the proper law under English common law conflict of

201 State Immunity Act 1978, s 9(1).
202 This must follow from the general principle that a party who seeks to protest the jurisdiction of the tribunal must either do so as soon as possible before the tribunal or the court or refrain from participating in the arbitration. A state cannot participate without raising state immunity and then seek to raise it at a later stage. It may be noted that a plea of state immunity is not an objection to substantive jurisdiction within the meaning of s 30 of the Arbitration Act 1996, which is silent on the issue.
203 So held by the Swiss Supreme Court in *Westland Helicopters (UK) v Arab Republic of Egypt* (1991) XVI YBCA 174. See Derains and Schwartz, *Guide to the New ICC Rules of Arbitration*, pp 95–97. See, to similar effect, the Institute of International Law Resolution on Arbitration Between States or State Entities and Foreign Enterprises 12 September 1989, XVI YBCA 236 (1991).
204 Lew, Mistelis and Kröll, *Comparative International Commercial Arbitration*, paras 27–54 ff.
205 State Immunity Act 1978, s 13(2),(4).
206 See *Fouchard, Gaillard, Goldman on Arbitration*, paras 550 ff; Lew, Mistelis, Kröll, *Comparative International Commercial Arbitration*, para 27–15.
207 It will be recalled that neither the Brussels Regulation on jurisdiction and enforcement nor the Rome Convention on the law applicable to contractual obligations applies to arbitration agreements and awards. But in an arbitration in England or elsewhere in the EU the law applicable to the primary agreement is normally to be determined by applying the rules of the Rome Convention.
208 See H-L Yu, 'Choice of law for arbitrators: 2 steps or 3?' (2001) 4 International Arbitration L Rev 152.

laws rules.[209] Also to be considered are the rules of what has become known as the new *lex mercatoria*, rules based on international usage as ascertained from a variety of sources – including expert evidence, international and regional restatements, and comparative law – and said by some scholars to be supranational in character. French scholars have been the leading exponents of the concept of the *lex mercatoria*, though what this encompasses remains a matter of debate.[210] To some it is a synonym for transnational commercial law, but this deprives us of a useful label for the law fashioned by merchants, the unwritten usages of trade that are the hallmark of the *lex mercatoria*, serving to distinguish it from rules that are binding as express terms of contracts, contractually incorporated uniform rules and international conventions, all of which, even if influenced by trade usage, change it in varying degree and constitute new and independent sources of obligation.[211]

It is widely, though not universally, accepted that there can be no rights or duties without law, and that while parties enjoy a high degree of freedom in selecting the rules which are to govern their relations, they cannot remove their contract from governing law or rules of law.[212] What is, however, undeniable is that in international commercial arbitration arbitral tribunals have, and not infrequently exercise, recourse to a wider range of sources than national judges. Their ability to do this stems from the delegation of authority by legislatures and courts, coupled with their self-imposed restrictions on judicial review of arbitral awards, including art V of the New York Convention. So there have been numerous arbitral awards in which the outcome has been determined or reinforced by the UNIDROIT Principles of International Commercial Contracts or the Principles of European Contract Law or by principles seen as common to relevant legal systems. The writer has identified elsewhere seven possible reasons why a tribunal might wish to avoid determining the applicable law under conflict of laws rules or relying on the law which would otherwise be applicable. They include situations in which the applicable law is insufficiently developed to answer the legal issues raised; the fact that the conflict rule would lead to the application of the law of one of the parties when the selection of a neutral law would be more responsive to sensitivities; the fact that the laws that come into consideration lead to the same result, so that no purpose is served by an elaborate exercise to determine which of them should be applied; and the fact that the choice between one legal system and another is so finely balanced that the tribunal finds it difficult to prefer one to the other. In policy terms most of these have at least some merit, though this is not true of a further reason for declining to apply the law found by the tribunal to be applicable under conflicts rules, namely that the tribunal does not favour the solution it offers. What we can say is that, in recognizing the wide powers enjoyed by arbitral tribunals and by the parties, it is neither desirable nor necessary to ascribe binding force to the will of the parties without dependence of any external legal order and thus to postulate some a-

---

209   For a full treatment of the subject see Merkin, *Arbitration Law*, ch 5.

210   One of the best discussions is to be found in that monumental comparative work *Fouchard, Gaillard, Goldman on International Commercial Arbitration*, paras 1443 ff.

211   See Roy Goode, 'Usage and Its Reception in Transnational Commercial Law' (1997) 46 ICLQ 1 at pp 2–3.

212   *Fouchard, Gaillard, Goldman*, para 1441.

national or autonomous law represented by the contract itself. To allow contracting parties to make their own law without reference to any external criteria for the validity of their agreement would be to subject them to any terms they chose to agree, however unreasonable or oppressive. No legal system could tolerate such a freedom.

(iii) Enforcement of foreign arbitral awards[213]

The Arbitration Act 1996 re-enacts provisions of the Arbitration Act 1975, giving effect in the United Kingdom to the 1958 New York Convention on the Recognition and Enforcement of Foreign Arbitral Awards. Under the Act awards made in the territory of a foreign state which is a party to the Convention[214] are recognized and enforceable in this country,[215] except in the cases mentioned in the Convention or set out in s 103 of the Act. These include the fact that recognition and enforcement would be contrary to English public policy, though this had to be construed in an international, not a purely domestic, sense. Where a vitiating factor such as illegality is relied on, the court will not usually entertain it if it is not apparent on the face of the award and could have been raised during the arbitration and was not, or if it has been unsuccessfully pursued in another forum.[216] The position is otherwise if the illegality is apparent on the face of the award.[217] Certain other foreign awards are registrable as judgments under Pt II of the Administration of Justice Act 1920 or Pt I of the Foreign Judgments (Reciprocal Enforcement) Act 1933 if they have become enforceable in the same manner as a judgment in the place they were given,[218] and an award by ICSID is registrable as a judgment pursuant to the Arbitration (International Investment Disputes) Act 1966. Foreign arbitral awards outside these categories are enforceable in the same way as domestic awards, namely by action on the award or by application to the court to enforce the award as a judgment pursuant to s 66 of the Arbitration Act 1996.

(iv) Recognition and enforcement of English awards in other states

A United Kingdom award will be recognized and enforceable abroad in states party to the New York Convention or receiving reciprocal treatment from the United Kingdom as described above. The Convention is one of the most successful ever to have been concluded, having now been ratified by some 134 states.[219] It is one of the major factors influencing parties in favour of arbitration rather than litigation, where the facilities for reciprocal enforcement of judgments are much more limited.

213 See Dicey and Morris, *Conflict of Laws* (13th edn, 2000), ch 16; D. Rhidian Thomas, 'International Commercial Arbitration Agreements and the Enforcement of Foreign Arbitral Awards – A Commentary on the Arbitration Act 1975' [1981] 1 LMCLQ 17.
214 Arbitration Act 1996, s 100(1).
215 Section 101.
216 *Westacre Investments Inc v Jugoimport-SPDR Holding Co Ltd* [1999] QB 740.
217 *Soleimany v Soleimany* [1999] QB 785.
218 Administration of Justice Act 1920, s 12(1); Foreign Judgments (Reciprocal Enforcement) Act 1933, s 10A.
219 As at 16 April 2004.

PART NINE
Envoi

40 Final Reflections

English commercial law is so vast, so complex, that it is all too easy for its structure to become buried in the detail of the common law rules and the statutory provisions. It is therefore necessary from time to time to throw off the shackles of rule and practice, of the latest case and the most recent business technique, and to examine the more durable abstract principles on which the network of case law is supported. In these last few pages we can stand back from the detail and reflect for a moment on the nature of English commercial law and on its future.

I. ARE THERE PRINCIPLES OF COMMERCIAL LAW?

Does commercial law exist? Are there unifying principles which bind the almost infinite variety of transactions in which businessmen engage, marking these off from other types of contract? The absence of anything resembling a commercial code makes this question harder to answer than might be imagined. If by commercial law we mean a relatively self-contained, integrated body of principles and rules peculiar to commercial transactions, then we are constrained to say that this is not to be found in England. The law affecting business transactions is not a seamless web, nor is it a jigsaw in which, with careful study and some luck, all the pieces can be fitted neatly together to make a harmonious whole. Rather it is a collocation of ill-assorted statutes bedded down on an amorphous mass of constantly shifting case law.

But if we view commercial law as the totality of the law's response to the needs and practices of the mercantile community, then, indeed, commercial law exists and flourishes in England, adapting itself constantly to new business procedures, new instruments, new demands.

This, then, is the essence of commercial law – the accommodation of rules, usages and documents fashioned by the world of business; the facilitation, rather than the obstruction, of legitimate commercial development. This is achieved not through ad hoc responses to particular problems but through the development of principles within a sound conceptual framework. Commercial law is rooted in principles of good faith, the sanctity of agreement, the recognition of trade usage as a source of contractual rights, and the maintenance of a fair balance between vested rights and the interests of third parties. It is part of the genius of the common law that despite the ritual and the formalism of its earlier life it has proved able to respond to the challenges of industrial growth. The significance of trade usage, the binding force of the documentary credit despite the absence of a deed or consideration, the concept of negotiability, the range and conceptual subtlety of the floating charge, all these bear witness to what Professor Harry Lawson happily called the rational strength of English law.

Thus commercial law is characterized primarily by those principles, rules and statutory provisions which are concerned to uphold and protect the acceptable customs and practices of merchants. And allied to the substantive law is its handmaiden, procedure, in which once again the creative role of the courts has shown itself, with such new weapons as the *Mareva* injunction (now called freezing injunction), the *Anton Piller* order (now labelled search order) and the non-liability declaration. Yet there remains the question whether, flexible and sophisticated as it is, this diffuse and uncodified body of law is today sufficient to meet the proper demands of the world of commerce.

2.   THE PHILOSOPHICAL FOUNDATIONS OF COMMERCIAL LAW[1]

No branch of law is a seamless web; each one embodies contradictions, competing policies, uncertainties and, on occasion, injustices. Commercial law too has its tensions, which are not easy to resolve. Where should the line be drawn between commercial law and commercial reality? The boundary between the two is increasingly blurred by a growth in the conferment of discretionary powers on courts and regulatory powers. How should the choice be made between rules, in which the law is laid down in advance and has simply to be applied by the judge, and standards, in which the law is given content only at the point of decision by a judge, a tribunal or an administrator, and through the exercise of a discretion? To what extent should the form of a transaction rather than its substance or function be the determinant of rights and duties? And to what extent should private rights be made to give way to public law and regulation?

Such tensions are unavoidable and are evidenced by swings in the judicial pendulum as the courts strive on the one hand to respect the autonomy of the parties and on the other to secure fairness and justice. For its part, the business community, understandably enough, would like to have its cake and eat it. Obviously, businessmen look to the law to produce results that in the typical case commend themselves as reasonable and as responsive to legitimate commercial needs and practices. What they also expect of the law is predictability in its application and thus in the outcome of disputes on legal issues. This, however, involves a paradox, for the higher the degree of predictability required, the greater the detail in which the principles and rules have to be expressed; yet businessmen also attach great importance to flexibility, to a legal environment which enables them to develop new commercial instruments, new business practices, confident in the knowledge that they will be upheld by the courts as producing their desired legal effects, and this militates in favour of broad principle and discretions and against a high degree of detail and the predictability that comes with it. So the legislature and the courts have to maintain a balancing act, providing sufficient predictability of the rules to

---

1   See Roy Goode, *Commercial Law in the Next Millennium* (1998), pp 12 ff.

generate the confidence on which business transactions so heavily depend while at the same time ensuring that the law is at once responsive to legitimate commercial needs, allowing leeway for the evolution of new markets and instruments without countenancing injustice and unfair dealing.

3. SHOULD COMMERCIAL LAW BE CODIFIED?

(i) Of codes in general

Codes are the staple diet of the civilian lawyer, and truly they have served him well. The expression of principle, uncluttered by rule or by detail, can combine clarity with flexibility, enabling the courts to keep the law in tune with social and economic development. The French Civil Code sets out the law of torts in a mere five articles,[2] of which four are no more than three lines of print.

But there are codes and codes, and their aims and style vary widely. The Prussian Code of Frederick the Great, the Allgemeine Landrecht of 1794, sought to solve every possible legal problem in a massive array of over 19,000 sections. By contrast, the Swiss Civil Code, the work of the outstanding Swiss jurist Eugen Huber, gets by with a mere 977 articles. Some countries, such as France and Germany, have a separate commercial code: others, such as Switzerland, include the dealings of merchants in their civil code. The codification of law, or of a particular branch of it, may be made to serve a number of different objectives: to unify, to improve (or even revolutionize), to systematize, to simplify and to make more accessible. The existence of a number of territorial units within one country has proved the initial motive-power for most of the great codes. This is as true of the American Uniform Commercial Code in the twentieth century as of the European codes in the nineteenth. In England, as a unitary jurisdiction, this motive-power is lacking. The task of unification was done long ago by the post-Norman Conquest itinerant judge.

The codes do not, of course, dispense with the need to refer to judge-made law. What they do provide is a systematic arrangement of principle which signposts the judge in the direction he should go; and the nature of a code is such that the courts are discouraged from excessive reliance on judicial precedent. The major weakness of judge-made law is its immense diffusion and the consequent difficulty of access to it. In England the function of codes in systematizing the law and making it accessible, at least to lawyers, is performed by textbooks, encyclopedic works and periodical literature. Even practitioners are not fully conscious of the degree of their dependence on these tools of the trade. Imagine the task of a barrister called upon to argue, or a judge to decide, a case on a point of law with which he was not familiar or which he had not had occasion to examine for some time if he were denied access to legal literature and were left simply with the law reports. How would he go about finding the principles involved and relating them to neighbouring principles? Where would he discover the detailed rules subsumed under the principles, the exceptions to the rules, the caveats and qualifications made by generations of judges? Left to trek

2 Articles 1382–1386.

through countless volumes of the law reports with no literature to guide him, his task would certainly be a thankless one.

The availability of legal literature, which is nowadays taken so much for granted, has had the effect of concealing the deficiencies of a non-code system, of enabling the English lawyer to take pride in the fact that we in England, with our commonsense, pragmatic approach, have no need of codes, that we get by perfectly well as we are and that conceptualism is for the theoretician, finding no place in the practical workings of the law.

Nothing could be further from the truth. Concepts matter; they matter enormously. Decision without principle is merely a reaction to a particular fact-situation, offering no guidance for the future, no indication to lawyers and their clients of the way in which a dispute over a different set of facts is likely to be resolved. Needless to say, English judges are fully conscious of the importance of theory and concepts. For intellectual rigour, subtlety and creative ingenuity they are certainly the equal of their civil law counterparts. But they also recognize that concepts must be our servants, not our masters, and that there are occasions on which established concepts must be modified to avoid injustice and when doctrinal purity must give way to commercial reality.

(ii)   The codification of commercial law[3]

That the difficulty of access to judge-made law is a serious problem in English jurisprudence is borne out by the partial codifications of commercial law in the nineteenth century by that outstanding draftsman Sir Mackenzie Chalmers. Reared on the Sale of Goods Act and the Bills of Exchange Act, we are prone to forget the problems of the nineteenth-century writer who had to delve for his law into a mass of undigested, often inconsistent, cases and then to impose his own system of arrangement, classification and statement of principle. But the textbook is not a code. The author does not create law, he merely expounds it; and the discursive nature of the modern textbook makes it too unwieldy, too diffuse, to serve as the equivalent of a code.[4] We lack even the closest common law equivalent to a code, the Restatement, one of America's greatest contributions to the systematization of the common law.

Whether commercial transactions or the affairs of merchants should be regulated in a separate commercial code or embodied in a broader civil code is a controversy we can leave to the civilians.[5] It need not trouble English lawyers, who at present have

---

3   See Roy Goode, 'The codification of commercial law' (the 1988 Wilfred Fullagar Memorial Lecture), (1988) Mon LR 135; Mary Arden, 'Time for an English commercial code?' (1997) 56 CLJ 516; Michael Bridge, 'The future of English private transactional law' in *Current Legal Problems 2002* (2002) 191. For a contrary view, see Malcolm Clarke, 'Doubts from the dark side: the case against codes' [2001] JBL 605.

4   An exception is Dicey's great work *The Conflict of Laws*, now (*sub nom* Dicey and Morris) in its 13th edition.

5   See, for example, Wolfram Muller-Freienfels, 'The Problem of Including Commercial Law and Family Law in a Civil Code' in *Problems of Codification* (ed S. J. Stoljar, 1977), especially at pp 103 ff.

neither the one nor the other. No one pretends that commercial law is a closed system, isolated from the general principles of civil law. Even in countries which have both a civil and a commercial code, the concepts of the latter derive from, and in turn give nourishment to, the former. But a commercial code can serve a useful purpose even if its provisions are not confined to dealings between merchants, a fact borne out by the striking success of the Uniform Commercial Code, a great part of which does not distinguish commercial transactions from contracts between a business enterprise and a private individual. What is important is that the preparation of a commercial code involves a restatement of principle, in the course of which many latent inconsistencies, irrational rules, and deficiencies in legal policy are brought to the surface. If this is true of the common law, it is even more true of legislation, which in the field of commercial law has developed piecemeal, lacking any coherent pattern and pulling several ways at once.

> Individual statutes drafted one by one over fifty years and more, by different persons under different circumstances and with different points of view, run of necessity in perplexingly different directions.[6]

Karl Llewellyn's strictures on American legislation, and his commendation of a commercial code, apply with equal force to English commercial law. The lack of integration, the absence of relationship between one statute and another, the verbiage and obscurity of present-day legislation, are lamentable. We have only to look at our statutes regulating security interests in personal property to see, as did the Crowther Committee,[7] how woefully inadequate is the statutory framework within which secured transactions operate. The Bills of Sale Acts, archaic in form and in content, have no link with credit legislation, with the Factors Acts or the Sale of Goods Act. The latter, though covering part of the same ground, have little relationship to each other. The general principles which unite sales law with that relating to negotiable instruments and to secured transactions are nowhere to be found in the legislation; they have to be extracted painfully from the cases. Our sales law itself remains largely in the form in which it was enacted over 100 years ago. Moreover, we lack a clear legal policy on the most fundamental questions. To what extent must remedies be exercised in good faith? How far do the principles of equitable obligation, in particular those delineating the concept of notice and the institution of the constructive trust, apply to commercial transactions? What constitutes value, and what is its significance?

It is not, of course, suggested that we in England should seek to codify the entirety of commercial law. Such an exercise would be both impracticable and pointless. There are many fields which can safely be left to existing statutes, case law and contractually incorporated trade rules, among them carriage of goods by sea, insurance, paper-based payment systems and documentary credits, and demand guarantees – in fact, all the fields which together generate the bulk of the work of

---

6 Karl Llewellyn, 'Why We Need the Uniform Commercial Code', 10 U Fla L Rev 367 (1957), at p 371.
7 *Report on Consumer Credit* (Cmnd 4596, 1971), ch 4.2. Despite subsequent endorsement of its principal recommendations in Professor Aubrey Diamond's report *Security Interests in Property* (1989), no steps have yet been taken to implement this part of the Committee's report.

the Commercial Court. What is advocated here is a code of the kind exemplified by the Uniform Commercial Code, restating, simplifying and modernizing the law in a small number of selected areas in order to make it more responsive to the practices and needs of modern commerce and finance while containing built-in mechanisms to allow for future development. Candidates for inclusion in such a code are the sale of goods, personal property security, electronic trading with particular reference to payment systems and dealings with goods in transit, interests in securities held with an intermediary and, perhaps, suretyship guarantees. Even codification in this restricted sense is not, of course, an easy task lightly undertaken.[8] On the contrary, it involves years of unremitting toil and a prodigious amount of time and resources. Several years ago the Law Commission began a project to codify the English law of contract but later abandoned it in favour of examination of a series of particular problems in contract law. But commercial law is narrower in compass, more readily reducible to principle and rule, and its codification, in the restricted sense in which this has been achieved by the Uniform Commercial Code, is an attainable goal. This would provide an opportunity not merely for restatement but for the fundamental reappraisal which is long overdue. It is ridiculous to imagine that statutes passed a century ago, when the volume and sophistication of commercial transactions were a fraction of what they are today, are still adequate for the needs of the commercial world. The technicality and rigour of negotiable instruments law, the property orientation of the Sale of Goods Act, require radical change if they are to accommodate the legitimate requirements of modern business and the effects of new technology on funds transfers and data interchange. Parties should not be expected to contract out of legislation with monotonous regularity; on the contrary, legislation should be so framed as to represent the typical solutions of the parties themselves. An excellent first stage, though not stated in terms of codification, is the Law Commission's project on the reform of personal property security law, using as a vehicle its remit to review the system on registration of company charges and to produce draft legislation.[9] Ideally, the Law Commission would have liked to produce a scheme not limited to security and quasi-security interests given by companies, but the exigencies of the parliamentary timetable have led it to accept that it is better to have half a loaf initially, with the prospect of the rest to come, rather than no loaf at all.

The gradual movement towards the harmonization of commercial law in Europe,[10] though creating additional problems for a purely national codification programme, also lends urgency to the task of restating the principles on which our own commercial law is based; and it has the additional advantage of providing an exportable product which can help to maintain, and indeed enhance, the influence of English law and English courts in international commercial transactions.

---

8   See generally, Stoljar, *Problems of Codification*, containing a series of thoughtful essays on the philosophy underlying some of the principal European civil and commercial codes.

9   See p 675.

10 See below.

4. TOWARDS A NEW *LEX MERCATORIA?*

A growing recognition that individual national laws are ill-suited to international transactions has resulted in a marked increase in international cooperation directed to the harmonization of law, particularly in the field of commercial transactions.[11] Among the commercial law harmonizing acts of recent times may be mentioned the Vienna Sales Convention,[12] the various transport conventions,[13] the Rome Convention on the Law Applicable to Contractual Obligations,[14] the EEC directives on unfair contract terms and commercial agents,[15] the UN Convention on the Assignment of Receivables in International Trade,[16] the UNCITRAL Model Law on International Commercial Arbitration,[17] the UNIDROIT Conventions on International Factoring,[18] International Financial Leasing and Mobile Equipment,[19] and, at the level of rules effectuated by contract, codifications of business practice by the International Chamber of Commerce, such as the Uniform Customs and Practice for Documentary Credits,[20] Incoterms,[21] and the Uniform Rules for Demand Guarantees.[22] A number of other prominent organizations are also concerned with this process, including the Council of Europe, the United Nations Commission on Trade and Development and, as regards conflicts of laws, the Hague Conference. Harmonizing measures take a variety of forms: an EC regulation or directive, a convention, a model law or set of uniform rules, a contractually incorporated codification of custom and usage or of trade terms, and model contracts and contractual conditions. More recently, scholars have turned their attention to general principles of the law of contract, with codifications such as the UNIDROIT *Principles of International Contracts* and a similar compilation, *Principles of European Contract Law*, prepared by the Commission on European contract law.[23] But whether the instrument of harmonization is permissive or mandatory, its objective is the same, namely to ensure as far as possible that in whatever state an issue is litigated the same law will be applied to determine the rights of the parties.

The ever-increasing volume and complexity of international trade have led to the resurgence of interest in a new *lex mercatoria*. The work of UNCITRAL and UNIDROIT directed to the progressive codification of substantive international trade law and of the Hague Conference on the unification of rules of private international law governing international commercial transactions indicates the revival of the spirit of internationalism which pervaded the old law merchant and reflects a willingness to

---

11 See generally Roy Goode, 'Reflections on the Harmonisation of Commercial Law' (1991) I Uniform Law Review 54, also published in *Commercial and Consumer Law* (eds Ross Cranston and Roy Goode, 1993), ch 1.
12 See ch 33.
13 See chs 32, 36.
14 See p 1095.
15 See pp 100, 173.
16 See p 16.
17 See p 1167.
18 See p 16.
19 See pp 16, 1107.
20 See p 951.
21 See p 867.
22 See p 1019.
23 See p 1181.

embark on the preparation of international conventions in fields at one time thought off limits, such as proprietary rights in tangible and intangible movables[24]. This process, already manifest in international commercial arbitration, will be accelerated by the steadily mounting volume of EU and EU-related law, such as the Rome Convention, the Brussels Regulation and the Insolvency Regulation, and by an increasing awareness that with the globalization of markets and transactions a move from domestic laws of international trade towards a more harmonizing transnational commercial law is essential. Professor Klaus Peter Berger, in a widely cited publication,[25] has analysed the doctrinal basis of the modern *lex mercatoria* and has sought to introduce a coherent and systematic framework of transnational commercial law.[26] Professor Joachim Bonell has gone a step further and advocated a global commercial code.[27]

We cannot, of course, hope to recapture the speed, the robustness and the pragmatism of the ancient merchant courts, nor to achieve within a measurable time-span more than a fraction of what would be necessary to produce a truly international commercial code. But if the labours now under way do no more than bring about a rapprochement between the common law and the civil law systems and create a greater understanding among states of the merits of each other's laws and institutions affecting commercial dealings, they will not be in vain.

It was his international approach to commercial law, his grasp of the civil law tradition, his absorbing interest in the universal customs of merchants that made Lord Mansfield one of the greatest commercial judges this country has ever known. It is fitting to conclude with a reference to *Luke v Lyde*,[28] in which in a single judgment he drew on Cicero, the Consolato del Mare, the Rhodian Laws, the Laws of Oléron, the Laws of Wisby, Roccius de Navibus et Naulo and the Ordinances of Louis XIV in order to resolve a disputed question of Admiralty law.

> The maritime law is not the law of a particular country but the general law of nations: '*non erit alia lex Romae, alia Athenis; alia nunc, alia posthac; sed et apud omnes gentes et omni tempore, una eademque lex obtinebit*'.[29]

24　See Roy Goode, 'The Protection of Interests in Movables in Transnational Commercial Law' 1998–2/3 Uniform Law Rev 453; J. H. Dalhuisen, 'European private law: moving from a closede to an open system of proprietary rights' (2001) 5 Edinburh L Rev 273.

25　*The Creeping Codification of the Lex Mercatoria* (1999).

26　Transnational commercial law, conceived as the product of the international harmonization process, whether through conventions, model laws, contractually incorporated trade rules, restatements or otherwise, has for several years been taught as a postgraduate course at Oxford University.

27　Michael Joachim Bonell, 'Do We Need a Global Commercial Code?, 2000–3 Uniform Law Rev 469.

28　(1759) 2 Burr 882.

29　The quotation is a somewhat inaccurate rendering of a passage from Cicero's *De Republica*, 3.22.33, which in fact reads: ' … *nec erit alia lex Romae, alia Athenis, alia nunc, alia posthac, sed et omnes gentes et omni tempore una lex et sempiterna et immutabilis continebit* … ' (… there shall not be one law at Rome, another at Athens, one now, another hereafter, but one everlasting and unalterable law shall govern all nations for all time …').

Index